ALSO FROM VISIBLE INK PRESS

Bud Collins' Tennis Encyclopedia

"Bud Collins, the walking tennis encyclopedia, has finally put himself between hard covers."
—**Mary Carillo, CBS-TV**

In this new edition, *Bud Collins' Tennis Encyclopedia*, considered the Bible of the tennis world, provides thorough statistics and presents a history of the sport from its country club beginnings in 1876 to the billion-dollar industry it is today.

Bud Collins and Zander Hollander   700 pages

Inside Sports College Basketball

"Sports fans everywhere will love the incredible amount of information contained in these books. We're proud to be associated with such terrific products."—**Jerry L. Croft, Publisher, *Inside Sports* magazine.**

Inside Sports College Basketball is the most comprehensive annual source on college basketball, covering not only the men's NCAA championship—the single biggest sporting event in America today—but every other aspect of the sport as well.

Michael Douchant   750 pages

Inside Sports World Series Factbook

Inside Sports World Series Factbook presents an exciting blow-by-blow description of every Series, from the first October Classic in 1903 through 1995. You'll get the scoop on competing teams, the final score for each game and a lively, detailed discussion of the managers, the "heroes and zeroes" and more.

George Cantor   600 pages

Inside Sports Hockey

In *Inside Sports Hockey*, exciting game action, vital stats, fascinating history, Stanley Cup highlights and much more are artfully combined for thorough coverage of one of America's favorite sports. This expanded new annual edition is updated with dozens of new lists such as all-time scores, all-time career leaders and all-time season leaders in points, goals, and assists.

Zander Hollander   725 pages

INSIDE
SPORTS MAGAZINE
GOLF

INSIDE SPORTS MAGAZINE
GOLF

Roger Matuz

VISIBLE INK PRESS

Detroit • New York • Toronto • London

Published by Visible Ink Press
A division of Gale Research
835 Penobscot Bldg.
Detroit, MI 48226-4094

Visible Ink Press is a trademark of Gale Research

Inside Sports Magazine © 1997, is a registered trademark of Inside Sports Inc.

Most Visible Ink Press books are available at special quantity discounts when purchased in bulk by corporations, organizations, or groups. Customized printings, special imprints, messages, and excerpts can be produced to meet your needs. For more information, contact the Special Markets Manager at the above address, or call 1-800-776-6265.

Art Director: Michelle DiMercurio
Front and back cover photographs: AP World Wide Photos, Inc.
All other photographs courtesy of the PGA and LPGA

Library of Congress Cataloging-in-Publication Data

Matuz, Roger.
    Inside sports golf / Roger Matuz.
        p. cm.
        Includes index.
        ISBN 1-57859-007-8
        1. Golf–Tournaments. I. Title.
        GV970.M386 1997
        796.352'66–dc21   97-12946
                                                                CIP

COURSE LAYOUT
(I.E. CONTENTS)

FORE WORD

I t's true: I laid my tee shot on the green on the 7th hole at Pebble Beach, and closed the day on 18 by driving one out over the ocean, finally turning that darn "natural slice" to an advantage, as the ball swung back over the rocks and sand, hit the fairway and bounded into a perfect approach position. Okay, so I three-putted the 7th and shanked the fairway shot on 18 into the rough, followed by a crisp iron straight and true and into a bunker. But moments like those two drives and always the glorious outdoor setting keeps you coming back to golf, despite countless strokes beyond par. And I still say that otter floating on his back in Carmel Bay was applauding the teeshot, not simply doing the otter thing of cracking crustaceans against the stone on his belly.

Just over one hundred years ago, the U.S. Open began play with the democratic notion that such an important tournament should not be dominated by a single golf course and that it should be open to anyone who could play well enough to qualify.

Nowadays, another kind of 'opening' is happening: excellent public courses compete in quality with more exclusive country clubs; more young people, more women, and more people of all kinds all over the world are playing golf, attending tournaments, and facing the same challenges that confound the most seasoned pro. Golf has entered a new age—more popular than ever as a game people play and watch, with dynamic young professionals like Tiger Woods and Karrie Webb helping further enthusiasm for the sport the world over.

A new age in golf calls for a new kind of golf guide, one that opens up to dynamic approaches—like a particularly challenging golf hole that seems to play a certain way, but after surveying the scene, you decide on a different approach. Unlike the individual decisions on the course, however, the approach for this book came from talking about golf and golf books with countless people, on the course, at tournaments, in clubhouses, and resulted from many generous and talented contributors.

A visit to Golf House at USGA Headquarters in Far Hills, New Jersey, and attending the 1996 U.S. Open at Oakland Hills impressed the need for an encyclopedia that can honor the sport's tradition and history and win respect from those who have followed and played the game for years. And playing regularly on public courses impressed the need for a golf book that is inviting to the multitudes who have begun playing over the past few years—the so-called baby boomers and Gen Xers, who are golf's fastest-growing demographic group.

In this encyclopedia we offer a course with 18 different looks, and something for everyone. There are statistics galore for fanatics and fantasy-league players; profiles of players on the three major tours, and of great golfers of the past; plenty of info on tournaments and public courses; a primer on golf course architecture that will help readers understand the logic of course design; descriptions of 100 of the greatest shots in tournament play—defining moments when a golfer achieved that rare stroke of perfection; many handy resources; a glossary of golf jargon; a series of common-sense tips by noted instructor Kip Puterbaugh that will help you get back to the basics; and a section that reflects ways in which golf is part of our popular culture, with contributions from Ann Liguori, host of *Conversations with Ann Liguori* on The Golf Channel.

Just about everything we could think of that might help you get to know and enjoy the game even more.

The following people made this publication possible:

Christopher Scanlon, Editor, Visible Ink Press, who plays a fine game of patience and persistence. Golfing partners Peter Gareffa and Dean Dauphinais, who contributed ideas and feedback all along the course, and we hereby continue the tradition of toasting Samuel Adams, brewer and patriot.

Marie McNee, for her links with and coverage of the LPGA; Eric Kinkopf, for ace contributions to the PGA Pro Files and 100 Greatest Shots; Robb Coleman, who's one committed golf fanatic, and Eric Patterson, western correspondent, for putting in on the PGA Pro Files; Dave Bianco, for carrying the Seniors and pitching in on the Glossary and the Hall of Fame sections; Bill Szumanski for his drive in completing the tour sections; Geoff Shackelford, for constructing an excellent primer on golf course architects; Ann Liguori for the stories from her many celebrity golfer interviews, and Dave Collins, Neil Walker, Don Boyden, and Cheryl MacDonald—among the many who helped whole-out the Golf and Pop Culture section by recalling even the most passing shots in film and book and song; and Kip Puterbaugh, who chipped in to help take the nonsense out of golf advice with a Top 10 list that can get you back to *your* game.

Kathy Dauphinais helped keep everything in order (with help from Sam and Joshua); Nancy Stulack and Patty Moran provided expert help at the USGA library; Ruth Martin and Chris Smith of the PGA, Karrie Felenz at the LPGA, and Pete Fontaine of SportsImages contributed illustrations and key information; and thanks to all in the galleries who offered their views and suggestions along the way, including Lynn Henning and Bradley Klein. Thanks also to Alex Micelli and the people at www.golf.com. (a great site where weekly statistical updates can be found) for various contributions. And friends . . . whom I have missed while being holed up during this round. Last but not least, all of the Matuzes, east and west.

Thanks to all at Visible Ink Press and Gale Research:

Martin Connors, Terri Schell, Judy Galens, Jim Craddock, Brad Morgan, Leslie Norback, Rebecca Nelson, Maria Franklin, and Kweli Jomo.

Roger Matuz

Manitou
Wordworks, Inc.

1

PRO FILES
MEN

JOHN ADAMS

Born: John Gregg Adams,
May 5, 1964

Birthplace: Scottsdale,
Ariz.

Ht: 6' 3" **Wt:** 220

Exempt Status: 74th on 1995
Money List

Q School: 1978, 1979, 1985

Through the 1996 season, Adams has played in 498 events without a win, losing his only playoff appearance to Jay Haas in the 1982 Hall of Fame Classic, when he bogeyed the second playoff hole at the famed Pinehurst No. 2 course. Adams finished second in the 1996 FedEx St. Jude Classic for his best recent showing. He earned more money in 1996 than in any of his previous 18 years on the Tour, collecting $257,842.

Adams is a long hitter who usually places in the top ten in driving distance, and he led the tour in Greens hit in Regulation (73.9%) in 1988. The son of a golf professional, Adams won the 1975 Arizona State amateur tournament.

• Second in driving distance in 1996 (286.7).

• Eighth in holes per eagle in 1996 (140.4).

• Had to regain Tour credentials after the 1994 season and did so by finishing just above the cut in the Qualifying Tournament.

YEAR	EVENTS	WINS	TOP 10	CUTS MADE	EARNINGS	RANK
1973	1			1	$511	267
1978	10			2	$2,025	196
1979	11			3	$1,785	224
1980	22		1	9	$19,895	125
1981	25		1	10	$17,898	140
1982	27		2	16	$54,014	86
1983	34		3	17	$59,287	87
1984	27		2	19	$73,567	80
1985	24			9	$9,613	181
1986	30		2	19	$64,906	124
1987	33			20	$51,976	149
1988	19		1	15	$64,341	140
1989	30		2	14	$106,824	120
1990	32		2	13	$127,733	122
1991	30		2	16	$117,549	125
1992	31		1	17	$173,069	89
1993	29		2	18	$221,753	78
1994	32		1	11	$106,689	151
1995	25		3	16	$243,366	74
1996	26		1	15	$257,842	86

BILLY ANDRADE

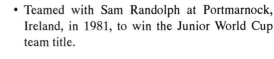

Born: William Thomas
Andrade, January 25, 1964

Birthplace: Fall River,
Mass.

Ht: 5' 8" **Wt:** 155

Residence: Bristol, R.I.
and Atlanta, Ga.

Q School: 1987, 1988

1996 Money Rank: 46th

Andrade is a journeyman-type player who had his best year in 1991, when he won his only two PGA events with back-to-back victories at the Kemper Open and Buick Classic. In doing so, he became the first player since John Fought in 1979 to win his first two PGA Tour events in consecutive weeks.

1996 was Andrade's second-best year, money-wise. He finished in the Top 10 three times and in the money in 18 of the 29 events he entered, winning $432,906. In 1991, he won $615,765. Andrade, an all-state high school basketball player in Rhode Island (Billy would be the first to remind you that Rhode Island is a *small* state), started golfing at age 5 and won his first golf tournament at age 11.

- Best finish in 1996 was a tie for second at the Motorola Western Open.

- Shot a final-round 67 at the 1993 Buick Southern Open to qualify for a five-man playoff won by John Inman.

- In '91 Kemper Open win, defeated Jeff Sluman on the first playoff hole after both golfers had carded tournament-record, 21-under-par 263s.

- A three-time All-American at Wake Forest and member of the Demon Deacon 1986 NCAA Championship team.

- Recipient of Arnold Palmer Scholarship to Wake Forest, Andrade graduated in 1987 with a degree in sociology.

- Teamed with Sam Randolph at Portmarnock, Ireland, in 1981, to win the Junior World Cup team title.

- Was No. 1-ranked junior player in nation in 1981.

YEAR	EVENTS	WINS	TOP 10	CUTS MADE	EARNINGS	RANK
1987	4			3	$4,001	235
1988	34		1	17	$74,950	134
1989	31		3	17	$202,242	69
1990	28		1	25	$231,362	64
1991	29	2	4	19	$615,765	14
1992	28		2	16	$202,509	76
1993	29		7	18	$365,769	40
1994	26		3	18	$342,208	48
1995	29		3	16	$276,294	69
1996	29		3	18	$432,906	46

EMLYN AUBREY

Born: Emlyn Aubrey,
January 28, 1964

Birthplace: Reading,
Penn.

Ht: 6' 2" **Wt:** 185

Residence: Austin, Tex.

Joined Tour: 1990

1996 Money Rank: 74th

In his second go-around on the PGA Tour, Emlyn Aubrey is indicating that this time he intends to stay. In 1996, Aubrey finished in the money in 13 out of 18 events to earn $296,005. His two top 10 finishes included a tie for second at the 1996 Greater Vancouver Open, where he fell short by just one stroke behind Guy Boros. Aubrey improved greatly from 1995, when he made just 5 cuts in 30 tournaments and ranked 140th.

Before rejoining the PGA Tour in 1995, Aubrey played on the NIKE Tour (1993-1994). By ranking tenth on the 1994 NIKE Tour money list with $113,919 in earnings, he gained his return to the PGA. Aubrey first played on the PGA Tour in

1990, when he ranked 126th. Aubrey apparently doesn't like hiring outside employees: his wife, Cindy, works as his caddie.

- Finished tied for second at the 1996 Greater Vancouver Open.

- Finished fourth at the 1996 Greater Greensboro Chrysler Classic.

- Finished tied for seventh at the 1990 H-E-B Texas Open.

- Finished tied for ninth at the 1995 AT&T Pebble Beach National Pro-Am.

- Finished tied for 24th at the 1996 PGA Championship.

- Ranked tenth on the 1994 NIKE TOUR money list.

- Won 1989 Philippines Open.

- Won 1994 Indian Open.

YEAR	EVENTS	WINS	TOP 10	CUTS MADE	EARNINGS	RANK
1990					$122,329	126
1991					$91,257	139
1992					$58,087	167
1995	30		1	5	$137,020	140
1996	18		2	13	$296,005	74

PAUL AZINGER

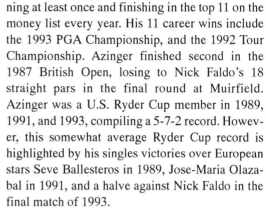

Born: Paul William Azinger, January 6, 1960

Birthplace: Holyoke, Mass.

Ht: 6' 2" **Wt:** 175

Q School: 1981, 1983, 1984

Exempt Status: 1993 PGA Champion

From 1987 to 1993, "Zinger" was one of the PGA Tour's best and most consistent golfers, win-

ning at least once and finishing in the top 11 on the money list every year. His 11 career wins include the 1993 PGA Championship, and the 1992 Tour Championship. Azinger finished second in the 1987 British Open, losing to Nick Faldo's 18 straight pars in the final round at Muirfield. Azinger was a U.S. Ryder Cup member in 1989, 1991, and 1993, compiling a 5-7-2 record. However, this somewhat average Ryder Cup record is highlighted by his singles victories over European stars Seve Ballesteros in 1989, Jose-Maria Olazabal in 1991, and a halve against Nick Faldo in the final match of 1993.

After the best year of his career in 1993, in which he had ten top 3 finishes (the most since Tom Watson in 1980), Azinger underwent treatment for lymphoma. Despite the pain in his shoulder from the treatments, he played well enough in 1995 to receive the Ben Hogan trophy from the Golf Writers Association of America for continuing in golf despite a physical handicap. His charity event, the Zinger Stinger Pro-Am, raised over $500,000 in two years for lymphoma research. He wrote a book, *Zinger*, about his bout with cancer.

Azinger is a determined competitor, a great wedge player, and is generally recognized as one of the best clutch putters in the game. He continued his comeback in 1996, moving from 100th to 95th on the money list. Azinger also has two European Tour victories at the BMW International, in 1990 and 1992.

- Finished second overall in earnings twice—1987 and 1993.

- Best 1996 finish was a tie for 8th at the Las Vegas Invitational.

- PGA Player of the Year in 1987.

- Tied for 6th in putts per green in regulation in 1996 (1.747) after tying for 7th in 1995.

- Won the 1993 Memorial Tournament by holing a sand shot on last hole.

YEAR	EVENTS	WINS	TOP 10	CUTS MADE	EARNINGS	RANK
1982	21			10	$10,655	174
1983	2					
1984	21			14	$27,821	144
1985	33		3	18	$81,179	93
1986	30		7	25	$254,019	29
1987	27	3	9	22	$822,481	2
1988	27	1	10	21	$594,850	11
1989	25	1	10	21	$951,649	3
1990	26	1	12	22	$944,731	4
1991	21	1	18	18	$685,603	9
1992	23	1	10	20	$929,863	7
1993	24	3	12	17	$1,458,456	2
1994	4				$13,422	242
1995	23		1	15	$182,955	100
1996	23		10	17	$231,420	95

CHIP BECK

Born: Charles Henry Beck, September 12th, 1956

Birthplace: Fayetteville, N.C.

Ht: 5' 10" **Wt:** 170

Exempt Status: 111th on 1995 money list

Q School: 1978

Beck's game features consistency marked by flashes of brilliance. His best year was 1988, when he won twice, had 11 Top Ten finishes, won the Vardon Trophy for the lowest scoring average, and finished in second place on the money list. Beck is one of two men in PGA Tour history (Al Geiberger was the other) to record a 59 in tournament play: at the 1991 Las Vegas Invitational, Beck made 13 birdies and had no bogeys on the par 72 layout. He received $500,000 from Hilton Hotels for the feat, and with the additional $500,000 designated for charity, he set up the Chip Beck Scholarship Fund.

Beck competed on Ryder Cup teams in 1989, 1991, and 1993, compiling an excellent 8-2-1 record, including 3-0 singles play. In the 1993 Ryder Cup, his better ball victory (with John Cook) over Nick Faldo and Colin Montgomerie in the Saturday afternoon match was viewed as "the heart of the U.S. Victory" by captain Tom Watson.

Beck's best and most famous finish in a major championship was his runner-up performance to Bernhard Langer in the 1993 Masters Tournament. In the final round, faced with a 240-yard second shot over water on the par 5 15th hole, Beck elected to lay up short of the water instead of hitting for the green and a possible eagle putt. This conservative play resulted in a par on the hole, leading many to second-guess him for not making a bolder play when he was behind. Unfairly perhaps, his decision came to be viewed as synonymous with laying up on a par five. Director Ron Shelton reportedly got the idea for the 1996 movie *Tin Cup* after viewing this tournament. In a different ending to the story, Kevin Costner, playing the lead, plunked five balls in the water instead of laying up in front of the 18th green, risking disqualification and blowing any chance of winning the U.S. Open.

- Won the 1989 and 1992 Merrill Lynch Shoot-Out Championships.

- Tied for 2nd at the 1986 U.S. Open at Shinnecock.

- Three-time All-American at the University of Georgia.

- Best 1996 finish was 2nd, at the Buick Open.

- Considered one of the more personable players on the Tour, perhaps because he earned a degree in journalism.

- Finished in the Top 10 on the Money list 3 consecutive years (1987-89) and in the Top 20 the following three years (1990-92), but 68th place in 1994 is his best since then.

YEAR	EVENTS	WINS	TOP 10	CUTS MADE	EARNINGS	RANK
1979	15			5	$4,166	197
1980	25		1	13	$17,109	134
1981	27		1	13	$30,034	112
1982	29		2	15	$57,608	77
1983	32		5	25	$149,909	33
1984	31		7	20	$177,289	34
1985	30		1	18	$76,038	97
1986	31		6	21	$215,140	39
1987	28		7	19	$523,003	9
1988	25	2	11	23	$916,818	2
1989	23		10	18	$694,087	9

1990	25	1	7	20	$571,816	17
1991	26		7	22	$578,535	16
1992	26	1	7	21	$689,704	17
1993	27		5	19	$603,376	25
1994	27		1	19	$281,131	68
1995	29		1	19	$170,081	111
1996	29		1	16	$228,127	98

AVERAGE STROKES PER ROUND

Rank	Name	Rounds	Strokes
1.	Tom Lehman	79	69.32
2.	Fred Couples	66	69.57
3.	Mark O'Meara	80	69.69
4.	Tom Watson	54	69.73
5.	Greg Norman	51	69.76
6.	Ernie Els	65	69.77
7.	Corey Pavin	81	69.79
8.	Davis Love III	80	69.81
9.	Nick Faldo	56	69.92
10.	Brad Faxon	82	69.94

RONNIE BLACK

Born: May 26th, 1958

Birthplace:
Lovington, N.M.

Ht: 6' 1" **Wt:** 180

Exempt Status: 30th in
1995 Q School

Q School: 1981, 1982, 1990, 1995

Black is a steady player (37 out of 54 cuts made in 1995-96) back on track after losing his exempt status in 1994. He has won two events, the 1983 Southern Classic and the 1984 Anheuser-Busch Classic. The A-B Classic win came via a final round 64 after he started the day seven shots off the lead. 1996 started and ended well for Black: he had a Top 10 finish in his first tournament, the Nortel Open, then after an undistinguished summer he finished in a tie for 8th at the Walt Disney World / Oldsmobile Classic and tied for 5th at the Las Vegas Invitational.

JAY DON BLAKE

Born: October 28, 1958
Birthplace:
St. George, Utah
Ht: 6' 2" **Wt:** 180
Residence: St. George, Utah
Q School: Fall 1986

Blake had his best year in 1991, when he captured his only Tour title at the Shearson Lehman Brothers Open, closing with consecutive 67s to edge Bill Sanders by two strokes. That finish catapulted him to his best-ever finish on the money list—21st, with $563,854. He also won the Argentina Open in 1991.

Blake's best 1996 performance and only Top Ten finish came at the Motorola Western Open, where he tied for second, winning $176,000. He finished in the money 20 out of 26 times in '96, earning $347,327.

Early in his career, Blake's strong suit was putting. He led the Tour in putting in 1991, averaging 1.733 putts per green in regulation and finished in the Top 10 in putting in 1992. In 1995, however, he finished tied for 105th with a 1.793 average. Blake is a racing aficionada who says he knew at age 12 that he wanted to be a golfer.

YEAR	EVENTS	WINS	TOP 10	CUTS MADE	EARNINGS	RANK
1982					$6,329	91
1983			1		$87,524	63
1984			1		$172,636	35
1985					$61,684	109
1986					$166,761	56
1987					$144,158	77
1988					$100,603	112
1989					$264,988	51
1990					$34,001	190
1991					$135,865	113
1992					$129,386	111
1993					$120,041	125
1994					$123,404	137
1995			1		$122,188	143
1996			3		$247,320	91

- In 1995, a disastrous 9 on the 16th hole in the final round of the LeCantera Texas Open, the final full-field event of the season, ruined a pair of earlier 67s, which had left Blake tied for second going into the third round. He finished tied for sixth, 13 strokes behind winner Duffy Waldorf.

- Ring him up, Ma: Blake finished tied for second with Steve Stricker, Vijay Singh and Loren Roberts at the 1994 Northern Telecom Open, second at the 1991 BellSouth Classic and tied for third at the 1989 BellSouth Atlanta Classic.

- Won the Utah State Open in 1988.

- Named College Player of the Year in 1981 at Utah.

- Won the 1980 NCAA Championship and finished second in 1981.

- Attended, with three fellow Tour members, a National Hot Rod Association driving school in Gainesville, Florida, in December 1995.

YEAR	EVENTS	WINS	TOP 10	CUTS MADE	EARNINGS	RANK
1987	31		1	19	$87,634	106
1988	31		2	24	$131,937	90
1989	27		3	16	$200,499	71
1990	30			16	$148,384	106
1991	27	1	6	23	$563,854	21
1992	24		4	15	$299,298	51
1993	26		3	15	$202,482	86
1994	25		2	20	$309,351	55
1995	26		3	17	$333,551	54
1996	26		1	20	$347,328	57

PHIL BLACKMAR

Born: Philip Arnold Blackmar, September 22, 1957

Birthplace: San Diego, Cal.

Ht: 6' 7" **Wt:** 245

Exempt Status: 121st on 1995 Money List

Q School: 1984, 1994

Blackmar has never matched his 1985 season, when he was Rookie of the Year on the PGA tour and won the Canon Sammy Davis, Jr. Greater Hartford Open with a birdie on the first playoff hole to beat Jodie Mudd and Dan Pohl. Blackmar's other win also came in a playoff when he defeated Payne Stewart (a fellow Missouri State Amateur Champion) at the 1988 Provident Classic. Blackmar rebounded to earn over $384,000 in 1995-96 after making only five cuts in 1994 and winning $28,159.

Blackmar was leading the 1991 Players Championship through 70 holes when his tee shot at the famous island green 17th hole found the water, drowning his chances and leading him to a tie for third place. In contention at the 1992 Players Championship at the same hole he again failed to find dry land with his tee shot, and finished in a tie for second place.

- Runner-up to Paul Azinger at the 1984 Q School.

- Second at the 1985 National Long Drive Championship.

- Father won the National Left-Handers Championship in 1965.

YEAR	EVENTS	WINS	TOP 10	CUTS MADE	EARNINGS	RANK
1984	1			1	$3,374	210
1985	27	1	4	16	$198,537	28
1986	29		4	17	$191,228	43
1987	32		1	19	$99,581	97
1988	29	1	1	9	$108,403	105
1989	27		2	15	$140,949	100
1990	30		2	15	$200,796	78
1991	27		3	13	$218,838	77
1992	24		2	17	$242,783	63
1993	30		2	17	$207,310	83
1994	30			5	$28,159	213
1995	24		1	15	$154,801	121
1996	27		3	19	$229,276	96

GUY BOROS

Born: Guy Donald Boros, September 4, 1964

Birthplace: Ft. Lauderdale, Fla.

Ht: 6' 2" **Wt:** 180

Joined Tour: 1990
1996 Money Rank: 75

Guy Boros notched his first PGA Tour victory in the inaugural 1996 Greater Vancouver Open. The win, worth $180,000, was Boros' only top 10 finish of the year; 17 in-the-money finishes, however, brought him $283,358. Boros fared better in 1995, notching four top 10 finishes to rank 62nd. Boros had a respectable rookie year in 1994, finishing in the top 10 four times, including a tied for third in the rain-shortened Deposit Guaranty Classic. Boros qualified in 1993 after playing four years on the Canadian Tour (where he notched two wins), two years on the Australian Tour, and one year (1993) on the Nike Tour.

Guy is the son of Julius Boros, the late two-time U.S. Open champion and popular Tour player. Guy was playing in the 1994 Southwestern Bell Colonial when his father died. After winning at Vancouver, Guy said: "Coming up the last hole, I thought about Dad. Hopefully, he was watching and was proud."

- Won the 1996 Greater Vancouver Open.

- Tied for third at the 1994 Deposit Guaranty Golf Classic (rain-shortened, 36 holes).

- Tied for fourth at the 1995 BellSouth Classic.

- Tied for fourth at the 1995 Buick Challenge.

- Tied for sixth at the 1995 AT&T Pebble Beach National Pro-Am.

- Won two Canadian Tour tournaments (1989 Atlantic Classic, 1991 B.C. Open).

YEAR	EVENTS	WINS	TOP 10	CUTS MADE	EARNINGS	RANK
1990	1					
1991	1					
1994	30		4	19	$240,775	76
1995	34	1	4	14	$303,654	62
1996	31	1	1	17	$283,358	75

MICHAEL BRADLEY

Born: Michael John Bradley, July 17, 1966
Birthplace: Largo, Fla.
Ht: 6' 0" **Wt:** 180
Residence: Valrico, Fla.
Q School: 1992
1996 Money Rank: 20th

Bradley, who lists pick-up basketball as one of his off-the-course pursuits, left the courts to the hoopsters in 1996 and fashioned the best year of his four-year career. The former two-time Oklahoma State All-American, who missed a month of the 1994 tour after injuring his elbow in a pick-up basketball game following the '94 Buick Open, won his first-ever Tour event in the rain-shortened 1996 Buick Challenge. He birdied the first playoff hole to defeat defending champion Fred Funk, John Maginnes, Davis Love III and Len Mattiace at Callaway Gardens in Pine Mountain, Georgia.

Bradley's impressive 1996 showings included a tie for second at the Doral-Ryder Open, a third-place finish at the Sprint International, and tie for third at the Michelob Championship at Kingsmill. A member of what some call the PGA's "youth brigade," Bradley has shown steady and determined progress each year of his career, moving up the Money List: 121st in 1993, 104th in 1994, 85th in 1995, and 18th in 1996. He finished in the money in 19 of the 26 events he entered in 1996, with six Top Ten finishes and a total of $766,825.

- Shot a 63 in the first round of the 1995 PGA Championship. The only previous first-round 63 in that event was carded by Ray Floyd in 1982.

- Before winning the Buick Challenge in '96, previous best career finish was a tie for third in the 1993 Kemper Open.

- In addition to his PGA Tour finishes, Bradley has won two Canadian Tour events, finished

52nd on the Austral/Asian Tour Order of Merit (1992) and once shot a 59 in the Willows Classic pro-am in Saskatoon, Saskatchewan.

- 1987-88 All-American at Oklahoma State.

YEAR	EVENTS	WINS	TOP 10	CUTS MADE	EARNINGS	RANK
1988	2			1	$1,664	281
1990	1					
1992	1					
1993	25		1	14	$126,160	121
1994	29		3	15	$175,137	104
1995	27		6	18	$214,469	85
1996	26	1	4	20	$820,825	20

MIKE BRISKY

Born: Michael Charles Brisky, May 28, 1965

Birthplace: Brownsville, Tex.

Ht: 6' 1" **Wt:** 185

Exempt Status: 92nd on 1995 money list

Q School: 1993, 1994

The best tournament of Brisky's career was the 1995 Buick Open: his four rounds in the 60's put him in a playoff with Woody Austin, but he lost on the first extra hole with a bogey. The Buick second-place paycheck ($129,600) more than doubled his career earnings. Brisky improved to 84th on the money list ranking in 1996, recording three Top 10 finishes, including a tie for 4th at the Motorola Western Open. Brisky tied for 14th place at the 1996 PGA Championship, his best finish in a major.

- Brisky's other 1996 Top 10s were a tie for 10th at the Greater Vancouver Open and a tie for 6th at the Canon Greater Hartford Open.

- Went back to the Qualifying Tournament after the 1994 season and regained his card by finishing 10th.

- Won the 1994 Nike Texarkana Open by 7 strokes.

- Nine Top 25 finishes in his career out of 34 cuts made.

YEAR	EVENTS	WINS	TOP 10	CUTS MADE	EARNINGS	RANK
1989	1					
1994	14			6	$38,713	200
1995	30		1	14	$194,874	92
1996	27		3	14	$260,360	84

MARK BROOKS

Born: Mark David Brooks, March 25, 1961

Birthplace: Fort Worth, Tex.

Ht: 5' 9" **Wt:** 150

Residence: Fort Worth, Tex.

Turned Professional: 1983

Q School: Fall 1983, 1984, 1985, 1987

1996 Money Rank: 3

A 14-year Tour pro and culinary enthusiast, Brooks cooked up the year of his career in 1996 by winning his first Major (the PGA championship in a playoff with Kenny Perry) to go along with victories in the Bob Hope Classic and the Shell Houston Open—finishing third overall in earnings with over $1.4 million.

The breakthrough year for Brooks, the father of two girls, almost occurred in 1995, when he narowly missed the playoff for the British Open, finishing third. He has four additional tour victories: the 1988 Canon Sammy Davis Jr. Greater Hartford Open; the 1991 Kmart Greater Greensboro Open; the 1991 Greater Milwaukee Open; and the 1994 Kemper Open.

A two-time All-American at the University of Texas, Brooks was introduced to golf by his grandfather at age eight. He hosts the Hall Brooks

Memorial Golf Tournament, an annual benefit for Brooks House, which provides counseling for teens. Both the tournament and the House were founded in memory of his father.

- In winning the PGA championship, took control of the playoff hole from the start with a drive down the center of the 18th fairway, the first sudden-death hole. Perry's drive found a miserable lie in the left rough and he pitched out with a wedge that also pulled to the left rough. Perry's third shot went over the green, and when his short pitch failed to reach the green, the match was all but over. Brooks, away with three putts to win, needed only two for a birdie four for the victory.

- Four regulation rounds included 23 birdies and 12 bogeys.

- PGA win made Brooks the third player from Fort Worth to win that championship, joining legendary greats Ben Hogan and Byron Nelson.

- In 1996, finished in the money in 22 of the 29 events entered.

- Does seem to have a flair for the dramatic. While winning the Greater Greensboro Open in 1991, fired an 8-under-par 64 on the final day to catch Gene Sauers, then defeated him on the third playoff hole. While recording his first Tour win in 1988, he sank a 10-foot birdie putt on a second extra hole for the win.

- Two-time All-American at University of Texas.

YEAR	EVENTS	WINS	TOP 10	CUTS MADE	EARNINGS	RANK
1983	6			2	$6,924	194
1984	35	1		17	$40,438	122
1985	32			11	$32,094	141
1986	32	1		19	$47,264	140
1987	32			17	$42,100	165
1988	30	1	2	22	$280,636	36
1989	30		1	15	$112,838	115
1990	33		5	23	$307,948	45
1991	30	2	5	24	$667,263	11
1992	29		11	24	$629,754	21
1993	31		3	19	$249,696	66
1994	33		4	23	$523,285	31
1995	29		3	17	$366,860	48
1996	31	3			$1,429,396	3

At the 1991 Las Vegas International, Mark Brooks teed up at the 17th hole in the third round, 12 under par. His tee shot landed in a tree. He needed only to find it to declare it unplayable (and not suffer a penalty stroke). He climbed the tree and found eight golf balls, but none were his, so he had to tee off again and ended up with a double-bogey 7.

OLIN BROWNE

Born: May 22, 1959

Ht: 5' 9" **Wt:** 175

Q School: 1995

Exempt Status:
8th in 1995 Q School

Belying the fact that his initials are common slang for "Out of Bounds," Browne tied for 10th in driving accuracy in 1996 (75.9% of fairways hit). After being off the tour in 1995, he bounced back in 1996 to finish 100th on the money list, with 3 Top 10 finishes and 20 cuts made in 27 events.

As winner of the 1993 Nike Monterrey (Mexico) Open, Browne pleased the crowd by giving his victory speech in Spanish. He attended Occidental College and has an interest in politics, giving him two things in common with 1996 Vice Presidential nominee Jack Kemp.

- Scored a rare double eagle at the 1994 Northern Telecom Open.

- Three Top 10 finishes in 1996: Greater Milwaukee Open (tied for 7th), Buick Open (tied for 7th), Michelob Championship at Kingsmill (tied for 9th).

YEAR	EVENTS	WINS	TOP 10	CUTS MADE	EARNINGS	RANK
1992					$84,152	84
1993					$2,738	290
1994					$101,580	154
1996	27			20	$223,703	100

BRAD BRYANT

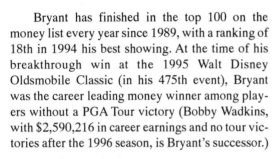

Born: Bradley Dub Bryant, December 11, 1954

Birthplace: Amarillo, Tex.

Ht: 5' 10" **Wt:** 170

Exempt Status 1995:
1995 Tournament Winner

Q School: 1978, 1987, 1988

Bryant has finished in the top 100 on the money list every year since 1989, with a ranking of 18th in 1994 his best showing. At the time of his breakthrough win at the 1995 Walt Disney Oldsmobile Classic (in his 475th event), Bryant was the career leading money winner among players without a PGA Tour victory (Bobby Wadkins, with $2,590,216 in career earnings and no tour victories after the 1996 season, is Bryant's successor.)

- Three Top 10 finishes in 1996: Buick Challenge (tied for 9th); Bob Hope Chrysler Classic (tied for 4th); Mercedes Championships (5th).

- Brother Bart Bryant is also a pro golfer.

- Led the tour in birdies in 1994 with 337.

- Nicknamed "Dr. Dirt" by CBS broadcaster Gary McCord.

- Tied for 7th in Greens in Regulation in 1996 (70.9%).

- After tying for 2nd at the 1982 Players Championship, he missed the cut in that event 5 of the next 6 years.

YEAR	EVENTS	WINS	TOP 10	CUTS MADE	EARNINGS	RANK
1978	11			7	$4,350	174
1979	29		5	21	$63,013	66
1980	32		3	24	$56,115	69
1981	29		3	19	$52,070	82
1982	29		4	18	$99,576	38
1983	30		2	20	$93,021	61
1984	31			16	$36,805	127
1985	16			2	$1,683	232
1986	20			8	$11,290	202
1987	7			4	$17,090	191
1988	26		2	15	$62,614	141
1989	32		1	22	$174,393	84
1990	31		5	15	$189,795	86
1991	29		1	9	$152,202	99
1992	33		3	26	$227,529	69
1993	30		3	21	$230,139	74
1994	32		6	25	$687,803	18
1995	31	1	5	20	$723,834	25
1996	27		3	17	$253,381	88

PATRICK BURKE

Born: Patrick Thomas Burke, March 17, 1962

Birthplace: Hollywood, Fla.

Ht: 5' 5" **Wt:** 165

1996 Money Rank: 79

Burke has been on the bubble for most of his PGA Tour career, but he will return to the Tour after having his best year in 1996. Though Burke finished in the top 10 just two times, he finished in the money in 14 tournaments to earn $265,083. In 1995, Burke also performed well, making the cut 16 times and earning $162,892 (ranking him 119th). 1995 marked the first time that Burke returned to the Tour without going through the Qualifying Tournament, as he did in 1989, 1991, and 1994.

In 1994, Burke did not play well on the PGA circuit, but he excelled on the Australian Tour. Burke won both the Victorian Open and the Optus Players Championship, the latter earning him a trip to the NEC World Series of Golf.

- Order of Merit earned him a berth in the 1995 British Open.

- Tied for sixth at the 1992 BellSouth Classic.

- Tied for seventh at the 1995 Walt Disney World/Oldsmobile Classic (rain-shortened, 54 holes).

- Won two Australian Tour tournaments (1994 Optus Players Championship, 1994 Victorian Open).

- Runner-up at the 1994 Alfred Dunhill Masters in Australia.

- Finished third in the 1994 Australian Order of Merit.

YEAR	EVENTS	WINS	TOP 10	CUTS MADE	EARNINGS	RANK
1990	23			3	$5,228	247
1992	28	1		19	$101,513	129
1993	17	1		11	$100,717	144
1994	10			2	$5,034	276
1995	24	1		16	$162,892	119
1996	24	2		14	$265,083	79

MARK CALCAVECCHIA

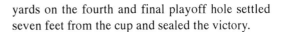

Born: June 12, 1960

Birthplace: Laurel, Neb.

Ht: 6' **Wt:** 200

Residence: West Palm Beach, Fla.

Q School: 1981, 1982, 1983

1996 Money Rank: 29

Fiery by nature, Calcaveccchia is capable of burying his putters as well as praising and naming them ("Billy," for example, is a favorite club). A golfing product of the University of Florida, Calcavecchia had the best year of his 16-year Tour career in 1995. He made his first 17 cuts and eight of his last 12, won the BellSouth Classic, narrowly missed making the Ryder Cup team, and enjoyed his biggest earnings year ever with $843,242.

In 1996, Calcavecchia finished in the money in 22 of 28 events, with six Top Ten results and a money total of $628,851. Calcavecchia's biggest career victory came in the 1989 British Open at Troon, where he defeated Wayne Grady and Greg Norman in a playoff. His five-iron shot from 190 yards on the fourth and final playoff hole settled seven feet from the cup and sealed the victory.

- Other career wins include the 1992 Phoenix Open; the 1989 Phoenix and Nissan Los Angeles opens; the 1988 Bank of Boston Classic; the 1987 Honda Classic, and the 1986 Southwest Golf Classic.

- Also has three international wins—the 1993 Argentine Open; the 1989 British Open, and the 1988 Australian Open.

- Was a playoff loser to Billy Mayfair in the 1993 Greater Milwaukee Open when Mayfair chipped in from 20 feet on the fourth extra hole.

- Tied for 7th in 1996 greens in regulation, achieving a 70.6% average.

- Has played on three Ryder Cup teams—1987, 1989 and 1991.

- Needed surgery in 1993 after a December skiing accident injured his knee (cartilage and ACL).

- First team All-SEC in 1979.

- Steve Elkington, who has partnered with Calcavecchia in the 1995 and 1996 Franklin Templeton Funds Shark Shootout team competition, stated "Mark has a different personality. He's very aggressive. Who knows what's going to happen? We may get into a fight or roll around on the ground."

YEAR	EVENTS	WINS	TOP 10	CUTS MADE	EARNINGS	RANK
1981	7			1	$404	313
1982	25		1	14	$25,064	135
1983	20		1	9	$16,313	161
1984	25		1	14	$29,660	140
1985	15			7	$15,997	162
1986	17		5	9	$155,012	58
1987	26	1	9	20	$522,398	10
1988	33	1	12	28	$751,912	6
1989	25	2	10	18	$807,741	5
1990	27		9	22	$834,281	7
1991	24		6	17	$323,621	50
1992	27	1	4	22	$377,234	39
1993	30		6	20	$630,366	21
1994	27		6	18	$533,201	30
1995	29	1	6	25	$843,552	13
1996	29		6	23	$628,851	29

JIM CARTER

Born: Jim Laver Carter,
June 24, 1961

Birthplace:
Spring Lake, N.C.

Ht: 6' 0" **Wt:** 175

Joined Tour: 1985

1996 Money Rank: 101

YEAR	EVENTS	WINS	TOP 10	CUTS MADE	EARNINGS	RANK
1985	1					
1987	32		1	20	$60,102	134
1988	30		5	19	$191,489	60
1989	32		6	22	$319,719	33
1990	32			12	$54,392	172
1991	7			1	$2,450	278
1993	1			1	$2,753	289
1994	1					
1995	30		1	19	$180,664	102
1996	32		2	25	$223,696	101

Jim Carter continued to make the most of his Tour comeback by earning $223,696 in 1996. Carter finished in the top 10 twice, including a tie for third at the 1996 Buick Open, following up a solid 1995, when he tied for third at the Anheuser-Busch Golf Classic and finished the year ranked 102nd.

Carter had an excellent year in 1989 when he earned $319,719 (ranking him 33rd) with six top 10 finishes. The next year, however, Carter fell to 172nd on the money list and lost his Tour Card. After four years (1991-1994) on the Nike Tour, Carter earned his return to the PGA Tour by ranking fourth on the 1994 Nike Tour money list, winning one tournament and finishing second in three others.

Carter capped a spectacular collegiate career at Arizona State University by winning the 1983 NCAA Championship. Arizona State honored Carter by inducting him into its Sports Hall of Fame in 1995.

- Tied for third at the 1989 AT&T Pebble Beach National Pro-Am.

- Tied for third at the 1995 Anheuser-Busch Golf Classic.

- Tied for third at the 1996 Buick Open.

- Shot a tournament record 11-under-par 61 during the second round of the 1989 Centel Classic.

- Won the 1994 Nike New Mexico Charity Classic.

- Won the 1983 NCAA Championship.

BRANDELL CHAMBLEE

Born: Brandell Eugene Chamblee, July 2, 1962

Birthplace: St. Louis, Mo.

Ht: 5' 10" **Wt:** 155

Exempt Status 1995:
86th on 1995 Money List

Q School: 1987, 1990, 1991, 1992

Chamblee has made steady progress up the money ranking list, improving every year from 1991 (163rd) to 1995 (86th), to go with a 94th place finish in 1996. In the 1990 inaugural season of the Hogan (now Nike) tour, Chamblee won the New England Classic as the only golfer under par. He had a strong NCAA career at the University of Texas, where he was a first-team All-American in 1983 (second-team in 1982 and 1984).

In an article he wrote for Golf World in 1995 detailing all of the free golf gear received by touring pros, Chamblee offered his slightly used golf shoes to readers. Due to the overwhelming response, Chamblee quickly became known as "8½ D".

- Two Top 10s in 1996: finished 2nd in the Bell-South Classic and tied for 10th in the Byron Nelson Classic.

- Led Texas to Southwest Conference Championship in 1983.

YEAR	EVENTS	WINS	TOP 10	CUTS MADE	EARNINGS	RANK
1983	1 (am)			1		
1984	1 (am)					
1985	1			1	$1,190	239
1987	4					
1988	29		1	10	$33,618	166
1989	4					
1991	30		1	12	$64,141	161
1992	28			15	$97,921	133
1993	29		2	13	$126,940	119
1994	27		1	20	$161,018	111
1995	25		3	13	$213,796	86
1996	22		2	10	$233,265	94

LENNIE CLEMENTS

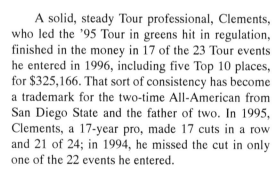

Born: Leonard Clyde Clements, January 20, 1957

Birthplace: Cherry Point, N.C.

Ht: 5' 8" **Wt:** 160

Residence: San Diego, Cal.

Q School: 1992

1996 Money Rank: 63

A solid, steady Tour professional, Clements, who led the '95 Tour in greens hit in regulation, finished in the money in 17 of the 23 Tour events he entered in 1996, including five Top 10 places, for $325,166. That sort of consistency has become a trademark for the two-time All-American from San Diego State and the father of two. In 1995, Clements, a 17-year pro, made 17 cuts in a row and 21 of 24; in 1994, he missed the cut in only one of the 22 events he entered.

Still, Clements is seeking his first Tour win (he did win the 1982 Timex Open in France). His closest call came at the 1994 Bob Hope Chrysler Classic, when he finished in a tie for second.

- In addition to that 1995 GIR title, ranked seventh in driving accuracy.

- Tied for 7th in driving accuracy in 1996 (76.2%).

- Top 10 finishes in 1996 were a tie for fifth at the Walt Disney World/Oldsmobile Classic; a tie for 10th at the Bellsouth Classic; a tie for fourth at the Freeport-McDermott; a tie for eighth at the Doral-Ryder Open; and a tie for third at the Buick Invitational of California.

- Best season of career came in 1994, when he finished 39th on the money list and posted six Top 10 finishes. Five of the Top 10s came in his first seven starts.

- Won the California High School Championship in 1975.

- Medalist at the 1979 California State Amateur and won 1979 Southwestern Amateur.

YEAR	EVENTS	WINS	TOP 10	CUTS MADE	EARNINGS	RANK
1980	1			1	$1,695	240
1981	24		1	12	$19,819	134
1982	23		2	12	$44,796	98
1983	29		1	14	$44,455	110
1984	31			13	$25,712	146
1985	24		1	16	$49,383	120
1986	28		4	19	$112,642	79
1987	25		3	15	$124,989	83
1988	33		3	21	$86,332	120
1989	29		1	13	$69,399	147
1990	29		1	12	$80,096	146
1991P	15			10	$62,827	163
1991N	6			5	$6,913	118
1992P	10			8	$30,121	198
1992N	13	1	6	12	$73,253	11
1993	25		2	16	$141,526	113
1994	22		6	21	$416,880	39
1995	24		4	21	$355,130	51
1996	24		1	17	$325,166	63

RUSS COCHRAN

Born: October 31, 1958

Birthplace: Paducah, Kan.

Ht: 6' **Wt:** 160

Q School: Fall 1982

1996 Money Rank: 62nd

A southpaw who started playing with ladies clubs as a youth because he couldn't find any lefties for his size, Cochran is a 14-year Tour veteran whose breakthrough year came in 1991, when he finished 10th on the money list. Things went downhill from there—46th, 59th, 77th and 131st, respectively, the next four years—until Cochran was forced back to Q School in '95, where he requalified for the 1996 Tour.

A graduate of the University of Kentucky and an ardent Wildcats hoops fan, Cochran, the father of four, bounced back in '96 to finish in the money in 14 of 26 events with two Top 10 finishes—a tie for fifth at the Greater Vancouver Open and second at the CVS Charity Classic—and $330,183 in prize money.

Cochran's oldest child, Ryan, scored a hole-in-one at age six, one of the youngest golfers ever to record an ace.

- Lone Tour victory came at the 1991 Centel Western Open.

- Best money finish came in '91, when he earned $684,851.

- Won two Tournament Players Series events in 1983—the Magnolia Classic and Greater Baltimore Open—finishing as the leading money winner and earning his PGA exemption for 1984.

- Won the 1975 Kentucky State High School Championships.

YEAR	EVENTS	WINS	TOP 10	CUTS MADE	EARNINGS	RANK
1983					$7,968	188
1984					$133,342	51
1985					$87,331	87
1986					$89,817	92
1987					$148,110	74
1988					$148,960	80
1989					$132,678	107
1990					$230,278	65
1991					$684,851	10
1992					$326,290	46
1993					$293,868	59
1994					$239,827	77
1995					$145,663	131
1996	28		1	14	$330,183	62

JOHN COOK

Born: John Neuman Cook, October 2, 1957

Birthplace: Toledo, Ohio

Ht: 6' **Wt:** 175

Residence: Rancho Mirage, Cal.

Q School: Fall 1979

1996 Money Rank: 19

A skiing enthusiast, Cook knows about doing downhill in golf, too. The career of the 17-year pro was headed that way in 1995 when Cook lingered above the cut line for most of the year, struggling with his game. In 26 events, Cook made only 16 cuts and finished 50th or worse seven times. Indeed, his earnings and money-list rank fell to their lowest levels since 1989, a season cut short by hand surgery. Only a rally at the end of the season—a tie for 15th at the Walt Disney and a 14th at the Las Vegas Invitational—gave him reason to hope.

But hope—and play on—he did, and Cook rebounded quite nicely in 1996 with a 26-under par that won the FedEX St. Jude Classic and gave him his first Tour win since 1992. A short time later, he became the fifth multiple winner on the 1996 PGA Tour with a three-stroke triumph at the CVS Charity Classic. All tolled, Cook finished in the money in 18 of 24 events, with five Top 10 finishes and a money total of $831,260. He finished 9th in greens in regulation (70%).

Born in Ohio, but raised in Southern California, Cook was convinced as a teen by Ohio State legends Jack Nicklaus and Tom Weiskopf to return to Ohio to golf for the Buckeyes in college. He became a three-time All-American there, helping the Buckeyes win the 1979 NCAA team championship.

- In addition to his two victories in 1996, finished eighth in the NEC World Series of Golf, ninth at the Sprint International, and tied for ninth at the Shell Houston Open.

- Cook's career victories include the 1992 Bob Hope Chrysler Classic (winning a five-man playoff with three birdies and an eagle over four holes), the 1992 United Airlines Hawaiian Open and the 1992 Las Vegas Invitational; the 1987 International; the 1983 Canadian Open (defeating Johnny Miller on the sixth playoff hole); and the 1981 Bing Crosby National Pro-Am (also in a five-man playoff).

- International wins include the 1995 Mexican Open and the 1982 Sao Paulo-Brazilian Open.

- Topped $1 million in earnings in 1992.

- Member of the 1993 Ryder Cup team.

- Teamed with Rex Caldwell to in 1983 World Cup.

- Won numerous amateur titles, including 1978 U.S. Amateur.

YEAR	EVENTS	WINS	TOP 10	CUTS MADE	EARNINGS	RANK
1980	30		2	19	$43,316	80
1981	30	1	3	23	$127,608	25
1982	28		3	21	$57,483	78
1983	28	1	7	27	$216,868	16
1984	28		1	20	$65,710	89
1985	29		1	17	$63,573	106
1986	30		6	20	$255,126	27
1987	32	1	6	19	$333,184	29
1988	29		2	21	$139,916	84
1989	12		1	6	$39,445	172
1990	27		4	20	$448,112	28
1991	25		8	21	$546,984	26
1992	21	3	8	18	$1,165,606	3
1993	23		5	19	$342,321	45
1994	24		6	16	$429,725	37
1995	27		1	17	$186,977	97
1996	26	2	5	19	$831,260	19

FRED COUPLES

Born: Frederick Stephen Couples, October 13, 1959

Birthplace: Seattle, Wash.

Ht: 5' 11" **Wt:** 185

Residence: Dallas, Tex.

Q School: Fall 1980

1996 Money Rank: 6

Couples is one of America's greatest and most volatile golf talents. Since turning pro in 1980, Couples has already totaled 12 PGA Tour victories (the latest being the 1996 Player's Championship), with the 1992 Masters the jewel in his crown. His strength is obviously his driving, for which he has earned the nickname "Boom Boom." He was third in average driving distance (285 yards) in 1996 and was the only golfer to win a million dollars while playing in less than 20 Tour events (he competed in 17).

Introduced to golf by his father, who worked in the Seattle Parks and Recreation Department, Couples had an off year in 1995 by his standards, but still managed to win the Dubai Classic and the Skins Game and missed only three cuts in 17 events while amassing $567,760 in PGA Tour earnings. He bounced back big in 1996, finishing in the money in 15 of the 17 events he entered—eight times in the Top 10—and earned $1.2 million.

Couples lists tennis, antiques, bicyling and vintage cars as his special interests and was a golfing teammate of CBS-TV sportcaster Jim Nantz at the University of Houston. His career year was 1992, when he won the Masters and more than $1.3 million in earnings and was named PGA Tour Player of the Year for the second consecutive year.

- Top 10 finishes in 1996 included: tied for 8th at the Las Vegas Invitational; tied for sixth at the Buick Challenge; tied for 7th at the British Open; fourth at the Mastercard Colonial; tied for fifth at the Bellsouth Classic; tied for second at the Nissan Open, and tied for seventh at the Bob Hope Chrysler Classic.

- In addition to '96 Player's and '92 Masters wins, victories include: the 1994 Buick Open; the 1993 Honda Classic; the 1992 Nissan Los Angeles Open and Nestle Invitational; the 1991 Federal Express St. Jude Classic and B.C. Open; the 1990 Nissan Los Angeles Open; the 1987 Byron Nelson Golf Classic; the 1984 Tournament Players Championship and the 1983 Kemper Open.

- International wins include: the 1995 Dubai Desert Classic and Johnnie Walker Classic; the 1994 World Cup; the 1991 Johnnie Walker World Championship.

- Began 1995 with back-to-back wins on the PGA European Tour, the first American since Charles Coody in 1975 to perform that feat.

- In 1996 Couples ranked 2nd in average strokes per round (69.57), 1st in average birdies per round (4.20), and first in greens in regulation (71.8% average).

- First Tour win came in a five-man playoff at the 1983 Kemper Open.

- Back problems, which have interrupted two seasons, diagnosed as the closing of the space between a disc and the spinal cord.

YEAR	EVENTS	WINS	TOP 10	CUTS MADE	EARNINGS	RANK
1981	25		4	19	$78,939	53
1982	28		2	18	$77,606	54
1983	30	1	7	23	$209,733	19
1984	26	1	9	24	$334,573	7
1985	26		7	23	$171,272	38
1986	26		1	16	$116,065	76
1987	27	1	9	21	$441,025	19
1988	27		10	25	$489,822	21
1989	24		9	21	$653,944	11
1990	22	1	9	17	$757,999	9
1991	21	2	9	20	$791,749	3
1992	22	3	12	20	$1,344,188	1
1993	19	1	9	17	$796,579	10
1994	15	1	4	15	$625,654	23
1995	15		4	12	$299,259	63
1996	18	1	2	16	$1,248,694	6

BEN CRENSHAW

Born: Ben Daniel Crenshaw, January 11, 1952

Birthplace: Austin, Tex.

Ht: 5' 9" **Wt:** 165

Joined Tour: 1973

1996 Money Rank: 119

In winning the 1995 Masters, Ben Crenshaw produced one of golf's most poignant memories. Just days after serving as pallbearer at the funeral of Harvey Penick, his friend and childhood mentor, Crenshaw played four rounds of brilliant golf; Penick's inspiration was his 15th club, he would say later. Upon clinching a one-stroke victory on Augusta's 18th green, Crenshaw collapsed in tears into the arms of his caddie. It was a career moment, yet Crenshaw has provided PGA Tour fans many more memories. The golfer nicknamed "Gentle Ben" for his even demeanor has won 19 PGA Tour events and ranks 10th on the all-time PGA money list.

Ben Crenshaw's first experience on a golf course came at age nine, when his father took him to the Austin (Texas) Country Club. Golf pro Harvey Penick took Ben out on a fairway, about 100 yards from the green, gave him a club, and told the youngster, who was already showing great talent as a little league baseball player, to hit the ball. Crenshaw hit it on to the green.

"That's fine, Ben," said Penick. "Now let's go up and see you knock it in the hole."

"Golly, Mr. Penick," replied Ben, confused, "why didn't you tell me that in the first place." Ben took another shot from the fairway and it landed in the cup.

Crenshaw had a spectacular collegiate golfing career at the University of Texas, where he won the NCAA championship three times (1971, 1972, and 1973). After an equally stellar amateur career, Crenshaw won the first tournament he entered as a PGA Tour pro—the 1973 San Antonio-Texas Open. Many great seasons followed. In 1976, Crenshaw won three tournaments, finished in the money 27 times out of 28 events (14 times in the top 10), and ranked second in earnings. In 1979, he finished in the top 10 nine times and ranked fifth. He followed in 1980 by finishing in the money in 24 events out of 26 entered and again placed fifth on the money list. In 1984, Crenshaw won his first Masters, by two strokes over Tom Watson. Then in 1987, Crenshaw again finished in the top 10 fourteen times to win $638,194, ranking him third among golfers.

A man with a reverence for the sport of golf, Crenshaw passionately studies both golf history and golf course architecture. He will serve as a golf analyst for CBS Sports for at least 10 events in 1997.

- Won 19 PGA Tour tournaments.

- Holds 10th place in all-time PGA career earnings.

- Received The Bob Jones Award (United States Golf Association's highest award) in 1991.

- Won the 1995 Masters Tournament.

- Won the 1984 Masters Tournament.
- Tied for third at the 1975 U.S. Open.
- Tied for second at the 1978 and 1979 British Open Championships.
- Finished second at the 1979 PGA Championship.
- Won the 1983 Byron Nelson Classic.
- Won the 1973 San Antonio-Texas Open (his first PGA tournament as a pro).
- Played on the 1981, 1983, 1987, and 1995 Ryder Cup teams.
- Won the 1971, 1972, and 1973 NCAA Championships.
- Also profiled in Course Designer section.

YEAR	EVENTS	WINS	TOP 10	CUTS MADE	EARNINGS	RANK
1973	5	1	3	5	$76,749	34
1974	27		6	22	$71,065	32
1975	28		6	20	$63,528	32
1976	28	3	14	27	$257,759	2
1977	24	1	6	19	$123,841	16
1978	27		5	24	$108,305	21
1979	25	2	9	20	$236,769	5
1980	26	1	10	24	$237,727	5
1981	25		9	20	$151,038	20
1982	22		2	15	$54,277	84
1983	21	1	9	18	$275,474	7
1984	24	1	9	20	$270,989	16
1985	22			8	$25,814	149
1986	26	2	5	22	$388,169	8
1987	24	1	14	19	$638,194	3
1988	26	1	8	25	$696,895	8
1989	23		5	18	$443,095	21
1990	21	1	2	15	$351,193	33
1991	21		4	10	$224,563	75
1992	24	1	4	19	$439,071	31
1993	22	1	1	15	$318,605	51
1994	24	1	6	20	$659,252	21
1995	23	1	4	17	$737,475	23
1996	18		1	11	$176,857	119

JOHN DALY

Born: John Patrick Daly, April 28, 1966

Birthplace: Carmichael, Cal.

Ht: 5' 11" **Wt:** 175

Joined Tour: 1989

1996 Money Rank: 121

John Daly, the longest driving pro on the PGA Tour (288.8 average yard per drive in 1996—more than two yards on average longer than anyone else), belongs to elite company. Along with Jack Nicklaus, Tom Watson, and Johnny Miller, Daly won two major tournaments before he turned 30. Unfortunately, Daly's play has suffered as he struggles to overcome alcoholism. In 1996, Daly finished in the top 10 once and earned $173,557. Daly had raised hopes in 1995 that his brilliant game was returning. Though he also finished in the top 10 only once, that finish was a win in the British Open, where Daly beat a hard-charging Costantino Rocca in a four-hole playoff.

Daly first wowed galleries as a last-second fill-in who won the 1991 PGA Championship. As the ninth and last alternate in the field, Daly saw the Crooked Stick course for the first time in the opening round. He toured it with a round of 69, then went on to win by three strokes over Bruce Lietzke. Daly also finished third in the 1991 Tour Championship to rank 17th for the year; as a result, he was named PGA Tour Rookie of the Year. But after a solid 1992, when he won the B.C. Open, Daly's game slipped because of his alcohol problems. In early 1994, Daly served a PGA Tour suspension, and in mid-1995, Daly suffered headaches related to his rehabilitation.

Daly remains a crowd favorite, particularly for his long driving. His 289.0 yard average in 1995 was the longest since the Tour started keeping records in 1980.

- Won the 1995 British Open.
- Won the 1991 PGA Championship.
- Won the 1994 BellSouth Classic.
- Won the 1992 B.C. Open.
- Tied for third at the 1993 Masters Tournament.
- Finished third at the 1991 THE TOUR Championship.
- Won the 1990 AECI Charity Classic (Africa).

- Won the 1990 Hollard Royal Swazi Sun Classic (Africa).

- Won the 1990 Utah Classic (NIKE TOUR).

YEAR	EVENTS	WINS	TOP 10	CUTS MADE	EARNINGS	RANK
1986	1					
1989	6			3	$14,689	200
1990	3			2	$10,000	230
1991	33	1	4	21	$574,783	17
1992	25	1	5	15	$387,455	37
1993	24		1	15	$225,591	76
1994	17	1	3	9	$340,034	49
1995	23	1	1	15	$321,748	57
1996	23		1	14	$173,557	121

- Regained his card after a poor 1994 performance by finishing 20th in his return trip to the Qualifying Tournament.

- Other two Tops 10 finishes: Buick Challenge (tied for 6th) and the CVS Charity Classic (tied for 4th).

YEAR	EVENTS	WINS	TOP 10	CUTS MADE	EARNINGS	RANK
1986	1			1	$2,080	249
1990	2			1	$2,154	272
1991	29		2	12	$96,756	137
1992	28		2	14	$113,464	123
1993	32		1	21	$120,462	124
1994	30		1	13	$121,025	139
1995	25		2	14	$261,214	71
1996	27		3	17	$259,326	82

MARCO DAWSON

Born: Marco Thomas Dawson, November 17th, 1963

Birthplace: Freising, Germany

Ht: 6' **Wt:** 195

Exempt Status: 71st on 1995 Money List

Q School: 1990, 1991, 1994

Dawson had his best year in 1995 when he finished 71st on the money list ($251,214), largely on the strength of a second place finish in the Greater Milwaukee Open and a tie for 6th at the Anheuser-Busch Classic. Defying all statistical odds, in 1995 Dawson ranked 166th in 3rd round scoring average and 1st in final round scoring average.

In 1996, Dawson had 3 Top 10 finishes, including a tie for third at the Buick Invitational. Dawson was the Florida Southern University teammate of both Lee Janzen and Rocco Mediate.

- Finished 33rd in 1996 Players Championship.

- Career low round of 61 in 1991 Chattanooga Classic.

GLEN DAY

Born: Glen Edward Day, November 16, 1965

Birthplace: Mobile, Ala.

Ht: 5' 10" **Wt:** 170

Joined Tour: 1994

1996 Money Rank: 73

Day hopes to regain the form of his stellar 1994 rookie year, when he earned $357,236 to rank 45th on the money list. Day had four top 10 finishes that year, including a second at the 1994 Anheuser-Busch Golf Classic. Day's play fell off in 1995, as he made 15 cuts in 32 events, finished only once in the top 10, and dropped to 91st on the money list. In 1996, however, Day rose to 73rd on the money list with $298,131 in earnings. He will return to the 1997 PGA Tour after finishing in the money 19 times, including a tied for fourth finish at the 1996 Motorola Western Open.

For Day, golf is often a family affair. Day's grandfather helped launch his pro career by co-signing a $20,000 loan. Day's father-in-law, Bob Ralston, competed against him in the 1995 FedEx St. Jude Classic. And whenever Day plays, a picture of his daughter, Whitney, is always clipped to his hat. Day sports an excellent short game, finishing fourth in 1996 in putting (1.744 per hole) and fourth in sand saves (63.2%).

- Finished second at the 1994 Anheuser-Busch Golf Classic.

- Finished tied for fourth, 1996 Motorola Western Open.

- Finished tied for seventh, 1995 Las Vegas Invitational.

- Finished tied for 15th, 1994 PGA Championship.

- Won the 1990 Benson & Hedges Malaysian Open.

YEAR	EVENTS	WINS	TOP 10	CUTS MADE	EARNINGS	RANK
1994	30		4	18	$357,236	45
1995	32		1	15	$201,809	91
1996	26		2	19	$298,131	73

DAVID DUVAL

Born: David Robert Duval, November 9, 1971

Birthplace: Jacksonville, Fla.

Ht: 6' **Wt:** 195

Residence: Ponte Vedra Beach, Fla.

1996 Money Rank: 10

If Duval's performance during his 1995 rookie year was, as some have noted, just short of miraculous, with second-place finishes at the AT&T National Pro-Am, the Bob Hope Chrysler Classic, and the Memorial, 1996 was a continuation. Duval finished second at the Bell Canadian Open, tied for second at the Memorial (again!), finished third at the Byron Nelson Classic and Shell Houston Open, tied for third at the Bellsouth Classic, and tied for fourth at the Players Championship. He finished in the money in 15 of the 23 events he entered.

The son and nephew of golf pros and one of three collegians to have been four-time Division I All-Americans (Phil Mickelson and Gary Hallberg were the others), Duval, who played collegiately at Georgia Tech, set a record for rookie earnings in 1995 with $881,436. Ernie Els had held the record at $684,440.

Duval began 1995 No. 437 on the Sony Ranking and made the fastest climb in history into the Top 50. He lists mountain biking and reading as his special interests.

- Finished 10th on the 1996 Money List, winning just over one million dollars, and tied for 6th in average birdies per round (3.93).

- Best Tour ranking in 1995 was fourth in all-around statistics; worst was a tie for 86th in driving accuracy. Finished ninth in total driving.

- Donated $5,000 check for winning the Bell-South Merrill Lynch Shoot-Out to Atlanta Golf Association.

- Was 1993 collegiate Player of the Year.

- Was American Junior Golf Association Player of the Year in 1989.

YEAR	EVENTS	WINS	TOP 10	CUTS MADE	EARNINGS	RANK
1993	5			4	$27,181	201
1993N	9	2	5	8	$85,882	11
1994	6		1	4	$44,006	195
1994N	22		10	17	$126,430	8
1995	26		8	20	$881,436	11
1996	23			16	$977,079	10

DAVID EDWARDS

Born: David Wayne Edwards, April 18, 1956

Birthplace: Neosho, Mo.

Ht: 5' 8" **Wt:** 165

Joined Tour: 1979

1996 Money Rank: 106

Edwards has been a consistent performer throughout his 18 PGA Tours, as consistent as his ability to land drives in the fairway: he finished third in that statistic in 1996 with a 77.5% accuracy rate. Edwards made the cut in 16 events and earned $201,974 in 1996. His play has fallen off since 1993, however, when he ranked 20th with $653,086 in earnings. His six top 10 finishes that year included a playoff victory over Rick Fehr in the 1993 MCI Heritage Classic. In 1992, Edwards ended an eight-year winless drought with a two-stroke victory in the 1992 Memorial Tournament, and finished the year ranked 27th on the money list.

After a splendid collegiate career, where he won the 1978 NCAA championship at Oklahoma State University, Edwards immediately made his mark as a pro. In 1980, he teamed with his brother Danny to win the 1980 Walt Disney World National Team Championship. In 1984, Edwards finished in the money 15 times in 19 events (including a win in the 1984 Los Angeles Open) to rank 23rd. Throughout the 1980s and 1990s, Edwards was consistent at finishing in the money—and often in the top 10.

You'll seldom find Edwards seated in a commercial jet; Edwards is an avid pilot who flies his own plane to most tournaments. He also has keen interests in cars, motorcycles, and radio-controlled miniature cars.

- Won the 1980 Walt Disney World National Team Championship (with Danny Edwards).

- Won the 1984 Los Angeles Open.

- Won the 1992 Memorial Tournament.

- Won the 1993 MCI Heritage Classic.

- Tied for third at the 1984 Masters Tournament.

- Tied for 11th at the 1993 U.S. Open.

- Won the 1978 NCAA Championship.

YEAR	EVENTS	WINS	TOP 10	CUTS MADE	EARNINGS	RANK
1979	27		4	18	$44,456	88
1980	28	1	4	12	$35,810	96
1981	27		4	17	$68,211	65
1982	21		4	13	$49,896	91
1983	25		5	18	$114,037	48
1984	19	1	5	15	$236,061	23
1985	26			12	$21,506	157
1986	24		4	16	$122,079	71
1987	21		3	14	$148,217	73
1988	23		1	16	$151,513	76
1989	27		2	17	$238,908	57
1990	22		4	13	$166,028	95
1991	27		5	20	$396,695	38
1992	26	1	4	21	$515,070	27
1993	21	1	6	17	$653,086	20
1994	23		6	20	$458,845	34
1995	22		2	15	$225,857	83
1996	24		2	16	$201,974	106

JOEL EDWARDS

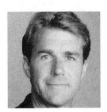

Born: November 22, 1961
Birthplace: Dallas, Tex.
Ht: 6' **Wt:** 165
Exempt Status: 149th on 1995 money list
Q School: 1988, 1989, 1990, 1995

Edwards had the best year of his career in 1996 after a trip to the Q School in 1995. He finished 90th on the money list rankings, his first time in the Top 100, and had two Top 10 finishes: a tie for 4th at the Freeport-McDermott Classic, and a tie for 6th at the Canon Greater Hartford Open. His career best finish is a tie for 2nd Place at the 1992 B.C. Open.

- 20 cuts made out of 27 events entered in 1996.

YEAR	EVENTS	WINS	TOP 10	CUTS MADE	EARNINGS	RANK
1989					$46,851	167
1990					$109,808	132
1991					$106,820	131
1992					$107,264	126
1993					$150,623	106
1994					$139,141	127
1995	31		1	16	$114,285	149
1996	27		2	20	$248,450	90

STEVE ELKINGTON

Born: Stephen John Elkington, December 8, 1962
Birthplace: Inverell, Australia

Ht: 6' 2" **Wt:** 190

Residence: Sydney, Australia and Houston, Tex.

Q School: Fall 1986

1996 Money Rank: 42

Reputed to have one of the most beautiful, fluid swings in golf, Elkington, a native of Australia with six Tour victories under his belt, has struggled on and off with medical ailments, most stemming from sinus problems which required surgery and a subsequent layoff during the 1994 season. Elkington won the PGA Championship in 1995, coming from six strokes down on the final day. He trailed Ernie Els going into the final round, but shot 31 going out and finished with a 64, forcing a playoff with Colin Montgomerie. He sank a 25-foot birdie putt to win.

In 1996, Elkington finished in the money in 15 of 21 events (earning $459,637), with five Top 10 finishes: tied for third at the PGA Championship, missing the playoff by an agonizingly unfaithful ten-foot putt; tied for eighth at the Motorola Western Open; tied for second at the Buick Classic, and tied for tenth at the Byron Nelson Classic and the Nissan Open. Elkington's boyhood hero was fellow Australian golfer Bruce Devlin, now on the Senior Tour. While attending college at the University of Houston, Elkington worked as an usher at The Summit sports arena. His hobbies include hunting, gardening, and character drawings.

- Ranked second on the 1995 PGA statistics both for scoring and sand saves.

- Other Tour wins include; the 1994 Buick Southern Open; the 1992 Infiniti Tournament of Champions; the 1991 Players Championship, and the 1990 Kmart Greater Greensboro Open.

- Lone international win came at the Australian Open in 1992.

- Made all 23 cuts in 1993.

- Rallied from seven strokes back for his first Tour victory at the 1990 Kmart Greater Greensboro Open.

Steve Elkington was penalized a stroke for picking a piece of grass and chewing on it while competing in the 1992 Swedish Open.

- Two-time All-American at Houston.

- Member of 1984 and 1985 NCAA championship teams.

- One of four PGA champion members at Champions GC in Houston, with Jack Burke, Jr., Jay Hebert and Dave Marr.

- Clubs were stolen in January 1996, contributing to his slow start: "I was disoriented for a few months."

YEAR	EVENTS	WINS	TOP 10	CUTS MADE	EARNINGS	RANK
1985	5			5	$9,897	180
1986	5			3	$12,705	194
1987	35		2	19	$75,738	118
1988	29		2	19	$149,972	79
1989	29		3	21	$231,062	61
1990	26	1	4	24	$548,564	18
1991	28	1	4	17	$549,120	25
1992	24	1	9	21	$746,352	12
1993	23		8	23	$675,383	17
1994	20	1	2	15	$294,943	62
1995	21	2	7	16	$1,254,352	5
1996	20			16	$459,637	42

ERNIE ELS

Born: Theodore Ernest Els, October 17, 1969

Birthplace: Johannesburg, South Africa

Ht: 6' 3" **Wt:** 210

Residence: Orlando, Fla.

Turned pro: 1989

Joined Tour: 1994

1996 Money Rank: 14

Els, an accomplished junior tennis player who turned his sole focus to golf at age 14, is, arguably, the world's most talented young player. The 1994 PGA Tour Rookie of the Year possesses one of the most faultless total games in recent memory and is already being compared to some of the game's all-time greats. Els missed only four cuts in 1995 and had eight top 10 finishes.

In 1996, after winning the Buick Classic, where he shot an even-par 71 on the final day and and cruised to an eight-stroke victory, he accomplished what no other golfing great has done—he became the first player to capture the World Matchplay title for a third successive year. Fellow pros on the same cusp—Gary Player in 1967, Hale Irwin in 1976 and Seve Ballesteros twice, in 1983 and 1986—had failed to achieve the feat.

Els, who began playing golf at age nine and completed 22 months of mandatory military service in the South African Army in 1988-89, was introduced in dramatic fashion to U.S. fans when he won the 1994 U.S. Open in a playoff over Loren Roberts and Colin Montgomerie.

- In 1996, finished in the money in 16 of 20 events, with the win at the Buick Classic and four other Top 10 finishes: tied for second at the British Open; tied for fifth at the U.S. Open; tied for sixth at the Memorial; tied for eighth at the Players Championship.

- Other Tour win was the 1995 GTE Byron Nelson Classic, where his 263 broke Sam Snead's 1957 tournament record by one stroke.

- Also in '95, after tieing for 13th at the Memorial and for 11th at the British Open, had three consecutive top three finishes.

- Other wins include the 1995 Lexington South African PGA Championship; 1995 Toyota World Match Play Championship; 1994 Dubai Desert Classic, Toyota World Match Play Championship, Johnnie Walker World Championship and Gene Sarazen World Open; 1993 Dunlop Phoenix Tournament, 1992 Protea Assurance South Africa Open, Lexington PGA Championship, South African Masters, Hollard Royal Swazi Sun Classic, First National Bank Players' Championship and Goodyear Classic.

- Best 1995 Tour statistical ranking was a tie for third in scoring; best 1996 ranking was sixth for average strokes per round, 69.77.

- At the end of his sensational rookie year, was ranked in the Top 20 of four of the world's tours—the PGA, the European Tour, the Austral/Asian Tour, and the South African Tour.

- In 1993, became the first player in the history of the British Open to record four rounds in the 60s.

- In 1992, became the only player besides Gary Player to win South African Open, South African PGA Championship and South African Masters in the same year.

YEAR	EVENTS	WINS	TOP 10	CUTS MADE	EARNINGS	RANK
1990	1					
1991	1			1	$2,647	274
1991N	8		1	5	$6,143	123
1992	3		2		$18,420	213
1993	6		1	2	$38,185	190
1994	11	1	4	10	$684,440	19
1995	18	1	6	14	$842,590	14
1996	18	1	5	17	$906,944	14

BRAD FABEL

Born: November 30th, 1955

Birthplace: Louisville, Ken.

Ht: 6' **Wt:** 195

Exempt Status: 10th on 1995 Nike Tour money list

Q School: N/A

In 1996, Fabel won the most money of any year of his career, placing 97th on the money list. He also had two Top 10 finishes in 1996. Taking a mid-career break from the PGA Tour, Fabel played the Nike Tour part-time in 1994 and full-time in 1995. His highest ranking on the money list occurred in 1992, when he placed 71st. His best career finish is a tie for 2nd at the 1990 Greater Hartford Open.

- Won two events on the Nike Tour, the 1994 Gateway Classic and the 1995 Shreveport Open.

- Won the 1974 Kentucky State Amateur Tournament.

YEAR	EVENTS	WINS	TOP 10	CUTS MADE	EARNINGS	RANK
1985					$74,425	100
1986					$25,634	165
1987					$90,024	104
1988					$112,093	101
1989					$69,823	146
1990					$165,876	96
1991					$147,562	103
1992					$220,495	71
1993					$59,672	175
1994					$33,812	205
1996	27	2		18	$227,648	97

NICK FALDO

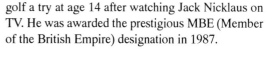

Born: Nicholas Alexander Faldo, July 18, 1957

Birthplace: Welwyn Garden City, England

Ht: 6' 3" **Wt:** 195

Residence: Orlando, Fla. and Windlesham, England

Turned professional: 1976

1996 Money Rank: 12

Considered one of the game's finest technicians, Faldo has won six Majors. He may be forever linked with Greg Norman's fateful collapse on the final day of the 1996 Masters, when The Shark lost a six-shot lead and Faldo played a masterful round of 67, finishing the tournament at 12-under and earning his third green jacket. His previous Masters win were in 1989 and 1990, and he has also won the British Open three times, 1987, 1990, and 1992.

In addition to his Majors titles, Faldo, whose off-the-fairway interests include fly fishing and flying helicopters, has won the 1995 Doral/Ryder Open, the 1984 Sea Pines Heritage Classic and 31 international tournaments dating back to 1977, when he was barely 20 years old. Faldo decided to give golf a try at age 14 after watching Jack Nicklaus on TV. He was awarded the prestigious MBE (Member of the British Empire) designation in 1987.

In 1996 Faldo won close to a million dollars while competing in only 17 PGA events. He ranked 2nd in driving accuracy (78%), 8th in putting (1.748 per hole), and 9th in average stokes per round (69.92).

- Best ranking in the 1995 Tour statistics was a tie for ninth place in driving accuracy.

- 1996 performance included 13 money finishes, the Masters win, and six other finishes in the Top 10: a tie for 10th at the NEC World Series of Golf; 9th at the Sprint International; fourth at the British Open; a tie for ninth at the Honda Classic; a tie for eighth at the Buick Invitational of California, and a tie for second at the Mercedes Championships.

- Finished second to Norman at the 1993 British Open: led after two rounds and tied for the lead with Corey Pavin after three, before losing to Norman by two strokes.

- Finished third to Paul Azinger in the 1993 PGA championship.

- In 1990 became the first foreign golfer to win the PGA Player of the Year award.

- Lost to Curtis Strange on a playoff at the 1988 U.S. Open.

- Won the British PGA Championship in 1978-80-81.

- Had 11 Top 10 finishes in 16 European Tour starts in 1983, compiling a 69.03 stroke average.

- Was the 1977 European Tour Rookie of the Year.

- His 1977 Ryder Cup victory over Tom Watson at Royal Lytham was the highlight of the beginning of his career.

- Won 1975 British Youths Amateur and English Amateur Championships.

YEAR	EVENTS	WINS	TOP 10	CUTS MADE	EARNINGS	RANK
1979	2			2	$2,613	214
1981	12		2	10	$35,349	102
1982	15		2	14	$56,667	80
1983	13		2	8	$67,851	79
1984	19	1	4	14	$166,845	38
1985	17		2	13	$54,060	117
1986	16		1	9	$52,965	135
1987	6		1	5	$36,281	169
1988	9		3	7	$179,120	64
1989	16	1	2	14	$327,981	31
1990	7	1	2	7	$345,262	37
1991	7		2	7	$127,156	117
1992	7		4	6	$345,168	42
1993	6		2	6	$188,886	91
1994	9		2	6	$221,146	83
1995	19	1	6	17	$790,961	19
1996	16	1	7	14	$942,641	12

BRAD FAXON, JR.

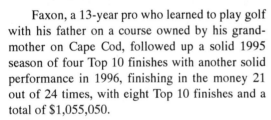

Born: Bradford John Faxon, Jr., August 1, 1961

Birthplace: Oceanport, N.J.

Ht: 6' 1" **Wt:** 170

Residence: Barrington, R.I.

Q School: Fall 1983

1996 Money Rank: 8th

Faxon, a 13-year pro who learned to play golf with his father on a course owned by his grandmother on Cape Cod, followed up a solid 1995 season of four Top 10 finishes with another solid performance in 1996, finishing in the money 21 out of 24 times, with eight Top 10 finishes and a total of $1,055,050.

His Top Ten finishes in 1996 included a tie for sixth at the Buick Challenge; second at the Sprint International; eighth at the Canon Greater Hartford Open; a tie for sixth at the Buick Classic; a tie for sixth at the Memorial; a tie for second at the Kemper Open; and second at the United Airlines Hawaiian Open. Faxon graduated in 1983 from Furman University with a degree in economics and is the father of three girls; he left the course during the second round of the Greater Milwaukee Open in 1995 to be with his wife, Bonnie, who was in labor with their third child, Sophie Lee.

- Over the last two years, has finished in the money 40 out of 48 times.
- Best 1995 Tour statistical rating was fifth, in putting; worst was a tie for 124th in total driving.
- Has four Tour Wins—the New England Classic and The International in 1992; the 1991 Buick Open, and the 1986 Provident Classic.
- Has one international win—the 1993 Heineken Australian Open.
- Slowed by rib cage injury in 1993.
- Lost 1992 playoffs at the Tournament of Champions and the Buick Open.
- Winner of 1983 Fred Haskins, Golf Magazine, and NCAA coaches Awards as nation's outstanding collegiate player.
- 1982-83 All-American.

YEAR	EVENTS	WINS	TOP 10	CUTS MADE	EARNINGS	RANK
1983	8		1	5	$16,526	160
1984	32		2	19	$71,688	82
1985	31		1	15	$46,813	124
1986	34	1	1	16	$92,716	90
1987	28		2	19	$113,534	90
1988	29		3	15	$162,656	74
1989	28		2	20	$222,076	63
1990	28		3	16	$197,118	81
1991	28	1	4	23	$422,088	34
1992	26	2	7	20	$812,093	8
1993	25		4	20	$312,023	55
1994	25		6	23	$612,847	24
1995	25		5	19	$471,887	37
1996	22		8	22	$1,055,050	8

RICK FEHR

Born: Richard Elliott Fehr August 28, 1962

Birthplace: Seattle, Wash.

Ht: 5' 11" **Wt:** 170

Joined Tour: 1985

1996 Money Rank: 78

Fehr continues to climb from the second valley in his pro career. In 1996, Fehr made the cut 14 times to earn $273,187 (ranking him 78th among golfers), a considerable improvement over 1995, when he ranked 126th. Before his 1995 fade, Fehr's play was outstanding. Between 1991 and 1994, Fehr won one tournament (the 1994 Walt Disney World/Oldsmobile Classic) and finished second in seven others. In 1993, he was in the money in 23 out of 26 events to earn $556,322 (ranking 28th). Fehr followed up in 1994 by ranking 27th.

Fehr had early success as a pro. In 1986, he finished in the money 20 times (including a win in the 1986 B.C. Open) to rank 61st. But Fehr's play dropped off in 1988 and 1989 (when he ranked 130th and 131st, respectively) before it came back to life in the 1990s.

An outstanding youth golfer, Fehr won the 1979 Washington State Junior and 1979 PGA National Junior Championships before becoming a two-time All-American at Brigham Young University.

- Won the 1994 Walt Disney World/Oldsmobile Classic.

- Won the 1986 B. C. Open.

- Finished second at the 1994 Sprint International.

- Finished second at the 1991 and 1993 Federal Express St. Jude Classic.

- Finished second at the 1992 and 1993 Bob Hope Chrysler Classic.

- Finished second at the 1992 Memorial Tournament.

- Finshed sixth at the 1993 THE TOUR Championship.

- Finished tied for ninth at the 1985 U.S. Open.

- Member of the 1983 Walker Cup team.

YEAR	EVENTS	WINS	TOP 10	CUTS MADE	EARNINGS	RANK
1985	15		1	11	$40,101	133
1986	28	1	4	20	$151,162	61
1987	24		3	8	$106,808	94
1988	28		1	11	$79,080	130
1989	21		1	16	$93,142	131
1990	28		2	17	$149,867	105
1991	26		3	14	$288,983	55
1992	26		4	18	$433,003	33
1993	26		6	23	$556,322	28
1994	25	1	4	16	$573,963	27
1995	24		2	14	$147,766	126
1996	22		3	14	$273,187	78

ED FIORI

Born: Edward Ray Fiori, April 21, 1953

Birthplace: Lynwood, Cal.

Ht: 5' 7" **Wt:** 190

Exempt Status: Special Medical Exemption

Q School: 1977

Fiori notched his fourth career win at the 1996 Quad City Classic, his first Tour victory in 14 years. The tournament became a media event focusing on whether Tiger Woods, the leader after 54 holes, could capture his first professional victory. An early quadruple-bogey 8 doomed Tiger's chances, and Fiori took some of the limelight with a two-stroke victory over Andrew Magee. The $216,000 first-place check was more than any single season earnings in Fiori's previous 18 campaigns. Fiori's three previous wins were at the 1979 Southern Open in a playoff over Tom Watson, the 1981 Western Open, and the 1982 Bob Hope Desert Classic in a playoff over Tom Kite. Before his rotator cuff troubles in 1994, Fiori had played in 25 or more Tour events for 16 straight years.

- Nicknamed "The Grip" due to overly strong grip.

- Member of the University of Houston's 1987 NCAA Championship Team.

YEAR	EVENTS	WINS	TOP 10	CUTS MADE	EARNINGS	RANK
1978	25		1	11	$19,846	109
1979	27	1	1	17	$64,428	65
1980	30		4	22	$79,488	52
1981	33	1	4	17	$105,510	48
1982	31	1	2	23	$91,599	45
1983	29		5	23	$175,619	26
1984	32			16	$41,582	119
1985	29		5	19	$116,002	71
1986	32		2	16	$70,828	119
1987	28		2	18	$104,570	95
1988	29		2	25	$193,765	58
1989	29		2	22	$188,637	77
1990	33		1	22	$108,816	133
1991	29			21	$120,722	123
1992	31		2	18	$124,537	115
1993	31		2	16	$117,617	127
1994	15		1	8	$108,259	150
1995	15			10	$83,852	170
1996	20	1	1	10	$262,292	83

DAN FORSMAN

Born: Daniel Bruce
Forsman, July 15, 1958

Birthplace:
Rhinelander, Wis.

Ht: 6' 4" **Wt:** 195

Joined Tour: 1983

1996 Money Rank: 123

Since a stellar season in 1992, Forsman's play has fallen off. In 1992, Forsman missed just one cut in 29 events, won the 1992 Buick Open, and finished runner-up in three other tournaments; his $763,190 in earnings ranked 10th. He followed in 1993 by ranking 36th, but in 1994 Forsman had no top 10 finishes. He again failed to finish in the top 10 in 1996, missed the cut 10 times in 22 events, and ranked 123rd with $170,197 in earnings.

Throughout the 1980s, Forsman enjoyed consistent success. Before 1992, his best seasons were 1988, when he had four top 10 finishes (including one second and two thirds) to rank 40th, and in 1990 he finished in the money 19 times (including a win at the 1990 Shearson Lehman Hutton Open) to rank 43rd.

Forsman enjoys many sports, both as a player and as a coach: In 1995, he took six weeks off from the Tour to help out his son's Little League baseball team.

- Won the 1992 Buick Open.
- Won the 1990 Shearson Lehman Hutton Open.
- Won the 1986 Hertz Bay Hill Classic (rainshortened).
- Won the 1985 Life Quad Cities Open.
- Finished second at the 1992 Federal Express St. Jude Classic.
- Finished second at the 1992 Chattanooga Classic.
- Finished second at the 1992 and 1993 Canon Greater Hartford Open.

- Tied for seventh at the 1993 Masters Tournament.
- Tied for seventh at the 1992 PGA Championship.

YEAR	EVENTS	WINS	TOP 10	CUTS MADE	EARNINGS	RANK
1982	1					
1983	30		1	14	$37,859	118
1984	32		2	16	$52,152	105
1985	26	1	4	16	$150,334	53
1986	27	1	2	16	$169,445	54
1987	33		1	29	$157,728	63
1988	35		4	26	$269,440	40
1989	30		4	15	$141,174	99
1990	26	1	4	19	$319,160	43
1991	26		2	19	$214,175	78
1992	29	1	8	28	$763,190	10
1993	25		6	19	$410,150	36
1994	23			13	$160,805	112
1995	23		2	18	$194,539	93
1996	22			12	$170,197	123

DAVID FROST

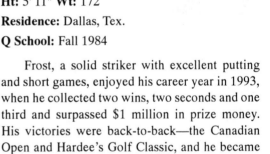

Born: David Laurence
Frost, September 11, 1959

Birthplace: Cape Town,
South Africa

Ht: 5' 11" **Wt:** 172

Residence: Dallas, Tex.

Q School: Fall 1984

Frost, a solid striker with excellent putting and short games, enjoyed his career year in 1993, when he collected two wins, two seconds and one third and surpassed $1 million in prize money. His victories were back-to-back—the Canadian Open and Hardee's Golf Classic, and he became the first golfer since Johnny Miller in 1975 to successfully defend one title after winning another tournament (he'd also won the Hardee's Classic in 1992.)

A rugby enthusiast given to hirsute stylings in the past (he was sporting a beard when he won the Hardee's Golf Classic in 1992, then shaved his trademark mustache in February 1993), Frost has nine Tour victories and eight international wins.

The biggest win of his career came at the 1989 NEC World Series of Golf, when his second-hole playoff victory over Ben Crenshaw earned him a 10-year Tour exemption.

In 1996, Frost finished in the money 14 times out of 23 tournaments, with four Top 10 finishes and $382,947. The Top 10 finishes were a tie for sixth at the Buick Classic; a tie for third at the Memorial; a tie for tenth at the Masters; and a tie for seventh at the Honda Classic.

- Best 1995 Tour rating was third in sand saves.

- International wins include: 1994 Lexington PGA Championship and Hong Kong Open; 1993 Kent Hong Kong Open; 1992 Million Dollar Challenge and Dunlop Phoenix; 1990 Million Dollar Challenge; 1989 Million Dollar Challenge, and the 1984 Air France Cannes Open.

- Tour wins include: 1994 Canon Greater Hartford Open; 1993 Canadian Open and Hardee's Golf Classic; 1992 Buick Classic and Hardee's Golf Classic; 1990 USF&G Classic; 1989 NEC World Series of Golf and 1988 Southern Open and Northern Telecom Tucson Open.

- His 259 at the 1992 Hardee's Classic was only two strokes off the 72-hole Tour record.

- Holed out from a bunker on the 72nd hole of the 1990 USF&G Classic to defeat Greg Norman.

- Shot a 60 in the second round of the 1990 Northern Telecom Open.

- First played in U.S. in 1981.

YEAR	EVENTS	WINS	TOP 10	CUTS MADE	EARNINGS	RANK
1983	1			1		
1985	28		3	18	$118,537	70
1986	28		6	20	$187,944	46
1987	27		12	24	$518,072	11
1988	25	2	11	18	$691,500	9
1989	26	1	8	23	$620,430	12
1990	26	1	4	15	$372,485	32
1991	28		2	18	$171,262	93
1992	25	2	6	16	$717,883	15
1993	22	2	9	15	$1,030,717	5
1994	23	1	6	20	$671,683	20
1995	21		3	15	$357,658	50
1996	23		4	15	$382,947	54

FAIRWAYS HIT IN REGULATION

Rank	Name	Rounds	Percent
1.	Fred Funk	108	78.7
2.	Nick Faldo	56	78.0
3.	David Edwards	82	77.5
4.	Tom Byrum	76	77.0
5.	Fulton Allem	54	76.8
6.	John Morse	94	76.7
T7.	Lennie Clements	83	76.2
T7.	Nick Price	52	76.2
9.	Jeff Hart	65	76.0
T10.	Olin Browne	94	75.9
T10.	Ed Fiori	61	75.9

FRED FUNK

Born: Frederick Funk, June 14, 1956
Birthplace: Takoma Park, Maryland
Ht: 5' 8" **Wt:** 165
Residence: Ponte Vedra Beach, Fla.
Q School: Fall 1988, 1989
1996 Money Rank: 21

A former golf coach at the University of Marlyand, Funk practices what he preached there—accuracy. A short driver, but the most accurate on the Tour in 1995 and 1996, Funk, also one of the busiest players on the Tour (he made 34 starts in 1993 and 30 in 1994), enjoyed his best season in 1996, with a win at the B.C. Open and seven other Top 10 finishes.

That '96 season followed a successful '95 Tour during which Funk won the Ideon Classic at Pleasant Valley and the Buick Challenge, finished in a tie for fourth at the Buick Classic, and tied for eighth at the Anheuser-Busch Golf Classic, winning $717,232 overall.

The "Other Fred" on the Tour to Fred ("Boom Boom") Couples, "Poof Poof" Funk, who majored in Law Enforcement at Maryland, has battled through a pair of debilitating injuries—a torn rotator cuff suffered in 1986 and a shoulder injury in 1991 that required surgery following a boogie board accident.

- Other PGA win was the 1992 Shell Houston Open.
- Lone international win was the 1993 Mexican Open.
- His Tour-leading driving accuracy in 1996 was 78.7%.
- Seven other Top 10 finishes in 1996 included a tie for second at the Buick Challenge; a tie for ninth at the Greater Milwaukee Open; a tie for tenth at the NEC World Series of Golf; a tie for seventh at the Buick Open; a tie for third at the Michelob Championship at Kingsmill; a tie for sixth at the Buick Classic, and a tie for third at the Nortel Open.
- Shot a 59 on the Desert Course at TPC of Scottsdale during a separate pro-am at the 1992 Phoenix Open.

YEAR	EVENTS	WINS	TOP 10	CUTS MADE	EARNINGS	RANK
1982	3			2	$1,779	251
1985	1			1	$6,345	196
1986	3					
1987	2			1	$2,400	255
1988	2			1	$1,552	285
1989	29		2	17	$59,695	157
1990	29		3	13	$179,346	91
1991	31		5	17	$226,915	73
1992	32	1	3	24	$416,930	34
1993	34		5	24	$309,435	56
1994	30		4	23	$281,905	67
1995	32	2	4	26	$717,232	26
1996	31	1	8	23	$814,334	21

JIM FURYK

Born: James Michael Furyk, May 12, 1970
Birthplace: West Chester, Penn.
Ht: 6' 2" **Wt:** 200
Residence: Ponte Vedra Beach, Fla.

Q School: 1993
1996 Money Rank: 26

Furyk, the man with the funky swing and cross-handed putting style learned from his father at age 7, had his best year in 1996, his third on the Tour, with one win and two other Top 10 finishes for a total of $674,349.

Furyk, a two-time All-American at the University of Arizona, will only take swing tips from his father. And why not? After all, the putting style learned from his dad placed Furyk No. 1 in putting (1.708 putts per GIR) in the 1995 Tour statistics and helped him finish in a tie for second in birdies, with 404. (In contrast, Furyk's quirky swing landed him in a tie for 161st in hitting the greens in regulation and 164th in total driving.)

- Has two Tour wins: 1996 Hawaiian Open, and 1995 Las Vegas Invitational.
- Other 1996 Top Ten finishes included: a tie for fifth at the U.S. Open, and a tie for seventh at the Greater Greensboro Chrysler Classic.
- Second-round 62 at the 1995 Buick Open at the Warwick Hills Country Club was a course record.
- Two-time All-American selection.

YEAR	EVENTS	WINS	TOP 10	CUTS MADE	EARNINGS	RANK
1993P	1					
1993N	25	1	3	13	$58,240	26
1994P	31		3	17	$236,603	78
1994N	1		1	1	$3,815	153
1995	31	1	3	22	$535,380	33
1996	28	1	3	24	$738,950	26

JIM GALLAGHER, JR.

Born: James Thomas Gallagher, Jr., March 24, 1961
Birthplace: Johnstown, Penn.

Ht: 6' 0" **Wt:** 195

Joined Tour: 1984

1996 Money Rank: 76

Gallagher had an off-year in 1996—he didn't win over a million dollars, as he did in 1993 and 1995. With just two top 10 finishes and $277,740 in 1996, Gallagher ranked 76th, off from 1995 when he earned $1,057,241 to rank eighth and won two tournaments, including the K-mart Greater Greensboro Open, where he made up a seven-stroke deficit in the final round. Gallagher first reached golf's million-dollar heights in 1993 by winning twice (including a two-stroke victory in The Tour Championship) and finishing in the top 10 six times. His $1,078,870 in earnings that year ranked him fourth.

Gallagher's career on the Tour started slowly. His breakthrough came in 1989, when he made the cut 24 times (including three top 10 finishes) to rank 50th. From there, Gallagher increased his yearly earnings (and ranking) by consistently finishing in the money and often in the top 10.

Golf's a family affair for Gallagher. Jim's father, a PGA pro in Marion, Ind., started Jim golfing at age two. Jim's sister, Jackie Gallagher-Smith, is a member of the LPGA; Jim's wife, Cissye, is a former LPGA member. And Jim's brother, Jeff, qualified for the 1996 PGA Tour.

- Won the 1995 FedEx St. Jude Classic.

- Won the 1995 K-mart Greater Greensboro Open.

- Won the 1993 Anheuser-Busch Golf Classic.

- Won the 1993 The TOUR Championship.

- Won the 1990 Greater Milwaukee Open.

- Tied for second at the 1992 PGA Championship.

- Finished third at the 1991 PGA Championship.

- Member of the 1993 Ryder Cup team.

- Member of the 1994 Presidents Cup team.

YEAR	EVENTS	WINS	TOP 10	CUTS MADE	EARNINGS	RANK
1984	25		2	13	$22,249	148
1985	16			8	$19,061	159
1986	36		3	21	$79,967	107
1987	36		1	17	$39,402	166
1988	19		1	14	$83,766	124
1989	34		3	24	$265,809	50
1990	34	1	5	25	$476,706	25
1991	32		6	25	$570,627	18
1992	28		7	25	$638,314	19
1993	27	2	6	18	$1,078,870	4
1994	27		4	16	$325,976	51
1995	27	2	6	22	$1,057,241	8
1996	25		2	15	$277,740	76

ROBERT GAMEZ

Born: Robert Anthony Gamez, July 21, 1958

Birthplace: Las Vegas, Nev.

Ht: 5' 9" **Wt:** 170

Exempt Status: 89th on 1995 money list

Q School: 1989

Gamez won in his first Tour Start, the 1990 Northern Telecom Open. Shortly thereafter, he became one of the many golfers to beat Greg Norman with a miraculous final shot when he holed his 176-yard 7-iron for an eagle deuce at the Nestle Invitational in 1990. This fast start, along with a top 30 money list ranking, earned him Rookie of the Year honors.

Gamez had a fine amateur career, winning the Jack Nicklaus award in 1989 as Collegiate Player of the Year, and was a member of the 1989 Walker Cup team. He hosts the annual Charity Tournament in Las Vegas to benefit the Robert Gamez foundation, which is run by his brother Randy, who caddied for his two tournament wins. His best finish at a major championship was a tie for 12th at the 1990 British Open.

- Career low round was a 61 at the 1991 Greater Milwaukee Open.

- Like countless duffers before him, Gamez put four balls in the water on the famous "Island

Green" 17th hole during the Players Championship at Sawgrass.

- In 1994 and 1995, finished in second place at the JC Penney Classic with Helen Alfredsson.

YEAR	EVENTS	WINS	TOP 10	CUTS MADE	EARNINGS	RANK
1988	1 (Am)				1	
1989	3			1	$4,827	
1990	25	2	2	16	$461,407	38
1991	27		3	13	$280,349	59
1992	25		3	13	$215,648	72
1993	25		3	15	$236,458	70
1994	23		5	15	$380,353	44
1995	27		3	13	$206,588	89
1996	25		2	12	$249,226	89

KELLY GIBSON

Born: Kelly Michael Gibson, May 2, 1964

Birthplace: New Orleans, La.

Ht: 5' 10" **Wt:** 175

Residence: New Orleans, La.

Q School: 1991, 1994

1996 Money Rank: 69th

With two Top 10 finishes in 1996 (a career-best tie for third at the Las Vegas Invitational and a tie for sixth at the Nissan Open) Gibson, a five-year Tour vet recorded his best money-list finish in his career with $307,228.

Gibson, who attended Lamar University and who casts himself as a die-hard fan of the New Orleans Saints, recorded his previous Tour-best finish at the rain-shortened 1992 Buick Southern Open, where he tied for fourth after an opening-round 67 that put him in a five-way tie for the lead.

- Ranked 7th on '96 Tour in average yards per drive—280.8.

- Finished fifth in the '95 Tour stats in driving (280.2), but tied for 174th in driving accuracy (61.8).

- Led the Tour in eagles in 1995 with 16.

- Lost his card in 1994, despite largest career payday at the Motorola Western Open, where he won $41,700, finishing with a 67 and in a tie for sixth, three strokes behind Nick Price.

- Finished 14th on 1991 Ben Hogan Tour money list.

- Four-year member of the Canadian Tour.

- Finished third on Canadian Tour Order of Merit in 1991.

- Led Canadian Tour in scoring average in 1991 (69.75).

YEAR	EVENTS	WINS	TOP 10	CUTS MADE	EARNINGS	RANK
1989	1			1	$502	298
1990P	2					
1990N	28		5	18	$33,550	26
1991P	2			1	$2,140	288
1991N	17	1	4	13	$50,098	14
1992P	33		3	14	$137,984	105
1992N	2					
1993	33			20	$148,003	110
1994	33		2	14	$134,841	129
1995	33		1	19	$173,425	109
1996	35			24	$307,228	69

PAUL GOYDOS

Born: Paul David Goydos, June 20, 1964

Birthplace: Long Beach, Cal.

Ht: 5' 9" **Wt:** 190

Residence: Long Beach, Cal.

Q School: 1992, 1993

1996 Money Rank: 44th

Jokingly nicknamed "Sunshine" because he always manages to find something negative in the most positive performance, Goydos captured his first Tour win in '96 with a tense, one-stroke victory over Jeff Maggert at the Bay Hill Invitational by Office Depot. His previous career-best was a tie for seventh at the 1994 B.C. Open.

A former high school teacher and a Long Beach State alum, Goydos, who was forced to withdraw from the '95 K-mart GGO with chicken pox, struggled with his overall Tour "health" in 1995, when he scrambled to retain his card (despite no Top 10 finishes) by winning $33,462 in his last two tournaments. He finished 129th on the '95 Tour money list.

- Finished in the money in 15 of 30 '96 events, with $438,111, including three other Top 10 finishes—tied for eighth at the Las Vegas Invitational; ninth at the Sprint International, and a tie for seventh at the Bob Hope Chrysler Classic.

- Thirty five Tour appearances in '95 tied him with Ted Tryba and Greg Kraft for most tournaments entered.

- Best finish in '95 Tour statistics was tenth in birdies (366); worst, ironically, was a tie for 169th in putting (1.816).

- Tied for 13th at 1993 Qualifying Tournament.

- Winner of 1992 Ben Hogan Yuma Open.

- No. 17 on 1992 Ben Hogan money list, with $61,104; 39th on '91 money list with $30,237.

- Winner of 1990 Long Beach Open.

- All-conference selection in Pacific Coast Athletic Association in 1985 and 1986.

Gump continues to resharpen his form after falling off the PGA Tour in 1994. Though Gump had no top 10 finishes in 1996, he made 20 cuts to earn $177,332. Gump's play dropped slightly from 1995, when he ranked 99th in his first year back on the Tour. His best season was his rookie year in 1991, when he finished in the top 10 twice (including a second place at the 1991 International) to rank 80th. From there, Gump's earnings declined until he fell off the tour in 1993, but a strong 1994 Nike Tour (where he ranked second in earnings) returned him to the PGA.

Gump has been tabbed with the nickname "Forest" after the popular 1994 movie, *Forest Gump*. Unlike the movie character, who attended the University of Alabama and was a football star, Scott Gump excelled in golf at the University of Miami, and it's not known whether he has likened golf to a box of chocolates.

- Tied for second at the 1991 International.

- Tied for tenth at the 1995 Motorola Western Open.

- Won the 1994 NIKE Monterrey Open.

- Won the 1994 NIKE Greater Greenville Classic.

- Ranked second on the 1994 Nike Tour money list.

YEAR	EVENTS	WINS	TOP 10	CUTS MADE	EARNINGS	RANK
1991	25		4	13	$30,237	39
1992	29	1	3	17	$61,104	17
1993P	30			18	$87,804	152
1993N	2			2	$615	246
1994	31		3	22	$241,107	75
1995	35			21	$146,423	129
1996	29	1	4	15	$438,111	44

YEAR	EVENTS	WINS	TOP 10	CUTS MADE	EARNINGS	RANK
1988	1					
1989	1					
1991	29		2	18	$207,809	80
1992	33		1	24	$148,696	102
1993	31			17	$96,822	147
1994	3			2	$4,181	286
1995	29		1	19	$184,828	99
1996	31			20	$177,332	118

SCOTT GUMP

Born: Scott Edward Gump, December 17, 1965
Birthplace: Rockledge, Fla.
Ht: 6' 2" **Wt:** 165
Joined Tour: 1991
1996 Money Rank: 118

JAY HAAS

Born: Jay Haas, December 1, 1963
Birthplace: St. Louis, Mo.
Ht: 5' 10" **Wt:** 180
Residence: Greenville, S.C.

Q School: Fall 1976
1996 Money Rank: 36th

Haas, a long-time Tour vet, had a very interesting year in '95, his career-best earnings year. When he wasn't missing cuts, he was racking up top-10 finishes. In the 18 cuts he made, he finished in the Top 10 a remarkable 11 times, winning $822,259 and finishing 16th on the money list. In 1996, he finished in the money in 21 of 27 events, with $523,019 and four Top 10s—tied for fifth at the Walt Disney World/Oldsmobile Classic; second at the LaCantera Texas Open; tied for eighth at the Players Championship; and tied for sixth at the Doral-Ryder Open.

The nephew of former Masters champ Bob Goalby and brother of Jerry, a past member of the Tour (Tour member Dillard Pruitt is Haas' brother-in-law), Haas, generally a model of consistency, has nine career Tour wins. He won his first trophy at the National Pee Wee Championships in Orlando at age 7.

The father of four, Haas won the 1975 NCAA Championship at Wake Forest, was that year's winner of the Fred Haskins Award as the outstanding collegiate player, and was a '75-76 All-American.

- Previous Tour wins include: 1993 H-E-B Texas Open; 1992 Federal Express St. Jude Classic; 1988 Bob Hope Chrysler Classic; 1987 Big "I" Houston Open; 1982 Hall of Fame Classic and Texas Open; 1981 Greater Milwaukee and B.C. opens; and the 1978 Andy Williams/San Diego Open.

- One international win came at the 1991 Mexican Open.

- Closed with consecutive 64s to win the 1992 FedEx St. Jude Classic.

- Opened with 63 en route to winning the '88 Bob Hope Chrysler Classic.

- Won 1987 Big "I" Houston Open by making a 70-foot putt on the 72nd hole, then defeating Buddy Gardner in a playoff.

- Captain's choice on 1994 U.S. President's Cup team, where his record was 3-2.

- Has $5,951,722 in career earnings.

YEAR	EVENTS	WINS	TOP 10	CUTS MADE	EARNINGS	RANK
1976	3			3	$1,882	205
1977	30		2	18	$32,326	77
1978	29	1	4	20	$77,176	31
1979	28		7	20	$102,515	34
1980	30		7	26	$114,102	35
1981	30	2	6	25	$181,894	15
1982	29	2	10	27	$229,746	13
1983	28		8	25	$191,735	23
1984	27		3	20	$146,514	45
1985	29		3	20	$121,488	69
1986	29		7	17	$189,204	45
1987	29	1	5	24	$270,347	37
1988	29	1	6	22	$490,409	20
1989	30		5	17	$248,831	54
1990	28		1	17	$180,023	89
1991	29		3	18	$200,637	84
1992	28	1	6	24	$632,628	20
1993	29	1	6	27	$601,603	26
1994	30		5	25	$593,386	25
1995	27		11	18	$822,259	16
1996	27		4	21	$523,019	36

DUDLEY HART

Born: August 4, 1968
Birthplace: Rochester, N.Y.
Ht: 5' 10" **Wt:** 175
Residence: Fort Lauderdale, Fla.
Q School: 1990, 1994, 1995
1996 Money Rank: 47th

After ping-ponging between the Tour and Q School the last few years, 1996 finally brought out the best in Hart, when he won his first Tour title (at the Canadian Bell Open) and managed two other Top 10 finishes in only 13 events.

Hart, a four-time All-American at the University of Florida, missed 10 weeks of the 1994 season with rib and back problems. The injuries seemed to be coincident with his slide in performance following decent years in 1992 and 1993, when he finished 61st and 52nd, respectively, on the money list. He made the cut in only 12 of 31 events in that injury-marred '94 season.

- Finished in the money in 10 of 13 events in 1996, with the Canadian Open win and $422,198 in total earnings, a tie for eighth at the Walt Disney World/Oldsmobile Classic, and a tie for ninth at the CVS Charity Classic.

- Previous to '96, best Tour finishes were a trio of ties for third—at the 1992 Greater Milwaukee Open, the 1993 Northern Telecom Open, and the 1993 K-mart Greater Greensboro Open.

- Despite making 18 of 29 cuts in '95, Hart slipped even further down the money list, finishing 148th, sending him back to Qualifying School.

- Best finishes in '95 were a pair of ties for 15th at the Canon Greater Hartford Open and the Ideon Classic at Pleasant Valley.

- Finished 6th at Q School on 1994 to earn his card for 1995.

- Won pro-am portion of 1994 AT&T Pebble Beach National Pro-Am with Raymond Floyd's son, Robert.

- After turning professional in 1990, won the Florida and Louisiana Opens.

YEAR	EVENTS	WINS	TOP 10	CUTS MADE	EARNINGS	RANK
1991					$126,217	120
1992					$254,903	61
1993					$316,750	52
1994					$126,313	135
1995	30				$116,334	148
1996	13	1	3	10	$422,198	47

NOLAN HENKE

Born: Nolan Jay Henke, November 25, 1964

Birthplace: Battle Creek, Mich.

Ht: 6' **Wt:** 165

Residence: Fort Myers, Fla.

Q School: Fall 1988, 1989

1996 Money Rank: 71st

After 28th, 45th and 31st money-list finishes in 1991 through '93, respectively, Henke, a jet-ski enthusiast and former Florida State University All-American, has hovered in the 70s the last three years. That's a good neighborhood when it comes to scoring, but not so great on the money rankings. He was 70th on the money list in '94, 78th in '95 and 71st in '96, with $302,726.

Henke finished in the money in 15 of 24 events in 1996, with three Top 10s—fourth at the Walt Disney World/Oldsmobile Classic; a tie for third at the Greater Milwaukee Open; and a tie for fourth at the Bob Hope Chrysler Classic. Henke, also an avid tennis player, has three Tour wins—the 1993 BellSouth Classic, 1991 Phoenix Open, and 1990 B.C. Open.

- Up and down effort at '95 MCI Classic ended with Henke losing a playoff with Bob Tway.

- Only two strokes off the lead through 36 at '95 Buick Invitational of California before third-round 73 dropped him into a tie for tenth.

- Best finish of '94 came in defense of BellSouth title, when he eagled the 72nd hole to tie Brian Henninger, one stroke behind John Daly.

- Led by four strokes at outset of final round at '91 Phoenix Open, but ended up having to make an 18-foot birdie putt on 18 to clinch victory over formidable trio of Tom Watson, Curtis Strange and Gil Moran at TPC of Scottsdale.

- First Tour win came at 1990 B.C. Open, where he defeated Mark Wiebe by three strokes.

- Won seven tournaments while at FSU.

- Winner of 1986 Porter Cup, 1987 American Amateur and 1987 Monroe Invitational.

YEAR	EVENTS	WINS	TOP 10	CUTS MADE	EARNINGS	RANK
1987	2			2	$9,072	208
1989	26		1	13	$57,465	159
1990	29	1	5	16	$294,592	48
1991	27	1	6	20	$518,811	28
1992	27		4	16	$326,387	45
1993	26	1	4	20	$502,375	31
1994	26		3	12	$278,419	70
1995	25		2	14	$237,141	78
1996	24		3	15	$302,726	71

TIM HERRON

Born: February 16, 1970
Birthplace: Minneapolis, Minn.
Ht: 5' 10" **Wt:** 210
Residence: Wayzata, Minn.
Q School: 1995
1996 Money Rank: 39th

Embarking upon his PGA Tour career in 1996, Herron, a two-time All-American at the University of New Mexico, had his first career win under his belt by early March, a four-stroke victory at the $1.3 million Honda Classic, becoming, in the process, the first player in nearly two years to lead a tournament from start to finish.

A former Walker Cup standout who won all three of his Cup matches in 1993 (as the U.S. won by its largest margin ever, 19-5), Herron began his professional career on the Nike Tour in 1995, where he finished 25th in total earnings. His best finish that year was a tie for third at the Nike Mississippi Gulf Coast Classic.

- Finished in the money in 22 of 32 Tour events in 1996, with $475,670. In addition to the Honda win, other Top 10 finishes were a tie for sixth at the LaCantera Texas Open and a tie for ninth at the Buick Classic.

- Braved steady rain to shoot final-round 3-under-par 69 at the TPC at Eagle Trace in Coral Springs at the '96 Honda Classic to become first golfer to go wire-to-wire since Bob Estes captured the 1994 Texas Open. 17-under 271 total was four shots better than Mark McCumber.

- Finished fifth on '96 Tour in average yards per drive (283.5).

- Special interests include fishing, pool and skiing.

YEAR	EVENTS	WINS	TOP 10	CUTS MADE	EARNINGS	RANK
1995	1					
1996	32	1	3	22	$475,670	39

SCOTT HOCH

Born: Scott Mabon Hoch, November 24, 1955
Birthplace: Raleigh, N.C.
Ht: 5' 11" **Wt:** 170
Residence: Orlando, Fla.
Q School: Fall 1979
1996 Money Rank: 9th

A playing partner of U.S. presidents Clinton, Bush and Ford, Hoch, a seven-time winner and ten-time bridesmaid in his 17-year Tour career, remains one of the best that the Tour has to offer. And no one knows better than Hoch the pain of nearly winning. At the 1995 Shell Houston Open, Hoch frittered away a seemingly insurmountable five-stroke lead, then made a miraculous putt to reach a playoff with Payne Stewart—which he lost. He also lost a Masters playoff to Nick Faldo in 1989. His dismay at missing a short putt in his duel with Faldo was a poignant image of the agony of defeat.

Hoch, who earned a communications degree from Wake Forest in 1978, donated $100,000 of his winner's share at the 1989 Las Vegas Invitational to the Arnold Palmer Children's Hospital in Orlando.

- Tour wins include a wire-to-wire win at the 1996 Michelob Championship; the 1995 Greater Milwaukee Open; the 1994 Bob Hope Chrysler Classic; the 1989 Las Vegas Invitational; the 1984 Lite Quad Cities Open and the 1980 Quad Cities Open.

- Six international wins include 1995 Heineken Dutch Open; 1991 Korean Open; 1990 Korean Open; 1986 Casio World Open; and the 1982 Pacific Masters and Casio World Open.

- Finished in the money in 23 of 28 events entered in '96 for $1,039,564. In addition to the Michelob Championship, he had seven other Top 10 finishes—tied for third at the Deposit Guaranty Golf Classic; tied for seventh at the U.S. Open; tied for second at the Kemper Open; third at the MCI Classic; tied for fifth at the Masters; third at the Bob Hope Chrysler Classic; and tied for second at the Mercedes Championships.

- Ranked second in '95 Tour statistics in putting (1.737) and ninth in birdies (371); worst finish was a tie for 127th in driving accuracy (67.3).

- Shot a 4-under-par 67 for a 72-hole total of 19-under 265 at the 1996 Michelob Championship, eclipsing the previous mark of 266 set by Lanny Wadkins in 1990, and equaled one year later by Mike Hulbert and Kenny Knox.

- Won 1995 Heineken Dutch Open, becoming the first American to do so since Stewart in 1991.

- Played in the "presidential foursome" during the first round of the Bob Hope Chrysler Classic title defense in 1995.

- Brother, Buddy, was a professional golfer; father was a baseball All-American at Wake.

- Has earned $6,505,462 on the Tour.

YEAR	EVENTS	WINS	TOP 10	CUTS MADE	EARNINGS	RANK
1980	18	1	1	6	$45,600	77
1981	31		2	19	$49,606	87
1982	28	1	8	23	$193,862	16
1983	25		7	20	$144,605	37
1984	26	1	7	22	$224,345	27
1985	30		6	24	$186,020	35
1986	28		6	23	$222,077	36
1987	27		8	23	$391,747	20
1988	31		10	26	$397,599	26
1989	27	1	6	21	$670,680	10
1990	26		7	19	$333,978	40
1991	31		9	26	$520,038	27
1992	16			13	$84,798	146
1993	28		6	18	$403,742	37
1994	28	1	7	21	$804,559	11
1995	28	1	8	23	$792,643	18
1996	27	1	8	23	$1,039,554	9

MIKE HULBERT

Born: Michael Patrick Hulbert, April 14th, 1958
Birthplace: Elmira, N.Y.
Ht: 6' **Wt:** 175
Exempt Status: 61st on 1995 Money List
Q School: 1984, 1985

After starting his career in 1985 by finishing 161st on the money list, Hulbert has enjoyed 11 straight years in the top 100. He has three tour wins: the 1986 Federal Express St. Jude Classic, the 1989 B.C. Open, and the 1991 Anheuser-Busch Classic.

Hulbert created interest in 1995 by going to a one-handed putting style, which helped him to 3 Top 10 finishes. In 1996, his best finishes were a tie for 3rd at the Nortel Open and a tie for 6th place at the Memorial. Hulbert also won the unofficial 1991 Ping Kapalua International tournament in a playoff over Davis Love III. An "Ironman" candidate, Mike has played in more than 30 events 11 straight years.

- Best friends with hometown pal (Horseheads, NY) and fellow tour pro Joey Sindelar.

- Best Major Championship finish was tie for 6th at 1992 U.S. Open.

YEAR	EVENTS	WINS	TOP 10	CUTS MADE	EARNINGS	RANK
1983	1					
1985	26			12	$18,368	161
1986	37	1	5	26	$276,687	21
1987	36		6	23	$204,375	49
1988	35		1	21	$127,752	94
1989	34	1	7	26	$477,621	18
1990	31		3	26	$216,002	67
1991	31	1	5	24	$551,750	24
1992	32		3	24	$279,577	55
1993	31			21	$193,833	89
1994	31		2	21	$221,007	84
1995	31		3	22	$311,005	61
1996	31		2	18	$235,131	93

JOHN HUSTON

Born: Johnny Ray Huston June 1, 1961
Birthplace: Mt. Vernon, Ill.
Ht: 5' 10" **Wt:** 155
Residence: Palm Harbor, Fla.
Q School: Fall 1987
1996 Money Rank: 37th

Huston had his career-best year in 1996, when he finished in the money in 18 of 24 events with six Top 10 finishes for $506,173. Born in Illinois, but raised in Florida, Huston, father of two and former collegiate golfer at Auburn University, is a true "homeboy": his three Tour victories have all come on Florida courses. Indeed, as a younger player, he enjoyed great success on Florida mini-tours, winning 10 events.

He loves the game and the competition so much that he says that he would compete as a mini-tour professional if he wasn't a member of the PGA Tour.

- Tour wins include: 1994 Doral-Ryder Open; 1992 Walt Disney World/Oldsmobile Classic; 1990 Honda Classic.

- 1996 Top 10 finishes included a tie for sixth at the LaCantera Texas Open; a tie for ninth at the FedEx St. Jude Classic; fifth at the Memorial Tournament; a tie for fifth at the Greater Greensboro Chrysler Classic; a tie for tenth at the Freeport-McDermott Classic; and second at the Bob Hope Chrysler Classic.

- 1995 was a tumultuous year, with three Top 10 finishes in his first four events, followed by struggles to make cuts throughout the rest of the year. His finish—64th on the money list—was his second-worst since joining the Tour in 1988.

- 1994 was Huston's biggest year in total earnings with $731,499.

- Lost playoff to Jim McGovern at 1993 Shell Houston Open.

- Carded a closing round of 62 to pass Mark O'Meara to win the 1992 Walt Disney World/ Oldsmobile Classic.

- Disney-winning 26-under was one stroke off all-time Tour record for most strokes under par.

- Won 1985 Florida Open.

YEAR	EVENTS	WINS	TOP 10	CUTS MADE	EARNINGS	RANK
1987	1			1	$1,055	287
1988	31		2	17	$150,301	78
1989	29		2	14	$203,207	68
1990	25	1	3	16	$435,690	30
1991	27		5	23	$395,853	40
1992	32	1	4	23	$515,453	26
1993	30		6	26	$681,441	15
1994	25	1	8	19	$731,499	16
1995	27		5	15	$294,574	64
1996	25		6	18	$506,173	37

LEE JANZEN

Born: Lee McLeod Janzen, August 28, 1964

Birthplace: Austin, Minn.

Ht: 6' **Wt:** 175

Residence: Orlando, Fla.

Q School: Fall 1989

1996 Money Rank: 31st

If Janzen, 1993 U.S. Open winner and owner of a marketing degree from Florida Southern, were putting together a PR campaign on his career, 1995 would take center stage. Seemingly in total command of his game that year, he won three titles on his way to reaching the seventh-highest money total in Tour history with $1,378,966.

And he did it in some drama. At the Sprint International, for example, Janzen, a protege of golfing guru Rick Smith, carded four birdies and a crucial par over the final five holes to beat a reeling Ernie Els.

Janzen began golfing at age 14, after his family moved from Maryland to Florida (baseball had been his sport until then). He has shown periods of brilliance throughout his professional career. He's placed in the Top 10 on the money list in three out of the last five years.

- Tour wins include: 1995 Tournament Players Championship, Kemper Open and Sprint International; 1994 Buick Classic; 1993 Phoenix and U.S. opens, and 1992 Northern Telecom Open.

- Finished in the money in 21 of 28 events in '96 with $540,916 and seven Top 10 finishes—a tie for ninth at the LaCantera Texas Open; a tie for second at the Greater Vancouver Open; a tie for eighth at the PGA Championship; a tie for eighth at the Motorola Western Open; a tie for third at the Nortel Open, and a tie for seventh at the Mercedes Championships.

AVERAGE BIRDIES PER ROUND

Rank	Name	Birdies
1.	Fred Couples	4.20
2.	Mark O'Meara	4.19
3.	Brad Faxon	4.02
T4.	Larry Nelson	3.96
T4.	Greg Norman	3.96
T6.	David Duval	3.93
T6.	Lee Janzen	3.93
8.	Gil Morgan	3.92
9.	Davis Love III	3.85
10.	Jeff Maggert	3.84

- Tied for sixth (with David Duval) in '96 Tour statistics in average birdies per round—3.93.

- Tied for sixth with Paul Azinger in '96 statistics for average strokes per hole—1.747.

- 1993 U.S. Open win came in head-to-head battle with Payne Stewart at Baltusrol.

- 272 in '93 Open tied Jack Nicklaus for lowest cumulative score in Open history.

- Enrolled, at the suggestion of wife Bev, in the Dave Pelz Short Game School after winning Players championship in 1995.

- Winner 1986 Division II national championship.

- First-team All-American in 1985-86.

- Won first tournament at 15 as a member of the Greater Tampa Junior Golf Association.

YEAR	EVENTS	WINS	TOP 10	CUTS MADE	EARNINGS	RANK
1985	1					
1988	2			1	$3,686	256
1989	2			1	$5,100	233
1990	30		2	20	$132,986	115
1991	33		2	23	$228,242	72
1992	32	1	6	21	$795,279	9
1993	26	2	7	23	$932,335	7
1994	26	1	2	19	$442,588	35
1995	28	3	4	22	$1,378,966	3
1996	27		7	21	$540,916	31

STEVE JONES

Born: Steven Glen Jones, December 27, 1958

Birthplace: Artesia, N.M.

Ht: 6' 4" **Wt:** 200

Residence: Phoenix, Ariz.

Q School: Fall 1981, 1984, 1986

1996 Money Rank: 22nd

Before a November 25, 1991, dirt bike accident sidelined him for almost three seasons, Jones, an all-state high school basketball player, had his career on the climb. His 1989 season included three tournament wins and he finished 8th on the money list.

In 1994, after two years of rehabilitation for ankle and shoulder problems and ligament damage in his left ring finger, Jones played in two PGA events, two Nike Tour tournaments, and finally in three European tournaments in August. His best finish of the season was a tie for 31st at the Hardee's Golf Classic—winning a paltry $8,740 and finishing 254th in winnings.

The following year was better for Jones—as he made 16 cuts and finished in the Top 10 twice. In '96, Jones' recovery was deemed complete when he won the U.S. Open with a two-putt par on the 72nd hole, holding off playing partner Tom Lehman. It was Jones' first appearance at a major since the 1991 British Open.

An avid fly fisherman, father of two and former University of Colorado Buffalo, Jones also ran track and played golf in high school before concentrating solely on golf at Boulder.

- In addition to the '96 U.S. Open, Tour wins include the 1988 AT&T Pebble Beach National Pro-Am and the 1989 MONY Tournament of Champions, Bob Hope Chrysler Classic and Canadian Open.

- 1996 Tour results: in the money in 18 of 26 events, winning $810,644, and additional Top 10 finishes included a tie for third at the Quad City Classic; a tie for ninth at the Canon Greater Hartford Open; a tie for sixth at the MasterCard Colonial; a tie for ninth at the Bay Hill Invitational by Office Depot, and a tie for tenth at the Phoenix Open.

- "I think every boy grows up dreaming of making a putt on the last green to win the U.S. Open," Jones said, after becoming the first qualifier to win the Open since Jerry Pate in 1976. Asked if he ever thought he would be in position to win, he responded, "Not in my wildest dreams."

- Said he drew inspiration for '96 Open win from a book on golf legend Ben Hogan that was sent to him during the week by a friend. "I don't think I would have won the tournament without reading that book," he said. "I looked at it and then couldn't put it down. I read it for three days. It really inspired me. No matter what the situation, this guy said, 'Always try to make a birdie, then focus on the next hole.'"

- Finished 10th in '96 Tour statistics in average yards per drive—280.0.

- The dirt bike accident had left Jones unable to properly grip a golf club; he developed a reverse overlapping grip to compensate.

- Made first appearance on comeback at '94 B.C. Open, shooting 67-70-70-74-281 for a tie for 40th.

- Opened breakthrough year of 1989 with back-to-back wins at MONY Tournament of Champions and Bob Hope Chrysler Classic.

- Second-team All-American at Colorado.

- Semi-finalist 1976 USGA Junior Championships.

YEAR	EVENTS	WINS	TOP 10	CUTS MADE	EARNINGS	RANK
1984	1			1	$788	264
1985	21		1	12	$43,379	129
1986	23		2	14	$51,473	136
1987	30		2	20	$154,918	66
1988	25	1	3	19	$241,877	45
1989	26	3	6	22	$745,578	8
1990	24		5	16	$350,982	34
1991	27		4	19	$294,961	54
1994P	2			2	$8,740	254
1994N	2		1	2	$5,195	140
1995	24		2	16	$234,749	79
1996	25	1	6	18	$810,644	22

PETE JORDAN

Born: Pete Jordan, June 10, 1964
Birthplace: Elmhurst, Ill.
Ht: 5' 11" **Wt:** 180
Joined Tour: 1995
1996 Money Rank: 110

Pete Jordan hopes to establish himself firmly on the PGA Tour after a 1996 season in which he finished in the money in just 10 of the 26 events he entered. Largely because of a second place finish at the 1996 B.C. Open, Jordan earned $191,240. Jordan's first year on the tour was 1994, when he ranked 132nd, and he followed up in 1995 by making the cut 12 times and had a third at the 1995 Deposit Guaranty Golf Classic. Before joining the PGA Tour, Jordan spent three years (1991-1993) on the Nike Tour.

- Finished second at the 1996 B.C. Open.

- Finished third at the 1995 Deposit Guaranty Golf Classic.

- Played in the 1993 U.S. Open, and though he finished way back in a tie for 72nd, he had played even with Jack Nicklaus and Nick Faldo.

- 1986 NCAA All-American at Texas Christian University.

YEAR	EVENTS	WINS	TOP 10	CUTS MADE	EARNINGS	RANK
1994					$128,960	132
1995	18		1	12	$143,936	134
1996	26		1	10	$191,240	110

JERRY KELLY

Born: Jerry Patrick Kelly, November 23, 1966
Birthplace: Madison, Wis.
Ht: 5' 11" **Wt.** 165
Residence: Madison, Wis.
Joined Tour: 1996
1996 Money Rank: 59th

A real-life "Happy Gilmore," Kelly was an all-city hockey player in high school and says that this background may have hurt his golf game in the past by making him too aggressive. Kelly came to the 1996 Tour as one of its most highly touted rookies, after finishing No. 1 on the 1995 Nike circuit with 15 Top 10 finishes and a Nike record $188,878 in earnings.

The 1989 University of Hartford grad (finance and insurance), Kelly, who lists surfing alongside hockey as his special interests, accounted nicely for himself in 1996 with four Top 10 finishes, including a "homecoming," second-place effort at the Greater Milwaukee Open.

Kelly's wife, Carol, whose brother, Jim Schuman, was a member of the Nike Tour from 1990-93, sometimes caddies for her husband.

• Finished in the money in 17 of 31 events in 1996, with $336,748.

• In addition to finishing second in Milwaukee, Kelly had three other Top 10 finishes: a tie for eighth at the Walt Disney World/Oldsmobile Classic; a tie for tenth at the BellSouth Classic; and a tie for fourth at the Doral-Ryder Open.

• Finished ninth in '96 Tour statistics in sand saves—61.2.

• Nike record earnings in '95 eclipsed Chris Perry's 1994 mark of $167,148.

• Led '95 Nike Tour in birdies and eagles and tied for lead in par breakers.

• Played in two PGA Tour events in 1995, missing the cut in the Motorola Western Open and tying for 34th in the Greater Milwaukee Open.

• Winner of 1992 and 1994 Wisconsin State Opens.

YEAR	EVENTS	WINS	TOP 10	CUTS MADE	EARNINGS	RANK
1991	1					
1992	1					
1993P	2					
1993N	28		3	15	$61,074	25
1994	26		8	19	$60,928	26
1995P	2			1	$4,733	306
1995N	28	2	15	22	$188,878	1
1996	31		4	17	$336,748	59

TOM KITE

Born: Thomas Oliver Kite, Jr., December 9, 1949

Birthplace: Austin, Tex.

Ht: 5' 8" **Wt:** 155

Residence: Austin, Tex.

Q School: Fall 1972

1996 Money Rank: 66th

Kite, a 25-year veteran, captain of the 1997 Ryder Cup Team and one of the country's finest all-around players (if his putter is working), is best known for his 19 career victories on the PGA Tour. Since joining the Tour in 1972, Kite has earned nearly $10 million, making him the Tour's second all-time money winner to Greg Norman. (He was first until passed by Norman in 1995.)

Kite, who started playing golf at age six and won his first tournament at 11, has two majors under his belt—the 1989 Players Championship and the 1992 U.S. Open. His most recent win of any kind, however, came at the 1993 Nissan Los Angeles Open. The victory drought is the longest of his career. Still he plays on with class and style, and many attribute his magnanimous character, not to mention his successful golf career, to his years of tutelage under the watchful eye of golfing guru Harvey Penick.

• Tour wins include: 1993 Bob Hope Chrysler Classic and Nissan Los Angeles Open; 1992 Bell-South Classic and U.S. Open; 1991 Infiniti Tournament of Champions; 1990 Federal Express St. Jude Classic; 1989 Nestle Invitational, The Players Championship and Nabisco Championships; 1987 Kemper Open; 1986 Western Open; 1985 MONY Tournament of Champions; 1984 Doral-Eastern Open and Georgia-Pacific Atlanta Classic; 1983 Bing Crosby National Pro-Am; 1982 Bay Hill Classic; 1981 American Motors-Inverrary Classic; 1978 B.C. Open, and 1976 IVB-Bicentennial Golf Classic.

• Has one international win—1980 European Open.

- 1996 performance included 15 money finishes in 22 events with one Top 10—second at the Canon Greater Hartford Open—for $319,326.

- Three of last four victories came on holidays: BellSouth Classic on Mother's Day; U.S. Open on Father's Day; Bob Hope Chrysler Classic on Valentine's day.

- Greatest victory came in 1992 U.S. Open at Pebble Beach, where an even-par 72 in tough Sunday conditions gave him a two-stroke win over Jeff Sluman.

- Got off to a blazing start in 1993 with two wins, a second and an eighth in five starts before a March back injury slowed him.

- Was untouchable in '93 Bob Hope Chrysler Classic, closing with rounds of 64-65-62 to set Tour record for most strokes under par (35) in 90-hole event.

- Owns two Arnold Palmer Awards as Tour's top money winner—1981 ($375,699) and 1989 ($1,395,278).

- 1989 PGA Player of the year.

- 1979 Bob Jones Award winner.

- 1973 Rookie of the Year.

- Co-winner, with Ben Crenshaw, of 1972 NCAA Championship.

- Member of 8 Ryder Cup teams.

- Has earned $9,654,760 on the Tour.

YEAR	EVENTS	WINS	TOP 10	CUTS MADE	EARNINGS	RANK
1972	3			3	$2,582	233
1973	34		2	31	$54,270	56
1974	28		8	27	$82,055	26
1975	26		9	21	$87,045	18
1976	27	1	8	25	$116,180	21
1977	29		7	27	$125,204	14
1978	28	1	8	25	$161,370	11
1979	28		11	24	$166,878	17
1980	26		10	22	$152,490	20
1981	26	1	21	26	$375,699	1
1982	25	1	15	24	$341,081	3
1983	25	1	8	21	$257,066	9
1984	25	2	10	21	$348,640	5
1985	24	1	6	21	$258,793	14
1986	26	1	9	24	$394,164	7
1987	24	1	11	21	$525,516	8
1988	25		10	21	$760,405	5
1989	23	3	10	23	$1,395,278	1
1990	22	1	9	21	$658,202	15
1991	25	1	4	19	$396,580	39
1992	23	2	9	22	$957,445	6
1993	20	2	8	14	$887,811	8
1994	23		8	18	$658,689	22
1995	25		1	21	$178,580	104
1996	21		1	15	$319,326	66

GREG KRAFT

Born: April 4, 1964
Birthplace: Detroit, Mich.
Ht: 5' 11" **Wt:** 170
Residence: Clearwater, Fla.
Q School: 1991, 1992
1996 Money Rank: 61st

Kraft, who has seven mini-tour victories to his credit, struggled mightily in 1995, missing 20 cuts in 35 events, finishing 139th on the money list (his worst finish since his first year in '92, when he was 140th). He lost his card in the process.

But the story, as usual, didn't end there. Kraft, who attended the University of Tampa, went back to Q School, finished at 14-under, re-earned his card, and came back in '96 to notch five Top 10 finishes and his second-best money-list finish. He was 60th in 1993.

- Best finishes on the Tour were a pair of seconds—at the 1993 Walt Disney World/Oldsmobile Classic and the 1994 Motorola Western Open.

- 1996 five Top 10 finishes (was in the money in 15 of 27 events, winning $331,708) included a tie for fourth at the LaCantera Texas Open; a tie for ninth at the Quad City Classic; a tie for third at the Deposit Guaranty Golf Classic; a tie for tenth at the Byron Nelson; and a tie for fifth at the Shell Houston Open.

- Finished third in the '96 Tour statistics in sand saves—63.3.

- Best 1995 finish was a tie for eighth at the Ideon Classic at Pleasant Valley.

- Won the unofficial 1993 Deposit Guaranty Golf Classic in Hattiesburg, Mississippi, birdieing the 72nd hole to defeat Morris Hatalsky and Tad Rhyan by one stroke.

- In 1992 Qualifying Tournament, birdied the last two holes to make the cut, then fired a 5-under-par 31 in final round at TPC at The Woodlands to earn his Tour membership.

YEAR	EVENTS	WINS	TOP 10	CUTS MADE	EARNINGS	RANK
1992					$88,824	140
1993					$290,581	60
1994					$279,901	69
1995	35		1		$137,655	139
1996	28		5	15	$331,708	61

NEAL LANCASTER

Born: Grady Neal Lancaster, September 13, 1962

Birthplace: Smithfield, NC

Ht: 6' 0" **Wt:** 170

Joined Tour: 1990

1996 Money Rank: 104

Though Lancaster didn't take his first formal golf lesson until 1992, he quickly became a PGA Tour mainstay. In 1996, Lancaster made 22 cuts (including a tie for fifth at the 1996 Deposit Guaranty Golf Classic) to earn $210,000. 1995 was a rockier year, when Lancaster had just one top 10 finish. But what a finish it was: a tie for fourth place at the U.S. Open, where Lancaster shot 29 on the final nine holes, a U.S. Open record. Lancaster's best year on the tour was 1994, when he ranked 58th. His only top 10 finish that year was a win in the rain-shortened GTE Byron Nelson Classic.

Lancaster first qualified for the Tour in 1989, having taught himself golf by studying pictures in golf magazines. Before taking his first golf lesson, Lancaster had been providing lessons to others as a club professional. But, Lancaster noted: "I kind of didn't know what I was doing."

- Won the 1994 GTE Byron Nelson Classic (rain-shortened, 36 holes).

- Tied for fourth at the 1995 U.S. Open.

- Tied for fifth at the 1991 Greater Milwaukee Open.

- Tied for fifth at the 1996 Deposit Guaranty Golf Classic.

- Tied for 20th at the 1991 The Players Championship.

- First player in U.S. Open history to shoot 29 for nine holes (1995).

YEAR	EVENTS	WINS	TOP 10	CUTS MADE	EARNINGS	RANK
1990	26		2	11	$85,769	142
1991	33		3	22	$180,037	90
1992	35		1	23	$146,867	103
1993	32		2	19	$149,381	107
1994	29	1	1	19	$305,038	58
1995	29		1	18	$182,219	101
1996	33		2	22	$210,000	104

TOM LEHMAN

Born: Thomas Edward Lehman, March 7, 1959

Birthplace: Austin, Minn.

Ht: 6' 2" **Wt:** 180

Residence: Scottsdale, Ariz.

1996 Money Rank: 1st

Possessor of one of the most solid all-around games on the Tour, Lehman had a truly awesome year in 1996, ending his season with a second victory (at the Tour Championship in Tulsa; the first came at the British Open) and $540,000 in first-place money, pushing him to a total of $1,780,159, edging Phil Mickelson's purse and point record. In addition, Lehman, the father of three who began golfing at age 5, wrapped up the best scoring average and PGA of America Player of the Year honors.

In '96, he also became the first American since Bobby Jones in 1926 to win the British Open at Royal Lytham. Lehman, who golfed collegiately at the University of Minnesota and who credits his marriage to wife, Melissa, with giving him focus for his game, has been taking the PGA Tour by storm since emerging from the ranks of the Ben Hogan Tour in 1991. He was third in the '93 Masters and second in '94.

- Entered 23 events in '96, finishing in the money 20 times with the two wins and 11 other Top 10 finishes: tied for seventh at the Bell Canadian Open; tied for tenth at the NEC World Series of Golf; tied for fifth at the Sprint International; tied for second at the U.S. Open; tied for second at the Buick Classic; tied for eighth at the Players Championship; tied for tenth at the Freeport-McDermott Classic; tied for ninth at the Bay Hill Invitational by Office Depot; tied for sixth at the Nissan Open; tied for fourth at the United Airlines Hawaiian Open; and tied for third at the Buick Invitational of California.

- In '96, finished out of the Top 20 only three times in 22 events.

- "The (1996) money title is nice," Lehman says, "but I've never put a lot of emphasis on money. I've always been more impressed by the guys who win the Vardon Trophy or are Player of the Year. Those are better indicators of who had a good year."

- Previous to winning the British Open, Lehman had failed on three prior occasions when he led going into the final round of a major. He led the 1994 Masters and each of the last two U.S. Opens after three rounds. "You never like to read that you can never win the big one," Lehman said after winning at Royal Lytham. "That's always been my biggest fear, to read it on your

gravestone—'Tom Lehman—He couldn't win the big one.'"

- In addition to '96 Tour Championship and British Open, Lehman has won the 1995 Colonial Invitational and '94 Memorial. The Memorial win was especially memorable: he shot 20 under par, beating the rest of the field by five strokes. "He played a game to which I am not accustomed," remarked Jack Nicklaus.

- Finished first in '96 Tour statistics in average strokes—69.32; finished fourth in greens in regulation—70.8.

- Has one international win—1993 Casio World Open.

- Previous best year came in 1994, when he had nine Top 10 finishes, including four 67s in a Memorial Tournament win over Greg Norman, and finishing second to Jose Maria Olazabal at the Masters.

- Mini-tours experiences include PGT, Dakotas, Golden State, South Florida and Carolinas.

- Is host to an annual tournament in Minneapolis to raise money for the Children's Cancer Research Fund.

- Two-time runner-up for Big Ten championship at the University of Minnesota.

- Lists hunting and church activities as his special interests.

YEAR	EVENTS	WINS	TOP 10	CUTS MADE	EARNINGS	RANK
1983	22			9	$9,413	182
1984	26			9	$9,382	184
1985	26			10	$20,232	158
1986	2					
1987	1					
1990P	1					
1990N	18	1	5	12	$41,338	17
1991	28	3	11	27	$141,934	1
1992	29		9	25	$579,093	24
1993	27		6	20	$422,761	33
1994	23	1	9	21	$1,031,144	4
1995	18	1	5	16	$830,231	15
1996	22	2	13	20	$1,780,159	1

JUSTIN LEONARD

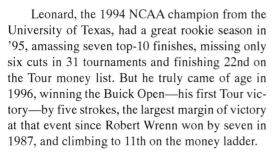

Born: Justin Charles Garret Leonard, June 15, 1972
Birthplace: Dallas, Tex.
Ht: 5' 9" **Wt:** 160
Residence: Dallas, Tex.
Joined Tour: 1994
1996 Money Rank: 11th

Leonard, the 1994 NCAA champion from the University of Texas, had a great rookie season in '95, amassing seven top-10 finishes, missing only six cuts in 31 tournaments and finishing 22nd on the Tour money list. But he truly came of age in 1996, winning the Buick Open—his first Tour victory—by five strokes, the largest margin of victory at that event since Robert Wrenn won by seven in 1987, and climbing to 11th on the money ladder.

Leonard, whose Tour mentors include fellow Longhorn alums Ben Crenshaw and Tom Kite and who is the only golfer in Southwest Conference history to win four consecutive conference championships, earned Tour privileges in 1994 without a trip to Q School by finishing 126th on the money list with $140,143. Leonard won the 1992 U.S. Amateur title.

- Finished in the money 23 of 30 times in 1996 for $943,140. In addition to Buick win, had seven other Top 10 finishes—a tie for sixth at the Tour Championship; fifth at the Sprint International; a tie for fifth at the PGA Championship; a tie for eighth at the Motorola Western Open; a tie for fourth at the FedEx St. Jude Classic; a tie for tenth at the MasterCard Colonial; and second at the Phoenix Open.

- By winning the Buick Open, Leonard joined Tim Herron, Paul Goydos, Scott McCarron, Paul Stankowski, Steve Stricker and Willie Wood as 1996 first-time winners.

- Finished fifth in '96 Tour statistics in sand saves (62.6).

- Finished first in '95 Tour ratings in all around (323).

- Played eight Tour events as an amateur, making the cut in five.

- Won 1994 NCAA title with 17-under 271, equaling NCAA record set by Phil Mickelson in 1992.

- First team All-American in 1993-94.

- Winner Texas 5A State Championship 1989-90.

YEAR	EVENTS	WINS	TOP 10	CUTS MADE	EARNINGS	RANK
1994	13		2	5	$140,413	126
1995	31		7	25	$748,793	22
1996	29	1	8	23	$943,140	11

WAYNE LEVI

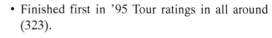

Born: Wayne John Levi, February 22, 1952
Birthplace: Little Falls, NY
Ht: 5' 9" **Wt:** 165
Joined Tour: 1977
1996 Money Rank: 108

After a terrible 1995 season by his career standards, Levi rebounded in 1996 to finish in the money 14 times (including two top 10s) to earn $194,999. Levi improved greatly from 1995, when he made the cut just six times and dropped to 208th on the money list.

Levi started playing on the tour in 1977. His breakthrough season came in 1979, when he made the cut 24 times out of 29 events (including a win) to rank 20th. Levi topped that season in 1982 when he had nine top 10 finishes (including two victories) and ranked 8th on the money list. Throughout the 1980s, Levi ranked among golf's top 60 players. Then in 1990, Levi had his career season: four tournament victories and $1,024,647 in earnings, ranking him second behind Greg Norman. After that, however, Levi's play dropped off until bottoming out in 1995.

When Levi isn't golfing, he prefers to be home with his wife and four children and to follow financial markets, where he has no doubt invested some of his $4.4 million in lifetime earnings.

- Won 12 PGA tournaments (won four tournaments in 1990).

- Fifth player in golf history to win over $1 million in one season (1990).

- Won the 1990 BellSouth Atlanta Classic.

- Won the 1990 Centel Western Open.

- Won the 1990 Canon Greater Hartford Open.

- Won the 1990 Canadian Open.

- Won the 1985 Georgia-Pacific Atlanta Classic.

- Won the 1984 B.C. Open.

- Won the 1983 Buick Open.

- Won the 1982 Hawaiian Open.

- Won the 1978 Walt Disney World National Team Play (with Bob Mann).

- Member of the 1991 Ryder Cup team.

YEAR	EVENTS	WINS	TOP 10	CUTS MADE	EARNINGS	RANK
1976	1			1	$1,412	217
1977	13			7	$8,136	159
1978	23	1	1	16	$25,039	99
1979	29	1	6	24	$141,612	20
1980	32	1	5	19	$120,145	32
1981	30		2	24	$62,177	69
1982	27	2	9	18	$280,681	8
1983	22	1	6	20	$193,252	22
1984	28	1	7	22	$252,921	20
1985	23	1	5	21	$221,425	22
1986	28		5	20	$154,777	59
1987	27		5	16	$203,322	53
1988	23		4	19	$190,073	61
1989	26		7	17	$499,292	16
1990	23	4	5	14	$1,024,647	2
1991	25		3	12	$195,861	87
1992	25		3	17	$237,935	65
1993	22		2	15	$179,521	95
1994	24		4	17	$200,476	91
1995	20			6	$46,095	208
1996	20		2	14	$194,999	108•

AVERAGE YARDS PER DRIVE

Rank	Name	Rounds	Yards
1.	John Daly	72	288.8
2.	John Adams	78	286.7
3.	Fred Couples	66	285.8
4.	Davis Love III	80	285.7
5.	Tim Herron	100	283.5
6.	Steve Stricker	82	281.8
7.	Kelly Gibson	114	280.8
T8.	Phil Mickelson	77	280.4
T8.	Carl Paulson	87	280.4
10.	Steve Jones	83	280.0

DAVIS LOVE III

Born: Davis Milton Love III, April 13, 1964

Birthplace: Charlotte, N.C.

Ht: 6' 3" **Wt:** 175

Residence: Sea Island, Geo.

Q School: Fall 1985

1996 Money Rank: 7th

Love, who was born shortly after his father competed in the 1964 Masters, vies with big hitters like John Daly and Fred Couples as one of the top drivers on the Tour. He won three tournaments in 1992 and has earned more than $1 million three times in his 11-year career. 1996 was a typically strong year for the consistent Love, as he won a tournament (the Buick Invitational) and had 10 other Top 10 finishes.

It hasn't been all roses, however. Love, who has distinguished himself as a Ryder Cup leader (and who won an unprecedented fourth consecutive World Cup title with Fred Couples in 1995), put himself in a deep hole in 1994 with a penalty stroke he called on himself at the Las Vegas Invitational. That error placed him in 33rd position on the money list and threatened to keep him out of the 1995 Masters. It took a dramatic, 11th hour playoff victory over Mike Heinen at the '95 Freeport-McMoRan Classic to garner an invitation. And Love, the father of two (including Davis Love IV), exploited the opportunity well, nearly winning the Masters on the strength of a heroic final round 66, falling one stroke short to winner and friend, Ben Crenshaw.

Love's father was a highly regarded teacher who died in a 1988 plane crash. Love is caddied by his brother, Mark.

- Tour wins include: 1996 Buick Invitational; 1995 Freeport MacMoRan Classic; 1993 Infiniti Tournament of Champions and Las Vegas Invitational; 1992 Players Championship, MCI Heritage Classic and K-mart Greater Greensboro Open; 1991 MCI Heritage Classic; 1990 International, and the 1987 MCI Heritage Classic.

- International wins: 1995 World Cup (individual title).

- Finished in the money in 19 of 24 events in 1996 for $1,211,139. Top 10 finishes (other than his win): second at the Las Vegas Invitational; tied for second at the Buick Challenge; tied for sixth at the NEC World Series of Golf; tied for second at the U.S. Open; tied for sixth at the Memorial Tournament; fifth at the MasterCard Colonial; fourth at the MCI Classic; tied for seventh at the Masters; tied for fourth at the Freeport-McDermott Classic; and sixth at the Mercedes Championship.

- 1996 Buick Invitational win gave Love at least one victory in six of the last seven years.

- Finished second in '96 Tour statistics in holes per eagle (120.0); fourth in average yards per drive (285.7); eighth in average strokes per round (69.81), and ninth in birdies per round (3.85).

- Ranked second in 1995 Tour in driving (284.6) and third in eagles (14).

- Won Tour driving distance titles in 1986 and 1994.

- Final 62 at K-mart Greater Greensboro Open in 1992 brought him from three strokes back for the win.

- Enjoys hunting and fishing, North Carolina basketball, Atlanta Braves baseball and stock car racing.

- Attended National Hot Rod Association driving school in Gainesville, Fla., in December 1995.

- Has earned $6,835,029 on the Tour.

YEAR	EVENTS	WINS	TOP 10	CUTS MADE	EARNINGS	RANK
1986	31		2	22	$113,245	77
1987	26	1	4	18	$297,378	33
1988	29		3	17	$156,068	75
1989	24		4	17	$278,760	44
1990	27	1	4	20	$537,172	20
1991	28	1	8	23	$686,361	8
1992	25	3	9	22	$1,191,630	2
1993	26	2	5	23	$777,059	12
1994	28		4	21	$474,219	33
1995	24	1	9	22	$1,111,999	6
1996	23	1	10	19	$1,211,139	7

ANDREW MAGEE

Born: Andrew Donald Magee, May 22, 1962
Birthplace: Paris, France
Ht: 6' **Wt:** 180
Residence: Paradise Valley, Ariz.
Q School: Fall 1984
1996 Money Rank: 60th

Born in Paris, where his father was working in the oil business, Magee, who lists "whistling" as one of his special interests (along with travel, swimming and fishing), enjoyed his best earnings year in 1991, when he won twice and finished fifth on the money list.

A three-time All-American at the University of Oklahoma and the father of three, Magee claimed his first Tour win at the 1988 Pensacola Open, where he rallied from four strokes back. In

1996 he finished in the money in 13 of 26 events in '96 with $332,504, and three Top 10 finishes—second at the Quad City Classic; tied for third at the Greater Milwaukee Open; and tied for tenth at the Greater Vancouver Open.

- Tour wins include: 1994 Northern Telecom Open, 1991 Nestle Invitational and Las Vegas Invitational, and 1988 Pensacola Open.

- Won 1994 Telecom with a closing 67 to defeat Loren Roberts, Vijay Singh, Jay Don Blake and Steve Stricker by two strokes.

- Posted a 31-under 329, then a PGA 90-hole Tour-record, to force a playoff with D.A. Weibring at the 1991 Las Vegas invitational. Defeated Weibring on the second extra hole at Las Vegas C.C.

- Won 1979 Doug Sanders Junior Invitational.

YEAR	EVENTS	WINS	TOP 10	CUTS MADE	EARNINGS	RANK
1984	3			1	$1,701	238
1985	30		4	18	$75,593	99
1986	33		1	17	$69,478	120
1987	33		2	18	$94,598	99
1988	30	1	4	17	$261,954	43
1989	33		3	19	$126,770	109
1990	30		3	22	$210,507	71
1991	28	2	7	19	$750,082	5
1992	28		3	21	$285,946	53
1993	25		2	14	$269,986	62
1994	25	1	3	20	$431,041	36
1995	27		3	18	$256,918	72
1996	26		3	13	$332,504	60

JOHN MAGINNES

Born: John Maginnes, July 14, 1968

Birthplace: Atlanta, Ga.

Ht: 6' 0" **Wt:** 210

Joined Tour: 1996

1996 Money Rank: 113

Maginnes had a respectable rookie season on the 1996 PGA Tour, making the cut 14 times out of 28 events—not half bad—and earning $184,065. His sole top 10 finish was strong: a tie for second (with Davis Love III, Fred Funk, and Len Mattiace) at the 1996 Buick Challenge. Maginnes qualified for the tour in 1995, then made the cut in the 1995 U.S. Open—his biggest thrill in golf, he said. Before making the PGA Tour, Maginnes played for two years (1994-1995) on the Nike Tour. In 1995, Maginnes ranked 16th on the Nike Tour money list, with $91,125, with one tournament victory and one runner-up finish.

- Finished tied for second at the 1996 Buick Challenge.

- Finished tied for 71st at the 1995 U.S. Open.

- Won the 1995 NIKE San Jose Open.

- Finished second at the 1995 NIKE TOUR Championship.

- Finished 16th on the 1995 NIKE TOUR money list.

YEAR	EVENTS	WINS	TOP 10	CUTS MADE	EARNINGS	RANK
1995	1			1	$2,807	324
1996	28		1	14	$184,065	113

DOUG MARTIN

Born: Douglas Allan Martin, December 8, 1966

Birthplace: Bluffton, Ohio

Joined Tour: 1992

1996 Money Rank: 103

After enduring some shaky seasons early in his career, Martin is performing consistently on the PGA Tour. In 1996, he made the cut 17 times (including a tie for fifth finish) to earn $210,667. Martin's play dropped slightly from his successful 1995 season, when he finished in the money 18 times and ranked 81st. His sole top 10 finish that year was a tie for second at the 1995 Buick Classic, where he lost to Vijay Singh in a playoff.

Martin had difficulty making the cut during his first years on the PGA Tour, so he played on the Nike Tour in 1991 and 1993 to sharpen his form. In 1993, Martin finished second on the Nike money list by winning one tournament, finishing runner-up in three others, and making the cut in 19 tournaments out of 20 entered.

Though he attended the University of Oklahoma, Martin is a rabid Notre Dame football fan. Several Saturday afternoons a year, he stood on the Fighting Irish sidelines as a guest of coach Lou Holtz.

- Tied for second at the 1995 Buick Classic.
- Tied for fourth at the 1993 Deposit Guaranty Classic.
- Tied for fifth at the 1996 Shell Houston Open.
- Finished second on the 1993 Nike money list.
- Won the 1993 Nike South Texas Open.

YEAR	EVENTS	WINS	TOP 10	CUTS MADE	EARNINGS	RANK
1989	1			1	$1,234	287
1990	2			1	$1,819	284
1992	32		1	12	$77,204	150
1993	5		1	4	$21,381	212
1994	33		1	8	$81,201	168
1995	29		1	18	$227,463	81
1996	30		1	17	$210,667	103

LEN MATTIACE

Born: October 15th, 1967

Birthplace: Mineola, N.Y.

Ht: 6' 1" **Wt:** 185

Exempt Status: 27th at 1995 Q-School; Nike 6-10 List

Q School: 1992, 1995

Mattiace had an excellent amateur career, highlighted by an NCAA Championship with Wake Forest in 1986 and All-American Status in 1987. After playing the Nike tour in 1995, he made a quantum leap to 92nd on the PGA Tour money list. Mattiace had 2 Top 10 finishes in 1996, and made 15 out of 29 cuts, including a tie for second at the Buick Challenge.

YEAR	EVENTS	WINS	TOP 10	CUTS MADE	EARNINGS	RANK
1994					$74,521	160
1996	29		2	15	$238,977	92

BILLY MAYFAIR

Born: William Fred Mayfair, August 6, 1966

Birthplace: Phoenix, Ariz.

Ht: 5' 8" **Wt:** 175

Residence: Scottsdale, Ariz.

Q School: Fall 1988

1996 Money Rank: 55th

Mayfair, winner of the 1987 Fred Haskins Award as the outstanding college player (Arizona State), showed the world and maybe even himself in 1995 how good a player he can be in his eighth year on the Tour. In 1995, he earned $1,542,191 (then the second-highest total in PGA history), had two wins and four other top-10 finishes, electrifying the golfing world with clutch putting and a tee-to-green game that was rock solid.

Mayfair has been up and down enough times on the Tour to know first-hand the fickle nature of the game of golf. In 1990, his second year on Tour, he was 12th on the Money List. The next year, he dipped to 89th. Two years later, he rose to 30th. Then, in 1994, he finished 113th, missed 14 cuts, and had only one top-10 finish.

A close friend of Houston Rockets forward Charles Barkley, Mayfair was a highly touted amateur after his wins at the 1986 U.S. Public Links and the 1987 U.S. Amateur. He was married on the 18th green at TPC at Las Colina in 1994.

- Tour wins include: the 1995 Motorola Western Open and Tour Championship, and the 1993 Greater Milwaukee Open.

- Finished in the money in 18 of 28 events in 1996, earning $357,654, with one Top 10 finish—a tie for second at the NEC World Series of Golf.

- Finished first in 1995 Tour statistics in sand saves (68.8).

- Holed out a 20-foot chip on fourth playoff hole for first Tour win '93 Greater Milwaukee Open, defeating Mark Calcavecchia.

- Lost twice in playoffs in 1990—to Jim Gallagher Jr., at the Greater Milwaukee Open and to Jodie Mudd in season-ending Nabisco Championships.

- About golf-course vows with wife, Tammy, he said: "We're going to be spending the rest of our lives on a golf course. We thought we might as well be married on one."

- 1985-87 Arizona Stroke Play champion.

- Member 1987 Walker Cup team.

- Four-time winner Arizona State Juniors.

YEAR	EVENTS	WINS	TOP 10	CUTS MADE	EARNINGS	RANK
1988	5			3	$8,433	220
1989	33			18	$111,998	116
1990	32		7	23	$693,658	12
1991	33		1	20	$185,668	89
1992	33		1	23	$191,878	79
1993	32	1	5	22	$513,072	30
1994	32		1	18	$158,159	113
1995	28	2	6	21	$1,543,192	2
1996	28		1	18	$357,654	55

BLAINE MCCALLISTER

Born: Blaine McCallister, October 17, 1958

Birthplace: Fort Stockton, Tex.

Ht: 5' 10" **Wt:** 190
Joined Tour: 1982
1996 Money Rank: 117

Though he finishes in the top 10 less often than he used to, Blaine McCallister continues to play a solid game of golf. In 1996, McCallister finished in the money 18 times to earn $179,427. His two top 10 finishes included a tie for fourth at the 1996 Freeport-McDermott Classic. McCallister's play has dropped off from 1994, however, when he had seven top 10 finishes and ranked 47th.

McCallister is a solid veteran of the tour. His first big year came in 1988, when he won his first PGA tournament, finished in the top 10 three times, and ranked 49th. McCallister followed up in 1989 with his career year. In earning $523,891 to rank 15th, McCallister won two tournaments (including a dramatic one-stroke victory over Brad Faxon in the 1989 Bank of Boston Classic) and finished in the top 10 five times. Throughout the 1990s, McCallister finished in the money consistently—and often in the top 10. He is an interesting golfer to watch: A natural lefthander, he putts southpaw but plays the fairways right-handed.

Because his wife Claudia suffers from a rare eye disease—pseudoxanthoma elasticum (PXE)—McCallister has been active in several eyesight organizations. McCallister has battled illness himself: In early 1990, he fought off mononucleosis, then came back in 1991 to win the H-E-B Texas Open.

- Won the 1993 B.C. Open.

- Won the 1991 H-E-B Texas Open.

- Won the 1989 Honda Classic.

- Won the 1989 Bank of Boston Classic.

- Won the 1988 Hardee's Golf Classic.

- Won the 1991 Vines Classic (Australia).

- Tied a PGA TOUR record by shooting middle rounds of 62-63—125 in the 1988 Hardee's Golf Classic.

YEAR	EVENTS	WINS	TOP 10	CUTS MADE	EARNINGS	RANK
1982	22			7	$7,894	186
1983	24			6	$5,218	201
1984	1					
1986	35		1	17	$88,732	94
1987	35		2	19	$120,005	87
1988	34	1	3	23	$225,660	49
1989	31	2	5	20	$523,891	15
1990	30		2	18	$152,048	103
1991	26	1	4	22	$412,974	36
1992	28		4	19	$261,187	59
1993	27	1	2	16	$290,434	61
1994	27		7	20	$351,554	47
1995	26		2	18	$238,847	77
1996	28		2	18	$179,427	117

SCOTT McCARRON

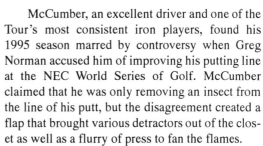

Born: Scott Michael McCarron, July 10, 1965

Birthplace: Sacramento, Cal.

Ht: 5' 10" **Wt:** 170

Residence: Rancho Murieta, Cal.

Q School: Fall 1994

1996 Money Rank: 49th

Making only 12 of 25 cuts in 1995, McCarron, who lists sky diving as special interest, was well on his way to a crash landing—back to the Tour Q School—when he began the first round at the Las Vegas Invitational. He was No. 212 on the money list. Five rounds later, he emerged with a third-place finish and a season-saving check for $108,000, good—coupled with a check for $4,620 the next week at the LaCantera Texas Open—for 128th on the list, saving his card by a mere $2,708.

Thus buoyed, McCarron, who was introduced to golf at age three by his father, stole his first PGA victory in 1996 at the Freeport-McDermott Golf Classic. McCarron's 72-hole total of 13-under 275 was five shots better than Tom Watson. McCarron, who owns a history degree from UCLA, also lists flying, mountain biking and skiing as recreational pursuits.

- Finished in the money in 16 of 27 events in '96, for $404,329, with win at the Freeport-McDermott Golf Classic and a tie for tenth at the Masters.

- Joined Tour in 1994 after finishing 31st at Qualifying Tournament.

- Was member of the Canadian Tour in 1993 and Hooters Tour in 1994.

- Won 1994 Long Beach Open.

- Was member of UCLA National Championship team in 1988.

YEAR	EVENTS	WINS	TOP 10	CUTS MADE	EARNINGS	RANK
1992	1			1	$720	268
1995P	25		1	12	$147,371	128
1995N	3			1	$1,950	204
1996	27	1	2	17	$404,329	49

MARK McCUMBER

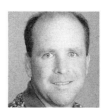

Born: Mark Randall McCumber, September 7, 1951

Birthplace: Jacksonville, Fla.

Ht: 5' 8" **Wt:** 170

Residence: Jacksonville, Fla.

Q School: Spring 1976

1996 Money Rank: 38th

McCumber, an excellent driver and one of the Tour's most consistent iron players, found his 1995 season marred by controversy when Greg Norman accused him of improving his putting line at the NEC World Series of Golf. McCumber claimed that he was only removing an insect from the line of his putt, but the disagreement created a flap that brought various detractors out of the closet as well as a flurry of press to fan the flames.

All the while, McCumber went about his business, making 14 of 19 cuts and posting three Top 10 finishes. He also advanced to the semi-finals of the Andersen Consulting World Series of Golf, where he came in third.

A golf course designer (the 1997 Honda Classic will be held at TPC at Heron Bay in Coral Springs, Fla., a course his firm designed), McCumber, a 19-year veteran, has Tour victories spanning three decades, beginning with the 1979 Doral-Eastern Open and ending, thus far, with three wins in 1994. McCumber's nephew, Josh McCumber, is an up-and-coming golfer at the University of Florida.

- Tour wins include: the 1994 Anheuser-Busch Classic, Hardee's Golf Classic and Tour Championship; the 1989 Beatrice Western Open; the 1988 Players Championship; the 1987 Anheuser-Busch Classic; the 1985 Doral-Eastern Open; the 1983 Western and Pensacola opens; and the 1979 Doral-Eastern Open.

- Finished in the money in 10 of 16 events in 1996 for $487,226, including four Top 10 finishes—a tie for seventh at the Buick Open; a tie for second at the British Open; a tie for ninth at the Michelob Championship at Kingsmill; and second at the Honda Classic.

- Won '94 Tour Championship by sinking a 40-foot birdie putt to defeat Fuzzy Zoeller on first playoff hole.

- With increased involvement in golf-course design projects affecting his game, made decision in 1993 to put full focus on tournaments during season. Decision paid immediate dividends with best money-list finish ever—third, with $1,208,209.

- Member 1989 Ryder Cup team and 1988 and 1989 World Cup squads.

- Won World Cup title with Ben Crenshaw in 1988.

- Golf course design firm is called Mark McCumber and Associates, an arm of McCumber Golf, a company he operates with his brothers.

YEAR	EVENTS	WINS	TOP 10	CUTS MADE	EARNINGS	RANK
1978	8		1	6	$6,948	160
1979	31	1	1	15	$67,886	60
1980	30		2	15	$36,985	88
1981	25		2	15	$33,363	103
1982	26		1	18	$31,684	119
1983	29	2	8	20	$268,294	8
1984	26		5	19	$133,445	50
1985	24	1	3	14	$192,752	32
1986	28		1	21	$110,442	80
1987	29	1	5	24	$390,885	22
1988	22	1	5	21	$559,111	13
1989	20	1	7	15	$546,587	14
1990	24		3	20	$163,413	97
1991	23		1	17	$173,852	92
1992	24		1	17	$136,653	106
1993	21		3	18	$363,269	41
1994	20	3	6	18	$1,208,209	3
1995	19		3	14	$375,923	47
1996	15		4	10	$487,226	38

ROCCO MEDIATE

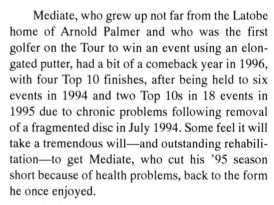

Born: Rocco Anthony Mediate, December 17, 1962

Birthplace: Greensburg, Penn.

Ht: 6' 1" **Wt:** 200

Residence: Ponte Vedra Beach, Fla.

Q School: Fall 1985, 1986

1996 Money Rank: 40th

Mediate, who grew up not far from the Latobe home of Arnold Palmer and who was the first golfer on the Tour to win an event using an elongated putter, had a bit of a comeback year in 1996, with four Top 10 finishes, after being held to six events in 1994 and two Top 10s in 18 events in 1995 due to chronic problems following removal of a fragmented disc in July 1994. Some feel it will take a tremendous will—and outstanding rehabilitation—to get Mediate, who cut his '95 season short because of health problems, back to the form he once enjoyed.

Both of Mediate's Tour victories came in playoffs. In '91 he birdied the 71st and 72nd holes at Doral to force a play-off with Curtis Strange, which he won with another birdie on the first hole of sudden death. The other victory came at the '93 Kmart Greater Greensboro Open, where he beat Steve Elkington on the fourth hole of their play-off.

- In addition to the two Tour wins, has one international win—the 1992 Perrier French Open.

- Finished in the money in 14 of 20 events in 1996 for $475,255, with four Top 10 finishes—tied for third at the MasterCard Colonial; tied for eighth at the MCI Classic; tied for fourth at the Players Championship; and tied for sixth at the Phoenix Open.

- In wake of back problems, Mediate developed bursitis in his hip and ankle, and, after Buick Open in July 1995, decided to shut down his season and pursue an aggressive therapy program to prepare for 1996.

- Received medical extension at end of season, giving him seven more tournaments in 1996 to earn the $40,741 he needed to finish in the Top 125 on the money list and retain his card.

- Finished 10th in '96 Tour statistics in greens in regulation (70.0).

- Played golf with Arnold Palmer for first time at age 19.

- Attended California (Pa.) State College before transferring to Florida Southern.

- Special interests include photography, music and collecting trading cards.

YEAR	EVENTS	WINS	TOP 10	CUTS MADE	EARNINGS	RANK
1985	2					
1986	27		1	10	$20,670	174
1987	32		1	19	$112,099	91
1988	32		1	25	$129,829	92
1989	30			23	$132,501	108
1990	27		3	17	$240,625	62
1991	25	1	7	19	$597,438	15
1992	25		6	17	$301,896	49
1993	24	1	6	22	$680,623	16
1994	6		1	4	$45,940	193
1995	18		2	8	$105,618	155
1996	21		4	15	$475,225	40

PHIL MICKELSON

Born: June 16, 1970
Birthplace: San Diego, Cal.
Ht: 6' 2" **Wt:** 190
Residence: Scottsdale, Ariz.

Joined Tour: June 1992
1996 Money Rank: 2nd

Mickelson, one of only four collegians to win the NCAA title in their freshman year (Ben Crenshaw, Curtis Strange and Billy Ray Brown were the others), enjoyed a breakthrough season in 1996 with four wins, four other Top 10 finishes and second-place earnings on the money list with $1,697,799.

By May of '96, Mickelson had won three times and had topped the $1 million mark in earnings. Noted as a very long driver as well as a marvelous short iron player and putter, Mickelson is right-handed in everything but golf. He began hitting golf balls before he was two by "mirroring" his father: dad was right-handed, and young Phil watched him and copied from his left side.

A fan favorite and one of the best young talents on the Tour, Mickelson won the World Series of Golf, Northern Telecom Open, Phoenix Open and Byron Nelson Classic in 1996. He finished in the money in 19 of 22 events, including four wins and four other Top 10 finishes— tied for eighth at the Las Vegas Invitational; tied for eighth at the PGA Championship; third at the Masters; and second at the Buick Invitational of California.

- Other tour wins: 1995 Northern Telecom Open; the 1994 Mercedes Championships; the 1993 Buick Invitational of California; and the 1991 Northern Telecom Open. Earned second and third titles in just second year on the Tour—but they were his first two as professional. His first win— while still playing at Arizona State University— came while he was an amateur. (He defeated Bob Tway and Tom Purtzer by one stroke).

- Finished tied for eighth in '96 Tour statistics in average yards per drive (280.4) and eighth in sand saves (61.3).

- 1995 win at Northern Telecom Open made him the first player in Tour history to win the same tournament as an amateur and as a professional.

- Was 3-0 in his first Ryder Cup in 1995.

- Turned professional at 1992 U.S. Open, where he failed to make the cut.

- Finished second in his third professional start at the 1992 New England Classic.

- Low amateur 1990-91 U.S. Opens and 1991 Masters.

- 1991 Golf World Amateur Player of the Year.

- Four-time first-team All-America at Arizona State University; only Gary Hallberg and David Duval have achieved the same feat.

- Winner 1989-90-91 NCAA Championships for ASU.

- Collegiate Player of the Year 1990-92.

- Only lefthander to win U.S. Amateur.

- Has earned $3,902,341 on the Tour.

YEAR	EVENTS	WINS	TOP 10	CUTS MADE	EARNINGS	RANK
1992	10		2	7	$171,714	90
1993	24	2	4	14	$628,735	22
1994	18	1	9	17	$748,316	15
1995	24	1	4	15	$655,777	28
1996	21	4	8	19	$1,697,799	2

LARRY MIZE

Born: Larry Hogan Mize, September 23, 1958

Birthplace: Augusta, Geo.

Ht: 6' **Wt:** 165

Residence: Columbus, Geo.

Q School: Fall 1981

1996 Money Rank: 67th

Mize is probably best known for his famous "impossible shot" Masters play-off win against Greg Norman in 1987, when he used a sand wedge on the second extra hole—No. 11—to chip in from 140 feet out.

A good driver and a superb putter (and a pianist), Mize, the father of three, played in only

NUMBER OF HOLES PLAYED PER EAGLE

Rank	Name	Rounds	Holes
1.	Tom Watson	54	97.2
2.	Davis Love III	80	120.0
3.	Carl Paulson	87	120.5
4.	Vijay Singh	90	124.6
5.	Curt Byrum	56	126.0
6.	Mark Calcavecchia	103	132.1
7.	Nick Price	52	133.7
8.	John Adams	78	140.4
9.	Omar Uresti	94	141.0
10.	Nolan Henke	80	143.8

22 events in 1993, '94 and '95 and 23 in '96, opting for more time with his family.

He's also something of a fast healer. Mize underwent arthroscopic knee surgery in March 1994—then finished in a tie for fifth the following week at the Nestle Invitational.

- In addition to the '87 Master, Tour wins include: 1993 Northern Telecom Open and Buick Open, and the 1983 Danny Thomas-Memphis Classic.

- Also has four international wins: 1993 Johnnie Walker World Championship; 1990 Dunlop Phoenix Open; 1989 Dunlop Phoenix Open; and 1988 Casio World Open.

- Finished in the money in 15 of 23 events in 1996 for $317,468, with three Top 10 finishes—a tie for eighth at the PGA Championship; a tie for eighth at the Kemper Open; and a tie for fourth at the United Airlines Hawaiian Open.

- Two wins in 1993 ended a drought following the '87 Masters.

- Birdied final hole in '87 Masters to force playoff with Norman and Seve Ballesteros. Ballesteros went out on the first playoff hole.

- Sank 25-foot birdie putt to win first Tour title at 1983 Danny Thomas-Memphis Classic, edging Fuzzy Zoeller, Sammy Rachels and Chip Beck.

- Lost playoffs to Norman at 1986 Kemper Open and to Payne Stewart at 1990 MCI Heritage Classic.
- Served as Player Director on the PGA Tour Policy Board from 1987-90.
- Member 1987 Ryder Cup team.
- Played three years No. 1 at Georgia Tech; captained team for two of those years.

YEAR	EVENTS	WINS	TOP 10	CUTS MADE	EARNINGS	RANK
1980	2			1	$1,189	251
1981	2					
1982	28		1	13	$28,787	125
1983	35	1	3	25	$146,325	35
1984	31		6	26	$172,513	36
1985	28		8	25	$231,041	17
1986	25		6	22	$314,051	17
1987	23	1	9	16	$561,407	6
1988	24		3	17	$187,823	62
1989	25		7	22	$278,388	45
1990	23		7	21	$668,198	14
1991	25		4	22	$279,061	60
1992	24		5	18	$316,428	47
1993	22	2	7	17	$724,660	13
1994	22		4	18	$386,029	42
1995	22		3	15	$289,576	67
1996	23		3	15	$317,468	67

COLIN MONTGOMERIE

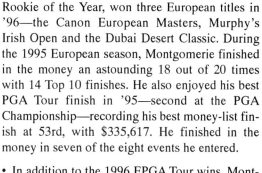

Born: June 23, 1963
Birthplace: Glasgow, Scotland
Ht: 6' 1" **Wt:** 205
Residence: Oxshott, Surrey, England
Turned professional: 1987
1996 Money Rank: 48th

Montgomerie played in only seven Tour events in 1996, concentrating instead—again—on defending his No. 1 position on the European Tour for the fourth consecutive year, a record previously equaled only by Englishman, Peter Oosterhuis from 1971 to 1974.

Montgomerie, a three-time All-American at Houston Baptist and the 1988 European Tour Rookie of the Year, won three European titles in '96—the Canon European Masters, Murphy's Irish Open and the Dubai Desert Classic. During the 1995 European season, Montgomerie finished in the money an astounding 18 out of 20 times with 14 Top 10 finishes. He also enjoyed his best PGA Tour finish in '95—second at the PGA Championship—recording his best money-list finish at 53rd, with $335,617. He finished in the money in seven of the eight events he entered.

- In addition to the 1996 EPGA Tour wins, Montgomerie has won the 1995 Volvo German Open and Trophee Lancome; the 1994 Peugeot Open de Espana, Murphy's English Open and Volvo German Open; 1993 Heineken Dutch Open and Volvo Masters; the 1991 Scandinavian Masters, and the 1989 Portuguese Open-TPC.
- Finished tied for second at the 1994 U.S. Open.
- PGA Tour playoff record is 0-2.
- Won the 1987 Scottish Amateur Championship.
- Won the 1985 Scottish Stroke Play Championship as an amateur.

YEAR	EVENTS	WINS	TOP 10	CUTS MADE	EARNINGS	RANK
1992					$98,045	132
1993					$17,992	221
1994					$213,828	87
1995	8				$335,617	53
1996	7		1	5	$421,011	48

GIL MORGAN

Born: Gilbert Bryan Morgan, September 25th, 1946
Birthplace: Wewoka, Okla.
Ht: 5' 9" **Wt:** 175
Exempt Status: 73rd on 1995 money list
Q School: 1973

Morgan has built a distinguished career the hallmark of which has been consistency. Since his first full-time season on the PGA Tour in 1974, Morgan never finished lower than 94th on the money list rankings. Morgan has seven PGA Tour wins, including the 1978 World Series of Golf, defeating Hubert Green in a playoff, the year in which he finished second on the money list behind Tom Watson. His best performances in the major championships are a third place finish at the 1983 U.S. Open, a third place finish at the 1990 PGA Championship, a tie for third at the 1984 Masters, and a tie for third in the 1980 PGA Championship. He reached 12 under par in the third round of the 1992 U.S. Open at Pebble Beach. Unfortunately, the wheels came off and he ended up in a tie for 13th place.

In October of 1996, in only the second start of his Senior PGA Tour career, Morgan became the Senior Tour's youngest winner (50 years, 11 days), with a victory over Chi Chi Rodriguez in the Ralph's Classic. Morgan waited until he obtained his Doctor of Optometry degree in 1972 (Southern College of Optometry) before he formally committed to professional golf, although he never practiced as an Optometrist.

• Earned the most money of his career in 1990, when he won the Kemper Open and finished in the top eight in seven straight tournaments.

• One of the few golfers to win in three consecutive decades, the 1970's, 1980's, and 1990's.

• Ryder Cup Member in 1979 and 1983.

YEAR	EVENTS	WINS	TOP 10	CUTS MADE	EARNINGS	RANK
1973	3			1	$3,800	204
1974	30		3	16	$23,880	94
1975	27		2	17	$42,772	60
1976	32		6	24	$61,372	42
1977	33	1	5	25	$104,817	24
1978	28	2	11	24	$267,459	2
1979	25	1	2	19	$115,857	29
1980	25		7	19	$135,308	28
1981	24		6	19	$171,184	18
1982	25		8	20	$139,652	26
1983	25	2	10	23	$306,133	5
1984	23		8	19	$281,948	13
1985	25		3	18	$133,941	62
1986	15		3	9	$98,770	84
1987	16		3	10	$133,980	81
1988	23		7	14	$288,002	34
1989	25		6	19	$300,395	39
1990	24	1	5	18	$702,629	11
1991	24	2	7	16	$232,913	70
1992	23		3	20	$272,959	56
1993	23		9	20	$610,312	24
1994	18		3	14	$309,690	54
1995	21		3	14	$255,565	73
1996	19		2	12	$259,776	85

JOHN MORSE

Born: John Paul Morse, February 16, 1958
Birthplace: Marshall, Mich.
Ht: 5' 10" **Wt:** 180
Residence: Casselberry, Fla.
Joined Tour: 1994
1996 Money Rank: 64th

Morse is nothing if not persistent. After failing six times to earn his card at the PGA Qualifying Tournament, Morse, a former all-conference high school basketball player, finally qualified for the Tour in 1994 by finishing fifth on the 1993 Nike money list.

He ended any suggestions that a sophomore jinx might send him packing in '95, when he won the United Airlines Hawaiian Open in the first week of the season. For the remainder of the '95 season, however, Morse, a former Big 10 champion at the University of Michigan, was far from impressive, making only 12 cuts in 23 attempts before rescuing his reputation with a tie for second at the Buick Challenge and then, two weeks later, a tie for third at the Texas Open to end his season.

Morse seems to have steadied his game in 1996, having finished in the money in 20 of 26 events, winning $322,090, and enjoying two Top 10 finishes—fourth at the U.S. Open and a tie for sixth at the United Airlines Hawaiian Open. A veteran of the Australasian Tour from 1989-92, Morse decided to cast his lot back home with the Nike tour in '93 following the birth of his daughter, Christina.

- Has four international wins in addition to '95 United Airlines Hawaiian Open: 1991 Air New Zealand/Shell Open, 1990 Australian Open and Nedlands Masters, and the 1989 Quebec Open.

- During one 15-start string in '95 posted no better than a tie for 56th.

- About winning the '95 United Airlines Hawaiian Open: "I have to admit it's nice when someone asks, 'Have you won a tournament before?' and you can answer them with a smile and a yes. To achieve champion status is why I am on the PGA Tour. That was one of my goals—and to have at least one of those goals in your pocket is satisfying."

- Won 1990 Australian Open in a playoff with Craig Parry.

YEAR	EVENTS	WINS	TOP 10	CUTS MADE	EARNINGS	RANK
1984	2					
1987	1					
1988	1					
1991	3			1	$9,117	230
1993N	26	1	9	19	$122,627	5
1994P	26		1	12	$146,137	122
1994N	2					
1995	24	1	3	12	$416,803	42
1996	27		2	21	$322,090	64

LARRY NELSON

Born: Larry Gene Nelson, September 10, 1947

Birthplace: Fort Payne, Ala.

Ht: 5' 9" **Wt:** 150

Residence: Marietta, Geo.

Q School: Fall 1973

1996 Money Rank: 70th

Nelson, a 24-year Tour vet who didn't begin playing golf until returning from military service in Vietnam (and broke 100 his first time out), became eligible for the Senior Tour in September 1996.

His 1995 season on the regular Tour was a disappointment (maybe even a disaster). He made only six cuts in 21 attempts (he twice missed three cuts in a row), but a tie for eighth at the Buick Challenge renewed his confidence and desire. "I know for sure I want to win, again, and I think it's only a matter of time," he said following that finish that placed him 214th on the money list, his worst finish since his abbreviated rookie season in 1973.

Though he didn't win in '96, there was improvement, with three Top 10 finishes and his best money-list ranking—70th—since his 25th-place finish in 1988.

- Has 10 Tour titles—1988 Georgia-Pacific Atlanta Classic; 1987 PGA Championship and Walt Disney World/Oldsmobile Classic; 1983 U.S. Open; 1981 Greater Greensboro Open and PGA Championship; 1980 Atlanta Classic and the 1979 Jackie Gleason-Inverrary Classic and Western Open.

- Also has four International wins: 1991 Dunlop Phoenix; 1989 Suntory Open; 1983 Dunlop International Open, and the 1980 Tokai Classic.

- Finished in the money in 16 of 21 events in 1996 for $305,083 and three Top 10 finishes: tied for eighth at the MCI Classic; tied for ninth at the Bay Hill Invitational by Office Depot; and tied for eighth at the Doral-Ryder Open.

- Finished tied for fourth (with Greg Norman) in '96 Tour statistics in birdies per round (3.96)

- With exception of 1979 Western Open and 1983 U.S. Open, all career victories have been achieved in the southeastern U.S.

- Last Tour victory—in 1988—came 300 yards from his house at the Atlanta Country Club.

- Finest year on the Tour occurred in 1987, when the won the PGA Championship in a playoff with Lanny Wadkins at Palm Beach Gardens.

- Former Player Director, PGA Tour Tournament Policy Board.

- Posted a 9-3-1 Ryder Cup record in three appearances—1979, 1981, 1987.

- Has earned $3,623,400 on the Tour.

YEAR	EVENTS	WINS	TOP 10	CUTS MADE	EARNINGS	RANK
1973	3			1	$356	287
1974	25		2	14	$24,022	93
1975	30		5	19	$39,810	66
1976	34		4	27	$66,482	41
1977	33		6	24	$99,876	26
1978	31		4	22	$65,686	45
1979	26	2	9	22	$281,022	2
1980	29	1	9	22	$182,715	11
1981	28	2	4	21	$193,342	10
1982	25		8	18	$159,134	21
1983	23	1	3	13	$138,368	40
1984	20	1	4	11	$154,689	42
1985	21		4	19	$143,993	54
1986	23		3	10	$124,338	69
1987	22	2	7	14	$501,292	14
1988	18	1	6	17	$411,284	25
1989	17		2	12	$186,869	79
1990	15		2	10	$124,260	124
1991	16		3	8	$160,543	96
1992	15		1	9	$94,930	135
1993	18			9	$54,870	177
1994	17		1	8	$66,831	175
1995	21		1	6	$40,689	214
1996	21		3	17	$305,083	70

FRANK NOBILO

Born: May 14th, 1960 in Auckland, New Zealand

Ht: 5' 11" **Wt:** 180

Exempt Status: None

Q School: N/A

Nobilo is a European PGA Tour player (23rd on the 1996 Order of Merit, the European version of the money list) who has performed well on his few visits to the U.S., especially in major championships. In a ranking based on average finish (missed cuts were assigned a 100th place finish) of all players who have played in at least 15 majors since 1980, Nobilo ranked ninth. In 1996, Nobilo finished fourth in the Masters and eighth in the PGA championship. Nobilo has won four European titles, three international titles, and the 1995 and 1996 Sarazen World Open titles in Braselton, Georgia, an unofficial PGA Tour event.

- Despite 100 degree heat at the U.S. Open at Oakmont in 1994, he dressed all in black for the final round.

- One of few tour players to list squash as a hobby.

- President's Cup team member for International team in both 1994 and 1996.

YEAR	EVENTS	WINS	TOP 10	CUTS MADE	EARNINGS	RANK
1992					$7,000	252
1993					$14,500	230
1994					$41,292	138
1995					$52,119	203
1996	8				$262,292	81

GREG NORMAN

Born: Gregory John Norman, February 19, 1955

Birthplace: Queensland, Australia

Ht: 6' **Wt:** 180

Residence: Hobe Sound, Fla.

Joined Tour: 1983

1996 Money Rank: 15th

One of the greatest golfers of the last quarter century and the all-time PGA Tour career money leader, Greg "The Shark" Norman has 69 Tour and International wins and several agonizing losses, including playoff losses in each of the Majors and his infamous collapse at the 1996 Masters. Norman went into the final round with a six-stroke lead, but a bogey on the 11th, double bogey on the famous par-3 12th, and another double-bogey on the par-3 16th left him, almost incomprehensibly four strokes behind Nick Faldo who played alongside the Shark with cool precision.

Norman followed a brilliant 1995 in which he was PGA Player of the Year with another outstanding year in 1996: he was in the money in 11 of 17 events in 1996, earned $891,237, won the Doral-Ryder Open and had four other Top 10 finishes: fifth at the NEC World Series of Golf; tied for seventh at the British Open; tied for tenth at the U.S. Open; and second at the Masters. A gallery favorite, Norman has been involved—win or lose—in some of golf's most memorable moments during the past two decades. He lost the 1987 Masters on the second playoff hole to Larry Mize, who made an incredible chip shot for a sudden, shocking victory; the year before, Bob Tway stole the PGA Championship from him by holing out from a bunker on the 72nd hole at Inverness.

- 16 Tour wins include: 1996 Doral-Ryder Open; 1995 Memorial, Greater Hartford Open, NEC World Series Of Golf; 1994 Players Championship; 1993 Doral-Ryder Open; 1992 Canadian Open; 1990 Doral-Ryder Open and Memorial Tournament; 1989 International and Greater Milwaukee Open; 1988 MCI Heritage Classic; 1986 Panasonic-Las Vegas Invitational and Kemper Open; 1984 Kemper and Canadian opens.

- 53 international wins include: 1995 Australian Masters; 1994 Johnnie Walker Asian Classic; 1993 British Open and Taiheyo Masters; 1990 Australian Masters; 1989 Australian Masters, PGA National Tournament Players Championship and Chunichi Crowns; 1988 Palm Meadows Cup, WSP Open, PGA National Tournament Players Championship and Panasonic New South Wales and Lancia Italian opens; 1987 Australian Masters and National Panasonic Australian Open; 1986 Stefan Queensland Open, National Panasonic New South Wales Open, West End Jubilee South Australian Open, National Panasonic Western Australian Open, European Open, British Open and Suntory World Matchplay Championship; 1985 Toshiba Australian PGA Championship and National Panasonic Australian Open; 1984 Victorian Open, Australian Masters and Toshiba Australian PGA Championship; 1983 Australian Masters, Stefan Queensland Open, National Panasonic New South Wales Open, Hong Kong Open, Cannes Invitational and Suntory World Match Play Championship; 1982 Dunlop Masters, State Express Classic and Benson & Hedges International; 1981 Australian Masters and Martini International, Dunlop Masters; 1980 Australian Open, French Open, Scandinavian Open and Suntory World Match Play Championship; 1979 Traralgon Classic, Martini International and Hong Kong Open; 1978 New South Wales Open, Traralgon Classic, Caltex Festival of Sydney Open and South Seas Classic; 1977 Martini International and Kuzuhz International, and 1976 Westlakes Classic.

- Awards include: 1986, 1990 and 1995 Arnold Palmer Award; 1995 PGA Tour Player of the Year.

- Wife arrived via helicopter with replacement driver during final round of '96 Doral-Ryder Open, after Norman discovered that the driver he used in all but two tournaments in 1995 "went dead," something apparently collapsing inside the metal head.

- Established a record in '96, when he won third tournament title in as many decades in the state of South Australia by winning the Ford South Australian Open by one stroke from Jean-Louis Guepy of France. Scored his first tournament win as a professional at the West Lakes Classic in South Australia in 1976.

- Finished tied for fourth (with Larry Nelson) in '96 Tour statistics in birdies per round (3.96), and fifth in average strokes per round (69.76).

- Difficult to imagine having a better year in golf than did Norman in 1995. Took the money title after entering 16 events and earning nine Top 10 finishes. Also selected PGA Player of the Year for 1995. Only he and Lee Janzen had three victories in 1995.

- Became PGA Tour's leading career money-winner after winning '95 NEC World Series of Golf.

- Finished first in 1995 Tour statistics in scoring (69.06), fourth in total driving (63) and ninth in sand saves (61.0).

- Didn't miss a cut in 1983, 1987, 1994 and 1995.

- Posted British Open record-tying 63 in Round Two of 1986 event at Turnberry. Even better in 1993, Norman became the first golfer ever to have four sub-70 rounds in the Open.

- 1993 PGA Championship playoff loss to Paul Azinger gave him the dubious distinction of losing playoffs in all four majors.

- Held lead in final round of all four majors in 1986.

- Suffered earlier back-to-back heartbreaks at the Masters, finishing tied for second in 1986 and losing a 1987 playoff to Larry Mize's 140-foot pitch for birdie.

- Has won in 13 countries.

- Back problems produced second-round withdrawal from 1995 MCI Classic and later at Colonial.

- Well known for charitable involvements, including annually playing host to Franklin Templeton Shark Shootout.

- Mantra for success comes from self-help book, *Zen and the Martial Arts.*

- Has earned $10,564,662 on the Tour.

YEAR	EVENTS	WINS	TOP 10	CUTS MADE	EARNINGS	RANK
1979	2			2	$3,653	205
1981	9		3	8	$54,272	77
1982	4		1	3	$22,671	142
1983	9		2	9	$71,411	74
1984	16	2	7	15	$310,230	9
1985	16		6	13	$165,458	42
1986	19	2	10	17	$653,296	1
1987	18		9	18	$535,450	7
1988	14	1	7	12	$514,854	17
1989	17	2	8	16	$835,096	4
1990	17	2	11	16	$1,165,477	1
1991	17		6	15	$320,196	53
1992	16	1	8	15	$676,443	18
1993	15	1	12	14	$1,359,653	3
1994	16	1	11	16	$1,330,307	2
1995	16	3	9	15	$1,654,959	1
1996	17	1	5	12	$891,237	15

DAVID OGRIN

Born: David Allen Ogrin, December 31, 1957

Birthplace: Waukeegan, Ill.

Ht: 6' **Wt:** 220

Residence: Garden Ridge, Tex.

Q School: Fall 1982, 1992

1996 Money Rank: 34th

The quintessential die-hard Chicago Cubs fan (Ogrin named his fourth child, a son, Clark Addison, after two streets adjoining Wrigley Field), Ogrin knows about waiting 'til next year in his career, too—at least until 1996. The 19-year veteran finally won his first title in '96, with a one stroke win over Jay Haas at the Texas Open at La Cantera.

A never-say-die story, Ogrin needed four tries to get through the Tour Qualifying Tournament (he did it in 1982). Then, he found himself back there 10 years later. Another product of a father's influence (Ogrin's dad put a set of sawed-off clubs in David's hands when he was two), golf eventually won out over Ogrin's youthful dream of becoming a switch-hitting catcher for the Cubbies, who haven't won the World Series of baseball since 1909.

- International wins include 1994 and 1988 Peru opens.

- Finished in the money in 21 of 31 events in 1996 for $537,225, with win in Texas and four other Top 10 finishes: a tie for ninth at the B.C. Open; a tie for seventh at the Greater Milwaukee Open; a tie for fifth at the Deposit Guaranty Golf Classic; and a tie for fourth at the United Airlines Hawaiian Open.

- Finished tied for second at the 1994 GTE Byron Nelson Classic, where he was part of a Tour-record six-man playoff won by Neal Lancaster.

- Before '96, finest season came in '89, with $234,196 and a second-place finish in the rain-shortened Hawaiian Open. Career seemed on an upswing at that juncture, but he failed to keep his card after placing 167th on the money list in 1990.

- Reached low point with just $8,024 in 1991.

- Did record an unofficial victory in 1987 Deposit Guaranty Golf Classic, edging Nick Faldo by one stroke.

- Winner of three collegiate events at Texas A&M, including the Harvey Penick Invitational.

YEAR	EVENTS	WINS	TOP 10	CUTS MADE	EARNINGS	RANK
1983	29			19	$36,003	121
1984	35			20	$45,461	113
1985	31		1	15	$76,294	95
1986	32		3	12	$75,245	113
1987	33		2	15	$80,149	110
1988	27		3	22	$138,807	86
1989	28		2	21	$234,196	59
1990P	31		1	9	$64,190	167
1990N	1			1	$1,600	172
1991P	15			4	$8,024	235
1991N	9			4	$3,338	152
1992P	28			11	$33,971	193
1992N	3			3	$3,174	160
1993P	28		3	18	$155,016	104
1993N	1		1	1	$9,375	110
1994	29		2	17	$199,199	92
1995P	30		3	14	$151,419	123
1995N	1			1	$2,830	184
1996	30	1	5	21	$537,225	34

MARK O'MEARA

Born: Mark Francis O'Meara, January 13, 1957

Birthplace: Goldsboro, N.C.

Ht: 6' **Wt:** 180

Residence: Windemere, Fla.

Q School: Fall 1980

1996 Money Rank: 5th

O'Meara, who has finished out of the Top 30 on the money list only twice in the last 13 seasons (43rd in '93 and 86th in '94), matched his previous best earnings rank in 1996, when he won two tournaments (for the fourth time in his career) and had six other Top 10 finishes, bringing home a career-high $1,255,749.

That effort followed a 1995 season in which O'Meara, who has won at Pebble Beach an astounding four times, also won twice, finishing 10th on the money list. A collegiate All-American at Long Beach State, O'Meara began playing golf at 13, when his family moved to a house near a golf course in California. He is an avid fund raiser for multiple sclerosis. Donny Wanstall, his long-time caddie, was diagnosed with the degenerative disease during the 1994 Players Championship.

- 12 Tour wins include: 1996 Mercedes Championships and Greater Greensboro Open; 1995 Honda Classic and Canadian Open; 1992 AT&T Pebble Beach National Pro-Am; 1991 Walt Disney World/Oldsmobile Classic; 1990 AT&T Pebble Beach National Pro-Am and H-E-B Texas Open; 1989 AT&T Pebble Beach National Pro-Am; 1985 Bing Crosby Pro-Am and Hawaiian Open; 1984 Greater Milwaukee Open.

- Five International wins include: 1994 Argentine Open; 1992 Tokai Classic; 1987 Lawrence Batley International; 1986 Australian Masters; and 1985 Fuji Sankei Classic.

- Finished in the money in 19 of 22 events in 1996 with the two wins and six other Top 10 finishes: a tie for third at the Memorial Tournament; a tie for second at the Kemper Open; second at the MCI Classic; a tie for fourth at the Bay Hill Invitational by Office Depot; sixth at the Honda Classic; and a tie for third at the Buick Invitational of California.

- Finished tied for first (with Fred Couples) in '96 Tour statistics for green in regulation (71.8); second in birdies per round (4.19); second in average strokes per hole (1.737); and third in average strokes per round (69.69).

- Key to 1995 season was victory at the '94 Argentine Open, which renewed his confidence in his ability to win after a two-year drought. The victory made him one of five players—Gary Player, David Graham, Hale Irwin and Bernhard Langer are the others—to win in the United

States, Europe, Japan, Australia and South America.

- 131 total after 36 holes at '95 PGA Championship equaled the Championship record.

- Of 12 Tour victories, five have come in pro-am events.

- Lost playoffs at 1990 and 1992 Bob Hope Chrysler Classics, also pro-ams. Part of five-man 1992 Hope playoff won by John Cook, and in the 1990 Hope he matched Corey Pavin at then-Tour record 29-under-par for 90 holes; Pavin chipped in to win on first extra hole.

- Came from four strokes off the pace with final-round 63 to capture the 1990 Texas Open.

- 1981 PGA Tour Rookie of the Year.

- Winner 1979 U.S. amateur, defeating John Cook. Also winner of 1979 California and Mexican amateurs.

- Has earned $7,382,215 on the Tour.

Exempt Status: 66th on 1995 money list
Q School: N/A

The youngest of the three golfing brothers—his older brothers are Masashi "Jumbo" Ozaki and Tateo "Jet" Ozaki—Joe Ozaki turned professional in 1977 and has won 25 tournaments (all in Japan) and over $9,000,000 worldwide, including almost one million on the PGA Tour. His best year on the Tour was 1995, with four Top 10 finishes and $290,001 in earnings.

In 1988, Joe earned four of the Ozaki Brothers' 12 titles on the Japanese tour. Ozaki led the PGA Tour in par breakers in 1995 (22.7 % of holes played under par), and tied for 6th in birdie conversion percentage at 33.1%. After the 1996 season, his Sony World Ranking is 75th.

- Five best PGA Tour finishes are all ties for 6th place, including the 1993 Players Championship.

- One of the few tour players to list Kareoke as a special interest.

YEAR	EVENTS	WINS	TOP 10	CUTS MADE	EARNINGS	RANK
1981	34		4	22	$76,063	55
1982	35		1	19	$31,711	119
1983	32		2	17	$69,354	76
1984	32	1	15	24	$465,873	2
1985	25	2	6	19	$340,840	10
1986	25		5	22	$252,827	30
1987	26		7	20	$327,250	30
1988	27		7	20	$438,311	22
1989	26	1	7	19	$615,804	13
1990	25	2	6	20	$707,175	10
1991	25	1	5	15	$563,896	20
1992	23	1	9	18	$759,648	11
1993	26		4	18	$349,516	43
1994	29		3	17	$214,070	86
1995	27	2	8	21	$914,129	10
1996	21	2	8	19	$1,255,749	5

JOE OZAKI

Born: Naomichi Ozaki, May 18th, 1956
Birthplace: Tokushima, Japan
Ht: 5' 8" **Wt:** 160

YEAR	EVENTS	WINS	TOP 10	CUTS MADE	EARNINGS	RANK
1985	2			1	$880	259
1989	2			1	$1,605	274
1990	8			5	$37,330	185
1991	2		1	1	$38,850	185
1992	7		1	5	$75,946	151
1993	12		1	8	$139,784	115
1994	17		1	15	$147,308	121
1995	20		4	13	$290,001	66
1996	23		1	13	$227,763	99

JESPER PARNEVIK

Born: Jesper Bo Parnevik, March 7, 1965
Birthplace: Stockholm, Sweden
Ht: 6' **Wt:** 175
Residence: South Palm Beach, Fla.

Joined Tour: 1993
1996 Money Rank: 53th

The son of Sweden's most famous comedian, Parnevik, a three-year Tour veteran, became the first Swede to win a European Tour event in his own country when he finished with a five-under-par 67 to take the 1995 Scandinavian Masters. Parnevik's best Tour finish was a tie for third at the 1996 Greater Milwaukee Open.

Like his father, young Parnevik has a knack for entertainment: he wears his golf cap in a trademark fashion, with bill turned up and a brand name stitched on the underside; and he turned a partially devastating mistake—his failure to read the 1994 Turnbury leader boards led to a misjudged shot selection and an 18th-hole bogey and subsequent loss to Nick Faldo at the British Open—into commercial appearances for a hotel chain that touts clearly visible signs and rates you can't possibly miss.

Parnevik, who first announced his intention to win the British Open at age 13, learned the game by hitting floating balls into the lake behind the family home in Osterskar and putting on a practice green in the backyard.

- International wins include 1996 Trophee Lancome; 1995 Scandinavian Masters; 1993 Scottish Open; 1990 Swedish Open; 1988 Odense and Raklosia opens.

- Finished in the money in 17 of 20 Tour events in 1996, with $389,266 and five Top 10 finishes: a tie for seventh at the Bell Canadian Open; a tie for third at the Greater Milwaukee Open; a tie for fifth at the PGA Championship; a tie for eighth at the Doral-Ryder Open; and a tie for 10th at the Buick Invitational of California.

- Finished third in '96 Tour statistics for greens in regulation (71.6) and seventh in sand saves (61.4).

- Moved to the PGA Tour in 1995 and played in 19 events, making the cut 15 times with two top-10 finishes.

- In just five 1994 European Tour events, Parnevik finished 26th on the money list with three Top 10s, including a second place finish at the British Open.

- Product of the Swedish national junior program, which has helped develop Anders Forsbrand, Joakim Haeggman, Liselotte Neumann, Helen Alfredsson and Annika Sorenstam.

- Played at Palm Beach Junior College from 1984-86 before qualifying for the European Tour.

- Winner of the 1985 Dixie Amateur.

YEAR	EVENTS	WINS	TOP 10	CUTS MADE	EARNINGS	RANK
1994	17		2	12	$148,816	120
1995	19		2	15	$222,458	84
1996	19		5	17	$389,266	53

CRAIG PARRY

Born: Craig David Parry, January 12, 1966
Birthplace: Sunshine, Victoria, Australia
Ht: 5' 6" **Wt:** 170
Residence: Sydney, Australia and Orlando, Fla.
Joined Tour: April 1992
1996 Money Rank: 43rd

Nicknamed "Popeye" for his huge forearms, Parry, a fan of cricket, rugby and Australian Rules Football, and owner of a strong, all-around game, has never won on the PGA Tour though he does have 13 International wins.

His closest call came at the 1995 Colonial, when he managed five birdies in six holes en route to a second-round 65 and a two-stroke 36-hole lead, only to fall one stroke short of victor, Tom Lehman.

A staunch supporter of the Australian PGA, Parry spoke out when countryman Robert Allenby was left out of the lineup of several Tour events.

PERCENTAGE OF GREENS IN REGULATION

Rank	Name	Rounds	Percent
T1.	Fred Couples	66	71.8
T1.	Mark O'Meara	80	71.8
3.	Jesper Parnevik	68	71.6
4.	Tom Lehman	79	70.8
T5.	Bob Tway	80	70.7
T5.	Fuzzy Zoeller	53	70.7
T7.	Brad Bryant	84	70.6
T7.	Mark Calcavecchia	103	70.6
9.	John Cook	89	70.1
10.	Rocco Mediate	69	70.0

- International wins include: 1995 Canon Challenge and Greg Norman's Holden classic; 1994 Australian Masters; 1992 Australian PGA Championship, New South Wales Open and Australian Masters; 1991 Italian and Scottish opens; 1989 German Open, Wang Four Stars Pro-Celebrity and Bridgestone ASO, and 1987 New South Wales Open and Canadian TPC.

- Finished in the money in 19 of 24 events in 1996 with $454,203, and three Top 10s—a tie for fourth at the Motorola Western Open; a tie for second at the Buick Classic, and second at the Byron Nelson Classic.

- Best 1995 Tour statistical finish was 29th in sand saves (58.0); worst was a tie for 121st in birdies (254).

- Had chance to win rain-shortened 1995 Walt Disney World/Oldsmobile Classic when career-best 64 put him two strokes off the pace after first round; third- and final-round 72 dashed hopes of first Tour victory.

- Tied for third at the 1993 U.S. Open, sharing first-round lead after opening 66; closed 69-68 to finish five strokes behind Lee Janzen.

- Tied with Ian Woosnam for 36-hole lead in 1992 Masters, then held third-round lead outright at 12-under 204, before skying to final-round 78 and a tie for 13th.

- Member of International Team in inaugural Presidents Cup match.

- Was low amateur at 1985 Australian Masters, Tasmanian and South African opens.

YEAR	EVENTS	WINS	TOP 10	CUTS MADE	EARNINGS	RANK
1987	1					
1988	1			1	$1,650	282
1990	8			6	$43,351	181
1991	6			6	$63,767	162
1992	13		4	11	$241,901	64
1993	23		6	16	$323,068	50
1994	20		3	15	$354,602	46
1995	24		2	16	$293,413	65
1996	25		3	20	$454,203	43

COREY PAVIN

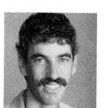

Born: Corey Allen Pavin, November 16, 1959

Birthplace: Oxnard, Cal.

Ht: 5' 9" **Wt:** 150

Residence: Orlando, Fla.

Q School: Fall 1983

1996 Money Rank: 18th

With his two stroke win at the 1995 U.S. Open, the gritty UCLA Bruin standout finally got the monkey off his back. No longer is he known as one of the best golfers never to win a major. His play at Shinnecock was superb, highlighted by a 228-yard 4-wood that landed five feet from the pin on the 72nd hole.

Pavin, who has been a dominant force on the PGA Tour the last six years (his worst money-list years were 18th-place finishes in '93 and '96), also won at the 1995 Nissan Los Angeles Open, successfully defending his title. He had nine Top 10 finishes in 1996, including his 14th Tour victory at the MasterCard Colonial. Pavin, a close friend of San Antonio Spurs basketball star David Robinson

(Robinson named his son Corey), possesses one of the greatest short games in golf.

- Finished in the money in 21 of 22 events in 1996 for $851,320. Top 10 finishes included the MasterCard win; ninth at the NEC World Series of Golf; a tie for ninth at the Buick Classic; a tie for tenth at the Kemper Open; a tie for sixth at the Byron Nelson Classic; a tie for seventh at the Masters; a tie for seventh at the BellSouth Classic, a tie for fourth at the Bay Hill Invitational by Office Depot; and a tie for seventh at the Mercedes Championships.

- Tour wins include the 1996 MasterCard Colonial; 1995 Nissan Los Angeles Open and U.S. Open; 1994 Nissan Los Angeles Open; 1992 Honda Classic; 1991 Bob Hope Chrysler Classic and BellSouth Atlanta; 1988 Texas Open; 1987 Bob Hope Chrysler Classic and Hawaiian Open; 1986 Hawaiian Open and Greater Milwaukee Open; 1985 Colonial National Invitation and 1984 Houston Coca-Cola Open.

- Nine international wins include: 1995 Asian Masters and Million Dollar Challenge; 1994 Tokai Classic; 1993 Toyota World Match Play Championship; 1984 and '85 New Zealand Opens; and the 1983 German Open, South African PGA Championship and Calberson Classic.

- Finished seventh in '96 Tour statistics in average strokes per round (69.79).

- Of '95 Open shot, said: "I can't think of any shot that I have hit better under pressure than that one."

- Recorded 4-1 mark for U.S. team in 1995 losing Ryder Cup effort.

- Won '95 Asian Masters by nine strokes.

- Earned $240,000 at '95 Skins Game, second to Fred Couples.

- Won 1995 Million Dollar Challenge in South Africa in December.

- Went 2-2-1 in five matches of inaugural Presidents Cup in 1994.

- Holed dramatic 136-yard 8-iron for eagle on final hole of 1992 Honda Classic to force a playoff with Fred Couples; won with birdie on second extra hole. Lost a playoff to Bruce Lietzke in 1992 Colonial.

- Won Arnold Palmer Award as tour's official money leader in 1991.

- Named 1991 PGA of America Player of the Year.

- Won two playoff victories in 1991—over Mark O'Meara in Bob Hope Chrysler Classic and Steve Pate in BellSouth Atlanta Classic.

- Scored victories in each of his first five years on the Tour, beginning with Houston Open in 1984.

- Captured 1988 Texas Open with 21-under-par 259, becoming the fifth player in Tour history to better 260.

- At 17, won Junior World title and became youngest winner of Los Angeles City Men's Crown.

- Winner 1981 North-South Amateur, Southwest Amateur, Maccabiah Games.

- Won 11 college tournaments at UCLA, including 1982 PAC-10 title.

- Has earned $8,031,052 on the Tour.

YEAR	EVENTS	WINS	TOP 10	CUTS MADE	EARNINGS	RANK
1983	3			1	$4,209	207
1984	29	1	5	26	$260,536	18
1985	27	1	13	23	$367,506	6
1986	28	2	6	23	$304,558	19
1987	26	2	7	17	$498,406	15
1988	26	1	3	17	$216,768	50
1989	28		1	23	$177,084	82
1990	29		6	26	$468,830	26
1991	25	2	10	24	$979,430	1
1992	25	1	7	20	$980,934	5
1993	24		6	21	$675,087	18
1994	20	1	9	16	$906,305	8
1995	22	2	6	18	$1,340,079	4
1996	22	1	9	21	$851,320	18

CHRIS PERRY

Born: September 27, 1961

Birthplace: Edenton, NC

Ht: 6' 1" **Wt:** 195

Joined Tour: 1985

1996 Money Rank: 112

In posting a solid 1996 season—his best since 1990— Perry made the cut 15 times to earn $184,171. His two top 10 finishes included a tie for third at the 1996 Quad City Classic. Perry's play improved from 1995, when he ranked 150th. That year, Perry finished in the money in 17 events—but did not finish once in the top 10.

Perry had a spectacular college career at Ohio State University and was named 1984 Collegiate Player of the Year. Perry's pro career has been uneven, however, though he has had some solid years. In 1987, he ranked 56th. In 1990, Perry had his best year to date, earning $259,108 to rank 58th. From there, Perry's play fell off until he resurrected his game on the 1994 Nike Tour. Perry finished atop the tour's money list with $167,148 in earnings and was named the 1994 Nike Tour Player of the Year and earned a return to the PGA Tour.

Perry's pedigree is in baseball rather than golf. His father, Jim Perry, pitched in the major leagues with four teams, and his uncle, Gaylord Perry, is a member of baseball's Hall of Fame.

- Tied for second at the 1987 Kemper Open.
- Tied for second at the 1990 Canon Greater Hartford Open.
- Tied for third at the 1996 Quad City Classic.
- Won the 1994 Nike Utah Classic.
- Was a three-time All-American (1982-1984).

YEAR	EVENTS	WINS	TOP 10	CUTS MADE	EARNINGS	RANK
1985					$60,801	110
1986					$72,212	114
1987					$197,593	56
1988					$85,546	121
1989					$206,932	67
1990					$259,108	58
1991					$116,105	126
1992					$53,943	171
1993					$25,332	202
1994					$14,840	237
1995	30			17	$113,632	150
1996	21		2	15	$184,171	112

KENNY PERRY

Born: James Kenneth Perry, August 10, 1960

Birthplace: Elizabethtown, Ken.

Ht: 6' 1" **Wt:** 190

Residence: Franklin, Ken.

Q School: Fall 1986

1996 Money Rank: 13th

He didn't win in '96, but Perry had nine Top 10 efforts, earned $925,079, and finished 11th on the money list, by far the best performance in his career. 1995 wasn't bad, either. After a tie for third at the AT&T Pebble Beach Pro-Am, Perry won the Bob Hope Chrysler Classic and then tied for second the following week at the Nissan Open. Two other top-10 finishes and 21 out of 25 cuts made nearly earned Perry a spot on the Ryder Cup roster, placed him 21st on the money list, and earned him a bid to the Tour Championship.

Perry possesses an unusual backswing, of which he says, "It's ugly going back, but from the top down, I'm as good as anyone." A member of the Western Kentucky University Sports Hall of Fame, Perry lists restoring old cars as a special interest, and he designed and built Country Creek GC, a public course that opened in his hometown in April 1995.

- Tour wins include: 1995 Bob Hope Chrysler Classic; 1994 New England Classic; and the 1991 Memorial.
- Finished in the money in 17 of 26 events in 1996, with nine Top 10 efforts: fourth at the Tour Championship; a tie for fifth at the Greater Vancouver Open; eighth at the Sprint International;

second at the PGA Championship; a tie for fourth at the CVS Charity Classic; third at the FedEx St. Jude Classic; a tie for fourth at the Freeport-McDermott Classic; a tie for tenth at the Phoenix Open; and a tie for seventh at the Bob Hope Chrysler Classic.

- His try for consecutive wins in '95 ended with an out-of-bounds shot on the 13th hole at Nissan Open after 36- and 54-hole leads.

- Started PGA Championship in 10th place in Ryder Cup standings but was bumped by Brad Faxon's fifth-place finish and Jeff Maggert's tie for third.

- Had to play catch-up late in the 1993 season to save his card, with back-to-back September Top 10s.

- Encouraged by his biggest fan, Kenny Perry, Sr., to start playing golf at age 7. His father used to sit for hours teeing golf balls up for him. First competition came at age 11.

- Attended National Hot Rod Association driving school in Gainesville, Florida, in December 1995.

YEAR	EVENTS	WINS	TOP 10	CUTS MADE	EARNINGS	RANK
1984	1					
1985	1					
1987	26		1	15	$107,239	93
1988	32		3	20	$139,421	85
1989	26		3	15	$202,099	70
1990	23		2	17	$279,881	50
1991	24	1	3	16	$368,784	44
1992	25		3	17	$190,455	81
1993	29		3	18	$196,863	88
1994	30	1	4	22	$585,941	26
1995	25	1	5	21	$773,388	21
1996	25		9	17	$925,079	13

NICK PRICE

Born: Nicholas Raymond Leige Price, January 28, 1957

Birthplace: Durban, South Africa

Ht: 6' **Wt:** 190

Residence: Hobe Sound, Fla.

Q School: Fall 1982

1996 Money Rank: 50th

A dominating driver and superb iron player, Price has 14 Tour wins and 16 International titles. From his breakthrough victory in 1992 PGA Championship through the end of 1994 Tour season, he totaled 17 worldwide wins. He captured six titles in 1994 alone, including the British Open crown and his second PGA championship, becoming the first golfer to win two majors in the same year since Nick Faldo in 1990 and only one of six players—Ben Hogan (who did it three times), Jack Nicklaus, Arnold Palmer, Lee Trevino and Tom Watson are the others—to win back-to-back majors since World War II. He entered only 15 Tour events in 1996 and finished in the money 12 times.

Price was born in South Africa to British parents, moved to Rhodesia (now Zimbabwe) at an early age, and served two years in the Rhodesian Air Force. He manages to keep things in perspective: when asked if 1995 was a disappointing season—he finished 30th on the money list while entering only 20 events and garnering seven Top 10 finishes, but no wins—he said: "I guess I've made around $800,000 around the world. If people want to call that a 'bad year,' I'll take bad years from here on out."

- 14 Tour wins include: 1994 Honda Classic, Southwestern Bell Colonial, Western Open, PGA Championship and Bell Canadian Open; 1993 Players Championship, Canon Greater Hartford Open, Sprint Western Open and Federal Express St. Jude Classic; 1992 PGA Championship and H-E-B Texas Open; 1991 GTE Byron Nelson Classic and Canadian Open; and the 1983 World Series of Golf.

- 16 International wins include: 1995 Alfred Dunhill Challenge, Hassan II Golf Trophy and Zimbabwe Open; 1994 British Open and ICL International; 1993 ICL International an Sun City Million Dollar Challenge; 1992 Air New Zealand/Shell Open;

1989 West End South Australian Open; 1985 Tro-phee Lancome and ICL International; 1982 Vaals Reef Open; 1981 Italian Open and South African Masters; 1980 Canon European Masters; and 1979 Asseng Invitational.

- Finished in the money in 12 of 15 events in 1996, with $402,467, and five Top 10s: a tie for eighth at the PGA Championship; a tie for fourth at the Byron Nelson Classic; a tie for fifth at the MCI Classic; a tie for third at the BellSouth Classic; and a tie for third at the Honda Classic.

- Shot a Master's record low 63 during the 1986 tournament, which was won by Jack Nicklaus.

- Finished seventh in '96 Tour statistics in holes per eagle (133.7).

- A cold cost him the chance to complete in the Wild Coast Classic in Port Edward, South Africa in 1996. Price suffered a rib injury when he tried to suppress a sneeze.

- Finished first in 1995 Tour statistics for total dri-ving rating (40).

- In '94, became the first golfer since Tom Watson in 1980 to win six times in one year. 10 victories in two years—1993-94—was best since Watson won 11 in 1979-80.

- Back-to-back winner of PGA Tour Player of the Year Award, 1993-94.

- Prior to 1994 win, was two-time runner-up in the British Open, 1982 and 1988.

- Has earned $7,740,586 on the Tour.

YEAR	EVENTS	WINS	TOP 10	CUTS MADE	EARNINGS	RANK
1983	21	1	2	14	$49,435	104
1984	19		4	15	$109,480	66
1985	20		2	14	$96,069	80
1986	25		6	17	$225,373	35
1987	25		7	19	$334,169	28
1988	24		4	20	$266,300	42
1989	27		7	22	$296,170	42
1990	28		6	22	$520,777	22
1991	23	2	9	18	$714,389	7
1992	26	2	13	24	$1,135,773	4
1993	18	4	8	17	$1,478,557	1
1994	19	6	8	14	$1,499,927	1
1995	18		5	15	$611,700	30
1996	16		5	13	$402,467	50

DICKY PRIDE

Born: Richard Fletcher Pride, III, July 15, 1969
Birthplace: Tuscaloosa, Ala.
Ht: 6' 0" **Wt:** 175
Joined Tour: 1994
1996 Money Rank: 125

Pride hopes to regain the form of his spectac-ular rookie season, when he stepped up and won the 1994 Federal Express St. Jude Classic. Enter-ing the tournament as the third alternate, Pride sank a 20-foot birdie putt on the final hole to force a playoff, then sank a 25-foot birdie putt on the first playoff hole to beat Hal Sutton and Gene Sauers. Pride's $305,769 in 1994 earnings ranked him 57th among golfers. But his play fell sharply in 1995, when he made only 12 cuts out of 31 events, finished in the top 10 just once, and fell to 161st. Pride improved in 1996, finishing in the top 10 twice, including a tie for third at the Canon Greater Hartford Open and earning $167,852.

- Won the 1994 Federal Express St. Jude Classic.

- Finished tied for third at the 1996 Canon Greater Hartford Open.

- Finished sixth at the 1996 Michelob Champi-onship at Kingsmill.

- Finished tied for eighth at the 1994 Deposit Guaranty Golf Classic.

- Finished tied for eighth at the 1995 Deposit Guaranty Golf Classic.

- Shot a hole-in-one at the 1994 Buick Southern Open, winning a Buick of his choice.

YEAR	EVENTS	WINS	TOP 10	CUTS MADE	EARNINGS	RANK
1992	1					
1994	27	1	2	12	$305,769	57
1995	31		1	12	$97,712	161
1996	27		2	14	$167,852	125

TOM PURTZER

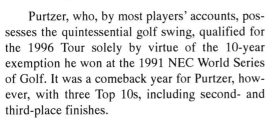

Born: Thomas Warren Purtzer, December 5, 1951

Birthplace: Des Moines, Iowa

Ht: 6' **Wt:** 180

Residence: Scottsdale, Ariz.

Q School: Spring 1975

1996 Money Rank: 51st

Purtzer, who, by most players' accounts, possesses the quintessential golf swing, qualified for the 1996 Tour solely by virtue of the 10-year exemption he won at the 1991 NEC World Series of Golf. It was a comeback year for Purtzer, however, with three Top 10s, including second- and third-place finishes.

In 1995, Purtzer, who played high school football before concentrating on golf, watched his game slip horribly. He had no Top 10 finishes and only four Top 25 efforts, while finishing 144th on the 1995 money list. The drop was precipitous for the golfer who had finished fourth on the money list in 1991, after winning the Southwestern Bell Colonial and the NEC World Series of Golf. Purtzer, whose brother, Paul, played briefly on the Tour, is a close friend of future baseball Hall of Famer, Robin Yount—an excellent golfer who chose to play baseball

- Other Tour wins: the 1988 Gatlin Brothers-Southwest Classic, 1984 Phoenix Open, and the 1977 Glen Campbell-Los Angeles Open.

- Finished in the money in 18 of 24 events in 1996, with $396,444 and three Top 10s: second at the Michelob Championship; a tie for ninth at the FedEx St. Jude Classic; and third at the Bay Hill Invitational by Office Depot.

- 1991 World Series victory came in playoff with Jim Gallagher Jr., and Davis Love III.

- Tied with Bob Tway in 1991 Northern Telecom Open, one stroke behind Phil Mickelson. Since Mickelson was an amateur and could not accept money, runners-up received $144,000, each.

- Won 1986 JC Penney Mixed Team Classic with Juli Inkster.

- Married wife, Lori, on Maui during 1994 Lincoln-Mercury Kapalua International.

- Father of three and graduate of Arizona State University (1973, business).

- Has earned $3,644,040 on the Tour.

YEAR	EVENTS	WINS	TOP 10	CUTS MADE	EARNINGS	RANK
1975	9			5	$2,093	194
1976	21		1	12	$26,682	82
1977	32	1	4	14	$79,337	37
1978	31		6	24	$58,618	55
1979	31		6	25	$113,270	30
1980	29		5	18	$118,185	34
1981	30		6	24	$122,812	27
1982	29		4	25	$100,118	36
1983	27		4	20	$103,261	55
1984	29	1	2	20	$164,244	39
1985	26			18	$49,979	119
1986	31		10	26	$218,280	37
1987	26		1	21	$123,287	85
1988	24	1	3	17	$197,740	57
1989	24		2	16	$154,868	88
1990	24		3	15	$285,176	49
1991	25	2	4	19	$750,568	4
1992	25		1	18	$166,722	93
1993	21		1	10	$107,570	136
1994	22		2	13	$187,307	94
1995	19			12	$120,717	144
1996	23		3	18	$396,444	51

LEE RINKER

Born: Lee Cross Rinker, November 10, 1960

Birthplace: Stuart, Fla.

Ht: 6' 0" **Wt:** 185

Joined Tour: 1984

1996 Money Rank: 111

After years of struggling to make it as a professional, Rinker will return to the PGA Tour for the third straight year. In 1996, Rinker earned $185,530, a slight drop off from 1995, when he finished in the top 10 three times (including a tie for sixth at the Greater Milwaukee Open) and ranked 96th. 1995 was Rinker's first successful year on the Tour. He excelled on the 1994 Nike circuit, where he finished tied for second in the 1994

 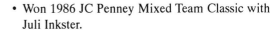

AVERAGE PUTTING STROKES PER HOLE

Rank	Name	Rounds	Strokes
1.	Brad Faxon	82	1.709
2.	Mark O'Meara	80	1.737
3.	Steve Stricker	82	1.740
4.	Glen Day	89	1.744
5.	Nolan Henke	80	1.746
T6.	Paul Azinger	77	1.747
T6.	Lee Janzen	92	1.747
8.	Nick Faldo	56	1.748
9.	Gil Morgan	61	1.749
10.	Payne Stewart	87	1.751

Nike Tour Championship, finished in the top 10 nine times, and ranked 12th in earnings. Before that, Rinker's only full year on any tour was the 1984 PGA Tour, when he made just 6 cuts in 17 events to rank 196th.

Golf runs in the Rinker family. Lee's sister, Laurie Rinker-Graham, has won several LPGA tournaments, and his brother, Larry, is also a PGA Tour veteran.

- Finished tied for sixth at the 1995 Greater Milwaukee Open.

- Finished tied for seventh at the 1995 Walt Disney World/Oldsmobile Golf Classic.

- Finished tied for ninth at the LaCantera Texas Open.

- Finished tied for second at the 1994 NIKE TOUR Championship.

- Ranked twelfth on the 1994 NIKE TOUR money list.

YEAR	EVENTS	WINS	TOP 10	CUTS MADE	EARNINGS	RANK
1984	17			6	$6,002	196
1985	2			2	$3,197	216
1991	1					
1992	1			1	$3,000	282
1993	1			1	$11,052	235
1995	29		3	18	$187,065	96
1996	32		1	20	$185,530	111

LOREN ROBERTS

Born: June 24, 1955
Birthplace: San Luis Obispo, Cal.
Ht: 6' 2" **Wt:** 190
Residence: Germantown, Tenn.
Q School: Fall 1980, 1982, 1983, 1986, 1987
1996 Money Rank: 27th

Nicknamed "Boss of the Moss" for his putting prowess and considered by his peers to be one of the hardest-working members of the Tour, Roberts followed up his 1994 4th-place money finish with solid years in '95 and '96, finishing 27th on the money list both years.

His win at the '94 Nestle Invitational shed him of the distinction of being the PGA Tour money leader without having won a tournament. But there was much more to that year: nine other Top Ten finishes, three of them in majors (a tie for fifth at the Masters, a tie for second at the U.S. Open and a tie for ninth at the PGA Championship).

Roberts, who achieved exempt status in 1984 and 1985, then lost his card each of the next two years, had a scare in '95, when he was forced to withdraw following the first round of the U.S. Open after hurting his back while marking his ball. The injury was later diagnosed as a bulging disc. He rebounded nicely with two wins in '96—at the Greater Milwaukee Open and at the MCI Classic.

- Other Tour victories include the 1994 and 1995 Nestle Invitationals.

- Finished in the money in 19 of 26 events in 1996 with $725,231 and one other Top 10 finish—a tie for ninth at the Quad City Classic.

- Performed admirably in first Ryder Cup in 1995, posting a 3-1 record in the losing U.S. effort.

- Was three strokes off the lead going in to the final round of his first Nestle win, but rallied to defeat Nick Price, Fuzzy Zoeller and Vijay Singh.

- With successful defense of '94 Nestle, became the first golfer since Calvin Peete (1979, 1982 Greater Milwaukee Open) to win the same event for his first two Tour victories.

- With his tie for 24th in the '94 British Open, had the best record of any Tour golfer in the majors that year. After missing a chance to win the '94 U.S. Open in regulation, he lost to Ernie Els on second sudden-death hole, following an 18-hole playoff.

- Donated $10,000 to Arnold Palmer Hospital for Women and Children after winning '94 Nestle.

YEAR	EVENTS	WINS	TOP 10	CUTS MADE	EARNINGS	RANK
1981	20			8	$8,935	177
1982	2					
1983	24			8	$7,724	189
1984	26		3	14	$67,515	87
1985	32		3	22	$92,761	83
1986	33		2	20	$53,655	133
1987	31			13	$57,489	138
1988	29		3	19	$136,890	89
1989	30		5	28	$275,882	46
1990	30		7	26	$478,522	24
1991	29		4	23	$281,174	58
1992	28		3	23	$338,673	43
1993	28		4	19	$316,506	53
1994	22	1	9	19	$1,015,671	6
1995	23	1	5	19	$678,335	27
1996	24	2	3	19	$725,231	27

CLARENCE ROSE

Born: December 8, 1957

Birthplace: Goldsboro, N.C.

Ht: 5' 8" **Wt:** 175

Residence: Goldsboro, N.C.

Q School: Spring 1981

1996 Money Rank: 41st

Rose, a 1980 All-American at Clemson and a pro since 1981, captured his first-ever Tour win in 1996 at the Sprint International. It was an astounding victory: he eagled 17 to take the lead, fell into a tie on 18, then eagled the first playoff hole to defeat Brad Faxon and become the eighth first-time winner on that year's Tour. The $288,000 first-prize purse was enough to eclipse Rose's best year's total on the Tour—$267,141 in 1989.

That's not to say that Rose, who has had more success on the Nike Tour (he finished 21st on the Nike money list in 1995), hasn't come close to breaking through earlier on the Tour. All of his previous best finishes have been as runner-up—at the 1985 Southern Open, the 1986 Los Angeles Open, the 1987 Greater Greensboro Classic, the 1988 GTE Byron Nelson Classic and the 1989 The International. He also had a tie for second at the 1986 Honda Classic.

- Finished in the money in 16 of 27 Tour events in 1996 with the win at the Sprint International and one of other Top 10 finish—a tie for ninth at the Shell Houston Open—and $461,899 in earnings.

- Entered only two Tour events in 1995, finishing in the money once—a tie for 20th in the Depository Guaranty Golf Classic.

- Had 22 points over the final two rounds of the Sprint, which scores on the Modified Stableford system, awarding eight points for a double-eagle, five for eagle, two for birdie and nothing for par. Players lose a point for a bogey and three points for a double-bogey or worse.

- Before the Sprint, had won just $69,926 during the 1990s.

- Winner 1995 Nike Pensacola Classic.

- Quarterfinalist, 1986 U.S. Amateur.

- Winner 1979 North Carolina Amateur.

YEAR	EVENTS	WINS	TOP 10	CUTS MADE	EARNINGS	RANK
1981					$965	233
1982					$41,075	100
1983					$45,271	109
1984					$62,278	92
1985					$133,610	63
1986					$189,387	44
1987					$173,154	59
1988					$228,976	48
1989					$267,141	49
1990					$25,908	202
1991					$9,564	228
1992					$10,488	240
1993					$6,823	251
1994					$2,992	295
1995	2				$7,061	283
1996	27	1	2	17	$461,899	41

HUGH ROYER III

Born: Hugh Royer III,
February 13, 1964
Birthplace: Columbus,
Ga.
Ht: 6' 1" **Wt:** 165
Residence:
Joined Tour: 1996
1996 Money Rank: 114

Royer had a solid rookie season on the 1996 PGA Tour, earning $183,066, making the cut in 16 events and finishing in the top 10 three times (including a tie for fifth at the 1996 Quad City Classic). Before joining the PGA Tour, Royer excelled on the Nike Tour, where he won several tournaments in 1993 and 1995. In 1995, Royer ranked in the top 10 on the NIKE Tour's money list.

Golf runs in Royer's family: His father, Hugh Royer, Jr., was a PGA Tour professional.

- Finished tied for fifth at the 1996 Quad City Classic.

- Finished tied for sixth at the 1996 B.C. Open.

- Finished tied for sixth at the 1996 Nissan Open.

YEAR	EVENTS	WINS	TOP 10	CUTS MADE	EARNINGS	RANK
1996	31		3	16	$183,066	114

SCOTT SIMPSON

Born: Scott William
Simpson, September 17,
1955
Birthplace: San Diego,
Cal.
Ht: 6' 2" **Wt:** 180
Residence: San Diego, Cal.
Q School: Fall 1978
1996 Money Rank: 68th

Simpson's game is on a level that places the 40-year-old veteran among the elite of the game. While he lacks the power to overwhelm courses, his accuracy and the completeness of his game make him a constant threat to break into the winner's circle. He won the 1987 U.S. Open in a dramatic back nine battle with Tom Watson, birdieing three holes and saving par on three others with excellent shots from off the green. He had top 10 finishes in the 1988 and 1989 Opens, and lost the 1991 Open in a playoff with Payne Stewart.

Though he slipped on the money list in 1996, one need look back no further than 1995 to understand the range of Simpson's talent. While he did not win in 1995, the Southern Cal grad enjoyed one of his best years ever, winning more money than ever before in his career—$795,798—and notching six Top 10 finishes in the process.

- Tour wins include: the 1993 GTE Byron Nelson Classic; 1989 BellSouth Atlanta Classic; 1987 Greater Greensboro and U.S. Opens; 1984 Manufacturers Hanover Westchester Classic; and the 1980 Western Open.

- International wins include: 1990 Perrier Invitational and the 1984 Chunichi Crowns and Dunlop Phoenix.

- Finished in the money in 14 of 23 events in 1996, with $309,648, and four Top 10 finishes: a tie for second at the Nissan Open; a tie for fourth at the United Airlines Hawaiian Open; a tie for third at the Buick Invitational of California; and a tie for sixth at the Phoenix Open.

- Claimed first win—1980 Western Open—in second year on the Tour.

- Won 1976-77 NACC Championships while at Southern Cal and was an All-American both years.

- Winner of California and San Diego junior titles.

- Winner of 1979, 1981 Hawaii State Opens.

- Traditionally takes family time away from the Tour late in the season and lists Bible study, family activities and exercise as special interests.

- Has earned $5,080,033 on the Tour.

YEAR	EVENTS	WINS	TOP 10	CUTS MADE	EARNINGS	RANK
1976	1			1		
1978	1			1	$3,100	186
1979	29		2	21	$53,084	74
1980	30	1	4	23	$141,323	24
1981	30		3	21	$108,793	34
1982	26		4	21	$146,903	24
1983	26		5	23	$144,172	38
1984	27	1	8	23	$248,581	22
1985	26		5	23	$171,245	39
1986	23		3	18	$202,223	41
1987	25	2	10	22	$621,032	4
1988	23		1	13	$108,301	106
1989	22	1	3	15	$298,920	40
1990	20		3	12	$235,309	63
1991	18		3	14	$322,936	51
1992	22		1	15	$155,284	97
1993	22	1	5	20	$707,166	14
1994	21		2	15	$307,884	56
1995	25		6	19	$795,798	17
1996	22		4	14	$309,648	68

JOEY SINDELAR

Born: Joseph Paul Sindelar, March 30, 1958
Birthplace: Fort Knox, NY
Ht: 5' 10" **Wt:** 200
Joined Tour: 1984
1996 Money Rank: 77

Sindelar continues to come back from a 1993 wrist injury that seriously threatened his career. In 1996, he made 18 cuts (including three top 10 finishes) to earn $275,531. Sindelar fractured a wrist bone during the 1993 PGA Championship; as a result, he struggled in 1994 and fell in rank to 145th. Since then, his game has recovered: In 1995, he had three top 10 finishes and ranked 90th.

Sindelar, a PGA Tour veteran, had his first big year in 1985, when he won two tournaments, finished in the money in 28 events, and ranked 12th. His career year came in 1988, when he won two tournaments (including the 1988 International), finished in the top 10 ten times, and earned $813,732, ranking third. That year, he finished in the money 27 times out of 30 tournaments. Though Sindelar never matched that season again, he consistently made the cut until he injured his wrist.

Sindelar had an outstanding collegiate career at Ohio State University, where he won 10 collegiate titles, was a three-time All-American, and a member of the 1979 NCAA Championship team. In honor, Ohio State inducted Sindelar into its Athletic Hall of Fame in 1992.

- Won the 1990 Hardee's Golf Classic.

- Won the 1988 Honda Classic.

- Won the 1988 International.

- Won the 1987 B.C. Open.

- Won the 1985 Greater Greensboro Open.

- Won the 1985 B.C. Open.

- Finished tied for sixth at the 1992 U.S. Open.

- Member of the 1979 NCAA Championship team at Ohio State University.

- Was a three-time All-American.

YEAR	EVENTS	WINS	TOP 10	CUTS MADE	EARNINGS	RANK
1982	2					
1983	3			2	$4,696	203
1984	33		3	23	$116,528	59
1985	33	2	7	28	$282,762	12
1986	35		7	29	$341,231	14
1987	33	1	4	25	$235,033	40
1988	30	2	10	27	$813,732	3
1989	28		3	20	$196,092	72
1990	27	1	3	15	$307,207	46
1991	28		2	19	$168,352	94
1992	32		6	22	$395,354	35
1993	22		5	14	$391,649	38
1994	22		1	12	$114,563	145
1995	24		3	14	$202,896	90
1996	29		3	18	$275,531	77

VIJAY SINGH

Born: February, 22, 1963
Birthplace: Lautoka, Fiji
Ht: 6' 2" **Wt:** 198
Residence: London, England and Ponte Vedra Beach, Fla.

Joined Tour: Spring 1983

1996 Money Rank: 17th

Singh, whose first name means "Victory" in Hindi, continues to live up to his reputation as one of the world's very best players—and one of the Tour's hardest workers. He plays various events in Asia and Europe while keeping his hat in the ring on the PGA Tour.

The son of an airplane technician who also taught golf, Singh, one of the longest drivers in the world (he combines this talent with deft putting, making him a formidable talent), was inspired by Tom Weiskopf as a youth. He left his birthplace, Fiji, to pursue his dream of becoming a professional golfer.

His best year on the Tour was in 1995, with victories at the Phoenix Open and the Buick Classic; he missed only five cuts in 23 events, had seven additional top-10 finishes, and placed 9th on the money list, with $1,018,713 in earnings. He followed that in 1996 by finishing in the money an astonishing 24 of 25 times, with another nine Top 10 finishes and $855,121 in earnings.

- In addition to his '95 titles, won 1993 Buick Classic.

- 16 International wins include: 1995 Passport Open; 1994 Scandinavian Masters and Trophee Lancome; 1993 Bells Cup; 1992 Turespana Masters Open de Andalucia and Malaysian and Volvo German opens; 1991 King Hassan Trophy; 1990 El Bosque Open; 1989 Volvo Open di Firenze and Ivory Coast, Nigerian and Zimbabwe opens; 1988 Nigerian Open and Swedish PGA, and the 1984 Malaysian PGA Championship.

- Nine Top 10 finishes in 1996: a tie for ninth at the Tour Championship; a tie for fifth at the PGA Championship; a tie for eighth at the Motorola Western Open; a tie for seventh at the U.S. Open; a tie for fifth at the MCI Classic; a tie for eighth at the Players Championship; a tie for ninth at the Honda Classic; a tie for second at the

Doral-Ryder Open, and a tie for eighth at the United Airlines Hawaiian Open.

- Finished fourth in '96 Tour statistics in holes per eagle (124.6).

- Best finish in the 1995 Tour statistics was fourth in driving (283.5).

- Tour Rookie of the Year in 1993, when he won the Buick Classic in a playoff with Mark Wiebe.

- Made cut in first 11 Tour events—last four of 1992 and first seven of 1993.

- Joined PGA European Tour in 1989, winning Volvo Open in rookie season.

- Has captured titles in Nigeria, Sweden, Zimbabwe, Spain, Germany, the Ivory Coast and Morocco.

- Led Order of Merit Safari tour in Africa in 1988.

- Only non-Swede to win the Swedish PGA (1988).

YEAR	EVENTS	WINS	TOP 10	CUTS MADE	EARNINGS	RANK
1992	4		1	4	$70,680	156
1993	14	1	6	12	$657,831	19
1994	21		3	16	$325,959	52
1995	22	2	9	17	$1,018,713	9
1996	24		9	24	$855,140	17

JEFF SLUMAN

Born: Jeffrey George Sluman, September 11, 1957

Birthplace: Rochester, N.Y.

Ht: 5' 7" **Wt:** 140

Residence: Chicago, Ill.

Q School: Fall 1982, 1984

1996 Money Rank: 28th

Sluman, who recorded one of the great finishing rounds in PGA Championship history when he came from three strokes down on the final day to win by three over Paul Azinger in 1988, has put together a pair of solid years in 1995-96 with nine Top 10s in '95 and seven in '96. But no wins, and that seems to highlight a sense of frustration that lingers about Sluman, whose only Tour victory remains that 1988 PGA title.

Sluman is a gritty competitor, much like that of close friend Bobby Rahal (1986 Indy 500 winner), whom he met when he was paired with the race-car driver at the 1987 AT&T Pebble Beach National Pro-Am. Because of his intensity and solid game, it's a good that the Florida State finance major, who dabbles in old cars, the stock market and raises Akitas, will find his way back into the winner's circle.

- Finished in the money in 23 of 31 events in 1996, with $650,128 and seven Top 10s: a tie for ninth at the Tour Championship; a tie for ninth at the B.C. Open; a tie for ninth at the Quad City Classic; second at the MasterCard Colonial; a tie for fourth at the Byron Nelson Classic; a tie for eighth at the Doral-Ryder Open, and a tie for eighth at the United Airlines Hawaiian Open.

- Finished second in '96 Tour statistics in sand saves (63.4) and second all-around (326) in 1995.

- Nearly won twice in 1991, losing playoff to Billy Andrade in the Kemper Open and finishing second by a stroke to Ted Schulz in the Nissan Los Angeles Open.

- 1992 season punctuated by remarkable accomplishments, including a final-round 71 and second-place finish in the U.S. Open at Pebble Beach (just one of four sub-par rounds that day), and a tie for fourth at the Masters, where he became the first player to ace the fourth hole as part of an opening-round 65 that earned him a tie for the lead.

- Held lead through first three rounds of 1994 B.C. Open, before closing with a 72 to finish four strokes behind Mike Sullivan.

- First close encounter with victory came in 1987 Tournament Players Championship, where he lost a three-hole playoff to Sandy Lyle.

- Winner 1980 Metro Conference Championship while at FSU.

YEAR	EVENTS	WINS	TOP 10	CUTS MADE	EARNINGS	RANK
1983	19			11	$13,643	171
1984	1			1	$603	282
1985	25		4	18	$100,523	78
1986	34		7	24	$154,129	60
1987	32		6	22	$335,590	27
1988	32	1	6	30	$503,321	18
1989	23		4	16	$154,507	89
1990	31		2	22	$264,012	56
1991	30		7	24	$552,979	23
1992	30		8	26	$729,027	14
1993	27		1	21	$187,841	93
1994	30		4	16	$301,178	59
1995	29		7	20	$563,681	31
1996	30		7	23	$650,128	28

TAYLOR SMITH

Born: June 28, 1967
Birthplace: Pensacola, Fla.
Ht: 6' 3" **Wt:** 185
Residence:
Joined Tour: 1996
1996 Money Rank: 102

In his first full year on the PGA Tour, Smith finished in the money in 15 tournaments to earn $221,517. His two top 10 finishes included a tie for second at the 1996 Greater Vancouver Open, where he finished just one stroke behind Guy Boros. Before joining the tour, Smith played on the Nike Tour (1992-1995). His best season came in 1992, when he won one tournament and ranked 12th among Nike golfers.

Smith turned pro at age 19 in 1987. He was an outstanding high school athlete who was an All-State selection in both soccer and basketball.

- Finished tied for second at the 1996 Greater Vancouver Open.

- Finished tied for third at the 1996 Bell Canadian Open.

- Won the 1992 NIKE Permian Basin Open.

- Ranked 12th on the 1992 NIKE TOUR money list.

YEAR	EVENTS	WINS	TOP 10	CUTS MADE	EARNINGS	RANK
1991					$1,980	300
1992					$2,232	298
1996	27		2	15	$221,517	102

CRAIG STADLER

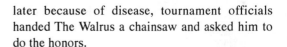

Born: Craig Robert Stadler, June 2, 1953

Birthplace: San Diego, Cal.

Ht: 5' 10" **Wt:** 210

Residence: Denver, Col.

Q School: Spring 1976

1996 Money Rank: 58th

Stadler enjoys the luxury of a 10-year exemption after his 1992 NEC World Series of Golf victory, which means that he is exempt until the year 2002 when he will be 49, and only one year away from the Senior Tour. And the prospect of seeing "The Walrus" on TV competing in a tournament suits most golf fans just fine.

Stadler's colorful nature and powerful swing are among the things that make professional golf so entertaining, but they can overshadow his marvelous talent. He won four tournaments in 1982, including the Masters, finished second on the money list ten years later in 1992, and won the Nissan Open in 1996, capturing his first Tour victory since 1994.

But the stories are sometimes the best. One example: Stadler was disqualified from a tournament at Torrey Pines in 1987 when he "built a stance" to hit from under a tree by kneeling on a towel. When it was time to fell the tree eight years

later because of disease, tournament officials handed The Walrus a chainsaw and asked him to do the honors.

- 12 Tour wins include: 1996 Nissan Open; 1994 Buick Invitational of California; 1992 NEC World Series of Golf; 1991 Tour Championship; 1984 Byron Nelson Classic; 1982 Joe Garagiola-Tucson Open, the Masters, Kemper Open and World Series Of Golf; 1981 Kemper Open and the 1980 Bob Hope Desert Classic and Greater Greensboro Open.

- Has four international wins—1992 Argentine Open; 1990 Scandinavian Enterprise Open; 1987 Dunlop Phoenix, and the 1985 Canon European Masters.

- Finished in the money in 12 of 18 events in 1996, with $336,820, and one Top 10 finish—the win at the Nissan Open.

- Played very well in 1995 missing only six cuts in the 21 events he entered and finishing 45th on the Money List.

- Captured the NEC World Series of Golf in 1992, on the 10th anniversary of his 1982 World Series win. Both victories carried 10-year exemptions.

- Start of his 1992 season was delayed by recuperation from an off-season skiing accident.

- Named 1982 PGA Tour Arnold Palmer Award recipient as the leading money-winner.

- Winner of the 1971 World Junior Championships and the 1973 U.S. Amateur at Inverness.

- Two-time All American at USC—1974-75.

- Has earned $6,337,638 on the Tour.

YEAR	EVENTS	WINS	TOP 10	CUTS MADE	EARNINGS	RANK
1976	9			5	$2,702	196
1977	29		4	19	$42,949	66
1978	27		5	20	$63,486	48
1979	33		4	24	$73,392	55
1980	24	2	7	21	$206,291	8
1981	28	1	8	21	$218,829	8
1982	25	4	11	23	$446,462	1

YEAR	EVENTS	WINS	TOP 10	CUTS MADE	EARNINGS	RANK
1983	27		11	20	$214,496	17
1984	22	1	8	20	$324,241	8
1985	24		8	20	$297,926	11
1986	26		8	17	$170,076	53
1987	22		6	17	$235,831	39
1988	21		5	16	$278,313	37
1989	22		4	20	$409,419	25
1990	19		5	16	$278,482	52
1991	21	1	7	16	$827,628	2
1992	25	1	4	18	$487,460	28
1993	24		5	17	$553,623	29
1994	22	1	4	15	$474,831	32
1995	21		4	15	$402,316	45
1996	18	1	1	12	$336,820	58

PAUL STANKOWSKI

Born: December 2, 1969

Birthplace: Oxnard, Cal.

Ht: 6' 1" **Wt:** 180

Residence: Flower Mound, Tex.

Q School: 1993, 1995

1996 Money Rank: 52nd

In his rookie year of 1994, Stankowski retained his exemption at the very last tournament of the year, the Las Vegas Invitational, by finishing in a tie for fifth and ending up 106th on the money list. Things weren't so dramatic in 1995. Losing his card (he made only 15 cuts in 31 attempts and posted only one top-10 finish) Stankowski, who attended the University of Texas-El Paso, finished in a tie for 15th at the Q-School tournament, on the strength of four rounds in the 60's, and made it back to the Tour.

Drama returned in '96. Stankowski, the last of six alternates included in the 1996 BellSouth Classic when several PGA Tour veterans withdrew to prepare for the Masters, birdied the first hole of a playoff with Brandel Chamblee to win his first Tour tournament, earned his first invitation to the Masters, and went on to enjoy a strong year.

- Finished in the money in 11 of 25 '96 tournaments, with the BellSouth win, $390,575 in total earnings, and two other Top 10 finishes—sixth at the FedEx St. Jude Classic and a tie for sixth at the Memorial.

- Captured the '96 Louisiana Open on the Nike Tour a week prior to BellSouth win.

- BellSouth playoff began at par-5 18th hole, with Chamblee's third shot landing in water for an eventual bogey; Stankowski put his second shot in the rough, but his third found the green. Holed birdie putt to become the fourth first-time winner on the 1996 Tour.

- Prior to BellSouth win, best previous Tour finish was a tie for fourth at the 1995 Shell Houston Open.

- Winner 1992 New Mexico Open and 1992 San Jaun Open.

- 1990 Western Athletic Conference champion at UTEP and three time All-American.

YEAR	EVENTS	WINS	TOP 10	CUTS MADE	EARNINGS	RANK
1994					$170,393	106
1995	31		1		$144,558	133
1996	25	1	3	11	$390,575	52

PAYNE STEWART

Born: William Payne Stewart, January 30, 1957

Birthplace: Springfield, Mo.

Ht: 6' 1" **Wt:** 180

Residence: Orlando, Fla.

Q School: Spring 1981

1996 Money Rank: 33rd

After a horrific 1994 season, when he finished 123rd on the money list, Stewart, who has nine career Tour wins and over $7 million in career earnings, seems on his way to resurrecting his game and regaining the form that won a PGA Championship and a U.S. Open and brought him three Top 5 PGA Tour money-list finishes (1986, 1989 and 1990).

His 1995 season featured flashes of his former brilliance, most notably his pursuit and subsequent defeat of Scott Hoch at the Shell Houston Open, where he came from seven strokes down on the final day. Stewart, a Southern Methodist University business grad, had five other Top-10 finishes in 1995 and missed only five cuts in 27 events. He had seven Top 10s in 1996, finished in the money in 18 of 26 events, and won $537,293. Stewart, whose greatest win came in the 1991 U.S. Open in an 18-hole playoff with Scott Simpson, is one of the most recognizable touring pros with his colorful outfits that feature old-fashioned knickers.

- Nine Tour wins include: 1995 Shell Houston Open; 1991 U.S. Open; 1990 MCI Heritage and GTE Byron Nelson classics; 1989 MCI Heritage Classic and PGA Championship; 1987 Hertz Bay Hill Classic; 1983 Walt Disney World Classic; and 1982 Quad Cities Open.

- Six international wins include: 1993 Hassan II Trophy; 1991 Heineken Dutch Open; 1990 World Cup; 1982 Coolangatta-Tweed Head Classic and the 1981 Indonesian and Indian opens.

- 1996 Top 10s: second at the Walt Disney World/Oldsmobile Classic; tie for tenth at the Kemper Open; tied for sixth at the MasterCard Colonial; tied for ninth at the Shell Houston Open; tied for fourth at the Freeport-McDermott Classic; tied for third at the Honda Classic; and tied for fourth at the Bob Hope Chrysler Classic.

- Finished tenth in '96 Tour statistics in average strokes per hole (1.751), and was sixth in putting (1.750) in 1995.

- Said of disappointing 1994 season, in which he finished 123rd on the money list: "The reason I had such a poor year was that I didn't dedicate myself."

- Runner up four times in 1993, including head-to-head battle with Lee Janzen in U.S. Open.

- Missed 10 weeks of 1991 season with a nerve problem in his neck.

- Was eight strokes off lead after first-round 74 at '89 PGA Championship, and rebounded to win by one stroke.

- Lost his knickers before a 1988 exhibition match at the Hercules Country Club in Wilmington, Delaware when he bet three women professionals he could beat their best ball, wagering his knickers against theirs (well, actually, their shorts).

- Winner All-Around category 1988 Nabisco Statistics and was scoring leader in '89 statistics.

- Third in Asian Tour Order of Merit in '91; third in Australian Order of Merit in '82.

- Three-time winner of Skins Games (1991-93).

- 1979 Southwest Conference co-champion.

- 1979 All-American.

- Donated 1987 Bay Hill Classic winner's check to Florida Hospital Circle of Friends in memory of father, who died two years earlier.

- Met and married wife, Tracey Ferguson of Australia, while in Malaysia.

- Lists hunting, fishing and cooking as special interests.

- Has earned $7,926,772 on the Tour.

YEAR	EVENTS	WINS	TOP 10	CUTS MADE	EARNINGS	RANK
1981	10		1	5	$13,400	160
1982	24	2	4	14	$98,686	39
1983	32	1	7	23	$178,809	25
1984	31		6	25	$288,795	11
1985	26		6	24	$225,729	19
1986	29		16	22	$535,389	3
1987	27	1	7	22	$511,026	12
1988	27		12	25	$553,571	14
1989	24	2	11	19	$1,201,301	2
1990	26	2	8	22	$976,281	3
1991	19	1	2	16	$476,971	31
1992	23		5	19	$334,738	44
1993	26		12	22	$982,875	6
1994	23		2	15	$145,687	123
1995	27	1	6	22	$866,219	12
1996	25		7	18	$537,293	33

SAND SAVE PERCENTAGE

Rank	Name	Rounds	Percent
1.	Gary Rusnak	78	64.0
2.	Jeff Sluman	106	63.4
3.	Greg Kraft	81	63.3
4.	Glen Day	89	63.2
5.	Justin Leonard	101	62.6
6.	Wayne Grady	64	61.7
7.	Jesper Parnevik	68	61.4
8.	Phil Mickelson	77	61.3
9.	Jerry Kelly	91	61.2
10.	Brad Faxon	82	61.1

DAVE STOCKTON, JR.

Born: David Bradley Stockton, Jr., July 31, 1968
Birthplace: Redlands, Cal.
Ht: 6' 2" **Wt:** 195
Joined Tour: 1994
1996 Money Rank: 120

In 1996, Stockton finished in the top 10 twice, including a tie for third at the 1996 Buick Open but made the cut in only 14 events out of 31 entered. Stockton had a flash of brilliance as he finished tied for second at the 1995 Canon Greater Hartford Open, two strokes behind Greg Norman. But by making the cut in just 15 events out of 32 entered, Stockton ranked only 124th and barely qualified for the 1996 tour.

Stockton had a fine—but also inconsistent—rookie year in 1994, when he ranked 96th. Though he finished in the money int half the tournaments he entered, Stockton had three top 10 finishes (including two tie for thirds). Before joining the tour, Stockton played on the Nike circuit (1993-1994), where he won two tournaments in 1993.

Stockton's father was himself a fine PGA Tour pro. Though Stockton is technically not a junior (his father and he have different middle names), Stockton took the Jr. to show his pride in his dad.

- Finished tied for second at the 1995 Canon Greater Hartford Open.

- Finished tied for third at the 1996 Buick Open.

- Finished tied for third at the 1994 Canon Greater Hartford Open.

- Finished tied for third at the 1994 Deposit Guaranty Golf Classic.

- Won the 1993 NIKE Connecticut Open.

- Won the 1993 NIKE Hawkeye Open.

- Finished runner-up in the 1989 NCAA Championship.

YEAR	EVENTS	WINS	TOP 10	CUTS MADE	EARNINGS	RANK
1994	31		3	15	$185,209	96
1995	32		1	15	$149,579	124
1996	31		2	14	$176,056	120

CURTIS STRANGE

Born: Curtis Northrop Strange, January 30, 1955
Birthplace: Norfolk, Vir.
Ht: 5' 11" **Wt:** 170
Joined Tour: 1977
1996 Money Rank: 116

Though not the dominant player he was in the 1980s, when he won back-to-back U.S. Open Championships, Strange still commands respect as a wily veteran. In 1996, Strange made 15 tournament cuts to earn $181,883. His play dropped off from 1995, when he finished in the top 10 four times (including a tie for third at the Bob Hope Chrysler Classic) and ranked 49th.

Strange's play in the 1990s, though solid, does not compare to his 1980s form. Between 1979 and 1989, he won 17 PGA Tournaments and was the tour's leading money winner in three seasons. His best season was in 1988, when he won four tournaments (including a playoff win over Nick Faldo in the U.S. Open) and became the first golfer to win over $1 million in one year. Strange also topped the money list in 1987, when he won three tournaments and finished in the top 10 eleven times, and in 1985, when he won three tournaments and finished runner-up in two others. Strange followed up his big 1988 by winning the 1989 U.S. Open and finishing second in the 1989 PGA Championship; with nine top 10 finishes in total, Strange ranked seventh.

Strange first played golf at age seven on the golf course his father owned—the White Sands CC in Virginia Beach, Virginia. Strange's identical twin brother, Allen, was a PGA Tour member.

- Won 17 PGA Tournaments.

- Won the 1989 U.S. Open.

- Won the 1988 U.S. Open.

- Was first golfer to win back-to-back U.S. Opens since Ben Hogan (1950-1951).

- Was first player to earn $1 million in one year (1988).

- Led the PGA TOUR money list three times (1985, 1987, 1988).

- Finished tied for second at the 1989 PGA Championship.

- Finished tied for second at the 1985 Masters Tournament.

- Won the 1987 NEC World Series of Golf.

- Won the 1983 Sammy Davis, Jr.-Greater Hartford Open.

- Won three international tournaments.

- Named to five Ryder Cup teams (1983, 1985, 1987, 1989, 1995).

- Wore the same red shirt on the final round of the 1989 Open as he did the previous year.

YEAR	EVENTS	WINS	TOP 10	CUTS MADE	EARNINGS	RANK
1976	1			1	$375	267
1977	18		2	11	$28,144	87
1978	28		3	16	$29,346	88
1979	34	1	9	24	$138,368	21
1980	30	2	9	27	$271,888	3
1981	28		12	23	$201,513	9
1982	29		12	26	$263,378	10
1983	28	1	6	22	$200,116	21
1984	26	1	9	23	$276,773	14
1985	25	3	7	22	$542,321	1
1986	25	1	6	19	$237,700	32
1987	26	3	11	23	$925,941	1
1988	24	4	6	21	$1,147,644	1
1989	21	1	9	20	$752,587	7
1990	20		6	17	$277,172	53
1991	20		3	13	$336,333	48
1992	17		2	13	$150,639	99
1993	24		5	16	$262,697	63
1994	23		5	18	$390,881	41
1995	24		4	17	$358,175	49
1996	23		1	15	$181,883	116

STEVE STRICKER

Born: Steven Charles Stricker, February 23, 1967

Birthplace: Edgerton, Wis.

Ht: 6' **Wt:** 185

Residence: Edgerton, Wis.

Q School: 1993

1996 Money Rank: 4th

A rising star with an excellent putting touch and overall consistency, Stricker finished 50th in the money list his 1994 rookie season, 40th in 1995 (with four Top 10 finishes), and rocketed to 4th in 1996. He had a spectacular year, winning twice (at the Kemper and Motorola Western opens) and finishing tied for second once, third once, and tied for third three times.

Caddied by his wife, Nicki, and taught by his father-in-law, Dennis Tizani, the golf coach at the University of Wisconsin, Stricker's golfing experience became even more of a family affair at the '95 Greater Milwaukee Open, when he was joined in the field by both his father-in-law and his brother-in-law, Mario Tizani. Stricker was recruited to play at Wisconsin by Dennis Tizani, but chose the University of Illinois, instead, where he was a two-time All-American in 1988-89.

- Has two International wins—1993 Canadian PGA and 1990 Victoria Open.

- Finished in the money in 19 of 24 events in 1996, with $1,383,739, and five other Top 10 finishes: third at the Tour Championship; tied for third at the Greater Milwaukee Open; tied for second at the NEC World Series of Golf; third at the Greater Greensboro Chrysler Classic; and third at the United Airlines Hawaiian Open.

- Of the Kemper win, his first, he said: "It went well. It was an emotional day. It creeps into your head about winning. After the sixth hole (on the final round) I didn't take too many chances. At the 13th I thought the time was now."

- At the Motorola Western, he was the only golfer to string together four rounds in the 60s, with a 72-hole total of 18-under 270 that was two strokes off the tournament record, set by Sam Snead in 1949, and the second-lowest score (just behind Nick Price's 269 in 1993) since the event moved to Cog Hill.

- Eight-shot Western win also equaled Ernie Els' mark for the largest victory margin on '95 PGA tour; it was also the biggest win at the Western Open since Tom Weiskopf beat Tom Watson by nine shots in 1982. The lead was so safe that he enjoyed a snack while walking up the 16th fairway.

- Finished third in '96 Tour statistics in average strokes per hole (1.740) and sixth in average yards per drive (281.8). Best finish in 1995 Tour statistics was 14th in driving.

- Made 26 consecutive cuts at one point in 1995, and missed only thee all season.

- Was fourth in rookie earnings in '94, behind Ernie Els, Mike Heinen and Glen Day.

- Finished tied for 18th at the 1993 Qualifying Tournament after failing to make the finals three years in a row.

- Tied for tenth at the 1990 Canadian TPC.

- Winner 1990 Payless/Pepsi and Wisconsin opens.

YEAR	EVENTS	WINS	TOP 10	CUTS MADE	EARNINGS	RANK
1990P	1			1	$3,974	255
1990N	2		1	2	$10,080	86
1991P	1					
1991N	12		1	7	$11,298	85
1992P	2			1	$5,550	261
1992N	1			1	$1,065	227
1993P	6		1	2	$46,171	186
1993N	3			1	$820	226
1994	26		4	22	$334,409	50
1995	23		4	20	$438,931	40
1996	22	2	7	19	$1,383,739	4

HAL SUTTON

Born: Hal Evan Sutton, April 28, 1958

Birthplace: Shreveport, La.

Ht: 6' 1" **Wt:** 185

Joined Tour: 1982

1996 Money Rank: 109

After suffering through two poor seasons that suggested he had reached the downside of his career, Sutton came back strong in 1994. He finished in the money 23 times (including four top 10 finishes) to rank 29th. He followed up in 1995 by again finishing in the top 10 four times (including a B.C. Open win, where he shot a final round 61) and ranking 32nd. Sutton played less sharply in 1996, however, when he finished in the money 17 times to earn $193,723.

After an outstanding collegiate career, including being named the *Golf Magazine* College Player of the Year, Sutton made a big splash in 1982, his first full year as a pro, finishing in the top 10 eight times (including an end-of-the-year win at the Walt Disney World Golf Classic) and ranked 11th. The next year marked the peak of Sutton's career: by winning two tournaments—The Tournament Championship and the PGA Championship—and finishing in the top 10 twelve times, Sutton finished atop the 1983 money list with $426,668 in earnings. In his remarkable PGA

Championship triumph, Sutton set a new two-round record low at 131, then held off a charging Jack Nicklaus by a single stroke.

Sutton had two more outstanding seasons. In 1985, he won two tournaments and ranked 7th in earnings, and in 1986, he again won two tournaments and ranked 6th in earnings. After that, Sutton played steady golf until his form suddenly dropped off in 1992 and 1993 (when he ranked 185th and 161st, respectively). For his return to form in 1994, Sutton received the Hilton Bounceback Award. Sutton credits his turnaround to returning to his old teacher, Jimmy Ballard.

- Won eight PGA Tournaments.

- Won the 1983 Tournament Players Championship.

- Won the 1983 PGA Championship.

- Won the 1985 St. Jude Memphis Classic.

- Won the 1986 Memorial Tournament.

- Won the 1995 B.C. Open.

- Won the 1982 Walt Disney World Golf Classic.

- Finished tied for fourth at the 1986 U.S. Open.

- Ranked first on the 1983 money list.

- Voted the 1983 PGA and Golf Writers Player of the Year.

- Won the 1994 Hilton Bounceback Award.

YEAR	EVENTS	WINS	TOP 10	CUTS MADE	EARNINGS	RANK
1981	4					
1982	31	1	8	25	$237,434	11
1983	30	2	12	25	$426,668	1
1984	26		11	23	$227,949	26
1985	26	2	7	23	$365,340	7
1986	28	2	9	23	$429,434	6
1987	25		6	20	$477,996	16
1988	27		1	16	$137,296	88
1989	30		7	20	$422,703	23
1990	28		4	18	$207,084	75
1991	28		5	23	$346,411	47
1992	29			8	$39,234	185
1993	29		1	13	$74,144	161
1994	29		4	23	$540,162	29
1995	31	1	4	17	$554,733	32
1996	29		1	17	$193,723	109

TOMMY TOLLES, JR.

Born: Thomas Louis Tolles, Jr., October 21, 1966
Birthplace: Fort Myers, Fla.
Ht: 6' 1" **Wt:** 195
Residence: Flat Rock, N.C.
Q School: 1994
1996 Money Rank: 16th

Tolles had an outstanding sophomore season on the PGA Tour, placing 16th on the money list with $871,589 in earnings. After making only 13 of 25 cuts the previous year but gaining an exemption by finishing 116th on the money list, Tolles played consistently strong in 1996: he made 21 of 26 cuts and had six Top 10 finishes, including a tie for second at the Players Championship and a tie for third at the PGA Championship. After getting used to being near the top, Tolles will look to break through in 1997.

Tolles spent four years on the Nike Tour; his best year was in 1994 when he finished 16th on the Nike money list. Tolles, who met his wife, Ilse, while playing the South African PGA Tour in 1989-90, attended the University of Georgia and lists fishing and boating as special interests.

- 1996 Top 10 finishes: a tie for third at the PGA Championship; a tie for sixth at the MasterCard Colonial; a tie for fifth at the Shell Houston Open; a tie for fifth at the BellSouth Classic; a tie for second at the Players Championship; and third at the Freeport-McDermott Classic.

- Made only 13 cuts in 25 events in 1995, but scored two Top 10 finishes.

- Best finish in 1995 Tour statistics was a tie for fifth in eagles (12); had three eagles during the second round of the '95 Bell Canadian Open, the first player to do so since Dave Stockton Jr. at the 1994 Walt Disney/Oldsmobile Classic.

- Qualified for and played in 1988 and 1991 U.S. Open, missing the cut in both.

- First professional victory came in the Nike Ozarks Open.

- Led the 1994 Nike Tour with 368 birdies.

- Ranked second to David Duval on the '94 Nike tour in par breakers at 24 percent; finished second in that category in '93.

YEAR	EVENTS	WINS	TOP 10	CUTS MADE	EARNINGS	RANK
1988	1					
1991P	2					
1991N	24		3	13	$20,480	61
1992N	24		3	15	$43,062	33
1993N	20	1	3	12	$61,391	24
1994N	26	1	7	18	$98,618	16
1995	27		2	13	$166,431	116
1996	25		6	21	$871,589	16

DAVID TOMS

Born: David Wayne Toms, January 4, 1967

Birthplace: Monroe, La.

Ht: 5' 10" **Wt:** 160

Joined Tour: 1992

1996 Money Rank: 105

After falling off the PGA Tour in 1994, Toms returned in 1996 with his best season, finishing in the top 10 twice (including a sixth place finish at the Kemper Open). It was a big improvement over 1994, when he made the cut in 16 tournaments out of 32 entered, did not finish once in the top 10, and lost his card by ranking 164th. Toms sharpened his form on the 1995 Nike TOUR, where he won two tournaments, finished in the top 10 ten times, and ranked third among Nike golfers.

Toms' first full year on the PGA Tour was in 1992, when he ranked 101st, and tied for third at the 1992 Northern Telecom Open, where he shot 63 in the final round. Toms has also played on the NIKE TOUR for four years (1990, 1991, 1993, 1995).

Toms has had some success playing courses without practice rounds. At the 1992 Kemper Open, he arrived near his tee time, having been married the previous Saturday and savoring it until the last second before work begins again. Without ever having played the TPC at Avenel course before, Toms shot a course-record-tying 63 during the opening round.

- Finished third at the 1992 Northern Telecom Open.

- Finished sixth at the 1996 Kemper Open.

- Shot a course-record-tying 63 at the 1992 Kemper Open.

- Won the 1995 NIKE Greater Greenville Classic.

- Won the 1995 NIKE Wichita Open.

- Ranked third on the 1995 NIKE TOUR money list.

- Was an All-American at Louisiana State University (1988-1989).

YEAR	EVENTS	WINS	TOP 10	CUTS MADE	EARNINGS	RANK
1989	5			1	$1,463	278
1990	3					
1992	30		1	14	$148,712	101
1993	32		3	12	$120,952	123
1994	32			16	$87,607	164
1996	29		2	16	$205,188	105

KIRK TRIPLETT

Born: Kirk Alan Triplett, March 29, 1962

Birthplace: Moses Lake, Wash.

Ht: 6' 3" **Wt:** 200

Residence: Nashville, Tenn.

Q School: Fall 1989

1996 Money Rank: 65th

A 1985 civil engineering grad from the University of Nevada, Triplett, whose wife, Cathi, occasionally caddies for him, slipped a bit in 1996 after a solid 1995, when he finished 29th on the money list with seven Top 10 finishes that included a pair of ties for second.

If the golfing experts are right, expect Triplett to fashion some highlights on the course during the next few years. He is second to Bobby Wadkins on the all-time money list among players yet to win a tournament, and finished in the money in 16 of 23 events in 1996.

The Washington state native played on the Australian, Asian and Canadian tours in 1987-89 and says of the experiences: "I wouldn't trade them for anything. I learned so much, not only about golf, but about myself. I'll be telling stories about Asia until the day I die."

- Has one International win—the 1988 Alberta Open.

- Three Top 10s in 1996: second at the Deposit Guaranty Golf Classic; a tie for ninth at the FedEx St. Jude Classic; and a tie for tenth at the Byron Nelson Classic.

- Made 24 of 27 cuts in 1995, when he earned $644,607 and tied for second at the Buick Invitational of California and the Greater Hartford Open. Was third in the all around category (339) and fourth in birdies (399) in 1995.

- Began the 1994 season with four Top 10 finishes in his first six starts.

- Placed third in Tour rookie earnings in 1990, trailing only Robert Games and Peter Persons.

YEAR	EVENTS	WINS	TOP 10	CUTS MADE	EARNINGS	RANK
1986	1					
1987	1					
1988	1					
1990	26		2	13	$183,464	88
1991	28			18	$137,302	112
1992	25		1	10	$175,868	85
1993	27		2	19	$189,418	90
1994	26		8	19	$422,171	38
1995	27		7	24	$644,607	29
1996	22		3	16	$321,714	65

BOB TWAY

Born: Robert Raymond Tway, May 4, 1959

Birthplace: Oklahoma City, Okla.

Ht: 6' 4" **Wt:** 180

Residence: Edmond, Okla.

Q School: Fall 1984

1996 Money Rank: 35th

After three years of struggle and poor play, Tway, who once recorded two aces at the same Tour tournament (the 1994 Memorial), finally bounced back in 1995 with one of his best years ever on the Tour—eight Top 10 finishes, including a win at the MCI classic, his first in almost five years.

"It was better than any other win I've ever had, because I was down so low," he said after the tournament. He was named 1995 PGA Comeback Player of the Year. 1996 was not as spectacular, but Tway kept his form, finishing in the money in 17 of 24 events in 1996, with five Top 10s and $529,456 in earnings.

The lift was just what Tway, the former PGA Champion who won four times in 1986 (his sophomore season on the Tour), needed after a dismal 1994 season in which he finished 146th on the money list and retained his eligibility only due to his 1986 PGA win. Some feel that the scare of losing his eligibility may have been just what was needed to bring the spark back into his game.

Tway, a three-time All-American at Oklahoma State, is best remembered by many as the one who stole the '86 PGA Championship from Greg Norman by holing out from a bunker on the 72nd hole at Inverness.

- Tour wins includes: 1995 MCI Heritage Classic; 1990 Las Vegas Invitational; 1989 Memorial Tournament; 1986 Shearson Lehman Brothers-Andy Williams Open, Manufacturers Hanover Westchester Classic, Georgia Pacific Atlanta Classic and PGA Championship.

- 1996 Top 10s: third at the Sprint International; a tie for seventh at the Buick Open; a tie for tenth at the Nissan Open; second at the Nortel Open and fourth at the Mercedes Championships.

- Finished tied for fifth (with Fuzzy Zoeller) in '96 Tour statistics in greens in regulation (70.7).

- Best finish in '95 Tour statistics was eighth in scoring (69.93).

- First player to record two aces in the same event ('94 Memorial) in 30 years.

- Fourth-round 67 at '95 MCI tied him with Nolan Henke and David Frost. Defeated Frost on second extra hole with a birdie after hitting a 7-iron to within three feet of the cup.

- Was tied for '95 U.S. Open lead through 63 holes before four bogeys dropped him to a tie for tenth.

- Named PGA '86 Player of the Year, finishing second on the money list, only $516 behind Greg Norman.

- Parred first playoff hole to edge John Cook in 1990 Las Vegas Invitational.

- Played mini-tours and in Asia before joining the Tour in 1985.

- Winner 1981 Fred Haskins Trophy as outstanding collegiate player.

- Member 1978 and 1980 NCAA Championship teams.

YEAR	EVENTS	WINS	TOP 10	CUTS MADE	EARNINGS	RANK
1981	2			1	$582	295
1982	9			7	$9,039	177
1983	8			6	$12,089	174
1984	2			1	$1,719	237
1985	25		4	14	$164,023	45
1986	33	4	13	28	$652,780	2
1987	27		7	19	$212,362	47
1988	30		4	25	$381,966	29
1989	28	1	4	19	$488,340	17
1990	29	1	5	20	$495,862	23
1991	24		5	15	$322,931	52
1992	21			12	$47,632	179
1993	25		2	11	$148,120	109
1994	29			13	$114,176	146
1995	27	1	8	22	$787,348	20
1996	25		5	17	$529,456	35

OMAR URESTI

Born: Omar Uresti, August 3, 1968

Birthplace: Austin, Tex.

Ht: 5' 6" **Wt:** 175

Residence:

Joined Tour: 1995

1996 Money Rank: 122

In his second year on the PGA TOUR, Uresti is striving for consistency. In 1995, his first full year on the tour, Uresti finished in the money 16 times (but never in the top 10) to rank 156th among golfers and barely maintain an exemption. He cracked the top 10 in 1996 (placing seventh at the Nortel Open and tenth at the Nissan Open) and finished the year ranked 122nd, but missed the cut in more than half the tournaments he entered. Before joining the tour, Uresti played on the Nike Tour, where he won the 1994 Nike Shreveport Open and ranked 30th on the 1994 Nike money list.

As if blasting out of sand traps weren't scary enough, Uresti enjoys reading Stephen King novels in his spare time.

- Finished seventh at the 1996 Nortel Open.

- Finished tenth at the 1996 Nissan Open.

- Finished twelfth at the 1995 Shell Houston Open.

- Won the 1994 Hollard Insurance Royal Swazi Sun Classic.

- Shot nine consecutive birdies at the 1994 NIKE Shreveport Open.

YEAR	EVENTS	WINS	TOP 10	CUTS MADE	EARNINGS	RANK
1995	31			16	$104,876	156
1996	33		2	15	$171,797	122

GRANT WAITE

Born: Grant Osten Waite, August 11, 1964
Birthplace: Palmerston, New Zealand
Ht: 6' **Wt:** 190
Residence: Palmerston North, New Zealand
Q School: Fall 1989, 1992
1996 Money Rank: 72nd

YEAR	EVENTS	WINS	TOP 10	CUTS MADE	EARNINGS	RANK
1988	3		1		$1,494	289
1990	27	1	11		$50,076	177
1991P	4	1	2		$9,307	229
1991N	2		2		$1,502	199
1992	2					
1993	30	1	4	16	$411,405	35
1994	25			13	$71,695	172
1995	26		2	16	$240,722	76
1996	26		2	14	$302,288	72

Selected by CBS Sports in 1993 as the "New Breed Player of the Year," Waite has been inconsistent since that breakthrough year when he won the Kemper Open in a head-to-head battle down the stretch with Tom Kite. Waite held first- and second- round leads before giving way to Kite at the 54-hole juncture, then beat him by one stroke.

The Kemper Open has been special for Waite: he won his only PGA tournament there in 1993, gave up the chance to defend his title in 1994 to be with his wife, Lea, when she gave birth to their first child, and recorded his best 1996 outing there—a tie for second. A wind-surfing, skiing and fitness buff, Waite was a three-time All-American at Oklahoma and two-time Australian Junior Champion.

- International wins include: 1992 New Zealand Open and Trafalgar Capital Classic.

- Finished in the money in only 12 of 26 events in 1996, with $302,288, two Top 10s—a tie for second at the Kemper Open and a tie for eighth at the Players Championship.

- Missed 10 cuts in 26 events in 1995, but two top-10 finishes brought him enough in winnings to be back on Tour in 1996. A tie for second at the Greater Hartford Open brought him $89,600.

- Was '93 Deposit Guaranty Golf Classic clubhouse leader following final-round 63, his career low, but ultimately finished in a tie for fourth.

- Prior to 1993, best finish had been a tie for sixth at the 1990 Hawaiian Open.

- Finished 25th in 1989 and tied for 20th in 1992 Qualifying Tournaments.

DUFFY WALDORF, JR.

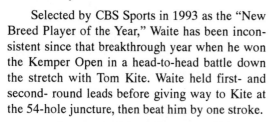

Born: James Joseph Waldorf, Jr., August 20, 1962
Birthplace: Los Angeles, Cal.
Ht: 5' 11" **Wt:** 225
Residence: Newhall, Cal.
Q School: Fall 1986, 1987, 1988, 1990
1996 Money Rank: 30th

Waldorf, the father of three, and a wine collector in his spare time, broke through in 1995 with his win at the LaCantera Texas Open, when he took a two-stroke lead with a six-under-par 66 in the second round and was never headed. He also had three other Top 10 finishes in '95 and placed 35th on the money list.

The 1985 UCLA psychology major followed that year up with a more-than-respectable 1996, with five Top 10 finishes, including a tie for second at the NEC World Series of Golf, a second-place finish at the Greater Greensboro Chrysler Classic, a tie for fifth at the Masters, and $604,382 in earnings, good for 30th on the winnings ladder.

Waldorf, a 10-year Tour veteran whose colorful shirt and cap combinations make him easy to spot on the course, was the 1985 College Player of the Year for the Bruins.

- Top 10 finishes in 1996: a tie for ninth at the Greater Milwaukee Open; the tie for second at the NEC World Series of Golf; second at the

Greater Greensboro Chrysler Classic; a tie for fifth at the Masters, and a tie for seventh at the Mercedes Championships.

- Ended 1995 season in the midst of a streak of 18 consecutive rounds of par or better, making his last 11 cuts.

- Six-stroke win over Justin Leonard at 1995 LaCantera was the largest margin of victory on the Tour since Nick Price's six-stroke win at the 1994 PGA Championship. After Lehman, the next closest competitor was 12 strokes back.

- Teamed with Tom Lehman in December of 1995 to win Diners Club matches.

- Turned potentially disastrous 1994 season around with three straight Top 10s in the midst of a season-ending string of eight consecutive finishes in the money.

- 1990 Qualifying medalist on his fourth time through Q School.

- Winner of 1984 California State Amateur.

YEAR	EVENTS	WINS	TOP 10	CUTS MADE	EARNINGS	RANK
1985	1					
1986	3					
1987	32		1	17	$52,175	148
1988	29		1	16	$58,221	143
1989	28		3	16	$149,945	94
1990	28		1	16	$71,674	157
1991	29		2	20	$196,081	86
1992	25		8	19	$582,120	23
1993	25		4	15	$202,638	15
1994	26		4	14	$274,971	71
1995	26	1	4	21	$525,622	35
1996	21		5	12	$604,382	30

TOM WATSON

Born: Thomas Sturges Watson, September 4, 1949

Birthplace: Kansas City, Mo.

Ht: 5' 9" **Wt:** 160

Residence: Mission Hills, Kan.

Q School: Fall 1971

1996 Money Rank: 25th

Watson made an extraordinary comeback in 1996, taking home his first PGA victory in nine years at the Memorial Tournament in May, and finishing in the money in 14 of 16 events and three other Top 10s. He led the '96 Tour in holes per eagle (97.2) and finished fourth in average strokes per round (69.73).

Watson is the holder of 33 PGA Tour victories, including 8 majors—two Masters, one U.S. Open and five British Opens. In '94 and '95 he missed only one cut per year and finished in the top 10 eight times. Watson won the Vardon Trophy in 1977, '78 and '79 and is a six-time PGA Player of the Year. He was elected to the World Golf Hall of Fame in 1988. Despite an ongoing battle with his putter, Watson continues to prove his greatness and his dogged work-ethic is legendary.

- 33 Tour wins include: 1996 Memorial Tournament; 1987 Nabisco Championships of Golf; 1984 Seiko-Tucson Match Play, MONY-Tournament of Champions and Western Open; 1982 Glen Campbell-Los Angeles Open, Sea Pines Heritage Classic and U.S. Open; 1981 Masters, USF&G-New Orleans Open and Atlanta Classic; 1980 Andy Williams-San Diego and Glen Campbell-Los Angeles opens, MONY-Tournament of Champions, New Orleans Open, Byron Nelson Classic and World Series of Golf; 1979 Sea Pines Heritage Classic, Tournament of Champions, Byron Nelson Golf Classic, Memorial Tournament and Colgate Hall of Fame Classic; 1978 Joe Garagiola-Tucson Open, Bing Crosby National Pro-Am, Byron Nelson Golf Classic, Colgate Hall of Fame Classic and Anheuser-Busch Classic; 1977 Bing Crosby National Pro-Am, Wickes-Andy Williams San Diego Open, Masters and Western Open; 1975 Byron Nelson Golf Classic, and 1974 Western Open.

- Eight International wins include: 1992 Hong Kong Open; 1984 Australian Open 1983, 1982,

1980, 1977 and 1975 British Opens, and the 1980 Dunlop Phoenix.

- Finished in the money in 14 of 16 events in 1996, with $761,238, the Memorial win and three other Top 10 finishes: tied for sixth at the Tour Championship; tied for fifth at the MCI Classic; and second at the Freeport-McDermott Classic.

- Had excellent early-season opportunity in '94 to end victory drought but his putter failed him during final round of AT&T Pebble Beach National Pro-Am, and he finished in a four-way tie for second, one stroke behind Johnny Miller, who was the Tour's leading money winner two years before Watson began an incredible string of four straight (1977-1980) money leads. During that streak Watson won 20 tournaments in the U.S. and two British Opens.

- Winner of 1994 Skins Game and $210,000 with playoff birdie. Holds Tour record for consecutive seasons with earnings over $100,000 (23).

- Captained U.S. to victory in 1993 Ryder Cup at The Belfry; was member of four other teams—1977, 1981, 1983 and 1989.

- Still seeks one major—the PGA Championship.

- Last player to win an event three consecutive times—the Byron Nelson Classic from 1978-80.

- Became first Tour player to earn $500,000 in a season (1980), when he won six Tour events, plus a third-place finish in the British Open.

- Has earned $7,822,588 on the Tour.

YEAR	EVENTS	WINS	TOP 10	CUTS MADE	EARNINGS	RANK
1971	3			3	$2,185	224
1972	30		1	20	$31,081	79
1973	30		7	22	$74,973	35
1974	29	1	10	27	$135,474	10
1975	25	1	12	22	$153,796	7
1976	23		11	22	$133,202	12
1977	25	4	17	22	$310,653	1
1978	24	5	15	22	$362,429	1
1979	21	5	15	20	$462,636	1
1980	22	6	16	22	$530,808	1
1981	21	3	10	19	$347,660	3
1982	20	3	12	19	$316,483	5
1983	17		10	16	$237,519	12

1984	20	3	9	17	$476,260	1
1985	19		7	17	$226,778	18
1986	19		9	17	$278,338	20
1987	20	1	5	15	$616,351	5
1988	19		6	15	$273,216	39
1989	18		2	13	$185,398	80
1990	17		5	13	$213,989	68
1991	16		6	12	$354,877	45
1992	15		5	12	$299,818	50
1993	16		4	14	$342,023	46
1994	15		5	14	$380,378	43
1995	16		3	14	$320,785	58
1996	15	1	4	14	$761,238	25

D.A. WEIBRING, JR.

Born: Donald Albert Weibring, Jr., May 25, 1953
Birthplace: Quincy, Ill.
Ht: 6' 1" **Wt:** 190
Residence: Plano, Tex.
Q School: Spring 1977
1996 Money Rank: 45th

One of the Tour's gurus of the short game, Weibring captured his greatest paycheck in his 21-year career at the 1996 Canon Greater Hartford Open where he brought home $270,000—and that after suffering from Bell's Palsy and pneumonia earlier in the year. The Hartford win broke a string of Illinois-only victories for the Illinois State alum. All four of his previous wins have taken place on Illini courses.

Weibring, who owns his own design and management company (The Golf Resources Group), has never broken the Top 20 on the money list. The flip side to that is that he's finished outside the Top 100 only twice in his 20-year Tour career—and one of those came in 1977, his first year, when he played in only nine tournaments.

- Five Tour wins: 1996 Canon Greater Hartford Open; 1995 Quad Cities Open; 1991 Hardee's Golf Classic; 1987 Beatrice Western Open; and the 1979 Quad Cities Open.

- Has two international wins—the 1985 Polaroid Cup and Shell-Air New Zealand Open.

- Finished in the money 11 of 17 times in 1996, with $436,275, and two Top 10 finishes—the win at Hartford and seventh place at the Sprint International.

- After winning at Hartford, Weibring, who had pneumonia in February, was afflicted by a case of Bell's palsy, which left his face partially paralyzed. "This was very emotional. My son (Matt, 17) was most affected during my illness and he was with me (at the tournament). I knew I could win. All the time I worked out (while recuperating) I had this moment in mind. I went into the final round trying to contain my emotions. I did not expect to get a win this soon, but I didn't expect to get sick so fast, either. The fear I had with the illness was looking into my son's eyes as he looked at me."

- Played consistently in '95, with four top-10 finishes, including a win at the Quad City Classic (holed an 18-foot birdie putt on the final hole for a one-stroke victory over Jonathan Kaye), making 18 cuts out of 24 attempts and finishing 36th on the money list.

- Finished in a tie for second at the 1995 Byron Nelson Classic, closing with a 65, despite receiving a cortisone injection prior to the tournament due to chronic wrist problems.

- Finest season came in 1991 when he won the Hardee's Golf Classic for the second time and lost a playoff to Andrew Magee in the Las Vegas Invitational. Finished Hardee's with a sizzling 64 to win by a stroke over Paul Azinger and Peter Jacobsen. In the Vegas tourney, Weibring shot a 31 under par—sharing a record for a 90-hole tournament with Magee.

- Co-winner of 1991 Hilton Bounceback Award for successful rebound from surgery on his right wrist in 1989.

- Lost 1989 Morocco Open playoff to Payne Stewart.

YEAR	EVENTS	WINS	TOP 10	CUTS MADE	EARNINGS	RANK
1977	9			3	$1,681	215
1978	27		4	17	$41,052	75
1979	33	1	2	20	$71,343	57
1980	28		4	20	$78,611	53
1981	30		6	21	$92,365	45
1982	30		7	26	$117,941	31
1983	23		3	14	$61,631	84
1984	28		4	21	$110,325	65
1985	24		1	14	$153,079	50
1986	24		3	19	$167,602	55
1987	26	1	5	19	$391,363	21
1988	25		5	17	$186,677	63
1989	24			17	$98,686	127
1990	22		2	13	$156,235	101
1991	24	1	5	20	$558,648	22
1992	24		3	19	$253,018	62
1993	22		2	18	$299,293	58
1994	20		3	14	$255,757	72
1995	24	1	4	18	$517,065	36
1996	17	1	2	11	$436,275	45

MARK WIEBE

Born: Mark Charles Wiebe, September 13, 1957
Birthplace: Seaside, Ore.
Ht: 6' 3" **Wt:** 225
Residence:
Joined Tour: 1984
1996 Money Rank: 107

Wiebe continues to play well on the PGA Tour after coming back from a severe shoulder injury in 1994, finishing in the top 10 two times in 1996 (including a tie for second at the Nissan Open). Wiebe missed most of 1994 after he broke and dislocated his shoulder in a skiing accident near Boulder, Colorado. He recovered nicely in 1995 by finishing in the top 10 three times and ranking 112th.

Wiebe has had a long and steady career. His breakthrough season came in 1985, when he won the Anheuser-Busch Golf Classic in a playoff over John Mahaffey, finished in the top 10 five times, and ranked 36th. In 1986, Wiebe again finished in the top 10 five times (including a win in the Hardee's Golf Classic) and ranked 25th. His biggest earnings year came in 1988: though he didn't win a tournament, Wiebe finished in the money in 27 out of 32 tournaments to earn $392,166, ranking him 28th.

Despite his career-threatening accident, Wiebe still enjoys skiing with his family.

- Won the 1986 Hardee's Golf Classic.

- Won the 1985 Anheuser-Busch Golf Classic.

- Finished tied for second at the 1996 Nissan Open.

- Finished tied for second at the 1993 Anheuser-Busch Golf Classic.

- Finished tied for twelfth at the 1989 PGA Championship.

- Won the 1986 Colorado Open.

- Was a second-team All-American at San Jose State.

YEAR	EVENTS	WINS	TOP 10	CUTS MADE	EARNINGS	RANK
1981	2			1	$2,538	222
1982	1					
1983	2			2	$6,628	197
1984	19		1	8	$16,257	166
1985	29	1	5	15	$181,894	36
1986	30	1	5	22	$260,180	25
1987	33		2	26	$128,651	82
1988	32		7	27	$392,166	28
1989	29		4	20	$296,269	41
1990	31		2	21	$210,435	72
1991	31		4	14	$100,046	136
1992	26		2	17	$174,763	86
1993	27		5	19	$360,213	42
1994	9			5	$16,032	233
1995	23		3	11	$168,832	112
1996	26		2	13	$201,058	107

WILLIE WOOD

Born: October 1, 1960

Birthplace: Kingsville, Tex.

Ht: 5' 7" **Wt:** 150

Exempt Status: Veteran Member

Q School: 1983, 1992

Wood registered the first tournament win of his 14-year career with a one-shot victory over Kirk Triplett in the 1996 Deposit Guaranty Clas-sic. Key to his victory was holing an 8-iron from 145 yards for birdie on the par four 13th hole in the final round. The first-place check of $180,000 was higher than any single season earnings total in Wood's career. Prior to his breakthrough win, he had three second place finishes to his credit. Wood was an accomplished amateur player, winning five major junior titles, including the 1977 USGA Junior title.

- Was the medalist at 1983 Q School.

- Sister Deanie has played on the LPGA Tour.

YEAR	EVENTS	WINS	TOP 10	CUTS MADE	EARNINGS	RANK
1983					$8,400	
1984					$115,741	
1985					$153,706	
1986					$172,629	
1987					$95,917	
1988					$53,064	
1989					$9,617	
1990					$179,972	
1991					$48,033	
1992					$57,748	
1993					$146,206	
1994					$87,102	
1995	11			8	$64,697	182
1996	11	1	1	9	$255,158	87

TIGER WOODS

Born: Eldrick Woods, July 21, 1976

Birthplace: Cypress, Cal.

Ht: 6'2" **Wt:** 150

Joined Tour: 1996

1996 Money Rank: 24

After a phenomenal amateur career that included titles at every age level, culminating with an unprecedented three-straight U.S. Amateur championships, Tiger Woods turned professional late in 1996 and promptly enjoyed the greatest debut in professional golf history—winning two tournaments in his first seven starts and amassing five Top 10 finishes. Woods has generated media and fan interest beyond anything the sport has experienced, and his mastery at such a young age recalls the rise of Bobby Jones, as well as Arnold Palmer and Jack Nicklaus—the excitement they stimulated and the charges of brilliant play that led to victories. Woods sports a complete game: he's a long and accurate driver, outdriving even John Daly, a strong irons player able to land approach shots to set up favorable putting spots, and as displayed in his 1996 Amateur championship victory, Woods is an excellent putter.

The1997 Tour will be another proving ground for Woods, but since turning pro in late August 1996 his dynamic presence has already been established: attendance tripled over previous levels at the Walt Disney/World Oldsmobile Classic, where Tiger scored his second Tour win, and conservative estimates count an additional 150,000 fans attending his first seven Tour appearances. With $790,594 in earnings, Tiger won his tour card for 1997, negating the $3,000 check he had already sent along with his application for the PGA Tour Qualifying Tournament.

• Won a record three straight U.S. Junior Amateur titles, 1991-1993.

• Won a record three straight U.S. Amateur tiles, 1994-1996.

• Member 1994 World Amateur Championship team.

• Member 1996 Walker Cup team.

• Won Las Vegas Invitational.

• Won Walt Disney World/Oldsmobile Classic.

• Finished second at the LaCantera Texas Open.

• Scored 14 eagles during his first seven tournaments as a professional.

YEAR	EVENTS	WINS	TOP 10	CUTS MADE	EARNINGS	RANK
1996	8	2	5	8	$790,594	24

Fuzzy Zoeller, comparing his early days on the tour to the 1990s: "The younger guys don't drink. They eat their bananas and drink their fruit drinks, then go to bed. It's a miserable way to live."

FUZZY ZOELLER

Born: Frank Urban Zoeller, November 11, 1951
Birthplace: New Albany, Ind.
Ht: 5' 10" **Wt:** 190
Residence: New Albany, Ind.
Q School: Fall 1974
1996 Money Rank: 56th

Irrepressible, light-hearted, eminently talented, Zoeller brings spontaneity and excitement to the putting green, the practice tee, the clubhouse, even the parking lot. Zoeller, who wears sunglasses and whistles while he works is one of four players to have won in their first Masters.

Troubled by a sore back in 1995, Zoeller was limited to 14 appearances. He made the cut in 12 of them but had only one top-10 finish, tieing for fifth in the Greater Hartford Open, dropping a big lead to Greg Norman in the final round. The 1996 season was only a bit better with three Top 10 finishes as he climbed to 56th on the winnings ladder.

The father of four who has been involved in golf course design (one of his projects is the TPC at Summerlin, host course for the Las Vegas Open), Zoeller has won 10 times on the PGA Tour, including the 1979 Masters and the 1983 U.S. Open.

• Tour wins include: The 1986 AT&T Pebble Beach National Pro-Am, Sea Pines Heritage Golf Classic and Anheuser-Busch Golf Classic; the 1985 Hertz Bay Hill Classic; the 1984 U.S. Open; the 1983 Sea Pines Heritage Classic and Las Vegas Pro-Celebrity Classic; the 1981 Colonial National Invitation, and the 1979 Wickes-Andy Williams San Diego Open and the Masters.

- Finished in the money in only nine of 17 events in 1996 with $347,629 and three Top 10 finishes: a tie for third at the Canon Greater Hartford Open; a tie for seventh at the Greater Greensboro Chrysler Classic; and a tie for fourth at the Players Championship.

- Finished tied for fifth (with Bob Tway) on the '96 Tour in green in regulation (70.7); best finish in 1995 was a tie for seventh in putting (1.751).

- Established Tour record in 1994 by earning $1,016,804 without winning a tournament. He finished second five times—the most runner-up finishes since Arnold Palmer and Jack Nicklaus had six apiece in 1964.

- Open win in '84 came in 18-hole playoff with Greg Norman at Winged Foot.

- '79 Masters win came on third hole of playoff with Ed Sneed and Tom Watson.

- Was hospitalized, barely able to move, the morning of the first round of the '84 PGA Championship. Underwent surgery for ruptured discs, returning to Tour in February 1985.

- Winner 1985-86 Skins Games.

- Winner 1973 Indiana State Amateur.

- 1972 Florida State Junior College champion.

- Has earned $5,266,277 on the Tour.

YEAR	EVENTS	WINS	TOP 10	CUTS MADE	EARNINGS	RANK
1975	21			10	$7,318	146
1976	27		4	18	$52,557	56
1977	32		7	24	$76,417	40
1978	28		5	23	$109,055	20
1979	24	2	6	20	$196,951	9
1980	22		7	19	$95,531	46
1981	25	1	4	19	$151,571	19
1982	25		6	20	$126,512	28
1983	28	2	12	23	$417,597	2
1984	21	1	3	15	$157,460	40
1985	21	1	7	18	$244,003	15
1986	20	3	4	16	$358,115	13
1987	21		5	16	$222,921	44
1988	22		4	18	$209,564	51
1989	19		4	14	$217,742	65
1990	20		2	13	$199,629	79
1991	16		3	12	$385,139	42
1992	18		1	11	$125,003	114
1993	18		4	17	$378,175	39
1994	19		6	16	$1,016,804	5
1995	15		1	12	$170,706	110
1996	16		3	9	$347,629	56

The following is a list of PGA Tour Members who did not finish in the top 125 earnings for 1996.

ADDITIONAL PGA TOUR MEMBERS

FULTON ALLEM

Born: Fulton Peter Allem, September 15, 1957
Birthplace: Kroonstad, South Africa
Ht: 5' 11" **Wt:** 215
Residence: Heathrow, Fla.
1996 Money Rank: 132
1996 Tournaments: 19
1996 Earnings: $162,515

STUART APPLEBY

Born: May 1, 1971
Birthplace: Cohuna, Australia
Ht: 6'1" **Wt:** 185
Residence: Sydney, Australia
1996 Money Rank: 130
1996 Tournaments: 31
1996 Earnings: $164,483

TOMMY ARMOUR, III

Born: October 8, 1959
Birthplace: Denver, Col.
Ht: 6' 2" **Wt:** 205
Residence: Irving, Tex.
1996 Money Rank: 178
1996 Tournaments: 22
1996 Earnings: $79,616

DAVE BARR

Born: March 1, 1952
Birthplace: Kelowna, British Columbia
Ht: 6' 1" **Wt:** 210
Residence: Richmond, Brithish Columbia
1996 Money Rank: 217

1996 Tournaments: 19
1996 Earnings: $31,810

ANDY BEAN

Born: March 13, 1953
Birthplace: Lafayette, Geo.
Ht: 6' 4" **Wt:** 238
Residence: Lakeland, Fla.
1996 Money Rank: 177
1996 Tournaments: 29
1996 Earnings: $80,849

SHANE BERTSCH

Born: March 3, 1970
Birthplace: Sheridan, Wyo.
Ht: 5' 7" **Wt:** 150
Residence: Sheridan, Wyo.
1996 Money Rank: 188
1996 Tournaments: 29
1996 Earnings: $65,517

BILLY RAY BROWN

Born: April 5, 1963
Birthplace: Missouri City, Tex.
Ht: 6' 3" **Wt:** 205
Residence: Missouri City, Tex.
1996 Money Rank: 185
1996 Tournaments: 27
1996 Earnings: $67,203

GEORGE BURNS

Born: George Burns, III, July 29, 1949
Birthplace: Brooklyn, N.Y.
Ht: 6' 2" **Wt:** 200
Residence: Boynton Beach, Fla.
1996 Money Rank: 339
1996 Tournaments: 10
1996 Earnings: $3,456

TOM BYRUM

Born: September 28, 1960
Birthplace: Onida, S.D.
Ht: 5' 10" **Wt:** 175
Residence: Sugarland, Tex.
1996 Money Rank: 126
1996 Tournaments: 26
1996 Earnings: $166,500

BRIAN CLAAR

Born: Brian James Claar,
July 29, 1959
Birthplace: Santa Monica, Cal.
Ht: 5' 8" **Wt:** 150
Residence: Palm Harbor, Fla.
1996 Money Rank: 127
1996 Tournaments: 33
1996 Earnings: $165,511

KEITH CLEARWATER

Born: September 1, 1959
Birthplace: Long Beach, Cal.
Ht: 6' **Wt:** 180
Residence: Orem, Utah
1996 Money Rank: 139
1996 Tournaments: 26
1996 Earnings: $137,617

JAY DELSING

Born: James Patrick Delsing,
October 17, 1960
Birthplace: St. Louis, Mo.
Ht: 6' 5" **Wt:** 200
Residence: St. Louis, Mo.
1996 Money Rank: 153
1996 Tournaments: 32
1996 Earnings: $117,246

ALLEN DOYLE

Born: Allen Michael Doyle, June 26, 1948
Birthplace: Woonsocket, R.I.
Ht: 6' 3" **Wt:** 210
Residence: La Grange, Geo.
1996 Money Rank: 140
1996 Tournaments: 28
1996 Earnings: $136,789

BRUCE FLEISHER

Born: October 16, 1948
Birthplace: Union City, Tenn.
Ht: 6' 3" **Wt:** 205
Residence: Ballen Isles, Fla.
1996 Money Rank: 136
1996 Tournaments: 15
1996 Earnings: $143,380

ROBIN FREEMAN

Born: Robin Lee Freeman, May 7, 1959
Birthplace: St. Charles, Mo.
Ht: 6' **Wt:** 185
Residence: Rancho Mirage, Cal.
1996 Money Rank: 144
1996 Tournaments: 36
1996 Earnings: $133,605

JEFF GALLAGHER

Born: December 29, 1964
Birthplace: Marion, Ind.
Ht: 6' **Wt:** 185
Residence: Jacksonville, Fla.
1996 Money Rank: 157
1996 Tournaments: 32
1996 Earnings: $114,001

BOB GILDER

Born: December 31, 1950
Birthplace: Corvallis, Ore.

Ht: 5' 9" **Wt:** 165
Residence: Corvallis, Ore.
1996 Money Rank: 156
1996 Tournaments: 28
1996 Earnings: $114,844

WAYNE GRADY

Born: Wayne Desmond Grady,
July 26, 1957
Birthplace: Brisbane, Australia
Ht: 5' 9" **Wt:** 160
Residence: Queensland, Australia
1996 Money Rank: 170
1996 Tournaments: 20
1996 Earnings: $94,338

KEN GREEN

Born: Kenneth J. Green, July 23, 1958
Birthplace: Danbury, Conn.
Ht: 5' 10" **Wt:** 175
Residence: West Palm Beach, Fla.
1996 Money Rank: 133
1996 Tournaments: 31
1996 Earnings: $161,663

MIKE HEINEN

Born: William Michael Heinen, Jr.,
January 17, 1967
Birthplace: Rayne, La.
Ht: 6' 1" **Wt:** 195
Residence: Lake Charles, La.
1996 Money Rank: 161
1996 Tournaments: 32
1996 Earnings: $102,588

DONNIE HAMMOND

Born: April 1, 1957
Birthplace: Frederick, Md.
Ht: 5' 10" **Wt:** 170

Residence: Winter Park, Fla.
1996 Money Rank: 165
1996 Tournaments: 22
1996 Earnings: $98,455

JEFF HART

Born: May 5, 1960
Birthplace: Pomona, Cal.
Ht: 5' 9" **Wt:** 150
Residence: Solana Beach, Cal.
1996 Money Rank: 186
1996 Tournaments: 24
1996 Earnings: $66,450

BRIAN HENNINGER

Born: Brian Hatfield Henninger,
October 19, 1962
Birthplace: Sacramento, Cal.
Ht: 5' 8" **Wt:** 155
Residence: Cal.nby, Ore.
1996 Money Rank: 142
1996 Tournaments: 29
1996 Earnings: $135,680

PETER JACOBSEN

Born: Peter Erin Jacobsen, March 4, 1954
Birthplace: Portland, Ore.
Ht: 6' 3" **Wt:** 200
Residence: Portland, Ore.
1996 Money Rank: 146
1996 Tournaments: 20
1996 Earnings: $127,197

STEVE JURGENSEN

Born: October 27, 1961
Birthplace: San Jose, Cal.
Ht: 5' 10" **Wt:** 160
Residence: Newport Beach, Cal.
1996 Money Rank: 152

1996 Tournaments: 32
1996 Earnings: $118,049

FRANK LICKLITER, JR.

Born: July 28, 1969
Birthplace: Middletown, Ohio
Ht: 6' 1" **Wt:** 180
Residence: Franklin, Ohio
1996 Money Rank: 138
1996 Tournaments: 30
1996 Earnings: $138,847

BRUCE LIETZKE

Born: Bruce Alan Lietzke,
July 18, 1951
Birthplace: Kansas City, Kan.
Ht: 6' 2" **Wt:** 185
Residence: Dallas, Tex.
1996 Money Rank: 150
1996 Tournaments: 16
1996 Earnings: $122,941

SANDY LYLE

Born: Alexander Walter Barr Lyle,
February 9, 1958
Birthplace: Shrewbury, England
Ht: 6' **Wt:** 187
Residence: West Linton, Scotland
1996 Money Rank: 168
1996 Tournaments: 16
1996 Earnings: $94,490

JOHN MAHAFFEY

Born: John Drayton Mahaffey,
May 9, 1948
Birthplace: Kerrville, Tex.
Ht: 5' 9" **Wt:** 160
Residence: Houston, Tex.
1996 Money Rank: 222

1996 Tournaments: 28
1996 Earnings: $30,016

ROGER MALTBIE

Born: June 30, 1951
Birthplace: Modesto, Cal.
Ht: 5' 10" **Wt:** 200
Residence: Los Gatos, Cal.
1996 Money Rank: 199
1996 Tournaments: 5
1996 Earnings: $48,800

JIM MCGOVERN

Born: James David McGovern,
February 5, 1965
Birthplace: Teaneck, N.J.
Ht: 6' 2" **Wt:** 195
Residence: Oradell, N.J.
1996 Money Rank: 154
1996 Tournaments: 32
1996 Earnings: $116,727

DAN POHL

Born: Danny Joe Pohl, April 1, 1955
Birthplace: Mt. Pleasant, Mich.
Ht: 5' 11" **Wt:** 175
Residence: Mt. Pleasant, Mich.
1996 Money Rank: 162
1996 Tournaments: 18
1996 Earnings: $100,562

MIKE REID

Born: Michael Daniel Reid,
July 1, 1954
Birthplace: Bainbridge, Md.
Ht: 5' 11" **Wt:** 160
Residence: Provo, Utah
1996 Money Rank: 134
1996 Tournaments: 24
1996 Earnings: $161,284

CHARLIE RYMER

Born: Charles Christopher Rymer,
December 18, 1967
Birthplace: Cleveland, Tenn.
Ht: 6' 4" **Wt:** 240
Residence: Atlanta, Geo.
1996 Money Rank: 145
1996 Tournaments: 30
1996 Earnings: $132,076

HISAYUKI SASAKI

Born: Hisayuki Sasaki,
November 27, 1964
Birthplace: Gumma, Japan
Ht: 6' 2" **Wt:** 180
Residence: Tokyo, Japan
1996 Money Rank: 159
1996 Tournaments: 20
1996 Earnings: $105,651

GENE SAUERS

Born: Gene Craig Sauers, August 22, 1962
Birthplace: Savannah, Geo.
Ht: 5' 8" **Wt:** 150
Residence: Savannah, Geo.
1996 Money Rank: 148
1996 Tournaments: 26
1996 Earnings: $123,904

MIKE STANDLY

Born: Michael Dean Standly,
May 19, 1964
Birthplace: Abilene, Tex.
Ht: 6' **Wt:** 200
Residence: Houston, Tex.
1996 Money Rank: 164
1996 Tournaments: 32
1996 Earnings: $99,034

MIKE SULLIVAN

Born: Michael James Sullivan, January 1, 1955
Birthplace: Gary, Ind.
Ht: 6' 2" **Wt:** 220
Residence: Greeneville, Tenn.
1996 Money Rank: 147
1996 Tournaments: 28
1996 Earnings: $126,069

KEVIN SUTHERLAND

Born: July 4, 1964
Birthplace: Sacrameto, Cal.
Ht: 6' 1" **Wt:** 185
Residence: Sacramento, Cal.
1996 Money Rank: 135
1996 Tournaments: 34
1996 Earnings: $144,828

TED TRYBA

Born: Ted Nickolas Tryba, January 15, 1967
Birthplace: Wilkes-Barre, Penn.
Ht: 6' 4" **Wt:** 205
Residence: Orlando, Fla.
1996 Money Rank: 131
1996 Tournaments: 37
1996 Earnings: $162,944

TRAY TYNER

Born: September 29, 1964
Birthplace: Anchorage, Alaska
Ht: 5' 10" **Wt:** 175
Residence: Humble, Tex.
1996 Money Rank: 197
1996 Tournaments: 18
1996 Earnings: $50,426

SCOTT VERPLANK

Born: Scott Rachal Verplank, July 9, 1964
Birthplace: Dallas, Tex.
Ht: 5' 9" **Wt:** 165
Residence: Edmond, Okla.
1996 Money Rank: 171
1996 Tournaments: 12
1996 Earnings: $88,801

LANNY WADKINS

Born: Jerry Lanston Wadkins, December 5, 1949
Birthplace: Richmond, Vir.
Ht: 5' 9" **Wt:** 170
Residence: Dallas, Tex.
1996 Money Rank: 189
1996 Tournaments: 21
1996 Earnings: $64,995

2

PRO FILES
WOMEN

AMY ALCOTT

Born: February 22, 1956

Birthplace: Kansas City, Mo.

Ht.: 5' 6"

Joined Tour: 1975

1996 Money Rank: 58

Alcott remains competitive in her the third decade on the LPGA Tour but continues winless since 1991. In 1996 she made the cut in 11 events and placed in the top 20 twice, tying for second at the Weetabix Women's British Open and for eleventh at the ShopRite LPGA Classic.

Alcott joined the LPGA in 1975 and had at least one win every season for her first dozen years on the Tour. She won four tournaments in both 1979 and 1980, and by 1983 she had become the Tour's sixth millionaire. Five years later, a victory at the Nabisco Dinah Shore helped her top the $2 million mark in career earnings, making her the third LPGA player to accomplish that feat. With 15 top-10 finishes in 1988, Alcott enjoyed her most lucrative season on the Tour.

Alcott had little experience on the amateur circuit prior to joining the LPGA. At 17 she did claim the 1973 USGA Junior Girls title. Alcott has garnered myriad honors and awards, including *GOLF Magazine* Player of the Year award in 1980, the 1980 Seagrams Seven Crowns of Sports Award and the 1983 YWCA Silver Achievement Award. Alcott is playing editor for *Golf Digest*.

- Tied for 2nd place at the Weetabix Women's British Open.

- Tied for 11th place at the 1996 ShopRite LPGA Classic.

- Tied for 5th place at the 1995 PING/Welch's Championship.

- Finished in 4th place at the 1994 Minnesota LPGA Classic.

- Registered a 12-year winning streak from 1975-1986.

- Posted three seasons with four tournament victories—in 1979, 1980 and 1984.

- Won three Nabisco Dinah Shore titles—in 1983, 1988 and 1991.

YEAR	EVENTS	BEST FINISH	EARNINGS	RANK	SCORING AVERAGE
1975	21	1	$26,798	15	73.52
1976	28	1	$71,122	7	73.54
1977	28	1	$47,637	14	73.57
1978	29	1	$75,516	9	73.06
1979	26	1	$144,838	3	72.43
1980	28	1	$219,887	3	71.51
1981	26	1	$149,089	7	72.33
1982	26	1	$169,581	6	72.27
1983	25	1	$153,721	8	73.05
1984	24	1	$220,412	5	72.34
1985	22	1	$283,111	4	71.78
1986	23	1	$244,410	4	71.99
1987	26	2	$125,831	17	72.57
1988	26	1	$292,349	7	71.71
1989	25	1	$168,089	18	72.16
1990	23	2	$99,208	42	73.12
1991	23	1	$258,270	13	72.43
1992	22	T8	$100,064	55	72.70
1993	22	T6	$60,518	76	72.91
1994	22	4	$154,183	35	72.13
1995	19	T5	$70,883	71	72.86
1996	20	2	$106,783	58	73.48

HELEN ALFREDSSON

Born: April 9, 1965

Birthplace: Goteborg, Sweden

Ht.: 5' 10"

Joined Tour: 1992

1996 Money Rank: 43

Sports Illustrated has described Alfredsson as a "fiery" athlete who "plays with emotional abandon that can lead her to impressive heights—but also to unpredictable breakdowns." Although not entirely a breakdown, Alfredsson's 1996 performance paled in comparison to her prior LPGA record. Failing the handsome purses of previous years, she settled into the 43rd position on the Money List—the first time she finished outside the top 20 on the money list. Not that 1996 was with-

Alcott, who has netted well over $3 million during her 22-year tenure on the Tour, has made a point of giving back to the sport that has treated her so well. A member of the Women's Sports Foundation, she has given the UCLA Women's Athletic Department a $50,000 endowment to establish scholarships for the women's golf program.

Additionally, the Amy Alcott Pro-Am for MS—an annual charity event—has brought in well over $750,000—to benefit the Multiple Sclerosis Society. In 1984, Alcott was honored with both the LPGA Good Samaritan Award and the National Multiple Sclerosis Achievement Award, and in 1986, she received the Founders Cup, an award that recognizes the altruistic contributions of LPGA members.

out its moments: Alfredsson had a second-place finish at the Samsung World Championship of Women's Golf, tied for sixth place at both the Fieldcrest Cannon Classic and the HealthSouth Inaugural, and managed a handful of other top-20 finishes before the season's end.

Alfredsson's winnings accompany an impressive resume. A member of the victorious European Solheim Cup team in 1992 and won that year's Rookie of the Year Award. In 1993, the Swedish native's free-swinging longball style paid of in nine top-10 finishes—including the Nabisco Dinah Shore, where she was recognized as a Rolex First-Time Winner. Also that year, she posted a 2nd-place tie at the U.S. Women's Open and 3rd-place ties at the McDonald's Championship and the Rochester International. Registering ten top-10 finishes the following season, she claimed her second LPGA title at the PING/Welch's Cup in Boston. And in 1995, she posted ten more top-10 finishes, crossing the $1 million mark in earnings a the Pinewild Women's Championship.

Having taken up the game at the age of 11, Alfredsson was a six-time Swedish National champion—from 1981 through 1984, and again in

The lowest single round ever recorded in the U.S. Women's Open was a 63, shot by Helen Alfredsson in 1994 at Indianwood Golf and Country Club in Lake Orion, Michigan, topping the Open record by two strokes.

1986 and 1988. In 1988, she graduated from the United States International University with a degree in International Business.

- Finished in 2nd place at the 1996 Samsung World Championship of Women's Golf.
- Tied for 6th place at the 1996 Fieldcrest Cannon Classic and HealthSouth Inaugural.
- Tied for 2nd place at the 1995 Friendly's Classic.
- Finished in 4th place at the 1995 Rochester International.
- Won the 1994 PING/Welch's Championship in Boston.
- Tied for 4th place at the 1994 Toray Japan Queens Cup.
- Was named the Rolex First-Time Winner at the 1993 Nabisco Dinah Shore.
- Tied for 2nd place at the 1993 U.S. Women's Open.
- Finished in 2nd place at the 1992 Mazda Japan Classic—having lost a four-hole sudden-death playoff to Betsy King.
- Won the 1991 Hennessy Cup, Queensland Open and Trophee Coconut Skol.
- Won the 1990 Weetabix Women's British Open.

YEAR	EVENTS	BEST FINISH	EARNINGS	RANK	SCORING AVERAGE
1992	24	2	$262,115	16	71.84
1993	22	1	$402,685	5	71.40
1994	23	1	$277,971	14	71.65
1995	22	T2	$260,596	20	71.84
1996	20	2	$143,631	43	73.00

DONNA ANDREWS

Born: April 12, 1967

Birthplace: Lynchburg, Vir.

Ht.: 5' 8"

Joined Tour: 1990

1996 Money Rank: 41

An improvement on her previous season's standings, Andrews settled into the 41st position on the 1996 Money List. Among the year's highlights were a tie for fifth place at the Star Bank LPGA Classic and a solo fifth-place finish at the Oldsmobile Classic. Andrews' 1995 season was far from her previous standard, as she earned only $25,346 in 25 events, dropping from fifth on the Money List in 1994 to 123rd. In 1994 she competed in 23 events with 12 top-10 finishes—which included victories at the PING/Welch's Championship in Tucson, the Nabisco Dinah Shore, and the ShopRite LPGA Classic.

A successful junior and amateur player, Andrews also won the 1989 Furman University Invitational for the University of North Carolina. Graduating with a B.S. in Business Administration, she joined the LPGA in October of 1985. Andrews claimed five top-20 finishes in her 1990 rookie season, and by 1993 was named Most Improved Player by *Golf Digest*. Building steam over the second half of the season, Andrews became a Rolex First-Time winner at the PING-Cellular One LPGA Golf Championship, and finished in the top-10 in seven of her final 11 starts.

- Finished in 5th place at the 1996 Oldsmobile Classic.
- Tied for 5th place at the 1996 StarBank LPGA Golf Championship.
- Tied for 20th at the Star Bank LPGA Classic in 1995.

- Won the 1994 PING/Welch's Championship, Nabisco Dinah Shore and ShopRite LPGA Classic.

- Was a member of the winning U.S. Solheim Cup team in 1994.

- Was a Rolex First-Time Winner at the 1993 PING-Cellular One LPGA Golf Championship.

- Finished in 2nd place at the 1993 McCall's LPGA Classic at Stratton Mountain and tied for second at the U.S. Women's Open Championship and the World Championship of Women's Golf.

- Finished in 2nd place at the 1992 Crestar-Farm Fresh Classic and tied for 2nd at the Phar-Mor in Youngstown.

- Finished in 2nd place in the 1990 Rookie of the Year race, behind Hiromi Kobayashi.

YEAR	EVENTS	BEST FINISH	EARNINGS	RANK	SCORING AVERAGE
1990	21	5	$52,430	75	73.43
1991	28	T4	$73,472	65	73.42
1992	26	2	$299,839	13	71.67
1993	23	1	$334,285	9	71.54
1994	23	1	$429,015	5	71.18
1995	24	T20	$25,346	123	74.54
1996	26	N/A	$155,231	41	72.09

TINA BARRETT

Born: June 5, 1966

Birthplace: Baltimore, Md.

Ht.: 5' 4"

Joined Tour: 1988

1996 Money Rank: 27

Barrett began to return to form in 1996 with a tie for second place at the JAL Big Apple Classic and a tie for fourth place at the Sprint Titleholders Championship. Suffering from tendinitis in her left wrist during the entire 1995 season, Barrett fell to the 85th spot on the Money List.

After joining the LPGA in October, 1988, Barrett soon established herself as a promising rookie, notching a Rolex First-Time victory at the Mitsubishi Motors Ocean State Open. Ranked among the top five rookies of 1989, she also carded her first hole-in-one at that year's SAFECO Classic. In 1991 she climbed to the 32nd spot on the Money List and had three top-10 finishes. A top-30 spot followed in 1992, and in 1993 she twice tied for second place—at the Nabisco Dinah Shore and at the PING/Cellular One LPGA Golf Championship.

Barrett is a former Eastern Amateur and Maryland State Amateur champion. Prior to graduating from Longwood College Cum Laude in 1988 with a degree in business administration, she was three times named Academic All-American and five times named to the Dean's list. Barrett—who took up the game as a 12-year-old—claimed seven collegiate titles, including consecutive Small College National Championships (in 1986 and 1987). Four times named a Division II All-American, she received an honorable mention as Division I All-American in 1988. Barrett married Dan Friedman in 1993.

- Tied for 2nd place at the 1996 JAL Big Apple Classic.

- Tied for 4th place at the 1996 Sprint Titleholders Championship.

- Tied for 7th place at the 1996 Betsy King LPGA Classic.

- Tied for 8th place at the 1995 GHP Heartland Classic.

- Tied for 5th place at the 1994 Lady Keystone Open.

- Tied for 2nd place at the 1993 Nabisco Dinah Shore.

- Tied for 2nd place at the 1993 PING/Cellular One LPGA Golf Championship.
- Was a Rolex First-Time Winner at the 1989 Mitsubishi Motors Ocean State Open.

YEAR	EVENTS	BEST FINISH	EARNINGS	RANK	SCORING AVERAGE
1989	27	1	$39,776	69	74.69
1990	27	T11	$17,867	121	74.81
1991	26	3	$138,232	32	72.86
1992	28	T3	$184,719	28	72.37
1993	25	T2	$261,491	19	71.87
1994	25	T5	$86,034	63	72.78
1995	23	T8	$52,251	85	73.45
1996	26	2	$209,167	27	72.64

AMY BENZ

Born: May 12, 1967

Birthplace: Rochester, N.Y.

Ht.: 5' 5"

Joined Tour: 1983

1996 Money Rank: 46

More than tripling her previous season's earnings in 1996, Benz settled back into a top-50 spot on the Money List, claiming the 46th position with $134,498 in season's earnings. Among her season's best finishes were a second place at the ShopRite LPGA Classic and an eighth-place tie at the Edina Realty LPGA. Suffering from tendinitis in her left elbow, Benz posted disappointing results for the 1995 season. She competed in 19 events, earning only $35,572—well behind her previous season's earnings of $124,189—and underwent surgery in September.

Benz had her best financial season in 1993, earning $166,968 thanks to six top-10 finishes. Tying for second at the Nabisco Dinah Shore and the ShopRite LPGA Classic, she posted a career-low scoring average of 72.25 that year. The fol-

lowing season, she placed third in the Oldsmobile Classic and tied for fourth at the Sara Lee Classic, and crossed the $1 million mark in career earnings. The former All-American registered her career-best finish in 1992 at the Sara Lee Classic, with a solo second place. Forcing a sudden-death playoff against Maggie Will and Brandie Burton, she won the playoff on the first extra hole—closing with a career-low round of 63.

Having taken up the game at the age of 13, Benz enjoyed an impressive showing as an amateur and collegiate player. In 1982, she won the AIAW National Championship and was the NCAA and AIAW All-American at Southern Methodist University.

- Finished in 2nd place at the 1996 ShopRite LPGA Classic.
- Tied for 8th place at the 1996 Edina Realty LPGA Classic.
- Finished in 3rd place at the 1995 Sara Lee Classic.
- Finished in 3rd place at the 1994 Oldsmobile Classic.
- Tied for 2nd place at the 1993 Nabisco Dinah Shore and the ShopRite LPGA Classic.
- Finished in 2nd place at the 1992 Sara Lee Classic.
- Finished in the top 10 three times in 1991.
- Tied for 2nd place at the 1990 Orix Hawaiian Ladies Open.
- Finished in the top 10 six times in 1989.

YEAR	EVENTS	BEST FINISH	EARNINGS	RANK	SCORING AVERAGE
1983	6	T5	$13,143	95	72.81
1984	29	T7	$41,014	54	74.08
1985	29	T5	$62,260	31	73.54
1986	26	3	$72,407	31	73.44
1987	24	T10	$42,870	57	73.44
1988	26	T3	$117,059	24	72.47
1989	27	T4	$98,129	35	72.44
1990	24	T2	$128,216	29	72.77
1991	23	T5	$96,248	51	72.91
1992	25	2	$141,673	40	72.55
1993	23	T2	$166,968	35	72.25
1994	25	3	$124,189	41	72.52
1995	19	T12	$35,572	107	73.37
1996	26	2	$134,948	46	73.36

NANCI BOWEN

Born: March 31, 1967

Birthplace:
Tifton, Ga.

Ht.: 5' 6"

Joined Tour: 1991

**1996 Money
Rank:** 61

Bowen had two top 20 finishes in 1996, a tie for third place at the Jamie Farr Kroger Classic and a tie for 14th place at the Sprint Titleholders Championship, she posted seven other top-30 finishes, taking home a check from a total of 14 events. Estill enjoyed her best season in 1995, when she was the Tour's 25th top earner. Competing in 24 events, she became a Rolex First-Time Winner at the Nabisco Dinah Shore and, one week later, tied for third place at the Pinewild Women's Championship.

Having first ventured onto the links as an eight-year-old, Bowen enjoyed a four-year tenure as the Georgia Girls State Junior champion (from 1981-1984). A semi-finalist in both the 1987 U.S. Women's Amateur and the 1988 Trans-National, she qualified for four U.S. Women's Open Championships as an amateur. Prior to graduating from the University of Georgia in 1989 with a degree in public relations, she enjoyed a successful collegiate career that included runner-up honors at the 1987 SEC Championship. In her final year as an undergraduate, the two-time All-American claimed sixth place in the 1989 NCAA Championship.

- Tied for 3rd place at the 1996 Jamie Farr Kroger Classic.

- Tied for 14th place at the 1996 Sprint Titleholders Championship.

- Was a Rolex First-Time Winner at the 1995 Nabisco Dinah Shore.

- Tied for 3rd place at the 1995 Pinewild Women's Championship.

- Tied for 3rd place at the 1994 JAL Big Apple Classic.

- Tied for 9th place at the 1994 GHP Heartland Classic.

- Was the Player of the Year on the 1993 Futures Tour.

YEAR	EVENTS	BEST FINISH	EARNINGS	RANK	SCORING AVERAGE
1991	24	T26	$21,583	122	74.86
1992	24	T24	$19,463	132	74.54
1993	DNP				
1994	23	T3	$88,302	61	73.02
1995	24	1	$228,137	25	73.10
1996	25	3	$100,717	61	72.96

PAT BRADLEY

Born: March 24, 1951

Birthplace: Marco Island, Fla.

Ht.: 5' 6"

Joined Tour: 1974

**1996 Money
Rank:** 19

Hall of Famer Bradley is one of the greats on the LPGA Tour, having won five Majors and placed in the top 10 more than half of the 600 tournaments in which she played. Bradley has topped the Tour's Money List twice in her career, in 1986 and 1981, and has claimed a top-20 earnings rating twenty times. In 1996, her twenty-third year of LPGA play, she held onto the 19th spot on the Money List, highlighted by a third place finish in the U.S. Women's Open.

Bradley's 1995 season was one for the record books. She collected nine top-10 finishes—eight of which were in the top four—including a victory at the HEALTHSOUTH Inaugural, her 31st win on the Tour. She topped the $5 million-mark in career earnings that year, making her the only LPGA play-

Pat Bradley's mother spends a lot of time ringing bells. Each time Pat bags a victory, her proud mother rings a bell on the back porch—no matter what time it is. At last count, Pat—a Hall of Famer who has netted well over $5 million in career earnings—had rung in a whopping 31 victories on the Tour.

Bradley's list of credits could fill a fat book. Here's a sample: Inducted into the LPGA Hall of Fame in 1992; 1992 Samaritan Award; 1991 Rolex Player of the Year; 1991 Vare Trophy; Led in four of the five statistical categories in 1991; 1991 Golf Writers Association of America's Ben Hogan Award; Was named one of *GOLF Magazine's* 100 heroes in 1988; 1989 National Golf Foundation's Jack Nicklaus Family of the Year Award; 1986 Rolex Player of the Year; 1986 Vare Trophy; Florida International University Hall of Fame.

er besides Betsy King to reach that level. On January 18, 1992, Bradley became the 12th inductee into the LPGA Hall of Fame. She served on the LPGA Executive Committee form 1993-1995.

Born in Massachusetts, Bradley first took up the game at the age of 11, under the tutelage of John Wirbal, head pro of the Nashua Country Club. At the age of 16, she snagged the New Hampshire Amateur title, a feat she repeated in 1969. She added two New England Amateur titles in 1972 and 1973 and was named an All-American during her collegiate career at Florida International University. She graduated in 1974 with a B.S. in physical education.

- Tied for 3rd place at the 1996 U.S. Women's Open.

- Tied for 5th place at the 1996 Chrysler-Plymouth Tournament of Champions.

- Finished in 7th place at the 1996 Sprint Titleholders Championship.

- Won the 1995 HEALTHSOUTH Inaugural.

- Has played in more than 600 tournaments since 1974 and has registered 309 top-10 finishes.

- Captured six major championship titles.

- Won 31 LPGA tournaments—including back-to-back wins at the 1991 SAFECO Classic and MBS LPGA Classic.

- Was inducted into the LPGA Hall of Fame in 1992.

YEAR	EVENTS	BEST FINISH	EARNINGS	RANK	SCORING AVERAGE
1974	26	5	$10,839	39	75.38
1975	24	2	$28,293	14	73.40
1976	29	1	$84,288	6	73.28
1977	26	1	$78,709	8	72.62
1978	29	1	$118,057	2	72.31
1979	28	2	$132,428	4	72.31
1980	31	1	$183,377	6	71.95
1981	31	1	$197,050	3	72.15
1982	29	4	$113,089	11	72.29
1983	29	1	$240,207	3	72.06
1984	28	2	$220,478	4	72.05
1985	28	1	$387,378	2	71.30
1986	27	1	$492,021	1	71.10
1987	23	1	$140,132	15	72.71
1988	17	T11	$15,965	109	75.19
1989	26	1	$423,714	4	71.00
1990	28	1	$480,018	5	71.13
1991	26	1	$763,118	1	70.66
1992	24	T2	$238,541	19	71.60
1993	25	T3	$188,135	27	71.96
1994	23	T2	$236,274	20	72.03
1995	25	1	$368,904	11	71.70
1996	22	3	$264,914	19	71.71

LAURIE BROWER

Born: November 12, 1963

Birthplace: Long Beach, Cal.

Ht.: 5' 6"

Joined Tour: 1992

1996 Money Rank: 66

Brower improved on her 1995 winnings of $33,633 by more than doubling her take in 1996—earning $96,911—to post her best financial season ever. Helping her to the 66th spot on the 1996 Money List were a handful of top-20 finishes, including a tie for fifth place at the JAL Big Apple Classic and a solo fourth-place finish at the

Youngstown-Warren LPGA Classic—her best results since joining the Tour. Competing in 18 events in 1995, she tied for sixth place at the PING-AT&T Wireless Services LPGA Golf Championship.

Following a successful collegiate career, which included capturing the California State Junior Championship and twice winning the Southern California Junior Championship, Brower went on to play collegiate golf at Texas Tech University, earning recognition as the All Southwestern Conference Player of the Year from 1983-1985. She graduated in 1985 with a degree in handicap recreation. An avid sportswoman, Bower began playing golf as a 12-year old, and her other interests include biking, bowling, swimming and water-skiing.

Brower joined the LPGA in October of 1991. Playing her first full season on the Tour in 1992, she managed a tie for 18th place at the Rail Charity Golf Classic. In 1993 she tied for 14th at the ShopRite LPGA Classic and for 26th at the U.S. Women's Open. Her 1994 season included a new career low round, a 66 for the first round of the Rochester International. She tied for 12th place in that event, and tied for ninth in that year's Lady Keystone Open.

- Finished in 4th place at the 1996 Youngstown-Warren LPGA Classic.

- Tied for 5th place at the 1996 JAL Big Apple Classic.

- Pocketed $33,633 in winnings in 1995, competing in 18 events.

- Tied for 6th place at the PING-AT&T Wireless Services LPGA Golf Championship.

- Tied for 9th place at the 1994 Lady Keystone Open.

- Tied for 12th place at the 1994 Rochester International and posted a new career low round of 66.

- Tied for 14th place at the 1993 ShopRite LPGA Classic and tied for 26th at the U.S. Women's Open.

YEAR	EVENTS	BEST FINISH	EARNINGS	RANK	SCORING AVERAGE
1992	23	T18	$17,957	134	74.62
1993	16	T14	$19,534	128	73.56
1994	9	T9	$22,889	126	72.68
1995	18	T6	$33,633	110	73.80
1996	24	N/A	$96,911	66	73.14

BRANDIE BURTON

Born: January 8, 1972

Birthplace: San Bernardino, Cal.

Ht.: 5' 7"

Joined Tour: 1991

1996 Money Rank: 14

While she didn't return to the winner's circle in 1996, Burton had her strongest season since 1993 with a solo second-place finish at the Friendly's Classic and a tie for second place at the Edina Realty LPGA Classic. Burton enjoyed her best financial season ever in 1993, when she brought in an impressive $517,741 to rank third on the Money List—less than $80k shy of Betsy King's first-place haul of $595,992. She also led the Tour in top-10 finishes that year, with 16, including three wins. Leading the Rolex Player of the Year standings on the eve of the season's final event, Burton was edged out of first place by Betsy King's victory. Also in '93, the California native registered her career-best scoring average of 71.02 and was named *Golf World's* Female Player of the Year.

Acquainted with the links since the age of nine, Burton quickly established herself as a talented amateur. She captured the 1987 and 1989 San Diego Junior World championships and reigned as both the 1988 PGA National champion and the 1989 USGA Junior titlist. Playing only one season of collegiate golf at Arizona State University, she medaled in six out of seven tournaments and was recognized as the nation's top women's collegiate golfer.

When Brandie Burton collected a $120,000 paycheck for winning the du Maurier Classic on October 29, 1993, she became the 35th LPGA player to join the Million Dollar Club. But that's not all. Having posted her first earnings—a modest $11,638—at the Orix Hawaiian Ladies Open in February, 1991, Burton became the fastest player in the LPGA's history to cross the million-dollar mark. And—at the tender age of 21—she was also the youngest. In 1996, however, Australian player Karrie Webb claimed the fastest LPGA million ever—collecting a seven-digit income during her rookie year on the Tour.

- Finished in 2nd place at the 1996 Friendly's Classic.

- Tied for 2nd place at the 1996 Edina Realty LPGA Classic.

- Tied for 3rd place at the 1995 Nabisco Dinah Shore.

- Tied for 3rd place at the 1995 Pinewild Women's Championship.

- Tied for 2nd place at the 1994 PING/Welch's Championship in Tucson.

- Tied for 5th place at the 1994 Chicago Challenge.

- Was a member of the winning 1994 U.S. Solheim team.

- Was a Rolex First-Time Winner at the 1992 PING/Welch's Championship in Tucson.

- Tied for 2nd place at the 1991 Rochester International.

- Was named 1991 LPGA Rookie of the Year.

YEAR	EVENTS	BEST FINISH	EARNINGS	RANK	SCORING AVERAGE
1991	24	T2	$176,412	22	71.96
1992	24	1	$419,571	4	71.30
1993	26	1	$517,741	3	71.02
1994	22	T2	$172,821	31	72.03
1995	24	T3	$214,455	27	71.96
1996	26	2	$313,175	14	71.67

DAWN COE-JONES

Born: Dawn Coe, October 19, 1960

Birthplace: Campbell River, B.C.

Ht.: 5' 7"

Joined Tour: 1983

1996 Money Rank: 54

Having enjoyed a top-25 spot on the money list for seven consecutive years, Coe-Jones dropped in earnings in 1996. Highlights of her relatively lackluster season included a tie for third at the Betsy King LPGA Classic and a tie for fifth at the Edina Realty LPGA Classic. The Canadian's previous season told another story: even though maternity leave restricted her to competing in only 16 events, she earned $268,665, climbing to the 18th spot on the Money List. Among that year's nine top-20 finishes was a six-stroke victory at the Chrysler-Plymouth Tournament of Champions, her third LPGA title.

Coe-Jones joined the LPGA in October, 1983, qualifying for the Tour on her first attempt. Progressing steadily through the ranks, she claimed the 33rd spot on the Money List by her fourth year on the Tour, and was honored that year with the first SCORE Award as Canada's top touring woman professional, an award she reclaimed in 1988. After having captured her first LPGA victory in 1992 at the Kemper Open, Coe-Jones enjoyed the most successful season of her career the following year, notching eight top-10 finishes, including a tie for second place at the Standard Register PING.

A native of British Columbia, Coe-Jones took to the links as a twelve-year-old and soon turned heads as an amateur player, laying claim to two consecutive British Columbia Amateur Championships (in 1982 and 1983) as well as the 1983 Canadian Amateur Championship. Prior to graduating from Lamar University with a degree in elementary education, she claimed the 1982 Dick McGuire and Husky Invitationals and was a 1983 first team All-American. In 1992, she married Jimmy Jones, and the couple's first child, James Richard, was born on October 17, 1995.

- Tied for 3rd place at the 1996 Betsy King LPGA Classic.

- Tied for 5th place at the 1996 Edina Realty LPGA Classic.

- Won the 1995 Chrysler-Plymouth Tournament of Champions.

- Finished in 4th place at the 1995 Star Bank LPGA Classic.

- Won the 1994 HEALTHSOUTH Palm Beach Classic.

- Finished in 2nd place at the 1994 Rochester International.

- Tied for 2nd place at the 1993 Standard Register PING.

- Finished in 3rd place at the 1993 du Maurier Ltd. Classic.

- Joined the LPGA's Million Dollar Club in 1992.

- Became a Rolex First-Time Winner at the 1992 Women's Kemper Open.

YEAR	EVENTS	BEST FINISH	EARNINGS	RANK	SCORING AVERAGE
1984	27	T12	$19,603	91	74.40
1985	25	9	$34,864	68	73.84
1986	26	T4	$54,332	47	73.26
1987	25	T3	$72,045	33	73.02
1988	25	T7	$52,659	58	73.54
1989	24	2	$143,423	19	72.91
1990	25	T2	$240,478	11	72.33
1991	25	3	$158,013	25	72.12
1992	25	1	$251,392	17	72.31
1993	25	T2	$271,978	16	71.71
1994	24	1	$230,388	21	72.10
1995	16	1	$268,665	18	72.06
1996	21	3	$120,618	54	73.00

JANE CRAFTER

Born: December 14, 1955

Birthplace: Perth, Australia

Ht.: 5' 4"

Joined Tour: 1981

1996 Money Rank: 42

Improving on her disappointing 1995 results, Crafter—whose nickname is "Crafty"—compiled impressive finishes at the McDonald's LPGA Championship Tied for third) and the Sara Lee Classic (tied for sixth).

Crafter's 1994 season was set back by a pulled rib cage muscle and knee surgery. Playing in 18 events, she managed to hold on to the 75th spot on the Money List, thanks, in part, to a fourth-place tie at the Sara Lee Classic, where she tied her career-low round of 64 during the opening round. Crafter registered her most lucrative season in 1993, when, with seven top-10 finishes and posted a career-low scoring average of 71.71.

Now the playing editor for *Golf Digest*, Crafter, who joined the LPGA in October, 1981, scored a number of weighty titles as an amateur. The runner-up at the 1977 Australian Amateur, she claimed the 1978 New Zealand Amateur and the 1980 Belgian Amateur, and she represented Australia ten times in international competition. Crafter is a pharmacist by trade.

- Tied for 3rd place at the 1996 McDonald's LPGA Championship.

- Tied for 6th place at the 1996 Sara Lee Classic.

- Tied for 7th place at the 1996 Rochester International.

- Tied for 14th place at the 1995 Friendly's Classic.

- Tied for 4th place at the 1994 Sara Lee Classic.

- Tied for 3rd place at the 1993 PING/Welch's Championship in Tucson.

- Tied for 3rd place at the 1993 LPGA Corning Classic.
- Finished in 2nd place at the 1992 PING/Cellular One LPGA Golf Championship.
- Became a Rolex First-Time Winner at the 1990 Phar-Mor at Inverrary.

YEAR	EVENTS	BEST FINISH	EARNINGS	RANK	SCORING AVERAGE
1981	7	T31	$1,617	135	75.84
1982	27	T18	$7,472	108	75.46
1983	26	T8	$37,433	43	73.67
1984	29	T2	$48,729	46	74.04
1985	28	2	$60,884	32	73.73
1986	27	3	$79,431	28	73.04
1987	28	2	$59,876	48	73.49
1988	24	T10	$32,733	73	73.90
1989	26	T3	$35,086	77	74.38
1990	27	1	$112,840	34	73.18
1991	23	T17	$34,168	101	73.56
1992	28	2	$155,485	35	72.41
1993	22	3	$187,190	29	71.71
1994	18	T4	$65,730	75	72.80
1995	19	T14	$60,133	79	73.03
1996	19	3	$147,159	42	72.86

STEFANIA CROCE

Born: May 17, 1970

Birthplace: Bergamo, Italy

Ht.: 5' 4"

Joined Tour: 1993

1996 Money Rank: 51

Croce had her best season in 1996 with a tie for third place at the Safeway LPGA Championship and over $100,000 in season's earnings— easily outearning her three previous seasons combined. Having taken up golf as a ten-year-old, Croce joined the LPGA in October, 1992, with a solid resume: eight-time Italian Junior champion, twice Spanish Junior champion, British Girls and the American Junior titlist (both in 1986), and French Junior Champion (1977). She won the American Tournament of Champions in 1988 and took individual first-place honors at the World Team Championships. Croce also competed on the Women Professional Golfers' European Tour, winning the 1992 Ford Ladies Classic in England.

- Tied for 3rd place at the 1996 Safeway LPGA Golf Championship.
- Tied for 9th place at the 1996 Sprint Titleholders Championship.
- Tied for 14th place at the 1996 U.S. Women's Open.
- Finished in 9th place at the 1995 JAL Big Apple Classic.
- Tied for 27th place at the 1994 Minnesota LPGA Classic.
- Tied for 13th place at the 1993 PING/Welch's Championship.

YEAR	EVENTS	BEST FINISH	EARNINGS	RANK	SCORING AVERAGE
1993	19	T13	$25,401	121	73.41
1994	15	T27	$11,423	151	74.18
1995	15	9	$42,915	93	73.35
1996	22	3	$125,829	51	72.74

BETH DANIEL

Born: October 14, 1956

Birthplace: Charleston, S.C.

Ht.: 5' 11"

Joined Tour: 1979

1996 Money Rank: 38

Daniel topped the $5 million mark in career earnings in 1996, a season that featured a tie for fifth at the Betsy King LPGA Classic as her best showing and three other top-20 finishes. These accomplishments are below her usual standards. In 1995, for example, Daniel posted ten top-10 finishes—including her 32nd career victory, at the Ping/Welch's Championship in Boston. Better yet, her 1994 season included runner-up honors on the Money List, four victories, her third Rolex Player of the Year Award and her third Vare Trophy.

Having turned pro in 1979, Daniel won a tournament in her first year on the Tour and was Rookie of the Year. In both 1980 and 1981, she was the Tour's leading money winner, for which she was hyped as "the next Nancy Lopez." By 1983, she had won 13 tournaments, and the following year she became the LPGA's eighth millionaire. Back trouble and mononucleosis sidetracked Daniel's juggernaut, but only briefly. From 1983 through 1988 she captured at least one title, and in 1989 she won big. Second on that year's Money List, she was also runner-up—behind Betsy King—in the Player of Year standings. Capturing four titles, she won the Vare Trophy (with a 70.38 scoring average) and became the seventh player to cross the $2 million in career earnings. Daniel duplicated her success the following year. With $863,578 in earnings (then a single-season earnings record) she grabbed top honors on the 1990 Money List, earning both the Rolex Player of the Year award and the Vare Trophy. Also that year, she set a record of consecutive rounds in the 60s, with nine, and won her first and only major, the Mazda LPGA Championship.

Daniel first drew notice as a collegian at Furman University in her home state. A physical education major, she was a star of a golf team that also included Betsy King and Sherri Turner. While all three future LPGA luminaries were at Furman, the tiny Baptist college won the 1976 NCAA golf championship. Daniel also won the women's amateur national titles in 1975 and 1977 and was a member of the U.S. Curtis Cup team in 1976 and 1978. Also in 1978, she was a member of the World Cup team. Daniel graduated in 1981 with a degree in education.

- Tied for 5th place at the 1996 Betsy King Classic.
- Tied for 6th place at the 1996 Friendly's Classic.
- Tied for 6th place at the 1996 Jamie Farr Kroger Classic.

- Posted 10 top-10 finishes in 1995, including a victory at the PING/Welch's Championship.
- Won the 1994 LPGA Corning Classic, Oldsmobile Classic, JAL Big Apple Classic and World Championship of Women's Golf .
- Won the 1991 Phar-Mor at Inverrary and the McDonald's Championship.
- Posted 18 top-10 finishes—including seven victories—in 1990.
- Won four titles in 1989, including the Greater Washington Open.
- Was the 1979 Rookie of the Year.

YEAR	EVENTS	BEST FINISH	EARNINGS	RANK	SCORING AVERAGE
1979	25	1	$97,027	10	72.65
1980	27	1	$231,000	1	71.59
1981	27	1	$206,977	1	71.87
1982	27	1	$223,624	5	71.66
1983	23	1	$167,403	6	72.29
1984	23	T2	$94,284	16	72.68
1985	27	1	$177,235	8	72.19
1986	24	T2	$103,547	21	72.71
1987	26	T2	$83,308	29	73.12
1988	18	2	$140,635	17	71.80
1989	25	1	$504,851	2	70.38
1990	23	1	$863,578	1	70.54
1991	18	1	$469,501	4	70.94
1992	23	2	$329,681	11	71.64
1993	23	T2	$140,001	40	72.25
1994	25	1	$659,426	2	70.90
1995	25	1	$480,124	6	71.33
1996	19	N/A	$163,592	38	72.09

LAURA DAVIES

Born: October 5, 1963

Birthplace: Coventry, England

Ht.: 5' 10"

Joined Tour: 1988

1996 Money Rank: 1

A powerhouse of natural talent, Laura Davies has been called the John Daly of the LPGA. She eschews practice, wields the club with an unortho-

Davies, an erstwhile bookie's assistant, has a penchant for fast cars—especially Ferraris. But after winning the 1994 McDonald's LPGA Championship, she had to settle for her second choice —a BMW 850CSi. A Ferrari Testarossa, it seems, doesn't have trunk room for clubs.

dox, self-taught swing, and is an inveterate gambler both on and off the fairway. She's never been accused of being either accurate or consistent. But in 1993, Charles Mechem Jr., then Commissioner of the LPGA, dubbed her "the greatest female golfer in the world."

And 1996 was a great year: Among the highlights were two majors among four victories—as she won the du Maurier Ltd. Classic, the McDonald's LPGA Championship, the Star Bank LPGA Classic, and the Standard Register PING. Davies outscored Webb to claim both the Rolex Player of the Year award and the Golf Writers Association Player of the Year award. She also led the Tour in scoring average, but, because she played only 68 rounds, was ineligible for the Vare trophy.

Davies received her first club—a five-iron— at the age of 10. Her parents, who had given older brother Tony his own set of clubs, wanted to give their daughter something to "swish about in the garden." Within four years she was a serious player and soon established a notable record as a junior and amateur player, winning the 1983 English Intermediate Championship in 1983, the Welsh Open Stroke Play Championship in 1984 as well as the 1983 and 1984 South Eastern Championships.

Her first years on the pro circuit were no less impressive, thanks to what *Sports Illustrated* has described as her "signature tri-level, two-time zone, to-be-continued drives." In 1985, her first year as a professional player, she lead the European Order of Merit—a feat she repeated in 1986. In 1987, playing her fourth tour in this country, she won the U.S. Women's Open, for which she was later granted automatic LPGA membership.

An aggressive player recognized for her creative approach to shots, Davies established herself as one of the strongest players ever on the Tour. By 1993, she had won five LPGA titles; the following year, posting $687,201 in winnings for the season, she earned first-place honors on the LPGA Money List. Competing in only 17 tournaments in the 1995 season, she notched seven top-10 finishes and two victories, topping the $2 million milestone in career earnings.

- Won the 1996 Star Bank LPGA Classic, du Maurier Ltd. Classic, McDonald's LPGA Championship and Standard Register PING.

- Finished in 2nd place at the 1996 Betsy King LPGA Classic.

- Successfully defended the Standard Register PING and the Chick-fil-A Charity Championship in 1995.

- Led the Tour in eagles in 1994, with 15.

- Won the 1993 McDonald's Championship with a five-under-par score—in spite of hitting four cart paths along the way.

- Was a member of the victorious European Solheim Cup team in 1992.

- Won the 1991 Inamori Classic.

- Won the 1989 Lady Keystone Open by birdying the final three holes.

- Won the Circle K LPGA Tucson Open and the Jamie Farr Toledo Classic as a rookie in 1988.

- Was named a Member of the British Empire (M.B.E.)—one of the highest honors accorded to British citizens—by Queen Elizabeth in 1988.

YEAR	EVENTS	BEST FINISH	EARNINGS	RANK	SCORING AVERAGE
1989	18	1	$181,574	13	71.87
1990	18	T2	$64,863	64	73.72
1991	23	1	$200,831	20	73.16
1992	21	2	$150,163	39	72.94
1993	16	1	$240,643	20	72.00
1994	22	1	$687,201	1	70.91
1995	17	1	$530,349	2	71.37
1996	18	1	$897,302	1	70.39

JUDY DICKINSON

Born: March 4, 1950

Birthplace: Akron, Ohio

Ht.: 5' 4"

Joined Tour: 1978

1996 Money Rank: 70

Dickinson has over $2 million in career earnings from her nineteen-year tenure on the Tour. A four-time champion, she posted four top-20 placings in 1996, claiming her best finish, a tie for fifth, at the McDonald's LPGA Championship. With $87,639 in winnings, she regained a top-70 spot on the Money List, up from the previous season's 126th position.

Dickinson posted her first victory in 1985, at the Boston Five Classic. She won two more tournaments the following year, the Rochester International and the SAFECO Classic, and posted her fourth and most recent win at the 1992 Inamori Classic. With three second-place finishes that year, she had her most lucrative season on the Tour, earning $351,559 to command the tenth spot on that year's Money List.

Previous to joining the LPGA Tour, Dickinson won the 1977 New Jersey Amateur title and graduated from Glassboro State College with a B.A. in history. She is married to former pro golfer Gardner Dickinson and served as President of the LPGA from 1990-1992.

- Tied for 5th place at the McDonald's LPGA Championship.
- Tied for 11th place at the 1996 Fieldcrest Cannon Classic.
- Tied for 13th place at the 1996 Standard Register Ping.
- Tied for 23rd place at the 1995 Youngstown-Warren LPGA Classic.

- Tied for 2nd place at the 1994 PING/Welch's Championship in Tucson.
- Won the 1992 Inamori Classic.
- Carded her second career hole-in-one at the 1990 PING-Cellular One LPGA Golf championship (during the third round).
- Won the 1986 Rochester International and the SAFECO Classic.
- Won the 1985 Boston Five Classic.

YEAR	EVENTS	BEST FINISH	EARNINGS	RANK	SCORING AVERAGE
1978	22	T11	$5,330	83	76.36
1979	25	4	$24,561	48	74.83
1980	29	T4	$30,648	46	74.06
1981	28	2	$42,570	36	74.23
1982	23	T4	$47,187	29	73.53
1983	28	T4	$69,091	23	73.50
1984	24	T2	$85,479	18	72.89
1985	28	1	$167,809	9	72.27
1986	25	1	$195,834	10	72.04
1987	17	T19	$19,602	96	73.86
1988	24	T2	$160,440	14	72.13
1989	11	T8	$23,460	96	73.64
1990	23	T4	$80,784	52	72.82
1991	28	T2	$251,018	14	72.21
1992	26	1	$351,559	10	71.90
1993	24	T2	$186,317	30	71.59
1994	26	T2	$246,879	18	71.73
1995	16	T23	$23,602	126	73.40
1996	19	N/A	$87,639	70	73.04

DANA DORMANN

Born: Dana Lofland, September 16, 1967

Birthplace: Oxnard, Cal.

Ht.: 5' 9"

Joined Tour: 1991

1996 Money Rank: 64

Improving on her previous season's results, which were affected by an early-season maternity leave, Dormann had two top 10 finishes in 1996, a tie for eighth at the du Maurier Ltd. Classic and a tie for tenth at the Jamie Farr Kroger

Classic. Dormann joined the LPGA in October, 1990, posting four top-20 finishes in her rookie season, including runner-up at that year's Oldsmobile LPGA Classic. The California native's best year came in 1992, when she had eight top-10 finishes and a victory at the Las Vegas LPGA International. The following season, Dormann posted her second Tour victory at the McCall's LPGA Classic at Stratton Mountain and five top-10 finishes.

Prior to turning professional, Dormann enjoyed an illustrious amateur career. In 1985 alone, when she was named top junior player by *GOLF Magazine*, she snagged the U.S. Junior Girls and the Optimist Junior World championships and was the runner-up in the PGA National Junior. A graduate of San Jose State University with a degree in business administration, Dormann played on the 1987 NCAA Championship team and was three times named All-American (1986-1988). An honors graduate who made the University's Dean's list, Dormann was Female Scholar Athlete of the Year in 1988. In 1990, she married John Dormann, and their son, William Martin, was born on March 11, 1995.

- Tied for 8th place at the 1996 du Maurier Ltd. Classic.

- Tied for 10th place at the 1996 Jamie Farr Kroger Classic.

- Tied for 18th place at the 1995 du Maurier Ltd. Classic.

- Tied for 7th place at the 1994 Chrysler-Plymouth Tournament of Champions.

- Won the 1993 McCall's LPGA Classic at Stratton Mountain.

- Was a Rolex First-Time Winner at the 1992 Las Vegas LPGA International.

- Finished in 2nd place at the 1991 Oldsmobile LPGA Classic.

YEAR	EVENTS	BEST FINISH	EARNINGS	RANK	SCORING AVERAGE
1991	27	2	$90,374	52	73.67
1992	28	1	$270,413	14	72.29
1993	26	1	$234,415	21	72.31
1994	25	T7	$101,715	54	73.07
1995	17	T18	$28,582	117	73.91
1996	23	N/A	$97,254	64	72.48

DALE EGGELING

Born: Dale Lundquist, April 21, 1954
Birthplace: Statesboro, Ga.
Ht.: 5' 5½"
Joined Tour: 1976
1996 Money Rank: 40

After more than twenty years on the Tour, Eggeling has settled into a consistent game and claimed a top-50 spot on the Money List in 1996. A frequent top-20 finisher, she posted a tie for fourth at the Fieldcrest Cannon Classic and a tie for third at the PING/Welch's Championship. 1995 was her best season, when, with a 19th spot on that year's Money List was her second victory, at the Oldsmobile Classic; in the first round of that tournament she registered a new career-low round of 63. Eggeling's second Tour victory came nearly 15 years after her first win—the 1980 Boston Classic—a record for the longest stretch between wins. Shelley Hamlin, the previous record-holder, waited 13 years and 6 months between victories. Eggeling's early career, most notable for its inconsistencies, nevertheless reached a watermark in 1993, when she crossed the $1 million mark in career earnings.

Eggeling attended Miami Dade Community College and the University of South Florida. As an amateur, she won the 1974 National Junior College title and was runner-up in that year's Eastern Amateur. Also that year, she was a semi-finalist in the Doherty Cup. She married Mike Eggeling, also a professional golfer, in December 1981, and their son, Dustin Elias, was born on March 1, 1988.

- Tied for 3rd place at the 1996 PING/Welch's Championship.
- Tied for 4th place at the 1996 Fieldcrest Cannon Classic.
- Tied for 8th place at the 1996 LPGA Corning Classic.
- Won the 1995 Oldsmobile Classic.
- Finished in 3rd place at the 1995 GHP Heartland Classic.
- Tied for 2nd place at the 1994 Chicago Challenge.
- Won the 1980 Boston Classic.

YEAR	EVENTS	BEST FINISH	EARNINGS	RANK	SCORING AVERAGE
1976	5	T46	$321	113	78.08
1977	21	T23	$5,859	70	76.14
1978	25	T5	$9,690	68	76.04
1979	29	T3	$21,333	55	75.01
1980	29	1	$45,335	27	74.38
1981	28	3	$50,594	23	73.88
1982	28	3	$57,691	26	73.92
1983	28	2	$52,967	29	74.02
1984	29	3	$53,355	37	74.44
1985	27	T5	$34,894	67	74.03
1986	28	T4	$52,684	50	73.71
1987	29	T9	$33,203	71	74.08
1988	17	T5	$32,203	74	74.20
1989	25	T8	$56,108	55	72.82
1990	29	2	$147,990	24	72.83
1991	28	T5	$78,386	61	73.21
1992	30	T2	$138,781	41	72.84
1993	26	T3	$145,789	38	71.93
1994	25	T2	$158,501	33	71.96
1995	27	1	$261,752	19	72.14
1996	29	3	$156,008	40	72.38

MICHELLE ESTILL

Born: November 1, 1962

Birthplace: Scottsdale, Ariz.

Ht.: 5' 8"

Joined Tour: 1991

1996 Money Rank: 57

Estill, who hasn't won a tournament since her rookie year on the Tour, slipped to the 57th spot on the 1996 Money List. Highlights included a tie for fourth at the Rochester International and a tie for eighth at the Edina Realty LPGA Classic. Her downward turn is reflected in her money ranking: 57th in 1996, 45th in 1995, and 34th in 1994.

An Arizona native, Estill enjoyed her best season on the Tour as a rookie in 1991. Having joined the LPGA in October 1990, having finished second in the Final Qualifying Tournament, she won her first Tour victory at the 1991 PING-Cellular One LPGA Golf Championship. Collecting three other top-10 finishes that year, she pocketed $171,475 in earnings to claim the 23rd spot on the Money List, finishing behind LPGA Rookie of the Year by less than $5,000.

A medalist in both the Publinks and the Trans-National, Estill was the runner-up in the 1986 NCAA Championship. Named to the Scholastic Academic Honor Roll from 1987-1989, she graduated from Arizona State University with a degree in management and real estate. Now a member of the LPGA Executive Committee, she competed on the Women Professional Golfers' European Tour before joining the LPGA. Estill won the Budget Service Award in 1994 in recognition of her involvement in the LPGA Urban Youth Golf Program.

- Tied for 4th place at the 1996 Rochester International.
- Tied for 8th place at the 1996 Edina Reality LPGA Classic.
- Tied for 9th place at the 1996 Cup Noodles Hawaiian Ladies Open.
- Tied for 7th place at the 1995 du Maurier Ltd. Classic.
- Finished in 2nd place at the 1994 ShopRite LPGA Classic.
- Tied for 2nd place at the 1994 SAFECO Classic.
- Tied for 2nd place at the 1992 Centel Classic.
- Was a Rolex First-Time Winner at the 1991 PING-Cellular One LPGA Golf Championship.

YEAR	EVENTS	BEST FINISH	EARNINGS	RANK	SCORING AVERAGE
1991	28	1	$171,475	23	73.13
1992	27	T2	$132,399	43	73.54
1993	24	T27	$21,428	124	74.48
1994	24	2	$155,667	34	72.78
1995	26	T7	$136,441	45	72.75
1996	26	N/A	$110,725	57	73.09

STEPHANIE FARWIG

Born: June 30, 1959

Birthplace: Milwaukee, Wis.

Ht.: 5' 6"

Joined Tour: 1982

1996 Money Rank: 63

Farwig turned in her most lucrative season in 1996, when, with close to $100,000 in winnings, she moved into the 63rd spot on the Money List and matched her best finish as runner-up in the Sara Lee Classic. It was a great improvement on Farwig's 1995 season, when she finished out of the top 100 on the Money List for the eighth time in her career, with a tie for seventh at the Fieldcrest Cannon Classic as her season's best placing. Having joined the Tour in July, 1982, Farwig enjoyed a stand-out 1983 season, taking Rookie of the Year honors in 1983. She was runner-up at that year's Elizabeth Arden Classic and placed 17th on the Money List, easily her best finish to date.

As an amateur, Farwig assembled an impressive resume that includes victories at the 1980 Wisconsin State Amateur in addition to three Wisconsin Public Links Championships (in 1977, 1979 and 1980). Before she graduated from Houston Baptist University in 1981 with a B.A. in Social Work/Art, she played four years of collegiate golf and was named a Southwest Regional All-American in her senior year. In 1984, the LPGA commissioned Farwig to sketch the Tour's award winners for promotional use.

- Tied for 2nd place at the 1996 Sara Lee Classic.

- Tied for 19th place at the 1996 Nabisco Dinah Shore.

- Tied for 7th place at the 1995 Fieldcrest Cannon Classic.

- Tied for 2nd place at the 1994 LPGA Corning Classic.

- Finished in 2nd place at the 1992 PING Welch's Classic.

- Was named the 1983 LPGA Rookie of the Year.

- Finished in 2nd place at the 1983 Elizabeth Arden Classic, United Virginia Bank Classic and Chrysler-Plymouth Classic.

YEAR	EVENTS	BEST FINISH	EARNINGS	RANK	SCORING AVERAGE
1982	9	T8	$11,801	89	73.48
1983	28	2	$80,627	17	73.53
1984	24	T30	$4,560	145	76.44
1985	29	T5	$39,568	56	74.36
1986	28	4	$26,893	77	74.94
1987	24	T35	$2,684	162	76.90
1988	20	T20	$9,557	138	75.35
1989	26	T47	$3,763	157	75.47
1990	22	T14	$11,757	139	74.71
1991	17	T30	$8,018	159	75.18
1992	18	2	$56,460	82	74.02
1993	24	T9	$29,192	115	73.84
1994	23	T2	$72,454	70	73.91
1995	24	T7	$28,070	118	74.88
1996	27	2	$98,363	63	73.56

VICKI FERGON

Born: September 29, 1955

Birthplace: Palo Alto, Cal.

Ht.: 5' 9"

Joined Tour: 1977

1996 Money Rank: 48

Fergon won the Heartland Classic in 1996, her first win in twelve years, and had a 10th place finish at the HEALTHSOUTH Inaugural, which helped

After knocking off an amazing 11 birdies at the 1984 San Jose Classic, Vicki Fergon—who credits sports psychologist Tom Hawes as having had a major influence on her career—posted an 11-under career-low round of 62. With that tally, the native Californian matched Hall of Famer Mickey Wright's best-ever career-low round. But she's not alone. Laura Davies fired off a 62 at the 1991 U.S. Women's Open and Hollis Stacy posted the magic number at the 1992 SAFECO Classic.

her to a top-50 spot on the Money List. The California native's 1995 season was comparable, with a tie for fourth at that year's Chick-fil-A Charity Championship and an eighth-place tie at the McCall's LPGA Classic among the year's highlights and a finish at 52nd position on the Money List.

A high school hurdler, Fergon joined the LPGA in July, 1977, and won her first tournament title, the Lady Stroh's, in 1979. With $57,205 in season's earnings, she clinched the 18th spot on the Money List, her highest ranking since joining the Tour. In 1991, her fifteenth year on the Tour, she enjoyed three top-10 finishes. Fergon, who, at 5'9" is nicknamed "Big Vic," joined the LPGA's Million Dollar Club in 1993. Elected to the 1993-1996 LPGA Tour Executive Committee, she was the organization's president from 1994-1996.

- Won the 1996 Heartland Classic.

- Tied for 10th place at the 1996 HEALTH-SOUTH Inaugural.

- Tied for 15th place at the 1996 Chick-fil-A Charity Championship.

- Tied for 4th place at the 1995 Chick-fil-A Charity Championship.

- Tied for 3rd place at the 1994 Cup Noodles Hawaiian Ladies Open.

- Tied for 5th place at the 1993 du Maurier Ltd. Classic.

- Tied for 2nd place at the 1992 SAFECO Classic.

- Won the 1984 S&H Classic.

- Won the 1979 Lady Stroh's.

YEAR	EVENTS	BEST FINISH	EARNINGS	RANK	SCORING AVERAGE
1977	8	T3	$4,113	81	74.90
1978	32	T7	$11,794	62	76.25
1979	31	1	$57,205	18	74.62
1980	30	5	$34,541	42	74.31
1981	26	T6	$30,817	48	74.22
1982	26	T10	$22,415	62	74.66
1983	26	3	$68,955	24	73.78
1984	29	1	$55,111	34	74.12
1985	26	T7	$37,483	60	74.19
1986	26	5	$50,324	52	74.36
1987	25	T13	$18,430	102	74.16
1988	28	T5	$79,313	37	72.78
1989	25	T2	$106,534	33	72.65
1990	27	T4	$101,049	40	73.06
1991	25	T6	$146,695	29	72.20
1992	27	T2	$99,617	56	72.94
1993	28	T5	$79,308	61	72.98
1994	24	T3	$109,635	51	72.41
1995	27	T4	$114,900	52	72.52
1996	27	1	$130,578	48	73.38

AMY FRUHWIRTH

Born: July 23, 1968

Birthplace: Cypress, Cal.

Ht.: 5' 2"

Joined Tour: 1993

1996 Money Rank: 29

Fruhwirth had a breakthrough year in 1996. With more than $200,000 in winnings—more than she had earned in her first three seasons on the Tour combined—she rocketed to a top-30 spot on the Money List. She had six top 10 finishes, which included runs at two majors—the du Maurier Ltd. Classic, where she finished tenth, and the Nabisco Dinah Shore, where she finished fifth. Her best showing was at the Rochester International, where she finished third.

Fruhwirth was a formidable amateur. In 1991, she won the California State Championship and the U.S. Women's Amateur Championship, and the following year she captured the Public Links Championship. Also that year, she was low amateur at the Nabisco Dinah Shore, placed second at the Broadmoor Invitational and was a member of the Curtis Cup team. Prior to graduating from Arizona State University in 1991 with a B.S. in general business, she three times earned All-America and All-Conference honors.

- Tied for 4th place at the 1995 McCall's LPGA Classic at Stratton Mountain.

- Tied for 9th place at the 1995 LPGA Corning Classic.

- Tied for 9th place at the 1995 Edina Realty Classic.

- Tied for 33rd at the 1994 PING-Cellular One LPGA Golf Championship.

- Tied for 12th at the 1993 Jamie Farr Classic.

YEAR	EVENTS	BEST FINISH	EARNINGS	RANK	SCORING AVERAGE
1993	18	T12	$22,949	123	73.50
1994	20	T33	$15,471	138	73.91
1995	20	T4	$112,469	53	72.04
1996	28	1	$201,855	29	72.47

JANE GEDDES

Born: February 5, 1960

Birthplace: Huntington, N.Y.

Ht.: 5' 5"

Joined Tour: 1983

1996 Money Rank: 11

A fourteen-year veteran of the Tour, Geddes continues to play near the top of her game. 1996 marked 13 consecutive seasons as a top-40 money-maker. Among the year's many top-20 placings were a solo third-place finish at the Cup

Not everyone can claim the U.S. Women's Open as her first LPGA title. In fact, Geddes is one of only 13 players to have won the Women's Open as her first Tour victory.

But Geddes didn't stop there. The week after she won the Open, she claimed the Boston Five Classic—distinguishing herself as one of only two players* in the history of the LPGA to win an event directly after her U.S. Open victory.

*Hall-of-Famer Louise Suggs followed her 1949 Women's Open triumph with a victory at the Western Open

Noodles Hawaiian Ladies Open and a tie for second place at the HealthSouth Inaugural. Earning $332,041 in 28 events, Geddes mounted an impressive campaign in 1995, posting ten top-10 finishes—as well as a new career-low scoring average of 71.62. What's more, she didn't miss a cut during the entire season. Geddes crossed the $2 million mark in career earnings in 1994 while collecting 14 top-20 finishes, including a victory at the Chicago Challenge. But Geddes has yet to better her 1987 season, when she collected five titles—the Mazda LPGA Championship among them—to finish third on the Money List.

Having played on Florida State University's 1981 AIAW national championship team, Geddes joined the LPGA in August, 1983. In 1985, she registered her career-low round of 65 at the du Maurier Ltd. Classic. A steady money-winner, she topped the $1 million mark in career earnings in 1989, becoming the 17th player in LPGA history to do so. In 1992, Geddes had her first career hole-in-one at that year's Welch's Classic.

- Tied for 2nd place at the 1996 HealthSouth Inaugural.

- Finished in 3rd place at the 1996 Cup Noodles Hawaiian Ladies Open.

- Finished in 3rd place at the 1995 McCall's LPGA Classic at Stratton Mountain.

- Finished in 5th place at the 1995 Sara Lee Classic and the SAFECO Classic.

- Won the 1994 Chicago Challenge.

- Finished in 2nd place at the 1989 Women's Kemper Open.

- Tied for 2nd place at the 1988 Boston Five Classic.

- Won the 1987 Mazda LPGA Championship, the Women's Kemper Open and the GNA/Glendale Federal Classic.

- Finished in 2nd place in the 1985 du Maurier Classic behind Pat Bradley.

YEAR	EVENTS	BEST FINISH	EARNINGS	RANK	SCORING AVERAGE
1983	6	T5	$13,755	94	73.90
1984	30	2	$53,682	36	73.84
1985	29	2	$108,971	17	73.20
1986	28	1	$221,255	5	72.39
1987	28	1	$396,818	3	71.64
1988	24	T2	$90,298	33	72.77
1989	25	2	$186,485	12	71.87
1990	28	T2	$181,874	16	72.33
1991	28	1	$315,240	10	72.13
1992	23	T6	$164,127	32	71.96
1993	23	1	$263,149	18	71.93
1994	24	1	$273,600	15	71.94
1995	28	3	$332,041	15	71.62
1996	25	2	$361,397	11	71.92

VICKI GOETZE

Born: October 17, 1972

Birthplace: Michicot, Wis.

Ht.: 5' 5"

Joined Tour: 1994

1996 Money Rank: 56

Goetze had her best financial season ever in 1996: pocketing $115,475 by year's end, she climbed to the 56th spot on the Money List. Season's highlights included a tie for fifth place at the Youngstown Warren LPGA Classic, a tie for ninth at the JAL Big Apple Classic, and a tie for 12th at the Heartland Classic. Goetze joined the Tour after qualifying on her first attempt in October of 1993. She earned $57,311 during her rookie season, recording four top-20 finishes on the LPGA Tour, a top-10 finish in the World Ladies in Japan and a fifth-place tie at the Evian Masters in France.

Now a Florida resident, Goetze began playing golf at the age of three and played in her first tournament when she was five. She played as an amateur in 11 professional tournaments, making the cut in nine events. Earning the U.S. Amateur title in both 1989 and 1992, she was also three-time A.J.G.A. Player of the Year (1988-1990). Playing for the University of Georgia, Goetze was twice named NCAA All-American (1992 and 1993) and was honored as NCAA Champion in 1992, competing on both the Curtis Cup and World Cup teams of that year.

- Tied for 5th place at the 1996 Youngstown-Warren LPGA Classic.

- Tied for 9th place at the 1996 JAL Big Apple Classic.

- Tied for 5th at the 1996 Youngstown Classic.

- Tied for 9th at the 1996 JAL Big Apple Classic.

- Finished in 3rd place at the 1995 PING-Cellular One LPGA Golf Championship—recording her first career hole-in-one.

- Posted four top-20 finishes on the LPGA Tour in 1994.

- Earned the Honda Broderick Award in 1993.

- Was named GOLFWEEK Amateur Player of the Year and Women's Collegiate Player of the Year in 1992.

YEAR	EVENTS	BEST FINISH	EARNINGS	RANK	SCORING AVERAGE
1994	22	11	$57,311	82	73.30
1995	25	3	$62,060	77	73.72
1996	21	N/A	$115,475	56	72.77

GAIL GRAHAM

Born: January 16, 1964

Birthplace: Vanderhoof, B.C.

Ht.: 5' 3"

Joined Tour: 1990

1996 Money Rank: 52

Coming off three consecutive seasons as a top-50 money winner, Graham fell to the 52nd spot on the Money List in 1996. Among her best finishes were fourth place at the PING/Welch's Championship and a tie for eighth place at the Fieldcrest Cannon Classic. Having been recognized as a Rolex First-Time Winner at the 1995 Fieldcrest Cannon Classic, where she recorded four rounds in the 60s, Graham registered her best season to date, winning $142,346 in 23 events. The same year, she tied for ninth at the HEALTH-SOUTH Inaugural and tied for 11th at the McCall's LPGA Classic at Stratton Mountain.

Graham's LPGA career got off to a slow start. In 1990, her rookie season, she suffered from rotator cuff tendinitis in her right shoulder. The following year, she tied for 13th place at the JAL Big Apple Classic and tied for 14th at the Phar-Mar in Youngstown. By 1992, however, with a sixth-place finish at that year's Women's Open Championship, her game began to improve. She had seven top 20 finishes in 1993. Playing in 24 events in 1994, she registered a new career-low score of 64 during the second round of the Sara Lee Classic, where she tied for ninth. Her best finish of the '94 season was a third-place tie at the State Farm Rail Classic. Graham became a member of the LPGA Executive Committee in 1994.

After taking up golf at the age of 13, Graham enjoyed some success as an amateur, winning the Manitoba Amateur title in both 1983 and 1985. A member of the Canadian Commonwealth Championship team in 1987, she was also the low amateur at that year's LPGA du Maurier Classic. In 1986, the year she graduated from Lamar University with a B.S. in Mass Communications, she was recognized as an NCAA Academic All-American. Graham's husband, Terry, is a CPGA Golf Professional.

- Finished in 4th place at the 1996 PING Welch's Championship.

- Tied for 8th place at the 1996 Fieldcrest Cannon Classic.

- Was a Rolex First-Time Winner at the 1995 Fieldcrest Cannon Classic.

- Tied for 9th place at the 1995 HEALTHSOUTH Inaugural.

- Tied for 3rd place at the 1994 State Farm Rail Classic.

- Tied for 6th place at the 1994 Nabisco Dinah Shore and PING Welch's Championship in Boston.

- Finished in 3rd place at the 1993 Sun-Times Challenge.

- Won the Manhattan Futures Classic in 1988, the year she turned professional.

- Was 1988 Canadian Ladies Professional Golf Association Champion.

YEAR	EVENTS	BEST FINISH	EARNINGS	RANK	SCORING AVERAGE
1990	28	T21	$10,948	143	75.36
1991	27	T13	$46,386	90	73.70
1992	29	T6	$58,938	79	73.64
1993	24	3	$126,048	45	72.49
1994	24	T3	$124,551	40	72.46
1995	23	1	$142,346	44	72.59
1996	19	N/A	$122,294	52	73.00

TAMMIE GREEN

Born: December 17, 1959

Birthplace: Somerset, Ohio

Ht.: 5' 8"

Joined Tour: 1987

1996 Money Rank: 39

Following on the heels of three strong seasons, Green settled for a top-40 spot on the Money List in 1996, with a tie for third place at the Safeco Classic and a tie for fifth place at the Youngstown-Warren LPGA Classic as her best finishes. She had eight top-10 finishes in 1995, with second place at the Fieldcrest Cannon Classic as her best, and finished sixth on the Money List in 1994, with eight top-10 finishes and three second places—at the Jamie Farr Toledo Classic, the U.S. Women's Open and the SAFECO Classic. Green posted two victories in 1993, including a win over JoAnne Carner on the first hole of a sudden-death playoff at the HEALTHSOUTH Palm Beach Classic. With $356,579 in season's earnings, she clinched the seventh spot on the 1993 Money List.

Prior to graduating from Marshall University with a degree in recreation, Green notched four collegiate titles—winning three of them in 1982, her senior year. And in 1981, she enjoyed low amateur honors at that year's LPGA Wheeling Classic. Green served on the LPGA Executive Committee from 1992-1994.

- Tied for 3rd place at the 1996 Safeco Classic.

- Tied for 5th place at the 1996 Youngstown-Warren LPGA Classic.

- Tied for 8th place at the 1996 U.S. Women's Open and the 1996 Chrysler-Plymouth Tournament of Champions.

- Finished in 2nd place at the Fieldcrest Cannon Classic.

- Finished in 4th place at the 1995 du Maurier Ltd. Classic.

- Won the 1994 Youngstown-Warren LPGA Classic.

- Won the 1993 HEALTHSOUTH Palm Beach Classic and the 1993 Rochester International.

- Was a Rolex First-Time Winner at the 1989 du Maurier Ltd. Classic.

- Was recognized as the Most Improved Player of 1989 by *Golf Digest*.

YEAR	EVENTS	BEST FINISH	EARNINGS	RANK	SCORING AVERAGE
1987	27	4	$68,346	39	73.38
1988	23	T2	$120,271	22	72.42
1989	23	1	$204,143	8	72.71
1990	24	4	$155,756	22	72.61
1991	27	T2	$237,073	15	72.16
1992	23	T2	$154,717	37	72.34
1993	23	1	$356,579	7	71.46
1994	24	1	$418,969	6	72.09
1995	23	2	$334,017	13	71.57
1996	17	3	$158,338	39	71.72

PENNY HAMMEL

Born: March 24, 1962

Birthplace: Decatur, Ill.

Ht.: 5' 5"

Joined Tour: 1984

1996 Money Rank: 20

Highlights of Hammel's 1996 season were a tie for second place at the Weetabix Women's British Open and a tie for third at the McDonald's LPGA Championship.

An Illinois native, Hammel joined the LPGA in October, 1984, and soon established herself as a promising rookie. Winning over $70,000 in her first season—good enough for the 27th spot on the Money List—she garnered the 1985 Rookie of the

Year Award. Highlighting that season was a victory at the Jamie Farr Toledo Classic, where she carded a career-low score of 65. Hammel enjoyed her second most successful season in 1989, when her second victory at the Toledo Classic helped her to 16th place on the Money List.

Having taken up the game at the age of seven, Hammel collected myriad victories as a junior, including the 1979 PGA Junior, the 1979 Junior Orange Bowl, the 1979 Illinois Junior and the 1979 USGA Junior. Low amateur in the 1983 Florida Women's Open, she was also a quarter-finalist in that year's Public Links. A student at the University of Miami, Hammel captured NCAA individual honors in 1983 and, the following year, was on the championship-winning team. A two-time All-American (1983 and 1984), she was also a member of the 1984 U.S. Curtis Cup team.

- Tied for 2nd place at the 1996 Weetabix Women's British Open.

- Tied for 3rd place at the 1996 McDonald's LPGA Championship.

- Tied for 8th place at the 1996 Heartland Classic.

- Tied for 18th place at the 1995 McCall's LPGA Classic at Stratton Mountain.

- Tied for 16th place at the 1994 Children's Medical Center LPGA Classic.

- Tied for 16th place at the 1993 Las Vegas LPGA at Canyon Gate.

- Won the 1991 Desert Inn LPGA International.

- Posted six top-10 finishes in 1990.

- Won the 1985 and 1989 Jamie Farr Toledo Classic.

YEAR	EVENTS	BEST FINISH	EARNINGS	RANK	SCORING AVERAGE
1985	27	1	$71,192	27	73.15
1986	27	T6	$62,135	38	73.56
1987	28	4	$85,737	25	73.31
1988	29	T5	$55,396	56	73.37
1989	30	1	$176,836	16	72.43
1990	29	T2	$128,753	28	72.74
1991	29	1	$87,270	55	75.18
1992	27	T35	$ 7,174	160	75.84
1993	24	T16	$ 8,048	150	75.09
1994	25	T16	$26,545	120	74.15
1995	28	T18	$27,490	119	74.36
1996	29	2	$243,359	20	72.45

TRACY HANSON

Born: October 28, 1971

Birthplace: Coeur D'Alene, Idaho

Ht.: 5' 7"

Joined Tour: 1995

Hanson improved slightly on her 1995 Rookie of the Year performance with $175,895 in winnings in 1996, thanks in part to a fourth-place finish at the Oldsmobile Classic, a fourth-place tie at the Sara Lee Classic, and top-10 finishes in the Jamie Farr Kroger Classic and Cup Noodles Hawaiian Ladies Open. Having pocketed $124,527 in 1995, Hanson finished in 51st place on the earnings ratings.

Hanson turned professional in August of 1993 and joined the LPGA in October of 1994. She competed in 26 events her rookie season, four times recording a career-low round of 67. Having tied for fourth at the GHP Heartland Classic, her best finish of 1995, Hanson placed second in the Rolex Rookie of the Year Award, only five points behind the winner, Pat Hurst.

A four-time All-American at San Jose State University, Hanson was named the Big West Player of the Year for three consecutive seasons. Her well-rounded resume as a junior and collegiate player also includes ten Collegiate tournament titles (four of which were consecutive), the 1989 Women's Western Junior Championship and the 1991 U.S. Public Links Championship. That same year, she was also the low amateur at the U.S. Women's Open. A member of the 1992 Curtis Cup Team, she also captained that year's National

Championship-winning San Jose Women's Golf Team. An avid rock climber and hiker, Hanson graduated from San Jose State with a degree in human performance in 1993.

- Finished in 4th place at the 1996 Oldsmobile Classic.
- Tied for 4th place at the 1996 Sara Lee Classic.
- Tied for 8th place at the 1996 Jamie Farr Kroger Classic.
- Tied for 4th place at the 1995 GHP Heartland Classic.
- Finished in 2nd place in the 1995 Rolex Rookie of the Year Award.
- Won the Indonesian Open and was first on the 1994 Ladies Asia Golf Circuit.
- Was named 1994 WPG European Tour Rookie of the Year.

YEAR	EVENTS	BEST FINISH	EARNINGS	RANK	SCORING AVERAGE
1995	26	T4	$124,527	51	72.47
1996	23	N/A	$175,895	37	72.01

MAYUMI HIRASE

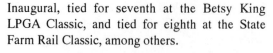

Born: October 30, 1969

Birthplace: Kumamoto, Japan

Ht.: 5' 7"

Joined Tour: 1996

1996 Money Rank: 17

In her first year on the LPGA Tour, Hirase quickly established herself as a talented newcomer, grabbing a top-20 spot on the Money List and an assortment of top-20 finishes. She tied for sixth at both the Sara Lee Classic and the HealthSouth

Inaugural, tied for seventh at the Betsy King LPGA Classic, and tied for eighth at the State Farm Rail Classic, among others.

Prior to joining the Tour, Hirase enjoyed a profitable career on the Japan LPGA, earning runner-up honors on the JLPGA money list in her final year. She joined the JLPGA in 1988, collecting 16 titles before joining the LPGA Tour in October, 1995. Having taken up golf at the age of 11, she was honored as the Japan Junior champion for three years running—from 1985 through 1987.

- Tied for 6th place at the 1996 Sara Lee Classic.
- Tied for 6th place at the 1996 HealthSouth Inaugural.
- Tied for 7th place at the 1996 Betsy King LPGA Classic.
- Tied for 8th place at the 1996 State Farm Rail Classic.
- Tied for 10th place at the 1996 Jamie Farr Kroger Classic.
- Tied for 10th place at the 1996 Chick-fil-A Charity Championship.
- Finished in 14th place in the 1995 LPGA Final Qualifying Tournament.

YEAR	EVENTS	BEST FINISH	EARNINGS	RANK	SCORING AVERAGE
1996	29	1	$266,272	17	72.41

CARIN HJ KOCH

Born: February 23, 1971

Birthplace: Kungalv, Sweden

Ht.: 5' 6"

Joined Tour: 1995

1996 Money Rank: 50

In only her second season on the Tour, Hj Koch managed to hold on to the 50th position on the 1996 Money List, with $128,772 in winnings. Highlights of the season included a second-place tie at the Edina Realty LPGA Classic and a tie for fifth place in the Cup Noodles Hawaiian Ladies Open. After joining the LPGA in October, 1994, Hj Koch posted six top-20 finishes during her rookie season in 1995, including a second-place tie at the JAL Big Apple Classic, where she carded her career-low round score of 65 during the third round. Taking home $129,313 in 22 events, she claimed 48th position on the Money List.

Prior to joining the LPGA Tour, Hj Koch played on the women Professional Golfers' European Tour and the Asian Tour. Turning pro in 1992, she notched several strong finishes, including second place at the 1994 Irish Open and the 1994 Taiwan Open, and third place at the 1993 Swedish Open and the Women's British Open. She also captured the 1992 Swedish Matchplay championship and placed fourth on the 1994 European Order of Merit.

Hj Koch took up the game at the age of nine and later became a member of the Swedish National Amateur Team. As an amateur, she won both the 1988 Swedish Girls Championship title and the 1990 European Team Junior Championship. Hj Koch was twice named Second Team All-American (1989-1990) as a collegiate player at the University of Tulsa.

- Tied for 2nd place at the 1996 Edina Realty LPGA Classic.

- Tied for 5th place at the 1996 Cup Noodles Hawaiian Ladies Open.

- Tied for 2nd place 1995 JAL Big Apple Classic.

- Tied for 7th place at the 1995 Pinewild Women's Championship.

- Finished in 2nd place in the 1994 Irish Open.

- Finished in 2nd place in the Republic of China Open.

- Finished in 3rd place in the 1993 IBM Ladies Open.

- Won three tournaments on the 1993 Swedish Golf Tour.

YEAR	EVENTS	BEST FINISH	EARNINGS	RANK	SCORING AVERAGE
1995	22	T2	$129,313	48	72.54
1996	22	2	$128,772	50	73.26

PAT HURST

Born: May 23, 1969

Birthplace: San Leandro, Cal.

Ht.: 5' 6"

Joined Tour: 1995

1996 Money Rank: 23

Improving on her success as a rookie, Hurst launched into a top-25 position on the 1996 Money List with more than $200,000 in earnings. Highlighting her year were a second place finishes at the Star Bank LPGA Classic and the Heartland Classic. A season of strong play in her first year on the Tour earned Hurst 49th place on the Money List—and the 1995 Rookie of the Year title. Making the cut in 17 out of 23 events, she posted four top-10 finishes, including fourth-place ties at both the Friendly Classic and the GHP Heartland Classic. Hurst also twice posted a career-low score of 67 during the final round of the Friendly's Classic and the first round of the State Rail Classic.

Prior to joining the Tour in October, 1994, Hurst notched five victories on the Players West mini-tour, and was a teaching pro at La Quinta Country Club. A regular on the links since she was 11 years old, the California native chalked up a series of wins as a junior. Honored as the 1986 USGA Junior Champion, she also collected the

1989 and 1990 USGA Amateur and was a member of the 1990 U.S. World Amateur team. As a collegiate player for San Jose University, Hurst garnered top NCAA honors in both the Individual and Team Championships (1989).

- Tied for 2nd place at the 1996 Star Bank LPGA Classic.

- Tied for 2nd place at the 1996 Heartland Classic.

- Finished in 5th place at the 1996 du Maurier Ltd. Classic.

- Finished in 5th place at the 1996 Friendly's Classic.

- Won the 1995 Rolex Rookie of the Year Award.

- Tied for 4th place at the 1995 Friendly's Classic.

- Tied for 4th place at the 1995 GHP Heartland Classic.

- Tied for 5th place at the 1995 Star Bank LPGA Classic in conjunction with the Children's Medical Center.

- Posted five wins on the Players West mini-tour.

YEAR	EVENTS	BEST FINISH	EARNINGS	RANK	SCORING AVERAGE
1995	23	T4	$124,989	49	72.69
1996	24	2	$226,440	23	72.34

JULI INKSTER

Born: Juli Simpson, June 24, 1960

Birthplace: Santa Cruz, Cal.

Ht.: 5' 7"

Joined Tour: 1983

1996 Money Rank: 22

Although not quite matching past standards, Inkster's 1996 season had its moments. She

improved on her previous year's earnings by picking up a handful of top-10 finishes, including solo fourth-place finishes at both the Star Bank LPGA and the Heartland Classic. Inkster garnered five top-10 finishes in 1995, including a second-place finish at the Star Bank LPGA Classic, third place at the du Maurier Classic, and a tie for third place at the Fieldcrest Cannon Classic.

Inkster played her best golf in 1986, when she won four tournament titles, twice posted her career-low score of 64, and finished third on the Money List. 1992 was also a banner year for the California native. With top-10 finishes in all four major championships—in addition to five other top-10 finishes—she held onto seventh place on the Money List, with $392,063.

Inkster was one of the great American amateur players. For three years running, she captured the U.S. amateur title (1980-1982). She was also a member of the U.S. Curtis Cup team in 1982 and played on the World Cup teams in 1980 and 1982. And playing for San Jose State, she was a four-time Collegiate All-American (1979-1982). Inkster's solid amateur record attracted a host of titles, including that of *Golf Digest's* top amateur (1981 and 1982).

- Finished in 4th place at the 1996 Star Bank LPGA Classic and Heartland Classic.

- Tied for 5th place at the 1996 Safeway LPGA Classic.

- Tied for 5th place at the 1996 McDonald's LPGA Championship.

- Finished in 2nd place at the 1995 Star Bank LPGA Classic.

- Finished in 3rd place at the 1995 du Maurier Classic.

- Tied for 3rd place at the 1995 Fieldcrest Cannon Classic.

- Posted eight top-20 finishes in 1994, including a tie for 2nd place at the PING Welch's Championship in Boston.

- Registered her first win at the 1983 SAFECO Classic—only her fifth event after joining the Tour.

YEAR	EVENTS	BEST FINISH	EARNINGS	RANK	SCORING AVERAGE
1983	8	1	$52,220	30	72.92
1984	26	1	$186,501	6	73.07
1985	26	1	$99,651	19	73.13
1986	23	1	$285,293	3	72.15
1987	24	T4	$140,739	14	72.27
1988	26	1	$235,344	10	71.78
1989	21	1	$180,848	14	72.98
1990	18	5	$54,251	73	73.32
1991	26	1	$213,096	17	72.28
1992	24	1	$392,063	7	71.43
1993	21	2	$116,583	47	72.50
1994	16	T2	$113,829	49	72.00
1995	20	2	$195,739	33	72.46
1996	21	N/A	229,660	22	71.78

CHRIS JOHNSON

Born: April 25, 1958

Birthplace: Arcata, Cal.

Ht.: 5' 11"

Joined Tour: 1980

1996 Money Rank: 31

Johnson's record since joining the Tour has been erratic—and her 1996 performance was no exception. On the strength of a second-place finish at the Safeway LPGA Golf Championship and a

handful of other top-20 finishes, she managed a top-30 spot on the Money List for the third consecutive year. The previous year, she competed in 24 events, claiming her seventh career victory at the Star Bank LPGA Classic.

Johnson joined the Tour in July, 1980, with a sturdy record as an amateur player. The 1975 Northern California Junior Girls champion, she was also a member of the Northern California International Junior Cup team. Prior to graduating from the University of Arizona in 1980 with a degree in accounting, she was twice named All-American (in 1979 and 1980). In 1985, she was inducted into the University's Hall of Fame. Johnson married Bill Shearman in 1990, and has been featured in *Fairway* magazine three times—in 1984, 1985 and 1992.

- Finished in 2nd place at the 1996 Safeway LPGA Golf Championship.

- Tied for 5th place at the 1996 State Farm Rail Classic.

- Tied for 5th place at the 1996 Chrysler-Plymouth Tournament of Champions.

- Won the 1995 Star Bank LPGA Classic.

- Tied for 2nd place at the 1995 Cup Noodles Hawaiian Ladies Open.

- Tied for 2nd place at the 1994 SAFECO Classic.

- Won the 1991 PING/Welch's Championship in Tucson.

- Won the 1990 Atlantic City Classic.

- Won the 1987 Columbia Savings LPGA National Pro-Am.

YEAR	EVENTS	BEST FINISH	EARNINGS	RANK	SCORING AVERAGE
1980	7	T17	$2,827	123	75.71
1981	30	T8	$25,182	55	74.49
1982	29	3	$60,449	24	73.62
1983	27	T4	$37,967	42	74.13
1984	26	1	$70,979	25	73.86
1985	25	T6	$67,123	29	73.11
1986	26	1	$200,648	8	72.26
1987	27	1	$197,722	8	72.19

1988	26	T6	$46,219	61	73.35
1989	26	T2	$97,195	37	72.47
1990	25	1	$187,486	14	72.94
1991	24	1	$135,416	33	72.65
1992	25	T5	$105,197	53	72.68
1993	23	T4	$111,027	50	72.66
1994	26	T2	$208,228	23	71.81
1995	24	1	$206,727	29	72.52
1996	23	2	$194,486	31	72.63

TRISH JOHNSON

Born: January 17, 1966

Birthplace: Bristol, England

Ht.: 5' 10"

Joined Tour: 1988

1996 Money Rank: 53

Johnson's performance since joining the LPGA in October, 1987 has had its peaks and valleys and 1996 was no exception. Highlighting the season was a victory at the Fieldcrest Cannon Classic—her third win on the Tour—but only top 10 finish. Johnson enjoyed what was easily her best season on the tour was 1993, when she finished in 10th spot on the Money List, won the Las Vegas LPGA at Canyon Gate and the Atlanta Women's Championship back-to-back, and posted ten top-10 finishes that season, outearning her first five seasons combined by more than $100,000. Having posted a new career-low round of 66 during the first round of the Sara Lee Classic, she managed a repeat at the second round of the Oldsmobile Classic, where she locked a tie for second place.

As an amateur, Johnson won both the 1985 English Match Play and the English Stroke Play Championships, and she captured third place at the 1986 World Cup. Competing for Great Britain and Ireland in that year's Curtis Cup Match, she established herself as the dominant point earner for both teams. Also that year, she made it to the quarter-finals of the U.S. Women's Amateur Championship. In 1987, on the strength of three wins on the WPGET, Johnson was voted European rookie of the year. Ranked fifth on that year's Order of Merit, she earned top honors in 1990, thanks to four wins on the European Tour.

- Won the 1996 Fieldcrest Cannon Classic.

- Tied for 14th place at the 1996 Friendly's Classic.

- Tied for 19th place at the 1996 Chick-fil-A Charity Championship.

- Tied for 9th place at the 1995 Sprint Championship.

- Was a Rolex First-Time Winner at the 1993 Las Vegas LPGA at Canyon Gate.

- Won the 1993 Atlanta Women's Championship.

- Tied for 3rd place at the 1991 du Maurier Ltd.

YEAR	EVENTS	BEST FINISH	EARNINGS	RANK	SCORING AVERAGE
1988	24	T6	$23,972	89	74.56
1989	16	14	$17,215	115	73.91
1990	15	7	$58,729	71	72.98
1991	19	T3	$85,639	57	73.57
1992	15	T19	$33,103	112	72.98
1993	16	1	$331,745	10	71.64
1994	15	T14	$42,750	102	74.33
1995	14	T9	$75,798	68	73.21
1996	18	1	$120,832	53	72.82

CATHY JOHNSTON-FORBES

Born: December 16, 1963

Birthplace: High Point, N.C.

Ht.: 5' 6"

Joined Tour: 1986

1996 Money Rank: 47

Johnston-Forbes claimed her second top-50 spot in 1996. Her second-place finish at the PING/Welch's Championship was her best since 1990, when she became a Rolex First-Time Winner at that year's du Maurier Ltd. Classic. In the first round of that tournament she carded her career-low round of 65.

Having first hit the links as a seven-year-old, Johnston-Forbes compiled a solid resume as an amateur, winning the 1980 Orange Bowl International Junior and the following year's PGA National Junior. As a collegiate player at the University of North Carolina, she captured the Memphis State Intercollegiate title and collected third-place honors at both the 1981 and 1983 Eastern Amateur championship.

- Finished in 2nd place a the 1996 PING/Welch's Championship.

- Tied for 8th place at the 1996 Safeway LPGA Golf Championship.

- Tied for 8th place at the 1996 Oldsmobile Classic.

- Tied for 4th place at the 1995 McCall's LPGA Classic at Stratton Mountain.

- Tied for 5th place at the 1994 Chicago Challenge.

- Tied for 8th place at the 1993 Mazda LPGA Championship.

- Was a Rolex First-Time Winner at the 1990 du Maurier Ltd. Classic.

- Tied for 2nd place at the 1986 MasterCard International.

YEAR	EVENTS	BEST FINISH	EARNINGS	RANK	SCORING AVERAGE
1986	26	T2	$23,969	82	75.51
1987	28	T2	$17,134	106	74.58
1988	29	T16	$20,846	98	74.37
1989	25	T18	$18,665	107	74.14
1990	26	1	$156,240	21	73.32
1991	25	T11	$22,829	119	74.27
1992	26	T19	$10,286	150	75.31
1993	25	T8	$53,623	84	73.43
1994	26	T5	$53,950	88	73.22
1995	25	T4	$69,475	72	73.47
1996	28	2	$132,161	47	73.20

ROSIE JONES

Born: November 13, 1959
Birthplace: Santa Ana, Cal.
Ht.: 5' 9"
Joined Tour: 1982
1996 Money Rank: 18

Although somewhat eclipsed by her previous season's earnings, Jones' 1996 results proved that she continues to be a top contender on the Tour. With a victory at the LPGA Corning Classic and a brace of other top-10 finishes, she ended the year with $275,592, in 18th place on the Money List. A member of the Tour since July, 1982, Jones mounted her most impressive season ever in 1995. Competing in 26 events, she collected $426,957, moving into a top-10 spot on the Money List for the first time in her LPGA career. Among the 12 top-10 finishes she posted that year was a sudden-death win over Dottie Mochrie (now Dottie Pepper) at the Pinewild Championship, her first win since 1991. Also that year, she tied for second place at the ShopRite LPGA Classic and for third place at the Standard Register PING.

Prior to 1995, Jones seemed destined to be a perennial runner-up. In 1994, for the fourth consecutive season, she tied for second place at the SAFECO Classic. For three seasons running, from 1992-1994, her season's best finish was inevitably second-best; in 1993 alone, she recorded three solo second-place finishes—at the Sprint Classic, the JAL Big Apple Classic, and the SAFECO Classic.

As a teen-aged player, Jones posted some impressive results, three times winning the New Mexico Junior (1974-1976) and once claiming the New Mexico State Championship (1979). Prior to graduating from Ohio State University in 1981 with a degree in education, she enjoyed a successful varsity career. In her final year, she was AIAW All-American and was the third low amateur at the U.S. Women's Open; also in 1981, she was a semi-finalist at the Trans-National and the U.S. Amateur.

- Won the 1996 LPGA Corning Classic.

- Tied for 4th place at the 1996 Chick-fil-A Charity Championship.

- Won the 1995 Pinewild Women's Championship.

- Tied for 2nd place at the 1995 ShopRite LPGA Classic.

- Tied for 3rd place at the 1995 Standard Register PING.

- Tied for 2nd place at the SAFECO Classic 1991-1994.

- Posted seven top-10 finishes in 1993.

- Posted nine top-10 finishes in 1992.

- Recorded eight top-10 finishes in 1991, including a victory at the Rochester International.

- Became the 20th player to cross the $1 million mark in career earnings in 1990.

YEAR	EVENTS	BEST FINISH	EARNINGS	RANK	SCORING AVERAGE
1982	7	T28	$2,869	127	74.50
1983	27	4	$64,955	27	73.57
1984	27	2	$81,793	19	73.27
1985	27	T5	$66,665	30	72.87
1986	22	7	$71,399	33	72.72
1987	26	1	$188,000	10	71.91
1988	27	1	$323,392	3	71.57
1989	25	T4	$110,671	32	72.45
1990	25	2	$353,832	6	71.48
1991	21	1	$281,089	12	71.87
1992	26	T2	$204,096	25	71.64
1993	24	2	$320,964	11	71.85
1994	21	T2	$123,683	42	72.22
1995	26	1	$426,957	10	71.64
1996	24	1	$266,092	18	71.76

TRACY KERDYK

Born: March 5, 1966

Birthplace: Coral Gables, Fla.

Ht.: 5' 8"

Joined Tour: 1989

1996 Money Rank: 25

Kerdyk enjoyed her richest season on the Tour in 1996, easily topping the $200,000 mark in season's earnings, with fourth place finishes at the Fieldcrest Cannon Classic and the Cup Noodles Hawaiian Ladies Open. Kerdyk first began to work her way up the ranks in 1995, when she registering five top-20 finishes and claimed her first career victory at the JAL Big Apple Classic.

Kerdyk joined the Tour in October, 1988, and, in her first season, was runner-up—behind Pam Wright—in the LPGA Rookie of the Year contest. She also turned heads her third year on the Tour, setting an LPGA record by posting three holes-in-one in a single season. A broken finger, however, forced her to sit out 10 events during the remainder of 1991. Also that year, Kerdyk was a guest columnist for the *Washington Post* during the Mazda LPGA Championship, a position she resumed for the 1992 championship.

A Florida native, Kerdyk took up golf at the age of 12. Four years later, she captured the 1982 American Junior Golf Classic, adding the PGA Junior Championship, the Junior Orange Bowl and the Doral Junior Championships the following year. As a collegiate player, Kerdyk was red-hot: prior to graduating from the University of Miami in 1988, she picked up 11 individual tournament titles and was twice recognized as first-team All-American. An honor student, she ended her collegiate career in the limelight. A member of that year's U.S. Curtis Cup team, she was named Player of the Year by both *Golfweek* magazine and the National Golf Coaches Association—*and* she was named the NCAA Collegiate Player of the Year.

- Finished in 4th place at the 1996 State Farm Rail Classic.

- Finished in 4th place at the 1996 Cup Noodles Hawaiian Ladies Open.

- Tied for 4th place at the 1996 Fieldcrest Cannon Classic.

- Tied for 7th place at the 1996 Weetabix Women's British Open and at the PING Welch's Championship.

- Became a Rolex First-Time Winner at the 1995 JAL Big Apple Classic.

- Tied for 3rd place at the 1994 Cup Noodles Hawaiian Ladies Open.

- Won the 1987 Canadian Amateur and Public Links Championship and was runner-up in that year's U.S. Women's Amateur.

YEAR	EVENTS	BEST FINISH	EARNINGS	RANK	SCORING AVERAGE
1989	27	T5	$64,644	51	73.02
1990	27	T16	$35,199	96	74.18
1991	21	5	$59,122	78	73.14
1992	30	T13	$63,732	72	74.26
1993	24	T4	$64,908	71	72.97
1994	26	T3	$84,145	65	73.41
1995	27	1	$182,600	38	73.01
1996	28	N/A	$221,053	25	72.18

BETSY KING

Born: August 13, 1955

Birthplace: Reading, Penn.

Ht.: 5' 6"

Joined Tour: 1977

1996 Money Rank: 45

For the first time in over a dozen years, King dropped out of the top 10 on the LPGA's Money List, settling for the 45th spot in 1996. She made the cut in 18 out of 26 events and claimed a solo fifth-place finish at the Heartland Classic as her season's best performance.

Having joined the LPGA in July, 1977, King initially struggled on the Tour, averaging 74.26 strokes per round through her first four years. In 1980, she sought the help of teaching pro Ed Old-field, who told her that her game would have to be "rebuilt from top to bottom": at the age of twenty-five, King had to relearn how to swing a golf club. The process was wrenching, and for months

During her twenty-year tenure on the Tour, King has acquired scores of titles and awards. Here's a sample: 1989 *Golf World's* Player of the Year; 1989 Mickey Wright Golf Writer's Association of America's Female Player of the Year; 1989 Founder's Cup Player of the Year;1987 Samaritan Award; 1987 *GOLF Magazine* and *Golf Illustrated's* Player of the Year; 1985 South Carolina's Professional Athlete of the Year; 1984 *Golf Digest's* Most Improved Player Award; 1977 Furman University Athlete of the Year and Scholar Athlete of the Year.

King's game deteriorated. Finally, in 1984, she posted her first victory on the Tour at the Kemper Open. Collecting two more wins, she led the LPGA in earnings that year and was named Rolex Player of the Year. In 1989, she collected six tournament victories, including the U.S. Women's Open, where she came back from an 11-stroke deficit to top Patty Sheehan. She posted three more victories the following year, including her second consecutive U.S. Women's Open title.

By 1994, King had 29 Tour victories—one shy of the 30 victories needed as one qualification for the LPGA Hall of Fame. Nine times in 1994 she held the lead in the final round of a tournament, failing each time to win. For the first time in 10 years, she ended the season without a single victory. King's slump lasted 20 months. Finally, in 1995, she captured the ShopRite LPGA Classic, with birdies on the two final holes, gaining entry into the LPGA Hall of Fame on November 11, 1995. At the time, she led the LPGA in career earnings, with $5,374,022. Also in 1995, she announced the addition of the Betsy King LPGA Classic to the 1996 roster.

Born in Reading, Pennsylvania, King began taking golf lessons at the age of 10. A gifted athlete—she was a star of her Exeter Township High School basketball team and batted .480 as a shortstop on the softball team—she did not focus on golf until a knee injury she sustained in a collegiate field hockey game prevented her from participating in more rigorous sports. As a student at Furman University, where she majored in physical education, she played collegiate golf on the same team as future LPGA pros Beth Daniel and Sherri Turner. In 1976, she played on the National Collegiate Championship team and was the low amateur at the U.S. Women's Open, where she finished in eighth place.

- Finished in 5th place at the 1996 Heartland Classic.

- Tied for 5th place at the 1996 State Farm Rail Classic.

- Posted her 30th career victory at the ShopRite LPGA Classic, thereby gaining a berth in the LPGA Hall of Fame.

- Became the first player to reach the $5 million mark in career earnings in 1995.

- Was runner-up at the 1994 Ping-Cellular One LPGA Golf Championship and the Toray Japan Queens Cup.

- Was a member of the 1994 winning Solheim Cup team.

- Won the unofficial JCPenney/LPGA Skins Game in 1994.

- Posted 29 official victories on the Tour between 1984 and 1993.

YEAR	EVENTS	BEST FINISH	EARNINGS	RANK	SCORING AVERAGE
1977	8	T15	$4,008	83	74.46
1978	29	T2	$44,092	20	73.90
1979	31	2	$53,900	19	74.15
1980	32	T5	$28,480	50	74.54
1981	31	2	$51,029	22	73.96
1982	30	T5	$50,563	28	73.71
1983	28	T2	$94,767	14	72.88
1984	30	1	$266,771	1	71.77
1985	28	1	$214,411	6	71.89
1986	28	1	$290,195	2	71.75
1987	28	1	$460,385	2	71.14
1988	28	1	$256,957	8	71.81
1989	25	1	$654,132	1	70.58
1990	28	1	$543,844	3	71.32
1991	26	1	$341,784	9	71.50
1992	28	1	$551,320	2	71.50
1993	26	1	$595,992	1	70.85
1994	27	2	$390,239	9	71.52
1995	26	1	$481,149	5	71.24
1996	26	N/A	$136,459	45	72.65

EMILEE KLEIN

Born: June 11, 1974

Birthplace: Santa Monica, Cal.

Ht.: 5' 4"

Joined Tour: 1995

1996 Money Rank: 9

Since joining the LPGA in October 1994, Klein has rocketed to the top 10 of the Tour's earning list. After being the highest money-ranking rookie of 1995, Klein posted an excellent 1996 season, clinching the ninth place on the LPGA Money List. This she accomplished through wins at the Weetabix Women's British Open and PING Welch's Championship, as well as a handful of other top-10 finishes, including a tie for third place at the Sacramento LPGA Classic and a tie for fourth place at the Sara Lee Classic.

Klein's rookie season earned her third place in the Rolex Rookie of the Year standings and augured things to come. Competing in 27 events, she notched six top-20 finishes, including second place at the SAFECO Classic. Losing to Mary Beth Zimmerman on the second hole of a sudden-death playoff, she also finished second in that year's State Farm Rail Classic.

A California native, Klein took up golf at the age of nine and enjoyed a successful amateur and collegiate career. As a 14-year-old, she earned kudos as California State Women's Amateur Champion. Between 1988 and 1991, she was a four-time Rolex Junior All American and was Rolex Junior Player of the Year in 1991. During her two years as a member of the Arizona State University golf team, she was recognized as a Collegiate All American (1993 and 1994), capturing the NCAA Individual Championship title and earning a place on the Curtis Cup Team during her final season as a non-professional.

- Won the 1996 Weetabix Women's British Open.

- Won the 1996 PING Welch's Championship.

- Tied for 3rd place at the 1996 Sacramento LPGA Classic.

- Tied for 4th place at the 1996 Sara Lee Classic.

- Finished in 2nd place at the 1995 SAFECO Classic and that year's State Farm Rail Classic.

- Was the only amateur to make the cut at the 1994 Nabisco Dinah Shore.

YEAR	EVENTS	BEST FINISH	EARNINGS	RANK	SCORING AVERAGE
1995	27	2	$179,803	40	72.66
1996	28	1	$403,793	9	71.91

HIROMI KOBAYASHI

Born: January 8, 1963

Birthplace: Fukushima, Japan

Ht.: 5' 8"

Joined Tour: 1990

1996 Money Rank: 26

Coming off three seasons of solid play, Kobayashi had a respectable 1996—posting a fifth place finish at the McDonald's LPGA Championship and a tie for sixth at the Sara Lee Classic. The previous year, she posted $233,125 in earnings—23rd on the Money List—to cross the $1 million mark in career earnings. Kobayashi's 1994 season was lucrative as well, thanks in part to a second-place finish at the Minnesota LPGA Classic and a tie for third place at the McDonald's LPGA Championship.

The Japanese player's fourth season on the Tour, however, eclipsed all others. With $347,060 in earnings, she rocketed to the eighth spot on the 1993 Money List, posting eight top-10 finishes. She collected two titles that year, including the Minnesota LPGA Classic—a victory she claimed on the first hole of a sudden-death playoff against Cindy Rarick.

Before joining the Tour in October, 1989, Kobayashi played in that year's Japan LPGA Tour, where she picked up five tournament titles. Also in 1989, she placed second behind Colleen Walker in the Nichirei Ladies Cup and captured the LPGA Final Qualifying Tournament. Kobayashi—who didn't take up the game until she was 18—garnered Rookie of the Year honors in 1990, when she posted four top-20 finishes. Despite having little amateur experience, she qualified for the Tour on her first attempt.

- Tied for 5th place at the 1996 McDonald's LOPGA Championship.

- Ted for 6th place at the 1996 Sara Lee Classic.

- Tied for 7th place at the 1996 Chick-fil-A Charity Championship.

- Tied for 8th place at the 1996 State Farm Rail Classic.

- Tied for 2nd place at the 1995 Cup Noodles Hawaiian Ladies Open.

- Tied for 2nd place at the 1995 Toray Japan Queens Cup.

- Finished in 2nd place at the 1994 Minnesota LPGA Classic.

- Was a Rolex First-Time Winner at the 1993 JAL Big Apple Classic.

- Won the 1993 Minnesota LPGA Classic.

YEAR	EVENTS	BEST FINISH	EARNINGS	RANK	SCORING AVERAGE
1990	28	T7	$66,325	60	73.54
1991	27	T4	76,582	63	73.58
1992	26	T8	$58,851	80	73.39
1993	24	1	$347,060	8	71.78
1994	25	2	$242,323	19	72.41
1995	28	T2	$233,125	23	72.43
1996	23	3	$220,450	26	72.18

JENNY LIDBACK

Born: March 30, 1963

Birthplace: Lima, Peru

Ht.: 5' 5"

Joined Tour: 1995

1996 Money Rank: 68

Lidback's 1996 season was tame compared with what seemed to be a breakthrough year in 1995, when she won the du Maurier Ltd. Classic; the major is her only win since joining the Tour in October, 1988.

Lidback—who speaks English, Spanish, Portuguese and Italian—took up golf at the age of 12 and soon racked up a dazzling amateur record. The runner-up in the 1978 USGA Junior Girls Championship, she had a great 1981, capturing the Future Legends, the Tournament of Champions and the All-American Junior Classic. Honored as that year's Player of the Year by *Golf Digest*, she garnered runner-up honors at the following year's Women's Western Amateur.

In her senior year at Louisiana State University, Lidback collected seven individual collegiate titles as well as All-America and Player of the Year honors. Prior to transferring to LSU, she was twice named All-American at Texas Christian University, where she played on the 1983 NCAA Championship team. After graduating from Louisiana State in 1986 with a degree in broadcast journalism, Lidback picked up eight tournament victories on the Futures Tour, clinching first place honors on the 1988 money list.

- Finished in 12th place at the 1996 U.S. Women's Open.

- Was a Rolex First-Time Winner at the du Maurier Ltd. Classic.

- Tied for 6th place at the 1995 Sara Lee Classic.

- Tied for 6th place at the Cup Noodles Hawaiian Ladies Open.

- Tied for 6th place at the 1993 SAFECO Classic.

- Tied for 5th place at the 1991 Atlantic City Classic.

- Tied for 5th place at the 1989 Women's Kemper Open.

YEAR	EVENTS	BEST FINISH	EARNINGS	RANK	SCORING AVERAGE
1989	24	T5	$42,418	68	73.42
1990	23	T14	$42,063	89	73.91
1991	26	T5	$58,362	80	73.44
1992	27	T13	$26,065	124	74.03
1993	17	T6	$82,136	60	72.02
1994	22	T6	$75,036	68	72.62
1995	25	1	$259,386	21	72.25
1996	25	N/A	$89,055	68	73.08

NANCY LOPEZ

Born: January 6, 1957

Birthplace: Torrance, Cal.

Ht.: 5' 7"

Joined Tour: 1977

1996 Money Rank: 28

A crowd favorite since she first burst onto the Tour almost twenty years ago, Lopez continued her reign as a top performer in 1996, although she failed to win a tournament for the third consecutive season. Top 10 finishes include a tie for second at the du Maurier Ltd. Classic and a tie for fifth place at the Star Bank LPGA Classic. Playing in only 17 events, she made the cut 14 times to end the season with $202,451 in earnings—just shy of her previous season's haul.

Lopez wasted no time establishing herself as one of the game's most gifted players. In 1978, her first full year on the Tour, she won eight titles and

"Nancy didn't just arrive on the tour, she burst upon it. It's difficult to comprehend the impact of a single individual on an entire sport. Miss Lopez had more pure charisma than any player since the Babe, and the game to go with it."

—Rhonda Glenn in *The Illustrated History of Women's Golf.*

posted an unprecedented five-tournament winning streak. And that's not all: she took top honors on that year's Money List, was named LPGA Rookie of the Year and Player of the Year, and her season's scoring average—71.76—garnered the prestigious Vare Trophy. Lopez duplicated her success the following season, winning nine out of nineteen tournaments in what *Sports Illustrated* described as "one of the most dominating sports performances in half a century." For a second consecutive season, she won the Vare trophy and was named LPGA Player of the Year. Lopez won at least one tournament between 1978 and 1993, except in 1986. To date, she has posted 47 victories on the LPGA Tour and has collected more than $4 million in winnings. In July, 1987, she was the 11th player inducted into the LPGA Hall of Fame, and two years later, was inducted into the PGA World Golf Hall of Fame.

Born in California, Lopez got an early start in golf. Coached by her father, who was convinced that his child was a prodigy, she ran away with a 110-stroke victory in her first pee-wee golf tournament at the age of nine. At the age of 12, she snatched the New Mexico Women's Amateur. She captured the USGA Junior Girls Championship in 1972 and again in 1974. Already a nationally ranked amateur In high school, she led her otherwise all-male golf team to the state championship. In 1975, as a senior in high school, she entered the U.S. Women's Open, finishing in a tie for third place. The following year, as a freshman at Tulsa University, she captured the AIAW National Championship and competed on the U.S. Curtis Cup and World Amateur teams. Named All-American, she was recognized as the university's female athlete of the year. Lopez turned professional after her sophomore year. She married baseball star Ray Knight in 1982 and has three children.

- Tied for 2nd place at the 1996 du Maurier Ltd. Classic.

- Tied for 5th place at the 1996 Star Bank LPGA Classic.

- Tied for 7th place at the 1996 Rochester International.

- Finished in 3rd place at the 1995 Youngstown-Warren LPGA Classic.

- Tied for 2nd place at the 1994 Chrysler-Plymouth Tournament of Champions.

- Posted her first career victory in 1978 and won at least one event every season for the next 15 years, with the exception of 1986.

- Won the Rolex Player of the Year Award four times, in 1978, 1979, 1985 and 1988.

- Set a record at the 1985 Henredon Classic, recording a tournament total of 268—20 under par.

- Won the Vare Trophy in 1978, 1979 and again in 1985, when her season's scoring average of 70.73 set a new LPGA record (broken by Beth Daniel in 1989).

- Was named Golfer of the Decade by *GOLF Magazine* for the years 1978-1987.

YEAR	EVENTS	BEST FINISH	EARNINGS	RANK	SCORING AVERAGE
1977	6	2	$23,138	31	73.24
1978	25	1	$189,813	1	71.79
1979	19	1	$197,488	1	71.20
1980	24	1	$209,078	4	71.81
1981	24	1	$165,679	6	72.10
1982	22	1	$166,474	6	72.10
1983	12	1	$91,477	15	72.59
1984	16	1	$183,756	7	72.00
1985	25	1	$416,472	1	70.73
1986	4	2	$67,700	35	70.29
1987	18	1	$204,823	7	71.91
1988	22	1	$322,154	4	71.40
1989	21	1	$487,153	3	70.73
1990	18	1	$301,262	8	71.33
1991	12	1	$153,772	26	71.69
1992	21	1	$382,128	8	71.05
1993	19	1	$304,480	14	70.83
1994	19	T2	$197,952	25	71.98
1995	18	3	$210,882	28	71.83
1996	17	2	$202,451	28	71.98

MEG MALLON

Born: April 14, 1963

Birthplace: Natick, Mass.

Ht.: 5' 6"

Joined Tour: 1987

1996 Money Rank: 6

Proving that there's still magic in her clubs, Mallon staked claim to the seventh spot on the 1996 Money List—turning in her sixth consecutive season as one of the Tour's top 15 money winners—and triumphs in the Sara Lee Classic and the Cup Noodles Hawaiian Ladies Open. With her year-end earnings topping the $500,000 mark, Mallon posted the second most prosperous season of her career. Seventh in the 1996 Rolex Player of the Year heat, she was fifth in the Vare Trophy scoring average standings, with 71.35.

Mallon, who joined the LPGA in October, 1986, first began to make a name for herself in 1990, when, on the strength of four top-10 finishes, she moved into the top 30 on the Money List. The following year proved that success to be no fluke: with $633,802, she won two majors, clinched the second spot on the Money List, and earned *Golf Digest's* Most Improved Player award. In addition to winning the Mazda LPGA Championship and the U.S. Women's Open, she took that year's Oldsmobile LPGA Classic and the Daikyo World Championship. In 1992 she had 14 top-10 finishes, joining the LPGA's Million Dollar Club in May, with the earnings from a fifth-place tie at the Centel Classic. Mallon crossed $2 million in career earnings in 1995, notching 11 top-10 finishes, including a solo second place in the U.S. Women's Open.

A Michigan Amateur champion (1983), Mallon twice garnered All-Conference honors as a collegiate player at Ohio State University (in 1984 and 1985). Also in 1985, she was runner-up in the Big 10 Championship.

- Won the 1996 Sara Lee Classic.

- Won the 1996 Cup Noodles Hawaiian Ladies Open.

- Tied for 2nd place at the 1996 Nabisco Dinah Shore.

- Posted 11 top-10 finishes in 1995, including 2nd place at the U.S. Women's Open.

- Posted nine top-10 finishes in 1994, including 2nd place at the Sara Lee Classic.

- Won the 1993 PING/Welch's Championship in Tucson and the Sara Lee Classic.

- Posted 14 top-10 finishes in 1992.

- Won the 1991 Oldsmobile LPGA Classic, the Mazda LPGA Championship, the U.S. Open and the Daikyo World Championship.

YEAR	EVENTS	BEST FINISH	EARNINGS	RANK	SCORING AVERAGE
1987	18	T62	$1,572	175	76.91
1988	21	21	$25,002	87	73.68
1989	25	T5	$42,574	67	73.36
1990	28	3	$129,381	27	72.71
1991	27	1	$633,802	2	71.37
1992	24	2	$400,052	6	70.99
1993	23	1	$276,291	15	72.74
1994	27	2	$353,385	10	71.43
1995	25	2	$434,986	8	71.28
1996	22	1	$503,209	6	71.30

MICHELLE MCGANN

Born: December 30, 1969

Birthplace: West Palm Beach, Fla.

Ht.: 5' 11"

Joined Tour: 1989

1996 Money Rank: 8

With several years of solid play, McGann has built a game that consistently places her on the podium. In 1996, her richest year on the Tour, she clinched the eighth spot on the Money List with three victories—the State Farm Rail Classic, the Youngstown-Warren LPGA Classic and the Oldsmobile Classic. Long recognized as a powerful hitter, placed first in the LPGA Birdies standings, third in Driving Distance, and also posted top-10 finishes in the Rolex Player of the Year and Vare Trophy race.

Having joined the LPGA at the age of 18, fresh from West Palm Beach's Rosarian Academy, McGann claimed her first victory on the Tour in 1995. Winning both the Sara Lee Classic and the Youngstown-Warren LPGA Classic among nine top-10 finishes, she banked $449,296 that year, which earned her the seventh spot on the Money List. But McGann, who loves to model flamboyant headgear on the links, hasn't always turned heads with her game: she didn't break into the top 40 on the Money List until 1992, when she posted 11 top-10 finishes. A year for the records, McGann's fourth year on the Tour also brought her top honors in driving distance, total eagles and total number of birdies.

McGann was a three-time Florida State Junior champion and snagged the 1987 USGA Junior Girls Championship en route to being named that year's AJGA Rolex Junior Player of the Year and a Rolex Junior First-Team All-American. Additionally, *Golf Magazine* and *Golf Digest* ranked her as the top player in 1987. The following year, McGann added a victory at the Doherty Cup Championship.

- Won the 1996 State Farm Rail Classic.

- Won the 1996 Youngstown-Warren LPGA Classic.

- Won the 1996 Oldsmobile Classic.

- Tied for 3rd place at both the 1996 ShopRite LPGA Classic and the PING/Welch's Championship.

- Won the 1995 Sara Lee Classic.

- Won the 1995 Youngstown-Warren LPGA Classic.

- Finished in 2nd place at the 1994 du Maurier Ltd. Classic.

- Tied for 2nd place at the 1993 World Championship of Women's Golf.

YEAR	EVENTS	BEST FINISH	EARNINGS	RANK	SCORING AVERAGE
1989	27	T19	$11,679	130	76.26
1990	19	T7	$34,846	98	73.41
1991	29	T4	$121,663	40	73.23
1992	29	T4	$239,062	18	71.76
1993	27	T2	$315,921	12	71.63
1994	25	2	$269,936	16	71.43
1995	23	1	$449,296	7	71.56
1996	25	1	$478,561	8	71.51

MISSIE MCGEORGE

Born: August 20, 1959

Birthplace: Pueblo, Col.

Ht.: 5' 7"

Joined Tour: 1983

1996 Money Rank: 36

McGeorge enjoyed one of her best seasons in 1996. With $176,248 in winnings, she clinched a top-40 spot on the Money List and crossed the $1 million mark in career earnings. Highlights include a fourth-place finish at the JAL Big Apple Classic and a tie for third place at the Chrysler-Plymouth Tournament of Champions.

The Colorado native played her best golf in 1993 and 1994, earning in excess of $180,000 both years. In 1993, she posted four top-10 finishes—including second place at the Las Vegas LPGA at Canyon Gate. The next year McGeorge won the PING-Cellular One LPGA Golf Championship, her only Tour victory so far.

Prior to joining the Tour in August, 1983, McGeorge compiled a solid record as an amateur. Crowned the Texas Junior champion in 1976, she was runner-up at the USGA Junior Girls Championship the following year. She graduated from Southern Methodist University with a B.A. in Physical Education in 1981, having enjoyed a successful collegiate career that included playing on the University's AIAW National Championship team in 1979. The following year, she captured the Texas A&M Invitational and was a semi-finalist in the Women's Western Amateur.

- Finished in 4th place at the 1996 JAL Big Apple Classic.

- Tied for 3rd place at the 1996 Chrysler-Plymouth Tournament of Champions.

- Finished in 6th place at the 1995 HEALTH-SOUTH Inaugural.

- Was a Rolex First-Time Winner at the 1994 PING-Cellular One LPGA Golf Championship.

- Tied for 5th place at the 1994 Lady Keystone Open.

- Finished in 2nd place at the 1993 Las Vegas LPGA Canyon Gate.

- Tied for 2nd place at the 1993 PING-Cellular One LPGA Golf Championship.

- Tied for 4th place at the 1991 Desert Inn LPGA International.

YEAR	EVENTS	BEST FINISH	EARNINGS	RANK	SCORING AVERAGE
1983	7	T16	$4,596	133	74.40
1984	26	T4	$20,117	89	74.77
1985	27	T13	$21,563	87	74.61
1986	28	T21	$23,436	83	74.48
1987	27	T5	$63,259	44	73.20
1988	27	2	$93,397	31	73.29
1989	28	T11	$68,493	48	73.01
1990	28	7	$93,721	45	73.02
1991	27	T4	$113,959	46	72.82
1992	26	T17	$30,248	118	73.70
1993	24	2	$180,311	32	72.17
1994	23	1	$181,281	30	72.14
1995	26	6	$92,885	61	72.96
1996	25	3	$176,248	36	72.43

MARIANNE MORRIS

Birthplace:
Middletown, Ohio

Ht.: 5' 5"

Joined Tour: 1990

1996 Money Rank: 16

Morris, who joined the Tour in October, 1989, posted her best season ever in 1996, with a second place finish at the Jamie Farr Kroger Classic and a tie for third place at the ShopRite LPGA Classic. The Ohio native first began to move up the ranks in 1995, earning $191,050—more than she had in her first four seasons combined. Competing in 26 events, she posted four top-10 finishes, including a tie for third place at the McDonald's LPGA Championship.

A golfer since the age of eight, Morris was a medalist in the 1985 U.S. Women's Open qualifier and was the Cincinnati Metropolitan champion the following year. Having posted one tournament victory during her collegiate career, Morris graduated from the University of South Carolina in 1988 with a degree in criminal justice.

- Finished in 2nd place at the 1996 Jamie Farr Kroger Classic.

- Tied for 3rd place at the 1996 ShopRite LPGA Classic.

- Tied for 3rd place at the 1995 McDonald's LPGA Championship.

- Registered eight top-20 finishes in 1995.

- Tied for 6th place at the 1994 Cup Noodles Hawaiian Ladies Open.

- Tied for 12th place at the 1993 Sun-Times Challenge.

- Posted seven wins on the Futures Tour prior to qualifying for the LPGA Tour.

YEAR	EVENTS	BEST FINISH	EARNINGS	RANK	SCORING AVERAGE
1990	15	T12	$13,511	133	74.14
1991	DNP				
1992	29	T21	$31,733	117	73.95
1993	22	T8	$56,615	82	72.53
1994	24	T6	$78,630	67	72.91
1995	26	T3	$191,050	36	72.18
1996	28	2	$293,188	16	71.86

BARB MUCHA

Born: December 1, 1961

Birthplace: Parma, Ohio

Ht.: 5' 6"

Mucha enjoyed her best season with the Tour in 1996, with seven top 10 finishes, and she broke into the top twenty on the Money List for the first time in her career. She won the Chick-fil-A Charity Championship and finished third at the Safeco Classic and the Sacramento LPGA Classic as her best showings.

Mucha's second most successful year came in 1992. Even though she suffered from tendonitis during the second half of the season, she managed 12 top-20 finishes, including a win at the Oldsmobile Classic. Carding a career-low round of 65 during the third round of that competition, Mucha claimed her second career title—her first win having come at the 1990 Boston Five Classic.

Now a Florida resident, Mucha graduated from Michigan State University in 1984 with a degree in personnel administration. A semi-finalist in that year's Women's Trans-National, she also received All-America honorable mention honors. As a collegiate player at Michigan State, Mucha collected two titles—the Illinois State Invitational and the Ohio State Invitational. Prior to joining the Tour in October, 1986, she collected six wins on the Futures Tour.

- Tied for 2nd place at the 1995 LPGA Corning Classic.

- Tied for 9th place at the 1995 HEALTHSOUTH Inaugural.

- Won the 1994 State Farm Rail Classic with three sub-par rounds (67-69-67).

- Tied for 12th place at the 1994 Sara Lee Classic.

- Tied for 6th place at the 1993 PING-Cellular One.

- Won the 1992 Oldsmobile Classic.

- Carded her first career hole-in-one at the 1991 U.S. Women's Open.

YEAR	EVENTS	BEST FINISH	EARNINGS	RANK	SCORING AVERAGE
1987	15	T21	$6,657	140	74.84
1988	DNP				
1989	18	T5	$47,849	60	72.88
1990	29	1	$149,972	23	72.82
1991	25	T4	$54,085	83	73.55
1992	26	1	$190,519	27	72.57
1993	23	T6	$91,806	56	72.56
1994	25	1	$152,685	36	73.05
1995	25	T2	$156,527	42	72.65
1996	26	1	$297,055	15	71.86

MARTHA NAUSE

Born: September 10, 1954

Birthplace: Sheboygan, Wis.

Ht.: 5' 5"

Joined Tour: 1978

1996 Money Rank: 59

A twenty-year veteran of the Tour, Nause has weathered occasional peaks, including the 1994 du Maurier Ltd. Classic, and winless valleys. With just over $100,000 in earnings in 1996, she moved up to the 59th spot on the Money List, thanks to a tie for second place at the HEALTHSOUTH Inaugural. The previous season, she managed to make the cut in 15 out of 22 starts, but settled for the 89th spot on the Money List, with only $49,525 in winnings at season's end.

Nause enjoyed her most lucrative season in 1994, when, with $212,130 in earnings, she moved up to the 22nd spot on the Money List and became the 49th player to join the LPGA's Million Dollar Club. Highlighting that year's play was a victory at the du Maurier Ltd. Classic, where she carded a 65 during the first round. Nause has two other career victories, in 1991 at the Chicago Sun-Times Shoot-Out—where she nailed an eagle-three at the final hole—and in 1988 at the Planters Pat Bradley International.

Apart from winning the Wisconsin Junior State Championship in 1972, Nause had little amateur experience. Having graduated from St. Olaf College in 1977 with a B.S. in biology, she became the first woman to be inducted into the school's sports Hall of Fame (in 1990), and in 1995 she was inducted into the Wisconsin Golf Hall of Fame.

- Tied for 2nd place at the 1996 HEALTHSOUTH Inaugural.

- Tied for 12th place at the 1996 Chrysler-Plymouth Tournament of Champions.

- Tied for 15th place at the 1995 Chrysler-Plymouth Tournament of Champions.

- Won the 1994 du Maurier Ltd. Classic.

- Won the 1991 LPGA Chicago Sun-Times Shoot-Out.

- Finished in 2nd place at the 1989 Red Robin Kyocera Inamori Classic.

- Won the 1988 Planters Pat Bradley International.

- Tied for 2nd place at the 1984 Lady Keystone Open.

- Finished in 2nd place at the 1981 Lady Keystone Open.

YEAR	EVENTS	BEST FINISH	EARNINGS	RANK	SCORING AVERAGE
1978	26	T28	$2,646	99	77.31
1979	25	T15	$5,151	97	77.14
1980	29	T22	$10,019	82	75.52
1981	25	2	$30,866	47	74.80
1982	26	T2	$27,206	57	75.03
1983	29	6	$41,760	37	74.13
1984	28	T2	$39,169	55	74.21
1985	24	T5	$25,211	79	74.42
1986	24	7	$37,850	63	73.90
1987	27	3	$69,412	38	73.33
1988	30	1	$138,490	19	73.20
1989	28	2	$138,639	21	72.30
1990	27	T11	$83,383	50	73.05
1991	28	1	$143,702	30	73.15
1992	19	T6	$64,810	71	72.77
1993	23	T16	$42,090	94	73.14
1994	24	1	$212,130	22	72.77
1995	24	T15	$49,525	89	73.53
1996	22	2	$103,958	59	72.88

LISELOTTE NEUMANN

Born: May 20, 1966

Birthplace: Finspang, Sweden

Ht.: 5' 7"

Joined Tour: 1988

1996 Money Rank: 4

Having long ago established herself as a major force on the Tour, Neumann was red hot in 1996, earning $618,633, more than she had any season since joining the LPGA in October, 1987. She won the Chrysler-Plymouth Tournament of Champions, the PING/Welch's Championship and the Edina Realty LPGA Classic, in addition to a second-place finishes at the Oldsmobile Classic and the Chick-fil-A Charity Championship. She also led LPGA standings with a season's putting average of 29.27 per round.

Neumann's 1994 season was nearly as impressive. Playing in 21 events, she collected $505,701, earning third-place honors on the Money List. She recorded a new career-low scoring average of 71.46 and posted three wins, at the

Minnesota LPGA Classic, the Weetabix Women's British Open and the GHP Heartland Classic, and a second-place finish at the Atlanta Women's Championship. Also that year, she was recognized as *Golf World's* Most Improved Golfer. Neumann's 1995 season, although less lucrative, had a number of highlights, including the Swede's second career hole-in-one, during the third round of the Star Bank LPGA Classic. Playing in 23 events, she posted nine top-10 finishes, to end the season with $405,167, for 16th place on the Money List.

Neumann assembled an impressive portfolio prior to joining the Tour in October, 1987. A fine amateur player, she notched two Swedish Amateur championships (1982 and 1983) and the Swedish Match Play championship (1983), among others. She won the European Open in 1985 and dominated the German Open from 1986-1988. In 1988, her rookie year, Neumann hit the Tour running— claiming that year's U.S. Open, the 12th LPGA player to post the Open as her first win. Also that year, she carded her first hole-in-one (at the Mazda Japan Classic) and won the LPGA Rookie of the Year Award.

- Won the 1996 Chrysler-Plymouth Tournament of Champions, PING/Welch's Championship and Edina Realty Classic.

- Finished in 2nd place at the 1996 Oldsmobile Classic.

- Tied for 2nd place at the 1996 Chick-fil-A Charity Classic.

- Finished in 2nd place at the 1995 Satake Japan Classic and du Maurier Classic.

- Finished in 2nd place at the 1994 Atlanta Women's Championship.

- Finished in 3rd place at the 1994 U.S. Women's Open.

- Tied for 3rd place at the 1994 McDonald's LPGA Championship.

YEAR	EVENTS	BEST FINISH	EARNINGS	RANK	SCORING AVERAGE
1988	22	1	$188,729	12	72.44
1989	22	T2	$119,915	30	72.66
1990	24	4	$82,323	51	73.74
1991	23	1	$151,367	27	72.91
1992	18	T2	$225,667	21	72.00
1993	16	T7	$90,776	57	72.54
1994	21	1	$505,701	3	71.46
1995	23	2	$305,157	16	71.79
1996	23	1	$618,633	4	70.88

ALISON NICHOLAS

Born: March 6, 1962

Birthplace: Gibraltar

Ht.: 5' 0"

Joined Tour: 1990

1996 Money Rank: 49

Playing in 16 LPGA events in 1996, Nicholas managed to hold on to a top-50 spot on the Money List, with a seventh-place finish at the Safeway LPGA Golf Championship and a tie for tenth place at the Chick-fil-A Charity Championship. She also posted some impressive finishes on the WPGET, including a win at the Irish Open, second place at the Trygg-Hansa Ladies Open and fourth at the Weetabix Women's British Open. 1995 was a rich year for Nicholas: competing in 17 events, she became a Rolex First-Time Winner at the LPGA Corning Classic, carding her season-low score of 66 during the third round. She posted her second career victory at the PING-AT&T Wireless Services LPGA Golf Championship, again carding a season-low score of 66 during the first round. Nicholas also finished third at the SAFECO Classic.

Although she didn't take up the game until she was 17, Nicholas enjoyed an impressive showing as an amateur in England. She won the 1982 and 1983 Northern Girls Amateur Open as well as the 1983 Yorkshire Ladies County Championship, and was the 1983 British Amateur Stroke Play champion.

- Tied for 4th place at the 1996 Weetabix Women's British Open.

- Finished 7th at the 1996 Safeway LPGA Golf Championship.

- Won the 1996 Irish Open.

- Became a Rolex First-Time Winner at the 1995 LPGA Corning Classic.

- Won the 1995 PING-AT&T Wireless Services Golf Championship.

- Won the 1995 Scottish Open.

- Tied for 15th place at the 1994 PGA Corning Classic and the JAL Big Apple Classic.

- Won her first career victory at the 1987 Weetabix British Open.

YEAR	EVENTS	BEST FINISH	EARNINGS	RANK	SCORING AVERAGE
1990	10	T14	$11,608	139	74.54
1991	DNP				
1992	DNP				
1993	16	2	$101,203	51	72.25
1994	15	T15	$37,651	111	73.23
1995	17	1	$231,660	24	72.56
1996	16	N/A	$130,556	49	72.38

CATRIN NILSMARK

Birthplace: Goteborg, Sweden

Ht.: 5' 11"

Joined Tour: 1995

1996 Money Rank: 34

After a lackluster 1995 rookie season on the tour, Nilsmark climbed the earnings ratings to finish in 34th place with $181,700 in 1996, with a third-place tie at the Jamie Farr Kroger Classic and a fourth-place tie at the Sprint Titleholder's Championship. Also in 1996, Nilsmark placed seventh in the U.S. Women's Open and tied for sixth at the Heartland Classic.

Having taken up the game at the age of 10, Nilsmark embarked on a promising amateur career, which included a win at the 1984 Orange Bowl as well as the title at that year's Swedish Junior Championship. She played one year of collegiate golf at the University of South Florida and competed on the Women Professional Golfers' European Tour (WPGET) en route to joining the LPGA Tour. Finishing second in the BMW European Masters in 1991, she garnered that year's Most Improved Player Award. The following season, she added a second-place finish in the European Ladies Open and competed on the European Solheim Cup team, where she holed the winning putt to edge out Meg Mallon.

- Tied for 3rd place at the 1996 Jamie Farr Kroger Classic.

- Tied for 4th place at the 1996 Sprint Titleholder's Championship.

- Tied for 14th place at the 1995 PING/Welch's Championship.

- Tied for 24th place at the 1995 McCall's LPGA Classic.

- Won the 1994 Ford Ladies Classic.

- Was a member of the 1994 European Solheim Cup team.

- Finished in 4th place in the European Ladies Golf Classic.

- Finished in 2nd place in the European Ladies Open.

- Was a member of the 1992 European Solheim Cup team.

YEAR	EVENTS	BEST FINISH	EARNINGS	RANK	SCORING AVERAGE
1995	22	T14	$25,329	124	73.68
1996	19	3	$181,700	34	72.22

KRISTAL PARKER-GREGORY

Born: February 7, 1965

Birthplace: Columbus, Ohio

Ht.: 5' 9"

Joined Tour: 1995

1996 Money Rank: 60

After a tough first year on the Tour, Parker-Gregory raised the level of her play in 1996 with a handful of top-20 finishes, including second-place at the Standard Register PING. With more than five times her previous season's earnings, the Ohio native moved into a top-100 position on the Money List.

No stranger to professional competitions, she competed in a number of tours prior to joining the LPGA Tour, including the Futures Tour (1988-1994), the LPGA Australia Tour (1990-1994) and the WPG European Tour (1991-1994). She also established herself as a bright junior player, capturing more than 30 titles—including the 1982 Junior World—before turning pro in August, 1987. As a collegiate player at UCLA, she notched four tournament wins and was three times recognized as an NCAA Division I All-American.

- Finished in 2nd place at the 1996 Standard Register PING.

- Tied for 2nd place at the 1996 Rochester International.

- Tied for 17th place at the 1996 LPGA Corning Classic.

- Tied for 20th place at the 1995 Cup Noodles Hawaiian Open.

- Tied for 32nd place at the 1995 State Farm Rail Classic.

- Tied for 9th place at the 1995 Final Qualifying Tournament.

- Finished in 3rd place at the 1994 Hennesy Cup.

- Finished in 3rd place at the 1993 BMW Italian Open.

- Finished in 7th place at the 1991 Women's British Open.

YEAR	EVENTS	BEST FINISH	EARNINGS	RANK	SCORING AVERAGE
1995	17	T20	$15,768	146	73.95
1996	23	2	$103,117	60	73.70

DOTTIE PEPPER

Born: Dottie Mochrie, August 17, 1965

Birthplace: Saratoga Springs, N.Y.

Ht.: 5' 6"

Joined Tour: 1987

1996 Money Rank: 5

Not once since joining the Tour in 1987 has Pepper failed to be among each year's top 30 money winners, and only twice has she been out of the top dozen. Earning $589,401 in 1996, she claimed a top-five spot on the Money List for the sixth consecutive season. And not without panache. Her year-end results included first-place honors at the Safeway LPGA Golf Championship, the Friendly's Classic, the ShopRite LPGA Classic, the Rochester International.

Despite having been sidelined for six weeks in early 1995 by rotator cuff and thoracic back sprain injuries, Pepper managed to finish fourth overall on the LPGA season Money List. She won both the PING/Welch's Championship and McCall's LPGA Classic at Stratton Mountain, bringing her career total of victories to 10 and crossing the $3 million mark in career earnings.

In her rookie season, Pepper notched seven top-10 finishes, to earn over $130,000. By 1992, she topped the season Money List with $693,335, winning both the Rolex Player of the Year Award and the Vare Trophy for having the lowest scoring average of the season (70.80). In 1993, Pepper, who travels the Tour with a chow-chow named Furman, notched a dozen top-10 finishes to top the $2 million mark in career earnings. The following year, she claimed 12 more top-10 finishes, winning the inaugural Chrysler-Plymouth Tournament of Champions. Pepper's resume includes a number of awards, including the 1993 ESPY Award and Jim Thorpe Award. In 1992, she was named the Golf Writers Association Player of the Year and was inducted into the Furman University Hall of Fame.

Pepper first made a name for herself as an amateur, capturing the 1981 New York State Amateur championship in 1981 as well as the 1981 and 1983 New York Junior Amateur championships, among others. As a student at Furman University, she was a three-time All-American, claiming five individual tournament titles.

- Won the 1996 Safeway LPGA Golf Championship, Friendly's Classic, ShopRite LPGA Classic and Rochester International.

- Tied for 2nd place at the 1996 Chick-fil-A Charity Championship.

- Won the 1995 PING/Welch's Championship and McCall's LPGA Classic at Stratton Mountain.

- Tied for 2nd place at the 1995 Sara Lee Classic.

- Posted 11 top-10 finishes out of 25 events in 1995.

- Won the inaugural Chrysler-Plymouth Tournament of Champions in 1994.

- Tied for 2nd place at the 1994 Weetabix Women's British Open.

- Won the 1993 World Championship of Women's Golf.

- Was a member of the 1992 winning LPGA team.

- Finished in 2nd place in the 1991 Nabisco Dinah Shore and Daikyo World Championship, and tied for 2nd in the Mazda Japan Classic.

- Won the 1990 Crestar Classic.

- Was a member of the U.S. Solheim Cup team in 1990, 1992 and 1994.

YEAR	EVENTS	BEST FINISH	EARNINGS	RANK	SCORING AVERAGE
1988	25	T2	$137,293	20	72.86
1989	24	1	$130,830	27	72.49
1990	28	1	$231,410	12	72.14
1991	29	2	$477,767	3	71.44
1992	26	1	$693,335	1	70.80
1993	26	1	$429,118	4	71.09
1994	27	1	$472,728	4	70.98
1995	25	1	$521,000	4	71.13
1996	22	1	$579,901	5	71.35

CAROLINE PIERCE

Born: August 2, 1963

Birthplace: Cheshire, England

Ht.: 5' 3"

Joined Tour: 1995

1996 Money Rank: 21

After settling for runner-up at the Big Apple Classic in 1995, Pierce posted her first Tour victory at the event in 1996, running away to a five-stroke win on the three final holes. Pierce's turnaround began in 1995, when, with seven top-10 finishes, she collected $196,722—twice her previous season's earnings—to claim a top-40 spot on the Money List. Tying for second place at that year's JAL Big Apple Classic, she posted a career-low scoring average of 72.10 for the season, twice carding her career-low round of 67 (during the second round of the PING/Welch's

Championship and the first round of the Edina Realty LPGA Classic).

A native of England, Pierce established an illustrious record as an amateur player. A semi-finalist in the 1979 English Girls Championship, she was twice crowned English Girls International champion (in 1980 and 1981). A semi-finalist in the 1986 British Amateur Championship, she was also selected for that year's Curtis Cup Team. Also that year, she graduated from Houston Baptist University with a degree in political science and history, having notched three wins as a collegiate player in addition to All-America honors (in 1983 and 1984). Pierce is a member of the LPGA Tour Executive Committee.

- Won the 1996 JAL Big Apple Classic.

- Tied for 5th place at the 1996 Betsy King LPGA Classic.

- Tied for 8th place at the 1996 HealthSouth Inaugural.

- Tied for 2nd place at the 1995 JAL Big Apple Classic.

- Tied for 4th place at the 1995 Weetabix Women's British Open.

- Tied for 3rd place at the 1994 ShopRite LPGA Classic.

- Posted a career-low round of 67 at the 1992 SEGA Women's Championship.

- Carded her first career hole-in-one at the 1990 Phar-Mor at Inverrary.

YEAR	EVENTS	BEST FINISH	EARNINGS	RANK	SCORING AVERAGE
1988	23	T41	$ 1,153	176	76.21
1989	26	T21	$24,545	94	74.06
1990	24	T21	$23,944	111	74.32
1991	27	T6	$56,813	82	73.46
1992	24	T7	$46,767	96	73.36
1993	25	8	$33,978	109	73.79
1994	22	T3	$84,756	64	72.91
1995	27	T2	$196,722	32	72.10
1996	27	1	$240,544	21	72.38

JULIE PIERS

Born: Julie Larsen, September 16, 1962

Birthplace: Westchester, N.Y.

Ht.: 5' 8"

Joined Tour: 1992

1996 Money Rank: 35

A second-place finish at the McDonald's LPGA Championship was the highlight of Piers' 1996 season. Finishing out of the top 20 throughout most of the season, she dropped in earnings but still managed to hold on to a top-50 spot on the Money List. The Florida resident had her most successful year in 1995, earning her first LPGA victory at the 1995 Edina Realty LPGA Classic and collecting four other top-10 finishes, including a tie for third place at the McDonald's LPGA Championship. Piers registered a career-low round of 66 during the opening rounds of both the 1995 Edina Realty and the PING Welch's Championship in Boston—having first carded a 66 in the first round of the previous year's Toray Japan Queens Cup.

Although Piers did not take up the game until she was 16, she enjoyed some success as an amateur. Having captured the 1982 Metropolitan Junior Championship, she qualified for the 1984 U.S. Women's Amateur Championship. She played four years of collegiate golf at Rollins College, graduating in 1984 with a degree in English. Prior to joining the LPGA Tour, she registered a number of impressive finishes on both the European and Asian Tours, including a second-place finish at the 1991 Thailand Open and a win at the 1990 Futures Team Classic.

- Finished in 2nd place at the 1996 McDonald's LPGA Championship.

- Tied for 21st place at the 1996 HealthSouth Inaugural.

- Tied for 23rd place at the 1996 Safeco Classic.

- Was a Rolex First-Time Winner at the 1995 Edina Realty LPGA Classic.

- Tied for 3rd place at the 1995 McDonald's LPGA Championship.

- Tied for 4th at the 1994 Toray Queens Cup.

- Finished in 3rd place at the 1993 Lady Keystone Open.

- Carded her first career hole-in-one in her rookie year, at the 1992 ShopRite LPGA Classic.

YEAR	EVENTS	BEST FINISH	EARNINGS	RANK	SCORING AVERAGE
1992	29	6	$45,445	97	73.94
1993	26	3	$83,532	59	72.85
1994	26	T4	$121,402	45	72.35
1995	28	1	$258,602	22	72.40
1996	29	2	$179,993	35	73.30

JOAN PITCOCK

Born: July 12, 1967

Birthplace: Fresno, Cal.

Ht.: 5' 4"

Joined Tour: 1988

1996 Money Rank: 32

Following on the heels of her most successful 1995, Pitcock enjoyed a lucrative 1996 season that included a third-place tie at the LPGA Corning Classic and a win at the Jamie Farr Classic—her first victory since joining the Tour in October, 1987. After losing a three-stroke lead on the back nine of the Highland Meadows Golf Club, she managed to regain the lead over Marianne Morris at the 16th hole—and then fell short of tying for first when a 20-foot birdie putt wouldn't fall.

Missing only four cuts in 24 starts in 1995, Pitcock posted ten top-20 finishes, including a tie for third place at the Standard Register PING. With $204,407 in winnings she crossed the $200,000 mark in season earnings for the first time in her career, to claim the 30th spot on the Money List. Pitcock registered her second-best finish as a rookie in 1988, when she tied for second place at the Mitsubishi Motors Ocean State Open; there she posted her career-low score of 63 during the second round of competition.

Prior to turning professional, Pitcock put together an impressive resume as a junior. The 1983 California State Junior champion, she also captured the 1984 Optimist Junior World Championship. Recognized as an AJGA All-American in both 1984 and 1985, she was low amateur in the 1986 Women's Open Championship.

- Won the 1996 Jamie Farr Kroger Classic.

- Tied for 3rd place at the 1996 LPGA Corning Classic.

- Tied for 3rd place at the 1995 Standard Register PING.

- Finished in 5th place at the 1995 HEALTHSOUTH Inaugural.

- Tied for 7th place at the 1995 Pinewild Women's Championship and the 1995 Oldsmobile Classic.

- Tied for 3rd place at the 1994 McCall's LPGA Classic at Stratton Mountain.

- Tied for 2nd place at the 1988 Mitsubishi Motors Ocean State Open.

YEAR	EVENTS	BEST FINISH	EARNINGS	RANK	SCORING AVERAGE
1988	29	T2	$22,766	93	74.72
1989	25	T8	$18,284	110	74.35
1990	27	T8	$44,067	88	73.87
1991	26	7	$79,837	60	73.12
1992	28	3	$91,359	58	73.11
1993	24	T11	$66,622	67	72.70
1994	25	T3	$114,735	47	72.59
1995	25	T3	$204,407	30	72.17
1996	25	1	$193,717	32	73.02

CINDY RARICK

Born: Cindy Flom,
September 12, 1959

Birthplace:
Glenwood, Minn.

Ht.: 5'8"

Joined Tour: 1985

**1996 Money
Rank:** 67

Rarick has been in a drought since her three-year streak of winning at least one tournament ended in 1992. With only one top-10 finish in 1996—a tie for eighth place at the U.S. Women's Open—she had her worst finish since 1986. Rarick's 1995 season was slightly better: making 19 cuts in 26 starts, the Minnesota native posted two top-10 finishes, including a tie for second at the PING/Welch's Championship in Tucson.

Rarick joined the LPGA in October, 1984 and first began to see her game pay off in 1987, when she snagged two victories and the Gatorade Most Improved Player Award. Also that year at the Nestle World Championship she carded the first of her three career hole-in-ones. Winning the 1989 Chrysler-Plymouth Classic, the 1990 Planters Pat Bradley International, and the 1991 Northgate Computer Classic (where she claimed a third-hole sudden-death victory over Beth Daniel), she enjoyed a top-20 spot on the Money List for three years running. Although a cyst in her wrist undermined the second half of her 1992 season, Rarick nevertheless managed to notch nine top-20 finishes—and a berth in the LPGA's Million Dollar Club.

Now a playing editor for *Golf for Women*, Rarick enjoyed some success as a junior player. The 1977 Arizona State Junior titlist, she also clinched the 1978 Hawaii Women's Match Play Championship and the 1979 Hawaii Stroke Play Championship.

- Tied for 8th place at the 1996 U.S. Women's Open.
- Tied for 2nd place at the 1995 PING/Welch's Championship in Tucson.
- Tied for 3rd place at the 1994 PING-Cellular One LPGA Golf Championship.
- Finished in 2nd place at the 1993 Minnesota LPGA Classic.
- Won the 1991 Northgate Computer Classic.
- Finished in 2nd place at the 1991 Women's Kemper Open.
- Won the 1990 Planters Pat Bradley International.
- Won the 1987 Gatorade Most Improved Player Award.

YEAR	EVENTS	BEST FINISH	EARNINGS	RANK	SCORING AVERAGE
1985	26	T5	$22,094	86	74.91
1986	27	10	$29,093	72	74.24
1987	31	1	$162,073	11	72.99
1988	26	T5	$63,699	49	73.44
1989	29	1	$196,611	11	72.03
1990	30	1	$259,163	10	72.18
1991	29	1	$201,342	19	72.65
1992	30	T3	$155,303	36	72.39
1993	26	2	$174,407	34	72.08
1994	25	T3	$82,848	66	72.29
1995	27	T2	$130,791	47	72.70
1996	26	N/A	$91,023	67	73.11

MICHELE REDMAN

Born: April 15, 1965

Birthplace:
Zanesville, Ohio

Ht.: 5' 8"

Joined Tour: 1992

**1996 Money
Rank:** 69

Having waged her most successful campaign in 1995, Redman faltered in 1996, with her best finishes coming at the Chick-fil-A Charity Championship (10th) and the PING Welch's Championship (16th). Redman's career-best finish came in 1995, when a par-saving putt at the 18th hole of the LPGA Star Bank Classic earned her third place.

Prior to joining the Tour in October, 1991, Redman played three seasons on the Futures Tour, collecting three titles and a number of top-10 finishes. Having taken up the game at the age of 11, she was a strong contender on the amateur circuit. The 1983 Ohio State Junior champion, she was a quarter-finalist in the 1986 U.S. Women's Amateur an was the second low amateur in that year's U.S. Women's Open. Prior to graduating from Indiana University in 1988 with a degree in public finance and management, Redman was twice named All-American and was four times recognized by All Big-Ten honors. She also notched one individual title, and was the 1987 Big-Ten Conference titlist.

- Tied for 10th place at the 1996 Chick-fil-A Charity Championship.

- Tied for 16th place at the 1996 PING Welch's Championship.

- Finished in solo 3rd place at the 1995 Star Bank LPGA Classic.

- Tied for 4th place at the 1995 ShopRite LPGA Classic.

- Tied for 4th place at the 1995 GHP Classic.

- Tied for 7th place at the 1994 Rochester International.

YEAR	EVENTS	BEST FINISH	EARNINGS	RANK	SCORING AVERAGE
1992	27	T13	$48,706	93	73.48
1993	24	T12	$64,518	73	72.61
1994	23	T7	$113,918	48	72.05
1995	26	3	$195,251	34	72.10
1996	26	N/A	$87,733	69	72.92

SUSIE REDMAN

Born: Susie Pager

Birthplace: April 17, 1966

Ht.: 6' 0"

Joined Tour: 1985

1996 Money Rank: 65

Redman had a creditable 1996, but her most inspired performance came the previous year, when she earned more than $100,000 in only 13 starts. Claiming the 46th spot on the Money List, Redman registered her career best finish in 1995—second place at the Nabisco Dinah Shore. Also that year, she carded a career-low season scoring average of 72.26. No doubt Redman would have had an even more spectacular season had it not been for the diagnosis of neuroblastoma in her son, Bo Jess, who was born December 28, 1994. Redman has two other sons, John Coyle, born in 1990, and Benjamin, born in 1993.

Redman joined the Tour in October, 1984, and enjoyed only moderate success prior to 1995. Earning less than $5,000 for her first two seasons combined, she lost her playing privileges in 1987. Highlights of her career include a career-low round of 65 during the fourth round of the 1989 Red Robin Kyocera Inamori Classic, a third-place finish at the 1992 Los Coyotes LPGA Classic, and a tie for fourth at the 1993 Itoki Hawaiian Ladies Open.

Redman also enjoyed some celebrity as an amateur. In 1984 alone, she captured the National High School All-American Tournament and the North-South Amateur Championship, was recognized as the AJGA Player of the Year—and was *Golf Digest's* Girls Junior Player of the Year.

- Tied for 14th place at the 1996 Oldsmobile Classic.

- Tied for 21st place at the 1996 ShopRite LPGA Classic.

- Finished in 2nd place at the 1995 Nabisco Dinah Shore.

- Tied for 12th place at the 1995 Chick-fil-A Charity Championship.

- Tied for 12th place at the 1994 SAFECO Classic.

- Tied for 4th place at the 1993 Itoki Hawaiian Ladies Open.

- Finished in 3rd place at the 1992 Los Coyotes LPGA Classic.

YEAR	EVENTS	BEST FINISH	EARNINGS	RANK	SCORING AVERAGE
1985	21	T40	$ 1,492	165	78.93
1986	28	26	$ 2,593	163	76.71
1987	DNP				
1988	24	T8	$21,736	97	74.35
1989	27	T16	$28,413	89	73.70
1990	8	T7	$24,574	110	73.63
1991	28	T12	$33,623	103	73.97
1992	28	3	$88,041	61	73.45
1993	16	T4	$36,426	102	73.77
1994	27	T12	$53,168	89	73.18
1995	13	2	$133,008	46	72.26
1996	30	N/A	$96,930	65	73.37

DEB RICHARD

Born: June 3, 1963

Birthplace: Abbeville, La.

Ht.: 5' 6"

Joined Tour: 1986

1996 Money Rank: 30

Although 1996 was not her most successful season on the Tour, Richard proved that she is still a dominant force on the links. With a sturdy, if not spectacular, roster of top-20 finishes—including a tie for 5th place at both the JAL Big Apple Classic and the Youngstown-Warren Classic—Richard climbed back into a top-30 spot on the Money List. Back surgery had prevented the Tour veteran from competing regularly during the previous season, but she nevertheless managed three top-20 finishes, including a tie for fourth at the Jamie Farr Toledo Classic.

Having burst onto the Tour in October, 1985, Richard earned almost $100,000 in her rookie season, thanks to six top-10 finishes. By 1992, years of steady play had helped her surpass the $1 million in career earnings—making her the 27th player to join the LPGA's Million Dollar Club. By 1994, she had four LPGA titles to her credit: the 1987 Rochester International, the 1991 Women's Kemper Open, the 1991 Phar-Mor in Youngstown

and the 1994 SAFECO Classic. That same year she was inducted into the University of Florida Hall of Fame and was awarded *Golf Digest's* Founders Cup Award.

Richard, who took up the game as an eleven-year old, easily established herself as a dominant player during her amateur campaign. A much-titled junior player, she claimed the 1984 U.S. Amateur Championship and garnered low individual honors at the World Cup Championship in Hong Kong. Prior to graduating from the University of Florida in 1986 with a degree in advertising, she collected seven tournament titles, and was the runner up at the 1985 NCAA Championship. That same year, she was honored with the Broderick Award as that year's outstanding collegiate woman golfer.

- Tied for 5th place at the 1996 JAL Big Apple Classic.
- Tied for 5th place at the 1996 Youngstown-Warren LPGA Classic.
- Tied for 7th place at the 1996 Weetabix Women's British Open.
- Tied for 4th place at the 1995 Jamie Farr Toledo Classic.
- Won the 1994 SAFECO Classic.
- Registered five top-10 finishes in 1993.
- Registered nine top-10 finishes in 1992 and was a member of that year's U.S. Solheim Cup team.
- Won the 1991 Women's Kemper Open and Phar-Mor in Youngstown.
- Registered eight top-10 finishes in 1990.
- Won the 1987 Rochester International.
- Registered six top-10 finishes in 1986, her rookie year.

YEAR	EVENTS	BEST FINISH	EARNINGS	RANK	SCORING AVERAGE
1986	27	2	$98,451	22	73.18
1987	29	1	$83,225	30	73.83
1988	28	T2	$112,647	26	72.89
1989	29	T3	$70,594	47	73.50

1990	28	2	$186,464	15	72.34
1991	27	1	$376,640	5	72.13
1992	26	2	$266,427	15	72.09
1993	23	3	$223,282	22	72.25
1994	24	1	$256,960	17	71.87
1995	16	T4	$62,658	76	72.48
1996	28	N/A	$197,245	30	72.44

KELLY ROBBINS

Born: September 29, 1969

Birthplace: Mt. Pleasant, Mich.

Ht.: 5' 9"

Joined Tour: 1992

1996 Money Rank: 7

During her third consecutive season as a top-10 dollar-winner, Robbins won the Sacramento LPGA Classic and had second-place finishes at the Sprint Titleholders Championship and the Nabisco Dinah Shore. 1995 was a also banner year for Robbins, who pocketed $527,655 in 24 competitions to top the $1 million mark in career earnings. Having joined the LPGA in October, 1991, she notched her third career victory by winning her first major—the 1995 McDonald's LPGA Championship.

A Michigan native, Robbins began playing golf at the age of eight. As a collegiate player at the University of Tulsa, she captured seven individual titles and was twice named a first team All-American. She credits Tulsa Women's Golf Coach Dale McNamara as a major figure in her career. Robbins collected seven top-20 finishes as a rookie in 1992 and became a Rolex First-Time Winner at the LPGA Corning Classic the following year. In 1994, she had 11 top-10 finishes and won the Jamie Farr Toledo Classic.

- Won the 1996 Sacramento LPGA Classic.

- Finished in 2nd place at the 1996 Sprint Titleholders Championship.

- Tied for 2nd place at the 1996 Nabisco Dinah Shore.

- Won the 1995 McDonald's LPGA Championship.

- Won the 1994 Jamie Farr Toledo Classic.

- Finished in 2nd place in the 1994 Sprint Championship.

- Was a member of the winning 1994 U.S. Solheim Cup team.

- Played all four rounds of the 1991 U.S. Women's Open Championship as an amateur.

- Was honored as the NCAA Co-Player of the Year in 1991.

- Qualified for the Tour on her first attempt.

YEAR	EVENTS	BEST FINISH	EARNINGS	RANK	SCORING AVERAGE
1992	26	T6	$90,405	59	73.28
1993	22	1	$200,744	24	71.59
1994	25	1	$396,778	8	71.64
1995	24	1	$527,655	3	71.66
1996	24	1	$502,458	7	70.54

KIM SAIKI

Born: January 24, 1966

Birthplace: Inglewood, Cal.

Ht.: 5' 4"

Joined Tour: 1992

1996 Money Rank: 33

Saiki hit the links running in 1996, grabbing a second-place finish at the Fieldcrest Cannon Classic. Adding another second-place finish at the Youngstown-Warren LPGA Classic and a tie for sixth place at the Friendly's Classic, she moved into a top-40 spot on the Money List for the first time in her career, outearning her combined earnings between 1992 and 1995. Saiki scored her previous career-best finish in 1994, when she tied for third place at the ShopRite LPGA Classic. Competing in 22 events that year, she broke into the top 100 on the Money List, claiming the 93rd spot.

A California native, Kim Saiki lists some of her interests as fitness, cooking . . . and mountain biking. Although the two sports may seem like strange bedfellows, Saiki's not alone in combining a passion for both dirt bikes and putting greens. In fact, a golfing sub-culture seems to have sprouted up in the professional mountain biking community, whose riders and team managers often find themselves with spare time at resorts that boast both gnarly ski hills and clear fairways.

Having taken up the game at the age of 11, Saiki knocked off some stunning victories as a junior. Winning both the USGA Junior girls Championship and the Junior World Championship in 1983, she also claimed back-to-back Broadmoor Invitational titles (1986 and 1987). Prior to graduating from the University of Southern California in 1988 with a degree in public administration, she was recognized as an NCAA All-American (1986) and was four times an All-Conference honoree.

- Finished in 2nd place at the 1996 Fieldcrest Cannon Classic.

- Finished in 2nd place at the 1996 Youngstown-Warren LPGA Classic.

- Tied for 6th place at the 1996 Friendly's Classic.

- Tied for 3rd place at the 1994 ShopRite LPGA Classic.

- Competed on the WPGET and Ladies Asian Tour in 1991.

- Claimed two wins on the 1990 Futures Tour.

- Claimed five wins on the Players West Golf Tour in 1989.

YEAR	EVENTS	BEST FINISH	EARNINGS	RANK	SCORING AVERAGE
1992	22	T25	$22,960	129	74.66
1993	DNP				
1994	22	T3	$50,817	93	73.29
1995	25	T22	$29,760	115	73.86
1996	22	2	$182,893	33	72.25

CINDY SCHREYER

Born: January 21, 1963
Birthplace: Forest Park, Geo.
Ht.: 5' 7"
Joined Tour: 1989
1996 Money Rank: 55

Schreyer eclipsed her previous Tour record in 1996, topping the $100,000-mark in season's earnings for the first time in her career. A Georgia native, Schreyer registered her second most lucrative season in 1993, when she climbed to the 54th spot on the Money List, with $95,343 in earnings. Her best finish of the season—and sole victory on the Tour—came at the Sun-Times Challenge, where she carded her career-low round of 66.

Although she didn't take up the game until she was 15, Schreyer waged an impressive campaign as a junior player, capturing the 1980 Georgia State championship and medaling in the 1981 USGA Junior Girls Championship. She also enjoyed a seven-year tenure as the Atlanta Amateur Champion (1978-1984) and, as a collegiate player at the University of Georgia, was the individual NCAA Women's Golf champion in 1984. The following year, she captured the Southeastern Conference Championship, and in 1986, the year she was selected for the U.S. Curtis Cup team, she also claimed the Public Links Championship. Schreyer married Cliff McCurdy in 1991.

- Tied for 5th place at the 1996 LPGA Corning Classic.

- Tied for 6th place at the 1996 Fieldcrest Cannon Classic.

- Tied for 6th place at the 1996 Sacramento LPGA Classic.

- Tied for 10th place at the 1996 Betsy King LPGA Classic.

- Tied for 18th place a the 1995 du Maurier Ltd. Classic.

- Tied for 9th place at the 1994 GHP Heartland Classic.

- Was a Rolex First-Time Winner at the 1993 Sun-Times Challenge.

- Tied for 2nd place at the 1991 Atlantic City Classic.

YEAR	EVENTS	BEST FINISH	EARNINGS	RANK	SCORING AVERAGE
1989	27	T28	$14,984	120	74.76
1990	25	T11	$20,156	114	74.81
1991	27	T2	$63,613	73	74.15
1992	30	T11	$50,513	89	74.09
1993	27	1	$95,343	54	73.74
1994	25	T9	$44,994	98	74.49
1995	27	T18	$42,688	94	74.49
1996	28	N/A	$119,846	55	72.83

PATTY SHEEHAN

Born: October 27, 1956

Birthplace: Middlebury, Ver.

Ht.: 5' 3"

Joined Tour: 1980

1996 Money Rank: 12

Ending the 1996 season with $342,391, Sheehan didn't post the best results of her 17-year tenure on the Tour, but nonetheless managed to claim a top-15 spot on the Money List for a whopping 16th consecutive season. This she did with brio, winning the Nabisco Dinah Shore (her fifth Major win) and finishing in second place at the Safeco Classic.

In 1993, having captured her 30th career victory at the Standard Register PING, Sheehan qualified for the LPGA Hall of Fame. That same year she crossed the $4 million mark in career earnings. Her accomplishments are immense and reflect perseverance as well as talent. After collecting an impressive list of Amateur titles—including the

1980 AIAW National Championship—Sheehan hit the Tour loaded with promise. She won two major titles, consecutive LPGA Championships in 1983 and 1984. In 1990, poised to collect the U.S. Women's Open title at the Atlanta Athletic Club, she saw her 11-shot lead in the final round dwindle to a second-place finish. What followed was even more disappointing: in the summer of 1991, a fluke accident at a birthday party damaged Sheehan's finger—and her prospects for the rest of the season.

Sheehan entered the 1992 Women's Open on the heels of victories at the Rochester International and Jamie Farr Toledo Classic. Forcing a playoff with a 15-foot birdie putt, she nailed the title with what was has been touted as possibly the greatest clutch finish in the history of the Open (see a description in the Taming the Monsters section). In 1993, she captured the Mazda LPGA Championship by one shot, having avoided a playoff by sinking a 4-foot putt on the 72nd hole. The following year, she collected her second U.S. Women's Open title in just three years, and in 1995, playing in 17 events, she added wins in the Rochester International and the SAFECO Classic.

- Won the 1996 Nabisco Dinah Shore.

- Finished in 2nd place at the 1996 Safeco Classic.

- Tied for 4th place at the 1996 HealthSouth Inaugural.

- Won the 1995 Rochester International and SAFECO Classic.

- Tied for 3rd place at the 1995 McDonald's LPGA Championship.

- Won the 1994 U.S. Open.

- Finished in 4th place in the 1994 Rochester International.
- Was a member of the victorious 1994 U.S. Solheim team.
- Won the 1993 Standard Register PING and the LPGA Championship.
- Won the 1992 Jamie Farr Toledo Classic, the Rochester International and U.S. Open.
- Won the 1991 Orix Hawaiian Ladies Open.
- Was rated as one of the top skiers in the country at age 13.

YEAR	EVENTS	BEST FINISH	EARNINGS	RANK	SCORING AVERAGE
1980	6	6	$17,139	63	72.86
1981	25	1	$118,463	11	72.52
1982	25	1	$225,022	4	71.72
1983	26	1	$250,399	2	71.72
1984	22	1	$255,185	2	71.40
1985	24	1	$227,908	5	71.59
1986	24	1	$214,281	7	72.17
1987	23	2	$208,107	6	71.83
1988	23	1	$326,171	2	71.56
1989	20	1	$253,605	5	71.24
1990	25	1	$732,618	2	70.62
1991	22	1	$342,204	8	71.49
1992	22	1	$418,622	5	71.30
1993	21	1	$540,547	2	71.04
1994	18	1	$323,562	13	71.65
1995	17	1	$333,147	14	71.69
1996	15	1	$332,891	12	71.47

VAL SKINNER

Born: October 16, 1960

Birthplace: Hamilton, Mont.

Ht.: 5' 6"

Joined Tour: 1983

1996 Money Rank: 10

A 14-year veteran of the Tour, Skinner shows no sign of slowing down and may even prove to have her best years of golf ahead of her. Finishing the season with $413,419, she was among the LPGA's top-dozen earners for the third consecutive

Skinner, who is interested in golf course architecture, is redesigning part of a course that she and her family purchased in Nebraska.

year. Among her several top-10 finishes were runner-up honors at both the LPGA Corning Classic and Sacramento LPGA Classic, and a third-place finish at the Sprint Titleholders Championship.

Considered to be one of the longest hitters on the Tour, Skinner captured her sixth career title in 1995 at the Sprint Championship. Turning in a second-round score of 65, she tied her career-low. Of the 26 events she entered during the 1995 season, she notched nine top-10 finishes, earning $430,248. Skinner's 1994 season was equally impressive, with nine top-10 finishes—including her fifth career title at the Atlanta Women's Championship—to bring in her third-best financial season at $328,021.

An avid golfer since childhood, Skinner claimed her first golf title at the age of seven. Before graduating from Oklahoma State University in 1982 with a degree in public relations, she was the 1980 and 1982 Big Eight champion, as well as the 1982 Outstanding Female Athlete of the Year. She was also named *GOLF Magazine's* 1982 Collegiate Player of the Year and was nominated for *Golf Digest's* Collegiate Player of the Year.

Skinner joined the LPGA the following year; in 1985, she was the runner-up at the Henredon Classic, coming in just behind Nancy Lopez's record 20-under-par finish. That year she recorded more than $100,000 in earnings, a feat she repeated in the following two seasons. With three top-10 finishes in 1991, Skinner captured her fourth LPGA career title at the 1993 Keystone Open. Skinner is an avid athlete who enjoys most sports, including surfing, water- and snow-skiing.

- Finished in 2nd place at the 1996 LPGA Corning Classic and Sacramento LPGA Classic.
- Finished in 3rd place at the 1996 Sprint Titleholders Championship.

- Finished in 5th place at the 1996 Safeco Classic.

- Won the 1995 Sprint Championship.

- Finished in 3rd place at the 1995 HEALTH-SOUTH Inaugural.

- Won the 1994 Atlanta Women's Championship.

- Tied for 3rd place at the 1994 Cup Noodles Hawaiian Ladies Open and the Lady Keystone Open.

- Won the 1993 Lady Keystone Open.

- Won the 1987 MasterCard International.

- Won the 1986 Mazda Classic.

- Won the 1985 Konica San Jose Classic.

- Was named NCAA and AIAW All-American in 1982.

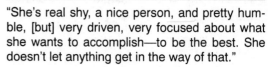

"She's real shy, a nice person, and pretty humble, [but] very driven, very focused about what she wants to accomplish—to be the best. She doesn't let anything get in the way of that."

—Leta Lindley, Sorenstam's teammate
and roommate at the University of Arizona.

Annika Sorenstam's younger sibling, Charlotta, is following in her older sister's footsteps: in 1993, Charlotta Sorenstam captured the NCAA golf championship.

YEAR	EVENTS	BEST FINISH	EARNINGS	RANK	SCORING AVERAGE
1983	24	T3	$29,485	57	74.26
1984	23	T6	$23,021	79	74.61
1985	28	1	$132,307	14	73.07
1986	24	1	$165,243	11	72.19
1987	26	1	$122,039	18	72.92
1988	23	3	$60,334	52	73.54
1989	27	2	$102,089	34	72.94
1990	23	T2	$66,577	59	74.09
1991	23	T3	$61,923	74	73.61
1992	24	T8	$41,651	100	73.95
1993	25	1	$129,665	43	73.10
1994	25	1	$328,021	12	71.65
1995	26	1	$430,248	9	71.94
1996	26	2	$413,419	10	71.85

ANNIKA SORENSTAM

Born: October 9, 1970

Birthplace: Stockholm, Sweden

Ht.: 5' 6"

Joined Tour: 1994

1996 Money Rank: 3

Sorenstam's 1995 season was a tough act to follow, but the Swedish player turned in a fine per-

formance in 1996. Taking an early lead in the 1996 Open, she ran away with her second consecutive title with a solid six-stroke lead. Having claimed the Corestates Betsy King Classic, she also finished second at the Rochester International and tied for second the Nabisco Dinah Shore.

In 1995, her second full season on the Tour, Sorenstam seemed blessed by a Midas touch. She captured the Rolex Player of the Year Award and Sweden's prestigious Athlete of the Year Award and also snagged first-place honors on the LPGA Money List. Topping the European Money List as well, she became the first player—male or female—to lead both earnings lists. She competed in 19 LPGA events that year, notching three victories—the first of which came at the U.S. Open at the Broadmoor (her first-ever LPGA victory), where she overcame Meg Mallon's third-round three-stroke lead. She also captured the GHP Heartland Classic with a 10-stroke lead and collected the Samsung World Championship title by managing a 45-foot chip-in on the first hole of a sudden-death playoff with Laura Davies. With an impressive total of 12 top-10 finishes, Sorenstam made every cut, maintaining a perfect record of 18 for 18.

Now a favorite among the fans, Sorenstam joined LPGA in October 1993, qualifying on her first attempt. Having taken up golf at the age of 12, she soon established herself as a dominant amateur, earning the 1992 World Amateur championship title as a member of the Swedish National Team (1987-1992). Sorenstam's collegiate resume is no less impressive: during her career at the University of Arizona, she collected seven collegiate titles and was named the 1991 College Player of the Year. Named NCAA champion in 1991, she also earned back-to-back NCAA All-American titles in 1991 and 1992 and was the 1992 PAC champion.

- Won the 1996 Samsung World Championship of Women's Golf, Corestates Betsy King Classic and U.S. Women's Open.

- Was awarded the 1996 ESPY Award for women's golf.

- Finished in 2nd place at the 1996 Rochester International.

- Tied for 2nd place at the 1996 Nabisco Dinah Shore.

- Won the 1995 Rolex Player of the Year Award.

- Won the 1995 Vare Trophy for lowest aggregate scoring average.

- Won the 1995 U.S. Women's Open, World Championship of Women's Golf and GHP Heartland Classic.

- Won the 1995 Hennesy Cup (Germany).

- Won the 1995 OVB Damen Open (Austria)— shooting 22 under par.

- Won the 1994 Holden Women's Australian Open.

- Won the 1994 LPGA Rolex Rookie-of-the-Year award.

- Tied for 2nd place in the 1994 British Women's Open.

- Was a member of the 1994 European Solheim Team.

YEAR	EVENTS	BEST FINISH	EARNINGS	RANK	SCORING AVERAGE
1994	18	T2	$127,451	39	71.90
1995	19	1	$666,533	1	71.00
1996	19	1	$792,311	3	70.48

SHERRI STEINHAUER

Born: December 27, 1962

Birthplace: Madison, Wis.

Ht.: 5' 7"

Joined Tour: 1986

1996 Money Rank: 62

Steinhauer slipped out of a top-50 spot on the Money List for the first time since 1989. Her best 1996 results included a tie for fourth at the Standard Register Ping, a tie for 17th at the Rochester International and a tie for 18th at the McDonald's LPGA Classic. The previous year, Steinhauer posted eight top-20 finishes—including second place at both the Rochester International and the Jamie Farr Toledo Classic.

A Wisconsin native, Steinhauer enjoyed her most successful year in 1994, when she grabbed seventh-place honors on the Money List. That year's eight top-10 finishes included a win at the Sprint Championship, her second career victory. Also that year, she lowered her career-best scoring average to 71.60, having carded a season-low score of 65 during the last round of the PING Welch's Championship in Boston. The previous season, 14 top-20 finishes—which included solo second place finishes at both the Atlanta Women's Championship and the McDonald's Championship—helped her to cross the $1 million mark in career earnings.

A three-time Wisconsin State Junior champion (1978-1980), Steinhauer also claimed the 1981 Wisconsin State Women's Amateur and the 1983 Women's Trans-National, and was low amateur on that year's U.S. Women's Open. Her impressive collegiate campaign at the University of Texas included five titles, All-America honors (in 1985) and MVP honors (in 1983 and 1985). Steinhauer was featured in the 1990 *Fairway* magazine.

- Tied for 4th place at the 1996 Standard Register PING.

- Finished in 2nd place at the 1995 Rochester International.

- Finished in 2nd place at the 1995 Jamie Farr Toledo Classic.

- Won the 1994 Sprint Championship.

- Finished in 3rd place at the 1994 Minnesota LPGA Classic.

- Posted 14 top-20 finishes in 1993.

- Became a Rolex First-Time Winner at the 1992 du Maurier Ltd. Classic.

YEAR	EVENTS	BEST FINISH	EARNINGS	RANK	SCORING AVERAGE
1986	27	23	$ 7,733	131	76.00
1987	7	T6	$45,741	54	74.02
1988	29	T4	$54,262	57	73.60
1989	27	T5	$44,825	64	73.65
1990	30	4	$109,407	37	73.19
1991	32	3	$165,568	24	72.53
1992	27	1	$315,145	12	71.82
1993	28	2	$311,967	13	71.64
1994	27	1	$413,398	7	71.60
1995	26	2	$216,897	26	72.15
1996	21	N/A	$98,406	62	73.06

KRIS TSCHETTER

Born: December 30, 1964

Birthplace: Detroit, Mich.

Ht.: 5' 7"

Joined Tour: 1988

1996 Money Rank: 13

Although she was edged out of claiming her second victory on the Tour, Tschetter enjoyed a profitable season in 1996, collecting more than $300,000 for the second consecutive year. She finished second at the U.S. Women's Open and fourth at the Samsung World Championship of Women's Golf.

Tschetter's game first began to pay off in 1995, when, with seven top-10 finishes, she drew $363,202 in earnings. Crossing both the $200,000 and the $300,000 milestones in season earnings for the first time since joining the Tour, she topped the $1 million mark in total career earnings. Helping her to a 12th-place spot on the Money List were a solo second place finish at the Sprint Championship, a tie for second place at the Cup Noodles Hawaiian Ladies Open and fourth-place ties at both the Friendly's Classic and the McCall's LPGA Classic at Stratton Mountain. Having joined the Tour in October, 1997, Tschetter claimed her only victory in 1992 at the Northgate Computer Classic.

Tschetter's amateur years yielded a number of wins, including the 1983 AJGA Tournament title and a four-year run of victories at the South Dakota State Women's Amateur Championship (1983-1986). Prior to graduating from Texas Christian University in 1987 with a degree in radio, T.V. and film, she finished ninth in the 1987 Women's NCAA Championship and was three times a member of the All-Southwest Conference team.

- Finished in 2nd place at the 1996 U.S. Women's Open.

- Tied for 4th place at the 1996 Samsung World Championship of Women's Golf.

- Tied for 6th place at the 1996 Oldsmobile Classic.

- Finished in 2nd place at the 1995 Sprint Championship.

- Tied for 2nd place at the 1995 Cup Noodles Hawaiian Ladies Open.

- Finished in 4th place at the 1994 Jamie Farr Toledo Classic.

- Tied for 2nd place at the 1993 Standard Register PING.

- Became a Rolex First-Time Winner at the 1992 Northgate Computer Classic.

YEAR	EVENTS	BEST FINISH	EARNINGS	RANK	SCORING AVERAGE
1988	28	T19	$ 7,590	145	75.96
1989	26	T14	$18,315	109	74.14
1990	27	T5	$39,469	91	74.00
1991	29	2	$129,532	38	73.19
1992	29	1	$157,436	33	72.90
1993	23	T2	$196,913	25	72.29
1994	26	4	$112,229	50	72.86
1995	27	2	$363,202	12	71.93
1996	26	2	$314,090	13	71.71

KARRIE WEBB

Born: December 21, 1974

Birthplace: Ayr, Queensland, Australia

Ht.: 5' 6"

Joined Tour: 1996

1996 Money Rank: 2

Webb's astonishing rookie performance in 1996 is unprecedented in professional golf: After qualifying for the Tour in October 1995 on her first attempt—finishing second at the LPGA Final Qualifying Tournament though she had an injured wrist—Webb burst onto the scene as a rookie with an enviable litany of wins and top-10 finishes. She won the 1996 SAFECO Classic, Sprint Titleholder's Championship and HEALTHSOUTH Inaugural as well as a one-stroke victory at the inaugural LPGA Tour Championship in Las Vegas.

Also in 1996, Webb posted second-place finishes at the PING Welch's Championship, Tournament of Champions, Cup Noodles Hawaiian Ladies Open (where she fell just one stroke shy of winner Meg Mallon), the JAL Big Apple Classic and the du Maurier Ltd. Classic. With more than twice the points of runner-up Mayumi Hirase, Webb ran away with the season's Rolex Rookie of the Year award. The runner-up in the 1996 Rolex Player of the Year race, she also placed third in both the Vare Trophy and Tour Birdies standings.

Having played golf since the age of eight, Webb turned professional in October of 1994 and competed on the Women Professional Golfers' European Tour (WPGET). The following year, having accumulated an impressive string of top finishes, she was recognized as the WPGET Rookie of the Year. That year's highlights included winning the Weetabix Women's British Open by six shots; capturing the Golden Flake/Golden Ocala Futures Classic; finishing second at the LPGA Final Qualifying School; and third place on the WPGET Final Order of Merit. As an amateur, Webb six times represented Australia in international competition from 1992-1994 and was the 1994 Australian Strokeplay champion.

- Won the 1996 SAFECO Classic, Sprint Titleholder's Championship and HEALTHSOUTH Inaugural.

- Finished in 2nd place at the 1996 Cup Noodles Hawaiian Ladies Open, PING Welch's Championship and Chrysler-Plymouth Tournament of Champions.

- Tied for 2nd place at the 1996 JAL Big Apple Classic and du Maurier Ltd. Classic.

- Won the 1995 Weetabix Women's British Open.

- Finished in 1st place at the 1995 Golden Flake/Golden Ocala Futures Classic.

- Finished in 2nd place at the 1995 LPGA Final Qualifying School.

- Was named 1995 WPGET Rookie of the Year.

- Finished in 2nd place at the 1994 Australian Ladies Masters.

YEAR	EVENTS	BEST FINISH	EARNINGS	RANK	SCORING AVERAGE
1996	24	1	$852,000	2	71.00

BARB WHITEHEAD

Born: Barb Thomas, January 22, 1961

Birthplace: Sibley, Iowa

Ht.: 5' 5"

Joined Tour: 1984

1996 Money Rank: 24

Having struggled through her first decade on the Tour, Whitehead enjoyed the second consecutive strong showing in 1996, which included a tie for second place at the State Farm Rail Classic and a tie for fourth place at the Rochester International. The previous year, five top-20 finishes, including a victory at the Cup Noodles Hawaiian Ladies Open, helped Whitehead to the 31st spot on the Money List. Pocketing $204,327 in 1995, Whitehead collected more than she had in the previous six seasons combined.

In 1983, the Arizona resident qualified for the Tour with panache, sinking a bunker shot on the final hole of the final LPGA Qualifying Tournament. Prior to joining the Tour, she established herself as a strong junior player, winning both the 1978 and 1979 Iowa Junior championships. Named All-American for Tulsa University in 1980, she took third place in the 1982 NCAA Championship and medaled in the 1980 Nancy Lopez and the 1983 Lamar invitationals. One of seven children, Whitehead was introduced to golf by her father when she was eight years old.

- Tied for 2nd place at the 1996 State Farm Rail Classic.

- Tied for 4th place at the 1996 Rochester International.

- Tied for 6th place at the 1996 Friendly's Classic.

- Was a Rolex First-Time Winner at the 1995 Cup Noodles Hawaiian Ladies Open.

- Tied for 6th place at the 1995 McDonald's LPGA Championship.

- Tied for 7th place at the 1993 Lady Keystone Open.

- Tied foe 2nd place at the 1986 United Virginia Bank Classic.

- Tied for 4th place at the 1985 Mazda Classic.

YEAR	EVENTS	BEST FINISH	EARNINGS	RANK	SCORING AVERAGE
1984	26	T8	$19,698	90	74.78
1985	27	T4	$38,285	59	74.11
1986	26	T2	$44,239	56	74.72
1987	27	T19	$ 7,777	133	76.65
1988	27	T25	$12,697	126	75.23
1989	20	T11	$31,403	84	73.70
1990	26	T12	$19,616	116	74.55
1991	25	T16	$21,524	123	74.63
1992	26	T17	$15,575	138	74.78
1993	20	T7	$63,052	74	72.48
1994	24	T11	$42,769	101	73.15
1995	25	1	$204,327	31	72.32
1996	27	2	$222,229	24	72.48

MAGGIE WILL

Born: November 22, 1964

Birthplace: Whiteville, N.C.

Ht.: 5' 4"

Joined Tour: 1989

1996 Money Rank: 44

1996 brought some measure of success to Will, who hasn't claimed an LPGA victory since she nailed a sudden-death playoff at the Children's Medical Center LPGA Classic 1994. With a tie for second at the Star Bank LPGA Classic, a tie for eighth at the Safeway LPGA Golf Championship and a couple of other top-20 finishes, she topped the $100,000 mark in season's earnings—something she had managed only two other times since joining the Tour in October, 1988.

Will's victory at the Children's Medical Center LPGA Classic—where she outplayed Alicia Dibos and Jill Bries-Hinton on the second hole of a sudden-death playoff—was the bright spot of her 1994 season. Will posted two other victories during her tenure on the Tour, the 1990 Desert Inn LPGA International and the 1992 Sara Lee Classic. In another sensational sudden-death playoff, she collected the latter victory in the first extra hole of a three-way playoff against Brandie Burton and Amy Benz.

Before she joined the LPGA Tour, Will competed on the Futures Tour and built a strong reputation as an amateur. Twice named the Carolinas PGA Junior champion (in 1981 and 1982), she was the 1986 North Carolina Women's Amateur titlist. Graduating from Furman University in 1987 with a degree in business, she was a member of that year's runner-up NCAA Championship team.

- Tied for 2nd place at the 1996 Star Bank LPGA Classic.

- Tied for 8th place at the 1996 Safeway LPGA Golf Championship.

- Tied for 14th place at the 1996 U.S. Women's Open.

- Finished in 6th place at the 1995 PING/Welch's Championship.

- Won the 1994 Children's Medical Center LPGA Classic.

- Won the 1992 Sara Lee Classic.

- Was a Rolex First-Time Winner at the 1990 Desert Inn LPGA Classic.

YEAR	EVENTS	BEST FINISH	EARNINGS	RANK	SCORING AVERAGE
1989	29	T3	$26,476	91	74.88
1990	30	1	$110,488	36	74.05
1991	27	T6	$61,227	75	73.59
1992	29	1	$126,428	46	73.45
1993	23	T12	$49,770	88	72.79
1994	25	1	$87,307	62	73.61
1995	23	6	$53,289	84	74.00
1996	24	2	$142,149	44	73.23

3

PRO FILES
SENIORS

TOMMY AARON

Born: Thomas D. Aaron,
February 22, 1937
Birthplace: Gainesville, Ga.
Ht: 6' 1" **Wt:** 185
Joined Tour: 1987
1996 Money Rank: 46

It was nearly 20 years between Aaron's 1973 Masters' victory on the PGA Tour and his next win at the 1992 Kaanapali Classic on the island of Maui. He entered 28 Senior Tour events in 1996 and was in the money in 27 of them, earning $313,323 (46th) with three top ten finishes.

Aaron had six top ten finishes in his rookie year on the Senior Tour in 1987. His best year on the Senior Tour was 1992, when he had his only victory plus eight top ten finishes. In 1995 a stomach virus kept him off the tour for about a month but he still managed three top ten finishes.

Aaron joined the PGA Tour in 1961 and was among the top 60 money winners from 1961 to 1973. Both of Aaron's PGA wins came in his native state of Georgia, the 1970 Atlanta Classic and the 1973 Masters Tournament. He won the Masters by shooting a final round 68 to edge J.C. Snead by one stroke.

• Only Senior Tour victory was the 1992 Kaanapali Classic.

• Two official PGA Tour victories, including the 1973 Masters Tournament. Also won the 1969 Canadian Open, then an unofficial event.

• Won the 1960 Western Amateur.

• Member of the 1959 Walker Cup team and the 1969 and 1973 U.S. Ryder Cup teams.

• Career Senior PGA Tour earnings: $2,210,778 (38th).

RICK ACTON

Born: Richard D. Acton,
January 5, 1946
Birthplace: Portland, Ore.
Ht: 5' 11" **Wt:** 215
Joined Tour: 1996
1996 Money Rank: 31

1996 was Acton's rookie year. He worked hard to earn his 1997 exemption, entering 36 tournaments and finishing 31st on the 1996 Senior Tour money list, with six top ten finishes, including third at the Royal Caribbean Classic toward the end of the 1996 season.

Acton turned professional in 1969 after graduating from the University of Washington in 1968. He never joined the PGA Tour, instead becoming a club and teaching pro in the Pacific Northwest. His last position prior to joining the Senior PGA Tour was Director of Golf at Sahalee Country Club in Seattle, Washington.

Acton qualified for exempt status by placing fifth in the Senior PGA Qualifying Tournament. His distinguished teaching career included recognition as a three-time Northwest PGA Teacher of the Year. He was also twice a member of the PGA Cup Team.

- Won $445,086 in 36 events to finish 31st on 1996 money list and earn an exemption for 1997.

- Won three Pacific Northwest Opens, four Pacific Northwest PGA titles, four Oregon Opens, three Washington Opens, and six Washington PGA titles.

Albus surprised the golf world in 1991, his first full year on the Senior Tour, when he won the Senior Players Championship at the TPC of Michigan. It was only his sixth Senior Tour start. In 1994 he became the first former club professional to win over $1 million in one year on the Senior Tour.

- Has five Senior Tour victories: 1995 SBC Dominion Seniors; 1994 Vantage at The Dominion; 1994 Bank of Boston Senior Classic; 1993 GTE Suncoast Classic; 1991 Mazda Senior Players Championship.

- Best year on the Senior Tour was 1994, when he earned $1,237,128, won two tournaments, and had 18 top ten finishes.

- Spent 14 years as head pro at the Piping Rock Club on Long Island before resigning to join the Senior Tour.

- Never played regularly on the PGA Tour, but participated in the old winter tour in 1977 and 1978.

- Played in six U.S. Opens and seven PGA Championships.

- In 1996 he entered more than 30 tournaments for the fifth year in a row.

JIM ALBUS

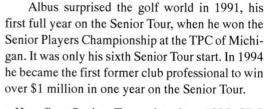

Born: James Christian Albus, June 18, 1940
Birthplace: Staten Island, N.Y.
Ht: 6' 2" **Wt:** 200
Joined Tour: 1991
1996 Money Rank: 56

Albus was one of the first former club professionals to perform well on the Senior Tour: he ranks 17th on the Tour in career earnings, with $3,575,311. His 1996 performance was not up to his usual standards, though, as he finished in the top ten only three times.

ISAO AOKI

Born: Isao Aoki, August 31, 1942
Birthplace: Abiko, Chiba, Japan
Ht: 6' 0" **Wt:** 170
Joined Tour: 1992
1996 Money Rank: 4

1996 was Aoki's best year on the Senior Tour. He won two tournaments and earned over $1 million for the second year in a row. In tour statistics he finished third overall, second in birdies (3.86 per round), and second in average strokes per round (70.04). Although he uses an unorthodox putting style, he considers it the strongest part of his game.

In 1980 Aoki shot a 274 in the U.S. Open, only to lose to Jack Nicklaus by two strokes. Aoki and Nicklaus relived their 1980 U.S. Open battle at The Tradition in 1995, when Aoki again finished second to Nicklaus, who prevailed by winning a playoff. Aoki has won six Senior Tour events, including the BellSouth Senior Classic and the Kroger Senior Classic in 1996.

Aoki is considered Japan's all-time greatest golfer, with 66 tournament victories worldwide. He joined the regular PGA Tour in 1981 and recorded his only victory in 1983, when he won the Hawaiian Open after holing a pitching wedge out of the rough from 128 yards for an eagle-3 on the 72nd hole.

- Has won six Senior Tour events: 1996 BellSouth Senior Classic; 1996 Kroger Senior Classic; 1995 Bank of Boston Senior Classic; 1994 Bank One Senior Classic; 1994 Brickyard Crossing Championship; 1992 Nationwide Championship.

- 1996 was best year on Senior Tour, with earnings of $1,162,581 (4th), two victories, and 16 top ten finishes out of 26 events entered.

- Earned $300,000 in his rookie year on the Senior Tour in 1992, more than twice what he earned in his best year on the PGA Tour.

- Nicknamed "Tower" after the Tokyo Tower because of his height.

- Has won on six different circuits: PGA Tour, Senior PGA Tour, PGA European Tour, Australasian Tour, Japan PGA Tour, and Japan Senior Tour.

- Was leading money winner five times on the Japan PGA Tour.

- Career Senior PGA Tour earnings: $3,719,638 (15th).

GEORGE ARCHER

Born: George William Archer, October 1, 1939
Birthplace: San Francisco, Cal.
Ht: 6' 6" **Wt:** 195
Joined Tour: 1989
1996 Money Rank: 67

Archer has 17 Senior Tour victories to go with his 12 victories on the regular PGA Tour that he earned between 1965 and 1984. Archer entered only 12 events in 1996, and it was only the second year in Archer's Senior career that he failed to win an official event. At 6'6" Archer is an imposing figure from tee to green, where he uses a short putter.

Archer became one of only four players to win their Senior Tour debut when he took the 1989 Gatlin Brothers Southwest Classic in a playoff against Orville Moody and Jimmy Powell. He went on to win four Senior Tour events in 1990, three in 1991, three in 1992, four in 1993, and two in 1995. His all-time Senior Tour earnings passed the $5 million mark in 1995.

Archer's degenerative hip may force him to retire soon. He had hinted at retiring early in 1995, but went on to win two tournaments that year, the Toshiba Senior Classic and the Cadillac NFL Golf Classic.

- Has 17 Senior PGA victories: 1995 Toshiba Senior Classic; 1995 Cadillac NFL Golf Classic; 1993 Ameritech Senior Open; 1993 First of America Classic; 1993 Raley's Senior Gold Rush; 1993 PING Kaanapali Classic; 1992 Murata Reunion Pro-Am; 1992 Northville Long Island Classic; 1992 Bruno's Memorial Classic; 1991 GTE North Classic; 1991 Raley's Senior Gold Rush; 1991 Northville Long Island Classic; 1990 MONY Tournament of Champions; 1990 Northville Long Island Classic; 1990 GTE Northwest Classic; 1990 Gold Rush at Rancho Murieta; 1989 Gatlin Brothers Southwest Classic.

- Won 12 tournaments on the PGA Tour, including the 1969 Masters, and finished among the top five money winners in 1968, 1971, and 1972.

- Two of his four 1993 Senior Tour victories were back-to-back, the Ameritech Senior Open followed by the First of America Classic, which he won in a playoff.

- Named Senior Tour Co-Player of the Year in 1991 along with Mike Hill.

- Hampered by injuries throughout his career, Archer has had surgery on his left wrist (1975), back (1979), and left shoulder (1987).

- Career Senior PGA Tour earnings: $5,264,385 (7th).

MILLER BARBER

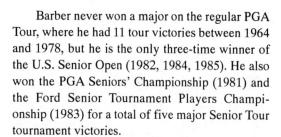

Born: Miller Westford Barber, Jr., March 31, 1931

Birthplace: Shreveport, La.

Ht: 5' 11" **Wt:** 210

Joined Tour: 1981

1996 Money Rank: 76

Barber never won a major on the regular PGA Tour, where he had 11 tour victories between 1964 and 1978, but he is the only three-time winner of the U.S. Senior Open (1982, 1984, 1985). He also won the PGA Seniors' Championship (1981) and the Ford Senior Tournament Players Championship (1983) for a total of five major Senior Tour tournament victories.

Barber's 24 wins on the Senior Tour are second only to Lee Trevino, who surpassed him in 1995. From 1992 through 1995 Barber won at least one Super Senior (age 60 and over) event each year. He entered 33 events in 1996 and finished in the money in 31 of them, earning $103,174 (76th) for the year.

AVERAGE BIRDIES PER ROUND

Rank	Name	Rounds	Stat
1.	Hale Irwin	74	4.05
2.	Isao Aoki	81	3.86
3.	Ray Floyd	74	3.82
4.	Bob Murphy	94	3.79
5.	Graham Marsh	88	3.74
6.	Jay Sigel	100	3.71
7.	Vicente Fernandez	60	3.70
8.	Jim Dent	106	3.63
9.	Jim Colbert	101	3.60
10.	Dave Stockton	91	3.58

Each of Barber's PGA Tour wins came in a different year, and from 1967 to 1974 he won at least one event every year. He was a member of the Ryder Cup team in 1969 and 1971. He became the tenth PGA Tour player to surpass the $1 million mark in official earnings on February 29, 1976.

- Has 24 Senior Tour victories, including five majors: 1989 MONY Tournament of Champions; 1989 Vintage Chrysler Invitational; 1988 Showdown Classic; 1988 Fairfield-Barnett Classic; 1987 Showdown Classic; 1987 Newport Cup; 1986 MONY Tournament of Champions; 1985 Sunrise Senior Classic; 1985 U.S. Senior Open; 1985 PaineWebber Seniors Invitational; 1984 Roy Clark Senior Challenge; 1984 U.S. Senior Open; 1984 Greater Syracuse Seniors; 1984 Denver Post Champions; 1983 Senior Tournament Players Championship; 1983 Merrill Lynch/Golf Digest Commemorative; 1983 United Virginia Bank; 1983 Hilton Head Seniors International; 1982 U.S. Senior Open; 1982 Suntree Senior Classic; 1982 Hilton Head Seniors International; 1981 Peter Jackson Champions; 1981 Suntree Senior Classic; 1981 PGA Seniors' Championship.

- 18 Super Senior (age 60 and over) victories.

- 11 PGA Tour victories in 11 different years.

- As captain, led the U.S. squad to victory in the 1991 and 1992 Chrysler Cup and DuPont Cup team competitions.

- Career Senior PGA Tour earnings: $3,627,184 (16th).

DON BIES

Born: Donald W. Bies, December 10, 1937
Birthplace: Cottonwood, Idaho
Ht: 6' 1" **Wt:** 170
Joined Tour: 1988
1996 Money Rank: 49

With one win on the PGA Tour and career earnings of $527,393, Bies had a respectable if not especially noteworthy career. He's done much better on the Senior Tour, winning two events in his rookie year (1988) and The Tradition in 1989. He entered 24 events in 1996, finishing in the money 23 times to earn $294,438 (49th) for the year.

Bies has seven Senior Tour victories to his credit. His best year on the Senior Tour was 1989, when he won three tournaments (two of them back-to-back) and earned $421,769 to finish in the top ten on the money list. His most recent victory came in 1995 at Raley's Senior Gold Rush, where he shot a final-round 68 to win by one over Lee Trevino.

Bies was a regular on the PGA Tour from 1968 to 1980. His only PGA Tour victory was the 1975 Sammy Davis, Jr.-Greater Hartford Open. He tied for fifth in the 1968 U.S. Open to earn an exemption for 1969.

- Has seven Senior Tour victories: 1995 Raley's Senior Gold Rush; 1992 PaineWebber Invitational; 1989 GTE Kaanapali Classic; 1989 Tradition at Desert Mountain; 1989 Murata Seniors Reunion; 1988 GTE Kaanapali Classic; 1988 Northville Invitational.

- Won the GTE Kaanapali Classic two years in a row (1988, 1989).

- Defeated Lee Trevino by one stroke to win the 1992 PaineWebber Invitational and did the same to win the 1995 Raley's Senior Gold Rush.

- Won back-to-back tournaments in 1989, the Murata Seniors Reunion and The Tradition at Desert Mountain.

- Career Senior PGA Tour earnings: $2,516,291 (30th).

JOHN BLAND

Born: John Louis Bland, September 22, 1945
Birthplace: Johannesburg, South Africa
Ht: 5' 9" **Wt:** 176
Joined Tour: 1995
1996 Money Rank: 3

Bland played in three Senior Tour events in 1995 after he turned 50 in September, winning one of them and finishing in the top ten in the other two. His winning ways continued in 1996. He captured four tournaments, finished in the top ten 17 times out of 35 events entered, and earned $1,357,987.

Bland never played on the PGA Tour. He turned professional in 1969, then went on to win numerous tournaments in his native South Africa following his first professional victory at the 1970 Transvaal Open. He played on the European PGA Tour from 1977 to 1994, where he won two tournaments, the 1983 Benson & Hedges International Open and the 1986 Suze Open at Cannes Mougin. In 1995 he won the London Masters.

Bland also represented South Africa in the 1975 World Cup and played on the 1991-1992 Dunhill Cup teams. He has made 17 holes-in-one in his career and once shot a 59 at a course in Johannesburg.

- Has five Senior Tour victories: 1996 Transamerica Senior Classic; 1996 Long Island Senior

Classic; 1996 Bruno's Memorial Classic; 1996 Puerto Rico Senior Tournament of Champions; 1995 Ralphs Senior Classic.

- He won his first Senior Tour victory, Ralphs Senior Classic, after qualifying on Monday.

- Bland developed a friendly rivalry with Jim Colbert after beating him by one stroke at the Puerto Rico Senior Tournament of Champions and by one at the Transamerica Senior Classic.

- Won South African Order of Merit four times (1977, 1978, 1984, 1986).

- Career Senior PGA Tour earnings: $1,542,853 (58th).

DRIVING ACCURACY

Rank	Name	Rounds	Stat
T1.	Deane Beman	41	79.6
T1.	Calvin Peete	72	79.6
3.	Hale Irwin	74	79.0
4.	Bob Murphy	94	78.4
5.	John Bland	110	78.0
T6.	Bud Allin	105	77.1
T6.	Isao Aoki	81	77.1
T6.	Bob E. Smith	103	77.1
9.	Graham Marsh	88	76.8

BILLY CASPER

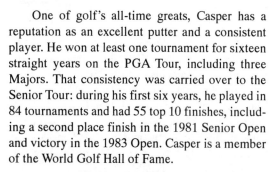

Born: William Earl Casper, Jr., June 24, 1931
Birthplace: San Diego, Cal.
Ht: 5' 11" **Wt:** 215
Joined SeniorTour: 1981
1996 Money Rank:

One of golf's all-time greats, Casper has a reputation as an excellent putter and a consistent player. He won at least one tournament for sixteen straight years on the PGA Tour, including three Majors. That consistency was carried over to the Senior Tour: during his first six years, he played in 84 tournaments and had 55 top 10 finishes, including a second place finish in the 1981 Senior Open and victory in the 1983 Open. Casper is a member of the World Golf Hall of Fame.

A two-time PGA Player of the Year (1966 and 1970), Casper was the second golfer to surpass $1 million in career earnings, and ranks sixth in career Tour victories, with 51. Casper won the Vardon Trophy five times and the Byron Nelson Award on three occasions. His 1959 Open win included only 114 putts, with 31 one-putts and only one three-putt. The 1966 Open, which has been called the most written about of all Opens, featured a late Casper charge in which he made up seven strokes to Arnold Palmer over the final nine holes, then defeated Palmer in a playoff. Casper's 1970 Master's title also came in a playoff over a fellow Hall of Famer, Gene Littler. Fittingly, Casper's Senior Open title also came in a playoff, as he defeated Rod Funseth.

- PGA Tour Victories: 1956 Labatt; 1957 Phoenix, Kentucky Derby; 1958 Bing Crosby, New Orleans, Buick; 1959 U.S. Open, Portland, Lafayette, Mobile; 1960 Portland, Hesperia, Orange County; 1961 Portland; 1962 Doral, Greesboro, "500" Festival, Bakersfield; 1963 Bing Crosby, Insurance City; 1964 Doral, Colonial, Seattle, Almaden; 1965 Bob Hope, Western, Insurance City, Sahara; 1966 San Diego, U.S. Open, Western, "500" Festival; 1967 Canadian, Carling; 1968 Los Angeles, Greensboro, Colonial, "500" Kaiser; 1973 Western, Hartford, 1975 New Orleans.

- PGA Tour Career Earnings: $1,691,584.

- Senior PGA Tour Victories: 1982 Shootout at Jeremy Ranch, Merrill Lynch/Golf Digest Commemorative Pro-Am; 1983 U.S. Senior Open; 1984 Senior PGA Tour Roundup; 1987 Del E, Webb Arizona Classic, Greater Gand Rapids Open; 1988 Vantage at The Dominion, Mazda

Senior TPC; 1989 Transamerica Senior Golf Championship.

- Ryder Cup teams: 1961-1975, and non-playing captain, 1979.

- Career Senior PGA Tour Earnings: $1,625,173

BOB CHARLES

Born: Robert James Charles, March 14, 1936
Birthplace: Carterton, New Zealand
Ht: 6' 1" **Wt:** 170
Joined Tour: 1986
1996 Money Rank: 12

With 23 Senior Tour victories, five PGA Tour wins, and numerous first-place finishes in other events, Charles has been a dominant force wherever he's played. He racked up 14 top ten finishes in 1996, including a repeat win at the Hyatt Regency Maui Kaanapali Classic, to earn $760,179. An exceptionally accurate driver (tied for tenth in 1996), the lanky lefthander finished tenth in overall Senior Tour statistics for 1996.

Charles was the most dominant golfer on the Senior Tour until Lee Trevino joined in 1990. After entering the Senior Tour full-time in 1986, he notched five victories each year in 1988 and 1989, with an amazing 22 top ten finishes each year. He also recorded two three-victory seasons in 1987 and 1993. 1993 was his best year on the Senior Tour, when he earned over $1 million.

In 1993 Charles won the Senior British Open, exactly 30 years after he won the British Open at the age of 26. He won the first of four New Zealand Opens in 1954 when he was 18.

- Has 23 Senior Tour victories: 1996 Maui Kaanapali Classic; 1995 Hyatt Regency Maui Kaanapali Classic; 1993 Doug Sanders Celebrity Classic; 1993 Bell Atlantic Classic; 1993 Quicksilver Clas-

sic; 1992 Raley's Senior Gold Rush; 1992 Transamerica Senior Golf Classic; 1991 GTE Suncoast Classic; 1990 Digital Seniors Classic; 1990 GTE Kaanapali Classic; 1989 GTE Suncoast Classic; 1989 NYNEX/Golf Digest Commemorative; 1989 Digital Seniors Classic; 1989 Sunwest Bank/Charley Pride Classic; 1989 Fairfield Barnett Space Coast Classic; 1988 NYNEX/Golf Digest Commemorative; 1988 Sunwest Bank Charley Pride Classic; 1988 Rancho Murieta Senior Gold Rush; 1988 Vantage Presents Bank One Classic; 1988 Pepsi Senior Challenge; 1987 Vintage Chrysler Invitational; 1987 GTE Classic; 1987 Sunwest Bank/Charley Pride Golf Classic.

- Won 11 unofficial senior events since 1986.

- Won five PGA Tour victories from 1963 to 1974.

- Other victories before turning 50 include the 1963 British Open four New Zealand Opens, three New Zealand PGAs, two Swiss Opens, and six other international events.

- Although golf fans consider Charles a left-hander, he actually does everything right-handed except sports requiring two hands.

- Charles was awarded the prestigious Order of the British Empire (OBE) by the Queen of England in 1972 and was named a Commander of the British Empire (CBE) in 1992.

- Career Senior PGA Tour earnings: $6,621,207 (2nd).

JIM COLBERT

Born: James Joseph Colbert, March 2, 1941
Birthplace: Elizabeth, N.J.
Ht: 5' 9" **Wt:** 165
Joined Tour: 1991
1996 Money Rank: 1

Colbert finished tied for third with a three-under 69 at the season-ending Energizer Senior

Tour Championship to edge Hale Irwin for the 1996 money title. It was a remarkable finish to Colbert's best year on the Senior Tour. He won five tournaments and took home $1,627,890 for the year, about $12,000 more than Irwin.

1996 was the third consecutive year that Colbert won over $1 million on the Senior Tour, and the second year in a row that he topped the senior money list. In 1995 he was named Player of the Year by his peers and the Golf Writers Association, when he had four victories and 17 top ten finishes. Colbert was the Senior Tour's Rookie of the Year in 1991. He won his first Senior Major in 1993 when he defeated Raymond Floyd by one shot at the Ford Senior Players Championship in Dearborn, Michigan. He notched his second major victory at the 1995 Energizer Senior Tour Championship.

Colbert joined the PGA Tour in 1966 and had seven victories in official PGA events. His best year on the PGA Tour was 1983, when he won two events, including the Colonial National Invitational.

- Has 18 Senior Tour victories: 1996 Raley's Gold Rush Classic; 1996 Vantage Senior Championship; 1996 Nationwide Championship; 1996 Las Vegas Classic; 1996 Toshiba Classic; 1995 Energizer Senior Tour Championship; 1995 Bell Atlantic Classic; 1995 Las Vegas Senior Classic; 1995 Senior Tournament of Champions; 1994 Southwestern Bell Classic; 1994 Kroger Senior Classic; 1993 Ford Senior Players Championship; 1993 Royal Caribbean Classic; 1992 Vantage Championship; 1992 GTE Suncoast Classic; 1991 First Development Kaanapali Classic; 1991 Vantage Championship; 1991 Southwestern Bell Classic.

- Won seven PGA Tour events.

- Named Senior Tour Rookie of the Year in 1991 and Player of the Year in 1995.

- Won the Arnold Palmer Award in 1995 and 1996 for most official earnings in a season.

- Won his first tournament in his adopted home-town when he took the 1995 Las Vegas Senior Classic.

- Spent several years as a color analyst for ESPN.

- Career Senior PGA Tour earnings: $6,570,797 (3rd).

FRANK CONNER

Born: Frank Joseph Conner, January 11, 1946
Birthplace: Vienna, Austria
Ht: 5' 10" **Wt:** 195
Joined Tour: 1996
1996 Money Rank: 20

Conner qualified the hard way for an exemption in 1996, his rookie year on the Senior Tour, by finishing in the top eight in the Senior PGA Tour National Qualifying Championship. He entered 35 Senior Tour events in 1996 and finished in the top ten six times, earning $561,465 and qualifying for a 1997 exemption.

Conner turned professional at the age of 26, then joined the PGA Tour in 1975. He played on the Nike Tour from 1990 through 1995, where he won two events in 1991 and finished in the top ten three times in 1995.

An avid tennis player, Conner is one of only two men to have played in the U.S. Open in both golf and tennis.

- Played in 26 Nike Tour events in 1995 and had three top ten finishes.

- Won two Nike Tour events in 1991, the Knoxville Open and the Tulsa Open.

- Qualified for a 1996 Senior Tour exemption by shooting 72-66-65-71 in the 1995 National Qualifying Tournament Finals.

- Placed 20th on the money list in his rookie year

on the Senior Tour. Tied for tenth in the Emerald Coast Classic and tied for sixth at the Energizer Senior Tour Championship to win nearly $95,000 in the last two events of the 1996 season.

- Career Senior PGA Tour earnings: $561,465 (93rd).

CHARLES COODY

Born: Billy Charles Coody, July 13, 1937
Birthplace: Stamford, Tex.
Ht: 6' 2" **Wt:** 195
Joined Tour: 1987
1996 Money Rank: 42

In 1996, his tenth year on the Senior Tour, Coody carded his fifth Senior Tour victory at the inaugural du Maurier Champions, also known as the Canadian Senior Open. The tall Texan entered 29 Senior Tour events in 1996 and had three top ten finishes, including his victory, to earn $328,054. Look for him to win some Super Senior events in 1997 after he turns 60 in July.

Coody's best years on the Senior Tour were 1990, when he won $762,901 (3rd), and 1991, when he won the NYNEX Commemorative and the Transamerica Senior Golf Championship. He had 14 top ten finishes in 1989 and 1990, and 13 in 1991. His 1996 victory was his first since 1991.

Coody had an outstanding amateur career, qualifying for the 1960 and 1961 U.S. Opens as an amateur and advancing to the semifinals of the 1962 U.S Amateur. He turned professional in 1963 and joined the PGA Tour that same year. The highlight of his three PGA Tour victories has to be the 1971 Masters Tournament, where he birdied two of the final four holes to beat Jack Nicklaus and Johnny Miller.

- Has five Senior Tour victories: 1996 du Maurier Champions (Canadian Senior Open); 1991 NYNEX Commemorative; 1991 Transamerica

Senior Golf Championship; 1990 Vantage Championship; 1989 General Tire Las Vegas Classic.

- Won the 1971 Masters Tournament and two other PGA Tour events.

- Won the 1971 World Series of Golf.

- Qualified for the U.S. open twice as an amateur (1960, 1961).

- Career Senior PGA Tour earnings: $3,183,235 (22nd).

BRUCE CRAMPTON

Born: Bruce Sidney Crampton, September 28, 1935
Birthplace: Sydney, Australia
Ht: 5' 9" **Wt:** 178
Joined Tour: 1986
1996 Money Rank: 43

After struggling through two difficult years in 1994 and 1995, the Australian Super Senior came back in 1996 to record two top ten finishes and earn $322,224. Crampton lived up to his "iron-man" reputation again by entering 35 Senior Tour events in 1996.

Crampton made quite a splash on the Senior Tour when he cruised to seven victories in 1986, his first full season on the Tour. He had 23 top ten finishes out of 27 events entered that year and finished at the top of the money list with $454,299 in earnings. He finished in the top 30 on the money list for eight consecutive years (1986-1993). He won four tournaments in 1987 and two each in 1988, 1989, and 1990.

Although he never won a major on the PGA Tour, he has 14 PGA Tour victories to his credit and earnings of $1,369,938. His first win in the

AVERAGE ROUNDS PERDRIVE

Rank	Name	Rounds	Stat
1.	Terry Dill	102	287.2
2.	John Jacobs	107	286.7
3.	Jay Sigel	100	283.4
4.	Jim Dent	106	277.3
5.	Tom Weiskopf	59	277.2
6.	David Graham	59	276.5
7.	DeWitt Weaver	95	275.5
8.	Jim Wilkinson	104	272.2
9.	Bruce Summerhays	119	272.1
10.	Brian Barnes	69	271.3

United States was the 1961 Milwaukee Open. In 1956 he won the Australian Open at the age of 20.

• Has 19 Senior Tour victories: 1992 GTE West Classic; 1991 Infiniti Senior Tournament of Champions; 1990 PaineWebber Invitational; 1990 Gatlin Brothers Southwest Senior Classic; 1989 MONY Arizona Classic; 1989 Ameritech Senior Open; 1988 United Hospitals Classic; 1988 GTE Northwest Classic; 1987 Vantage Presents Bank One Seniors; 1987 MONY Syracuse Seniors Classic; 1987 Greenbrier/American Express Championship; 1987 Denver Champions of Golf; 1986 Shearson Lehman Brothers Seniors; 1986 Las Vegas Senior Classic; 1986 Pepsi Senior Challenge; 1986 PaineWebber World Seniors Invitational; 1986 GTE Northwest Classic; 1986 MONY Syracuse Senior Classic; 1986 Benson & Hedges Invitational at The Dominion.

• Won 17 PGA Tour events between 1961 and 1975, including three in 1965 and four in 1973.

• Retired from the PGA Tour in 1977.

• Had seven victories in his rookie year on the Senior Tour (1986).

• Known as an "ironman" for number of Senior Tour events entered each year.

• Career Senior PGA Tour earnings: $4,000,892 (12th).

JIM DENT

Born: James Lacey Dent, May 9, 1939

Birthplace: Augusta, Ga.

Ht: 6' 3" **Wt:** 224

Joined Tour: 14

1996 Money Rank: 1989

Dent had 11 top ten finishes in 1996 and took home $707,655 , a better-than-average year for him. He won $120,000 and a victory at the Bank of Boston Senior Classic. The powerful Dent is one of the Senior Tour's longest drivers with a 277.3-yard average (4th) in 1996.

Dent has ranked among the top 20 money winners every year since he joined the Senior Tour in 1989, when he had two victories and 12 top ten finishes in his rookie year. He won four tournaments the next year and earned $693,214 (6th), but his best earnings year was 1994, when he took home $950,891 (7th).

Dent grew up in Augusta, Georgia, where he caddied at both the Augusta National Golf Club and the Augusta Country Club. He joined the PGA Tour in 1970, where his best finish was tied for second behind Jack Nicklaus in the 1972 Walt Disney World Classic. He won three consecutive Florida PGA titles (1976-78) and was one of the PGA Tour's longest drivers in the 1970s.

• Has 10 Senior Tour victories: 1996 Bank of Boston Senior Classic; 1995 BellSouth Senior Classic; 1994 Bruno's Memorial Classic; 1992 Newport Cup; 1990 Vantage at The Dominion; 1990 MONY Syracuse Senior Classic; 1990 Kroger Senior Classic; 1990 Crestar Classic; 1989 MONY Syracuse Senior Classic; 1989 Newport Cup.

• Was Senior Tour's longest driver from 1989 through 1994.

• Earned $565,245 on the PGA Tour without an official victory.

• Won the Florida PGA Championship three consecutive years (1976-78).

- Nicknamed "Big Boy" by other pros for his size and power.
- Career Senior PGA Tour earnings: $4,901,863 (9th).

DALE DOUGLASS

Born: Dale Dwight Douglass, March 5, 1936
Birthplace: Wewoka, Okla.
Ht: 6' 2" **Wt:** 160
Joined Tour: 1986
1996 Money Rank: 45

After falling out of the top 31 money winners in 1995 for the first time since he joined the Senior Tour in 1986, Douglass came back with his first victory in three years when he took the 1996 Bell Atlantic Classic on the third playoff hole. He finished the year with $318,507 and two top ten finishes including his victory.

Douglass had an outstanding rookie year on the Senior Tour in 1986, winning four tournaments, including the U.S. Senior Open. He notched 16 top ten finishes out of 23 events entered and earned $309,760 (3rd). His best earnings year was 1992, when he had two victories, 16 top ten finishes, and earnings of $694,564 (6th).

Douglass joined the PGA Tour in 1963 and won his first PGA tournament in 1969, the Azalea Open Invitational. He was also a member of the Ryder Cup team that year.

- Has 11 Senior Tour victories: 1996 Bell Atlantic Classic; 1993 Ralphs Senior Classic; 1992 NYNEX Commemorative; 1992 Ameritech Senior Open; 1991 Showdown Classic; 1990 Bell Atlantic Classic; 1988 GTE Suncoast Classic; 1986 Vintage Invitational; 1986 Johnny Mathis Senior Classic; 1986 U.S. Senior Open; 1986 Fairfield-Barnett Senior Classic.

- Won three PGA Tour events in 1969-70.
- Douglass and Charles Coody won the unofficial Liberty Mutual Legends of Golf in 1990 and 1994.
- Has won one Senior Major (1986 U.S. Senior Open) and finished second or tied for second in four other major senior tournaments (1994 The Tradition, 1987 PGA Seniors' Championship, 1990 and 1992 Energizer Senior Tour Championship).
- Shot a final-round 61 at the 1994 Ralphs Senior Classic to become the fourth player to shoot the Senior Tour's lowest score.
- Won the inaugural Merrill Lynch Shoot-Out Championship (unofficial event) in 1989.
- Served on the Senior PGA Tour Division Board as a Player Director, 1990-1994.
- Career Senior PGA Tour earnings: $4,773,830 (10th).

VICENTE FERNANDEZ

Born: Vicente Fernandez, April 5, 1946
Birthplace: Corrientes, Argentina
Ht: 5' 7" **Wt:** unknown
Joined Tour: 1996
1996 Money Rank: 20

After playing regularly on the European PGA Tour, Fernandez joined the Senior Tour in 1996 when he turned 50 in April. He went on to garner ten top ten finishes out of the 20 events he entered, including a victory in the Burnet Senior Classic worth $187,500. His season earnings of $605,251 on the Senior Tour earned him an exemption for 1997.

Fernandez is an experienced international professional. In 1995 he finished fourth in the

British Masters and placed 71st in the Order of Merit that year. He has five European PGA Tour victories to his credit. He won the Argentine Open eight times between 1968 and 1990 and the Brazil Open three times.

- Has one Senior Tour victory: 1996 Burnet Senior Classic.

- Has five European PGA Tour victories: 1992 Murphy's English Open; 1990 Tenerife Open; 1979 Colgate PGA Championship; 1975 Benson & Hedges Festival; 1970 Dutch Open.

- Has 12 other victories to his credit: 1990 Argentine Open; 1987 Argentine Open; 1986 Argentine Open; 1985 Argentine Open; 1984 Brazil Open, Argentine Open; 1983 Brazil Open; 1981 Argentine Open; 1977 Brazil Open; 1972 Marcaibo Open; 1969 Argentine Open; 1968 Argentine Open

- Career Senior PGA Tour earnings: $605,251 (90th).

JIM FERREE

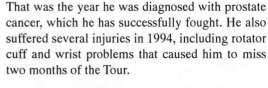

Born: Purvis Jennings Ferree, Jr., June 10, 1931
Birthplace: Pine Bluff, N.C.
Ht: 5' 9" **Wt:** 165
Joined Tour: 1981
1996 Money Rank: 90

Super Senior Ferree has had better years on the Senior Tour than 1996, when he entered only 18 events and won just $47,124. His best year was 1993, when he won nine Super Senior titles and $255,550 (unofficial earnings), the most money won by someone 60 or over in one year. He continued to play well in 1994 and 1995, finishing eighth on the Super Senior money list in 1994 with $152,000 and eighth again in 1995 with $169,410.

Ferree was just 15 days shy of his 60th birthday when he won the 1991 Bell Atlantic Classic.

That was the year he was diagnosed with prostate cancer, which he has successfully fought. He also suffered several injuries in 1994, including rotator cuff and wrist problems that caused him to miss two months of the Tour.

Ferree played full-time on the PGA Tour from 1956 to 1966, with one victory in the 1958 Vancouver Open. He also had three victories on the Caribbean Tour in the early 1960s.

- Has two Senior Tour victories: 1991 Bell Atlantic Classic; 1986 Greater Grand Rapids Open.

- Joined Senior Tour in 1981 after turning 50 in June.

- Finished among the top 31 money winners from 1983 to 1989 and again in 1991 and 1993.

- Received the Hilton Bounceback Award from his fellow professionals in 1993.

- Received the Mathews Foundation Man of the Year Award for his willingness to go public with his fight against prostate cancer.

- Captain/player of the 1993 U.S. DuPont Cup team.

- Known as a sharp dresser on the golf course, where he sports plus-fours and a Hogan-style cap.

- Career Senior PGA Tour earnings: $2,343,487 (34th).

RAYMOND FLOYD

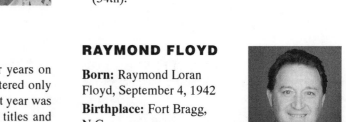

Born: Raymond Loran Floyd, September 4, 1942
Birthplace: Fort Bragg, N.C.
Ht: 6' 1" **Wt:** 200
Joined Tour: 1992
1996 Money Rank: 8

1996 marked the third year in a row that Floyd won more than $1 million in official Senior Tour events. Add to that total $240,000 that he won in

> At the 1987 T.P.C., Ray Floyd's caddie left his golf bag unattended in the fairway. Floyd hit a drive into his own bag and was penalized two strokes.

the 1996 Senior Skins Game, not to mention his winnings from the 1996 Senior Slam, a two-day event that brings together the previous year's winners of the Senior Tour's four major championships. He added another senior major to his list of victories when he won the 1996 Ford Senior Players Championship.

Floyd's early September birthday allowed him to compete in seven Senior Tour events toward the end of 1992 and finish with $436,991 (14th) in earnings. Since then he's finished among the top ten money winners on the Senior Tour every year. Except for the U.S. Senior Open, he's won every major Senior Tour tournament, including The Tradition in 1994 and the 1995 PGA Seniors' Championship. He also won the 1992 and 1994 Energizer Senior Tour Championship.

Floyd amassed 22 PGA Tour victories over a span of 30 years (1963-1992) and is the only other player in PGA history beside Sam Snead to have won a PGA Tour event in each of four decades. His major tournament victories include the 1969 and 1982 PGA Championships, the 1976 Masters Tournament, and the 1986 U.S. Open. He was also a three-time winner at Doral (1980, 1981, and 1992).

- Has 13 Senior Tour victories: 1996 Ford Senior Players Championship; 1995 PGA Seniors Championship; 1995 Burnet Senior Classic; 1995 Emerald Coast Classic; 1994 The Tradition; 1994 Las Vegas Senior Classic; 1994 Cadillac NFL Golf Classic; 1994 Golf Magazine Senior Tour Championship; 1993 Gulfstream Aerospace Invitational; 1993 Northville Long Island Classic; 1992 GTE North Classic; 1992 Ralphs Senior Classic; 1992 Senior Tour Championship.

- Won 22 official PGA Tour events between 1963 and 1992.

- Won three straight Senior Skins Games (1994-96) to earn $960,000 (unoffical event).

- In 1992 became the first player to win on both the Senior PGA Tour and the regular PGA Tour in the same year when he won the PGA's Doral-Ryder Open and then the Senior's GTE North Classic.

- Career Senior PGA Tour earnings: $4,995,515 (8th).

AL GEIBERGER

Born: Allen Lee Geiberger, September 1, 1937
Birthplace: Red Bluff, Cal.
Ht: 6' 2" **Wt:** 185
Joined Tour: 1987
1996 Money Rank: 36

Geiberger ended his three-year victory drought by winning the 1996 Greater Naples IntelliNet Challenge, beating Isao Aoki by one stroke after a birdie on the 17th hole on Sunday. It was his tenth Senior Tour victory and capped his comeback from a torn rotator cuff in 1994. He had three other top ten finishes in 1996 and earned $372,301.

The tall, lanky Geiberger joined the Senior Tour toward the end of 1987 and finished his rookie year with three wins and seven top ten finishes out of only ten events entered. He was among the top ten money winners for his first three years on the Senior Tour and among the top twenty for the next four years.

Geiberger joined the PGA Tour in 1960 and has 11 PGA Tour victories to his credit, including the 1966 PGA Championship. He earned the nickname, "Mr. 59," when he shot the first-ever sub-60 round in an official PGA Tour event to win the Danny Thomas-Memphis Classic in 1977. He carded 11 birdies and one eagle to shoot a 59 that day.

- Has 10 Senior Tour victories: 1996 Greater Naples IntelliNet Challenge; 1993 Infiniti Tournament of Champions; 1993 GTE West Classic; 1992 Infiniti Tournament of Champions; 1991 Kroger Senior Classic; 1989 GTE Northwest Classic; 1988 Pointe/Del E. Webb Arizona Classic; 1987 Vantage Championship; 1987 Hilton Head Seniors International; 1987 Las Vegas Senior Classic.

- Won 11 official PGA Tour Events, including the 1966 PGA Championship.

- Member of the 1967 and 1975 Ryder Cup teams.

- Won the unofficial Liberty Mutual Legends of Golf with Harold Henning in 1989.

- Was known for winning on tough courses on the PGA Tour, including the Firestone Country Club, the Colonial Country Club, and Butler National.

- Was 1954 National Jaycee Champion.

- Always carries a peanut butter sandwich in his bag for snacking.

- Career Senior PGA Tour earnings: $3,843,368 (14th).

GIBBY GILBERT

Born: C.L. Gilbert, Jr., January 14, 1941

Birthplace: Chattanooga, Tenn.

Ht: 5' 9" **Wt:** 175

Joined Tour: 1991

1996 Money Rank: 30

Gilbert ended a three-year victory drought when he won the inaugural Boone Valley Classic in 1996, beating Hale Irwin on the first playoff hole after making birdie on the 18th. The win was worth $180,000, helping to make 1996 a good year for Gilbert, who had four top ten finishes and earnings of $446,307.

Gibby joined the Senior Tour in 1991 and was among the top 20 money winners for his first three years on the Tour. His first two victories came in 1992 with back-to-back wins at the Southwestern Bell Classic and the Kroger Senior Classic. He won three tournaments that year and had eight top ten finishes to earn $603,630 (8th). His best earnings year was 1993, when he had one victory, ten top ten finishes, and earnings of $661,378 (11th).

Gilbert was a regular on the PGA Tour from 1967 to 1985, where he won two tournaments and earned more than $1 million. He earned exemptions for 14 of his years on the PGA Tour, and in 1980 finished tied for second behind Seve Ballesteros in the Masters Tournament.

- Has five Senior Tour victories: 1996 Boone Valley Classic; 1993 Las Vegas Senior Classic; 1992 Southwestern Bell Classic; 1992 Kroger Senior Classic; 1992 First of America Classic.

- Won two consecutive tournaments in 1992, the Southwestern Bell Classic and the Kroger Senior Classic.

- Led the 1992 Southwestern Bell Classic after shooting a 62 in the first round, which turned out to be the lowest round of the year on the Senior Tour. His victory margin of nine strokes was the largest 54-hole margin ever on the Senior Tour, and his 54-hole score of 193 equaled a Senior Tour numerical record.

- With a combined 3-1 record, Gilbert does well in playoffs. On the PGA Tour he defeated Bruce Crampton to win the 1970 Houston Champions International. On the Senior Tour he beat J.C. Snead to take the 1992 Kroger Senior Classic, and he defeated Hale Irwin on the first playoff hole to win the 1996 Boone Valley Classic.

- Won the 1988, 1989, and 1990 Tennessee Opens after retiring from the PGA Tour.

- Career Senior PGA Tour earnings: $2,817,655 (26th).

LARRY GILBERT

Born: Lawrence Allen Gilbert, November 19, 1942
Birthplace: Fort Knox, Ken.
Ht: 6' 0" **Wt:** 192
Joined Tour: 1993
1996 Money Rank: 26

Gilbert hasn't won a Senior Tour event since he scored two victories in 1994, but his steady play and good showings in major tournaments earned him $480,975 in 1996. He had nine top ten finishes out of 32 events entered, including a tie for fourth at the Cadillac NFL Golf Classic.

Gilbert earned an exemption for the 1993 Senior Tour as low professional at the 1992 Senior Tour National Qualifying Tournament with rounds of 70-68-66-72. He had 13 top ten finishes in his rookie year and has been among the top 31 money winners every year through 1996. His only Senior Tour victories came in 1994, when he won a career-high $848,544 (9th). He experienced back problems in 1995 and finished the year with a one-stroke higher average than the previous year.

Gilbert joined the PGA Tour in 1972, but his best finish there was 25th in the 1982 World Series of Golf. He did rather well as a club professional, winning the PGA Club Professional Championship in 1981, 1982, and 1991.

- Has two Senior Tour victories: 1994 Dallas Reunion Pro-Am; 1994 Vantage Championship.

- $225,000 paycheck for winning the 1994 Vantage Championship was the biggest of his career.

- Won ten Kentucky PGA Championships, three Kentucky Opens, one Tennessee Open, and one Tennessee PGA Championship.

- Career Senior PGA Tour earnings: $2,335,371 (35th).

HAROLD HENNING

Born: Harold Ralph Henning, October 3, 1934
Birthplace: Johannesburg, South Africa
Ht: 6' 0" **Wt:** 175
Joined Tour: 1984
1996 Money Rank: 68

The South African Super Senior is still competitive among the over-60 crowd on the Senior Tour and taking home unofficial Super Senior paychecks, even though he won only $158,708 in official earnings in 1996 with two top ten finishes overall. In 1995 he won the $15,000 first-place money in four Super Senior competitions.

Henning joined the Senior Tour at the end of the 1984 season and improved steadily throughout the 1980s, earning a career-high $453,163 (6th) in 1989 with 18 top ten finishes. His first Senior Tour victory came in the 1985 Seiko/Tucson Match Play Championship, where he beat Dan Sikes 4-3 in the final round.

Henning first came to the United States in 1954 to compete professionally, arriving on the same flight as another famous South African, Gary Player. He played intermittently on the PGA Tour and won one event, the 1966 Texas Open Invitational. He has more than 50 international titles to his credit, including victories in Australia, New Zealand, Germany, Italy, Denmark, and Switzerland.

- Has three Senior Tour victories: 1991 First of America Classic; 1988 GTE Classic; 1985 Seiko/Tucson Match Play Championship.

- Ranked among the top 20 money winners in each of his first seven years on the Senior Tour (1985-1991).

- Teamed with Al Geiberger to win the 1989 Liberty Mutual Legends of Golf (unofficial event) and also won the same event in 1993, the only year it was a solo competition.

- Career Senior PGA Tour earnings: $3,337,227 (20th).

MIKE HILL

Born: Michael Joseph Hill, January 27, 1939

Birthplace: Jackson, Mich.

Ht: 5' 10" **Wt:** 170

Joined Tour: 1989

1996 Money Rank: 22

After winning the 1996 Bank One Classic, Hill finished 1996 with strong showings at the Emerald Coast Classic, where he tied for second with three others after Lee Trevino won a five-man playoff, and the Energizer Senior Tour Championship (tied for 10th). He had seven top ten finishes out of only 19 events entered and earned $528,130.

Hill joined the Senior Tour in 1989 and won his first Senior Tour event a year later—the 1990 GTE Suncoast Classic. He won five tournaments that year and again in 1991, when he was the Senior Tour's leading money winner with $1,065,657 in earnings. He had more than 20 top ten finishes three years in a row (1990-1992) and has a seven-year winning streak in progress of at least one victory every year since 1990.

Hill joined the PGA Tour in 1968 and has three PGA Tour victories to his credit, including the 1970 Doral-Eastern Open Invitational.

- Has 18 Senior Tour victories: 1996 Bank One Classic; 1995 Kroger Senior Classic; 1994 IntelliNet Challenge; 1993 Better Homes & Gardens Real Estate Challenge; 1993 PaineWebber Invitational; 1992 Vintage ARCO Invitational; 1992 Doug Sanders Kingwood Celebrity Classic; 1992 Digital Senior Classic; 1991 Doug Sanders Kingwood Celebrity Classic; 1991 Ameritech Senior Open; 1991 GTE Northwest Classic; 1991 Nationwide Championship; 1991 New York Life Champions; 1990 GTE Suncoast Classic; 1990 GTE North Classic; 1990 Fairfield Barnett Space Coast Classic; 1990 Security Pacific Senior Classic; 1990 New York Life Champions.

- Teamed with Lee Trevino to win the Liberty Mutual Legends of Golf (unofficial event) an unprecedented four times, 1991, 1992, 1995, and 1996.

- Has three PGA Tour victories: 1977 Ohio Kings Island Open; 1972 San Antonio Texas Open; 1970 Doral-Eastern Open Invitational.

- Mike's younger brother Dave also plays on the Senior Tour.

- Won the Arnold Palmer Award in 1991 for most earnings in a single season when he became the second Senior Tour player to top $1 million in a single season. Career Senior PGA Tour earnings: $5,658,265 (6th).

SIMON HOBDAY

Born: Simon Hobday, June 23, 1940

Birthplace: Mareking, South Africa

Ht: 5' 11" **Wt:** 170

Joined Tour: 1991

1996 Money Rank: 34

Hobday's winless 1996 season ended a three-year streak for the South African. For the first time since he joined the Senior Tour in 1991 he also failed to finish among the top 31 money winners. He had six top ten finishes and earned $388,217, his lowest earnings since his rookie year.

Hobday posted 28 top ten finishes on the Senior Tour before winning his first Senior tournament, the 1993 Kroger Senior Classic. His most notable win on the Senior Tour was the 1994 Senior Open, where he hung on to win despite shooting a final-round 75. Hobday also captured the season-ending Senior Tour Championship in 1993.

Hobday played on the European PGA Tour from 1969 to 1986, where he had two career wins. He also played on South Africa's Safari circuit, where he won four events.

- Has five Senior Tour victories: 1995 Brickyard Crossing Senior Golf Championship; 1994 U.S. Senior Open; 1994 GTE Northwest Classic; 1993 Kroger Senior Classic; 1993 Hyatt Senior Tour Championship.

- Won six international tournaments, including the 1971 South African Open, the 1976 German Open, the 1976 and 1977 Rhodesian Opens, the 1979 Madrid Open, and the 1985 TrustBank Tournament.

- His choice of clothes and casual appearance earned him the nickname "Scruffy" from his Senior Tour colleagues.

- Career Senior PGA Tour earnings: $2,905,280 (25th).

HALE IRWIN

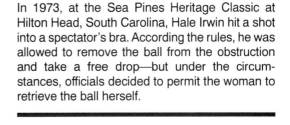

Born: Hale Irwin, June 3, 1945

Birthplace: Joplin, Mo.

Ht: 6' 0" **Wt:** 180

Joined Tour: 1995

1996 Money Rank: 2

Irwin's duel with Jim Colbert for the 1996 money title brought added drama to the end of the 1996 season. Irwin went into the Senior Tour's final event with a $66,000 lead for the top money spot. When the Energizer Tour Championship was over, Irwin had tied for tenth and lost the money title to Jim Colbert by about $12,000. Nonetheless, Irwin had an outstanding year in his first full season on the Senior Tour, with 21 top ten finishes in

In 1973, at the Sea Pines Heritage Classic at Hilton Head, South Carolina, Hale Irwin hit a shot into a spectator's bra. According the rules, he was allowed to remove the ball from the obstruction and take a free drop—but under the circumstances, officials decided to permit the woman to retrieve the ball herself.

the 23 Senior Tour events he entered, including victories at the PGA Seniors' Championship and the American Express Invitational.

Irwin joined the Senior Tour midway in 1995, after he turned 50 in June. He entered 12 events that year, finished in the top ten eleven times, ranked tenth on the money list, and won two tournaments to earn Rookie of the Year honors. His first Senior Tour victory, the Ameritech Senior Open, came in only his fifth start. He also played in 14 official PGA Tour events in 1995 and had two top ten finishes.

Irwin was a force to be reckoned with during his 27-year PGA Tour career, especially during the 1970s when he won 11 of his 20 PGA Tour titles. From 1975 through 1978 he played in 86 tournaments without missing a cut, the third-longest streak in PGA history. He is a three-time U.S. Open champion, winning at Winged Foot (1974), Inverness (1979), and Medinah (1990).

- Has four Senior Tour victories: 1996 American Express Invitational; 1996 PGA Senior's Championship; 1995 Ameritech Senior Open; 1995 The Vantage Championship.

- Led the 1996 Senior Tour in overall statistics, birdies (4.05 average per round), scoring (69.47 average), and greens in regulation.

- His first and last official tour PGA Tour wins were at the MCI Heritage Classic—in 1971 (when it was known as the Sea Pines Heritage Classic) and in 1994.

- Became the oldest person to win the U.S. Open at age 45 in 1990.

- Outstanding in both golf and football at the University of Colorado, where he was the 1967 NCAA Champion in golf and a two-time Big Eight selection as a football defensive back.

- Played on five Ryder Cup teams (1975, 1977, 1979, 1981, 1991).

- Represented the United States twice in the World Cup (1974, 1979) and earned the individual title in the 1979 World Cup.

- Captained the U.S. team to victory in the inaugural President's Cup Match in 1994.

- Career Senior PGA Tour earnings: $2,414,944 (31st).

- Won the 1995 Senior Series Gulfport Open (unofficial event).

- Has four international victories: 1991 Republic of China Open; 1986 Singapore Rolex Open; 1984 Dunlop International; 1984 Republic of China Open.

- Won over 100 Long Drive Championships in his career.

- John's brother Tommy Jacobs is a veteran on the PGA Tour.

- Career Senior PGA Tour earnings: $522,866 (96th).

JOHN JACOBS

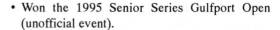

Born: John Alexander Jacobs, March 18, 1945
Birthplace: Los Angeles, Cal.
Ht: 6' 3" **Wt:** 220
Joined Tour: 1996
1996 Money Rank: 23

In his first full year on the Senior Tour the long-hitting Jacobs carded eight top ten finishes in 34 events to earn $510,263. His best finish was second at the Brickyard Crossing Championship, good for $66,000 and his biggest paycheck on the Senior Tour. He was second to Terry Dill on the Senior Tour in driving distance with an average of 286.7 yards.

Jacobs played in three 1995 Senior Tour events through Monday qualifying. He qualified for the 1996 Senior Tour by finishing tied for second in the Senior Tour National Qualifying Tournament with rounds of 67-70-68-67.

Jacobs played on the PGA Tour from 1968 though 1980 without scoring a victory. During the 1980s he played extensively in Asia and in 1984 became the first American to win the Asian Golf Circuit Order of Merit.

DON JANUARY

Born: Donald Ray January, November 20, 1929
Birthplace: Plainview, Tex.
Ht: 6' 0" **Wt:** 175
Joined Tour: 1980
1996 Money Rank: 77

January played in only 17 events in 1996, his 17th year on the Senior Tour. His best finish was a tie for eighth at the Vantage Championship, worth $45,000 in official earnings. Starting with the 1990 season, January was eligible to compete with the Super Seniors (age 60 and over). He has won a record 33 Super Senior competitions through the end of the 1995 season.

One of the original members of the Senior Tour Players Advisory Council, Janaury won the very first Senior Tour event, the 1980 Atlantic City Senior International. He has 22 Senior Tour victories to his credit, his last one the 1987 MONY Senior Tournament of Champions.

January joined the PGA Tour in 1956 and won the Dallas Centennial Open that year. He amassed 10 PGA Tour victories in his 20+ years on the PGA Tour, including the 1967 PGA Championship. He was runner-up in the 1960 PGA.

- Has 22 Senior Tour victories: 1987 MONY Senior Tournament of Champions; 1986 Senior Players Reunion Pro-Am; 1986 Greenbrier/American Express Championship; 1986 Seiko/Tucson Match Play Championship; 1985 Senior Tour Roundup; 1985 The Dominion Seniors; 1985 United Hospitals Senior Golf Championship; 1985 Greenbrier/American Express Championship; 1984 Vintage Invitational; 1984 du Maurier Champions; 1984 Digital Middlesex Classic; 1983 Gatlin Brothers Senior Classic; 1983 Peter Jackson Champions; 1983 Marlboro Classic; 1983 Denver Post Champions; 1983 Citizens Union Senior Classic; 1983 Suntree Seniors Classic; 1982 Michelob Classic; 1982 PGA Seniors Championship; 1981 Michelob-Egypt Temple; 1981 Eureka Federal Savings; 1980 Atlantic City Senior International.

- First player to surpass the $1 million mark in career Senior Tour earnings (August 4, 1985).

- Won first Senior Tour event, the 1980 Atlantic City Senior International.

- Holds the record for most wins (33) in Super Senior competitions.

- Topped the Senior Tour money list in 1983 with $237,571 in official earnings, then repeated in 1984 with $328,597.

- Career Senior PGA Tour earnings: $3,016,549 (24th).

JACK KIEFER

Born: Leo Charles Kiefer, January 1, 1940

Birthplace: Columbia, Penn.

Ht: 5' 10" **Wt:** 175

Joined Tour: 1991

1996 Money Rank: 17

1996 was former club pro Kiefer's best year on the Senior Tour since he joined in 1990. He entered a workmanlike 34 events and had eight top ten fin-

ishes to earn $662,697. He finished third or tied for third four times and picked up his biggest paycheck of the season for $81,000 when he tied for fourth at the Ford Senior Players Championship. Kiefer is one of the Tour's longer and more accurate drivers.

Kiefer's Senior career began by qualifying on Mondays for five Senior Tour events in 1990, then earned his exemption at the National Qualifying Finals. His only Senior Tour victory came in the 1994 Ralphs Senior Classic in Los Angeles, when he shot a 63 on Sunday. Prior to 1996 his best earnings year was 1994, when he had nine top ten finishes and earned $532,467 (21st). He entered 37 events in 1995 but lost the "ironman" title to John Paul Cain, who played three more rounds in the same number of events.

Kiefer spent his entire career as a club pro until he joined the Senior Tour. His wife Jan is also a golf professional.

- Has one Senior Tour victory: 1994 Ralphs Senior Classic.

- Took up golf in the early 1960s after trying out for the Detroit Tigers baseball team in 1961.

- Career Senior PGA Tour earnings: $2,346,886 (33rd).

LARRY LAORETTI

Born: Larry Phillip Laoretti, July 11, 1939
Birthplace: Mahopac, NY
Ht: 5' 11" **Wt:** 185
Exempt Status: Top 31 on All-Time Senior Tour Money List (otherwise not exempt)

After finishing 29th on the money list in 1995, Laoretti had an off year in 1996. He scored only one top ten finish out of 35 events entered in 1996 and earned $231,541 (58th) for the year. His best finish was a tie for eighth at the Pittsburgh Senior Classic.

Since joining the Senior Tour full-time in 1990, Laoretti has only one Senior Tour victory, but it was a major. He won the 1992 U.S. Senior Open by four strokes over Jim Colbert, shooting a bogie-free 68 on Sunday. 1992 was also his best year on the Senior Tour, with nine top ten finishes and earnings of $444,385 (13th).

Rarely seen without his trademark cigar, Laoretti never played on the PGA Tour. He spent 28 years as a club professional before leaving Indian Creek Country Club in Jupiter, Florida to prepare for the Senior Tour. He usually travels in a large motorhome and stays at campgrounds across the country.

- Has one Senior Tour victory: 1992 U.S. Senior Open.

- Has played in 30 or more events every year he's been on the Senior Tour.

- Career Senior PGA Tour earnings: $2,012,600 (43rd).

GENE LITTLER

Born: Gene Alec Littler, July 21, 1930
Birthplace: San Diego, Cal.
Ht: 5' 9" **Wt:** 160

Joined Tour: 1954
1996 Money Rank: 54

Littler has enjoyed a long career in golf, in which he has found success and made important contributions on all levels, including helping to found the Senior Tour. He was the 1953 U.S. Amateur champion, won his first pro tournament in 1954 as an amateur, then turned pro with much fanfare and was hailed as the next great golfing superstar. He finished second in the 1954 U.S. Open, missing a 7-foot putt on the final hole that would have put him in a playoff with Ed Furgol. Littler won three tournaments in 1955, four more in 1956, and became known as "Gene the Machine" for his consistent, fluid swing. Littler was the U.S. Open champion in 1961 and was involved in two thrilling playoffs in Majors, finishing runner up to Billy Casper in the 1970 Masters and to Lanny Wadkins in the 1977 PGA Championship.

In 1972, Littler underwent surgery for cancer, then recovered and returned to the Tour in 1973, when he won the Bobby Jones and Ben Hogan awards for contributions to golf and for his courageous comeback. Littler joined the Senior Tour in 1981 and won seven events from 1983 through 1987, placing in the top 10 in earnings each year. He was slowed by a rotator cuff injury in 1993. Littler was elected into the World Golf Hall of Fame in 1990.

- PGA Tour Victories: 1954 San Diego (as amateur); 1955 Los Angeles, Phoenix Tournament of Champions, Labatt; 1956 Texas, Tournament of Champions, Palm Beach Round Robin; 1957 Tournament of Champions; 1959 Phoenix, Tucson, Arlington Hotel, Insurance City, Miller Open; 1960 Oklahoma City, Eastern; 1961 U.S. Open; 1962 Lucky International, Thunderbird; 1965 Canadian Open; 1969 Phoenix, Greensboro; 1971 Monsanto, Colonial; 1973 St. Louis; 1975 Bing Crosby ProAm, Danny Thomas-Memphis, Westchester; 1977 Houston.

- Joined Senior Tour in 1981.

- Senior PGA Tour Victories: 1983 Daytona Beach Senior Classic, Greater Syracuse Classic; 1984 Seiko/Tucson Match Play; 1986 Sunwest Bank/Charley Pride Senior Classic, Bank One Senior Classic; 1987 NYNEX/Golf Digest Commemorative, Gus Machado Classic; 1989 Aetna Challenge.

- Played on Ryder Cup teams from 1961 through 1975.

- Career Senior PGA Tour Earnings: $2,044,991.

GRAHAM MARSH

Born: Graham Vivian Marsh, January 14, 1944
Birthplace: Kalgoorlie, Australia
Ht: 5' 11" **Wt:** 187
Exempt Status: Top 31 on 1996 Senior Tour Money List

The Australian's third year on the Senior Tour was his best thus far with 16 top ten finishes, including victories at the 1996 Franklin Quest Championship and the 1996 PaineWebber Invitational worth $120,000 each. He was one of nine Senior Tour players to earn more than $1 million in official earnings in 1996. His 1996 Senior Tour statistics bear out his reputation for accuracy, where he finished in the top ten in driving accuracy (9th), greens in regulation (2nd), scoring (5th, 70.34 stroke average), birdies (5th), and all-around (9th).

Marsh has improved steadily since joining the Senior Tour in 1994, when he earned $492,402 (24th). The next year he won his first Senior Tour event, Bruno's Memorial Classic, on his way to 14 top ten finishes and earnings of $849,350 (8th).

In addition to his three Senior Tour victories, Marsh has won 56 events in international competition, including 24 on the Japan PGA Tour, 16 on the Australasia Tour, 15 on the PGA European Tour, and the 1977 Heritage Classic on the PGA Tour. He was among the top ten on the Australasian Order of Merit for seven consecutive seasons (1978-1984).

- Has three Senior Tour victories: 1996 Franklin Quest Invitational; 1996 PaineWebber Invitational 1995 Bruno's Memorial Classic.

- Best finish in a senior major was a tie for second in the 1994 U.S. Senior Open.

- Actively participates in his own junior golf foundation in Australia.

- Honored as a Member of the British Empire (MBE) by the Queen of England.

- Nicknamed "Swampy" by his fellow golfers.

- Career Senior PGA Tour earnings: $2,366,041 (32nd).

ORVILLE MOODY

Born: Orville J. Moody, December 9, 1933
Birthplace: Chickasha, Okla.
Ht: 5' 10" **Wt:** 210
Exempt Status: Top 31 on All-Time Senior Tour Money List (otherwise not exempt)

Moody has played a full calendar of Senior Tour events since undergoing heart bypass surgery prior to the start of the 1995 season. In 1995 he won $116,635 (12th) in Super Senior events (unofficial earnings) to go with his $70,771 (79th) in official earnings. He ended the 1996 season by finishing second to Bob Charles in the second annual MasterCard Grandmaster competition at the Energizer Senior Tour Championship with rounds of 74-71-70.

Moody was a familiar figure in the Senior Tour winner's circle in the late 1980s. He won three tournaments in 1988, a career-high. The next year he won two senior majors, the Mazda Senior TPC and the U.S. Senior Open, on his way to earning a career-high $647,985 (2nd).

Moody joined the PGA Tour in 1967 and won his only official PGA Tour event in 1969, the U.S. Open at Champions Golf Club in Houston. He later won that year's World Series of Golf, then an unofficial event, which matched the year's four major tournament winners.

• Has 11 Senior Tour victories: 1992 Franklin Showdown Classic; 1991 PaineWebber Invitational 1989 Mazda Senior TPC; 1989 U.S. Senior Open; 1988 Vintage Chrysler Invitational; 1988 Senior Players Reunion; 1988 Greater Grand Rapids Open; 1987 Rancho Murieta Senior Gold Rush; 1987 GTE Kaanaplai Classic; 1984 Daytona Beach Seniors Classic; 1984 MONY Tournament of Champions

• Teamed with Bruce Crampton to win the 1987 and 1988 Liberty Mutual Legends of Golf (unofficial event).

• Has five international titles to his credit, including two Australian PGA Championships (1986, 1987).

• Switched to a long putter in the fall of 1985.

• Nicknamed "Sarge" for his 14-year Army career.

• Career Senior PGA Tour earnings: $3,191,894 (21st).

WALTER MORGAN

Born: Walter Morgan, May 31, 1941
Birthplace: Haddock, Ga.
Ht: 5' 9" **Wt:** 205
Exempt Status: Top 31 on 1996 Senior Tour Money List

In his best year yet on the Senior Tour, cigar-smoking Morgan entered a career-high 37 events, finished tenth on the 1996 money list with $848,303 in official earnings, and passed the $1 million mark in career Senior Tour earnings. His two-stroke victory at the Ameritech Senior Open earned him the $165,000 first prize, and his win at the FHP Healthcare Classic was worth $120,000.

After struggling to maintain his exemption for four years, Morgan finished second at the 1994 National Qualifier and entered 35 Senior Tour events in 1995. He scored his first Senior Tour victory in the 1995 GTE Northwest Classic and earned $423,756 (27th) that year.

Morgan spent 20 years in the Army and was the All-Service champion in 1975 and 1976. He left the military in 1980 and was a club professional until joining the Senior Tour in 1991.

• Has three Senior Tour victories: 1996 Ameritech Senior Open; 1996 FHP Health Care Classic 1995 GTE Northwest Classic.

• Missed qualifying for the PGA Tour by one-stroke at Q-school after leaving the military in 1980.

• Cousin of baseball Hall of Famer Joe Morgan.

• Took up golf at age 25.

• Career Senior PGA Tour earnings: $1,549,669 (57th).

BOB MURPHY

Born: Robert J. Murphy, Jr., February 14, 1943
Birthplace: Brooklyn, N.Y.
Ht: 5' 10" **Wt:** 200
Exempt Status: Top 31 on 1996 Senior Tour Money List

"Murph" passed the $5 million mark in combined career earnings from the PGA and Senior PGA Tours in 1996. With 18 top ten finishes, including victories at the Royal Caribbean Senior Golf Classic and the Cadillac NFL Golf Classic, and season earnings of $1,067,188 (7th), Murphy nearly equaled his career-best performance of 1995, when he had four victories, 20 top ten finishes, and $1,241,524 (4th) in earnings.

Murphy was the second player to win Rookie of the Year honors on both the PGA Tour (1968) and the Senior Tour (1993). Since 1993, when he left his job as a television golf announcer to join the Senior Tour, he's had at least two victories and finished among the top ten in earnings every year.

Murphy has five PGA Tour victories to his credit. He won two PGA tournaments in his rookie year, and his last victory came at age 43 in the 1986 Canadian Open, where he finished ahead of Greg Norman by three strokes.

- Has 10 Senior Tour victories: 1996 Royal Caribbean Classic; 1996 Cadillac NFL Classic; 1995 VFW Senior Championship; 1995 Nationwide Championship; 1995 PaineWebber Invitational; 1995 IntelliNet Challenge; 1994 Raley's Senior Gold Rush; 1994 Hyatt Regency Maui Kaanapali Classic; 1993 Bruno's Memorial Classic; 1993 GTE North Classic.

- In 1995 established a Senior Tour record with 24 straight sub-par rounds.

- Has five PGA Tour victories: 1986 Canadian Open; 1975 Jackie Gleason Inverrary Classic; 1970 Greater Hartford Open Invitational; 1968 Philadelphia Golf Classic; 1968 Thunderbird Classic.

- Member of the 1966 U.S. World Amateur Cup team, the 1967 Walker Cup team, and the 1975 Ryder Cup team.

- Left the ESPN broadcast booth to join the Senior Tour at the urging of Lee Trevino.

- Overcame severe arthritis to continue his golf career.

- Career Senior PGA Tour earnings: $3,933,317 (13th).

JACK NICKLAUS

Born: Jack William Nicklaus, January 21, 1940
Birthplace: Columbus, Ohio
Ht: 5' 11" **Wt:** 185
Exempt Status: Top 31 on All-Time Senior Tour Money List (otherwise not exempt)

Approaching the 40th year of his remarkable golf career, Nicklaus continued to establish records on the Senior Tour in 1996. With his victory at The Tradition, he became the first player in the history of the Senior Tour to win the same tournament four times. At the GTE Suncoast Classic he overcame a five-shot deficit on Sunday to win his second 1996 tournament. Devoting more time to other interests, Nicklaus entered only seven Senior Tour and seven PGA Tour events in 1996.

Since he joined the Senior Tour in 1990, Nicklaus has generally limited his participation to the top senior tournaments. In his rookie year he won The Tradition, his first Senior Tour event, and the Mazda Senior TPC. Then in 1991 he took The Tradition again and won the U.S. Senior Open and the PGA Seniors' Championship. He won The Tradition again in 1995 and 1996 and captured his second U.S. Senior Open in 1993.

Nicklaus' accomplishments on the PGA Tour and before that as an amateur add up to the most impressive resume of any golfer. He played in his first U.S. Open in 1957, and forty years later was granted a special exemption to play in the 1997 U.S. Open at the Congressional Country Club. In between he won four U.S. Opens (1962, 1967, 1972 and 1980), six Masters Tournaments (1963, 1965, 1966, 1972, 1975, 1986), five PGA Championships (1963, 1971, 1973, 1975, 1980) and three British Opens (1966, 1970, 1978). It's no wonder that Sports Illustrated named him "Golfer of the Century."

- Has ten Senior Tour victories: 1996 GTE Suncoast Classic; 1996 The Tradition; 1995 The Tradition; 1994 Mercedes Championships; 1993 U.S. Senior Open; 1991 The Tradition at Desert; Mountain; 1991 PGA Seniors' Championship; 1991 U.S. Senior Open; 1990 The Tradition at Desert Mountain; 1990 Mazda Senior TPC.

- Has 70 PGA Tour victories.

- Five-time winner of the World Series of Golf (1962, 1963, 1967, 1970, 1976).

- Six-time winner of the Australian Open (1964, 1968, 1971, 1975, 1976, 1978).

- Won the U.S. Amateur and NCAA Championship in 1961 as well as the 1959 U.S. Amateur.

- Nicknamed the "Golden Bear."

- One of the world's leading golf course acrhitects.

- Career Senior PGA Tour earnings: $2,143,249 (41st).

ARNOLD PALMER

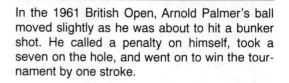

Born: Arnold Daniel Palmer, September 10, 1929

Birthplace: Latrobe, Penn.

Ht: 5' 10" **Wt:** 185

Exempt Status: Special exemption

Palmer was a golf legend long before he joined the Senior Tour in 1980 and continues to be a popular public figure and ambassador for the game. Much of his time now is devoted to an active business schedule that includes designing golf courses and overseeing their construction and development. Palmer dropped out of the top 31 all-time Senior Tour money winners after the 1996 season, when he won only $48,192 (89th) in 16 events. Palmer hasn't won a Senior Tour event since 1988, but in 1995 he shot a 66 on his 66th birthday in the final round of the GTE Northwest Classic.

In the 1961 British Open, Arnold Palmer's ball moved slightly as he was about to hit a bunker shot. He called a penalty on himself, took a seven on the hole, and went on to win the tournament by one stroke.

It was Palmer's participation in the first Senior Tour season of 1980 that gave the circuit a measure of credibility. He is one of a handful of Senior Tour players to win the first Senior Tour event he entered. In Palmer's case it was a major senior event, the 1980 PGA Seniors' Championship. Other major victories include the 1981 U.S. Senior Open, a repeat win at the 1984 PGA Seniors' Championship, and back-to-back wins at the 1984 and 1985 Senior Tournament Players Championships.

- Has 10 Senior Tour victories: 1988 Crestar Classic; 1985 Senior Tournament Players; Championship; 1984 PGA Seniors' Championship; 1984 Senior Tournament Players Championship; 1984 Quadel Senior Classic; 1983 Boca Grove Senior Classic; 1982 Marlboro Classic; 1982 Denver Post Champions; 1981 U.S. Senior Open; 1980 PGA Seniors' Championship.

- Won 60 official PGA Tour events, including four Masters Tournaments (1958, 1960, 1962, 1964), two British Opens (1961, 1962), and one U.S. Open (1960).

- Joined the PGA Tour in 1955 after winning the 1954 U.S. Amateur.

- Has more victories in Ryder Cup matches, 22-8-2, than anyone else.

- The awards for leading money winners on the PGA Tour and the Senior Tour are named after him.

- The fans who followed him from tee to green in golf tournaments became known as "Arnie's Army."

- Career Senior PGA Tour earnings: $1,634,966 (55th).

GARY PLAYER

Born: Gary Jim Player,
November 1, 1935
Birthplace: Johannesburg,
South Africa
Ht: 5' 7" **Wt:** 147
Exempt Status: Top 31 on
1996 Senior Tour Money List

Although winless in 1996, Player had one of his best years on the Senior Tour, with seven top ten finishes and earnings of $494,714 (24th). His tie for second at the 1996 Vantage Championship was worth $110,000. He also played in the 1996 British Open and the Masters Tournament.

The only years Player earned more than he did in 1996 were 1989 and 1990, when he topped the $500,000 mark both years. In 1988 he had a career-high five Senior Tour victories and finished in the top ten in 16 out of 20 events entered to take home $435,914 (2nd). Playing the Senior Tour full-time since 1986, Player finished among the top ten money winners for each of his first five years. He's a three-time winner of the PGA Seniors' Championship (1986, 1988, 1990), a two-time U.S. Senior Open winner (1987, 1988), and he won the Mazda Senior TPC once (1987).

Player has had a remarkable professional golf career, achieving legendary status on the strength of his major tournament victories. He is one of only four players to have won the four major PGA championships in his career: Masters Tournament (1961, 1974, 1978), U.S. Open (1965), British Open (1959, 1968, 1974), and PGA Championship (1962, 1972). Gene Sarazen, Ben Hogan, and Jack Nicklaus are the others.

• Has 18 Senior Tour victories: 1995 Bank One Classic; 1993 Bank One Classic; 1991 Royal Caribbean Classic; 1990 PGA Seniors' Championship; 1989 GTE North Classic; 1989 RJR Championship; 1988 General Foods PGA Seniors' Championship; 1988 Aetna Challenge; 1988 Southwestern Bell Classic; 1988 U.S.

In one of his first tournaments, Gary Player was knocked unconscious by his own shot.

Senior Open; 1988 GTE North Classic; 1987 Mazda Senior TPC; 1987 U.S. Senior Open; 1987 PaineWebber World Seniors Invitational; 1986 General Foods PGA Seniors' Championship; 1986 United Hospital Classic; 1986 Denver Post Champions; 1985 Quadel Seniors Classic.

• Has 21 PGA Tour victories.

• Won more than 120 tournaments internationally.

• Has traveled more miles than any other athlete.

• Career Senior PGA Tour earnings: $4,269,992 (11th).

JIMMY POWELL

Born: Jimmy Dale Powell,
January 17, 1935
Birthplace: Dallas, Tex.
Ht: 6' 1" **Wt:** 200
Exempt Status: Top 31 on
1996 Senior Tour Money List

Powell had one of his best years on the Senior Tour in 1996. He earned $576,382 (19th), second only to his total in 1994, and had nine top ten finishes. He captured his fourth Senior Tour victory at the 1996 Brickyard Crossing Championship, taking home $112,500 for first place.

Powell joined the Senior Tour in 1985 and carded his first Senior Tour victory in 1990 at the Southwestern Bell Classic. His best year was 1994, when he had 12 top ten finishes and earned $588,378 (14th). In 1995 he took the First of America Classic to become the first Senior Tour player over 60 to win both a Super Senior competition and an overall event.

Powell is a former club pro who played intermittently on the PGA Tour, never winning a PGA Tour event. In 1980, at age 45, he became the oldest player to qualify for the PGA Tour through the Q-School.

- Has four Senior Tour victories: 1996 Brickyard Crossing Championship; 1995 First of America Classic; 1992 Aetna Challenge; 1990 Southwestern Bell Classic.

- Three-time winner of the Southern California PGA Championship (1968, 1970, 1975).

- First Senior Tour player to win an overall event and the Super Seniors competition in the same tournament.

- Former head pro at Stevens Park Golf Club in Dallas, the same course where he learned to play golf.

- Career Senior PGA Tour earnings: $2,791,994 (27th).

CHI CHI RODRIGUEZ

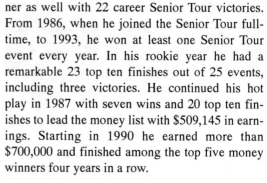

Born: Juan Rodriguez, October 23, 1935

Birthplace: Rio Pedras, Puerto Rico

Ht: 5' 7" **Wt:** 132

Exempt Status: Top 31 on All-Time Senior Tour Money List (otherwise not exempt)

Rodriguez rebounded from an off year in 1995, when he had only one top ten finish and dropped out of the top 31 money winners for the first time in his Senior Tour career, to score six top ten finishes in 1996 and earn $390,900 (33rd). His last Senior Tour victory came in 1993, when he won the inaugural Burnet Senior Classic near Minneapolis.

A popular golfer who performs crowd pleasing theatrics, Rodriguez has a reputation as a winner as well with 22 career Senior Tour victories. From 1986, when he joined the Senior Tour full-time, to 1993, he won at least one Senior Tour event every year. In his rookie year he had a remarkable 23 top ten finishes out of 25 events, including three victories. He continued his hot play in 1987 with seven wins and 20 top ten finishes to lead the money list with $509,145 in earnings. Starting in 1990 he earned more than $700,000 and finished among the top five money winners four years in a row.

Rodriguez earned more than $1 million and had eight victories in his PGA Tour career from 1960 to 1981. He has also received numerous awards and been inducted into the World Golf Hall of Fame and the World Humanitarian Sports Hall of Fame.

- Has 22 Senior Tour victories: 1993 Burnet Senior Classic; 1992 Ko Olina Senior Invitational; 1991 GTE West Classic; 1991 Vintage ARCO Invitational; 1991 Las Vegas Senior Classic; 1991 Murata Reunion Pro-Am; 1990 Las Vegas Senior Classic; 1990 Ameritech Senior Open; 1990 Sunwest Bank/Charley Pride Senior Golf Classic; 1989 Crestar Classic; 1988 Doug Sanders Kingwood Classic; 1988 Digital Seniors Classic; 1987 General Foods PGA Seniors' Championship; 1987 Vantage at The Dominion; 1987 United Hospitals Classic; 1987 Silver Pages Classic; 1987 Senior Players Reunion; 1987 Digital Seniors Classic; 1987 GTE Northwest Classic; 1986 Senior TPC; 1986 Digital Seniors Classic; 1986 United Virginia Bank Seniors.

- Won the Senior Skins Game in 1988 and 1989 (unofficial event).

- Won eight PGA Tour events.

- An active supporter of junior golf, Chi Chi received the Card Walker Award from the PGA Tour in 1986 for his outstanding contributions.

- Won the Bobby Jones Award in 1989, the USGA's highest honor.

- Other awards include the Ambassador of Golf Award (1981), the National Puerto Rico Coalition Life Achievement Award (1987), Old Tom Morris Award (1988) and Herb Graffis Award (1993).

- Career Senior PGA Tour earnings: $5,696,544 (5th).

JOHN SCHROEDER

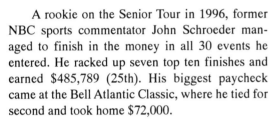

Born: John Lawrence Schroeder, November 12, 1945

Birthplace: Great Barrington, Mass.

Ht: 5' 10" **Wt:** 170

Exempt Status: Top 31 on 1996 Senior Tour Money List

A rookie on the Senior Tour in 1996, former NBC sports commentator John Schroeder managed to finish in the money in all 30 events he entered. He racked up seven top ten finishes and earned $485,789 (25th). His biggest paycheck came at the Bell Atlantic Classic, where he tied for second and took home $72,000.

Schroeder earned his exemption for the 1996 season by finishing eighth in the 1995 Senior Tour National Qualifying Open. He tied with four others for the last qualifying spot with rounds of 70-67-69-71, then went on to win the eighth spot with a birdie on the first extra hole.

Schroeder played on the PGA Tour from 1969 to 1982, where he had one victory at the 1973 U.S. Professional Match Play. He was an NBC sports commentator from 1982 until he joined the Senior Tour after turning 50 in November of 1995.

- Son of Ted Schroeder, winner of the 1949 Wimbledon tennis championship.

- An All-American selection in golf at the University of Michigan in 1968.

- Had over $500,000 career earnings on the PGA Tour.

- Career Senior PGA Tour earnings: $485,789 (99th).

JAY SIGEL

Born: Robert Jay Sigel, November 13, 1943

Birthplace: Narberth, Penn.

Ht: 6' 1" **Wt:** 208

Exempt Status: Top 31 on 1996 Senior Tour Money List

Sigel finished his third and best year on the Senior Tour with a two-stroke victory at the season-ending Energizer Senior Tour Championship. His first-place prize of $280,000 was the largest on the 1996 Senior Tour. Together with a season total of 15 top ten finishes, it brought his yearly earnings to more than $1 million (6th), a mark topped by nine golfers on the Senior Tour in 1996.

Sigel earned Rookie of the Year honors on the Senior Tour in 1994. He won the GTE West Classic that year with a remarkable come-from-behind victory. Ten strokes down going into the final round, he shot a 62 to catch Jim Colbert, then won it on the fourth playoff hole. He also had a stunning finish at the 1994 season-ending Senior Tour Championship, where he shot a final-round 63 that included an eagle and a rare double eagle to finish third and take home his largest paycheck to date, $115,000.

Sigel was one of the best amateur golfers in history and only turned pro in 1993. He has captured numerous amateur titles and was low amateur in the Masters Tournament three times and also in the 1980 British Open and the 1984 U.S. Open.

- Has two Senior Tour victories: 1996 Energizer Senior Tour Championship; 1994 GTE West Classic.

- One of the country's finest amateur golfers, Sigel never played on the PGA Tour and only turned professional after he turned 50 in 1993.

- His amateur titles include the 1982 and 1983 U.S. Amateurs, three U.S. Mid-Americas, and the 1979 British Amateur.

- Holds the record for the most appearances and total points in the prestigious Walker Cup competitions.

- Has won many honors and awards, including the Bobby Jones Award and Ben Hogan Award in 1984, among many others.

- Career Senior PGA Tour earnings: $2,296,317 (36th).

J.C. SNEAD

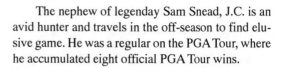

Born: Jesse Carlyle Snead, October 14, 1940

Birthplace: Hot Springs, Vir.

Ht: 6' 2" **Wt:** 200

Exempt Status: Top 31 on 1996 Senior Tour Money List

Snead had another great year in 1996, following his career-best 1995 season on the Senior Tour. Although winless in 1996, he garnered ten top ten finishes, including a tie for second at the Burnet Senior Classic worth $100,000, to earn $763,382 (11th) for the year. He also had a second-place finish at the GTE Suncoast Classic.

Snead almost earned $1 million in 1995, his fifth full year on the senior circuit, despite a six-week layoff due to broken ribs. He had two victories, including a major at the Ford Senior Players Championship, where he defeated Jack Nicklaus on the first playoff hole. He also had a playoff victory over Raymond Floyd at the Royal Caribbean Classic and scored 12 top ten finishes to take home $978,137 (6th) that year. Snead captured his first Senior Tour victory in 1993 at the Vantage at The Dominion.

The nephew of legenday Sam Snead, J.C. is an avid hunter and travels in the off-season to find elusive game. He was a regular on the PGA Tour, where he accumulated eight official PGA Tour wins.

- Has three Senior Tour victories: 1995 Ford Senior Players Championship; 1995 Royal Caribbean Classic; 1993 Vantage at the Dominion.

- Won eight official PGA Tour events: 1987 Manufacturers Hanover-Westchester Classic; 1981 Southern Open; 1976 Andy Williams San Diego Open; 1976 Kaiser International; 1975 Wickes-Andy Williams San Diego Classic; 1972 Philadelphia Classic; 1971 Doral-Eastern Open 1971 Tucson Open.

- Joined the PGA Tour in 1968.

- Member of the Ryder Cup team in 1971, 1973, and 1975.

- Played professional baseball in the Washington Senators farm system before becoming a professional golfer in 1964.

- Career Senior PGA Tour earnings: $3,547,362 (18th).

DAVE STOCKTON

Born: David Knapp Stockton, November 2, 1941

Birthplace: San Bernardino, Cal.

Ht: 5' 11" **Wt:** 180

Exempt Status: Top 31 on 1996 Senior Tour Money List

Stockton earned more than $1 million on the Senior Tour in 1996 for the fourth season in a row. He won the U.S. Senior Open, beating Hale Irwin by two strokes, and the First of America Classic. He was part of a five-man playoff in the Emerald Coast Classic, won by Lee Trevino on the first sudden death playoff hole.

GREENS IN REGULATION

Rank	Name	Rounds	Stat
1.	Hale Irwin	74	74.7
2.	Graham Marsh	88	72.6
3.	Brian Barnes	69	72.1
4.	Jay Sigel	100	71.8
5.	Ray Floyd	74	71.5
6.	John Bland	110	70.8
7.	Isao Aoki	81	70.6
8.	Dave Stockton	91	69.4
9.	Mike Hill	58	69.1
T10.	Bob Charles	93	68.9
T10.	Bob Murphy	94	68.9

Stockton joined the Senior Tour full-time in 1992 and won his first major that year, the Mazda Senior Players Championship in Dearborn, Michigan. He has finished among the top ten money winners every year since joining the Senior Tour. He took the Arnold Palmer Award for top money winner in 1993 and 1994 and was named the 1994 Player of the Year by the Golf Writers Association. He had more than 20 top ten finishes for three years in a row (1993-1995) and nailed five victories in 1993.

Stockton joined the PGA Tour in 1964 and is best-remembered as a two-time winner of the PGA Championship, in 1970 and 1976, his final PGA Tour victory.

• Has 13 Senior Tour victories: 1996 First of America Classic; 1996 U.S. Senior Open; 1995 GTE Suncoast Classic; 1995 Quicksilver Classic; 1994 Nationwide Championship; 1994 Ford Senior Players Championship; 1994 Burnet Senior Classic; 1993 Muratec Reunion Pro-Am; 1993 Southwestern Bell Classic; 1993 Franklin Quest Championship; 1993 GTE Northwest Classic; 1993 The Transamerica; 1992 Mazda Senior Players Championship.

• Named Senior Tour Rookie of the Year (1992), Senior Tour Player of the Year (1993), and Player of the Year (1994).

• First Senior Tour player to post four straight $1 million seasons.

• Captain of the victorious 1991 U.S. Ryder Cup team.

• Career Senior PGA Tour earnings: $5,781,417 (4th).

BOBBY STROBLE

Born: December 4, 1944 in Albany, Ga.

Ht: 6' 1" **Wt:** 227

Exempt Status: Top 31 on 1996 Senior Tour Money List

Stroble earned full exempt status for the 1996 Senior Tour after qualifying through the Senior PGA Tour National Qualifying Tournament with rounds of 69-67-68-68. He did well in his rookie year, entering 35 events and finishing in the top ten nine times to earn $464,648 (27th). His best finish was third at the Transamerica, where he took home his biggest paycheck of the year, $50,400.

Stroble has played intermittently on the PGA Tour since 1967 and more recently on the Nike Tour (1990-91) and the mini-tour Senior Series, where he won two events in 1995 and finished in the top ten in 13 tournaments.

• Stroble appeared in three 1995 Senior Tour events through Monday qualifying. He qualified for the U.S. Senior Open, but after opening rounds of 77-74 he missed the cut.

• Best 1996 Senior Tour finish was third at the 1996 Transamerica.

• Finished 27th on the 1996 Senior Tour money list to earn another exemption for 1997.

• Career Senior PGA Tour earnings: $473,628 (100th).

BRUCE SUMMERHAYS

Born: Bruce Patton Summerhays, February 14, 1944

Birthplace: St. Louis, Mo.

Ht: 5' 9" **Wt:** 170

Exempt Status: Top 31 on 1996 Senior Tour Money List

Although winless after two full seasons on the Senior Tour, Summerhays finished among the top 31 money winners in both 1995 and 1996. He entered 38 Senior Tour events in 1996 and managed five top ten finishes to take home $449,659 (29th). His best finish was fourth at the BellSouth Senior Classic, worth $72,000.

Summerhays's strong performance in 1995 earned him a nomination for Senior Tour Rookie of the Year honors. He carded 14 top ten finishes in 36 events and earned $729,021 (13th). He came close to scoring victories at the Nationwide Championship, where he opened with a 63, and at The Transamerica, where he led with six holes to play.

Primarily a teaching pro, Summerhays never played on the PGA Tour. He earned a reputation as one of the top players in the Utah PGA Section prior to joining the Senior Tour, and was named Rocky Mountain PGA Section Player of the Year twice. He was an assistant pro at the Olympic Club in San Francisco from 1968 through 1976 and golf coach at Stanford University in 1978-79.

- A long hitter, he averaged 272.1 years per drive in 1996 (9th).

- Led the Senior Tour in birdies in 1995 with 411.

- As a teaching pro he won numerous regional events in California and Utah.

- Qualified for four U.S. Open Championships and four PGA Championships.

- Career Senior PGA Tour earnings: $1,199,391 (66th).

ROCKY THOMPSON

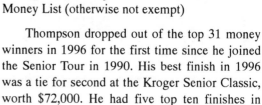

Born: Hugh Delane Thompson, October 14, 1939

Birthplace: Shreveport, La.

Ht: 5' 11" **Wt:** 172

Exempt Status: Top 31 on All-Time Senior Tour Money List (otherwise not exempt)

Thompson dropped out of the top 31 money winners in 1996 for the first time since he joined the Senior Tour in 1990. His best finish in 1996 was a tie for second at the Kroger Senior Classic, worth $72,000. He had five top ten finishes in 1996 and earned $385,719 (35th).

The inventor of the "Killer Bee" driver, Thompson joined the Senior Tour in 1989 after turning fifty in October and played his first full season in 1990. His first Senior Tour victory came at the 1991 MONY Syracuse Senior Classic, after he shot a course-record opening round of 62 and went wire-to-wire to win. His best earnings year was 1995, when he took home $666,521 (14th) and had nine top ten finishes.

Thompson joined the PGA Tour in 1964 but never earned an exemption. He was successful in so many qualifying events for PGA tournaments, though, that caddies nicknamed him "King Rabbit." His best PGA Tour finish was second at the 1969 Western Open. In his career he has won 12 junior titles, 25 amateur events, and 23 professional events.

- Has three Senior Tour victories: 1994 GTE Suncoast Classic; 1991 Digital Seniors Classic; 1991 MONY Syracuse Senior Classic.

- A steady putter, Thompson finished among the top ten putters on the Senior Tour in 1995 and 1996.

- Designed the "Killer Bee" driver, which comes in varying lengths between 46 and 56 inches.

- Career Senior PGA Tour earnings: $3,347,943 (19th).

LEE TREVINO

Born: Lee Buck Trevino, December 1, 1939

Birthplace: Dallas, Tex.

Ht: 5' 7" **Wt:** 180

Exempt Status: Top 31 on 1996 Senior Tour Money List

Trevino saved his winning streak and made it seven years in a row that he has won at least one tournament on the Senior Tour when he captured the next-to-last event, the 1996 Emerald Coast Classic. The win became possible after Dave Stockton bogeyed the final hole to force a five-way playoff, the first time that many players have been in a playoff in Senior Tour history. Trevino birdied the first playoff hole and took home the $157,500 first prize. The win also made him eligible for the season-ending Energizer Senior Tour Championship, where he finished 16th.

With 27 Senior Tour victories since he joined in 1990, Trevino has been a dominant force. Of the senior's top tournaments, he won the U.S. Senior Open in his rookie year and is a two-time winner of the PGA Seniors' Championship (1992, 1994). In his rookie year he became the first senior to earn more than $1 million. He had seven victories that year, 26 top ten finishes out of 28 events entered, topped the money list, and took the Byron Nelson Award with an average score of 68.89 per round, the lowest in Senior Tour history. He was also named Senior Tour Rookie of the Year.

Trevino was also a star on the PGA Tour, where he was named Rookie of the Year in 1967. He was the PGA Tour's leading money winner in 1970 and was named Player of the Year in 1971. Among his 27 PGA Tour victories are the 1968 and 1971 U.S. Opens, 1974 and 1984 PGA Championships, and 1980 Tournament Players Championship.

- Has 27 Senior Tour victories: 1996 Emerald Coast Classic; 1995 Northville Long Island Classic; 1995 The Transamerica; 1994 Royal Caribbean Classic; 1994 PGA Seniors' Championship; 1994 PaineWebber Invitational; 1994 Bell Atlantic Classic; 1994 BellSouth Senior Classic; 1994 Northville Long Island Classic; 1993 Cadillac NFL Classic; 1993 Nationwide Championship; 1993 Vantage Championship; 1992 Vantage at The Dominion; 1992 The Tradition; 1992 PGA Seniors' Championship; 1992 Las Vegas Senior Classic; 1992 Bell Atlantic Classic; 1991 Aetna Challenge; 1991 Vantage at The Dominion; 1991 Sunwest Bank/Charley Pride Senior Classic; 1990 Royal Caribbean Classic; 1990 Aetna Challenge; 1990 Vintage Chrysler Invitational; 1990 Doug Sanders Kingwood Celebrity Classic; 1990 NYNEX Commemorative; 1990 U.S. Senior Open; 1990 Transamerica Senior Golf Championship.

- Won the PGA Championship in 1974 and 1984, and in 1994 won the PGA Seniors' Championship.

- Trevino and Mike Hill have teamed together to win the Liberty Mutual Legends of Golf (unoffical event) an unprecedented four times, 1991, 1992, 1995, 1996.

- Finished in the top five money winners from 1990 through 1994 and won the Arnold Palmer Award twice (1990, 1992) for most earnings in a season.

- All-time leading money winner on the Senior Tour, and the first player to earn more than $1 million in a single season.

- Named Senior Tour Player of the Year three times (1990, 1992, 1994).

- Career Senior PGA Tour earnings: $6,715,649 (1st).

TOM WARGO

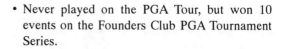

Born: Amos Tom Wargo, September 16, 1942,

Birthplace: Marlette, Mich.

Ht: 6' **Wt:** 200

Exempt Status: Top 31 on 1996 Senior Tour Money List

Although winless in 1996 for the first time since joining the Senior Tour in 1993, Wargo had three ties for second among his ten top ten finishes and earned $695,705 (15th). The former club professional finished tied for second at the Bank of Boston Senior Classic to earn $64,000, the Bell Atlantic Classic (worth $72,000), and the Paine-Webber Invitational (worth $64,000).

Wargo was a rookie surprise on the Senior Tour with his playoff victory over Bruce Crampton in the 1993 PGA Seniors' Championship. In 1994 he was the Senior Tour's "ironman," entering 36 events and playing 112 rounds. He took one week off that year to win the British Senior Open at Royal Lytham & St. Anne's. He earned over $1 million that year with 25 top ten finishes, including a win at the Doug Sanders Celebrity Classic.

An outstanding club professional, Wargo never played on the PGA Tour. He was named 1992 PGA Club Professional of the Year. In 1992 and 1993 he was the low club professional in the PGA Championship.

- Has three Senior Tour victories: 1995 Dallas Reunion Senior Pro-Am; 1994 Doug Sanders Celebrity Classic; 1993 PGA Seniors' Championship.

- Never played on the PGA Tour, but won 10 events on the Founders Club PGA Tournament Series.

- Member of the PGA Cup squad from 1988 through 1992.

- Took up golf at the age of 25 and taught himself how to play.

- Previous jobs prior to golf include iron worker, assembly line autoworker, and bartender.

- Career Senior PGA Tour earnings: $3,103,007 (23rd).

TOM WEISKOPF

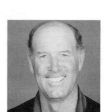

Born: Thomas Daniel Weiskopf, November 9, 1942

Birthplace: Massillon, Ohio

Ht: 6' 3" **Wt:** 190

Exempt Status: Top 31 on 1996 Senior Tour Money List

Entering only about half of the Senior Tour events in 1996, Weiskopf managed to win two tournaments and take home $454,584 (28th). He carded victories at the Pittsburgh Senior Classic and the SBC Dominion Seniors and had two other top ten finishes.

Weiskopf joined the Senior Tour in 1993 and won his first event in 1994, the Franklin Quest Championship. In 1995, his best year on the Senior Tour, he shot four rounds in the 60s to take the U.S. Senior Open at the Congressional Country Club by four strokes. He had eight top ten finishes that year and took home official earnings of $580,137 (18th).

Weiskopf was a strong, if erratic, player on the PGA Tour for many years. His best year came in 1973, when he won four official PGA Tour events as well as the British Open. He was a four-time runner up at the Masters Tournament and finished tied for second at the 1976 U.S. Open.

- Has four Senior Tour victories: 1996 SBC Dominion Seniors; 1996 Pittsburgh Senior Classic; 1995 U.S. Senior Open; 1994 Franklin Quest Championship.

- Has 15 PGA Tour Victories and PGA Tour career earnings of more than $2.2 million.

- Won the 1973 British Open.

- Member of the 1973 and 1975 Ryder Cup teams.

- Won the 1963 Western Amateur.

- Career Senior PGA Tour earnings: $1,646,272 (54th).

year. He won two PGA Tour events over the course of his career. As an amateur he led the University of Houston to an NCAA Championship in 1962 and was medalist that year.

- Has one Senior Tour victory: 1994 The Transamerica.

- Won two official PGA Tour Events: 1970 Canadian Open; 1968 Kaiser International Open Invitational.

- Interest in bible studies led him to establish the PGA Tour Bible Study group in 1965. Also wrote three books on religion and world affairs in the 1980s.

- Son Michael and daughter Christine alternate as his caddie during the season.

- Career Senior PGA Tour earnings: $2,537,394 (29th).

KERMIT ZARLEY

Born: Kermit Millard Zarley, Jr., September 29, 1941
Birthplace: Seattle, Wash.
Ht: 6' 0" **Wt:** 175
Exempt Status: Top 31 on 1996 Senior Tour Money List

Zarley ended a winless 1996 on a high note by finishing all alone in second place at the season-ending Energizer Senior Tour Championship. It was worth $180,000 and brought his season's earnings to a career-high $710,110 (13th). He also had one other second place finish along with two ties for second in his quest for a second Senior Tour victory.

Zarley joined the Senior Tour full-time in 1992 and has finished among the top 31 money winners every year. His lone Senior Tour win came in 1994 at The Transamerica, where he defeated Isao Aoki on the first playoff hole.

Zarley played on the PGA tour from 1963 through 1987, with 1982 being his last full-time

WALT ZEMBRISKI

Born: Walter J. Zembriski, May 24, 1935
Birthplace: Matwah, N.J.
Ht: 5' 8" **Wt:** 160
Exempt Status: Top 31 on All-Time Senior Tour Money List (otherwise not exempt)

With only one top ten finish in 1995 and 1996, Zembriski now competes primarily with other Super Seniors (age 60 and over). In 1995 he won three Super Senior competitions and finished tenth on the Super Senior money list with $157,142 (unofficial earnings).

Zembriski joined the Senior Tour in 1985 and carded his first Senior Tour victory in 1988 at the Newport Cup. He then surprised the golf world by taking the 1988 Vantage Championship, worth $135,000. He had 16 top ten finishes that year and earned a career-high $348,531 (7th) in what has been his best year on the Senior Tour.

Zembriski is a real late bloomer, with the blossom coming on the Senior Tour. He played briefly on the PGA Tour, but only earned $2,203. He was also a construction worker for several years before qualifying for the Senior Tour.

- Has three Senior Tour victories: 1989 GTE West Classic; 1988 Vintage Championships; 1988 Newport Classic.

- Qualified for the 1978 and 1982 U.S. Opens.

- Won 10 tournaments on the 1982 Space Coast mini-tour in Florida.

- Career Senior PGA Tour earnings: $2,698,906 (28th).

4

PRO FILES
HALL OF FAME

The sport of golf will have an internationally-recognized and definitive Hall of Fame in 1998. The World Golf Village resort, set to begin opening in phases during 1998, will have as its centerpiece the World Golf Hall of Fame, a 75,000-foot building designed with high vaulted ceilings, broad windows, and large porches to reflect the airy, outdoor nature of the sport. The World Golf Hall of Fame will feature a permanent shrine, honoring the history and greats of the sport, as well as interactive exhibits for instruction and pleasure. All major golf organizations worldwide support the World Golf Village, and each provided a representative on the World Golf Hall of Fame Advisory Board.

The initial inductees to the World Golf Hall of Fame were adopted from the PGA Hall of Fame, previously housed at Pinehurst, and the LPGA Hall of Fame. Additional inductees will have met specific criteria, which are outlined below. Johnny Miller, who won 24 Tour titles and two majors, became in 1996 the first player elected under the World Golf Hall of Fame inclusion guidelines.

The sections in this chapter contain information about the World Golf Village and the Hall of Fame election guidelines; a list of individuals included in the World Golf Hall of Fame; career profiles of those Hall of Fame tournament golfers deceased or no longer competing; and an outline of the election process for PGA, Senior PGA, International, and Special Distinction categories for female golfers; the LPGA Hall of Fame criteria continues to govern their induction.

The World Golf Hall of Fame

Beginning in 1974, the Golf Writers of America (GWA) became responsible for electing inductees to the World Golf Hall of Fame by voting on individuals previously selected under various criteria to the PGA Hall of Fame and the LPGA Hall of Fame; additionally, the GWA was given responsibility for acknowledging excellent ambassadors and administrators for the sport who did not necessarily compete in professional or amateur tournaments. Sixty-four male and female golfers from the PGA Hall of Fame were "grandfathered in" by GWA voting from 1974 through 1992, when voting was suspended; voting resumed in 1996 under the present World Golf Hall of Fame guidelines. In addition to the 64 members voted into the World Golf Hall of Fame, seven LPGA Hall of Famers who were not in the PGA Hall of Fame were voted in—since the very strict LPGA guidelines were adopted for the World Golf Hall of Fame—for a grand total of 71 honorees, plus 1996 inductee Johnny Miller.

Listed below are those inducted into the World Golf Hall of Fame since 1974, followed in alphabetical order by career profiles of golfing greats of the past.

1974
Patty Berg
Walter Hagen
Ben Hogan
Robert T. (Bobby) Jones
Byron Nelson
Jack Nicklaus—active: see
    Pro Files: Seniors
Francis Ouimet
Arnold Palmer—active: see
    Pro Files: Seniors
Gary Player—active: see
    Pro Files: Seniors
Gene Sarazen
Sam Snead
Harry Vardon
Babe Zaharis

1975
Willie Anderson
Fred Corcoran—PGA Administrator
Joseph C. Dey—PGA Administrator
Chick Evans
Young Tom Morris
John H. Taylor
Glenna C. Vare
Joyce Wethred

1976
Tommy Armour
James Braid

Old Tom Morris
 Jerome Travers
Mickey Wright

1977
Bobby Locke
John Ball
Herb Graffis—PGA Historian
Donald Ross—see Course Designers

1978
Billy Casper—active: see
    Pro Files: Seniors
Harold Hilton
Dorothy Campbell
Bing Crosby—see Golf and
    Popular Culture
Cliford Roberts—Masters Tournament
    Administrator

1979
Louise Suggs
Walter Travis

1980
Lawson Little Henry Cotton

1981
Lee Trevino—active: see
    Pro Files: Seniors
    Ralph Guldhal

World Golf Hall of Fame

1982
Julius Boros
Kathy Whitworth

1983
Bob Hope—see Golf and Popular Culture
Jimmy Demaret

1985
JoAnne Carner—active: see
    Pro Files: Women

1986
Cary Middlecoff

1987
Robert Trent Jones—see Course Designers
Betsy Rawls

1988
Tom Watson—active: see
    Pro Files: Men
Peter Thomson
Bob Harlow—PGA Administrator
1989
Raymond Floyd—active: see
    Pro Files: Seniors
Nancy Lopez—active: see
    Pro Files: Women

Roberto De Vicenzo
Jim Barnes

1990

William C. Campbell
Paul Runyan
Gene Littler—active: see
   Pro Files: Seniors
Horton Smith

1992

Hale Irwin—active: see
   Pro Files: Seniors
Chi Chi Rodriguez—active: see
   Pro Files: Seniors
Richard Tufts—Administrator
Harry Cooper

From LPGA Hall of Fame

Pat Bradley—active: see
   Pro Files: Women
Sandra Haynie
Betty Jameson
Betsy King—active: see
   Pro Files: Women
Carol Mann
Patty Sheehan—active: see
   Pro Files: Women
Dinah Shore—see Golf and Popular Culture

1996

Johnny Miller

WILLIE ANDERSON

1878?–1910

A Scotsman who emigrated to the United States just before the turn of the century, Anderson was the first four-time U.S. Open winner (1901, 1903, 1904, 1905), a feat since equaled by three other Hall of Famers—Bobby Jones, Ben Hogan, and Jack Nicklaus. Anderson is the only man to win the Open three years in a row and he had several other close calls as well. He finished second in 1897 when Joe Lloyd, one of the long drivers of the time, eagled 18—the only Open to be won by an eagle on the final hole. Anderson's Open record includes finishing third, fourth twice, and fifth three times. He set scoring records, including the first-ever 72 score (par) for a round at the Open (1901).

Anderson, born in North Berwick, was a modest man, though often brooding, and a heavy drinker, according to some sources. In addition to his accomplishments on the course, he led protests against second-class treatment of professionals by some of the exclusive golf clubs: at the 1901 Open, for example, professionals who were not members of the host Myopia Hunt Club (near Boston) were assigned to eat in the kitchen, but Anderson's agitation resulted in special tents being raised for the pros.

Anderson's skills began fading early; in 1910 he played a series of exhibition matches to supplement dwindling tournament winnings. Anderson died very young (somewhere between the age of 30 and 32), two days after a 36-hole exhibition match with fellow pro Gil Nicholls against Amateur Champions of 1910 and 1906—a match won by the amateurs when one of them sank a chip shot on the final hole.

TOMMY ARMOUR

1896–1968

Armour was one of the best-known golfers during the 1920s and 1930s and a respected instructor through his death in 1968. The "Silver Scot" won three Majors—the 1927 U.S. Open (in a playoff against future Hall of Famer Harry Cooper), the 1930 PGA Championship, and the 1931 British Open, where he came from 5 shots behind in the final round. He accomplished these feats after having lost an eye when his tank was hit by enemy artillery during World War I.

Armour moved to America after the war and has the distinction of playing both for and against the U.S. in international competition: he played for the United Kingdom in the first official Walker Cup Match (1921) and for the U.S. with a team of touring pros in a 1926 exhibition match against professionals from the United Kingdom at Wentworth Surrey, a competition that officially became the Ryder Cup in 1927. He teamed with Bobby Jones during mid-20s to win a series of seven exhibition matches against fellow professionals, and played in the first Masters in 1934.

Armour became equally renowned as a golf instructor. His book, *How to Play Your Best Golf All the Time* (1953), was for many years the biggest-selling publication on golf. Armour's philosophy can be summed up in a phrase—"Hit the hell out of the ball with your right hand"—that reflects his blunt and straightforward approach to golf and life in general. For example, on having scored 25 aces during his career Armour remarked, "I never felt the [hole-in-one] shot was anything but pure luck."

Armour occasionally suffered putting problems and coined the term "yips" to describe negative feelings that overcome golfers as they attempt to hole short putts. He introduced a thin-blade putter that was very popular during the 1960s.

JOHN BALL

Dec. 24, 1861–1940

The most prominent English amateur of the late-nineteenth century through World War I, Ball won eight British Amateur Championship titles, with a 24-year span between his first title in 1888 and his last in 1912, when he triumphed after being five strokes down with seven holes to play. He was competitive in amateur tournaments from his mid-teens through his last appearance in the British Amateur at age 60 in 1921. In 1890 he became the first Englishman to win the British Open, and in 1892 the first man to win the Amateur and Open championships in the same year.

The phrase "postage-stamp green" was coined by Tommy Armour who stated that the eighth green at Royal Troon was so small it was harder to hit than a postage stamp.

Ball also had two second-place finishes in the Amateur and was runner-up in the 1892 British Open. He had a couple of memorable duels with Freddie Tait, a two-time winner of the Amateur: in the 1899 tournament, Ball won on the first playoff hole after Tait made a miraculous save on 17 from standing water in a deep bunker, while Tait won a match later that year by coming from four down with 12 holes to play. Ball once won a bet with the stipulation that he must shoot under 90 and not lose a ball while playing in a dense fog. He shot an 81, using a black ball that was easier to track in the murk.

JIM BARNES

April 8, 1886–May 26, 1966

Long Jim Barnes won four Majors: the 1916 and 1919 PGA Championships, the 1921 U.S. Open, and the 1925 British Open, where he came from 5 strokes back on the final day to defeat MacDonald Smith, the third-round leader, by three strokes. Barnes was presented his U.S. Open trophy by President Warren G. Harding, a golf fan who remarked, "I'd give anything to be in your shoes today."

Born in Lelant, in the Cornwall region of England, Barnes emigrated to the United States in 1904. He won his first tournament in 1914 and his last in 1937, among the top 6 longest spans between a player's first and last wins in PGA history, and the 1937 win at age 51 made him the oldest player ever to win a PGA tournament until 52-year-old Sam Snead won in 1965. Barnes led or tied for the lead for most tournament wins in a year four times: 3 wins in 1916 tied with Walter Hagen;

2 in 1917 tied with Mike Brady; and he led outright with 5 in 1919 and 3 in 1921.

Barnes played with Willie Chisolm the day Chisolm took a then-record 18 strokes on a par 3, 185-yard hole at the 1919 U.S. Open; he helped the inebriated Chisolm count the strokes, although Chisolm claimed a few that Barnes counted were actually echoes.

PATTY BERG
Born Feb. 13, 1918

A leading player on the LPGA Tour and one of its founding members, Berg won an estimated 83 tournaments from the mid 1930s through the early 1960s. She has made immense contributions to women's professional golf as a player and leader, having organized the LPGA tour in 1948 with Babe Zaharias and Betty Jameson and serving as LPGA president from 1949-1952. She has been elected to numerous Halls of Fame, and her importance to golf is perhaps best exemplified by the annual Patty Berg Award, which was established by the LPGA in 1978 to recognize outstanding contributions to women's golf.

Berg first came to national attention by reaching the final of the 1935 U.S. Women's Amateur, losing to Glenna Collett Vare in the final Amateur victory of Vare's illustrious career. Berg reached the final again in 1937 and won the Amateur in 1938. She won the inaugural U.S. Women's Open in 1946 and a total of 41 events on the LPGA and WPGA tours, including the 1953, 1957, and 1958 Western Opens and the 1955 and 1957 Titleholders, considered majors at the time. She was runner-up in the 1957 Open at Winged Foot and the 1956 and 1959 LPGA Championships. Berg was the first woman to top $100,000 in earnings and led the LPGA in earnings in 1954, 1955, and 1957.

A great athlete, Berg played football as a youngster on a hometown Minneapolis team—the Fifteenth Street Tigers—organized by Bud Wilkin-

son, who would go on to become one of the all-time college football coaching greats at the University of Oklahoma. She was also an accomplished speed skater and took up golf at 13, winning the Minneapolis City Championship three years later. Injuries slowed her career, including an 18-month layoff following a car crash in 1941. In 1951 Berg was one of several American professional women golfers who challenged accomplished British male amateurs to a match; after a lunch break following the opening round in which the women were far behind, Berg led the women to victory—beginning with a lunch-ending statement to her teammates: "all those who expect to win their singles, follow me."

JULIUS BOROS
Born March 3, 1920

Boros was a late-bloomer in golf, joining the PGA Tour at age 30 in 1950 but quickly establishing himself as a major player by winning the 1952 U.S. Open and finishing that year as the Tour's leading money winner and its Player of the Year. He was also the leading money winner in 1955. Boros later won the 1963 U.S. Open (in a playoff over Arnold Palmer and Jacky Cupit, whom he beat by 6 and 3 strokes, respectively) and the 1968 PGA Championship, becoming at age 48 the oldest player ever to win a major. Boros captured the PGA Seniors Championship in 1971 and was a four-time Ryder Cup member. He won 18 PGA Tour events in all, placing him in the top 40 all-time in tournament wins, and his total career earnings exceeded $1 million.

Boros was an especially proficient sand player, frequently using a 9-iron from the bunker. In preparation for turning professional, he took driving instruction from Hall of Famer Tommy Armour, but could never master Armour's "hit the hell out of the ball with your right hand" philosophy. After Boros shanked a few drives Armour dismissed his chances of making it as a pro, but advised, "aim for the bunkers and you might make it."

JAMES BRAID

Feb. 6, 1870–Nov. 27, 1950

The Scottish-born Braid was a member of the Great Triumvirate with J.H. Taylor and Harry Vardon, who collectively won the British Open an astounding 16 times between 1894 and 1914. Braid won five Opens—1901, 1905, 1906, 1908, and 1910—the first to achieve that feat. He was runner-up in 1897 and 1909 and finished in the top five 15 times. Braid also won four British PGA championships (1903, 1905, 1907 and 1911) as well as the 1910 French Open. Braid first drew notice in 1895 when as an amateur he tied Open champion Taylor in an exhibition match.

Braid's 1901 British Open victory began and ended in notable fashion; his first drive hooked over a stone wall and landed out of bounds, and his wooden iron shattered on his tee shot at the final hole of the tournament: the ball still made it to the green 200 yards away, carrying twice as far as the severed club head. Braid lost the 1902 Open by a stroke to Sandy Herd, who had switched from the gutty ball to the Haskell on the first day of the tournament and immediately popularized the new rubber-cored golf ball.

MIKE BRADY

April 15, 1887–Dec. 3, 1972

Brady is among the greatest golfers never to win a major. He lost celebrated playoffs twice in the U.S. Open—to John McDermott in 1911 and to Walter Hagen in 1919. In 1917 he tied for the lead in Tour wins and in 1919 he succeeded Hagen as club pro at Oakland Hills, where he won the Western Open in 1917.

In the 1911 playoff, Brady lost to McDermott, who at age 19 became the youngest ever to win the Open. In the 1919 Open, Brady led Hagen by 5 strokes going into the final round, but shot an 80 and sweated the outcome in the clubhouse. Hagen

reached the 18th hole tied with Brady and made a beautiful approach shot that stopped eight feet short of the cup. While he walked to the green Hagen sent word ahead to Brady, inviting him to watch the tournament-winning putt. As Brady watched, the putt lipped the cup, and Hagen settled for a tie. During the playoff Hagen proved very resourceful: at one point he recommended to Brady that he roll down his shirt sleeves because "everyone can see your forearms quavering;" later, when an errant shot lie mired in muck, Hagen claimed the right to identify the ball, picked it up, wiped it and placed it back softly for a more favorable lie. Hagen won the playoff by a single stroke.

BILLY BURKE

Dec. 14, 1902–April 19, 1972

Burke had a solid career punctuated by an excellent 1931 season, when he won the U.S. Open, reached the semi-finals of the PGA Championship, won three other tournaments, and won both of his matches for the U.S. champion Ryder Cup team. His win at the Open came in a marathon 72-hole playoff against George von Elm: the two were tied after regulation and still tied after 36 playoff holes, forcing another 36 to be played, which Burke won by one stroke.

JACK BURKE, JR.

Born Jan. 29, 1923

A leading golfer of the 1950s, Burke won 15 PGA tournaments in his career, 41st on the all-time list, including a half-slam with the 1956 Masters and PGA championships. In the Masters he made up an eight-stroke deficit in the final round to overcome amateur Ken Venturi. He was PGA Player of the Year in 1956 and led the Tour in wins in 1952. After Burke's career was cut short by injuries, he teamed with Jimmy Demaret to build the Champions Club near Houston.

Burke first gained attention with two lopsided victories in the 1951 Ryder Cup matches. He also played on the 1953 and 1955 teams, captained the squad in 1957, and served as non-playing captain in 1973. Perhaps his most famous match was his nine-hour, 40-hole quarterfinal loss to Cary Middlecoff in the 1955 PGA Championship, which still used a match play format at the time.

WILLIAM C. CAMPBELL

1929–

Among the great American amateur golfers, Campbell achieved some notable tournament success but is as well respected for sportsmanship and as one of the sport's great international ambassadors. He competed in 37 U.S. Amateurs and 18 Walker Cup matches, winning the U.S. Amateur in 1964 after having moved through at least four rounds on six previous occasions dating back to a semifinal defeat in 1949 to that year's winner, C.R. Coe. Campbell reached the finals of the 1954 British Amateur and finished as runner up.

Campbell represented the United States on eight Walker Cup teams, 6 of which were triumphant, and another tied. In 18 matches, Campbell won 11 and halved three others, and he holds the all-time Walker Cup singles record with seven wins, one halve, and no losses. Campbell won the 1956 Bobby Jones Award, given annually by the USGA for distinguished sportsmanship—"the demonstration of personal qualities esteemed in sport: fair play, self-control and perhaps self-denial; generosity of spirit towards the game as a whole, and the manner of playing or behaving so as to show respect for the game and the people in it."

JOANNE CARNER

Born April 4, 1939

Still Competing. See Pro Files: Women.

HARRY COOPER

Born August 6, 1904

"Lighthorse" Cooper, so named for his quick pace, was a master of precision and a top touring pro of the 1920s and 1930s who never broke through in the Majors.

He had seven top ten finishes in the U.S. Open, including second place in 1927, when he lost in a playoff to Tommy Armour, and 1936, when he finished two strokes behind Tony Manero. Cooper also placed second in the 1936 Masters, losing by a stroke to Horton Smith, and was almost an annual quarterfinalist in the PGA Championship.

Cooper won 31 titles on the PGA Tour, placing him in the top 15 of all-time in tournament wins. He captured 8 tournament championships in 1937 and was awarded the first Vardon Trophy. Cooper won the Canadian Open in 1932 and 1937.

HENRY COTTON

Born Jan. 26, 1907

Cotton brought the British Open crown back to Great Britain by winning the 1934 Open, the first time in 11 years that it was won by an Englishman. He was in the prime of his excellent career, which featured two other Open wins (1937 and 1948), when World War II intervened. Cotton's 1934 Open triumph included a record second round 65 that featured 11 birdies, in which the longest putt he faced was 9 feet—reflective of his masterful skill with irons. The popular Dunlop 65 ball was named after the score he attained in that round. He had a ten stroke lead going into the final round, but was headed for a major collapse before closing with 4 pars and a 5 stroke victory. The final round of Cotton's 1937 win was concluded in a torrential rain, but he still managed to shoot 70. Great precision characterized his 1948 championship, as Cotton hit 53 of 56 fairways, and won by five strokes, becoming the first man from Great Britain to achieve three Open championships since the Great Triumvirate of Vardon, Taylor, and Braid.

Cotton's first career triumph was at the 1926 Kent Open, his first appearance in the Ryder Cup was in 1929, and he was a runner-up in the British PGA Championship in 1930. He captured many European titles: in 1937 alone, Cotton won the British, French and Czechoslovakian Opens and was selected for the Ryder Cup matches. Cotton served as captain of the Ryder Cup team in 1947 and 1953. Cotton also became a noted course designer.

BOBBY CRUICKSHANK
Nov 16. 1894–Aug. 27, 1975

Of Scottish birth, Cruickshank was prominent on the PGA Tour during the years between the World Wars, winning 17 tour events (among the Top 50 all-time) and being involved in several excruciating near-misses in the Majors. He reached the finals of the 1922 and 1923 PGA Championships, losing both times to Gene Sarazen, was runner-up in the 1923 and 1932 U.S. Opens, and led the 1934 Open until he was undone by his own expression of elation. On the 11th hole of the final round of that Open at Merion Golf Course in Philadelphia, Cruickshank sent an approach shot that was dipping into a water hazard when it miraculously skipped off the surface and rolled on to the green. Cruickshank threw up his arms and the iron in jubilation, and the club came down and conked him on the head, knocking him out. He finished the round dizzily and ended up third. Cruickshank's greatest year was 1927, when he won the Los Angeles and Texas Opens and finished as the leading money winner for the year. He last won on the Tour in 1935.

Among Cruickshank's celebrated and agonizing near-misses was the 1923 U.S. Open. Bobby Jones had the tournament in hand during the final round until finishing bogey, bogey, double bogey, while Cruikshank made a marvelous approach shot to the 18th green, carrying over a lagoon and stopping within six feet of the hole to set up a tournament-tying birdie putt. During the playoff, the two golfers came to 18 still tied. Cruikshank hooked his drive behind a tree, then had to lay up before the lagoon, while Jones sliced his drive into the rough, 200 yards from the green. It was Jones' turn for a marvelous approach, his shot landing six feet from the cup, and he parred it for his first Major championship. A few years later, Crickshank made legal bets in Scotland that Jones would win the Grand Slam in 1930, and when Jones completed the Slam Cruickshank pocketed $10,000; *The New York Times* mistakenly estimated the winnings at $100,000, leading to an Internal Revenue Service audit that eventually cleared Cruickshank. Cruickshank was a World War I hero, who witnessed his brother's death by an enemy shell, was captured and made a prisoner of war, and escaped through enemy lines to rejoin the fighting.

JIMMY DEMARET
May 24, 1910–Dec. 28, 1983

Demaret was among the most colorful members of the PGA as a golfer and announcer. He won 31 events (ranking in the Top 15 all-time) and was the first three-time winner of the Masters (1940, by a then-record 4 strokes, 1947, and 1950). Demaret peaked from 1940 to 1950, leading the Tour with 6 wins in 1940, taking 3 Masters, leading the Tour in earnings and winning the Vardon Trophy in 1947, and finishing second to Ben Hogan in both the 1948 U.S. Open and the PGA Championship. He reached the semi-finals of the PGA Championship four times, was unbeaten in Three Ryder Cup appearances, and represented the U.S. in the 1961 World Cup. As his career wound down in the 1950s, although he was still winning tournaments, like the 1952 Crosby, he became a popular television announcer and was the original host of Shell's Wonderful World of Golf in the early 1960s. The over-70s groupings on the PGA

Senior Tour are known as the Friends of Demaret, in his honor.

Demaret's freewheeling personality is exemplified in a couple of incidents. As a TV announcer he covered the 1953 World Championship of Golf, which typically drew an excellent field because of its large purse. This was the first coast-to-coast broadcast of a golf tournament, and it ended dramatically with a shot that at that point was seen by more people than any in golf history. Lew Worsham sent a 100 yard wedge shot to the green and it rolled into the hole for a tournament-winning eagle; as the ball fell into the hole, Demaret exclaimed, "the son-of-a-bitch holed it!" On another occasion, being told Ben Hogan had said that if Demaret practiced as hard as Hogan he would win every tournament, Demaret raised his glass and replied, "I'll drink to that."

ROBERTO DE VICENZO
Born April 14, 1923

One of the greatest international golfers, De Vicenzo won over 200 tournaments worldwide, including four on the PGA Tour and the 1967 British Open. De Vicenzo was making his 19th Open appearance that year without much previous success; during the final round he held off charges by two of the hottest golfers of the time—Jack Nicklaus and Gary Player, both future Hall of Famers—to win the tournament at age 44, the oldest Open winner in modern times. A second Major, the 1968 Masters, eluded the Argentine-born golfer in perhaps the most unfortunate mistake in the history of professional golf, when he signed an incorrect scorecard and was disqualified.

DeVicenzo found great success in the early days of the PGA Senior Tour, winning the Liberty Mutual Legends of Golf three times and the inaugural U.S. Senior Open in 1980. He also won the 1974 PGA Seniors Championship and represented Argentina 17 times in the Canada and World Cups.

De Vicenzo's final round in the 1968 Masters was especially spectacular, beginning with an eagle 2 and a front nine 31, five under par. Birdies at 12 and 15 put him 7 under par; his approach on 17 landed within five feet of the hole, and he put it in for another birdie. A bogey at 18, though, left him tied for the lead. Unfortunately, Tommy Aaron, who was keeping De Vicenzo's score for the round, marked a 4 instead of a 3 on 17, and when Di Vicenzo signed the scorecard, 66 became his official score for the round, instead of the correct, tournament-tying 65. He was disqualified—the mistake costing him a chance at a playoff with Bob Goalby for the green jacket, but De Vicenzo accepted this fate with utmost sportsmanship. Still, he gained a small bit of revenge a couple years later on writers who mocked his plight.

When presented the William D. Richardson Award for significant contributions to golf, he held the trophy up and noted in his best English to a packed ballroom, "Golf writers make three mistakes spelling my name on the trophy. Maybe I not the only stupid."

LEO DIEGEL
April 27, 1899–May 5, 1951

Diegel was am excellent player of the 1920s and early 1930s, winning 11 PGA Tour events, including 5 in 1925—most of any player that year. He won the PGA Championship in 1928 and 1929, ending the four-year winning streak of Walter Hagen by defeating him in the quarter-final in 1928 to avenge defeats by Hagen in the 1925 quarter-finals and the 1926 final. Hagen had a different form of revenge: he misplaced the PGA Championship Trophy, which was found a couple years later in a Detroit factory, carefully wrapped within a beaten-up storage crate that had passed from a bankrupt golf-equipment manufacturer in Florida to one in Detroit. The temporary replacement trophy with which Diegel was presented in 1928 was subsequently lost by the PGA.

Diegel won the Canadian Open four times, (1924-25, 1928-29) and played on the inaugural 1927 Ryder Cup team as well as the 1929, 1931 and 1933 squads. He was runner-up to Bobby Jones at the British Open in 1930, falling two strokes shy of denying Jones one part of his Grand Slam.

Diegel was a high-strung man who frequently had to battle for self-control, a struggle he most often won, as indicated by his success. In order to calm himself on the green Diegel developed a distinctive, bird-like putting style: he spread his arms outward from the grip—elbows and forearms parallel to the ground. This method usually served him well, but it failed him on the 18th green of the 1933 British Open, where he needed one putt to win, two to force a three-man playoff. His first putt stopped within two feet of the hole, but he whiffed on the next one, holing out in three to tie with two others for third place. In the nerve-wracking 1920 U.S. Open, Diegel was the final-round leader at 14 after Harry Vardon and Ted Ray bogeyed holes ahead. An excited friend broke Diegel's concentration as he prepared to drive on 14 by informing him of the good news and an exasperated Diegel fell apart, double-bogeying 14 and bogeying 16 and 17, finishing in a tie for second with Vardon, one stroke behind Ray.

ED DUDLEY
Feb. 19, 1901–Oct. 25, 1963

Dudley was another golfing great who never won a major. A 15-time winner on the Tour during the years between the World Wars, which places him among the Top 50 all-time, Dudley had his best showing in 1933, when he was a quarter-finalist in the PGA Championship and won selection to the Ryder Cup team. He won two key matches in the 1937 Ryder Cup to help the United States capture the competition for the first time on English turf. A steady if not spectacular player, Dudley was one of only two professionals to break par at the Pine Valley Invitational during the late 1930s, covering 450 rounds of golf: Craig Wood did it in 1938 and Dudley in 1939.

OLIN DUTRA
Jan. 17, 1901–May 5, 1983

Dutra won 19 tournaments during the late 1920s and 1930s, including the 1932 PGA Championship, where he played 196 holes and finished an astounding 19 under par, and the 1934 U.S. Open, where he held off Gene Sarazen by one stroke. Dutra tied for the lead in tournaments won in 1932 and played in the 1933 and 1935 Ryder Cup matches.

CHARLES EVANS, JR.
July 18, 1890–Nov. 6, 1979

Chick Evans was the greatest American amateur golfer before Bobby Jones. He competed in a record 50 consecutive U.S. Amateurs, winning in 1916 and 1920 and finishing second three times. He won the U.S. Open in 1916, becoming the first golfer to win the Amateur and Open in the same year, and he finished second in the 1914 Open. He was selected to the Walker Cup team in 1922, 1924, and 1928.

Evans was particularly skilled in the short game. In the 1914 U.S. Open he needed an eagle on the par 4, 277 yard 18th hole to tie Walter Hagen. After nearly driving the green, he chipped to the cup, falling short of the tying eagle by less than a foot. He finished the job in 1916. Evans led after three rounds, but Jock Hutchison finished his final round with a 68 and a 288 72-hole total, which broke the Open record by two strokes. But Evans played with precision and closed two strokes better at 286—an Open record that stood for twenty years despite enormous improvements in clubs and golf balls. Evans' victory in the U.S. Amateur that year against defending champion Bob Gardner was equally dramatic, as Gardner whittled Evans' 3-stroke first round lead to one before Evans pulled away on the back nine. Evans played his last nine holes in 1978 at age 88, burying a 25-yard pitch shot on the final hole to go out with style.

JOHNNY FARRELL
Born April 1, 1901

Farrell had a mighty run of success from the mid-1920s through the early-30s, winning 22 tournaments, including seven in 1927 alone. He ranks in the Top 25 all-time in tournament wins.

Farrell won the U.S. Open in 1928 in a tight, 36-hole playoff with Bobby Jones, and in 1929 he was runner-up at both the British Open (to Walter Hagen) and the PGA Championship (to Leo Diegel). Farrell was a key member of the first Ryder Cup team in 1927 and played in the 1929 and 1931 matches as well. His career declined in the 1930s, but Farrell reappeared in the 1950s when he competed in several PGA Seniors Championships.

DOUG FORD
Born August 6, 1922

Ford was the top player on the tour during the mid-1950s and prior to the arrival of Arnold Palmer and Jack Nicklaus. He won 19 PGA Tour titles, ranking in the Top 40 all-time, including the 1955 PGA Championship and the 1957 Masters, where he outdueled three-time winner Sam Snead. In addition to the Masters, Ford's 1957 season included wins at the Los Angeles Open and the Western Open. Ford was on the Ryder Cup team between 1955-61 and was named PGA Player of the Year in 1955.

Ford continued to be a strong threat on tour through the early 1960s, winning the Canadian Open in 1959 and 1963, the 1962 Crosby, and finishing fifth in the 1961 and 1962 PGA Championships. Ford managed several top-20 finishes in the PGA Seniors Championship in the 1970s and won two unofficial Seniors events in 1981.

VIC GHEZZI
Oct. 19, 1912–May 30, 1976

Ghezzi was an overnight sensation at 22 with a playoff victory over future Hall of Famer Johnny Revolta in the 1935 Los Angeles Open. His career had several other bright moments but was interrupted as well by World War II. Ghezzi won the 1941 PGA Championship at Cherry Hills in a playoff over Byron Nelson and lost the 1946 U.S. Open in a playoff with Lloyd Mangrum; Byron Nelson, whose caddy slipped on a green during the third round and accidentally kicked Nelson's ball, resulting in a penalty stroke, was also in that 36-hole playoff that Mangrum won by a single stroke. Ghezzi was selected for the 1939 and 1941 Ryder Cup teams but the matches were canceled due to the war. He reached the semifinals of the 1947 PGA Championship and later played in PGA Seniors Championships during the 1960s.

RALPH GULDAHL
Born Nov. 22, 1911

Guldahl won 16 tournaments (ranking in the Top 45, all-time) during the 1930s and early 1940s, overcoming fits of erratic putting and an early retirement at age 22. He first rose to prominence as a runner-up in the 1933 U.S. Open, battling fellow 20-year-old Johnny Goodman to the end before bogeying the final hole. His game began faltering during the next two seasons and in 1935 Guldahl quit the Tour, returning to his hometown of Dallas. His son had developed health problems, and Guldahl moved his family to the California desert where the dry air was better for his son's health. He began playing golf there occasionally with movie executive Ralph Woolsey and actor Rex Bell. They lent him $100 to restart his career in early 1936. He placed in the money in a few tournaments, winning enough cash to keep trying, then won the Western Open and ended up with the best average score per round on the Tour that year.

1937 was a year of agony and ecstasy for Guldahl. He enjoyed a comfortable lead at the turn in the final round of the Masters, but he double bogeyed the par three 12th hole and bogeyed the par five 13th; meanwhile, Byron Nelson birdied and eagled those holes, respectively, creating a six-stroke turnaround. Nelson went on to win the tournament by two-strokes and achieved a bit of revenge as well. Ten years earlier, when both Nelson and Guldahl were sixteen, Guldahl crushed the already competing amateur Nelson in a 72-hole caddie tournament that was ceded after 54 holes because Guldahl had an 18-stroke lead. A few weeks after the Masters disaster, however, and while Sam Snead was in the clubhouse accepting congratulations for a sure victory in the U.S. Open, Guldahl followed a front nine 33 with a 36 coming in, winning the Open with a record low score 281. Guldahl also keyed the 1937 Ryder Cup triumph by winning both his matches.

In 1938, Guldahl again finished second in the Masters, but became only the fourth man ever to win consecutive Opens—finishing ahead by six strokes—and he also won the second of three straight Western Opens titles. Guldahl also had a stellar 1939 campaign, winning the Masters (again Snead finished as runner-up) and the Greensboro Open, and he reached the semifinals of the PGA Championship in 1940. After reaching the quarterfinals in the 1941 PGA Championship, Guldahl did not have any more significant success.

Guldahl once gave golf lessons to Howard Hughes, and Hughes once kept him on the phone for hours as he prepared meticulously, hole-by-hole and under varying conditions, for a club tournament. Hughes won the tournament, and Guldahl received a $10,000 check in the mail a few days later.

WALTER HAGEN
Dec. 21, 1892–Oct. 6, 1969

A flamboyant and colorful personality on and off the course, Hagen dominated professional golf in the 1910s and 1920s. He set a record for winning consecutive matches (22) in PGA Championships while capturing four consecutive titles from 1924 through 1927; he won his first PGA in 1921. He tied for the most wins on the PGA Tour

After playing in the 1928 Tijuana Open, Walter Hagen and Joe Kirkwood made a $50 bet on who could hit a ball back to their hotel in the fewest strokes. Hagen got there first but was unable to get his ball into the toilet, which had been designated as the official "hole." Kirkwood nailed his porcelain wedge shot on the first try.

five times—1916, 1918, 1922, 1923, and 1924. It was his victory in the 1914 U.S. Open at the age of 21 that convinced Hagen to turn to golf full-time. He later won the 1919 U.S. Open, when it was resumed after World War I. His record of 11 major championship victories has been exceeded only by Jack Nicklaus and Bobby Jones, and his career total of 40 PGA tournament victories places him tied for seventh with Cary Middlecoff on the list of all-time Tour winners.

Hagen is regarded as a pioneer for having helped improve the standing of professional golfers, especially in Great Britain, where Hagen was a four-time winner of the British Open (1922, 1924, 1928, 1929) and the first American-born player to win an Open. His antics there helped break down barriers for the pros. For example, host clubs like Royal St. George's and Troon wouldn't allow professional golfers to use their clubhouse facilities to eat or change. Hagen customarily hired a limousine, which he used as a changing room, and had it park outside the clubhouse, where he had a lavish meal served on a portable table.

He reputedly referred to the Duke of Windsor as "Eddie" when they played golf together.

Hagen was the first American golfer to earn a living as a touring professional, but he knew he would have to supplement his tournament winnings with exhibition matches. He played as many as 125 exhibitions a year, often with Australian trick-shot artist Joe Kirkwood. Hagen later became the first professional golfer to establish his own equipment manufacturing company.

The extroverted Hagen influenced the life of future golf professionals in other ways, too. On the course he dressed for style and color. After Hagen played in vibrant pullover or cardigan sweaters and plus-fours, golf fashion became less conservative and coats virtually disappeared as golfing attire. He also popularized black-and-white golf shoes. In business matters, Hagen was the first golf professional to employ a manager.

SANDRA HAYNIE

Born June 4, 1943

After winning several amateur events as a teenager in the 1950s, including the 1957 and 1958 Texas amateurs and the 1960 Trans-Mississippi, Haynie turned pro in 1961. She became one of the best LPGA players of the 1960s and 1970s, winning a total of 42 LPGA tournaments in her career. Her final Tour championship victory came in the 1982 Peter Jackson Classic.

Haynie won the LPGA Championship in 1965 and 1974 and the U.S. Women's Open in 1974. Winning the only two designated major championships in 1974 gave Haynie the honor of being the only golfer along with Babe Zaharias to have won all the LPGA Majors in a given year. Fellow Hall of Famer JoAnne Carner led the field by two strokes in the 1974 Women's Open with nine holes to play, but Haynie outdueled her and two other golfers, finishing with birdies on the final two holes to win the championship by a stroke. Haynie won ten tournaments spanning 1974 and 1975 and tied for the LPGA Tour lead in victories both of those years.

HAROLD HILTON

1869–1942

Harold Horace Hilton was one of the great amateur golfers as well as a bit of an eccentric character. He played in white sneakers with some-what rumpled clothes, a small hat perched back on his head and a cigarette dangling from his lips; some claimed he smoked up to 50 cigarettes during a round of golf. He was small in stature and played with an extremely aggressive style—his feet sometimes leaving the ground while uncorking drives.

He had an immediate impact, finishing as runner-up in the 1891 British Amateur, losing on the second playoff hole; repeated as runner up the next year. But in 1892 he became only the second amateur to win the British Open. In his usually quirky manner, Hilton showed up the morning of the final practice round fresh from an all-night train ride and left on the train immediately following the tournament. He had his third second-place finish in the Amateur in 1896 and won his second British Open in 1897 at his home course of Holyoke. He came close in two other Opens, finishing third in 1898, 2 strokes behind Harry Vardon and had a fourth-place finish in 1901.

After three second-place finishes, Hilton started winning the British Amateur, first in 1900 and then defending his title in 1901. He also won the British Amateur in 1911 and 1913. Hilton also won the U.S. Amateur in 1911, becoming the first man to win both the British and American Amateurs in the same year. His 1911 U.S. Amateur was memorable: he blew a six-hole lead and ended up tied with Fred Herreshoff. Herreshoff outdrove Hilton on the first playoff hole, a par 4, 377 yard hole with a green elevated high above the fairway and bordered on the left by a mound studded with rocks. Hilton's approach shot was off target, veering left, but hit a soft spot on the mound and rolled down on to the green for a tap in. Herreshoff couldn't recover.

Having accumulated four British Amateur titles and seven top-2 finishes, a U.S. Amateur, and two British Opens, Hilton began concentrating on other golf pursuits. He served as an editor of *Golf Monthly* and *Golf Illustrated* and became a respected golf course designer.

BEN HOGAN
Born Aug. 13, 1912

Generally considered one of the top golfers of all time, Hogan's road to golf success and fame was not an easy one. He turned pro at the age of 17 but was plagued by a snap-hook. He worked on developing the perfect swing but didn't win his first tournament until he was 25. Then he had to wait another eight years before winning his first major, the 1946 PGA Championship. In 1948 he scored the first of his four U.S. Open victories and notched his second PGA Championship.

After dominating the PGA Tour in the 1940s, where he was the leading money winner in 1940-42, 1946, and 1948 and led in victories in 1942 and 1946-48, Hogan suffered a near-fatal automobile accident in February of 1949 when his car ran head-on into a bus in Texas. His legs were severely damaged in the accident, and many thought he would be lucky to be able to walk again, let alone play golf. Remarkably, Hogan recovered, underwent an arduous rehabilitation, and was competing professionally by January of 1950.

Hogan mounted an inspired comeback in the 1950s, winning the U.S. Open in 1950, 1951, and 1953. He won his first Masters Tournament in 1951 and repeated in 1953. In 1953 Hogan also won his first and only British Open at Carnoustie. That made three majors in one year. Unfortunately, Hogan was unable to compete in the 1953 PGA Championship because of a scheduling conflict with the British Open. Hogan remained competitive throughout the 1950s, finishing second in the 1955 and 1956 U.S. Opens and third in 1960.

After his professional career declined, rather than competing in Senior events, Hogan concentrated on managing his highly successful golf equipment company, the Ben Hogan Company. He also wrote one of the classics of golf instruction, *Five Lessons*. In 1967 he served as nonplaying captain of the U.S. Ryder Cup team, the same year he made a run at the Masters.

BOB HOPE

See Golf and Popular Culture.

BETTY JAMESON
Born May 19, 1919

Jameson was dominant as an amateur and then as a professional during the formative years of women's professional golf. She won back-to-back titles in the U.S. Women's Amateur in 1939 and 1940 and took ten LPGA titles in the 1940s and 1950s, including a victory in the 1947 U.S. Women's Open. She had finished as runner-up in the 1946 Open, but dominated play in 1947 and won by six strokes. In 1948 she joined Babe Zaharias and Patty Berg to organize the original American Women's Professional Tour, which consisted of eight events in its first year.

In the 1950s Jameson finished runner-up in the 1952 U.S. Women's Open and won the 1954 Western Open, then considered a major championship. She went on to win three LPGA titles in 1955.

ROBERT T. JONES
March 17, 1902–Dec. 18, 1971

For the greatest amateur golfer of all time, a Grand Slam consisted of winning the U.S. and British Open and Amateur titles. It was this feat that Bobby Jones set out to accomplish in 1930. A Grand Slam year would be the fitting end to a spectacular amateur career. Going into 1930, Jones had won nine major championships since 1923: three U.S. Opens, four U.S. Amateur titles, and three British Opens. A teenage phenomenon, Jones qualified for the 1916 U.S. Amateur when he was only 14 years old, then reached the final of the 1919 U.S. Amateur. He won the Amateur in 1924, 1925, 1927 and 1928. Jones won two British Opens in a row 1926 and 1927, the 1926 victory coming on a great shot on the 71st hole. He finished second to 20-year-old Gene Sarazen, who shot a final-round 68,

> "If I ever needed an eight-foot putt and every-
> thing I owned depended on it, I would want
> Arnold Palmer to putt it for me."
>
> —Bobby Jones

in the 1922 U.S. Open and took the first two of his four Opens in 1923 and 1926. The 1923 win came in a playoff over Bobby Cruickshank, who made a spectacular final-round comeback. In 1929, Jones blew a four-stroke lead over Al Espinosa with four holes to play, but whipped Espinosa by 23 strokes in a 36-hole playoff.

In 1930 Jones won the first leg of his Grand Slam bid when he took the British Amateur on the Old Course at St. Andrews. He then captured the British Open at Royal Liverpool with 291, two strokes ahead of Leo Diegel and Macdonald Smith. Back in the United States, Jones shot 287 at the Interlachen Country Club in Minneapolis, Minnesota, to win the U.S. Open by two strokes over Mac Smith. He completed his Grand Slam with a victory in the U.S. Amateur at Merion. At the end of his amateur career at age 28, Jones had won 13 major championships, a feat only surpassed by Jack Nicklaus. In addition to capturing four U.S. Opens, he finished second four times, and won three of the four British Opens in which he participated.

Jones held degrees in engineering, law and literature from the Atlanta School of Technology and Harvard University. He began planning the Augusta National Golf Course in the early 1930s. Having been greatly impressed with the design of Cypress Point, which he played in the 1929 U.S. Amateur at Pebble Beach, he hired its architect, Alister MacKenzie to design the Augusta course. New York financier Clifford Roberts selected the site and arranged the financing. Construction of Augusta was completed in 1932. Jones and Roberts wanted to show off their new course with a tournament, and after Augusta failed to land a U.S. Open, they decided to stage their own invitational tournament based primarily on golfers that

Jones had played against. Originally to be called the Augusta National Invitational, the tournament became the Masters and was first held in 1934.

See also his profile in the Course Designers chapter.

W. LAWSON LITTLE
June 23, 1910–Feb. 1, 1968

Little showed great potential as the leading amateur of the 1930s. After reaching the semifinals of the U.S. Amateur in 1933, he was rewarded with a spot on the Walker Cup team in 1934. Little and Johnny Goodman won the Walker Cup for the United States, soundly defeating Britain's best, Roger Wethered and Cyril Tolley. Little proceeded to win the 1934 British Amateur before returning to the States and winning the U.S. Amateur. He solidifed his reputation by successfully defending both titles in 1935.

After 1935 Little joined the PGA Tour. His decision to turn professional was as important in the mid-1930s as similar moves in later years by Arnold Palmer, Jack Nicklaus, and Tiger Woods. Little won the 1936 Canadian Open, the first of seven PGA Tour victories. He also won the 1940 U.S. Open, defeating two-time winner Gene Sarazen by three strokes in a playoff.

GENE LITTLER
Born July 21, 1930

Still Competing. See Pro Files: Seniors.

BOBBY LOCKE
(ARTHUR D'ARCY LOCKE)
1917–1987

Locke became the first golfer to fashion his own international tour, maintaining a presence on the PGA Tour as well as in South Africa and Great Britain during the 1940s and 1950s. The South

African golfer first came to attention before World War II, when he won the New Zealand Open. After the war he quickly established himself as a force in the United States and Europe. He won 11 events on the PGA Tour between 1947-50, including the 1947 Tournament of Champions and Canadian Open and the 1948 Phoenix Open.

After finishing second to Sam Snead in the 1946 British Open, Locke captured his first of four Opens in 1949, defeating Harry Bradshaw in a playoff at Sandwich.

He successfully defended his title in 1950 at Troon with a record-setting score of 279, the first-ever sub-280 four-round total in a British Open. He won again in 1952 at Royal Lytham. His victory in 1957 is probably his most famous, where he again shot 279, this time at St. Andrews. It was the first year the British Open was televised, and on the final hole Locke inadvertently misplaced his ball on the green. His error went unnoticed until it was later seen on a news film, but it was decided that since he gained no benefit and the tournament was over, the victory would stand. He had won by three strokes, anyway.

During the 1950s Locke took home the national championships of South Africa, Germany, France, Switzerland, and Egypt. He was allowed to compete for England in the 1953 Canada Cup, but afterwards represented South Africa. His final Canada Cup appearance was in 1960, where he teamed with Gary Player to lead South Africa to a fifth-place finish.

NANCY LOPEZ

Still Competing. See Pro Files: Women.

CAROL MANN

Born February 3, 1941

Mann was a giant on the LPGA Tour during the 1960s and 1970s, with 38 career tournament victories and a height of 6' 3". She started out on the junior amateur circuit, winning the 1958 Western and Chicago Juniors. After she won the 1960 Chicago Amateur, Mann turned professional.

Mann's most important win was the 1965 U.S. Women's Open; she fell behind by seven strokes after the first round but rallied to take command in the middle rounds and won the tournament by two strokes. The final round was the first nationally-televised women's tournament competition. Mann fell by one stroke in her Open title defense in 1966. She enjoyed excellent years in 1968 and 1969. In 1968 she won three consecutive tournaments and ten overall, tieing for the lead with Kathy Whitworth, and was awarded the Vare Trophy for lowest scoring average. She led the LPGA Tour in victories in 1969 with eight and was the Tour's leading money winner. Mann again tied for the Tour lead in wins in 1975 with four.

CARY MIDDLECOFF

Born Jan. 6, 1921

Middlecoff's 40 PGA Tour victories between 1947 and 1961 place him tied for seventh with Walter Hagen on the list of all-time PGA Tour winners. His dentist's degree earned him the nickname "Doc" on the Tour. After winning some amateur tournaments and the 1945 North and South Open, the only time an amateur won that event, Middlecoff was invited to play on the 1947 Walker Cup team for the United States but decided to turn professional instead. He won his first professional tournament that year, then finished second to Claude Harman in the 1948 Masters.

Middlecoff led the PGA Tour in victories three times, starting in 1949 with seven wins. That year at Medinah he won his first U.S. Open, shooting a course-record 67 in the second round to make up for his first-round 75, which had him in 38th place. Middlecoff was a nervous man who calmed himself on the course by playing very methodically, and while sweating out his 1949 Open win in the clubhouse as others finished their rounds, he bet against himself as the eventual winner. In 1951 he again led the PGA Tour with wins (6), including the Colonial. In 1953 he was selected for the U.S. Ryder Cup team. His best year came in 1955, when he won the Masters and the Western Open on his way to a Tour-leading six victories. His seven-stroke margin over Ben Hogan in the 1955 Masters was a dominant performance. That year he also finished second in the PGA Championship, losing to Doug Ford, and was selected for the second time to play on the U.S. Ryder Cup team.

Still at the top of his game in 1956, Middle-coff captured his second U.S. Open victory, this time at Oak Hill, where he sweated out missed opportunities by Ben Hogan (a 30-inch putt that couldn't find the cup on 17) and Julius Boros (an in-and-out 15-footer on 18), beating them both by a stroke. Defending his Open crown in 1957, Middlecoff made up 8 strokes during the final two rounds to tie Dick Mayer, but lost to Mayer by 7 strokes in a playoff, where Meyer brought along a folding chair to rest on while Middlecoff studied and prepared for his shots.

Middlecoff played on the U.S. Ryder Cup team for the third time in 1959. After being one of the dominant players of the 1950s, "Doc" captured his final tour victory in 1961 at Memphis, Tennessee, not far from where he was raised.

JOHNNY MILLER

Born 1947–

Miller enjoyed his greatest success during the 1970s, when he won two Majors among 17 Tour victories. He was capable of brilliant runs, highlighted by long iron approaches that set up birdie putts—as he displayed in the 1973 U.S. Open, when he shot a record low 63 in the final round at Oakmont to win the championship. During the following two years he had 12 Tour victories, was

named PGA Player of the Year in 1974, and finished first and second, respectively, on the money list. In 1976, he won the British Open.

As a 19-year-old, Miller wanted desperately to be part of the U.S. Open, which was being held in his hometown of San Francisco at the Olympic Club. He signed up to caddy and also tried his luck in the qualifying tournament: he shot 143 and won a player badge. In the Open, Miller was tied with Jack Nicklaus, 5-strokes behind the lead, after two rounds, and finished tied for eighth place. Miller joined the PGA Tour in 1969 and won his first event, the Southern Open, in 1971. At the 1972 British Open at Muirfield, Miller displayed the dazzle of things to come: facing the 570-yard 5th hole during the third round, Miller drove his ball about 290 yards on the hard fairway, leaving him about 280 yards to the pin, which was tucked back, into the right corner. He hit a three-iron that landed just short of the green, rolled up and continued rolling until trickling into the cup for the double-eagle. For the round, Miller carded a course-record, three-under 66, which put him into contention on the final day.

During the final round of his 1973 U.S. Open win, which he entered tied for thirteenth place six strokes behind, Miller hit every green in regulation and took only 29 putts; ten of his approach shots with irons stopped within 15-feet of the hole, five of those within six feet. He won by a stroke. The next year Miller won 8 events and was the PGA Player of the Year; he won four more events in 1975, and took the 1976 British Open by six strokes. Prior to his 1973 Open win, Miller had a reputation for running hot and cold, as in the 1971 Masters, when he lost a two-stroke lead on the final four holes. He cooled off after 1976 and began curtailing his appearances, broadening his family activities as well as his interests in course architecture and broadcasting. Still, he won four events from 1980 to 1983 and was in the top 20 in earnings from 1981-1983. He won the 1987 AT&T Pebble Beach National Pro-Am in 1987, then came back and won it again in 1994 for the third time and on the twentieth anniversary of his first win in the tournament.

Miller was also a three time winner of the Tucson Open (1974-1976) and twice played on Ryder Cup teams (1975, 1981). Still playing occasional tournaments and widely recognized as a broadcaster for NBC, Miller has 24 tournament wins to date and 49 top-three finishes.

TOM MORRIS, JR.
1851–Dec. 25, 1875

"Young Tom," son of British Open champion and St. Andrews greenskeeper "Old Tom" Morris, was a dominant player of the late 1860s and early 1870s until his untimely death on Christmas Day, 1875, at the age of 24. His feat of winning four consecutive British Open titles has never been matched, and likely never will be. More than being a dominant golfer, Young Tom was innovative as well. He introduced the use of the niblick, or five-iron, for approach shots, and used the cleek, previously used only for run-up shots, for pitching; he is said to have been the first golfer to use backspin.

In winning four consecutive British Opens, Young Tom brought scoring to a new level. A careful and meticulous putter, Young Tom won his first British Open in 1868 at the age of 17, succeeding his father as the Open champ. His score was 157 (36-hole format), five strokes under the previous record, and he is credited as having shot the first ace in championship play on Prestwick's 8th hole. Begun in 1860, the British Open was played at Prestwick every year until a rotation was established with St. Andrews and Musselburgh in 1873. The tournament consisted of three rounds played over Prestwick's 12-hole links, for a 36-hole total. In 1869 Young Tom improved his score to 154, beating his father, who finished second, by two strokes, and then shot a 149 in 1870, winning his third consecutive Open by a whopping 12 strokes; his 18-hole average score of 74.5 stood for 34 years and was never beaten with the gutta-percha ball.

Under the terms of the tournament, anyone who won three consecutive Opens was entitled to take permanent possession of the Challenge Belt, made of genuine red Morocco leather embellished with silver ornaments. Since Young Tom owned the belt after his third victory, the Open was discontinued in 1871. When it was resumed in 1872, with a cup as the prize, Young Tom promptly won his fourth Open. It would be his last Open victory, although he continued to play money matches.

Young Tom was teamed with his father in the midst of one of their money matches in September of 1875, when he received word that his wife had died in childbirth. Heartbroken, he only played in two more matches to honor previous commitments, then died three months later on Christmas Day.

TOM MORRIS, SR.
June 16, 1821–1908

Old Tom Morris was the most widely influential golfing figure during the time when golf became organized into the modern game. In addition to being a leading professional golfer and the first four-time winner of the British Open, Old Tom brought expert skill to such areas as greenskeeping, golf course architecture, and the manufacturing of clubs and balls. From his stoop at Old Tom's Golf Shop at St. Andrews he mentored many of the men who would bring further improvements and innovations to the game (see also Old Tom's profile in the Golf Course Designers section for further information). Old Tom began his career in his native St. Andrews as an apprentice to Allen Robertson, then a leading manufacturer of "feathery" golf balls. He teamed with Robertson and won a series of great victories in the 1840s against Willie and Jamie Dunn. Old Tom left St. Andrews and the employ of Allen Robertson in 1851, moving to Prestwick on the west coast of Scotland. He and Robertson reportedly argued over the new gutta-percha golf balls, which Old Tom preferred.

Old Tom was 39 and already living in Prestwick when the first British Open was held there; Prestwick was site for the first twelve Opens. Old Tom finished second to Willie Park that year, but came back to win his first Open in 1861 and then again in 1862, where his 13-stroke victory margin still stands as a record. He won again in 1864 and 1867 and placed second three times, including a runner-up finish to his son, Young Tom, in 1869. Old Tom played in his last British Open when he was 75 years of age.

Old Tom left Prestwick and returned to St. Andrews in 1864, where he became the town's first golf professional and greenskeeper. He laid out many courses during the late nineteenth century and remodeled others, including Royal Dornoch. His design apprentices included Donald Ross and Charles Balir Macdonald, and his influence is greatly evidenced in their work and in American golf course architecture in general.

BYRON NELSON

Born Feb. 4, 1912

Nelson confirmed legendary status with his remarkable performance on the PGA Tour in 1944 and 1945. The top money winner in both of those years, Nelson won 13 of 23 tournaments in 1944 to lead the Tour. He astounded the golf world in 1945 with a record 19 victories, including a streak of 11 tournament wins that extended from March 11 to August 4. Although many top players were away on war service, Nelson's statistics that year stand on their own merit. He carded 19 consecutive sub-70 rounds and won the Vardon Trophy with a stroke average of 68.33. When his hemophilia made him ineligible to serve in the armed forces, Nelson staged a number of war bond exhibitions as he devoted the war years to golf.

Nelson's 52 PGA Tour victories place him fifth on the all-time Tour winners list behind Sam Snead, Jack Nicklaus, Ben Hogan, and Arnold Palmer. More remarkable is that he won those events over only 11 full-time seasons (1935-1946), an average of nearly five wins per year. Nelson won his first of five Majors in 1937 with a thrilling comeback. He opened with a record-setting 66 but trailed Ralph Guldahl by four strokes on the final nine. He made up the deficit on the 12th and 13th holes, shooting 2 and 3 to Guldahl's 5 and 6, and won by two strokes. Later that year he defeated major championship winners Leo Diegel, Johnny Farrell, and Craig Wood at the PGA Championship before losing in the quarterfinals. He was also a member of the 1937 U.S. Ryder Cup, the first to win on British soil.

In addition to the 1937 Masters, Nelson won the 1942 Masters over Ben Hogan in a thrilling playoff. Nelson had been ahead of Hogan by 8 strokes after two rounds. He fell behind in the playoff by 3 strokes after five holes, but birdied his way through Amen Corner while playing the 6th through the 13th in a whopping 6 under par. Nelson won the U.S. Open in 1939 in a 36-hole playoff over Craig Wood and Densmore Shute (who was eliminated after 18 playoff holes), highlighted by his double eagle on the 94th hole. Interestingly, he would lose the 1946 U.S. Open at Canterbury to Lloyd Mangrum in another 36-hole playoff. Nelson was a five-time finalist in the PGA Championship between 1940 and 1945, when it was a match play event. He lost to Henry Picard late in the 1939 championship, then won late himself in 1940 over Sam Snead, taking two of the final four holes. Vic Ghezzi, in turn, rallied late on Nelson in 1941, making up a three-hole deficit on the final nine. Nelson in 1944 lost for the third time in the PGA championship final round when Bob Hamilton protected a one-hole lead by sinking a birdie putt on the final hole. Nelson won the 1945 PGA during his 19-victory year.

Nelson reduced his schedule in 1946 and retired from full-time competition after the 1946 season. He continued his involvement with golf, playing on the 1947 U.S. Ryder Cup team and serving as the nonplaying captain of the victorious 1965 U.S. Ryder Cup team. He occasionally appeared in Tour events during the 1950s and won the 1951 Crosby.

He declined to compete on the Senior circuit in later years, restricting himself to hosting the Byron Nelson Classic and offering expert analysis on Tour events broadcast by ABC Television.

JACK NICKLAUS

Still Competing. See Pro Files: Seniors.

FRANCIS OUIMET
May 8, 1893–Sept. 2, 1967

Ouimet, America's first golf celebrity and a dominant amateur until the rise of Bobby Jones in the 1920s, seemingly came out of nowhere to snatch victory in the 1913 U.S. Open from the two top British professionals of the day, Harry Vardon and Ted Ray. Vardon and Ray had tied at the end of 72 holes and were expecting to meet in a playoff, when Ouimet sank a fifteen-foot downhill birdie putt on the 17th hole. Ouimet finished at 304 and tied Vardon and Ray. The next day, the 20-year-old Ouimet defeated the two British pros with a 72 to Vardon's 77 and Ray's 78 and became the first amateur to win a U.S. Open.

Ouimet grew up in Brookline, Massachusetts, just across the street from The Country Club where the 1913 U.S. Open was held. He learned golf as a young boy, frequently sneaking onto the course at The Country Club and also caddying there. He also played at the Franklin Park public course, but

getting there involved a mile-and-a-half walk with his golf clubs, three street car changes, and another walk of a mile to the course. Only 13 at the time, he would play 54 holes there and then come home.

Ouimet won the 1909 Boston Interscholastic championship when he was 16. He failed to qualify for the U.S. Amateur for three years before finally making it in 1913, just prior to the U.S. Open. He gave eventual winner Jerry Travers a good match in the second round but finally lost, 2-3. His play was observed by Robert Watson, president of the USGA, who asked Ouimet to enter the U.S. Open at The Country Club in Brookline. Ouimet was reluctant to enter because he had already taken time off work to play in the U.S. Amateur. Enter he did, though, and his understanding boss gave him the necessary time off.

Ouimet followed up his surprise victory in the U.S. Open with a win in the 1914 U.S. Amateur. His career was disrupted when the USGA revoked his amateur status because of a business association with a sporting goods company. The outcry over Ouimet's banishment caused the USGA to rescind the ban in 1918, and Ouimet returned to amateur competition. He reached the finals of the U.S. Amateur in 1920 and took his second victory in the 1931 U.S. Amateur. Ouimet was a member of the Walker Cup team in 1922 and played on eight Walker Cup teams between 1922 and 1934. He also served as nonplaying captain of the Walker Cup team five times between 1936 and 1949. He was subsequently elected captain of the Royal & Ancient in 1951, the first American to hold the post.

ARNOLD PALMER

Still Competing. See Pro Files: Seniors

GARY PLAYER

Still Competing. See Pro Files: Seniors

BETSY RAWLS
Born May 4, 1928

Rawls was one of the star attractions on the LPGA Tour that helped make it a success in the 1950s and 1960s before it was televised. She rose through the amateur ranks in the late 1940s and won the 1949 Trans-National. In 1950 she finished second to Babe Zaharias in the U.S. Women's Open. She turned pro in 1951 and won her first U.S. Women's Open with a five-stroke triumph.

Rawls was a consistent winner on the LPGA Tour throughout the 1950s. She quickly rose to the top rank of the LPGA in 1952, her second year on the Tour, winning six events including the Western Open. She scored major championship victories in the 1953 and 1957 U.S. Women's Open. The 1953 win came in a playoff, where she defeated Jacqueline Pung by six strokes. Rawls' 1957 win also came at Pung's expense when Pung signed an incorrect scorecard; her marker missed a stroke, and Pung signed the incorrect scorecard leading to a disqualification. Rawls closed out the decade with victories in the 1959 Western Open and LPGA Championship.

Rawls captured a record fourth U.S. Women's Open in 1960 at the peak of her career. She had led or tied for first in LPGA Tour wins in 1952, 1957, and 1959 and was the leading money winner in 1952 and 1959. She finished as runner-up in the 1961 U.S. Women's Open, and won her last Major with the 1969 LPGA Championship. Rawls capped her brilliant amateur and professional career by serving as the Tournament Director for the LPGA.

CHI CHI RODRIGUEZ

Still Competing. See Pro Files: Seniors

DONALD ROSS

See the Course Designers chapter.

PAUL RUNYAN
Born July 12, 1908

Runyan racked up 29 PGA Tour victories during the 1930s, placing him tied for 16th with Gene Littler on the list of all-time Tour winners. He was a small man with an excellent short game that served him well when he came up against more powerful opponents. He won his first major tournament in 1934 at the age of 24 when he defeated Craig Wood on the second playoff hole of the PGA Championship, then a match-play event. That was a great year for Runyan, who won a Tour-leading nine events and played on the U.S. Ryder Cup team.

Runyan again led the Tour in victories with seven in 1935 and finished the year as the Tour's leading money winner. His next major victory came in the 1938 PGA Championship. Playing against the powerful Sam Snead in the final round, he demolished Swinging Sam with his short game, winning by 8 and 7, the largest victory margin during the PGA's matchplay format.

Although there was no Ryder Cup competition from 1939 to 1945, Runyan was among the players selected to phantom teams in 1939 and 1941. He also had a fine career as a senior player: he twice won the PGA Seniors Championship (1961, 1962) and was runner-up in 1959 and 1960.

GENE SARAZEN
Born Feb. 27, 1902

When he won the 1935 Masters Tournament, Sarazen became the first player to record a career Grand Slam. In a dramatic turnaround at the par-five 15th hole of the final round, Sarazen holed his four-wood second shot for a rare albatross and went on to finish regulation play tied with Craig Wood, then defeated Wood in a 36-hole playoff by five shots. Sarazen's albatross is considered one of the greatest shots in golf history, but by then Sarazen had already won fame as a golfer and had been courted by Hollywood. Sarazen's 38 PGA Tour victories place him ninth on the list of all-time Tour winners.

Sarazen won the first of seven major titles at the 1922 U.S. Open at the age of 20, shooting a final-round 68 to overcome a 4-stroke deficit to Bobby Jones. It would be ten years before he won another U.S. Open in 1932, a decade in which Jones win four Opens, but in 1932 Sarazen followed Jones as the second man ever to win the U.S. and British Opens in the same year. Sarazen captured the first of three PGA Championships in 1922 at Oakmont, then repeated in 1923 by defeating Walter Hagen in the first-ever PGA Championship playoff. Hagen would go on to set a record for consecutive match play victories and take the next four PGA Championships from 1924 to 1927. After finishing runner-up in a tight and dramatic final in 1930, when Tommy Armour sank a 14-foot putt on the last hole, Sarazen won his third PGA Championship in 1933.

Sarazen won the British Open in 1932, the only time it was held at Prince's, Sandwich. British fans who may not remember that victory were thrilled in 1973 when Sarazen returned to Troon to celebrate the 50th anniversary of his first entry into the British Open. Playing with two other ex-champions, Fred Daly and Max Faulkner, the 71-year-old Sarazen stepped up to the tee at the par-3 eighth hole, known as the Postage Stamp, and shot a hole-in-one. Fortunately, television cameras were there to record it. Sarazen led that 1932 Open all the way and shot 283, a record-low total that stood until 1950.

In later years Sarazen played in senior competitions and won the 1954 and 1958 PGA Seniors Championship. He remained an active golf personality, reaching new generations of golfers in his role as host of "Shell's Wonderful World of Golf." In the early 1990s he was associated with the Sarazen World Championship of Golf, a tournament played at Chateu Elan in Georgia, where he was a course design consultant.

HORTON SMITH
May 22, 1908–Oct. 15, 1963

Smith came to the attention of the golfing world when he reached the semifinals of the 1928 PGA Championship as a 20-year-old. He won eight of nine events in 1929 to lead the Tour in victories, a performance that earned him a spot on the 1929 U.S. Ryder Cup team captained by Walter Hagen. Smith won his singles match, but the U.S. lost to Great Britain. Smith went on to have a brilliant Ryder Cup record and never lost a Ryder Cup singles match.

Smith was a leading player on the PGA Tour of the 1930s, but is perhaps best remembered as the winner of the first Masters Tournament in 1934. He captured his second Masters two years later, coming from six strokes back after 36 holes. He led the PGA Tour in earnings in 1936 as well. His career total of 32 PGA Tour victories places him tied for 11th with Tom Watson on the list of all-time Tour winners. Smith's best finish in the U.S. Open came in 1930, when he finished third after leading the eventual winner, Bobby Jones during his Grand Slam year, by two strokes after two rounds.

SAM SNEAD
Born May 27, 1912

Snead won more official PGA Tour events (81) than anyone else. His victories include seven major championships, though Snead is the best player never to win the U.S. Open. Later in his career, Snead won numerous major senior tournaments and was one of the founders of the PGA Senior Tour in 1980.

Snead won his first tournament in 1936 at the age of 24, then joined the PGA Tour in 1937. He won five events that year, including the Crosby, and played on the Ryder Cup team. His 1938 campaign was even better. He led the tour in number of victories (8) and in earnings. He finished second in the U.S. Open, the first of four runner-up finishes in that event. He also won the Vardon Trophy for lowest scoring average.

In 1958, on a goodwill tour of South America, Sam Snead was getting ready to hit a bunker shot when he was attacked by an ostrich. The bird, the club mascot, clamped down on his hand so hard that Snead was unable to play golf for two weeks.

Snead's career was somewhat overshadowed in the late 1930s and 1940s by his long-time rivals, Ben Hogan and Byron Nelson. He won twelve more tournaments in 1939-41 before capturing his first major in 1942, the PGA Championship. By then Snead had accumulated an impressive record in the majors: runner-up in the 1938 and 1940 PGAs; runner-up in the 1937 U.S. Open to Ralph Guldahl's record low-total; and runner up in the 1939 Masters, where he was bested again by Guldahl. Snead limited his appearances during World War II and in 1945 returned to an active schedule. He won six tournaments, including the British Open, in 1946. Snead slumped by his standards in 1947 and 1948, including a case of the yips in the 1947 U.S. Open—missing a 3-footer on the final hole to lose by a stroke. In this case, Snead's yips may have been induced by his opponent, Lew Worsham. Both Snead and Worsham faced three-footers, with Snead seeming a bit further away, but just as he prepared to putt, Worsham asked for a measurement. Snead was proven to be away, but perhaps Worsham's strategic time-out had proven fateful.

Snead came back with the best year of his career in 1949, winning the Vardon Trophy, playing on the winning Ryder Cup team, and winning his first Masters and second PGA Championship. The Masters victory included shooting 134 over the final two rounds, 14 strokes better than his first two-round total, and the PGA victory came in front of adoring fans in his home state of Virginia. He also finished second in the U.S. Open again. Snead continued his strong form in 1950 with 11 Tour victories (a total not equaled since).

Snead won his third PGA Championship in 1951, and his last major victory came at the 1954 Masters in a playoff over Ben Hogan, as both Hall of Famers withstood an amazing performance by virtual unknown Billy Joe Patton. Snead entered the final round of the 1957 Masters ahead by 3 strokes over Doug Ford, but Ford shot an amazing closing-round 66, a new record low, and beat Snead by 3 strokes.

Snead played or captained the U.S. Ryder Cup team in four decades, starting in 1937. He played on the winning team in 1949, 1953, and 1955. He captained the winning team in 1959 and was undefeated in two matches. He captained the U.S. team to an historic tie in the 1969 Ryder Cup matches.

During the 1960s Snead became the first golfer to successfully play in both senior and regular competition. He became the oldest golfer, at 52 years and 10 months, to win a PGA event when he captured the Greater Greensboro Open in 1965 for a PGA Tour-record eighth time. This occurred six months after his first senior victories in the PGA Seniors Championship and the World Seniors. Snead's highly successful senior career included six PGA Seniors Championships between 1963 and 1973 and five World Seniors titles between 1964 and 1973. In 1974 he finished tied for third in the PGA Championship behind Lee Trevino and Jack Nicklaus. In 1979 he became the first Tour player in history to shoot his age or better when he fired rounds of 67 and 66 in the Quad Cities Open. It was the last year he won money in a Tour event.

LOUISE SUGGS
Born Sept. 7, 1923

A founding member of the LPGA and one of the key players who helped boost the tour's appeal and recognition, Suggs was a leading amateur of the 1940s before turning pro in 1947. She first came to prominence with two stunning victories as an amateur in 1946, taking the Titleholders and the Western Open, both considered majors at the time. She won the 1947 Women's Amateur after finishing as medalist in qualifying. She also recorded three North and South Amateur titles before turning professional.

Suggs found almost immediate success in the newly formed Women's Professional Golf Association (WPGA) with major championships in the 1947 and 1949 Western Opens. In 1949 she had a commanding victory in the 1949 U.S. Women's Open, shooting a record 291 and topping runner-up Babe Zaherias by 14 strokes. Suggs joined the newly chartered LPGA as a founding member in 1950.

The 1950s turned out to be Suggs best decade. She won six LPGA events in 1952, including the 1952 U.S. Women's Open, where she set a new record-low total at 284, seven strokes better than her 1949 low. She took five more major LPGA tournaments before the end of the 1950s, including the 1957 LPGA Championship, 1953 Western Open, and the 1954, 1956, and 1959 Titleholders. She was also a four-time runner-up in the U.S. Women's Open (1955, 1958, 1959, and 1963), and in the 1967 Open she made up eight of a nine-stroke deficit in the final round, before falling back.

Suggs was a frequent tournament winner on the regular LPGA Tour circuit. She led or tied for the lead for tournament wins in 1949 and 1952 through 1954, recording 50 career wins. In 1957 she was awarded the Vare Trophy for lowest scoring average, and she was the LPGA Tour's leading money winner in 1953 and 1960. Suggs maintained a steady, if less spectacular, pace in the 1960s, winning an average of two tournaments a year for the first half of the decade.

JOHN H. TAYLOR
March 19, 1871–February, 1963

It was fitting that one of the greatest English professionals of the day should win his first British Open the first time the event was held outside of Scotland, at Sandwich in Kent, in 1894. It was also the first time an Englishman won the coveted event. Taylor successfully defended his title in 1895 at St. Andrews. Altogether, he won five British Opens, the next being at St. Andrews again in 1900, then at Deal in 1909 and at Hoylake in 1913.

Taylor was one of the "Great Triumvirate," consisting of Harry Vardon, Taylor, and James Braid, that dominated golf between 1900 and the outbreak of World War I in the mid-teens. His 1894 and 1895 British Open victories made him the first of the trio to achieve national golfing success. Braid, another five-time British Open winner, took the event in 1901, 1905-06, 1908, and 1910. Vardon, a six-time British Open winner, won in 1896, 1898-99, 1903, 1911, and 1914. Taylor was the runner-up in 1896 and then for four years straight, from 1904 to 1907 before winning again in 1909. His final-round 68 in 1904 stood as a record-low Open round for 30 years.

During his best decade Taylor also won the 1904 and 1907 British PGAs as well as the 1907 and 1909 French Opens. Taylor's age began to affect his game, but he won the 1913 British Open and finished second to Vardon in 1914. Taylor also won the 1912 German Open. With the outbreak of World War I, Taylor concluded his active career as a player. In 1921 he played in the first America vs. Great Britain match, and in 1933 he captained the winning Ryder Cup team for Great Britain. Taylor was a founding member of the PGA in 1901 and served as both its chairman and captain.

PETER THOMSON
Born Aug. 23, 1929

Considered the best Australian golfer until Greg Norman came on the scene, Thomson is a five-time British Open winner. Together with Bobby Locke, Thomson dominated the British Open in the 1950s. After runner-up finishes in 1952 and 1953, Thomson won the first of three consecutive British Opens in 1954 at Royal Birkdale. He successfully defended his crown at St. Andrews in 1955, then became the first player since the 1880s to win three consecutive British Opens with a victory at Hoylake in 1956. His other British Open wins came in 1958 at Royal Lytham and in 1965 at Southport.

Thomson's first tournament victory was the 1950 New Zealand Open, which he won eight times. In his career he also won three Australian Opens and the national championships of Germany, Hong Kong, Holland, Spain, and Italy. An advocate of an international tour, Thomson never seemed to feel at ease on the PGA Tour, perhaps because he preferred the smaller ball used in international competition. He did win the Texas Open in 1956 and finished fourth in the U.S. Open that year.

Ironically, Thomson achieved some success on the PGA Senior Tour after he turned 50 in 1979. In 1985 he scored five victories on the Senior circuit.

JEROME S. TRAVERS
May 19, 1887–March 30, 1951

Travers was a leading American amateur in the first decades of the twentieth century. He achieved fame in 1915 when he became one of the few amateurs to win the U.S. Open, which was held at Balustrol that year. His first victories came in the U.S. Amateur, which he won in 1907 at Euclid and again in 1908 at Garden City. He again won back-to-back Amateurs in 1912-13, making him the first player to win four U.S. Amateur titles. He nearly won a third consecutive U.S. Amateur in 1914, when he lost the final match to Francis Ouimet, who had won the 1913 U.S. Open.

Travers' U.S. Open was excruciating. On the 10th hole of the final round, he drove out-of-bounds and shot next into the rough, leaving a difficult approach shot to a green surrounded by water; he executed an excellent shot, the ball settling within 30 inches of the hole. He topped his

tee shot on the next hole, then hit a great approach from heavy rough, leaving a pitch shot and a putt for par. He settled down and parred the remaining holes before an enthusiastic crowd.

That year, 1915, he set a record for widest victory margin in the first round of the U.S. Amateur (14-13 over 36 holes) but did not win the event. After losing the Metropolitan Amateur that year, he announced his retirement at age 28, frustrated with his ability to play amateur golf and make ends meet. He did not defend his Open title.

WALTER TRAVIS
1862–1927

Australian-born Travis was the first dominant U.S. amateur player in the first decade of the twentieth century. He became the first player to ever win the U.S. Amateur three times, in 1900, 1901, and 1903, and nearly won the 1902 U.S. Open, finishing second to Laurie Auchterlonie of Great Britain.

Travis had already won his three U.S. Amateur titles when he went to England in 1904 to try and win the British Amateur title. He met Edward Blackwell in the final round and despite being out-driven, won the match 4-3 on the strength of his putting. He used a center-shafted putter, called the Schenectady after the city in which it was manufactured. Travis's victory was not a popular one in Great Britain, and shortly afterwards the Royal and Ancient banned the use of center-shafted clubs.

Travis founded the *American Golfer* magazine in 1905 and edited the magazine while continuing to play in tournaments as an amateur. He also became involved in designing golf courses (see his profile in the Course Designers section). He again found himself in a controversy when his amateur status was revoked because of off-course professional activities relating to golf, but was later reinstated.

LEE TREVINO

Still Competing. See Pro Files: Seniors

HARRY VARDON
May 9, 1870–March 20, 1937

The only six-time winner of the British Open, Vardon was one of the best British professionals of the late nineteenth and early twentieth century. He became so popular the he was the first golfer to be able to support himself as a full-time professional and live off his prize earnings and exhibition fees.

Vardon did not become a serious golfer until he was 20, when he was inspired by the success of his brother, Tom. His first British Open appearance came in 1893, his first victory in 1896 at Muirfield, when he defeated J.H. Taylor in a playoff by four strokes to end Taylor's quest for his third consecutive Open title. After the amateur Harold Hilton won it in 1897, Vardon captured two consecutive Open titles in 1898, with the first-ever four sub-80 rounds, and 1899. In 1900 he won the U.S. Open at Chicago while on an exhibition tour of the United States, again edging Taylor. Vardon took his fourth British Open title in 1903, with brother Tom finishing as runner up, but became ill during the tournament. His health declined, and he spent a great deal of time under treatment for tuberculosis. After he regained his health, Vardon won two more British Opens, including a playoff victory in 1911 and in 1914, where Taylor finished second again. Vardon finished second in the 1912 British Open and in the famous 1913 U.S. Open, won by amateur Francis Ouimet. His last effective run at a second U.S. Open title came up short, when he finished tied for second in 1920 at the age of 50.

Vardon had a great impact on the technical aspect of golf. He developed a grip, now known as the Vardon grip, that compensated for the slimmer handles of the hickory-shafted clubs that replaced thicker-shafted clubs. His upright swing took full advantage of the characteristics of the rubber-core ball and attracted many imitators. Vardon was known for the accuracy of his shots, especially his fairway woods, and it is fitting that the Vardon Trophy for lowest scoring average on the PGA Tour was named for him.

GLENNA COLLETT VARE
Born June 20, 1903

Glenna Collett Vare began her amateur career in the 1920s and by the end of the decade was considered the top American player. She won four U.S. Women's Amateur titles (1922, 1925, 1928, and 1929) and the 1923 and 1924 Canadian Ladies title. In 1929 she met top British amateur Joyce Wethred in the final match of the British Amateur at St. Andrews, only to lose 1-3 in what was billed as the unofficial world championship. She never won the British title, finishing as runner-up again in 1930 and making her last attempt in 1936.

Vare continued to win championships in the 1930s, with two more victories in the U.S. Women's Amateur (the last in 1935) for a career total of six national championships, and she was runner-up in 1931 and 1932. Her six victories and eight appearances in the Amateur final are not likely to be matched. In addition, Vare was a six-time winner of the prestigious North and South championship. She played on three Curtis Cup teams in the competitions between the United States and Great Britain and Ireland. She also served as captain of the Curtis Cup team in 1948 and as non-playing captain in 1950.

The LPGA trophy for lowest scoring average is named after this outstanding amateur golfer.

JOYCE WETHRED
Born Nov. 7, 1901

From a casual beginning in golf in 1918 to an early retirement at age 24 and a triumphant return, Joyce Wethred was an outstanding golfer, acclaimed by Bobby Jones as the best golfer he'd ever seen. She was encouraged by her brother, Roger Wethred, an accomplished amateur, to try golf during a family vacation when she was seventeen. Two years later she qualified for the English Ladies Amateur Championship, reportedly playing in the event to keep a friend company. She won the tournament over defending champion Cecil Leitch and began an amazing run of success that she ended early, as Jones would, with almost nothing left to win.

Wethred repeated as English Amateur champion in 1921 and finished runner-up to Leitch in that year's Ladies British Open Amateur Championship. In 1922 and 1924 she won both events. Wethered also won the 1923 English Ladies Amateur, her fourth straight title in that event. After taking the Ladies British Open Amateur Championship again in 1925, Wethred retired from competition. She made a triumphant return in the 1929 British Ladies Amateur at St. Andrews, defeating Glenna Colett Vare, who was in the prime of a career in which she won the U.S. Women's Amateur six times. Wethred also played in the inaugural Curtis Cup match in 1932.

In her first English Ladies Amateur championship, Wethred outdueled defending champion Cecil Leitch, winning on the final hole with a clutch putt while a locomotive chugged by. Asked later if the train had affected her concentration at all, Wethred replied, "What train?" Leitch and Wethred had several more momentous battles. After finishing runner-up to Leitch in the 1921 Ladies British Open Amateur Championship, Wethred defeated her in 1922 by the largest margin (9 and 7) ever in the final and topped Leitch again in a one-hole playoff the following year.

KATHY WHITWORTH

Born Sept. 27, 1939

The all-time leader in tournament wins, Whitworth was a dominant player on the LPGA circuit from 1962, when she won her first tournament, through the 1970s, becoming the first female with career earnings over one million dollars in 1981 and passing Mickey Wright for most career wins in 1982. In 1965, when she ended Wright's five-year streak of most tournament wins, Whitworth began her own four-year streak, taking 35 tournaments in that span and never winning less than eight in a single year. She won The Titleholders in 1965 and 1966 and took the Western Open and LPGA Championship in 1967. She also won the Vare Trophy four times (1965-67 and 1969).

The 1970s were also triumphant for Whitworth. She led in tournament wins three more times (1971-1973) and was the LPGA Tour's leading money winner from 1970 through 1973, repeating her four-year streak from 1965 through 1968. Whitworth had twenty-eight tour victories during the 1970s, including the 1970 and 1975 LPGA Championships, and won the Vare Trophy from 1970-72. She was less dominant when reaching her mid-30s in the mid-1970s, but Whitworth continued to be a strong presence on the LPGA Tour. She won at least one tournament per season from 1981 through 1985.

Like her career tournaments-won counterpart on the PGA Tour, Sam Snead, who never won the U.S. Open, Whitworth's success does not include a U.S. Women's Open triumph. She was runner-up in 1971, tied the record for the lowest total of the first two rounds with a 139 in 1981, and finished in the top 10 thirteen times.

MICKEY WRIGHT

Born Feb. 14, 1935

A shy and retiring person who shunned the spotlight, Wright's outstanding performances on the LPGA Tour in the late 1950s and 1960s are credited with bringing women's professional golf to national attention. Her 82 career wins place her among the top professional women golfers of all time. She shares a record four victories in the U.S. Women's Open with Betsy Rawls. Other accomplishments include four-time leading money winner, six-time leading tournament winner, and five-time Vare Trophy winner for lowest stroke average. Her 62 in the 1964 Midland, Texas, tournament is an LPGA Tour record.

As Mary Kathryn Wright she reached the final round of the 1950 U.S. Girls Junior Amateur at the age of 15, and won it in 1952. In 1954 she took the World and All-American Amateur titles and finished fourth in the U.S. Women's Open. After losing the final match of the 1954 Women's Amateur, Wright turned professional. Her first professional victory came in 1956, followed by three wins in 1957.

Wright began her conquest of majors in 1958, winning both the U.S. Women's Open, where she led all the way and finished ahead by five stokes, and the LPGA Championship. She successfully defended her U.S. Women's Open title in 1959 with a record-low 287 on the way to five wins that year. Wright's best years on the LPGA Tour came in the 1960s, however, as she won 50 tournaments over five years, 1960-1964. After six wins in 1960, including the LPGA Championship, Wright became the Tour's leading money winner in 1961, taking a record three of the four major championships, failing to win only the LPGA. She repeated as the leading money winner in 1962 and won an astonishing ten events, including four in a row and the Titleholders and the Western Open, both considered majors then. Her 1963 campaign was the most spectacular of all, with an unmatched thirteen wins, including victories in the LPGA and the Western Open. Her 1964 season was only slightly less spectacular, when she took the money title for the fourth straight year and won eleven events, including a twelfth major and her fourth U.S. Women's Open to tie Rawls' record for most victories in the Open. The 1964 win came at a course she played often, the San Diego Country Club, in a playoff over Ruth Jensen, whom she beat by two strokes.

Plagued by injuries, Wright sharply reduced her schedule in 1965.

Although less dominant, Wright managed to capture her thirteenth major with a win in the 1967 Western Open. Through the end of the decade she stretched her streak of winning at least one tournament a year to 14 years. Starting in 1970, Wright became a part-time player on Tour. In 1979 she made one last run at a title but lost to Nancy Lopez in the Coca-Cola Classic.

MILDRED "BABE" ZAHARIAS
June 26, 1911–September 27, 1956

Born Mildred Didrikson, she became better known as "Babe," nicknamed for her penchant for hitting long drives that wowed spectators, similar to baseball's Babe Ruth. A remarkable all-around athlete, Babe excelled at basketball, earning All-American honors in 1930 and 1932, and track and field. She won six of the eight track and field events she entered in the 1932 AAU Championships and took a record five gold medals at the 1932 Olympic Games in Los Angeles.

Babe didn't take golf seriously until she was in her twenties, winning the Texas Amateur in 1935. It was said she could drive the ball over 250 yards and sometimes as far as 300. She lost her amateur status in 1935 because of her professional activities in other sports and would not regain it until 1943. By then she had married wrestler George Zaharias and had tried and given up tennis. In 1946 and 1947 she is said to have won 17 consecutive golf tournaments. She took both the 1946 U.S. Amateur at Tulsa and the British Amateur at Gullane in Scotland. Soon after she turned professional.

Zaharias and Patty Berg reorganized the struggling Women's Professional Tour and set up eight events in 1948, three of which Zaharias won, including the U.S. Women's Open by 8 strokes. She was the leading money winner from 1948 to 1951 and was the biggest draw on the Tour. In

1950 she completed the Slam by winning the Women's Open (tieing the then record-low total and triumphing by nine strokes), the Titleholders, and the Western Open in one year.

In 1953 Zaharias underwent a major operation for cancer. She made an astounding comeback in 1954, winning five events. She won her tenth and final major with her third U.S. Women's Open championship (by 12 strokes) and also won the Vare Trophy. Her cancer reappeared in 1955 and limited her schedule to eight events. She won her final two victories in competitive golf that year, then died of cancer in 1956 while still in the top rank of female American golfers.

5

MAJOR CHAMPIONSHIPS
MEN

THE MASTERS

The following is a list of the top finishers at the Masters tournament held at Augusta National Golf Club in Georgia from its inception. Included are the competitors, their daily scores, and total scores.

March 22-25, 1934

Horton Smith	70	72	70	72	284
Craig Wood	71	74	69	61	285
Billy Burke	72	71	70	73	286
Paul Runyan	74	71	70	71	286
Ed Dudley	74	69	71	74	288
Willie MacFarlane	74	73	70	74	291
Harold McSpaden	77	74	72	69	292
Al Espinosa	75	70	75	72	292
Jimmy Hines	70	74	74	74	292
Macdonald Smith	74	70	74	74	292

April 4-8, 1935

Gene Sarazen	68	71	73	70	282
Craig Wood	69	72	68	73	282
Sarazan won playoff 147 to 149					
Olin Dutra	70	70	70	74	284
Henry Picard	67	68	76	75	286

Denny Shute	73	71	70	73	287
Lawson Little, Jr.	74	72	70	72	288
Paul Runyan	70	72	75	72	289
Vic Ghezzi	73	71	73	73	290
Jimmy Hines	70	70	77	74	291
Byron Nelson	71	74	72	74	291
B. Cruickshank	76	70	73	72	291
Joe Turnesa	73	71	74	73	291

April 2-6, 1936

Horton Smith	74	71	68	72	285
Harry Cooper	70	69	71	76	286
Gene Sarazen	78	67	72	70	287
B. Cruickshank	75	69	74	72	290
Paul Runyan	76	69	70	75	290
Ray Mangrum	76	73	68	76	293
Ed Dudley	75	75	70	73	293
Ky Laffoon	75	70	75	73	293
John Dawson	77	70	70	77	294
Henry Picard	75	72	74	73	294

April 1-4, 1937

Byron Nelson	66	72	75	70	283
Ralph Guldahl	69	72	69	76	285
Ed Dudley	70	71	71	74	286

The defending champion of the Masters is required to host an opening-night dinner for all the former champions.

Harry Cooper	73	69	71	74	287
Ky Laffoon	73	70	74	73	290
Jimmy Thomson	71	73	74	73	291
Al Warrous	74	72	71	75	292
Tommy Amour	73	75	73	72	293
Vic Ghezzi	72	72	72	77	293
Jimmy Hines	77	72	68	77	294
Leonard Dodson	71	75	71	77	294

April 1-4, 1938

Henry Picard	71	72	72	70	285
Ralph Guldahl	73	70	73	71	287
Harry Cooper	69	77	71	71	287
Paul Runyan	71	73	74	70	288
Byron Nelson	73	74	70	73	290
Ed Dudley	70	69	77	75	291
Felix Serafin	72	71	78	70	291
Dick Metz	70	77	74	71	292
Jimmy Thomson	74	70	76	72	292
Jimmy Hines	75	71	75	72	293
Vic Ghezzi	75	74	70	74	293
Lawson Little, Jr.	72	75	74	72	293

March 30 - April 2, 1939

Ralph Guldahl	72	68	70	29	279
Sam Snead	70	70	72	68	280
Billy Burke	69	72	71	70	282
Lawson Little, Jr.	72	72	68	70	282
Gene Sarazen	73	66	72	72	283
Craig Wood	72	73	71	68	284
Byron Nelson	71	69	72	75	287
Henry Picard	71	71	76	71	289
Ben Hogan	75	71	72	72	290
Toney Penna	72	75	72	72	291
Ed Dudley	75	75	69	72	291

April 4-7, 1940

Jimmy Demaret	67	72	70	71	280
Lloyd Mangrum	64	75	71	74	284
Byron Nelson	69	72	74	70	285

Ed Dudley	73	72	71	71	287
Harry Cooper	69	75	73	70	287
Willie Goggin	71	72	73	71	287
Henry Picard	71	71	71	75	288
Craig Wood	70	75	67	76	288
Sam Snead	71	72	69	76	288
Toney Penna	73	73	72	72	290
Ben Hogan	73	74	69	74	290

April 3-6, 1941

Craig Wood	66	71	71	72	280
Byron Nelson	71	69	73	70	283
Sam Byrd	73	70	68	74	285
Ben Hogan	71	72	75	68	286
Ed Dudley	73	72	75	68	288
Sam Snead	73	75	72	69	289
Vic Ghezzi	77	71	71	70	289
Lawson Little, Jr.	71	70	74	75	290
Lloyd Mangrum	71	72	72	76	291
Harold McSpaden	75	74	72	70	291
Willie Goggin	71	72	72	76	291

April 9-13, 1942

Byron Nelson	68	67	72	73	280
Ben Hogan	73	70	67	70	280
Nelson won playoff 69 to 70					
Paul Runyan	67	73	72	71	283
Sam Byrd	68	68	75	74	285
Horton Smith	67	73	74	74	287
Jimmy Demaret	70	70	75	75	290
E. J. Harrison	74	70	71	77	292
Lawson Little, Jr.	71	74	72	75	292
Sam Snead	78	69	72	73	292
Gene Kunes	74	74	74	71	293
Chick Harbert	73	73	72	75	293

April 4-7, 1946

Herman Keiser	69	68	71	74	282
Ben Hogan	74	70	69	70	283
Bob Hamilton	75	69	71	72	287
Ky Laffoon	74	73	70	72	289
Jimmy Demaret	75	70	71	73	289
Jim Ferrier	74	72	68	75	289
Sam Snead	74	75	70	71	290
Clayton Heafner	74	69	71	76	290

| Byron Nelson | 72 | 73 | 71 | 74 | 290 |
| Chick Harbert | 69 | 75 | 76 | 70 | 290 |

April 3-6, 1947

Jimmy Demaret	69	71	70	71	281
Byron Nelson	69	72	72	70	283
Frank Stranahan	73	72	70	67	283
Ben Hogan	75	68	71	70	284
Harold McSpaden	74	69	70	71	284
Henry Picard	73	70	72	71	286
Jim Ferrier	70	71	73	72	286
Ed Oliver, Jr.	70	72	74	71	287
Chandler Harper	77	72	68	70	287
Lloyd Mangrum	76	73	68	70	287
Toney Penna	71	70	75	71	287
Dick Metz	72	72	72	71	287

April 8-11, 1948

Claude Harmon	70	70	69	70	279
Cary Middlecoff	74	71	69	70	284
Chick Harbert	71	70	70	76	287
Jim Ferrier	71	71	75	71	288
Lloyd Mangrum	69	73	75	71	288
Ed Furgol	70	72	73	74	289
Ben Hogan	70	71	77	71	289
Byron Nelson	71	73	72	74	290
Harry Todd	72	67	80	71	290
Herman Keiser	70	72	76	73	291
Bobby Locke	71	71	74	75	291
Dick Metz	71	72	75	73	291

April 7-10, 1949

Sam Snead	73	75	67	67	282
Johnny Bulla	74	73	69	69	285
Lloyd Mangrum	69	74	72	70	285
Johnny Palmer	73	71	70	72	286
Jim Turnesa	73	72	71	70	286
Lew Worsham, Jr.	76	75	70	68	289
Joe Kirkwood, Jr.	73	72	70	75	290
Jimmy Demaret	76	72	73	71	292
Clayton Heafner	71	74	72	75	292
Byron Nelson	75	70	74	73	292

April 6-9, 1950

| Jimmy Demaret | 70 | 72 | 72 | 69 | 283 |
| Jim Ferrier | 70 | 67 | 73 | 75 | 285 |

Sam Snead	71	74	70	72	287
Ben Hogan	73	68	71	76	288
Byron Nelson	75	70	69	74	288
Lloyd Mangrum	76	74	73	68	291
Clayton Heafner	74	77	69	72	292
Cary Middlecoff	75	76	68	73	292
Lawson Little, Jr.	70	73	75	75	293
Fred Haas, Jr.	74	76	73	71	294
Gene Sarazen	80	70	72	72	294

April 5-8, 1951

Ben Hogan	70	72	70	68	280
Skee Riegel	73	68	70	71	282
Lloyd Mangrum	69	74	70	73	286
Lee Worsham, Jr.	71	71	72	72	286
Dave Douglas	74	69	72	73	288
Lawson Little, Jr.	72	73	72	72	289
Jim Ferrier	74	70	74	72	290
Johnny Bulla	71	72	73	75	291
Byron Nelson	71	73	73	74	291
Sam Snead	69	74	68	80	291

April 3-6, 1952

Sam Snead	70	67	77	72	286
Jack Burke, Jr.	76	67	78	69	290
Al Besselink	70	76	71	74	291
Tommy Bolt	71	71	75	74	291
Jim Ferrier	72	70	77	72	291
Lloyd Mangrum	71	74	75	72	292
Julius Boros	73	73	76	71	293
Fred Hawkins	71	73	78	71	293
Ben Hogan	70	70	74	79	293
Lew Worsham, Jr.	71	75	73	74	293

April 9-12, 1953

Ben Hogan	70	69	66	69	274
Ed Oliver, Jr.	69	73	67	70	279
Lloyd Mangrum	74	68	71	69	282
Bob Hamilton	71	69	70	73	283
Tommy Bolt	71	75	68	71	285
Chick Harbert	68	73	70	74	285
Ted Kroll	71	70	73	72	286
Jack Burke, Jr.	78	69	69	71	287
Al Besselink	69	75	70	74	288
Julius Boros	73	71	75	70	289

| Chandler Harper | 74 | 72 | 69 | 74 | 289 |
| Fred Hawkins | 75 | 70 | 74 | 70 | 289 |

April 8-12, 1954

| Sam Snead | 74 | 73 | 70 | 72 | 289 |
| Ben Hogan | 72 | 73 | 69 | 75 | 289 |

Snead won playoff 70 to 71

Billy Joe Patton	70	74	75	71	290
E. J. Harrison	70	79	74	68	291
Lloyd Mangrum	71	75	76	69	291
Jerry Barber	74	76	71	71	292
Jack Burke, Jr.	71	77	73	71	292
Bob Rosburg	73	73	76	70	292
Al Besselink	74	74	74	72	294
Cary Middlecoff	73	76	70	75	294

April 7-10, 1955

Cary Middlecoff	72	65	72	70	279
Ben Hogan	73	68	72	73	286
Sam Snead	72	71	74	70	287
Bob Rosburg	72	72	72	73	289
Mike Souchak	71	74	72	72	289
Julius Boros	71	75	72	71	289
Lloyd Mangrum	74	73	72	72	291
E. Harvie Ward, Jr.	77	69	75	71	292
Stan Leonard	77	73	69	74	292
Dick Mayer	78	72	72	71	293
Byron Nelson	72	75	74	72	293
Arnold Palmer	76	76	72	69	293

April 5-8, 1956

Jack Burke, Jr.	72	71	75	71	289
Ken Venturi	66	69	75	80	290
Cary Middlecoff	67	72	75	77	291
Lloyd Mangrum	72	74	72	74	292
Sam Snead	73	76	72	71	292
Jerry Barber	71	72	76	75	294
Doug Ford	70	72	75	77	294
Shelley Mayfield	68	74	80	74	296
Tommy Bolt	68	74	78	76	296
Ben Hogan	69	78	74	75	296

April 4-7, 1957

Doug Ford	72	73	72	66	283
Sam Snead	72	68	74	72	286
Jimmy Demaret	72	70	75	70	287
E. Harvie Ward, Jr.	73	71	71	73	288
Peter Thomson	72	73	73	71	289
Ed Furgol	73	71	72	74	290
Jack Burke, Jr.	71	72	74	74	291
Dow Finsterwald	74	74	73	70	291
Arnold Palmer	73	73	69	76	291
Jay Herbert	74	72	76	70	292

April 3-6, 1958

Arnold Palmer	70	73	68	73	284
Doug Ford	74	71	70	70	285
Fred Hawkins	71	75	68	71	285
Stan Leonard	72	70	73	71	286
Ken Venturi	68	72	74	72	286
Cary Middlecoff	70	73	69	75	287
Art Wall	71	72	70	74	287
Billy Joe Patton	72	69	73	74	288
Claude Harmon	71	76	72	70	289
Jay Herbert	72	73	73	71	289
Billy Maxwell	71	70	72	76	289
Al Mengert	73	71	69	76	289

April 2-5, 1959

Art Wall, Jr.	73	74	71	66	284
Cary Middlecoff	74	71	68	72	285
Arnold Palmer	71	70	71	74	286
Dick Mayer	73	75	71	68	287
Stan Leonard	69	74	69	75	287
Charles R. Coe	74	74	67	73	288
Fred Hawkins	77	71	68	73	289
Julius Boros	75	69	74	72	290
Jay Herbert	72	73	72	73	290
Gene Littler	72	75	72	71	290
Billy Maxwell	73	71	72	74	290
Billy Joe Patton	75	70	71	74	290
Gary Player	73	75	71	71	290

April 7-10, 1960

Arnold Palmer	67	73	72	70	282
Ken Venturi	73	69	71	70	283
Dow Finsterwald	71	70	72	71	284
Billy Casper	71	71	71	74	287
Julius Boros	72	71	70	75	288
Walter Burkemo	72	69	75	73	289

Ben Hogan	73	68	72	76	289
Gary Player	72	71	72	74	289
Lionel Herbert	74	70	73	73	290
Stan Leonard	72	72	72	74	290

April 6-10, 1961

Gary Player	69	68	69	74	280
Charles R. Coe	72	71	69	69	281
Arnold Palmer	68	69	73	71	281
Tommy Bolt	72	71	74	68	285
Don January	74	68	72	71	285
Paul Harney	71	73	68	74	286
Jack Burke, Jr.	76	70	68	73	287
Billy Casper	72	77	69	69	287
Bill Collins	74	72	67	74	287
Jack Nicklaus	70	75	70	72	287

April 5-9, 1962

Arnold Palmer	70	66	69	75	280
Gary Player	67	71	71	71	280
Dow Finsterwald	74	68	65	73	280

Palmer won playoff 68 to 71 and 77

Gene Littler	71	68	71	72	282
Mike Souchak	70	72	74	71	287
Jimmy Demaret	73	73	71	70	287
Jerry Barber	72	72	69	74	287
Bill Maxwell	71	73	72	71	287
Ken Venturi	75	70	71	72	288
Charles R. Coe	72	74	71	71	288

April 4-7, 1963

Jack Nicklaus	74	66	74	72	286
Tony Lema	74	69	74	70	287
Julius Boros	76	69	71	72	288
Sam Snead	70	73	74	71	288
Dow Finsterwald	74	73	73	69	289
Ed Furgol	70	71	74	74	289
Gary Player	71	74	74	70	289
Bo Winninger	69	72	77	72	290
Don January	73	75	72	71	291
Arnold Palmer	74	73	73	71	291

April 9-12, 1964

Arnold Palmer	69	68	69	70	276
Dave Marr	70	73	69	70	282
Jack Nicklaus	71	73	71	67	282

Bruce Devlin	72	72	67	73	284
Billy Casper	76	72	69	69	286
Jim Ferrier	71	73	69	73	286
Paul Harney	73	72	71	70	286
Gary Player	69	72	72	73	286
Dow Finsterwald	71	72	75	69	287
Ben Hogan	73	75	67	72	287
Tony Lema	75	68	74	70	287
Mike Souchak	73	74	70	70	287

April 8-11, 1965

Jack Nicklaus	67	71	64	69	271
Arnold Palmer	70	68	72	70	280
Gary Player	65	73	69	73	280
Mason Rudolph	70	75	66	72	283
Dan Sikes	67	72	71	75	285
Gene Littler	71	74	67	74	286
Ramon Sota	71	73	70	72	286
Frank Beard	68	77	72	70	287
Tommy Bolt	69	78	69	71	287
George Knudson	72	73	69	74	288

April 7-11, 1966

Jack Nicklaus	68	76	72	72	288
Tommy Jacobs	75	71	70	72	288
Gay Brewer, Jr.	74	72	72	70	288

Nicklaus won playoff 70 to 72 and 78

Arnold Palmer	74	70	74	72	290
Doug Sanders	74	70	75	71	290
Don January	71	73	73	75	292
George Knudson	73	76	72	71	292
Raymond Floyd	72	73	74	74	293
Paul Harney	75	68	76	74	293
Billy Casper	71	75	76	72	294
Jay Herbert	72	74	73	75	294
Bob Rosburg	73	71	76	74	294

April 6-9, 1967

Gay Brewer, Jr.	73	68	72	67	280
Bobby Nichols	72	69	70	70	281
Bert Yancey	67	73	71	73	284
Arnold Palmer	73	73	70	69	285
Julius Boros	71	70	70	75	286
Paul Harney	73	71	74	69	287
Gary Player	75	69	72	71	287

Tommy Aaron	75	68	74	71	288
Lionel Herbert	77	71	67	73	288
R. De Vicenzo	73	72	74	71	290
Bruce Devlin	74	70	75	71	290
Ben Hogan	74	73	66	77	290
Mason Rudolph	72	76	72	70	290
Sam Snead	72	76	71	71	290

April 11-14, 1968

Bob Goalby	70	70	71	66	277
R. De Vicenzo	69	73	70	66	278
Bert Yancey	71	71	72	65	279
Bruce Devlin	69	73	69	69	289
Frank Beard	75	65	71	70	281
Jack Nicklaus	69	71	74	67	281
Tommy Aaron	69	72	72	69	282
Raymond Floyd	71	71	69	71	282
Lionel Herbert	72	71	71	68	282
Jerry Pittman	70	73	70	69	282
Gary Player	72	67	71	72	282

April 10-13, 1969

George Archer	67	73	69	72	281
Billy Casper	66	71	71	74	282
George Knudson	70	73	69	70	282
Tom Weiskopf	71	71	69	71	282
Charles Coody	74	68	69	72	283
Don January	74	73	70	66	283
Miller Barber	71	71	68	74	284
Tommy Aaron	71	71	73	70	285
Lionel Hebert	69	73	70	73	285
Gene Littler	69	75	70	71	285

April 9-13, 1970

| Billy Casper | 72 | 68 | 68 | 71 | 279 |
| Gene Littler | 69 | 70 | 70 | 70 | 279 |

Casper won playoff 69 to 74

Gary Player	74	68	68	70	280
Bett Yancey	69	70	72	70	281
Tommy Aaron	68	74	69	72	283
Dave Hill	73	70	70	70	283
Dave Stockton	72	72	69	70	283
Jack Nicklaus	71	75	69	69	284
Frank Beard	71	76	68	70	285
Bob Lunn	70	70	75	72	287
Chi Chi Rodriguez	70	76	73	68	287

April 8-11, 1971

Charles Coody	66	73	70	70	279
Johnny Miller	72	73	68	68	281
Jack Nicklaus	70	71	68	72	281
Don January	69	69	73	72	283
Gene Littler	72	69	73	69	283
Gary Player	72	72	71	69	284
Ken Still	72	71	72	69	284
Tom Weiskopf	71	69	72	72	284
Frank Beard	74	73	69	70	286
R. De Vicenzo	76	69	72	69	286
Dave Stockton	72	73	69	72	286

April 6-9, 1972

Jack Nicklaus	68	71	73	74	286
Bruce Crampton	72	75	69	73	289
Bobby Mitchell	73	72	71	73	289
Tom Weiskopf	74	71	70	74	289
Homero Blancas	76	71	69	74	290
Bruce Devlin	74	75	70	71	290
Jerry Heard	73	71	72	74	290
Jim Jamieson	72	70	71	77	290
Jerry McGee	73	74	71	72	290
Gary Player	73	75	72	71	291
Dave Stockton	76	70	74	71	291

April 5-9, 1973

Tommy Aaron	68	73	74	68	283
J. C. Snead	70	71	73	70	284
Jim Jamieson	73	71	70	71	285
Jack Nicklaus	69	77	73	66	285
Peter Oosterhuis	73	70	68	74	285
Bob Goalby	73	70	71	74	288
Johnny Miller	75	69	71	73	288
Bruce Devlin	73	72	72	72	289
Masashi Ozaki	69	74	73	73	289
Gay Brewer, Jr.	75	66	74	76	291
G. Dickinson	74	70	72	75	291
Don January	75	71	75	70	291
Chi Chi Rodriguez	72	70	73	76	291

April 11-14, 1974

Gary Player	71	71	66	70	278
Dave Stockton	71	66	70	73	280
Tom Weiskopf	71	69	70	70	280
Jim Colbert	67	72	69	73	281

Hale Irwin	68	70	72	71	281
Jack Nicklaus	69	71	72	69	281
Bobby Nichols	73	68	68	73	282
Phil Rodgers	72	69	68	73	282
M. Bembridge	73	74	72	64	283
Hubert Green	68	70	74	71	283

April 10-13, 1975

Jack Nicklaus	68	67	73	68	276
Johnny Miller	75	71	65	65	277
Tom Weiskopf	69	72	66	70	277
Hale Irwin	73	74	71	64	282
Bobby Nichols	67	74	72	69	282
Billy Casper	70	70	73	70	283
Dave Hill	75	71	70	68	284
Hubert Green	74	71	70	70	285
Tom Watson	70	70	72	73	285
Tom Kite	72	74	71	69	286
J. C. Snead	69	72	75	70	286
Lee Trevino	71	70	74	71	286

April 8-11, 1976

Raymond Floyd	65	66	70	70	271
Ben Crenshaw	70	70	72	67	279
Jack Nicklaus	67	69	73	73	282
Larry Ziegler	67	71	72	72	282
Charles Coody	72	69	70	74	285
Hale Irwin	71	77	67	70	285
Tom Kite	73	67	72	73	285
Billy Casper	71	76	71	69	287
Roger Maltbie	72	75	70	71	288
Graham Marsh	73	68	75	72	288
Tom Weiskopf	73	71	70	74	288

April 7-10, 1977

Tom Watson	70	69	70	67	276
Jack Nicklaus	72	70	70	66	278
Tom Kite	70	73	70	67	280
Rik Massengale	70	73	67	70	280
Hale Irwin	70	74	70	68	282
David Graham	75	67	73	69	284
Lou Graham	75	71	69	69	284
Ben Crenshaw	71	69	69	76	285
Raymond Floyd	71	72	71	71	285
Hubert Green	67	74	72	72	285

Don January	69	76	69	71	285
Gene Littler	71	72	73	69	285
John Schlee	75	73	69	68	285

April 6-9, 1978

Gary Player	72	72	69	64	277
Rod Funseth	73	66	70	69	278
Hubert Green	72	69	65	72	278
Tom Watson	73	68	68	69	278
Wally Armstrong	72	70	70	68	280
Bill Kratzert	70	74	67	69	280
Jack Nicklaus	72	73	69	67	281
Hale Irwin	73	67	71	71	282
Joe Inman	69	73	72	69	283
David Graham	75	69	67	72	283

April 12-15, 1979

Fuzzy Zoeller	70	71	69	70	280
Ed Sneed	68	67	69	76	280
Tom Watson	68	71	70	71	280
Zoeller won playoff 4-3 to 4-4 and 4-4
Jack Nicklaus	69	71	72	69	281
Tom Kite	71	72	68	72	283
Bruce Lietzke	67	75	68	74	284
Lanny Wadkins	73	69	70	73	285
L. Thompson	68	70	73	74	285
Craig Stadler	69	66	74	76	285
Hubert Green	74	69	72	71	286
Gene Littler	74	71	69	72	286

April 10-13, 1980

Seve Ballesteros	66	69	68	72	275
Gibby Gilbert	70	74	68	67	279
Jack Newton	68	74	69	68	279
Hubert Green	68	74	71	67	280
David Graham	66	73	72	70	281
Gary Player	71	71	71	70	283
Ben Crenshaw	76	70	68	69	283
Ed Fiori	71	70	69	73	283
Tom Kite	69	71	74	69	283
Larry Nelson	69	72	73	69	283
Jerry Pate	72	68	76	67	283

April 9-12, 1981

| Tom Watson | 71 | 68 | 70 | 71 | 280 |
| Johnny Miller | 69 | 72 | 73 | 68 | 282 |

Jack Nicklaus	70	65	75	72	282
Greg Norman	69	70	72	72	283
Tom Kite	74	72	70	68	284
Jerry Pate	71	72	71	70	284
David Graham	70	70	74	71	285
Ben Crenshaw	71	72	70	73	286
Raymond Floyd	75	71	71	69	286
John Mahaffey	72	71	69	74	286

April 8-11, 1982

| Craig Stadler | 75 | 69 | 67 | 73 | 284 |
| Dan Pohl | 75 | 75 | 67 | 67 | 284 |

Stadler won playoff 4 to 5

Seve Ballesteros	73	73	68	71	285
Jerry Pate	74	73	67	71	285
Tom Kite	76	69	73	69	287
Tom Watson	77	69	70	71	287
Larry Watson	79	71	70	69	289
Curtis Strange	74	70	73	72	289
Raymond Floyd	74	72	69	74	289
Andy Bean	75	72	73	70	290
Mark Hayes	74	73	73	70	290
Fuzzy Zoeller	72	76	70	72	290
Tom Weiskopf	75	72	68	75	290

April 7-11, 1983

Seve Ballesteros	68	70	73	69	289
Ben Crenshaw	76	70	70	68	284
Tom Kite	70	72	73	69	284
Raymond Floyd	67	72	71	75	285
Tom Watson	70	71	71	73	285
Hale Irwin	72	73	72	69	286
Craig Stadler	69	72	69	76	286
Gil Morgan	67	70	76	74	287
Dan Pohl	74	72	70	71	287
Lanny Wadkins	73	70	73	71	287

April 12-15, 1984

Ben Crenshaw	67	72	70	68	277
Tom Watson	74	67	69	69	279
David Edwards	71	70	72	67	280
Gil Morgan	73	71	69	67	280
Larry Nelson	76	69	66	70	281
Ronnie Black	71	74	69	68	282
David Graham	69	70	70	73	282

Tom Kite	70	68	69	75	282
Mark Lye	69	66	73	74	282
Fred Couples	71	73	67	72	283

April 11-14, 1985

Bernhard Langer	72	74	68	68	282
Seve Ballesteros	72	71	71	70	284
Raymond Floyd	70	73	69	72	284
Curtis Strange	80	65	68	71	284
Jay Haas	73	73	72	67	285
Gary Hallberg	68	73	75	70	286
Bruce Lietzke	72	71	73	70	286
Jack Nicklaus	71	74	72	69	286
Craig Stadler	73	67	76	70	286
Fred Couples	75	73	69	70	287
David Graham	74	71	71	71	287
Lee Trevino	70	73	72	72	287
Tom Watson	69	71	75	72	287

April 10-13, 1986

Jack Nicklaus	74	71	69	65	279
Tom Kite	70	74	68	68	280
Greg Norman	70	72	68	70	280
Seve Ballesteros	71	68	72	70	281
Nick Price	79	69	63	71	282
Tom Watson	70	74	68	71	283
Jay Haas	76	69	71	67	283
Payne Stewart	75	71	69	69	284
Bob Tway	70	73	71	70	284
Tommy Nakajima	70	71	71	72	284

April 9-12, 1987

Larry Mize	70	72	72	71	285
Greg Norman	73	74	66	72	285
Seve Ballesteros	73	71	70	71	285

Mize won playoff 4-3 to 4-X and 5-X

Ben Crenshaw	75	70	67	74	286
Roger Maltbie	76	66	70	74	286
Jodie Mudd	74	72	71	69	286
Jay Haas	72	72	72	73	289
Bernhard Langer	71	72	70	76	289
Jack Nicklaus	74	71	73	70	289
Tom Watson	71	72	74	72	289
D. A. Weibring	72	75	71	71	289

April 7-10, 1988

Sandy Lyle	71	67	72	71	281
Mark Calcavecchia	71	69	72	70	282
Craig Stadler	76	69	70	68	283
Ben Crenshaw	72	73	67	72	284
Fred Couples	75	68	71	71	285
Greg Norman	77	73	71	64	285
Don Pooley	71	72	72	70	285
David Frost	73	74	71	68	286
Bernhard Langer	71	72	71	73	287
Tom Watson	72	71	73	71	287

April 6-9, 1989

| Nick Faldo | 68 | 73 | 77 | 65 | 283 |
| Scott Hoch | 69 | 74 | 72 | 69 | 283 |

Faldo won playoff 5-4 to 5-X

Ben Crenshaw	71	72	70	71	284
Greg Norman	74	75	68	67	284
Seve Ballesteros	71	72	73	69	285
Mike Reid	72	71	71	72	286
Jodie Mudd	73	76	72	66	287
Chip Beck	74	76	70	68	288
J. M. Olazabal	77	73	70	68	288
Jeff Sluman	74	72	74	68	288

April 5-8, 1990

| Nick Faldo | 71 | 72 | 66 | 69 | 278 |

Faldo won playoff 4-4 to 4-X

Raymond Floyd	70	68	68	72	278
John Huston	66	74	68	75	283
Lanny Wadkins	72	73	70	68	283
Fred Couples	74	68	72	69	284
Jack Nicklaus	72	70	69	74	285
Seve Ballesteros	74	73	68	71	286
Bill Britton	68	74	71	73	286
Bernhard Langer	70	73	69	74	286
Scott Simpson	74	71	68	73	286
Curtis Strange	70	73	71	72	286
Tom Watson	77	71	67	71	286

April 11-14, 1991

Ian Woosnam	72	66	67	72	277
J. M. Olazabal	68	71	69	70	278
Lanny Wadkins	67	71	70	71	279
Tom Watson	68	68	70	73	279
Ben Crenshaw	70	73	68	68	279
Steve Pate	72	73	69	65	279
Jodie Mudd	70	70	71	69	280
Andrew Magee	70	72	68	70	280
Ian Baker-Finch	71	70	69	70	280
Tommy Nakajima	74	71	67	69	281
Hale Irwin	70	70	75	66	281

April, 1992

Fred Couples	69	67	69	70	275
Raymond Floyd	69	68	69	71	277
Corey Pavin	72	71	68	67	278
Mark O'Meara	74	67	69	70	280
Jeff Sluman	65	74	70	71	280
Nick Price	70	71	67	73	281
Ian Baker-Finch	70	69	68	74	281
Nolan Henke	70	71	70	70	281
Steve Pate	73	71	70	67	281
Larry Mize	73	69	71	68	281

April, 1993

Bernhard Langer	69	70	69	70	277
Chip Beck	72	67	72	70	281
Steve Elkington	71	70	71	71	283
Lanny Wadkins	69	72	71	71	283
John Daly	70	71	73	69	283
Tom Lehman	67	75	73	68	283
Dan Forsman	69	69	73	73	284
Jose Maria Olazabal	70	72	74	68	284
Brad Faxon	71	70	72	72	285
Payne Stewart	74	70	72	69	285

April, 1994

Jose Maria Olazabal	74	67	69	69	279
Tom Lehman	70	70	69	72	281
Larry Mize	68	71	72	71	282
Tom Kite	69	72	71	71	283
Jim McGovern	72	70	71	72	285
Loren Roberts	75	68	72	70	285
Jay Haas	72	72	72	69	285
Corey Pavin	71	72	73	70	286
Ernie Els	74	67	74	71	286
Ian Baker-Finch	71	71	71	74	287

April 6-9, 1995

Ben Crenshaw	70	667	69	68	274
Davis Love III	69	69	71	66	275
Greg Norman	73	68	68	68	277
Jay Haas	71	64	72	70	277
David Frost	66	71	71	71	279
Steve Elkington	73	67	67	72	279
Phil Mickelson	66	71	70	73	280
Scott Hoch	69	67	71	73	280
Curtis Strange	72	71	65	73	281
Fred Couples	71	69	67	75	282
Brian Henninger	70	68	68	76	282

April 11-14, 1996

Nick Faldo	69	67	73	67	276
Greg Norman	63	69	71	78	281
Phil Mickelson	65	73	72	72	282
Frank Nobilo	71	71	72	69	283
Duffy Waldorf	72	71	69	72	284
Scott Hoch	67	73	73	71	284
Corey Pavin	75	66	73	71	285
Jeff Maggert	71	73	72	69	285
Davis Love III	72	71	74	68	285

―――――

U.S. OPEN CHAMPIONSHIP

The following is a list of the top finishers at the U.S. Open from its inception. Included is the year, the tournament's location, the competitors, their daily scores, and total scores.

1895, Newport Golf Club
Newport, RI

Horace Rawlins	45	46	41	41	173
Willie Dunn	43	46	44	42	175
James Foulis	46	43	44	43	176
A.W. Smith	47	43	44	42	176
W.F. Davis	45	49	42	42	178
Willie Campbell	41	48	42	48	179
John Harland	45	48	43	47	183
John Patrick	46	48	46	43	183
Samuel Tucker	49	48	45	43	185
John Reid	49	51	55	51	206

1896, Shinnecock Hills Golf Club
Southampton, NY

James Foulis	78	74	152
Horace Rawlins	79	76	155
Joe Lloyd	76	81	157
George Douglas	79	79	158
A.W. Smith	78	80	158
John Shippen	78	81	159
H.J. Whigham	82	77	159
Willie Tucker	78	82	160
R.B. Wilson	82	80	162
Alfred Ricketts	80	83	163

1897, Chicago Golf Club
Wheaton, IL

Joe Lloyd	83	79	162
Willie Anderson	79	84	163
Willie Dunn	87	81	168
James Foulis	80	88	168
W.T. Hoare	82	87	169
Bernard Nicholls	87	85	172
Alfred Ricketts	91	81	172
David Foulis	86	87	173
Horace Rawlins	91	82	173
H.J. Whigham	87	86	173

1898, Myopia Hunt Club
South Hamilton, MA

Fred Herd	84	85	75	84	328
Alex Smith	78	86	86	85	335
Willie Anderson	81	82	87	86	336
Joe Lloyd	87	80	86	86	339
Willie Smith	82	91	85	82	340
W.B. Hoare	84	84	87	87	342
Willie Dunn	85	87	87	84	343
J. Jones	83	84	90	90	347
H.C. Leeds	81	84	93	89	347
R.G. McAndrews	85	90	86	86	347
Bernard Nicholls	86	87	88	86	347

1899, Baltimore CC (Roland Course)
Baltimore, MD

Willie Smith	77	82	79	77	315
Val Fitzjohn	85	80	79	82	326
George Low	82	79	89	76	326

W.H. Way	80	85	80	81	326
Willie Anderson	77	81	85	84	327
Jack Park	88	80	75	85	328
Alex Smith	82	81	82	85	330
Henry Gullane	81	86	80	84	331
Laurie Auchterlonie	86	87	82	78	333
Peter Walker	84	86	77	86	333

1900, Chicago Golf Club
Wheaton, IL

Harry Vardon	79	78	76	80	313
J.H. Taylor	76	82	79	78	315
David Bell	78	83	83	78	322
Laurie Auchterlonie	84	82	80	81	327
Willie Smith	82	83	79	83	327
George Low	84	80	85	82	331
Tom Hutchinson	81	87	81	84	333
Harry Turpie	84	87	79	84	334
Stewart Gardner	85	78	84	89	336
Val Fitzjohn	84	83	89	82	338

1901, Myopia Hunt Club
South Hamilton, MA

| Willie Anderson | 84 | 83 | 83 | 81 | 331 |
| Alex Smith | 82 | 82 | 87 | 80 | 331 |

Willie Anderson beat Alex Smith in a
playoff- Anderson 85 Smith 86

Willie Smith	84	86	82	81	333
Stewart Gardner	86	82	81	85	334
Laurie Auchterlonie	81	85	86	83	335
Bernard Nicholls	84	85	83	83	335
David Brown	86	83	83	84	336
Alex Campbell	84	91	82	82	339
George Low	82	89	85	85	341
Jack Park	87	84	85	85	341

1902, Garden City Golf Club
Garden City, NY

Laurie Auchterlonie	78	78	74	77	307
Stewart Gardner	82	76	77	78	313
Walter Travis	82	82	75	74	313
Willie Smith	82	79	80	75	316
Willie Anderson	79	82	76	81	318
John Shippen	83	81	75	79	318
Charles Thorn	80	82	80	77	319

Harry Turpie	79	85	78	78	320
Donald Ross	80	83	78	81	322
Alex Ross	83	77	84	79	323

1903, Baltusrol G.C. (Original Course)
Springfield, NJ

| Willie Anderson | 73 | 76 | 76 | 82 | 307 |
| David Brown | 79 | 77 | 75 | 76 | 307 |

Willie Anderson beat David Brown in a
playoff- Anderson 82 Brown 84

Stewart Gardner	77	77	82	79	315
Alex Smith	77	77	81	81	316
Donald Ross	79	79	78	82	318
Jack Campbell	76	83	83	77	319
Laurie Auchterlonie	75	79	84	83	321
Findlay Douglas	77	79	82	84	322
Jack Hobens	76	81	82	84	323
Alex Ross	83	82	78	80	323

1904, Glen View Club
Golf, IL

Willie Anderson	75	78	78	72	303
Gilbert Nicholls	80	76	79	73	308
Fred MacKenzie	76	79	74	80	309
Laurie Auchterlonie	80	81	75	78	314
Bernard Nicholls	80	77	79	78	314
Percy Barrett	78	79	79	80	316
Stewart Gardner	75	76	80	85	316
Robert Simpson	82	82	76	76	316
James Foulis	83	74	78	82	317
Donald Ross	80	82	78	78	318

1905, Myopia Hunt Club
South Hamilton, MA

Willie Anderson	81	80	76	77	314
Alex Smith	76	80	80	80	316
Percy Barrett	81	80	77	79	317
Peter Robertson	79	80	81	77	317
Stewart Gardner	78	78	85	77	318
Alex Campbell	82	76	80	81	319
Gilbert Nicholls	82	76	84	79	321
Jack Hobens	82	80	81	78	321
George Cummings	85	82	75	81	323
Arthur Smith	81	77	80	86	324

1906, Onwentsia Club
Lake Forest, IL

Alex Smith	73	74	73	75	295
Willie Smith	73	81	74	74	302
Laurie Auchterlonie	76	78	75	76	305
James Maiden	80	73	77	75	305
Willie Anderson	73	76	74	84	307
Alex Ross	76	79	75	80	310
Stewart Gardner	80	76	77	78	311
H. Chandler Egan	79	78	76	80	313
Gilbert Nicholls	79	81	77	79	316
Jack Hobens	75	84	76	79	314

1907, Philadelphia Cricket Club
(St. Martins Course)
Chestnut Hill, PA

Alex Ross	76	74	76	76	302
Gilbert Nicholls	80	73	72	79	304
Alex Campbell	78	74	78	75	305
Jack Hobens	76	75	73	85	309
George Low	78	76	79	77	310
Fred McLeod	79	77	79	75	310
Peter Robertson	81	77	78	74	310
David Brown	75	80	78	78	311
Bernard Nicholls	76	76	81	78	311
Donald Ross	78	80	76	78	312

1908, Myopia Hunt Club
South Hamilton, MA

Fred McLeod	82	82	81	77	322
Willie Smith	77	82	85	78	322

Fred McLeod beat Willie Smith in a
playoff- McLeod 77 Smith 83

Alex Smith	80	83	83	81	327
Willie Anderson	85	86	80	79	330
John Jones	81	81	87	82	331
Jack Hobens	86	81	85	81	333
Peter Robertson	89	84	77	83	333
Percy Barrett	94	80	86	78	338
Jock Hutchison	82	84	87	85	338
Richard Kimball	84	86	83	86	339

1909, Englewood Golf Club
Englewood, NJ

George Sargent	75	72	72	71	290
Tom McNamara	73	69	75	77	294

Alex Smith	76	73	74	72	295
Willie Anderson	79	74	76	79	299
Jack Hobens	75	78	72	74	299
Isaac Mackie	77	75	74	73	299
Tom Anderson, Jr.	78	74	75	73	300
H.H. Barker	75	79	73	73	300
Andrew Campbell	71	75	77	77	300
Tom Peebles	76	73	73	78	300

1910, Philadelphia Cricket Club
(St. Martins Course)
Chestnut Hill, PA

Alex Smith	73	73	79	73	298
John McDermott	74	74	75	75	298
Macdonald Smith	74	78	75	71	298

Alex Smith beat John McDermott &
Mcdonald Smith in a playoff-
Alex Smith 71 - John McDermott -
Mcdonald Smith 77

Fred McLeod	78	70	78	73	299
Tom McNamara	73	78	73	76	300
Gilbert Nicholls	73	75	77	75	300
Jack Hobens	74	77	74	76	301
Tom Anderson, Jr.	72	76	81	73	302
H.H. Barker	75	78	77	72	302
Jock Hutchison	77	76	75	74	302

1911, Chicago Golf Club,
Wheaton, IL

John McDermott	81	72	75	79	307
Mike Brady	76	77	79	75	307
George Simpson	76	77	79	75	307

John McDermott beat Mike Brady &
George Simpson in a playoff-
McDermott 80 - Brady 82 -
Simpson 86

Fred McLeod	77	72	76	83	308
Jock Hutchison	80	77	73	79	309
Gilbert Nicholls	76	78	74	81	309
H.H. Barker	75	81	77	78	311
George Sargent	76	77	84	74	311
Peter Robertson	79	76	78	79	312
Alex Ross	74	75	81	82	312

1912, Country Club of Buffalo
Buffalo, NY

John McDermott	74	75	74	71	294
Tom McNamara	74	80	73	69	296
Mike Brady	72	75	73	79	299
Alex Smith	77	70	77	75	299
Alex Campbell	74	77	80	71	302
George Sargent	72	78	76	77	303
Jack Dowling	76	79	76	74	305
Otto Hackbath	77	77	75	76	305
C.R. Murray	75	78	77	76	306
Tom Anderson, Jr.	75	76	81	75	307

1913, The Country Club
Brookline, MA

Francis Ouimet	77	74	74	79	304
Harry Vardon	75	72	78	79	304
Edward Ray	79	70	76	79	304

Francis Ouimet beat Harry Vardon & Edward Ray in a playoff- Ouimet 72 - Vardon 77 - Ray 78

James Barnes	74	76	78	79	307
Walter Hagen	73	78	76	80	307
Macdonald Smith	71	79	80	77	307
Louis Tellier	76	76	79	76	307
John McDermott	74	79	77	78	308
Herbert Strong	75	74	82	79	310
Pat Doyle	78	80	73	80	311

1914, Midlothian C.C.
Blue Island, IL

Walter Hagen	68	74	75	73	290
Charles Evans, Jr.	76	74	71	70	291
Fred McLeod	78	73	75	71	297
George Sargent	74	77	74	72	297
Mike Brady	78	72	74	74	298
James Donaldson	72	79	74	73	298
Francis Ouimet	69	76	75	78	298
Louis Tellier	72	75	74	78	299
John McDermott	77	74	74	75	300
Arthur Smith	79	73	76	72	300

1915, Baltusrol G.C. (Revised Course)
Springfield, NJ

Jerome Travers	76	72	73	76	297
Tom McNamara	78	71	74	75	298
Bob MacDonald	72	77	73	78	300
James Barnes	71	75	76	79	301
Louis Tellier	75	71	76	79	301
Mike Brady	76	71	75	80	302
George Low	78	74	76	75	303
Jock Hutchison	74	79	76	76	305
Fred McLeod	74	76	76	79	305
Alex Campbell	76	75	74	81	306

1916, Minikahda Club
Minneapolis, MN

Charles Evans, Jr.	70	69	74	73	286
Jock Hutchison	73	75	72	68	288
James Barnes	71	74	71	74	290
Gilbert Nicholls	73	76	71	73	293
Wilfred Reid	70	72	79	72	293
George Sargent	75	71	72	75	293
Walter Hagen	73	76	75	71	295
Bob MacDonald	74	72	77	73	296
Mike Brady	75	73	75	74	297
J.J. O'Brien	76	72	73	76	297

1919, Brae Burn Country Club
West Newton, MA

Walter Hagen	78	73	75	75	301
Mike Brady	74	74	73	80	301

Walter Hagen beat Mike Brady in a playoff- Hagen 77 Brady 78

Jock Hutchison	78	76	76	76	306
Tom McNamara	80	73	79	74	306
George McLean	81	75	76	76	308
Louis Tellier	73	78	82	75	308
John Cowan	79	74	75	81	309
Fred McLeod	78	77	79	78	312
George Bowden	73	78	75	86	312
Charles Evans, Jr.	77	76	82	78	313

1920, Inverness Club
Toledo, OH

Edward Ray	74	73	73	75	295
Jack Burke, Sr.	75	77	72	72	296
Leo Diegel	72	74	73	77	296
Jock Hutchison	69	76	74	77	296
Harry Vardon	74	73	71	78	296
James Barnes	76	70	76	76	298

Charles Evans, Jr.	74	76	73	75	298
Bobby Jones	78	74	70	77	299
Willie MacFarlane	76	75	74	74	299
Bob MacDonald	73	78	71	78	300

1921, Columbia Country Club
Chevy Chase, MD

James Barnes	69	75	73	72	289
Walter Hagen	79	73	72	74	298
Fred McLeod	74	74	76	74	298
Charles Evans, Jr.	73	78	76	75	302
Emmett French	75	77	74	77	303
Bobby Jones	78	71	77	77	303
Alex Smith	75	75	79	74	303
George Duncan	72	78	78	77	305
Clarence Hackney	74	76	78	77	305
Emil Loeffler, Jr.	74	77	74	81	306

1922, Skokie Country Club
Glencoe, IL

Gene Sarazen	72	73	75	68	288
John Black	71	71	75	72	289
Bobby Jones	74	72	70	73	289
William Mehlhorn	73	71	72	74	290
Walter Hagen	68	77	74	72	291
George Duncan	76	73	75	72	296
Leo Diegel	77	76	73	71	297
Mike Brady	73	75	74	76	298
John Golden	73	77	77	71	298
Jock Hutchison	78	74	71	75	298

1923, Inwood Country Club
Inwood, NY

| Bobby Jones | 71 | 73 | 76 | 76 | 296 |
| Bobby Cruickshank | 73 | 72 | 78 | 73 | 296 |

Bobby Jones beat Bobby Cruickshank in a
playoff- Jones 76 - Cruickshank 78

Jock Hutchison	70	72	82	78	302
Jack Forrester	75	73	77	78	303
Johnny Farrell	76	77	75	76	304
Francis Gallett	76	72	77	79	304
W.M. Reekie	80	74	75	75	304
Leo Diegel	77	77	76	76	306
William Mehlhorn	73	79	75	79	306
Al Watrous	74	75	76	81	306

1924, Oakland Hills Country Club
Birmingham, MI

Cyril Walker	74	74	74	75	297
Bobby Jones	74	73	75	78	300
William Mehlhorn	72	75	76	78	301
Bobby Cruickshank	77	72	76	78	303
Walter Hagen	75	75	76	77	303
Macdonald Smith	78	72	77	76	303
Abe Espinosa	80	71	77	77	305
Peter O'Hara	76	79	74	76	305
Mike Brady	75	77	77	77	306
Charles Evans, Jr.	77	77	76	77	307

1925, Worcester Country Club
Worcester, MA

| Willie MacFarlane | 74 | 67 | 72 | 78 | 291 |
| Bobby Jones | 77 | 70 | 70 | 74 | 291 |

Willie MacFarlane beat Bobby Jones in a
playoff- MacFarlane 75-72=147
Jones 75-73=148

Johnny Farrell	71	74	69	78	292
Francis Ouimet	70	73	73	76	292
Walter Hagen	72	76	71	74	293
Gene Sarazen	72	72	75	74	293
Mike Brady	74	72	74	74	294
Leo Diegel	73	68	77	78	296
Laurie Ayton	75	71	73	78	297
Al Espinosa	72	71	74	80	297

1926, Scioto Country Club
Columbus, OH

Bobby Jones	70	79	71	73	293
Joe Turnesa	71	74	72	77	294
Leo Diegel	72	76	75	74	297
Johnny Farrell	76	79	69	73	297
William Mehlhorn	68	75	76	78	297
Gene Sarazen	78	77	72	70	297
Walter Hagen	73	77	74	74	298
Willie Hunter, Jr.	75	77	69	79	300
Tommy Amour	76	76	74	75	301
Willie Klein	76	74	75	76	301

1927, Oakmont Country Club
Oakmont, PA

| Tommy Amour | 78 | 71 | 76 | 76 | 301 |
| Harry Cooper | 74 | 76 | 74 | 77 | 301 |

Tommy Amour beat Harry Cooper
in a playoff- Amour 76 Cooper 79

Gene Sarazen	74	74	80	74	302
Emmett French	75	79	77	73	304
William Mehlhorn	75	77	80	73	305
Walter Hagen	77	73	76	79	308
Archie Compston	79	74	76	79	308
Johnny Farrell	81	73	78	76	308
John Golden	83	77	75	73	308
Harry Hampton	73	78	80	77	308

1928, Olympia Fields CC (No. 4 Course)
Mateson, IL

Johnny Farrell	77	74	71	72	294
Bobby Jones	73	71	73	77	294

Johnny Farrell beat Bobby Jones in a play-
off- Farrell 70-73=143 Jones 73-71=144

Roland Hancock	74	77	72	72	295
Walter Hagen	75	72	73	76	296
George Von Elm	74	72	76	74	296
Henry Ciuci	70	77	72	80	299
Waldo Crowder	74	74	76	75	299
Ed Dudley	77	79	68	75	299
Bill Leach	72	74	73	80	299
Gene Sarazen	78	76	73	72	299

1929, Winged Foot Golf Club
Mamaroneck, NY

Bobby Jones	69	75	71	79	294
Al Espinosa	70	72	77	75	294

Bobby Jones beat Al Espinosa in a playoff-
Jones 72-69=141 Espinosa 84-80=164

Gene Sarazen	71	71	76	78	296
Denny Shute	73	71	76	76	296
Tommy Armour	74	71	76	76	297
George Von Elm	79	70	74	74	297
Henry Ciuci	78	74	72	75	299
Leo Diegel	74	74	76	77	301
Peter O'Hara	74	76	73	78	301
Horton Smith	76	77	74	75	302

1930, Interlachen Country Club
Minneapolis, MN

Bobby Jones	71	73	68	75	287
Macdonald Smith	70	75	74	70	289

Horton Smith	72	70	76	74	292
Harry Cooper	72	72	73	76	293
Johnny Golden	74	73	71	76	294
Tommy Armour	70	76	75	76	297
Charles Lacey	74	70	77	77	298
Johnny Farrell	74	72	73	80	299
William Mehlhorn	76	74	75	75	300
Craig Wood	73	75	72	80	300

1931, Inverness Club
Toledo, OH

Billy Burke	73	72	74	73	292
George Von Elm	75	69	73	75	292

Billy Burke beat George Von Elm in
a playoff, July 5- Burke 73-76=149 Von
Elm 75-74=149. A tie forced another 36
hole playoff, July 6- Burke 77-71=148
Von Elm 76-73=149

Leo Diegel	75	73	74	72	294
Wiffy Cox	75	74	74	72	295
William Mehlhorn	77	73	75	71	296
Gene Sarazen	74	78	74	70	296
Mortie Dutra	71	77	73	76	297
Walter Hagen	74	74	73	76	297
Philip Perkins	78	76	73	70	297
Al Espinosa	72	78	75	74	299

1932, Fresh Meadow Country Club
Flushing, NY

Gene Sarazen	74	76	70	66	286
Bobby Cruickshank	78	74	69	68	289
Philip Perkins	76	69	74	70	289
Leo Diegel	73	74	73	74	294
Wiffy Cox	80	73	70	72	295
Jose Jurado	74	71	75	76	296
Billy Burke	75	77	74	71	297
Harry Cooper	77	73	73	74	297
Olin Dutra	69	77	75	76	297
Walter Hagen	75	73	79	71	298

1933, North Shore Country Club
Glenview, IL

Johnny Goodman	75	66	70	76	287
Ralph Guldahl	76	71	70	71	288
Craig Wood	73	74	71	72	290

Tommy Armour	68	75	76	73	292
Walter Hagen	73	76	77	66	292
Mortie Dutra	75	73	72	74	294
Olin Dutra	75	71	75	74	295
Gus Moreland	76	76	71	72	295
Clarence Clark	80	72	72	72	296
Johnny Farrell	75	77	72	72	296

1934, Merion Cricket Club (East Course)
Ardmore, PA

Olin Dutra	76	74	71	72	293
Gene Sarazen	73	72	73	76	294
Harry Cooper	76	74	74	71	295
Wiffy Cox	71	75	74	75	295
Bobby Cruickshank	71	71	77	76	295
Billy Burke	76	71	77	72	296
Macdonald Smith	75	73	78	70	296
Tom Creavy	79	76	78	66	299
Ralph Guldahl	78	73	70	78	299
Jimmy Hines	80	70	77	72	299

1935, Oakmont Country Club
Oakmont, PA

Sam Parks, Jr.	77	73	73	76	299
Jimmy Thomson	73	73	77	78	301
Walter Hagen	77	76	73	76	302
Ray Mangrum	76	76	72	79	303
Denny Shute	78	73	76	76	303
Alvin Krueger	71	77	78	80	306
Henry Picard	79	78	70	79	306
Gene Sarazen	75	74	78	79	306
Horton Smith	73	79	79	75	306
Dick Metz	77	76	76	78	307

1936, Baltusrol G.C. (Upper Course)
Springfield, NJ

Tony Manero	73	69	73	67	282
Harry Cooper	71	70	70	73	284
Clarence Clark	69	75	71	72	287
Macdonald Smith	73	73	72	70	288
Wiffy Cox	74	74	69	72	289
Ky Laffoon	71	74	70	74	289
Henry Picard	70	71	74	74	289
Ralph Guldahl	73	70	73	74	290
Paul Runyan	69	75	73	73	290
Denny Shute	72	69	73	77	291

1937, Oakland Hills C.C.
Birmingham, MI

Ralph Guldahl	71	69	72	69	281
Sam snead	69	73	70	71	283
Bobby Cruickshank	73	73	67	72	285
Harry Cooper	72	70	73	71	286
Ed Dudley	70	70	71	76	287
Al Brosch	74	73	68	73	288
Clarence Clark	72	75	73	69	289
Johnny Goodman	70	73	72	75	290
Frank Strafaci	70	72	77	72	291
Charles Kocsis	72	73	76	71	292

1938, Cherry Hills Country Club
Denver, CO

Ralph Guldahl	74	70	71	69	284
Dick Metz	73	68	70	79	290
Harry Cooper	76	69	76	71	292
Toney Penna	78	72	74	68	292
Byron Nelson	77	71	74	72	294
Emery Zimmerman	72	71	73	78	294
Frank Moore	79	73	72	71	295
Henry Picard	70	70	77	78	295
Paul Runyan	78	71	72	74	295
Gene Sarazen	74	74	75	73	296

1939, Philadelphia Country Club
(Spring Mill Course)
Philadelphia, PA

Byron Nelson	74	73	71	68	284
Craig Wood	70	71	71	72	284
Denny Shute	70	72	70	72	284

Byron Nelson beat Craig Wood & Denny Shute in a playoff- July 11 Nelson 68 Wood 68 Shute 76 - was eliminated July 12 Nelson 70=138 Wood 73=141

Bud Ward	69	73	71	72	285
Sam Snead	68	71	73	74	286
Johnny Bulla	72	71	68	76	287
Ralph Guldahl	71	73	72	72	288
Dick Metz	76	72	71	69	288
Ky Laffoon	76	70	73	70	289
Harold McSpaden	70	73	71	75	289

1940, Canterbury Golf Club
Cleveland, OH

Lawson Little	72	69	73	73	287
Gene Sarazen	71	74	70	72	287

Lawson Little beat Gene Sarazen in a
playoff Little 70 Sarazen 73

Horton Smith	69	72	78	69	288
Craig Wood	72	73	72	72	289
Ralph Guldahl	73	71	76	70	290
Ben Hogan	70	73	74	73	290
Lloyd Mangrum	75	70	71	74	290
Byron Nelson	72	74	70	74	290
Dick Metz	75	72	72	72	291
Ed Dudley	73	75	71	73	292

1941, Colonial Country Club
Fort Worth, TX

Craig Wood	73	71	70	70	284
Denny Shute	69	75	72	71	287
Johnny Bulla	75	71	72	71	289
Ben Hogan	74	77	68	70	289
Herman Barron	75	71	74	71	291
Paul Runyan	73	72	71	75	291
Dutch Harrison	70	82	71	71	294
Harold McSpaden	71	75	74	74	294
Gene Sarazen	74	73	72	75	294
Ed Dudley	74	74	74	73	295

1946, Cantebury Golf Club
Cleveland, OH

Lloyd Mangrum	74	70	68	72	284
Vic Ghezzi	71	69	72	72	284
Byron Nelson	71	71	69	73	284

Lloyd Mangrum beat Vic Ghezzi and Byron
Nelson in a playoff- Mangrum 72, Ghezzi
72, Nelson 72. A tie forced another playoff-
Mangrum 72=144, Ghezzi 73=145, Nelson
73=145

Herman Barron	72	72	72	69	285
Ben Hogan	72	68	73	72	285
Jimmy Demaret	71	74	73	68	286
Edward Oliver, Jr.	71	71	74	70	286
Chick Harbert	72	78	67	70	287
Dick Metz	76	70	72	69	287
Dutch Harrison	75	71	72	70	288

1947, St. Louis Country Club
St. Louis, MO

Lew Worsham	70	70	71	71	282
Sam Snead	72	70	70	70	282

Lew Worsham beat Sam Snead in a
playoff Worsham 69 Snead 70

Bobby Locke	68	74	70	73	285
Edward Oliver, Jr.	73	70	71	71	285
Bud Ward	69	72	73	73	287
Jim Ferrier	71	70	74	74	289
Vic Ghezzi	74	73	73	69	289
Leland Gibson	69	76	73	71	289
Ben Hogan	70	75	70	74	289
Johnny Palmer	72	70	75	72	289

1948, Riviera Country Club
Pacific Palisades, CA

Ben Hogan	67	72	68	69	276
Jimmy Demaret	71	70	68	69	278
Jim Turnesa	71	69	70	70	280
Bobby Locke	70	69	73	70	282
Sam Snead	69	69	73	72	283
Lew Worsham	67	74	71	73	285
Herman Barron	73	70	71	72	286
Johnny Bulla	73	72	75	67	287
Toney Penna	70	72	73	72	287
Smiley Quick	73	71	69	74	287

1949, Medinah C.C. (No. 3 Course)
Medinah, IL

Cary Middlecoff	75	67	69	75	286
Clayton Heather	72	71	71	73	287
Sam Snead	73	73	71	70	287
Bobby Locke	74	71	73	71	289
Jim Turnesa	78	69	70	72	289
Dave Douglas	74	73	70	73	290
Buck White	74	68	70	78	290
Pete Cooper	71	73	74	73	291
Claude Harmon	71	72	74	74	291
Johnny Palmer	71	75	72	73	291

1950, Merion Golf Club (East Course)
Ardmore, PA

Ben Hogan	72	69	72	74	287
Lloyd Mangrum	72	70	69	76	287

George Fazio	73	72	72	70	287

Ben Hogan beat Lloyd Mangrum & George
Fazio in a -playoff Ben Hogan 69 - Lloyd
Mangrum 73 - George Fazio 75

Dutch Harrison	72	67	73	76	288
Jim Ferrier	71	69	74	75	289
Joe Kirkwood, Jr.	71	74	74	70	289
Henry Ransom	72	71	73	73	289
Bill Nary	73	70	74	73	290
Julius Boros	68	72	77	74	291
Cary Middlecoff	71	71	71	79	292

1951, Oakland Hills C.C.
Birmingham, MI

Ben Hogan	76	73	71	67	287
Clayton Heather	72	75	73	69	289
Bobby Locke	73	71	74	73	291
Julius Boros	74	74	71	74	293
Lloyd Mangrum	75	74	74	70	293
Al Besselink	72	77	72	73	294
Dave Douglas	75	70	75	74	294
Fred Hawkins	76	72	75	71	294
Paul Runyan	73	74	72	75	294
Al Brosch	73	74	76	72	295

1952, Northwood Club
Dallas, TX

Julius Boros	71	71	68	71	281
Edward Oliver, Jr.	71	72	70	72	285
Ben Hogan	69	69	74	74	286
Johnny Bulla	73	68	73	73	287
George Fazio	71	69	75	75	290
Dick Metz	70	74	76	71	291
Tommy Bolt	72	76	71	73	292
Ted Kroll	71	75	76	70	292
Lew Worsham	72	71	74	75	292
Lloyd Mangrum	75	74	72	72	293

1953, Oakmont C.C.
Oakmont, PA

Ben Hogan	67	72	73	71	283
Sam Snead	72	69	72	76	289
Lloyd Mangrum	73	70	74	75	292
Pete Cooper	78	75	71	70	294
Jimmy Demaret	71	76	71	76	294
George Fazio	70	71	77	76	294

Ted Kroll	76	71	74	74	295
Dick Metz	75	70	74	76	295
Marty Furgol	73	74	76	73	296
Jay Hebert	72	72	74	78	296

1954, Baltusrol GC (Lower Course)
Springfield, NJ

Ed Furgol	71	70	71	72	284
Gene Littler	70	69	76	70	285
Lloyd Mangrum	72	71	72	71	286
Dick Mayer	72	71	70	73	286
Bobby Locke	74	70	74	70	288
Tommy Bolt	72	72	73	72	289
Fred Haas	73	73	71	72	289
Ben Hogan	71	70	76	72	289
Shelley Mayfield	73	75	72	69	289
Billy Joe Patton	69	76	71	73	289

1955, Olympic Club
San Francisco, CA

Jack Fleck	76	69	75	67	287
Ben Hogan	72	73	72	70	287

Jack Fleck beat Ben Hogan in a playoff-
Jack Fleck 69 Ben Hogan 72

Tommy Bolt	67	77	75	73	292
Sam Snead	79	69	70	74	292
Julius Boros	76	69	73	77	295
Bob Rosburg	78	74	67	76	295
Doug Ford	74	77	74	71	296
Bud Holscher	77	75	71	73	296
Harvie Ward	74	70	76	76	296
Jack Burke	71	77	72	77	297

1956, Oak Hill Country Club
Rochester, NY

Cary Middlecoff	71	70	70	70	281
Julius Boros	71	71	71	69	282
Ben Hogan	72	68	72	70	282
Ed Furgol	71	70	73	71	285
Ted Kroll	72	70	70	73	285
Peter Thomson	70	69	75	71	285
Arnold Palmer	72	70	72	73	287
Ken Venturi	77	71	68	73	289
Jerry Barber	72	69	74	75	290
Wes Ellis	71	70	71	78	290

1957, Inverness Club
Toledo, OH

Dick Mayer	70	68	74	70	282
Cary Middlecoff	71	75	68	68	282

Dick Mayer beat Cary Middlecoff in a
playoff- Mayer 72 Middlecoff 79

Jimmy Demaret	68	73	70	72	283
Julius Boros	69	75	70	70	284
Walter Burkemo	74	73	72	65	284
Fred Hawkins	72	72	71	71	286
Ken Venturi	69	71	75	71	286
Roberto DeVicenzo	72	70	72	76	290
Chick Harbert	68	79	71	72	290
Billy Maxwell	70	76	72	72	290

1958, Southern Hills Country Club
Tulsa, OK

Tommy Bolt	71	71	69	72	283
Gary Player	75	68	73	71	287
Julius Boros	71	75	72	71	289
Gene Littler	74	73	67	76	290
Walter Burkemo	75	74	70	72	291
Bob Rosburg	75	74	70	72	291
Jay Herbert	77	76	71	69	293
Don January	79	73	68	73	293
Dick Metz	71	78	73	71	293
Ben Hogan	75	73	75	71	294

1959, Winged Foot Golf Club
Mamaroneck, NY

Billy Casper	71	68	69	74	282
Bob Rosburg	75	70	67	71	283
Claude Hamon	72	71	70	71	284
Mike Souchak	71	70	72	71	284
Doug Ford	72	69	72	73	286
Arnold Palmer	71	69	72	74	286
Ernie Vossler	72	70	72	72	286
Ben Hogan	69	71	71	76	287
Sam Snead	73	72	67	75	287
Dick Knight	69	75	73	73	290

1960, Cherry Hills Country Club
Denver, CO

Arnold Palmer	72	71	72	65	280
Jack Nicklaus	71	71	69	71	282
Julius Boros	73	69	68	73	283
Dow Finsterwald	71	69	70	73	283
Jack Fleck	70	70	72	71	283
Dutch Harrison	74	70	70	69	283
Ted Kroll	72	69	75	67	283
Mike Souchak	68	67	73	75	283
Jerry Barber	69	71	70	74	284
Don Cherry	70	71	71	72	284

1961, Oakland Hills C.C.
Birmingham, MI

Gene Littler	73	68	72	68	281
Bob Goalby	70	72	69	71	282
Doug Sanders	72	67	71	72	282
Jack Nicklaus	75	69	70	70	284
Mike Souchak	73	70	68	73	284
Dow Finsterwald	72	71	71	72	286
Doug Ford	72	69	71	74	286
Eric Monti	74	67	72	73	286
Jacky Cupit	72	72	67	76	287
Gardner Dickinson	72	69	71	75	287

1962, Oakmont Country Club
Oakmont, PA

Jack Nicklaus	72	70	72	69	283
Arnold Palmer	71	68	73	71	283

Jack Nicklaus beat Arnold Palmer
in a playoff- Jack Nicklaus 71
Arnold Palmer 74

Bobby Nichols	70	72	70	73	285
Phil Rodgers	74	70	69	72	285
Gay Brewer	73	72	73	69	287
Tommy Jacobs	74	71	73	70	288
Gary Player	71	71	72	74	288
Doug Ford	74	75	71	70	290
Gene Littler	69	74	72	75	290
Billy Maxwell	71	70	75	74	290

1963, The Country Club
Brookline, MA

Julius Boros	71	74	76	72	293
Jacky Cupit	70	72	76	75	293
Arnold Palmer	73	69	77	74	293

Julius Boros beat Jacky Cupit & Arnold
Palmer in a playoff-

Julius Boros 70 - Jacky Cupit 73 - Arnold Palmer 76

Paul Harney	78	70	73	73	294
Bruce Crampton	74	72	75	74	295
Tony Lema	71	74	74	76	295
Billy Maxwell	73	73	75	74	295
Walter Burkemo	72	71	76	77	296
Gary Player	74	75	75	72	296
Dan Sikes	77	73	73	74	297

1964, Congressional Country Club
Bethesda, MD

Ken Venturi	72	70	66	70	278
Tommy Jacobs	72	64	70	76	282
Bob Charles	72	72	71	68	283
Billy Casper	71	74	69	71	285
Gay Brewer	76	69	73	68	286
Arnold Palmer	68	69	75	74	286
Bill Collins	70	71	74	72	287
Dow Finsterwald	73	72	71	72	288
Johnny Pott	71	73	73	72	289
Bob Rosburg	73	73	70	73	289

1965, Bellerive Country Club
St. Louis, MO

| Gary Player | 70 | 70 | 71 | 71 | 282 |
| Kel Nagle | 68 | 73 | 72 | 69 | 282 |

Gary Player beat Kel Nagle in a playoff-
Gary Player 71 Kel Nagle 74

Frank Beard	74	69	70	71	284
Julius Boros	72	76	70	70	287
Al Geiberger	70	76	70	71	287
Bruce Devlin	72	73	72	71	288
Ray Floyd	72	72	76	68	288
Tony Lema	72	74	73	70	289
Gene Littler	73	71	73	72	289
Dudley Wysong	72	75	70	72	289

1966, Olympic Club
San Francisco, CA

| Billy Casper | 69 | 68 | 73 | 68 | 278 |
| Arnold Palmer | 71 | 66 | 70 | 71 | 278 |

Billy Casper beat Arnold Palmer in a play-off- Billy Casper 69 Arnold Palmer 73

Jack Nicklaus	71	71	69	74	285
Tony Lema	71	74	70	71	286
Dave Marr	71	74	68	73	286
Phil Rodgers	70	70	73	74	287
Bobby Nichols	74	72	71	72	289
Wes Ellis	71	75	74	70	290
Johnny Miller	70	72	74	74	290
Mason Rudolph	74	72	71	73	290

1967, Baltusrol G.C. (Lower Course)
Springfield, NJ

Jack Nicklaus	71	67	72	65	275
Arnold Palmer	69	68	73	69	279
Don January	69	72	70	70	281
Billy Casper	69	70	71	72	282
Lee Trevino	72	70	71	70	283
Deane Beman	69	71	71	73	284
Gardner Dickinson	70	73	68	73	284
Bob Goalby	72	71	70	71	284
Dave Marr	70	74	70	71	285
Kel Nagle	70	72	72	71	285

1968, Oak Hill Country Club
Rochester, NY

Lee Trevino	69	68	69	69	275
Jack Nicklaus	72	70	70	67	279
Bert Yancey	67	68	70	76	281
Bobby Nichols	74	71	68	69	282
Don Bies	70	70	75	69	284
Steve Spray	73	75	71	65	284
Bob Charles	73	69	72	71	285
Jerry Pittman	73	67	74	71	285
Gay Brewer	71	71	75	69	286
Billy Casper	75	68	71	72	286

1969, Champions GC (Cypress Creek)
Houston, TX

Orville Moody	71	70	68	72	281
Deane Beman	68	69	73	72	282
Al Geiberger	68	72	72	70	282
Bob Rosburg	70	69	72	71	282
Bob Murphy	66	72	74	71	283
Miller Barber	67	71	68	78	284
Bruce Crampton	73	72	68	71	284
Arnold Palmer	70	73	69	72	284
Bunky Henry	70	72	68	75	285
George Archer	69	74	73	70	286

1970, Hazeltine National G.C.
Minneapolis, MN

Tony Jacklin	71	70	70	70	281
Dave Hill	75	69	71	73	288
Bob Charles	76	71	75	67	289
Bob Lunn	77	72	70	70	289
Ken Still	78	71	71	71	291
Miller Barber	75	75	72	70	292
Gay Brewer	75	71	71	76	293
Billy Casper	75	75	71	73	294
Bruce Devlin	75	75	71	73	294
Lee Trevino	77	73	74	70	294

1971, Merion Golf Club (East Course)
Ardmore, PA

| Lee Trevino | 70 | 72 | 69 | 69 | 280 |
| Jack Nicklaus | 69 | 72 | 68 | 71 | 280 |

Lee Trevino beat Jack Nicklaus in a play-off- Lee Trevino 68 Jack Nicklaus 71

Jim Colbert	69	69	73	71	282
Bob Rosburg	71	72	70	69	282
George Archer	71	70	70	72	283
Johnny Miller	70	73	70	70	283
Jim Simons	71	71	65	76	283
Ray Floyd	71	75	67	71	284
Gay Brewer	70	70	73	72	285
Larry Hinson	71	71	70	73	285

1972, Pebble Beach Golf Links
Pebble Beach, CA

Jack Nicklaus	71	73	72	74	290
Bruce Crampton	74	70	73	76	293
Arnold Palmer	77	68	73	76	294
Homero Blancas	74	70	76	75	295
Lee Trevino	74	72	71	78	295
Kermit Zarley	71	73	73	79	296
Johnny Miller	74	73	71	79	297
Tom Weiskopf	73	74	73	78	298
Chi Chi Rodriguez	71	75	78	75	299
Cesar Sanudo	72	72	78	77	299

1973, Oakmont Country Club
Oakmont, PA

| Johnny Miller | 71 | 69 | 76 | 63 | 279 |
| John Schlee | 73 | 70 | 67 | 70 | 280 |

Tom Weiskopf	73	69	69	70	281
Jack Nicklaus	71	69	74	68	282
Arnold Palmer	71	71	68	72	282
Lee Trevino	70	72	70	70	282
Julius Boros	73	69	68	73	283
Jerry Heard	74	70	66	73	283
Lanny Wadkins	74	69	75	65	283
Jim Colbert	70	68	74	72	284

1974, Winged Foot Golf Club
Mamaroneck, NY

Hale Irwin	73	70	71	73	287
Forrest Fezler	75	70	74	70	289
Lou Graham	71	75	74	70	290
Bert Yancey	76	69	73	72	290
Jim Colbert	72	77	69	74	292
Arnold Palmer	73	70	73	76	292
Tom Watson	73	71	69	79	292
Tom Kite	74	70	77	72	293
Gary Player	70	73	77	73	293
Brian Allin	76	71	74	73	294

1975, Medinah C.C. (No. 3 Course)
Medinah, IL

| Lou Graham | 74 | 72 | 68 | 73 | 287 |
| John Mahaffey | 73 | 71 | 72 | 71 | 287 |

Lou Graham beat John Mahaffey in a playoff- Lou Graham 71 John Mahaffey 73

Frank Beard	74	69	67	78	288
Ben Crenshaw	70	68	76	74	288
Hale Irwin	74	71	73	70	288
Bob Murphy	74	73	72	69	288
Jack Nicklaus	72	70	75	72	289
Peter Oosterhuis	69	73	72	75	289
Pat Fitzsimons	67	73	73	77	290
Arnold Palmer	69	75	73	73	290

1976, Atlanta Athletic Club
Atlanta, GA

Jerry Pate	71	69	69	68	277
Al Geiberger	70	69	71	69	279
Tom Weiskopf	73	70	68	68	279
Butch Baird	71	71	71	67	280
John Mahaffey	70	68	69	73	280

Only one player has scored a double eagle in the U.S. Open—Tze-Chung Chen of Taiwan, in the opening round of the 1985 championship at Oakland Hills Golf Club in Bloomfield Hills, Michigan. In the closing round he had a double-hit on the 5th hole, took an 8, lost a four-stroke lead, and finished tied for second.

Hubert Green	72	70	71	69	282
Tom Watson	74	72	68	70	284
Ben Crenshaw	72	68	72	73	285
Lyn Lott	71	71	70	73	285
Johnny Miller	74	72	69	71	286

1977, Southern Hills Country Club
Tulsa, OK

Hubert Green	69	67	72	70	278
Lou Graham	72	71	68	68	279
Tom Weiskopf	71	71	68	71	281
Tom Purtzer	69	69	72	72	282
Jay Haas	72	68	71	72	283
Gary Jacobsen	73	70	67	73	283
Lyn Lott	73	72	71	67	283
Terry Diehl	69	68	73	74	284
Tom Watson	74	72	71	67	284
Rod Funseth	69	70	72	74	285

1978, Cherry Hills Country Club
Denver, CO

Andy North	70	70	71	74	285
J.C. Snead	70	72	72	72	286
Dave Stockton	71	73	70	72	286
Hale Irwin	69	74	75	70	288
Tom Weiskopf	77	73	70	68	288
Andy Bean	72	72	71	74	289
Bill Kratzert	72	74	70	73	289
Johnny Miller	78	69	68	74	289
Jack Nicklaus	73	69	74	73	289
Gary Player	71	71	70	77	289

1979, Inverness Club
Toledo, OH

Hale Irwin	74	68	67	75	284
Jerry Pate	71	74	69	72	286

Gary Player	73	73	72	68	286
Larry Nelson	71	68	76	73	288
Bill Rogers	71	72	73	72	288
Tom Weiskopf	71	74	67	76	288
David Graham	73	73	70	73	289
Tom Purtzer	70	69	75	76	290
Keith Fergus	70	77	72	72	291
Jack Nicklaus	74	77	72	68	291

1980, Baltusrol GC (Lower Course)
Springfield, NJ

Jack Nicklaus	63	71	70	68	272
Isao Aoki	68	68	68	70	274
Keith Fergus	66	70	70	70	276
Lon Hinkle	66	70	69	71	276
Tom Watson	71	68	67	70	276
Mark Hayes	66	71	69	74	280
Mike Reid	69	67	75	69	280
Hale Irwin	70	70	73	69	282
Mike Morley	73	68	69	72	282
Andy North	68	75	72	67	282

1981, Merion Golf Club (East Course)
Ardmore, PA

David Graham	68	68	70	67	273
George Burns	69	66	68	73	276
Bill Rogers	70	68	69	69	276
John Cook	68	70	71	70	279
John Schroeder	71	68	69	71	279
Frank Conner	71	72	69	68	280
Lon Hinkle	69	71	70	70	280
Jack Nicklaus	69	68	71	72	280
Sammy Rachels	70	71	69	70	280
Chi Chi Rodriguez	68	73	67	72	280

1982, Pebble Beach Golf Links
Pebble Beach, CA

Tom Watson	72	72	68	70	282
Jack Nicklaus	74	70	71	69	284
Bobby Clampett	71	73	72	70	286
Dan Pohl	72	74	70	70	286
Bill Rogers	70	73	69	74	286
David Graham	73	72	69	73	287
Jay Haas	75	74	70	68	287

Gary Koch	78	73	69	67	287
Lanny Wadkins	73	76	67	71	287
Bruce Devlin	70	69	75	74	288

1983, Oakmont Country Club
Oakmont, PA

Larry Nelson	75	73	65	67	280
Tom Watson	72	70	70	69	281
Gil Morgan	73	72	70	68	283
Seve Ballesteros	69	74	69	74	286
Calvin Peete	75	68	70	73	286
Hal Sutton	73	70	73	71	287
Lanny Wadkins	72	73	74	69	288
David Graham	74	75	73	69	291
Ralph Landrum	75	73	69	74	291
Chip Beck	73	74	74	71	292

1984, Winged Foot Golf Club
Mamaroneck, NY

| Fuzzy Zoeller | 71 | 66 | 69 | 70 | 276 |
| Greg Norman | 70 | 68 | 69 | 69 | 276 |

Fuzzy Zoeller beat Greg Norman in a playoff-
Fuzzy Zoeller 67 Greg Norman 75

Curtis Strange	69	70	74	68	281
Johnny Miller	74	68	70	70	282
Jim Thorpe	68	71	70	73	282
Hale Irwin	68	68	69	79	284
Peter Jacobsen	72	73	73	67	285
Mark O'Meara	71	74	71	69	285
Fred Couples	69	71	74	72	286
Lee Trevino	71	72	69	74	286

1985, Oakland Hills C.C.
Birmingham, MI

Andy North	70	65	70	74	279
Dave Barr	70	68	70	72	280
T.C. Chen	65	69	69	77	280
Denis Watson	72	65	73	70	280
Seve Ballesteros	71	70	69	71	281
Payne Stewart	70	70	71	70	281
Lanny Wadkins	70	72	69	70	281
Johnny Miller	74	71	68	69	282
Rick Fehr	69	67	73	74	283
Corey Pavin	72	68	73	70	283

1986, Shinnecock Hills G.C.
Southampton, NY

Ray Floyd	75	68	70	66	279
Chip Beck	75	73	68	65	281
Lanny Wadkins	74	70	72	65	281
Hal Sutton	75	70	66	71	282
Lee Trevino	74	68	69	71	282
Ben Crenshaw	76	69	69	69	283
Payne Stewart	76	68	69	70	283
Bernhard Langer	74	70	70	70	284
Mark McCumber	74	71	68	71	284
Jack Nicklaus	77	72	67	68	284

1987, Olympic Club
San Francisco, CA

Scott Simpson	71	68	70	68	277
Tom Watson	72	65	71	70	278
Seve Ballesteros	68	75	68	71	282
Ben Crenshaw	67	72	72	72	283
Bernhard Langer	69	69	73	72	283
Larry Mize	71	68	72	72	283
Curtis Strange	71	72	69	71	283
Bobby Wadkins	71	71	70	71	283
Lennie Clements	70	70	70	74	284
Tommy Nakajima	68	70	74	72	284

1988, The Country Club
Brookline, MA

| Curtis Strange | 70 | 67 | 69 | 72 | 278 |
| Nick Faldo | 72 | 67 | 68 | 71 | 278 |

Curtis Strange beat Nick Faldo in a playoff-
Curtis Strange 71 Nick Faldo 75

Mark O'Meara	71	72	66	71	280
Steve Pate	72	69	72	67	280
D.A. Weibring	71	69	68	72	280
Paul Azinger	69	70	76	66	281
Scott Simpson	69	66	72	74	281
Bob Gilder	68	69	70	75	282
Fuzzy Zoeller	73	72	71	66	282
Fred Couples	72	67	71	73	283

1989, Oak Hill Country Club
Rochester, NY

| Curtis Strange | 71 | 64 | 73 | 70 | 278 |
| Chip Beck | 71 | 69 | 71 | 68 | 279 |

Mark McCumber	70	68	72	69	279
Ian Woosnam	70	68	73	68	279
Brian Claar	71	72	68	69	280
Jumbo Ozaki	70	71	68	72	281
Scott Simpson	67	70	69	75	281
Peter Jacobsen	71	70	71	70	282
Paul Azinger	71	72	70	70	283
Hubert Green	69	72	74	68	283

1990, Medinah C.C. (No. 3 Course)
Medinah, IL

| Hale Irwin | 69 | 70 | 74 | 67 | 280 |
| Mike Donald | 67 | 70 | 72 | 71 | 280 |

Hale Irwin beat Mike Donald in a playoff-
Hale Irwin 74 Mike Donald 74. With both
players tied it forced a sudden-death playoff
with Irwin making birdie 3 on the first hole.

Billy Ray Brown	69	71	69	72	281
Nick Faldo	72	72	68	69	281
Mark Brooks	68	70	72	73	283
Greg Norman	72	73	69	69	283
Tim Simpson	66	69	75	73	283
Scott Hoch	70	73	69	72	284
Steve Jones	67	76	74	67	284
Jose Maria Olazabal	73	69	69	73	284

1991, Hazeltine National G.C.
Minneapolis, MN

| Payne Stewart | 67 | 70 | 73 | 72 | 282 |
| Scott Simpson | 70 | 68 | 72 | 72 | 282 |

Payne Stewart beat Scott Simpson in a play-
off- Payne Stewart 75 Scott Simpson 77

Fred Couples	70	70	75	70	285
Larry Nelson	73	72	72	68	285
Fuzzy Zoeller	72	73	75	67	286
Scott Hoch	69	71	74	73	287
Nolan Henke	67	71	77	73	288
Ray Floyd	73	72	76	68	289
Jose Maria Olazabal	73	71	75	70	289
Corey Pavin	71	67	79	72	289

1992, Pebble Beach G.L.
Pebble Beach, CA

Tom Kite	71	72	70	72	285
Jeff Sluman	73	74	69	71	287
Colin Montgomerie	70	71	77	70	288

Nick Faldo	70	76	68	77	291
Nick Price	71	72	77	71	291
Billy Andrade	72	74	72	74	292
Jay Don Blake	70	74	75	73	292
Bob Gilder	73	70	75	74	292
Mike Hulbert	74	73	70	75	292
Tom Lehman	69	74	72	77	292

1993, Baltusrol Golf Club
Springfield, NJ

Lee Janzen	67	67	69	69	272
Payne Stewart	70	66	68	70	274
Paul Azinger	71	68	69	69	277
Craig Parry	66	74	69	68	277
Scott Hoch	66	72	72	68	278
Tom Watson	70	66	73	69	278
Ernie Els	71	73	68	67	279
Ray Floyd	68	73	70	68	279
Fred Funk	70	72	67	70	279
Nolan Henke	72	71	67	69	279

1994, Oakmont Country Club
Oakmont, PA

Ernie Els	69	71	66	73	279
Colin Montgomerie	71	65	73	70	279
Loren Roberts	76	69	64	70	279

Ernie Els beat Colin Montgomerie & Loren
Roberts in a playoff- Ernie Els 74 - Colin
Montgomerie 78 - Loren Roberts 74.
With Els and Roberts tied, they went into
sudden-death and Els won with a par on the
second hole.

Curtis Strange	70	70	70	70	280
John Cook	73	65	73	71	282
Tom Watson	68	73	68	74	283
Greg Norman	71	71	69	72	283
Clark Dennis	71	71	70	71	283
Frank Nobilo	69	71	68	76	284
Jeff Sluman	72	69	72	71	284

1995, Shinnecock Hills G.C.
Southhampton, NY

Corey Pavin	72	69	71	68	280
Greg Norman	68	67	74	73	282
Tom Lehman	70	72	67	74	283

Neal Lancaster	70	72	77	65	284
Jeff Maggert	69	72	77	65	284
Bill Glasson	69	70	76	69	284
Jay Haas	70	73	72	69	284
Davis Love III	72	68	73	71	284
Phil Mickelson	68	70	72	74	284
Frank Nobilo	72	72	70	71	285
Bob Tway	69	69	72	75	285
Vijay Singh	70	71	72	72	285

1996, Oakland Hills C.C.
Bloomfield Hills, MI

Steve Jones	74	66	69	69	278
Davis Love III	71	69	70	69	279
Tom Lehman	71	72	65	71	279
John Morse	68	74	68	70	280
Jim Furyk	72	69	70	70	281
Ernie Els	72	67	72	70	281
Scott Hoch	73	71	71	67	282
Ken Green	73	67	72	70	282
Vijay Singh	71	72	70	69	282
Lee Janzen	68	75	71	69	283

BRITISH OPEN CHAMPIONSHIP

The following is a list of the top finishers at the British Open from its inception. Included is the year, the tournament's location, the competitors, their total scores or daily and total scores.

1860, Prestwick

Willie Park	174
Tom Morris Sr.	176
Andrew Strath	180
Robert Andrew	191
George Brown	192
Charles Hunter	195

1861, Prestwick

| Tom Morris Sr. | 163 |
| Willie Park | 167 |

William Dow	171
David Park	172
Robert Andrew	175
Peter McEwan	178

1862, Prestwick

Tom Morris Sr.	163
Willie Park	176
Charles Hunter	178
William Dow	181
*James Knight	186
*J. F. Johnston	208

1863, Prestwick

Willie Park	168
Tom Morris Sr.	170
David Park	172
Andrew Strath	174
George Brown	176
Robert Andrew	178

1864, Prestwick

Tom Morris Sr.	167
Andrew Strath	169
Robert Andrew	175
Willie Park	177
William Dow	181
William Strath	182

1865, Prestwick

Andrew Strath	162
Willie Park	164
William Dow	171
Robert Kirk	173
Tom Morris Sr.	174
*William Doleman	178

1866, Prestwick

Willie Park	169
David Park	171
Robert Andrew	176
Tom Morris Sr.	178
Robert Kirk	180
Andrew Strath	182
*William Doleman	182

1867, Prestwick

Tom Morris Sr.	170
Willie Park	172
Andrew Strath	174
Tom Morris Jr.	175
Robert Kirk	177
William Doleman	178

1868, Prestwick

Tom Morris Jr.	157
Robert Andrew	159
Willie Park	162
Robert Kirk	171
John Allan	172
Tom Morris Sr.	176

1869, Prestwick

Tom Morris Jr.	154
Tom Morris Sr.	157
*S. Mure Fergusson	165
Robert Kirk	168
David Strath	169
J. Anderson	173

1870, Prestwick

Tom Morris Jr.	149
Bob Kirk	161
David Strath	161
Tom Morris Sr.	162
*William Doleman	171
Willie Park	173

1871, No Competition

1872, Prestwick

Tom Morris Jr.	166
David Strath	169
*William Doleman	177
Tom Morris Sr.	179
David Park	179
Charlie Hunter	189

1873, St. Andrews

Tom Kidd	179
Jamie Anderson	180
Tom Morris Jr.	183

Bob Kirk	183
Davie Strath	187
Walter Gourlay	188

1874, Musselburgh

Mungo Park	159
Tom Morris Jr.	161
George Paxton	162
Bob Martin	164
Jamie Anderson	165
David Park	166
W. Thomson	166

1875, Prestwick

Willie Park	166
Bob Martin	168
Mungo Park	171
Robert Ferguson	172
James Rennie	177
David Strath	178

1876, St. Andrews

Bob Martin	176
David Strath	176

(Martin was awarded the title when Strath refused to playoff)

Willie Park	183
Tom Morris Sr.	185
W. Thomson	185
Mungo Park	185

1877, Musselburgh

Jamie Anderson	160
Bob Pringle	162
Bob Ferguson	164
William Cosegrove	164
Davie Strath	166
William Brown	166

1878, Prestwick

Jamie Anderson	157
Bob Kirk	159
J. O. F. Morris	161
Bob Martin	165
John Ball	165

Phil Mickelson became the youngest PGA player to earn $1 million in a season in `96 with a Tour-high four victories and a 2nd-place showing on the money list with $1,697,799.

Willie Park	166
William Cosegrove	166

1879, St. Andrews

Jamie Anderson	169
James Allan	172
Andrew Kirkaldy	172
George Paxton	174
Tom Kidd	175
Bob Ferguson	176

1880, Musselburgh

Bob Ferguson	162
Peter Paxton	167
Ned Cosgrove	168
George Paxton	169

Bob Pringle	169
David Brown	169

1881, Prestwick

Bob Ferguson	170
Jamie Anderson	173
Ned Cosgrove	177
Bob Martin	178
Tom Morris Sr.	181
W. Campbell	181
Willie Park Jr.	181

1882, St. Andrews

Bob Ferguson	171
Willie Fernie	174
Jamie Anderson	175
John Kirkaldy	175
Bob Martin	175
*Fitz Boothby	175

1883, Musselburgh

Willie Fernie	159
Bob Ferguson	159
(Fernie won playoff 158-159)	
W. Brown	160
Bob Pringle	161
W. Campbell	163
George Paxton	163

1884, Prestwick

Jack Simpson	160
David Rollan	164
Willie Fernie	164
Willie Campbell	169
Willie Park Jr.	169
Ben Sayers	170

1885, St. Andrews

Bob Martin	171
Archie Simpson	172
David Ayton	173
Willie Fernie	174
Willie Park Jr.	174
Bob Simpson	174

1886, Musselburgh

David Brown			157
Willie Campbell			159
Ben Campbell			160
Archie Simpson			161
Willie Park Jr.			161
Thomas Gossett			161
Bob Ferguson			161

1887, Prestwick

Willie Park Jr.			161
Bob Martin			162
Willie Campbell			164
*Johnny Laidlay			166
Ben Sayers			168
Archie Simpson			168

1888, St. Andrews

Jack Burns			171
David Anderson Jr.			172
Ben Sayers			172
Willie Campbell			174
*Leslie Balfour			175
Andrew Kirkaldy			176
David Grant			176

1889, Musselburgh

Willie Park Jr.			155
Andrew Kirkaldy			155
(Playoff Park 158 to Kirkaldy 163)			
Ben Sayers			159
*Johnny Laidlay			162
David Brown			162
Willie Fernie			164

1890, Prestwick

*John Ball	82	82	164
Willie Fernie	85	82	167
A. Simpson	85	82	167
Willie Park, Jr.	90	80	170
Andrew Kirkaldy	81	89	170
*Horace Hutchinson	87	85	172

1891, St. Andrews

Hugh Kirkaldy	83	83	166
Willie Fernie	84	84	168
Andrew Kirkaldy	84	84	168
S. Mure Fergusson	86	84	170
W. D. More	84	87	171
Willie Park, Jr.	88	85	173

1892, Muirfield

*Harold Hilton	78	81	72	74	305
* John Ball, Jr.	75	80	74	79	308
James Kirkaldy	77	83	73	75	308
Sandy Herd	77	78	77	76	308
J. Kay	82	78	74	78	312
Ben Sayers	80	76	81	75	312

1893, Prestwick

Willie Auchterlonie	78	81	81	82	322
*Johnny E. Laidlay	80	83	80	81	324
Sandy Herd	82	81	78	84	325
Hugh Kirkaldy	83	79	82	82	326
Andrew Kirkaldy	85	82	82	77	326
J. Kay	81	81	80	85	327
R. Simpson	81	81	80	85	327

1894, Sandwich

J. H. Taylor	84	80	81	81	326
Douglas Rolland	86	79	84	82	331
Andrew Kirkaldy	86	79	83	84	332
A. Toogood	84	85	82	82	333
Willie Fernie	84	84	86	80	334
Harry Vardon	86	86	82	80	334
Ben Sayers	85	81	84	84	334

1895, St. Andrews

J. H. Taylor	86	78	80	78	322
Sandy Herd	82	77	82	85	326
Andrew Kirkaldy	81	83	84	84	332
G. Pulford	84	81	83	87	335
Archie Simpson	88	85	78	85	336
Willie Fernie	86	79	86	86	337
David Brown	81	89	83	84	337
David Anderson	86	83	84	84	337

1896, Muirfield

Harry Vardon	83	78	78	77	316
J. H. Taylor	77	78	81	80	316
(Vardon won playoff 157 to 161)					
*Freddie G. Tait	83	75	84	77	319

Willie Fernie	78	79	82	80	319
Sandy Herd	72	84	79	85	320
James Braid	83	81	79	80	323

1897, Hoylake

*Harold H. Hilton	80	75	84	75	314
James Braid	80	74	82	79	315
*Freddie G. Tait	79	79	80	79	317
G. Pulford	80	79	79	79	317
Sandy Herd	78	81	79	80	318
Harry Vardon	84	80	80	76	320

1898, Prestwick

Harry Vardon	79	75	77	76	307
Willie Park	76	75	78	79	308
*Harold H. Hilton	76	81	77	75	309
J. H. Taylor	78	78	77	79	312
*Freddie G. Tait	81	77	75	82	315
D. Kinnell	80	77	79	80	316

1899, Sandwich

Harry Vardon	76	76	81	77	310
Jack White	79	79	82	75	315
Andrew Kirkaldy	81	79	82	77	319
J. H. Taylor	77	76	83	84	320
James Braid	78	78	83	84	322
Willie Fernie	79	83	82	78	322

1900, St. Andrews

J. H. Taylor	79	77	78	75	309
Harry Vardon	79	81	80	78	317
James Braid	82	81	80	79	322
Jack White	80	81	82	80	323
Willie Auchterlonie	81	85	80	80	326
Willie Park, Jr.	80	83	81	84	328

1901, Muirfield

James Braid	79	76	74	80	309
Harry Vardon	77	78	79	78	312
J. H. Taylor	79	83	74	77	313
*Harold H. Hilton	89	80	75	76	320
Sandy Herd	87	81	81	76	325
Jack Whiteq	82	82	80	82	326

1902, Hoylake

Sandy Herd	77	76	73	81	307
Harry Vardon	72	77	80	79	308
James Braid	78	76	80	74	308
R. Maxwell	79	77	79	74	309
Tom Vardon	80	76	78	79	313
J. H. Taylor	81	76	77	80	314
D. Kinnell	78	80	79	77	314
*Harold Hilton	79	76	81	78	314

1903, Prestwick

Harry Vardon	73	77	72	78	300
Tom Vardon	76	81	75	74	306
Jack White	77	78	74	79	308
Sandy Herd	73	83	76	77	309
James Braid	77	79	79	75	310
R. Thompson	83	78	77	76	314
A. H. Scott	77	77	83	77	314

1904, Sandwich

Jack White	80	75	72	69	296
James Braid	77	80	69	71	297
J. H. Taylor	77	78	74	68	297
Tom Vardon	77	77	75	72	301
Harry Vardon	76	73	79	74	302
James Sherlock	83	71	78	77	309

1905, St. Andrews

James Braid	81	78	78	81	318
J. H. Taylor	80	85	78	80	323
R. Jones	81	77	87	78	323
J. Kinnell	82	79	82	81	324
Arnaud Massy	81	80	82	82	325

1906, Muirfield

James Braid	77	76	74	73	300
J. H. Taylor	77	72	75	80	304
Harry Vardon	77	73	77	78	305
J. Graham, Jr.	71	79	78	78	306
R. Jones	74	78	73	83	308
Arnaud Massy	76	80	76	78	310

1907, Hoylake

Arnaud Massy	76	81	78	77	312
J. H. Taylor	79	79	76	80	314
Tom Vardon	81	81	80	75	317
G. Pulford	81	78	80	78	317
Ted Ray	83	80	79	76	318
James Braid	82	85	75	76	318

1908, Prestwick

James Braid	70	72	77	72	291
Tom Ball	76	73	76	74	299
Ted Ray	79	71	75	76	301
Sandy Herd	74	74	79	75	302
Harry Vardon	79	78	74	75	306
D. Kinnell	75	73	80	78	306

1909, Deal

J. H. Taylor	74	73	74	74	295
James Braid	79	73	73	74	299
Tom Ball	74	75	76	76	301
C. Johns	72	76	79	75	302
T. G. Renouf	76	78	76	73	303
Ted Ray	77	76	76	75	304

1910, St. Andrews

James Braid	76	73	74	76	299
Sandy Herd	78	74	75	76	303
George Duncan	73	77	71	83	304
Laurie Ayton	78	76	75	77	306
Ted Ray	76	77	74	81	308
W. Smith	77	71	80	80	308
J. Robson	75	80	77	76	308

1911, Sandwich

Harry Vardon	74	74	75	80	303
Arnaud Massy	75	78	74	76	303

(Playoff; Massy conceded at the 35th hole)

Harold Hilton	76	74	78	76	304
Sandy Herd	77	73	76	78	304
Ted Ray	76	72	79	78	305
James Braid	78	75	74	78	305
J. H. Taylor	72	76	78	79	305

1912, Muirfield

Ted Ray	71	73	76	75	295
Harry Vardon	75	72	81	71	299
James Braid	77	71	77	78	303
George Duncan	72	77	78	78	305
Laurie Ayton	74	80	75	79	308
Sandy Herd	76	81	76	76	309

1913, Hoylake

J. H. Taylor	73	75	77	79	304
Ted Ray	73	74	81	84	312

Harry Vardon	79	75	79	80	313
M. Moran	76	74	89	74	313
Johnny J. McDermott	75	80	77	83	315
T. G. Renouf	75	78	84	78	315

1914, Prestwick

Harry Vardon	73	77	78	78	306
J. H. Taylor	74	78	74	83	309
H. B. Simpson	77	80	78	75	310
Abe Mitchell	76	78	79	79	312
Tom Williamson	75	79	79	79	312
R. G. Wilson	76	77	80	80	313

1920, Deal

George Duncan	80	80	71	72	303
Sandy Herd	72	81	77	75	305
Ted Ray	72	83	78	73	306
Abe Mitchell	74	73	84	76	307
Len Holland	80	78	71	79	308
Jim Barnes	79	74	77	79	309

1921

Jock Hutchison	72	75	79	70	296
*Roger H. Wethered	78	75	72	71	296

(Hutchison won playoff 150 to 159)

T. Kerrigan	74	80	72	72	298
Arthur G. Havers	76	74	77	72	299
George Duncan	74	75	78	74	301

1922, Sandwich

Walter Hagen	76	73	79	72	300
George Duncan	76	75	81	69	301
Jim Barnes	75	76	77	73	301
Jock Hutchison	79	74	73	76	302
Charles A. Whitcombe	77	79	72	75	303
J. H. Taylor	73	78	76	77	304

1923, Troon

Arthur G. Havers	73	73	73	76	295
Walter Hagen	76	71	74	75	296
Macdonald Smith	80	73	69	75	297
Joe Kirkwood	72	79	69	78	298
Tom R. Fernie	73	78	74	75	300

George Duncan	79	75	74	74	302
Charles A. Whitcombe	70	76	74	82	302

1924, Hoylake

Walter Hagen	77	73	74	77	301
Ernest R. Whitcombe	77	70	77	78	302
Macdonald Smith	76	74	77	77	304
F. Ball	78	75	74	77	304
J. H. Taylor	75	74	79	79	307
George Duncan	74	79	74	81	308
Aubrey Boomer	75	78	76	79	308

1925, Prestwick

Jim Barnes	70	77	79	74	300
Archie Compston	76	75	75	75	301
Ted Ray	77	76	75	73	301
Macdonald Smith	76	69	76	82	303
Abe Mitchell	77	76	75	77	305

1926, Royal Lytham

*Bobby T. Jones, Jr.	72	72	73	74	291
Al Watrous	71	75	69	78	293
Walter Hagen	68	77	74	76	295
George von Elm	75	72	76	72	295
Abe Mitchell	78	78	72	71	299
T. Barber	77	73	78	71	299

1927, St. Andrews

*Bobby T. Jones, Jr.	68	72	73	72	285
Aubrey Boomer	76	70	73	72	291
Fred Robson	76	72	69	74	291
Joe Kirkwood	72	72	75	74	293
Ernest R. Whitcombe	74	73	73	73	293
Charles A. Whitcome	74	76	71	75	296

1928, Sandwich

Walter Hagen	75	73	72	72	292
Gene Sarazen	72	76	73	73	294
Archie Compston	75	74	73	73	295
Percy Alliss	75	76	75	72	298
Fred Robson	79	73	73	73	298
Jose Jurado	74	71	76	80	301

Aubrey Boomer	79	73	77	72	301
Jim Barnes	81	73	76	71	301

1929, Muirfield

Walter Hagen	75	67	75	75	292
John Farrell	72	75	76	75	298
Leo Diegel	71	69	82	77	299
Abe Mitchell	72	72	78	78	300
Percy Alliss	69	76	76	79	300
Bobby Cruickshank	73	74	78	76	301

1930, Hoylake

*Bobby Jones, Jr.	70	72	74	75	291
Leo Diegel	74	73	71	75	293
Macdonald Smith	70	77	75	71	293
Fred Robson	71	72	78	75	296
Horton Smith	72	73	78	73	296
Archie Compston	74	73	68	82	297
Jim Barnes	71	77	72	77	297

1931, Carnoustie

Tommy D. Armour	73	75	77	71	296
Jose Jurado	76	71	73	77	297
Percy Alliss	74	78	73	73	298
Gene Sarazen	74	76	75	73	298
Macdonald Smith	75	77	71	76	299
John Farrell	72	77	75	75	299

1932, Prince's

Gene Sarazen	70	69	70	74	283
Macdonald Smith	71	76	71	70	288
Arthur G. Havers	74	71	68	76	289
Charles A. Whitcombe	71	73	73	75	292
Percy Alliss	71	71	78	72	292
Alf H. Padgham	76	72	74	70	292

1933, St. Andrews

Densmore Shute	73	73	73	73	292
Craig Wood	77	72	68	75	292
Sid Easterbrook	73	72	71	77	293
Gene Sarazen	72	73	73	75	293
Leo Diegel	75	70	71	77	293
Olin Dutra	76	76	70	72	294

1934, Sandwich

Henry Cotton	67	65	72	79	283
Sid F. Brews	76	71	70	71	288
Alf H. Padgham	71	70	75	74	290
Macdonald Smith	77	71	72	72	292
Joe Kirkwood	74	69	71	78	292
Marcel Dallemagne	71	73	71	77	292

1935, Muirfield

Alf Perry	69	75	67	72	283
Alf Padgham	70	72	74	71	287
Charles Whitcombe	71	68	73	76	288
Bert Gadd	72	75	71	71	289
Lawson L. Little	75	71	74	69	289
Henry Picard	72	73	72	75	292

1936, Hoylake

Alf H. Padgham	73	72	71	71	287
Jimmy Adams	71	73	71	73	288
Henry Cotton	73	72	70	74	289
Marcel Dallemagne	73	72	75	69	289
Percy Alliss	74	72	74	71	291
T. Green	74	72	70	75	291
Gene Sarazen	73	75	70	73	291

1937, Carnoustie

Henry Cotton	74	72	73	71	290
Reg A. Whitcombe	72	70	74	76	292
Charles Lacey	76	75	70	72	293
Charles A. Whitcombe	73	71	74	76	294
Bryon Nelson	75	76	71	74	296
Ed Dudley	70	74	78	75	297

1938, Sandwich

Reg A. Whitcombe	71	71	75	78	295
Jimmy Adams	70	71	78	78	297
Henry Cotton	74	73	77	74	298
Alf H. Padgham	74	72	75	82	303
Jack J. Busson	71	69	83	80	303
Dick Burton	71	69	78	85	303
Allan Dailey	73	72	80	78	303

1939, St. Andrews

Dick Burton	70	72	77	71	290
Johnny Bulla	77	71	71	73	292

Johnny Fallon	71	73	71	79	294
Bill Shankland	72	73	72	77	294
Alf Perry	71	74	73	76	294
Reg A. Whitcombe	71	75	74	74	294
Sam L. King	74	72	75	73	294

1946, St. Andrews

Sam Snead	71	70	74	75	290
Bobby Locke	69	74	75	76	294
Johnny Bulla	71	72	72	79	294
Charlie H. Ward	73	73	73	76	295
Henry Cotton	70	70	76	79	295
Dai J. Rees	75	67	73	80	295
Norman von Nida	70	76	74	75	295

1947, Hoylake

Fred Daly	73	70	78	72	293
Reg W. Horne	77	74	72	71	294
*Frank R. Stranahan	76	74	75	70	295
Bill Shankland	76	74	75	70	295
Dick Burton	77	71	77	71	296
Charlie Ward	76	73	76	72	297
Sam L. King	75	72	77	73	297
Arthur Lees	75	74	72	76	297
Johnny Bulla	80	72	74	71	297
Henry Cotton	69	78	74	76	297
Norman von Nida	74	76	71	76	297

1948, Muirfield

Henry Cotton	71	66	75	72	284
Fred Daly	72	71	73	73	289
Norman von Nida	71	72	76	71	290
Roberto de Vicenzo	70	73	72	75	290
Jack Hargreaves	76	68	73	73	290
Charlie Ward	69	72	75	74	290

1949, Sandwich

Bobby Locke	69	76	68	70	283
Harry Bradshaw	68	77	68	70	283
(Locke won playoff 135 to 147)					
Roberto de Vicenzo	68	75	73	69	285
Sam King	71	69	74	72	286
Charlie Ward	73	71	70	72	286
Arthur Lees	74	70	72	71	287
Max Faulkner	71	71	71	74	287

1950, Troon

Bobby Locke	69	72	70	68	279
Roberto de Vicenzo	72	71	68	70	281
Fred Daly	75	72	69	66	282
Dai J. Rees	71	68	72	71	282
E. Moore	74	68	73	68	283
Max Faulkner	72	70	70	71	283

1951, Royal Portrush

Max Faulkner	71	70	70	74	285
Tony Cerda	74	72	71	70	287
Charlie Ward	75	73	74	68	290
Fred Daly	74	70	75	73	292
Jimmy Adams	68	77	75	72	292
Bobby Locke	71	74	74	74	293
Bill Shankland	73	76	72	72	293
Norman Sutton	73	70	74	76	293
Harry Weetman	73	71	75	74	293
Peter W. Thomson	70	75	73	75	293

1952, Royal Lytham

Bobby Locke	69	71	74	73	287
Peter W. Thomson	68	73	77	70	288
Fred Daly	67	69	77	76	289
Henry Cotton	75	74	74	71	294
Tony Cerda	73	73	76	73	295
Sam L. King	71	74	74	76	295

1953, Carnoustie

Ben Hogan	73	71	70	68	282
*Frank R. Stranahan	70	74	73	69	286
Dai J. Rees	72	70	73	71	286
Peter W. Thomson	72	72	71	71	286
Tony Cerda	75	71	69	71	286
Roberto de Vicenzo	72	71	71	73	287

1954, Royal Birkdale

Peter W. Thomson	72	71	69	71	283
Sid S. Scott	76	67	69	72	284
Dai J. Rees	72	71	69	72	284
Bobby Locke	74	71	69	70	284
Jimmy Adams	73	75	69	69	286
Tony Cerda	71	71	73	71	286
J. Turnesa	72	72	71	71	286

1955, St. Andrews

Peter W. Thomson	71	68	70	72	281
Johnny Fallon	73	67	73	70	283
Frank Jowle	70	71	69	74	284
Bobby Locke	74	69	70	72	285
Tony Cerda	73	71	71	71	286
Ken Bousfield	71	75	70	70	286
Harry Weetman	71	71	70	74	286
Bernard J. Hunt	70	71	74	71	286
Flory van Donck	71	72	71	72	286

1956, Hoylake

Peter W. Thomson	70	70	72	74	286
Flory van Donck	71	74	70	74	289
Roberto de Vicenzo	71	70	79	70	290
Gary Player	71	76	73	71	291
John Panton	74	76	72	70	292
Henry Cotton	72	76	71	74	293
E. Bertolino	69	72	76	76	293

1957, St. Andrews

Bobby Locke	69	72	68	70	279
Peter W. Thomson	73	69	70	70	282
Eric C. Brown	67	72	73	71	283
Angel Miguel	72	72	69	72	285
David C. Thomas	72	74	70	70	286
Tom B. Haliburton	72	73	68	73	286
*W. Dick Smith	71	72	72	71	286
Flory van Donck	72	68	74	72	286

1958, Royal Lytham

Peter W. Thomson	66	72	67	73	278
David C. Thomas	70	68	69	71	278
(Thomson won playoff 139 to 143)					
Eric C. Brown	73	70	65	71	279
Christy O'Connor	67	68	73	71	279
Flory van Donck	70	70	67	74	281
Leopoldo Ruiz	71	65	72	73	281

1959, Muirfield

Gary Player	75	71	70	68	284
Flory van Donck	70	70	73	73	286
Fred Bullock	68	70	74	74	286
Sid S. Scott	73	70	73	71	287
Christy O'Connor	73	74	72	69	288

*Reid R. Jack	71	75	68	74	288
Sam L. King	70	74	68	76	288
John Panton	72	72	71	73	288

1960, St. Andrews

Kel D. G. Nagle	69	67	71	71	278
Arnold Palmer	70	71	70	68	279
Bernard J. Hunt	72	73	71	66	282
Harold R. Henning	72	72	69	69	282
Roberto de Vicenzo	67	67	75	73	282
*Guy B. Wolstenholme	74	70	71	68	283

1961, Royal Birkdale

Arnold Palmer	70	73	69	72	284
Dai J. Rees	68	74	71	72	285
Christy O'Connor	71	77	67	73	288
Neil C. Coles	70	77	69	72	288
Eric C. Brown	73	76	70	70	289
Kel D. G. Nagle	68	75	75	71	289

1962, Troon

Arnold Palmer	71	69	67	69	276
Kel D. G. Nagle	71	71	70	70	282
Brian Huggett	75	71	74	69	289
Phil Rodgers	75	70	72	72	289
Bob Charles	75	70	70	75	290
Sam Snead	76	73	72	71	292
Peter W. Thomson	70	77	75	70	292

1963, Royal Lytham

Bob Charles	68	72	66	71	277
Phil Rodgers	67	68	73	69	277
(Charles won playoff 140 to 148)					
Jack Nicklaus	71	67	70	70	278
Kel D. G. Nagle	69	70	73	71	283
Peter W. Thomson	67	69	71	78	285
Christy O'Connor	74	68	76	68	286

1964, St. Andrews

Tony Lema	73	68	68	70	279
Jack Nicklaus	76	74	66	68	284
Roberto de Vicenzo	76	72	70	67	285
Bernard J. Hunt	73	74	70	70	287
Bruce Devlin	72	72	73	73	290

Christy O'Connor	71	73	74	73	291
Harry Weetman	72	71	75	73	291

1965, Royal Birkdale

Peter W. Thomson	74	68	72	71	285
Christy O'Connor	69	73	74	71	287
Brian Huggett	73	68	76	70	287
Roberto de Vicenzo	74	69	73	72	288
Kel D. G. Nagle	74	70	73	72	289
Tony Lema	68	72	75	74	289
Bernard J. Hunt	74	74	70	71	289

1966, Muirfield

Jack Nicklaus	70	67	75	70	282
David C. Thomas	72	73	69	69	283
Doug Sanders	71	70	72	70	283
Gary Player	72	74	71	69	286
Bruce Devlin	73	69	74	70	286
Kel D. G. Nagle	72	68	76	70	286
Phil Rodgers	74	66	70	76	286

1967, Hoylake

Roberto de Vicenzo	70	71	67	70	278
Jack Nicklaus	71	69	71	69	280
Clive A. Clark	70	73	69	72	284
Gary Player	72	71	67	74	284
Tony Jacklin	73	69	73	70	285
Sebastian Miguel	72	74	68	72	286
Harold Henning	74	70	71	71	286

1968, Carnoustie

Gary Player	74	71	71	73	289
Jack Nicklaus	76	69	73	73	291
Bob J. Charles	72	72	71	76	291
Billy Casper	72	68	74	78	292
Maurice Bembridge	71	75	73	74	293
Brian Barnes	70	74	80	71	295
Neil C. Coles	75	76	71	73	295
Gay Brewer	74	73	72	76	295

1969, Royal Lytham

Tony Jacklin	68	70	70	72	280
Bob J. Charles	66	69	75	72	282
Peter W. Thomson	71	70	70	72	283
Roberto de Vicenzo	72	73	66	72	283
Christy O'Connor	71	65	74	74	284

| Jack Nicklaus | 75 | 70 | 68 | 72 | 285 |
| Denis M. Love, Jr. | 70 | 73 | 71 | 71 | 285 |

1970, St. Andrews

| Jack Nicklaus | 68 | 69 | 73 | 73 | 283 |
| Doug Sanders | 68 | 71 | 71 | 73 | 283 |

(Nicklaus won playoff 72 to 73)

Harold Henning	67	72	73	73	285
Lee Trevino	68	68	72	77	285
Tony Jacklin	67	70	73	76	286
Neil C. Coles	65	74	72	76	287
Peter A. Oosterhuis	73	69	69	76	287

1971, Royal Birkdale

Lee Trevino	69	70	69	70	278
Lu Liang Huan	70	70	69	70	279
Tony Jacklin	69	70	70	71	280
Craig de Foy	72	72	68	69	281
Jack Nicklaus	71	71	72	69	283
Charles Coody	74	71	70	68	283

1972, Muirfield

Lee Trevino	71	70	66	71	278
Jack Nicklaus	70	72	71	66	279
Tony Jacklin	69	72	67	72	280
Doug Sanders	71	71	69	70	281
Brian W. Barnes	71	72	69	71	283
Gary Player	71	71	76	67	285

1973, Troon

Tom Weiskopf	68	67	71	70	276
Neil C. Coles	71	72	70	66	279
Johnny Miller	70	68	69	72	279
Jack Nicklaus	69	70	76	65	280
Bert Yancey	69	69	73	70	281
Peter J. Butler	71	72	74	69	286

1974, Royal Lytham

Gary Player	69	68	75	70	282
Peter Oosterhuis	71	71	73	71	286
Jack Nicklaus	74	72	70	71	287
Hubert M. Green	71	74	72	71	288
Danny Edwards	70	73	76	73	292
Lu Liang Huan	72	72	75	73	292

1975, Carnoustie

| Tom Watson | 71 | 67 | 69 | 72 | 279 |
| Jack Newton | 69 | 71 | 65 | 74 | 279 |

(Watson won playoff 71 to 72)

Bobby Cole	72	66	66	76	280
Jack Nicklaus	69	71	68	72	280
Johnny Miller	71	69	66	74	280
Graham Marsh	72	67	71	71	281

1976, Royal Birkdale

Johnny Miller	72	68	73	66	279
Jack Nicklaus	74	70	72	69	285
Severiano Ballesteros	69	69	73	74	285
Raymond Floyd	76	67	73	70	286
Mark James	76	72	74	66	288
Hubert Green	72	70	78	68	288
Christy O'Connor, Jr.	69	73	75	71	288
Tom Kite	70	74	73	71	288
Tommy A. Horton	74	69	72	73	288

1977, Turnberry

Tom Watson	68	70	65	65	268
Jack Nicklaus	68	70	65	66	269
Hubert Green	72	66	74	67	279
Lee Trevino	68	70	72	70	280
Ben Crenshaw	71	69	66	75	281
George Burns	70	70	72	69	281

1978, St. Andrews

Jack Nicklaus	71	72	69	69	281
Simon Owen	70	75	67	71	283
Ben Crenshaw	70	69	73	71	283
Raymond Floyd	69	75	71	68	283
Tom Kite	72	69	72	70	283
Peter Oosterhuis	72	70	69	73	284

1979, Royal Lytham

Severiano Ballesteros	73	65	75	70	283
Jack Nicklaus	72	69	73	72	286
Ben Crenshaw	72	71	72	71	286
Mark James	76	69	69	73	287
Rodger Davis	68	68	75	78	289
Hale Irwin	68	68	75	78	289

1980, Muirfield

Tom Watson	68	70	64	69	271
Lee Trevino	68	67	71	69	275
Ben Crenshaw	70	70	68	69	277
Jack Nicklaus	73	67	71	69	280
Carl Mason	72	69	70	69	280

1981, Royal St. George's

Bill Rogers	72	66	67	71	276
Bernhard Langer	73	67	70	70	280
Mark James	72	70	68	73	283
Raymond Floyd	74	70	69	70	283
Sam Torrance	72	69	73	70	284
Bruce Lietzke	76	69	71	69	285
Manuel Pinero	73	74	68	70	285

1982, Royal Troon

Tom Watson	69	71	74	70	284
Nick Price	69	69	74	73	285
Peter Oosterhuis	74	67	74	70	285
Nick Faldo	73	73	71	69	286
Des Smyth	70	69	74	73	286
Tom Purtzer	76	66	75	69	286

1983, Royal Birkdale

Tom Watson	67	68	70	70	275
Andy Bean	70	69	70	67	276
Hale Irwin	69	68	72	67	276
Graham Marsh	69	70	74	64	277
Lee Trevino	69	66	73	70	278
Seve Ballesteros	71	71	69	68	279

1984, St. Andrews

Seve Ballesteros	69	68	70	69	276
Tom Watson	71	68	66	73	278
Bernhard Langer	71	68	68	71	278
Fred Couples	70	69	74	68	281
Lanny Wadkins	70	69	73	69	281
Greg Norman	67	74	74	67	282
Nick Faldo	69	68	76	69	282

1985, Royal St. George's

Sandy Lyle	68	71	73	70	282
Payne Stewart	70	75	70	68	283
Jose Rivero	74	72	70	68	284
Christy O'Connor, Jr.	64	76	72	72	284
Mark O'Meara	70	72	70	72	284
David Graham	68	71	70	75	284

1986, Turnberry

Greg Norman	74	63	74	69	280
Gordon Brand	71	68	75	71	285
Bernhard Langer	72	70	76	68	286
Ian Woosnam	70	74	70	72	286
Nick Faldo	71	70	76	70	287
Seve Ballesteros	76	75	73	64	288

1987, Muirfield

Nick Faldo	68	69	71	71	279
Paul Azinger	68	68	71	73	280
Rodger Davis	64	73	74	69	280
Ben Crenshaw	73	68	72	68	281
Payne Stewart	71	66	72	72	281
David Frost	70	68	70	74	282

1988, Royal Lytham & St. Anne's

Seve Ballesteros	67	71	70	65	273
Nick Price	70	67	69	69	275
Nick Faldo	71	69	68	71	279
Fred Couples	73	69	71	68	281
Gary Koch	71	70	72	68	281
Peter Senior	70	73	70	69	282

1989, Royal Troon

Mark Calcavecchia	71	68	68	68	275
Wayne Grady	68	67	69	71	275
Greg Norman	69	70	72	64	275
Tom Watson	69	68	68	72	277
Jodie Mudd	73	67	68	70	278
Fred Couples	68	71	68	72	279

1990, St. Andrews

Nick Faldo	67	65	67	71	270
Payne Stewart	68	68	68	71	275
Mark McNulty	74	68	68	65	275
Jodie Mudd	72	66	72	66	276
Ian Woosnam	68	69	70	69	276
Ian Baker-Finch	68	72	64	73	277

1991, Royal Birkdale

Ian Baker-Finch	71	71	64	66	272
Mike Harwood	68	70	69	67	274
Mark O'Meara	71	68	67	69	275
Fred Couples	72	69	79	64	275
Bob Tway	75	66	70	66	277
Eamonn Darcy	73	68	66	70	277

1992, Muirfield

Nick Faldo	66	64	69	73	272
John Cook	66	67	70	70	273
Jose Maria Olazabal	70	67	69	68	274
Steve Pate	64	70	69	73	276
Malcolm Mackenzie	71	67	70	71	279
Robert Karisson	70	68	70	71	279

1993, Royal St. George's

Greg Norman	66	68	69	64	267
Nick Faldo	69	63	70	67	269
Bernhard Langer	67	66	70	67	270
Peter Senior	66	69	70	67	272
Corey Pavin	68	66	68	70	272
Nick Price	68	70	67	69	274

1994, Turnberry

Nick Price	69	66	67	66	268
Jesper Parnevik	68	66	68	67	269
Fuzzy Zoeller	71	66	64	70	271
Anders Forsband	72	71	66	64	273
Mark James	72	67	66	68	273
David Feherty	70	69	66	70	273

1995, St. Andrews

John Daly	67	71	73	71	282
Costantino Rocca	69	70	70	73	282
Steven Bottomley	70	72	72	69	283
Mark Brooks	70	69	73	71	283
Michael Campbell	71	71	65	76	283
Vijay Singh	68	72	73	71	284

1996, Royal Lytham & St. Anne's

Tom Lehman	67	67	64	73	271
Mark McCumber	67	69	71	66	273
Ernie Els	68	67	71	67	273
Nick Faldo	68	68	68	70	274
Jeff Maggert	69	70	72	65	276
Mark Brooks	67	70	68	71	276

* indicates player was an amateur

THE PGA CHAMPIONSHIP

The following is a list of the top finishers at the PGA Championship from its inception. Included is the year, the tournament's location, the competitors, and the result. Beginning in 1958, the tournament was decided by strokeplay. To reflect this change in format, the competitors, their daily scores, and total scores are listed.

1916, Siwanoy C.C.
Bronxville, NY
James M. Barnes beat Jock Hutchison 1 up

1917 No Championship

1918 No Championship

1919, Engineers C.C.
Roslyn, NY
James M. Barnes beat Fred McLeod 6 and 5

1920, Flossmoor C.C.
Flossmoor, IL
Jock Hutchison beat J. Douglas Edgar 1 up

1921, Inwood C.C.
Far Rockawaw, NY
Walter Hagen beat Jim M. Barnes 3 and 2

1922, Oakmont C.C.
Oakmont, PA
Gene Sarazen beat Emmet French 4 and 3

1923, Pelham C.C.
Pelham, NY
Gene Sarazen beat Walter Hagen 1 up

1924, French Lick C.C.
French Lick, IN
Walter Hagen beat Jim M. Barnes 2 up

1925, Olympia Fields C.C.
Olympia Fields, Illinois
Walter Hagen beat Bill Mehlhorn 6 and 5

1926, Salisbury G.C.
Westbury, NY
Walter Hagen beat Leo Diegel 5 and 3

1927, Cedar Crest C.C
Dallas, TX
Walter Hagen beat Joe Turnesa 1 up

1928, Baltimore C.C.
Five Farms, MD
Leo Diegel beat Al Espinosa 6 and 5

1929, Hillcrest C.C.
Los Angeles, CA
Leo Diegel beat John Farrell 6 and 4

1930, Fresh Meadow
Flushing, NY
Tommy Armour beat Gene Sarazen 1 up

1931, Wannamoisett C.C.
Rumford, RI
Tom Creavy beat Densmore Shute 2 and 1

1932, Keller G.C.
St. Paul, MN
Olin Dutra beat Frank Walsh 4 and 3

1933, Blue Mound C.C.
Milwaukee, WI
Gene Sarazan beat Willie Goggin 5 and 4

1934, Park C.C.
Williamsville, NY
Paul Runyan beat Craig Wood at 38th

1935, Twin Hills C.C.
Oklahoma City, OK
Johnny Revolta beat Tommy Armour 5 and 4

1936, Pinehurst C.C.
Pinehurst, NC
Densmore Shute beat Jimmy Thomson
3 and 2

1937, Pittsburgh C.C.
Aspinwall, PA
Densmore Shute beat Harold McSpaden
at 37th

1938, Shawnee C.C.
Shawnee, PA
Paul Runyan beat Sam Snead 8 and 7

1939, Pomonok C.C.
Flushing, NY
Henry Picard beat Byron Nelson at 37th

1940, Hershey C.C.
Hershey, PA
Byron Nelson beat Sam Snead 1 up

1941, Cherry Hills C.C.
Denver, CO
Vic Ghezzi beat Byron Nelson at 38th

1942, Seaview C.C.
Atlantic City, NJ
Sam Snead beat Jim Turnesa 2 and 1

1943 No Championship

1944, Manito G. & C.C.
Spokane, WA
Bob Hamilton beat Byron Nelson 1 up

1945, Morraine C.C.
Dayton, OH
Byron Nelson beat Sam Byrd 4 and 3

1946, Portland G.C.
Portland, OR
Ben Hogan beat Porky Oliver 6 and 4

1947, Plum Hollow C.C.
Detroit, MI
Jim Ferrier beat Chick Harbert 2 and 1

1948, Norwood Hills C.C.
St. Louis, MO
Ben Hogan beat Mike Turnesa 7 and 6

1949, Hermitage C.C.
Richmond, VA
Sam Snead beat John Palmer 3 and 2

1950, Scioto C.C.
Columbus, OH
Chandler Harper beat Henry Williams Jr 4 and 3

1951, Oakmont C.C.
Oakmont, PA
Sam Snead beat Walter Burkemo 7 and 6

1952, Big Spring C.C.
Louisville, KN
Jim Turnesa beat Chick Harbert 1 up

1953, Birmingham C.C.
Birmingham, MI
Walter Burkemo beat Felice Torza 2 and 1

1954, Keller G.C.
St. Paul, MN
Chick Harbert beat Walter Burkemo 4 and 3

1955, Meadowbrook C.C.
Detroit, MI
Doug Ford beat Cary Middlecoff 4 and 3

1956, Blue Hill C.C.
Boston, MA
Jack Burke beat Ted Kroll 3 and 2

1957, Miami Valley G.C.
Dayton, OH
Lionel Herbert beat Dow Finsterwald 2 and 1

(Decided by strokeplay hereafter)

1958, Llanerch C.C.
Havertown, PA

Dow Finsterwald	67	72	70	67	276
Billy Casper	73	67	68	70	278
Sam Snead	73	67	67	73	280

1959, Minneapolis G.C.
St. Paul, MN

Bob Rosburg	71	72	68	66	277
Jerry Barber	69	65	71	73	278
Doug Sanders	72	66	68	72	278

1960, Firestone C.C.
Akron, OH

Jay Herbert	72	67	72	70	281
Jim Ferrier	71	74	66	71	282
Sam Snead	68	73	70	72	283
Doug Sanders	70	71	69	73	283

1961, Olympia Fields C.C.
Olympia, IL

Jerry Barber	69	67	71	70	277
Don January	72	66	67	72	277
(Barber won playoff 67 to 68)					
Doug Sanders	70	68	74	68	280

1962, Aronimink G.C.
Aronimink, PA

Gary Player	72	67	69	70	278
Bob Goalby	69	72	71	67	279
Jack Nicklaus	71	74	69	67	281
George Bayer	69	70	71	71	281

1963, Dallas Athletic C.C.
Dallas, TX

Jack Nicklaus	69	73	69	68	279
Dave Ragan	75	70	67	69	281
Dow Finsterwald	72	72	66	72	282
Bruce Crampton	70	73	65	74	282

1964, Columbus C.C.
Columbus, OH

Bobby Nichols	64	71	69	67	271
Arnold Palmer	68	68	69	69	274
Jack Nicklaus	67	73	70	64	274

1965, Laurel Valley G.C.
Ligonier, PA

Dave Marr	70	69	70	71	280
Billy Casper	70	70	71	71	282
Jack Nicklaus	69	70	72	71	282

1966, Firestone C.C.
Akron, OH

Al Gieberger	68	72	68	72	280
Dudley Wysong	74	72	66	72	284
Billy Casper	73	73	70	70	286
Gene Littler	75	71	71	70	286
Gary Player	73	70	70	73	286

1967, Columbine C.C.
Littleton, CO

| Don January | 71 | 72 | 70 | 68 | 281 |
| Don Massengale | 70 | 75 | 70 | 66 | 281 |

(January won playoff 69-71)

| Jack Nicklaus | 67 | 75 | 69 | 71 | 282 |
| Dan Sikes | 69 | 70 | 70 | 73 | 282 |

1968, Pecan Valley C.C.
San Antonio, TX

Julius Boros	71	71	70	69	281
Bob Charles	72	70	70	70	282
Arnold Palmer	71	69	72	70	282

1969, NCR G.C.
Dayton, OH

Ray Floyd	69	66	67	74	276
Gary Player	71	65	71	70	277
Bert Greene	71	68	68	71	278

1970, Southern Hills C.C.
Tulsa, OK

Dave Stockton	70	70	66	73	279
Bob Murphy	71	73	71	66	281
Arnold Palmer	70	72	69	70	281

1971, PGA National G.C.
Palm Beach Gardens, FL

Jack Nicklaus	69	69	70	73	281
Billy Casper	71	73	71	68	283
Tommy Bolt	72	74	69	69	284

1972, Oakland Hills G.C.
Birmingham, MI

Gary Player	71	71	67	72	281
Tommy Aaron	71	71	70	71	283
Jim Jamieson	69	72	72	70	283

1973, Canterbury Club
Cleveland, OH

Jack Nicklaus	72	68	68	69	277
Bruce Compton	71	73	67	70	281
Mason Rudolph	69	70	70	73	282
Lanny Watkins	73	69	71	69	282
Jesse C. Snead	71	74	68	69	282

1974, Tanglewood G.C.
Winston-Salem, NC

Lee Trevino	73	66	68	69	276
Jack Nicklaus	69	69	70	69	277
Bobby Cole	69	68	71	71	279
Hubert Green	68	68	73	70	279
Dave Hill	74	69	67	69	279
Sam Snead	69	71	71	68	279

1975, Firestone C.C.
Akron, OH

Jack Nicklaus	70	68	67	71	276
Bruce Crampton	71	63	75	69	278
Tom Weiskopf	70	71	70	68	279

1976, Congressional C.C.
Bethesda, MD

Dave Stockton	70	72	69	70	281
Raymond Floyd	72	68	71	71	282
Don January	70	69	71	72	282

1977, Pebble Beach
Pebble Beach, CA

| Lanny Wadkins | 69 | 71 | 72 | 70 | 282 |
| Gene Littler | 67 | 69 | 70 | 76 | 282 |

(Wadkins won sudden-death
playoff at 3rd hole)

| Jack Nicklaus | 69 | 71 | 70 | 73 | 283 |

1978, Oakmont C.C.
Oakmont, PA

John Mahaffey	75	67	68	66	276
Jerry Pate	72	70	66	68	276
Tom Watson	67	69	67	73	276

(Mahaffey won sudden-death
playoff at 2nd hole)

1979, Oakland Hills
Birmingham, MI

David Graham	69	68	70	65	272
Ben Crenshaw	69	67	69	67	272

(Graham won sudden-death playoff
at 3rd hole)

Randy Caldwell	67	70	66	71	274

1980, Oak Hill C.C.
Rochester, NY

Jack Nicklaus	70	69	66	69	274
Andy Bean	72	71	68	70	281
Len Hinkle	70	69	69	75	283
Gil Morgan	68	70	73	72	283

1981, Atlanta Athletic Club,
Duluth, GA

Larry Nelson	70	66	66	71	273
Fuzzy Zoeller	70	68	68	71	277
Dan Pohl	69	67	73	69	278

1982, Southern Hills C.C.
Tulsa, OK

Raymond Floyd	63	69	68	72	272
Lanny Wadkins	71	68	69	67	275
Fred Couples	67	71	72	66	276

1983, Riviera C.C
Pacific Palisades, CA

Hal Sutton	65	66	72	71	274
Jack Nicklaus	73	65	71	66	275
Peter Jacobsen	73	70	68	65	276

1984, Shoal Creek
Birmingham, AL

Lee Trevino	69	68	67	69	273
Gary Player	74	73	69	71	277
Lanny Wadkins	68	69	68	72	277

1985, Cherry Hills C.C.

Hubert Green	67	69	70	72	278
Lee Trevino	66	68	75	71	280
Andy Bean	71	70	72	68	281

1986, Inverness Club
Toledo, OH

Bob Tway	72	70	64	70	276

Greg Norman	65	68	69	76	278
Peter Jacobsen	68	70	70	71	279

1987, PGA National
Palm Beach Gardens, FL

Larry Nelson	70	72	73	72	287
Lanny Wadkins	70	70	74	73	287

(Nelson won sudden-death playoff)

Scott Hoch	74	74	71	69	288

1988, Oak Tree G.C.
Edmond, OK

Jeff Sluman	69	70	68	65	272
Paul Azinger	67	66	71	71	275
Tommy Nakajima	69	68	74	67	278

1989, Kemper Lakes G.C.
Hawthorn Woods, IL

Payne Stewart	74	66	69	67	276
Andy Bean	70	67	74	66	277
Mike Reid	66	67	70	74	277

1990, Shoal Creek
Birmingham, AL

Wayne Grady	72	67	72	71	282
Fred Couples	69	71	73	72	285
Gil Morgan	77	72	65	72	286

1991, Crooked Stick G.C.
Carmel, IN

John Daly	69	67	69	71	276
Bruce Lietzke	68	69	72	70	279
Jim Gallagher, Jr.	70	72	72	67	281

1992, Bellerive C.C.
St. Louis, MO

Nick Price	70	70	68	70	278
John Cook	71	72	67	71	281
Jim Gallagher, Jr.	72	66	72	71	281
Gene Sauers	67	69	70	75	281
Nick Faldo	68	70	76	67	281

1993, Inverness Club
Toledo, OH

Paul Azinger	69	68	69	68	272
Greg Norman	68	68	67	69	272

(Azinger won sudden-death playoff)

| Nick Faldo | 68 | 68 | 69 | 68 | 273 |

1994, Southern Hills C.C.
Tulsa, OK

Nick Price	67	65	70	67	269
Corey Pavin	70	67	69	69	275
Phil Mickelson	68	71	67	70	276

1995, Riviera C.C.
Pacific Palisades, CA

| Steve Elkington | 68 | 67 | 68 | 64 | 267 |
| Colin Montgomerie | 68 | 67 | 67 | 65 | 267 |

(Elkington won sudden-death playoff)

Ernie Els	66	65	66	72	269
Jeff Maggert	66	69	65	69	269
Brad Faxon	70	67	71	63	271
Mark O'Meara	64	67	69	73	273
Bob Estes	69	68	68	68	273

1996, Valhalla G.C.
Louisville, KY

| Mark Brooks | 68 | 70 | 69 | 70 | 277 |
| Kenny Perry | 66 | 72 | 71 | 68 | 277 |

(Brooks won sudden-death playoff)

| Tommy Tolles | 69 | 71 | 71 | 67 | 278 |
| Steve Elkington | 67 | 74 | 67 | 70 | 278 |

6

MAJOR CHAMPIONSHIPS
WOMEN

THE U.S. WOMEN'S OPEN CHAMPIONSHIP

YEAR	SITE	WINNER	SCORE	RUNNER-UP
1946	Spokane C.C. Spokane, WA	Patty Berg	5 and 4	Betty Jameson
1947	Starmount Forest C.C. Greensboro, NC	Betty Jameson	295	Sally Sessions
1948	Atlantic City C.C. Northfield, NJ	Babe Zaharias	300	Betty Hicks
1949	Prince Georges G. & C.C. Landover, MD	Louise Suggs	291	Babe Zaharias
1950	Rolling Hills C.C. Wichita, KS	Babe Zaharias	291	Betsy Rawls
1951	Druid Hills G.C. Atlanta, GA	Betsy Rawls	293	Louise Suggs
1952	Bala G.C. Philadelphia, PA	Louise Suggs	284	Marlene Bauer
1953	C.C. of Rochester Rochester, NY	*Betsy Rawls	302	Jacqueline Pung
1954	Salem C. C. Peabody, MA	Babe Zaharias	291	Betsy Hicks
1955	Wichita C.C. Wichita, KS	Fay Crocker	299	Louise Suggs
1956	Northland C.C. Duluth, MN	*Kathy Cornelius	302	Barbara McIntire
1957	Winged Foot G.C. (East Course) Mamaroneck, NY	Betsy Rawls	299	Patty Berg
1958	Forest Lake C.C. Bloomfield, MI	Mickey Wright	290	Louise Suggs
1959	Churchill Valley C.C. Pittsburgh, PA	Mickey Wright	287	Louise Suggs
1960	Worcester C.C Worcester, MA	Betsy Rawls	292	Joyce Ziske
1961	Baltusrol G.C. Springfield, NJ	Mickey Wright	293	Betsy Rawls
1962	Dunes G.& B. Club Myrtle Beach, SC	Murle Lindstrom	301	Ruth Jesen
1963	Kenwood C.C. Cincinnati, OH	Mary Mills	289	Sandra Haynie
1964	San Diego C.C. Chula Vistas, CA	*Mickey Wright	290	Ruth Jesen
1965	Atlantic City C.C. Northfield, NJ	Carol Mann	290	Kathy Cornelius
1966	Hazeltine Nat. G.C. Chaska, MN	Sandra Spuzich	297	Carol Mann
1967	Virginia Hot Springs G. & T.C. (Cascades) Hot Springs, VA	Catherine Lacoste	294	Susie Maxwell
1968	Moselem Spring G.C. Fleetwood, PA	Susie Maxwell Berning	289	Mickey Wright
1969	Scenic Hills G.C. Pensacola, FL	Donna Caponi	294	Peggy Wilson
1970	Muskogee C.C. Muskogee, OK	Donna Caponi	287	Sandra Haynie
1971	Kahkwa Club Erie, PA	JoAnne Carner	288	Kathy Whitworth
1972	Winged Foot G.C. (East Course) Mamaroneck, NY	Susie Maxwell Berning	299	Kathy Ahern
1973	C.C. of Rochester Rochester, NY	Susie Maxwell Berning	290	Shelly Hamlin
1974	La Grange C.C. La Grange, IL	Sandra Haynie	295	Beth Stone
1975	Atlantic City C.C. Northfield, NJ	Sandra Palmer	295	Nancy Lopez
1976	Rolling Green G.C. Springfield, PA	*JoAnne Carner	292	Sandra Palmer
1977	Hazeltine Nat. G.C. Chaska, MN	Hollis Stacy	292	Nancy Lopez
1978	C.C. of Indianapolis Indianapolis, IN	Hollis Stacy	289	JoAnne Carner

A game of golf is called a "round" because at one time all courses were built in a circular pattern, with the first hole starting at the clubhouse and the 18th taking a player back there.

1979	Brooklawn C.C. Fairfield, CT	Jerilyn Britz	284	Debbie Massey
1980	Richland C.C. Nashville, TN	Amy Alcott	280	Hollis Stacy
1981	La Grange C.C. La Grange, IL	Pat Bradley	279	Beth Daniel
1982	Del Paso C.C. Sacramento, CA	Janet Alex	283	Sandra Haynie
1983	Cedar Ridge C.C. Tulsa, OK	Jan Stephenson	290	JoAnne Carner
1984	Salem C.C. Peabody, MA	Hollis Stacy	290	Rosie Jones
1985	Baltusrol G.C. (Upper Course) Springfield, NJ	Kathy Guadagnino	280	Judy Clark
1986	NCR C.C. Kettering, OH	*Janes Geddes	287	Sally Little
1987	Plainfield C.C. Edison, NJ	*Laura Davies	285	Ayako Okamoto
1988	Baltimore C.C. (Five Farms East) Baltimore, MD	Liselotte Neumann	277	Patty Sheehan
1989	Indianwood G. & C.C. (Old/East Course) Lake Orion, MI	Betsy King	278	Nancy Lopez
1990	Atlanta A.C. (Riverside Course) Duluth, GA	Betsy King	284	Patty Sheehan
1991	Colonial C.C. Fort Worth, TX	Meg Mallon	283	Pat Bradley
1992	Oakmont C.C. Oakmont, PA	*Patty Sheehan	280	Juli Inkster
1993	Crooked Stick G.C. Carmel, IN	Laurie Merten	280	Helen Alfredsson
1994	Indianwood G. & C.C. (Old/East Course) Lake Orion, MI	Patty Sheehan	277	Tammie Green
1995	The Broadmoor C.C. (East Course) Colorado Springs, CO	Annika Sorenstam	278	Meg Mallon
1996	Pine Needles Lodge & G.C. Southern Pines, NC	Annika Sorenstam	272	Kris Tschetter

MAZDA LPGA CHAMPIONSHIP

YEAR	SITE	WINNER	SCORE	RUNNER-UP
1955	Orchard Ridge C.C. Ft. Wayne, IN	Beverly Hanson	220	Louise Suggs
1956	Forest Lake C.C. Detroit, MI	Marlene Hagge	291	Patty Berg
1957	Churchill Valley C.C. Pittsburgh, PA	Louise Suggs	285	Wiffi Smith
1958	Churchill Valley C.C. Pittsburgh, PA	Mickey Wright	288	Fay Crocker
1959	Sheraton Hotel C.C. French Lick, IN	Betsy Rawls	288	Patty Berg
1960	Sheraton Hotel C.C. French Lick, IN	Mickey Wright	292	Louise Suggs
1961	Stardust C.C. Las Vegas, NV	Mickey Wright	287	Louise Suggs
1962	Stardust C.C. Las Vegas, NV	Judy Kimball	282	Shirley Spork
1963	Stardust C.C. Las Vegas, NV	Mickey Wright	294	Mary Lena Faulk
1964	Stardust C.C. Las Vegas, NV	Mary Mills	278	Mickey Wright
1965	Stardust C.C. Las Vegas, NV	Sandra Haynie	279	Clifford A. Creed
1966	Stardust C.C. Las Vegas, NV	Gloria Ehret	282	Mickey Wright
1967	Pleasant Valley C.C. Sutton, MA	Kathy Whitworth	284	Shirley Englehorn
1968	Pleasant Valley Valley C.C. Sutton, MA	*Sandra Post	294	Kathy Whitworth
1969	Concord G.C. Kiamesha Lake, NY	Betsy Rawls	293	Susie Berning
1970	Pleasant Valley C.C. Sutton, MA	Shirley Englehorn	285	Kathy Whitworth
1971	Pleasant Valley C.C. Sutton, MA	Kathy Whitworth	288	Kathy Ahern
1972	Pleasant Valley C.C. Sutton, MA	Kathy Ahern	293	Jane Blalock
1973	Pleasant Valley C.C. Sutton, MA	Mary Mills	288	Betty Burfeindt
1974	Pleasant Valley C.C. Sutton, MA	Sandra Haynie	288	JoAnne Carner
1975	Pine Ridge G.C. Baltimore, MD	Kathy Whitworth	288	Sandra Haynie
1976	Pine Ridge G.C. Baltimore, MD	Betty Burfeindt	287	Judy Rankin
1977	Bay Tree Golf Plantation N. Myrtle Beach, SC	Chako Higuchi	279	Pat Bradley
1978	Jack Nicklaus G.C. Kings Island, OH	Nancy Lopez	275	Amy Alcott
1979	Jack Nicklaus G.C. Kings Island, OH	Donna Caponi	279	Jerilyn Britz
1980	Jack Nicklaus G.C. Kings Island, OH	Sally Little	285	Jane Blalock
1981	Jack Nicklaus G.C. Kings Island G.C.	Donna Caponi	280	Jerilyn Britz
1982	Jack Nicklaus G.C. Kings Island, OH	Jan Stephenson	279	JoAnne Carner
1983	Jack Nicklaus G.C. Kings Island, OH	Patty Sheehan	279	Sandra Haynie
1984	Jack Nicklaus G.C. Kings Island, OH	Patty Sheehan	272	Beth Daniel
1985	Jack Nicklaus G.C. Kings Island, OH	Nancy Lopez	273	Alice Miller
1986	Jack Nicklaus G.C. Kings Island, OH	Pat Bradley	277	Patty Sheehan
1987	Jack Nicklaus G.C. Kings Island, OH	Jane Geddes	275	Betsy King
1988	Jack Nicklaus G.C. Kings Island, OH	Sherri Turner	281	Amy Alcott

1989	Bethesda C.C. Bethesda, MD	Nancy Lopez	274	Ayako Okamoto
1990	Bethesda C.C. Bethesda, MD	Beth Daniel	280	Rosie Jones
1991	Bethesda C.C. Bethesda, MD	Meg Mallon	274	Pat Bradley
1992	Bethesda C.C. Bethesda, MD	Betsy King	267	JoAnne Carner
1993	Bethesda C.C. Bethesda, MD	Patty Sheehan	275	Laurie Merten
1994	DuPont C.C. Wilmington, DE	Laura Davies	279	Alice Ritzman
1995	DuPont C.C. Wilmington, DE	Kelly Robbins	274	Laurie Davies
1996	DuPont C.C. Wilmington, DE	Laura Davies	213	Julie Piers

NABISCO DINAH SHORE

**MISSIONS HILLS COUNTRY CLUB
RANCHO MIRAGE, CA**

YEAR	WINNER	SCORE	RUNNER-UP
1972	Jane Blalock	213	Carol Mann
1973	Mickey Wright	284	Joyce Kamierski
1974	*JoAnne Prentice	289	Jane Blalock
1975	Sandra Palmer	283	Kathy McMullen
1976	Judy Rankin	285	Betty Burfiendt
1977	Kathy Whitworth	289	JoAnne Carner
1978	*Sandra Post	283	Penny Pulz
1979	Sandra Post	276	Nancy Lopez
1980	Donna Caponi	275	Amy Alcott
1981	Nancy Lopez	277	Carolyn Hill
1982	Sally Little	278	Hollis Stacy
1983	Amy Alcott	282	Beth Daniel
1984	*Juli Inkster	280	Pat Bradley
1985	Alice Miller	275	Jan Stephenson
1986	Pat Bradley	280	Val Skinner
1987	*Betsy King	283	Patty Sheehan
1988	Amy Alcott	274	Colleen Walker
1989	Juli Inkster	279	Tammie Green
1990	Betsy King	283	Kathy Postlewait
1991	Amy Alcott	273	Dottie Mochrie
1992	*Dottie Mochrie	279	Juli Inkster
1993	Helen Alfredsson	284	Amy Benz
1994	Donna Andrews	276	Laura Davies
1995	Nanci Bowen	285	Susie Redman
1996	Patty Sheehan	281	Kelly Robbins

Pat Bradley shoots from the fairway at the Twelve Bridges Classic.

DU MAURIER LTD. CLASSIC

YEAR	SITE	WINNER	SCORE	RUNNER-UP
1973	Montreal G.C. Montreal, PQ	*Jocelyne Bourassa	214	Sandra Haynie
1974	Candiac G.C. Montreal, PQ	Carole Jo Callison	208	JoAnne Carner
1975	St. George's C.C. Toronto, ON	JoAnne Carner	214	Carol Mann
1976	Cedar Brae G.&C.C. Toronto, ON	*Donna Caponi	212	Judy Rankin
1977	Lachute G.&C.C. Montreal, PQ	Judy Rankin	214	Pat Meyers
1978	St. George's C.C. Toronto, ON	JoAnne Carner	278	Hollis Stacy
1979	Richelieu Valley C.C. Montreal, PQ	Amy Alcott	285	Nancy Lopez
1980	St. George's C.C. Toronto,ON	Pat Bradley	277	JoAnne Carner
1981	Summerlea C.C. Dorion, PQ	Jan Stephenson	278	Nancy Lopez

1982	St. George's C.C. Toronto, ON	Sandra Haynie	280	Beth Daniel
1983	Beaconsfield G.C. Montreal, PQ	Hollis Stacy	277	JoAnne Carner
1984	St. George's G.&C.C. Toronto, ON	Juli Inkster	279	Ayako Okamoto
1985	Beaconsfield C.C. Montreal, PQ	Pat Bradley	278	Jane Geddes
1986	Board of Trade C.C. Toronto, ON	*Pat Bradley	276	Ayako Okamoto
1987	Islemere G.C. Laval, PQ	Jody Rosenthal	272	Ayako Okamoto
1988	Vancouver G.C. Coquitlam, BC	Sally Little	279	Laura Davies
1989	Beaconsfield G.C. Montreal, PQ	Tammie Green	279	Pat Bradley
1990	Westmount G.&C.C. Kitchener, ON	Cathy Johnson	276	Patty Sheehan
1991	Vancouver G.C. Coquitlam, B.C.	Nancy Scranton	279	Debbie Massey
1992	St. Charles C.C. Winnipeg, Manitoba	Sherri Steinhauer	277	Judy Dickinson
1993	London Hunt and C.C. London, ON	*Brandie Button	277	Betsy King

Shortly after completing the first round of the 1994 Youngstown-Warren Classic LPGA tournament in Ohio, Kim Williams was accidentally shot by someone taking target practice a mile away. Even though she had a bullet lodged in her ribcage, Williams played in the Jamie Farr Toledo Classic the next week and shot a 68 in the first round.

1994	Ottawa Hunt & G.C. Ottawa, ON	Martha Nause	279	Michelle McGann
1995	Beaconsfield G.C. Pointe-Claire, PQ	Jenny Lidback	280	Liselotte Neumann
1996	Edmonton C.C. Atlanta, GA	Laurie Davies	277	Nancy Lopez

* indicates playoff victory

7

MAJOR CHAMPIONSHIPS
SENIORS

THE U.S. SENIOR OPEN CHAMPIONSHIP

YEAR	SITE	WINNER	SCORE	RUNNER-UP
1980	Winged Foot G.C. Mamaroneck, NY	Roberto De Vincenzo	285	William C. Campbell
1981	Oakland Hills C.C. Birmingham, MI	*Arnold Palmer	289	Bob Stone, Billy Casper
1982	Portland G.C. Portland, OR	Miller Barber	282	Gene Littler
1983	Hazeltine National G.C. Chaska, MN	*Billy Casper	288	Rod Funseth
1984	Oak Hills C.C. (East Course) Rochester, NY	Miller Barber	286	Arnold Palmer
1985	Edgewood Tahoe G.C. Stateline, NV	Miller Barber	285	Roberto DeVicenzo
1986	Scioto C.C. Columbus, OH	Dale Douglas	279	Gary Player
1987	Brooklawn C.C. Fairfield, CT	Gary Player	270	Doug Sanders
1988	Medinah C.C. (No. 3 Course) Medinah, IL	*Gary Player	288	Bob Charles
1989	Laurel Valley G.C. Ligonier, PA	Orville Moody	279	Frank Beard
1990	Ridgewood C.C. (Center and West nines) Paramus, NJ	Lee Trevino	275	Jack Nicklaus
1991	Oakland Hills C.C. (South Course) Birmingham, MI	*Jack Nicklaus	282	Chi Chi Rodriguez
1992	Saucon Valley C.C. (Old Course) Bethlehem, PA	Larry Laoretti	275	Jim Colbert
1993	Cherry Hills C.C. Englewood, CO	Jack Nicklaus	278	Tom Weiskopf
1994	Pinehurst C.C. Pinehurst, NC	Simon Hobday	274	Graham Marsh
1995	Congressional C.C. Bethesda, MD	Tom Weiskopf	275	Jack Nicklaus
1996	Canterbury G.C. Beachwood, OH	Dave Stockton	277	Hale Irwin

SENIOR PGA CHAMPIONSHIP

YEAR	SITE	WINNER	SCORE	RUNNER-UP
1937	Augusta National G.C.	Jock Hutchinson	233	George Gordon
1938	Augusta National G.C.	*Fred McLeod	154	Otto Hackharth
1939	No Championship			
1940	North Shore C.C.	*Otto Hackharth	146	Jock Hutchinson
1941	Sarasota Bay C.C.	Jack Burke, Sr.	142	Eddie Williams
1942	Ft. Myers G. & C.C.	Eddie Williams	138	Jock Hutchinson
1943	No Championship			
1944	No Championship			
1945	PGA National Dunedin	Eddie Williams	148	Jock Hutchinson
1946	PGA National Dunedin	*Eddie Williams	146	Jock Hutchinson
1947	PGA National Dunedin	Jock Hutchinson	145	Ben Richter
1948	PGA National Dunedin	Charles McKenna	141	Ben Richter
1949	PGA National Dunedin	Marshall Crichton	145	Louis Chiapetta

The reason golf clubs have grooves is to prevent the ball from sliding up and over the face of the club on impact. The grooves hold the ball on the club and help propel it forward.

1950	PGA National Dunedin	Al Warrous	142	Bill Jeliffe
1951	PGA National Dunedin	*Al Warrous	146	Jock Hutchinson
1952	PGA National Dunedin	Ernie Newnham	146	Al Warrous
1953	PGA National	Harry Schwab	142	Charles McKenna
1954	PGA National Dunedin	Gene Sarazen	214	Perry Del Vecchio
1955	PGA National	Morrie Dutra	213	Mike Murra
1956	PGA National	Pete Burke	215	Ock Willoweir
1957	PGA National Dunedin	*Al Warrous	210	Bob Stupple
1958	PGA National Dunedin	Gene Sarazen	288	Charles Sheppard
1959	PGA National Dunedin	Willie Groggin	284	Leland Gibson
1960	PGA National Dunedin	Dick Metz	284	Tony Longo
1961	PGA National Dunedin	Paul Runyan	278	Jimmy Denaret
1962	PGA National Dunedin	Paul Runyan	278	Errie Ball
1963	Port St. Lucie C.C.	Herman Baron	272	John Barnum
1964	PGA National Dunedin	Sam Snead	279	John Barnum
1965	Ft. Lauderdale C.C.	Sam Snead	278	Joe Lopez, Sr.
1966	PGA National JDM C.C.	Freddie Haas	286	John Barnum
1967	PGA National JDM C.C.	Sam Snead	279	Bob Hamilton
1968	PGA National JDM C.C.	Chandler Harper	279	Sam Snead
1969	PGA National JDM C.C.	Tommy Bolt	278	Pete Fleming
1970	PGA National JDM C.C.	Sam Snead	290	Freddie Haas
1971	PGA National JDM C.C.	Julius Boros	285	Tommy Bolt
1972	PGA National JDM C.C.	Sam Snead	286	Tommy Bolt
1973	PGA National JDM C.C.	Sam Snead	268	Julius Boros
1974	Port St. Lucie C.C.	Roberto DeVicenzo	273	Julius Boros
1975	Walt Disney World Magnolia	*Charlie Sifford	280	Fred Wampler
1976	Walt Disney World Magnolia	Pete Cooper	283	Fred Wampler
1977	Walt Disney World Magnolia	Julius Boros	283	Freddie Haas
1978	Walt Disney World Magnolia	*Joe Jimenez	286	Joe Cheves
1979	Walt Disney World Magnolia	*Jack Fleck	289	Bob Erickson
1979	Turnbery Isle C.C.	Don January	270	George Bayer

1980	Turnbery Isle C.C.	*Arnold Palmer	289	Paul Harney
1981	Turnbery Isle C.C.	Miller Barber	281	Arnold Palmer
1982	PGA National Champions Course	Don January	288	Julius Boros
1983	No Championship			
1984	PGA National Champions Course	Arnold Palmer	282	Don January
1984	PGA National Champions Course	Peter Thomson	286	Don January
1985	No Championship			
1986	PGA National Champions Course	Gary Player	281	Lee Elder
1987	PGA National Champions Course	Chi Chi Rodriguez	282	Dale Douglas
1988	PGA National Champions Course	Gary Player	284	Chi Chi Rodriguez
1989	PGA National Champions Course	Larry Mowry	281	Miller Barber
1990	PGA National Champions Course	Gary Player	281	Chi Chi Rodriguez
1991	PGA National Champions Course	Jack Nicklaus	271	Bruce Crampton
1992	PGA National Champions Course	Lee Trevino	278	Mike Hill
1993	PGA National Champions Course	*Tom Wargo	275	Bruce Crampton
1994	PGA National Champions Course	Lee Trevino	279	Jim Colbert
1995	PGA National Champions Course	Ray Floyd	277	John Paul Cain
1996	PGA National Champions Course	Hale Irwin	280	Isao Aoki

![black bar]

THE TRADITION

DESERT MOUNTAIN G.C., COCHISE COURSE

YEAR	WINNER	SCORE
1989	Don Bies	275
1990	Jack Nicklaus	206
1991	Jack Nicklaus	277
1992	Lee Trevino	274
1993	Tom Shaw	269
1994	*Raymond Floyd	271
1995	Jack Nicklaus	276
1996	Jack Nicklaus	272

FORD SENIOR PLAYERS CHAMPIONSHIP

YEAR	SITE	WINNER	SCORE
1983	Canterbury G.C. Cleveland, OH	Miller Barber	278
1984	Canterbury G.C. Cleveland, OH	Arnold Palmer	276
1985	Canterbury G.C. Cleveland, OH	Arnold Palmer	274
1986	Canterbury G.C. Cleveland, OH	Chi Chi Rodriguez	206
1987	Sawgrass C.C. Ponte Verda, FL	Gary Player	280
1988	Players Club at Sawgrass Valley Ponte Verda, FL	Billy Casper	278
1989	Players Club at Sawgrass Valley Ponte Verda, FL	Orville Moody	271
1990	Dearborn C.C. Dearborn, MI	Jack Nicklaus	261

At age 13, Jack Nicklaus suffered from a mild case of polio. Obviously, he recovered with no loss of muscle strength or coordination.

1991	Dearborn C.C. Dearborn, MI	Jim Albus	279
1992	Dearborn C.C. Dearborn, MI	Dave Stockton	277
1993	Dearborn C.C. Dearborn, MI	Jim Colbert	278
1994	Dearborn C.C. Dearborn, MI	Dave Stockton	271
1995	Dearborn C.C. Dearborn, MI	J.C. Snead	272
1996	TPC of Michigan Dearborn, MI	Raymond Floyd	275

* indicates playoff victory

8

MAJOR CHAMPIONSHIPS
INTERNATIONAL TEAM EVENTS

THE RYDER CUP

This is a three-day 12-man team competition which includes foursomes, best ball, and singles play.

YEAR	SITE	WINNER	SCORE
1927	Worcester C.C., U.S.	U.S.	9.5-2.5
1929	Moortown G.C., England	Great Britain	7-5
1931	Scioto C.C., U.S.	U.S.	9-3
1933	Southport & Ainsdale G.C.,	England	6.5-5.5
1935	Ridgewood C.C., U.S.	U.S.	9-3
1937	Southport & Ainsdale G.C.,	England	8-4
1947	Portland G.C., U.S.	U.S.	11-1
1949	Ganton G.C., England	U.S.	7-5
1951	Pinehurst C.C., U.S.	U.S.	9.5-2.5
1953	Wentworth G.C., England	U.S.	6.5-5.5
1955	Thunderbird G.& C.C., U.S.	U.S.	8-4
1957	Lindrick G.C., England	Great Britain	7.5-4.5
1959	Eldorado C.C., U.S.	U.S.	8.5-3.5
1961	Royal Lytham & St. Anne's, England	U.S.	14.5-9.5
1963	East lake C.C., U.S.	U.S.	23-9
1965	Royal Birkdale G.C., England	U.S.	19.5-12.5
1967	Champions G.C., U.S.	U.S.	23.5-8.5
1969	Royal Birkdale G.C., England	Tie	16-16
1971	Old Warson C.C., U.S.	U.S.	18.5-13.5
1973	Muirfield, Scotland	U.S.	19-13
1975	Laurel Valley G.C., U.S.	U.S.	21-11
1977	Royal Lytham & St. Anne's, England	U.S.	12.5-7.5
1979	The Greenbrier, U.S.	U.S.	17-11
1981	Walton Heath G.C., England	U.S.	18.5-9.5
1983	PGA National G.C., U.S.	U.S.	14.5-13.5
1985	The Belfry, England	Europe	16.5-11.5
1987	Muirfield Village G.C.,	U.S.	15-13
1989	The Belfry, England	Tie	14-14
1991	The Ocean Course, U.S.	U.S.	14.5-13.5
1993	The Belfry, England	U.S.	15-13
1995	Oak Hill G.C., U.S.	Europe	14.5-13.5

THE SOLHEIM CUP

This is a three-day 10-woman team competition between the U.S. and Europe which includes foursomes, best ball, and singles play.

YEAR	SITE	WINNER	SCORE
1990	Lake Nona G.C. Orlando, FL	U.S.	284
1992	Dalmahoy G. & C.C. Edinburgh, Scotland	Europe	282
1994	The Greenbrier G.C. White Sulphur Springs, WV	U.S.	13-7
1996	Chepstow, Wales	U.S.	17-11

THE WORLD CUP

This is a two-man international team competition which features stroke play. Until 1966, it was known as the Canada Cup.

The Swilken Golf Company of St. Andrews produced 7,500 sets of manganese-aluminum-bronze clubs from a propeller of the luxury liner Queen Elizabeth II.

YEAR	SITE	WINNER	TEAM MEMBERS
1953	Montreal	Argentina	Roberto de Vincenzo, Antonio Cerda
1954	Canada	Australia	Peter Thompson, Kel Nagle
1955	Washington, D.C.	United States	Ed Furgol, Chick Harbert
1956	Wentworth (UK)	United States	Ben Hogan, Sam Snead
1957	Tokyo	Japan	Torakichi Nakamura, Koichi Ono
1958	Mexico City	Ireland	Harry Bradshaw, Christy O'Connor
1959	Melbourne	Australia	Peter Thompson, Kel Nagle
1960	Dublin	United States	Sam Snead, Arnold Palmer
1961	Dorado (Puerto Rico)	United States	Sam Snead, Jimmy Demaret
1962	Buenos Aires	United States	Sam Snead, Arnold Palmer
1963	Paris	United States	Jack Nicklaus, Arnold Palmer
1964	Maui	United States	Jack Nicklaus, Arnold Palmer
1965	Madrid	South Africa	Gary Player, Harold Henning
1966	Tokyo	United States	Jack Nicklaus, Arnold Palmer
1967	Mexico City	United States	Jack Nicklaus, Arnold Palmer
1968	Rome	Canada	Al Balding, George Knudson
1969	Singapore	United States	Lee Trevino, Orville Moody
1970	Buenos Aires	Australia	David Graham, Bruce Devlin
1971	Palm Beach (U.S.)	United States	Jack Nicklaus, Lee Trevino
1972	Melbourne	Rep. of China	Hsieh Min-Nan, Lu Liang-Huan
1973	Marbella, Spain	United States	Johnny Miller, Jack Nicklaus
1974	Caracas	South Africa	Bobby Cole, Dale Hayes
1975	Bangkok	United States	Johnny Miller, Lou Graham
1976	Palm Springs	Spain	Manuel Pinero, Steve Ballesteros
1977	Manila	Spain	Antonio Garrido, Steve Ballesteros
1978	Kauai	United States	John Mahaffey, Andy North
1979	Athens	United States	John Mahaffey, Hale Irwin
1980	Bogota	Canada	Dan Halldorson, Jim Nelford
1981	No Tournament		
1982	Acapulco	Spain	Manuel Pinero, Jose Canizares
1983	Jakarta	United States	Rex Caldwell, John Cook
1984	Rome Spain	Jose Canizares, Jose Rivero	
1985	La Quinta	Canada	Dave Barr, Dan Halldorson
1986	No Tournament		
1987	Maui	Wales	Ian Woosnam, David Llewellyn
1988	Melbourne	United States	Ben Crenshaw, Mark McCumber
1989	Marbella, Spain	Australia	Peter Fowler, Wayne Grady
1990	Orlando	Germany	Bernhard Langer, Torsten Giedeon
1991	Rome	Sweden	Per-Ulrik Johansson, Anders Forsbrand
1992	Madrid	United States	Fred Couples, Davis Love III
1993	Orlando	United States	Fred Couples, Davis Love III
1994	France	United States	Fred Couples, Davis Love III
1995	Beijing	United States	Fred Couples, Davis Love III
1996	South Africa	South Africa	Ernie Els, Wayne Westner

INDIVIDUAL TROPHY

YEAR	COUNTRY	WINNER
1953	Argentina	Antonio Cerda
1954	Canada	Stan Leonard
1955	United States	Ed Furgol
1956	United States	Ben Hogan
1957	Japan	Torakichi Nakamura
1958	Spain	Angel Miguel
1959	Canada	Stan Leonard
1960	Belgium	Flory Van Donck
1961	United States	Sam Snead
1962	Argentina	Roberto de Vicenzo
1963	United States	Jack Nicklaus
1964	United States	Jack Nicklaus
1965	South Africa	Gary Player
1966	Canada	George Knudson
1967	United States	Arnold Palmer
1968	Canada	Al Balding
1969	United States	Lee Trevino
1970	Argentina	Roberto de Vicenzo
1971	United States	Jack Nicklaus
1972	Rep. of China	Hsieh Min-Nan
1973	United States	Johnny Miller

1974	South Africa	Bobby Cole
1975	United States	Johnny Miller
1976	Mexico	Ernesto Acosta
1977	South Africa	Gary Player
1978	United States	John Mahaffey
1979	United States	Hale Irwin
1980	Scotland	Sandy Lyle
1981	No Tournament	
1982	Spain	Manuel Pinero
1983	Canada	Dave Barr
1984	Spain	Jose Canizares
1985	England	Howard Clark
1986	No Tournament	
1987	Wales	Ian Woosnam
1988	United States	Ben Crenshaw
1989	Australia	Peter Fowler
1990	United States	Payne Stewart
1991	Wales	Ian Woosnam
1992	Australia	Brett Ogle
1993	Germany	Bernhard Langer
1994	U.S.	Fred Couples
1995	U.S.	David Love III
1996	South Africa	Ernie Els

A golf ball stays on the face of a persimmon wood for only .0036 seconds.

1987	England	Scotland
1988	Ireland	Australia
1989	U.S.	Japan
1990	Ireland	England
1991	Sweden	South Africa
1992	England	Scotland
1993	U.S.	England
1994	Canada	U.S.
1995	Scotland	England
1996	U.S.	New Zealand

THE ALFRED DUNHILL CUP

This is a three-man international team competition held at the Old Course, St. Andrews, Scotland, and features round-robin matches.

YEAR	WINNER	RUNNER-UP
1985	Australia	U.S.
1986	Australia	Japan

THE PRESIDENT'S CUP

This is a three-day 12-man team competition which pits the U.S. against an international team which includes foursome, best ball, and singles play.

YEAR	SITE	WINNER	SCORE
1994	Robert Trent Jones G.C. Manassas, VA	U.S.	20-12
1996	Robert Trent Jones G.C. Manassas, VA	U.S.	17.5-16.5

9

MAJOR CHAMPIONSHIPS
AMATEURS

U.S. MEN'S AMATEUR CHAMPIONSHIP

YEAR	SITE	WINNER
1895	Newport	Charles Blair McDonald
1896	Shinnecock	H.J. Whigham
1897	Chicago	H.J.Whigham
1898	Morris County	Findlay S. Douglas
1899	Onwentsia	H.M. Harriman
1900	Garden City	Walter J. Travis
1901	C.C. of Atlantic City	Walter J. Travis
1902	Glen View	Louis N. James
1903	Nasau	Walter J. Travis
1904	Baltusrol	H. Chandler Egan
1905	Chicago	H. Chancler Egan
1906	Englewood	Eben M. Byers
1907	Euclid	Jerome D. Travers
1908	Garden City	Jerome D. Travers
1909	Chicago	Robert A. Gardner
1910	The Country Club	William C. Fownes Jr.
1911	Apawamis	Harold H. Hilton
1912	Chicago	Jerome D. Travers
1913	Garden City	Jerome D. Travers
1914	Ekwanok	Francis Quimet
1915	C.C. of Detroit	Robert A. Gardner
1916	Merion	Chick Evans
1917	No Tournament	
1918	No Tournament	
1919	Oakmont	S. Davidson Herron
1920	Engineers	Chick Evans
1921	St. Louis	Jesse P. Guilford
1922	The Country Club	Jess W. Sweetser
1923	Rossmoor	Max R. Marston
1924	Merion	Robert T. Jones Jr.
1925	Oakmont	Robert T. Jones Jr.
1926	Baltusrol	George Von Elm
1927	Minikahda	Robert T. Jones Jr.
1928	Brae Burn	Robert T. Jones Jr.
1929	Pebble Beach	Harrison R. Johnston
1930	Merion	Robert T. Jones Jr.
1931	Beverly	Francis Quimet
1932	Baltimore	C. Ross Somerville
1933	Kenwood	George T. Dunlap Jr.
1934	The Country Club	W. Lawson Little Jr.
1935	The Country Club (O.)	W. Lawson Little Jr.
1936	Garden City	John W. Fischer
1937	Alderwood	John Goodman
1938	Oakmont	William P. Turnesa
1939	North Shore	Marvin H. Ward
1940	Winged Foot (West)	Richard D. Chapman
1941	Omaha Field	Marvin H. Ward
1942	No tournament	
1943	No tournament	
1944	No tournament	
1945	No tournament	
1946	Baltusrol (Lower)	Ted Bishop
1947	Pebble Beach	Skee Riegel
1948	Memphis	William P. Turnesa
1949	Oak Hill (East)	Charles R. Coe
1950	Minneapolis	Sam Urzetta
1951	Saucon Valley	(Old) Billy Maxwell
1952	Seattle	Jack Westland
1953	Oklahoma City	Gene Littler
1954	C.C. of Detroit	Arnold Palmer
1955	C.C. of Virginia (James R.)	E. Harvie Ward Jr.
1956	Knollwood	E. Harvie Ward Jr.

An "average" golfer will shoot in the high 90s on a Par-72 course. Only one player in twelve will break 80 with any consistency.

1957	The Country Club	Hillman Robbins Jr.
1958	Olympic (Lake)	Charles R. Coe
1959	Broadmoor (East)	Jack Nicklaus
1960	St. Louis	Deane Berman
1961	Pebble Beach	Jack Nicklaus
1962	Pinehurst (No.2)	Labron E. Harris Jr.
1963	Wakonda	Deane Berman
1964	Canterbury	William C. Campbell
1965	Southern Hills	Robert J. Murphy Jr.
1966	Merion (East)	Gary Cowan
1967	Broadmoor (West)	Robert B. Dickson
1968	Scioto	Bruce Fleisher
1969	Oakmont	Steven N. Melnyk
1970	Waverly	Lanny Wadkins
1971	Wilmington (South)	Gary Cowan
1972	Charlotte Marvin	Giles III
1973	Inverness	Craig Stadler
1974	Ridgewood	Jerry Pate
1975	C.C. of Virginia	Fred Ridley
1976	Bel Air	Bill Sander
1977	Aronimink	John Fought
1978	Plainfield	John Cook
1979	Canterbury	Mark O'Meara
1980	C.C.. of N. Carolina	Hal Sutton
1981	Olympic (Lake)	Nathaniel Crosby
1982	The Country Club	Jay Sigel
1983	North Shore	Jay Sigel
1984	Oak Tree	Scott Verplank
1985	Montclair	Sam Randolph
1986	Shoal Creek	Buddy Alexander
1987	Jupiter Hills	Bill Mayfair
1988	Va. Hot Spt. (Cascades)	Eric Meeks
1989	Merion (East)	Chris Patton
1990	Cherry Hills	Phil Mickelson
1991	The Honors	Mitch Voges
1992	Muirfield Village	Justin Leonard
1993	Champion (Cypress Cr.)	John Harris
1994	TPC at Sawgrass	Eldrick (Tiger) Woods
1995	Newport	Eldrick (Tiger) Woods
1996	Pumpkin Ridge	Eldrick (Tiger) Woods

U.S. MEN'S MID-AMATEUR CHAMPIONSHIP

YEAR	SITE	WINNER
1981	Bellerive	Jim Holtgrieve
1982	Knollwood	William Hoffer
1983	Cherry Hills	Jay Sigel

1984	Atlanta A.C.	Michael Podolak
1985	The Vintage Club	Jay Sigel
1986	Annadale	Bill Loeffler
1987	Brook Hollow	Jay Sigel
1988	Prairie Dunes	David Eger
1989	Crooked Stick	James Taylor
1990	Troon	Jim Stuart
1991	Long Cove	Jim Stuart
1992	Detroit	Danny Yates
1993	Eugene	Jeff Thomas
1994	Hazeltine National	Tim Jackson
1995	Caves Valley	Jerry Courville
1996	Tumble Brook C.C.	John "Spider" Williams

U.S. MEN'S SENIOR AMATEUR CHAMPIONSHIP

YEAR	SITE	WINNER
1955	Belle Meade	J. Wood Platt
1956	Somerset	Frederick J. Wright
1957	Ridgewood	J. Clark Espie
1958	Monterey Peninsula	Thomas C. Robbins
1959	Memphis	J. Clark Espie
1960	Oyster Harbours	Michael Cestone
1961	Southern Hills	Dexter H. Dabiels
1962	Evanston	Merrill L. Carlsmith
1963	Sea Island	Merrill L. Carlsmith
1964	Waverly	William D. Higgins
1965	Fox Chapel	Robert B. Kiersky
1966	Tucson National	Dexter H. Daniels
1967	Shinnecock Hills	Ray Palmer
1968	Atlanta C.C.	Curtis Person Sr.
1969	Wichita	Curtis Person Sr.
1970	California	Gene Andrews
1971	Sunnybrook	Tom Draper
1972	Sharon	Lewis W. Oehmig
1973	Onwentsia	William Handyman III
1974	Harbour Town	Dale Morey
1975	Carmel Valley	William F. Colm
1976	Cherry Hills	Lewis W. Oehmig
1977	Salem	Dale Morey
1978	Pine Tree	Keith K. Compton
1979	Chicago	William C. Campbell
1980	Virginia Hot Springs	William C. Campbell
1981	Seattle	Edgar R. Updegraff
1982	Tucson	Alton Duhon
1983	Crooked Stick	William Handyman III
1984	Birmingham	Robert Rawlins
1985	Wild Dunes	Lewis W. Oehmig
1986	Interlachen	R.S. Williams
1987	Saucon Valley	John Richardson
1988	Milwaukee	Clarence Moore
1989	Lochinvar	R.S. Williams
1990	Desert Forest	Jackie Cummings
1991	Crystal Downs	Bill Boshard

1992	Loxahatchee	Clarence Moore
1993	Farmington	Joe Ungvary
1994	Champions	O. Gordon Brewer
1995	Prairie Dunes	James Stahl Jr.
1996	Taconic G.C.	O. Gordon Brewer

WALKER CUP

This bienniel competition pits amateur men of the United States against those of Great Britain and Ireland.

YEAR	SITE	SCORE
1922	National Golf Links of America	U.S. 8, Great Britain & Ireland 4
1923	St. Andrews (Old)	U.S. 6, Great Britain 5
1924	Garden City G.C.	U.S. 9, Great Britain & Ireland 3
1926	St. Andrews (Old)	U.S. 6, Great Britain & Ireland 5
1928	Chicago G.C.	U.S. 11, Great Britain & Ireland 1
1930	Royal St. George's G.C.	U.S. 10, Great Britain & Ireland 2
1932	The Country Club (Mass.)	U.S. 8, Great Britain 1
1934	St. Andrews (Old)	U.S. 9, Great Britain & Ireland 2
1936	Pine Valley G.C.	U.S. 9, Great Britain & Ireland 0
1938	St. Andrews (Old)	Great Britain & Ireland 7, U.S. 4
1940-46		No competition
1947	St. Andrews (Old)	U.S. 8, Great Britain & Ireland 4
1949	Winged Foot G.C. (West)	U.S. 10, Great Britain & Ireland 2
1951	Birkdale G.C. U.S. 6,	Great Britain & Ireland 3
1953	The Kittansett Club	U.S. 9, Great Britain & Ireland 3
1955	St. Andrews (Old)	U.S. 10, Great Britain & Ireland 2
1957	Minikahda Club	U.S. 8, Great Britain & Ireland 3
1959	Muirfield	U.S. 9, Great Britain & Ireland 3
1961	Seattle G.C.	U.S. 11, Great Britain & Ireland 1
1963	Turnberry (Ailsa)	U.S. 12, Great Britain & Ireland 8
1965	Baltimore C.C. (Five Farms)	U.S. 11, Great Britain & Ireland 11
1967	Royal St. George's G.C.	U.S. 13, Great Britain & Ireland 7
1969	Milwaukee C.C.	U.S. 10, Great Britain & Ireland 8
1971	St. Andrews (Old)	Great Britain & Ireland 13, U.S. 11
1973	The Country Club (Mass.)	U.S. 14, Great Britain & Ireland 10

Ken Nagle took a 35-stroke penalty in the second round of the 1969 Alcan Golfer of the Year Tournament in Portland, Oregon. He was in second place in the tournament when he inadvertently entered his nine-hole total in the space for the ninth-hole score. After he signed the scorecard, he was forced to add 35 strokes to his score.

1975	St. Andrews (Old)	U.S. 15½, Great Britain & Ireland 8½
1977	Shinnecock Hills	U.S. 16, Great Britain & Ireland 8
1979	Muirfield	U.S. 15½, Great Britain & Ireland 8½
1981	Cypress Point Club	U.S. 15, Great Britain & Ireland 9
1983	Royal Liverpool G.C.	U.S. 13½, Great Britain & Ireland 10-1/2
1985	Pine Valley G.C.	U.S. 13, Great Britain & Ireland 11
1987	Sunningdale G.C.	U.S. 16½, Great Britain & Ireland 7½
1989	Peachtree G.C.	Great Britain & Ireland 12½, U.S. 11½
1991	Portmarnock G.C.	U.S. 14, Great Britain & Ireland 10
1993	Interlachen C.C.	U.S. 19, Great Britain & Ireland 5
1995	Royal Porthcawl	Great Britain & Ireland 14, U.S. 10

U.S. WOMEN'S AMATEUR CHAMPIONSHIP

YEAR	SITE	WINNER
1895	Meadow Brook	Mrs. Charles S. Brown
1896	Morris County	Beatrix Hoyt
1897	Essex County	Beatrix Hoyt
1898	Ardsley	Beatrix Hoyt
1899	Philadelphia	Ruth Underhill
1900	Shinnecock Hills	Frances C. Griscom
1901	Baltrusol	Genevieve Hecker
1902	The Country Club	Genevieve Hecker
1903	Chicago	Bessie Anthony
1904	Merion	Georgianna M. Bishop
1905	Morris County	Pauline Mackay
1906	Brae Burn	Harriot S. Curtis
1907	Midlothian	Margaret Curtis
1908	Chevy Chase	Katherine C. Harley
1909	Merion	Dorothy I. Campbell

In his 21 years on the Tour, Fuzzy Zoeller has won 10 tournaments and amassed $5,266,400 in earnings.

Year	Location	Winner
1910	Homewood	Dorothy I. Campbell
1911	Baltusrol	Margaret Curtis
1912	Essex County	Margaret Curtis
1913	Wilmington	Gladys Ravenscroft
1914	Nassau	Katherine Jackson
1915	Onwentsia	Florence Vanderbeck
1916	Belmont Springs	Alexa Stirling
1917	No tournament	
1918	No tournament	
1919	Shawnee	Alexa Stirling
1920	Mayfield	Alexa Stirling
1921	Hollywood	Marion Hollins
1922	Greenbrier	Glenna Collett
1923	Westchester-Biltmore	Edith Cummings
1924	Rhode Island	Dorothy C. Hurd
1925	St. Louis	Glenna Collett
1926	Merion	Helen Stetson
1927	Cherry Valley	Miriam Burns Horn
1928	Va. Hot Springs	Glenna Collett
1929	Oakland Hills	Glenna Collett
1930	Los Angeles	Glenna Collett
1931	C.C. of Buffalo	Helen Hicks
1932	Salem	Virginia Van Wie

Year	Location	Winner
1933	Exmoor	Virginia Van Wie
1934	Whitemarsh Valley	Virginia Van Wie
1935	Interlachen	Glenna Collett Vare
1936	Canoe Brook	Pamela Barton
1937	Memphis	Estelle Lawson Page
1938	Westmoreland	Patty Berg
1939	Wee Burn	Betty Jameson
1940	Pebble Beach	Betty Jameson
1941	The Country Club	Elizabeth Hics Newell
1942-45	No tournament	
1946	Southern Hills	Babe Zaharis
1947	Franklin Hills	Louise Suggs
1948	Pebble Beach	Grace S. Lenczyk
1949	Merion	Dorothy Porter
1950	Atlanta A.C.	Beverly Hanson
1951	Town & Country	Dorothy Kirby
1952	Waverly	Jacqueline Pung
1953	Rhode Island	Mary Lena Faulk
1954	Allegheny	Barbara Romack
1955	Myers Park	Patricia Lesser
1956	Meridian Hills	Marlene Stewart
1957	Del Paso	JoAnne Gunderson
1958	Wee Burn	Anne Quast
1959	Congressional	Barbara McIntire
1960	Tulsa	JoAnne Gunderson
1961	Tacoma	Anne Quast Decker
1962	C.C. of Rochester	JoAnne Gunderson
1963	Taconic	Anne Quast Welts
1964	Prairie Dunes	Barbara McIntire
1965	Lakewood	Jean Ashley
1966	Birmingham	JoAnne Carner
1967	Annandale	Mary Lou Dill
1968	Birmingham	JoAnne Carner
1969	Las Colinas	Catherina Lacoste
1970	Wee Burn	Martha Wilkinson
1971	Atlanta C.C.	Laura Baugh
1972	St. Louis	Mary Budke
1973	Montclair	Carol Semple
1974	Broadmoor	Cynthia Hill
1975	Brae Burn	Beth Daniel
1976	Del Paso	Donna Horton
1977	Cincinatti	Beth Daniel
1978	Sunnybrook	Cathy Sherk
1979	Memphis	Carolyn Hill
1980	Prairie Dunes	Juli Inkster
1981	Waverly	Juli Inkster
1982	Broadmoor	Juli Inkster
1983	Canoe Brook	Joanne Pacillo
1984	Broadmoor	Deb Richard
1985	Fox Chapel	Mickiko Hattori
1986	Pasatiempo	Kay Cockerill
1987	Rhode Island	Kay Cockerill
1988	Minikahda	Pearl Sinn
1989	Pinehurst No.2	Vicki Goetze
1990	Canoe Brook	Pat Hurst
1991	Prairie Dunes	Amy Fruhwirth
1992	Kemper Lakes	Vicki Goetze
1993	San Diego	Jill McGill
1994	Cascades	Wendy Ward
1995	The Country Club	Kelli Kuehne
1996	Firethorn G.C.	Kelli Kuehne

U.S. WOMEN'S MID-AMATEUR CHAMPIONSHIP

YEAR	SITE	WINNER
1987	Southern Hills	Cindy Scholefield
1988	Amelia Island	Martha Lang
1989	The Hills of Lakeway	Robin Weiss
1990	Allegheny	Carol Semple Thompson
1991	Desert Highlands	Sarah LeBrun Ingram
1992	Old Marsh	Marion Maney-McInerny
1993	Rochester	Sarah LeBrun Ingram
1994	Tacoma	Maria Jemsek
1995	Essex	Ellen Port
1996	Mission Hills C.C.	Ellen Port

U.S. WOMEN'S SENIOR AMATEUR CHAMPIONSHIP

YEAR	SITE	WINNER
1962	Manufacturers'	Maureen Orcutt
1963	C.C. of Florida	Marion Choate
1964	Del Paso	Lorna Smith
1965	Exmoor	Lorna Smith
1966	Lakewood	Maureen Orcutt
1967	Atlantic City	Marge Mason
1968	Monterey Peninsula	Carolyn Cudone
1968	Ridgelea	Carolyn Cudone
1970	Coral Ridge	Carolyn Cudone
1971	Sea Island	Carolyn Cudone
1972	Manufacturers'	Carolyn Cudone
1973	San Marcos	Gwen Hibbs
1974	Lakewood	Justine B. Cushing
1975	Rhode Island	Alberta Bower
1976	Monterey Peninsula	Cecile Maclaurin
1977	Dunes Club	Dorothy Porter
1978	Rancho Bernardo	Alice Dye
1979	Herdscrabble	Alice Dye
1980	Sea Island	Dorothy Porter
1981	Spring Lake	Dorothy Porter
1982	Kissing Camels	Edean Ihlanfeldt
1983	Gulph Mills	Dorothy Porter
1984	Tacoma	Constance Guthrie
1985	Sheraton Savannah	Marlene Street
1986	Lakewood	Constance Guthrie
1987	Manufacturers'	Anne Sander
1988	Sea Island	Lois Hodge
1989	TPC at The Woodlands	Anne Sander
1990	Del Rio	Anne Sander
1991	Pine Needles	Phyllis Preuss
1992	Tucson	Rosemary Thompson
1993	Preakness Hills	Anne Sanders

The odds of an amateur golfer making a hole-in-one on any given hole are about 12,600 to 1. The chances of a touring professional hitting a hole-in-one are about 3,708 to 1.

1994	Sea Island	Nancy Fitzgerald
1995	Somerset	Jean Smith
1996	Broadmoor G.C.	Gayle Borthwick

CURTIS CUP

This bienniel competition pits amateur women of the U.S. against those of Great Britain and Ireland.

YEAR	SITE	SCORE
1932	Wentworth	U.S. 5½, Great Britain & Ireland 3½
1934	Chevy Chase	U.S. 6½, Great Britain & Ireland 2½
1936	Gleneagles	U.S. 4½, Great Britain & Ireland 4-1/2
1938	Essex	U.S. 5½, Great Britain & Ireland 3-1/2
1940-46		No competition
1948	Birkdale	U.S. 6½, Great Britain & Ireland 2½
1950	C.C. of Buffalo	U.S. 7½, Great Britain & Ireland 1-1/2
1952	Muirfield	U.S. 5, Great Britain & Ireland 4
1954	Merion	U.S. 6, Great Britain & Ireland 3
1956	Prince's	U.S. 5, Great Britain & Ireland 4
1958	Brae Burn	U.S. 4½, Great Britain & Ireland 4½
1960	Lindrick	U.S. 6½, Great Britain & Ireland 2½
1962	Broadmoor	U.S. 8, Great Britain & Ireland 1
1964	Royal Porthcawl	U.S. 10½, Great Britain & Ireland 7-1/2
1966	Virginia Hot Springs	U.S. 13, Great Britain & Ireland 5
1968	Royal County Down	U.S. 10½, Great Britain & Ireland 7½
1970	Brae Burn	U.S. 11½, Great Britain & Ireland 6½
1972	Western Gailes	U.S. 10, Great Britain & Ireland 8
1974	San Francisco	U.S. 13, Great Britain & Ireland 5
1976	Royal Lytham & St. Anne's	U.S. 11½, Great Britain & Ireland 6-1/2

Year	Site	Result
1978	Apawamis Club	U.S. 12, Great Britain & Ireland 6
1980	St. Pierre	U.S. 13, Great Britain & Ireland 5
1982	Denver	U.S. 14½, Great Britain & Ireland 3½
1984	Muirfield	U.S. 9½, Great Britain & Ireland 8½
1986	Prairie Dunes	Great Britain & Ireland 13, U.S. 5
1988	Royal St. George's	Great Britain & Ireland 11, U.S. 7
1990	Somerset Hills	U.S. 14, Great Britain 4
1992	Royal Liverpool	Great Britain & Ireland 10, U.S. 8
1994	The Honors Course	U.S. 13, Great Britain & Ireland 5
1996	Killarney G. & F.C.	Great Britain & Ireland 11.5, U.S. 6.5

1978	Pacific Harbour G.&C.C, Fiji	U.S.
1980	Pinehurst, U.S.	U.S.
1982	Lausanne G.C., Switzerland	U.S.
1984	Royal Hong Kong G.C., Hong Kong	Japan
1986	Laguinta, Venezuela	Canada
1988	Ullna G.C., Sweden	Great Britain & Ireland
1990	Christchurch G.C., New Zealand	Sweden
1992	Capilano G.&C.C., Canada	New Zealand
1994	La Boulie, France	U.S.

MEN'S WORLD AMATEUR TEAM CHAMPIONSHIP

YEAR	SITE	WINNER
1958	St. Andrews, Scotland	Australia
1960	Merion G.C., U.S.	U.S.
1962	Fuji G.C., Japan	U.S.
1964	Olgiata G.C., Italy	Great Britain & Ireland
1966	Club de Golf, Mexico	Australia
1968	Royal Melbourne, Australia	U.S.
1970	Real Club de la Purta de Hierro, Spain	U.S.
1972	Olivos G.C., Argentina	U.S.
1974	Campo de Golf, Dominican Rep.	U.S.
1976	Pennina G.C., Portugal	Great Britain & Ireland

WOMEN'S WORLD AMATEUR TEAM CHAMPIONSHIP

YEAR	SITE	WINNER
1964	St. Germain G.C., France	France
1966	Mexico City G.C., Mexico	U.S.
1968	Victoria G.C., Australia	U.S.
1970	RSHE Club de Campo, Spain	U.S.
1972	The Hindu C.C., Argentina	U.S.
1974	Campo de Golf, Dominican Rep.	U.S.
1976	Vilamoura G.C., Portugal	U.S.
1978	Pacific Harbour G.&C.C.	Australia
1980	Pinehurst, U.S.	U.S.
1982	Geneva G.C., Switzerland	U.S.
1984	Royal Hong Kong G.C., Hong Kong	U.S.
1986	Lagunita C.C., Venezuela	Spain
1988	Drottningholm G.C., Sweden	U.S.
1990	Russley G.C., New Zealand	U.S.
1992	Marine Drive G.C., Canada	Spain
1994	La Boulie, France	U.S.
1996	St. Elena G.C., Philippines	South Korea

10

TOURNAMENTS OF THE PGA TOUR

AT&T PEBBLE BEACH NATIONAL PRO-AM

Pebble Beach Golf Links
Poppy Hills Golf Club
Spyglass Hill Golf Course
Pebble Beach, CA

Date: January 30 – February 2, 1997

TV: USA/CBS

Tickets: AT&T Pebble Beach National Pro-Am
P.O. Box 869
Monterey, CA 93942

To play: All three courses are open to the public.

About the tournament and courses:

• Pebble Beach is arguably the most famous course outside of Georgia, with two of the most famous par-3s anywhere: the 107-yard 7th, where tournament golfers have been known to use just about any club in their bag depending on wind conditions in an effort to avoid the "Cliffs of Doom;" and the 209-yard 17th, scene of Tom Watson's memorable chip in the 1982 U.S. Open on his way to beating Jack Nicklaus. Ten years earlier, Nicklaus hit the stick on 17 with his drive, leading to victory in the first U.S. Open ever at Pebble Beach.

• Number 17 could very well be the most photographed hole on the circuit. The Pacific Ocean abuts the large, two-tiered green on two sides.

• The field is split among the three courses for the first three days of the tournament, while everyone heads to Pebble for the final round.

• Spyglass Hill has a reputation for being even tougher, and to some players better, than Pebble Beach. Players have to limber up quickly at Spyglass, as the first hole stretches a whopping 600 yards. Between teeing off in the woods and hitting the approach shot to an island green, however, the player does get a break with a wide fairway.

• Poppy Hills, known for tight landing areas and large greens, has replaced Cypress Point as one of the three host courses.

1996 Leaderboard

Tournament canceled due to rain.

Tournament History

Bing Crosby Professional-Amateur

1937	Sam Snead	68
1938	Sam Snead	139
1939	Dutch Harrison	138
1940	Ed Oliver	135
1941	Sam Snead	136
1942	Tie-Lloyd Mangrum	
	Leland Gibson	133
1943-46	No Tournaments 1947	
	Tie-Ed Furgol	
	George Fazio	213
1948	Lloyd Mangrum	205
1949	Ben Hogan	208
1950	Tie-Sam Snead	
	Jack Burke, Jr.	
	Smiley Quick	
	Dave Douglas	214
1951	Byron Nelson	209
1952	Jimmy Demaret	145

The Bing Crosby Professional- Amateur Invitational 1953

Lloyd Mangrum		204
1954	Dutch Harrison	210
1955	Cary Middlecoff	209

Bing Crosby National Professional- Amateur Golf Championship

1956	Cary Middlecoff	202
1957	Jay Heber	217
1958	Billy Casper	277

Bing Crosby National

1959	Art Wall	279
1960	Ken Venturi	286
1961	Bob Rosburg	282
1962	*Doug Ford	286
1963	Billy Casper	285

Bing Crosby National Professional-Amateur

1964	Tony Lema	284
1965	Bruce Crampton	284
1966	Don Massengale	283
1967	Jack Nicklaus	284
1968	*Johnny Pott	285
1969	George Archer	283
1970	Bert Yancey	278
1971	Tom Shaw	278
1972	*Jack Nicklaus	284
1973	*Jack Nicklaus	282
1974	#Johnny Miller	208
1975	Gene Littler	280
1976	Ben Crenshaw	281
1977	Tom Watson	273
1978	*Tom Watson	280
1979	Lon Hinkle	284
1980	George Burns	280
1981	*#John Cook	209
1982	Jim Simons	274
1983	Tom Kite	276
1984	*Hale Irwin	278
1985	Mark O'Meara	283

AT&T Pebble Beach National Pro-Am

1986	#Fuzzy Zoeller	205
1987	Johnny Miller	278
1988	*Steve Jones	280
1989	Mark O'Meara	279
1990	Mark O'Meara	281
1991	Paul Azinger	274
1992	*Mark O'Meara	275
1993	Brett Ogle	276
1994	Johnny Miller	281
1995	Peter Jacobsen	271
1996	Tournament canceled due to rain	

BAY HILL INVITATIONAL
Bay Hill Club
Orlando, FL

Date: March 20-23, 1997

TV: USA/NBC

Tickets: PGA Tournament Office Bay Hill Club and Lodge
9000 Bay Hill Blvd.
Orlando, FL 32819

To play: The three 9 hole courses at the Bay Hill Club are open to the public year-round.

About the tournament and courses:

- Arnold Palmer has owned and operated Bay Hill, and hosted the event since 1976. Palmer remodeled the course in 1981, and his Golf Academy takes up residence here.

- Players get a taste of what's in store right out of the clubhouse. The first hole is a 401-yard par 4 with bunkers along the far side of the dogleg left. The second shot is to a small green surrounded by four traps.

- Bay Hill's finishing hole is usually a test of nerves as well. The 441 yard par-4's wickedness kicks in on the approach shot. Water on the right side and a deep, narrow green sloped, of course, to the water.

- Then a tour rookie, Robert Gamez tamed number 18 in 1990, when he holed his approach from 176 yards for an eagle, and victory.

HOLE	1	2	3	4	5	6	7	8	9	OUT
YARDS	401	218	395	530	365	543	197	424	467	3580
PAR	4	3	4	5	4	5	3	4	4	36

HOLE	10	11	12	13	14	15	16	17	18	IN
YARDS	400	428	570	364	206	425	481	219	441	3534
PAR	4	4	5	4	3	4	5	3	4	36

TOTALS	
YARDS	7114
PAR	772

Tournament History

Florida Citrus Open Invitational

1966	Lionel Herbert	279
1967	Julius Boros	274
1968	Dan Sikes	274
1969	Ken Still	278
1970	Bob Lunn	271
1971	Arnold Palmer	270
1972	Jerry Heard	276
1973	Brian Allin	265

1974	Jerry Heard	273
1975	Lee Trevino	276
1976	*Hale Irwin	270
1977	Gary Koch	274
1978	Mac McLendon	271

Bay Hill Citrus Classic

1979	*Bob Byman	278

Bay Hill Classic

1980	Dave Eichelberger	279
1981	Andy Bean	266
1982	*Tom Kite	278
1983	*Mike Nicolette	283
1984	*Gary Koch	274

Hertz Bay Hill Classic

1985	Fuzzy Zoeller	275
1986	#Dan Forsman	202
1987	Payne Stewart	264
1988	Paul Azinger	271

Bay Hill Invitational

1989	*Tom Kite	278
1990	Robert Gamez	274
1991	#Andrew Magee	203
1992	Fred Couples	269
1993	Ben Crenshaw	280
1994	Loren Roberts	275
1995	Loren Roberts	272
1996	Paul Goydos	275

B.C. OPEN
En-Joie Golf Club
Endicott, NY

Date: September 25-28, 1997

TV: The Golf Channel

Tickets: B.C. Open
P.O. Box 5571 Union Station
Endicott, NY 13763-5571

To play: En-Joie is a public course open from April to December.

About the tournament and course:

- This municipal course, built in the late 1920's, has matured into a shotmaker's delight. The scorecard reads 37-34=71, with five par-3s averaging slightly over 200 yards each.

- The front nine features par-5s of 554, 565, and 553 yards, while three of the last five holes are par-3s.

- The hometown flavor of this stop is evident in that there is no name sponsor—all monies are raised locally, and some of the activities sponsored by the event. On Friday evening, a concert is held on the 18th green. Past entertainers have included Tanya Tucker, The Kingston Trio, and Chuck Mangione.

- On the Monday following the event, caddies get to try out their swings in their own annual Classic.

Tournament History

Broome County Open

1971	*Claude Harmon, Jr.	69

B.C. Open

1972	Bob Payne	136
1973	Hubert Green	266
1974	*Richie Karl	273
1975	Don Iverson	274
1976	Bob Wynn	271
1977	Gil Morgan	270
1978	Tom Kite	267
1979	Howard Twitty	270
1980	Don Pooley	271
1981	Jay Hass	270
1982	Calvin Peete	265
1983	Pat Lindsey	268
1984	Wayne Levi	275
1985	Joey Sindelar	274
1986	Rick Fehr	267
1987	Joey Sindelar	266
1988	Bill Glasson	268
1989	*Mike Hulbert	268
1990	Nolan Henke	268
1991	Fred Couples	269
1992	John Daly	266
1993	Blaine McCallister	271
1994	Mike Sullivan	266
1995	Hal Sutton	269
1996	*#Fred Funk	197

BELL CANADIAN OPEN
Glen Abbey Golf Club Oakville, Ontario, Canada

Date: September 4-7, 1997

TV: ESPN

Tickets: Bell Canadian Open
c/o Royal Canadian Golf Association Golf House
Oakville, Ontario, Canada L6J 4Z3

To play: Glen Abbey is open to the public between late April and early November.

About the tournament and course:

- Having been in existence since 1904, with the exceptions of the war years, the Canadian Open is one of the oldest national championships around.

- Glen Abbey, Jack Nicklaus's first solo try at golf course design, is a public course and the home of the Royal Canadian Golf Association. The long hitters enjoy this course, partly due to the four par-5s which all range between 508 and 529 yards.

- The finishing hole is always a challenge, as the tee shot landing area at the 508-yard par-5 is guarded by nine bunkers, and the narrow green has more bunkers on the left as well as water on the right and in front.

HOLE	1	2	3	4	5	6	7	8	9	OUT
YARDS	435	414	156	417	527	437	197	433	458	3474
PAR	4	4	3	4	5	4	3	4	4	35

HOLE	10	11	12	13	14	15	16	17	18	IN
YARDS	443	452	187	529	426	141	516	436	508	3638
PAR	4	4	3	5	4	3	5	4	5	37

TOTALS	
YARDS	7112
PAR	72

Tournament History

Year	Winner	Score
1904	J.H. Oke	156
1905	George Cumming	148
1906	Charles Murray	170
1907	Percy Barrett	306
1908	Albert Murray	300
1909	Karl Keller	309
1910	Daniel Kenny	303
1911	Charles Murray	314
1912	George Sargent	299
1913	Albert Murray	295
1914	Karl Keller	300
1915-18	No tournament	
1919	J. Douglas Edgar	278
1920	*J. Douglas Edgar	298
1921	W.H. Trovinger	293
1922	Al Watrous	303
1923	C.W. Hackney	295
1924	Leo Diegel	285
1925	Leo Diegel	295
1926	Mac Smith	283
1927	Tommy Armour	288
1928	Leo Diegel	282
1929	Leo Diegel	274
1930	*Tommy Armour	273
1931	*Walter Hagen	292
1932	Harry Cooper	290
1933	Joe Kirkwood	282
1934	Tommy Armour	287
1935	Gene Kunes	280
1936	Lawson Little	271
1937	Harry Cooper	285
1938	*Sam Snead	277
1939	Harold McSpaden	282
1940	*Sam Snead	281
1941	Sam Snead	274
1942	Craig Wood	275
1943-44	No tournament	
1945	Byron Nelson	280
1946	*George Fazio	278
1947	Bobby Locke	268
1948	C.W. Congdon	280
1949	Dutch Harrison	271
1950	Jim Ferrier	271
1951	Jim Ferrier	273
1952	John Palmer	263
1953	Dave Douglas	273
1954	Pat Fletcher	280
1955	Arnold Palmer	265
1956	Doug Sanders	271
1957	George Bayer	271
1958	Wesley Ellis, Jr.	267
1959	Doug Ford	276
1960	Art Wall, Jr.	269
1961	Jacky Cupit	270
1962	Ted Kroll	278
1963	Doug Ford	280
1964	Kel Nagle	277
1965	Gene Littler	273
1966	Don Massengale	280
1967	*Billy Casper	279
1968	Bob Charles	274
1969	*Tommy Aaron	275
1970	Kermit Zarley	279
1971	*Lee Trevino	275
1972	Gay Brewer	275
1973	Tom Weiskopf	278
1974	Bobby Nichols	270
1975	*Tom Weiskopf	274
1976	Jerry Pate	267
1977	Lee Trevino	280
1978	Bruce Lietzke	283
1979	Lee Trevino	281
1980	Bob Gilder	274
1981	Peter Oosterhuis	280
1982	Bruce Lietzke	277
1983	*John Cook	277
1984	Greg Norman	278
1985	Curtis Strange	275
1986	Bob Murphy	280
1987	Curtis Strange	276
1988	Ken Green	275
1989	Steve Jones	271
1990	Wayne Levi	278
1991	Nick Price	273
1992	*Greg Norman	280
1993	David Frost	279
1994	Nick Price	275
1995	Mark O'Meara	274
1996	#Dudley Hart	202

BELLSOUTH CLASSIC

Atlanta Country Club
Marietta, GA

Date: May 8-11, 1997

TV: CBS

Tickets: The BellSouth Classic
380 Interstate North, Suite 160
Atlanta, GA 30339

To play: Atlanta is a private club open to members and their guests.

About the tournament and course:

- The last few years, the 9th and 15th holes have been the toughest in tournament play. The par 4, 421-yard 9th is a dogleg left with a well-placed bunker left of the landing area and a two-tiered green. The 452-yard, par-4 15th is a dogleg right with a creek running the entire right side of the hole and a green guarded in front by two bunkers.

- Big hitters can flourish at Atlanta. For instance, the 499-yard, par-5 finishing hole may look ominous with two large ponds and a dogleg, but this hole is prone to birdies and the occasional eagle.

- In 1995's final round, John Daly almost holed his drive at the 335-yard, par-4 14th.

- In 1995, Mark Calcavecchia came home with a 31, including an eagle on 11 and birdies on four of the last six holes, to win the tournament by two strokes.

HOLE	1	2	3	4	5	6	7	8	9	OUT
YARDS	407	563	188	427	432	190	340	550	421	3518
PAR	4	5	3	4	4	3	4	5	4	36

HOLE	10	11	12	13	14	15	16	17	18	IN
YARDS	457	548	426	156	335	452	206	421	499	3500
PAR	4	5	4	3	4	4	3	4	5	36

TOTALS
YARDS 7018
PAR 72

1996 Leaderborad

1-Paul Stankowski (*)	−8, 280	$234,000
2-Brandel Chamblee	−8, 280	$140,400
t3-Nick Price	−6, 282	$75,400
t3-David Duval	−6, 282	$75,400

Tournament History

Atlanta Classic

1967	Bob Charles	282
1968	Bob Lunn	280
1969	*Bert Yancey	277
1970	Tommy Aaron	275
1971	*Gardner Dickinson	275
1972	Bob Lunn	275
1973	Jack Nicklaus	272
1974	Hosted TPC	
1975	Hale Irwin	271
1976	Hosted U.S. Open	
1977	Hale Irwin	273
1978	Jerry Heard	269
1979	Andy Bean	265
1980	Larry Nelson	270
1981	*Tom Watson	277

Georgia-Pacific Atlanta Golf Classic

1982	*Keith Fergus	273
1983	#*Calvin Peete	206
1984	Tom Kite	269
1985	*Wayne Levi	273
1986	Bob Tway	269
1987	Dave Barr	265
1988	Larry Nelson	268

BellSouth Atlanta Golf Classic

1989	*Scott Simpson	278
1990	Wayne Levi	275
1991	*Corey Pavin	272

BellSouth Classic

1992	Tom Kite	272
1993	Nolan Henke	271
1994	John Daly	274
1995	Mark Calcavecchia	271
1996	*Paul Stankowski	280

BRITISH OPEN CHAMPIONSHIP
Royal Troon Golf Club
Troon, Scotland

Date: July 17-20, 1997

TV: ABC/ESPN

Tickets: Royal and Ancient Golf Club
Championship Department
St. Andrews Fife, Scotland KY16 9JD

To play: Royal Troon is a semi-private club.
Guests may play by providing a letter of introduction from their home course and a handicap certification of less than 20.

About the tournament and course:

- This will be the Open's seventh visit to Troon, the last being in 1989. Greg Norman set the Troon tournament record that year with a final round 64 to tie Mark Calcavecchia and Wayne Grady, forcing a playoff, which Calcavecchia won.

- Bunkers are everywhere at Troon, and usually not visible from the tee. Legend has it there are 365 traps on the course, one for each day of the year. Water is everywhere, also. The first five and the last six holes run along the coastline.

- Troon features both the longest and the shortest holes in the Open's course rotation. The par-5 sixth hole runs 577 yards, while number 8 is only 126 yards.

- The eighth hole is also known as the "Postage Stamp," because the green is so small. Missing the green can not be high on any golfer's list, as small bunkers, mounds, and valleys encircle the area. This was the scene of a heartwarming story in 1973 when 71-year-old Gene Sarazen aced the Postage Stamp in front of thousands of cheering fans.

- During the 1989 Open Championship, all ten of the par-4s played over par. Numbers 9, 10, and 15 all recorded averages of 4.25 and above. The four par-5's, however, all came in under par for the tournament.

- The toughest hole to score on in 1989 was the par-3 17th, with an average of 3.27 strokes.

For past results, see Chapter 5, Major Championships: Men.

BUICK CHALLENGE
Callaway Gardens Resort –
Mountain View Course
Pine Mountain, GA

Date: October 2-5, 1997

TV: ESPN

Tickets: Buick Challenge
P.O. Box 2056
Columbus, GA 31902

To play: Callaway Gardens is a year-round
public resort.

About the tournament and course:

- Formerly the Southern Open Invitational and the Buick Southern Open, the first Buick Challenge was held in 1996.

- Well manicured with plenty of bunkers, the Mountain View course has been home to this tour stop since 1990.

- The 1996 Challenge was shortened to 36 holes due to rain. Michael Bradley sank a 15-foot birdie putt on the first playoff to break a five-way tie at the top.

1996 Leaderboard

1-Michael Bradley*	–10, 134	$180,000
John Maginnes	–10, 134	$66,000
Fred Funk	–10, 134	$66,000
Davis Love III	–10, 134	$66,000
Len Mattiace	–10, 134	$66,000

Tournament History

Green Island Open Invitational

1970	Mason Rudolph

Southern Open Invitational

1971	Johnny Miller	267
1972	*DeWitt Weaver	276
1973	Gary Player	270
1974	Forrest Fezler	271
1975	Hubert Green	264
1976	Mac McClendon	274
1977	Jerry Pate	266
1978	Jerry Pate	269
1979	*Ed Fiori	274
1980	Mike Sullivan	269
1981	*J.C.Snead	271
1982	Bobby Clampett	266
1983	*Ronnie Black	271
1984	Hubert Green	265
1985	Tim Simpson	264
1986	Fred Wadsworth	269
1987	Ken Brown	266
1988	*David Frost	270
1989	Ted Schulz	266

Buick Southern Open

1990	*Kenny Knox	265
1991	David Peoples	276
1992	#Gary Hallberg	206
1993	*John Inman	278
1994	*#Steve Elkington	200
1995	Fred Funk	

Buick Challenge

1996	*#Michael Bradley	134

BUICK CLASSIC
Westchester Country Club-West Course
Rye, NY

Date: June 16-22, 1997

TV: Thursday and Friday – USA Network
Saturday and Sunday – CBS

Tickets: The Buick Classic
P.O. Box 200
Rye, NY 10580

To play: Westchester Country Club is a private club.

About the tournament and course:

- The first Classic had Jack Nicklaus truly "weathering" the storm. After rainouts Friday, Saturday, and Sunday, the final round wasn't played until Wednesday of the following week. Dan Sikes shot an amazing 62 in the second round only to lose to Jack Nicklaus by one stroke.

- Bruce Crampton won the 1970 Classic despite playing without his favorite driver for most of the final round. Jack Nicklaus and Larry Hinson each eagled the 72nd hole, but Crampton held them off by one shot.

- The final round of 1973's Classic was a thriller. Bobby Nichols eagled number 18 to tie Bob Murphy, then birdied the first extra hole to win the first Classic to end in a playoff.

- The finishing hole was the site of another great scorecard mark, this time during 1982's third round. Bob Gilder, leading by four shots coming to the 18th on Saturday, hit driver/3-wood to the uphill green. Not being able to see his second shot, it wasn't until he reached the green himself that Gilder realized he had dropped a double-eagle. Gilder's 261 total remains the all-time tournament record.

- Vijay Singh's second Classic win was a grueling affair. The 1993 and 1995 victor gave away three shots to Doug Martin during the final round, only to birdie the fifth playoff hole for first prize.

- Ernie Els may be the Westchester player of the 1990s. Having only played in the last three Buick Classics, Els finished second in 1994 and tied for fourth the following year before a 13-under par win in 1996. During those three years, Els had only one round over par.

- One of only two regular PGA stops to begin with a par-3, Westchester's West Course also boasts one of the most difficult par 4 holes on tour. The

476 yard 12th requires the player to carry a hill with their tee shot, only to be normally faced with a downhill lie for the second shot. To finish, the small green slopes left to right. This hole had the highest stroke average over par on the tour in both 1992 and 1993, and was rated the third most difficult hole in 1994.

HOLE	1	2	3	4	5	6	7	8	9	OUT
YARDS	192	386	419	422	573	133	333	455	505	3418
PAR	3	4	4	4	5	3	4	4	5	36

HOLE	10	11	12	13	14	15	16	17	18	IN
YARDS	314	444	476	381	154	477	204	376	535	3361
PAR	4	4	4	4	3	4	3	4	5	35

TOTALS
YARDS 6779
PAR 71

Tournament History

Westchester Classic

1967	Jack Nicklaus	272
1968	Julius Boros	272
1969	Frank Beard	275
1970	Bruce Crampton	273
1971	Arnold Palmer	270
1972	Jack Nicklaus	270
1973	*Bobby Nichols	272
1974	Johnny Miller	269
1975	*Gene Littler	271

American Express Westchester Classic

1976	David Graham	272
1977	Andy North	272
1978	Lee Elder	274

Manufacturer's Hanover Westchester Classic

1979	Jack Renner	277
1980	Curtis Strange	273
1981	Ray Floyd	275
1982	Bob Gilder	261
1983	Seve Ballesteros	276
1984	Scott Simpson	269
1985	*Roger Maltbie	275
1986	Bob Tway	272

1987	*J.C.Snead	276
1988	*Seve Ballesteros	276
1989	*Wayne Grady	277

Buick Classic

1990	Hale Irwin	269
1991	Billy Andrade	273
1992	David Frost	268
1993	Vijay Singh	280
1994	Lee Janzen	268
1995	*Vijay Singh	278
1996	Ernie Els	271

BUICK INVITATIONAL OF CALIFORNIA
Torrey Pines Golf Courses
La Jolla, CA

Date: February 6-9, 1997

TV: ESPN/NBC

Tickets: Century Club of San Diego Jack Murphy Stadium 9449 Friars Blvd., Gate P San Diego, CA 92108-1771

To play: The Torrey Pines North and South courses are open to the public year-round.

About the tournament and courses:

- Torrey Pines Golf Courses lie adjacent the Pacific Ocean, where the strong winds come consistently into play.

- The tournament field is split between the North and South course for the first two rounds, then shifts to the South course exclusively for the final two rounds of play.

- The seventh hole on each course usually play tough. On the North course, the uphill 400 yard par 4 combines a dogleg flanked by a canyon and trees, a small green well-guarded by traps. On the South side, the wind is normally a factor on number 7, a 453-yard par 4 dogleg with a hillside green.

- The South course's finishing hole is a par-5, 498 yard test, with the green guarded by a pond in front, and traps to each side. The final round in 1975 is an example of the trickiness of this hole. Bruce Devlin fell from 3 shots back to 30th place after hitting his approach into the pond. Jack Nicklaus eagled this hole during the final round in 1982 on his way to a course record 8-under, 64.Johnny Miller, leading by seven shots going into the last 18 holes, dropped his needed par for victory.

- Many fans will remember this stop as the Andy Williams, whose name the tournament bore from 1968-88.

South Course

HOLE	1	2	3	4	5	6	7	8	9	OUT
YARDS	447	365	173	453	404	535	453	171	536	3537
PAR	4	4	3	4	4	5	4	3	5	36

HOLE	10	11	12	13	14	15	16	17	18	IN
YARDS	373	207	468	535	398	356	203	425	498	3463
PAR	4	3	4	5	4	4	3	4	5	36

TOTALS
YARDS 7000
PAR 72

1996 Leaderborad

1-Davis Love III	−19, 269	$216,000
2-Phil Mickelson	−17, 271	$129,600
t3-Tom Lehman	−16, 272	$54,120
t3-Mark O'Meara	−16, 272	$54,120
t3-Scott Simpson	−16, 272	$54,120
t3-Marco Dawson	−16, 272	$54,120

Tournament History

San Diego Open

1952	Ted Kroll	276
1953	Tommy Bolt	274
1954	#Gene Littler	274

Convair-San Diego Open

1955	Tommy Bolt	274
1956	Bob Rosburg	270

San Diego Open Invitational

1957	Arnold Palmer	271
1958	No Tournament	
1959	Marty Furgol	274
1960	Mike Souchak	269
1961	*Arnold Palmer	271
1962	*Tommy Jacobs	277
1963	Gary Player	270
1964	Art Wall	274
1965	*Wes Ellis	267
1966	Billy Casper	268
1967	Bob Goalby	269

Andy Williams-San Diego Open Invitational

1968	Tom Weiskopf	273
1969	Jack Nicklaus	284
1970	*Pete Brown	275
1971	George Archer	273
1972	Paul Harney	275
1973	Bob Dickson	278
1974	Bobby Nichols	275
1975	*J.C.Snead	279
1976	J.C.Snead	272
1977	Tom Watson	269
1978	Jay Hass	278
1979	Fuzzy Zoeller	282
1980	*Tom Watson	275

Wickes/Andy Williams San Diego Open

1981	*Bruce Lietzke	278
1982	Johnny Miller	270

Isuzu/Andy Williams San Diego Open

1983	Gary Hallberg	271
1984	*Gary Koch	272
1985	*Woody Blackburn	269

Shearson Lehman Brothers Andy Williams Open

1986	*#Bob Tway	204
1987	George Burns	266

Shearson Lehman Hutton Andy Williams Open

1988	Steve Pate	269

Shearson Lehman Hutton Open

| 1989 | Greg Twiggs | 271 |
| 1990 | Dan Forsman | 275 |

Shearson Lehman Brothers Open

| 1991 | Jay Don Blake | 268 |

Buick Invitational of California

1992	#Steve Pate	200
1993	Phil Mickelson	278
1994	Craig Stadler	268
1995	Peter Jacobsen	269
1996	Davis Love III	269

CANON GREATER HARTFORD OPEN

TPC at River Highlands
Cromwell, CT

Date: July 24-27, 1997

TV: ESPN/CBS

Tickets: Canon Greater Hartford Open
One Financial Plaza Second Floor
Hartford, CT 06103-2601

To play: TPC at River Highlands is a private club open to members and their guests.

About the tournament and course:

- This event carried singer Sammy Davis, Jr.'s name for almost two decades before changing name sponsors in 1989.

- Adjacent holes 16 and 17 both require shots over a lake. The tee shot at the par-3, 171-yard 16th must carry the water to a green flanked by four bunkers. Number 17 is a 420-yard affair with a dogleg right. The second shot is also over water, to an unguarded, yet small green.

- Nearly one hundred bunkers dot the landscape at River Highlands. The 574-yard 6th hole, for instance, has over a dozen traps alone, only one greenside.

1996 Leaderborad

1-D.A. Weibring	−10, 270	$270,000
2-Tom Kite	−6, 274	$162,000
t3-Dicky Pride	−5, 275	$78,000
t3-Mark Calcavecchia	−5, 275	$78,000
t3-Fuzzy Zoeller	−5, 275	$78,000

Tournament History

Insurance City Open

1952	Ted Kroll	273
1953	Bob Toski	269
1954	*Tommy Bolt	271
1955	Sam Snead	269
1956	*Arnold Palmer	274
1957	Gardner Dickinson	272
1958	Jack Burke, Jr.	268
1959	Gene Littler	272
1960	*Arnold Palmer	270
1961	*Billy Maxwell	271
1962	*Bob Goalby	271
1963	Billy Casper	271
1964	Ken Venturi	273
1965	*Billy Casper	274
1966	Art Wall	266

Greater Hartford Open Invitational

1967	Charlie Sifford	272
1968	Billy Casper	268
1969	*Bob Lunn	268
1970	Bob Murphy	267
1971	*George Archer	268
1972	*Lee Trevino	269

Sammy Davis Jr. Greater Hartford Open

1973	Billy Casper	264
1974	Dave Stockton	268
1975	*Don Bies	267
1976	Rik Massengale	266
1977	Bill Kratzert	265
1978	Rod Funseth	264
1979	Jerry McGee	267
1980	*Howard Twitty	266
1981	Hubert Green	264
1982	Tim Norris	259
1983	Curtis Strange	268

1984	Peter Jacobsen	269
1985	*Phil Blackmar	271

Canon Sammy Davis Jr. Greater Hartford Open

1986	*Mac O'Grady	269
1987	Paul Azinger	269
1988	*Mark Brooks	269

Canon Greater Hartford Open

1989	Paul Azinger	267
1990	Wayne Levi	267
1991	*Billy Ray Brown	271
1992	Lanny Wadkins	274
1993	Nick Price	271
1994	David Frost	268
1995	Greg Norman	267
1996	D.A. Weibring	270

———

DEPOSIT GUARANTY GOLF CLASSIC

Annandale Golf Club
Madison, MS

Date: July 17-20, 1997

TV: The Golf Channel

Tickets: Deposit Guaranty Golf Classic
P.O. Box 1939
Madison, MS 39130

To play: Annandale is a private club.

About the tournament and course:

- Held the same weekend as the British Open, this event allows the lesser known players to excel.

- Water comes into play on eight holes at Annandale, including three of the four finishing holes.

- Annandale is yet another Jack Nicklaus design, and has been home to the Deposit Guaranty Classic since the event received full PGA status in 1994.

1996 Leaderborad

1-Willie Wood	−20, 268	$180,000
2-Kirk Triplett	−19, 269	$108,000

t3-Scott Hoch	−17, 271	$58,000
t3-Greg Kraft	−17, 271	$58,000

Tournament History

Magnolia State Classic

1968	*B.R. McLendon	269
1969	Larry Mowry	272
1970	Chris Blocker	271
1971	Roy Pace	270
1972	Mike Morey	269
1973	Dwight Nevil	268
1974	#Dwight Nevil	133
1975	Bob Wynn	270
1976	Dennis Meyer	271
1977	Mike McCullough	269
1978	Craig Stadler	278
1979	Bobby Walzel	272
1980	#*Roger Maltbie	65
1981	*Tom Jones	268
1982	Payne Stewart	270
1983	#Russ Cochran	203
1984	#*Lance Ten Broeck	201
1985	#*Jim Gallagher, Jr.	131

Deposit Guaranty Classic

1986	Dan Halldorson	263
1987	David Ogrin	267
1988	Frank Conner	267
1989	#*Jim Booros	199
1990	Gene Sauers	268
1991	*Larry Silveira	266
1992	Richard Zokol	267
1993	Greg Kraft	267
1994	#*Brian Henninger	135
1995	Ed Dougherty	272
1996	Willie Wood	268

———

DORAL-RYDER OPEN

Doral Resort and Country Club-
Blue Course
Miami, FL

Date: March 6-9, 1997

TV: Thursday and Friday – USA Network
Saturday and Sunday – CBS

Tickets: Doral-Ryder Open
P.O. Box 522927
Miami, FL 33152

To play: The Doral Resort and Country Club boasts 6 golf courses, all year round facilities open to the public.

About the tournament and course:

- Nicknamed the Blue Monster, Doral's Blue Course is almost 7,000 yards, with 10 man made lakes and more than 100 traps.

- Winds from the Atlantic Ocean come into play consistently

- The 18th hole is the toughest on the course, and Ray Floyd, the only player to win this tournament three times, calls it the most difficult par 4 "in the world". The 425-yard finishing hole has a dogleg left with water running the entire left side of the hole and wind that usually makes the hole run longer.

- The Blue Monster favors a long hitter, but one who can control their shots to avoid the penalties. One example is Jack Nicklaus, a two-time winner who also has five second place finishes to his credit.

HOLE	1	2	3	4	5	6	7	8	9	OUT
YARDS	514	355	398	237	371	427	415	528	163	3408
PAR	5	4	4	3	4	4	4	5	3	36

HOLE	10	11	12	13	14	15	16	17	18	IN
YARDS	563	348	591	246	418	174	360	406	425	3531
PAR	5	4	5	3	4	3	4	4	4	36

TOTALS
YARDS 6939
PAR 72

1996 Leaderborad

1-Greg Norman	–19, 269	$324,000
t2-Vijay Singh	–17, 271	$158,400
t2-Michael Bradley	–17, 271	$158,400

Tournament History

Doral CC Open Invitational

1962	Billy Casper	283
1963	Dan Sikes	283
1964	Billy Casper	277
1965	Doug Sanders	274
1966	Phil Rodgers	278
1967	Doug Sanders	275
1968	Gardner Dickinson	275
1969	Tom Shaw	276

Doral-Eastern Open Invitational

1970	Mike Hill	279
1971	J.C.Snead	275
1972	Jack Nicklaus	276
1973	Lee Trevino	276
1974	Brian Allin	272
1975	Jack Nicklaus	276
1976	Hubert Green	270
1977	Andy Bean	277
1978	Tom Weiskopf	272
1979	Mark McCumber	279
1980	*Ray Floyd	279
1981	Ray Floyd	273
1982	Andy Bean	278
1983	Gary Koch	271
1984	Tom Kite	272
1985	Mark McCumber	284
1986	*Andy Bean	276

Doral-Ryder Open

1987	Lanny Wadkins	277
1988	Ben Crenshaw	274
1989	Bill Glasson	275
1990	*Greg Norman	273
1991	*Rocco Mediate	276
1992	Ray Floyd	271
1993	Greg Norman	265
1994	John Huston	274
1995	Nick Faldo	272
1996	Greg Norman	269

FEDEX ST. JUDE CLASSIC

TPC at Southwind
Memphis, TN

Date: June 26-29, 1997

TV: CBS

Tickets: FedEx St. Jude Classic
3325 Club at Southwind
Memphis, TN 38125

To play: TPC at Southwind is a private course open to members and guests only.

About the tournament and course:

- Starting out as the Memphis Classic in 1958, this tournament was host to the greatest round in PGA history—Al Geiberger's famous 59 in 1977.

- The 1996 event was also a record breaker. John Cook's blistering 263, a 26-under par performance, crushed the previous all-time tournament mark by five shots.

- TPC at Southwind has been home to the St. Jude since 1989. This Ron Pritchard, Fuzzy Zoeller, Hubert Green design features greens that are either quite large or quite small, as well as deep rough bordering the fairways.

1996 Leaderborad

1-John Cook	−26, 258	$243,000
2-John Adams	−19, 265	$145,800
3-Kenny Perry	−18, 266	$91,800

Tournament History

Memphis Invitational Open

1958	Billy Maxwell	267
1959	*Don Whitt	272
1960	*Tommy Bolt	273
1961	Cary Middlecoff	266
1962	*Lionel Hebert	267
1963	*Tony Lema	270
1964	Mike Souchak	270
1965	*Jack Nicklaus	271
1966	Bert Yancey	265
1967	Dave Hill	272
1968	Bob Lunn	268
1969	Dave Hill	265

Danny Thomas Memphis Classic

1970	Dave Hill	267
1971	Lee Trevino	268
1972	Lee Trevino	281
1973	Dave Hill	283
1974	Gary Player	273
1975	Gene Littler	270
1976	Gibby Gilbert	273
1977	Al Geiberger	273
1978	*Andy Bean	277
1979	*Gil Morgan	278
1980	Lee Trevino	272
1981	Jerry Pate	274
1982	Ray Floyd	271
1983	Larry Mize	274
1984	Bob Eastwood	280

St. Jude Memphis Classic

1985	*Hal Sutton	279

Federal Express St. Jude Classic

1986	Mike Hulbert	280
1987	Curtis Strange	275
1988	Jodie Mudd	273
1989	John Mahaffey	272
1990	*Tom Kite	269
1991	Fred Couples	269
1992	Jay Hass	263
1993	Nick Price	266
1994	*Dicky Pride	267
1995	Jim Gallagher, Jr.	267
1996	John Cook	258

FREEPORT-MCDERMOTT CLASSIC

English Turn Golf and Country Club
New Orleans, LA

Date: April 3-6, 1997

TV: NBC

Tickets: Freeport-McDermott Classic
110 Veterans Blvd., Suite 170
Metairie, LA 70005

To play: English Turn is a private club open to members and their guests.

About the tournament and course:

- In addition to water hazards on every hole, this 1988 design has one major Jack Nicklaus attribute: players must be able to hit the greens accurately with long irons.

- The toughest hole on the course is the par-4 18th. Water runs the entire left side of this 471 yard finishing hole, and a waste bunker squeezes itself between the water and the left side of the fairway. To the right of the landing area sit five more bunkers, and the green is surrounded by sand, with the exception of the approach. This hole was rated the most difficult on the 1991 PGA Tour.

- The 542-yard, par-5 15th hole is another attention grabber. The green sits on an island lightly to the right at the end of the fairway.

HOLE	1	2	3	4	5	6	7	8	9	OUT
YARDS	398	519	200	349	463	557	445	176	370	3477
PAR	4	5	3	4	4	5	4	3	4	36

HOLE	10	11	12	13	14	15	16	17	18	IN
YARDS	420	550	158	380	469	542	442	207	471	3639
PAR	4	5	4	3	4	4	3	4	5	36

TOTALS
YARDS 7116
PAR 72

1996 Leaderborad

1-Scott McCarron	−13, 275	$216,000
2-Tom Watson	−8, 280	$129,600
3-Tommy Tolles	−7, 281	$81,600

Tournament History

Greater New Orleans Open Invitational

1938	Harry Cooper	285
1939	Henry Picard	284

1940	Jimmy Demaret	286
1941	Henry Picard	276
1942	Lloyd Mangrum	281
1943	No tournament	
1944	Sammy Byrd	285
1945	*Byron Nelson	284
1946	Byron Nelson	277
1947	No tournament	
1948	Bob Hamilton	280
1949-57	No tournament	
1958	*Billy Casper	278
1959	Bill Collins	280
1960	Dow Finsterwald	270
1961	Doug Sanders	272
1962	Bo Wininger	281
1963	Bo Wininger	279
1964	Mason Rudolph	283
1965	Dick Mayer	273
1966	Frank Beard	276
1967	George Knudson	277
1968	George Archer	271
1969	*Larry Hinson	275
1970	*Miller Barber	278
1971	Frank Beard	276
1972	Gary Player	279
1973	*Jack Nicklaus	280
1974	Lee Trevino	267

First NBC New Orleans Open

1975	Billy Casper	271
1976	Larry Ziegler	274
1977	Jim Simons	273
1978	Lon Hinkle	271
1979	Hubert Green	273

Greater New Orleans Open

1980	Tom Watson	273

USF&G New Orleans Open

1981	Tom Watson	270

USF&G Classic

1982	#Scott Hoch	206
1983	Bill Rogers	274
1984	Bob Eastwood	272

1985	#Seve Ballesteros	205
1986	Calvin Peete	269
1987	Ben Crenshaw	268
1988	Chip Beck	262
1989	Tim Simpson	274
1990	David Frost	276
1991	*Ian Woosnam	275

Freeport-McMoran Classic

1992	Chip Beck	276
1993	Mike Standly	281
1994	Ben Crenshaw	273
1995	Davis Love III	274
1996	Scott McCarron	275

———

GREATER MILWAUKEE OPEN

Brown Deer Park Golf Course
Milwaukee, WI

Date: August 28-31, 1997

TV: ABC

Tickets: Greater Milwaukee Open
4000 W. Brown Deer Road
Milwaukee, WI 53209

To play: Brown Deer Park Golf Course is open to the public from April to November.

About the tournament and course:

- After 21 years at Tuckaway Country Club, the Greater Milwaukee moved to the recently remodeled, all-public Brown Deer in 1994.

- Not your typical public course, Brown Deer lets golfers know immediately what lies ahead with a pair of par 4s. The 447-yard first is straight, but tree-lined. The 417-yard dogleg left second hole is considered the toughest on the course. More mature trees line the fairway, and bunkers guard the approach to the green.

- After making the turn, number ten is no picnic. A good tee shot must split the trees along each side

of the fairway. A dogleg right, the hole demands a second shot through more trees to a green with bunkers on either side.

1996 Leaderborad

1-Loren Roberts (*)	-19, 265	$216,000
2-Jerry Kelly	-19, 265	$129,600
t3-Andrew Magee	-18, 266	$57,600
t3-Steve Stricker	-18, 266	$57,600
t3-Nolan Henke	-18, 266	$57,600
t3-Jesper Parnevik	-18, 266	$57,600

Tournament History

Greater Milwaukee Open

1968	Dave Stockton	275
1969	Ken Still	277
1970	Deane Beman	276
1971	Dave Eichelberger	270
1972	Jim Colbert	271
1973	Dave Stockton	276
1974	Ed Sneed	276
1975	Art Wall	271
1976	Dave Hill	270
1977	Dave Eichelberger	278
1978	*Lee Elder	275
1979	Calvin Peete	269
1980	Bill Kratzert	266
1981	Jay Haas	274
1982	Calvin Peete	274
1983	*Morris Hatalsky	275
1984	Mark O'Meara	272
1985	Jim Thorpe	274
1986	*Corey Pavin	272
1987	Gary Hallberg	269
1988	Ken Green	268
1989	Greg Norman	269
1990	*Jim Gallagher, Jr.	271
1991	Mark Brooks	270
1992	Richard Zokol	269
1993	Billy Mayfair	270
1994	Mike Springer	268
1995	Scott Hoch	269
1996	Loren Roberts	265

GTE BYRON NELSON CLASSIC

**TPC at Las Colinas and
Cottonwood Valley Golf Course
Irving, TX**

Date: May 15-18, 1997

TV: USA/ABC

Tickets: GTE Byron Nelson Classic
c/o Salesmanship Club of Dallas
350 Union Station 400 South Houston St.
Dallas, TX 75202-4811

To play: The TPC at Las Colinas is open to the
public year-round.

About the tournament and the courses:

- The Byron Nelson Classic is the only tournament named for a player, having changed from the Dallas Open in 1968.

- The TPC at Las Colinas has been home to the Nelson since 1986. Designer Jay Morrish, with consulting help from Nelson himself, as well as Ben Crenshaw, accounted for the southerly Texas winds by approximately one third of the holes each heading downwind, upwind, and crosswind.

- The 409-yard, par-4 14th is generally one of the toughest holes. The tee shot is into the wind onto a mounded fairway, and the second shot is over water to a small green.

TPC at Las Colinas

HOLE	1	2	3	4	5	6	7	8	9	OUT
YARDS	385	176	490	425	176	396	533	457	439	3477
PAR	4	3	4	4	3	4	5	4	4	35

HOLE	10	11	12	13	14	15	16	17	18	IN
YARDS	447	347	426	183	409	445	554	196	415	3422
PAR	4	4	4	3	4	4	5	3	4	35

TOTALS
YARDS 6899
PAR 70

1996 Leaderborad

1-Phil Mickelson	−15, 265	$270,000
2-Craig Parry	−13, 267	$162,000
3-David Duval	−12, 268	$102,000

Tournament History

Dallas Open

1944	Byron Nelson	276
1945	Sam Snead	276
1946	Ben Hogan	284
1947-55	No tournaments	
1956	Don January	268
1956a	*Peter Thomson	267
1957	Sam Snead	264
1958	*Sam Snead	272
1959	Julius Boros	274
1960	*Johnny Pott	275
1961	Earl Stewart, Jr.	278
1962	Billy Maxwell	277
1963	No tournament	
1964	Charles Coody	271
1965	No tournament	
1966	Roberto DeVicenzo	276
1967	Bert Yancey	274

Byron Nelson Golf Classic

1968	Miller Barber	270
1969	Bruce Devlin	277
1970	*Jack Nicklaus	274
1971	Jack Nicklaus	274
1972	*Chi Rodriguez	273
1973	*Lanny Wadkins	277
1974	Brian Allin	269
1975	Tom Watson	269
1976	Mark Hayes	273
1977	Ray Floyd	276
1978	Tom Watson	272
1979	*Tom Watson	275
1980	Tom Watson	274
1981	*Bruce Lietzke	281
1982	Bob Gilder	266
1983	Ben Crenshaw	273
1984	Craig Stadler	276

1985	*Bob Eastwood	272
1986	Andy Bean	269
1987	*Fred Couples	266

GTE Byron Nelson Golf Classic

1988	*Bruce Lietzke	271
1989	*Jodie Mudd	265
1990	#Payne Stewart	202
1991	Nick Price	270
1992	#*Billy Ray Brown	199
1993	Scott Simpson	270
1994	#*Neal Lancaster	132
1995	Ernie Els	263
1996	Phil Mickelson	265

HONDA CLASSIC
TPC at Heron Bay
Ponte Verde, FL

Date: March 13-16, 1997

TV: USA/NBC

Tickets: Honda Classic
2608 Country Club Way
Fort Lauderdale, FL 33332

To play: TPC Heron Bay is a year-round public course.

About the tournament and course:

• The Honda Classic moved to the Mark McCumber-designed TPC at Heron Bay for the 1996 tournament, appropriately won by Tim Herron.

• The course boasts over 100 bunkers and water running along just about every hole.

• This tournament carried comedian Jackie Gleason's name for most of the 1970s

1996 Leaderborad

| 1-Tim Herron | −17, 271 | $234,000 |
| 2-Mark McCumber | −13, 275 | $140,400 |

t3-Nick Price	−12, 276	$67,600
t3-Payne Stewart	−12, 276	$67,600
t3-Lee Rinker	−12, 276	$67,600

Tournament History

Jackie Gleason's Inverrary Classic

| 1972 | Tom Weiskopf | 278 |

Jackie Gleason's Inverrary National Airlines Classic

| 1973 | Lee Trevino | 279 |

Jackie Gleason's Inverrary Classic

1974	Leonard Thompson	278
1975	Bob Murphy	273
1976	Hosted Tournament Players Championship	
1977	Jack Nicklaus	275
1978	Jack Nicklaus	276
1979	Larry Nelson	274
1980	Johnny Miller	274

American Motors Inverrary Classic

| 1981 | Tom Kite | 274 |

Honda Inverrary Classic

| 1982 | Hale Irwin | 269 |
| 1983 | Johnny Miller | 278 |

Honda Classic

1984	*Bruce Lietzke	280
1985	*Curtis Strange	275
1986	Kenny Knox	287
1987	Mark Calcavecchia	279
1988	Joey Sindelar	276
1989	Blaine McCallister	266
1990	John Huston	282
1991	Steve Pate	279
1992	*Corey Pavin	273
1993	*#Fred Couples	207
1994	Nick Price	276
1995	Mark O'Meara	275
1996	Tim Herron	271

KEMPER OPEN

TPC at Avenel
Potomac, MD

Date: June 5-8, 1997

TV: CBS

Tickets: Kemper Open
10000 Oaklyn Dr.
Potomac, MD 20854

To play: TPC at Avenel is a private club open to members and their guests.

About the tournament and course:

- Although the Kemper boasts the longest run with the same title sponsor, it has moved up and down the east coast a few times. Massachusetts to North Carolina to Congressional, outside of Washington, D.C. Since 1987, the Kemper has been hosted by the TPC at Avenel, also in suburban D.C.

- Like so many other PGA stops, Avenel's toughest hole is number 18. This 444-yard par-4 dogs to the right with a bunker just to the left of the turn. More bunkers await the approach shot, to the right and rear of the green.

- Billy Andrade's course record 263 in 1991 was a thing of beauty, as only one other Kemper winner carded a sub-270 tournament, that being a 268 by Tom Byrum in 1989.

1996 Leaderborad

1-Steve Stricker	−14, 270	$270,000
t2-Grant Waite	−11, 273	$99,000
t2-Brad Faxon	−11, 273	$99,000
t2-Mark O'Meara	−11, 273	$99,000
t2-Scott Hoch	−11, 273	$99,000

Tournament History

Kemper Open

1968	Arnold Palmer	276
1969	Dale Douglass	274
1970	Dick Lotz	278
1971	*Tom Weiskopf	277
1972	Doug Sanders	275
1973	Tom Weiskopf	271
1974	*Bob Menne	270
1975	Ray Floyd	278
1976	Joe Inman	277
1977	Tom Weiskopf	277
1978	Andy Bean	273
1979	Jerry McGee	272
1980	John Mahaffey	275
1981	Craig Stadler	270
1982	Craig Stadler	275
1983	*Fred Couples	287
1984	Greg Norman	280
1985	Bill Glasson	278
1986	*Greg Norman	277
1987	Tom Kite	270
1988	*Morris Hatalsky	274
1989	Tom Byrum	268
1990	Gil Morgan	274
1991	*Billy Andrade	263
1992	Bill Glasson	276
1993	Grant Waite	275
1994	Mark Brooks	270
1995	*Lee Janzen	272
1996	Steve Stricker	270

KMART GREATER GREENSBORO OPEN

Forest Oaks Country Club
Greensboro, NC

Date: April 24-27, 1997

TV: CBS

Tickets: Kmart Greater Greensboro Open
c/o Greensboro Jaycees
401 N. Greene St.
Greensboro, NC 27401

To play: Forest Oaks is a private club open to members and their guests.

About the tournament and course:

- Sam Snead won eight of the first 25 Greater Greensboro Open tournaments.

- The third hole is not only quite a test for the Greater Greensboro competitors, it is also one of the toughest holes on the PGA Tour. The 409-yard par-4 has a good sized pond that stretches down the right side of the fairway beginning at the tee shot landing area, then bisects the fairway near the approach to the green. And what a green it is: two-tiers, with bunkers left, right and back.

- Large is the operative word at Forest Oaks. Large fairway bunkers, large greenside bunkers, and large greens with plenty of movement can easily make for a large scorecard.

HOLE	1	2	3	4	5	6	7	8	9	OUT
YARDS	411	523	409	179	420	393	379	221	584	3519
PAR	4	5	4	3	4	4	4	3	5	36

HOLE	10	11	12	13	14	15	16	17	18	IN
YARDS	400	392	185	521	439	559	414	198	435	3543
PAR	4	4	3	5	4	5	4	3	4	36

TOTALS
YARDS 7062
PAR 72

1996 Leaderborad

1-Mark O'Meara	−14, 274	$324,000
2-Duffy Waldorf	−12, 276	$194,400
3-Steve Stricker	−10, 278	$122,400

Tournament History

Greater Greensboro Open

1938	Sam Snead	272
1939	Ralph Guldahl	280
1940	Ben Hogan	270
1941	Byron Nelson	276
1942	Sam Byrd	279
1943-44	No tournaments	
1945	Byron Nelson	271
1946	Sam Snead	270
1947	Vic Ghezzi	286
1948	Lloyd Mangrum	278
1949	*Sam Snead	276
1950	Sam Snead	269
1951	Art Doering	279
1952	Dave Douglas	277
1953	*Earl Stewart	275
1954	*Doug Ford	283
1955	Sam Snead	273
1956	*Sam Snead	279
1957	Stan Leonard	276
1958	Bob Goalby	275
1959	Dow Finsterwald	278
1960	Sam Snead	270
1961	Mike Souchak	276
1962	Billy Casper	275
1963	Doug Sanders	270
1964	*Julius Boros	277
1965	Sam Snead	273
1966	*Doug Sanders	276
1967	George Archer	267
1968	Billy Casper	267
1969	*Gene Littler	274
1970	Gary Player	271
1971	*Bud Allin	275
1972	*George Archer	272
1973	Chi Chi Rodriguez	267
1974	Bob Charles	270
1975	Tom Weiskopf	275
1976	Al Geiberger	268
1977	Danny Edwards	276
1978	Seve Ballesteros	282
1979	Ray Floyd	282
1980	Craig Stadler	275
1981	*Larry Nelson	281
1982	Danny Edwards	285
1983	Lanny Wadkins	275
1984	Andy Bean	280
1985	Joey Sindelar	285
1986	Sandy Lyle	275
1987	Scott Simpson	282

Kmart Greater Greensboro Open

1988	*Sandy Lyle	271
1989	Ken Green	271
1990	Steve Elkington	282

1991	*Mark Brooks	275
1992	Davis Love III	272
1993	*Rocco Mediate	281
1994	Mike Springer	275
1995	Jim Gallagher, Jr.	274
1996	Mark O'Meara	274

LA CANTERA TEXAS OPEN
La Cantera Golf Club
San Antonio, TX

Date: September 18-21, 1997

TV: The Golf Channel

Tickets: La Cantera Texas Open
San Antonio Golf Association
70 N.E. Loop 410, Ste. 370
San Antonio, TX 78216

To play: La Cantera is a year-round public course.

About the tournament and course:

- For the most part, the Texas Open has been a mainstay on the tour since 1922. Rotated among several courses until La Cantera's 1996 opening, it was at Brackenridge Park Golf Course that Mike Souchak made history in 1957. There, Souchak shot a PGA best 27-under par 257, a record that stands to this day.

- Jay Haas put on a show in 1993 with birdies on 3 of the last four regulation holes, as well as another on the first playoff hole for victory.

- The new design by Tom Weiskopf and Jay Morrish starts with a bang. The 665-yard par-5 first hole features a tree-lined fairway, four bunkers on the approach to the green, and a large pond to the rear of the green, but the tee box is over 100 feet above the rest of the hole.

- Weiskopf and Morrish used scores of trees, almost 70 bunkers, and over 7100 yards to create this challenging course.

Only one golfer has scored consecutive holes-in-one in tournament play: Bob Hudson, who aced the 11th and 12th holes in the Martini International at Norwich, England, in 1971.

1996 Leaderborad

1-David Ogrin	–13, 275	$216,000
2-Jay Haas	–12, 276	$129,600
3-Tiger Woods	–11, 277	$81,600
t4-Greg Kraft	–10, 278	$52,800
t4-Len Mattiace	–10, 278	$52,800

Tournament History

Texas Open

1922	Bob MacDonald	281
1923	Walter Hagen	279
1924	Joe Kirkwood	279
1925	Joe Turnesa	284
1926	Mac Smith	288
1927	Bobby Cruikshank	272
1928	Bill Mehlhorn	297
1929	Bill Mehlhorn	277
1930	Denny Shute	277
1931	Abe Espinosa	281
1932	Clarence Clark	287
1933	No tournament	
1934	Wiffy Cox	283
1935-38	No tournament	
1939	Dutch Harrison	271
1940	Byron Nelson	271
1941	Lawson Little	273
1942	*Chick Harbert	272
1943	No tournament	
1944	Johnny Revolta	273
1945	Sam Byrd	268
1946	Ben Hogan	264
1947	Ed Oliver	265
1948	Sam Snead	264
1949	Dave Douglas	268
1950	Sam Snead	265
1951	*Dutch Harrison	265
1952	Jack Burke, Jr.	260
1953	Tony Holguin	264

1954	Chandler Harper	259
1955	Mike Souchak	257
1956	Gene Littler	276
1957	Jay Hebert	271
1958	Bill Johnston	274
1959	Wes Ellis	276
1960	Arnold Palmer	276
1961	Arnold Palmer	270
1962	Arnold Palmer	273
1963	Phil Rodgers	268
1964	Bruce Crampton	273
1965	Frank Beard	270
1966	Harold Henning	272
1967	Chi Rodriguez	277
1968	No tournament	
1969	*Deane Beman	274

San Antonio Texas Open

1970	Ron Cerrudo	273
1971	No tournament	
1972	Mike Hill	273
1973	Ben Crenshaw	270
1974	Terry Diehl	269
1975	*Don January	275
1976	*Butch Baird	273
1977	Hale Irwin	266
1978	Ron Streck	265
1979	Lou Graham	268
1980	Lee Trevino	265

Texas Open

1981	*Bill Rogers	266
1982	Jay Hass	262
1983	Jim Colbert	261
1984	Calvin Peete	266
1985	*John Mahaffey	268

Vantage Championship

| 1986 | #Ben Crenshaw | 196 |

Nabisco Championships of Golf

| 1987 | Tom Watson | 268 |

Texas Open Presented by Nabisco

| 1988 | Corey Pavin | 259 |
| 1989 | Donnie Hammond | 258 |

H-E-B Texas Open

1990	Mark O'Meara	261
1991	Blaine McCallister	269
1992	*Nick Price	263
1993	Jay Hass	269
1994	Bob Estes	265
1995	Duffy Waldorf	268

La Cantera Texas Open

| 1996 | David Ogrin | 275 |

LAS VEGAS INVITATIONAL
TPC at Summerlin
Las Vegas, NV

Date: October 22-26, 1997

TV: ESPN

Tickets: Las Vegas Invitational
801 S. Rancho Dr.
Las Vegas, NV 89106

To play: TPC at Summerlin is a private club open to members and their guests.

About the tournament and course:

- The Las Vegas is a 90 hole pro-am event held on various courses with the TPC at Summerlin hosting the final round.

- The site of a senior tour stop as well, the TPC at Summerlin plays more than 7200 yards at a par of 72. Six traps flanking the green make the 239-yard par-3 eighth hole the course's most difficult.

- One of the local courses in the pro-am rotation is Sunrise Golf Club, where Chip Beck shot a 59 in 1991's third round.

1996 Leaderborad

1-Tiger Woods (*)	−27, 332	$297,000
2-Davis Love III	−27, 332	$178,000
t3-Kelly Gibson	−26, 333	$95,700
t3-Mark Calcavecchia	−26, 333	$95,700

Tournament History

Panasonic Las Vegas Pro-Celebrity Classic

| 1983 | Fuzzy Zoeller | 340 |

Panasonic Las Vegas Invitational

1984	Denis Watson	341
1985	Curtis Strange	338
1986	Greg Norman	333
1987	#Paul Azinger	271
1988	#Gary Koch	274

Las Vegas Invitational

1989	*Scott Hoch	336
1990	*Bob Tway	334
1991	*Andrew Magee	329
1992	John Cook	334
1993	John Inman	331
1994	Bruce Lietzke	332
1995	Bruce Lietzke	346
1996	*Tiger Woods	332

LINCOLN-MERCURY KAPALUA INTERNATIONAL
**Kapalua Resort Courses
Lahaina, HI**

Date: November 6-9, 1997

TV: ESPN/ABC

Tickets: The Lincoln Mercury
Kapalua International
Kapalua Land Company, Ltd.
500 Bay Dr. Lahaina, Maui, HI 96761

To play: Kapalua's Bay and Plantation Courses are public courses open year-round.

About the tournament and course:

- An unofficial event, the Kapalua is a pro-am boasting one course with Ben Crenshaw's signature and another with the name Arnold Palmer as designer.

- Trees, trees, trees. One look at the layout of either course reveals the success the designers

had in maintaining as much of the natural attributes of the land.

- The final two rounds are played exclusively at Plantation, a 7200-plus yard with a par of 73. The toughest hole generally is number 17, a 486-yard par-4 which features a 150-foot downhill elevation change.

Tournament History

Kapalua International

| 1983 | Greg Norman | 268 |
| 1984 | Sandy Lyle | 266 |

Isuzu Kapalua International

1985	Mark O'Meara	275
1986	Andy Bean	278
1987	Andy Bean	267
1988	Bob Gilder	266
1989	*Peter Jacobsen	270
1990	David Peoples	264

Ping Kapalua International

| 1991 | *Mike Hulbert | 276 |

Lincoln-Mercury Kapalua International

1992	Davis Love III	275
1993	Fred Couples	274
1994	Fred Couples	279
1995	Jim Furyk	271
1996	Paul Stankowski	269

MASTERCARD COLONIAL
**Colonial Country Club
Fort Worth, TX**

Date: May 22-25, 1997

TV: USA/CBS

Tickets: The MasterCard Colonial
3735 Country Club Circle
Fort Worth, TX 76109

To play: Colonial is a private club open to members and their guests.

About the tournament and course:

- Colonial is Ben Hogan's home course, as evidenced by his 5 wins in the first 12 tournaments, including the first two Colonials. The clubhouse is home to Hogans' trophy room.

- The toughest part of the course each year may very well be the "horrible horseshoe," holes 3, 4, and 5. First is a 476-yard par 4, a dogleg left with bunkers just to the left of the landing area. Next is a 246-yard, par-3 with a small green. And number 5 is another long par 4, 459 yards with trees along the right of the fairway and a green almost surrounded by bunkers.

- Only a par-70, Colonial favors the long-iron player who can control the urge to go for broke.

HOLE	1	2	3	4	5	6	7	8	9	OUT
YARDS	565	400	476	246	459	393	420	192	391	3542
PAR	5	4	4	3	4	4	4	3	4	35

HOLE	10	11	12	13	14	15	16	17	18	IN
YARDS	404	599	433	178	426	430	188	383	427	3468
PAR	4	5	4	3	4	4	3	4	4	35

TOTALS
YARDS 7010
PAR 70

1996 Leaderborad

1-Corey Pavin	–8, 272	$270,000
2-Jeff Sluman	–6, 274	$162,000
3-Rocco Mediate	–5, 275	$102,000

Tournament History

Colonial National Invitational Tournament

1946	Ben Hogan	279
1947	Ben Hogan	279
1948	Clayton Heafner	272
1949	No tournament	
1950	Sam Snead	277
1951	Cary Middlecoff	282
1952	Ben Hogan	279

Forged irons are made by stamping red-hot metal bars between a pair of dies. Cast irons are made by pouring molten metal into a mold and allowing it to harden.

1953	Ben Hogan	282
1954	Johnny Palmer	280
1955	Chandler Harper	276
1956	Mike Souchak	280
1957	Roberto DeVicenzo	284
1958	Tommy Bolt	283
1959	*Ben Hogan	285
1960	Julius Boros	280
1961	Doug Sanders	281
1962	*Arnold Palmer	281
1963	Julius Boros	279
1964	Billy Casper	279
1965	Bruce Crampton	276
1966	Bruce Devlin	280
1967	Dave Stockton	278
1968	Billy Casper	275
1969	Gardner Dickinson	278
1970	Homero Blancas	273
1971	Gene Littler	283
1972	Jerry Heard	275
1973	Tom Weiskopf	276
1974	Rod Curl	276
1975	Hosted TPC	
1976	Lee Trevino	273
1977	Ben Crenshaw	272
1978	Lee Trevino	268
1979	Al Geiberger	274
1980	Bruce Lietzke	271
1981	Fuzzy Zoeller	274
1982	Jack Nicklaus	273
1983	*Jim Colbert	278
1984	*Peter Jacobsen	270
1985	Corey Pavin	266
1986	*#Dan Pohl	205
1987	Keith Clearwater	266
1988	Lanny Wadkins	270

Southwestern Bell Colonial

1989	Ian Baker-Finch	270

1990	Ben Crenshaw	272
1991	Tom Purtzer	267
1992	*Bruce Lietzke	267
1993	Fulton Allem	264
1994	*Nick Price	266
1995	Tom Lehman	271
1996	Corey Pavin	272

THE MASTERS TOURNAMENT
Augusta National Golf Club
Augusta, GA

Date: April 10-13, 1997

TV: CBS/USA

Tickets: P.O.Box 2086
Augusta, GA 30913

To play: Augusta National is a private club open to members and their guests.

About the tournament and course:

- The picture is etched in every television-watching golfer's mind—the magnolias, azaleas and other flowering plants blooming in mid-April. It's time for The Masters.

- Augusta National was built on the site of an old nursery, hence the beautiful scenery. Each hole has a nickname, describing the variety of landscaping prevalent on that hole. Most fans know of Amen Corner, the 11th, 12th and 13th holes, but how many know the nicknames of each hole?

- Number 11 is "White Dogwood." This 455 yard par-4 leads the prayers at Amen Corner. The approach shot is to a narrow green guarded by water on the left and traps right and back.

- The 12th is called "Golden Bell," and may be the most famous, visually. This 155-yard par 3 requires a flawless tee shot over Rae's Creek to a green bunkered once to the front and twice to the rear. Many a golfer has made the walk over Ben Hogan Bridge lying three after hitting a first shot into the creek.

- Then there's "Azalea," the 465-yard, par-5 13th hole. This dogleg left requires concentration due to the quick turn in the fairway, and the narrow, fast green with bunkers and water.

- The 15th hole, "Firethorn," has seen it's share of great shots. In 1935, Gene Sarazen holed a fairway wood for double-eagle, or albatross as some remember it, on his way to beating Craig Wood in a playoff the next day.

- Jack Nicklaus won his record sixth green jacket in 1986 by dropping a 12-footer for eagle on 15. Nicklaus' final round of 65 edged him past Greg Norman and Tom Kite.

For past results, see Chapter 5, Major Championships: Men.

MCI CLASSIC
Harbour Town Golf Links
Hilton Head, S.C.

Date: April 17-20, 1997

TV: CBS

Tickets: MCI Classic
71 Lighthouse Rd., Suite 414
Hilton Head Island, SC 29928

To play: Sea Pines Resort is a year-round resort open to the public. Harbour Town Golf Links is joined by the Ocean course and Sea Marsh.

About the tournament and course:

- The picturesque finishing hole at Harbour Town is also challenging. Running 478 yards, this par-4 has a waste bunker along the final 80 yards of the left side of the fairway, marshes to be carried on both of the player's first two shots, and a bunker on the long side of a small green. The famous red and white lighthouse sits majestically off to the back right of the final green.

- Designed by Pete Dye and Jack Nicklaus for a 1969 opening, Harbour Town's smallish greens and numerous trees, combined with winds from the Atlantic Ocean, favor the shotmaker.

- Hale Irwin and Davis Love III are the only three-time winners of the Classic and Irwin owns the course record, an 18-under 266 in 1994

HOLE	1	2	3	4	5	6	7	8	9	OUT
YARDS	414	505	411	198	535	419	180	466	337	3465
PAR	4	5	4	3	5	4	3	4	4	36

HOLE	10	11	12	13	14	15	16	17	18	IN
YARDS	436	438	413	378	165	575	376	192	478	3451
PAR	4	4	4	4	3	5	4	3	4	35

TOTALS
YARDS 6916
PAR 71

1996 Leaderborad

1-Loren Roberts	−19, 265	$252,000
2-Mark O'Meara	−16, 268	$151,200
3-Scott Hoch	−14, 270	$95,200

Tournament History

Heritage Classic

1969	Arnold Palmer	283
1970	Bob Goalby	280

Sea Pines Heritage Classic

1971	Hale Irwin	279
1972	Johnny Miller	281
1973	Hale Irwin	272
1974	Johnny Miller	276
1975	Jack Nicklaus	271
1976	Hubert Green	274
1977	Graham Marsh	273
1978	Hubert Green	277
1979	Tom Watson	270
1980	*Doug Tewell	280
1981	Bill Rogers	278
1982	*Tom Watson	280
1983	Fuzzy Zoeller	275

1984	Nick Faldo	270
1985	*Bernhard Langer	273
1986	Fuzzy Zoeller	276

MCI Heritage Classic

1987	Davis Love III	271
1988	Greg Norman	271
1989	Payne Stewart	268
1990	*Payne Stewart	276
1991	Davis Love III	271
1992	Davis Love III	269
1993	David Edwards	273
1994	Hale Irwin	266
1995	*Bob Tway	275
1996	Loren Roberts	265

MEMORIAL TOURNAMENT
Muirfield Village Golf Club
Dublin, OH

Date: May 29 – June 1, 1997

TV: ESPN/ABC

Tickets: The Memorial Tournament
P.O. Box 396
Dublin, OH 43017

To play: Muirfield Village is a private club open to members and their guests.

About the tournament and course:

- If this is Ohio, it must be a Jack Nicklaus design. Designing the course in 1974 along with Desmond Muirhead, Nicklaus created a 7100-yard layout rich in trees, ponds and quick greens.

- Nicklaus has tasted victory twice in the Memorial, the first coming in 1977. His hunger for a second win would not be satisfied until 1984 when during the final round, Jack's tee shot on number 17 ended up under a picnic table. No word on whether he was able to clean and place his ball after the ants swarmed around. Nicklaus eventually beat Andy Bean in a playoff.

- Tom Lehman was a model of consistency in 1994, shooting four 67s for the course record of 268.

- The ten par 4s average over 424 yards each, and the finishing hole is generally regarded as the toughest. The 437-yard dogleg right has a narrow landing area with sand on the right and water on the left. The green has more sand, this time right, left and back.

HOLE	1	2	3	4	5	6	7	8	9	OUT
YARDS	446	452	392	204	531	430	549	189	410	3603
PAR	4	4	4	3	5	4	5	3	4	36

HOLE	10	11	12	13	14	15	16	17	18	IN
YARDS	441	538	156	442	363	490	204	430	437	3501
PAR	4	5	3	4	4	5	3	4	4	36

TOTALS
YARDS 7104
PAR 72

1996 Leaderborad

1-Tom Watson	–6, 274	$324,000
2-David Duval	–4, 276	$194,000
t3-David Frost	–2, 278	$104,000
t3-Mark O'Meara	–2, 278	$104,000

Tournament History

Memorial Tournament

1976	*Roger Maltbie	288
1977	Jack Nicklaus	281
1978	Jim Simons	284
1979	Tom Watson	285
1980	David Graham	280
1981	Keith Fergus	284
1982	Ray Floyd	281
1983	Hale Irwin	281
1984	*Jack Nicklaus	280
1985	Hale Irwin	281
1986	Hal Sutton	271
1987	Don Pooley	272
1988	Curtis Strange	274
1989	Bob Tway	278
1990	#Greg Norman	216
1991	*Kenny Perry	273

1992	*David Edwards	273
1993	Paul Azinger	274
1994	Tom Lehman	268
1995	Greg Norman	269
1996	Tom Watson	274

——————

MERCEDES CHAMPIONSHIPS
La Costa Resort and Spa
Carlsbad, CA

Date: January 9-12, 1997

TV: ESPN/ABC

Tickets: Mercedes Championship
c/o La Costa Resort and Spa
2100 Costa del mar Rd. Carlsbad, CA 92009

To play: The North and South courses are open to resort guests and to the public.

About the tournament and course

- The season opener, only the preceding year's tour winners are invited to the Mercedes.

- Formerly known as the Tournament of Champions, this tour stop has been hosted by La Costa since 1969.

- In 1953, the First Tournament of Champions was held at the Desert Inn in Las Vegas. Tournament winner Al Besselink was paid $10,000, all in silver dollars.

- The North course has 9 water hazards and almost 80 bunkers, while the South side claims 12 water holes and 84 traps.

- The best 18 holes from the two courses are combined to make the tournament track.

- "Golf's longest mile," the four finishing holes run almost 1,800 yards into a two club wind.

1996 Leaderborad

1-Mark O'Meara	–17, 271	$180,000
t2-Scott Hoch	–14, 274	$88,000
t2-Nick Faldo	–14, 274	$88,000

Tournament History

Mony Tournament of Champions

1953	Al Besselink	280
1975	*Al Geiberger	277
1954	Art Wall	278
1976	Don January	277
1955	Gene Littler	280
1977	*Jack Nicklaus	281
1956	Gene Littler	281
1978	Gary Player	281
1957	Gene Littler	285
1979	Tom Watson	275
1958	Stan Leonard	275
1980	Tom Watson	276
1959	Mike Souchak	281
1981	Lee Trevino	273
1960	Jerry Barber	268
1982	Lanny Wadkins	280
1961	Sam Snead	273
1983	Lanny Wadkins	280
1962	Arnold Palmer	276
1984	Tom Watson	274
1963	Jack Nicklaus	273
1985	Tom Kite	275
1964	Jack Nicklaus	279
1986	Calvin Peete	267
1965	Arnold Palmer	277
1987	Mac O'Grady	278
1966	*Arnold Palmer	283
1988	#Steve Pate	202
1967	Frank Beard	278
1989	Steve Jones	279
1968	Don January	276
1969	Gary Player	284

Infiniti Tournament of Champions

1970	Frank Beard	273
1990	Paul Azinger	272
1971	Jack Nicklaus	279
1991	Tom Kite	272
1972	*Bobby Mitchell	280
1992	*Steve Elkington	279
1973	Jack Nicklaus	276
1993	Davis Love III	272
1974	Johnny Miller	280

Mercedes Championships

1994	*Phil Mickelson	276
1995	*Steve Elkington	278
1996	Mark O'Meara	271

___

MICHELOB CHAMPIONSHIP AT KINGSMILL

**Kingsmill Golf Club – River Course
Williamsburg, VA**

Date: October 9-12, 1997

TV: TBD

Tickets: Michelob Championship
328 McLaws Circle
Williamsburg, VA 23185

To play: Kingsmill is a year-round resort.

About the tournament and course:

- Established in 1968 and played at Silverado Country Club in Napa, California until 1980, the tournament then moved to Anheuser-Busch's own Kingsmill resort in Virginia.

- Neighboring James River, from where the River Course gets its name, is not the only water coming into play on the course. Kingsmill Pond borders the fairway on the third hole, just about where the second shots are dropping, then the pond meanders to bisect holes four and five.

- The 413-yard, par-4 eighth hole is usually the toughest. The tee shot heads for a sloped landing area, the approach shot to a bi-level green flanked by bunkers.

- Kingsmill resident Curtis Strange has his own cheering section during this tournament— boaters in the James River nicknamed "Curtis Strange's Navy".

1996 Leaderborad

1-Scott Hoch	−19, 265	$225,000
2-Tom Purtzer	−15, 269	$135,000
t3-Michael Bradley	−12, 272	$65,000
t3-Ted Tryba	−12, 272	$65,000
t3-Fred Funk	−12, 272	$65,000

Tournament History

Kaiser International Open Invitational

1968	Kermit Zarley	273
1969	#Miller Barber	135
1969+	*Jack Nicklaus	273
1970	*Ken Still	278
1971	Billy Casper	269
1972	George Knudson	271
1973	*Ed Sneed	275
1974	Johnny Miller	271
1975	Johnny Miller	272
1976	J.C. Snead	274

Anheuser-Busch Golf Classic

1977	Miller Barber	272
1978	Tom Watson	270
1979	John Fought	277
1980	Ben Crenshaw	272
1981	John Mahaffey	276
1982	#Calvin Peete	203
1983	Calvin Peete	276
1984	Ronnie Black	267
1985	*Mark Wiebe	273
1986	Fuzzy Zoeller	274
1987	Mark McCumber	267
1988	*Tom Sieckmann	270
1989	*Mike Donald	268
1990	Lanny Wadkins	266
1991	*Mike Hulbert	266
1992	David Peoples	270
1993	Jim Gallagher	269
1994	Mark McCumber	267
1995	Ted Tryba	272

Michelob Championship

1996	Scott Hoch	265

MOTOROLA WESTERN OPEN

**Cog Hill Golf and Country Club –
Cog Hill No. 4
Lemont, Il**

Date: July 3-6, 1997

TV: USA/CBS

Tickets: Motorola Western Open
Western Golf Association
One Briar Rd.
Golf, IL 60029

To play: The four courses at Cog Hill are open to the public year-round.

About the tournament and course:

- Having been an annual stop since 1899, the Western Open is the second longest running event on tour.

- Cog Hill No. 4 (Dubsdread) and its nearly 100 bunkers, has been home to the Western since 1991. The green alone at the 192-yard par-3 14th is surrounded by 6 bunkers.

- During the 1994 Western Open, players recorded scoring averages over par on 12 of the 18 holes.

- The 452 yard finishing hole is traditionally the toughest during the event. A narrow landing area guarded by bunkers on either side awaits the tee shot, while the second shot must avoid water to the left and bunkers to the right of the green.

- Since 1930, the Western Open has contributed to the Evans Scholarships, a program formed by 1910 winner Chick Evans and designed to help caddies pay for college.

HOLE	1	2	3	4	5	6	7	8	9	OUT
YARDS	420	177	415	416	525	213	410	378	568	3522
PAR	4	3	4	4	5	3	4	4	5	36

HOLE	10	11	12	13	14	15	16	17	18	IN
YARDS	372	564	209	446	192	519	409	388	452	3551
PAR	4	5	3	4	3	5	4	4	4	36

TOTALS
YARDS 7073
PAR 72

1996 Leaderborad

1-Steve Stricker	−18, 270	$360,000
t2-Billy Andrade	−10, 278	$176,000
t2-Jay Don Blake	−10, 278	$176,000

Tournament History

Western Open

Year	Player	Score
1899	*Willie Smith	156
1900	No tournament	
1901	Laurie Auchterlonie	160
1902	Willie Anderson	299
1903	Alex Smith	318
1904	Willie Anderson	304
1905	Arthur Smith	278
1906	Alex Smith	306
1907	Robert Simpson	307
1908	Willie Anderson	299
1909	Willie Anderson	288
1910	Chick Evans, Jr.	6&5
1911	Robert Simpson	2&1
1912	Mac Smith	299
1913	John McDermott	295
1914	Jim Barnes	293
1915	Tom McNamara	304
1916	Walter Hagen	286
1917	Jim Barnes	283
1918	No tournament	
1919	Jim Barnes	283
1920	Jock Hutchinson	296
1921	Walter Hagen	287
1922	Mike Brady	291
1923	Jock Hutchinson	281
1924	Bill Mehlhorn	293
1925	Mac Smith	281
1926	Walter Hagen	279
1927	Walter Hagen	281
1928	Abe Espinosa	291
1929	Tommy Armour	273
1930	Gene Sarazen	278
1931	Ed Dudley	280
1932	Walter Hagen	287
1933	Mac Smith	282
1934	*Harry Cooper	274
1935	John Revolta	290
1936	Ralph Guldahl	274
1937	*Ralph Guldahl	288
1938	Ralph Guldahl	279
1939	Byron Nelson	281
1940	*Jimmy Demaret	293
1941	Ed Oliver	275
1942	Herman Barron	276
1943-45	No tournament	
1946	Ben Hogan	271
1947	Johnny Palmer	270
1948	*Ben Hogan	281
1949	Sam Snead	268
1950	Sam Snead	282
1951	Marty Furgol	270
1952	Lloyd Mangrum	274
1953	Dutch Harrison	278
1954	*Lloyd Mangrum	277
1955	Cary Middlecoff	272
1956	*Mike Fetchick	284
1957	*Doug Ford	279
1958	Doug Sanders	275
1959	Mike Souchak	272
1960	*Stan Leonard	278
1961	Arnold Palmer	271
1962	Jacky Cupit	281
1963	*Arnold Palmer	280
1964	Chi Rodriguez	268
1965	Billy Casper	270
1966	Billy Casper	283
1967	Jack Nicklaus	274
1968	Jack Nicklaus	273
1969	Billy Casper	276
1970	Hugh Royer	273
1971	Bruce Crampton	279
1972	Jim Jamieson	271
1973	Billy Casper	272
1974	Tom Watson	287
1975	Hale Irwin	283
1976	Al Geiberger	288
1977	Tom Watson	283
1978	*Andy Bean	282
1979	*Larry Nelson	286
1980	Scott Simpson	281
1981	Ed Fiori	277

1982	Tom Weiskopf	276
1983	Mark McCumber	284
1984	*Tom Watson	280
1985	#Scott Verplank	279
1986	*Tom Kite	286

Beatrice Western Open

1987	#D.A. Weibring	207
1988	Jim Benepe	278
1989	*Mark McCumber	275

Centel Western Open

1990	Wayne Levi	275
1991	Russ Cochran	275
1992	Ben Crenshaw	276

Sprint Western Open

1993	Nick Price	269

Motorola Western Open

1994	Nick Price	277
1995	Billy Mayfair	279
1996	Steve Stricker	270

NEC WORLD SERIES OF GOLF
Firestone Country Club – South Course
Akron, OH

Date: August 21-24, 1997

TV: Thursday and Friday – USA Network
Saturday and Sunday – CBS

Tickets: NEC World Series of Golf
445 E. Warner Rd.
Akron, OH 44319

To play: Firestone is a private club open to members and their guests.

About the tournament and course:

- Over 50 professionals, the previous year's tournament winners from around the world, meet at Firestone for the World Series.

- The World Series began in 1962 as an exhibition match between the winners of the most recent Masters, British and U.S. Opens, and the PGA Championship. Since 1976, the NEC World Series of Golf has been the exclusive visit of the PGA tour each season.

- Firestone hosted the PGA Championship in 1960, 1966 and 1975. The Rubber City Open and American Golf Classic also called the course home between 1954 and 1976.

- This 7139 yards, par 70 course favors a good long-iron player, like Jack Nicklaus, who won the event 5 times in the first 15 years.

- The par 4, 458-yard fourth hole is generally considered the toughest on the course. The fairway slopes from right to left and the teardrop shaped green is guarded by traps front-right and front-left.

HOLE	1	2	3	4	5	6	7	8	9	OUT
YARDS	399	497	442	458	200	469	219	450	470	3604
PAR	4	5	4	4	3	4	3	4	4	35

HOLE	10	11	12	13	14	15	16	17	18	IN
YARDS	410	370	178	457	418	221	625	392	464	3535
PAR	4	4	4	4	3	4	3	4	5	35

TOTALS
YARDS 7139
PAR 70

1996 Leaderboard

1-Phil Mickelson	–6, 274	$378,000
t2- Duffy Walforf	–3, 277	$156,800
t2-Steve Stricker	–3, 277	$156,800
t2-Billy Mayfair	–3, 277	$156,800
5 Greg Norman	–2, 278	$84,000

Tournament History

World Series of Golf

1962	Jack Nicklaus	135
1963	Jack Nicklaus	140
1964	Tony Lema	138
1965	Gary Player	139

1966	Gene Littler	143
1967	Jack Nicklaus	144
1968	Gary Player	143
1969	Orville Moody	141
1970	Jack Nicklaus	136
1971	Charles Coody	141
1972	Gary Player	142
1973	Tom Weiskopf	137
1974	Lee Trevino	139
1975	Tom Watson	140

NEC World Series of Golf

1976	Jack Nicklaus	275
1977	Lanny Wadkins	267
1978	*Gil Morgan	278
1979	Lon Hinkle	272
1980	Tom Watson	270
1981	Bill Rogers	275
1982	*Craig Stadler	278
1983	Nick Price	270
1984	Denis Watson	271
1985	Roger Maltbie	268
1986	Dan Pohl	277
1987	Curtis Strange	275
1988	*Mike Reid	275
1989	*David Frost	276
1990	Jose Maria Olazabal	262
1991	*Tom Purtzer	279
1992	Craig Stadler	273
1993	Fulton Allem	270
1994	Jose Maria Olazabal	269
1995	*Greg Norman	278
1996	Phil Mickelson	274

NISSAN OPEN
Riviera Country Club
Pacific Palisades, CA

Date: February 27 – March 2, 1997

TV: USA/CBS

Tickets: Nissan Open
c/o Los Angeles Junior Chamber of Commerce
350 Bitel St., Suite 100
Los Angeles, CA 90017

To play: Riviera Country Club is a private course.

About the tournament and course:

- Riviera Country Club has hosted the 1948 U.S. Open as well as the 1983 and 1995 PGA Championships, and the course has holes that show up on many tour professional's list of classics.

- Among the toughest holes is the par 4 number 2, a 460-yard effort normally a par 5 for members. The drive travels into a cutting wind onto a narrow fairway, and bunkers line the approach to a small green.

- Other quality holes include the 170-yard par 3 6th with its bunker in the middle of the green; and the 311-yard par 4 10th, a double dogleg with traps around the green.

1996 Leaderborad

1-Craig Stadler	−6, 278	$216,000
t2-Mark Brooks	−5, 279	$79,200
t2-Fred Couples	−5, 279	$79,200
t2-Scott Simpson	−5, 279	$79,200
t2-Mark Wiebe	−5, 279	$79,200

Tournament History

Los Angeles Open

1926	Harry Cooper	279
1927	Bobby Cruikshank	282
1928	Mac Smith	284
1929	Mac Smith	285
1930	Densmore Shute	296
1931	Ed Dudley	285
1932	Mac Smith	281
1933	Craig Wood	281
1934	Mac Smith	280
1935	*Vic Ghezzi	285
1936	Jimmy Hines	280
1937	Harry Cooper	274
1938	Jimmy Thomson	273
1939	Jimmy Demaret	274
1940	Lawson Little	282
1941	Johnny Bulla	281

1942	*Ben Hogan	282
1943	No Tournament	
1944	Harold McSpaden	278
1945	Sam Snead	283
1946	Byron Nelson	284
1947	Ben Hogan	280
1948	Ben Hogan	275
1949	Lloyd Mangrum	284
1950	*Sam Snead	280
1951	Lloyd Mangrum	280
1952	Tommy Bolt	289
1953	Lloyd Mangrum	280
1954	Fred Wampler	281
1955	Gene Littler	276
1956	Lloyd Mangrum	272
1957	Doug Ford	280
1958	Frank Stranahan	275
1959	Ken Venturi	278
1960	Dow Finsterwald	280
1961	Bob Goalby	275
1962	Phil Rodgers	268
1963	Arnold Palmer	274
1964	Paul Harney	280
1965	Paul Harney	276
1966	Arnold Palmer	273
1967	Arnold Palmer	269
1968	Billy Casper	274
1969	*Charles Sifford	276
1970	*Billy Casper	276

Glen Campbell Los Angeles Open

1971	*Bob Lunn	274
1972	*George Archer	270
1973	Rod Funseth	276
1974	Dave Stockton	276
1975	Pat Fitzsimons	275
1976	Hale Irwin	272
1977	Tom Purtzer	273
1978	Gil Morgan	278
1979	Lanny Wadkins	276
1980	Tom Watson	276
1981	Johnny Miller	270
1982	*Tom Watson	271
1983	Gil Morgan	270

Los Angeles Open

1984	David Edwards	279
1985	Lanny Wadkins	264
1986	Doug Tewell	270

Los Angeles Open Presented by Nissan

| 1987 | *Tze-Chung Chen | 275 |
| 1988 | Chip Beck | 267 |

Nissan Los Angeles Open

1989	Mark Calcavecchia	272
1990	Fred Couples	266
1991	Ted Schulz	272
1992	*Fred Couples	269
1993	#Tom Kite	206
1994	Corey Pavin	271

Nissan Open

| 1995 | Corey Pavin | 268 |
| 1996 | Craig Stadler | 278 |

NORTEL OPEN
Tucson National Golf Resort
Starr Pass Golf Club
Tucson, AZ

Date: February 20-23, 1997

TV: ESPN

Tickets: NorTel Open
Tucson Conquistadores
6450 E. Broadway Blvd.
Tucson, AZ 85710

To play: Both Tucson National and Starr Pass courses are open to the public year round.

About the tournament and course:

- Both courses host the first two rounds of play, while the final two rounds are the exclusive domain of Tucson National's Orange/Gold combination of nine hole layouts.

- The finishing holes of those two nine are high on the challenge scale. The Orange 9th hole is a

440-yard, par-4 affair with a lake on the right and trees on the left of the landing area. The 9th hole on the Gold layout, the 18th hole in tournament play, runs 465 yards, uphill. The second shot at this par-4 is to a green guarded by two traps on the front and another to the back.

- Normally a par-5, the 10th hole at Tucson National is a 456-yard tournament par-4 dogleg with a bunkered green. Also watch the 15th hole, a 663-yard monster with 4 bunkers in front, and two in back of the green. Over at Starr Pass, the par-4 fourth hole is only 396 yards, but the small, elevated green provides the tough challenge.

- As an Arizona State junior, then 20-year old Phil Mickelson birdied the final hole to win in 1991 to become the youngest amateur ever to win a Tour event.

Tucson National Course

HOLE	1	2	3	4	5	6	7	8	9	OUT
YARDS	410	495	377	170	395	426	202	528	440	3443
PAR	4	5	4	3	4	4	3	5	4	36

HOLE	10	11	12	13	14	15	16	17	18	IN
YARDS	456	515	182	406	405	663	427	186	465	3705
PAR	4	5	3	4	4	5	4	3	4	36

TOTALS
YARDS 7148
PAR 72

1996 Leaderborad

1-Phil Mickelson	−14, 273	$225,000
2-Bob Tway	−12, 275	$135,000
t3-Fred Funk	−11, 276	$60,000
t3-Lee Janzen	−11, 276	$60,000
t3-Bob Estes	−11, 276	$60,000
t3-Mike Hulbert	−11, 276	$60,000

Tournament History

Tucson Open

1945	Ray Mangrum	268
1946	Jimmy Demaret	268
1947	Jimmy Demaret	264
1948	Skip Alexander	264
1949	Lloyd Mangrum	263
1950	Chandler Harper	267
1951	Lloyd Mangrum	269
1952	Henry Williams	274
1953	Tommy Bolt	265
1954	No tournament	
1955	Tommy Bolt	265
1956	Ted Kroll	264
1957	Dow Finsterwald	269
1958	Lionel Herbert	265
1959	Gene Littler	266
1960	Don January	271

Home of the Sun Invitational

1961	*Dave Hill	269
1962	Phil Rodgers	263
1963	Don January	266
1964	Jack Cupit	274
1965	Bob Charles	271
1966	*Joe Campbell	278
1967	Arnold Palmer	273

Tucson Open

1968	George Knudson	273
1969	Lee Trevino	271
1970	*Lee Trevino	275
1971	J.C.Snead	273
1972	Miller Barber	273
1973	Bruce Crampton	277

Dean Martin Tucson Open

1974	Johnny Miller	272
1975	Johnny Miller	263

NBC Tucson Open

1976	Johnny Miller	274

Joe Garagiola Tucson Open

1977	Bruce Lietzke	275
1978	Tom Watson	276
1979	Bruce Lietzke	265
1980	Jim Colbert	270
1981	Johnny Miller	265
1982	Craig Stadler	266
1983	*Gil Morgan	271

Seiko-Tucson Match Play Championships

1984	Tom Watson	2 &1
1985	Jim Thorpe	4 &3
1986	Jim Thorpe	6 &7

Seiko-Tucson Open

| 1987 | Mike Reid | 268 |

Northern Telecom Tucson Open

1988	David Frost	266
1989	No Tournament	
1990	Robert Gamez	270

Northern Telecom Open

1991	Phil Mickelson	272
1992	Lee Janzen	270
1993	Larry Mize	271
1994	Andrew Magee	270
1995	Phil Mickelson	269
1996	Phil Mickelson	273

———

PGA CHAMPIONSHIP
Winged Foot Golf Club
Mamaroneck, NY

Date: August 14-17, 1997

TV: CBS/TBS

To play: Both courses at Winged Foot are private and open to members and their guests.

About the tournament and course:

- The course begins with hole number 1, or "Genesis," a 446-yard par 4. A large fairway bunker sits in the crook of the dogleg about 200 yards out. The undulating green has large, long traps on either side.

- The fourth hole is named "Sound View." When the course was built in the 1920's, Long Island Sound could be seen from this hole. Mature trees have grown over the view on this 465-yard par-4.

- Finishing up the front is "Meadow," a long, tough par-4. Number nine runs 469 yards with trees down both sides of the fairway. The elevated green is surrounded by a narrow approach and five traps.

- After the turn is the course's signature hole. Number 10, "Pulpit," is 190 yards to a three-tiered green. Hit the green, because what traps front, left and right don't get, trees to the long side will.

- Four great finishing holes await. "Pyramid" at 15 requires some thought. 417 yards seems fine, but a creek spanning the fairway at 270 yards awaits. The elevated narrow green slopes toward the approach shot.

- "Hells Bells" is exclaimed at 16. Willow trees to the right and left of the landing area make accuracy mandatory on this 457-yard par-4. The fairway then dogs to the left onto a three-trapped green.

- The 17th hole may not be "Well Well" for some. Bunkers are positioned short and right of the dogleg right on this 444-yard par-4. The fun begins, however, on the long, narrow green. Traps on either side mimic the shape of the green, which slopes from the middle to the front.

- Finishing up is "Revelations," which features a generous landing area, setting up an approach iron to a fat green. Overshooting the dance floor here means sand traps.

For past results, see Chapter 5, Major Championships: Men.

———

PHOENIX OPEN
TPC of Scottsdale
Scottsdale, AZ

Date: January 23-26, 1997

TV: ESPN

Tickets: The Thunderbird
7226 N. 16th St., Suite 100
Phoenix, AZ 85020

To play: TPC of Scottsdale is a public course open year-round.

About the tournament and course:

- Co-designed by local resident Tom Weiskopf, the TPC of Scottsdale has been home to the Phoenix Open since 1987.

- The stadium layout of the TPC of Scottsdale means large grassy mounds aid tournament viewing.

- In 1988's sudden death playoff, Fred Couples hit his tee shot into the lake on the 18th hole, the third playoff hole. Couples carded a 6, while Sandy Lyle bogeyed the hole for victory.

- Although less than 7,000 yards, the more than 70 bunkers, water on the back nine, and variable winds make this course a must for placement shots.

- The par 4 11th hole measures 469 yards with water running the entire length of the left side. The slight dogleg right, variable winds, and large approach bunker make this a difficult hole.

- The 15th hole combines a lake down the left side of the fairway, a dogleg right, and an island green with two traps on the approach side. However, this 501 yard par-5 is reachable in regulation.

- Johnny Miller carded an amazing 260 at the Phoenix Country Club during the 1975 tournament to win by 14 strokes.

1996 Leaderborad

1-Phil Mickelson (*)	−15, 269	$234,000
2-Justin Leonard	−15, 269	$140,400
3-Tom Scherrer	−14, 270	$88,400

Tournament History

Phoenix Open

1935	Ky Laffoon	281
1936-38	No Tournament	
1939	Byron Nelson	198
1940	Ed Oliver	205
1941-43	No Tournament	
1944	*Harold McSpaden	273
1945	Byron Nelson	274

1946	*Ben Hogan	273
1947	Ben Hogan	270
1948	Bobby Locke	268
1949	Jimmy Demaret	278
1950	*Jimmy Demaret	269
1951	Lew Worsham	272
1952	Lloyd Mangrum	274
1953	Lloyd Mangrum	272
1954	*Ed Furgol	272
1955	Gene Littler	275
1956	Cary Middlecoff	276
1957	Billy Casper	271
1958	Ken Venturi	274
1959	Gene Littler	268
1960	*Jack Fleck	273
1961	*Arnold Palmer	270
1962	Arnold Palmer	269
1963	Arnold Palmer	273
1964	Jack Nicklaus	271
1965	Rod Funseth	275
1966	Dudley Wysong	278
1967	Julius Boros	272
1968	George Knudson	272
1969	Gene Littler	263
1970	Dale Douglass	271
1971	Miller Barber	261
1972	Homero Blancas	273
1973	Bruce Crampton	268
1974	Johnny Miller	271
1975	Johnny Miller	260
1976	Bob Gilder	268
1977	*Jerry Pate	277
1978	Miller Barber	272
1979	#Ben Crenshaw	199
1980	Jeff Mitchell	272
1981	David Graham	268
1982	Lanny Wadkins	263
1983	*Bob Gilder	271
1984	Tom Purtzer	268
1985	Calvin Peete	270
1986	Hal Sutton	267
1987	Paul Azinger	268
1988	*Sandy Lyle	269
1989	Mark Calcavecchia	263
1990	Tommy Armour III	267

1991	Nolan Henke	268
1992	Mark Calcavecchia	264
1993	Lee Janzen	273
1994	Bill Glasson	268
1995	*Vijay Singh	269
1996	*Phil Mickelson	269

THE PLAYERS CHAMPIONSHIP
TPC at Sawgrass-Stadium Course
Ponte Vedra Beach, FL

Date: March 27-30, 1997

TV: ESPN/NBC

Tickets: The Players Championship
P.O. Box 829
103 TPC Blvd.
Ponte Vedra Beach, FL 32082

To play: TPC at Sawgrass is a public course and resort.

About the tournament and course:

- Held two weeks before the Masters, The Players Championship boasts a strong field, year after year.

- The TPC at Sawgrass was the first in the string of stadium-style TPC courses. Tournament viewing is aided by strategically placed grassy mounds throughout the course. Some of the mounds are high enough to prevent the high winds from becoming too much of a factor during play.

- When the course first opened in 1982, some players reacted less than favorably. Jack Nicklaus said of the greens, "I've never been very good at stopping a 5-iron on the hood of a car."

- Some of the greens were remodeled after that first year, possibly to save wear and tear on clothes.

- After winning that first tournament, Jerry Pate threw both course architect Pete Dye and then-

PGA Commissioner Deane Beman into the lake next to the 18th hole.

- Numbers 17 and 18 may just be the two toughest finishing holes on tour. The 132-yard par-3 17th has an island green that slopes back to front, right into a bunker. The par-4 440-yard 18th has water bordering the entire left side of the hole, tee to well-guarded green.

1996 Leaderborad

1-Fred Couples	–18, 270	$630,000
t2-Colin Montgomerie	–14, 274	$308,000
t2-Tommy Tolles	–14, 274	$308,000

Tournament History

The Tournament Players Championship

1974	Jack Nicklaus	272
1975	Al Geiberger	270
1976	Jack Nicklaus	269
1977	Mark Hayes	289
1978	Jack Nicklaus	289
1979	Lanny Wadkins	283
1980	Lee Trevino	278
1981	*Ray Floyd	285
1982	Jerry Pate	280
1983	Hal Sutton	283
1984	Fred Couples	277
1985	Calvin Peete	274
1986	John Mahaffey	275
1987	*Sandy Lyle	274

The Players Championship

1988	Mark McCumber	273
1989	Tom Kite	279
1990	Jodie Mudd	278
1991	Steve Elkington	276
1992	Davis Love III	273
1993	Nick Price	270
1994	Greg Norman	264
1995	Lee Janzen	283
1996	Fred Couples	270

QUAD CITY CLASSIC
**Oakwood Country Club
Coal Valley, IL**

Date: July 10-13, 1997
TV: The Golf Channel
Tickets: Quad City Classic
P.O. Box 9249
 Moline, IL 61265-9249
To play: Oakwood is a private club open
to members and their guests.

About the tournament and course:

- With water on only one hole and approximately
  35 bunkers, Oakwood is considered one of the
  easiest courses on tour.

- Running slightly less than 6800 yards, Oakwood
  favors a player who can accurately maneuver
  their way around the course.

- A par-5 for club members, the 460-yard fourth
  hole becomes a par-4 for the pros. The dogleg
  left challenge ends with trees to both sides of a
  narrow green.

1996 Leaderborad

1-Ed Fiori	−12, 268	$216,000
2-Andrew Magee	−10, 270	$129,600
t3-Chris Perry	−9, 271	$69,600
t3-Steve Jones	−9, 271	$69,600

Tournament History

Quad Cities Open

1972	Deane Beman	279
1973	Sam Adams	268
1974	Dave Stockton	271

McMahon-Jaycees Quad City Open

1975	Roger Maltbie	275
1976	John Lister	268
1977	Mike Morley	267
1978	Victor Regalado	269
1979	D.A. Weibring	266

Quad Cities Open

1980	Scott Hoch	266
1981	*Dave Barr	270

Miller High-Life Quad Cities Open

1982	Payne Stewart	268
1983	*Danny Edwards	266
1984	Scott Hoch	266

Lite Quad Cities Open

1985	Dan Forsman	267

Hardee's Golf Classic

1986	Mark Wiebe	268
1987	Kenny Knox	265
1988	Blaine McCallister	261
1989	Curt Byrum	268
1990	*Joey Sindelar	268
1991	D.A. Weibring	267
1992	David Frost	266
1993	David Frost	259
1994	Mark McCumber	265
1995	#D.A. Weibring	197
1996	Ed Fiori	268

SHELL HOUSTON OPEN
**TPC at the Woodlands
The Woodlands, TX**

Date: May 1-4, 1997
TV: ABC
Tickets: Shell Houston Open
Houston Golf Association
1830 South Millbend Dr.
The Woodlands, TX 77380
To play: TPC at The Woodlands is a
public course.

About the tournament and course:

- With its large Bermuda grass greens, water on
  half the holes, and fairway bunkers on even

more holes, the TPC at the Woodlands allows the shotmaker the chance to excel.

- TPC at the Woodlands is yet another course where the two finishing holes can be the toughest. The 17th runs only 383 yards, but the landing area on this par-4 is to a very narrow part of the fairway guarded on the left by water. The second shot is to a green surrounded on the better part of three sides by more water along with scattered sand traps on the far side. To finish up, number 18 cards out at a par-4 and 445 yards. Water runs the second half of the fairway's right side and the green is nestled comfortably inside a bevy of bunkers on the left and water on the right.

- PGA players stay close on this track. The last three tournaments, and eight of the last 11, have been playoff affairs.

HOLE	1	2	3	4	5	6	7	8	9	OUT
YARDS	515	365	165	413	457	577	413	218	427	3550
PAR	5	4	3	4	4	5	4	3	4	36

HOLE	10	11	12	13	14	15	16	17	18	IN
YARDS	428	421	388	525	195	530	177	383	445	3492
PAR	4	4	4	5	3	5	3	4	4	36

TOTALS
YARDS 7042
PAR 72

1996 Leaderborad

1-Mark Brooks (*)	–14, 274	$270,000
2-Jeff Maggert	–14, 274	$162,000
3-David Duval	–13, 275	$102,000

Tournament History

Tournament of Champions

1946	Byron Nelson	274
1947	Bobby Locke	277
1948	No tournament	
1949	John Palmer	272

Houston Open

1950	Cary Middlecoff	277
1951	Marty Furgol	277
1952	Jack Burke, Jr.	277
1953	*Cary Middlecoff	283
1954	Dave Douglas	277
1955	Mike Souchak	273
1956	Ted Kroll	277
1957	Arnold Palmer	279
1958	Ed Oliver	281

Houston Classic

1959	*Jack Burke, Jr.	277
1960	*Bill Collins	280
1961	*Jay Hebert	276
1962	*Bobby Nichols	278
1963	Bob Charles	268
1964	Mike Souchak	278
1965	Bobby Nichols	273

Houston Champion International

1966	Arnold Palmer	275
1967	Frank Beard	274
1968	Roberto DeVicenzo	274
1969	Hosted U.S. Open	
1970	*Gibby Gilbert	282
1971	*Hubert Green	280

Houston Open

1972	Bruce Devlin	280
1973	Bruce Crampton	277
1974	Dave Hill	276
1975	Bruce Crampton	273
1976	Lee Elder	288
1977	Gene Littler	276
1978	Gary Player	270
1979	Wayne Levi	268

Michelob Houston Open

1980	*Curtis Strange	266
1981	#Ron Streck	198
1982	*Ed Sneed	275

Houston Coca-Cola Open

| 1983 | David Graham | 275 |
| 1984 | Corey Pavin | 274 |

Houston Open

1985	Ray Floyd	277
1986	*Curtis Strange	274

Big I Houston Open

1987	*Jay Hass	276

Independent Insurance Agent Open

1988	*Curtis Strange	270
1989	Mike Sullivan	280
1990	*#Tony Sills	204
1991	Fulton Allem	273

Shell Houston Open

1992	Fred Funk	272
1993	*#Jim McGovern	199
1994	Mike Heinen	272
1995	*Payne Stewart	276
1996	*Mark Brooks	274

THE SPRINT INTERNATIONAL
Castle Pines Golf Club
Castle Rock, CO

Date: July 31- August 3, 1997

TV: ESPN/CBS

Tickets: The Sprint International
1000 Hummingbird Dr.
Castle Rock, CO 80104

To play: Castle Pines is a private club open to members and their guests.

About the tournament and course:

- The Sprint is unique as it uses a modified Stablefors scoring system. Under par equals plus points: a double eagle is worth 8 points, eagles are 5 points, birdies are 2 points. Par brings zero points, a bogey is worth –1, and double-bogeys and worse cost –3 points.

- At first look, the 644-yard first hole and the 7559 yards on the scorecard overall may open a

golfer's eyes, but remember the thin air. The 14th hole is also over 600 yards, and usual par 5 numbers (the 10th hole at 485 and the finishing hole at 480) both 4 pars.

- In the 1996 Sprint International, Clarence Rose earned his first tour victory with an eagle at the 17th hole in regulation. Rose then came back and eagled 17 in a playoff with former champion Brad Faxon for the first place check.

1996 Leaderborad

1-Clarence Rose (*)	–31	$288,000
2-Brad Faxon	–31	$172,000
t3-Bob Tway	–30	$92,800
t3-Michael Bradley	–30	$92,800

Tournament History

1986	Ken Green	Plus 12
1987	John Cook	Plus 11
1988	Joey Sindelar	Plus 17
1989	Greg Norman	Plus 13
1990	Davis Love III	Plus 14
1991	Jose Maria Olazabal	Plus 10
1992	Brad Faxon	Plus 14
1993	Phil Mickelson	Plus 45
1994	Steve Lowery	Plus 35
1995	Lee Janzen	Plus 34
1996	*Clarence Rose	Plus 31

UNITED AIRLINES HAWAIIAN OPEN
Waialae Country Club
Honolulu, HI

Date: February 13-16, 1997

TV: ABC

Tickets: United Airlines Hawaiian Open
677 Ala Mouna Blvd. Suite 207
Honolulu, HI 96813

To play: Waialae is a private course open to club members and their guests.

About the tournament and course:

- Scenes from the 1950 movie *From Here to Eternity* were shot at Waialae.

- Well guarded greens break mostly toward the ocean.

- The 5th Hole, "Auwai," or "Two Ditches," is generally regarded as the toughest on the course. This 460-yard par 4 has streams crossing through two breaks in the tree lined fairway, wind coming down the "ditches" like it wants to play through and a three-bunkered, heavily contoured green.

- In 1983, Isao Aoki holed a 126 yard wedge on the finishing hole to become the first Japanese player to win a PGA Tour event.

1996 Leaderborad

1-Jim Furyk (*)	–11, 277	$216,000
2-Brad Faxon	–11, 277	$129,600
3-Steve Stricker	–10, 278	$81,600

Tournament History

Hawaiian Open

1965	*Gay Brewer	281
1966	Ted Makalena	271
1967	*Dudley Wysong	284
1968	Lee Trevino	272
1969	Bruce Crampton	274
1970	No tournament	
1971	Tom Shaw	273
1972	*Grier Jones	274
1973	John Schlee	273
1974	Jack Nicklaus	271
1975	Gary Groh	274
1976	Ben Crenshaw	270
1977	Bruce Lietzke	273
1978	*Hubert Green	274
1979	Hubert Green	267
1980	Andy Bean	266
1981	Hale Irwin	265
1982	Wayne Levi	277
1983	Isao Aoki	268
1984	*Jack Renner	271
1985	Mark O'Meara	267
1986	Corey Pavin	272
1987	*Corey Pavin	270
1988	Lanny Wadkins	271
1989	#Gene Sauers	197
1990	David Ishii	279

United Hawaiian Open

1991	Lanny Wadkins	270

United Airlines Hawaiian Open

1992	John Cook	265
1993	Howard Twitty	269
1994	Brett Ogle	269
1995	John Morse	269
1996	*Jim Furyk	277

U.S. OPEN

**Congressional Country Club
Bethesda, MD**

Date: June 12-15, 1997

TV: NBC/ESPN

Tickets: The U.S.G.A.
P.O.Box 708
Far Hills, NJ 07931

To play: Congressional is a private club open to members and their guests.

About the tournament and course:

- Congressional is no stranger to the Majors crowd, having hosted the 1964 U.S. Open, the 1976 PGA Championship, and the 1995 U.S. Senior Open.

- Part of the course had been a training ground for the OSS during World War II. After the war, the course was revamped and reopened.

- The last time the Open was played here, one of golf's truly great stories happened. The then 33-

year old Ken Venturi's game had deteriorated to a point where he had to qualify to play. At the turn of the first round, Venturi almost quit because of his poor performance. His playing partners talked him into staying, and he responded with a third round 66, including a sparkling 30 on the front. In those days, the final two rounds were played on the last day. With temperatures over 100 degrees, Venturi added a 70 to his earlier 66, totaled 276, and proved to the golf world his game was back.

- The finishing hole has a waterfall in the middle of the fairway.

For past results, see Chapter 5, Major Championships: Men.

Tiger Woods exploded onto the scene winning two PGA tournaments in as many months after rewriting the record books as an amateur.

WALT DISNEY WORLD/ OLDSMOBILE CLASSIC

Walt Disney World Resort Magnolia, Palm and Lake Buena Vista Golf Courses

Lake Buena Vista, FL

Date: October 16-19, 1997

TV: The Golf Channel

Tickets: Walt Disney World/ Oldsmobile Golf Classic
4510 N. Fort Wilderness Trail
Lake Buena Vista, FL 32830

To play: Walt Disney World Resort is a year-round public resort.

About the tournament and course:

- Tiger Woods won the 1996 Classic after Taylor Smith was disqualified for using an illegal grip on his putter. Smith had just sunk a birdie putt on the 18th hole that would have forced a sudden-death playoff when officials ruled his putter's grip had a flat edge on one of two putter grips.

Woods, who finished 23rd on the money list, eagled the par-5 fourth hole to go along with seven birdies and three bogeys.

- The "Magic Linkdom," as the Disney resort is sometimes called, is also home to the LPGA's HealthSouth Classic.

- The first three days of tournament play are held on the Lake Buena Vista, Palm and Magnolia courses, while Magnolia gets the nod for the final round.

- The finishing hole at Magnolia is a 455-yard par-4 with bunkers on either side of the landing area. The sloped green has three more traps to test shotmaking skills.

1996 Leaderborad

1-Tiger Woods	–21, 267	$216,000
2-Payne Stewart	–20, 268	$129,600
3-Robert Gamez	–19, 269	$81,600
4-Nolan Henke	–18, 270	$57,600
t5-Jay Haas	–17, 271	$43,800
t5-Rick Fehr	–17, 271	$43,800
t5-Lennie Clements	–17, 271	$43,800

Tournament History

Walt Disney World Open Invitational

1971	Jack Nicklaus	273
1972	Jack Nicklaus	267
1973	Jack Nicklaus	275

Walt Disney World National Team Championship

1974	Hubert Green & Mac McClendon	255
1975	Jim Colbert & Dean Refram	252
1976	Woody Blackburn & Bill Kratzert	260
1977	Gibby Gilbert & Grier Jones	253
1978	Wayne Levi & Bob Mann	254
1979	George Burns & Ben Crenshaw	255
1980	Danny Edwards & Dave Edwards	253
1981	Vince Heafner & Mike Holland	275

Walt Disney World Golf Classic

1982	*Hal Sutton	269
1983	Payne Stewart	269
1984	Larry Nelson	266

Walt Disney World Oldsmobile Classic

1985	Lanny Wadkins	267
1986	*Ray Floyd	275
1987	Larry Nelson	268
1988	*Bob Lohr	263
1989	Tim Simpson	272
1990	Tim Simpson	264
1991	Mark O'Meara	267
1992	John Huston	262
1993	Jeff Maggert	265
1994	Rick Fehr	269
1995	#Brad Bryant	198
1996	Tiger Woods	267

* Won in playoff
# Shortened tournament

11

TOURNAMENTS OF THE LPGA TOUR

CHICK-FIL-A CHARITY CHAMPIONSHIP

Eagles Landing Country Club
Stockbridge, GA

Date: April 25-27, 1997

TV: The Golf Channel

Tickets: Chick-fil-A Charity Championship
100 Eagles Landing Way
Stockbridge, GA 30281

To play: Eagles Landing is a private club
open to members and their guests.

About the tournament and course:

- This Tom Fazio design generally favors players with strong short games. Quick, undulating greens can sometimes be tough to get to because of the 35 or so greenside bunkers.

- The par-4 15th is generally regarded as the toughest hole at Eagles Landing. Into the wind, this 404-yard effort has water on the left and bunkers to the right of the fairway. The geeen is protected by more sand on the right and wetlands to the left.

1996 Leaderboard

1-Barb Mucha	–8, 208	$82,500
t2-Liselotte Neumann	–6, 210	$44,282
t2-Dottie Pepper	–6, 210	$44,282

Tournament History

Sega Women's Championship

1992	Dottie Mochrie	277

Atlanta Women's Championship

1993	Trish Johnson	282
1994	Val Skinner	206

Chick-Fil-A Charity Championship

1995	Laura Davies	201
1996	Barb Mucha	208

CHRYSLER-PLYMOUTH TOURNAMENT OF CHAMPIONS

Weston Hills Country Club
Ft. Lauderdale, FL

Date: January 9-12, 1997

TV: SportsChannel/NBC

Tickets: Chrysler-Plymouth
Tournament of Champions
c/o Weston Hills Country Club
2608 Country Club Way
Ft. Lauderdale, FL 33332

To play: Weston Hills is a private club open to members and their guests.

About the tournament and course:

• Invitations are sent to tournament winners of the past two years, as well as LPGA Hall of Fame members to participate.

• The Chrysler/Plymouth is the season opener, and 1996 winner Liselotte Neumann started that year with quite a bang. She cruised to an 11-stroke victory, setting the Grand Cypress course record with a second round 66, and her 13 under total smoked the old tournament record by six strokes. During the final round, Pat Bradley tied Neumann's two-day-old course record with her own 6-under 66, but Bradley finished 16 shots behind the leader.

• The 1997 event moves from Orlando to Fort Lauderdale, and the Weston Hills Country Club. Par at number 5 is considered a good score. This 174-yard par-3 has water left and front of the green. Combine that with the prevailing cross wind, and club selection is critical.

1996 Leaderboard

1-Liselotte Neumann	−13
2-Karrie Webb	−2
3-Laura Davies	−1

In 1986, the Los Angeles City Council introduced legislation requiring foursomes to finish 9 holes in 2 hours and 20 minutes or be forced off of city golf courses.

Tournament History

1994	Dottie Mochrie	287
1995	Dawn Coe Jones	281
1996	Liselotte Neumann	275

CORE STATES/ BETSY KING CLASSIC

Berkleigh Country Club
Kutztown, PA

Date: October 2-5, 1997

TV: TBD

Tickets: Core States/Betsy King Classic
P.O.Box 248
Kutztown, PA 19530

To play: Berkleigh is a private club open to members and their guests.

About the tournament and course:

• In 1996, Annika Sorenstam had four rounds in the 60's and breezed to an eight-shot victory in the inaugural Betsy King Classic. Sorenstam began the day with a three-shot lead, then birdied four holes on the front nine to seal the victory.

• The tournament is named in honor of King, who grew up in nearby Limekiln. She has 30 career wins and was inducted into the LPGA Hall of Fame last year, but missed Friday's cut.

• Another course that saves the toughest for last, Berkleigh's finishing hole is a par-5, uphill, dog-leg left with a tricky green.

1996 Leaderboard

1-Annika Sorenstam	−18, 270	$90,000
2-Laura Davies	−10, 278	$55,855
t3-Dawn Coe-Jones	−5, 283	$36,230
t3-Liselotte Neumann	−5, 283	$36,230

Tournament History

1996	Annika Sorenstam	270

DU MAURIER LTD. CLASSIC

Glen Abbey Golf Club
Oakville, Ontario, Canada

Date: July 31- August 3, 1997

TV: ESPN

Tickets: du Maurier Classic
855 rue Irene
Montreal, Quebec, Canada H4C 2P2

To play: Glen Abbey is a public course.

About the tournament and course:

- This 1974 Jack Nicklaus design features two personalities. The front nine is flatter and more open than it's counterpart, while holes 11-15 on the back traverse a gorge. On top of the ridge sits the Abbey, home of the Royal Canadian Golf Association.

- The third hole is one of nine on the course where water comes into play. The tee shot at this 156-yard par-3 is entirely over water to a deep, narrow green trapped twice. Rumor has it that over 15,000 balls are retrieved from the lake each year.

- The ninth hole runs 458 yards and measures a par of 4. Trees on both sides of the landing area, along with a bunker to the right set up an approach over more water.

- Things generally get tougher on the back. The elevated tee at number 11 forces a shot to a treed landing area some 120 feet below. The approach is over a creek to a bunkered green.

- The toughest par-3 is usually number 12. This 187-yard beauty has water and three traps along the front of the green, and another trap to the back.

- Need a break? Not at 13. This 529-yard par-5 has a creek that cuts in and out of the playing area. Those who choose to lay up in front of the creek with their second shot, usually need an accurate wedge shot to the trapped green.

For past results, see Chapter 6, Major Championships: Women.

FIELDCREST CANNON CLASSIC

Peninsula Country Club
Charlotte, NC

Date: September, 25-28, 1997

TV: TBD

Tickets: Fieldcrest Cannon Classic
P.O.Box 33367
Charlotte, NC 28233-3367

To play: Peninsula is a private club open to members and their guests.

About the tournament and course:

- Trish Johnson set the course record of 64, finishing the 1996 tournament at 18-under 270. Johnson birdied eight holes, four on each side during the roundincluding dropping a putt from 60 feet out on the ninth hole.

- Number 9 is a par-5, 441-yard test with a straight, bunkered fairway and an offset green guraded by water. Another tough par 5 is the 18th, a 499-yard effort with yet another offset green. Like the ninth, this green is also fronted by water, forcing a choice of whether to go for the dance floor in two.

1996 Leaderboard

1-Trish Johnson	−18, 270	$75,000
2-Kim Saiki	−15, 273	$46,546
3-Dottie Pepper	−14, 274	$33,966

Tournament History

1995	Gail Graham	
1996	Trish Johnson	270

────

FIRST BANK PRESENTS THE EDINA REALTY LPGA CLASSIC

Rush Creek Golf Club
Maple Grove, MN

Date: June 13-15, 1997
TV: Regional/Midwest Sports Channel
Tickets: The Edina Realty LPGA Classic
7820 County Road 101
Maple Grove, MN 55311
To play: Rush Creek is a public course.

About the tournament and course:

- In 1997, the Edina Realty event moves to a new home, Rush Creek Golf Club. Rush Creek opened in June of 1996 and features marshes, maple and oak trees, and 50 bunkers to test strategy.

- The finishing holes on each nine are regarded as the toughest for their respective sides. Number nine measures 418 yards, and the second shot must negotaite a narrow approach corridor with a large pond to the right. The 18th hole runs 530 yards with a dogleg left. The tee shot carries water, as does the second shot for all but the mightiest drivers.

- For the seven years previous to the move, this event was held at Edinburgh USA Golf Course. Of those seven tournaments, three, including 1996, were decided by sudden-death playoffs. That year, Liselotte Neumann knocked in a 45-foot putt on the third extra hole to break a four-way tie. She entered the final round five shots out of the lead but rallied with a 5-under 65 to force the playoff.

1996 Leaderboard

1-Liselotte Neumann(*)	−9, 207	$82,500
t2-Brandie Burton	−9, 207	$39,208
t2-Suzanne Strudwick	−9, 207	$39,208
t2-Carin Hj Koch	−9, 207	$39,208

Tournament History

Northgate Classic1

1990	Beth Daniel	203

Northgate Computer Classic

1991	*Cindy Rarick	211
1992	Kris Tschetter	211
1993	Hiromi Kobayashi	205

Minnesota LPGA Classic

1994	Liselotte Neumann	205

Edina Realty Classic

1995	Julie Larsen	205
1996	*Liselotte Neumann	207

────

FRIENDLY'S CLASSIC

Crestview Country Club
Agawam, MA

Date: August 7-10, 1997
TV: The Golf Channel
Tickets: Friendly's Classic
1855 Boston Road
Wilbraham, MA 01095
To play: Crestview is a private club open to members and their guests.

About the tournament and course:

- Talk about distance off the tee! During the 1995 Friendly's classic, both Noeiie Daghe and Moira

Dunn made holes in one across state lines at the 14th hole. Crestview is unique in that 15 holes are in Massachusetts and three are in Connecticut. Number 14's tee box is in the former and the green is in the latter. An accountants nightmare for the winner.

- Players at Crestview have to account for water hazards on eight holes and over 60 bunkers. The fast greens are usually tiered and well guarded.

- The toughest hole on the course is probably number 4. This par-4 only runs 372 yards, but the fairway bunkers force a well-placed tee shot. The second shot is to a green fronted by traps left and right, as well as a large trap to the rear.

- During the 1996 event, Dottie Pepper teed off at the par-4 18th hole trailing Brandi Burton by one shot, then birdied that final hole while Burton carded a bogey, giving Pepper a one-stroke victory.

1996 Leaderboard

1-Dottie Pepper	−9, 279	$75,000
2-Brandie Burton	−8, 280	$46,546
3-Mardi Lunn	−7, 281	$33,966

Tournament History

| 1995 | Becky Iverson | 276 |
| 1996 | Dottie Pepper | 279 |

About the tournament and course:

- Formerly the Youngstown-Warren Classic, this event takes on a title sponsor in 1997, the Giant Eagle.

- Michelle McGann became this event's first two-time champion with back-to-back titles in 1995 and 1996, the latter win a record setting 16 under par, 200. After a sluggish start (4 over after 7 holes in the first round), McGann played the next 47 holes at 20 under, including scorching the course for 64 and 65 in the final two rounds.

1996 Leaderboard

1-Michelle McGann	−16, 200	$90,000
2-Kim Saiki	−13, 203	$55,855
3-Kelly Robbins	−11, 205	$40,759

Tournament History

Phar-Mor in Youngstown

1990	*Beth Daniel	207
1991	*Deb Richard	207
1992	*Betsy King	209

Youngstown-Warren LPGA Classic

1993	Nancy Lopez	203
1994	Tammie Green	206
1995	*Michelle McGann	205
1996	Michelle McGann	200

GIANT EAGLE LPGA CLASSIC

Avalon Lakes
Warren, OH

Date: July 25-27, 1997
TV: The Golf Channel
Tickets: Giant Eagle LPGA Classic
One American Way
Warren, OH 44484
To play: Avalon Lakes is a public course open year-round.

JAL BIG APPLE CLASSIC

Wykagyl Country Club
New Rochelle, NY

Date: July 17-20, 1997
TV: NBC
Tickets: JAL Big Apple Classic
1266 E. Main St., 7th Floor
Stamford, CT 06902
To play: Wykagyl is a private club open to members and their guests.

About the tournament and course:

- Majestic trees and large, bunkered greens—must be Donald Ross. The legendary designer was one of five men to remodel this course in it's 90-plus year history.

- The origin of the interesting name Wykagyl was shrouded in mystery for many years. The commonly accepted version now is a Native American, probably Algonquin, meaning "country of the birch bark."

- The annual list of the tour's 50 toughest holes usually contains at least one from Wykagyl. At top of the course's own list would most likely be the doglegged number 14. The 377-yard par-4 requires most golfers to lay up short of a creek, then hit to a smallish, trapped green.

1996 Leaderboard

1-Caroline Pierce	−2, 211	$108,750
t2-Tina Barrett	+3, 216	$58,371
t2-Karrie Webb	+3, 216	$58,371

Tournament History

1990	Betsy King	273
1991	Betsy King	279
1992	Juli Inkster	273
1993	Hiromi Kobayashi	278
1994	*Beth Daniel	276
1995	Tracy Kerdyk	273
1996	Caroline Pierce	211

JAMIE FARR KROGER CLASSIC

Highland Meadows Golf Club
Sylvania, OH

Date: July 3-6, 1997

TV: The Golf Channel

Tickets: Jamie Farr Kroger Classic
600 Jefferson Avenue
One Lake Erie Center
Toledo, OH 43604

ROLEX PLAYER OF THE YEAR

1.	Laura Davies	250.50
2.	Karrie Webb	223.00
3.	Annika Sorenstam	191.50
4.	Dottie Pepper	154.61
5.	Liselotte Neumann	148.90
6.	Michelle McGann	120.66
7.	Meg Mallon	120.50
8.	Kelly Robbins	104.11
9.	Emilee Klein	89.41
10.	Patty Sheehan	83.75

To play: Highland Meadows is a private club open to members and their guests.

About the tournament and course:

- Over 60 bunkers and numerous mature trees give this 1928 course a true Donald Ross feel. No wonder, since designer Sandy Alves was a student of the legendary Ross.

- The round finishes on a pair of par 5 holes. The 17th is a 513-yard slight dogleg left with large bunkers to the left and right of the green. The final hole, another dogleg left, measures 532 yards. The tee shot landing area is flanked by two bunkers to the right and a clump of trees on the left. The angled green has two more traps standing guard.

- In 1996, Joan Pitcock entered the final round of the Jamie Farr with a three-shot lead, a lead she promptly lost by the turn. However, Marianne Morris bogeyed the 16th hole, allowing Pitcock to capture her first LPGA tour victory.

1996 Leaderboard

1-Joan Pitcock	−9, 204	$86,250
2-Marianne Morris	−8, 205	$53,528
t3-Catrin Nilsmark	−7, 206	$31,345
t3-Mitzi Edge	−7, 206	$31,345
t3-Nanci Bowen	−7, 206	$31,345

Tournament History

1984	Lauri Peterson	278
1985	Penny Hammel	278
1986	No tournament	
1987	Jane Geddes	280
1988	Laura Davies	277
1989	Penny Hammel	206
1990	Tina Purizer	205
1991	*Alice Miller	205
1992	Patty Sheehan	209
1993	Brandi Burton	201
1994	*Kelly Robbins	204
1995	Kathryn Marshall	205
1996	Joan Pitcock	204

JCPENNEY/LPGA SKINS GAME

Stonebriar Country Club
Frisco, TX

Date: May 24-25, 1997

TV: ABC

Tickets: JCPenney Skins Game
c/o JCPenney Co.
P.O.Box 10001
6501 Legacy Dr.
Plano, TX 75024-3698

To play: Stonebriar is a private club open to members and their guests.

About the tournament and course:

- While the rest of the tour heads to New York this weekend, four players travel to Texas for this high stakes shootout. Holes 1 through 6 are worth $20,000 each, the next 6 holes will bring $30,000 each, and the final 6 holes are worth $40,000 each. If a hole is halved, the skin carries over to the next hole.

- Laura Davies established the standard in 1996, winning $340,000 on 12 skins.

- Finishing up either nine at Stonebriar can be tough. The 9th hole measures 405 yards, but just shy of the landing area water starts to line the fairway on either side. Wind plays a factor here as well as on number 18, a 490-yard, par-5 test. This dogleg right finishing hole also has water on both sides of the fairway, as well as numerous fairway bunkers.

1996 Leaderboard

Player	Skins	Total
Laura Davies	12	$340,000
Dottie Pepper	3	$100,000
Annika Sorenstam	3	$100,000
Beth Daniel	0	$0

Tournament History

1990	Jan Stephenson	6 skins
1991	No tournament	
1992	Pat Bradley	8 skins
1993	Betsy King	7 skins
1994	Patty Sheehan	11 skins
1995	Dottie Mochrie	8 skins
1996	Laura Davies	12 skins

LPGA CORNING CLASSIC

Corning Country Club
Corning, NY

Date: May 22-25, 1997

TV: The Golf Channel

Tickets: LPGA Corning Classic
P.O. Box 1048
Corning, NY 14830-1480

To play: Corning is a private club open to members and their guests.

About the tournament and course:

- First hole jitters are not acceptable at Corning. The first hole, a 402-yard par-4, was rated sixth

ROLEX ROOKIE OF THE YEAR

1.	Karrie Webb	1527
2.	Mayumi Hirase	609
3.	Jill McGill	411
4.	Wendy Ward	350
5.	Wendy Doolan	276
6.	Susan Veasey	185
7.	Lorie Kane	134
8.	Cindy Haley	84
9.	Jean Bartholomew	65
T10.	Shani Waugh	64
	Leslie Spalding	64

1983	Patty Sheehan	272
1984	JoAnne Carner	281
1985	Patti Rizzo	272
1986	Laurie Rinker	278
1987	Cindy Rarick	275
1988	Sherri Turner	273
1989	Ayako Okamoto	272
1990	Pat Bradley	274
1991	Betsy King	273
1992	Colleen Walker	276
1993	*Kelly Robbins	277
1994	Beth Daniel	278
1995	Alison Nicholas	275
1996	Rosie Jones	276

most difficult on the tour in 1995, and the most difficult in 1994. This dogleg right has a small green guarded by bunkers to the front-left and rear-left.

- Strategy and shotmaking are the best tools to have on this mature course. Tight fairways and small greens leave little room for error.

- At the winner's ceremony on the 18th green, tournament victors have given thanks to various family members and other inspirations, but 1996 winner Rosie Jones had a new spin. "I owe this one to my dog Cory," said Jones, who did not arrive until Wednesday and had no practice round. Seems she had a court appearance after her dog was accused of biting someone.

1996 Leaderboard

1-Rosie Jones	−12, 276	$90,000
2-Val Skinner	−10, 278	$55,855
t3-Joan Pitcock	−9, 279	$36,230
t3-Nancy Ramsbottom	−9, 279	$36,230

Tournament History

1979	Penny Pulz	284
1980	Donna Caponi	281
1981	Kathy Hite	282
1982	Sandra Spuzich	280

MCDONALDS LPGA CHAMPIONSHIP

DuPont Country Club
Wilmington, DE

Date: May 15-18, 1997

TV: CBS

Tickets: McDonalds LPGA Championship
601 Rockland Road
P.O. Box 394
Rockland, DE 19732

To play: DuPont is a private club open to members and their guests.

About the tournament and course:

- The seventh hole proves tough each and every year. This 391-yard, par-4 doglegs to the right with a large bunker in the turn. Four more bunkers guard the approach to the green.

- DuPont is recognized as the largest private golf club in the U.S. with almost 8,000 members.

- Laura Davies has owned this event in recent memory, winning in 1994 and 1996, while placing second in 1995. The course favors long hit-

Annika Sorenstam putts at the LPGA Tour Championship. Sorenstam had another outstanding year, finishing 3rd on the '96 money list.

MICHELOB LIGHT HEARTLAND CLASSIC

Forest Hills Country Club
St. Louis, MO

Date: May 29- June 1, 1997

TV: The Golf Channel

Tickets: MetroTix outlets

To play: Forest Hills is a private club open to members and their guests.

About the tournament and course:

- During the 1995 event, Annika Sorenstam was the only golfer who broke par during the 72-hole tournament, finishing with a four round total of 278. Jan Stephenson was next at even par, 10 shots back.

- Accuracy is crucial at Forest Hills. Water, trees, narrow fairways and over 50 bunkers keep the golfer thinking.

- Considered one of the tougher holes on tour, the par-4 sixth looks benign enough. The hole measures only 349 yards with a straight fairway, but the approach is the difficult part. The sloped green is flanked by a handful of bunkers guarding the left and front right.

ters like Davies, but the small greens will keep everyone honest.

- The 18th is a tough finishing hole. It runs only 399 yards, but features a severe dogleg left with an approach over a creek. The green is bunkered front-left and front-right.

For past results, see Chapter 6, Major Championships: Women.

1996 Leaderboard

1-Vicki Fergon	−12, 276	$82,500
t2-Patti Liscio	−8, 280	$44,282
t2-Pat Hurst	−8, 280	$44,282

Tournament History

1994	Liselotte Neumann	278
1995	Annika Sorenstam	278
1996	Vicki Fergon	276

NABISCO DINAH SHORE

Mission Hills Country Club
Rancho Mirage, CA

Date: March 27-30, 1997

TV: ABC/ESPN2

Tickets: The Dinah Shore
2 Racquet Club Dr.
Rancho Mirage, CA 92270

To play: Mission Hills is a private club open to members and their guests.

About the tournament and course:

- The finishing hole at the Old Course is so very typical of what championship golf drama can be. This 526-yard, par-5 has water running the entire left side and a series of bunkers to the right. Want to go for the green in two? Think again. The small green is on an island with palm trees to the left and back.

- In 1995, Nancy Lopez hit her approach into the water on 18. Laura Davies missed putts that would have forced playoffs in both 1994 and 1995.

- Hole number six can also cause fits. The fairway at this 352-yard par-4 bulges in and out of a lake running along the left side. The hole can be shortened by hitting the second shot over the lake, but the green is dotted with traps on all four sides.

- Not to leave out the par threes at Mission Hills, number 14 will force a player to take an extra practice swing. This hole only measures 148 yards, but water abuts the putting surface on the right-front, the right, and the right-rear. Three wide bunkers stack up along the left side of the green, and a smaller trap sits to the left-rear.

- This ladies major is a testament to the influence of the late Dinah Shore. Not only is Shore the only non-player to be elected to the LPGA Hall of Fame, the tournament just celebrated 25 years of existence, the last 15 as a major.

For past results, see Chapter 6, Major Championships: Women.

OLDSMOBILE CLASSIC

Walnut Hills Country Club
East Lansing, MI

Date: June 5-8, 1997

TV: ESPN

Tickets: Oldsmobile Classic
P.O. Box 12240
Lansing, MI 48901

To play: Walnut Hills is a private club open to members and their guests.

About the tournament and course:

- Michelle McGann rolled in a 12-foot birdie putt on the par-4 18th, the third hole of a sudden-death playoff, to beat Liselotte Neumann.

- Walnut Hills is one of the older tour courses, a 1920's layout with many trees, narrow fairways and well-bunkered, small greens. The ninth hole is generally regarded as the toughest on the course. Measuring 385 yards along a narrow fairway, this par-4 plays to an elevated, sloped green bordered by three traps.

1996 Leaderboard

1-Michelle McGann (*)	−16, 272	$90,000
2-Liselotte Neumann	−16, 272	$55,855
3-Meg Mallon	−15, 273	$40,759

Tournament History

1992	Barb Mucha	276
1993	Jane Geddes	277

1994	Beth Daniel	268
1995	Dale Eggeling	274
1996	*Michelle McGann	272

PING/WELCH'S CHAMPIONSHIP

**Blue Hill Country Club
Canton, MA**

Date: September 18-21, 1997

Tickets: PING/Welch's Championship
1320 Centre St., Ste. 206
Newton Center, MA 02159

To play: Blue Hill is a private club open
to members and their guests.

About the tournament
and course:

• Two-time NCAA champion Emilee Klein captured her first career victory in the 1996 event,
beating Karrie Webb by two strokes. She fired a
7-under-par 65 for a four-round total of 15-under
273. Klein started the final round two shots
behind Webb, but birdied three of the first four
holes to take the lead for good.

• The long par-4 first hole is the toughest on the
course, and one of the toughest on tour. The
landing area usually leaves a golfer with a downhill lie shooting to a green with bunkers front left
and front right.

• Designed by Skip Wogan, a student of Donald
Ross, Blue Hill has a true Ross feel. Large trees
and uneven fairways are common, as are
medium-plus sized greens trapped in front.

1996 Leaderboard

1-Emilee Klein	−15, 273	$75,000
2-Karrie Webb	−13, 275	$46,546
3-Meg Mallon	−12, 276	$33,966

LOW SCORING AVERAGE: VARE TROPHY

**1.	Laura Davies	70.32
2.	Annika Sorenstam	70.47
3.	Karrie Webb	70.87
4.	Liselotte Neumann	70.94
5.	Meg Mallon	71.35
6.	Dottie Pepper	71.37
7.	Kelly Robbins	71.41
8.	Michelle McGann	71.43
9.	Patty Sheehan	71.49
10.	Brandi Burton	71.57

** Not eligible for Vare Trophy—must complete
70 rounds to be eligible; Davies completed 68
rounds.

Tournament History

Boston Five Classic

1980	Dale Eggeling	276
1981	Donna Caponi	276
1982	Sandra Palmer	281
1983	Patti Rizzo	277
1984	Lauri Rinker	286
1985	Judy Dickinson	280
1986	Jane Geddes	281
1987	Jane Geddes	277
1988	Colleen Walker	274
1989	Amy Alcott	272
1990	*Barb Mucha	277

LPGA Bay State Classic

| 1991 | Juli Inkster | 275 |

Welch's Classic

| 1992 | Dottie Mochrie | 278 |

PING/Welch's Championship

1993	*Missie Berteotti	276
1994	Helen Alfredsson	274
1995	Beth Daniel	271
1996	Emilee Klein	273

ROCHESTER INTERNATIONAL

Locust Hill Country Club
Pittsford, NY

Date: June 19-22, 1997

Tickets: Locust Hill Country Club
2000 Jefferson Rd.
Pittsford, NY 14534

To play: Locust Hill is a private club open to members and their guests.

About the tournament and course:

- Dottie Pepper had what she termed a "perfect day—golf from sun-up to sundown" on the final day of the 1996 tournament. Having already been shortened to 54 holes due to rain on the first day, many players didn't finish the second round on Saturday, also because of rain. So it was a marathon on Sunday for Pepper as she shot 66-71 to edge Annika Sorenstam by two strokes, even though Sorenstam birdied three of the final six holes.

- Narrow, treed fairways and small greens are the norm here at Locust Hill, where Robert Trent Jones, Sr. has his name on nine of the holes.

- Don't lick your chops seeing the 158-yard fifth hole on the scorecard. The three-tiered kidney shaped green is uphill from the tee, has one large bunker to the left and another to the right. First impressions can be deceiving.

1996 Leaderboard

1-Dottie Pepper#	−10, 206	$90,000
2-Annika Sorenstam	−8, 208	$55,855
3-Amy Fruhwirth	−5, 211	$40,759

Tournament History

Bankers Trust Classic

1977	Pat Bradley	213
1978	Nancy Lopez	214

Sarah Coventry

1979	Jane Blalock	280
1980	Nancy Lopez	283
1981	Nancy Lopez	285

Rochester International

1982	*Sandra Haynie	276
1983	Ayako Okamoto	282
1984	*Kathy Whitworth	281
1985	Pat Bradley	280
1986	Judy Dickinson	281
1987	Deb Richard	280
1988	*Mei-chi Cheng	287
1989	*Patty Sheehan	278
1990	Patty Sheehan	271
1991	Rosie Jones	276
1992	Patty Sheehan	269
1993	Tammie Green	276
1994	Lisa Kiggens	273
1995	*Patty Sheehan	278
1996	#Dottie Pepper	206

SAFECO CLASSIC

Meridian Valley Country Club
Kent, WA

Date: September 11-14, 1997

TV: Regional/KSTW-TV

Tickets: SAFECO Classic
P.O.Box 6488
Kent, WA 98064

To play: Meridian Valley is a private club open to members and their guests.

About the tournament and course:

- The 16th hole is the toughest at Meridian. This dogleg right measures 371 yards and finishes on an elevated green protected by three traps. During the 1995 tournament, the average score for this par 4 was 4.209.

- Three-time winner Patty Sheehan holds the tourney record at 270 from her 1990 victory. No other golfer has come within three strokes of that total in the other 14 years of this event.

- In the 15 year history of this event, Sheehan has finished in the top ten an amazing ten times!

1996 Leaderboard

1-Karrie Webb	−11, 277	$82,500
2-Patty Sheehan	−9, 279	$51,201
t3-Barb Mucha	−8, 280	$33,211
t3-Tammie Green	−8, 280	$33,211

Tournament History

1982	Patty Sheehan	276
1983	Juli Inkster	283
1984	Kathy Whitworth	279
1985	JoAnne Carner	279
1986	Judy Dickinson	274
1987	Jan Stephenson	277
1988	Juli Inkster	278
1989	Beth Daniel	273
1990	Patty Sheehan	270
1991	*Pat Bradley	280
1992	Colleen Walker	277
1993	Brandi Burton	274
1994	Deb Richard	276
1995	Patty Sheehan	274
1996	Karrie Webb	277

SAFEWAY LPGA GOLF CHAMPIONSHIP

**Columbia-Edgewater Country Club
Beaverton, OR**

Date: September 5-7, 1997

TV: Regional/KPDX

Tickets: Safeway LPGA Golf Championship
6775 SW 111th St., Ste. 100
Beaverton, OR 97008-5378

To play: Columbia-Edgewater is a private club open to members and their guests.

About the tournament and course:

- The 17th hole was the toughest during the 1996 event, with a scoring average of 4.349. Off the left side of the fairway sit trees and out-of-bounds, while more trees and a hidden pond lurk to the right.

- This event celebrated its 25th year as an LPGA regular stop in 1996, although 1977-1982 were unofficial team events.

- 1996 winner Dottie Pepper shattered the tounament record by 5 strokes, carding a 202 total. The previous record had been held by three golfers.

1996 Leaderboard

1-Dottie Pepper	−14, 202	$82,500
2-Chris Johnson	−12, 204	$51,201
t3-Karrie Webb	−8, 208	$33,211
t3-Stefania Croce	−8, 208	$33,211

Tournament History

Portland LPGA Classic

1972	Kathy Whitworth	212
1973	#Kathy Whitworth	144
1974	JoAnne Carner	211
1975	Jo Ann Washam	215
1976	*Donna Caponi	217

Portland PING Team Championships

1977	*JoAnne Carner & Judy Rankin	202
1978	*Donna Caponi & Kathy Whitworth	203
1979	Nancy Lopez & Jo Ann Washam	198
1980	Donna Caponi & Kathy Whitworth	195
1981	*Donna Caponi & Kathy Whitworth	203
1982	*Sandra Haynie & Kathy McMullen	196

Portland PING Championship

1983	*JoAnne Carner	212
1984	Amy Alcott	212
1985	Nancy Lopez	215

Ping-Cellular One Golf Championship

1986	Ayako Okamoto	207
1987	Nancy Lopez	210
1988	Betsy King	213
1989	M. Spencer-Devlin	214
1990	Patty Sheehan	208
1991	Michelle Estill	208
1992	*Nancy Lopez	209
1993	Donna Andrews	208
1994	Missie McGeorge	207
1995	Alison Nicholas	207

Safeway LPGA Golf Championship

1996	Dottie Pepper	202

SARA LEE CLASSIC

Hermitage Golf Course
Old Hickory, TN

Date: May 9-11, 1997

Tickets: Sara Lee Classic
3939 Old Hickory Blvd.
P.O.Box 390
Old Hickory, TN 37138

To play: Hermitage is a public course
open year-round.

About the tournament and course:

- The Hermitage is named after Andrew Jackson's birthplace, only a few miles away in this northern Tennessee setting. The course features water on 13 holes, a myriad of traps, and twisted fairways everywhere.

- Meg Mallon birdied the 17th hole during 1996's final round for some breathing room, winning by

two strokes. Mallon was also victorious here in 1993, and just missed a chance at a playoff with winner Laura Davies in 1994.

- The 520-yard, par-5 16th hole is a serpentine affair that first bends left, the landing area guarded by water on both sides and two good-sized traps to the right. The fairway then narrows between the ponds and bends right to a green bounded by three traps.

1996 Leaderboard

1-Meg Mallon	−6, 210	$90,000
2-Stephanie Farwig	−4, 212	$48,307
3-Pam Wright	−4, 212	$48,307

Tournament History

1988	*Patti Rizzo	207
1989	Kathy Postlewait	203
1990	Ayako Okamoto	210
1991	Nancy Lopez	206
1992	*Maggie Will	207
1993	*Meg Mallon	205
1994	Laura Davies	203
1995	Michelle McGann	202
1996	Meg Mallon	210

SHOPRITE LPGA CLASSIC

Greate Bay Resort and Country Club
Somers Point, NJ

Date: June 27-29, 1997

TV: Regional/WMGM-WPVI-WABC

Tickets: ShopRite LPGA Classic
599 Shore Rd., Ste. 202
Somers Point, NJ 08244

To play: Greate Bay is a public course
open year-round.

About the tournament and course:

- Dottie Pepper set the new 54 hole standard in 1996 with an 11-under, 202. Near the turn on the final day, Pepper was tied with Amy Benz. Pepper then birdied the 11th, 12th and 14th holes to go to 13-under, a lead adequate enough that a couple of late bogeys didn't matter.

- From the comfortable lead department: Donna Andrews played the final 4 holes in 1994 at 4 over par and still won by two shots. First and second round scores of 67 and 66 respectively were the difference.

- Wind swirling off Egg Harbor Bay keeps the golfer thinking on many holes. The finishing hole is one of them. This 390-yard par-4 dogleg right not only requires adjustment for the wind, but the approach shot must negotiate a pair of greenside bunkers.

1996 Leaderboard

1-Dottie Pepper	–11, 202	$112,500
2-Amy Benz	–7, 206	$69,819
t3-Annika Sorenstam	–6, 207	$40,885
t3-Michelle McGann	–6, 207	$40,885
t3-Marianne Morris	–6, 207	$40,885

Tournament History

Atlantic City Classic

1986	Juli Inkster	209
1987	Betsy King	207
1988	*Juli Inkster	206
1989	Nancy Lopez	206
1990	Chris Johnson	275
1991	Jane Geddes	208

ShopRite LPGA Classic

1992	Anne-Marie Palli	207
1993	Shelley Hamlin	204
1994	Donna Andrews	207
1995	Betsy King	204
1996	Dottie Pepper	202

TOTAL NUMBER OF BIRDIES

1.	Michelle McGann	327	
2.	Liselotte Neumann	324	
3.	Karrie Webb	323	
4.	Brandie Burton	316	
T5.	Val Skinner	306	
T5.	Kris Tschetter	306	
7.	Barb Mucha	291	
8.	Kelly Robbins	288	
T9.	Jane Geddes		286
T9.	Deb Richard	286	

SPRINT TITLEHOLDERS CHAMPIONSHIP

**LPGA International
Daytona Beach, FL**

Date: May 1-4, 1997

TV: CBS

Tickets: Tournament Headquarters
101 Corsair Dr., Ste. 202
Daytona Beach, FL 32114

To play: The LPGA International is a public course open year-round.

About the tournament and course:

- While the winds off the Atlantic Ocean tempt the golfer to compensate, bunkers on every fairway and water on almost every hole can reign in that temptation.

- This links course features large shared fairways in two instances, both dotted with fairway bunkers. Quick, contoured greens are also the norm at this 1994 Rees Jones design.

- The 16th hole plays uphill and into the wind with four fairway and four greenside traps. Number 18 is a par-5, 452-yard dogleg left with water on the left and a large bunker in the middle of the fairway just shy of the landing area.

LONGEST AVERAGE DRIVING DISTANCE (YDS.)

1.	Michelle McGann	327
1.	Laurie Davies	262.3
2.	Jean Bartholomew	255.6
3.	Michelle McGann	255.5
4.	Kelly Robbins	254.0
5.	Jane Geddes	252.7
6.	Tania Abitbol	249.9
T7.	Karrie Webb	249.6
T7.	Beth Daniel	249.6
9.	Annette DeLuca	249.3
10.	Helen Alfredsson	249.0

1996 Leaderboard

1-Karrie Webb	−16, 272	$180,000
2-Kelly Robbins	−15, 273	$111,711
3-Val Skinner	−14, 274	$81,519

Tournament History

Centel Classic

1990	Beth Daniel	271
1991	Pat Bradley	278
1992	Dan'le Ammaccapane	208

Sprint Championship

1993	Kristi Albers	279
1994	Sherri Steinhauer	273
1995	Val Skinner	273
1996	Karrie Webb	272

STANDARD REGISTER PING

Moon Valley Country Club
Phoenix, AZ

Date: March 20-23, 1997

TV: ESPN

Tickets: Standard Register PING
1441 N. 12th St.
Phoenix, AZ 85006

To play: Moon Valley is a private club open to members and their guests.

About the tournament and course:

- Moon Valley Country Club most famous member may just be it's owner, PING founder Karsten Solheim.

- Three-in-a-row. Laura Davies completed that impressive feat with a one shot victory in 1996. Moon Valley suits Davies' game just fine. The course is long and generally flat, but wind, trees and rough keep everyone honest.

- After making the turn, the difficult 10th hole awaits. This 530-yard, par-5 features a narrow fairway flanked by bunkers. Some players can cut the corner on this dogleg left, but a large ditch will easily swallow errant shots.

1996 Leaderboard

1-Laura Davies	−8, 284	$105,000
2-Kristal Parker-Gregory	−7, 285	$65,165
3-Kelly Robbins	−6, 286	$47,553

Tournament History

Sun City Classic

1980	Jan Stephenson	275
1981	Patty Hayes	277
1982	*Beth Daniel	278

Samaritan Turquoise Classic

1983	Anne-Marie Palli	205
1984	Chris Johnson	276
1985	*Betsy King	280

Standard Register Turquoise Classic

1986	M.B. Zimmerman	278
1987	Pat Bradley	276
1988	Ok-Hee Ku	281
1989	Allison Finney	282
1990	Pat Bradley	280

Standard Register Ping

1991	Dan'le Ammaccapane	283
1992	Dan'le Ammaccapane	279
1993	Patty Sheehan	275
1994	Laura Davies	277
1995	Laura Davies	280
1996	Laura Davies	284

THE STAR BANK LPGA CLASSIC

Country Club of the North
Beavercreek, OH

Date: August 18-24, 1997

Tickets: The Star Bank LPGA Classic
One Prestige Place, Ste. 530
Miamisburg, OH 45342

To play: Country Club of the North is a private club open to members and their guests.

About the tournament and course:

• According to GolfWeek Magazine, the finshing hole at Country CLub of the North was the toughest hole on the LPGA tour during the 1995 season. The 436-yard par-4 had a scoring average for that year of 4.61.

• That 18th hole, a dogleg right, has wetlands coming into play on the first two shots. The long, narrow green features a deep bunker that stretches along the back and the right side.

• As with many Jack Nicklaus designs, this course favors the long hitter. Fairly generous landing areas and large greens are the norm and only three greens have as many as three sand traps.

1996 Leaderboard

1-Laura Davies	−12, 204	$82,500
t2-Maggie Will	−9, 207	$44,282
t2-Pat Hurst	−9, 207	$44,282

Tournament History

1994	*Maggie Will	210
1995	Chris Johnson	210
1996	Laura Davies	204

STATE FARM RAIL CLASSIC

Rail Golf Club
Springfield, IL

Date: August 30 – September 1, 1997

TV: ESPN2

Tickets: State Farm Rail Classic
427 E. Monroe St., Ste. 301
Springfield, IL 62701

To play: The Rail is a public course open March through December.

About the tournament and course:

• Having been a regular stop since 1976, the Rail is the second longest running tournament on the LPGA tour.

• The 16th is the number one handicap hole at Rail. The green at this 167-yard par-3 is extremely narrow, with water in front and along the right side. Sitting between the putting surface and the lake are bunkers on all sides.

• This Robert Trent Jones, Jr. design yields some low scores, but numerous water hazards still inflate some scorecards.

1996 Leaderboard

1-Michelle McGann(*)	−14, 202	$86,250
t2-Barb Whitehead	−14, 202	
t2-Laura Davies	−14, 202	

Tournament History

Jerry Lewis Muscular Dystrophy Classic

1976	*Sandra Palmer	213

Rail Golf Classic

1977	Hollis Stacy	271
1978	Pat Bradley	276
1979	Jo Ann Washam	275
1980	Nancy Lopez	275
1981	JoAnne Carner	205
1982	JoAnne Carner	202
1983	*Lauri Peterson	210
1984	Cindy Hill	207
1985	Betsy King	205
1986	*Betsy King	205
1987	Rosie Jones	208
1988	Betsy King	207
1989	Beth Daniel	203
1990	Beth Daniel	203
1991	Pat Bradley	197
1992	*Nancy Lopez	199

State Farm Rail Classic

1993	*Helen Dobson	203
1994	Barb Mucha	203
1995	Mary Beth Zimmerman	206
1996	Michelle McGann	202

U.S. WOMEN'S OPEN

Pumpkin Ridge Golf Club
Cornelius, OR

Date: July 10-13
TV: NBC
Tickets: 1-800-295-2094
To play: Call ahead (503-647-9977), at least a week in advance by phone, six days in advance in person.

About the tournament and course:

- The Ghost Creek Course opened in 1992 and was named Best New Public Course of 1992 by *Golf Digest.*

- Host of the 1996 U.S. Amateur, where Tiger Woods won his third-straight championship with a thrilling, come from-behind victory.

- The course rewards straight play on its thick fairways, and strong course management is needed to play its various looks; those who stay out of trouble and take advantage of opportunities when presented will survive.

- Seems ideal for long straight slingers like Anika Sorenstam, who'll be gunning for her third-straight Open championship. Karrie Webb will challenge if she's on target, and veterans like Patty Sheehan and Laura Davies might discover a secret or two and take charge.

- Robert Cupp design (see his profile in the course designers section), featuring shallow, grassed-face bunkers that can turn wayward approaches into sudden double bogeys.

For past results, see Chapter 6, Major Championships: Women.

WELCH'S/CIRCLE K CHAMPIONSHIP

Randolph North Golf Course
Tucson, AZ

Date: March 13-16, 1997
Tickets: Tucson Parks Foundation
900 S. Randolph Way
Tucson, AZ 85716
To play: Randolph Park is open to the public year-round.

About the tournament and course:

- Mature trees and numerous water hazards greet the golfer at Randolph Park. The lack of fairway bunkers is evident, but greenside traps dot the landscape at all but two holes.

- The most difficult hole is generally number 4. To master this 402-yard, par-4 venture, golfers must avoid the trees on the right side of the landing area, and traps front-right and front-left of the green.

LOW PUTTING AVERAGE (PER ROUND)

1.	Liselotte Neumann	29.27
2.	Cindy Schreyer	29.38
3.	Danielle Ammaccapane	29.45
T4.	Dottie Pepper	29.49
T4.	Brandie Burton	29.49
6.	Carolyn Hill	29.68
7.	Jennifer Wyatt	29.70
8.	Barb Whitehead	29.71
9.	Jenny Lidback	29.72
10.	Tammie Green	29.74

• Chris Johnson is not only the event's only two-time winner, but she also holds the tournament record (along with Meg Mallon) at 16-under, 272.

1996 Leaderboard

1-Liselotte Neumann	−12, 276	$67,500
2-Cathy Johnson-Forbes	−11, 277	$41,891
t3-Karen Weiss	−9, 279	$24,530
t3-Michelle McGann	−9, 279	$24,530
t3-Dale Eggeling	−9, 279	$24,530

Tournament History

Arizona Copper Classic

1981	Nancy Lopez	278
1982	*Ayako Okamoto	281

Tucson Conquistadores Open

1983	Jan Stephenson	207
1984	Chris Johnson	272

Circle K LPGA Tucson Open

1985	Amy Alcott	279
1986	Penny Pulz	276
1987	Betsy King	281
1988	Laura Davies	278
1989	Lori Garbacz	274
1990	Colleen Walker	276

Ping/Welch's Championship (Tucson)

1991	Chris Johnson	273
1992	Brandi Burton	277
1993	Meg Mallon	272
1994	Donna Andrews	276
1995	Dottie Mochrie	278
1996	Liselotte Neumann	276

* Won in playoff
\# Shortened tournament

12

TOURNAMENTS OF THE SENIOR PGA TOUR

AMERICAN EXPRESS INVITATIONAL

TPC at Prestancia
Sarasota, FL

Date: February 21-23, 1997

TV: ESPN

Tickets: TPC at Prestancia
4409 TPC Dr.
Sarasota, FL 34238

To play: TPC at Prestancia is a private club open to members and their guests.

About the tournament and course:

• The TPC at Prestancia gives the golfer quite a variety. Some of the earlier holes have a bit of elbow room, while closer to the end of the course things tighten up a bit. A putter on fire can really do some damage here.

• The inaugural event saw Hale Irwin set three season marks for 1996. His 54 hole total of 197 was tops for the year, as was his five shot winning margin. Irwin's final round 64 was best finish by a winner for the season.

Tournament History

American Express Invitational

| 1996 | Hale Irwin | 197 |

AMERITECH SENIOR OPEN

Kemper Lakes Golf Club
Long Grove, Il

Date: May 30-June 1, 1997

TV: CBS

Tickets: Ameritech Senior Open
30 S. Wacker Drive
Chicago, IL 60606

To play: Kemper Lakes is a public course.

About the tournament and course:

• Long recognized as one of the best public tracks in the country, Kemper Lakes has hosted the last two Ameritech Senior Opens, as well as the 1989 PGA Championship.

- Numerous hazards dot the landscape here, including fairway traps on number nine which narrow the landing area. The uphill second shot is to a narrow green.

- Walt Morgan set the course record at 63 in 1996's opening round on his way to a two shot win. Morgan is a cousin of baseball great Joe Morgan.

1996 Leaderboard

1-Walt Morgan	–11, 205	$165,000
2-John Bland	–9, 207	$96,800
3-Bob Murphy	–8. 208	$79,200

Tournament History

1989	Bruce Crampton	205
1990	Chi Chi Rodriguez	203
1991	Mike Hill	200
1992	Dale Douglass	201
1993	George Archer	133
1994	John Paul Cain	202
1995	Hale Irwin	267
1996	Walt Morgan	205

BANK OF BOSTON CLASSIC
Nashawtuc Country Club
Concord, MA

Date: August 1-3, 1997
TV: ESPN
Tickets: Bank of Boston Senior Classic
1861 Sudbury Rd.
Concord, MA 01742
To play: Nashawtuc is a private club open to members and their guests.

About the tournament and course:

- Jim Dent won the 1996 event when Tom Wargo bogeyed number 16 and missed a short birdie putt on the final hole.

- This almost-40 year old course is known on Tour for its birdies. Wide fairways and greens without too many tricks make the difference here.

- The seventh hole has heavy rough on both sides of the fairway. At 454 yards, this hole requires a long second shot to a well-trapped green.

1996 Leaderboard

1-Jim Dent	–12, 204	$120,000
t2-Jay Sigel	–11, 205	$64,000
t2-Tom Wargo	–11, 205	$64,000

Tournament History
Marlboro Classic

1981	Bob Goalby	208
1982	Arnold Palmer	276
1983	Don January	273

Digital Middlesex Classic

1984	Don January	209

Digital Seniors Classic

1985	*Lee Elder	208
1986	Chi Chi Rodriguez	203
1987	Chi Chi Rodriguez	198
1988	Chi Chi Rodriguez	202
1989	Bob Charles	200
1990	Bob Charles	203
1991	Rocky Thompson	205
1992	#*Mike Hill	136

Bank of Boston Classic

1993	Bob Betley	204
1994	Jim Albus	203
1995	Isao Ozaki	204
1996	Jim Dent	204

BELL ATLANTIC CLASSIC
Chester Valley Golf Club
Malvern, PA

Date: May 23-25, 1997
TV: ESPN

Tickets: Bell Atlantic Classic
P.O.Box 506
Malvern, PA 19355

To play: Chester Valley is a private club open to members and their guests.

About the tournament and course:

- Chester Valley annually places a handful of holes on the Tour's top 50 list of difficulty. In 1994, the field averaged over 4 strokes to the bad on this par 70 layout.

- The 6th stands out as the toughes of the tough. The 411-yard has a creek cutting through the fairway which usually keeps the driver in the bag.

- In 1996, Dale Douglass birdied the third playoff hole to beat John Schroeder and Tom Wargo. Schroeder held a one-shot lead going to number 18 in regulation, but he bogeyed it, while Wargo missed a 20-foot birdie attempt for the victory. Thus, the door was opened for the playoff, and Douglass.

1996 Leaderboard

1-Dale Douglass(*)	−4, 206	$135,000
t2-John Schroeder	−4, 206	$72,000
t2-Tom Wargo	−4, 206	$72,000

Tournament History

United Hospitals Senior Golf Championship

1985 #Don January		135
1986 Gary Player		206
1987 Chi Chi Rodriguez		202

United Hospitals Classic

1988 *Bruce Crampton		205

Bell Atlantic/St. Christopher's Classic

1989 *Dave Hill		206

Bell Atlantic Classic

1990	*Dale Douglass	204
1991	Jim Ferree	208
1992	Lee Trevino	205

As a boy learning golf in his native Spain, Seve Ballesteros learned to pitch, chip, and drive the ball with an old three iron. It was the only club he owned.

1993	Bob Charles	204
1994	Lee Trevino	206
1995	Jim Colbert	207
1996	Dale Douglass	206

BELLSOUTH SENIOR CLASSIC AT OPRYLAND

Springhouse Golf Club
Nashville, TN

Date: June 6-8, 1997

TV: NBC

Tickets: BellSouth Senior Classic at Opryland
18 Springhouse Lane
Nashville, TN 37214

To play: Springhouse is a public course.

About the tournament and course:

- Springhouse has its name show up on the tough hole list each year. One of the usual suspects is number 11, a 435 yard par-4. The Cumberland River is to the right of the fairway, a large trap to the left. More traps around the narrow green keep the golfer on his toes for the second shot, also.

- Number 4 is no picnic on the banks of a river, either. Water along the entire left side of the fairway, and a green that slopes down to that water make this hole tough.

- PGA Golfer Larry Nelson designed this course for a 1990 opening. Nelson kept a large area of wetlands intact, allowing a natural habitat for many flying creatures.

1996 Leaderboard

1-Isao Aoki	202
t2-Jay Sigel	203
t2-Graham Marsh	203
4-Bruce Summerhays	204

Tournament History

1994	Lee Trevino	199
1995	Jim Dent	203
1996	Isao Aoki	202

BRICKYARD CROSSING CHAMPIONSHIP

Brickyard Crossing
Indianapolis, IN

Date: September 19-21, 1997

TV: ABC/ESPN

Tickets: Brickyard Crossing Championship
P.O. Box 24486
Indianapolis, IN 46224

To play: Brickyard Crossingis a public course.

About the tournament and course:

- Jimmy Powell and John Jacobs both shot final round 66 in 1996's rain shortened event. The problem for Jacobs? He was one behind at the start of the day. Powell carded eight birdies and two bogeys on the day.

- The black cloud seems to have been following this event lately, literally. Three of the last four championships have been shortened to 36 holes by rain.

- This course shares ground with one of the world's most popular sporting events, the Indianapolis 500. The racetrack actually cuts through the course, with four holes on the infield and the rest outside the track.

1996 Leaderboard

1-Jimmy Powell	−10, 134	$112,500
2-John Jacobs	−9, 135	$66,000
3-Bud Allin	−8, 136	$54,000

Tournament History

GTE North Classic

1988	Gary Player	201
1989	#Gary Player	135
1990	*Mike Hill	201
1991	George Archer	199
1992	Ray Floyd	199
1993	#Bob Murphy	134

Brickyard Crossing Championship

1994	#Isao Aoki	133
1995	Simon Hobday	204
1996	#Jimmy Powell	134

BRUNO'S MEMORIAL CLASSIC

Greystone Golf Club
Birmingham, AL

Date: May 2-4, 1997

TV: ESPN

Tickets: Bruno's Memorial Classic
1200 Corporate Dr., Ste. 410
Birmingham, AL 35242

To play: Greystone is a private club open to members and their guests.

About the tournament and course:

- This long course favors those hitters that can control their length. Three of the last six holes are par-5s at 526, 526, and 531 yards. The course totals over 7,000 yards.

- Number 3 runs 453 yards with a dogleg to the right. The rut off to the right side of the fairway at the landing area can result in a gutter ball. The approach from the left side of the fairway is over water. The architects then squeezed a trap between water and the right side of the green.

1996 Leaderboard

1-John Bland(*)	208
t2-John Paul Cain	208
t2-Kermit Zarley	208
4-Isao Aoki	209

Tournament History

1992	George Archer	208
1993	Bob Murphy	203
1994	Jim Dent	201
1995	Graham Marsh	201
1996	John Bland	208

BURNET SENIOR CLASSIC

Bunker Hills Golf Club
Coon Rapids, MN

Date: July 18-20, 1997

TV: ESPN

Tickets: Burnet Senior Classic
P.O.Box 33218
Coon Rapids, MN 55433-0218

To play: Bunker Hills is a public course.

About the tournament and course:

- In 1996, Vicente Fernandez qualifed on Monday, then proceeded to win the tournament, only the fifth player in Seniors history to do just that. Second-round leader Jim Dent paved the way for Fernandez' win by shooting 36-38=74 for the final round, falling way back.

- Tall trees, some water, and numerous bunkers give this track its character. Long hitters can flourish here as the layout measures almost 6900 yards. The four par-3s run 180, 180, 200 amd 215.

- The 14th lists as the toughest hole at Bunker Hills. The 430 yard par 4 has trees along the fairway and a green trapped on both sides.

1996 Leaderboard

1-Vicente Fernandez	−11, 205	$187,500
t2-Bruce Crampton	−10, 206	$100,000
t2-J.C. Snead	−10, 206	$100,000

Tournament History

1993	Chi Chi Rodriguez	201
1994	Dave Stockton	203
1995	Ray Floyd	201
1996	Vincente Fernandez	205

CADILLAC NFL GOLF CLASSIC

Upper Montclair Country Club
Clifton, NJ

Date: May 16-18, 1997

TV: ESPN

Tickets: Cadillac NFL Golf Classic
1266 E. Main St., 7th Fl.
Stamford, CT 06902

To play: Upper Montclair is a private club open to members and their guests.

About the tournament and course:

- Combining Senior Tour stars with NFL stars has success written all over it. And in four short years, this event has done just that. During the first event, in 1993, almost 80,000 fans walked through the turnstiles.

- Pro-am events, along with long drive contests for the footballers and, oh yeah, a seniors tournament make this a busy week for all.

- This relatively short course dates back to 1901, with a late-1950's remodeling job by Robert Trent Jones. Number 9 is the toughest, a dogleg right with the landing area is flanked by three bunkers. Overall measurement is 420-yards, the second shot of which is uphill to a small green.

In the 1977 Tournament Players Championship, a strong wind blew J.C. Snead's hat off his head and onto the green. There it hit his ball and cost him a two-stroke penalty.

1996 Leaderboard

1-Bob Murphy	202
2-Jay Sigel	204
3-Tommy Aaron	206

Tournament History

1993	Lee Trevino	209
1994	Ray Floyd	206
1995	George Archer	205
1996	Bob Murhpy	202

EMERALD COAST CLASSIC

The Moors Golf Club
Milton, FL

Date: September 26-28, 1997

TV: TBD

Tickets: Emerald Coast Classic
25 W. Cedar Street, Ste. 620
Pensacola, FL 32501

To play: The Moors is a public course open year-round.

About the tournament and course:

- Lee Trevino dropped a 30 foot birdie putt on the first playoff hole to win the 1996 stop. Dave Stockton held a one-stroke lead entering the final hole in regulation, but an 18th hole bogey forced the four-way playoff.

- The ninth hole ususally plays tough. Out-of-bounds runs the right side of the fairway, and the second shot is over water to a large green trapped twice at the back.

1996 Leaderboard

1-Lee Trevino(*)	−3, 207	$157,500
t2-Bob Eastwood	−3, 207	$70,350
t2-Mike Hill	−3, 207	$70,350
t2-David Graham	−3, 207	$70,350
t2-Dave Stockton	−3, 207	$70,350

Tournament History

1996	Lee Trevino	207

FIRST OF AMERICA CLASSIC

Egypt Valley Country Club –
Ridge and Valley Courses
Ada, MI

Date: August 15-17, 1997

TV: TBD

Tickets: First of America Classic
233 E. Fulton St., Ste. 104
Grand Rapids, MI 49503

To play: Egypt Valley is a private club open to members and their guests.

About the tournament and course:

- Dave Stockton went 69-69 over the last two rounds in 1996 to beat Bob Murphy by one stroke. Stockton, who began the final day four strokes off the pace, carded five birdies on this tough track. "This is a thinking course. If you're a pessimist, this course will eat your lunch," Stockton said.

- This event moved to Egypt Valley in 1994, taking holes from both Arthur Hills-designed courses for tournament play. Players with good short games can flourish here.

- The front nine finishes on a 426 yard par-4. This dogleg right ends up on a small, bi-level green with plenty of hazards.

1996 Leaderboard

1-Dave Stockton	−10, 206	$125,000
2-Bob Murphy	−9, 207	$74,800
t3-Tom Wargo	−8, 208	$56,100
t3-Jimmy Powell	−8, 208	$56,100

Tournament History

Greater Grand Rapids Open

1986	*Jim Ferree	204
1987	Billy Casper	200
1988	Orville Moody	203
1989	John Paul Cain	203
1990	#Don Massengale	134

First of America Classic

1991	*Harold Henning	202
1992	Gibby Gilbert	202
1993	*George Archer	199
1994	#Tony Jacklin	136
1995	Jimmy Powell	201
1996	Dave Stockton	206

FORD SENIOR PLAYERS CHAMPIONSHIP

TPC of Michigan
Dearborn, MI

Date: July 10-13, 1997

TV: ABC/ESPN

Tickets: Ford Senior Players Championship
15550 Rotunda
Dearborn, MI 48120

To play: TPC of Michigan is a private club open to members and their guests

About the tournament and course:

- Once again in 1996, the 14th hole proved up the toughest. This 429-yard par-4 is a dogleg left with water down the left side. Players wishing to try the shortest route have to deal with that water, and everyone has to deal with carrying a swamp on approach. The green is narrow and unforgiving.

- Before getting to the 14th, a couple of tests await. The 166-yard, par-3 12th hole requires an accurate mid-iron to an odd-shaped green. Water snakes along the front and to the right of the green.

- The two par-5s on the back side, numbers 13 and 17, run alongside each other, creating a nice viewing area. The tee shot at 13 is over a small creek to a fairway that doglegs left. The green can be reached in two on this 506-yarder, but beware the surrounding seven or so traps.

- The other par-5 on the back, the 17th, runs 521 yards. The second half of the fairway narrows considerably as water squeezes the left side. The incredibly narrow green is tucked around the side of the lake, and is flanked by traps on either side.

- Course architect Jack Nicklaus has patterned a championship layout around wetlands and water. The wet stuff comes into play on the first six holes, as well as numbers 10-13 and 17 and 18.

For past results, see Chapter 7, Major Championships: Seniors.

FRANKLIN QUEST CHAMPIONSHIP

Park Meadows
Park City, UT

Date: July 25-27, 1997

TV: ESPN

Tickets: Franklin Quest Championship
2200 W. Parkway Blvd.
Salt Lake City, UT 84119

To play: Park Meadows is a public course.

About the tournament and course:

- Graham Marsh shot 67 during 1996's final round to card a two stroke win. Marsh began the day two shots off the lead, but birdied the 14th, 15th and 17th holes for a strong back nine.

- This Jack Nicklaus course was designed on old mining grounds at the foot of the Wasatch mountain range. The open, treeless track features over 100 bunkers and numerous streams, along with the usual tough Nicklaus greens.

- The ninth hole runs 451 yards with a dogleg right, three fairway bunkers and four greenside traps. The green slopes away from those four traps making the apporach that much more difficult.

1996 Leaderboard

1-Graham Marsh	–14, 202	$120,000
2-Kermit Zarley	–12, 204	$70,400
3-Jack Kiefer	–11, 205	$57,600

Tournament History

The Shootout at Jeremy Ranch

1982	Billy Casper	279
1983	Bob Goalby & Mike Reid	256
1984	Don January & Mike Sullivan	250
1985	Miller Barber & Ben Crenshaw	257

Showdown Classic

1986	Bobby Nichols & Curt Byrum	249
1987	Miller Barber	210
1988	Miller Barber	207
1989	Tom Shaw	207
1990	Rives McBee	202
1991	Dale Douglass	209

Franklin Showdown Classic

| 1992 | *#Orville Moody | 137 |
| 1993 | Dave Stockton | 197 |

Franklin Quest Championship

1994	Tom Weiskopf	204
1995	Tony Jacklin	206
1996	Graham Marsh	202

GTE SUNCOAST CLASSIC

TPC of Tampa Bay at Cheval Lutz, FL

Date: February 14-16, 1997

TV: ESPN

Tickets: GTE Suncoast Classic 16002 N. Dale Mabry, 2nd Fl. Tampa, FL 33618

To play: TPC of Tampa Bay at Cheval is a public course open year-round.

About the tournament and course:

- Yet another stadium-style TPC course, Cheval attracts some of the largest crowds each year.

- Water everywhere swallows up errant shots. Number 15, for example. The entire left side of this 425-yard par 4 is liquid, and the approach shot must not only consider the water, but traps on both sides of the green, as well.

- Rocky Thompson's victory in 1994 was a result of a final round 61, aided by 10 birdies.

1996 Leaderboard

1-Jack Nicklaus	211
2-J.C. Snead	212
3-Bob Murphy	213
4-Simon Hobday	214

Tournament History

GTE Suncoast Seniors Classic

| 1988 | Dale Douglass | 210 |
| 1989 | *Bob Charles | 207 |

GTE Suncoast Classic

1990	Mike Hill	207
1991	Bob Charles	210
1992	*Jim Colbert	200
1993	Jim Albus	206
1994	Rocky Thompson	201
1995	Dave Stockton	204
1996	Jack Nicklaus	211

At the 1986 Senior TPC Al Chandler whiffed three times.

KROGER SENIOR CLASSIC

**The Golf Center at Kings Island – Grizzly Course
Mason, OH**

Date: July 4-6, 1997
TV: ESPN
Tickets: Kroger Senior Classic
P.O.Box 499
Mason, OH 45040
To play: All facilities at Kings Island are public.

About the tournament and course:

- The Grizzly course was designed in 1971 by Jack Nicklaus and Desmond Muirhead, the same two that built the famous Muirfield course, home of the PGA's Memorial tournament.

- Water on 10 holes and lots of sand is offset by normally flat greens at the Grizzly.

- Isao Aoki carded a 66 in 1996's final round for the win. After missing some short putts during the second round, Aoki hit the practice green before the final round. His final round of 5 under was the result of his practice.

1996 Leaderboard

1-Isao Aoki	−15, 198	$135,000
t2-Rocky Thompson	−10, 203	$72,000
t2-Mike Hill	−10, 203	$72,000

Tournament History

1990	#Jim Dent	133
1991	Al Geiberger	203
1992	*Gibby Gilbert	203
1993	Simon Hobday	202
1994	Jim Colbert	199
1995	Mike Hill	196
1996	Isao Aoki	198

LAS VEGAS SENIOR CLASSIC

**TPC at The Canyons
Las Vegas, NV**

Date: April 25-27, 1997
TV: ESPN
Tickets: Las Vegas Senior Classic
801 S. Rancho Dr., Ste. C3
Las Vegas, NV 89134
To play: TPC at The Canyons is a private club open to members and their guests.

About the tournament and course:

- The 18th hole is a real challenge. The tee shot at this 433-yard, par-4 must carry a large wasteland to a fairway with a pair of bunkers on the far side. The second shot is over water to a small, irregularly shaped green.

- The PGA stops at Summerlin as well as the Seniors. PGA golfers play the par 3 eigth at 239 yards and very tough, but it is scaled down to 190 yards for the Seniors.

1996 Leaderboard

1-Jim Colbert(*)	207
t2-Dave Stockton	207
t2-Bob Charles	207
4-Hale Irwin	208

Tournament History

Las Vegas Senior Classic

1986	Bruce Crampton	206
1987	Al Geiberger	203

General Tire Las Vegas Classic

1988	Larry Mowry	204
1989	*Charles Coody	205

Las Vegas Senior Classic

1990	Chi Chi Rodriguez	204
1991	Chi CHi Rodriguez	204

1992	Lee Trevino	206
1993	Gibby Gilbert	204
1994	Ray Floyd	203
1995	Jim Colbert	205
1996	Jim Colbert	207

LIBERTY MUTUAL LEGENDS OF GOLF

PGA West – Stadium Course
La Quinta, CA

Date: March 21-23, 1997

TV: ABC

Tickets: Liberty Mutual Legends of Golf
55920 PGA Blvd.
La Quinta, CA 92253

To play: There are two public and two private courses on the resort grounds.

About the tournament and course:

- Two-man, better ball format makes this tremendously difficult course at bit easier. Architect Pete Dye's marching orders on this course were to make it the "hardest...in the world."

- The event is open only to players with at least 5 wins on either the PGA or Senior tours.

- Bunkers that never seem to end prevail on the course. On the par-5 number 16, long, deep bunkers come into play on each shot.

1996 Leaderboard

1-Lee Trevino/Mike Hill	198
t2-Chi Chi Rodriguez/ Harold Henning	200
t2-Jack Nicklaus/Gary Player	200
t2-Jimmy Powell/ Orville Moody	200
5-Simon Hobday/ George Archer	201

Tournament History

Legends of Golf

1978	Sam Snead & Gardner Dickinson	193
1979	Julius Boros & Roberto DeVicenzo	195

Liberty Mutual Legends of Golf

1980	Tommy Bolt & Art Wall	187
1981	Gene Littler & Bob Rosburg	257
1982	#Sam Snead & Don January	183
1983	Rod Funseth & Roberto DeVicenzo	258
1984	Billy Casper & Gay Brewer	258
1985	Don January & Gene Littler	257
1986	Don January & Gene Littler	255
1987	Bruce Crampton & Orville Moody 2	51
1988	*Bruce Crampton & Orville Moody	254
1989	Harold Henning & Al Geiberger	251
1990	Dale Douglass & Charles Coody	249
1991	Lee Trevino & Mike Hill	252
1992	Lee Trevino & Mike Hill	251
1993	*Harold Henning	204
1994	Dale Douglass & Charles Coody	188
1995	Mike Hill & Lee Trevino	195
1996	Lee Trevino & Mike Hill	198

A bronze plaque at the Rancho Park Golf Course commemorates Arnold Palmer's 12-stroke final hole at the 1961 Los Angeles Open.

NATIONWIDE CHAMPIONSHIP
Golf Club of Georgia – Lakeside Course
Alpharetta, GA

Date: June 20-22, 1997

TV: ESPN

To play: Both courses at the Golf Club of Georgia are private and open to members and their guests.

About the tournament and course:

- The Arthur Hills-designed Lakeside Course was named best new private course in 1991 by Golf Digest.

- Holes 11 through 15 play along Lake Windward. The greens at all these holes but 15 abut the lake, and the par-3 13th is completely over water to an odd-shaped green.

- Number 11 is the toughest on the course. A par-5 measuring 587 yards, the landing area is flanked by a large tree on one side, and severe rough on the left. The green is the first look at the large lake, and any long approach shot has the possibility of getting wet.

1996 Leaderboard

1-Jim Colbert	206
2-Isao Aoki	209
3-Hale Irwin	210

Tournament History

1991	Mike Hill	212
1992	Isao Aoki	208
1993	Lee Trevino	205
1994	Dave Stockton	198
1995	Bob Murphy	203
1996	Jim Colbert	206

NORTHVILLE LONG ISLAND CLASSIC
Meadow Brook Club
Jericho, NY

Date: August 8-10, 1997

TV: ESPN

Tickets: Northville Long Island Classic
25 Melville Park Rd. Melville, NY 11747

To play: Meadow Brook is a private club open to members and their guests.

About the tournament and course:

- John Bland shot a pair of 66s for the final two rounds in 1996 for the victory. The abundance of right-to-left holes fit Bland's game, and he carded only one bogey for the entire tournament.

- Very few holes on the course are straight, and the 17th hole is a double-dogleg. The track was cut into an old hunt club in the early 1950's by Dick Wilson, and the mature trees are evident on the front nine.

- The ninth hole is always one of the toughest on Tour. The par-4, 417 yarder is a dogleg right onto a trapped green. The course is unusual in that it finishes on a par-3. The 167-yard finishing hole is a perfect site to watch the players come home.

1996 Leaderboard

1-John Bland	−14, 202	$120,000
2-Jim Colbert	−11, 205	$70,400
3-Raymond Floyd	−10, 206	$57,600

Tournament History

The Northville Invitational

1988 Don Bies		202

Northville Long Island Classic

1989	#*Butch Baird	183
1990	George Archer	208

1991	George Archer	204
1992	George Archer	205
1993	Ray Floyd	208
1994	Lee Trevino	200
1995	Lee Trevino	202
1996	John Bland	202

PGA SENIORS CHAMPIONSHIP

PGA National Resort and Spa
Palm Beach Gardens, FL

Date: April 17-20, 1997

TV: NBC/ESPN

Tickets: PGA Seniors Championship
100 Avenue of the Champions
Palm Beach Gardens, FL 33418

To play: All courses at the National are part of the resort.

About the tournament and course:

• Making the turn at the Champion Course can raise your heart rate. Holes number 11, 15, 16 and 17 annually rank very high on the toughest-on-tour list. As a matter of fact, in 1992 the 15th was second toughest on tour, while the 16th ranked number 4 on the list and the 17th hole placed seventh.

• The 11th is a 412 yard, par 4 with a body of water that begins near the tee shot landing area. The second shot is a mid-to long iron to a green that offers little relief—just ask Bruce Crampton. In 1996, he three-putted No. 11 in the final round to allow Jack Nicklaus a ten shot lead.

• Number 15 offers a golfer the chance to change his or her mind, a lot. Over water to a 36 yard deep green with the wind always in play, this 164-yarder averaged 3.706 strokes in 1990's tournament, and 3.565 strokes two years later.

• Next is a 412 yard test that doesn't let up. A fairway bunker along the right side, water past the bunker as well as on the approach, and a two-

tiered green trapped to the right all prove difficult here.

• The 17th hole is another par-3, this time 152 yards directly into the wind, over water. Raymond Floyd has said this hole reminds him of number 12 at Augusta.

For past results, see Chapter 7, Major Championships: Seniors.

PITTSBURGH SENIOR CLASSIC

Quicksilver Golf Club
Midway, PA

Date: August 29-31, 1997

TV: TGC

Tickets: Pittsburgh Senior Classic
2000 Quicksilver Road
Midway, PA 15060

To play: Quicksilver is a public course.

About the tournament and course:

• In 1996, Tom Weiskopf started the final round with a three stroke lead, shot two-under, and finished the round with a three shot win. Along the way, he set a new tournament record of 11 under for the weekend.

• On the site of an old coal strip mine, Quicksilver is constantly rated among the toughest courses anywhere. Of the 239 rounds played during the three day 1996 tournament, only 21 were under 70.

• The tenth hole eats up stray shots. Out of bounds runs the entire right side of the fairway, and extends up close to the green. This 423 yard par 4 also requires an accurate approach to avoid the two traps front of the green.

1996 Leaderboard

1-Tom Weiskopf	−11, 205	$165,000
2-Brian Barnes	−8, 208	$88,000
3-J.C. Snead	−8, 208	$88,000

Tournament History

1993	Bob Charles	207
1994	Dave Eichelberger	209
1995	Dave Stockton	208
1996	Tom Weiskopf	205

RALEY'S GOLD RUSH CLASSIC

Serrano Country Club
El Dorado Hills, CA

Date: October 24–26, 1997

TV: TBD

Tickets: Raley's Gold Rush Classic
991 Governor Dr., Ste. 101
El Dorado Hills, CA 95762

To play: Serrano is a private club open to members and their guests.

About the tournament and course:

- Number 2 at this newer Robert Trent Jones Jr. layout is nicknamed the "Delta Breeze" because of the stiff wind usually found here. This par 4 runs only 375 yards, but combine the wind with a green that has two distinct personalities, and golfers have a very difficult test.

- In 1996, the first year for this stop at Serrano CC, Jim Colbert sailed to a comfortable victory by dropping six birdies on the back nine. Colbert's total of 202 was five shots ahead of Dave Stockton.

- The previous tournaments were held at Rancho Murieta through 1995. That year, Lee Trevino bogeyed the final hole to lose out to Don Bies. Trevino's bogey was familiar to all hackers—a three-putt.

1996 Leaderboard

1-Jim Colbert	−14, 202	$120,000
2-Dave Stockton	−9, 207	$70,400

t3-Jack Kiefer	−8, 208	$52,800
t3-Butch Baird	−8, 208	$52,800

Tournament History

Rancho Murieta Senior Gold Rush

1987	Orville Moody	205
1988	Bob Charles	207
1989	Dave Hill	207

Gold Rush at Rancho Murieta

1990	George Archer	204

Raley's Senior Gold Rush

1991	George Archer	206
1992	Bob Charles	201
1993	George Archer	202
1994	Bob Murphy	208
1995	Don Bies	205
1996	Jim Colbert	202

ROYAL CARIBBEAN CLASSIC

The Links at Key Biscayne
Key Biscayne, FL

Date: January 31-February 2, 1997

TV: ESPN

Tickets: Royal Caribbean Classic
1000 Crandon Blvd.
Key Biscayne, FL 33149

To play: The Links at Key Biscayne is a public course open year-round.

About the tournament and course:

- The first full field tournament for the seniors is held each year here at one of Florida's finest public courses.

- The seventh hole is generally regarded as the toughest for tournament play. This 434-yard dogleg right has traps to the left and water to the right of the landing area, the same water that must be carried on the way to a kidney shaped green trapped three times.

1996 Leaderboard

1-Bob Murphy	203
2-Hale Irwin	207
3-Rick Acton	208
t4-Ray Floyd	209
t4-Mike Hill	209

Tournament History

Gus Machado Senior Classic

1987	Gene Littler	207
1988	Lee Elder	202
1989	No tournament	

Royal Carribean Classic

1990	Lee Trevino	206
1991	Gary Player	200
1992	Don Massengale	205
1993	Jim Colbert	199
1994	*Lee Trevino	205
1995	*J.C.Snead	209
1996	Bob Murphy	203

SAINT LUKE'S CLASSIC

**Loch Lloyd Country Club
Belton, MO**

Date: August 22-24, 1997

TV: ESPN

Tickets: Loch Lloyd Country Club
16750 Country Club Dr.
Belton, MO 64012

To play: Loch Lloyd is a private club open to members and their guests.

About the tournament and course:

- After making the turn, golfers have a short par-3 at number 10, then the fun starts. The elbow room of the front nine is gone as the course is transformed into a series of narrow fairways and water on most of the last eight holes.

- The 17th is probably the toughest for tournament play. This 383-yard par-4 starts low then runs uphill with water along the left side of the fairway. The multi-level green poses more problems at the end.

- In 1996, Dave Eichelberger came home with birdies on 15 and 18 to post a two-shot win over Jim Colbert. Dave Stockton tied for third with Lee Trevino at the same time Dave Stockton, Jr. was finishing third at the PGA's Buick Open.

1996 Leaderboard

1-Dave Eichelberger	–10, 200	$135,000
2-Jim Colbert	–8, 202	$79,200
t3-Lee Trevino	–6, 204	$59,400
t3-Dave Stockton	–6, 204	$59,400

Tournament History

Silver Pages Classic

1987 Chi Chi Rodriguez	200

Southwestern Bell Classic

1988 *Gary Player	203
1989 *Bobby Nichols	209
1990 Jimmy Powell	208
1991 Jim Colbert	201
1992 Gibby Gilbert	193
1993 Dave Stockton	204
1994 Jim Colbert	196

VFW Senior Championship

1995 Bob Murphy	195
1996 Dave Eichelberger	200

SENIOR SKINS GAME

**Mauna Lani Resort – South Course
Kohala Coast, HI**

Date: January 25-26, 1997

TV: ABC

Tickets: Senior Skins Game
Mauna Lani Resort
68-150 Ho'Ohana St.
Kohala Coast, HI 96743
To play: The two courses are part of the resort.

About the tournament and course:

- The course is built on the Kaniku lava flow, and the lava is evident on tee boxes and fairways everywhere.

- Number 3 has all the right touches for torture – 601 yards; dogleg; water to the left and traps top the right of the tee shot landing area; and a tricky, sloped green.

- A sports fanatic's dream weekend, this event shares the spotlight with the Super Bowl.

Tournament History

1988	Chi Chi Rodriguez	$300,000
1989	Chi Chi Rodriguez	$120,000
1990	Arnold Palmer	$240,000
1991	Jack Nicklaus	$310,000
1992	Arnold Palmer	$205,000
1993	Arnold Palmer	$190,000
1994	Ray Floyd	$240,000
1995	Ray Floyd	$420,000
1996	Ray Floyd	$240,000

SOUTHWESTERN BELL DOMINION

**The Dominion Country Club
San Antonio, TX**

Date: March 28-30, 1997
TV: ESPN
Tickets: Dominion Seniors
1 Dominion Dr.
San Antonio, TX 78257
To play: The Dominion is a private club open to members and their guests.

About the tournament and course:

- The wind is always a consideration here at The Domninion, which has been host to this event continually since 1985. Other hazards give the course its fair cshare of tough holes.

- The finishing hole is a dogleg left, 508-yard par-5. The tee shot landing area is pocked by three bunkers, and the green has water immediately to the left and more traps to the right.

- Number 8 is only 153 yards, but one mistake hurts bad. The green on this par-3 has a horeshoe shaped pond on three sides, and traps front-left and right, as well as back-left and right.

1996 Leaderboard

1-Tom Weiskopf	207
t2-Gary Player	209
t2-Bob Dickson	209
t2-Graham Marsh	209
5-Tom Shaw	211

Tournament History

The Dominion Seniors

1985	Don January	206

Benson & Hedges Invitational at The Dominion

1986	Bruce Crampton	202

Vantage at The Dominion

1987	Chi Chi Rodriguez	203
1988	Billy Casper	205

RJR at The Dominion

1989	Larry Mowry	201

Vantage at The Dominion

1990	Jim Dent	205
1991	#Lee Trevino	137
1992	Lee Trevino	201
1993	J.C.Snead	214
1994	Jim Albus	208

SBC Presents The Dominion Seniors

| 1995 | Jim Albus | 205 |
| 1996 | Tom Weiskopf | 207 |

THE TRADITION

Desert Mountain Golf Club—Cochise Course
Scottsdale, AZ

Date: April 3-6, 1997
TV: ABC/ESPN
Tickets: The Tradition
6263 N. Scottsdale Rd., Ste. 215
Scottsdale, AZ 85250
To play: All five courses at Desert Mountain are private and open only to members and their guests.

About the tournament and course:

• Familiarity breeds success? Or something like that. Jack Nicklaus designed the Cochise Course at Desert Mountain, The Tradition has been played there since 1989, and Nicklaus has won half of the eight tournaments since.

• In 1996, Nicklaus blistered the course with a pair of 7-under 65s, including his first double-eagle in 31 years, this one at the 511-yard 12th hole during the third round. Second place finisher Hale Irwin said about Nicklaus, "Those of us who buried him two or three years ago better put our shovels back in the garage."

• The 14th hole has "Nicklaus designed me" written all over it. Fairway bunkers to the left of a narrow landing area; a long iron to a narrow, sloped green.

• A double green hosts shots from the seventh and 15th holes. The former proves tough at 194 yards over water, while 15, at 524 yards, is the longest hole on the back side. Trying to reach the dance floor in two can be costly since the water comes right up to the front edge of the green.

For past results, see Chapter 7, Major Championships: Seniors.

U.S. SENIOR OPEN

Olympia Fields Country Club
Chicago, IL

Date: June 26-29
TV: NBC
Tickets: 1-800-861-3191
To play: Olympia Fields is a private club open to members and their guests.

• Opened in 1924 and designed by Willie Park, Jr., one of Scotland's finest early professionals and a two-time British Open champ (1887 and 1889), who became just as well known for his golf writing and architecture.

• Fabled Olympia Fields was the site of the 1925 and 1961 PGA Championships, won by Walter Hagen and Jerry Barber, respectively, and the 1928 U.S. Open, where 21-year old Roland Hancock came to the final two holes needing 10 strokes or less to win, then took a pair of sixes. Johnny Farrell beat Bobby Jones in a playoff.

• Course hasn't changed much through the years; par could take a severe beating if the players learn her secrets early.

For past results, see Chapter 7, Major Championships: Seniors.

WORLD INVITATIONAL

TPC at Piper Glen
Charlotte, NC

Date: May 9-11, 1997
TV: ESPN
Tickets: TPC at Piper Glen
4300 Piper Glen Dr.
Charlotte, NC 28277
To play: TPC at Piper Glen is a private club open to members and their guests.

About the tournament and course:

- The long par-4 13th hole has a narrow, snaked fairway and a bi-level green bordered on the approach by three greens.

- If number 13 wasn't enough, the 14th hole measures 389 yards and features a creek down the left side and a pond in front of, and to the right of the green.

1996 Leaderboard

1-Graham Marsh	206
t2-Tom Wargo	207
t2-Brian Barnes	207
4-Jack Kiefer	208

Tournament History

World Seniors Invitational

1980	*Gene Littler	211
1981	Miller Barber	282
1982	Gene Littler	280
1983	Doug Sanders	283

WBTV World Seniors Invitational

1984	Peter Thomson	81

PaineWebber World Seniors Invitational

1985	Miller Barber	277
1986	Bruce Crampton	279
1987	*#Gary Player	207

PaineWebber Invitational

1988	Dave Hill	206
1989	Tournament canceled due to weather	
1990	Bruce Crampton	205
1991	Orville Moody	207
1992	Don Bies	203
1993	Mike Hill	204
1994	Lee Trevino	203
1995	Bob Murphy	203
1996	Graham Marsh	206

* Won in playoff
# Shortened tournament

13

THE 200-COURSE
'ROUND THE WORLD TOUR

L isted below are 200 courses open to the public to help plot your next vacation or world tour. Each listing provides phone numbers, tee time information, and a fee rating. Resort courses are duly noted in the fee rating, which reflects the greens fees for registered guests.

The 200 sites were selected from a composite of sources that rate world and U.S. courses. The sources are listed at the end of the chapter. Be sure to check the index for other references to the courses in this encyclopedia. If a course hosts a 1997 PGA event, a reference will lead you to the course profile in one of the 1996 Review/1997 Preview sections.

Fee Ratings: 1 = under $75
2 = $75 to $125
3 = $125 to $225
4 = over $225

NORTHEAST

The Balsams Resort

Dixville Notch, NH
(603)255-3400
(800)255-0600

Year opened: 1912

Rating: 73.9/69.9
Slope: 136/124
Tee Time Info: Guests can call 7 days ahead, others 3 days ahead.
Fee Rating: 1

Donald Ross, tight from tee to small greens, thickly wooded.

The largest single green on any golf course is on the fifth hole of the International Golf Club in Bolton, Massachusetts. It has an area of more than 28,000 square feet, big enough for three average suburban houses, including their yards.

Bethpage (Black)

Farmingdale, NY

(516)293-8899

Year opened: 1935

Rating: 75.4/78.9

Slope: 144/146

Tee Time Info: Call one week in advance.

Fee Rating: 1

Classic Tillinghast course. Rolling layout; walking only.

The Captains

Brewster, MA

(508)896-5100

Year opened: 1985

Rating: 72.7/70.5

Slope: 130/117

Tee Time Info: Call two days prior or prepay.

Fee Rating: 1

Cornish and Silva design. Heavily wooded.

The Concord Resort

Kiamesha Lake, NY

(914)794-4000

(800)-431-3850

Year opened: 1963

Rating: 76.4/78.5

Slope: 142/144

Tee Time Info: Call year round with credit card.

Fee Rating: 2

45 holes, The Monster is best. Rolling, demands accuracy.

Crumpin-Fox Club

Bernardston, MA

(413)648-9101

Year opened: 1978

Rating: 73.8/71.5

Slope: 141/131

Tee Time Info: Two days in advance, as far in advance for dinner guests and club members.

Fee Rating: 1

Hilly, water, trees, and traps, then long greens. Robert Trent Jones, Sr., and Roger Rulewich design.

Eagle's Landing Golf Course

Berlin, MD

(410)213-7277

Year opened: 1991

Rating: 74.3/69.3

Slope: 126/115

Tee Time Info: 90 days in advance

Fee Rating: 1

Links in wetlands.

Gleneagles Golf Course

Manchester, VT

(802)362-3223

Year opened: 1926

Rating: 71.3/65.2

Slope: 129/117

Tee Time Info: 2 days in advance

Fee Rating: 1

Hog Neck

Easton, MD

(410)822-6079

Year opened: 1976

Rating: 73.8/71.1

Slope: 125/118

Tee Time Info: Call on Saturday for upcoming week.

Fee Rating: 1

Out along the ocean, in through the forest.

Hominy Hill

Colts Neck, NJ

(908)462-9222

Year opened: 1964

Rating: 74.4/73.9

Slope: 132/128

Tee Time Info: Call one week in advance.

Fee Rating: 1

Tough: need distance, heavily bunkered (100+), rough rough. Robert Trent Jones, Sr. design.

Howell Park

Farmingdale, NJ

(908)938-4771

Year opened: 1972

Rating: 73.0/72.5

Slope: 128/125

Tee Time Info: Call one week in advance.

Fee Rating: 1

A great public course—heavily used but well maintained. Robert Trent Jones, Sr., design; long, many bunkers.

Montauk Downs

Montauk, NY

(516)668-1100

Year opened: 1968

Rating: 73.3/75.9

Slope: 133/135

Tee Time Info: Call nine days in advance.

Fee Rating: 1

Long Island, near ocean. Design by Robert Trent Jones, Sr., with Rees Jones. Very scenic, open to elements.

New Seabury (Blue)

New Seabury, MA

(508)477-9110

Year opened: 1964

Rating: 75.3/73.8

Slope: 130/128

Tee Time Info: Resort guests can reserve one day in advance.

Fee Rating: 1

Rolling layout on Cape Cod, water play.

Quicksilver Golf Club

Midway, PA

See Review/Preview, SPGA, Quicksilver Classic.

Richter Park

Danbury, CT

(203)792-2552

Year opened: 1971

Rating: 73.0/72.8

Slope: 130/122

Tee Time Info: Nonresidents call Thursday 9 a.m. for weekend.

Fee Rating: 1

Scenic and challenging, wooded and hilly.

Samoset

Rockport, ME

(207)594-1431

(800)341-1650

Year opened: 1978

Rating: 69.3/69.1

Slope: 125/117

Tee Time Info: Resort—Call well in advance.

Fee Rating: 1

Along ocean; wind often comes into play.

Spook Rock

Ramapo, NY

(914)357-3085

Year opened: 1970
Rating: 73.3/70.9
Slope: 129/118
Tee Time Info: Call Sunday after 6 p.m. for weekdays and Thursday after 7 a.m. for weekends.
Fee Rating: 1
Rolling, championship layout—strategic placements an optimum.

Sugarloaf

Carrabassett Valley, ME
(207)237-2000 x 6806
(800)843-5623
Year opened: 1986
Rating: 70.8/73.7
Slope: 137/136
Tee Time Info: Resort—call two weeks in advance.
Fee Rating: 1
Robert Trent Jones, Jr., design. Thickly wooded mountainside, very tight.

SOUTH

Bay Hill

Orlando, FL
See Review/Preview PGA Nestle Invitational.

Callaway Gardens (Mountain View)

Pine Mountain, GA
See Review/Preview, PGA Buick Challenge

Colony West

Tamarac, FL
(419)331-2951

Year opened: 1950
Rating: 69.8/67.9
Slope: N/A
Tee Time Info: Call anytime.
Fee Rating: 1
Championship layout.

Doral (Blue)

Miami, FL
See Review/Preview, PGA Doral Open

Eastwood

Fort Myers, FL
(813)275-4848
Year opened: 1977
Rating: 72.0/72.1
Slope: 130/128
Tee Time Info: Call four days in advance.
Fee Rating: 1
Wooded out, bunkered in.

Fall Creek Falls

Pikeville, TN
(615)881-5706
Year opened: 1934
Rating: 71.2/67.7
Slope: 129/118
Tee Time Info: Call one week in advance.
Fee Rating: 1
In a mountain state park. Trees and bunkers.

Golden Ocala

Ocala, FL
(904)622-0198
(800)251-7674
Year opened: 1986
Rating: 72.2/72.2
Slope: 132/124
Tee Time Info: Call one week in advance.

Fee Rating: 1

Replica holes of Augusta, St. Andrews, Troon, and others.

Golden Horseshoe

Williamsburg, VA

(804)220-7696

(800)447-8679

Year opened: 1963

Rating: 73.1/66.2

Slope: 137/120

Tee Time Info: Resort, make tee times when making reservations; call one week in advance.

Fee Rating: 1 to 2

Gold: Robert Trent Jones, Sr. design, hilly; Green: Rees Jones design.

Grand Cypress (North/South)

Orlando, FL

(407)239-1904

(800)835-7377

Year opened: 1984

Rating: 73.9/74.4/73.9

Slope: 130/132/130

Tee Time Info: Guests only (the Villas of Grand Cypress or the Hyatt Regency Grand Cypress). One tee time in advance.

Fee Rating: 1 to 2

Jack Nicklaus-designed links course.

Grenelefe

Haines City, FL

(812)422-7511

(800)237-9549

Year opened: 1978

Rating: 72.5/69.2

Slope: 123/114

Tee Time Info: Package guests may make reservations one year ahead (Champions package) and 90 days ahead (Classic package).

"Cypress Point is the Sistine Chapel of golf."
—Sandy Tatum, former USGA president.

Fee Rating: 1 to 2

West course designed by Robert Trent Jones, Sr.

Harbour Town

Hilton Head Island, SC.

See Review/Preview, PGA MCI Classic

Heather Glen

Little River, SC

(803)249-9000

(800)868-4536

Year opened: 1987

Rating: 72.4/72.4/72.4

Slope: 130/130/127

Tee Time Info: Call anytime.

Fee Rating: 1

Scottish-style, with trees and elevations.

Heritage

Pawleys Island, SC

(803)237-3424

(800)377-2315

Year opened: 1986

Rating: 74.2/71.0

Slope: 137/125

Tee Time Info: Call up to nine months in advance. Deposit required during high season.

Fee Rating: 1

Variety of natural settings.

The Homestead (Cascades)

Hot Springs, VA

(703)839-7994

Year opened: 1923

Rating: 72.9/72.9
Slope: 136/137 Season: April-October
Tee Time Info: Call
Fee Rating: 1
Robert Trent Jones design within a sprawling 230+ year-old retreat.

Hunter's Creek

Orlando, FL
(407)240-4653
Year opened: 1986
Rating: 75.2/72.5
Slope: 127/120
Tee Time Info: Call three days in advance.
Fee Rating: 1
Long, flat, open—a great public.

Innisbrook

Tarpon Springs, FL
See Review/Preview, LPGA J.C. Penney Classic

Jones Creek

Evans, GA
(706)860-4228
Year opened: 1986
Rating: 73.8/72.4
Slope: 137/130
Tee Time Info: Call on Friday for following week and weekend.
Fee Rating: 1
Rees Jones design, near Augusta.

Lagoon Park

Montgomery, AL
(334)271-7000
Year opened: 1978
Rating: 71.1/69.6
Slope: 124/113

Tee Time Info: Call Thursday a.m. for weekend tee times. No reserved times during week.
Fee Rating: 1
Well-maintained public; demands accuracy.

Links at Key Biscayne

Key Biscayne, FL
See Review/Preview SPGA Royal Carribbean Classic

Long Point

Amelia Island, FL
(904)277-5907
(800)874-6878
Year opened: 1987
Rating: 72.9/69.1
Slope: 129/121
Tee Time Info: During reservation at Amelia Island Plantation Resort..
Fee Rating: 2
Oceanfront course.

Oceanside Marriott's Bay Point (Lagoon Legend)

Panama City Beach, FL
(909)234-3307
Year opened: 1986
Rating: 75.3/69.8
Slope: 152/127
Tee Time Info: Resort; call computerized tee times (904)235-6909.
Fee Rating: 1
Water and bunker play.

Marsh Harbour

Calabash, NC
(910)579-3161
(800)377-2315
Year opened: 1980

Rating: 72.4/67.7

Slope: 134/115

Tee Time Info: Call up to nine months in advance. Deposit required during high season.

Fee Rating: 2

Water and trees.

Oak Hollow

High Point, NC

(910)883-3260

Year opened: 1972

Rating: 71.6/67.4

Slope: 124/114

Tee Time Info: Call 48 hours in advance for weekdays. Call Thursday for upcoming weekend.

Fee Rating: 1

Early Pete Dye. Challenging.

The Ocean Course

Kiawah Island, SC

(803)768-7272

Year opened 1991

Rating: 76.9/72.9

Slope: 149/133

Tee Time Info: Resort: Call 60 days in advance

Fee Rating: 2

Pete Dye oceanside course; once a Ryder Cup site.

Osprey Point

Kiawah Island, SC

(803)768-2121

(800)845-2471

Year opened: 1988

Rating: 71.8/69.6

Slope: 124/120

Tee Time Info: Resort; may call five days in advance.

Fee Rating: 1

Tom Fazio design; close to ocean, good round opportunity.

A local rule at a golf course in Tientsin, China, laid out in a cemetery, states that a ball rolling into an open grave may be lifted without penalty.

Oyster Bay

Sunset Beach, NC

(516)364-3977

Year opened: 1989

Rating: 71.5/70.4

Slope: 131/126

Tee Time Info: First come, first serve.

Fee Rating: 1

Many marshes.

Palm Beach Polo (Dunes)

West Palm Beach, FL

(407)798-7401

Year opened: 1984

Rating: 73.6/71.4

Slope: 132/122

Tee Time Info: Must be a registered resort guest, guest of a member or member of another private country club arranged through their golf pro.

Fee Rating: 1 to 2

Challenging layout.

Pinehurst (No. 2)

Pinehurst, North Carolina

(910)295-8141

(800)795-4653

Year opened: 1901

Rating: 74.1/74.2

Slope: 131/135

Tee Time Info: Resort, call (800)-ITS-GOLF

Fee Rating: 4

Donald Ross course; one of the very best.

> The Ndola Golf Club in Zambia features 20-foot high termite mounds all over the course.

Pinehurst (No. 7)

Pinehurst, NC
(910)295-8141
(800)795-4653
Year opened: 1986
Rating: 75.6/69.7
Slope: 145/124 Season: Year-round
Tee Time Info: Resort, call 800-ITS-GOLF
Fee Rating: 2
Rees Jones design; one of the best.

The Pit

Pinehurst, NC
(910)944-1600
(800)574-4653
Year opened: 1985
Rating: 72.3/68.4
Slope: 139/121
Tee Time Info: Call 800-574-4653.
Fee Rating: 1
Quirky and wild.

PGA National (Champion)

Palm Beach Gardens, FL
(407)627-1800
(800)633-9150
See Preview/Review SPGA

Sea Island (Plantation/Seaside)

St. Simons Island, GA
(912)638-5118
(800)732-4752
Year opened: 1927
Rating: 73.2/69.1
Slope: 134/115

Tee Time Info: Resort, all.
Fee Rating: 1
Travis/Colt/Alison 9-hole, renovated by Rees Jones, combine with other 9-holes.

Stonehenge

Fairfield Glade, TN
(615)484-3731
(800)624-8755
Year opened: 1984
Rating: 71.5/70.2
Slope: 131/124 Season: Year-round
Tee Time Info: Resort, write, 30 days in advance: Central Tee Times, PO Box 2000, Fairfield Glade, TN 38558; Then call 5 days in advance.
Fee Rating: 1
Heavily forested, varying elevations.

Stone Mountain (Stonemont/Woodmont)

Stone Mountain, GA
(404)498-5715
Year opened: 1971/1987
Rating: 72.6/69.1 / 71.6/69.4
Slope: 133/121 / 130/120
Tee Time Info: Call Tuesday for following weekend and holidays starting at 9 a.m. For weekdays call one week in advance.
Fee Rating: 1
Rolling and wooded.

Tanglewood Park (Championship)

Clemmons, NC
(910)766-5082
See Preview/Review, SPGA Vanatage Championship

TPC at Sawgrass (Stadium)

See Review/Preview, PGA Player's Championship

Walt Disney World Resort (Palm)

Lake Buena Vista, FL
(407)824-2288
See Review/Preview, PGA Walt Disney World/Oldsmobile Classic.

West Palm Beach

West Palm Beach, FL
(407)582-2019
Year opened: 1947
Rating: 72.8/73.3
Slope: 124/126
Tee Time Info: Lottery system. One person per foursome enters names evening before day of play at 7 p.m. As slips are drawn golfer gets choice of available times. Or call starter after lottery or day of play to secure a time. Saturday and Sunday double crossover lottery. Wed. evening for Sat. and Thurs. for Sund. at 7:30 p.m.
Fee Rating: 1
Lots of trees and sand.

Wild Dunes (Links)

Isle of Palms, SC
(803)886-2180
(800)845-8880
Year opened: 1980
Rating: 72.7/69.1
Slope: 131/121 Season: Year-round
Tee Time Info: Call pro shop
Fee Rating: 1 to 2
Tom Fazio links design along the Atlantic.

MIDWEST

Blue Ash

Blue Ash, OH
(513)745-8577

"The man who doesn't feel emotionally stirred when he golfs at Pinehurst beneath those clear blue skies and with the pine fragrance in his nostrils is one who should be ruled out of golf for life."

—Tommy Armour

Year opened: 1979
Rating: 72.6/70.3
Slope: 127/124
Tee Time Info: Nonresidents call five days in advance.
Fee Rating: 1
Kidwell/Hurdzan design, hilly and thickly wooded.

Boyne Highlands (Heather)

Harbor Springs, MI
(616)526-3029 x 182
(800)462-6963
Year opened: 1985
Rating: 73.4/68.5
Slope: 132/119
Tee Time Info: Resort, call anytime.
Fee Rating: 1
Robert Trent Jones, Sr., course—Scottish with lots of heather. Donald Ross Memorial course also strong.

Edinburgh, USA

Brooklyn Park, MN
(612)424-7060
See LPGA Review/Preview, Edina Realty Open

Brown County

Oneida, WI
(414)497-1731
Year opened: 1957
Rating: 72.1/72.7

At the Port Sudan Country Club in Africa, a course rule states that balls may be removed from camel skeletons or cactuses and replaced on the course no nearer the hole.

Slope: 133/127

Tee Time Info: Call one day in advance for weekdays. Call Monday at 6 p.m. for upcoming weekend and holidays.

Fee Rating: 1

Challenging public course, well-maintaned.

Cantigny

Wheaton, IL

(708)668-3323

Year opened: 1989

Rating: 72.4/71.1/72.2

Slope: 130/126/125

Tee Time Info: Call up to seven days in advance.

Fee Rating: 1

Woods, water on 12 holes; on the McCormick estate.

Cog Hill

Lemont, IL

See Review/Preview, PGA Motorola Western Open

Eagle Creek

Indianapolis, IN

(317)297-3366

Year opened: 1974

Rating: 74.6/68.2

Slope: 139/116

Tee Time Info: Call one week in advance for weekdays and Monday for the following weekend.

Fee Rating: 1

Early Pete Dye; very challenging—a gem that needs polishing.

Eagle Ridge (North, South)

Galena, IL

(815)777-5200

800 892-2269

Year opened: 1984

Rating: 72.9/72.4

Slope: 133/128

Tee Time Info: Resort, non guests call one week in advance.

Fee Rating: 2

Varying elevations, water and trees—demands accuracy. North course opened 1977.

Golf Club of Indiana

Zionsville, IN

(317)769-6388

Year opened: 1974

Rating: 73.2/72.7

Slope: 140/122

Tee Time Info: Call pro shop.

Fee Rating: 1

Very open, many bunkers and water hazards.

Grand Haven

Grand Haven, MI

(616)842-4040

Year opened: 1965

Rating: 71.9/71.4

Slope: 124/119

Tee Time Info: Weekday: as far in advance as possible. Weekend: one week in advance.

Fee Rating: 1

Pine-lined, well-bunkered.

Grand Traverse (Bear)

Acme, MI

(616)938-1620

800 748-0303

Year opened: 1965

Rating: 71.9/71.4

Slope: 124/119

Tee Time Info: Resort, one week in advance for weekend..

Fee Rating: 1

Nicklaus design, open with varying natural looks.

The Greenbrier

White Sulphur Springs, WV

(304)273-3396

Call Resort for further information.

MacDonald/Raynor design.

High Pointe

Williamsburg, MI

(616)267-9000

(800)753-7888

Year opened: 1989

Rating: 72.9/69.6

Slope: 135/121

Tee Time Info: Call.

Fee Rating: 1

Early Tom Doak, Scottish style with trees.

Hulman Links

Terre Haute, IN

(812)877-2096

Year opened: 1978

Rating: 74.9/73.4

Slope: 144/134

Tee Time Info: Call anytime for weekday play. Call Wednesday for following weekend.

Fee Rating: 1

Rolling with many different looks.

Kemper Lakes

Hawthorn Woods, IL

(708)320-3450

Year opened: 1979

Rating: 75.7/67.9

Be sure to hit your shots straight at Stanley Golf Club in the Falkland Islands. Unexploded land mines are thought to remain in the out of bounds.

Slope: 140/125

Tee Time Info: Call two weeks in advance.

Fee Rating: 1

Rolling, lake area; greens well protected; site of 1989 PGA.

Lick Creek

Pekin, IL

(309)346-0077

Year opened: 1976

Rating: 72.8/72.9

Slope: 128/125

Tee Time Info: Call one week in advance.

Fee Rating: 1

Very tight, must be good with irons.

Otter Creek

Columbus, IN

(812)579-5227

Year opened: 1964

Rating: 74.2/72.1

Slope: 137/116

Tee Time Info: Call as far in advance as needed. Credit card necessary to hold reservation.

Fee Rating: 1

Robert Trent Jones, Sr. design; long and rolling and many bunkers.

Pine Meadow

Mundelein, IL

(708)566-4653

Year opened: 1985

Rating: 74.4/70.9

Slope: 131/121

Tee Time Info: Call up to six months in advance. Prepayment of green fee is necessary from May 15th to Oct. 1st.

Fee Rating: 1

Havily wooded, with water flowing into play.

SentryWorld

Stevens Point, WI

(715)345-1600

Year opened: 1981

Rating: 74.5/71.6

Slope: 144/130

Tee Time Info: Call pro shop.

Fee Rating: 1

Wooded, tough, Robert Trent Jones, Jr., design.

Shanty Creek (Legend)

Bellaire, MI

(616)533-8621

(800)678-4111

Year opened: 1985

Rating: 73.6/69.4

Slope: 137/121 Season: April-October

Tee Time Info: Hotel guests: with reservations; Non-guests: One month ahead (for Monday to Thursday), two weeks (Friday to Sunday).

Fee Rating: 1 to 2

Palmer/Seay design, hilly and heavily wooded.

Timber Ridge

East Lansing, MI

(517)339-8000

(800)874-3432

Fred Couples looks to continue his resurgence in 1997 after finishing 6th on the '96 money list with $1,248,694.

Year opened: 1989

Rating: 72.7/70.4

Slope: 137/129

Tee Time Info: Call seven days prior for a foursome. Groups of eight or more may book in advance.

Fee Rating: 1

Woods, need good iron play.

Treetops Sylvan

Gaylord, MI

(517)732-6711

(800)444-6711

Year opened: 1987

Rating: 75.8/70.2

Slope: 146/124

Tee Time Info: Call.

Fee Rating: 2

Robert Trent Jones, Sr., wooded, hilly.

PLAINS

Alvamar

Lawrence, KS

(913)842-1907

Year opened: 1968

Rating: 75.0/N/A

Slope: 135/N/A

Tee Time Info: Call seven days in advance.

Fee Rating: 1

Tight fairways demand accuracy.

Amana Colonies

Amana, IA

(319)622-6222

(800)383-3636

Year opened: 1989

Rating: 73.3/69.7

Slope: 136/115

Tee Time Info: 30 days in advance, with credit card.

Fee Rating: 1

Up and downhill, wooded.

To play golf in Arkansas City, Kansas, you must sign a release form absolving the city from liability in case of a snakebite.

Barton Creek

Austin, TX

(512)329-4001

Year opened: 1986

Rating: 74.0/69.4

Slope: 135/120 Season: Year-round

Tee Time Info: Must be an overnight resort guest, member or conference guest.

Fee Rating: 2

3 courses: Tom Fazio, Arnold Palmer, Crenshaw/Coore designs—lush, dramatic.

Bear Creek (Masters)

Houston, TX

(713)855-4720

Year opened: 1972

Rating: 74.1/72.1

Slope: 133/125

Tee Time Info: Call seven days in advance.

Fee Rating: 1

Distance and accuracy needed; tree-lined fairways.

Horseshoe Bay (Ram Rock)

Horseshoe Bay, TX

(210)598-6561

Year opened: 1981

Rating: 73.9/71.4

Slope: 137/121

Tee Time Info: Resort, seven days in advance.

Fee Rating: 1

Three Robert Trent Jones, Sr., courses, all demanding precision.

Heritage Hills Golf Course

McCook, NE
(308)345-5032
Year opened: 1981
Rating: 72.7/71.1
Slope: 130/127
Tee Time Info: 7 days in advance.
Fee Rating: 1
Tough, with blind shots.

Lodge of Four Seasons

Lake Ozark, MO
(314)365-8532
(800)843-5253
Year opened: 1991
Rating: 71.4/71.0
Slope: 130/118
Tee Time Info: Resort; call pro shop.

Meadowbrook

Rapid City, SD
(605)394-4191
Year opened: 1976
Rating: 73.0/71.1
Slope: 138/130
Tee Time Info: Call 24 hours in advance or by advance booking.
Fee Rating: 1
Heavily wooded and bunkered.

Pecan Valley

San Antonio, TX
(210)333-9018
(800)336-3418
Year opened: 1963
Rating: 73.9/71.3
Slope: 136/113
Tee Time Info: Call two weeks in advance with credit card or one month in advance through hotel.
Fee Rating: 1
Press Maxwell design in critical state of maturation.

___

WEST

Arrowhead

Littleton, CO
(303)973-9614
Year opened: 1978
Rating: 70.9/70.0
Slope: 134/123
Tee Time Info: Call seven days in advance with credit card.
Fee Rating: 1
Spectacular rocky setting, not the most challenging course.

The Boulders (North)

Carefree, AZ
(602)488-9028
Year opened: 1984
Rating: N/A
Slope: 135/113
Tee Time Info: Resort, N/A
Fee Rating: N/A
Desert layout, long fairways, large greens, well-placed bunkers.

The Broadmoor (East and West)

Colorado Springs, CO
(719)577-5790
(800)634-7711
Year opened: 1918
Rating: 73.0/71.6
Slope: 133/122
Tee Time Info: Resort, call pro shop.
Fee Rating: 2
Courses by Donald Ross, Robert Trent Jones, Sr., Palmer/Seay, in spectacular mountain setting,

Cochiti Lake

Cochiti Lake, NM
(505)465-2239

Year opened: 1981
Rating: 71.2/70.6
Slope: 131/121
Tee Time Info: Call up to seven days in advance.
Fee Rating: 1
Robert Trent Jones, Jr., design with assorted challenges.

Coeur d'Alene Resort

Coeur d'Alene, Idaho
(208)667-4653
(800)688-5253
Year opened: 1991
Rating: 69.9/70.3
Slope: 121/118 Season: April-October
Tee Time Info: Resort, may call up to one year in advance
Fee Rating: 2
Many bunkers, a floating par 3 controlled by a computer.

Desert Dunes

Palm Springs, CA
(619)251-5367
(800)766-2767
Year opened: 1989
Rating: 73.8/70.7
Slope: 142/122
Tee Time Info: Call seven days in advance.
Fee Rating: 1
Robert Trent Jones, Jr., windy links type in a desert setting.

Desert Inn

Las Vegas, NV
(702)733-4290
(800)634-6909
Year opened: 1952
Rating: 73.9/72.7

Slope: 124/121
Tee Time Info: Resort, call.
Fee Rating: 2 to 3
Many water and bunker challenges.

Eastmoreland

Portland, OR
(503)775-2900
Year opened: 1921
Rating: 71.7/71.4
Slope: 123/117
Tee Time Info: Call six days in advance.
Fee Rating: 1
Mature course very park like.

Edgewood Tahoe

Stateline, NV
(702)588-3566
Year opened: 1968
Rating: 75.1/71.5
Slope: 136/130
Tee Time Info: Call two weeks, to the day, in advance.
Fee Rating: 2
George Fazio design, overlooking Lake Tahoe. Bunkers, trees, water in crucial spots.

Heron Lakes (White/Blue)

Portland, OR
(503)289-1818
Year opened: 1971
Rating: 73.6/69.8
Slope: 132/120
Tee Time Info: Call Tee Time Inc. at (503)292-8570
Fee Rating: 1
Robert Trent Jones, Jr., design; water and trees.

> Glen Canyon Golf Course, Page Arizona: "If your ball lands within a club's length of a rattlesnake, you are allowed to move the ball."

Highland Hills Golf Course

Westminster, CO

(210)692-3752

Year opened: 1974

Rating: 70.4/66.8

Slope: 124/109

Tee Time Info: Call in advance.

Fee Rating: 1

Thickly tree-lined, well-kept municipal course.

Indian Canyon

Spokane, WA

(509)747-5353

Year opened: 1935

Rating: 70.7/65.9

Slope: 126/115

Tee Time Info: Call as far in advance as needed.

Fee Rating: 1

Charles Egan design, traditional with many different challenges; finesse required.

Jackson Hole

Jackson Hole, WY

(307)733-3111

Year opened: 1967

Rating: 72.3/73.2

Slope: 133/125

Tee Time Info: Call anytime with credit card.

Fee Rating: 1

Robert Trent Jones, Sr., course with the Tetons as a stunning backdrop.

Kapalua Golf Club (3 Courses)

Kapalua, Maui, Hawaii

(808)669-8820

Year opened: 1975

Rating: 71.7/69.6

Slope: 138/121

Tee Time Info: Resort guests reserve tee times one week in advance; Non guests call four days in advance

Fee Rating: 2

Plantation (1991): beautiful ocean view, blind spots on course. Village (1980): windier and tighter. Bay (1975): beautiful and more forgiving.

Kauai Lagoons (Kiele)

Lihue, Kauai, Hawaii

(808)241-6000

Year opened: 1988

Rating: 73.7/66.5

Slope: 137/123

Tee Time Info: Resort, call within 30 days

Fee Rating: 2

Nicklaus design, challenges risktaking.

Kayak Point

Stanwood, WA

(360)652-9676

(800)562-3094

Year opened: 1977

Rating: 72.7/72.8

Slope: 133/129

Tee Time Info: Call one week in advance for weekdays. Weekend tee times are given on Monday morning.

Fee Rating: 1

Tight, up-down, penal course.

Keystone Ranch

Keystone, CO

(303)468-4250

Year opened: 1980

Rating: 71.4/70.7

Slope: 130/129

Tee Time Info: Resort, call seven days in advance.

Fee Rating: 1 to 2

Mountain course, a journey through woods, links, and a valley.

Ko Olina

Ewa Beach, Oahu, Hawaii

(808)676-5300

See Review/Preview, LPGA Cup Noodles Hawaiian Open

La Paloma (Ridge/Canyon)

Tucson, AZ

(602)299-1500

(800)222-1249

Year opened: 1984

Rating: 74.2/74.2/74.8

Slope: 152/150/151

Tee Time Info: Resort guests up to 60 days in advance.

Fee Rating: 1 to 2

Nicklaus design in foothills, demands hitting targets.

La Quinta Resort and Club (Dunes)

La Quinta, CA

(619)564-5729

(619)564-7686

Year opened: 1981

Rating: 73.1/68.0

Slope: 137/114

Tee Time Info: Hotel guests may make tee times up to one year in advance. Nonguests three days in advance. Call for all advance tee times.

Fee Rating: 1 to 2

Challenging Dye desert layout, wild scenery.

The country of Naura, between the Marshall and Solomon Islands, has a golf course made entirely of sand.

Mauna Kea Beach Golf Course

Kohala Coast, Hawaii

(808)880-3480

Year opened: 1965

Rating: 73.6/65.8

Slope: 135/109 Season: Year-round

Tee Time Info: Guests four days in advance; non guests, two days in advance

Fee Rating: 1 to 2

Jewel of green, blue and black (lava).

McCormick Woods

Port Orchard, WA

(206)895-0130

Year opened: 1988

Rating: 74.1/71.1

Slope: 135/122

Tee Time Info: Call 30 days in advance if out of state; homeowners call seven days in advance; general public call five days in advance beginning at 9 a.m.

Fee Rating: 1

Thick with trees, pristine; water, mounds.

Moreno Valley Ranch (Mountain/Lake/Valley)

Moreno Valley, CA

(909)924-4444

Year opened: 1988

Rating: 73.1/74.1

Slope: 139/138

Tee Time Info: Call seven days in advance.

Fee Rating: 1

Three Pete Dye nines, play a combo with different looks and targets.

A golf course in Zimbabwe allows players to remove their ball from elephant dung and play a dropping of their own without penalty, provided their ball is placed nowhere closer to the hole.

Pasatiempo

Santa Cruz, CA
(408)459-9155
Year opened: 1929
Rating: 72.9/73.6
Slope: 138/135
Tee Time Info: Call seven days for weekdays. Call Monday for upcoming weekend at 10 a.m.
Fee Rating: 2
Alister Mackenzie classic, spectacular views, constant challenges.

PGA West (Stadium)

See Review/Preview, SPGA Liberty Mutual Legends of Golf

PGA West (Nicklaus Resort)

La Quinta, CA
(619)564-7170
Year opened: 1987
Rating: 75.5/69.0
Slope: 138/116
Tee Time Info: Resort; call.
Fee Rating: 1 to 2
Nicklaus design demanding accuracy; punishing bunkers.

Pole Creek

Winter Park, CO
(303)726-8847
Year opened: 1984
Rating: 73.1/67.9
Slope: 135/119
Tee Time Info: Call up to seven days in advance.
Fee Rating: 1
Rockies course with rustic feel, need accuracy.

Port Ludlow

Port Ludlow, WA
(206)437-0272
(800)732-1239
Year opened:1975
Rating: 73.6/73.1/72.7
Slope: 138/138/131
Tee Time Info: Resort guests make tee times at room confirmation. Non guests call one week in advance.
Fee Rating: 1
Overlooking Puget Sound, demands accuracy.

Priceville Resort
Prince Golf & Country Club

Princeville, Kauai, Hawaii
(800)826-5000
Year opened: 1991
Rating: 75.6/70.0
Slope: 144/127
Tee Time Info: One month in advance
Fee Rating: 4
Terrors with the beauty.

Princeville Resort
Princeville Makia
(Ocean/Lakes)

Princeville, Kauai, Hawaii
(800)826-4400
Year opened: 1973
Rating: 72.7/72.7/72.3
Slope: 133/134/129
Tee Time Info: Resort; call one month in advance.
Fee Rating: 1 to 2
Scenic and forgiving.

Sun Valley Resort Golf Course

Sun Valley, ID

(208)622-3300

Year opened: 1975

Rating: 72.4/69.2

Slope: 133/120

Tee Time Info: Resort; public two days in advance or 30 days in advance with credit card.

Fee Rating: 1

Tight, Sun Valley setting.

Riverdale (Dunes)

Brighton, CO

(303)659-6700

Year opened: 1985

Rating: 72.1/67.5

Slope: 129/109

Tee Time Info: Call two days in advance for weekday. Call Monday at 5:30 p.m. for Saturday and Tuesday at 5:30 p.m. for Sunday.

Fee Rating: 1

Dye design demanding course management, long hits.

Salishan Golf Links

Gleneden Beach, OR

(503)764-3632

(800)452-2300

Year opened: 1928

Rating: 69.6/70.0

Slope: 118/N/A

Tee Time Info: Call two days in advance for weekdays, or Monday for the upcoming weekend.

Fee Rating: 1

Rough links course, windy.

Sandpiper

Goleta, CA

(805)968-1541

Year opened: 1972

Rating: 74.5/73.3

Slope: 134/125

Tee Time Info: Call one week in advance.

Fee Rating: 1

Long, high along ocean; forgiving in calm weather.

Semiahmoo

Blaine, WA

(206)371-7005

(800)770-7992

Year opened: 1986

Rating: 74.5/71.6

Slope: 130/126 Season: Year-round

Tee Time Info: Call 72 hours in advance Monday-Friday; 24 hours in advance for Saturday and 48 hours in advance for Sunday; Guests can call 90 days in advance through hotel.

Fee Rating: 1

Palmer/Seay design; rolling—bunkered, contoured greens a challenge.

Spanish Bay, Spyglass Hill

See Review/Preview, PGA AT&T Pebble Beach Pro Am

Sunriver (North)

Sunriver, OR

(503)593-1221

Year opened: 1981

Rating: 73.0/70.3

Slope: 131/118 Season: April-October

Tee Time Info: Guests may make tee time at time of reservation; Non-guests call 30 days in advance.

Fee Rating: 1

Mountain views, different looks; Robert Trent Jones, Jr. design.

Tamarron

Durango, CO

(303)259-2000

(800)678-1000

> "Pebble Beach is Alcatraz with grass."
>
> —Bob Hope

Year opened: 1975
Rating: 73.0/71.9
Slope: 144/127
Tee Time Info: Resort guests call two days in advance; Non guests call one day in advance.
Fee Rating: 2
Course management in mountain setting; bunkers, water, large greens more difficult than they appear.

Teton Pines Country Club and Resort

Jackson, WY
(307)733-1733
(800)238-2223
Year opened: 1987
Rating: 74.2/70.8
Slope: 137/117
Tee Time Info: Call anytime during the year.
Fee Rating: 2
Palmer/Seay design, ranch with lots of water and challenges.

Tokatee

Blue River, OR
(503)822-3220
(800)452-6376
Year opened: 1966
Rating: 72.0/71.2
Slope: 126/115
Tee Time Info: Call in advance.
Fee Rating: 1
Cascade foothills; forgiving beauty.

Torrey Pines (North/Soth)

LaJolla, CA
(619)452-3226
(800)985-4653
See Review/Preview, PGA Buick Invitational of California

TPC of Scottsdale (Stadium)

Scottsdale, AZ
See PGA Review/Preview, PGA Phoenix Open

Ventana Canyon Golf and Racquet Club (Mountain/Canyon)

Tucson, AZ
(602)577-4061
(800)828-5701
Year opened: 1984
Rating: 74.2/68.3
Slope: 146/117
Tee Time Info: Call seven days in advance.
Fee Rating: 2
Tom Fazio designs; desert mountain layouts, mistakes very costly.

Wailea Golf Club (Blue/Gold)

Wailea, Maui, Hawaii
(808)875-5111
Year opened: 1972
Rating: 71.6/72.0
Slope: 130/117
Tee Time Info: Resort guests call five days in advance.
Fee Rating: 1
Robert trent Jones, Jr., designs; open and short, heavily bunkered.

Waikola Beach Resort (King's Course)

Waikoloa, Hawaii
(808)885-6060

Year opened: 1981
Rating: 71.5/69.4
Slope: 133/119 Season:Year-round
Tee Time Info: Call or fax 30 days in advance with credit card to guarantee.
Fee Rating: 2
Open, long; toughens with wind.

Waialua

Kauai, Hawaii
(808)245-8092
Year opened: 1963
Rating: 73.0/73.1
Slope: 136/122
Tee Time Info: Call one week in advance, minimum two players.
Fee Rating: 1
Strong public, tricky; hosted several USGA Public Links championships (1996 included).

——

CANADA/CARRIBEAN

Algonquin

St. Andrews, New Brunswick
(506)529-3062
Year opened: 1984
Rating: 69.3/73.0
Slope: 114/N/A
Tee Time Info: Open
Fee Rating: 1
Two Donald Ross designs—Seaside and Woodlands; windy, rough.

Banff Springs

Banff, Alberta
(403)762-6833
Year opened: 1928

Rating: N/A
Slope: N/A
Tee Time Info: Call ahead
Fee Rating: 1
Mountain setting with spectacular views; 3 9-hole courses, with original design by Stanley Thompson; rewards the long and straight.

Cape Breton Highlands Golf Links

Ingonish Beach, Nova Scotia
(902)285-2600
Year opened: 1942
Rating: 73.7/73.3
Slope: 139/131
Tee Time Info: Advance notice except if lodging.
Fee Rating: 1
Mountainside, with long fairways.

Deerhurst Resort

Huntsville, Ontario
(705)789-2381
Year opened: 1990
Rating: 74.5/71.2
Slope: 140/125
Tee Time Info: Resort; week in advance.
Fee Rating: 1
Long hitters course, open/densely wooded mix.

Gallagher's Canyon

Kelowna, British Columbia
(604)861-4240
Year opened: 1980
Rating: 73.5/73.8
Slope: 136/131
Tee Time Info: Call ahead.
Fee Rating: 1
Various elevations, long.

Glen Abbey Golf Club

Oakville, Ontario
See Review/Preview, PGA Bell Canadian Open

Jasper Park Golf Course

Jasper, Alberta
(403)852-6089
Year opened: 1925
Rating: 70.5/73.5
Slope: 121/N/A
Tee Time Info: Open
Fee Rating: 1
Old favorite aging gracefully; bunkers restored to original Stanley Thompson design.

Kananaskis Country Golf Club (Mt. Kidd/Mt. Lorette)

Kananaskis Village, Alberta
(403)591-7070
Year opened: 1983
Rating: 72.8/71.5
Slope: 134/N/A
Tee Time Info: Call in advance to secure.
Fee Rating: 1
Two tough Robert T. Jones, Sr., courses; mountains, streams, demands course management.

Lionhead Golf and Country Club

Brampton, Ontario
(905)455-4900
Year opened: 1991
Rating: 77.0/74.0
Slope: 151/137
Tee Time Info: Call in advance.
Fee Rating: 1
2 courses, Legends long and more challenging, tight fairways.

Mill River

O'Leary, Prince Edward Island
(800)367-8337
Year opened: 1971
Rating: 75.0/70.5
Slope: 132/127
Tee Time Info: Open
Fee Rating: 1
Tight, hilly, long in remote locale; scenic and tricky.

Northview Golf and Country Club (Ridge)

Surrey, British Columbia
(604)576-4653
Year opened: 1994
Rating: 73.4/N/A
Slope: 142/124
Tee Time Info: Call in advance.
Fee Rating: 1
Palmer/Seay course, with tight fairways, opening to broad greens.

Twin Rivers Golf Club

Port Blanford, Newfoundland
(709)543-2626
Year opened: 1984
Rating: 71.9/72.5
Slope: 116/121
Tee Time Info: Open
Fee Rating: 1
Scenic ocean setting, tough on and around greens.

Whistler Golf Club

Whistler Village, British Columbia
(604)932-3280
(800)944-7853
Year opened: 1982
Rating: 71.3/70.5
Slope: 128/120

Tee Time Info: Hotel guests get priority; call ahead.

Fee Rating: 1

Palmer/Seay course: mountain scenery has that getaway feel, but the course makes you think and plan.

Carambola Beach Golf Club

Kingshill, St. Croix, Virgin Islands

(809)773-2100

Year opened: 1966

Rating: 72.7/71.0

Slope: 131/123

Tee Time Info: Non-resort guests 24 hours in advance

Fee Rating: 1

Pleasureable, not difficult for straight shooters.

Casa de Campo Resort and Country Club

La Romano, Dominican Republic

(809)523-3333

Year opened: 1970

Rating: 74.1/72.9

Slope: 140/130

Tee Time Info: Call/Fax

(809)523-8800

Fee Rating: 2

2 courses, a links and Teeth of the Dog, one of the world's best; dreamy, but winds and bunkers play havoc.

Hyatt Dorado Beach Resort (East/West)

Dorado, Puerto Rico

(809)796-8961

Year opened: 1958

Rating: 72.8/72.6

Slope: 127/124

Robert Trent Jones, Sr., courses, demands hitting targets; scenic ocean views.

EUROPE

Ballybunion Golf Club

Ballybunion

County Kerry

Ireland

Founded 1893

(353)6827 146

Tee Time Information: Open, book in advance for weekends.

Two courses, both links with varying looks, many sublime.

The Belfry

North Warwickshire

England

Founded 1977

0675-470301

Tee Time Information: Open.

Two 18 hole courses. Peter Aliss and Dave Thomas design, very American: long, water play, large greens.

Blairgowrie Golf Club

Blairgowrie

Scotland

Founded 1889

0250 872594

Tee Time Information: Check restrictions in advance.

Two 18-hole courses: Rosemount more thickly wooded and heathered, Landowne tighter. Very green.

Campo de Golf El Saler

El Saler

Spain

Founded 1968

(346) 161 1186

> I've got a lawn mower back in Texas. I'll send it over"
>
> —Ben Hogan, playing the British Open at Carnoustie in 1953.

Tee Time Information: Open

Javier Arana-design; Scottish links-like, with interesting array of dunes, scrub, and well-placed individual trees.

Carnoustie Golf Links

Carnoustie
Scotland
Founded ca 1500
0241-853789

Tee Time Information: Pre-arrange and must have handicap.

On a comeback; flat, pit bunkers, various challenges—wind, water, and always menacing rough.

Corfu

Ropa Valley
Ermones Beach
Greece
Founded 1971
(30) 661 94 220

Tee Time Information: Open to visitors, March-October season.

Harradine design, with sudden challenges, rewards careful play. Amid eucalyptus and birch, exotic wildlife.

Falsterbo Golfklub

Falsterbo
Sweden
Founded 1909
(46)4047 00 78

Tee Time Information: Book in advance.

Classic links course, plus natural water hazards throughout.

Golfclub Beuerberg

Gut Sterz
Germany
Founded 1982
(49) 81 79 617

Tee Time Information: Weekdays only; Open April-November.

Donald Harradine design. At the edge of foothills of the Alps; water and bunkers to avoid, mountains rising above and a stream winding through.

Golf Club Hubbelrath

Dusseldorf
Germany
Founded 1961
(49) 21 047 2178

Tee Time Information: Weekdays, with member only on weekends.

Accuracy off the tee and careful putting on sloping greens needed. Water and bunkers, thickly treed.

Golf Club du Touquet

Le Touquet
France
Founded 1904
(33) 21 05 6847

Tee Time Information: Open; handicap limit of 24; just south of Calais.

2 courses—a classic rough links, and a flatter, woodsy, parkland style

Golf de Chantilly

Chantilly
France
Founded 1906
(33) 44 57 0443

Tee Time Information: Open Tuesdays and Wednesday; restrictions on weekends. Just over 20 miles north of Paris.

Tom Simpson design, restored after damage in WW II. Thickly carpeted and treed, many bunkers and demands accuracy. 2 courses.

Golf de Fontainbleau

Fontainebleau

France

Founded 1909

(33)64 22 2295

Tee Time Information: Open; closed Tuesdays.

Mixture of tough holes and different looks—plays long, lush with oaks and pines.

Golf and Country Club Gut Altentan

Henndorg am Wallersee

Founded 1986

Austria

(43) 62 14 6026

Tee Time Information: Weekdays only; open April-October. Within 10 miles of Salzburg. American-typle layout, with hills, lakes and streams; Nicklaus design.

Holstebro Golfklub

Rasted

Denmark

Founded 1970

(45) 97 48 5155

Tee Time Information: Open; Near Idom.

Heath course, with trees and heather accepting wayward shots.

Kennemer Golf & Country Club

Zandvoort

Holland

Founded 1910

(31) 25 07 12 836

Pubic: Advanced booking.

Three 9-hole natural links courses (Pennink, Colt, Van Hengel), wind, with dunes and gorse off the rolling fairways.

Lahinch

County Clare

Ireland

> "Say, that looks like an old, abandoned golf course. What did they call it?"
>
> —Sam Snead, on first seeing St. Andrews, 1946.

Founded 1893

(353)658 1003

Tee Time Information: Open.

Two Alister Mackenzie courses. Not long, but punishing dunes, and plateau greens run fast.

Modena Golf and Country Club

Colombaro di Formiginiei

Italy

Founded 1987

(39) 59 55 34 82

Tee Time Information: Open.

Bernhard Langer layout. Short, but heavily bunkered, water play and rolling greens.

The Old Course, St. Andrews

St. Andrews Fife

Scotland

Founded ca. 1400

0334-75757

Tee Time Information: Reserve time; need handicap certificate; lottery in summer; not open on Sundays.

Classic seaside links, many double greens, treacherous bunkers, some hidden. Many famous holes.

Portmanock Golf Club

County Dublin

Ireland

Founded 1894

(353) 1846 2968

Tee Time Information: Book ahead.

Peninsula open to elements; bracken and dunes. Moody, but not long or terribly punishing, depending on weather.

Quinto Do Lago

Almansil

Portugal

Founded 1974

(351) 89 396 0023

Tee Time Information: Book in advance.

Four 9-hole courses, each different in play but following the rolling land and meandering water, with well-placed bunkers.

Real Golf El Prat

Llobregat

Spain

Founded 1956

(343)379 0278

Tee Time Information: Open; just south of Barcelona.

Tropic-like course, with a full host of trouble to find; water, trees, bunkers—various looks.

Royal Birkdale

Southport, Merseyside

England

Founded 1889

0704-567920

Tee Time Information: Open Monday-Friday.

Willow scrub, dunes; now playing more tame, but tough.

Royal County Down Golf Club

Newcastle

County Down

Ireland

Founded 1889

03967-23314

Tee Time Information: Open except Saturdays.

Blind shots, tight fairways, sand and heather, well-placed bunkers.

Royal Darnoch

Dornoch

Scotland

Founded 1877

0862-810219

Tee Time Information: Open, must have handicap certificate.

Subtly serpentine links course, lulling, until the wind, bunkers, valleys and the odd bunker come into play, and gorse, of course.

Royal Liverpool

Merseyside

England

Founded 1869

051-632 3101

Tee Time Information: Limited times, call ahead. 10 miles south of Liverpool.

Very tough holes, pot bunkers; hosted 10 Opens but no longer in rotation.

Royal Lytham & St. Annes

Lancashire

England

Founded 1869

0253-724206

Tee Time Information: Mid-morning and mid-afternoon tee times most days; very limited Tuesday and weekends.

Links-type course with dunes, urban.

Royal Porthcawl

Porthcawl

Wales

Founded 1891 0656-782251

Tee Time Information: Open, with handicap certificate; restricted times weekends.

Tightly-bunkered with small greens, treeless and windy, short but plenty of trouble.

Royal St. Georges

Sandwich

England

Founded 1897

0304-613090

Tee Time Information: Call well ahead. Men up to 18 handicap, Women 15.

Links, dunes, pot bunkers; in the Open rotation.

Royal Troon Golf Club

Troon

Scotland

Founded 1878 0292-311555

Tee Time Information: Book ahead.

Two 18-hole courses. Endlessly deep bunkers, protected fast greens, windy, mixes short and long.

Royal Waterloo

Vieux Chemin De Wavre

Belgium

Founded: 1869

(02) 63 31 850

Tee Time Information: Open. South of Brussels

45 holes, Fred Hawtree design. Rolling, heavily wooded, excellent strategic design.

Sunningdale

Ascot

Berkshire

England

Founded 1900

0344-21681

Tee Time Information: Prior arrangement only: submit letter of introduction and handicap.

Two courses (old/new). Hilly, deep-bunkered, runs fast in summer.

Turnberry Golf Course

Ayshire

Scotland

Founded 1906

0655-31000

Tee Time Information: Book well in advance, begin with written application.

2 courses, oceanside, rocky, rolling, windy.

Valderamma Golf Club

Sotogrande

Cadiz

Spain

Founded 1975

(34) 56 795 775

Tee Time Information: Advanced booking, noon to 2.

Robert Trent Jones, Sr., design and restoration. Sloping fairways, many-bunkered, varying elevations, sometimes open, sometimes woodsy.

Wentworth

Surrey

England

Founded 1924

0344 842201

Tee Time Information: Weekdays by prior arrangement; with member only on weekend.

Long, heathland course, designed by Colt. Fir-lined.

14

THE GREAT DESIGNERS

"Every golfer worthy of the name should have some acquaintance with the principles of golf course design, not only for the betterment of the game, but for his own selfish enjoyment. Let him know a good hole from a bad one and the reasons for a bunker here and another there, and he will be a long way towards pulling his score down to respectable limits. When he has taught himself to study a hole from the point of view of the man who laid it out, he will be much more likely to play it correctly."

—Bobby Jones

CHARLES HUGH ALISON
(1882–1952)

The often forgotten member of H.S. Colt's architecture firm, C.H. Alison was a prolific designer displaying much of his best work in the Far East. A fine player and member of the Oxford and Cambridge Golfing Society, Alison met Colt while he was constructing London's Stokes Pages course in 1908. Alison eventually joined Colt's firm, first as a construction superintendent and later as his associate.

While working with Colt (and briefly with Alister Mackenzie as a partner in the firm), Alison was involved with most of the firm's projects, including original designs for Sunningdale and Wentworth and redesigns at two British Open rotation members, Royal St. George's and Royal Lytham and St. Anne's. Alison is most noted for his solo work while on his Far East swing in the early 1930s, creating such world renowned courses as Kasumigaseki and Kawana Golf Clubs in Japan.

Alison co-authored *Some Essays on Golf Architecture* with Colt, published in 1920. He also wrote numerous magazine articles and shared many of the same bold opinions as his associates, Colt and Mackenzie. In an article published in the 1920s, Alison expressed his views on hazards and probably echoed the feelings of many a high handicap golfer: "Hazards should be visible. In general, they should not penalize to the extent of more than one stroke, provided that the stroke out of them is properly played. They should not be so severe as to discourage bold play. In placing hazards it is vital to keep the course navigable for the duffer. It is perfectly possible to do this, and yet to render it interesting and testing for the first-class player."

public appearance except on the darkest nights. Therefore, I believe it is safer, right at the beginning, to call in the specialist—the golf architect—and place on him the major responsibility for the designing and building of the course."

CHARLES BANKS
(1883–1931)

Longtime construction assistant of Seth Raynor and Charles Blair Macdonald, Charles Banks was involved in ten projects before starting his own firm. Banks met Raynor soon after he graduated from Yale and later helped in the construction of his alma mater's course, a Raynor/Macdonald masterpiece to this day.

In his solo work, Banks designed and redesigned over thirty courses with the trademark Macdonald/Raynor look—squared off edges to his greens, grass-faced bunkering and green placements based on the basic principles used for the great holes of Scotland. Like his mentors, Banks always included a version of the "Redan" and other renowned holes in his designs. Banks' layouts of note include Forsgate Country Club, East, and Essex Country Club (New Jersey), Tamrack (New York), and his last design, Castle Harbour (Bermuda).

Banks also wrote several articles on construction, his specialty, as well as design, and he was one of the first architects to advocate using heavy equipment for bold earthmoving. In his writings, Banks was eloquent and certainly not afraid to express an opinion. In this excerpt from his 1931 essay, "Golf Course Design and Construction," Banks discusses why a professional architect is necessary: "Building a golf course and then calling in a golf architect afterwards to remedy the defects is like 'building' your own suit of clothes and then calling in a tailor to give them style and reinforce the seams so that they won't rip in vital spots. The way some golf courses rip after being built is appalling. Some courses cannot safely put in a

BILLY BELL
(1886-1953)

Soft-spoken and modest by those who knew him, Billy Bell never received the credit he deserved for his remarkable bunker shaping, his ingenuity in constructing courses, or his influence on the outcome of George Thomas's design work. Born on April 19, 1886, in Canonsburg, Pennsylvania, Bell moved to California in 1910, but did not know Thomas or the "Philadelphia gang" of aspiring architects during his years in Pennsylvania. With a background in agriculture, Bell worked first as a caddymaster at Annandale Golf Club, later as the greenskeeper at Pasadena Golf Club, and briefly as a construction foreman for Southern California's most prominent golf course architect at the time, Willie Watson.

In 1920 Bell ventured into the design business on his own and quickly won contracts in California's booming golf course development industry. Among his first designs were the Balboa Park Golf Course and San Diego Country Club. Though the exact time is unclear, Bell met George Thomas sometime around 1922 and asked for Thomas's endorsement of his design of Candlewood Country Club in northern California. Thomas was impressed and asked Bell to serve as construction foreman on several Thomas designs. In photographs of Thomas courses where Bell administered construction, one can see the dramatic, rugged-edged, "baseball glove" sand traps that later became known as "Thomas bunkers." Significantly, photographs of Thomas's early solo work do not show this kind of bunkering, but photographs of Bell's work in the late 1920s and 1930s reveal the spirited bunker design.

Thomas and Bell worked together on such classic courses as Bel-Air Country Club, Ojai Valley Inn, Los Angeles Country Club, Stanford Golf Club, and their masterpiece, Riviera Country Club. Bell went on to design many fine courses in the western United States, always with his trademark bunker sculpturing. Sadly, much of the original character of those bunkers has been lost through years of weather, explosion shots and the use of motorized edgers.

As well as having had a major impact on Thomas's work, Bell designed or redesigned over 100 courses on his own. He was a charter member of the American Society of Golf Course Architects and served as its President in 1952. Bell briefly formed a partnership with A.W. Tillinghast after "Tillie's" move to California in 1936. They worked on two projects together, a redesign of the Brookside municipal courses that surrounds the Rose Bowl and Virginia Country Club in Long Beach.

TOM BENDELOW
(1872–1936)

One of the very first professional American architects, Tom Bendelow was a course designing machine responsible for over 400 courses at a time when travel was extremely difficult. Bendelow got his start in the New York area when he laid out a course for the wealthy Platt family in the early 1900s. He continued to receive requests for design work in the area and was responsible for several of the earliest American courses.

Bendelow later joined the sporting goods division of the A.G. Spalding Company, traveling the country selling Spalding products and all the while staking out courses with the company's support. But Bendelow's early work left a lot to be desired. He only visited many sites once and most of those were subsequently redesigned when better earth moving equipment became available and golfers' standards became higher.

In 1920, Bendelow left Spalding to take over William Langford's vacated spot with the American Park Builders and focused his attention on courses in Illinois. Having settled there, Bendelow was able to focus on the details of design, leading to several fine creations, the most noted being the three courses of Medinah Country Club. Medinah, No. 3, has hosted two United States Opens and will be in the spotlight again in 1999 when it plays host to the PGA Championship.

JAMES BRAID
(1870–1950)

A five-time British Open Champion in the early 1900s, James Braid first learned to play at age four and as a teenager worked at St. Andrews as an apprentice carpenter. Because of his status as a golfer (see his sketch in the Hall of Fame section), Braid was commissioned to design a few courses during his heyday, when he was sharing the spotlight with J.H. Taylor and Harry Vardon. The three golfers combined won 16 of 21 British Opens between 1894 and 1914 and were nicknamed "the Great Triumvirate."

Braid was the busiest golf designer in the British Isles after his retirement from playing, creating or redesigning over 200 courses. Afraid to travel, especially overseas, Braid rarely designed courses outside of Scotland and England. He is responsible for such classics as Carnoustie, Gleneagles (Kings and Queen's courses), North Berwick (East Links), and Musselburgh Country Club, all in Scotland. Braid was also responsible for St. Enodoc in England, a redesign of Ballybunion (Old), and some minor work at the Old Course of St. Andrews.

HARRY S. COLT
(1869–1951)

A Cambridge graduate who practiced law for a number of years, H.S. Colt was a fine player who became so interested in golf course design that he dropped his law practice altogether and became a full time architect. His first design was in London during the early 1900s, and many other pre-World War I projects followed.

His workload became so heavy that Colt added several fine associates. First was his lifelong partner in design, C.H. Alison, and later a brief partnership was formed with Alister Mackenzie, whom Colt met while working at Mackenzie's home course, Alwoodley, in England. Colt was perhaps the first prolific, full-time golf course designer. He presented drawings, wrote articles on the subject, penned *Golf Course Architecture* with C.H. Alison, and was the first to actually plan tree-planting schemes, even though Colt considered trees "a fluky and obnoxious hazard."

Colt's list of important design and redesign work is staggering in terms of quality courses. He was the most important assistant to George Crump in building Pine Valley. He redesigned and created the modern versions of Sunningdale and Wentworth, England's two most noted inland courses. And he was responsible for Muirfield—what many consider to be perhaps the best course architecturally in all of Scotland. These gems show that Colt was a master at routing courses and was a brilliant strategist.

BILL COORE (B. 1945) AND BEN CRENSHAW (B. 1952)

With the 1995 unveiling of Sand Hills Golf Club, Bill Coore and Ben Crenshaw introduced perhaps the finest natural and strategic new course since the work of their mentors from the "Golden Age" of architecture. Coore and Crenshaw both share an affinity for classic design and are two of the most serious students of golf architecture.

Crenshaw's fascination with architecture began at the age of sixteen, when he left his homestate of Texas and played the U.S. Junior at The Country Club in Brookline, Massachusetts. It was the first

time Crenshaw had been exposed to traditional architecture and it was the beginning of his lifelong passion for the history of the game. Since then Crenshaw has compiled one of the finest private golf book collections in the world and has written several fine essays on all facets of the game.

Bill Coore's passion for architecture began while playing Perry Maxwell's Old Town Club and Donald Ross's Pinehurst during his college days at Wake Forest in North Carolina. Like so many other talented architects in the business today, Coore joined Pete Dye and Associates, working there for ten years before starting his own firm in 1982. After several highly-regarded efforts, including Rockport Country Club in Texas and Golf du Medoc in France, Coore joined forces with Crenshaw, his fellow Austin, Texas, native, in 1986.

In addition to their idylic design at Sand Hills (*Golf Digest's* best new private course in 1995), Coore and Crenshaw have taken their strategic design style to the Plantation Course at Kapalua, Hawaii, 18-holes at Barton Creek in Austin, and a 9-hole addition to historic Southern Hills in Tulsa, Oklahoma. They have also undertaken several high profile restorations, including A.W. Tillinghast's Brook Hollow in Dallas and George Thomas's Riviera Country Club in Pacific Palisades, California.

GEOFFREY CORNISH
B. 1914

A former trainee under Canadian Stanley Thompson, Geoffrey Cornish established his own practice in 1952, becoming one of the busiest golf architects and helping expand appreciation for the golf design profession. Cornish designed or redesigned over 400 courses, most in the northeastern United States.

Few architects have worked as hard as Cornish to further the profession of golf course design and few have been as successful in generating the average golfer's respect for the architect and his work. In addition to many articles in various publications, Cornish has co-authored two major books on golf course architecture: *Golf Course Design: An Introduction* (1975), a primer on design written with his former partner, William Robinson, and *The Golf Course* (1981), written with former lawyer Ronald Whitten. Cornish and Whitten's remarkable research into the lives and work of every golf architect was a monumental event for the profession, leading many clubs to more greatly appreciate the historical significance of courses and designers.

GEORGE CRUMP
(1871–1918)

Despite only having one course to his credit, George Crump is one of golf architecture's most important figures. Fifteen miles from his native Philadelphia, Crump created his dream course amongst once barren scrubland of New Jersey and called it Pine Valley. Since its inception, Pine Valley has been considered one of America's finest golf courses, if not the very best in the land—ranking at the top of *Golf Magazine's 100 Greatest Courses in the World* (1993). What makes Crump's design at Pine Valley so special? For starters, it is one of the finest properties ever used for a golf course, combining virtually every element and environmental factor imaginable for a challenging round: sand, trees, water, wind and rolling, sometimes hilly terrain. Pine Valley also reflects Crump's application of advice from his friends, many of whom were fine players who would go on to have their own successful architecture careers. The list of advisors to Crump is a "who's who" of golf architecture: H.S. Colt, A.W. Tillinghast, Hugh Wilson, George Thomas, William Flynn, Walter Travis, C.H. Alison, Robert Hunter, W.C. Fownes, and many others. Of the group, Colt had the greatest influence and appropriately shares design credit with Crump.

George Thomas, a founding member of Pine Valley, explains why Pine Valley is so special:

"Every true golfer loves Pine Valley. It may be measured by some as very difficult, especially recovery from the rough; yet its charm is the lure of diversity coupled with the thrill surmounting its varied hardships. Pine Valley is for superlative play. While its heroic carries are in the minority, nevertheless there is not always a safe path for the short player. Its hazards penalize severely, and its strategy compels finesse." Thomas concludes: "To my mind, Pine Valley is the acme of golf in this country, and any club which expects to build a fine test of golf should, if possible, have members of its committee carefully inspect Pine Valley."

Sadly, Crump died suddenly in 1918 before the completing the course, and the final four holes were finished by Hugh and Alan Wilson, with help from H.S. Colt and C.H. Alison.

ROBERT CUPP
B. 1939

Jack Nicklaus' assistant for over fourteen years, Bob Cupp created his own design firm in 1985 after a one-course stint with another Nicklaus employee, Jay Morrish. Cupp's strong opinions and writing talent quickly moved him into the upper tier of architects during the building boom of the late 1980s.

Working with a plethora of Tour players, including Jerry Pate, Hubert Green, Tom Kite, Fred Couples, Fuzzy Zoeller and John Fought, Cupp has focused his design philosophy on building difficult courses with a variety of aesthetic looks. His work ranges from the classic sand-faced bunkering seen in his early work, to the shallower grassed-face bunkers at his best-known design, Pumpkin Ridge in Cornelius, Oregon (co-design with John Fought). Pumpkin Ridge hosted Tiger Wood's triumphant 1996 U.S. Amateur victory and will also host the 1997 U.S. Women's Open. Look for Pumpkin Ridge to host the first men's United States Open ever played in the Pacific Northwest in the near future.

> "[The TPC at Sawgrass] is *Star Wars* golf. The place was designed by Darth Vader."
>
> —Ben Crenshaw

Cupp has also ventured into bizarre territory only previously explored by another former Nicklaus designer, Desmond Muirhead. His Palmetto-Hall (Cupp Course) on Hilton Head Island features odd-looking, computer generated trapezoidal and linear forms for bunkers, greens, and teeing areas that have been well-received by the low-handicap players of South Carolina. Other notable designs by Cupp include the highly acclaimed Settindown Creek in Woodstock, Georgia, and Old Waverly in West Point, Mississippi. Cupp has also overseen the softening of several greens at Augusta National Golf Club to accommodate modern green speeds. Cupp collaborated at Augusta with the club's former superintendent, Billy Fuller, now one of the nations foremost consulting agronomists.

TOM DOAK
B. 1961

Tom Doak received a Bachelor of Science Degree, majoring in Landscape Architecture, at Cornell University in 1982. He also received the Architecture Department's William F. Deer Award to study golf course architecture in the British Isles; during 1982-83, he visited 170 golf courses and had a two-month caddying stint on The Old Course at St. Andrews.

Doak continued what Ben Crenshaw has called "one of the finest educations of anyone in golf architecture" with a four-year apprenticeship under Pete Dye. In 1989 he started Renaissance Golf Design and has since assembled a talented supporting team, including associates Bruce Hepner, Jim Urbina, and Tom Mead. In addition to several highly-regarded restorations, Doak's original design work has earned rave reviews from archi-tecture experts. Relying on a style truly inspired by the classic designers from the "Golden Age" of architecture, Doak's Stonewall design in Philadelphia has quickly become one of that area's best courses with its sound strategy and bold sand-faced bunkering. His authentic links course at The Legends at Myrtle Beach is the most sophisticated design in the South Carolina resort town, while his strongest work to date may be his first design, the daily-fee High Pointe Golf Club in Doak's hometown of Traverse City, Michigan.

Doak is also a prolific writer and perhaps the most astute scholar in the architecture business today. He has contributed to several books, and his two personal efforts, *The Anatomy of a Golf Course* and *The Confidential Guide to Golf Courses*, have been landmark efforts in the recent design renaissance. Doak's *Confidential Guide*, a critical review of golf courses around the world, includes many of his own photographs and is the definitive golf course guide for architecture students as well as a handy guide for the duffer.

PETE DYE
B. 1925

Discussed for his eccentric and controversial work, Pete Dye is the man most responsible for changing the direction of golf course design over the last thirty years. With new courses becoming more ordinary during the 1960s, Dye injected consideration for shotmaking and strategy back into the game with his bold style, and he virtually started the design renaissance.

A former insurance salesman who was a fine player in his homestate of Indiana, Dye generated immediate interest with such early works as Crooked Stick (Indiana) and The Golf Club (outside of Columbus, Ohio). They were the first Dye designs after his important trip to Scotland, when he and his wife, Alice, cultivated many of the ideas that would later become Pete Dye design trademarks (railroad ties, use of native grasses, deep grass-faced bunkers and vast wastes areas). Though both courses are low-profile by Dye standards today, they were a bold deviation from the other work of the 1960s, including those by Trent Jones, Dick Wilson and George Fazio.

Dye's next works further expressed his eccentric ideas. Casa De Campo (1971), which sits on a stunning coastline in the Dominican Republic, is Dye's personal favorite, while Harbour Town (1969) and Oak Tree Golf Club (1976) remain as Dye's most popular work with Tour pros. These three designs marked Dye's first extensive use of features that were completely opposite of what was considered proper at the time. While Robert Trent Jones was building 10,000 square foot greens with 50-yard long tees and flat fairways, Dye came along and put bumps in the landing areas, built tiny greens and created numerous teeing options on each hole. And just when the golf world thought it had seen everything from Dye, along came the first Tournament Players Course, in Sawgrass, Florida. Though it was widely criticized (Jack Nicklaus stated, "I'm not good at landing a 5-iron on the hood of a car"), the TPC at Sawgrass has evolved into a favorite of tour players and has helped elevate The Players Championship into one of golf's elite tournaments.

The list of honored and revered Dye courses has continued to lengthen: La Quinta Hotel's three courses, Long Cove Club, The Honors Course, PGA West (Stadium), Blackwolf Run, The Ocean Course at Kiawah Island, Medalist Club, and his West Virginia masterpiece, Pete Dye Golf Club.

Dye has been one of the most giving of architects. Alice Dye has made immeasurable contributions to his designs and has been a major influence on improving "ladies," or front tees on golf course designs. Unlike most modern designers who simply place the tees at the front of the driving area, the Dyes have worked to design the front tees on their courses to play as strategically as the championship tees. Dye has also trained many promising young architecture students. Among those who got their start with Dye: his sons Perry and P.B., Tom Doak, Lee Schmidt, Bill Coore, Bobby Weed, and John Harbottle.

GEORGE FAZIO
(1912–1986)

A respected golfer who finished runner-up with a playoff loss to Ben Hogan in the 1951 U.S. Open at Merion, George Fazio retired from competitive golf in 1959. Before venturing into course design, Fazio served as resident pro at several prestigious clubs, including Pine Valley and Hillcrest Country Club in Los Angeles.

In 1959 he redesigned Langhorne Golf Club in Pennsylvania for a friend and it spawned a successful design career. Fazio had done quite well in the car business and his architecture venture began as fun "side project," but his adeptness proved that he would receive many requests for his services over the next three decades. His experience as a fine player and at Pine Valley bred a design style based on difficulty and bold natural hazards. Among his most popular designs is Butler National, the all-men's club that hosted the PGA Tour's Western Open for many years.

Other notable Fazio designs include Moselem Springs (site of a U.S. Women's Open), the Jackrabbit Course at Champions Golf Club in Houston, and Fazio's personal favorite, Jupiter Hills in Florida. Fazio died in 1986 while still practicing architecture, more than ten years after his nephew Tom had left the firm and started his own successful business. Tom Fazio credits much of his success to the opportunities and education given to him by his uncle.

TOM FAZIO
B. 1945

Emphasizing playability, naturalness and detailed construction work, Tom Fazio has established himself as the most popular golf architect of the 1990s. Fazio ranked behind only Mackenzie, Ross, and Tillinghast in a recent *Golf Digest* readers poll of favorite designers.

Fazio has taken a far different route than the most popular architects of the previous two decades (Robert Trent Jones in the 70s and Pete Dye in the 80s), emphasizing a "look hard, play easy" design philosophy. The result is a portfolio of some of the most popular course designs in recent years. In Florida, Fazio's work at the 36-hole World Woods, Lake Nona Golf Club, and Black Diamond Ranch have garnered numerous awards, and his design at Pelican Hill Golf Club is strongly acclaimed. His home club, Wade Hampton in the Blue Ridge Valley of North Carolina, was voted *Golf Digest's* Best New Private Course in 1987.

Perhaps his most noted design is the garish, ultra-private Shadow Creek Golf Club in Las Vegas, Nevada. Built at a cost of $20 million for Mirage Hotel creator Steve Wynn, Shadow Creek was a barren desert property transformed into an incredible oasis of 23,000 trees, with creeks and lakes amid strategic sandy reaches. Though it has dropped in the rankings since its stunning *Golf Digest* debut as the 8th best course in the United States, Shadow Creek remains one of the most remarkable design accomplishments.

WILLIAM S. FLYNN
(1890–1945)

Another member of the Philadelphia School of Design, William Flynn got his start working under Hugh Wilson at Merion. There, Flynn supervised construction of the club's famed East course, and some years later, carried out a renovation after Wilson had passed away.

Following World War I Flynn created a partnership with construction specialist Howard Toomey and the two went on to create some of America's finest courses, including the modern version of Shinnecock Hills (New York), Cascades (Virginia), Atlantic City G.C. (New Jersey), Philadelphia Country Club in his home state, and Cherry Hills (Colorado). Like the Philadelphia tandem of George Thomas and Billy Bell, Flynn handled the design and public relations side while Toomey supervised the construction.

Flynn's style was simple and remarkably similar to his colleagues from Philadelphia. He believed in strategic design and an emphasis on using natural features. He has written: "Natural topographical features should always be developed in presenting problems in the play. As a matter of fact, such features are much more to be desired than man made tests for they are generally much more attractive."

In describing his ideas about design strategy, Flynn writes: "The best way to whet the appetite and improve the game of any golfer is to offer an incentive and provide a reward for high class play, and by high class play is meant simply the best of which each individual is capable. Placing a premium on accuracy with due consideration for length should be the aim of all men who design courses, for accuracy in the play signifies skill, and skill is generally the master of brute force."

Flynn is perhaps the least known of the great American architects. He was an accomplished golfer, an expert on turf and course maintenance, and an excellent tennis player. Flynn and Toomey trained several fine architects, including Dick Wilson, William Gordon, and Robert Lawrence.

HERBERT FOWLER
(1856–1941)

Described by legendary British golf writer and authority Bernard Darwin as one of the most gifted architects of his time, Herbert Fowler was a quick thinker who often insulted clients because of his swift judgments about the potential of their course. Fowler's first design effort possibly proved to be his finest—the Old Course at Walton

Heath. Between 1902 and 1904 he built the Surrey, England, course for friends of his wealthy father, who commissioned him because of his successful amateur golf career.

Fowler's triumphant design at Walton Heath led to more work in the British Isles, especially with many new course properties popping up in the expanding Heathlands region. His redesign work at Royal North Devon and Royal Lytham and St. Anne's won praise, and Fowler soon branched out to the United States. Joining his design firm at the time was the eccentric Tom Simpson, who would later write one of the finest books on golf course design and construction, *The Architectural Side of Golf*. Simpson focused on the firm's contracts in the British Isles, while Fowler traveled overseas to America.

Fowler's most noted work in the United States was at Eastward Ho! (Massachusetts) and a 1921 redesign of Los Angeles Country Club. There, Fowler expanded and completely rebuilt the club's course into 36-holes, with LACC member George C. Thomas, Jr., supervising the construction. Some years later, Thomas would object to Fowler's "geometric" and penal style of design by convincing his fellow members to allow him to redesign the now world-renowned North Course. Fowler and Simpson designed few courses together, though their 1926 creation of Cruden Bay in Scotland is considered one of the true hidden gems in the world of golf.

HENRY FOWNES (1856–1935) AND WILLIAM FOWNES (1878–1950)

Responsible for one of America's truly great golf courses, Henry and William Fownes created and groomed Oakmont Country Club for over fifty years. Situated in the suburbs of Pittsburgh, Pennsylvania, Oakmont is one of the most prolific tournament courses in America, not to mention one of the elite golf clubs in the golf rich state of Pennsylvania.

> "[Oakmont] is a course where good putters worry about their second shot before they hit the first one."
>
> —Lew Worsham

Henry Fownes formed Oakmont in 1903 after selling his steel company to Carnegie Steel. Fownes routed and designed the original course and over the years his son William tinkered with the design, creating the monster that Oakmont is today. Even in the early days, Oakmont was known for its lightning fast greens and ferocious bunkers, a product of William's constant concern for the course and consultation with legendary Oakmont greenskeeper, Emil Loeffler. William was a fine player, winning the 1910 U.S. Amateur and captaining the first Walker Cup team in 1922. He also served as USGA President from 1925-26.

WILLIAM (1893–1973) AND DAVID GORDON (B. 1922)

William Gordon was first introduced to golf course design while working with the Peterson Seed Company, where he met and worked with architects Willie Park, Jr., Devereux Emmet, and Donald Ross, among others. Eventually, he joined the firm of Toomey and Flynn, assisting on many important Flynn designs.

Gordon started his own business in 1941 and designed over one hundred courses during a thirty year career, including Stanwich Country Club, ranked in the top 100 in the United States by *Golf Digest* magazine. In 1947, David Gordon, his son, joined the firm and oversaw construction of most Gordon designs until 1952, when his father made him a partner in the firm.

David Gordon was an Air Force pilot during World War II, then he continued studies in turfgrass, graduating from Penn State's prestigious agricultural program in 1947. David Gordon continued working until the mid 1980s after his father's retirement in 1974.

GIL HANSE
B. 1965

Hanse is a rising young architect who bases his work on the principles of classic design. He started his own design firm in 1993 and is quickly garnering an impressive resume. In 1996, Hanse became just the third American architect to build a course in Scotland, crafting the 18-hole Craighead Golf Links for the Crail Golfing Society, the seventh oldest golf club in the world. Due to open in 1997, Crail's second links sits on the cliffs overlooking the North Sea and is sure to be one of the most talked about new courses in years.

Before starting his own company, Hanse worked under Tom Doak at Renaissance Golf Design. Hanse attended Cornell and, like Doak, was awarded the William F. Deer Award, allowing him to travel all over Scotland to study the links. Hanse shaped many of the bunkers and was involved in several aspects of the design at two highly-touted Doak courses, Stonewall in Pennsylvania and Wilderness Valley in Gaylord, Michigan.

Hanse has also been involved in several important restoration and long-range planning projects. He has begun to lay out a master plan for Merion, near his home in Philadelphia, as well as overseeing restoration at several other classic courses, including Kittansett Club in Massachusetts, William Flynn's underrated Lancaster Country Club in Pennsylvania, and Herbert Strong's Engineers Country Club in New York.

ARTHUR HILLS
B. 1930

A former landscape architect and college golfer at Michigan State, Arthur Hills has established himself as one of America's most popular architects with several high profile projects throughout the country. Hills stresses a traditional approach to design, listing Pinehurst #2, Cypress Point, Prairie Dunes, Merion and Inverness among his most admired courses.

In his most noted designs, Hills has gained national acclaim for building playable, strategic, and attractively built courses. Several of his courses have been selected to host championships, including The Champions in Lexington, Kentucky (1993 NCAA Men's Championship), Bighorn (Skins Game, 1992–1995), and The Golf Club of Georgia (Nationwide Championship, Senior PGA Tour). To date, Hills has designed over 150 courses and overseen renovation at another 100. Hills oversaw subtle improvements at Oakland Hills before the 1996 U.S. Open and at his home club, Inverness, in Toledo, Ohio, in preparation for the 1993 PGA Championship.

Hills also consulted at Oakmont Country Club in Pennsylvania for the 1994 U.S. Open. The Oakmont preparation was praised by architecture traditionalists: Hills worked with the club to remove nearly 1000 trees, opening up lost vistas and allowing the design to more closely resemble the intentions of club founders, Henry and William Fownes.

Hill's devotion to his project at Ironhorse in Florida was documented in John Strawn's fascinating book, *Driving the Green*, the only book to ever document the design and building of a golf course during its construction.

DR. MICHAEL HURDZAN
B. 1943

One of architecture's most innovative figures, Dr. Michael Hurdzan has a resume of over 150 course designs along with major contributions to the recent scientific advances in course construction. With a Ph.D. in environmental plant physiology, he has been a pioneer in the study of environmental impacts of golf courses, and as a response to excesses of the 1980s, Hurdzan created many successful methods for developers to lower course construction and maintenance costs while still building attractive designs.

His recent book, *Golf Course Architecture*, is the most comprehensive ever written on the subject, with detailed discussion of subjects ranging from the obvious, "Hazards," to the seminal, "Site Feasibility Studies." For the first time in a text, *Golf Course Architecture* gracefully covers all of the subjects that make modern golf architecture a challenging and difficult business. Dr. Hurdzan also draws great inspiration from the classic books on design and has accumulated the world's finest collection of golf architecture books at his Columbus, Ohio, office.

Hurdzan's field work has drawn strong reviews from several golf publications, with his Devil's Paintbrush and Devil's Pulpit designs in Caledon, Ontario, receiving the highest praise. Hurdzan is one of a select group of architects trying to lead a renaissance in course design, attempting to return to the strategic school of design. Hurdzan skillfully explained the reason for this renaissance in *Golf Course Architecture*: "Few modern golf architects understand the subtle nuances of strategic design, and thus couldn't skillfully apply them. But today, the beauty and natural-looking complexity of such strategic courses have been meeting with far more acceptance."

ROBERT HUNTER
(1874–1942)

One of the most fascinating characters in early twentieth century golf architecture, Robert Hunter never actually designed a golf course on his own. His golf course architecture career was limited to assisting Dr. Alister Mackenzie on such noted courses as Cypress Point, The Meadow Club, and The Valley Club of Montecito—all in California. A native of Indiana, Hunter also contributed to some minor redesign work at Monterey Peninsula Country Club's underrated Dunes Course and the Pebble Beach Golf Links in 1928. Hunter was primarily responsible for luring Mackenzie to California, and the two formed a design firm with two-time U.S. Amateur Champion H. Chandler Egan.

Hunter wrote a brilliant work on golf architecture, *The Links*, four best-selling books dealing with social ills, and once ran for public office in Connecticut as a Socialist. More remarkably, Hunter was a multimillionaire when he was in the midst of his Socialist campaigning.

The depth of *The Links* might persuade even a beginning student of golf course architecture that Hunter significantly shaped Mackenzie's widely respected philosophy. But Mackenzie's 1920 book, *Golf Architecture* is a concise explanation of architecture, and his long-lost 1934 manuscript, *The Spirit of St. Andrews* (published in 1996) is a much more profound and refined book on the subject. In between the publication of those books, Mackenzie was exposed to many interesting thinkers, including Hunter. Hunter's greatest influence on Mackenzie surely came at Cypress Point, where, with the help of Marion Hollins, the three crafted what many call the most "perfect" golf course design.

ROBERT TYRE JONES, JR.
(1902–1971)

Robert Tyre Jones, or "Bobby" as he was popularly called (though he hated it), influenced American golf architecture as much as any player in the history of the game. Though he never practiced architecture, Jones worked with Alister Mackenzie in the original design of Augusta National and later with Robert Trent Jones at the exclusive Peachtree Golf Club in Atlanta.

Jones's collaboration on Augusta is well documented and was lauded by Mackenzie. Jones emphasized many of his favorite principles from Scottish courses on Augusta, including firm turf, boldly contoured greens and holes designed with numerous playing options. The strategic design of Augusta has been and always will be its finest attribute, and Mackenzie himself was adamant about Jones's influence on the original layout. Though Mackenzie would have difficulty recognizing much of his original design, it was Jones who maintained the spirit of the original during the ensuing years when the Masters gained momentum and changes in the ball and equipment precipitated alterations to the design.

Jones envisioned the par-3 course at Augusta, with George Cobb; his endorsement of "short courses" started a nationwide boom in par-3 courses during the 1950s and 60s. He was also a prolific writer who frequently commented on architecture. In his Foreword to Mackenzie's *The Spirit of St. Andrews*, Jones eloquently summarized why it is important for all golfers to understand at least the basic principles of course design: "Every golfer worthy of the name should have some acquaintance with the principles of golf course design, not only for the betterment of the game, but for his own selfish enjoyment. Let him know a good hole from a bad one and the reasons for a bunker here and another there, and he will be a long way towards pulling his score down to respectable limits. When he has taught himself to study a hole from the point of view of the man who laid it out, he will be much more likely to play it correctly."

REES JONES
B. 1941

Always compared to his father, the legendary designer Robert Trent Jones, Rees Jones has established himself as one of America's premier golf architects with a more "user-friendly" style. After an ten-year apprenticeship, Rees left his dad's firm in 1974 to venture on his own. Even with many solid solo efforts in the early years, Jones struggled to escape from his father's immense shadow. But in the mid-eighties he was commissioned to restore The Country Club in Brookline, Massachusetts, in preparation for the 1988 US Open. Jones's subtle and sensitive restoration returned The Country Club to prominence and revolutionized the course restoration business, forcing his con-

temporaries to carefully research classic courses before making any substantial design changes.

After his restoration success, Jones's career flourished with several nationally prominent designs, including Pinehurst #7, Haig Point in South Carolina, Ocean Forest in Georgia and Atlantic Golf Club in Long Island. Jones's work will be very prominent in major championship golf over the next few years, with his redesign of Congressional in the spotlight during the 1997 U. S. Open and major modifications underway at 1998 PGA Championship host, Sahallee Country Club.

Perhaps no architect has worked harder in the last ten years to improve courses for the average player while maintaining challenges for the low-handicap golfer. This emphasis of Rees Jones marks a substantial change from his father's "easy bogey, difficult par" philosophy, which frustrates many a beginning golfer. Rees, on the other hand, defines his course strategy more clearly and believes in rewarding the well-hit shot with a reasonable birdie opportunity. There is no question that his emphasis on strategic, playable courses and his belief in low-profile earth-moving has moved Rees Jones into an elite group, bringing comparisons to his favorite designer, A. W. Tillinghast.

ROBERT TRENT JONES, JR.
B. 1939

The most eccentric of the Jones trio, Robert Trent "Bobby" Jones, Jr., has defined his design career with several renowned projects throughout the world, particularly in the western United States. Jones was a member of the Yale University Golf team and later enrolled at Stanford to pursue a law career. He lasted one year before wisely joining his father's design firm to head up the elder Jones's California office. Bobby co-designed several courses with his father before starting his own firm in 1972.

Since that time, Bobby has followed many of the design principles that his father used with great success, though there are several subtle differences in their styles. Bobby's designs tend to lean toward the strategic school, as opposed to his father's self-titled "heroic" school of design, meaning you will find Bobby's courses more playable with fewer forced carries required. His versatility as an architect is evident at Jones Jr.'s two designs inside the Monterey Peninsula: Poppy Hills and Spanish Bay. The latter, designed with Tom Watson and Sandy Tatum, incorporates many of the same shot characteristics as the great links of Scotland. While at Poppy Hills, Jones crafted a distinctly American parkland test with his trademark bunkering style, patterned after those at his home course, San Francisco Golf Club.

In addition to his architecture business, Bobby Jones is avidly involved in international relations and various environmental committees in his home-state of California. He has consulted with President Clinton on international matters and restored Dwight Eisenhower's original putting green for The White House. Jones authored *Golf By Design*, the only book ever devoted to the art of interpreting course designs for the betterment of the game.

ROBERT TRENT JONES, SR.
B. 1906

The first designer to actually study to become a course architect, Robert Trent Jones, Sr., has a career spanning seven decades, and after working on over 500 courses is among the most prolific designers of all time. Born in England, Jones moved with his family to the United States in 1911 and worked as a club pro and teacher before studying a variety of subjects at Cornell.

In 1930 Jones joined Canadian architect Stanley Thompson and collaborated on such noted courses as Banff and Capilano. After World War II, Jones went on his own and his business flourished. An accomplished speaker and salesman, Trent Jones also quickly became an interna-

> "God builds golf courses. Men just go out and find them."
>
> —Robert Trent Jones

tional designer, with courses that include the highly acclaimed Valderama in Spain, which hosts the 1997 Ryder Cup.

Besides his brilliant sales capabilities, Jones's business also flourished because of several high profile "redesigns." Later to become known as "The Open Doctor" (a title now unofficially held by his son Rees), Trent Jones oversaw pre-tournament fine-tuning at many of the world's best golf courses. Augusta National, Oakland Hills, Olympic Club, Oak Hill, Southern Hills, and Baltusrol are just some of the giants to have called on Trent for help. At Augusta, Jones created the current sixteenth hole along with major revisions to the eleventh—the first leg of Amen Corner.

His original design work deserves mention as well. Relying on his self proclaimed philosophy of "easy bogey, hard par," Trent Jones built some of the most difficult courses. Many critics will claim his work lacks charm and character, but Jones catered to customers who knew what they were getting when inquiring for his services. The list of notable original designs by Trent Jones is impressive. Among some of the most celebrated are Peachtree in Atlanta, Point O'Woods in Michigan, Hazeltine National in Minnesota, Spyglass Hill in Pebble Beach, and Ohio's Firestone.

Trent Jones' style was consistent: he built penal holes that punished wayward shots and rewarded well-played, aerial approaches. He continued the "Golden Age" style of sand-faced style bunkering, but deviated in the strategic sense, building only a few holes with interesting playing options. Jones called these "heroic" because they rewarded precision and punished poorly played shots.

WILLIAM LANGFORD
(1887-1977)

A fine golfer who played on three NCAA Championship teams at Yale and who reached the semi-finals of the U.S. Amateur, William Langford was an outstanding designer of courses throughout the Midwest. Educated as an engineer, he formed his own design firm in 1918 with Theodore Moreau.

Like many of his contemporaries during the 1920s and 30s, Langford was a strategic designer emphasizing the short game with boldly undulating greens and deep, grass-faced bunkering. He designed or remodeled some 250 courses during his career and later renovated some of his own courses because of changes in equipment and his fear that they would become obsolete.

Langford's design at Wakonda Club in Iowa remains as one of his most acclaimed, and recently his writings on design were discovered. Langford wrote several fine essays for a Chicago area publication, focusing his thoughts on construction and methods to create more cost-effective designs while maintaining enough interest to build a fine course.

HERBERT LEEDS
(1854-1930)

A true "Renaissance (sports)man," Leeds graduated from Harvard where he was an outstanding athlete in baseball and football. As Leeds grew older, he became a noted yachtsmen and wrote three books, one detailing his exploits as a crew member on a competitive yachting team, the other two on the art of card-playing.

His first design effort, for the Myopia Hunt Club in Massachusetts, was his masterpiece. Like Donald Ross at Pinehurst, Leeds lived near the course and constantly refined Myopia in a quest for perfection. As Tom Doak explained in *Golf in America: The First One Hundred Years:* "The strength of Myopia's layout derived from the placement of its hazards: they presented difficul-

ties for the better players (Leeds often marked the spot where an accomplished visitor's poor drive had come to rest and built a bunker there afterward) while leaving the weaker members an open, if narrow path to the hole."

Leeds also designed Essex Country Club and Bass Rocks Golf Club, both in Massachusetts. The influence of Leeds on American architecture cannot be underestimated, since so many architects were influenced by Myopia and its abundance of hazards. Although Leeds may have been excessive in his use of bunkers (Harry Vardon complained about them in *My Golfing Life*), designers like Donald Ross, A.W. Tillinghast and George Thomas were informed by Leeds' careful placement of hazards.

CHARLES BLAIR MACDONALD
(1856-1939)

The son of a native Scotsman who had moved to Chicago, C.B. Macdonald was sent to Scotland by his father at age sixteen for two years of study at the University of St. Andrews. Soon after young C.B.'s arrival, his grandfather, a member of the Royal and Ancient Golf Club and a St. Andrews resident, took young Charles to Old Tom Morris' Golf Shop to be fitted for a new set of clubs.

Over the next two years, Macdonald's love for St. Andrews flourished and his relationship with the Morrises—Old Tom, Young Tom, and Jamie—helped him become an expert player and authority on golf. He became close friends with Young Tom and kept a locker at Old Tom's Golf Shop. Macdonald quickly developed into a scratch player and joined the group of fine golfers in the area, playing most of his matches with the Morrises. During these competitions, Macdonald absorbed the strategy and subtlety of the Old Course and several of the other nearby links.

After his two year study abroad, Macdonald returned in 1878 to an America that found little interest in golf. For almost fifteen years, Macdonald was forced to play most of his golf on business trips to

Patty Sheehan with a sand save at the Chrysler-Plymouth Tournament of Champions.

and little-known architectural masterpieces.

The nation's premier amateur golfer at one point, Macdonald, through his influence and persistence, led the creation of the United States Golf Association in 1895. He spent most of the next ten years fostering the USGA and playing competitive golf before turning his focus toward creating charismatic and brilliant golf courses. The opening of The National Golf Links in 1911 marked the beginning of the twenty-year "Golden Age" of American golf architecture, the most productive period in the United States for distinguished golf course designs.

To build The National Golf Links, Macdonald personally formed a syndicate and purchased the rolling land in 1907, setting out to design a course that would embody the best elements of the great links of Scotland and England. It included holes built on the principle of Macdonald's favorites from North Berwick, St. Andrews, Prestwick, and Royal St. George's, and also incorporated many other architectural elements that Macdonald learned from Old Tom Morris and the Scottish links. Macdonald introduced several original strategic and aesthetic elements at The National, including enormous greens and water hazards on a scale never before seen in the United States.

England at Royal Liverpool. Then in 1892, with golf finally catching on in the States, he built the first nine holes of the original Chicago Golf Club. Macdonald later persuaded the club to buy a more suitable piece of property in Wheaton, Illinois, where he would construct a 200-acre masterpiece. Macdonald's longtime design associate, Seth Raynor, later made significant changes to the design, but Chicago Golf Club remains one of America's most enduring

The National Golf Links became and still is America's version of the Old Course—a national treasure every golf architect should visit before practicing design. Macdonald himself obsessed over every detail at the National, nurturing it for several years. And when members or guests had complaints about the course, Macdonald was known to patiently listen and often implement the changes. Then he would send the critic a bill for the cost of making the suggested change.

Other Macdonald design gems (all built and co-designed under the devoted supervision of Seth Raynor) are the Yale University Course, Piping Rock and The Creek (New York), Camargo (Ohio), and Mid Ocean (Bermuda), as well as the now defunct Lido Golf Club. Macdonald's book, *Scotland's Gift*: *Golf,* is basically an autobiography with one chapter presenting his golf course design philosophy. The "Architecture" chapter is without question the most concise and entertaining description of golf architecture fundamentals ever published. Its timeless appeal and Macdonald's ability to concisely describe the principles of good architecture is unsurpassed.

DR. ALISTER MACKENZIE
(1870–1934)

Born in Yorkshire, England, Mackenzie spent many of his summers as a young man in the highlands of Scotland. He studied at Cambridge and earned degrees in medicine, natural science, and chemistry before serving as a field surgeon in the Boer War, where he developed many theories on camouflage. Mackenzie studied how the Boer soldiers hid themselves in the treeless fields and later applied his observations to golf course design.

Following the war, Mackenzie practiced medicine in Leeds, England, and in his spare time created models of greens and bunkers while serving as Green Committee Chairman at Alwoodley Golf Club. H.S. Colt, an established architect at the time, visited the Leeds area in 1907 and stayed at Mackenzie's residence, where the two evidently discovered many philosophic similarities. Colt then requested Mackenzie's assistance in the redesign of Alwoodley. They eventually worked on several other projects together. In 1914 Mackenzie achieved fame when his submission of a par-4 hole drawing won first prize in C.B. Macdonald's *Country Life Magazine* contest. The contest-winning hole, judged by Horace Hutchison, Herbert Fowler, and Bernard Darwin, was later constructed by C.B. Macdonald and Seth Raynor at the now defunct Lido Golf Club on Long Island, New York.

Mackenzie's medical practice had been dissolved and he was dabbling in architecture, but war broke out again (the same day it was announced he had won the *Country Life* contest) and the British Army called on his services. This time Mackenzie was assigned to the Royal Engineers in World War I, where he expanded on his camouflage techniques that were eventually credited with saving thousands of British lives.

After the war, Mackenzie formed a partnership with Colt and C.H. Alison. Just two years later, Dr. Mackenzie published his first book, *Golf Architecture*, a concise and wonderful text that was the first description of the fundamentals of design. Interestingly, Colt and Alison came out with a book at the same time called *Some Essays on Golf Architecture*, which included a brief essay by Mackenzie on golf course construction, maintenance, and labor-saving practices.

Not long after the books were published, their partnership deteriorated and Mackenzie began to work independently. Evidently, there were some philosophical differences of opinion mixed with a serious case of Mackenzie's Scottish stubbornness. During the 1920s Mackenzie made an extended trip through South Africa, New Zealand, and Australia, designing courses but rarely overseeing their construction. Two Australian courses, Royal Melbourne and the highly touted redesign of Kingston Heath, are the most noted layouts from this period of Mackenzie's work.

The late 1920s marked Mackenzie's most influential work in America, where he formed two notable but brief design partnerships, first with Robert Hunter and H. Chandler Egan and later with

Perry Maxwell. Among his finer courses in America were his collaborations with Hunter at The Valley Club of Montecito, Meadow Club, and Cypress Point in 1928, and a solo effort at Pasatiempo in 1929. Mackenzie won the design job for Augusta National Golf Club (over a disappointed Donald Ross) sometime in late 1930 and began the two-year design process. In 1933 he completed what many say is his least known but perhaps best effort, Crystal Downs Golf Club in Michigan, where Perry Maxwell carried out the construction.

Mackenzie died in Santa Cruz, California, in 1934, and his ashes were spread over the Pasatiempo golf course by plane. Living those final years in Santa Cruz beside the sixth fairway, Mackenzie wrote a second book on architecture, *The Spirit of St. Andrews*, a manuscript thought lost until almost sixty years later when his step-grandson discovered it buried in a chest full of papers. Mackenzie also had plans to expand on his camouflage theories and their relationship to golf course design in book form, but only got around to writing two articles for the *Army War College Journal*.

PERRY MAXWELL
(1879–1952)

A successful banker who took up golf at the age of 30, Perry Maxwell became one of America's most important and yet least-known architects. His resume is mightily impressive, with two midwestern gems in Southern Hills and Prairie Dunes, not to mention major redesign work at Augusta National and Colonial along with minor work at Pine Valley and The National Golf Links.

Maxwell was one of the first architects to promote the need for and practicality of grass greens in the Midwest, where sand or oil greens were the norm well into the 1920s, and in later years would be best known for the brilliant contouring of greens in his design work. The "Maxwell green" could best be described as large with bold swales and quirky rolls adding interest to otherwise flat midwestern terrain.

Some of Maxwell's creativity may have stemmed from a brief but successful collaboration with Alister Mackenzie in Michigan. Maxwell oversaw construction at the University of Michigan Golf Club and at Mackenzie's brilliant Crystal Downs, where the two giants of architecture crafted some of the boldest green contours and designs. In 1946, Maxwell's right leg was amputated but he continued to take on design projects, with his son, Press, overseeing the on-site work.

OLD TOM MORRIS
(1821–1908)

At the age of 30, Old Tom Morris became the pro at Prestwick in Scotland, where he eventually won three of his four British Open Championships. He had apprenticed under Allan Robertson at St. Andrews before moving over to Prestwick, learning the art of golf club and ball manufacturing. In 1867 Old Tom returned to St. Andrews permanently as its pro and over the next twenty years would teach many young men the crafts of playing golf, ball and club manufacturing, greenskeeping, and golf architecture.

Having established himself as the first official golf architect, Old Tom received requests from many towns and clubs to consult on course creation or renovation. One of those courses was Dornoch, in the northernmost part of Scotland. A few years later, Old Tom would teach one of Dornoch's finest young players, Donald Ross. Other future architects to visit Old Tom were C.B. Macdonald, Alister Mackenzie and A.W. Tillinghast.

Old Tom created the basic routings and design of Muirfield, Prestwick and Dornoch, and he redesigned the Old Course at St. Andrews, Carnoustie and Machrihanish, all landmarks in Scotland. Not bad for someone who regarded his design work as a hobby and who never charged more than one pound. The impact of Old Tom Morris was best summarized by British golf writer Horace Hutchison: "Old Tom is the most remote point to which we can carry back our genealogical inquiries into the golfing style, so that we may virtually accept him as the common golfing ancestor who has stamped the features of his style most distinctly on his descendants."

JAY MORRISH (B. 1936) AND TOM WEISKOPF (B. 1942)

1996 marked the end of a ten-year run for the team of Jay Morrish and Tom Weiskopf, with each moving on in the architecture business. The partnership started triumphantly in 1987 with Troon Golf and Country Club in Scottsdale, Arizona. Troon quickly joined *Golf Digest's* Top 100 list of America's best courses, immediately establishing Morrish (Jack Nicklaus's former top design associate) and Weiskopf (1973 British Open Champion and four-time Masters runner-up) as a force in course design.

Since Troon opened, they have completed such high profile and well-regarded projects as the TPC at Scottsdale (perhaps the Tour's most popular TPC), Forest Highlands in Flagstaff, Arizona (ranked 40th in the United States by *Golf Digest*), Troon North (another Top 100), Double Eagle (which features several bold alternate holes) and Loch Lomond in Scotland. Weiskopf and Morrish are still under contract at the Olympic Club to rework its Ocean Course. They also built the 9-hole par-3 Cliffs Course at Olympic and refurbished the Lake Course's short par-3 fifteenth hole. Olympic hosts the United States Open in 1998. Morrish now works out of Dallas with his son, Carter, focusing on 2 to 3 projects a year, while Weiskopf is continuing projects worldwide with a new partner, David Porter.

JACK NEVILLE (1895-1978) AND DOUGLAS GRANT (1887-1981)

Widely considered the most beautiful course in the world, Pebble Beach Golf Links has a sound design in a picturesque environment, and much of the credit goes to its original architects, amateur golfers Jack Neville and Douglas Grant. A real estate salesman by trade, Jack Neville was asked to design Pebble Beach in 1915 by Samuel Morse, who owned all of the land now known as the Seventeen Mile Drive. Morse hired Neville because of his status as a multiple winner of the California State Amateur, and Neville in turn asked Grant, a friend and former California Amateur Champion, to assist in the design. Though many changes have been made to Pebble Beach during the years, including Chandler Egan's conversion of the 18th into a par 5, Neville and Grant's brilliant original routing prevails.

Blessed with this site, many architects might have sent the first nine holes through the Monterey Cypress forest and swung the course back in along the cliffs of the Pacific Ocean, creating what surely would have been an incredible finish. Instead, Neville and Grant opted to tease the golfer with a stretch of holes bordering the Pacific in the middle of the round, then turning inland before a dramatic seaside return on the 17th and 18th holes. Not only did this ingenious routing give us the brilliant stretch from 7 through 10, it created an incredibly diverse golf course where many different looks and conditions can exist in just one round of golf.

Neville was involved in a few other projects, including Bel-Air Country Club in Los Angeles, where he helped his friends, George Thomas and Billy Bell. Grant on the other hand was not involved in any other designs except for some consulting at Pebble Beach many years after the course opened.

JACK NICKLAUS
B. 1940

Preaching a return to the strategic school, Nicklaus is one of the few modern day designers who looks to enhance the strategic aspects of his designs. Often criticized for high maintenance standards and costly construction work, Nicklaus has established a highly successful architecture career to augment his many other business activities. Nicklaus has been unfairly criticized and much of the fine work he has done has been overlooked.

After starting as an assistant to Pete Dye at Harbour Town, Nicklaus worked with Desmond Muirhead for several years before starting his own firm in 1974. In his early design work, Nicklaus had a very traditional approach, with sand faced bunkering and minimal earth moving. During the 1980s, Nicklaus was ridiculed for many of his innovative design ideas, some of which were successful, and others which weren't. Nicklaus has never been afraid to try a double fairway hole or to force a long carry.

With over 100 courses to his credit, Nicklaus appears to be moving back toward his early years style, with less earthmoving, and smaller, less severe putting surfaces. When architecture students review Nicklaus's work, they always return to the site of his first triumph: Muirfield Village. Built with Muirhead, it remains his finest work and one of America's truly great parkland tests. Known for its slick greens and difficult par 4s, Muirfield stands out as the site of Nicklaus's most interesting strategic design work, with all of the par 5s reachable in two shots and providing all sorts of playing options.

Nicklaus has also nurtured many other successful architects. In the 1980s, Jay Morrish and Bob Cupp left Nicklaus to create their own respective businesses, while in recent years Jack's three sons, Jack II, Steve and now Gary, have all joined the family business and are active in the design side.

ARNOLD PALMER (B. 1929) AND ED SEAY (B. 1938)

A talented team that has built a wide variety of golf courses worldwide, Arnold Palmer and Ed Seay have been designing together since 1971. With over 140 courses to their credit, the jetsetting Palmer has built courses with Seay in all parts of

the world and even dared several years ago to venture into new golf regions, like China and Taiwan.

Palmer's impact on the sport is well documented, but his course design business has long gone unnoticed. Palmer is one of the few player-architects who has devoted himself to building courses that are attractive, but, more importantly, playable for the average golfer.

Seay was a former associate of Ellis Maples when he joined Palmer and has headed the firm's design department since he joined Palmer Course Design. Seay has been an active member of the American Society of Golf Course Architects since 1976 and has been the driving force behind Palmer design. The firm has always prided itself on developing a host of different course design "looks," most recently building dramatic "fingered" bunkers at Hapuna on Maui and at Empire Lakes in Southern California in the spirit of classic architects like Tillinghast and Billy Bell.

WILLIE PARK, JR.
(1864–1925)

One of Scotland's finest early players, Willie Park, Jr., won the British Open in 1887 and 1889 before retiring and devoting his attention to writing and golf architecture. His two books, *The Game of Golf* and *The Art of Putting*, stand out as some of the finest early golf books written, and his golf architecture work wasn't far behind. Park was the son of four-time British Open winner Willie Park, Sr., and his uncle, Mungo Park, won the Open in 1874.

Park built or redesigned over 200 courses starting in England before emigrating to America. Here, he built such fine country club courses as Hot Springs in Arkansas, Olympia Fields in Illinois (site of the 1997 U.S. Senior Open), and Pawtuckett in Rhode Island. Park was also responsible for the original designs of two fine courses in England, Sunningdale and Huntercombe.

SETH RAYNOR
(1874–1926)

A Southhampton surveyor and landscape engineer, Seth Raynor was hired in 1908 by amateur design great C.B. Macdonald to consult on Macdonald's pride and joy, The National Golf Links. The two got along so well, despite Raynor never having played golf before or after, that Macdonald hired Raynor for other projects.

Raynor's association with Macdonald led to several impressive solo designs. Camargo in Ohio, Fishers Island in New York, Shoreacres in Chicago and Yeaman's Hall in South Carolina are just a few of the Raynor gems. And at each, as his mentor Macdonald always did, Raynor built a collection of "replica" holes, patterned after the great holes of Scotland (which Raynor had never seen), including the Redan (15th at North Berwick), the Eden (11th at St. Andrews), and the Alps (17th at Prestwick).

Raynor's collaboration with Macdonald resulted in such wonderful gems as Yale University Golf Course, the Mid-Ocean Club in Bermuda, and several New York courses, including The Creek Club, Piping Rock, Sleepy Hollow, and Lido Golf Club (defunct). Raynor also oversaw a complete revision of the Chicago Golf Club, a Macdonald original, and he was working on a routing for Cypress Point when he died in 1926.

DONALD ROSS
(1872–1948)

Donald Ross went to St. Andrews in the early 1890's and worked with Old Tom Morris on all facets of the game, but architecture and greenskeeping proved his two greatest areas of interest. In 1893, Ross returned to his home course, Royal Dornoch, as the club's greenskeeper. There, his tutoring continued under the watchful eye of John Sutherland, a noted player who had redesigned Old Tom's original layout at Dornoch.

Ross emigrated to America at the turn of the century and took a position as pro and greenskeeper at Oakley Country Club, in Watertown, Massachusetts. He soon converted the rather benign and dull layout into a sporty test of golf, which so impressed James Tufts and his wealthy family that Ross was invited to become the pro and course designer for the Tufts's family resort being built in Pinehurst, North Carolina. Word spread quickly about Ross's plans for Pinehurst, and he soon became known as an architect worthy of hire. Over the next forty-plus years, Ross designed or remodeled over 400 courses, including several of America's most revered tournament sites—Oakland Hills outside of Detroit, Inverness in Toledo, and Oak Hill in Rochester, New York—and continued to refine his beloved Pinehurst #2 until his death in 1948.

Ross was a soft-spoken, humble gentleman whose designs reflect his personality (as it seems with so many other architects). His background in Scotland, particularly Dornoch, can still be felt in his work. Ross rarely strayed from his roots, building simple but strategically designed holes with bold green contours reminiscent of Dornoch. Ross was the first architect to travel extensively, and he was the first to design courses after only one or two site visits, and in a few cases, no site visits. But Ross gave elaborate sketches and instructions to his well-trained construction supervisors, and the results showed careful attention to detail. Variety, strategy and naturalness are the most consistent traits in Ross designs. He instilled these traits in the many architects he tutored. His courses were all quite different, contrary to popular belief. Ross displayed versatility in design, ranging from punch bowl to crowned greens, from sand faced bunkers to deeper, grass-faced ovals like some at Dornoch. A compilation of his commentaries on architecture, *Golf Has Never Failed Me*, was discovered and published in 1996.

TOM SIMPSON
(1877–1964)

One of golf architecture's most mysterious figures, Tom Simpson was a fine player and member of the Oxford and Cambridge Golfing Society. With enormous family wealth, Simpson studied law but was more fascinated with golf, playing most of his games at Woking in England. Though he had started his own law practice, Simpson closed out to pursue golf course design with Herbert Fowler in 1910. After developing a small portfolio of designs with Fowler, Simpson joined forces with Phillip Mackenzie Ross and famous golfer Molly Gourlay. During the 1930s Simpson collaborated with Ross and Gourlay on several designs and redesigns. Simpson was responsible for a great deal of sensitive restoration work to various courses in the British Isles that had deteriorated during World War II, including modifications or restoration to Ballybunion's Old Course, Muirfield, Sunningdale's New Course, and Royal Lytham and St. Anne's.

Simpson was also a brilliant artist and writer. In 1929 he co-wrote (with H.N. Wethered) *The Architectural Side of Golf*, one of the most interesting books on course design. The chapter on strategy is perhaps the most convincing ever written on the subject. In it, Simpson and Wethered succinctly describe the importance of strategy in design: "A golf course is a field of maneuver and action, employing, as it were, the military and engineering side of the game. It opens up a series of tactical and strategical opportunities, the implications of which it would be well for every golfer to grasp, whether he happens to approve or disapprove of the conclusions we have ventured to put forward. It is important to emphasize the necessity for the golfer to use his head as much as his hands; or, in other words, to make his mental agility match his physical ability."

STEVE SMYERS
B. 1953

Perhaps the strongest player among non-PGA Tour architects today, Steve Smyers has taken his playing ability and combined it with a brilliant artistic eye to establish himself as one of the more exciting new architects. A member of the 1973 University of Florida golf team that captured the NCAA Championship, Smyers has reached the match play rounds of several important events, including the U.S. and British Amateurs.

Smyers worked briefly with Ron Garl before creating his own firm in 1984. His recent success can be attributed to one simple philosophy: build traditional, strategic, and well constructed courses. Though many a modern architect preaches these same values, Smyers is among only a very small handful of designers who actually know how to go about creating such a course.

His most stunning work to date is Wolf Run, just north of Indianapolis. With angled cross bunkers and strategic routes on each hole, Smyers has created one of the best new courses in years that remains playable for all levels of golfer, despite numerous hazards. Wolf Run also features small greens and beautifully sculptured bunkers that reflect the "irregular" look of the old-style works by Alister Mackenzie and George Thomas.

Other highly touted work by Smyers include Southern Dunes in Haines City, Florida, and his co-design with Nick Faldo at Chart Hills in Kent, England. He has recently joined forces with another Nick, Zimbabwe's Nick Price, and the two figure to have a major influence in sustaining the renaissance in golf course design over the next twenty years.

HERBERT STRONG
(1879–1944)

Once the golf professional at St. George's in England, Herbert Strong moved to the Rye, New York, area in 1905 to become the professional at Apawamis Club. He subsequently switched to Inwood Golf Club and supervised the complete remodeling of the course that would later host the 1921 PGA Championship and the 1923 U.S. Open.

Strong gave up being a club pro to focus his attention on architecture. His work is best exemplified in three American gems—Engineers Golf Club (Long Island), Saucon Valley's Old Course (Bethlehem, Pennsylvania), and Canterbury Golf Club (near Cleveland)—all of which display the bold green contours that are his design signatures. Like many others, Strong was forced to abandon the design field during the Depression, and he returned to other aspects of the golf business until his death in 1944.

GEORGE C. THOMAS JR.
(1873–1932)

One of the games' great amateur architects, George Thomas was another product of the informal "Philadelphia School of Design," the group who nurtured Pine Valley and Merion during course construction. Thomas was one of 150 founding members of Pine Valley. With his low handicap, Thomas met and played with some of the finer golfers in the Philadelphia area, including George Crump, Hugh Wilson, William Flynn, and fellow Philadelphia Cricket Club member, A.W. Tillinghast. After three moderately successful designs on the East coast, Thomas moved west in 1920, where he created some of the finest strategic golf courses.

Upon arriving at his new home of Beverly Hills, Thomas joined Los Angeles Country Club and quickly became involved in their 36-hole renovation under Herbert Fowler's supervision. Thomas continued his architecture work at several area courses, including the 36-hole public facility at Griffith Park, which Thomas helped to complete with his own money. In 1925 he embarked on the difficult terrain of Bel-Air Country Club, where he introduced several of his now trademark design traits. Included were a double-fairway hole, a green complex guarded by two large mounds and named after buxom film star Mae West, and a modified Redan par-3. Bel-Air is widely regarded as one of the most masterfully routed courses in America because of Thomas' ability to weave play

in and out of three canyons without making the course feel like a mountain-climbing contest.

In 1926, Thomas and Billy Bell, his longtime associate, began their most endearing design, Riviera Country Club. Built between the walls of Santa Monica Canyon, Riviera incorporated Thomas design trademarks: bold bunkering and a layout that requires a balance of shots and provides numerous options for strategic play on each hole. Riviera has proven to be one of America's best strategic designs and has played host to the 1948 U.S. Open, two PGA Championships and over 35 Los Angeles Opens.

During the same period, Thomas was publishing his classic book, *Golf Architecture in America* (1927), and he and Bell undertook a bold renovation of the North Course at Los Angeles Country Club, where they incorporated several interesting concepts, including a variety of tees to create four completely different courses within the 18-hole design. Thomas completed his design career at Stanford Golf Club, where he laid the holes out on paper and Bell supervised construction. Thomas was too ill to travel and see the finished product.

Thomas also wrote two books on roses and is credited with having bred over forty varieties of roses. He also wrote a book on Pacific game fishing and served as an Army captain during World War I.

STANLEY THOMPSON
(1894–1952)

Canada's equivalent to Robert Trent Jones, Stanley Thompson was an artistic genius who trained many fine architects while churning out an impressive list of courses during the 1920s and 30s. Best known for his early work at the breathtaking Banff Springs Hotel course and at Jasper Park Golf Club in Alberta, Thompson created a style based on the strategic school of design popular in the United States at the time and incorporated elements of the penal, or heroic school, surely influenced by his partner in the early days, Robert Trent Jones.

Thompson was a fine tournament player who believed that the strategic school was the only true form of golf course design. In addition to his two courses in Alberta, St. George's in Ontario and the Ladies Golf Club of Toronto stand out as his best examples of strategic design. Among the future architects who would train under Thompson were Geoffrey Cornish, Robert Moote, Howard Watson, Norman Woods and, of course, Trent Jones.

ALBERT W. TILLINGHAST
(1874–1942)

A.W. Tillinghast, who became one of America's most prolific architects, didn't start designing courses until he was in his early thirties. To that point, Tillie had been a well-established player, receiving his first golf lesson from Old Tom Morris during a stay at St. Andrews in the mid–1890s. His playing career included a 25th place finish in the 1910 U.S. Open, held at his home course, the Philadelphia Cricket Club. Tillie also played in the U.S. Amateur from 1905 to 1912 and turned pro in 1914.

In 1916 Tillinghast helped establish the PGA of America, the very first organization dedicated to golf professionals, and, to date, the only such group of its kind. In the later years of his life, Tillinghast served as a consultant to the PGA and its members on golf course maintenance and design. Like his friend and fellow Philadelphia Cricket Club member, George C. Thomas, Jr., Tillie grew up in a wealthy Philadelphia suburb and received his first design job through a family friend, Charles Worthington. Worthington reasoned that because of Tillinghast's playing ability, he could design a golf course. And he was right, as exemplified in Shawnee-on-the-Delaware, which became a popular Poconos resort due in large part

> "To match par on [Winged Foot] you've got to be luckier than a dog with two tails."
>
> —Sam Snead

to its Tillinghast-designed golf course. After years of spending his family's money and concentrating on billiards, polo, and cricket, Tillinghast had finally discovered a profession he was good at. Tillie devoted much of his time to Shawnee, drawing several routings and spending considerable energy overseeing its construction.

Soon after the opening of Shawnee, Tillie started his own design company and by the 1920s it was flourishing. During his most successful years, Tillinghast traveled extensively throughout the country and kept an office on 42nd Street in Manhattan. He would travel to the city by limousine from his home in Harrington Park, New Jersey. Long before his days of great success in the architecture business, Tillinghast pursued other creative interests, including photography and writing. The articles and columns Tillinghast authored range from the basics of golf architecture to tournament updates and other important golf topics of the day. But Tillie had a less serious side. His columns on golf fashion and his humorous golfing tales (fiction and non-fiction) revealed the fun-loving, wild side to Tillinghast. He never actually published a book on golf architecture, but he did self-publish two books of his fictional stories, *Cobble Valley Golf Yarns* in 1915 and *The Mutt* in 1925. His architecture essays were compiled in 1996 for *The Course Beautiful*, a book devoted solely to Tillinghasts' writings.

After the Tillinghast/Trent Jones-designed Baltusrol Golf Club opened in 1922, New York Athletic Club officials commissioned Tillinghast to design a "man-sized course" on their attractive Westchester County property. Tillie actually gave them two man-sized courses at Winged Foot, the East and West. The West has been the scene of ten major championships, but the East is considered by some just as excellent and having more character. By the late 1920s, Tillinghast was a millionaire due in large part to his marketing talent and the unusual method he used in assessing design fees. He commonly charged clients as much as ten percent of the construction cost, a remarkable sum in those days. By 1930 his resume of classic courses was impressive: Ridgewood, Baltusrol and Somerset Hills in New Jersey; Winged Foot, Sleepy Hollow, Quaker Ridge in New York; Brook Hollow in Texas; and redesigns of Newport in Rhode Island and Brooklawn in New York.

His final design effort, the four municipal courses at Bethpage Park, was completed in 1936; many consider this the finest municipal golf complex in the United States. The Black Course at Bethpage will host the 2002 US Open. Arguably, Tillie's most perfect design may be the San Francisco Golf Club, built in 1917. It combines nearly every feature a golf course could possess: strategy, variety, diverse and rolling terrain, beauty, and superlative hazards. San Francisco Golf Club remains virtually unchanged from his original design, a tribute to the club's steadfast respect for the original.

Once the Bethpage courses were complete, Tillie retired from architecture, except for his consulting with the PGA of America and the USGA Green Section, which he also helped found. He served as editor of *Golf Illustrated* until 1934, when the Depression forced it out of business and propelled the onset of Tillinghast's own bankruptcy. In 1937 Tillie moved to George Thomas's former hometown of Beverly Hills, California (Thomas died in 1932), where he and his wife Lillian set up an antique shop. Tillie briefly advertised a design partnership with Billy Bell but the sluggish market in California, combined with Tillinghast's well-known alcoholism, allowed only a few collaborations. Tillie suffered a major heart attack in 1940 and he and Lillian moved to their daughter's home in Ohio. In May of 1942 he died from his second heart attack. None of the national golf publications noticed, with the only mention of his passing appearing in a local Ohio newspaper.

WALTER TRAVIS
(1862–1927)

Even though he didn't take up the game until he was thirty-five, Australian Walter Travis was one of the great players in the early 20th century, winning the U.S. Amateur in 1900, 1901 and 1903. He also won the 1904 British Amateur and contended in several early U.S. Opens before turning his attention to other aspects of the game.

A prolific author, Travis wrote two of the earliest instruction books, *The Art of Putting* and *Practical Golf*, and founded *The American Golfer* magazine, which he edited for many years. Included in the *The American Golfer* were articles on golf design, some of which were not exactly complimentary of British style golf architecture. However, Travis's finest design effort, a 1922 overhaul of the Garden City Golf Club, an all men's club just outside of New York City, contains many of the features found in the prominent inland British courses, including rugged native grasses, windblown sand pits and a few deep pot bunkers, forcing a full variety of shots and making Garden City one of America's most charming courses.

Travis also supervised the original 1922 design of Westchester Country Club, host to the annual Buick Classic. His favorite design was a collaboration with his mentor, John Duncan Dunn, at Ewanok Golf Club in Vermont.

HARRY VARDON
(1870–1937)

Plagued by health problems throughout his career, Harry Vardon still won six British Open Championships and made a lasting impression on all aspects of golf, including having introduced the Vardon Grip. Vardon designed several fine links in England and Ireland. Perhaps his best work were redesigns in 1908 and again in 1919 at Royal County Down. The Northern Ireland course is a terrible beauty—widely regarded as one of the world's sternest tests of golf in one of its most sublime settings.

Vardon, along with James Braid and J.H. Taylor, was one of the first golf professionals to convince the British that golf was an honorable profession. His brilliant writings in *The Complete Golfer* and *How to Play Golf* solidified his place in golfing lore. He summed up the brilliance of the natural links as well as any architect or writer ever has: "Seaside links are made by Nature herself, and generally as regards their chief features they must be taken or left as the golfer decides. A new hazard may be thrown up here and there, but usually the part of the constructor of a seaside course is to make proper use of those that are there are ready made for him, and which are frequently better than any that could be designed by man."

ROBERT C. WEED
B. 1955

After building a practice bunker and green on his father's farm, young Bobby Weed met Pete and Alice Dye during summer work at Amelia Island Plantation and has since become the most influential man in the PGA Tour's TPC chain of courses. Dye hired Weed in 1980 to work on Long Cove Club on Hilton Head Island; Tom Doak was another member of the Long Cove construction crew.

At Long Cove, Weed learned the various aspects of the business that made Dye successful and was influential in the "grow-in" aspect of the golf course. Soon after, he was hired as superintendent at the TPC at Sawgrass, where Weed would work over several years to soften and improve the original TPC design that had received a lukewarm response from tour pro's during the early years.

His work at Sawgrass led to a promotion by the PGA Tour to construction superintendent for all TPC courses, and just a few years later Weed was spending all of his time as lead designer of the future TPC courses. Among the TPCs Weed

designed with various tour pros: TPC at Tampa Bay, his widely praised TPC at River Highlands, a co-design with Pete Dye on the TPC at Sawgrass-Valley Course, and two courses at the TPC at Summerlin in Las Vegas. Weed has since left the Tour to create his own design and restoration business.

HUGH WILSON
(1879–1925)

A member of the Merion Cricket Club, Wilson took an early part in the Merion's golf interests and assumed many responsibilities in the club's search for a new golf course site. Concerned that the new Haskell ball might make their course obsolete, Merion Cricket Club sent Wilson to England and Scotland to research ideas for a new, modern course. The president of a successful insurance business in Philadelphia, Wilson went first to the National Golf Links in Long Island, New York, to prepare for his design effort at Merion. C.B. Macdonald, architect of The National Golf Links, gave young Hugh suggestions about his trip abroad and on golf course design in general. Upon his return to the United States, Wilson began the design of Merion's new courses.

Wilson's freshly acquired knowledge and philosophy, most of which he procured during his seven month stay overseas, made a major impact on other Philadelphians, namely William Flynn and George Thomas. Thomas wrote of Wilson, "I always considered Hugh Wilson, of Merion, Pennsylvania, as one of the best of our golf architects, professional or amateur. He taught me many things at Merion and the Philadelphia Municipal; and when I was building my first California courses, he kindly advised me by letter when I wrote him concerning them." Wilson is perhaps best known for making hazards perfectly visible to the golfer and for criticizing blind or pot bunkers, features he frequently observed in the British Isles. Wilson was so obsessed with making bunkers visible that he had his construction superintendent, Joe Valen-

tine, spread white bed sheets on the site of proposed bunkers so that Wilson could be sure the
hazard would be visibile from the tee. Like C.B.
Macdonald, Wilson borrowed the traits of the better holes in Scotland and England. Among those
which Wilson emulated at Merion were the Redan
from North Berwick and the Valley of Sin at St.
Andrews. With Alan Crump and H.S. Colt, Wilson
later helped finish Pine Valley after George Crump
died. Sadly, Wilson passed away in 1925 at the age
of forty-five, after completing only two courses at
Merion, a municipal course in Philadelphia and
four holes at Pine Valley.

DICK WILSON
(1904-1965)

Another Philadelphia-born golf architect,
Dick Wilson continued the area's rich design tradition with over 100 courses to his credit. Wilson
served under William Flynn and Howard Toomey,
contributing to some of their most important golf
course constructions.

After graduating from the University of Vermont, Wilson worked on the revision of Merion in
the mid-20s and on Flynn's compete overhaul of
Shinnecock Hills in 1930. Wilson moved to Florida and disappeared from the architecture scene
until after World War II. In 1945 he created his
own course design firm. Business was so steady
that within a few years Wilson became Robert
Trent Jones's chief rival during the golf course
boom of the 1950s and 60s.

Among his most noted designs in the early
days were NCR Country Club (Dayton, Ohio) and
West Palm Beach Country Club. Joe Lee joined
Wilson in the early 60s and the two collaborated
on several classic courses, including Bay Hill Golf
Club and Pine Tree in Florida, La Costa Resort in
California, the "Dubsdread" No. 4 course at Cog
Hill, Callaway Gardens in Georgia, and Laurel
Valley in Pennsylvania.

GOLF COURSE DESIGN TERMS

Approach—Can be used two different ways,
either as a description of the area immediately in
front of a green that may or may not be used to
bounce the ball up to the putting surface, or,
approach can define the shot to the green.

Crowned green or fairway—Land that is
highest at its center point, with drainage and
slopes moving out from the center point. Donald
Ross is generally regarded as someone who built
crowned greens, and he did so at Pinehurst #2,
though it was certainly not the only style he used.

Golden Age of Design—Generally regarded
as the period between the opening of C.B. Macdonald's National Golf Links in 1911 and the opening
of Augusta National in 1934. The most creative and
productive period in the history of course design, as
most of the truly classic courses were constructed
during this period, including designs by Alister
Mackenzie, Donald Ross, A.W. Tillinghast, Macdonald, William Flynn, Perry Maxwell, George
Thomas, and others.

Grow-in—Describes the time period after a golf
course is seeded or sodded before its opening.
Many wonderful courses have seen turf problems
for years because a proper "grow-in" period was
not allowed for.

Heroic—Term created by Robert Trent Jones Sr.,
to describe his style of design, a combination of
the Penal and Strategic schools. A heroic hole is
one where the more of a hazard the player cuts off,
the greater the reward. Similar to Strategic, except
that players failing on Heroic holes face a greater
penalty should they fail.

Links—Seaside Scottish terrain with sandy soil
and odd dune shapes created by wind, weather and
tides. In reality, only a few properties with golf
courses can be called links, but the term is often
misused to refer to courses near the ocean or those
that have tall grass and mounds.

Penal—Design where carries are forced, as opposed to having optional routes of play. Best exemplified in some of Pete Dye's work, and in earlier times, C.B. Macdonald courses.

Philadelphia School of Design—Informal title cast upon five golf architects who grew up in the Philadelphia area between 1870 and 1930. They were A.W. Tillinghast, George Crump, Hugh Wilson, William Flynn, and George Thomas. Crump's work at Pine Valley and Wilson's work at Merion united the men, with Flynn, Tillinghast and Thomas all producing several of American's finest courses themselves, basing much of their philosophy on the influence of Merion and Pine Valley.

Punch Bowl green—A "collection" style green, where the lowest point is at the center and where balls hitting on the edges will likely funnel towards the middle. Rarely used in modern design, but punch bowl greens were prevalent in the years before irrigation was common, or at courses in dry climates where greens needed to collect as much water as possible.

Redan—Name given to the par-3 15th hole at North Berwick's West Links. The hole was first emulated by C.B. Macdonald at The National Golf Links, and has subsequently been reproduced hundreds of times by architects all over the world. Usually a medium-length hole guarded by bunkers in the front left and short right areas, with a green generally tilted from southeast to northwest. The genius of the best Redans is in the strategy and contouring of the green. The intelligent player will use the contours on the right half of the green with a low, right-to-left shot, while the sloppy play is to go directly at the pin and risk not being able to hole the putt.

Redesign—Term to describe the rebuilding and altering of a golf hole. Not to be confused with restoration.

Renaissance—Term given to recent design trend of less earth moving, more strategic holes and an emphasis on naturalness, in a tribute to the "Golden Age of Design," when the same principles guided architects.

Restoration—Term to describe the repairing of a classic course. Does not include the addition of new features; instead, restoration is an attempt to reestablish a course to its original design, playing, and aesthetic characteristics. Many courses were neglected during World War II for obvious reasons, and, therefore, many features lost that would add to a current layout. Many courses were also overplanted with trees in the post-war years, requiring a restoration of playing characteristics.

Routing—The layout, position and order of the holes, as dictated by the architect. The best architects were almost always masters at routing the course and attaining the most great natural locations for holes in a piece of property.

Strategic—Style of design that provides alternate shot options and routes, with differing rewards depending on the shot that is carried out. Different from the Heroic school in that penalties for miss-hit shots are not as severe. Best examples of the Strategic style of design include Augusta National, San Francisco Golf Club, Riviera Country Club and, most of all, the Old Course at St. Andrews, where most of the holes have as many as five different playing options from the tee.

GOLF ARCHITECTURE BOOKS OF NOTE

Bauer, Aleck. *Hazards, Those Essential Elements in a Golf Course Without Which the Game Would Be Tame and Uninteresting.* Grant Books, 1994 (reprint of 1913 edition).

Christian, Frank. *Augusta National and The Masters.* Sleeping Bear Press, 1996.

Colt, H.S., and C.H. Alison. *Some Essays on Golf Architecture.* Charles Scribners and Sons, 1920 (also, Grant Books, 1990).

Cornish, Geoffrey S., and Ronald E. Whitten. *The Architects of Golf.* Harpers and Collins Publishers, 1993.

Crockford, Claude. *The Complete Golf Course: Turf and Design.* Thomson, Wolveridge and Associates, 1993.

Darwin, Bernard. *The Golf Courses of the British Isles.* Duckworth and Co., 1919 (reprinted by The Classics of Golf, 1985)

Doak, Tom. *The Anatomy of a Golf Course.* Lyons and Burford, 1992.

Doak, Tom. *The Confidential Guide to Golf Courses.* Sleeping Bear Press, 1996.

Grant, Donald. *Donald Ross of Pinehurst and Royal Dornoch.* The Sutherland Press, 1973.

Hawtree, Fred W. *Colt and Co.* Cambuc Archive, 1991.

Hunter, Robert. *The Links.* Charles Scribner's Sons, 1926 (reprinted by the United States Golf Association, 1994)

Kroeger, Robert. *The Golf Courses of Old Tom Morris.* Heritage Communications, 1995.

Macdonald, Charles Blair. *Scotland's Gift: Golf.* Charles Scribners and Sons, 1928 (reprinted by The Classics of Golf, 1985).

Mackenzie, Dr. Alister. *Golf Architecture.* Simpkin, Marshall, Hamilton, Kent and Co., 1920 (reprinted by Grant Books, 1987, and The Classics of Golf, 1985).

Mackenzie, Dr. Alister. *The Spirit of St. Andrews.* Sleeping Bear Press, 1995.

Ross, Donald J. *Golf Has Never Failed Me.* Sleeping Bear Press, 1996.

Shackelford, Geoff. *The Captain, George C. Thomas Jr. and his Golf Architecture.* Captain Fantastic Publishing, 1996.

Sutton, Martin H. F., editor. *The Book of the Links.* W. H. Smith and Sons, 1912.

Thomas Jr., George C. *Golf Architecture in America: Its Strategy and Construction.* Times Mirror Press, 1927 (reprinted by Sleeping Bear Press, 1997)

Tillinghast, Albert W. *The Course Beautiful, A Collection of Original Articles and Photographs on Golf Course Design.* Treewolf Productions, 1996.

Wethered, H. N. and T. Simpson. *The Architectural Side of Golf.* Longmans, Green and Co., 1929 (reprinted by Grant Books, 1995).

Profiles, Terms and Bibliography compiled by Geoff Shackelford

Geoff Shackelford is author of *The Riviera Country Club: A Definitive History* and *The Captain: George C. Thomas Jr. and his Golf Architecture.* He is a member of the Golf Writer's Association of America, the Donald Ross Society and the Golf Collector's Society. Mr. Shackelford is also an avid photographer, providing all the illustrations for *The Riviera Country Club: A Definitive History.* His photo work has also appeared in *The Major* series and *Executive Golfer* magazines. Shackelford is a graduate of Pepperdine University, where he played on the Men's Golf Team.

15

TAMING THE MONSTERS
THE 100 GREATEST GOLF SHOTS

"I'm glad I brought this course, this monster, to its knees."

—*Ben Hogan, following his victory at the 1951 U.S. Open at Oakland Hills*

Drama on the field of play, like the stage or the course, usually revolves around one of three great conflicts—man *vs.* man, man *vs.* nature, or man against himself—and the resolution of the conflict is often a moment of personal triumph, even a moment of perfection in sports.

Described below are 100 defining moments in golf tournament play, covering the Men's and Women's professional and amateur Majors, with three non-Major triumphs included as well. Each short recounting focuses on a defining moment, usually ending in victory; but not every triumph results in victory as measured by fewest strokes or other means, and so these reports, above all, salute the valiant effort that is the essence and reward of athletic competition.

TOMMY AARON

Tournament: 1973 Masters
Site: Augusta National
Defining Moment: Final Round, 15th Hole

Aaron, the tall, gentlemanly, bespectacled Southerner with a well-earned reputation as a "bridesmaid" finds himself in a final-round pack with J.C. Snead, Jack Nicklaus, Peter Oosterhuis and Jim Jamieson going into the last four holes. His approach shot on the 15th flies 25 yards over the green, and he has that and about 45 feet of putting surface to work with for a chance at birdie and a route to victory; he needs a stroke of pure magic—a perfectly spun chip shot to a lightning fast, down-sloped 15th green that bleeds anything with speed into the water. If he strokes the ball too hard he'll end up all wet and if he doesn't strike hard enough he will probably have to settle for a bogey.

Aaron makes his pitch with a sand iron: the ball plops and holds about four feet below the hole.

He would later call the pitch the greatest shot of his career. He putts for the birdie and pars the remaining holes. The birdie gives Aaron a marvelous 68 on the final day for a 283 total and a one-stroke win over Snead.

The win was his greatest Tour victory. Oosterhuis (who began the day ahead of Aaron by 4 strokes), Jamieson, and Nicklaus, who charged to a final-day 66, finished two back, while J.C. Snead finished a stroke behind.

JAMIE ANDERSON

Tournament: 1878 British Open
Site: Prestwick
Defining Moment: Final Round, 9th-12th Holes

Jamie Anderson, the defending British Open champion, is on the brink with four holes to go. J.O.F. Morris, youngest son of Old Tom and brother to Young Tom, who between them won 8 British Opens, has finished at 161. With four holes to go (Opens at Prestwick are played in three rounds of 12 holes), Anderson stands at 144 with no room for error: in the greatest round ever played at Prestwick, Young Tom Morris in 1870 needed 16 strokes to cover the final four holes.

Anderson begins by holing his approach shot from off the green on 9 for a three, then barely reaches the green with his third shot on 10, but he holes his putt from over 30 feet for a four. Now he's in better position, 10 strokes back with two holes to play. Getting excited, he inadvertently tees up ahead of the marker on 11, and just as he is about to address a disqualification, he realizes his error and re-tees. The ball flies over the green, hits a mound, bounces up, falls into the mound's slope and trickles back, rolling on to the green and pulling toward the cup, which it finds and drops in for an ace.

After what amounts to having gone eagle, birdie, eagle, Anderson closes with a five, finishing an astonishing four strokes ahead of youngest Morris. But it ain't over. Bob Kirk, playing in the group behind Anderson, reaches the final green with a chance to tie—if he sinks a long putt. Kirk strokes the putt with nothing left to spare, and it finds the back of the cup, but spits out. Anderson's thrilling finish wins the Open, by four over Morris, and by two over Kirk, who botches the tap-in after having come so close in his attempt to tie.

GEORGE ARCHER

Tournament: 1969 Masters
Site: Augusta National
Defining Moment: Final Round, 15th Hole

Going into the final round, Billy Casper leads the 1969 Masters field by one stroke; Archer is one back, and George Knudson and Tom Weiskopf are three back. Charles Coody charges into the lead after 15 holes but bogeys the last three. Weiskopf and Knudson stay close but can't break through. All five are vying for the Green Jacket as they reach 15, all within a stroke of each other.

On 15 Archer looks finished. His second shot finds the famed water hazard, and he has to drop with a penalty stroke. His next shot, though, is masterful, reaching the green and stopping within six feet of the cup. Always an excellent putter, Archer puts it in to salvage par and remain in the running. He pars the remaining holes and sweats out the finish in the clubhouse. Casper's approach shot to the 18th green rolls 40 feet past the cup, and even Casper, one of the game's greatest putters, can't negotiate the long, tournament-tying putt. Archer has his green jacket.

TOMMY ARMOUR

Tournament: 1930 PGA Championship
Site: Fresh Meadow
Defining Moment: Final Round, 18th Hole

Tommy Armour coined the term "yips" to describe short putts that seem to veer off course because of negative vibes rather than from misreading diabolically contoured hole placements. The "Silver Scot" was one of the most successful golfers in the Roaring 20s and an especially proficient driver and irons player. In the 1930 PGA Championship final he faced Gene Sarazen, a two-time PGA champ playing on his home course, in a 36-hole matchplay format.

Sarazen and Armour are close all the way in a thrilling final: Sarazen's up by one stroke after 9, Armour by one after 18; they're all even after 27, and are tied going to the final hole, having matched stroke for stroke. Sarazen hooks his tee shot into the rough, while Armour finds the fairway. Sarazen's approach is off target and lands in a bunker by the side of the green. Keeping par with the script, Armour joins him in the bunker. The evenness continues, as Sarazen explodes out and the ball stops 12 feet past the cup; Armour explodes out and the ball stops 14 feet past the cup, but at least Armour seems to be out of yipsville range. Or is he? He stoops over his putt, then backs off, disturbed by a photographer. The address begins again, and Armour coaxes the putt, which dies on the lip and then topples in. This time Sarazen can't match him.

SEVE BALLESTEROS

Tournament: 1976 British Open
Site: Royal Birkdale
Defining Moment: Final Round, 18th Hole

Sometimes a great shot makes a statement about maturing excellence. Johnny Miller didn't win the 1972 British Open, but his overall play and a gutsy shot on the 5th hole of the third round won him a lot of respect and attention as well as self-confidence; four years later he triumphed in the 1976 British Open. The big story of the 1976 Open is 20-year-old Seve Ballesteros, who is announc-ing his presence in the English-speaking golf world after whirlwind success throughout Europe.

Ballesteros makes an immediate impact, sharing the first-round lead with a 69. After some early trouble in the second round, he finishes with another 69 and ties Miller for the lead. He hits only four fairways in the third round—already showing his forte as a big, if somewhat errant driver and an approach-shot *afficion*—and settles for a 73, still two shots ahead of Miller. Ballesteros makes it a three-stroke lead after the first hole of the final round, but stumbles just as Miller catches fire; with 5 holes left Ballesteros trails by 8 strokes. The wild cheering has turned to polite applause, as in "nice going, kid." But Seve revs it up again: a birdie on 14, an eagle on 17, and now, on 18, while Miller putts in for victory and waves to the crowd, Seve finds a slim chance to flare the panache that serves notice in this tournament and will win Majors in the future.

His lie in two is in the rough on the left side of the green, behind adjacent bunkers. The pin is just off the fringe and the greens are lightning-fast—even a delicate lob over the bunkers is going to roll past the hole. But there is a yard of turf between the bunkers that has tantalizing possibilities—a very slim opening to try a soft pitch-and-run through the rough, with the two bunkers ready to accept anything less than perfect execution and greens ready to run away with a shot hit too firmly. With a 9-iron opened slightly and the ball parallel to his back foot, Ballesteros bumps the ball through the rough, where it skips three times, rubs through the fringe and drifts to the hole, stopping there for a tap in. He'll win his first British Open in 1979, and by 1984 will have three Open and two Masters titles.

SEVE BALLESTEROS

Tournament: 1980 Masters
Site: Augusta National
Defining Moment: Final Round

Perhaps it was a coincidence that Seve Ballesteros celebrated his 23rd birthday on the opening day of the 1980 Masters. The tournament seemed one big birthday party for the Spaniard, who finished 66, 69, 68 for the first three rounds, and even as he grew older he could become the youngest Masters champion ever.

Not that there weren't a few obstacles. From a seemingly unassailable 10-stroke lead over Gibby Gilbert with nine holes to play, Ballesteros' margin dwindles to two: he takes three putts for a bogey on the 10th, is in the water on the 12th and takes a double-bogey five, and is in the water again at 13 and took a double-bogey six.

At 14 his drive finds the rough, but he rights with a fine approach and manages a birdie, once again taking command. At 15 he rips a 4-iron second shot to the green and birdies again. Ballesteros finishes with a 72 on the final day and ends up winning by four strokes, completing the final five holes in 1-under par. He'll win The Masters by four strokes in 1983, too.

PATTY BERG

Tournament: 1935 U.S. Women's Amateur

Site: Interlachen Golf Club

Defining Moments: Quarterfinal and Semifinal, 18th Hole

Patty Berg is 18, playing in her first major championship and the event is being held in her hometown. It's the quarterfinals and she's one up on seasoned amateur Peggy Chandler with one hole to go. The final hole plays 400 yards downhill then up to an elevated green; if you don't reach the green with your second shot, it comes rolling back, away from the hole. Both Berg and Chandler miss the green, then both sneak on with their third shots. Berg is away at 75 feet, and her plan is simply to get close to the cup then finish for victory. Much to her surprise, her putt is strong and true, rushing up a rise, riding smooth, then breaking, breaking right

and disappearing into the hole for a stunning exclamation point for her upset victory.

In the semifinal round, Berg is playing against Charlotte Glutting, who holds a one-stroke lead going into 18. Berg chips on in three, a bit closer than the day before—about 60 feet away, and Glutting pitches to within 15 feet of the cup, but faces a tricky putt. Again Berg hits the putt strong; again it rides the incline, rolls steady and breaks, breaks right and lands in the cup. The crowd explodes with delight—her brother, Herman, aged 12, falls out of the tree from where he's watching the outcome, and a man faints in the gallery and has to be rushed away to the hospital. Glutting misses her putt, taps in for a tie, but Berg beats her on the third extra hole.

On the next day, Berg plays in the championship against Glenna Collett Vare—the 18-year-old hometown kid against the five-time U.S. Amateur winner. She plays well but doesn't get the chance to work the magic again on 18, as Vare takes the last of her six U.S. Amateur titles. There will be plenty more to come from Berg: another final loss in 1937, Amateur Champion in 1938, and a Hall of Fame career as a professional in the LPGA.

PATTY BERG

Tournament: 1957 Titleholders Championship

Site: Augusta National

Defining Moment: Final Round, 5th Hole

Hunting for a seventh Titleholders title (then a Major on the LPGA Tour), Berg is two shots behind tournament leader Anne Quast entering the final round. She begins with par, birdie, eagle, par, leading to the 5th hole, a short Par 5, dogleg right. A big hitter, Berg knows that she has another chance for birdie if she can just stay away from the right side of the fairway—it's lined with tall trees beyond which looms No Man's Land, a 100-foot drop into a ravine from where there is almost no escape.

Well, she can't. Her tee shot never even smiles at the fairway, and when Berg gets to her ball in the ravine she realizes her options are limited. She can't go for the green because of the trees. Her only escape is the low road to the fairway, requiring her to whack the ball up the slope of the ravine and under the lowest hanging branches of the trees. She chooses a 4-iron, and her shot stays low and true, reaching the center of the fairway; she follows with a 3-iron to the green and putts for par. Suddenly, Berg is ready, once, again, to roll for that seven.

Berg later credits that shot for keeping her confidence—and her round—intact; she finishes the front nine with a 33, turns in a 36 on the back, and wins the tournament by three strokes for her record seventh Titleholders championship.

SUSIE BERNING

Tournament: 1972 U.S. Women's Open
Site: Winged Foot
Defining Moment: Final Round, 17th Hole

A late-bloomer to golf, Berning took up the game at 15 and promptly won three Oklahoma high school championships while competing against boys, then was the first woman to receive a golf scholarship to Oklahoma City University, competing on the men's team. You don't blaze trails like those without some guts.

She relies on that feistiness when challenging the small green on the 200-yard, Par-3 17th to just about clinch her second U.S. Women's Open title. Under normal conditions, the green was a good 4-wood for the women. On this day, however, the ladies face a headwind that is too much for the 4-wood, though not strong enough to dictate use of a driver. Berning, who had started the final round four back and who didn't carry a 3-wood in her bag, gambles, selecting a high-cut driver that she'd previously used only in practice. Well, the practice must've made perfect, because her drive ends up about 20 feet from the pin. She makes a birdie putt

for a roll-the-dice deuce, giving her the chance to cop her second U.S. Women's Open title. Not surprisingly, Berning began using the special driver on a regular basis.

JULIUS BOROS

Tournament: 1968 PGA Championship
Site: Pecan Valley
Defining Moment: Final Round, 18th hole

It was as much a victory over the course as over the elements, Father Time, and Arnie. Carrying an umbrella for protection against a burning sun, 48-year-old Julius Boros enters the final round at Pecan Valley tied with Arnold Palmer, and is still tied at the turn, but now Marty Fleckman and Bob Charles have made it a foursome in the fray. Boros stands at the tee on the 460-yard 18th on the day after confiding to friends that the course was too hilly and the conditions too stifling for an old man to win. He is one stroke up, having taken a two-stroke lead on 16 but dropping a shot right back on 17.

Palmer isn't giving in. Arnie hits one of the great approach shots of his career—a 3-wood to within eight feet of the flag—to set up a birdie putt. He misses. Still, Boros, an expert at self-deprecation regarding his golf game, needs par to win. Unable to get on in two, he works his specialty shot—a short pitch that bites and holds—and it settles four feet from the pin. He knocks in the putt to earn par, defeating Arnie and Bob Charles by a stroke and earning a victory over Father Time by becoming the oldest golfer (48 years and four months) ever to win a Major.

PAT BRADLEY

Tournament: 1986 du Maurier Classic
Site: Board of Trade Country Club
Defining Moment: Fourth Round, 18th Hole

Pat Bradley had been a top performer on the tour with top 10 finishes in earnings for a decade leading into her historic 1986 season. That summer, she has already won the Nabisco Dinah Shore and the LPGA Championship, and is trying to become the first woman since Mickey Wright (1961) to win three Majors in a year. It would also be her third du Maurier title, having won the previous year and in 1980.

Bradley leads Ayako Okamoto by two going into the final round, and they both trail Chris Johnson, but it quickly becomes a two-women match, as both Bradley and Okamoto birdie five of the first six holes. Okamoto stays hot coming in, while Bradley gives up three strokes and comes to the 18th, a par 5, trailing by one. She is off the green after two, in thick rough facing a small landing area on an uphill green: too soft a chip and she'll face a difficult putt, too far and she risks passing the hole and going off the green. The chip is clean, as it hits and rolls to within six feet; Bradley then putts in for a birdie that ties her with Okamoto.

The first playoff hole is a par 3. Bradley hits a 6-iron to within 10 feet of the hole and faces a subtle uphill route to the cup, while Okamoto reaches the green 12 feet beyond the pin and faces a more difficult downhill slide. Okamoto can't quite negotiate her putt, and Bradley rises to the occasion and holes her putt, matching the great Mickey Wright and Babe Zaharias as the only women to win three Majors in a year.

MARK CALCAVECCHIA

Tournament: 1989 British Open
Site: Royal Troon
Defining Moment: Final Round, 12th Hole

On the wind-blasted heaths of Scotland, weather is as much an adversary to golfers as are opponents and hairy roughs, but the 1989 British Open is played in fast conditions—the course has been dried out by a summer drought that affects all of Great Britain, the weather warm and calm, with not a trace of rain or bluster in the air. The conditions are ideal for low scoring, and the pros take full advantage. But the ideal conditions also serve as an equalizer, and the man who makes the best shots most often is still going to be the winner. It comes down to a three-way tie and the first three-man playoff in British Open history, played in a new format: four holes, lowest aggregate score wins.

Wayne Grady was the third round leader, but he closes with an ordinary 71 to finish at 275—13-under par. Greg Norman starts the final round seven strokes back, but by the time the leaders tee up he's in the thick of things by birdieing the first six holes. He makes the turn at 31 and adds three more birdies on the back nine, to finish at 64, then sits back to see if anyone can catch him. Mark Calcavecchia is five shots off the pace going into the back nine. Things get thornier for Calcavecchia on the 11th hole, as he extracts his second shot from the bramble, and gets on in four, then he comes through with a whopping 40-foot putt to save par. It's even a tougher challenge to mettle on the par-4 12th, as Calcavecchia's weak second shot falls 50 yards short of the green and settles in a small dent in the dried turf. But Calcavecchia comes through brilliantly, lofting a smooth wedge shot toward the flag: it descends, hits the stick and drops in for a birdie, putting him at 11-under. Late birdies on 15 and 18 put him at 13-under, and he joins Norman in the lead, and then Grady makes it three for the playoff.

On the first of the four playoff holes (par 4, 1st Hole), Norman takes the lead with a birdie to pars for Grady and Calcavecchia. On the second hole, Calcavecchia comes up with another amazing shot —a 35-foot putt from the fringe; Norman also birdies the hole, and Grady falls two back with another par. The third hole (par-3, 17th Hole) proves tricky, as all three golfers miss the green: Calcavecchia hits a nice chip from 50 feet that just misses going in, and he taps for par; Norman's chip runs 10 feet past the hole, and he can't convert the putt, finishing with a bogey and slips back into a tie with Calcavecchia. Grady remains two back.

On the 18th Hole, Calcavecchia's drive finds the fairway, but Norman unleashes a mighty blow—the ball travels more than 300 yards, but it finds a bunker that usually swallows up weak second shots. Then, Calcavecchia comes up with another beautiful shot—a 4-iron from just over 200 yards that rolls to within seven feet of the cup.

A stunning shot on a final hole is nothing new to Norman—in fact, it's getting rather old: a 1986 PGA Championship loss to Bob Tway, who holed out from a bunker, and the 1987 Masters ended with a pitch-and-run from just under 50 yards by Larry Mize. Norman tries desperately to match Calcavecchia from the bunker, but his approach finds another bunker, then his next shot sails over the green and out of bounds. Calcavecchia putts in for a victory in which he made several amazing shots, but almost didn't stick around for the finish. With his wife near her due date for their first child, he had been preparing to withdraw from the Open. The child came into the world two weeks after the British Open win, and is named Brittany.

JOANNE CARNER

Tournament: 1976 U.S. Women's Open
Site: Rolling Green Country Club
Defining Moment: Playoff Round

JoAnne Carner came to the LPGA with impressive credentials: five U.S. Women's Amateur titles and a U.S. Junior Girls Title. She joined the tour in 1970 and won a tournament that year, then became the U.S. Women's Open champ the following year. She is tested tough, as is her opponent during a dramatic final round at the 1976 Open—Sandra Palmer, who is the defending U.S. Open champ. The 1976 Open is played on a short but tricky course in wet conditions; the scores are high, and the final round begins after a rain delay.

Palmer leads Carner by two strokes going into the final round. They battle back and forth, with Palmer needing a short but tricky putt for par to tie

Carner on 18. She makes it, and the give-and-take struggle is repeated head-to-head in a playoff. Carner takes the lead with a birdie on the 1st hole and leads by two strokes after nine. Palmer cuts the lead to one on the 10th, then falls back by four by bogeying the 11th through 13th against Carner's par. But then Carner goes off track with three bogies against two Palmer birdies and a par, giving Palmer the lead by one. Then it's Palmer's turn to go off track; as Carner safely plays the par-5 17th hole, Palmer hooks her second shot, landing it in a bunker, and she ends up with a bogey, tying the tournament once again.

The 18th is also a par 5, and by now the clouds are returning and the wind is whipping up. Carner's drive veers left and ends up near the woods of the tree-lined fairway; Palmer goes even further left, and her drive is slapped down by a tree. Carner recovers into the fairway, makes it to the green, and two-putts from over 60 feet. This time, Palmer can't match her, taking three to reach the green and two more to hole out.

BILLY CASPER

Tournament: 1966 U.S. Open
Site: Olympia Country Club
Defining Moment: Final Round, 17th Hole

Arnold Palmer is famous for great charges to victory, but Billy Casper enjoyed a major charge over Arnie and his Army during the final nine holes in the 1966 Open. Casper trails by seven strokes with nine holes to play, and is still down by four after the 14th. Casper sinks a 15-foot birdie on 15, which Arnie bogeys. The lead is two going to the 17th hole. There will be many dramatic moments to come, with Casper's sweet pitch on 17 setting the stage.

On 17, Casper pitches from the edge of the fairway to the green and it rolls to the pin, leaving a birdie tap-in that gives him a chance. Arnie bogeys again, tying the golfers going into 18. Both make excellent and agonizing putts on 18, Palmer from 40 feet, Casper from 20.

In an 18-hole playoff the next day, Palmer again holds the early lead and watches as Casper who makes the winning charge. Down two strokes on 11, Casper sinks a 25-foot birdie putt, and then sinks a 35-footer for another bird on 12, taking a one-stroke lead. Palmer begins a bogey run, and Casper finishes calmly and consistently for the Open championship.

HENRY COTTON

Tournament: 1934 British Open
Site: Royal St. George's Sandwich
Defining Moment: Second Round

Some athletes have candy bars named after them in honor of their accomplishments. Henry Cotton's record-setting second round in the 1934 British Open was so astounding that a new golf ball —the Dunlop 65—was christened to commemorate the achievement. In bringing the championship trophy back to Great Britain as the first Englishman to win the Open since the American invasion began in 1922, Cotton dispensed with drama: the 65 remained a record until 1977, and his two-round total of 132 still hasn't been beaten. His closest competitor after two rounds was nine strokes back, seven after three rounds, and Cotton won by five shots, despite ballooning to a final-round 79.

Cotton's remarkable round begins on the second hole, as he drives 300 yards, wedges from 70 yards to within 12 feet of the pin and putts in for a birdie. A putt on 4 is left hanging on the lip, but he still scores a birdie, and a birdie putt under 12 feet is missed on 5. He makes the turn at 33 and the fun really begins. On 11 he hits a mashie niblick with great backspin to set up a birdie; on 14 he's on in two (520 yards), misses a tough 10-footer, and birdies; on the 423-yard 17th he approaches with a spade mashie to within three feet of the pin and putts for a three; and on 18, his 2-iron approach lands within seven feet and he putts for another birdie—closing with three threes. Despite a couple of near-miss putts, Cotton needs only 28 putts for the round, and all putts he holed were within 12 feet.

BEN CRENSHAW

Tournament: 1995 Masters
Site: Augusta National
Defining Moment: Final Round, 16th, 17th and 18th Holes

Ben Crenshaw's victory in the 1995 Masters was an emotional and dramatic triumph, and above all, it seemed right. A great student of the game, Crenshaw particularly admired renowned instructor Harvey Penick, who played and wrote about and lived the game with a sense of grace. Penick died just before the Masters, and Crenshaw flew to Austin, Texas, to attend the funeral. He returned to Augusta and played inspired golf, though he doesn't remember how. Penick died shortly after watching Davis Love III, another of his students, win a tournament that qualified him for the Masters. Love also played an emotionally-charged tournament for Penick and contended with Crenshaw for the Masters title.

Crenshaw shoots a first-round 70 and Love a 69, fine scores considering the circumstances, and are in the hunt after David Frost and his chilling 66. Crenshaw rises to a stroke off the pace following his solid second-round 67, putting him one behind Scott Hoch and one ahead of Love, and a 69 in the third round ties him for the lead with Brian Henninger, with Love three strokes off the pace. The story that's hoped for unfolds in the fourth round, as the play of the two students pays tribute to the teacher.

Crenshaw's playing a strong final round, but is losing strokes to Love and is in trouble on the par-5 15th when his approach lands in the gallery; a firm chip shot to the green turns his fortunes, however, and leaves him only a short putt for par, tying him with Love. On the par-3 16th, with its treacherous carry over water, Crenshaw hits an inspired 6-iron shot that easily clears the water and the runoff at the front of the green; it hits 30 feet beyond the hole, but spins back to within five feet of the cup. He putts for a birdie and the lead, and a surge seems to run through the gallery and through Crenshaw. On 17 his approach lands within seven feet of the cup, and he negotiates a wicked curling line for another birdie and a safe two-stroke lead. Maybe on 18, especially during the ovation that greets him as he comes to the green, the weight of the last few days begins to affect him; he closes with a bogey, but is never in danger and finishes with a one-stroke victory over Love, whose 66 is the best final round of the day. Crenshaw's 72-hole total 274 is the lowest score to win the tournament since Ray Floyd's 271 in 1976, when Crenshaw was runner-up.

"I had a 15th club in the bag," said Crenshaw following the tournament, "and it was my friend, Harvey Penick." Love, who had a one-stroke lead over Crenshaw and Greg Norman before three-putting for bogey on the 16th hole, added, "I'm as happy as anyone for Ben. There couldn't be a better end for Harvey Penick's life than for Ben Crenshaw to win the Masters the week he died."

BOBBY CRUICKSHANK

Tournament: 1923 U.S. Open
Site: Inwood Country Club
Defining Moment: Final Round, 18th Hole

The 18th Hole at Inwood in the 1923 U.S. Open was the stage for several dramatic shots, culminating with a playoff winner by Bobby Jones that remains among the most legendary in the history of the sport. Jones had finished regulation with a bogey, bogey, double-bogey but still seemed to have the championship at hand, even though he walked off after 72 holes saying, "I didn't finish like a champion. I finished like a yellow dog." Cruickshank's late heroics during that final round would ensure that the winner would indeed finish like a champion.

Cruickshank enters the final round three strokes back and is down by four after the 5th hole, but a birdie, eagle, birdie (on the 6th through 8th holes) ties him with Jones coming in. He cools off with bogey, double bogey, bogey (13th through 15th), then birdies 17 and comes to 18 with a 270, with Jones in the clubhouse at 273. A fine tee shot down the middle leaves Cruickshank about 170 yards from the green, which is fronted by a lagoon. Cruickshank's approach carries the water hits the green, bounds and brakes within five feet of the cup. He putts in to tie Jones.

Cruickshank and Jones reach the 18th hole of the playoff tied again, and again the 18th plays host to a dramatic finish. Cruickshank's drive hooks behind a tree, while Jones slices into the rough. Cruickshank has to lay up, while Jones takes a chance and goes for the green. That legendary shot is described below; Cruickshank doesn't have a chance to catch Jones this time, and finishes as a runner-up, as he had in the 1922 PGA Championship and will again in the 1923 PGA Championship.

Cruickshank would remember Jones' brilliance. In 1930 he made legal bets in Scotland that Jones would win the Slam that year (U.S. and British Opens and Amateurs), and when Jones completed the Slam Cruickshank pocketed $10,000; *The New York Times* mistakenly estimated the winnings at $100,000, leading to an Internal Revenue Service audit that eventually cleared Cruickshank. Cruickshank was also a World War I hero, who witnessed his brother's death by an enemy shell, was captured and made a prisoner of war, and escaped through enemy lines to rejoin the fighting.

JOHN DALY

Tournament: 1991 PGA Championship
Site: Crooked Stick
Defining Moment: Third Round, 4th-6th Holes

It's a dreamy scenario every athlete has imagined: an unknown steps into a major sporting event, plays fantastically to a cheering crowd, and roars to victory in legendary fashion. It was near midnight on Wednesday when John Daly checked into an Indianapolis hotel to spend the night and to see if by some miracle he was going to get an invite to the PGA Championship starting the next morning in the city. As the ninth alternate he had a slim chance, and when he took off from Memphis that evening on his way to the next Tour stop after the PGA, Indianapolis wasn't too far out of the way. A message awaits him: an invitation to play. Several alternates had declined because of the late timing and because the course was none too inviting—second longest in PGA Championship history. Jack Nicklaus would say later that it was the most difficult course he had ever played, and Curtis Strange didn't say much that he wants repeated, as he packed it in after an opening round 81.

But length doesn't pose a problem for Daly, not nearly as challenging for him as hitting fairways and making cuts: he ranks first in the PGA in driving length in 1991, but 185th in driving accuracy and he's made the cut just over half the time—13 times in 24 events. Daly is long and on target right from the first tee in the PGA, however, shooting an opening round 69 and finishing two off the lead. He gets even better in the second round, shooting a 67, and he finishes the round with a one-stroke lead over Bruce Lietzke, the only other golfer with two sub-70 rounds. The story's out now. During the third round Daly has a huge gallery following, marveling at the way he way he pulls his club so far back and the powerful uncoiling that launches rockets from the tee. But the irons shots are long and straight, too, and his putting game is on as well.

Now comes the third-round proving ground, and Daly meets the test early. On the par-4, 456-yard 4th hole, he hits a monster drive and follows with a long, high 8-iron shot that hits within a foot of the hole and leaves an easy birdie. On the 609-yard, par-5 5th, his long drive fades into the rough, but he follows with a screeching iron clip that falls just 10 yards short of the green; he chips right to the hole, but it doesn't fall for an eagle, so he taps in for

another birdie; the par 3, 199-yard 6th is no contest—a long loping five iron drive hits the green and rolls three yards past the pin for an easy downhill birdie putt. The gallery resounds with each shot; seeking superlatives, television announcers conjure up this one: Daly's uncoil is so fast it can't be captured in slow-motion. The stuff of legend.

Daly ends the third round leading by three strokes and keeps right on driving long and sure to the finish, winning by three strokes. And it ends the way good dreams do: "I can tell you one thing," says Daly, after the tournament: "I've done this thing my way."

LAURA DAVIES

Tournament: 1987 U.S. Women's Open
Site: Plainfield Country Club
Defining Moment: Playoff, 14th and 15th Holes

The final round and playoff of the 1987 Women's Open offered a great study in contrasting styles: power driver Laura Davies contending with Ayako Okamoto, a finesse shooter, and JoAnne Carner, who was known for her long, accurate shots with her irons. It would come down to a putting contest—and a triumph over the elements, as heavy rains and hot, humid temperatures made for a soggy and stifling six-day event: Sunday's final round was canceled because of rain, and late heroics on Monday necessitated a playoff on Tuesday.

Okamoto finesses her way to a three-stroke lead in the final round, then inexplicably four-putts the ninth hole, allowing Davies to catch her. Then Okamoto three-putts the 13th, beginning with a missed four-footer. Carner catches Davies on 15 with a birdie, then a birdie on 17 gives her a one-stroke lead, but she has a tough lie against the collar of the 18th green and three-putts back into a tie, while Okamoto finds her putting stroke again and joins them for a three-woman playoff.

Davies birdies the 4th by outdriving Okamoto and Carner, playing a closer approach, and putting in. Davies has a two-stroke lead wiped out, however, when Carner birdies 9 and Davies bogeys 10. Davies plays steady through 13, taking a two-stroke lead over Carner and one over Okamoto, then wins the battle on the 14th and 15th greens. On 14 she holes a 20-foot birdie, and on 15 she holes a 35-foot birdie, then finishes with par putts to win by two over Okamoto and by three over Carner. For the 23-year-old Englishwoman it is her first LPGA victory in the U.S., and follows her earlier triumph in the British Women's Open, making Davies the first woman to win both events in the same year.

ROBERTO DE VICENZO

Tournament: 1968 Masters
Site: Augusta National
Defining Moment: Final Round, 17th Hole

The globetrotting golfer Roberto de Vicenzo is a gallery favorite on five continents, and the past summer he became the British Open champion after having been a top-three finisher five times in 19 previous tries. He enters the final round of the 1968 Masters two strokes back but sets a record pace that slows only on the 18th hole and then is catastrophically undone *after* the round is over.

De Vicenzo's great round begins immediately. His long, sweet drive on the 400-yard first hole leaves him with a 9-iron shot to the green, where the pin is placed at the front edge just beyond a bunker; his second shot just clears the bunker, hops toward the cup and slides in for an eagle. He birdies the 2nd hole, then leaves an approach within a foot of the third cup and putts for another birdie. As he makes his way through the front nine in five-under par with the gallery becoming increasingly fervid, de Vicenzo takes the lead by one over Bruce Devlin and by two over Bob Goalby, both playing a few twosomes back. It's looking like a great birthday celebration for de Vicenzo (it's at least his 45th).

On 10 he saves par with an explosion that leaves him four feet from the hole; he challenges the water on 11 with his approach and leaves the

ball within three yards of the cup, but misses a birdie putt and settles for par; on the par-3 12th hole his tee shot stops within 12 feet of the cup, and this time he pars for a birdie. Back on the front nine, Devlin falls back, but Goalby is keeping pace, still two behind. De Vicenzo gets another birdie on 15, blasting from the bunker then putting from 10 feet to go 11-under for the tournament, but Goalby has actually gained a stroke and moved to 10-under. De Vicenzo wedges a beautiful approach to the par-4 17th, then putts in from three feet for a birdie at the same instant that Goalby putts for an eagle on 15 and ties the tournament. De Vicenzo stumbles with a bogey on 18, and Goalby finishes with a chance to win (see Goalby's progress below).

Goalby and de Vicenzo end tied. Their momentous struggle, which unfolded simultaneously on separate stages during the final round, will be played over again, head-to-head, in a playoff round on Monday. But 20 minutes after the round, the playoff is canceled. That beautiful three by de Vicenzo on 17 was mistakenly marked as a four on his scorecard by playing partner Tommy Aaron, and without examining it de Vicenzo signed the card—thereby officially validating the round as scored. The extra stoke, according to the rules (Rule 38, Paragraph 4), clearly finalizes de Vicenzo as having finished one stroke behind Goalby. Officials look for a loophole, Goalby offers to play the playoff anyway, but the rule is clear and de Vicenzo graciously accepts his fate. The outcome stands: Goalby is the Masters champion.

JIMMY DEMARET

Tournament: 1947 Masters
Site: Augusta National
Defining Moment: Third Round, 13th Hole

Tied with Byron Nelson after the first round and ahead by one stroke after two, the dapper Demaret, aiming for his second green jacket, feels victory slipping away in the third round, when he finds himself four over par after 12 holes. Worse, his drive on 13 leaves him with a difficult downhill lie about 260 yards from the green. He is fading fast.

His first instinct is to play the downhill lie safe, lay up short of the water in front of the green with an iron, then go for birdie or a definite par. The water often sucks in the overly-ambitious. But being four over, he decides to go for broke; he rifles a 2-wood shot that carries the water, finds the green and rolls to within one foot of the hole. He sinks the putt for an eagle and is back in front. Perhaps more importantly, his flagging confidence is restored: he wins back four more strokes on the back nine and turns from four-over after 12 to two-under for the round.

Demaret's eagle turned a round going bad into a good one, enabling him to take a three-stroke lead into the final round. The following day, he won the second of his three Masters titles.

LEO DIEGEL

Tournament: 1928 PGA Championship
Site: Five Farms
Defining Moment: Quarterfinal Match

Leo Diegel was an interesting character on the course—a high-strung man whose biggest battles seemed to be against his own nervous energy. For example, Diegel was the final-round leader at the 14th hole of the 1920 U.S. Open after Harry Vardon and Ted Ray bogeyed holes ahead. An excited friend broke Diegel's concentration as he prepared to drive on 14 by informing him of the good news and an exasperated Diegel fell apart, double-bogeying 14 and bogeying 16 and 17, finishing in a tie for second. Diegel developed a distinctive, bird-like putting style in order to calm himself on the green: he spread his arms outward from the grip, elbows and forearms parallel to the ground. This method usually served him well, but it failed him on the 18th green of the 1933 British Open, where he needed one putt to win, two to force a three-man playoff. His first putt stopped within two feet of the

hole, but he whiffed on the next one, then holed out in three to tie with two others for third place.

But Diegel had plenty of triumphs, and several major ones occurred in the 1928 PGA Championship. In the quarterfinals he beat four-time defending champion Walter Hagen, ending Hagen's incredible PGA victory string at 22 matches. Diegel finished the front nine five up on Hagen, but Hagen made up three holes by the end of the round. In the final, Hagen rallied from three down to pull within one going into the 35th hole, a par-3. Both players reach the green, but it is Diegel, with his awkward putting style, who sinks a 15-foot birdie and clinches victory. Diegel then beats Gene Sarazen, a two-time PGA Champion, in the semifinal and whips Al Espinosa 6 and 5 to take the championship.

Diegel defended his championship in 1929. His quarterfinal win in 1928 over Hagen avenged defeats by Hagen in the 1925 quarterfinals and the 1926 final. Hagen had a different form of revenge in 1928: he had misplaced the PGA Championship Trophy, which he held for four years. It was finally found a year later in a Detroit factory, carefully wrapped within a beaten-up storage crate that had passed from a bankrupt golf-equipment manufacturer in Florida to one in Detroit. And the temporary replacement trophy with which Diegel was presented in 1928 was subsequently lost by the PGA.

GEORGE DUNCAN

Tournament: 1922 British Open
Site: Royal St. George's Sandwich
Defining Moment: Final Round, 16th Hole

George Duncan won the 1920 British Open by making up a 13-stroke deficit to Abe Mitchell over the third round, then broke away from a pack of five bunched within two strokes in the final round (he was tied for third going in, two strokes back) to win by two strokes. This time he's down by six to Jock Hutchison going into the final round; what's more, the clouds are getting heavier and the wind rougher as the day progresses, and the leaders are off first, ahead of the storm. Hutchison has a poor round, but Walter Hagen, who had been two strokes back, finishes with a strong 72 and sits out the outcome as leader with a 300 aggregate score.

Duncan makes turn at 265, comes up with three 4s (277), then begins a brilliant stretch over final six holes. He birdies the 13th (par 4, 439 yards), takes a 5 for par on the 14th;, makes a beautiful approach on 15 but misses a short birdie try; on 16, his approach stops 10 feet from the pin and he holes it for a birdie 3, for an aggregate 292 score. On the 17th he gets his par 4 and needs one more 4 to tie. After a fine tee shot, he hits a brassie that's heading for the flag but tails at the last second, falling and rolling into a hollow beside the green. The crowd had been following his progress coming in and is now in a frenzy over his chance to win, and Hagen is looking on. But the hollow is formidable, and Duncan shreds some grass with a little pitch and run and that leaves the ball 15 feet short of the hole; then, his putt to tie falls short, as does his second glorious comeback. That small indentation off the 18th green was soon dubbed Duncan's Hollow, and it would have significance again in future British Opens.

CHICK EVANS

Tournament: 1914 U.S. Open
Site: Midlothian Country Club
Defining Moment: Final Round, 18th Hole

Three of the four U.S. Opens from 1913 through 1916 were won in spectacular fashion by amateurs, and in the other an amateur finished second by a stroke. Evans was the winner in 1916 and a runner-up in 1914, falling just shy of turning in one of the most miraculous shots in Open history.

Evans didn't seem to have much of a chance after barely making the Open field in the pre-tournament qualifying round, and he was playing on a bum leg that ached anew as he made his way

through each round. He carded a 76 in the first round and made no progress on a 8-stroke deficit to Walter Hagen in the second, and Hagen had turned in an excellent first-round 68 despite jitters brought on by eating too many oysters the night before. Evans managed to cut the deficit in half after the third round and was among a handful of golfers with a prayer left for catching Hagen. Hagen finished his final round, learned that all prayers were being unanswered back on the course, and retired to the clubhouse trying not to even think of oysters. His stomach got a jolt, though, when he heard that Evans reached the 18th tee two strokes off the lead. The 18th is a par 4 of only 277 yards, and Hagen himself had birdied it four times—still the only time a champion has birdied the finishing hole in all four rounds of an Open. So he left the clubhouse to watch the action and found a large and boisterous crowd gathered near the 18th green cheering on Evans, who needs an eagle just to force a tie.

Evans nearly drives the green and as he approaches his lie the crowd cheers loudly, then falls into complete silence—so quiet you can hear a wedge click. Evans pitches toward the hole and it rolls straight, stopping within a foot on the right side of the cup. The crowd shares the agony of the near-miss, then applauds Evans' great effort. His last two rounds set a new 36-hole record total for the Open.

NICK FALDO

Tournament: 1990 Masters
Site: Augusta National
Defining Moment: Playoff

Nick Faldo is the defending Masters champion, having won in 1989 when Scott Hoch missed a two-foot putt on the first playoff hole, and then Faldo outplayed him on the second hole of sudden death. He's back in 1990, trying to become only the second man to defend a Masters title: two others came very close, Ben Hogan and Gary Player, but they both lost in playoffs.

Faldo is battling Raymond Floyd in the final round in 1990. He trails Floyd by three strokes coming in, and Floyd makes it a four-stroke cushion with a 20-foot birdie putt on 12. But just as he would six years later against Greg Norman, Faldo birdies the back nine par-5s— the 13th and 15th holes—and follows with a birdie on 16 to move within one. While Faldo is holing out with a par on 18, Floyd three-putts 17, and the two are tied. Floyd comes to 18 needing par to tie, but is in trouble when his drive finds a fairway bunker, then his approach falls into a greenside bunker on the right. Always a great wedge player, Floyd explodes out to within five feet and putts in to tie the tournament.

The first playoff hole is a repeat of 1989. Faldo hits a weak drive off the right side of the fairway, then lands his approach in a greenside bunker. Floyd, like Hoch, hits a good drive and almost as perfect an approach, a 7-iron that stops fifteen feet below the hole. But Faldo rights himself again, as he did in 1989, with a great bunker blast within four feet of the cup. Floyd's birdie can't finish the climb to the hole, and both he and Faldo putt for par. On the second playoff hole, as in 1989, Faldo's drive finds the fairway, while Floyd, like Hoch, is off target, and then his trusty 7-iron sends the ball left of the flag, where it sinks into the water guarding the left of the green. This is Faldo's moment to seize and he does, as in 1989: his 8-iron from the fairway stops eighteen feet short of the hole, permitting a leisurely two-putt for victory.

Nick Faldo has won both the Masters and the British Open 3 times each, but has yet to win either the U.S. Open or the PGA Championship.

NICK FALDO

Tournament: 1996 Masters
Site: Augusta National
Defining Moment: Final Round

Nick Faldo's tournament victories don't send sportswriters into adjective frenzies. Intense, focused, and doggedly consistent, Faldo's victories are usually triumphs of man over course, as he targets-in on spots that provide favorable lies and birdie opportunities, like a chess or billiards player planning ahead even as he skillfully executes the play at hand. The 1996 Masters might be remembered most for Greg's Norman's gargantuan and painful fall from sure victory, but Faldo played with the characteristic precision he showed in five previous victories in the Majors, shot five-under for the final round—the best showing of the field and his third sub-70 round, the only such feat in the tournament—then showed a touch of class as the tournament ended. Faldo enters the final round six strokes back of Norman. Norman loses a stroke on the 1st hole (missing the fairway with his drive and the green with his approach) and the 4th hole, gets one back on the 5th, and loses it back on 6; after seven holes he still has a four-stroke lead. It's gone by 11: while Faldo is methodically parring his way toward Amen Corner, Norman's approach falls short on 9 and runs back down a hill, and he has to hit back up for a bogey; his chip on 10 goes left of the green, and he bogeys; he lies above the pin on 11 and three-putts for bogey. Faldo hits his targets on each of the holes—reaching the greens with his approaches and placing below the pin for the best putting opportunity on 11. On 12, he plays to a safe spot on the notorious par 3, while Norman goes for the flag. Norman's shot doesn't carry the water fronting the green, and splish-splash he's taking a bath and trailing Faldo by two strokes. Faldo seizes the moment with a birdie on 13 and another on 15, and Norman matches him both times to stay alive. Then at 16, while the Shark treads water again, Faldo shoots four precise shots for a par and a four-stroke lead.

It was probably over on 12, but Faldo's birdies on 13 and 15 make it a sure thing. Norman's troubles on 16, another double bogey, is painful to watch—the overkill of bathos. Faldo goes out with style, birdieing 18, and the draining drama ends. Faldo approaches Norman, who is looking numbed by the day's events, and embraces him. "He looked like he needed a hug," Faldo would say later.

WILLIE FERNIE

Tournament: 1883 British Open
Site: Musselburgh
Defining Moment: Playoff Round, 36th Hole

Bob Ferguson is close to joining Young Tom Morris as a four-time winner of the British Open. He had survived the Great Storm of 1881, which hit late in that Open and forced several golfers off the course, but he was comfortably ahead back then; this time he has to overcome a 10 on a first-round hole and struggle back into contention; he closes with three straight threes to tie Willie Fernie and set up 36-hole playoff.

Ferguson and Fernie duel through the playoff, coming to the final hole with Ferguson ahead by one, in command of his game, and set to join legendary Young Tom. And he hits a fine drive. Then Fernie steps up and wallops one: it soars past Ferguson's drive, hits the fairway and bounces on to the green, a tremendous hit but still over 40 feet from the hole. Ferguson weathers the storm and chips to the green, leaving himself with a chance at a 3, but certainly a sure 4. Then Fernie does it again: he sends a screaming putt over bumps and hollows that slides into the hole for a 2. Now Ferguson is suddenly putting for a tie and he can't quite convince it to fall; in a stunning reversal of fortune, Fernie's two perfect shots help him steal away the Open crown.

JACK FLECK

Tournament: 1955 U.S. Open
Site: Olympic Club of San Francisco
Defining Moment: Final Round, 18th Hole

So sure were golf cognoscenti that Ben Hogan was the winner of his fifth U.S. Open with his final-round 70, that he was proclaimed the winner on TV as he presented his ball to a representative of the USGA's Golf Museum. But Fleck, a little-known professional who ran a pair of public courses in Davenport, Iowa, was just making the turn and calculating his chances. He needed a 34 on the back nine for a 67 and a tie with Hogan.

A clutch birdie putt on 17 gave him an opening, and a birdie on 18 would tie the score. Things got bleak before they got better, as Fleck drove into the rough. But he had a decent lie and took advantage of it. Fleck hit a 7-iron sharply, and the ball found the green, stopping within eight feet of the cup. He then judged the break of a fast putt perfectly and birdied to tie Hogan.

Hearing the crowd roar, Hogan, who was packed and ready to leave, understood the news, retrieved his clubs and faced Fleck in a playoff, which wasn't nearly as dramatic as the fourth-round finish. The backstage pro from Davenport finished off the come-from-behind win and beat the master by three strokes.

RAYMOND FLOYD

Tournament: 1976 Masters
Site: Augusta National
Defining Moment: Third Round, 13th Hole

Floyd led the 1976 Masters from wire to wire, winning by a record eight shots and setting two- and three-round records (65, 66 for 131, and 70 for a 201). Though he was never seriously challenged, Hubert Green had closed to within three after Floyd had recorded his only double-bogey of the tournament on 11 in the third round. When Floyd's tee shot on 13, a right-to-left dogleg, went slightly right and came to rest at the base of two tall Georgia pines on a steep sidehill lie, with the ball nearly a foot above his stance, it was decision time.

Floyd has to decide whether to go for the green, trying to carry Rae's Creek more than 200 yards along to reach a bunker and play from there for par or birdie, or to play a middle iron short of the creek, then wedge on for a surer par. Because he's been hitting his 5-wood, which he had spe-

cially manufactured just a few weeks earlier, so well, Floyd goes for what he would later characterize as the most ambitious approach of his career. When he swung, he at first thought that he'd hit the ball too well and that it would carry the bunker and land in heavy grass. But his ball barely reaches the bunker, where Floyd, one of the Tour's finest sand players, wedges up, then one-putts for a birdie.

Suddenly, Floyd's lead was back to five, and it would only grow from there. When he later saw replays of the shot, Floyd would tell reporters that he couldn't believe it—not only that he'd made such a superb 5-wood shot, but that he'd even chanced it. He'd just been that confident, he said. And it showed, all week.

DOUG FORD

Tournament: 1957 Masters
Site: Augusta National
Defining Moment: Final Round, 18th Hole

When asked by sports writers before the 1957 Masters Tournament to pick his five favorites, Ford picked only one—himself. Things didn't go so smoothly, however, especially after Ford put himself in bad shape in the third round with a 6 on the 15th hole. Though he was still second entering the final day, he trailed Sam Snead by three strokes.

But he caught and passed Snead, a three-time Masters winner (1949, 1952, 1954) during the last round by shooting a then-record 66—capping the charge by holing out from a bunker on 18. After burying a 7-iron approach shot in the sand, Ford played a closed-face explosion shot to the left of the hole. The ball wafted out softly and rolled 15 feet in a big arc into the cup for a birdie-3.

Ford finished 5-under for the tournament, beating Snead by three strokes. And, oh, yes, remember that pre-tournament interview? Besides telling the scribes that he would win, Ford also said that he would shoot a 283. Which he did, precisely.

ED FURGOL

Tournament: 1954 U.S. Open
Site: Baltusrol, Lower Course
Defining Moment: Final Round, 18th Hole

A sequence of shots Ed Furgol selected and played in the 1954 U.S. Open are among the most interesting in Open history. The selection and his perseverance in following through on them is reflective, perhaps, of Furgol's character, as he had persevered over a severe arm injury to realize his dream of becoming a professional golfer. Furgol had a wicked fall on a playground when he was 12: trying to swing from one parallel bar to another, he missed and fell, landing on his left elbow and suffering a compound fracture. He had several operations and the arm was finally put in a cast that held it over his head for six weeks. When the doctors removed the cast, it was days before he could begin returning his arm to his side and the arm was locked permanently at a 45-degree angle. Furgol was able to restore some flexibility and began his quest to become a professional golfer, achieving a good measure of success on the PGA Tour in the post-World War II years.

Furgol keeps close in the Open—two back after each of the first two rounds—then rises to the lead by one over Dick Mayer and by three over three others, including Gene Littler, who has a terrible third-round 76. Furgol holds the lead during the tough final round against an unrelenting course: he has two bogeys and 15 pars, but no one is making headway. He comes to the final hole still ahead by a stroke and tries some strategy to protect his lead.

The closing holes of Baltusrol's Upper and Lower courses run parallel, separated by a stream lined with tall trees. The 18th hole on the Lower Course, where the Open is being held, has a slight dogleg left, and Furgol decides to drive to the left side of the fairway to cut some distance to the green, but the shot hooks a bit and falls in among the trees. His only angle back to the fairway is a short safe pitch that will leave him two shots from the green. But, there is a small window of opportunity among the trees on the left, to shoot through and clear them and land on a fairway: sure, it's a fairway on Baltusrol's Upper Course, but it's a much better landing area and has a clear shot at the 18th green on the Lower Course. After checking to make sure that the Upper fairway is not out of bounds, Furgol yanks the ball out of a hairy lie with his 8-iron, sending it through the trees and it lands on the Upper fairway about 150 yards from the Lower 18th green. Furgol then hits a 7-iron, and strikes it well, but maybe it's more than 150 yards from this fairway to that green—there are no markers when you improvise—and the ball lands short of the green. But Furgol chips it to within five feet of the cup, then holes the putt for par and a one-stroke victory over Littler.

JANE GEDDES

Tournament: 1986 U.S. Women's Open
Site: NCR Golf Course
Defining Moment: Playoff Round, 13th Hole

"Fire and Rain" could have been the theme song for the 1986 Open. Throw in an earthquake for another measure (4.2 on the Richter scale), a quartet playing an exciting final eight, and a rousing point-counterpoint playoff finale—and you have the Open that had it all, and then some. When a forty-four car train derailed early on near the course, a phosphorous tank car erupted into a major fire; then violent thunderstorms swept in and out, delaying each of the first three rounds; and the second round was shaken up by the earthquake. That was just the opening acts.

By Sunday the storms and shakes and fire danger have passed, and coming in during the final round three golfers have a chance to win—third-round leaders Betsy King and Ayako Okamato; Sally Little has caught them, but up ahead Jane Geddes makes a late charge. Geddes birdies the 12th, 14th, and 17th holes, then pars the 18th and is in safely, tied with Little, with King and Okamato a stroke back. Little hits a fine approach to 18, but the ball bites immediately and leaves her a thirty-foot putt for the lead. She comes agonizingly close, then taps in for a tie. King and Okamato also reach the greens in regulation but neither can hole a tournament-tying birdie putt.

Little takes a three-stroke lead during the playoff by birdieing the 4th through 6th holes. Then she bogeys the 8th hole, to Geddes' birdie, and double bogeys the 9th, to Geddes' par, and Geddes has a one-stroke lead coming in. Little ties things up again with a birdie on 12. 13 brings a final twist of fortune: Geddes is trying to save par from off the green, while Little is on and within 15 feet of a birdie and the lead. Geddes pushes a chip on to the green, it rolls to the cup, and falls for her par; Little's putt lips the hole and stays out. Still tied, but Geddes has heated up: she birdies the 14th, and then Little bogeys the 15th, and the final three holes are played out evenly. Geddes wins by two. The Open that had it all and then some had one more story: it is Geddes' first professional tournament win.

BOB GOALBY

Tournament: 1968 Masters
Site: Augusta National
Defining Moment: Final Round, 15th Hole

In seven previous Masters, Bob Goalby had never finished better than 25th, but he stuck close to the leaders through three rounds and saved his best golf and sportsmanship for the final round, when the Masters championship unexpectedly came his way.

Goalby is among 16 golfers bunched within four strokes after 54 holes, but Robert de Vicenzo charges ahead of the pack and almost everyone ahead of him on the board and playing behind him begins to fall back: Don January, Raymond Floyd, Gary Player, Frank Beard, and then Bruce Devlin, until only Goalby is left to challenge de Vicenzo.

Goalby birdies the 5th, 6th, and 8th holes, then he pars 9 and makes the turn trailing by two strokes.

Goalby holes a putt on 13 for a birdie to move within one. On the par 5, 15th hole— 520 yards with a green guarded by a pond, Goalby drives the fairway deep, then hits a marvelous 3-iron shot that carries the water, heads straight at the flag, hits softly on the front of the green and rolls to within eight feet of the cup. At almost the same instant, de Vicenzo is reaching the green for a birdie try on the fateful 17th hole. They putt almost simultaneously, de Vicenzo for birdie, Goalby for eagle, and as both putts fall, the competitors are tied at 11-under. De Vicenzo finishes his great round out of character, with a bogey on 18, and Goalby comes to 17 needing two pars to win. His tee shot finds the green on 17, but the ball stops 45 feet away from the cup and he takes three putts to hole out, bogeying back into a tie. Then come almost simultaneous twists of fate: at about the time de Vicenzo is signing his scorecard, which proves to be incorrectly marked, Goalby gets lucky when his tee shot on 18 goes screaming toward the woods like an irate banshee but careens off a tree and bounds back to the fairway; he hits a 2-iron to the green but the ball bounds 50 feet past the pin to back of the green, and it takes him two careful putts to tie and set up a playoff.

The playoff never happens. De Vicenzo is disqualified for signing an incorrect scorecard (details in de Vicenzo's profile above). Goalby offers to continue the playoff anyway, since the error was a mistake that added a stroke to de Vicenzo's score. But the rules are clear, and Goalby wins a well-earned green jacket.

DAVID GRAHAM

Tournament: 1981 U.S. Open
Site: Merion
Defining Moment: Final Round, 14th-16th Holes

Australian David Graham had humble golf beginnings, playing with left-handed clubs until he earned enough money at age sixteen from a golf shop job to trade for a set of righties, and later taking a position as a golf pro at a nine-hole course in Tasmania. But by the time he was 24 he helped Australia win the 1970 World Cup. Then came a couple of international tournament wins in 1971, before he joined the PGA Tour in 1972 and showed the ability to play sustained, brilliant runs. His play over the final 18 holes at the 1981 U.S. Open has been has been viewed as one of the prestigious tournament's most perfect rounds.

As the tournament moves into the final round, George Burns holds a three-stroke lead over Graham, with whom he is paired. Graham misses the first fairway with his drive, but it will be the only fairway he will miss that day; he reaches the green in regulation, and sinks a birdie putt. Only three times will Graham miss reaching a green in regulation during the round, and on all three occasions his ball ends up on the green's collar, from which he putts for one birdie and two pars. Another birdie on the 2nd hole puts him one stroke behind, and he ties Burns on the 10th hole with another birdie. On the par-4 14th hole, both men drive into the fairway and are faced with approaches to a small green gaurded on the front by a trough: Burns' second shot sails over the green, while Graham hits a seven iron that lands just beyond the trough and rolls to within seven feet of the cup. He putts for a birdie, while Burns saves par. On the 15th hole Graham gains another stroke when his 8-iron approach lands within eight feet and he negotiates another birdie putt. On 16 Graham's approach carries a dangerous quarry to an upsloped green, lands safely and rests within ten feet of the cup; though Graham misses his birdie putt, Burns bogeys the hole and Graham goes three up, which ends as the winning margin.

RALPH GULDAHL

Tournament: 1939 Masters
Site: Augusta National
Defining Moment: Final Round, 13th Hole

Lost in the aura of contemporaries such as Byron Nelson, Sam Snead, Ben Hogan, and Jimmy Demaret, Guldahl enjoyed a spectacular string from 1936 to 1939, when he won two consecutive U.S. Open titles, one Masters, and three consecutive Western Opens. But it was the 1939 Masters that produced his most dramatic moment.

As Guldahl passes from the 9th green to the 10th tee at Augusta, he hears the announcer inform the crowd that Sam Snead has just finished his final round in 68 for a record-low 280 total. Guldahl, who had been two strokes ahead going into the final round, knows he needs a 33 on the back nine for the win. His 36 on the front nine isn't very encouraging, but a birdie three on the 10th and a safe tour through the 11th and 12th holes gives him some momentum.

His drive on the 13th carries about 225 yards down the middle, but leaves him a slightly downhill, slightly sidehill, snug lie, still 245 yards from the flag. He needs a second shot that will travel about 235 yards to carry Rae's Creek. He first thinks of playing short, then pitching up for a possible birdie, but concludes that in order to catch Snead, he has to go for broke. And he does. Using a 3-wood and cutting across the ball to get it up in the air, Guldahl launches a shot dead on the pin: it lands 10 feet beyond the creek and stops within six feet of the hole to the astonished screams of the gallery. From there, Guldahl putts for an eagle-3. Five holes later, which he covers in par, he has his green jacket.

WALTER HAGEN

Tournament: 1922 British Open
Site: Royal St. Georges' Sandwich
Defining Moment: Final Round, 15th Hole

Making the turn on the final round, Hagen is vying to become the first native-born American to win the British Open. He estimates that if he can finish the back nine in even par, he will win the title. Everything is going according to plan until the 15th, a short par 4, when his second shot drifts into a wide stretch of sand known as Cross Bunker, the ball approximately 100 feet from the pin. Hagen has two options: explode the ball high, a heavy shot that would probably run out of steam well before it reached the cup, or hit a chip shot aimed at reaching the cup, a far more risky stroke. The first option is the safer of the two but it would mean a sure bogey and be a stroke that he would have to recapture.

Many who saw him play said that most of Hagen's most impressive shots were those played from seemingly hopeless situations. Well, this sure seemed like one. Indeed, Hagen studies the shot for what seems like an eternity, changing clubs several times—wedge to mid-iron, back to wedge, back to mid-iron, back to wedge—before finally settling on the mid-iron. Then, with a concise, clipped, perfectly purposeful stroke, he lops the ball off the top of the sand. It carries as intended and comes to rest less than a foot from the cup.

Hope recaptured, Hagen saves par on 15, makes par on each of the final three holes, and wins the title by a single stroke. None of the five other contenders (separated by only two strokes) going into the final round makes par, and only George Duncan, who trails by four strokes, breaks par—with the first sub-70 round in the Open since 1904.

WALTER HAGEN

Tournament: 1927 PGA Championship
Site: Cedar Crest Country Club
Defining Moment: Semifinal, 36th Hole

Walter Hagen has won three straight PGA Championships and is in the midst of a 22-match winning streak spanning from the 1925 to 1928 PGAs, but he is challenged all the way through to the final in 1927. He came from four down after 18 holes of the 36-hole matchplay format during his first match and ended up winning 3 and 2. In the

quarterfinal he needs a hot putter to stave off Tommy Armour, winning 4 and 3. In the semifinal, Al Espinosa wins the 35th hole to go one up, then is safely on the green on the final hole, while Hagen is chipping back after a heavy approach shot carried the green.

Hagen was a fierce competitor not above employing tactics that might give him an edge. In the 1919 U.S. Open, for example, Mike Brady led Hagen by 5 strokes going into the final round but shot an 80 and sweated the outcome in the clubhouse. Hagen reached the 18th hole tied with Brady and made a beautiful approach shot that stopped eight feet short of the cup. While he walked to the green Hagen sent word ahead to Brady, inviting him to watch the tournament-winning putt. As Brady watched, the putt lipped the cup, and Hagen settled for a tie. During the playoff Hagen proved resourceful: at one point he recommended to Brady that he roll down his shirtsleeves because "everyone can see your forearms quavering;" later, when an errant shot lie mired in muck, Hagen claimed the right to identify his ball, picked it up, wiped it and placed it back softly for a more favorable lie. Hagen won the playoff by a single stroke. But that was then, and Hagen has been on his best behavior in this tournament: why, he's even conceded every putt from three-feet and under that Espinosa has faced in this match.

Hagen's in big trouble now, past the green with his second shot while Espinosa lies within 25 feet. Always one to come up with the great shot when he most desperately needs it, Hagen strokes a beautiful chip that bounds on the green and rolls to within a foot of the cup. As Hagen approaches the putt, Espinosa concedes it—one good turn deserves another. Espinosa lines up his putt and strokes it, but the birdie attempt stops three feet shy, leaving him that much for victory. He looks up at Hagen, expecting him to concede again, but Hagen smiles, turns his back, and begins talking with someone in the gallery. Espinosa addresses his first gimme of the day, and is yipped. He has to putt again to tie the tournament. Then on the 37th hole, Espinosa three-putts again, and Hagen is in the final.

In the final, Hagen was three-down after 19, came back and tied the match with a birdie on the 29th hole, then went ahead when Joe Turnsea bogeyed the 31st. For some reason, Turnsea suddenly loses his putting stroke, missing several short ones over the final five holes, including a tournament-tying bid on the 36th that is left hanging on the lip of the cup. Hagen wins his fourth straight PGA Championship by that much.

MARLENE HAGGE

Tournament: 1956 LPGA Championship
Site: Forest Lake Country Club
Defining Moment: Playoff, 1st Hole

In the first-ever playoff in an LPGA Major, two of the Tour's founding members are battling for victory, and the better chip shot will win. Hagge is only 22 but she's a wily veteran, having taken her first LPGA victory in 1952 at the age of 18, still the youngest tournament winner ever on the LPGA Tour. That same year Patty Berg won the first-ever U.S. Women's Open. Berg seemed headed for the LPGA championship, leading Hagge by two with three strokes to play, but she can't produce a great shot, bogeying 16 and 17 while Hagge pars them and moves into a tie. The 18th hole doesn't produce a winner, so they move to a sudden death playoff.

As they had throughout the tournament, Hagge and Berg match strokes, and both have approach shots that just barely miss reaching the green. Berg chips to within seven feet of the hole and the pressure turns to Hagge. She delivers a better chip, straight at the cup and just over a foot away. When Berg can't hole her seven-footer, Hagge taps in for victory.

The tournament reflected a change at the top in the LPGA. Berg had led the Tour in victories in 1954, for the third time in her career, and had led the tour in earnings the previous two seasons. Hagge claimed both titles in 1956, with the LPGA championship proving the difference. Berg reclaimed the top spot in 1957, however.

HAROLD HILTON

Tournament: 1911 U.S. Amateur
Site: Apawamis
Defining Moment: First Playoff Hole

Hilton was one of the more colorful characters in the game—an outstanding amateur player, an editor of *Golf Monthly* and *Golf Illustrated*, and a course designer. He was recognizable in tournaments: though he eventually dropped his signature white sneakers, he always played with a cigarette dangling from his lips and often wore a thin-brimmed, beanie-like hat perched back on his head. He pretty much summarized his outlook on life when he said, "I could fight pretty well if I saw the humor of it." He was small in stature, had an aggressive swing, and was daring on the course, taking great pleasure in challenges, but even he must have been dumbfounded and endlessly amused by his incredible victory shot in the 1911 U.S. Amateur.

He had already won his third of four British Amateurs in 1911 and is bidding to become the first man to win both the British and American Amateurs in the same year. Things are going well enough, as he reaches the finals and is blowing away Fred Herreshoff by six strokes with 15 holes to play. But Hilton blows the lead and ends up tied with Herreshoff after 36 holes, forcing a continuation of play.

Herreshoff outdrives Hilton on the first extra hole, a par-4, 377-yarder with an elevated green bordered on the left by a mound studded with rocks. Hilton's approach shot is off target, veering left to the rocky mound, but it lands in a soft spot on the mound, twists down to the green, rolls and settles near the hole for a tap in. Herreshoff can't recover, taking two shots to the green, where he is still away at 20 feet, and taking two more strokes before Hilton can tap for victory.

BEN HOGAN

Tournament: 1950 U.S. Open
Site: Merion
Defining Moment: Final Round, 18th Hole

Ben Hogan had already won U.S. Open (with a record-setting score), the PGA, and a place on the Ryder Cup team when he was almost killed in a car accident in 1949. Doctors were amazed that he was still alive. They thought he would probably never walk again. No one dared speculate on the chances of his ever playing golf. But Hogan did come back. It is a round of golf that turns out to be a profile in courage. Leading by three strokes with six holes to play, Hogan, his legs bandaged from ankle to groin in an effort to relieve the nearly debilitating, still-lingering pain from the auto accident that had side-lined him for all of that season, feels his legs giving out and confides to a friend that he isn't sure he can finish the round. Indeed, he is hitting the ball pure-ly on instinct; his playing partner, Cary Middlecoff, is marking his ball for him on the greens, and his caddie picks it up out of the holes.

His skills flagging with his spirit, Hogan loses those three buffer strokes through 17 and needs par on the 18th to force a playoff. Standing on the 18th fairway after his tee shot, he considers two options: try to cut a 4-wood for a birdie possibility or hit a straight 1-iron for a more certain four. He chose the 1-iron, figuring that if he forces a play-off, he will have a day to rest. From a slightly hanging lie, while summoning the courage to somehow fight through the blinding pain, Hogan strikes skillfully: the ball reaches the green, setting up a two-putt finish and a next-day playoff with Lloyd Mangrum and George Fazio.

Hogan, after a night of rest, not only survives the playoff, but triumphs as well, shooting a 69 to beat Mangrum's 73 and Fazio's 75.

BEN HOGAN

Tournament: 1951 U.S. Open
Site: Oakland Hills
Defining Moment: Final Round

If the 1950 Open was a testament to Hogan's courage, the '51 version was testimony to his unparalleled golf skills. Oakland Hills, scripted by legendary golf architect Robert Trent Jones, had fairways so narrow that the only tactic available was to aim for the middle, disallowing the possibil-ity to open up the green and the flag for the second shot. The course was a monster, made even tougher by "the Open Doctor," which is what Jones was nicknamed for his pre-tournament fine-tuning.

After respectfully playing defensively for two days and carding a 76 and 73, respectively, Hogan makes the turn in the third round in 32 and looks to be headed towards a 67 before he fritters several shots away and rises to a 71, two strokes down to Lloyd Mangrum. Still, Hogan feels there is a sub-70 round in him. And there is.

Unleashing a series of superb strokes in the final round, Hogan brings home a 67, only the sec-ond sub-70 round of the week and the lowest to Mangrum's earlier 69. He beats Clayton Heafner by two strokes. In the end, it is a successful defense of his 1950 title, accomplished by an aggressive offense. After going out in par, he birdies 10 and 13, bogeys 14 but birdies 15, then climaxes his triumph with a 6-iron approach shot to 18 that stops within 20 feet of the cup. He putts in for another birdie.

BEN HOGAN

Tournament: 1953 British Open
Site: Carnoustie
Defining Moment: Final Round, 5th hole

By 1953, Hogan's comeback was in full swing. He won the Masters with a four-round total of 274 and the U.S. Open at Oakmont with a 283. The one Major Hogan had never won was the British Open, a tournament he had never even entered. Thus the stage is set when Hogan enters the open at Carnoustie, where the weather turns cold and damp before the tournament, spelling trouble for his continually troubled back. To make matters worse, he has the flu; his temperature is rising and his blood pressure dropping as play begins. Still, Hogan attacks the course, shooting an opening qualifying-round 70. By the second qualifying round, however, his health has worsened, and he slumps to a 75. Hogan begins tournament play with a 73 and follows on the second day with a respectable 71, but the final 36 holes are to be played in a single day, and there are those who doubt that Hogan's body will be up to the challenge.

Hogan arrives at the course bundled in two sweaters and begins his charge. His iron play is phenomenal, and despite poor putting, he turns in a 70 for the first 18 holes. After eating lunch on the course, he begins the afternoon round, one in which he is to play some of the finest golf of his career. On the fifth hole, his second shot lands in a bunker, 50 feet from the cup. It would take an outstanding approach just to get close, but Hogan holes it, causing the crowd to go wild. From that point on, he plays careful, methodical golf, protecting his lead and winning the British Open to secure the Triple Sweep and cap a comeback story that is one of the greatest achievements in the history of sports.

HALE IRWIN

Tournament: 1974 U.S. Open
Site: Winged Foot
Defining Moment: Final Round, 18th Hole

It was the year that Winged Foot devastated the field: Jack Nicklaus opening with four straight bogeys? Johnny Miller with a seven on a Par 3? Tom Watson with a final-round 79? It was mostly

a matter of survival. And Hale Irwin did just that—he survived. When questioned, Irwin likes to say that his greatest golf shot was actually a succession of shots—a 12-foot putt for par on 17; a perfect tee shot on 18, and a succeeding 2-iron to the green. If forced to choose, however, most aficionados would cite the 2-iron into the teeth of one of the toughest finishing holes in the world. Some have described Irwin's shot as majestic. If not that, it did at least manage to momentarily tame the Winged Foot course.

Unsure of whether he is alone in first place or tied with the pesky, 23-year-old Forrest Fezler, Irwin tees up on 18 and his drive splits the fairway, coming to rest 215 yards from the hole. As he addresses the ball for his second shot, Irwin knows exactly what he needs: a high, straight, powerful shot that will have to stop quickly once it reaches the slippery, fiercely-sloping green. Irwin's shot lands on the green, hops a couple of times, then comes safely to rest 20 feet behind the pin.

Irwin takes two putts for his par and a 72 total of 287, a stocky seven over par, but good enough, on this course, for a two-stroke victory—over Fezzler and over Winged Foot.

TONY JACKLIN

Tournament: 1969 British Open
Site: Royal Lytham
Defining Moment: Final Round, 18th Hole

As he stands at the final tee, Jacklin knows that he needs only a par 4 to beat Bob Charles, his closest competitor and playing partner. "Only," however, seems to be a pretty daunting challenge. Though only about 400-yards long, the 18th hole features a narrow fairway with bunkers on the left, one on the right, and a bunker in front of the green that challenges the wisdom of laying up. Then there are the bushes. And the hopes of the gallery: a citizen of Great Britain hasn't won the British Open for 18 years, the longest such drought. What does it take to get into position for par on that devilish finishing hole? A helluva swat with a driver.

Which is exactly what Jacklin produces. Thinking only of his mechanics and shutting out everything else with a moment of steely concentration—never once, he would later say, did he consider the do-or-die situation he was facing—Jacklin produces the tee shot of his life, which sets him up for a 7-iron to the green (a safe carry over the front bunker) and a two-putt for the title.

He won two titles: shortly after his win, Jacklin was knighted by the Queen.

BOBBY JONES

Tournament: 1923 U.S. Open
Site: Inwood Country Club
Defining Moment: Playoff, 18th Hole

One mark of a champion is to seize the lead in a close battle and never relinquish it, and another is to momentarily lose command but summon back the qualities that make a champion. Bobby Jones has a three-stroke lead over Bobby Cruickshank going into the final round of the 1923 Open. He doesn't play a particularly good round, opening with a front nine 39, but shoots the next six holes in two-under par, and his lead seems safe. But just as Cruickshank begins a run (see his profile above), Jones begins to lose command: a tee shot lands in a parking lot off of the 16th hole, and Jones scrambles for a bogey; on 17 another bogey; on 18 he lands in the gallery, and holes out with a double bogey. Cruickshank cools off and it looks like Jones may have backed in, but Cruickshank ties it up with a stirring birdie on the final hole.

Cruickshank and Jones are close all the way in the playoff and come to the 18th hole tied. Cruickshank hooks his tee shot behind a tree, Jones slices into the rough; as Jones is pondering whether to go for the green, Cruickshank makes his only play by laying up before a pond. Jones decides to go for

the green, staking the tournament on an all-or-nothing shot of just over 200 yards that has to carry the pond. He drills a 2-iron that streaks toward the flag, carries the pond, hits the green and rolls to within eight feet of the cup. He'd almost backed in during regulation, but he stormed to victory in the playoff.

BOBBY JONES

Tournament: 1926 British Open
Site: Royal Lytham
Defining Moment: Final Round, 17th Hole

Bobby Jones' "legendary season" usually refers to 1930, when he won the Slam of his time —Open and Amateur championships of the U.S. and Great Britain in a span of six months. But the 1926 British Open was the first leg of another incredible journey that would see Jones get to the fifth round of the British Amateur, finish second in the U.S. Amateur and win the U.S. Open. Some call 1926 Jones' "other" awesome season. Others, still, simply considered it a necessary prelude to the spectacular run in 1930.

In any event, it wasn't easy in the British Open. Jones catches Al Watrous, called by many the greatest golfer never to win a major championship, when Watrous three-putts on the 14th and 15th greens to lose his two-stroke edge coming in. But Jones is the one who cracks next. After both golfers par the 16th, Jones' tee shot at the 411-yard 17th hole sails too far left too soon, landing in unraked sand at the corner of a dogleg. Watrous drives straight and shorter, then plops his approach on the green.

In his book, *Down The Fairway*, Jones described his predicament: "I had to hit a shot with a carry of close to 175 yards and hit it on a good line and stop the ball very promptly when it reached the green—if it reached the green. This, off dry sand." Selecting the equivalent of a four-iron, Jones makes the shot he needed, and a little better. His ball not only stops on the green, it comes to rest in a closer and better spot than Watrous' ball, unnerving Watrous, who three-putts for a bogey while Jones salvages par. Jones pars 18 while Watrous bogies, again, giving Jones a two-stroke win. He would later admit that he'd won the title with a single shot. A plaque was laid off the 17th fairway, near to the bunker where Jones' ball lay, commemorating the great shot.

BOBBY JONES

Tournament: 1930 U.S. Open
Site: Interlachen
Defining Moments: Second Round, 9th Hole, Final Round, 18th Hole

Jones was to make 1930 the most famous year in the history of the game. He scrambled his way to victory in the British Amateur at venerable St. Andrews. He followed with a win in the British Open at Hoylake and returned to America to find that the sports pages were already full of talk of a first-ever Grand Slam. The pressure was on.

Jones is one stroke behind after the first round of the Open, two strokes behind after the second. In the second round a little luck comes Jones' way. His tee shot on the 9th hole (par 5, 485 yards) slices into the rough, but he decides to go for the green, which demands a carry of over 225 yards to clear a pond fronting the green. The shot streaks for the green but begins to descend too soon—it doesn't clear the water, but it miraculously skips off the surface and lands safely before the green; he pitches and then strokes a birdie putt. On the third day of the tournament, Jones comes alive. He shoots a startling 68 and moves ahead by five strokes.

It isn't over. His lead is one coming to 18, and he's on the green in two on the par-4, 402-yard hole, 40 feet from the cup. He hopes to get it close, but instead actually holes it and wins the Open by two strokes.

The 1930 U.S. Amateur at Merion, outside Philadelphia, is almost an anticlimax. In the match-play event, Jones methodically eliminates each opponent he faces and becomes the only golfer in history to achieve the Grand Slam. Two months later, Bobby Jones announced his retirement from golf at the age of 28.

BETSY KING

Tournament: 1987 Nabisco Dinah Shore
Site: Mission Hills
Defining Moment: Fourth Round and Playoff, 16th Hole

Betsy King had been an almost instant success on the LPGA Tour, joining in 1984 and winning eight tournaments prior to the 1987 Nabisco Dinah Shore. Add a Major to the mix and you have one of the most formidable players on the Tour. She has a chance for the Major entering the final round, but she's tied with Pat Bradley and the two are soon joined by Patty Sheehan, who began the round three strokes back and is playing ahead and applying pressure.

Sheehan opens with three straight birdies, but King matches her. Sheehan gets in another birdie at the 6th Hole, and Bradley starts making headway by birdieing the 5th and 8th. King reaches the turn one ahead of Bradley and two ahead of Sheehan, but Sheehan birdies the 10th and 11th holes, and Bradley makes it a three-way tie with a birdie at 10. King takes back the lead with a birdie at the 12th, while Bradley bogies, then Sheehan ties King again with a birdie at the 14th. But King bogeys 13, while Bradley birdies, and Sheehan bogeys 15—all tied again.

There's more: Sheehan's under a tree with her drive on 16, but she clips a 6-iron that flies to the green and lands withing 15 feet of the cup. She putts for a birdie. When King reaches the 16th, she's down by one and heading for big trouble: her tee shot hooks into the rough, and then her second shot crosses the fairway and plops into a greenside bunker. King steadies herself in the bunker, focuses in, and explodes out; the ball bails out of its loft, hits the green running, and rolls the final 20 feet into the cup—King holes out from 45 feet to tie the tournament once again. King follows Sheehan's lead by parring the final two holes, setting up a playoff, as Bradley finishes third, short on the dramatics.

King is in trouble again on the first playoff hole, a par 4 with a narrow, tree-lined fairway. She has to chip safely back in the fairway, leaving 100 yards to the green. Using a wedge she lofts a high shot that floats along the fairway falls to the green and stops five feet short of the cup. Sheehan gets up and down, and King putts to tie. On to the 16th, where both players pulled out of trouble in the final round to save their chances. This time they drive well and hit approaches that land on the green. Both players miss putts from 20 feet, Sheehan falling three feet short, King half better, and when Sheehan's next putt slides by agonizingly close, King putts in for victory on the same 16th hole where she found a winning shot from the sand.

TOM KITE

Tournament: 1992 U.S. Open
Site: Pebble Beach
Defining Moment: Final Round, 7th Hole

During his 20 years on the PGA Tour, Tom Kite had won just about everything—Rookie-of-the-Year, 16 tournament titles and over $7 million in career earnings (the most ever at that time)—but was becoming known as the greatest golfer never to have won a major. The 1992 Open seems no different, as he stands eight strokes back of second-round leader Gil Morgan. The Pebble Beach course is playing remarkably easy; by the 8th hole of the third round, Morgan is an amazing 12-under par. But the course suddenly becomes more characteristically demanding on Morgan, and no one is

Scores for the last three twosomes playing the wind-whipped final round of the 1992 Open:

Nick Faldo	77
Joey Sindelar	78
Tom Kite	72
Mark Brooks	84
Ian Woosnam	79
Gil Morgan	81

spared when weather becomes a factor during the final round.

Morgan's birdies on 16 and 18 save his one-stroke lead after three rounds over Kite, Ian Woosnam, and Mark Brooks. Their reward for placing in the top four is to bear the brunt of the blustery weather—the final round is played in increasingly tough, gusting winds: almost a third of the field shoots in the 80s, including Morgan and Brooks, and only four break par—Colin Montgomerie, who teed off two-and-a-half hours before Kite, Jeff Sluman and Nick Price (both of whom teed off an hour before Kite), and Tray Tyner, who teed off before Montgomerie. Kite birdies the first hole, falls back with a double-bogey on four as the wind settles into an unrelenting fury, and comes back with a par on six by sinking a 25-foot putt. On the 107-yard, 7th hole in the teeth of a 35 mph wind, Kite uses a six iron (yes, a six iron to reach 107 yards), and like 15 of the 16 golfers before him, misses the green. He has plenty of green to work with, but his lie is in thick rough with a bunker yawning before him. Using a wedge, Kite teases the bunker with a short arcing shot that hits the green rolling, speeds across, hits the flagstick and drops in the hole.

Kite then endures a constant struggle with the elements on the links—the ocean holes—of Pebble Beach, playing par, and then takes advantage of opportunities as they happen: a 30-foot putt on 12, a wedge to within two feet of the cup on 14 for a birdie four. With a gutsy par in an all-out gust on the 18th hole, where he refuses to back off, Kite wins by two strokes.

BERNHARD LANGER

Tournament: 1985 Masters
Site: Augusta National
Defining Moment: Third Round, 13th Hole

Some call them the twitches. Some refer to them as the yips. Others just say, simply, putting woes. And Bernhard Langer had them, in triplicate. Oftentimes so bad that fellow golfers would turn away in pain rather than watch; or they would yawn, as Langer became methodical in preparing for his putts. Thus, Langer's '85 Masters win was as much a triumph of mental discipline as anything. Still, Langer wasn't even in the running until the 13th hole of the third round, after opening with a 72 and 74.

Even then, it takes some luck. Langer's drive off the tee isn't exceptional, but he decides to take a chance and try to carry Rae's Creek and go for the green with his second shot. Using a 3-wood, Langer swings and almost immediately, his heart sinks. He knows the ball is never going to carry the water. Then luck steps in. Langer's ball bounces the burn and skips to the green. Langer holes the ensuing putt for an eagle-3, giving him a tremendous psychological boost.

Still, Curtis Strange leads the field by six with six holes to play in the final round. But as Strange falters, Langer keeps up his charge and eventually wins, conquering his putting woes in the process with birdie putts of 14 feet on the 3rd hole, 18 feet at the 5th, 13 feet at the 12th, 4 feet at the 13th and 15th, and 14 feet at the 17th. Yips, begone!

JOE LLOYD

Tournament: 1897 U.S. Open
Site: Chicago Golf Club
Defining Moment: Final Round, 18th Hole

Few people watched Joe Lloyd make one of the greatest final shots in U.S. Open history. It was fitting, somehow, for Lloyd was a mysterious man who kept out of the little limelight golf afforded in the U.S. at the turn of the century, choosing to play occasional competitions and mostly in New England. He then disappeared from the golf scene as his skills waned and he was not heard from again. It is known that he was born in England and emigrated to the United States, where he became a club pro in Massachusetts while spending his winters in France.

18-year-old Willie Anderson is the big story of the 1897 Open, which is being played in one day with two 18-hole rounds. Going into the final round, defending Open champ James Foulis is one back of Andreson, while Lloyd is three back. Lloyd goes out in one of the early groups in the afternoon, and most people stick around to follow the leaders. Lloyd plays the front nine in 40 and adds 28 strokes over the next six holes. Meanwhile, Foulis shoots a 45 on the front nine and adds a 43 coming in—he will finish tied for third—and Anderson, shooting 131 after 30 holes, seems headed for victory. But Anderson runs cold, playing the next three holes in 17 strokes, totaling 148 to Lloyd's 151 after each played 33 holes. The final three holes make the difference, but Anderson is young with greatness to come: he will later win four U.S. Opens. Anderson plays the final three in 15 strokes to finish at 163; Lloyd plays them in 11 strokes, each hole more spectacular than the one before it, to finish at 162 and claim victory.

Lloyd plays the 543-yard 16th hole perfectly: solid straight drive, long iron to the fringe, chip to within 10 feet, putt for four. On the 432-yard 17th, he hits a long straight drive, then an iron to the green, but he putts twice for four. Again on the 461-yard 18th, Lloyd rips the gutty ball long down the fairway, then plays a brassy true—the ball hits just before the green, bounces on and rolls to within eight feet of the cup. Lloyd holes it for a three and the winning margin. Pars weren't used back then, but considering the 461-yard 18th hole is fourth longest on the course and taking into account the ball and the equipment, the hole could be considered a par 5, which would make Lloyd's three an eagle and the 1897 tournament the only Open to have been won with an eagle on the final hole. While that can be debated, the three did indeed win the tournament.

NANCY LOPEZ

Tournament: 1978 LPGA Championship
Site: Grizzly Course, King's Island
Defining Moment: Final Round, 2nd Hole

Nancy Lopez's triumph at the 1978 LPGA Championship wasn't a total surprise: she had won the three tournaments leading up to the LPGA and two others earlier on the '78 Tour. And she already had two runner-up finishes in the U.S. Women's Open—in 1975 as a fresh-out-of high school, 18-year old amateur, and in 1977 in her first tournament as a professional. Still, she is a rookie on the 1978 Tour, and some big names—Amy Alcott, Judy Rankin, and JoAnne Carner—are ready to break her five-stroke lead. Lopez seems to be providing them the chance: a poor approach to the 2nd hole is followed by a weak chip from the rough that leaves her 16 feet away, facing a tricky right-to-left putt. She reads it well, as the ball starts away and then comes on line for the hole and falls for par. The same scenario is played out on the 7th hole, and again she comes through with a right-to-left-breaking ten-footer for par. She pars the first nine holes, in fact, then shoots two-under coming in, and any chance for a rookie collapse is vanquished. The crowded, enthusiastic galleries and media throng get the story they want, and women's golf has a bright, young, vibrant superstar.

Lopez set an LPGA Championship record-low aggregate score, breaking the mark of 278 that was set in 1964. It was only one of several feats for Lopez during the year: she won nine tournaments, and no rookie previously in the LPGA or PGA had ever won more than two; she earned almost $190,000, breaking the rookie earnings record established in the PGA by Jerry Pate in 1976; and

her string of five-straight victories (of which the LPGA was fourth) set a new LPGA record, passing the previous mark of four held by three others, including Hall of Famers Mickey Wright and Kathy Whitworth. It was a major step in Lopez's own Hall of Fame career. Lopez's nine victories in 1978 included the U.S. Open, the Nabisco Dinah Shore, and the du Maurier Classic (nee Peter Jacobsen Classic)—which, with the LPGA Championship, form the contemporary LPGA Grand Slam. The du Maurier was designated as a Major in 1979, the Dinah Shore in 1983. Lopez was LPGA Player of the Year and the Vare Trophy winner in 1978 and 1979 and won 17 tournaments during that two-year span.

SANDY LYLE

Tournament: 1985 British Open
Site: Royal St. George's, Sandwich
Defining Moment: Final Round

For 16 years, the courses of the British Open had been conquered by non-British golfers. And things looked no different going into the final round at Royal St. George's, Sandwich. Bernhard Langer of West Germany and David Graham of Australia share the lead, three strokes up. Then, Sandy Lyle appears. A strapping man of great natural strength, Lyle paced quietly along in his usual manner and bit by bit takes advantage of Langer and Graham miscues until he is atop the leaderboard after birdies on 14 and 15. A four at 18 would certainly give him the win, just as a four would have served British golfer George Duncan in 1922, who came charging after Walter Hagen.

But in 1922, Duncan was undone by a depression at the bottom of a steep slope just off the 18th green, the soon-to-be-named Duncan's Hollow. Duncan's chip didn't have quite enough oomph to climb the steep slope and he ended up with a five, losing to Hagen. Lyle found the Hollow, too, with his second shot, then sank to his knees in despair when his chip failed to mount the crest of the green and rolled back almost to his feet. He gathered himself, however, and salvaged a Duncan-like five.

But this time—perhaps it was some sort of poetic justice—five was good enough. Langer and Graham couldn't catch Lyle, and, after an agonizing wait, the UK finally had another British champion in the British Open.

SANDY LYLE

Tournament: 1988 Masters
Site: Augusta National
Defining Moment: Final Round, 18th Hole

Vying to become the first Briton to win the Masters, Lyle enters the final round—after 71, 67, 72—with a two-stroke lead, then improves upon that on the fourth hole of the final round, where he chips in after hitting his tee shot clean through the back of the green. But after a quick succession of problems on the 11th (three putts), 12th (Rae's Creek), and 13th (a long pitch into a bunker behind the green), Lyle is trailing Mark Calcavecchia. He needs a par on 18 for a tie, and a birdie for the win.

Lyle bunkers his 18th tee shot, despite using a safe 1-iron, and is left with a 150-yard shot from the sand uphill to the green. A little luck is with him, however: he has a clean lie, his ball on a slight upslope. He goes for it, hitting a staggering shot that drops beyond the flag then screws back to within eight feet of the cup as the crowd roars. He has the birdie try he needed for victory, and he completes it.

JOHN MAHAFFEY

Tournament: 1978 PGA
Site: Oakmont
Defining Moment: Final Round

Mahaffey had endured his share of troubles in the years before the tournament. After losing the 1975 U.S. Open playoff to Lou Graham, he suffered a succession of elbow, finger, and hand injuries as well as a divorce and drinking troubles. Things certainly didn't look much sunnier, at least professionally, at the 1978 PGA. Entering the final round, Mahaffey is a very distant seven strokes behind Tom Watson. There seems to be no way that Watson, who is playing superlative golf, can lose.

But just when things seem so absolutely certain, Watson begins to falter on the back nine, and his two playing partners, Mahaffey and Jerry Pate (who trails by five at the start of Day Four), begin to make up ground. Once the bleeding starts, Watson can't stop it. Indeed, stepping to the 17th tee, he is, incredibly, a stroke behind Mahaffey and Pate, who are now tied for the lead. A birdie there ties Watson with Mahaffey, but Pate birdies, too, and Watson and Mahaffey need a flubbed short putt by Pate on the 18th to force a playoff. They get it—and Mahaffey takes advantage of the opportunity, winning the tournament with a birdie on the second extra hole. After the win, some would say that it was destiny—and some measure of poetic justice—that allowed the down-on-his-luck Mahaffey to win the PGA title.

CAROL MANN

Tournament: 1965 U.S. Women's Open
Site: Atlantic City Country Club
Defining Moment: Final Round, 16th, 17th, 18th Holes

Carol Mann is only 24 in 1965, inexperienced in major professional competition, and finds herself leading the U.S. Women's Open by four strokes. Then disaster tries to bully her. After six holes on the final day, with her father, mother, and all four brothers in from Baltimore to see the finish, Mann loses her lead and finds herself three over par. Worse, she's never faced this type of pressure.

She fights back, eventually regaining a one-stroke lead through 15, then unleashes a streak of superb shots through the final four holes. Those shots are almost a coming out party for Mann, who will go on to demonstrate poise and excellence as a golfer and strong leadership of the LPGA over the next decades. First, a strong 12-foot putt hits the back of the cup, pops up and plops in on 16 for a saving par. A blast from a bunker on 17 falls lightly and stops within four feet of the cup. On 18, a dead-center 4-wood off the tee to within 30 yards of the flag, pitch to within five feet of the hole, and birdie putt. She picks up a stroke in the process to win by two.

The win is Mann's first major in what would turn into a spectacular professional golfing career. She calls it her greatest win.

DAVE MARR

Tournament: 1965 PGA Championship
Site: Laurel Valley
Defining Moment: Final Round, 15th-18th Holes

Dave Marr enters the final round of the PGA Championship tied for the lead with Tommy Aaron, two strokes ahead of Billy Casper and Jack Nicklaus. Of the four Marr seems least likely to win the title. He had not won since 1962, he blew a tournament late three weeks before the PGA, and he is somehow viewed as too thoughtful, too sensitive, too intelligent, as if his ever-inquisitive mind will overwhelm his execution of the immediate task at hand; he's a thinker in a sport that rewards full attention. But Marr prevails through thirteen, maintaining his two-stroke lead over Casper, and has moved three up on Nicklaus; Aaron has fallen out of contention. Then the thinking starts to move beyond the task at hand, and maybe the thinking on Marr is correct.

On the 190 yard par-3 14th, Marr's lead begins to crack: his tee shot flies left of the hole, and he loses a stroke to Casper by bogeying the hole. On 15 he selects a 2-iron off the tee to make sure he hits the narrow fairway, then faces a long approach to a small green sandwiched by bunkers;

his approach lands between them and brakes quickly—within seven feet of the hole, and then he putts in for a birdie and is back on top by two. On 16 he hits a great fairway drive, then has a long shot to a heavily-bunkered green, with the pin placed near bunkers on the right: he hits a 4-iron that stays left and finds a bunker, but he uses the ample green space to explode out, with the ball stopping within two feet of the cup. He seems safe, but misses the two-footer, and his lead over Casper falls to one, with Nicklaus two strokes back.

On the 17th hole, a 230-yard par 4, Marr hits a 4-wood to the left of the pin on a green that slopes wickedly left to right. Jack Nicklaus, his playing partner, pushes it further left, then watches in horror as his soft pitch runs on the slope, passes the cup by eighteen feet and stops on the fringe. Nicklaus steps up to the challenge, however, and holes out with an excellent, firm 7-iron punch of pitch shot. Marr's turn, and he taps the putt after having watched Nicklaus' careful pitch run wild, but Marr's putt gathers momentum and slides eight feet past the hole. However, Nicklaus' great pitch shot revealed a subtle slope near the hole; Marr putts to that same slope and the ball angles into the hole. He still leads Nicklaus by two, and Casper has bogeyed 18, falling two strokes back.

On 18, Marr has room for a bogey, but Nicklaus puts the pressure on. Nicklaus hits a long drive and is rewarded with an excellent target at the top, flat area where the pin stands on an abruptly terraced green. Marr finds a fairway bunker, and perhaps a bogey won't be enough after Nicklaus' great tee shot. Marr gets back into the fairway from the bunker, then lobs a nine-iron shot dead for the flag, hitting the center of the green and bouncing up to within three feet of the cup. It helps Marr save par, as he putts in for a one-stroke victory over Nicklaus, who birdies the hole. It was a thinking man's triumph, both for the strategy and execution Marr employed and for willing back command when his execution was failing, as he made up for a muffed two-footer and a drive into the bunker.

JOHN MCDERMOTT

Tournament: 1911 U.S. Open
Site: Chicago Golf Club
Defining Moment: Playoff

McDermott was America's first great home-grown professional and the first American-born golfer to win the U.S. Open; he won it at the age of 19—still the youngest man ever to win the Open (he successfully defended his title the next year). Seemingly on his way to a fabulous career, McDermott met with a series of unfortunate incidents that cut short his golf career at the age of 23.

At the tournament in Chicago, Mike Brady and local hero George Simpson post identical scores, round by round, while McDermott runs hot and cold: behind by five after the first round, tied for the lead after 36 holes, ahead by four going into the final round, then falling back and needing a birdie on the 72nd hole to tie for a three-way play-off. He bogeys the first and third playoff holes, then rights himself and leads Brady by four after nine, with Simpson playing out heroically over an attack of inflammatory rheumatism. By the 13th, McDermott and Brady are tied, and after a Brady bogey on 15 they reach 18 with McDermott ahead by one. McDermott wins with a great approach that rolls to within 10 feet of the hole. Brady can't match it, and McDermott ends up winning by two.

McDermott defended his championship in 1912, continued to work hard at his game but was beset by a series of unfortunate incidents. He lost most of his money in the stock market in 1913. In 1914, McDermott missed connections from a ferry to a train and arrived too late for the qualifying round of the British Open. The ship he traveled on for his return to the United States collided with another ship in a dense fog and sank. McDermott was saved, but his performance in the 1914 U.S. Open showed distress. He began to suffer blackouts later that year, spent time in rest homes, which would recur throughout the remainder of his life, and never played competitive golf again. Six weeks before he died, McDermott was spotted inconspicuously attending the 1971 U.S. Open.

JOHNNY MILLER

Tournament: 1972 British Open
Site: Muirfield
Defining Moment: Third Round, 5th Hole

Miller wouldn't win the '72 British Open, but with one shot, on the 5th hole of the third round, he would give the golfing world an indication of what was to come two years later when he would take the Tour by storm, winning the first three tournaments of the 1974 season and earning comparisons to Nicklaus, Palmer, Hogan, and other heroes of the sport.

Facing the 570-yard hole, Miller drives his ball about 290 yards on the hard fairway, leaving 280 yards to a pin that is tucked back into the right corner. He grabs a 3-wood from his bag and swings as hard as he can swing. The ball hits just short of the green, rolls up and continues rolling, trickling into the cup for the rare double-eagle.

The shot helps Miller card a course-record, three-under 66, which puts him into contention on the final day. It proves to be too little, too late, however, as Lee Trevino wins the tournament.

JOHNNY MILLER

Tournament: 1973 U.S. Open
Site: Oakmont
Defining Moment: Final Round, 15th Hole

Johnny Miller expected to make a quick getaway from the 1973 Open. He enters the final round tied for thirteenth place, six strokes off the lead (held by John Schlee, Jerry Heard, and a couple of former Open champions, Arnold Palmer and Julius Boros) and is playing in the eighth from last group—a full two hours before the leaders will tee off. He's also coming off of a third-round 76. But that was then. He begins the final round by birdieing the first four holes, then his streak seems to run out on the 8th, where he three-putts for bogey. But he comes back with birdies on the 9th, 11th, and 13th holes, and just misses another on 14. As he tees up on the 453-yard par-4 15th hole, generally considered the toughest on the course, he is tied for the lead.

Miller's drive on 15 covers the first 280 yards, then he hits a splendid 4-iron to within ten feet of the hole, and finishes off a tough putt for birdie. He pars the remaining holes. His seven-under par 63 is the best round ever in the U.S. Open. Miller hit every green in regulation and took only 29 putts; ten approach shots with irons stopped within 15-feet of the hole, five of those within six feet. One by one, those who were so far ahead fell behind on the back nine, and only John Schlee finished within a stroke.

LARRY MIZE

Tournament: 1987 Masters

Site: Augusta National

Defining Moments: Final Round, 18th Hole, and Playoff

Augusta-native Larry Mize was practically playing in his backyard at the Masters and was a natural crowd favorite, but it was mostly a show of sentiment considering he had only one career title —the 1983 Danny Thomas Memphis Classic, which ended dramatically with his 25-foot tournament-winning birdie putt. Mize as a Cinderella story at the Masters seems unlikely with the formidable competition atop the leaderboard entering the final round: Ben Crenshaw (1984 Masters champ) and Roger Maltbie tied for the lead, Bernhard Langer (1985 Master champ) and Greg Norman (1986 British Open champ and Masters runner-up) a stroke back, and Seve Ballesteros (1980 and 1983 Masters champ) two strokes back.

Mize is also two strokes back and playing ahead of this pack. He has a strong final in a high-scoring Masters, heading for his third-straight par round, but he comes to life on 18: Mize blasts his drive long down the fairway, hits the green with a 9-iron, and putts for a birdie. One by one those playing behind him can't match his pace and fall from contention, except for Ballesteros and Norman, perhaps the two best golfers in the world at the time. They are tied with Mize as each approaches 18. Ballesteros' approach lands in a bunker, and he saves with a smooth sand shot and putts for par. Norman's walk to the green, where his second shot lies, seems a victory march. But his winning putt on 18 veers left at the last possible second and narrowly misses the hole, setting up a three-man, sudden death playoff between Ballesteros, a five-time Majors winner, Norman, who's been ahead in the final round of five straight Majors, and Mize, a journeyman playing near home.

On the first playoff hole, Ballesteros is off-target all the way and three-putts out of the playoff. On the second hole, the 11th, Norman reaches the green in two, with a long putt ahead, while Mize is in the fairway just under 50 yards out. He has a choice of lofting a shot, but with a wide field of green before him, Mize opts for a pitch-and-run: it takes off in good speed toward the green, bounces a couple of times, reaches the green and roles directly into the cup. It's a stunning and totally unexpected ending—sudden victory in the truest sense of the term, Cinderella with a different kind of ending: instead of a shoe, the hometown golfer fits into a green jacket.

YOUNG TOM MORRIS

Tournament: 1870 British Open

Site: Prestwick

Defining Moment: Opening Round, First Hole

There are no official histories or reports that describe exactly how Young Tom conquered

Prestwick right from the first tee in 1870, and some flat-out figures will have to do, but it sets him racing to the greatest tournament score ever recorded with the gutty ball—a total of 149 covering the three-rounds-of-12-holes format. There wasn't a formal system for rating holes, but an informal measure of perfection had been set up and Young Tom's total reflected 2 strokes "in excess of absolutely faultless play"—which is a lot tougher standard than par.

The first hole at Prestwick course, which is set up in a criss-cross pattern, is a monsterous 578 yards. Young Tom covers it in three. It can be assumed that his drive covered over 250 yards, carrying the double green (5th and 11th holes) in the middle area of the 1st hole, and landed before the swale called "The Pill Box" (at about 400 yards) and the mound beyond it called "Cardinal's Nob," and that he avoided them on the second shot. Young Tom went on to cover five other holes in 3s, including "Tunnel" (the 6th, 350 yards) and "Lunch House" (the 10th, 290 yards), and closed the first round of 12 holes at 47. Young Tom follows that performance with 51s—a 149 total, winning his third consecutive Open by a whopping 12 strokes.

BYRON NELSON

Tournament: 1939 U.S. Open
Site: Philadelphia Country Club
Defining Moment: Second Playoff Round, 4th Hole

Nelson had many spectacular moments in his 15-year career, especially considering that he won 11 consecutive tournaments and 18 overall in 1945. But it was a single shot in 1939 that he recalls as his greatest single golfing feat. After the final round of the 1939 Open, Nelson is tied with Craig Wood and Denny Shute. The first 18-hole playoff eliminated Shute, but Nelson and Wood tied again,

with 68s. The following day, Nelson and Wood face off, again.

On the fourth hole, a 460-yarder, Nelson leaves his tee shot on a plateau on the left, the best place to land a drive, about 240 yards from the hole. Next, he hits a 1-iron that never leaves the line of the flag. Nelson would later say that a bullet couldn't come from a rifle any straighter. And he was right. The ball hits the green about 20 feet from the cup and rolls in for an albatross.

There was more golf to be played that day, of course, but the shot gave Nelson a four-stroke lead and he went on to win 70 to 73 over Wood. The 1939 Open also included one of golf's greatest collapses. Sam Snead, finishing just behind Nelson, suffered an 8 on the 72nd hole. He thought he needed a birdie to tie and took a chance on reaching the green with a long approach but landed in a bunker. The 8 included a whiff in the bunker, a near-miss thirty-foot putt that would have given him a bogey and a tie, then a brokenhearted miss from very close.

BYRON NELSON

Tournament: 1951 Crosby
Site: Cypress Point
Defining Moment: Second Round, 17th Hole

Coaxed out of his formal retirement of five years, Nelson is leading the 1951 Crosby through the first two rounds, but that lead is in jeopardy with his tee shot off 17, which skirts the frothing Pacific but lands in a thicket of large, gnarly cypress trees 250 yards out. The only worse lie would've been in the ocean. Initially, Nelson plans to play his next shot safe—pitch short over the trees to the fairway, pitch to the green, and one-putt for a workingman's par. Then, he gets another idea, a risky one—the "intentional hook."

Nelson sizes up the strong wind blowing in off the Pacific and ignores the screams of his playing partner, Eddie Lowery, who is amazed by his colleague's bout of temporary insanity. Ignoring Lowery, Nelson crafts a huge hook—not a simple fade along the water's edge, but an all-out hook launched over the water and curving back—figuring that the gale winds will turn the ball back hard and fast enough to catch the green; it works, with the ball stopping just shy of the green.

If it hadn't, Nelson would've taken at least a six. But he pars the hole and goes on to win the tournament by one stroke. It is the last of his 54 career victories.

JACK NICKLAUS

Tournament: 1962 U.S. Open
Site: Oakmont
Defining Moment: Playoff, 4th Hole

The year was 1962, and a youngster named Jack Nicklaus had just turned pro, placing himself in contention with the best in the game, including Tour superstar Arnold Palmer. The U.S. Open that year was held at Oakmont, the home course of Palmer, who was heavily favored to win the tournament.

Nicklaus and Palmer are partnered for the first two rounds, which means Jack is forced to play in front of the large and vocal group of admirers known as "Arnie's Army," who have broken the concentration of many older and more experienced pros. But Nicklaus is no ordinary golfer. His powers of concentration are legendary, and he plays one of the steadiest and most consistent games in the history of golf. He turns in a first-round 72 to Palmer's 71. After the second round, Nicklaus stands at 142, while Palmer is tied with Bob Rosburg at 139. The third round leaves Nicklaus at 214, Palmer at 212, and Rosburg out of the contest. In the last two rounds, both played on the final day of the tournament, Nicklaus plays his usual steady, methodical game and ties Palmer with five holes to go. The two men shoot par golf until the 18th,

where Nicklaus two-putts, giving Palmer the chance to win with a birdie. But he misses a 12-foot putt, forcing a playoff.

The course is packed for the 18-hole playoff, with almost the entire crowd pulling for Palmer, the local hero. Nicklaus is not intimidated. He pars the first hole, where his opponent takes a bogey. The lead stays at one until the fourth hole, a 544-yard, par-5. There Nicklaus hits into the rough and is outdriven for the first time. Jack hits a 3-iron safely onto the fairway, but he has a tricky 100 yards to go, and the green is protected by a huge sand trap. He blasts a wedge shot that just clears the sand, hits the green cleanly, and rolls to within six feet of the cup. The birdie putt is practically a tap-in.

Palmer pars that fourth hole and is down by two strokes. In the next four holes, Nicklaus picks up two more strokes. Then Palmer begins one of his patented late charges, birdying the 9th, 11th, and 12th holes. The crowd is electrified, and for a brief time it appears that once again Palmer will snatch a victory from almost certain defeat. But Nicklaus, though young, shows the poise that will become a hallmark of his career. He plays rock-solid and steady, while Arnie runs into trouble as he is forced to play a more aggressive game. Palmer finishes the playoff with a 74, while Nicklaus shoots a 71, making him—at 22—the youngest U.S. Open winner since Bobby Jones in 1923.

JACK NICKLAUS

Tournament: 1970 British Open
Site: St. Andrews
Defining Moment: Playoff, 18th Hole

One of Nicklaus' career-long ambitions had been to win at St. Andrews, the Home of Golf. Now, the day after catching Doug Sanders in the final round, he has a four-stroke advantage through the first extra 13 holes. Then, his lead begins to dwindle, and as he and Sanders stand at the tee at 18, the final green 358 yards away, his lead is one. Sanders, hitting first, places his ball beautifully in the middle of the fairway just short of the depression named the Valley of Sin, only 30 yards shy of the green. Now, Nicklaus seems uncertain. He has a decision: power drive to the green (he'd done it three days in a row), challenging the fences and buildings lining the fairway, or play it safe with a cautious 4-wood. After all, a par probably will beat Sanders.

But Nicklaus has the heart of a champion. As he removes his sweater, all who are watching know that he's made the champion's decision. He grabs his driver, lines himself up and swings. As soon as he hits the ball his fears of inaccuracy fade —and a new one emerges: he worries that he's hit the ball too well. And he has. The ball, blasted prodigiously, reaches the green, scoots past the pin toward the gallery, and stops in heavy rough a few feet short of out-of-bounds.

But fate often shines brightest on those with the courage to test her, and, moments later, following a brilliant comeback pitch, both he and Sanders are within five feet of the hole. Nicklaus holes a slippery downhiller for a birdie, his win at St. Andrews, and his second British Open victory.

JACK NICKLAUS

Tournament: 1972 U.S. Open
Site: Pebble Beach
Defining Moment: Final Round, 17th Hole

Sometimes it's not perfection that yields the greatest golf moments, and Jack Nicklaus will attest to that. On the way to his second U.S. Open title in 1972, Nicklaus' dramatic near hole-in-one on the 17th begins with a poor swing.

With a comfortable lead but a discomfiting wind threatening swift disaster, Nicklaus is hoping to keep the ball low. He pulls the 1-iron back inside his normal swing pattern and slightly closes the face of the club. Quickly sensing the problem, he cor-

rects, coming through cleanly and ends up with a great shot. The ball hits about four inches from the hole, bounces off the flagstick, and settles six inches away. Nicklaus would later say that it was the best shot he'd ever hit that began with a bad swing.

Interestingly enough, three of the shots that Nicklaus lists among his greatest came with the 1-iron. And Pebble Beach, where he won his 1961 Amateur title and two Crosby pro-ams (including that year's tournament) and which he calls his favorite course, would be the stage 10 years later for his dramatic showdown with Tom Watson, where, again, the 17th hole would prove climactic.

JACK NICKLAUS

Tournament: 1986 Masters
Site: Augusta National
Defining Moment: Final round

Nicklaus, with five green jackets in his closet already, is in a multiple tie for ninth place, four strokes off the lead, going into the final round of the 1986 tournament. Greg Norman holds the lead, as he did in all the major championships that year, and no one expects what is about to happen.

Nicklaus never paid much attention to what was supposed to be. He just played consistent golf with major charges for glory. This day would be no different—for the final 10 holes, he plays the game almost as well as anyone possibly could. After a rather routine 35 going out, he birdies 10 and 11, but bogeys 12, then holes a wondrous putt for an eagle on 15, birdies 16 and birdies 17. By the time Nicklaus is finished with his charge, Norman needs a birdie to win and a par to tie. So unnerved is he by Nicklaus' attack and the emotional charge from the gallery that the Shark, having difficulty even choosing the correct club to use, takes a five for the loss.

With the win, Nicklaus, who'd won his first green jacket in 1963 and his fifth more than a decade later in 1975, had become the oldest Master's champion—by nearly four years. His walk up the fairway to the rousingly applauding gallery on the 72nd hole was itself a moment of pure triumph.

GREG NORMAN

Tournament: 1986 British Open
Site: Turnberry
Defining Moment: Second Round

Greg Norman is nicknamed The Shark for his attacking, aggressive play through which he became the all-time money winner on the PGA Tour. The attacking style makes him a constant threat and is his greatest strength; some believe that its his greatest fault—a form of *hubris*, excessive pride that keeps him on the attack even during times when laying up or playing for more makeable targets seems a surer route to victory . He was all attack in 1986, leading all four majors at some time during the final rounds that year. But the detractors will point out that two big-hitters who also play with great finesse—Jack Nicklaus and Raymond Floyd—bested Norman in the Masters and US Open, respectively, that year, and Bob Tway became part of a growing contingent that beat Norman late by finessing a magic shot, winning from a bunker in the PGA Championship.

Norman's response to very tight fairways, despairing roughs, and a blustery wind in the 1986 Open is to attack, attack, attack. From a 74 opening round he shoots a record-tying 63 in the second round, beginning with three birdies (2nd through 4th holes), then after bogeying the 5th hole, he birdies the 7th; on the 10th hole he hits a 6 iron to within 5 feet, then birdies; his tee shot on the 177-yard 11th hole stops one foot from the pin; a drive and 3-iron leave him within 3 feet at the 440-yard 14th; he birdies the 15th through 17th, just missing an eagle on 17. The marvelous performance leaves him with a two-stroke lead. He shoots a 74 in relentless gusts on Saturday, but still holds the lead by a stroke, then finishes with a 69 for a 5-stroke victory.

FRANCIS OUIMET

Tournament: 1913 U.S. Open
Site: The Country Club
Defining Moment: Final Round, 17th hole

In the early years of the twentieth century, golf in America was still in its infancy; the game belonged to the British, the Scots, and the French. And it was expected that the 1913 U.S. Open would be won by one of the two top British entrants, the legendary Harry Vardon, master of the finesse shot, or Ted Ray, the long driver. If these titans of the game were to be beaten, surely it would be by one of the top Americans or perhaps another Brit or a Frenchman. Certainly, a 20-year-old American amateur named Francis Ouimet didn't even belong in the field, let alone stand a chance of winning. To everyone's surprise, Ouimet survived the first three rounds by playing unspectacular, steady golf, while the heroes of the game were beaten by the course at key moments.

In the final round, Ouimet continues his consistent, methodical play and finds himself needing one birdie in the last two holes for a tie. His drive on the Par-4 17th, a dogleg to the right, settles neatly into the middle of the fairway, and his approach shot leaves him a 20-foot putt for birdie. It has rained for the entire fourth round, and the greens are getting slower by the minute. Ouimet gives the ball a firm smack. It holds against the sidehill grain and drops straight into the cup. A routine par on the 18th ensures a three-way tie.

The rain continues for the 18-hole playoff the next day. But while the soggy conditions—not to mention the unexpected tie by the young unknown —may have dampened the spirits of his opponents, Ouimet is unaffected by the weather. The front nine is relatively uneventful; the deadlock remains. But Vardon three-putts the 10th, and Ray does the same. Ray self-destructs even further on the 15th, and Vardon hooks badly on the 17th. Ouimet wins the championship by three strokes and goes on to become one of the best-known and most popular golfers in history.

ARNOLD PALMER

Tournament: 1960 Masters
Site: Augusta National
Defining Moments: 17th and 18th Holes

Arnold Palmer, a true legend of the game and one of the tour's first big-money winners, helped make golf a national spectator sport with his patented final-round charges that seemed tailor-made for television audiences. The first televised Palmer charge took place in the 1960 Masters. Going into the final round, Arnie is well back of Ken Venturi, who finishes the tournament with a 283. As Palmer approaches the 17th tee, Venturi is, in fact, already in the clubhouse being fitted for the winner's green jacket and briefed by the television crew for his upcoming interview.

Palmer arrives at the 400-yard, par-4 17th needing a birdie on one of the final two holes to tie. He drives long to the center of the fairway, and then hits an 8-iron shot that stops up short, 25 feet from the pin. The green is long and undulating, fast and intimidating. Palmer strokes the putt sharply; it rolls to the cup and hesitates for a second before dropping in.

At the 18th hole, Palmer needs a par to tie Venturi. He drives 260 yards into a strong wind and then punches a 6-iron shot low and hard; it bites and stops five feet from the hole. With millions of fans watching on television sets around the world, he studies the putt briefly before giving it an authoritative ride straight into the hole for a birdie and the outright win.

ARNOLD PALMER

Tournament: 1960 U.S. Open
Site: Cherry Hills Country Club
Defining Moment: Final Round, Front Nine

In 1960 Jack Nicklaus was still in college, and Arnold Palmer—having won the 1954 U.S. Amateur, as well as the 1958 and 1960 Masters—was well on his way to superstardom. However, in the first three rounds of the 1960 Open, Arnie had turned in a respectable, but not spectacular, 72-71-72 that left him seven strokes behind the tournament leader, Mike Souchak.

Palmer starts out the fourth round in dynamic fashion—by driving the green on the 346-yard, par-4 1st hole; he misses the eagle putt but leaves a tap-in for birdie. On the 410-yard 2nd, he hits another long drive, just misses the green with his pitch, but chips in for another birdie. Palmer smashes his tee shot again on the next hole, a 348-yard dogleg left, and puts a wedge shot a foot from the pin: birdie. His fourth consecutive birdie comes on the 426-yard 4th hole when he sinks an 18-foot putt. He settles for a par on the par-5 5th, but comes back with a 25-foot putt for another birdie on the par-3 6th. On the 411-yard, par-4, 7th hole, Palmer stops a wedge shot six feet from the stick and holes out for his sixth birdie in seven holes. Parring the 8th and 9th, he turns in a 30 for the front nine and solidifies his reputation for final-round charges.

Even after this spectacular performance, Palmer's win is far from a done deal. At this point in the tournament, Souchak is tied for the lead and several other players have a chance to win the Open, including young Nicklaus and the legendary Ben Hogan, who are playing together two groups ahead of Palmer. Arnie arrives at the 17th needing pars on the last two holes to win. He plays the par-5 17th conservatively, laying up short of the water with his second shot and ensuring the par. Then, although he misses the green with his second shot on the par-4 18th, his neat little chip and four-foot putt win the Open. Palmer's final-round 65 (30 for the front and 35 on the back) is the lowest ever shot by an Open winner on the last round of the tournament.

ARNOLD PALMER

Tournament: 1968 PGA Championship
Site: Pecan Valley
Defining Moment: Final Round, 18th hole

It is what some have come to regard as the single-most electrifying shot of Palmer's storied career. And it comes during the one Major he had yet to win. With one hole to play and one stroke behind Julius Boros, who is playing behind him, Palmer faces the 470-yard dogleg right that has, over the four days, yielded only 19 birdies. The hole forces even the best players to lay up on the drive, then rattle a long iron to the elevated, blind green.

Arnie is going for broke, and, perhaps addressing his final drive with too much fury, Palmer hooks into the heavy rough, 230 yards from the green. From there he faces an almost impossible assignment: move the ball out of the grass, carry a creek and a hill to drop down on the green in position for a birdie three. But Palmer, who utterly depends upon his daring style of play, calmly swings a 3-wood and uncorks a massive shot, ripping the ball out of the grass and up the fairway, riding low and sure with a slight fade. His ball lands just short of the green, bounds forward, hits the pin and caroms eight feet past the hole. Arnie's Army erupts in glee.

Alas, the cheers soon turn to groans of disappointment, however. For although Palmer is so close, he misses the birdie putt: he expects a slight break, but the ball never wavers, and Boros hangs on to win.

SANDRA PALMER

Tournament: 1975 U.S. Women's Open
Site: Atlantic City Country Club
Defining Moment: Final Round, 11th Hole

Six players are bunched within a stroke going into the final round of the 1975 Open: Sandra Palmer, Sandra Post, and Sally Little are ahead of JoAnne Carner and a couple of longshots—Debbie Austin and Nancy Lopez, an 18-year old amateur who charms the gallery and the media with her excellent play and spirited personality. The best line of the day comes from a spectator in the gallery, who describes an excellent sequence of saves by

Carner on the first three holes of the back nine as "the mother of all pars," and the best story is Lopez. Facing the pressure of the Open with bright cheer, she was homesick nevertheless, but was greeted in the morning by her parents, who were flown in from New Mexico to watch the final round after having to pass over the Open because finances were low.

But it's Sandra Palmer's year, so far, as the leading money winner coming to the Open. She makes a move on the par-3 3rd hole, landing her tee shot safely on the green and negotiating a 16-foot par for a birdie. On the 6th hole, Lopez holes a six-footer for birdie and ties Palmer and Post with the lead, but then she falls back with bogeys on the 7th and 8th holes. Lopez would make six bogeys on the first thirteen holes and four birdies, with only three pars. Post, too, would have more bogeys than birdies, and on the very tough course the winner will have to play par during the final round. Through ten, Palmer has three birdies, three bogeys and four pars, then on the 11th hole her approach lands in a greenside bunker. Palmer recovers with the shot of the day, an explosion that touches down and heads right for the hole, stopping three inches short; making par is an achievement, and she saves it. She makes five pars on the back nine to balance with two bogeys and two birdies—a steadiness that brings her the Open Championship. It's Palmer's greatest moment, her first and only major coming in the year she tops the LPGA money list, beating a couple of past champions (Carner, 1971 Open champ, and Post, 1968 LPGA champ), and Lopez, who had the best finish (tied for second) of an amateur in the Open since Catherine LaCoste won it in 1967.

JERRY PATE

Tournament: 1976 U.S. Open
Site: Atlanta Athletic Club
Defining Moment: Final Round, 18th Hole

Pate, 22, a rookie seeking his first professional win, hit what some aficionados argue is the finest golf shot ever made under maximum pressure. Pate is 194 yards out on his second shot, in heavy grass, facing a tiny green fronted by a lake. Tom Weiskopf and Al Geiberger, playing ahead, are already finished, having sunk 7- and 20-foot putts, respectively. Pate needs a par to beat them.

He picks a 5-iron from his bag and the crowd murmurs its disapproval. Most fans expect Pate to try to hit a hard 4-iron or a soft 3 from that distance. But, adrenaline pumping, Pate uses the 5. And the moment he hits the ball he knows that he's not only hit his greatest shot ever, but that he's also won the tournament. The ball flys high into the blue Georgia sky, carries over the water, then plummets to earth, stabbing the green and stopping barely three feet from the hole. From there, Pate putts for the birdie to win by two strokes.

With the win, Pate became the first player since Jack Nicklaus in 1962 to win both the U.S. Open and U.S. Amateur crowns. In the first round on that same 18th hole, Pate barely cleared the water, then didn't: a frog jumped on his ball and sent it rolling into the lake. The day after the Open, Pate was in Iowa for a Pro-Am tournament. He was invited to play poker by country singers Charley Pride and Roy Clark, to whom he announced that he didn't care about the stakes—he'd just won the Open—and that he wasn't much of a card player. He later admitted the Open champ lost a few thousand dollars of his winnings in that card game.

COREY PAVIN

Tournament: 1995 U.S. Open
Site: Shinnecock Hills
Defining Moment: Final Round, 18th Hole

There is price for success in golf for those who win all but four tournaments. A number of great golfers through time have proven themselves consistent winners only to bear the label "best golfer never to win a Major." Corey Pavin assumed the unwanted title soon after Tom Kite shed it by winning the 1992 U.S. Open. And one of the men he battles against in the final round of the 1995 Open, Greg Norman, has assumed another silly title, a three-quarter nickname: best player never to win an American major.

Norman shoots a blistering 135 over the first two rounds, finishing with a birdie on the 36th hole. Then he goes birdieless for 32 holes. He starts the final round tied with Tom Lehman, leading Bob Tway and Phil Mickelson by a stroke, with Pavin three off. But Pavin, playing ahead, whittles away the lead, while everyone playing behind and leading him struggles against the course to make par: the course wins. Lehman trails Pavin by one stroke on the 16th, then finds disaster when his chip shot rolls back down a ridge and stops at his feet; he takes a double-bogey and is done for. Tway, who briefly shares the lead with Pavin, Norman and Lehman during the round, collapses on the back nine: bogeys on the 10th and 14th holes and a three-straight-bogey finish for a 5-over 75. Norman is still matching Pavin, but he bogeys the 17th to fall to 2-over for the day. Only Pavin is hot, but he needs to place added pressure on those playing and chasing him from behind by coming to terms with Shinnecock Hills. Victory is delivered in magnificent fashion when his approach to the par-4 18th stops within five feet of the cup. Pavin birdies for a 2-under-par 68 and is the only golfer to finish at par for the tournament—the first player to win the U.S. Open without breaking par since Hale Irwin had an even-par 284 at Inverness in 1979.

GARY PLAYER

Tournament: 1972 PGA Championship
Site: Oakland Hills
Defining Moment: Final Round, 16th Hole

Some call it the most electrifying recovery shot in the history of professional golf. Others, with a shake of the head, simply call it impossible.

Player begins the final round with a three-stroke lead, but falters, bogeying three of the first four holes of the final round and allowing a dozen golfers to take pursuit. Still struggling through the next 12 holes, he arrives at 16, a 408-yard dogleg right with a large, menacing pond, tied with journeyman Jim Jamieson.

Player's drive is poorly struck and placed, falling short of the pond and lodging in deep damp rough smack behind a large weeping willow. Player needs to hit his approach high enough to clear the tree yet long enough (150 yards) to reach a green guarded by deep bunkers with a dangerous runoff. Neither a 7-iron nor an 8 will provide the needed loft. Player uses a 9-iron and swings with all his might. Only the gallery can see the ball skim the very top of the tree, sail along in the gray sky, land on the green, and hold four feet from the hole. Player is unable to see the flag until he lays on the ground to peer beneath the skirt of the willow after taking the shot. Moments later, Player sinks the birdie putt for a two-stroke lead and the eventual margin of victory.

GARY PLAYER

Tournament: 1978 Masters
Site: Augusta National
Defining Moment: Final Round

Player's third and final Masters championship was as much a testament to his spirit as his superb golfing abilities. Player had an indominitable work ethic, was fanatic about fitness and devoted to health foods. He would wear black one day to absorb the heat and white the next day to reflect it. His first and last Masters' titles came 17 years apart. There is no doubt that he saved the best for last.

Seven back of leader Hubert Green, and trailing a list of others, too, going into the final round, someone jokes to the 42-year-old Player that he needs eight birdies for any sort of chance to climb back into contention. Well, Player says that he will

get them—then does that one better. He cards nine birdies, seven over the last 10 holes for a back-nine 30 and a final-round 64. The back-nine, record-tying charge requires consistent excellence; Player considers the difficult, 12-foot, downhill putt on 18 the greatest of those 30 strokes. It is fast enough to challenge him to win with a birdie, with the danger that a miss might sweep past far enough to endanger his ability to come back and tie.

The putt gives Player a one-stroke win over Green, Tom Watson, and Rod Funseth. The finish is not without some controversy, however. After a magnificent second shot to within a yard of the flag, Green, as he prepares to putt, is apparently undone by a TV commentator's voice and backs away from the shot. He tries to gather himself, but misses the putt. When asked about the distraction, Green dismisses it, blaming only himself for the loss.

SANDRA POST

Tournament: 1968 LPGA Championship
Site: Pleasant Valley
Defining Moment: Playoff, 15th Hole

Don't ask Sandra Post how her ball got into the cup on the 15th hole at Pleasant Valley. She says that she doesn't know and was too excited to ask. Her shot on the 15th gave her the momentum to win the playoff with LPGA great and defending champion Kathy Whitworth in what many call the most thrilling LPGA Championship ever.

Post, 19, had hit her drive on 15 into the bank of a creek and is facing a 110-yard shot to an elevated green. Her nerves jangle. A Tour rookie, she's never been in a position like this, having to make the perfect shot to beat an LPGA star in the prestigious LPGA Championship. She takes a wedge and, as she has described, hits the ball the best she could. The swing feels good, the ball rises, and, seconds later, the rolling thunder from the gallery gives Post cause to suspect she's reached the green, and maybe even hope a little that she's holed out. As she approaches the green, the crowd's cheers grow even louder. Her ball is nowhere in sight, and she finds it in the hole.

Post would say later that the shot completely changed her approach to the rest of the match, boosting her confidence and aggressiveness, and, eventually, leading to her win by seven strokes. A star was born.

NICK PRICE

Tournament: 1994 British Open
Site: Turnberry
Defining Moment: Final Round, 17th Hole

Nick Price was gaining a reputation as the best golfer in the world, but it wasn't based on performances in the British Open titles. In 1982 he lost a three-stroke lead over the final six holes, and he entered the final round in 1988 atop the leaderboard by two strokes, but didn't win that one either. He had won the 1992 PGA and fifteen Tour events since then, but he did nothing in two earlier Majors in 1994.

And this Open doesn't seem much different. Price is playing behind Jesper Parnevik, who's in command on the back nine of the final round, while Price is teetering near disaster and barely saving a chance to catch Parnevik. On 14, he's in a patch of dry rough near a television tower, and the green ahead slopes away quickly from the front pin position. While Marshals hold up cable wires, Price chops the ball and it rumbles along the bumpy terrain catching the downslope of a small mound and riding down to the green for a short putt to save par. On 16, trailing by three strokes with three holes to go, Price holes a tough 12-footer to close within two.

Meanwhile, Parnevik goes through the most agonizingly misinformed stroke since Sam Snead played himself out of the 1939 U.S. Open. Unaware that he has a two-stroke lead and thinking he needs a birdie to win, Parnevik chooses to go for the green after his drive lands in the rough off the right of the fairway; the pin is placed in the front left side of the green, a small target area bordered by thick clumps of gnarly grass. Parnevik's shot lands short and in the grass, and he takes a short chip and two putts to finish with a bogey.

Price, playing behind Parnevik trails by two after he birdies 16, but Parnevik doesn't know that and his bogey reduces his lead to one. On the par-5 17th, Price hits an excellent long and straight tee shot and follows up by reaching the green with an iron, but the ball still lies 50 feet from the cup with a ridge in between on the green. Prices aims a firm putt to the right of hole: it climbs the ridge, pulls toward the hole, seems about to stop at any moment but reaches the cup and falls in for an eagle. One ahead, and well aware of it, Price needs only to make par on 18, but he's bogeyed the hole each of the first three rounds. Price hits a three iron to the center of fairway, plops a 7-iron within a yard of the cup, and putts in for victory. Now, he can be rightly considered the best player of the time, and he seals that honor by winning the 1994 PGA Championship a few weeks later.

BETSY RAWLS

Tournament: 1953 U.S. Women's Open
Site: Country Club of Rochester
Defining Moment: Final Round, 18th Hole

In 1953, the USGA assumed administration of the U.S. Women's Open and brought their characteristic toughening of Open venues into play. They kept it simple—moving the tees back, so that tournament played like an endurance course. Patty Berg established the early pace, leading by eight strokes after two rounds. By the end of the third round the pack was catching up, as her lead was whittled to three strokes, but she was managing to keep ahead—two strokes up with three to play. Then, she couldn't finish it off, bogeying each of the last three holes. Jacqueline Pung had passed her on the 17th, then with a chance to win, she, too, bogeyed 18, tying her with Betsy Rawls and forcing a playoff.

Rawls is one of the star attractions of the LPGA Tour, at that time in its seventh season. In 1950, as an amateur, she finished second to Babe Zaharias in the U.S. Women's Open. She turned pro in 1951 and won the Open by five-strokes. She quickly rose to the top rank of the LPGA in 1952, her second year on the Tour, winning six events including the Western Open. Rawls had managed to make her way safely through the final three holes, parring the 16th and 17th, and on 18, unlike Berg and Pung, she reached the green of the long par-4 in two—fitting that on a long course, a long iron to the green would prove crucial to victory. Still, though she's on the green, she faces a 60-foot putt: Rawls runs it up in good speed, leaving a safe putt for par that would secure her place in the playoff.

Pung and Rawls would have an interesting history together in the Open. Rawls won outright, head to head, in their 1953 playoff, shooting a brilliant 34 on the front nine and finishing up with a six-stroke victory. In the 1957 Open, she also finished strong but needed a bogey by Pung to force a playoff. Pung didn't oblige this time, and enjoyed an emotional triumph at Winged Foot. However, it wasn't over: Pung had incorrectly marked a 5 for her fourth hole score when she actually took a 6, and even though her total on the card was correct, the lower reported score on the hole was grounds for her disqualification, and Rawls became champion. Coincidentally, Rawls, a four-time Open winner, later became the first woman to serve on the Rules Committee for the U.S. Open, and another Hall of Famer, Betty Jameson, who was playing with Pung that fateful day, also mistakenly marked a five on her scorecard, though she had scored a six, also had the correct total incorrectly added, and was also disqualified.

GENE SARAZEN

Tournament: 1935 Masters
Site: Augusta National
Defining Moment: Final Round, 15th Hole

The Masters was in only its second year of existence, so less than two dozen people were in the gallery when Sarazen made this legendary shot. Trailing leader Craig Wood, who was already in the clubhouse, by three shots, Sarazen confers with his caddie, Stovepipe. The two figure that Sarazen will need a birdie four on 15, birdie two on 16, then a birdie three on either 17 or 18 for a tie. Sarazen figures he had a decent chance, until he sees his lie in the rough after his drive on 15. It is, as he says in his book, *Thirty Years of Championship Golf*, "None too good." He and his caddy huddle again and he decides on hitting a 4-wood, the close lie eliminating his 3-wood from consideration. What occurrs next has been called "the Shot Heard Round the World" and is considered by some as the most spectacular shot in the history of golf.

With the flag 220 yards away, Sarazen is concerned about the possible loss of yardage with the 4-wood and toes the club in to decrease loft and seek the extra distance. He tears into the shot with everything he has and the ball rises no more than 30 feet off the ground, heading straight for the flag. Sarazen begins running to watch the flight and sees the ball hit the green on perfect line. When he hears the tiny crowd explode in cheers, he knows he's scored an albatross.

That shot wipes out the 3-stroke deficit and Sarazen plays the final three holes in par to force a playoff, then takes the 36-hole playoff by five strokes.

PATTY SHEEHAN

Tournament: 1994 U.S. Women's Open
Site: Indianwood Golf and Country Club
Defining Moments: Third and Fourth Rounds, 16th Hole

Over a ten year span, Patty Sheehan has 10 Top-2 finishes in the Women's Majors—four wins and six times runner-up. The worst of those second-place finishes was probably the 1990 U.S. Open, where she led by nine-strokes after 36 holes and lost ten of them to Betsy King over the final 36, finishing second by a stroke. She's playing ahead of Helen Alfredsson during the third round, and though she won't witness Alfredsson's collapse, she's been there. So has Alfredsson, who lost the previous year's Open by a stroke after taking a two-stroke lead into the final round.

Alfredsson has finished seven holes with a seven stroke lead during the third round, while Sheehan's up ahead, playing well, but she's lost two strokes during the round. On the 16th hole, Sheehan's fortunes change, suddenly, while Alfredsson has lost command of her game by bogeying the 8th, 9th, and 14th holes. Sheehan's facing a 50-foot putt on 16 and she reads it perfectly—a long snaking line that goes to the heart of the cup. Then, on 18, she birdies while Alfredsson double bogeys the 17th, and when Alfredsson bogeys 18, Sheehan has the lead by a stroke. Alfredsson's fortunes get worse in the final round, and she ends up an astounding eight strokes behind when it's all over. On the 16th hole of the final round, Sheehan is tied with Tammie Green, but another winding putt finds the hole and becomes the one-stroke margin of victory.

SAM SNEAD

Tournament: 1946 British Open

Site: St. Andrews

Defining Moment: Final Round, 5th Hole

Sam Snead hadn't planned to play the 1946 British Open. Hogan wasn't competing. Neither was Nelson. After being dominated by Americans between the wars and having closed down during World War II, the British Open seemed to have a lowered status. But Snead went, and it was lucky for the golfing world. For while championship golfers often are called upon to play at least one daring or dangerous shot in a final round, it is almost inconceivable that one would face three on a single hole!

Tied for the lead after three rounds with Johnny Bulla, Dai Rees, and Bobby Locke, Snead feels confident that if he can avoid major mistakes, he can win. But after the first four holes, hs is three over and about to face his biggest challenge on the 567-yard 5th hole. Hooking his first shot into Hell Bunker, he faces a high-lipped ridge. He explodes out nicely, but the wind takes hold and dashes his ball across the fairway into a thick clump of gorse. When he gets to the spot, he finds his ball perched a foot off the ground, being blown back and forth in the wind like a pendulum. From there, he hits a low 6-iron into The Eyes, a bunker 140-yards out from the green. Bad, again, with worse to come. As he addresses the ball, the lip of the bunker is higher than his trademark hat.

Although he has a decent lie, it is comparable to hitting up a hillside: Snead needs the ball to climb straight up and then sail 150 yards. Daunted, but amazingly still not undone, he grabs a 9-iron and swings, following through as high as he can. The ball shaves the grass at the lip of the bunker, skies high, carries well, and finally comes to rest about 20 feet from the green. From there, Snead two-putts for the most welcome six of his life. Fully armed, now, with a gallows-like confidence that he has weathered the worst, Snead fashions a four-shot victory.

SAM SNEAD

Tournament: 1954 Masters

Site: Augusta National

Defining Moment: Final Round and Playoff

It was the last great Masters match-up of rivals Ben Hogan and Snead, who were both born in 1912, whose careers paralleled one another's, and whose greatest rivalries took place on the grounds of Augusta National. Between 1949 and 1953, Snead and Hogan combined to win the tournament four times, including the three years leading up to 1954. The two were tied, 2-2, in Masters victories, but, for a time, all eyes were on an amateur named Billy Joe Patton. Patton leads the field through 36 holes, drops five behind Hogan going into the final round, then makes a late charge.

Though Patton doesn't catch Hogan, his rally contributs to the undoing of Snead's archrival. Hearing the cheers from the gallery, Hogan learns that Patton has scored an ace on the 6th hole and birdied the eighth and ninth. But unaware that Patton has carded a seven on 13, Hogan makes an uncharacteristic error in judgement on the 11th, hitting into the water on an attempt for the flag instead of laying up. The decision probably costs him the title outright.

Though he beats Patton by a stroke, Hogan ends tied with Snead, and the two face off in a playoff. For nine holes there is nothing separating them. Then, Snead chips in at the 10th, Hogan gets the stroke back at the 11th and Snead edges back in front on 13. A single stroke separates them at 16, where Hogan has the better tee shot, but comes up short on a five-foot putt. He takes the 18th, but Snead wins the playoff, 70 to 71, in the last of their Masters duels.

ANIKKA SORENSTAM

Tournament: 1995 U.S. Women's Open
Site: The Broadmoor
Defining Moment: Final Round

The U.S. Women's Open is the oldest and most prestigious women's professional golf tournament and the one that should be most nerve-wracking, but on eight occasions a player's first win on the LPGA tour has come in an Open. At the 50th U.S. Women's Open championship in 1995,

Meg Mallon enters the final round with a solid three-stroke lead and has experience (1991 Open and LPGA championships) on her side, but 24-year old Annika Sorenstam, who has been making her way up the leaderboards in her third full year on the LPGA Tour, is in contention, and, what's more, she hasn't yet won on the LPGA Tour.

Mallon's three-shot lead is gone after the fourth hole, and it's almost anyone's tournament. Sorenstam makes a bid with four birdies and seems able to coast to victory coming in, with a three-stroke lead over Mallon, but she is going to have to demonstrate the will of a champion. She finds a greenside bunker on the 15th and makes bogey. The lead over Mallon is down to two. On the par-three sixteenth, a weak approach leaves her 45 feet away from the pin, and she takes three putts to get there. Her lead is down to one and she needs a victory stroke.

On the 544-yard par-five 17th, the long-hitting Sorenstam has a proper stage to showcase her talent. But she drives into the right rough. Then, trying to reach the green with an iron, she catches the long grass and sends the ball skidding across the fairway into the left rough, over 150 yards out. Her approach finishes hole high, but off the green, and she chips six feet past the hole. Sorenstam makes her putt for par and also pars the 18th for a 68 and an aggregate 278.

Sorenstam sweats it out in the clubhouse: Mallon, two groups back, misses a 12-footer for birdie on the par-three sixteenth, lays up well in front of the green on the 17th but her chip shot goes astray and she settles for a two-putt par. On 18, a brilliant four-iron from 180 yards rolls to within 15 feet, but she pulls the putt left. No one catches Sorenstam—her victory comes about by playing the best final round of the field, and she becomes the ninth woman to have a U.S. Open as her first win. She will repeat the triumph in 1996 in much more dominant fashion.

JEROME TRAVERS

Tournament: 1915 U.S. Open
Site: Baltusrol
Defining Moment: Final Round, 10th and 11th Holes

Travers' U.S. Open in 1915 would be his last major tournament. Frustrated by trying to make ends meet as an amateur and beaten later that year in a tournament by his arch-rival, Walter Travis, Travers retired from golf at 28. He had already won four U.S. Amateur titles and missed a fifth in a final loss to Francis Ouimet in 1914. He mysteriously dropped out of amateur competition for a few years when he was at the top of his game, and there were rumors of drinking problems. The match play format of the Amateur seemed to favor his character: he thrived in direct competition and had much less success in stroke play. On the final back nine in the 1915 Open he seemed to be competing only with himself.

Travis enters the final round atop the leaderboard, but there are five players bunched behind him within two strokes. Travers is out in 39 and begins to fret over his game. Always erratic from the tee, he decides to go with a driving iron on 10 and promptly whacks the ball out of bounds (not a penalty stroke at that time). His second drive on the 314-yard hole ends up in the rough, leaving a tricky shot to a green surrounded by water, but he turns the trick with a high floater that plops on the green and rests two feet from the hole, then taps in for a lead-preserving par. His next tee shot finds heavy rough, and he seems on the brink of losing command, but he pulls out a high approach that lands just in front of the green, then pitches and putts for another saving par. Twice getting himself out of trouble that he created steadies Travers, and he pars the three remaining holes for a one-stroke victory. And it's a rousing triumph, as Travers' fans from his nearby hometown of New York raise him to their shoulders and carry him to the clubhouse. Yet Travers retires later that year and remains the only Open champion not to defend his title.

LEE TREVINO

Tournament: 1972 British Open
Site: Muirfield
Defining Moment: Third Round, 16th, 17th Holes

Trevino would win his second British Open title by one stroke over Jack Nicklaus, but it was Tony Jacklin who was matching the Merry Mex for two days and seemed ready to move ahead late in round three. Distracted by a loosened grip on the 16th tee, then flustered by a TV cameraman's movement on the 17th, Trevino found the concentration and moxie to pull off a pair of miraculous shots and remain in the lead.

Trevino pushes his 6-iron approach shot to 16 into a bunker and a treacherous downhill lie, 30 feet from the cup. He explodes out of the sand, and the ball bounces once on the green and skips into the cup. On the 17th tee, unnerved by the cameraman, he hits into a fairway bunker, hits out, then pulls a 3-wood into a hill of heavy rough, 50 feet short and left of the green; Trevino then wedges through the green and several feet up a grassy bank. Jacklin stands to gain at least one shot, maybe two and possibly three. But Trevino steps up to his ball, gives it a nudge, and watches it flop onto the edge of the green, trickle forward, and drop smack into the center of the cup for a par five.

Stunned, Jacklin, who faces a 20-foot birdie putt, three-putts for a bogey. Trevino, faced with losing three strokes, has gained one.

BOB TWAY

Tournament: 1986 PGA Championship
Site: Inverness
Defining Moment: Final Round, 18th Hole

Ahead by four strokes with nine to play, Greg Norman looked like a winner and would later say that he felt comfortable. And why not? He'd played the first three rounds in 65, 68, 69, and, for a few missed putts, would've been even further ahead. Ever the picture of composure, Norman, who was paired with Tway, seemed totally unaffected, too, that his Sunday round had been delayed a day by heavy rains on the first hole.

Then, things began to change, so suddenly as they always seem to do. Norman takes a six on 11, Tway birdies 13, Norman drops a third stroke on 14, and just that fast the two are tied. They are still tied for the lead at 18, with Norman just off the green in two (he'd pitched on, but with such fierce backspin that the ball dragged back to the fringe). Tway, already the winner of three tournaments in his only second year on the Tour, is deep in the rough off the tee and can only manage to get his ball to the bunker just below the green on his second shot.

Most assume that Tway is beaten as he screws his feet into the sand for his third shot, hoping to save par and for Norman to falter. His next shot, instead, sends a dagger into Norman's heart. With head down and a precise swing, Tway holes the shot for a birdie three. The win for Tway adds yet another entry to long list of miraculous shots or comebacks that have plagued Norman throughout his career.

HARRY VARDON

Tournament: 1896 British Open
Site: Muirfield
Defining Moment: Final Round, 18th Hole

Harry Vardon was among the greatest contributors to the game: he promoted the overlapping grip (or Vardon Grip) that became most commonly used, and as a member of the Great Triumverate, he dominated golf with J.H. Taylor and James Braid from the mid 1890s until World War II. His tours of the United States helped popularize the game, and he participated in three famous Opens: he was the chief figure of interest and won the 1900 Open as part of a 65-match whirlwind swing through the States, where he posted 52 victories; the 1913 Open was a turning point for golf in America, when little-known amateur Francis Ouimet beat the 43-year-old Vardon and Ted Ray in a playoff; and in 1920 he was playing for victory in the final round at Inverness when a stiff wind came lashing through and proved too much—he was 50-years-old and had been treated years before for tuberculosis—the gathering storm affected his play. Vardon had many great victories, beginning with his first British Open triumph in 1896, where he got by with a little help from a friend.

In 1896, Taylor is the two-time defending champ and is up by six after two rounds, but Vardon cuts it to three after 3 rounds and is tied with Taylor coming to 18 in the final round; Taylor has finished, Vardon needs four to win, five to tie. The Muirfield finishing hole is long (equivalent to a par 5) with an elevated green guarded by a trough of a bunker, where a sheer wall rises up to the overhanging lip of the green. A good drive still leaves Vardon 200 yards away; he debates whether or not to go for the green and victory, while landing short and in the bunker will be catastrophic. He continues to think it over—checks the wind, rechecks the distance, and weighs the risks: make a stand here or lay up and play for a playoff. He can't decide. But he spots a friend up ahead about 20 yards in front of the bunker tapping his toe to indicate a good area to lay up. Vardon agrees, lays up, and gets in with a tie.

The significance of the decision is revealed in the playoff, which Vardon leads by two on the 18th. Taylor faces the same predicament Vardon had, only the option is gone—he has to go for the green. Taylor lets loose his best shot and it sails well but descends and knocks against the wall of the bunker; he ends up taking a six and loses by four stokes to Vardon.

KEN VENTURI

Tournament: 1964 U.S. Open
Site: Congressional Country Club
Defining Moment: Final Round

Ken Venturi burst onto the professional golf scene in the mid-1950s when, as a brash young rookie, he made a habit of regularly challenging the tour's seasoned veterans. It worked—he won 10 tournaments in his first four years. But Venturi suffered a pinched nerve in his side early in the 1962 season, a condition that was to plague him for many years and at one point almost paralyzed the right side of his body. After undergoing every kind of treatment imaginable, he spent two years trying to rebuild his game from the grip up. Upon re-entering the pro tour in 1964, he finished in a tie for fifth in the Thunderbird Open and then qualified for the U.S. Open at Congressional Country Club, then the longest course in the history of that tournament.

The biggest factor in the 1964 Open, however is not the course's length but the heat. Temperatures in Washington soar well into the 90s, with plenty of humidity. Venturi shoots a 72 in the first round, tied with Jack Nicklaus and four shots back of Arnold Palmer, who leads the field with an opening-round 68. On the second day of the Open, Venturi turns in a score of 70; Palmer shoots 69, and Tommy Jacobs jumps into the lead with a 64, putting him one stroke ahead of Palmer. As is not uncommon at the time, the last 36 holes of the tournament are to be shot on the final day, a day when the thermometer is hovering at 100 degrees. Palmer, in trouble all the way, shoots a 75 in the morning, while Jacobs hits 70; despite the heat, Venturi moves to within two strokes of the leader with an unbelievable 66. But Venturi has not eaten breakfast and has neglected to take his salt tablets. By lunchtime, he is practically unconscious. The head of the USGA assigns a doctor to look after the stricken Venturi. The physician gives him tea and salt tablets and orders him to bed between rounds.

Venturi starts the final round with the doctor at his side, administering ice bags and keeping a close watch on his patient. At times it seemed that Venturi will pass out, but he not only plays the round, he plays it brilliantly. He pars the first five holes, bogeys the sixth, but then comes back with a birdie on the seventh. At the same time, Jacobs is faltering, going three over par in the first two holes and taking bogeys on the ninth and tenth. Venturi strokes an 18-foot putt for birdie on 13, which puts him four strokes in the lead. By the time he reaches 18, he is in bad shape, stumbling and almost falling twice. But he pars the hole from 10 feet, holding on to win the Open before heading back to the clubhouse and collapsing. The next year, before the 1965 U.S. Open, the USGA concluded that the 36-hole final-round could be dangerous for golfers and certainly did nothing for the quality of play. From that year on, the 72-hole championship was spread out over four days, rather than three.

LANNY WADKINS

Tournament: 1977 PGA Championship
Site: Pebble Beach
Defining Moment: Final Round, 18th Hole

Three former U.S. Amateur champions battle during the final round of the 1977 PGA Championship. Gene Littler, who won the Amateur in 1953 while in the Navy, has led since the first round and is up by five strokes with 9 holes to play, but Lanny Wadkins is hot, having scored two eagles on the front nine. Wadkins was the 1970 Amateur champ, which he won in a thriller by a stroke over Tom Kite. Jack Nicklaus, Amateur champion in 1959 and in 1961 when he won at this same Pebble Beach course, is making a late charge. Littler's resume also features the 1954 U.S. Open, which he lost by one stroke as an amateur, the 1961 Open, which he won by one stroke, and the 1970 Masters, where he finished runner-up in a playoff; Nicklaus's resume is simply the best ever for a professional golfer; Wadkins hasn't won anything in four years.

Littler has a five-stroke lead coming in, but the next six holes are his undoing, as he loses the lead to Nicklaus after the 15th. Wadkins, playing steady up ahead, finds himself a stroke off the pace. Littler's and Nicklaus' fortunes reverse on 17, as Nicklaus bogeys to fall one back and Littler pars for the lead. Up ahead on the par-5 18th, which Nicklaus calls the greatest finishing hole in golf, Wadkins has to come up with some magic.

Wadkins hits a sharp drive that opens up possibilities. His next shot carries well, almost reaching the green, and he's able to get up and down in two, finishing with a birdie and a 282 total; Littler pars and matches the 282, but Nicklaus' par leaves him a stroke shy of the playoff, which Wadkins wins on the third extra hole.

TOM WATSON

Tournament: 1977 British Open
Site: Turnberry
Defining Moment: Final Round

Some consider it the greatest head-to-head match up in golf history—Watson, the heir to the golfing throne, against Jack Nicklaus, the king who refuses to abdicate. So locked in struggle were they, that the rest of the field seemed a memory. Indeed, Hubert Green, who finished a distant third, called himself "the winner of the other tournament."

Both shoot opening-round 68s, leaving them two strokes behind the leader, John Schroeder. Both shoot 70s in the second round, putting them a stroke behind Roger Maltbie, the leader after 36 holes. Both shoot 65s on the third day and share the lead, three strokes ahead of the field.

On the final day, Nicklaus quickly pulls ahead of Watson by two after two holes and by three after

four, but Watson gains them back by the 8th hole, then falls back by one at the turn. Nicklaus goes up by two at the 12th. Watson gets one stroke back at 14. At the par-3, 15th, Nicklaus reaches the green while Watson is just off in parched grass, He chooses to putt from that lie, 60 feet out, sending a firm hit rolling onto the green, straight at the hole —it hits the flagstick and drops in for a tying birdie. On the par-5, 17th hole, Watson's approach reaches the green and settles within 15 feet of the cup, while Nicklaus comes up short. However, Nicklaus' pitch rolls to within five feet of the cup, while Watson misses an eagle opportunity. Nicklaus fails to negotiate his five-footer, and Watson takes the lead by one with a birdie. Then, Nicklaus gets himself in serious trouble, finding the long grass with his drive on 18. Watson has an excellent drive and follows it with a stunning, 7-iron approach that stops within two feet of the cup. Nicklaus uses an 8-iron to tear through the tall grass and floats one to the green, where it holds about 30 feet from the cup.

All but defeated, Nicklaus has given himself a chance and follows it up by holing the 30-footer. Watson sinks his short putt, which suddenly seems longer than two feet, and matches Nicklaus' birdie —besting him in the round, and the tournament, with a 65.

TOM WATSON

Tournament: 1982 U.S. Open
Site: Pebble Beach Golf Links
Defining Moment: Final Round, 17th hole

The 1982 U.S. Open mirrored the 1977 British Open when it came down to a monumental battle between Watson and Jack Nicklaus; the pair provided one of the most dramatic and thrilling finishes in Open history. Nicklaus, who had won four Opens, including one at Pebble Beach in 1972, had played some of the best golf of his career on this course. Watson had never won the tournament in eight attempts, but by all accounts he was at the top of his game and was primed for victory.

Both men play steady golf through the first three rounds, and on the last day Watson finds himself tied for the lead with a total of 212, while Nicklaus is three strokes back at 215. Nicklaus starts off the final round with a bogey but then sinks a long putt on the 3rd hole for a birdie, which sets off a string of four more birdies followed by a bogey on the eighth. He finishes the front nine one stroke behind the leader, Bill Rogers, amd tied with Watson, who had started the day at four under par and is still four-under. At this point in the round, Rogers begins a downward slide, and it becomes a two-man match. Nicklaus three-putts the 11th green, leaving Watson one stroke in the lead. But on the 16th Watson misses the fairway for the first time that day, landing his tee shot in a fairway bunker a foot away from its vertical wall. He is forced to hit out sideways, wasting a stroke and goes into the final two holes tied with Nicklaus.

Watson walks to the 17th tee just as Nicklaus is leaving the 18th green, the deadlock intact. The 209-yard par-3, 17th at Pebble Beach is one of the most famous holes in all of golf. The green is extremely wide, very shallow from front to back, and devilishly guarded by bunkers, rocks, and the ocean. Watson hooks his 2-iron and ends up pin-high but eight feet left of the green, in very thick rough. He opens the face of his sand wedge and cuts under and across the ball, which rises only two feet, lands on the edge of the green, follows the contour of the putting surface, and rolls all the way into the cup for a birdie and the lead.

Watson, only needing a par on the 548-yard 18th to win the tournament, tees off with a 3-wood, lays up with a 7-iron to the center of the fairway, and hits a solid 9-iron to the green, 20-feet from the pin. All he wants to do was get close and tap it in. But, in fact, he sinks the long putt for a two-stroke win.

KARRIE WEBB

Tournament: 1996 LPGA Tour Championship
Site: Desert Inn Golf Course
Defining Moment: Final Round, 16th Hole

It was fitting that the fiftieth anniversary year of the women's professional golf tour should end with a historic event. The women's tour, as we now know it, began in 1946 with a few scattered events and the first U.S. Women's Open, all organized by the Women's Professional Golf Association. The fledgling tour was in trouble by 1947, but three prominent female professionals—Babe Zaharias, Patty Berg, and Louise Suggs, along with Babe's personal manager, Fred Corcoran—formed the Ladies Professional Golf Association in 1948, and it gradually took hold and prospered. It wasn't until 1981 that a women attained $1 million in career earnings, but by 1996 two women had a chance to earn that much in a single year. It was somehow fitting, as well, that the contending golfers were not American—symbolizing the international flavor in players and tournament sites that makes the LPGA Tour a world event.

The two contenders for the million-dollar honor are Laura Davies, who has won her third and fourth Majors in 1996 and has spent a portion of the season on the LPGA European Tour, and Karrie Webb, a *rookie* from Australia. After two rounds they are tied at 139, one-stroke behind Juli Inkster, but Webb takes command during the third round with a 65 and opens up a three-stroke lead over an honor-roll host of competitors—Nancy Lopez, Brandee Burton, Davies and Inkster. Lopez shoots 66 in the final round, Burton, Davies and Inkster all shoot 67s, and Kelly Robbins, who entered the round four strokes back shoots a 65, all in contention at the turn.

The rookie responds to the challenge from those playing ahead by birdieing the 10th, 11th, and 13th holes and reaches the par-5 16th hole with a two-stroke lead. The hole becomes a reflection of Webb's skill and determination. She launches a long, straight fairway drive, followed by an approach that reaches the green, followed by a putt for an eagle. Webb matches the low-round (65) for the day, tying the course record, and wins the tournament by four strokes.

JOYCE WETHRED

Tournament: 1929 Ladies British Open Amateur Championship
Site: St. Andrews
Defining Moment: Final Round

Golf seemed to come easy and naturally for Joyce Wethred. She started playing the sport at age 17 during a family holiday after seeing the excitement with which her brother, Roger, and his friends approached the game. Roger Wethred was already on his way to becoming one of the great British amateur players. On the course she was a picture of calm and fluidity, with an ability to become absorbed in the circumstances. That seeming coolness masked a deep intensity: she usually needed a week or two to wind down once a major tournament was concluded.

Karrie Webb thanks the gallery at the LPGA Tour Championship. Webb won an amazing three tournaments during in rookie year in 1996.

The intensity and the fact that she won almost everything possible for a woman golfer at that time led her into early retirement at age 24, when she could distance herself from the rigors of competition and enjoy the sport again. From 1919 through 1925 she had won four English Amateurs and two Ladies British Open Amateur

Championships, the final Open coming in 1925 over the great American amateur Glenna Collett Vare at Troon, where she shot the final 10 holes in six-under par. Wethred came out of retirement to play in the 1929 Ladies British Open Amateur at St. Andrews, and again she meets Vare, then a four-time U.S. Women's Amateur champion, in the final match that is billed as the unofficial world championship.

As in the 1925 match, Vare is in excellent form, shooting a 34 on the first nine of 36 holes and taking a five-hole lead. Then Wethred gets hot. Beginning on the 12th hole, when she cuts the lead to four, and continuing through the front nine on the final day of play, Wethred takes command of the match: over the stretch of 18 holes, covering the back nine of the first round and the front nine of the second, Wethred shoots an excellent 73 on the Old Course. The final nine are anticlimactic, as Wethred takes the championship, 3 and 1.

TIGER WOODS

Tournament: 1996 U.S. Amateur
Site: Pumpkin Ridge Golf Club
Defining Moment: Final Round, 17th hole

In 1994 Eldrick "Tiger" Woods became the youngest U.S. Amateur champion, when he took the title as a 17-year old at TPC Sawgrass in Florida. He continued to dominate the amateur scene in 1995, when he was the first player in twelve years to successfully defend the crown. But no one had ever won three U.S. Amateurs in a row—not even the great Bobby Jones.

The media was all but handing the 1996 Amateur to Woods before the tournament even started. But University of Florida sophomore Steve Scott had other ideas. Scott took a three-hole lead after the first nine of the 36-hole final round. He increased his lead to five after eighteen holes.

Tiger Woods begins one of his patented, final-round charges with a birdie at the 16th hole. But it is a spectacular 35-foot putt on the 17th that ties the match and forces a playoff. In the playoff, Woods' signature length off the tee gives him a huge advantage on the 463-yard, par-4 9th hole; his drive lands a full 70 yards ahead of Scott's shot. But both players land their second shots on the green, and both two-putt. On the final hole, a 194-yard Par 3, Woods hits a six-iron within seven feet of the hole, while Scott catches some nasty rough. He fails to get up and down, and Woods two-putts to win his record third straight U.S. Amateur Championship.

MICKEY WRIGHT

Tournament: 1964 U.S. Women's Open
Site: San Diego Country Club
Defining Moment: Final Round, 18th Hole

The San Diego Country Club is home for Wright—where she learned to master the game, and now she's coming home a celebrated champion. Playing a familiar course with hometown fans and family rooting her on, it almost seems foretold that she will win. That and the unprecedented streak she's been playing for years: she has won thirty-nine tournaments over the four previous seasons, leading the tour each year, and has won three previous Opens. But her place at the top of the LPGA is being threatened by Ruth Jessen. Wright has recorded eight tournament wins in 1964 to Jensen's six, the two-win difference coming in playoffs taken by Wright. Now Wright's coming to the final hole needing a birdie to beat Jensen and a par to tie and force another playoff.

The 18th is a 395-yard par 4; Wright hits a 2-iron approach, trying for that birdie win, but it's seeming disaster instead, as the ball bleeds into a bunker on the right side of the green. As she reaches the bunker she discovers why the crowd's groan at her shot continues to murmur: the ball rests at a severe downhill lie at the extreme right of the bunker, with the pin about 35 yards away near the very top edge of the green. If she doesn't catch the ball well it will die short of the hole, as will her chances, and if she clips it too well the ball will roll past the pin and off the green, where another bunker waits. Standing parallel to the slope with the ball at left heel, Wright whacks and the explosion is high and soft—the ball floats, almost suspended, beyond the sand shrapnel, falls lightly and stops five feet from the hole. From the silence after the clubhead struck the ball to its fall and rest on the green, the crowd watches and now it roars with delight. Wright pars the hole, then wins the championship in a playoff, shooting 70 to Jessen's 72.

BABE ZAHARIAS

Tournament: 1954 US Women's Open
Site: Salem Country Club
Defining Moment: Final Round

Babe Zaharias' athletic accomplishments are legendary: gold medals in track and field at the 1932 Olympics, impressive showings as a baseball player and as a long driver on golf exhibition tours with the most famous male golfers of the time. She won the U.S. and British Amateur Championships (the first American to win the British Women's Amateur) and has thirty-one tournament titles on the LPGA Tour she helped found, including two U.S. Women's Opens. In 1953, however, she was diagnosed with cancer and underwent an operation and extended recuperation. She's back in 1954, hoping that her game is still intact and that the cancer has stopped. She still has her athletic gift, but it would be her last Open (she died in 1956) and she gave a commanding final performance.

Babe is in true form. After two rounds she's at 143, seven strokes ahead of the field. It is one of her most dominant performances, from first tee to final green—long drives followed by strong irons followed by firm putts. Her final round 75 is simply an extended victory tour, as she finishes up twelve strokes ahead of the field.

FUZZY ZOELLER

Tournament: 1979 Masters
Site: Augusta National
Defining Moment: Final Round and Playoff

Fuzzy Zoeller, a Masters rookie who'd just shot a final-round 70, was in the clubhouse, now, nursing a beer, watching Ed Sneed complete what most had assumed would be his inevitable victory. After all, Sneed led by five going into the day and still led by three with three holes to play. But still led means that there was still some golf to play. And Zoeller, who'd trailed by six going into the final round, watched as things began to unravel.

First, Sneed took three putts on 16, then another three on 17. Now, at 18, he needed par to win; Tom Watson, his playing partner, needed a birdie to tie. Sneed's six-foot putt stops on the lip of the cup and hangs there, like a cold kiss. Watson tied him. Suddenly, amazingly, Zoeller, resurrected by Sneed's final-round 76, was back among the living and into sudden death.

All three men have tough birdie putts on the 10th—the first extra hole—but miss. And Sneed makes an heroic attempt on a recovery shot from a bunker on 11, nearly holing the shot. Zoeller follows a huge drive with an 8-iron shot to the green, then putts the tournament-winning birdie, becoming the first man to win the Masters on his first try since the first man to win the first Masters.

Bibliography

The following sources were consulted to form the list of 100 great moments in tournament play:

Books: *Down the Nineteenth Fairway: A Golfing Anthology*, by Peter Dobreiner 1983; *Following Through: Writings on Golf*, by Herbert Warren Wind, expanded edition, 1995; *Golf Anecdotes*, by Robert T. Sommers, 1995; *Golf's Greatest Shots by the World's Greatest Players*, by Nevin Gibson and Tommy Kouzmanoff, 1971; *Golf's Supershots: How the Pros Played Them— How You Can Play Them*, by George Peper, 1982; *Grand Slam Golf*, by *. 1992; *Great Moments in Golf*, by Dave Klein, 1971; *Guiness Golf: Record Facts & Champions*, Donald Steel, editor, 1987; *The Official U.S. Open Almanac*, by Salvatore Johnson, 1995. **Magazines:** Various issues of *Golf, Golf Digest, Inside Sports, The New York Times, Sports Illustrated,* and *USA Today.*

16

GOLF AND POPULAR CULTURE

"Stick out your fanny, Mr. President."

—Sam Snead's friendly advice to President Eisenhower.

THEY ALSO PLAY(ED) THE GAME

AGNEW, SPIRO T.
U.S. Vice President, 1968–1973

Agnew and Gerald Ford, the man who succeeded him as Vice-President, often played in celebrity Pro-Am tournaments, where both established reputations as golfers to watch, or watch out for. Tales of their errant shots and the spectators they found became regular items in news reports and provided endless material for stand-up comics. The veeps even got into the stand-up act: "Sanders won $200 in the tournament, and that just paid for the medical attention he required," said Agnew, following a round in the Bob Hope Desert Classic in which pro golfer Doug Sanders was hit with one of Agnew's shots.—*Golf Digest*, 1970.

ANTON, SUSAN
Model, actress

Anton starred in a golf movie (*Spring Fever*, 1983), sports a 16-handicap, and once outdrove John Daly during a pro-am.

"There are just so many levels of golf. Every time you get out there, I think you learn a new life lesson. You've got to play what the moment is—you can't be ahead or behind, you've really got to appreciate things at the time you're there. Also, I love that you always need to look around and see where you are. It's the only game that you play in God's arena. Golf teaches you patience and acceptance; you never know what the day's going to bring you."—from *Conversations with Ann Liguori*, The Golf Channel.

BARKLEY, CHARLES
Basketball superstar

Barkley is known as a ferocious competitor and an outspoken, eminently quotable athlete, chasing an elusive NBA championship in 1996-97 with the Houston Rockets.

On what he likes about golf: "There's nobody here bugging me, asking for autographs and stuff. Most of the people at these country clubs are stuck up so they leave me alone. I have a good time."—from *Conversations with Ann Liguori*, The Golf Channel.

BEHRENS, SAM
Actor

"When Harry (Belafonte, his father in law), found out that I was playing golf he sat me down and warned me in his Godfather voice, 'I'm warning you, I have friends that gave up everything to play golf.' He was really concerned. But you know what they say; if you can't beat them, join them."—from *Conversations with Ann Liguori*, The Golf Channel.

BELAFONTE, SHARI
Actress

She and husband Sam Behrens planned a cross-country trip with a route that would allow them to play top golf courses along the way. "At one point we thought we would be moving back east because Sam had done a pilot and the question was whether we'd be picking everything up and moving. We actually started planning how we would plot golf courses along the way in order to get across the country."—from *Conversations with Ann Liguori*, The Golf Channel.

BENNY, JACK
Comedian

Benny was a casual golfer who reportedly made money on golf courses by borrowing quarters to mark his lies, and then keeping the quarters. He wasn't totally committed to golf:

"Give me golf clubs, the fresh air and a beautiful partner and you can keep my golf clubs and the fresh air."

BRODIE, JOHN
Pro football player and golfer

The former San Francisco 49er quarterback great joined the Senior Tour not long after his retirement from the grid iron. He won more than $600,000 on the Senior circuit and then turned his focus to celebrity, pro-am, and charity tournaments.

"I never thought golf was a game of the most intelligent people in the world or the guys who are winning every week wouldn't be winning."—from *Conversations with Ann Liguori*, The Golf Channel.

BUSH, GEORGE
U.S. President, 1988–1992

Bush is a good golfer, and in 1996 he won a round of golf with ex-president Gerald Ford and Bush's successor, Bill Clinton.

The Bush family has strong ties to organized golf. The trophy for the Walker Cup was donated by George Herbert Walker, the maternal grandfather of Bush. Bush's father, Prescott Bush, was a United States senator, and before that he was a USGA-sanctioned referee. Prescott Bush made a controversial ruling in favor of Bobby Jones late in the final round of the 1930 U.S. Open at the Interlachen Country Club that may have saved Jones a stroke or two. Jones' drive at the long par 3 (262 yards), 17th hole, veered right, hit off a tree and then couldn't be found. Jones turned to Bush for a ruling, and Bush concluded that the ball landed in a dried up swamp that was filled with reeds. He permitted Jones to drop with a penalty stroke in the fairway—a good lie in a good place for such a bad shot. The swamp hadn't been listed as a hazard, so many people felt Jones should have been made to hit again from the tee. Jones won the tournament by two strokes as the third victory of his grand slam year.

CAPONE, AL
American gangster

Not surprisingly, Capone is one of the few golfers who ever took a shot (as opposed to making one) on the golf course. He always carried a pistol in his golf bag. When playing the Burnham Woods course near Chicago one day in 1928, his caddie dropped the bag and the pistol went off, wounding Capone in the foot.

CARMICHAL, HOAGY
Musician

After an ace at Pebble Beach: "I think I've got the idea now."

CARNEGIE, ANDREW
American Industrialist

The largest business deal in American history at one point was arranged at the St. Andrews Golf Club in Yonkers, New York. Andrew Carnegie, who golfed regularly, was playing with Charles Schwab, who was making a bid to purchase Carnegie Steel. During the round, Schwab worked on convincing Carnegie to sell his firm and when Carnegie seemed ready Schwab asked Carnegie's price. After playing a few shots and thinking about it, Carnegie came up with a figure and jotted it down on a scorecard—$480 million. Schwab agreed, and such was the birth of U.S. Steel.

> "The devoted golfer is an anguished soul who has learned a lot about putting just as an avalanche victim has learned a lot about snow."
>
> —author Dan Jenkins

CARSON, JOHNNY
Entertainer

Carson always ended his monologues on the *The Tonight Show* with a golf swing as the band began playing. However, he didn't play or watch golf nearly as much as he did tennis, his favorite sport.

CHURCHILL, WINSTON
British Prime Minister

In addition to being one of Great Britain's most beloved politicians and a member of an association of druid enthusiasts, Churchill was a fairly avid golfer who played primarily for enjoyment, rather than competition.

"Playing golf was like chasing a quinine pill around a pasture."

"Golf is a game whose aim is to hit a very small ball into an even smaller hole, with weapons singularly ill-designed for the purpose."

CLINTON, BILL
United States President, 1992—present

Clinton sports a 13-handicap and plays regularly. In a major policy decision, he had the putting green restored on the White House grounds; it was originally installed for President Eisenhower. The restoration was done by renowned golf architect Robert Trent Jones, Jr., a graduate of Yale, who has consulted with Clinton on international economic matters.

> "Golf is an open exhibition of overweening ambition, courage deflated by stupidity, skill soured by a whiff of arrogance . . . These humiliations are the essence of the game."
>
> — Alistair Cooke

Before attending a trade summit in Asia in 1996, Clinton visited Australia and played a round of golf with Greg Norman. Clinton also used Norman's quick and sudden fall from a seemingly insurmountable final-round lead at the 1996 Masters as an example to inspire his aides to continue working diligently during the presidential campaign even as polls showed that Clinton had a healthy lead over Bob Dole.

Hillary Clinton often golfs with her husband but hasn't taken to the game. "I have to confess, I have just never gotten there," she said. She has taken two sets of golf lessons. P.G. Wodehouse once remarked that the ideal wife is one who would spend the winter nights listening to her husband recounting his golfing for the year, round by round, hole by hole. "(Bill's) exhilarated from playing 18 holes. He tells me about every hole he's played in great detail."—Interview with Michael Jackson of Los Angeles radio station KABC.

CONNERY, SEAN
Actor

Connery is an excellent golfer and acted in one of the finer golfing scenes in film (see the review of *Goldfinger* in the *Golf in Film* section). He teamed with Hale Irwin to win the 1996 Lexus Pro-Am Challenge, and regularly plays well in the Pebble Beach Pro-Am.

Connery is a member of the Royal and Ancient, plays St. Andrews regularly, where he always carries his own clubs, and participated in the annual golf marathon at the Old Course. "I played 14 straight days at St. Andrews in the autumn meeting (in 1996). The meeting lasts for 21 days and consists of 36 holes a day. I've played in the event every year since I became a member at St. Andrews over 20 years ago."—*USA Today*, December 23, 1996.

COOKE, ALISTAIR
Historian and television host

Cooke is an excellent golf writer, whose recounting of the 1967 Crosby Tournament ("King Lear at Pebble Beach") played in blasts of rain and wind is an often anthologized piece. He is also a decent player and witty observer on the game.

"You must expect anything in golf. A stranger comes through, he's keen for a game, he seems affable enough, and on the eighth fairway he turns out to be an idiot."

"Golf was just what the Scottish character had been seeking for centuries, namely, a method of self-torture."

COOPER, ALICE
Rock star

Alice (his stage name) is the King of Shock Rock, who was dominant on the concert tour during the 1970s. He plays in celebrity and pro-am tournaments, sporting an impressive 5-handicap.

"I'm not totally accepted (in the golf world), which is kind of good. I think that that's part of the fun of it—the fact that a lot of the older stodgy guys aren't really around anymore. Golf cuts through lines of everything, it cuts right through social lines. It doesn't matter if you're a hard rocker or a diplomat, when it comes to golf it's the common denominator. Besides, if you can go out there and play well no one can really say anything about you."—from *Conversations with Ann Liguori*, The Golf Channel.

"Golf is hipper now than when I was a kid. When Alice Cooper started playing, the walls were broken down."—Loudon Wainwright, III, *Billboard*, September 14, 1996.

COSTNER, KEVIN
Actor

Costner took to the game when preparing for *The Tin Cup*, arguably the best golf movie ever made, an opinion held by those who feel *Bull Durham* is the best baseball movie. But Costner claims both movies are mostly about relationships: romance, golf, baseball, what more is there to life?

Despite only having played golf a short time, Costner shoots in the 80s. He performed all of Roy McAvoy's swings in *Tin Cup*.

CROSBY, BING
Singer, actor, and golfer

Bing Crosby is in the World Golf Hall of Fame for his work as an ambassador for and promoter of the sport, including helping establish the longest-running annual Pro-Am, which celebrates its 60th anniversary in 1997. Now known as the AT&T Pebble Beach Pro-Am, it still carries the mystique of the Crosby, when Bing brought along a few Hollywood friends to the Rancho Santa Fe to mingle with the pros and have some fun. The Crosby moved to Pebble Beach in 1947.

Crosby was an excellent golfer. He was among 150 golfers who won regional matches and win invitations to compete in the U.S. Amateur Championship qualifying tournament in 1940. The 36-hole tournament at Winged Foot in New York determined the final 64 entrants to the Amateur Championship. Somewhat distracted by a large crowd that came to see him play, Crosby shot an 83 on the first day; he had a 70 going into the final hole of the second round when groups of people broke through restraints and swarmed him. It took police 15 minutes to clear the teeing area and the fairway. Crosby needed an eagle to qualify on that last hole but made it in 7 and missed the cut by 5 strokes.

Crosby always cherished the bronze medallion player badge given to those who reach the U.S. Amateur Championship Qualifying round. After he died, Katherine Crosby, his widow, had the medallion made into a necklace, and in 1981, their son, Nathaniel, wore it around his neck when he played in and won the U.S. Amateur.—*Golf Anecdotes*, Robert T. Sommers.

"Bing Crosby invented the pipe, the shirt worn outside the pants, the cocked hat. He is so rich even his caddies subscribe to *Fortune*." — Bob Hope

DANIELS, JEFF
Actor

The titles of two movies in which Daniels has starred have taken on additional meaning. The Purple Rose Theatre, a venue he owns and operates in his hometown of Chelsea, Michigan, was named after one movie, and he uses another, *Dumb and Dumber*, to describe his golf game, though it's not that bad.

"In airplanes, it's the mile high club. In golf, I don't know what you would call it. But there's a green on the sixth hole at a club near Jackson, Michigan, that is a very special place. I looked at her and said, 'it's you and me on the sixth green.' She was so into it. It was like going to Scotland. You've got to go to Scotland and you've got to make love on the golf course at least once, or otherwise you really can't call yourself a golfer. I really recommend it. I don't know if it's the chemicals they put on the green or something, but it heightens everything. It's really beautiful—golf's equivalent to the mile high club."—from *Conversations with Ann Liguori*, The Golf Channel.

DEDMAN, ROBERT
CEO of ClubCorp International

"There are 168 hours in a week. If you put 56 hours in bed, you still have 112 waking hours out of bed. So, if you spend 80 hours in gainful endeavor, you still have 32 hours to play golf, tennis, and make love, go to church, dance and do all of those things. You can do a whole lot in 32 hours a week if you time-budget it."—from *Conversations with Ann Liguori*, The Golf Channel.

DEVANE, WILLIAM
Actor

Devane practices golf on his ranch, driving out to a field and hitting approaches and pitches back to the lawn.

"I can't get (the ball) to go right to left, but that's about control. But as Gary McCord said, 'Billy listen. You have the perfect golf game; you never have to worry about the left side of the golf course, just the right.' So I aim for the condos and drop it on the fairway."—from *Conversations with Ann Liguori*, The Golf Channel.

EASTOOD, CLINT
Actor

Eastwood is the former mayor of Carmel by the Sea, which is adjacent to Pebble Beach. Eastwood is a member of the Board of Directors for the annual AT&T Pebble Beach Pro-Am.

EBAN, ABBA
Israeli statesman

"Playing the game, I have learned the meaning of humility. It has given me an understanding of the futility of human effort."

EISENHOWER, IKE
U.S. President, 1952–1960

Eisenhower was the most visible presidential golfer, and golfing stories involving him are numerous. He not only had a putting green put in place on the White House grounds, he often practiced putting in the oval office. A favorite course of his was Augusta National, and he was asked once, after a heart attack, what could be done to improve the course. He replied that a particular tree should be removed, an oak on the 17th hole that always seemed to block his approach. Of course, that was the purpose of having the tree there, and it still remains.

Eisenhower once claimed his happiest moment occurred on February 6, 1968, when at age 77 he aced a par 3, 104-yard hole at the Seven Lakes Country Club in Palm Springs, using a 9-iron, for his first and only hole-in-one.

FAIRBANKS, DOUGLAS
Actor

Fairbanks was a strong golfer who often participated in the Gold Vase Tournament, a celebrity charity event. Asked how he performed in the 1930 Gold Vase Tournament: "Like a motorboat: putt, putt, putt, putt."

FARINA, DENNIS
Actor

"I was playing with a friend. I noticed some smoke in the distance when we teed off. I say, 'hey, look, smoke,' and he's like 'don't worry about it.' Well, we're playing and I'd swear the smoke was getting closer. We get to the fifth hole and we're hearing fire engines, we look up and see a helicopter ready to throw water on the fire. The fire is about 15 yards from us at that point, and they're turning the sprinklers on us. It didn't bother us, though, we planned on playing through it. The funny thing was, we were the only ones on the golf course and we were smoking cigars—they thought that we started the fire."—from *Conversations with Ann Liguori*, The Golf Channel.

FIELDS, W.C.
Comedian

Fields was a good golfer, but pretty much approached the game in the same grumbling, wisecracking manner as he did life in general. He offers one of the better cinematic comic turns on golf in *The Golf Specialist* and a smaller sequence in *The Dentist* (see reviews of these movies in the *Golf in Film* section).

On why he carried a bottle of whiskey in his golf bag: "I always keep a supply of stimulants handy in case I see a snake, which I also keep handy."

"W.C. Fields was fond of playing the course sideways with his pal, Oliver Hardy. He liked being in the trees where he could drink without scandalizing the natives."—Jim Murray, *Golf Digest*, 1973.

FORD, GERALD R.
U.S. President, 1973–1976

Ford brought the same grace and style to the course that he displayed when disembarking from airplanes. He never could quite master control of his golfswing and was perhaps best suited to play offensive lineman, as he did at the University of Michigan, where you are supposed to hit people.

"I know I'm getting better at golf because I'm hitting fewer spectators."

"President Ford waits until he hits his first drive to know what course he's playing that day."—Bob Hope.

FRANZ, DENNIS
Actor

"You'd think I'd be a good golfer with how much I like it, but I just don't have the time. When I do I really had a pretty-together game. But it's that whole thing about actors and handicaps. When your handicap is low, then you're not working much and when it gets back up there that means you're too busy to play. It's rising up there so I'm glad on that level. I have an excuse these days."—from *Conversations with Ann Liguori*, The Golf Channel.

FREY, GLEN
Singer

Frey is a best-selling artist with *The Eagles* and as a solo performer. He frequently golfs in celebrity charity events.

"I'm a grinder. And I tell you, what I've learned to do is not to beat myself to death when I'm playing. You really learn a lot about yourself through golf because there are just so many ups and downs. You have to deal with the disappointments all the time. In tennis, you get a second serve; in golf, you are punished for every mistake you make. When I'm skiing I know I can't fly down the slopes like the pros; in tennis when I'm playing I know I'm not returning a 120 mph serve. But when you hit your sand wedge 105 yards and it lands near the pin—now that's the equivalent of a professional shot. It's great."—from *Conversations with Ann Liguori*, The Golf Channel.

GILL, VINCE
Country music star

Gill hosts a celebrity pro-am tournament in Nashville called "The Vinny."

"I have an evil twin that shows up when I play golf, and so I try to compensate for the evil side. Nobody ever sees anything positive about the emotion of anger. All my emotions are pretty much right here on my sleeve, you know, whether I cry, whether I laugh, whether I'm sad, and anger is another one of your emotions. That's the reason I try to do so much nice stuff for folks, raise money and do tournaments, because they know how evil I am on the golf course."—from *Conversations with Ann Liguori*, The Golf Channel.

GIRADOUX, JEAN
Author

"A golf course is the epitome of all that is purely transitory in the universe, a space not to dwell in, but to get over as quickly a possible," *The Enchanted*, 1933.

GLEASON, JACKIE
Comedian

Gleason was a fine golfer and did a good comic turn on golf with Art Carney in an episode of *The Honeymooners*. He also helped organize an promote the Jackie Gleason Inverrary Classic.

Gleason was fond of comparing golf to an unpromising woman: "You know you're not going to wind up with anything but grief, pal, but you can't resist the impulse."—*Golf Digest*, 1977.

GRAHAM, REV. BILLY
Evangelist

Graham has prayed and played golf around the world, but rarely mixes the two: "Prayer never seems to work for me on the golf course. I think this has something to do with my being a terrible putter."

"I never pray on the golf course. Actually, the Lord answers my prayers everywhere except on the course."—*Golf Magazine*, 1970.

GRANT, AMY
Singer

Grant first won fame as singer of Christian music. She was once teamed in a tournament with Alice Cooper, forming the "heaven and hell" twosome.

"To pick up golf in your thirties, which I'm sure a lot of people do, you just don't realize by that time in life you're pretty much doing things you're good at. Why put yourself out? I took a lot of lessons before I went out the first time, and it was so much harder than I dreamed it was going to be . . . (On my first day) I got stuck in a sand trap and couldn't get out. Days later, they sent in food and water."—from *Conversations with Ann Liguori*, The Golf Channel.

GUMBEL, BRYANT
Television host

Gumbel, an excellent golfer, retired from the *Today* show in January of 1997. Previously, he had been a sports host for several events, including golf.

On having killed a seagull with a golf ball on the 17th hole at Pebble Beach in 1994: "The thing I'm always amused about is that people suspect I'm embarrassed. I'm not. I'd be embarrassed if I'd of hooked it into a seagull that was sitting on the ground. I'd be embarrassed if the seagull was sitting on a fence and I sliced it and knocked him off the fence. The shot I hit was pure. The seagull was flying in the center of the fairway. It's one of those zillion-to-one shots. It hit the poor creature and killed it."—from *Conversations with Ann Liguori*, The Golf Channel.

HARDING, WARREN G.
U.S. President

Harding was a fair golfer who loved the game and had a penchant for walking to his ball almost immediately after finishing his swing, regardless of how many others playing with him still had to hit. It backfired once when he played a round with a foursome that included writer Ring Lardner. Lardner's drive hit a tree, severing a branch that fell on Harding.—*Golf Anecdotes*, by Robert T. Sommers.

"I'd give anything to be in your shoes today." —President Harding, presenting the U.S. Open Trophy to Jim Barnes in 1921.

HARRELSON, KEN
Baseball star

Harrelson was a baseball star with the Boston Red Sox who considered giving up his baseball career for a shot at the pro golf circuit.

"In baseball you hit a home run over the right-field fence, the left-field fence, the center-field fence. In golf everything has got to be right over second base."

HARVEY, PAUL
Radio commentator

On artificial-heart-transplant patient Barney Clark: "I've just heard that soon he might be well enough to play golf. Hasn't the man suffered enough?"

"Golf is a game in which you yell Fore, shoot six, and write down five,"—*Golf Digest*, 1979.

HOOTIE AND THE BLOWFISH (DARIUS RUCKER, MARK BRYAN AND DEAN FELBER)
Rock stars

"Playing golf is a prerequisite to joining Hootie and the Blowfish."—Darius Rucker.

HOPE, BOB
Comedian

Bob Hope is a member of the World Golf Hall of Fame. He often carried a golf club around while doing his monologues, particularly in performance tours for American troops stationed overseas. He helped organize and promote the Bob Hope Pro-Am, which is still part of the PGA Tour (see the tournament profile in the Men's Tournament Review/Preview section).

"Hope invented the nonbody turn, the interlocking grip on a money clip, the fast backswing and a good short game—off the tee."—Bing Crosby.

HORNSBY, ROGERS
Baseball player

"When I hit a ball, I want someone else to go chase it."

HUGHES, HOWARD
Businessman

Not surprisingly, Hughes was fanatical when it came to golf. He hired touring pros to give him lessons and played rounds for money and to make business deals.

Hughes was also a great pilot, but once had to land a damaged plane on a golf course. On another occassion, in order to keep a tee time with Katherine Hepburn, Hughes flew a single-engine plane from Santa Barbara to the Bel-Air Country Club in

Los Angeles and landed the plane on the eighth fairway, making the time by five minutes. When the Club's Board of Governors assessed Hughes a fine for the deed, Hughes resigned from the club.

KENNY G
Musician

Kenny G promises to play the sax for the gallery if he makes the cut at Pebble Beach and to serenade his pro partner as he putts.

"When I'm on the golf course I don't think about music. I don't think about anything in my life: I just think about my golf game and enjoy the comraderie—that is the main thing in golf. I come back to my concert refreshed and ready to go. I play my saxophone better now that I'm a golfer."—from *Conversations with Ann Liguori*, The Golf Channel.

KERNS, JOANNA
Actress

"My work as an actress is on the mark when I'm not really thinking about it. It's the same as golf. You take lessons and you have some technique and you practice. Then when you get out to play the game you should just be playing the game, you shouldn't be thinking about any of that other stuff. That's where it's similar to acting. You have to erase everything you're thinking about: just be clear and in the moment and you can usually hit a pretty good shot."—from *Conversations with Ann Liguori*, The Golf Channel.

KING, ALAN
Comedian and actor

"Don't give lessons . . . I go out there, and a guy's hitting the ball like he's playing hockey or polo—he just keeps moving and hitting the ball. All

of a sudden, I whiff the ball and this guy turns to me and says, 'you gotta keep your head balanced and swing slower.' The man can't play; I'm like, 'why are *you* giving me lessons?"—from *Conversations with Ann Liguori*, The Golf Channel.

KNIEVEL, EVEL
Stuntman

Knievel was a dare-devil motorcycle stuntman until 1980; he retired from that career, which included many amazing jumps as well as over three-years recuperation time from injuries. He now plays high-stakes golf games around the world.

"They say we all have two sides to us as human beings. I think it's the serenity I find out here. I love it. I really have gone through quite a change of life since I quit performing. This has been a wonderful thing for me. I love golf. Sometimes when I look at these golf courses I say to myself, 'I just wish I could live another thousand years so I could play every course in the world.' Life's too short."—from *Conversations with Ann Liguori*, The Golf Channel.

KNIGHT, RAY
Cincinnati Reds manager

Knight was a former third baseman who topped his strong career by being named the World Series MVP in the New York Mets' 1986 championship. Knight is married to golfing great Nancy Lopez.

On caddying for Nancy: "Nancy always listened to me in our marriage, and all of a sudden she's treating me like I'm the guy that's from the local . . . whatever. I just all of a sudden didn't feel any respect; one time she asked for a tee and I gave her a pencil. It was just too close.

We're both great competitors, there was just no way it could work. But the thing that really irritated me is that people said she fired me. But she

Nancy Lopez lines up a putt at the Nabisco Dinah Shore Championship

the time. . . . You know how guys check out women to see if they are wearing a wedding ring?—I look to see who has a white left hand and a tanned right hand because I know I have something to talk to them about—golf."

LARDNER, RING
Writer

"One reward golf has given me, and I shall always be thankful for it, is introducing me to some of the world's most picturesque, tireless and bald-faced liars."—*Out of the Bunker and Into the Trees*, 1960.

LEMON, JACK
Actor

Lemmon is one of the crowd favorites at the annual Pebble Beach Pro-Am tournament, where he has failed to make the cut in his 30 tries, but not for lack of trying, or concentration. He was preparing to drive on the 15th tee one year when a scruffy dog broke from the gallery and ran right through his legs during his address. When announcer Jimmy Demaret complimented him on keeping his composure as a dog ran through his legs, Lemmon replied with absolute surprise, "you mean that was a real dog?"

couldn't have fired me because she never paid me anything."—from *Conversations with Ann Liguori*, The Golf Channel.

LADD, CHERYL
Actress

"(Golf) gets under your skin. It really becomes part of your life. It's something I look forward to all

Lemmon took several strokes to reach a green at Pebble Beach, then as reached the green he noticed that a television camera came on to record his putt. He tried to look skillful, reading the green, assessing the break, and whispered to his caddy,

The youngest golfer to score a hole-in-one was 4-year-old Scott Statler, who aced the seventh hole at a Par-3 course in Greensburg, Pennsylvania, in 1962.

"which way do you think she'll break?" The caddy replied, "who cares?"

"I'd rather play *Hamlet* with no rehearsal than play golf on television."

LENDL, IVAN
Tennis great

Lendl, who held the #1 ranking for a record 270 weeks and won every major tournament except Wimbledon, is now a six-handicap lefty golfer on the Celebrity Golf Association tour.

On his first golf outing: "I remember slipping, falling face-down a few times. I figured it's just sitting there, how much easier it must be than a tennis ball. You don't have to chase it."—from *Conversations with Ann Liguori*, The Golf Channel.

LEONARD, SUGAR RAY
Boxing great

Leonard was an Olympic gold medalist and professional champion in five different weight divisions. He started golfing after retiring from boxing (either the third or eighth retirement), already has a hole-in-one (14th at the Las Vegas TPC), and has learned that when he tries to out-muscle the ball, the ball out-muscles him.

"I love the game so much. For me, it's therapy. You challenge yourself . . . there's always room for improvement. There's always room to learn something new. I'm just having a great time. I just wish I found this sport years ago. My life would have been a lot easier, too."—from *Conversations with Ann Liguori*, The Golf Channel.

LINDON, HAL
Actor and singer

Lindon won two Emmys for the *Barney Miller* TV series and a Tony Award, has played clarinet with Leonard Bernstein, sang with the Mormon Tabernacle Choir, and danced with Ginger Rogers, but still feels incomplete: "I wanna make the cut at Pebble Beach."

"I played a course on the Safe Shell Islands—there was cattle grazing between the fairways. If you hooked into the cattle, you left it there. In Malaysia, there were monkeys coming out of the trees. And in Jakarta, there was a sign that said 'Beware of cobras.' I didn't go after my ball there either."—from *Conversations with Ann Liguori*, The Golf Channel.

MANTEGNA, JOE
Actor

In addition to playing is such acclaimed films as *Godfather III* and *Waiting for Bobby Fisher*, Mantegna appeared in the Broadway production of *Hair* ("millions of people have seen all of me"). He plays golf as much as possible after having had to do without it during the long winters of Chicago, where he grew up.

On his 15 handicap: "That's only when the moon is right and everything is in line with Aquarius."—from *Conversations with Ann Liguori*, The Golf Channel.

MARX, GROUCHO
Comedian

Groucho was an inconsistent golfer, who once got so frustrated he threw his clubs off a cliff and left a golf course, vowing to never play again. It lasted a short while.

When asked about the most difficult shot: "I find it to be the hole-in-one."

MARX, ZEPPO
Comedian

Zeppo played in the original Crosby Pro-Am and was a gallery favorite.

"The hardest shot is a mashie at ninety yards from the green, where the ball has to be played against an oak tree, bounces back into a sandtrap, hits a stone, bounces on the green and then rolls into the cup. That shot is so difficult I have only made it once."

MCCONAUGHY, MATTHEW
Actor

McConaughy has won some respect (and more work) for his role in *A Time to Kill.* That might lead to less time for golf, but also has a positive side: "Now that I have some money I'll be able to lose golf balls and not care."

MCKINLEY, WILLIAM
U.S. President

McKinley is credited as being the first president to play golf.

MEAT LOAF
Rock star

Mr. Loaf is known as the "King of Excess" for his spirited and theatrical performances. His best-known acting role is *The Rocky Horror Picture Show.*

"(Golf) is a different, different ballgame. I mean if I was Greg Norman then I would play with that intensity, but this is not my job. I come out to ride around on a cart and talk to rabbits. That's what I was doing out on the eighth hole: there was a little rabbit and he came hopping out of the woods. He stopped and he looked at me and he hopped closer to me, and I stood there and talked to him. I go, 'what are you doing, rabbit?' The people come over to me and go, 'what are you doing, Meat?' . . . and I'm talking to a rabbit."—from *Conversations with Ann Liguori,* The Golf Channel.

MURRAY, BILL
Actor

Murray is a clown on the links. At Pebble Beach he's worn outrageous outfits, including a wool hat with a pin and flag sticking out and a little white golf ball attached to it. He's danced in a sand trap with an elderly lady (they took a spill) and had a memorable scene in *Caddyshack,* pretending to be a "Cinderella story" at the Masters, loping off flowers while making one incredible shot after another.

He takes golf seriously, however, and after a bad outing at a pro-am took instructions from noted golf teacher Kip Puterbaugh. "His game is much improved, and if he only took it more seriously . . . but why?"

MURRAY, ANNE
Singer

Murray's passion for tennis and golf are not a secret to fans, who leave her cans of tennis balls and sleeves of golf balls on the stage during her performances. She has broken 90 for a round.

"In golf, it's for the moment. In my music career, (success) is more lasting. Golf is more fleeting because you're on to your next game trying to do better. I liken a golf game to an album because every one you do you want better than the one before."—from *Conversations with Ann Liguori,* The Golf Channel.

NELSON, WILLIE
Singer

On the course he purchased near Austin, Texas, "Par is anything you want it to be. For instance, this hole here is a par forty-seven. And yesterday I birdied the sucker."

O'DONNELL, CHRIS
Actor

O'Donnell, who played Robin, the Boy Wonder, in *Batman Forever*, sports a 15-handicap.

"(Golf's) the only thing I do when I'm working; when I work I tend not to go out. When I worked on a film in Vienna and in Ireland, whenever I had a free day I was always on the golf course. I'd work six days a week and on my day off I'd play golf, because no matter wherever you are in the world, if you get on the golf course it makes you feel like you're home again."—from *Conversations with Ann Liguori*, The Golf Channel.

O'ROURKE, P.J.

"Golf combines two favorite American pastimes: taking long walks and hitting things with a stick."—*Modern Manners*, 1983.

PESCI, JOE
Actor

Pesci is one of the most active celebrity golfers and usually finishes in the top 10 in pro-am team events.

"Golf is a whole way of life. I play for relaxation and to take my mind off everything else in life. I don't think about anything except trying to play golf. A lot of people I know in my situation or even who are more successful in my business— they see psychologists and psychiatrists and ana-

lysts all the time. I don't have to do that. I go to a golf course and that's my equalizer."—from *Conversations with Ann Liguori*, The Golf Channel.

POSTON, TOM
Comedian and actor

On his most frustrating moment of a golf course: "I lost a tee once and it ruined my whole day."—from *Conversations with Ann Liguori*, The Golf Channel.

QUAYLE, DAN
U.S. Vice-President, 1988–1992

A very low-handicap golfer, Quayle, along with his predecessor, George Bush, made galleries a safe place again to watch golfing Republican veeps.

"Golf is a little bit more brutal to me than politics has been, if you can believe that. Because if you go out and try to break par, shoot par, that's pretty tough to do. I can do it every once in awhile, but not very often, and that's always the goal. In politics, what you do is go out and take your opponent on, and you tackle the issues. You take your case to the American people and they decide. In golf, you're the judge because it's you and the golf course. Nobody else has a say in it. You post a number and that's it."—from *Conversations with Ann Liguori*, The Golf Channel.

ROBINSON, BROOKS
Baseball great

A Hall of Fame third baseman who played his entire career with the Baltimore Orioles, back when players played their entire career with one team, Robinson is perhaps best remembered for several amazing plays during the 1970 World Series, for which he was MVP.

"Growing up, I'd see guys playing golf and tennis when I was playing baseball. I'd say, 'hey, what are they doing? Are these guys crazy?' Now, 40 years later, I'm beating my head in trying to play golf and tennis. Life is upside down."—from *Conversations with Ann Liguori*, The Golf Channel.

RUTH, BABE
Baseball legend

Ruth never could master golf, but one he uttered a statement to pro J.A. Buchanan all duffers can relate to: "Yeah, no more golf for me. But I tell you, Buchanan, maybe if you aren't busy tomorrow we could meet on the first tee at nine tomorrow morning, because if I'm going to quit I might as well get in one more game."

SAMPRAS, PETE
Tennis champion

"I was playing with Jerry West and Mitch Kupchak of the Lakers. I had asked Jerry about his clubs. He had some old-looking drivers. I asked if I could hit one of them. He's been hitting this driver for 25 years and loves it. I took a big whack at it because I always do that and it broke the club, the head flew 100 yards into the fairway. He took it pretty well, but I could tell he was pissed."—from *Conversations with Ann Liguori*, The Golf Channel.

SCHULZ, CHARLES
Cartoonist

Although Schulz's "Peanuts" gang are best known for their baseball playing, they have appeared on the course numerous times. Snoopy, of course, is an all-around, great athlete: as well as being a great shortstop, Snoopy once played in the Masters. Schulz calls golf a perfect sport for cartoons and gets ideas for scripts Every time he plays.

"It's hard to tell whether golf or income tax had made the American people bigger liars."

—Will Rogers

On which character best exemplifies his own golf game: "Snoopy, because he gets so terribly angry and upset. We all do. Golf is like women. Golf leads us on. You hit a perfect drive—a 3-wood right up there near the green, and you're thinking birdie all the way up. And then you chunk your approach shot and get a bogey or double bogey. So you've been led on and turned down again."—from *Conversations with Ann Liguori*, The Golf Channel.

SHAW, GEORGE BERNARD
Writer

"To that man, age brought only golf instead of wisdom."

"Golf is a typical capitalist lunacy of upper-class Edwardian England."

SHOW, GRANT
Actor

Show plays Jake Hanson on TV's *Melrose Place*. Several people involved with *Melrose Place* use free time to drive golf balls into an empty field behind the studio where the show is filmed.

"The reason why I started playing golf was my father and I had, as many people do . . . when they first leave home, not the greatest relationship. I wanted to get to know him a little better. And he was playing golf. I thought, 'well, hey—this is great. I get to spend five hours with my dad, and I don't really have to talk to him, because we don't have anything to talk about.' So, I started playing. I started taking some lessons, and going to the driving range, and after about six months I said, 'Dad, let's go play golf.' I got addicted, and I've been playing ever since."

SMITH, WILL
Actor

The Fresh Prince has a goal of beating Michael Jordan in a round of golf.

STACK, ROBERT
Actor

Stack was Eliot Ness in *The Untouchables* TV series and is a television host for one of those mystery shows, but did you know that he is a member of the Skeet Shooting Hall of Fame?

"I'm continually trying to be someone I'm not (on the course). It's a very difficult game. Someone said, 'I'm humiliated enough in my profession and I get paid for it. I come out on the golf course and do it for free."—from *Conversations with Ann Liguori*, The Golf Channel.

STALLONE, SYLVESTER
Actor

"(Golf) is a game of imperfection, and when you happen to have a momentary slice of glory, you almost feel immortal for a few seconds. You just savor it because it is so much work and the mere fact that this is an extraordinary experience. It's like the stars ad the planets are aligned perfectly. And it all works. It's such a relief, such a validation . . ."

"I've worked harder at (golf) than any other facet of my career, which is a sad statement, but it's true. I really have found myself to be absorbed by the psychology of the game and, really, that's what it's all about."—from *Conversations with Ann Liguori*, The Golf Channel.

TAFT, W.H.
U.S. President

Taft shot in the mid 90s and often played with Todd Lincoln, Abraham Lincoln's oldest son.

THOMAS, DAVE
Businessman

Thomas is the founder of Wendy's Hamburgers and a popular spokesman in television ads for the firm. He owns a golf course, which he obtained in a trade for a yacht, and played recently with Arnold Palmer, of which Thomas reports, "he beat me."

"I was playing with President Ford and Jim McDonald, who was the president of General Motors. Jim McDonald said to the President, 'I never thought I'd be playing with a Ford,' and I said, 'Jim, I never thought I'd be playing with a McDonald.'"—from *Conversations with Ann Liguori*, The Golf Channel.

UPDIKE, JOHN
Writer

Updike has written on golf in fiction and nonfiction (see the Golf in Literature section). Here's his fictional character, Henry "Rabbit" Angstrom connecting on a tee shot: "Very simply, he brings the clubhead around his shoulder into it. The sound has a hollowness, a singleness he hasn't heard before. His arms force his head up and his ball is hung way out, lunarly pale against the beautiful black blue of storm clouds . . . It hesitates, and Rabbit thinks it will die, but he's fooled, for the ball makes its hesitation the ground of a final leap:

with a kind of visible sob takes a last bite of space before vanishing in falling. That's it!" he cries.

"I'm happy on the golf course. I don't know why, since my play is often not so happy . . . It's a lovely day . . . The fairways are very inviting. It's a shame we're not making much use of them."—Interview with Mike Snider, *USA Today*, September 6, 1996.

WAGNER, JACK
Actor and singer

Wagner is one of the better celebrity golfers and plays regularly on the Celebrities Golf Association tour.

"(Golfers) used to be the people with money—actors, producers. People who you would never think play, play now. Golf is something everyone can play, and that nobody can perfect. Everybody is equal. I think that's what's really caught on with golf. We all have the same problems, the same frustrations."—from *Conversations with Ann Liguori*, The Golf Channel.

WILSON, WOODROW
U.S. President

Playing one day Bannockburn in suburban Maryland, a man rushed on the course and grabbed Wilson's caddy, began leading him off the course by the ear. Seems the caddy was skipping school. He was allowed to finish the round with the president, then had to go back to stay after school. The caddy, Al Houghton, later became vice president at the PGA.

WULH, ROBERT
Actor

Wuhl, who plays an agent in the *Arliss* TV series, likes playing Pebble Beach because they allow him to take his dog, who runs along on a long leash attached to the golf cart.

"The least thing upset him on the links. He missed short putts because of the uproar of butterflies in the adjoining meadows."

—P.G. Wodehouse, from
"The Unexpected Clicking of Cuthbert."

Comparing the rhythm of comedy with the rhythm of a good golf swing: "You get into a tempo. Golf is a rhythm and a tempo, and there's music to it." "Tempo and rhythm is everything. I think it's the same thing in comedy. The best comedians I know . . . are all musically inclined, whether it's Woody Allen or Mel Brooks or Steve Martin . . . There is a rhythm and tempo to comedy , or even to Shakespeare . . . Anybody who is an artist at what they do, I see for most of them there is some musical correlation."—from *Conversations with Ann Liguori*, The Golf Channel.

Wuhl had an ace at the 1996 Lexus Pro-Am Challenge on the Citrus Course at La Quinta Resort, using a wedge on the 119-yard 7th hole.

ZIMBALIST, EFREM, JR.
Actor

Zimbalist starred in the TV series *77 Sunset Strip* and *The FBI*. His first round of golf was at a club in the Redwood Forest: "I remember the cathedral sound—bung, wung, boo—those shots hitting the trees, it was like gongs."

"I had a very interesting experience in Australia. I was invited to play in a pro-am. I went out and shot a snappy 115; I had no business being there. The next day I'm looking in the morning paper and what had happened the night before when we left the golf course, the safe was rifled and they took $5000. There's a cartoon on the front page of the paper—it's the manager of the golf course and me. The smoking safe is in the background and he looks at me and says, 'you were in the FBI, can't you do something about it?' I'm holding my scorecard and say, 'as soon as I finish adding this up.' The card showed 115!"—from *Conversations with Ann Liguori*, The Golf Channel.

In addition to her show on the Golf Channel, Ann Ligouri produces and hosts *Sports Innerview with Ann Ligouri,* broadcast nationally, and *Hey Ligouri, What's the Story?,* a weekly sports talk show on WFAN-NY radio. A collection of Ann's celebrity interviews will be published in 1997 by Taylor Publishing. She regularly participates in pro-am and charity events and has hosted VH-1's *Fairway to Heaven* golf competition.

GOLF IN FILM

Included below are references to 50 films and television episodes with golf content, spanning full-length films that can be considered golf movies to movies and television episodes with a brief golf connection.

The Majors section includes summaries and ratings of films with more significantly-developed golf themes; Passing Shots describes films with more limited golf content or references; TV Comedies lists seven top television episodes.

Golf content rating

♀♀♀♀ = Excellent golf scenes

♀♀♀ = Up to par

♀♀ = Funny, but review the Golf Etiquette section

♀ = A bogey all around, even with golf content

The Majors

Babe! (1975) Credible made-for-TV movie on the life of Babe Deidrickson Zaharias, starring Susan Clark as Babe and Alex Karras as her husband, George Zaharias. Intelligent treatment of real-life heroism and mortality, the kind of drama TV usually reduces to schlock. Babe was an excellent all-around athlete—an Olympic Gold medalist in track and field and a skilled, powerful, and charismatic golfer who struggled to help establish the LPGA and to promote respect for women's golf. She was stricken with cancer and died while still in the prime of her life. Fair amount of golf content in the context of much larger issues. ♀♀♀

The Caddy (1953) Jerry Lewis plays a frantic caddy prone to slapstick against Dean Martin's smooth professional golfer with a drive for singing. Mostly a series of Martin and Lewis sketches that frequently land in the rough. Introduces several songs, including a classic Martin and Lewis rendition of "That's Amore." Look for cameos by a host of professional golfers and some very good golf scenes amid the slapstick comedy. ♀♀♀

Caddyshack (1980) Inspired performances by Bill Murray and Rodney Dangerfield drive this sublimely moronic comedy onto the green. The action takes place at Bushwood Country Club, where caddy O'Keefe is bucking to win the club's college scholarship. Characters involved in various sophomoric set pieces include an obnoxious club president (Ted Knight), a playboy who is too laid back to keep his score (Chevy Chase), a loud, vulgar, and extremely rich golfer (Dangerfield), and Murray as a filthy gopher-hunting groundskeeper. Occasional dry moments are followed by scenes of pure (and tasteless) anarchy, so its best to enjoy the movie with someone immature: like, way cool is Murray's scene where he pretends to be a "Cinderella story" at the Masters. The golfing by duffers is realistic and there's a memorable gopher who's inspired many a clubhead cover. ♀♀♀♀

Caddyshack II (1988) Obligatory sequel to *Caddyshack*, minus Bill Murray, who wisely avoided further encroachment of gopher holes, and director Harold Ramis, who opted for the screen-writing chore and gets a penalty stroke. Jackie Mason is the star of the show as a crude self-made millionaire who tangles with the snobs at the country club, and as in his comedy act Mason occasionally earns a side-splitting chuckle. *Shack 2* has significantly fewer guffaws than the original, proving once again that funny guys are always undone by lousy scripts and weak direction. ♀

Carefree (1938) A screwball comedy with music. Love triangle develops between Ginger Rogers, Ralph Bellamy, and Fred Astaire. When Rogers can't make up her mind about beau Bellamy, he sends her to analyst Astaire. She dreams she's in love with the Astaire, who hypnotically suggests that she really loves Bellamy. Fred stops dancing just long enough to realize he's in love with Ginger. The dancing extravaganzas include a golf-swing routine to the tune "Since They Turned Loch Lomond into Swing" and a rousing finale, where Astaire drives golf balls while keeping time with the music. ♀♀♀

Change of Heart (1938) Golfing lady teams with a handsome pro, which makes her non-golfing husband take up the sport, and he improves from doofus to duffer. ♀♀

Dead Solid Perfect (1988) Randy Quaid stars as a golf pro whose life on the PGA tour is handicapped by his taste for scotch and his eye for the ladies. Faithful rendition of the book by Dan Jenkins. Because of its less than pure portrayal of the pro tour it did not receive the blessings of the PGA. Still, the golf scenes are strong and Quaid plays the role and the game well. ♀♀♀

Follow the Sun (1951) Excellent telling of the Ben Hogan story, with a strong performance by Glenn Ford. Released in the year Hogan won his second straight U.S. Open and two years after Hogan's near-fatal automobile accident. His determined recovery from the accident forms a major part of the film. ♀♀♀

The youngest golfer to score a hole-in-one was 4-year-old Scott Statler, who aced the seventh hole at a Par-3 course in Greensburg, Pennsylvania, in 1962.

Follow Thru (1930) Romance, golf, golf, romance—this movie has it all. Woman club champ loses a match to another club champ. A good-looking pro and his goofy friend arrive on the scene; the woman takes lessons from the pro and soon they begin to swing in sync while her friend falls for the pro's duffing sidekick. It's love on the links, as the foursome golf happily ever-after. ♀♀♀

A Foozle at the Tee Party (1915) An early *Caddyshack*, as a mischievous man enters an exclusive golf club after pickpocketing one of the members and initiates farce and frenzy. ♀♀

Goldfinger (1962) Ian Fleming's James Bond, Agent 007, attempts to prevent international gold smuggler Goldfinger and his pilot Pussy Galore from robbing Fort Knox. Features villainous assistant and erstwhile caddy Oddjob and his deadly bowler hat. The third in the series is perhaps the most popular. Great golfing scene, where James Bond takes on Goldfinger in a round with a gold bar as the wager. Bond is as resourceful as ever, begging the age-old question of whether cheating at golf for the sake of the goodness of humankind still demands disqualification.

Ian Fleming, author of the 007 books, was an excellent golfer: he was especially proficient with his 007 iron and once sported an 007 handicap. He was a member of the Royal St. George club; the club's course is carefully described in the golf scene in the book version. Sean Connery, the only real James Bond, is also an avid golfer and is a member of the Royal and Ancient. Connery teamed with pro Hale Irwin to win the 1996 Lexus Pro-Am Challenge. ♀♀♀♀

The Golf Specialist (1930) W.C. Fields' first sound film has the golf course for his stage and clubs for his props. Great slapstick fun and mutterings by Fields, who wrote the script. A house detective's flirty wife and a stumbling bumbling caddy contribute to the mayhem. ♀♀♀

Happy Gilmore (1996) Skating-impaired hockey player Gilmore (Sandler) translates his slap shot into a 400-foot tee shot and joins the pro golf tour. His unique style brings a new, less refined breed of fan to the game and upsets the reigning tour hotshot (McDonald). Sandler swears at or beats up about 90% of the supporting cast, including Bob Barker in a charity pro-am. Unfortunately, it won't make anyone forget *Caddyshack II*. ♀♀

The Man with the Perfect Swing (1995) Middle-aged ex-baseball player-turned-business entrepreneur Anthony "Babe" Lombardo (Black) is deep in debt and having trouble with the IRS even as he schemes to find success with his latest endeavor—designing specialty golf equipment. Babe's latest design is a radically new golf swing (combining putting with his baseball expertise) featured in a how-to video with a budding PGA star. Naturally, given Babe's woeful record, the money just doesn't seem to be coming his way. ♀

My Bunny Lies Over the Sea (1948) Filmed back when Bugs Bunny played golf with a Scotsman instead of hoops with Air Jordan. Hilarious opening where Bugs pops his head out of the ground and mistakes a kilted man playing the bagpipes for a lady being attacked by a foul-sounding monster; Bugs rushes to "her" aid and slays the bagpipes, then has to make amends by competing with the enraged Kiltster in a game of golf. "Trrrrrrrrrrrrry and top that!" says the man after expert shots, and Bugs does. ♀♀♀

Den ofrivillige golfaren (1992) Swedish golf farce in which a quarreling woman drives in the ultimate put-down of her boyfriend, betting him that any non-golfer in the world can beat him after just one week of practice. Ooooh. A hapless man nearby becomes the chosen one and ineptly works his way through practice and a showdown with the boyfriend on the course. ♀♀♀

Pat and Mike (1952) Another great Tracy–Hepburn war of the sexes rages in this comedy about a leathery sports promoter who isn't above fixing events and an athletically-gifted woman who counters all his moves. Tracy and Hepburn have fine chemistry, but supporting players contribute too. Watch for cameos by several professional golfers, including Babe Dedrickson. The golf scenes are done well. ♀♀♀

Should Married Men Go Home? (1928) When Laurel visits Hardy their tomfoolery gets them tossed out of the house by Hardy's missus. Naturally, they head for the golf course, where they try to impress two young women and end up annoying other golfers, culminating with a mud fight. ♀♀

Spring Fever (1983) A shipping clerk (Carling Bassett) who's a fine golfer is taken by his boss to an exclusive country club as the boss seeks tips to improve his game. The clerk catches the eye of a rich girl (Susan Anton) and then tries to impress her by pretending he is wealthy, spilling the truth only after they are married. Back on his own again, he continues to play, turns pro, wins a big prize, but can he win her back? ♀

Three Little Beers (1935) The Three Stooges in one of their better rounds, as beer delivery men who consistently botch the job. Learning of an upcoming company golf outing, they go to the course for some practice and end up riling other golfers and pretty much destroying the course. Great climax when they flee an angry mob in their beer truck and launch barrels down a steep hill to cover their escape. ♀♀

Tin Cup (1996) You've got your romantic triangle, you got your sports, you've got Kevin Costner reteamed with Ron Shelton—*Bull Durham* on a golf course? Roy "Tin Cup" McAvoy (Costner) is a West Texas golf hustler who had the ability to be on the pro tour. McAvoy decides on a last-ditch effort to qualify for the U.S. Open in hopes of winning over a psychologist (Rene Russo in an excellent comic turn as a novice golfer) who comes to Costner's range for lessons, and to beat her love interest, Don Johnson, a pro who was Costner's archrival as an amateur. The excellent U.S. Open scenes were filmed at Houston's Kingwood Country Club and the actors hit their own shots. 🏌🏌🏌

Passing Shots

The Big Broadcast of 1938 (1938) Dueling ocean liners: W.C. Fields enters his ship in a race against a scheming opponent who summons his brother to disrupt Fields' plans, but the brother is delayed by a golf game and then becomes a catalyst for farce. Bob Hope, in his first feature film, gets to sing his Oscar-winning signature tune "Thanks for the Memories."

Blood & Donuts (1995) Hungry vampire, who's just been awakened from a slumber of several years by a wildly hit golf ball, is looking for a rat snack when he stumbles across an all-night donut shop where pretty cashier and a friendly cabbie seek his help with a local crime boss. Mild horror mixed with comedy and limited gore and not enough golf.

Call Me Bwana (1963) Pure cornpone with Bob Hope as a bumbling explorer sent with CIA agent Edie Adams to track down a lost American space capsule in deepest Africa. Enemy agents try to make things difficult. In one scene, Hope is sneaking through the dense jungle and runs into Arnold Palmer, who's facing a terrible lie.

Convict 13 (1920) Too bad there isn't more of Buster Keaton playing golf. He gets knocked out on the course and falls into the rough as an escaped convict steals his clothes. Keaton, dressed in the convict's clothes, is mistakenly arrested and taken to prison. He manages to change clothes with a prison guard just as a riot breaks out and the prisoners go after the guards. And there's more.

The Dallas Connection (1994) Three of the four scientists working on a microchip for a satellite weapons system are deleted by a trio of scantily clad assassin terrorists. Strictly a T&A flick, with some of the Teeshots and Assassins revealed on the golf course, where one of the vicious beauties exhibits an inexcusably bad golf swing and one of their victims falls for the old exploding golf ball trick.

Dallas Doll (1994) Sandra Bernhard stars in this Australian wacko comedy about a touring golfer who brings sexual chaos to a suburban Sydney household as she tries to seduce each member of a family.

The Dentist (1932) W.C. Fields treats several oddball patients in his office. After watching the infamous tooth-pulling scene, viewers will be sure to brush regularly. The iceman with the melting heart is an excellent supporting character. Fields' dentist raising havoc on the golf course is a fair way to appreciate his comedic skills, but a whole round's worth (as in *The Golf Specialist*) is a better approach.

Doorway to Hell (1930) A mob boss tries to retire to Florida for quality time on the course and with his family, but the syndicate he brought together—by encouraging thugs to work with each other— is splitting apart, and he is made an offer to return that he shouldn't refuse. As in life, work gets in the way of golf.

Goof Balls (1987) The tourist denizens of a island golf resort putt and cavort about, and golf isn't all that's on their minds or scorecards. Nothing's good here—not the golf, not the acting, not the script, not the film.

The Great Gatsby (1974) Adaptation of F. Scott Fitzgerald's novel of the idle rich in the 1920s. A key scene occurs on the course, when narrator Nick Carraway catches Jordan Baker (his love interest and a professional golfer) cheating in a tournament, thereby illustrating the decadence and immorality of the Jazz Age, or something. Interesting to see the authentic style of clothes women golfed in back then.

The Idle Class (1921) The tramp in the country club: Charlie Chaplin sneaks into an exclusive golf resort. He meets a woman who's arguing with her drunken husband (also played by Chaplin). Farce arises when the woman later mistakes the tramp for her husband, which leads to some hilarity but we could have had more of Chaplin applying his great comedic talents to golf.

In Like Flint (1967) Agent Flint is summoned from retirement when the president of the U.S. is kidnapped during a round of golf and replaced with an actor, of all things. Imagine that. Sequel to *Our Man Flint* sees our dapper spy confronting an organization of women endeavoring to take over the world.

The Lady Consents (1936) Married doctor plans to run off with lady pro golfer. Wife says he'll regret it. Doctor runs off and comes to regret it.

M*A*S*H (1970) Hilarious, irreverent, and well-cast black comedy about a group of surgeons and nurses at a Mobile Army Surgical Hospital in Korea. Loosely adapted from the novel by the pseudonymous Richard Hooker (Dr. H. Richard Hornberger) and William Heinz. Subsequent hit TV series moved even further from the source novel. Both the film and the TV series showed doctors relieving tension by driving golfballs into no-man's lands, as indeed some troops have done.

National Lampoon's Animal House (1978) Set in 1962 and responsible for defining cinematic food fights. Every college tradition from fraternity rush week to the homecoming pageant is irreverently and relentlessly mocked in this wild comedy about Delta House, a fraternity on the edge. The golf scene is typical: young turks drive golf balls at military types.

Off and Running (1991) Struggling actress Cyd (Cyndi Lauper) is working as a mermaid at a Miami hotel lounge when her horse trainer boyfriend Woody is suddenly murdered by a psycho thug (Richard Belzer). Turns out he's after a key hidden in a necklace now in Cyd's possession. Cyd goes on the run and gets some help from failed golf pro as they try to stay one step ahead of the killer and discover what the key unlocks.

Ordinary People (1980) Powerful, well-acted story of a family's struggle to deal with one son's accidental death and the other's subsequent guilt-ridden suicide attempt. Features strong performances as well as Robert Redford's directorial debut. Based on the novel by Judith Guest. Excellent golf course scene where the marriage of Donald Sutherland and Mary Tyler Moore begins to unravel—filled with tension and great acting.

The Philadelphia Story (1940) A woman's plans to marry again go awry when her dashing ex-husband arrives on the scene. Matters are further complicated when a loopy reporter—assigned to spy on the nuptials—falls in love with the blushing bride. Classic comedy, with trio of Katherine Hepburn, Cary Grant, and James Stewart all swinging true. Very brief golf content, but we've all experienced it: the beginning scene has Hepburn tossing Grant's golf clubs out the door—hate when that happens.

The Seduction of Joe Tynan (1979) Political drama about a young senator (Alan Alda) torn between his family, his political career, and his mistress (Meryl Streep). Alda also wrote the thin screenplay, which reportedly is loosely based on the remarkable life of Ted Kennedy. Relatively shallow treatment of the meaty themes of power, hypocrisy, sex, and corruption in our nation's capital. Alda and Streep use a golf course as a rendezvous for playing around.

Stealing Home (1988) A washed-up baseball player learns his former babysitter (who was also his first love and inspiration), has committed suicide. Their bittersweet relationship is told through flashbacks. Jodie Foster's superb performance steals the show in this quiet sleeper. In one scene, Jonathan Silverman (*The Single Guy* on TV) gets teed off at his best friend, grabbing clubs from his golf bag and flinging them down the fairway while emphatically accusing his best friend of promiscuity: (one club per word) "You—had—sex—with—my—prom—date!"

The Two Jakes (1990) Ten years have passed and Jake Gittes is still a private investigator in this sequel to 1974's *Chinatown*. Includes a golf course scene but it doesn't show Jack Nicholson hacking away.

Zorro Rides Again (1937) The great Zorro's grandson is called on when Mexican banditos disrupt construction of the Baja-California railroad. The nephew is much better at golf than being a superhero, but he gives up the pullcart for a horse and saves the day.

And Seven Television Episodes

The Dick Van Dyke Show Laura tells Rob not to play golf the morning that she's planned an evening dinner party. Rob plays, becomes ill, tries to make it through the party, and collapses. Laura's "I told you so" becomes moot when a house-calling doctor says Rob had a virus and golf had nothing to do his illness, and everything's fine again with the Petries. Whew.

Get Smart! Maxwell Smart creates chaos on the course while attempting to stop Kaos golfer/agents from spreading evil. Features assassin golfers able to strike their victims with expert shots from over a hundred and fifty yards out, something a couple of 1970s vice-presidents were also capable of doing.

The Honeymooners Ralph and Ed take up golf. Classic comic take off on golf instruction, beginning with the address the ball bit. Norton leaning over and saying, "Hello, ball," will get you every time.

I Love Lucy Lucy's let loose on a golf course.

The Munsters While the other Munsters try to gain entry into a country club, Herman plays a round of golf and destroys the course. You gotta laugh when he trods on greens and leaves footprints behind.

Seinfeld (2) For a show supposedly about nothing, here are a couple mini-plots with golf themes: Kramer uses a beach for a driving range, whacking balls into the ocean; later, George is on the same beach pretending he's a marine biologist to impress a woman. They encounter a beached whale; George is encouraged to give aid (being a marine biologist) and does so by removing a golf ball from the whale's spout, but in confessing the truth he loses the girl and then bores everyone with the story ("The sea was angry that day, my friends . . ."). In another episode, Kramer gains entrance into a prestigious golf course by bribing the Starter with Cuban cigars. Later, when Kramer's remaining cigars are wiped out in a cabin fire he inadvertently started by leaving behind a lit cigar, he shows up at the Cuban embassy and makes a slightly illegal cigar/golf/overcoat deal.

GOLF IN FICTION

The following bibliography lists stories, poems, plays, and novels with golf references and themes meant as creative fictional works. Works cited in the Anthologies section reprint many of the short pieces listed in Golf Fiction.

Anthologies

Bartlett, Michael. *The Golf Book*. New York: Arbor House, 1980.
> Pieces of many different kinds on golf.

Dobreiner, Peter. *Down the Nineteenth Fairway*. New York: Atheneum, 1983.
> Over 60 pieces from golf historians, players, and commentators, with a few fictional stories as well

Hall, Holworthy. *Dormie One and Other Golf Stories*. London: Century, 1917.
> Collection of pieces by one of the first golf storytellers.

Hallberg, William. *Perfect Lies: A Century of Great Golf Stories*. New York: Fireside, 1989.
> Excellent collection of stories, including some previously published only in magazines.

Updike, John. *Golf Dreams*, New York: Alfred A. Knopf, 1996.
> Writings on golf by the Pulitzer Prize winning novelist and critic, from observations on the game to excerpts from his fiction.

Van Loan, Charles. *Fore!* London: P.P. Collier & Son. 1914.
> A mostly humorous collection involving an odd collection of golfing characters.

Wind, Herbert Warren. *The Complete Golfer*. New York: Simon & Schuster, 1954.
> Collects fiction and non-fiction pieces.

Wodehouse, P. G. *The Golf Omnibus*. London: Barrie & Jenkins, 1973; *Fore! The Best of Wodehouse on Golf*. New York: Ticknor & Fields, 1983.
> The best golf in fiction, funny and poignant.

Fiction

Abbott, Lee K. "The Valley of Sin." *Strangers in Paradise*. New York: Putnam, 1986.
> The tale of Dillon Ripley, Deming Golf Club's "most ardent" duffer, and his sudden separation from the game.

Adams, Herbert. *The Body in the Bunker*. New York: Lippincott, 1935.
> Murder mystery.

Allerton, Mark. *The Girl on the Green*. London: Metheun, 1914.
> Light romance.

Allis, Peter. *The Duke*. London: New English Library, 1983.
> Alliss is a prolific and accomplished golf writer trying his hand here at fiction.

Anderson, Robert. *A Funny Thing Happened on the Way to the Clubhouse* London: Arthur Baker, 1971.
> Humorous observations on the ways of golfers.

Baert, Raymond. *The Adventures of Monseiur DuPont, Golf Champion*. London: Laurence & Jellicoe, 1913.
> Light reading.

Ball, Brian. *Death of a Low Handicap Man*. New York, Walker, 1974.
> Mystery.

Banes, Ford. *Right Down Your Fairway*. New York: A.S. Barnes, 1947.
> Lightly comic.

Bentley, E.C. *Trent Intervenes*. London: Curtis Brown, 1938.
> Interesting mystery in the parlor-murder vein extended to a clubhouse and golf course.

Brown, Horace. *Murder in the Rough*. London: T.V. Boardman, 1948.

More murder on the course.

Brown, Kenneth. *Putter Perkins*. Boston: Houghton Mifflin, 1923.

Light, cute fare.

Bruff, Nancy. *The Country Club*. New York: Bartholomew House, 1969.

Romance.

Canin, Ethan. "The Year of Getting to Know Us." *Emperor of the Air*. New York, Houghton-Mifflin Company, 1988.

Golf becomes a way for a wayward father to try and connect with his son.

Christie, Agatha. *Murder on the Links*. London: John Lane, 1923.

Murder and golf by the eminent mystery writer. After a body is discovered on a golf course, ace detective questions several suspects, searching for a hole in one's alibi.

Compston, Archie, and Stanley Anderson. *Love on the Fairway: A Romance of the Open Championship*. London: T Werner Laurie, 1936.

Clean—no divots, no grass-stains in this romance.

Darwin, Bernard. "The Wooden Putter." *

A fictional piece by one of the sport's most noted chroniclers.

Dickinson, Charles. "My Livelihood." *With or Without*. New York: Afred A. Knopf, 1982.

Lackadaisical man finds a sense of meaning in golf.

Dubus, Andre. "An Afternoon with the Old Man." *Adultery and Other Choices*. New York: Godine, 1977.

Father and son find some connection through golf.

Faulkner, William. *The Sound and the Fury*. New York: Eandom House, 1929.

The opening scene presents Benjy's impressions as he watches golfers and keeps an eye on his siblings, culminating with Benjy getting struck by a golf ball.

Fleming, Ian, *Goldfinger*. *

Secret agent James Bond duels with gold-hoarder Goldfinger (and his razor-brimmed caddy Oddjob) on a golf course patterned after Royal St. George, where Fleming was a member.

Fitzgerald, F. Scott. "Winter Dreams." *All the Sad Young Men*. New York: Charles Scribner's Sons, 1922.

Small-town caddy interacts with the country club set and a wealthy girl.

Fitzgerald, F. Scott. *The Great Gatsby*. *

A passing golf scene, as narrator Nick Carroway observes his love interest cheating during a tournament.

Frome, David. *Murder on the Sixth Hole*. London: Metheun & Company, 1931.

Murder mystery.

Gault, William Campbell. *The Long Green*. New York: E.P. Dutton, 1965.

By the author of the golf story "Gallery Shy."

Giradoux, Jean. *The Enchanted: A Comedy in Three Acts*. New York: S. French, 1950.

A play first staged in 1933. Has a great line: "A golf course is the epitome of all that is purely transitory in the universe, a space not to dwell in, but to get over as quickly a possible."

Hallberg, William. *The Rub of the Green*. New York: Doubleday & Co., 1988.

The ups and downs of Ted Kendall, who grows up within driving range of a golf course (errant shots occassionally smash through windows of his family's home) and later tries to build a couple of golf holes on prison grounds.

Jenkins, Dan. *Dead Solid Perfect*. New York: Price, Stern and Sloan, 1986.

Life on the Tour with a golfer distracted by women and booze and a caddy who helps him along. Like Jenkins' golf reporting, it's straight and tough with some soft edges.

Lardner, Ring. "A Caddy's Diary." *How to Write Short Stories*. New York: Charles Scribners and Sons, 1922.

Diary of a sincere 16-year-old caddy that contains hilarious recountings of the ways golfers improve their game through creative interpretations of rules and outright cheating.

Leacock, Stephen. "Mathematics for Golfers." *Feasts of Stephen: A Cornucopia of Delights*. Toronto: McClelland and Stewart, 1991.

Hilarious observations on scoring golf.

Links, Bo. *Follow the Wind*. New York: Simon & Schuster, 1995.

Fantasy where golfers of the past come to life for fun and to confront some unfinished business.

Lowry, Malcolm. *Under the Volcano*. New York: Reynal & Hitchcock, 1947.

Excellent novel about a self-destructive British diplomat in Mexico. Contains a brief golf metaphor that describes the main character's condition: "Who holds the flag while I hole out in three? Who hunts my Zodiac Zone [a golf ball brand] along the shore? And who, upon the last and final green, though I hole out in four, accepts my ten and three score . . . though I have no more?"

Marshall, Robert. *The Haunted Major*. New York: Stokes, 1920.

Also published as *The Enchanted Golf Clubs*.

Milne, A. A. *A Holiday Round*. *

Contains several golf tales by Milne, best known as the creator of Winnie the Pooh, and Tigger, too.

Murphy, Michael. *Golf in the Kingdom*. New York: Viking, 1972.

Transcendent mystery and parable about a man who travels to Scotland and meets the legendary linksmaster, Shivas Irons.

Nash, Ogden, "The Strange Case of the Ambitious Caddie." *The Selected Poems of Ogden Nash*. New York: Modern Library, 1947.

Light comic verse about Robin, a miserably downtrodden young man, who will end up caddying for Ogden Nash.

Olson, Toby. *Seaview*. New York: New Directions, 1983.

The goings-on in the small community of Seaview, including a very funny passage on golf tourists.

Patterson, James and Peter De Jonge. *Miracle on the 17th Green*. Boston: Little Brown and Company, 1996.

50-ish man down on his life and bored with his family discovers a secret stroke during a round on Christmas day, then devotes himself to making it on the senior tour.

Percy, Walker. "Sunday Under Par." *The Second Coming*. New York: Farrar, Strauss and Giroux, 1980.

Man undergoes deep self-reflection after a couple of events on a golf course. Funny and revealing work by a master of fiction.

Pressfield, Steven. *The Legend of Bagel Vance*. New York: Avon Books, 1995.

Drops a local legend in on the Walter Hagen-Bobby Jones exhibition match in Georgia that took place in the early 1930s.

Shaw, Joseph T. *Out of the Rough*. New York: Windward House, 1932.

Another tale combining redemption and golf.

Steele, Chester K. *The Golf Course Mystery*. Cleveland: International Fiction Library, 1919.

One of many golf course murder mysteries.

Sutphen, W.G. *The Golficide and Other Tales of the Fair Green*. New York: Harper, 1898.

More crime on the course, some of it social, some against good sportsmanship.

Travers, Ben. *The Temptation of Admiral Juddy*. *
Sane man meets his opposites on the course.

Updike, John *Rabbitt Run* (1960), *A Month of Sundays* (1975), and *Rabbit at Rest* (1990)—all published by Knopf.

One of America's most honored writers since the late 1950s has angst-ridden protagonists working on their game, finding some frustrations and some redemption.

West, Henry Lichtfield (editor). *Lyrics of the Links*. New York: The MacMillan Company, 1921.
    Collects historical verse on the ancient game.

Wind, Herbert Warren *On the Tour With Harry Sprague*. New Haven: Ticknor and Fields, 1983.
    Fictional player on the Tour story by one of the best golf writers.

Wynne, Anthony. *Death of a Golfer*. Philadelphia: Lippencott, 1937.
    For mystery reading golfers.

For books on Golf Architecture, see the chapter on Course Designers.

GOLF IN MUSIC

"It's Mother Nature with a manicure"—from "Back Nine," Loudon Wainwright, III

Alabama, *Press it Down*, Elektra. "Golf"

Joe Beck, *Friends*, Digital Music Products. "Golf Swing"

Oscar Brand and the Sandtrappers, *Fore*, Elecktra.
    A whole album's worth by the folksinger, including "Larceny on the Links," "Golf Widow," "Golf Bum," "My Caddy," and "Old Golfers Never Die."

Archie Campbell, *Best of Archie Campbell*, RCA Victor. "Golf, Golf, Golf"

Frank Capelli, *On Vacation*, A&M Records. "Golf"

The Chieftains, *The Grey Fox*, DRG Records "A Golf Waltz"

Larry Clinton, *Music for Tired Golfers*, MGM.
    Instrumentals.

Cousin Bubba, Rhinestone Plowboy, MCA. "Golf."

Bing Crosby, *Top Hat, White Tie, Golf Shoes, Tap Time*. Title song; with Fred and Ginger.

Flying Scotsmen, *Scottish Dance Time*, RCA Victor. "South Uist Golf Club"

Don Hays, *New Course Record*, Teed Off Records. Whole album of new and old songs.

The Mulligans, *In the Leather*, Beserkely Records. New songs—"Swing," "Scramble," "Back and Through, Straight and True," plus old favorites.

Pete and Fred Shoemaker, *Extraordinary Golf*, Teed Off Records. The most prolific golf songwriters, with "Bogey Bob" and "Hey Dad," plus many others.

Ross Talbot, *Bermuda is Paradise*, Audio Fidelity. "Golf Time in Bermuda."

Joe Timmer, *Polka Hit Parade*, Fiesta. "Golfer's Polka."

Loudon Wainwright, III, *Final Exam*, Arista, and *More Love Songs*, Rounder Records. "Golfin' Blues" appears on Exam, "Back Nine" on More Love Songs.

Various Artists, *Golf's Greatest Hits*, Teed Off Records. J.F. Knoblach's "Golf's a Bitch, and Then You Die" and many of the above.

Various Artists, *Tin Cup*, Epic Soundtraxx. Contains "Big Stick," by Bruce Hornsby and "Double Bogey Blues," by Mickey Jones.

Martha Wright, *Love Honor & All That Jazz*, RCA Victor. "The Golf Widow."

Henny Youngman, *Take My Album, Please*, Waterhouse. "Golf & Football."

See "Music of the Spheres," by Richard Skelly, USGA Journal, January-February, 1994, pp. 14-18, for more information on golf in popular song.

17

GETTING STARTED

THE DUFFER'S QUALIFYING SCHOOL

This chapter presents information directed primarily at new golfers but is useful for every player to increase enjoyment of the game for themselves and others. The chapter is divided into four sections: 1) basic, common-sense tips on the golf swing from acclaimed instructor Kip Puterbaugh; 2) handy information on basic rules; 3) a primer on golf etiquette; and 4) a glossary on golf jargon.

GOLF INSTRUCTION: "WHAT YOU KNOW CAN DEFINITELY HURT YOU," BY KIP PUTERBAUGH.

Kip Puterbaugh has been a golf instructor since the mid-1980s after having competed with the University of Houston's championship teams in the late 1960s and serving as a golf pro at clubs in Chicago and California. In the mid-1980s he turned his focus to instruction, first at the Golf University at Pala Mesa Golf Club, then as Owner and Director of Instruction at Kip Puterbaugh's Aviara Golf Academy. The Aviara Academy ranks as one of the top instructional facilities in the world, and Puterbaugh was named one of the top 50 golf instructors in *Golf* magazine's report on golf instruction. He has contributed articles to all of the major golf publications and produced a 1990 video, *The Natural Swing*, that won a 4-star rating from *Golf* magazine. Scott Simpson and Larry Mize are among the professionals Puterbaugh has tutored, and Bill Murray and Charles Schwab are among the golfing celebrities, but his proudest accomplishment is "teaching the average player to play the game better."

The following passage, "What You Know Can Definitely Hurt You," focuses on the importance of the body, as opposed to the hands and arms, in initiating and completing a smooth and successful golf swing. This philosophy is expressed within the context of the ten most frequent golf tips you are likely to hear that can hurt your game. The passage is taken from a work-in-progress on golf mechanics.

"What You Know Can Definitely Hurt You."

Golf can be a tremendously complex and confusing game and has generated more instructional books and videos than any other sport. The environment and pace of the game encourage ongoing analysis and instruction, especially by amateurs. After you hit a series of bad shots, the conversation inevitably turns to the golf swing.

Amateur instruction can be lumped into a Top Ten list—a list of items you are most likely to hear and which I encourage, for the sake of your golf game, to ignore. Look at and enjoy the scenery if any of these suggestions is offered—they can definitely hurt you:

1. Keep your head still and your eye on the ball.

2. Keep your left arm straight.

3. Keep your right elbow in close during the back swing.

4. Your left side controls the swing; you are using your right hand too much.

5. Keeping your left heel on the ground will solidify your back swing turn.

6. During the back swing, focus on cocking your wrist to set up the correct angle for the downswing.

7. Start the downswing by pulling your right arm and elbow into your side.

8. You want to delay the uncocking of the wrist on the downswing until the last possible moment.

9. You want to watch the club head strike the ball.

10. You want your hands and arms in a nice high position in the follow-through.

If any of these well-intentioned bits of advice is a priority in your swing, your chances of a good stroke are minimal. If more than three of these are in your mental preparation to swing the club, you are headed for trouble.

1. Keep your head still and your eye on the ball.

If you keep your head still you cannot create the proper body rotation, arm swing and extension, and sequence of motion necessary for a good swing. The upper body must move to initiate the swing in order for the club head to move back from the ball properly. There is simply no way for the chest area to start to the right while the head remains still. By trying to keep your head still you are stuck with a hands- and arms-dominated swing.

Remember Harvey Penick's line from *The Little Red Book of Golf Instruction*: In 75 years of teaching he had to tell 2 students to keep their head more stable.

2. Keep your left arm straight.

The more you tense-up your left arm the more your grip pressure will increase. This build up of pressure creates a much stronger chance of club-head movement being initiated with the hands and arms instead of the torso, thus destroying the correct sequence of motion.

Keep both arms equal in pressure and relaxed; the proper sequence will create the centrifugal force that keeps the club head swinging out and around from the center of motion. Your arms stay relatively extended without tension.

3. Keep your right elbow in close on the back swing.

Great golfers at the waist-high position of the back swing have between 3 to 5 inches of space between the inside joint of the elbow and the right rib cage. The average golfer at the same position often has the right elbow brushing against the ribs.

If you attempt to keep the right elbow close you are encouraging a quicker reaction of your hands relative to the body turn, placing the whole swing motion out of sequence. The more the elbow stays close to the body the faster the club head travels relative to body rotation, and the back swing will go too far inside of the swing plane.

4. Keep your left side in control of the swing; or, you use too much right hand.

Dr. Frank Jobe, a pioneer in Orthopedic surgery, led a two-year study of professional golfers to determine what muscles are most involved in the swing. The conclusion: the golf swing is bi-lateral, meaning that the right and left side are equally involved in both the backswing and the downswing.

Many amateurs try to pull their left arm down on the downswing. The moment someone pulls either arm down to initiate the downswing the arms begin moving too fast, relative to the body rotation. In good swings the body initiates the downswing, with the hips shifting weight and rotating, bringing the hands and arms around.

5. Keeping your left heel on the ground will solidify your back swing turn.

The left heel and foot do nothing to initiate the swinging motion. The swing starts with the upper body moving and turning to the right, the arms staying free and away from the torso so the clubhead is pulling out from center. The lower portion of the body is merely following the movement of the upper body.

Movement of the left foot is an *effect* of the proper turn, it does not *cause* the correct turn.

6. You need to cock your wrist at the precise time at the correct angles to be ready for the downswing.

If you have the correct grip (allowing for the hinging of both hands as one unit), the correct arm tension (really a lack of tension), and the right grip pressure, the hinging of the wrist on the back swing is a totally natural process as the club swings on arc.

The hands need to stay relaxed and calm, especially as the upper body starts its movement to the right and starts to rotate. The hands, if they stay quiet, should stay out in front and away from the torso. The quicker you cock your wrists, the faster

the arms pull into the body, and the less likely you will be able to rotate your torso correctly.

7. You start the downswing by pulling your right arm and elbow into your side.

The main problem with worrying about the right elbow is that it concentrates on the effect of the right arm and elbow, not the cause. If your hands take the club back too quickly—relative to body motion—it leads to a top of the back swing position where the body has not completed a successful turn, and you will have no recourse but to lead and hit with your hands and arms.

The correct rotation in the back swing allows the body to initiate the forward swing, with the hands and arms following; this is what allows the right elbow to return to a correct downswing position.

8. You want to delay the un-cocking of the wrist on the downswing until the last possible moment.

The hands and arms follow the body into driving the golf ball, and the wrists turn naturally during the process of hitting the ball. Attempting to control the un-cocking of the wrists pulls the arms into the body and disrupts the ability to rotate your torso correctly.

9. Your eyes should watch the club head strike the ball.

The center of the body must keep turning to allow the clubhead to stay free and on its arc, allowing the club head to reach the bottom of its swing arc with the radius at maximum and full extension. Trying to watch the club hit the ball will freeze the center from turning: the head locks so that the eyes can stare at the ball.

10. You want to have a follow through with your hands and arms in a nice high position.

As a general rule, the higher the hands and arms finish relative to your shoulders, the more weight you will have back on your right foot at the completion of your swing. The higher you swing the arms the less you can rotate the torso.

A good thought on the follow through is to let your head and shoulders rotate freely up into what I call "Up and Out": your head should be one-head forward from your starting position, and ½ to 1 head higher. Your body should be at its natural height with nearly 100% of your weight on your left foot. Your torso should feel high, not your hands and arms.

RULES OF THE GAME

The United States Golf Association and the Royal and Ancient Golf Club of St. Andrews publish the *Rules of Golf*, the definitive source on all rules pertaining to the game. Excerpts, summaries, and more basically-worded sources are abundantly available as well. In this section, some of the basic and most useful rules are explained.

The Society of St. Andrews Golfers was the first group to seriously attempt to codify the rules of golf. Their "Thirteen Basic Rules of Golf" was spelled out in 1754, and although some of rules and wording are archaic and downright funny today, the "Thirteen Basic Rules" do provide a framework in which to present contemporary rules that cover the most common situations novice golfers will confront. For your enjoyment and best interest, the original "Thirteen Basic Rules of Golf" is printed below, followed by a modernized list of basic rules as of 1997.

The Thirteen Basic Rules of Golf by The Society of St. Andrews Golfers, 1754

1. You must tee your ball within a club length of the hole.

2. Your tee must be on the ground.

3. You are not to change the ball which you strike off the tee.

4. You are not to remove stones, bones, or any break-club for the sake of playing your ball, except upon the fair green, and that only within a club length of your ball.

5. If your ball come among water or any watery filth, you are at liberty to take out your ball and throw it behind the hazard six yards at least; you may play it with any club, and allow your adversary a stroke for so getting out your ball.

6. If your balls be found anywhere touching one another, you are to lift the first ball until you play the last.

7. At holing you are to play your ball honestly for the hole, and not to play upon your adversary's ball, not lying in your way to the hole.

8. If you should lose your ball by its being taken up or any other way, you are to go back to the spot where you struck last and drop another ball and allow your adversary a stroke for the misfortune.

9. No man at holing his ball is to be allowed to mark his way to the hole with his club or anything else.

10. If a ball is stopped by any person, horse, dog or anything else, the ball so stopped must be played where it lies.

11. If you draw your club in order to strike and proceed so far with your stroke as to be bringing down your club, if then your club should break in any way, it is to be counted a stroke.

12. He whose ball lies farthest from the hole is obliged to play first.

13. Neither trench, ditch, nor dike made for the preservation of the links, nor the Scholar's Holes, nor the Soldier's Line shall be counted a hazard, but the ball is to be taken out, teed, and played with an iron club.

Thirteen Basic Rules of Golf, Modernized, 1997

1. You must tee your ball within a club length of the hole.

You must tee your ball within two club-lengths of the markers that form the tee box, and you can't use a tee for any other shot on the course.

If you tee off outside the tee box, you are assessed a two stroke penalty and must begin the hole again by teeing off from the proper area.

2. *Your tee must be in the ground.*

Your tee must be placed in the ground when teeing off. Until the wood tee was invented in the 1920s, golfers teed their ball on a small mound of sand supplied near the teeing area.

3. *You are not to change the ball which you strike off the tee.*

You are not to change the ball that you strike off the tee, and you can only touch it if you need to identify that it is yours. When the ball reaches the green, however, you are allowed to pick it up and mark its lie, and you can clean the ball.

4. *You are not to remove stones, bones, or any break-club for the sake of playing your ball, except upon the fair green, and that only within a club length of your ball.*

You can remove twigs, bones, teeth and other natural objects that aren't growing, fixed in place, or stuck to the ball (like a wet leaf)—provided your ball doesn't move in the process. If the ball moves you are assessed a penalty stroke.

On the fair green you are allowed to repair ball marks and remove obstacles, but you are not allowed to repair spike marks (spike marks aren't repairable, and attempting to fix them damages the green).

Natural objects that aren't growing or fixed in place are called Loose Impediments. Man-made objects are called Obstructions, and rules pertaining to them are included below.

5. *If your ball comes upon water or any watery filth, you are at liberty to take out your ball and throw it behind the hazard six yards at least; you may play it with any club, and allow your adversary a stroke for so getting out your ball.*

If your ball splashes into a water hazard or pond scum, you are free to play it or drop a new ball at a point on land near to where the ball crossed over the water. Throwing the ball has been replaced by the drop: hold your new ball out and drop it from shoulder height. You can play your next shot with any club, and you must take a penalty stroke.

6. *If your balls be found anywhere touching one another, you are to lift the first ball until you play the last.*

If the ball you are playing is in the putting line of another player, pick up the ball and mark its spot on the green. You can request to another player to mark their ball as well and they are obliged to do so. It's a two-stroke penalty if your putt hits another ball on the green, or if you deflect your own shot or someone else's.

7. *At holing you are to play your ball honestly for the hole, and not to play upon your adversary's ball, not lying in your way to the hole.*

Your only shot on the putting green is to try and stroke the ball into the hole. The "stymie," a putt designed to leave the shooter's ball in a spot where it obstructs his opponent's line to the hole, was outlawed in 1951.

8. *If you should lose your ball by its being taken up or any other way, you are to go back to the spot where you struck last and drop another ball and allow your adversary a stroke for the misfortune.*

It is a penalty stroke for the misfortune of losing your ball, and you may drop a new one into play at the point where the shot crossed an out-of-bounds marker, passed into a hazard, or was "taken up."

9. *No man at holing his ball is to be allowed to mark his way to the hole with his club or anything else.*

Don't touch the line of your putt except to remove loose impediments or to repair ball marks, and you can't test the putting surface by scraping it or rolling a ball.

10. If a ball is stopped by any person, horse, dog or anything else, the ball so stopped must be played where it lies.

If your stroke hits a tree, a cow, a building, or some other vegetable/animal/mineral object and is still in bounds, you must play the ball where it lies. And you can't improve your lie by bending or breaking anything on which the ball rests or improve your shot outside of the normal swing area.

It's a one stroke penalty for these infractions, and two strokes if you play the wrong ball (plus, you have to go back and replay your shot from the original lie).

11. If you draw your club in order to strike and proceed so far with your stroke as to be bringing down your club, if then your club should break in any way, it is to be counted a stroke.

Once you begin your downswing you are officially taking a stroke, pal.

If your ball is in a bunker or water hazard, you can't touch the ground with the club before striking the ball. Touching the clubhead to the ground is called "grounding," and you can't ground the club in a bunker or water hazard.

12. He whose ball lies farthest from the hole is obliged to play first.

The person "away" (furthest from the hole) always shoots next. On the tee, a lottery can determine the first person to tee off. The person with the lowest score on the previous hole or the most recent low score has the honor of teeing off on the remaining holes, followed by ascending order of scores.

13. Neither trench, ditch, nor dike made for the preservation of the links, nor the Scholar's Holes, nor the Soldier's Line shall be counted a hazard, but the ball is to be taken out, teed, and played with an iron club.

Man-made objects that interfere with play, not including objects used as out-of-bounds markers, are called obstructions. Obstructions can be moved without penalty, or you can drop your ball within one club length of the nearest open spot without penalty. If you encounter an obstruction in a bunker or on the green, drop within one club length while remaining in the bunker or on the green. If your ball is in casual water (not designed to be part of the course), ground under repair, or in a hole made by a burrowing animal, you can drop within one club length without a penalty.

GOLF ETIQUETTE

- Silence is golden—don't talk, move around, or stand too close to a player taking a shot.

- Don't play until the group ahead is out of the way.

- Leave the green as soon as all players in your group have holed out.

- Allow faster players to play through.

- Replace divots, smooth out bunkers.

- Don't step on the line of another player's putt.

- Repair ball marks on the green, and don't drop clubs on the putting surface.

- The best you can do is to leave the course in the condition in which you found it.

- Play well, have fun.

GLOSSARY OF GOLF JARGON

ace—hitting the ball in the hole from the driving area; also a *hole-in-one*.

address—the golfer's position when preparing to strike the ball just before beginning the backswing.

aggregate—the total number of strokes for all holes completed by a golfer.

air shot—a stroke in which the player completely misses the ball. Same as a *whiff*.

albatross—three strokes under par for a hole; also a *double eagle*.

amateur—in golf, a nonprofessional player, someone who is not paid for playing. The complete "Rules of Amateur Status" appear as an appendix to the *Rules of Golf* (USGA).

american ball—the USGA requires that a golf ball must conform to requirements concerning maximum weight, minimum size, spherical symmetry, initial velocity, and overall distance. The USGA also issues a List of Conforming Golf Balls. Historically, American balls have tended to be somewhat larger than those used in Great Britain and internationally. Compare with *British ball*.

approach—a shot from the fairway or the rough to the green, and also the strategy selected to land a shot on a particular area of the green.

approach putt—a cautious putting stroke designed to ensure the ball will stop at a spot from which the golfer can easily hole out, avoiding the possibility of holing out in one but reducing the risk of facing another difficult putt. Compare with *lag putt*.

apron—the area of close-cropped grass outlining the green. Shots made from the apron are not considered putts, even though a putter may be used. Players may not pick up their ball and clean it when it is on the apron. See also *fringe, frog hair,* and *collar*.

architect—the designer of a golf course.

architecture—the design of a course and the discipline of designing golf courses.

arnie—successfully making par after having driven off the fairway.

The odds of making an albatross have been put at 1 in 5.85 million. John Cook did it on the 14th hole (475-yard par 5) at the Ocean Course on Hilton Head Island using a 3 Wood and an 8 Iron. That was in the morning; in the afternoon he did it again on the same hole, using a 3 Wood and a Wedge.

---

attack—to play aggressively.

away—the ball furthest from the hole. The phrase "you're away" is spoken to the person who shoots next; "you're still away" is one of the worst things to hear on a golf course.

baffie—an old club similar to a 3-iron; from "baff," a Scottish word meaning to put the ball in the air.

backspin—reverse rotation of a ball in flight. Players impart backspin to the ball to make it fly up more steeply and to make it stop upon landing. Excessive backspin can cause the ball to literally spin back toward the player after landing.

backstroke—same as *backswing*.

backswing—that part of the golf swing that begins with the takeaway and ends with the start of the downswing.

bail out—when the weight of the body pulls away from the ball during a stroke, drawing the shot along the side the golfer swings from.

balata—golf ball cover material made from by-product of the rubber tree. Balata balls spin faster but don't travel as far and tend to be easily cut.

ball—in addition to referring to the golf ball with which golf is played, a ball may also refer to the ball as a shot, as in "Good ball!"—meaning good shot. Ball may also refer to a golfer's score, so that the best ball on a hole means the lowest score.

The practice of using the word "birdie" to describe a score of one stroke under par was begun in the United States. Supposedly, A.H. Smith of Atlantic City holed out in one under par and said, "That's a bird of a shot," and the term stuck.

ball mark—the mark left by a ball when it hits the surface of the green. Golf etiquette demands that players repair their ball marks, usually with a tee or repair tool. When putting, a player may repair a ball mark in his or her line without penalty.

ball marker—the coin or other flat object used to mark one's ball on the green.

banana ball—an outrageous slice, where the trajectory of the ball resembles a banana's curve.

bank shot—when the backswing is impeded by a wall or a tree, a golfer might turn his back to the hole and bank his shot off the impediment for a better chance at moving the ball nearer to the hole. More commonly, a bank shot is played into a bank surrounding a green, so that the ball bounces against the bank and rolls down to the putting surface.

barkie—successfully making par after hitting a tree on the approach shot.

baseball grip—a grip in which the hands function independently, similar to the way most players hold a baseball bat; unlike the *overlapping* grip or the *interlocking* grip. See also *Vardon* grip.

bent—a finely textured strain of grass used for putting greens. See also *Bermuda*.

bermuda—coarser than bent grass, Bermuda is typically used in fairways as well as greens in hot, humid climates. The coarser Bermuda grain can affect the line of a putt and needs to be taken into account.

best ball—team format in which the lowest individual score on a hole becomes the team's score in a best-ball match.

birdie—scoring one-under par for a hole. "Nice bird" is always good to hear.

birdieable—expression of confidence that a hole can be stroked under par; something usually said by those who also say "do-able."

bird's-nest—a hole that proves easy to break par on.

bisque—a handicap stroke that can be used at any time during a match.

bite—a term usually implored on an approach shot to catch hold and stop on the green.

blade—the bottom edge on the clubface of an iron; a narrow, forged iron; to *scull.*

blade putter—a style of putter where the shaft is attached to one end of the head of the putter, with the head usually made of iron. Compare with *center-shafted putter, mallet-head putter.*

blast—an *explosion* from the bunker that floats up and lands on the green with strong backspin.

blind—a blind shot is one where the golfer cannot see the ball land, often caused by strategically placed hills and trees that obstruct the player's view. Similarly, a blind green is one that is obstructed from view even from the teeing area or the fairway.

bogey—holing the ball in one over par. Before par came into use early in the twentieth century, shooting bogey golf was considered a standard for the average player. Additional strokes on a hole are called double-, triple-, and quadruple bogies, then only the number can adequately convey the horror.

borrow—when putting across a slope, the borrow is the amount of compensation required to play the break in lining up the putt. A player or a ball may be said to borrow (some land) from the slope of the green.

bramble—gnarly brush.

brassie or brassy—a club similar to the two-wood, with a brass plate on the sole. Not used much after the mid-twentieth century.

break—the slope of a green that putters try to read in planning their shots.

british ball—the Royal and Ancient Club of St. Andrews, the British rulemaking body, requires that a golf ball must conform to requirements concerning maximum weight and minimum size, among other things. British balls have tended to be somewhat smaller than those used in the United States. Compare *American ball.*

bump and run—a low shot from the fairway, usually under 70 yards and executed with a shortened back-swing in which the golfer attempts to bounce the ball onto the green, rather than lofting it. Usually used in windy conditions or on dry, fast courses.

bunker—the official and authorized term for a hole in the ground, sometimes a crater, filled with sand, and designated as a hazard. From the Scottish. The term "sand trap" isn't recognized by the USGA.

bye—in match play, refers to those holes left after the match has been decided. If a match ends at 4-3, the final three holes are called bye holes.

The term "bogey" comes from the Great Yarmouth Golf Club in England, where a member, Major Charles Wellman, referred to a failure to achieve par as "getting caught by the bogey man." Club members created an imaginary Colonel Bogey, who allegedly would go around the course in one stroke over par for each hole.

caddie/caddy—from the French word *cadet* name for assistants in royal courts; Mary Queen of Scots, generally acknowledged as the first woman golfer, brought French cadets (called pages in English courts) to Great Britain, and among other duties they lugged her golf clubs. Caddies carry and care for players' equipment and many have become essential associates for professional golfers.

calcutta—a form of gambling on a match or tournament where bets placed on the competitors are put into a pool and distributed to the winning players and bettors.

callaway system—a means of scoring for players who lack an established handicap (see the handicapping section in this chapter).

card—as a noun it refers to the scorecard, which in tournaments must be verified and signed. Signing an incorrect card is grounds for disqualification. As a verb it means to score, or make and record a score, as in, "She carded a par 72 in the final round."

carry—the distance a shot remains aloft; also used as a verb to describe the distance needed for a successful shot ("you'll need to carry the water and the bunker if you aim directly for the pin").

casual water—a puddle not designed for the course, resulting from rain or excessive moisture. A ball lying in casual water may be picked up and dropped without penalty on a dryer spot but not nearer to the hole. Compare *water hazard.*

After Walter Travis, an American, won the British Amateur in 1904 using a center-shafted putter called a Schenectady, the Royal and Ancient banned the use of center-shafted putters from 1909 to 1952.

center-shafted—a club with the shaft attached some distance from the heel of the clubface. Such clubs are not legal under the rules of golf, except for putters.

charge—a series of excellent shots in tournament play that closes the score between competitors; Arnold Palmer, Jack Nicklaus, and Tiger Woods have frequently won tournaments with late charges.

chili-dip—a weak shot resulting from the clubhead striking the ground before the ball and unearthing a small tract of land.

chip, chip shot, chip and run—a shortened or softer stroke with a partial swing near the green, where a player uses an iron to keep the ball low and have it roll toward the hole.

chip in—to hole the ball from a short distance outside the putting surface using a chip shot.

cleek—a nineteenth-century club that was characteristically a lightweight narrow-bladed iron club. Various models were used for long shots to the green (similar to a present-day 1- or 2-iron), for playing from sand and rough, for approaching, and for putting. See also *putting cleek.*

cleekmaker—a nineteenth-century term for someone who made iron clubs by hand. See also *cleek.*

closed stance—a stance where the golfer moves his or her back foot away from the line of play. Closed stances are favored for shots where the player desires to keep the ball low and possibly to draw the ball from right to left (for a right-handed player). See also *open stance, square stance.*

club professional—a professional golfer who derives income from affiliation with a particular country club, rather than from competing regularly in tournaments. Compare *playing professional.*

clubface (also face)—the area on the *clubhead* designed for striking the ball. Specifically, the flat part of the club-head that makes contact with the ball. The clubface is typically grooved or scored, although the rules of golf prohibit certain types of grooves in the clubface. The sweet spot is also located on the clubface.

clubhead (also head)—that part of the club at the opposite end of the grip that makes contact with the ball. Golfers like to talk about generating clubhead speed for greater distance.

club-length—obviously the length of a club, which was once an allowable distance away from a hole for using a tee in rough terrain; on the putting green, players use the club length to mark their ball if the lie is in directly line with another player's putt.

clubshaft (also shaft)—the long part of the club that connects the grip with the club head. Players may choose from clubshafts made of different materials, such as titanium, steel, or graphite, and of differing flexibility.

collar—an area of slightly longer grass that borders the edge of the putting green. Shots made from the collar are not considered putts, even though a putter may be used. Players may not pick up their ball and clean it when it is on the collar. Same as *apron* or *fringe.*

come back, come-backer—a ball that lands with backspin that causes it to spin back, or the putt one makes after having passed the hole with a previous putt.

coming in—the back nine of an 18-hole course, which returns the golfer to the clubhouse.

compression—refers to the hardness or resilience of a golf ball, which affects how the ball reacts to the impact of a golf club. Balls come in a range of compressions, form high to low.

concede—to give to one's opponent. In match play a competitor may concede an opponent's putt. They may even concede a hole when it is clear there is no chance of winning it. No shots can be conceded in medal play.

cop or cop bunker—an obsolete term referring to a knoll or bank regarded as a hazard or obstacle.

course management—refers to a player's ability to direct his or her play in terms of what the course offers. An example of good course management would be to try for a par on a hole that is too difficult to birdie, or to aim a shot to a landing area on the left when there is a water hazard to contend with on the right.

course rating—the average score a *scratch handicap* (zero handicap) golfer would score on a particular course, as sanctioned by golf's governing bodies. See *slope rating*.

croquet—a form of putting where a player stands behind the ball and strokes in the manner of croquet shots; now outlawed.

cross-bunker—a bunker that stretches across the fairway, rather than running parallel to it, like the one on the second hole at Pebble Beach.

Sam Snead changed his putting stroke to the croquet style after suffering from the yips in the 1966 PGA Championship

---

cross-handed—a type of putting grip in which the hands are reversed from their normal position.

cup—same as *hole*. Refers to the cup placed inside the hole on the putting green to reinforce the sides of the hole. A fellow golfer might say, "Put it in the cup," as encouragement to hole out the putt.

cut shot—a special shot that a player hits in such a way as to make the ball fade. The shot typically has a high trajectory and carries extra backspin and is executed with an open clubface.

the cut—a score demarcation line after two rounds that narrows the number of players in a tournament for the final two rounds by eliminating those with higher scores. Professional golfers have to make the cut in order to be eligible for tournament money.

dance floor—the putting surface.

deuce—a two, same as in cards. Most deuces are scored on par-three holes, where they are birdies. A deuce on a par-four would be an eagle.

dimple—dimples appear on the surface of a golf ball. Different dimple patterns can affect the trajectory of the ball, hence ball manufacturers may designate different ball models as "high trajectory" or "tour trajectory" and so forth.

divot—the scar left on the ground when a golf club hits beneath the ball and excavates some turf. Divot is actually a Scottish word for a piece of turf. Remember to repair your divots.

Gene Sarazen scored a rare deuce on the par-five fifteenth in the 1935 Masters to catch leader Craig Wood, then won the tournament in a playoff. Sarazen's deuce was an albatross, or double eagle.

dogleg or dog-leg—a fairway that runs partway straight and partway angled off, similar to the shape of a dog's hind leg. Also used as a verb, as in "this hole doglegs right."

dormie—used in match play to describe a situation where a player cannot lose but has not yet clinched victory, like being four holes ahead with four left to play.

double-eagle—a more common term than *albatross* to describe a three-under par hole.

downhiller—a putt that picks up speed as its goes downhill toward the hole. The opposite of an "uphiller."

downswing—that part of the golf swing that begins at the top of the backswing and ends with ball contact.

draw—a shot that spins right to left (and vice versa for lefties) purposefully to avoid or compensate for an obstacle and reach a desired lie, as opposed to a *hook*—an unintentionally curved shot that turns on the golfer's side.

drive—the initial shot on a hole, played from a tee.

driver—the club with the least loft, used for striking off the tee. Used to be called the play club.

driving cleek—see *cleek*.

driving iron—may refer to a modern-day one-iron or to iron clubs, no longer in use, that were used for various shots through the green.

driving mashie—an obsolete iron club with less loft than a mashie-iron that was used for driving and long shots to the green.

driving putter—a nineteenth-century wooden club with little or no loft that was used for driving low shots, especially into the wind.

driving range—an area where golfers practice their drives and other shots. It may be an area set aside from the course itself, or a commercial location where players may hit golf shots for practice.

drop—refers to dropping the ball, usually from shoulder height, under certain conditions specified in the rules of golf. "He's allowed a drop" or "He'll have to drop" means the player may drop his ball as specified in the rules of golf. To drop a putt means to hole it.

dub—to dub a shot means to mishit it, especially a shot that doesn't go very far. May also refer to a player who consistently dubs his or her shots.

duck-hook—an especially sharp hook to the left (for a right-handed golfer).

duff—a mishit, especially one that involves hitting behind the ball and then topping it.

duffer—a casual, part-time golfer, not as bad as a *hack*.

eagle—two stokes below par for a hole.

executive course—a short-yardage golf course consisting mainly of par-three holes.

explode—to swing with full might with a severely lofted club at a ball in a bunker or deep rough and loft it out to land, preferably, on the green.

explosion or explosion shot—a full-swing shot used in the sand to make the ball "explode" upward out of the bunker.

face (also clubface, or club face)—the flat part of the club-head that makes contact with the ball. The face is typically grooved or scored, although the rules of golf prohibit certain types of grooves in the face. The sweet spot is also located on the face.

fade—a shot designed to veer away from the side where the golfer hits in order to avoid an obstacle and reach a desired lie. Compare *slice, draw,* and *hook.*

fair green—an early term for the putting surface.

fairway—closely-cropped grass along the center line of a hole that provides the best surface from which to hit. Usually runs 30 to 50 yards wide.

fairway wood—a club with a larger head than an iron used for longer-distance shots from the fairway.

fat—hitting behind the ball unintentionally, resulting in a lusty swing with little distance to show.

featherie—a ball made of tightly-wrapped feathers within a leather covering. Used from the earliest times to the mid-nineteenth century, when the *guttie* came into use.

fescue—a type of grass widely used on golf courses.

flag—same as *flagstick.* The flag typically has the number of the hole printed on it. Some courses use different colored flags to indicate whether the pin placement is toward the front of the green, in the middle, or toward the back.

flagstick—used to mark the spot where the hole is. See also *pin.*

flange—the bottom part of the iron clubhead that projects backward from the clubface. The flange on a sand wedge is somewhat larger than on other clubs, which prevents the club from digging in too deeply into the sand.

flat—can be used in golf as an adjective to describe holding a golf club; a type of swing; or a golf course layout. A golf club is held flat when it is held at a wide angle to the ground. A flat swing is one that moves more horizontally than vertically. A flat course is one with relatively few hills and valleys.

flex—refers to the relative flexibility or stiffness of the shaft of a golf club. Today's clubs come in a range of flexes, from super stiff to highly flexible.

flip or flip shot—a short, delicate approach shot played with a lofted club. Generally used when a player has little green to work with and doesn't want the ball to roll a lot. Compare *flop shot.*

flip wedge—a *flip shot* played with a wedge.

floater—an obsolete term referring to a golf ball that would float in water, as opposed to a *sinker.*

flop shot—a delicate approach shot from the rough, where the player opens the clubface to allow the club to move through the heavy grass without digging into the ground. Compare *flip shot.*

flub—to mishit a shot, or a mishit shot.

fly—to fly the green means to air one's shot over the green. The term can also be used with other designated objects, such as a hazard or tree, meaning to make the ball fly over them.

The word Fore! may have derived from a phrase, "beware before," that British artillery men yelled to warn the infantry that a volley of cannonballs were about to be discharged at the enemy.

flyer—a shot that travels farther in the air than was intended by the golfer. Flyers often occur on shots from the rough.

follow through or follow-through—that part of the golf swing that occurs after contact is made with the ball. A good follow-through is an important part of an effective golf swing.

fore—a word called out to warn other golfers that a ball is headed their way.

forecaddie or forecaddy—a non-club-carrying assistant who goes ahead of the players to indicate the position of their balls during play.

four-ball—a match between two teams of two players, in which each team plays its better ball against the better ball of the other. In four-ball stroke play, the lower score of the partners is their score for the hole.

foursome—a match in which two play against two, and each side plays one ball. Once the term came to be used to mean a four-ball match, or any group of four golfers, the term *Scotch foursome* was used to distinguish a foursome from a four-ball match.

fried-egg—a ball half-buried in a sand trap.

fringe—a common expression for the area of slightly longer grass around a putting green. See also *apron, collar,* and *frog hair.*

frog hair—a colloquial expression for the area of slightly longer grass around a putting green.

frosty—another cute name, like *snowman,* to describe an ugly 8 score on a hole.

gallery—the spectators who follow and watch the players.

galleryite—someone who is a member of the gallery.

game—the game of golf. May also refer to a round of golf, as in "Nice game," or to a player's level of performance, as in "She plays a good game." A player's short game refers to his or her performance around the greens, while a player's long game refers to their driving and long approach shots.

gimme—a putt, usually two inches or less, conceded to a player.

globe (miss the globe)—an archaic phrase meaning to make a stroke without hitting the ball, or globe. See also *air shot, whiff.*

gobble—an archaic term used to describe a hard-hit putt that goes in the hole.

going out—the front nine holes of a golf course that leads the player away from the clubhouse; coming in is the back nine.

glove or golf glove—most golfers wear a soft, tight-fitting glove when driving and hitting other shots, but rarely on or around the green.

golf lawyer—someone who frequently quotes the rules of golf and invokes them on perhaps too many occasions.

golf widow—the poor spouse of a dedicated golfer who's on a golf course more often than he's at home.

golf widower—the poor spouse of a dedicated golfer who's on a golf course more often than she's at home.

goose-neck or goose-necked—describes an older type of golf club that had a curved neck, making the heel slightly offset from the line of the shaft.

gorse—a type of evergreen found chiefly on British courses.

grain—the angle of grass on or around a green, which a player must take into account when putting and chipping.

green—the putting surface. Also used to indicate the whole course, which is why course superintendents are called greenskeepers.

greenie—a bet won by the golfer who hits the ball closest to the pin.

green committee—usually a group of members at a golf club who are responsible for the maintenance of the golf course. Sometimes erroneously referred to as the greens committee.

green fee (also greens fee)—the fee charged by a golf course to play a round of golf. The green fee usually does not include the cost of a golf cart.

greenkeeper or green-keeper (also greenskeeper)—an employee of a golf club who takes care of the greens and other parts of the course. The head greenkeeper may also be called the course superintendent.

grip—the position of the hands and fingers on the shaft. See *baseball grip, overlapping grip, interlocking grip*, and *Vardon grip*.

groove—scored lines that appear on the clubfaces of woods and irons. Certain types of grooves may be ruled illegal.

The word "golf" comes from the German word *kolbe*, meaning club. The first written reference to golf was in an Act of Scottish Parliament in 1457 forbidding the playing of the game, because Scotland and England were at war, and the country's leaders didn't want young men neglecting their military service.

---

gross or gross score—a player's score before handicap strokes are added or subtracted.

ground—to settle the head of a club into the playing surface around the ball. Clubs cannot be ground in a bunker.

ground under repair—designated unplayable areas undergoing reconditioning; a player is allowed to drop away from such areas without penalty.

gutta percha—a type of golf ball common in the late nineteenth century. Made of a hard substance derived from the sap of Malaysian trees. First used in 1848 and subsequently replaced by rubber-cored balls around the turn of the century.

guttie, gutty—the gutta percha ball, made of solid rubber and developed in the mid-nineteenth century. Replaced the *feathery* and was in turn replaced by the rubber-cored *Haskell ball*.

hack/hacker—a wild swinging player, generally, a poor golfer.

halve—in match play, a hole is said to be halved when both sides make the same score.

handicap—an average of scores that indicates the amount of strokes over par a golfer is likely to have after 18 holes. Handicaps were developed to improve competition between players of various skill levels.

Golfing tradition has it that a player who scores a hole-in-one is obligated to buy a drink for everyone in the clubhouse.

haskell ball—the first rubber-cored golf ball, first manufactured by Coburn Haskell and J.R. Gammeter around 1898-1900.

hazard—refers to a *bunker* or a *water hazard*. Playing from a hazard is usually restricted in some way, such as not being allowed to ground your club in a bunker, or sand trap.

head (also clubhead or club-head)—that part of the club at the opposite end of the grip that makes contact with the ball. Golfers like to talk about generating clubhead speed for greater distance.

heel—the area of the clubhead directly beneath the shaft.

heroic architecture—a type of golf course layout that presents players with the opportunity to make "heroic" shots and score well provided they do not fail the test.

hickory—wood that was used to make golf shafts during the nineteenth and early twentieth centuries. A hickory is a club with such a shaft.

high or hole-high or pin-high—an approach shot that stops even with the hole, but usually some distance away to either side.

hit—to make contact with the ball.

hitter—a type of player who hits the ball hard, making maximum contact with the ball.

hog's back or hogback—refers to the contour of a green or fairway with a single ridge down the center.

hold—greens are said to hold when they are on the soft side and absorb the impact of the golf ball. Such shots to the green have little bounce or roll after impact.

holding—See *hold.*

hole—the object of the game is to put the ball in the hole with as few strokes as possible. Also refers to the eighteen tee-to-green subdivisions of a golf course, as in the "tenth hole." See also *cup.* For use as a verb, see *hole out.*

holeable—a variation on "makeable." Means that a putt, while long, can be made. May also refer to chip shots around the green.

holed—to sink a putt, to finish the hole. A ball is said to be holed when it is in the cup. See also *hole out.*

hole-high—even with the hole. Same as *pin-high.*

hole-in-one—completing a hole in only one shot. Most commonly occurs on a par-three hole, although holes-in-one have happened on short par-fours. Prizes are usually awarded to a player who scores a hole-in-one, and many clubhouses display the names of the players who have scored holes-in-one. Also called an *ace.*

hole out—to complete a hole by hitting the ball into the hole. Failure to hole out in medal play is grounds for disqualification. In match play, a player is not required to hole out if his or her competitor concedes the shot.

holer—someone who is a good putter.

home—although golfers are away from home a lot, the word itself has many positive meanings on the golf course. To "get home" can mean to get in the hole or on the green. To "come home" means to play the incoming nine holes, just as the "home nine" means the final nine holes of an eighteen-hole course. The "home hole" refers to the eighteenth hole.

home-and-home—refers to a match or tournament that is played on the home courses of both sides in the competition.

honor or honour—the person who scores lowest on a hole has the honor of teeing off first on the next one.

hood—a hooded clubface is one that is held in such a way as to reduce its loft. Somewhat different from closing the face of club, which involves turning the clubface at an angle from the intended line of flight.

hook—a ball is said to hook when it travels sharply from right to left (for a right-handed golfer), or left to right for a left-handed player. A hook is basically an out-of-control draw.

hooker—someone who habitually hooks the ball.

hosel—the socket where the shaft of the club is attached to the clubhead.

impediment—according to the USGA's *Rules of Golf,* "Loose impediments are natural objects such as stones, leaves, twigs, branches and the like, dung, worms and insects and casts or heaps made by them, provided they are not fixed or growing, are not solidly imbedded and do not adhere to the ball." Loose impediments may be moved without penalty, except when both the loose impediment and ball lie in or touch the same hazard. If the ball moves when removing an impediment, a one-stroke penalty should be assessed unless the ball is on the green, in which

case there is no penalty "provided the movement of the ball or the ball-marker is directly attributable to the removal of the loose impediment." Compare *obstruction.*

inland—used to describe a golf course that is not located near the ocean or other large body of water, hence not a classic Scottish seaside links-type course.

inside—to be inside your opponent means to be closer to the hole.

interlocking grip—a way of holding the golf club so that the little finger of the right hand interlocks with the forefinger of the left hand (for a right-handed player).

iron—an iron, as distinguished from a *wood,* is any club from a one-iron to a wedge. Players who use an iron off the tee are willing to sacrifice distance for greater accuracy.

jigger—an iron club, no longer in use, that had moderate loft and was used primarily for approach shots.

kick—same as bounce. A ball may "kick left" or "kick right" when it lands. When a ball takes a particularly favorable bounce, a player might say, "Nice kick!"

knockdown shot—a shot that is hit intentionally low, usually played under windy conditions so as to minimize the effect of the wind on the shot.

lag—to play a long putt intentionally short to avoid the risk of going too far past the hole and three-putting.

lag putt—a long putt that comes up just short of the hole, within makeable range.

laid back—the club face is laid back when a player opens the face to achieve greater loft.

lay—refers to hitting a shot with good results, especially on and around the green, as when a player lays his approach shot close to the hole.

lay back—to open the clubface to achieve greater loft.

layout—a term used to refer to the arrangement of holes on a golf course.

lay up—to play a drive or other shot intentionally short, either to keep it away from a hazard or for position on the next shot.

layup—a shot that is laid up, or played intentionally short.

length—golfers have length when they are able to hit the ball consistently far. Such players are known as long hitters. The length of a golf club may refer to the physical length of its shaft as well as to the distance of the shots hit with the club.

lie—a lie can refer to the position of the golf ball at rest on the ground and is usually described either as a good lie or a bad lie. As a verb it is used when asking or stating how many shots a player has taken to a certain point on a hole, as in "How many do you lie?," or as an answer, "I'm lying three."

lift—to pick up one's ball. Under certain wet conditions, tournament players may be allowed to lift, clean, and place their ball in the fairway to give them the opportunity to remove mud and other debris from the ball. Under normal playing conditions, players may lift their ball without penalty only when on the green.

line—on the green, the line is an imaginary line from the ball to the hole. From tee to green, or

through the green, the line is an imaginary line in the fairway running from the tee to the hole. It's basically where a golfer wants the ball to go.

line up—golfers line up their putts by standing behind the ball and imagining a line from the ball to the hole, taking into account the speed and contour of the green. Golfers playing without the benefit of a forecaddie sometimes line up their ball with a tree or other landmark after hitting it to make it easier to find.

links—although commonly misused today to refer to any type of golf course, it originally referred to courses in Scotland where the holes were laid out end to end, often along the coastline. In a links course the holes appear as "links" in a chain.

linksland—terrain typical of the classic Scottish seaside links courses. Linksland conditions also include the winds that frequently occur on Scottish seaside links.

linksman—another term for a golfer.

lip—the edge of the cup or hole. Putts are said to lip out when they fail to drop in the hole after skirting the lip of the cup.

loft—to loft the ball means to hit it higher than normal.

loft—the loft of a club refers to the angle of the clubface. Standard loft on a driver is about 12 degrees, 47 degrees for a nine-iron.

lofted—a lofted club is one with a relatively steep loft, or angle, on the clubface. Lofted clubs are used to hit the ball high and short rather than low and far.

lofter or lofting iron—an iron club used in the nineteenth and early twentieth century chiefly for approach shots.

The PGA Championship was held as a match play event until it became a strokeplay event in 1958. Many international competitions, such as the Ryder Cup, are conducted as match play events.

long driving—hitting drives that go a long distance. Some tournaments feature a long-driving contest, in which the winner is the player who can hit the ball the farthest with a driver.

long irons—those irons that are used primarily for distance, as opposed to the short irons that are used for accuracy. Long irons are generally one-through three-irons, middle irons are four-through six-irons, and short irons include seven-through nine-irons and wedges.

loop—another term for a round of golf.

loose impediments—according to the USGA's *Rules of Golf,* "Loose impediments are natural objects such as stones, leaves, twigs, branches and the like, dung, worms and insects and casts or heaps made by them, provided they are not fixed or growing, are not solidly imbedded and do not adhere to the ball." Loose impediments may be moved without penalty, except when both the loose impediment and ball lie in or touch the same hazard. If the ball moves when removing an impediment, a one-stroke penalty should be assessed unless the ball is on the green, in which case there is no penalty "provided the movement of the ball or the ball-marker is directly attributable to the removal of the loose impediment." Compare *obstruction.*

LPGA—Ladies Professional Golf Association.

mallet or mallet-head— a type of putter with a wider and heavier head than a blade putter. They come in many variations and styles.

marker—can mean one of three things on a golf course. A fellow competitor or any person other than a referee designated to keep score is a marker. The two objects placed on the teeing ground, between which players must tee off from, are markers. The coin or other flat object used to mark one's ball on the green is also a marker, though most commonly referred to as a *ball marker.*

marshal—a tournament official whose duty is to control the movement of the gallery and to keep them quiet if need be.

mashie—term for a lofted iron club used in the nineteenth century, comparable to a five iron.

mashie-iron—term for a lofted iron club used in the nineteenth century, comparable to a four iron.

mashie-niblick—term for a lofted iron club used in the nineteenth century, comparable to a six or seven iron.

match—in golf, a contest between two sides or teams, played under the rules of *match play.*

match play—in match play, players or teams compete on a hole-by-hole basis rather than going by their total score for eighteen holes. The winner in match play is determined by who had the lowest score on the most holes. A winning score of 4-3, for example, means that the winner was up by four holes with only three holes left to play. Rules governing match play are somewhat different from those governing medal, or stroke, play.

match player—a golfer known for his or her ability in *match play.* Jerome Travers won four U.S. Amateurs and generally excelled in match-play events but had much less success in stroke-play tournaments, though he did win the 1914 U.S. Open.

In part to accommodate the needs of today's television audience, nearly all official PGA Tour, Senior PGA Tour, and LPGA Tour events are conducted as medal play events.

medal—the low qualifying score for a match-play event. The player with such a score is said to be the medalist for that event.

medal play—same as stroke play. Players compete on the basis of who had the lowest score for a particular number of holes, usually in multiples of 18 holes.

middle spoon or mid-spoon—a nineteenth-century wooden club with loft comparable to a three wood. There were also long spoons and short spoons.

mid-iron—refers to one of three types of clubs: an iron, used in the nineteenth and early twentieth century, with somewhat more loft than a driving iron; a two iron; or the middle irons (four through six irons) in between the long and short irons.

mid-mashie—another term for a three iron.

military golf— "left-right, left-right;" play similar to the cadence call in a military march.

misclub—a player is said to misclub when he or she selects the wrong club to use, with the result that the shot is either too long or too short. Usually the result of misjudging the distance and failing to take into account other conditions, such as the wind speed and direction.

misread—when a putt doesn't follow the line a player thought it would, then the player is said to have misread the putt. Also used as a noun, as in "That looked like a misread."

mulligan—although not allowed under the rules of golf, a Mulligan refers to replaying a shot, so that a player counts only one stroke when two were taken. A Mulligan is most commonly taken on a tee shot, although it is not clear whether the Mulligan refers to the first or second shot taken. Players usually seek or receive permission from their playing companions before taking a Mulligan.

nassau—a three-part contest or wager in golf, with winners designated for the first nine holes, the back nine, and the overall eighteen holes.

neck—that part of the club head that is tapered and holds the hosel.

net or net score—a player's score after handicap strokes are added or subtracted. Can refer to the score on a single hole, as in a net birdie, or for a full round.

niblick—wooden and iron niblicks were used in Scotland in the nineteenth century. The wooden niblick was a short-headed, steeply lofted club used primarily for hitting out of ruts and other tight spots. The iron niblick was also steeply lofted, with a concave face, and was also used for hitting out of ruts, divots, and other tight lies. The iron niblick developed into a steeply-lofted, deep-bladed club that was used in the rough and in sand. Niblick later became an alternate term for a nine iron.

nine—nine holes of a golf course. The front nine consists of the first nine holes of an eighteen-hole layout, the back nine being the final nine holes.

nineteenth hole—the clubhouse, where players meet for food, refreshment, and camaraderie after playing a round of eighteen holes.

observer—someone appointed to assist a referee during a tournament. May help decide questions of fact and report rules violations.

obstruction—as described in the USGA's *Rules of Golf,* an obstruction is "anything artificial, including the artificial surfaces and sides of roads and paths and manufactured ice." Exceptions include walls, fences, stakes, and railings used to define out of bounds. Also excepted is any construction deemed to be an integral part of the course. The rules provide for relief without penalty from obstructions.

offset—usually refers to a putter with a the clubhead set slightly off the line of the shaft.

on—short for "on the green," as in "I'm on in two."

one-putt—to finish a hole with only one putt. Since par assumes two putts per hole, a one-putt green can help a player make up a stroke on par or score a birdie.

one-shot—a one-shot hole is one whose green can be reached from the tee in one shot. Hence, it usually refers to a par-three or short par-four hole.

one up—in match play, to be ahead of one's opponents by one hole. In medal play, to have a lead of one stroke, as in "He's one up on the field."

one-wood—same as a driver.

open—a golf tournament open to any player who has won qualifying tournaments or has met other criteria.

open—a type of course without many trees.

open stance—an open stance is one where the golfer moves his or her forward foot back from the line of play. Open stances are favored for shorter shots requiring greater loft and accuracy, such as wedge shots, and when the player wants to fade the ball from left to right (for a right-handed player). See also *closed stance, square stance.*

out of bounds—any ground on which play is prohibited. According to the USGA's *Rules of Golf,* "A ball is out of bounds when all of it lies out of bounds."

outside agency—refers to a person or other type of agency that is not part of the match or, in stroke play, not part of the competitor's side. Includes referees, markers, observers, and forecaddies. Wind and water are not considered outside agencies.

overclub—to overclub is to take too much club. That is, to use too long of a club on a shot, with the result that the ball goes too far.

overlapping grip—a way of holding the golf club so that the little finger of the right hand overlaps the space between the forefinger and the second finger of the left hand (for a right-handed player). Also known as the *Vardon grip.*

overspin—same as topspin. Desirable on drives and putts, as it makes the ball travel farther and more likely to drop into the hole.

pair—two golfers playing as partners in a match or playing together in medal play.

pairing—the grouping of two competitors together in medal play.

par—the number of strokes a good golfer can be expected to make on each hole. Instead of reporting their scores in raw numbers, golfers may say they are so many strokes over or under par, or they shot even par.

par-five—the longest holes on a golf course are the par-fives. A good golfer is expected to reach the green in three shots and take two putts. There are usually two to four par-five holes on an eighteen-hole course.

Guidelines for par according to distance: Par 3...
up to 250 yards for men, 210 for women Par 4...
251 to 470 yards for men, 211 to 400 for women
Par 5...over 470 for men, 401 to 575 for women

par-four—most of the holes on a golf course are par-fours, where a player is expected to reach the green in two strokes and take two putts.

par-three—the shortest holes on a golf course are the par-threes, where players can reach the green with their tee shots. The challenge of the par-threes is selecting the proper club to use off the tee.

par-three course—a short-yardage golf course where all of the holes are par-threes. Some players practice on these courses to improve their accuracy. Also known as an *executive course.*

park or parkland—a type of course with trees and water that still retains a sense of openness, as opposed to having tree-lined fairways.

partner—a golfer who is teamed with another in a match or other type of competition. May also refer to the other golfer in a group of two in medal play. See also *playing partner.*

pawky—a pawky player is one who is considered cunning or tricky. From the Scottish term for trick or ruse.

peg—same as a *tee.*

penal—refers to a type of golf course architecture popular in the early twentieth century that penalizes poor shots with difficult lies and hazards.

penalty stroke—an extra stroke that is added to the score of a player or team under certain rules, such as for a lost ball or for a ball hit into a water hazard.

PGA—Professional Golf Association.

pick up—a player is said to pick up when he or she fails to hole out. In match play, a player may pick up their ball to signal they are conceding the hole to their opponent, or their opponent has conceded the putt. In medal play, to pick up means disqualification.

pill—another term for a golf ball.

pin—same as *flagstick.* Used to mark the spot where the hole is. Hitting the pin with a putt incurs a penalty stroke. A player may ask someone to "hold the pin" while he or she is putting, or "pull the pin" prior to putting. If the pin is being held, it must be pulled so that the ball does not touch it. The pin may be left in when chipping or putting from off the green.

pin-high—even with the hole. A shot that is pin-high is one that went the correct distance but is off-line.

pin placement or pin position—the location of the hole with respect to the front, back, or sides of the green. During the course of a tournament, the pin placements are generally changed each day.

pinsetter—the official or course employee responsible for *pin placement.*

pinsetting—same as *pin placement.*

pitch (also pitch shot)—used around the green to get the ball close to the hole, pitch shots are executed with a partial swing motion to loft the ball high into the air with little roll after the ball lands. See also *pitch-and-run* and *chip shot.*

pitch-and-putt—refers to a short-yardage golf course where most of the shots are short pitch shots to the green. Same as a *par-three course* or *executive course*.

pitch-and-run—this shot has a higher trajectory than a chip shot, but not so high as a full pitch. The ball is expected to roll toward the hole after landing.

pitch-in—when a pitch or pitch-and-run goes in the hole.

pitching irons—generally, those irons other than a pitching wedge that can be used for pitch or pitch-and-run shots around the green. Could be anything from a five-iron to a nine-iron, depending on the amount of loft desired and how much the player wants the ball to run after landing.

pitching wedge—a pitching wedge is distinguished from a sand wedge by less of an angle on the clubface, less weight, and a smaller flange projecting backwards from the face. Players typically use a pitching wedge around the green. A full swing with a pitching wedge can cause the ball to travel 100 yards or more.

pivot—refers to the rotation of the body, especially the shoulders, upper body, and hips, during the golf swing. Used as both a noun and verb.

placement—refers to the location of shots, especially as to where the ball ends up. Courses may be said to be designed for placement rather than for power, meaning that accuracy is rewarded more than distance.

plateau—refers to an area of raised ground on the golf course with a flat surface, usually a putting green.

plateaued—a plateaued green is one that is set on raised ground.

play—this versatile term is used by golfers in many different ways, but they always seem to know what it means. It can mean to make a stroke, to use a particular club in making a stroke, or the act of golfing in general. A golf course may be said to play long or in some other manner. A ball is "in play" as soon as it has been hit. Scoring systems are designated as types of play, as in match play or medal play.

playable—refers to the lie of a golf ball, meaning that the ball can be played. Compare *unplayable*.

playing partner—in medal or stroke play, the fellow competitor in a group of two.

playing professional—a golf pro who plays in tournaments, especially in one of the major tours. Compare *club professional*.

play through—to go ahead of the group in front. A faster group of players is sometimes, but rarely, allowed to play through a group of slower players.

playoff—additional holes played to determine the winner of a tournament when two or more players are tied at the end of regulation play. Playoffs may be of the "sudden death" variety, where the winner is the player who first wins a playoff hole. In some cases, such as the U.S. Open and other major tournaments, the playoff may consist of an additional round of 18 holes, to be played the next day.

plus fours—knickers, or knickerbockers, that are longer than shorts but shorter than full-length trousers. The term "plus fours" refers to the extra four inches added to shorts to make the knickers come over the knee. Although not widely worn these days, some touring professionals have made them their trademark.

pop—a pop shot is a short shot that is hit so as to make the ball come up sharply and quickly. To pop the ball is to make such a shot. Comparable to the baseball term, pop-up.

pot bunker—a type of bunker that is typically small and deep, very difficult to get out of. More common on Scottish links-type courses than in the United States.

preferred lies—to play preferred lies means to play under Winter Rules that allow golfers to improve the lie of their ball through the green.

president—refers to a nineteenth-century iron golf club that had a hole in the clubface to make it easier to play out of water.

press—golfers are said to press when they are trying too hard or put too much effort into a shot.

press—another completely different meaning of the term is its use in wagering on the course. A press bet is an additional bet made during the round, usually by the competitor who is losing, in order to have a chance to make up the original bet.

pro—same as *professional*.

pro-am—a golfing event that involves amateurs and professionals playing together, often held in conjunction with a professional tournament.

professional—golfers who earns their livelihood from golf, either through employment at a golf club or by entering tournaments and other competitive events to win money and other prizes.

pronate—a physiological term referring to the turning of the wrists from a palm-upward position to a palm-downward position.

pronation—see *pronate*.

pro side—to putt the ball away from the cup to a slope that will lead the ball toward the cup, as opposed to sucker side, which is to have the putt turn away from the hole by incorrectly reading the slope.

provisional ball—a second ball that is played when the first ball may be out of bounds or lost outside a water hazard. Players must announce they are hitting a provisional ball. If the first ball is subsequently found, the provisional ball is picked up without penalty.

public links—a golf course that is open to the public.

publinx—a shortened form of the term, "public links," that is used to refer to players not affiliated with a private golf club.

pull—a shot that is off-line to the left (for a right-handed player). The opposite of a push. Also used as a verb, meaning to make the ball go to the left of the intended line. See also *hook, pull-hook*.

pull cart—a two-wheel device that players use to carry their golf clubs. They are usually available for rent at a golf course. The British call them *trolleys*.

pull-hook—a shot that is not only off-line to the left, but also has the characteristics of a hook shot. It would tend to go farther left than a simple pull shot.

punch shot—a shot where the golfer attempts to "punch" the ball to keep it low, especially into the wind. The ball is usually positioned back in the stance, and the swing is a three-quarter one with lots of acceleration through the ball. Compare *knockdown shot*.

punchbowl—a descriptive term for a green that is contoured and shaped into a hollow, like a punchbowl.

Laura Davies eyes a putt at the Chrysler-Plymouth Tournament of Champions where she finished third.

are counted; shots made with a putter from off the putting surface are not considered putts. Two putts per hole is considered average. Also used as a verb, as in "She putts very well."

putter—the club used for putting on the green. There are countless models of putter, with the most recent innovation being the long-shafted putter. Most putters may be categorized as either a mallet-head or a blade-type putter, with either a center shaft or a shaft that is attached to one end of the putter head.

putting cleek—a nineteenth-century club that was characteristically a lightweight, narrow-bladed iron club used for putting. See also *cleek*.

putting green—the area of short grass around the hole, usually mowed and rolled to achieve the smoothest possible surface. The edge of the green may be bordered by a *collar* or *apron* of slightly longer grass. Specific rules govern play on the putting green, such as being able to pick up one's ball and clean it without penalty.

push—a shot that is off-line to the right (for a right-handed player). The opposite of a pull. Also used as a verb, meaning to make the ball go to the right of the intended line. See also *slice*.

putt—a shot made on the green with a putter, originally from the Scottish term meaning to push gently or nudge. When tabulating the number of putts, only those shots made on the putting surface

putt out—to finish putting, even when one is not farthest from the hole. In match play, the player closest to the hole may not putt out without permission from his or her opponent.

quail-high—a picturesque expression for a shot hit low to the ground, without much height. Useful for playing into an oncoming wind.

> The word "putt" comes from "put." On the green, the object is to "put" the ball into the hole.

quarter shot—a phrase no longer used much that refers to short chip shots and the like that are taken with less than a half swing.

rake—term for a club no longer in use that had vertical slots similar to a rake and was used for playing from sand or water. Today, when golfers refer to a rake, they mean an actual rake that is to be used for smoothing out the sand after playing from a sand trap. The rake should be place outside of the trap, where it is least likely to obstruct an oncoming ball.

read—players are said to "read" their putts, meaning to take into account the contour and speed of the green when lining up a putt. "Nice read," she said, meaning the ball rolled as intended and ended up in or near the cup. Players sometimes can get a "read" from another player whose putt is on the same line as theirs.

recover—even the best of golfers make mistakes and hit errant shots. When a golfer plays a good shot after a bad one, they are said to have recovered. The ability to recover from one's bad shots is essential to good scoring.

recovery— a recovery shot is one taken from the rough or a bunker or some other bad position that ends up in a good position.

regulation—to reach the green in regulation means to reach it in the number of strokes it would take to make par with two putts. For example, to reach a par four in regulation means to reach the green in two strokes. Also refers to the number of holes to be played in a tournament or competition. If two or more players are tied after regulation, they must determine the winner in a playoff.

relief—the rules of golf permit players to seek relief under certain conditions, which means they can move their ball and drop or place it without penalty.

reverse overlap—a type of grip in which the forefinger of the left hand overlaps the little finger of the right hand (for a right-handed player).

ribbed—refers to a clubface with prominently featured grooves and ribs. Such clubs are now illegal under the rules of golf. Grooves in the clubface must meet certain specifications, and markings in the impact area must not have sharp edges or raised lips.

rifle—a rifled shot is one that is hit hard, far, and accurately, as if it were shot from a rifle.

rim—to rim the cup means to roll one's putt around the edge of the cup, so the ball either goes past the hole or drops in.

rim out—to roll one's putt around the edge of the cup, so that the ball fails to drop in the hole.

roll—what the golf ball does after landing, or a putt does after being stroked. Depending on course conditions, the ball will tend to roll more or less than usual.

roll in—to sink a putt.

rough—the area along the sides of the fairway where the grass is allowed to grow longer. Courses may have two or three cuts of rough, with the grass being a different length in each one.

round—today a round of golf consists of playing eighteen holes, but that was not always the case. The British Open, for example, consisted of three rounds of twelve holes each when it was played at Prestwick from 1860 to 1872.

royal and ancient—a shortened version of The Royal and Ancient Golf Club of St. Andrews, which was so named in 1834 with the permission of King William IV. Also known as the "R & A," the rule-making body of international golf. Can also be used simply to refer to the game of golf itself, as in "a royal and ancient game."

rub of the green—refers to anything accidental that happens to the ball during the course of play, such as hitting a spectator or taking an unusual bounce off a cart path. The rules of golf provide no relief from a rub of the green; from the British expression, "that's the rub."

rubbercore—a ball with a rubber core, which replaced the gutta percha ball around the turn of the century.

rubber-cored—see *rubbercore*.

rules of golf—the official rules of golf, which are codified and published in the United States by the United States Golf Association (USGA) and in Great Britain by the Royal and Ancient Golf Club of St. Andrews.

run—the distance the ball travels after hitting the ground. May also refer to a shot hit along the ground. May also be used as a verb, meaning to play the ball along the ground. Compare *pitch and run*.

run down—a colorful way of making a putt.

run in—to run in a putt or chip means to hole it.

run up—to run up a shot means to play a short, low approach shot that bounces and runs onto the green.

rut iron or rutter or rutting iron or rutting niblick—different terms that refer to an iron club, no longer used, that was used primarily for hitting out of ruts and divots. Compare *niblick*.

sammy—an iron club, no longer in use, that made by twisting the head of a cleek. It is similar

Courses that host the U.S. Open each year prepare for the tournament by letting their roughs grow much longer than usual. This has the effect of keeping the scores high, so that each year there tend to be fewer subpar rounds in the U.S. Open than in other tournaments.

to a jigger but had a rounded back and was used for approach shots. Reportedly named after someone who worked in the shop in St. Andrews where the club was first made.

sand—short for *sand trap*. Players may discuss the different types of sand used in such traps, ranging from fine white sand to coarse brown sand.

sand-blaster—a sand wedge.

sand iron—may refer to a sand wedge or to a nineteenth-century club no longer in use that was used for playing from bunkers.

sand trap—*Bunker* is the officially recognized term.

sand wedge—has more loft than a pitching wedge and a longer flange, or bottom edge of the clubface, to keep the club from going too deep into the sand in a bunker. Sand wedges may also be used on grass.

schenectady or schenectady putter—a center-shafted putter with a mallet-type head, named after the city in New York where it was patented and manufactured.

scoop—a fault to be avoided when striking the ball is the tendency to scoop the ball instead of striking it cleanly.

scorecard—the card on which scores for each hole and the entire round are recorded, so named for the card stock out of which it is made. Players generally keep track of their own score, or a mark-

> Whatever happens to a ball by accident must be reckoned a rub of the green."
>
> —from the 1812 code of the Royal and Ancient.

er in each group may be designated to keep score. Scorecards must be signed and verified after each round of a tournament, and signing an incorrect scorecard is grounds for disqualification.

score play—an out-of-date term for stroke play.

scoring—lines or grooves that appear on the clubfaces of woods and irons.

scotch foursome—technically, a foursome competition means two teams of two players each playing one ball. With the term "foursome" frequently used to indicate a four-ball match, the term "Scotch foursome" was used to distinguish a foursome from a four-ball match.

scramble—has become the most popular format for corporate golf outings, since it tends to equalize players of different skill levels. In a scramble format, players on the same team each hit a shot. They choose the best result, then each player hits a shot from within one club length of where the best shot landed.

scrambling—players are said to be scrambling when they are struggling to make par, or find themselves playing a lot of *recovery shots*. A scrambling score is a good score that is made despite erratic play.

scratch—a scratch player is one with a zero handicap, that is, someone who usually shoots par or better. The term's origin lies in nineteenth-century athletics, where a scratch line indicated the start of a race. Runners with no handicap had to start from the scratch, while those with handicaps started ahead of the scratch.

scuff—to scuff a shot means to mishit it, especially by hitting the ground behind the ball before making contact with the ball. Compare *dub*.

scull—to scull (or skull) a ball means to hit it so that is travels along the ground without getting up in the air. Specifically, to hit the ball above its center or top half with the leading edge of an iron. Happens frequently with wedge shots and shots from the sand. Similar to topping the ball.

second—the second shot, taken after the drive or tee shot, as in "he hit a good second to the green."

setup—the way a player positions his or her body with respect to the ball and the intended line of flight before striking the ball.

set up—to set up means to position oneself for the golf swing.

shaft or clubshaft—the long part of the club that connects the grip with the club head. Players may choose from shafts made of different materials, such as titanium, steel, or graphite, and of differing flexibility.

shank—to hit the ball with the hosel, or shank, of an iron club, causing the ball to travel far right of the intended line; also, to hit a poor shot, as in "I shanked it."

shoot—to make or play a certain score, as in "What did you shoot?" May also mean to play, as in "Let's go shoot some golf."

short—a ball is said to be short when it fails to travel as far as intended, especially putts and approach shots. A ball that is short of a hazard is one that failed to travel the full distance to the hazard, and hence is in good shape.

short course—can refer to any layout that is less than full length. Compare *par-three course* and *executive course*.

short hole—generally used to refer to the par-three holes on a course, but may refer to any hole that is easy to reach in regulation because of its length.

short irons—those irons that are used primarily for accuracy, as opposed to the long irons that are used for distance. Short irons include seven-through nine-irons and wedges.

shot—what one does with a golf club and ball. In golf, frequently used interchangeably with *stroke*.

shotgun start—courses will resort to shotgun starts in special events and on other occasions to be able to accommodate more players. Under a shotgun start, groups of players start play at a designated time from different tees on the course, as opposed to a normal start when everyone begins play on the first hole. Thus, one group may start their round on the fifteenth hole and finish up on the fourteenth hole. When possible, the tees after par-three holes are left open at the start so as to avoid delays.

shotmaker—an accomplished golfer who can execute a variety of special shots, such as intentional fades and draws, knockdown shots, and bunker shots.

shotmaking—the ability to make a variety of special shots.

shut—another term for closed, as in closed face. To turn the club forward relative to the line of play.

shut-faced—a shut-faced club is one that is held so that the face is turned forward relative to the line of play.

side—a side may refer to one of two competing teams or entities, or it may refer to half of a full round of golf on a course.

sidehill—a sidehill lie is one where the ball is either above or below the golfer's feet. If the ball

---

"Schlaff" is one of the oldest terms in golf. Probably Scottish in origin, it refers to a mishit in which the clubhead strikes the ground before making contact with the ball.

---

is above the feet, it will tend to go left when struck. If below the player's feet, the ball tends to travel further right than usual.

sidehiller—usually refers to a putt than has to travel along the side of a hill or rise in the green.

single—a single match is one between only two players.

sink—another term for holing a putt.

sinker—an obsolete term referring to a golf ball that would sink in water, as opposed to a *floater.*

sit down—what players tell a ball to do when they want it to stop bouncing or rolling.

sit up—players hope their ball will sit up in the rough or wherever it comes to rest, making it easier to strike.

skull—to skull (or scull) a ball means to hit it so that is travels along the ground without getting up in the air. Specifically, to hit the ball above its center or top half with the leading edge of an iron. Happens frequently with wedge shots and shots from the sand. Similar to topping the ball.

sky—to sky a ball means to hit it very high into the air, with little distance. A type of mishit.

slice—a ball in flight is said to slice when it travels sharply from left to right (for a right-handed golfer), or right to left for a left-handed player. A slice is basically an out-of-control fade.

slicer—someone who habitually slices the ball.

One PGA Tour event, the Sprint International, uses a modified Stableford scoring system.

slope rating—a number assigned to a golf course that allows for the comparison of scores made on different courses. The slope rating is calculated by dividing the average score of "bogey golfers" by the average score of scratch players. Compare *course rating*.

smother—to smother the ball means to strike down on it so that it travels a short distance along the ground. A type of mishit cause by closing the clubface too soon before impact.

snake—a serpentine putt, or one that breaks more than once on its way to the hole.

snap-hook—an especially ugly type of hook shot, where the ball ends up on a right-to-left path (left to right for a left-handed player) nearly at a ninety degree angle to the fairway.

snowman—term used to describe a score of eight (8) on a hole. Same as a *frosty*.

socket—see *hosel*.

sole—the bottom surface of an iron or wood that generally rests on the ground when addressing the ball.

sole plate—a metal plate screwed to the sole of a wood.

spade or spade-mashie—an iron club, no longer in use, that has more loft than a mashie.

spoon—early wooden clubs were called spoons, and depending on their loft may have been called short spoons, long spoons, and middle spoons. In the twentieth century spoons were woods with more loft than brassies, and the term came to mean a three-wood.

spooned—an obsolete term meaning lofted. The spoon of a clubface meant its loft.

spray—players are said to spray their shots when they go in all different directions, without any apparent consistency.

spring—refers to the flexibility of the shaft of a golf club.

square or all-square—a match is square or all-square when it is tied, or even. To square a match means to bring both sides to the position of being even.

square stance—a square stance is one that is neither open nor closed, that is, it is parallel to the intended line of flight. See also *closed stance, open stance*.

stableford—a scoring system invented in 1931 by Dr. Frank Stableford of Liverpool, England. Under the Stableford system, points are won for scores in relation to a fixed score (par) on each hole, on a scale of one to five points: five points for a score of three under the fixed score (par), four points for two under, three points for one under, two points for even, and one point for one over. Higher scores receive no points.

stance—refers to the position of the golfer's body when addressing the ball, especially the feet in relation to the intended line of flight. See also *closed stance, open stance, square stance*.

stick—slang for a golf club, as in "Bring your sticks. We're going to play some golf." Also short for *flagstick*, as in "It hit the stick."

stiff—to knock a ball stiff means to hit it very close to the hole.

stipulated round—the playing of eighteen holes in sequence.

stop—a noun meaning the same as backspin, so that a pitched ball stops quickly upon landing. A golfer might say, "I need to put stop on the ball."

straight—a golfer who is straight hits consistently straight drives. Compare *hooker* and *slicer.*

straightaway—a hole is straightaway when there is a direct line from tee to green without any *doglegs.*

strategic architecture—a style of golf course architecture that emphasizes presenting options to golfers, causing them to weigh the risks and rewards of a particular shot. It is the most dominant form of golf course architecture today.

stroke—three meanings: the act of striking a ball which counts toward a player's score whether or not it is successful; the score of a stroke added to a player's score as a penalty or subtracted as a handicap. As a verb it refers to an especially smooth swing, especially in putting.

stroke play—same as medal play. Players compete on the basis of who had the lowest score for a particular number of holes, usually in multiples of eighteen holes.

stymie—abolished by the rules of golf in 1951, a stymie occurred on the putting green when one player's ball was in the line of another player's ball. Prior to the new rule, players were not allowed to lift and mark their ball on the green, so a player that was stymied had to play around it. Stymie may also refer to any type of obstacle, such as a tree, on the golf course that stands in line between a player and the hole.

sudden death—a type of playoff format where the winner of the tournament is the golfer who first wins a playoff hole.

superintendent—same as *greenkeeper.*

During the back nine of the 1928 PGA Championship, Leo Diegel twice set up a stymie—where his putt came to rest on a line between his opponent's ball and the cup—and both times Johnny Farrell, that year's U.S. Open champ, knocked Diegel's ball into the cup.

supinate—a physiological term meaning to rotate the wrists so that the palms face upward.

supination—the rotation of the wrists so that the palms face upward.

swale—refers to the contour of the ground on a golf course, specifically a contoured depression or hollow.

sweet spot or sweetspot—that part of the clubface where it is most desirable to make contact with the ball.

swing—refers to the entire act of hitting the ball, including taking the club away from the ball, the backswing, the downswing, and the follow through. Golfers who are "working on their swing" are trying to improve their ability to hit the ball in a consistent fashion.

swingweight—a way of measuring the weight of a golf club for the purpose of manufacturing a set of clubs with a consistent swingweight. Calculating the swingweight involves correlating the weight of the shaft and that of the clubhead.

swipe—to take a swipe at the ball means to swing at it.

takeaway—the beginning of the backswing, or that part of the swing where the club is "taken away" from the ball.

tap in—to complete a very short putt.

tap-in—a very short putt that can literally be tapped in without too much thought.

tee—the wooden peg used to elevate the ball when driving from the teeing ground. May not be used elsewhere on the golf course. May refer to the teeing ground as well, as in "The group ahead of us is already on the next tee." "You're on the tee" means it's your turn to tee off.

tee-box—before the advent of wooden tees, tees were improvised with mounds of sand. The tee-box was a box of sand placed near the teeing area for the purpose of making tees.

teed or teed up—through the green a ball is said to be teed up when it is sitting up, as opposed to its being buried.

teeing ground—the starting point for each hole on a golf course. Markers placed on the teeing ground indicate where players are supposed to tee off. Players must tee off from between the markers and no farther than two club lengths behind the markers.

tee off—to begin a hole by taking the first shot from the teeing ground. May also mean to start a round of golf, as in "What time do we tee off?"

tee-shot—any shot taken from the teeing ground, whether or not an actual tee was used.

tee up—to place the ball on a tee prior to making a tee-shot.

tempo—refers to the pace and timing, or rhythm, of a player's golf swing.

texas wedge—slang golfing terminology for a putter, when a putter is used for a shot from off the putting surface.

thin—to hit the ball thin means to catch the ball slightly above center.

three-putt—players don't like to three-putt a green, which means taking three putts to finish the hole. Since par is based on two putts per green, three-putting is a good way to blow a par after hitting the green in regulation.

three-ball match—a match where three players each play their own ball, and each player is in competition against the other two. Compare *threesome*.

three-quarter shot—a shot made with less than a full swing, usually referring to an approach shot.

threesome—a match in which one plays against two, and each side plays one ball.

through the green—according to the USGA's *Rules of Golf*, "The whole area of the course, except: a) The teeing ground and putting green of the hole being played; and b) All hazards on the course."

tight—a tight hole or golf course is one with characteristically narrow fairways. A tight lie is one where the ball sits directly on hard ground.

toe—the end of the clubhead, opposite the heel, that is farthest from the shaft.

top—to top the ball means to hit the ball above its center. The result is usually a shot that dribbles along and doesn't go very far.

topspin—same as *overspin*. Desirable on drives and putts, as it makes the ball travel farther and more likely to drop into the hole.

torque—in golf, refers to the tendency of the club to twist on impact.

torsion—in golf, same meaning as *torque*.

touch—refers to a golfer's ability to make difficult shots with delicate accuracy.

tour—a series of scheduled tournaments for professional golfers. In the United States, the major tours include the PGA Tour, PGA Senior Tour, and LPGA Tour.

touring—a touring professional is one who plays regularly on one of the major tours.

tournament—golfing competitions held over one or more days in which many players compete for money and/or prizes.

track iron—a primitive club used to hit out of ruts and divots. Alternate name for a rut iron or iron niblick.

trap or sand trap—casual term used instead of the official term, "bunker."

trapped—a player is said to be trapped when his or her ball lies in a sand trap, or bunker. A course is said to be well-trapped when it has a lot of sand traps.

trolley—British term for a *pull cart*.

trouble—on a golf course, any type of difficulty, such as a hazard, out of bounds, trees, etc. It's easy to get into trouble on a golf course.

turn—the turn is the halfway point in a round of golf, after nine holes have been played. The turn also refers to the turn of the hips and upper body in a golf swing. See also *pivot*.

two-putt—to finish a hole with two putts. Since par is based on two putts per hole, most players consider two putts nothing to complain about.

Sam Snead on the yips: "I've gotten rid of the yips four times, but they hang in there. You know, those two-foot downhill putts with a break. I'd rather see a rattlesnake."

---

twosome—a group of two golfers playing together in stroke play, where each plays their own ball.

uncock—refers to the straightening of the wrists in the downswing, after they have been cocked at the top of the backswing.

uncork—to hit an exceptionally long shot.

underclub—to use less club than was needed to cover the necessary distance.

underspin—another term for *backspin*.

unplayable lie—a terrible lie, so bad the player elects to repent and take a penalty stroke (dropping within two club-lengths).

up—a "nice up" can refer to an approach shot or a long putt that ends up well. To be up in a match means to be winning. Up can also mean to be on the green, as in "She was up in two."

up and down—most commonly used to describe reaching the green and holing out with one shot (up) and one putt (down). Used most often with reference to approach shots and especially bunker shots from around the green. A confident player might approach a bunker shot by saying, "I can get up and down from here."

upswing—alternate term, not used much these days, for *backwsing*.

USGA—United States Golf Association, the rule-making body in the United States.

vardon grip—same as *overlapping grip.* Named after six-time British Open winner Harry Vardon, who developed the grip to compensate for the slimmer handles of the hickory-shafted clubs that replaced the thicker-shafted clubs around the turn of the century.

waggle—at *address,* moving the club back and forth behind the ball to help set timing and concentration.

waste area—most precisely referring to a sandy area where the player is allowed to ground his club, unlike the rules governing bunkers. Becoming commonly used in reference to patches of bramble or heather or temporary disposal areas where duffers find themselves.

water hazard—according to the USGA's *Rules of Golf,* "A water hazard is any sea, lake, pond, river, ditch, surface drainage ditch or other open water course (whether or not containing water) or anything of a similar nature." The boundaries of a water hazard are usually defined by yellow stakes, which are considered obstructions and are part of the hazard. A lateral water hazard, usually defined by red stakes, is one that sits so that a player could not drop a ball behind the hazard. Compare *casual water.*

water club—now illegal, water clubs were in use from around 1880 to 1930 and generally had holes or other spaces in the clubface to make it easier to hit the ball from water.

wedge—wedges are the irons with the most loft, or angle. Properly-hit wedge shots have a high trajectory. Many wedge shots are executed around the green with a partial swing. See also *pitching wedge, sand wedge, Texas wedge.*

whiff—a stroke in which the player completely misses the ball.

windcheater—a shot played low against the wind. Compare *knockdown shot* and *punch shot.*

winter rules—local rules that allow players to clean their ball or improve their lies during play in off-season months. Not endorsed by the USGA's *Rules of Golf* and usually promoted by courses more interested in turning a buck on diehards than in allowing the course to weather the effects of winter.

wood—clubs originally with a large wooden head designed for long distance shots. These power clubs are still referred to as woods, though metal heads are more commonly used nowadays, replacing the long-favored persimmon wood heads. The mix of modern technology and traditional nomenclature leads to the oxymoron, "metal woods."

yips—that shakey feeling you get when trying to hole a very short putt. Coined by Tommy Armour.

18

RESOURCES

U.S. ORGANIZATIONS

183-Happy Hackers

c/o Parkville Post 183 American Legion
1700 Kennoway Rd.
Baltimore, MD 21234-5206

All-American Collegiate Golf Foundation

555 Madison Ave., 12th Fl.
New York, NY 10022
Phone: (212)751-5170
Fax: (212)755-3762
Contact: William Denis Fugazy, Chm.
Description: Promotes collegiate golf by providing donations to youth-oriented charities and student scholarship funds. Presents achievement awards. Maintains All-American Collegiate Golf Hall of Fame.

Altadena Men's Golf Club

c/o Manuel P. Lopez
1616 W. Chetney Dr.
West Covina, CA 91790-1537

Amelia County Golf

PO Box 254
Amelia, VA 23002-0254

American Golf Association

P.O. Box 8606
Lexington, KY 40533
Phone: (606)278-7095
Contact: Tim Self, Pres.

American Golf Sponsors

4 Sawgrass Village, Ste. 220A
Ponte Vedra Beach, FL 32082
Phone: (904)282-4222
Fax: (904)273-5726
Contact: Barry Palm
Description: Sponsors of the major professional golf tournaments held on the regular PGA Tour in the United States and Canada each year. Provides forum for exchange of information and ideas.

American Junior Golf Association

2415 Steeplechase Ln.
Roswell, GA 30076

Phone: (404)998-4653

Fax : (404)992-9763

Contact: Stephen A. Hamblin, Exec.Dir.

Description: Golfers aged 13-18; sponsors are former members, corporations, and interested individuals. Seeks to upgrade the caliber of competitive junior golf events. Facilitates communication between junior golfers and collegiate golf coaches through mailings of tournament results. Sponsors AJGA tournament schedule consisting of 36 national junior golf events and 17 qualifying tournaments; annually names Rolex Junior All-American teams and Compaq Scholastic teams.

American Medical Golf Association

38 Kemp Rd. E.

Greensboro, NC 27410

Contact: Dr. William Forest

Description: Members must have a Doctor of Medicine degree and must be licensed to practice. Promotes fitness in the medical community through participation in golf. Operates Medical Golf Classics, which offer continuing medical education courses at famed U.S. golf resorts.

Anchorage Women's Golf Association

c/o Sherryl K. Nelson

9416 Noblewood St.

Anchorage, AK 99515-1307

Antelope Hills Golf Club Association

PO Box 10726

Prescott, AZ 86304

Phone: (520)445-0583

Anthon Golf Club

c/o Mark J. Groth

106 E Main St.

Anthon, IA 51004-0000

Arizona Golf Association

7226 N 16th St., Ste. 200

Phoenix, AZ 85020

Phone: (602)944-3035

Austin Women's City Golf Association

PO Box 163297

Austin, TX 78716

Phone: (512)328-5175

Avondale Golf Club

75800 Avondale Dr.

Palm Desert, CA 92260-7024

Bayou Golf Association

c/o Robert Myers

PO Box 2088

Texas City, TX 77592-2088

Bayshore Golf Club

c/o Hisanori Watanabe

2217 Springfield Way

San Mateo, CA 94403-1534

Bayview Golf Club

c/o Richard H. Higgs

PO Box 64210

Sunnyvale, CA 94088-4210

Bayville Golf Club

Dominion Tower 2100

999 Waterside Dr.

Norfolk, VA 23510-0000

Bechtel Procurement and Suppliers Golf Club

50 Beale St.

PO Box 193965

San Francisco, CA 94119-3965

Blackledge Men's Golf Association

180 West St.

Hebron, CT 06248-1257

Bobby Jones Open Committee

1408 Kirkway Rd.
Bloomfield, MI 48302-1317

Briarmeade Golf Club

PO Box 5265
Glencoe, AL 35905-0265

**Brookside Country Club
Men's Golf Association**

3603 St. Andrews Dr.
Stockton, CA 95219-1868

Bryan Park Mens Golf Association

PO Box 38394
Greensboro, NC 27438-8394

Burbank Men's Golf Club

PO Box 1254
Burbank, CA 91507-1254

Caddy Shack

5615 Chevrolet Blvd.
Parma, OH 44130-1406

**Carolinas Golf Course
Superintendents Association**

108 4 Frontage Rd.
Clemson, SC 29631-1671

Carolinas PGA

3852 Highway No. 9 East
PO Box 709
North Myrtle Beach, SC 29597-0709
Phone: (803)399-2742

Cayman Golf Association

P.O. Box 2314
Winter Haven, FL 33883
Phone: (813)324-1300
Fax : (813)325-0384
Contact: Bob Stine, Exec.Dir.
Description: Proponents of short golf courses and modified golf; manufacturers of golf products; interested individuals. Promotes modified golf. (Modified golf uses a less lively golf ball and is played on a smaller golf course.) Encourages the sale and manufacture of modified balls and other golf equipment. Sponsors tournaments.

Cazenovia Golf Club

PO Box 314
Cazenovia, NY 13035-0314

Central Georgia Open

PO Box 7646
Macon, GA 31209-7646

**Central New York Section
of the PGA**

822 State Fair Blvd.
Syracuse, NY 13209
Phone: (315)468-6812

Chambersburg Golf Club

PO Box 159
Scotland, PA 17254-0159

Charity Celebrity Classics

PO Box 4684
Spokane, WA 99202-0684

**Charleston Chapter of
the National Golf Course
Owners Association**

14 Exchange St.
Charleston, SC 29401-2554

Chevron Golf Club San Ramon

2000 Rockspring Pl.
Walnut Creek, CA 94596-6160

**Chicago Women's District
Golf Association**

c/o E. Winkler
10339 S Kildare Ave.
Oak Lawn, IL 60453-4803

Chip Beck Invitational Golf Tournament

PO Box 1789
Fayetteville, NC 28302-1789

Christian Golf Club of Central California

3142 Willow, Ste. 101
Clovis, CA 93612-4714

Cimarron Valley Golf Association

c/o Russell Winter
PO Box 698
Satanta, KS 67870-0698

Clayton Golf Club

Box 4
Clayton, NM 88415-0004

Club at PGA West Men's Golf Association

c/o Don Troy
55955 PGA Blvd.
La Quinta, CA 92253-0000

Colorado Golf Association

5655 South Yosemite, Ste. 101
Englewood, CO 80111
Phone: (303)779-GOLF

Columbus Golf Association

c/o Randy Amour
PO Box 711
Columbus, TX 78934-0711

Columbus Womens District Golf Association

c/o Mary Pinkley
2063 Springhill Dr.
Columbus, OH 43221-1201
Phone: (614)451-5893

Contra Costa Bell Golf Club

6385 Benner Ct.
Pleasanton, CA 94588-3920

Coto De Caza Women's Golf Association

25291 Vista Del Verde
Coto De Caza, CA 92679-4900

Cottonwood Golf Club

c/o Leone Strandemo
PO Box 84
Steele, ND 58482-0084

Cypress Golf Club

5853 Pistoia Way
San Jose, CA 95138-2352

Dayton District Women's Golf Association

c/o Cathy A. Jefferson
6320 Jason Ln.
Centerville, OH 45459-2537

Desert Men's Golf Association

PO Box 840
La Quinta, CA 92253-0840

Discover Golf on Michigan's Sunrise Side

1361 Fletcher St.
National City, MI 48748-9666
Phone: (517)469-4231

Door County Golf Association

1029 Bennie View Dr.
Sturgeon Bay, WI 54235-1150

Dunn County Golf Association

Box 549
Killdeer, ND 58640-0549

Eagles Mere Country Club

One Country Club Ln.
Eagles Mere, PA 17731-9999

**Eastern Maine Seniors
Golf Association**

c/o Lewis A. Crowell
32 W Broadway
Bangor, ME 04401-4541
Phone: (207)945-9701

Eastwood Mens Golf Club

Eastwood Rd. SE
Rochester, MN 55904
Phone: (507)289-9031

Ebony Ladies Golf League

c/o Louise B. Horne
300 Park Ave. No. 338
Calumet City, IL 60409-5027

Echo Mesa Men's Golf Association

20349 Echo Mesa Dr.
Sun City West, AZ 85375-5591

Edelweiss Chalet Country Club

PO Box 311
New Glarus, WI 53574-0311

El Segundo Golf Club

c/o Floyd Carr
PO Box 5
El Segundo, CA 90245-0005
Phone: (310)322-3782

Elite Golf Club

c/o Jesse Turner
PO Box 8474
Pittsburg, CA 94565-8474

**Emerald Coast Military
Golf Association**

PO Box 501
Valparaiso, FL 32580-0501

Estill County Golf Course

Old Pike, Box 392
Irvine, KY 40336-1290

**Executive Women's Golf League—
Chicago Chapter**

9108 Devon Ridge Dr.
Burr Ridge, IL 60521-8340

F & H Golf Club

PO Box 51
Haxtun, CO 80731-0051

Fairway Network/Chicago Chapter

PO Box 81414
Chicago, IL 60681-0414
Phone: (815)462-1393

Fallon Mens Golf Association

c/o Mert Mickelson
1175 Wood Dr.
Fallon, NV 89406-8937

Florida State Golf Association

5714 Draw Ln.
Sarasota, FL 34238
Phone: (941)921-5695

Fore Dearborn

15544 Michigan Ave.
Dearborn, MI 48126-2996
Phone: (313)584-3277

**Fountain of the Sun Country Club—
Ladies 18 Hole Golf Association**

500 S. 80th St.
Mesa, AZ 85208-6400
Phone: (602)986-3128

Fox Hollow Golf Club

c/o James F. Kenyon
PO Box 280464
Lakewood, CO 80228-0464

Franklin Park Golf Club

1 Circuit Dr.
Dorchester, MA 02121-0000

Gaylord Golf Mecca

PO Box 3069
Gaylord, MI 49735
Phone: (517)732-6333

Georgia State Golf Association

121 Village Pkwy., Bldg. 3
Marietta, GA 30067-4061
Phone: (404)955-4272

Georgia Women's Golf Association

c/o Helen V. Kirbo
1111 Eighth Ave.
PO Box 70519
Albany, GA 31708-0519

Glenmaura National Golf Club

Glenmaura National Blvd.
Moosic, PA 18507

Glenrock Golf Club

PO Box 1391
Glenrock, WY 82637-1391

Golf Coaches Association of America

Ohio State University
3605 Tremont Rd.
Columbus, OH 43221
Phone: (800)925-1687
Contact: Jim Brown, Mgr.
Description: Golf coaches of four-year colleges and universities who are members of the National Collegiate Athletic Association (see separate entry). Supervises college golf so that it will be administered in accordance with the definition of amateurism and the principles of amateur sports; has responsibility for collegiate golf tournaments as set forth by the NCAA; promotes intercollegiate and intramural golf participation; encourages

adoption of strict eligibility rules. Selects first, second, and third All-American Golf Teams. Conducts research into conditions and types of competitive golf play.

Golf Course Superintendents Association of New Jersey

66 Morris Ave., Ste. 2-A
Springfield, NJ 07081
Phone: (201)379-1100

Golf 4 Fun

c/o Bob Nelson
PO Box 5304
Englewood, CO 80155
Phone: (303)985-3403

Golf Writers Association of America

25882 Orchard Lake Rd.
Farmington Hills, MI 48336
Phone: (810)442-1481
Contact: Jack Berry, Sec.-Treas.
Description: Editors and writers covering golf for newspapers, magazines, and news services.

Goodyear Golf Club

c/o Larry L. Oliver
922 E. Meighan Blvd.
Gadsden, AL 35903-1922

Grand Traverse Area Junior Golf Association

10090 East Pickwick Ct.
Traverse City, MI 49684-5218

Grant City Golf Club

c/o Nancy Hill
PO Box 37
Grant City, MO 64456-0037

Greater Jackson Golf Association

c/o Charlene Haglund
11800 Trist Rd.
Grass Lake, MI 49240-9256

Grenora Golf Club Association

c/o Sandra K. Peterson
HC 1, Box 34
Grenora, ND 58845-9739

GTE Suncoast Classic Association

16002 N Dale Mabry Hwy., 2nd Fl.
Tampa, FL 33618-1330

Harbour Pointe Men's Golf Club

PO Box 1400
Mukilteo, WA 98275-1400

Hatherly Golf Club

PO Box 449
North Scituate, MA 02060-0449

**Hawaii State Women's
Golf Association**

350-D Kaelepule Dr.
Kailua, HI 96734-3303
Phone: (808)262-2428

Hawaiian Golf Club

c/o Dennis H. Kudo
16646 Evergreen Circle
Fountain Valley, CA 92708-2311

Hawks Nest Golf Club

6005 Old Dixie Hwy.
Vero Beach, FL 32967-7528

Hearne Golf Association

PO Box 26
Hearne, TX 77859-0026

Hi-Line Golf Association

c/o Mary Lou Winheim
PO Box 276
Bertrand, NE 68927-0276

**Hidden Valley Womens
Golf Association**

c/o Kay Wilhelm
PO Box 83286
Lincoln, NE 68501-3286

Highland Palms Ladies' Golf Club

30777 Butia Palm Ave.
Homeland, CA 92548-9515

Highland Palms Men's Golf Club

30777 Butia Palm
Homeland, CA 92548-9515

**Hollybrook Women's 9 Hole
Golf Association**

900 Hollybrook Dr.
Pembroke Pines, FL 33025-1554

**Huntington Landmark
Golf Foundation**

20880 Oakridge Ln.
Huntington Beach, CA 92646-5605

Inland Impire Open

c/o Robert W. Klemme
PO Box 20321
Riverside, CA 92516-0321

International Golf Association

7442 Jager Ct.
Cincinnati, OH 45230
Phone: (513)624-2100
Fax : (513)624-2110
Contact: Burch R. Riber, Exec.Dir.
Description: Sponsors World Cup and International Trophy Matches, with teams from 32 nations competing annually.

Jet Golf Club

c/o Katsuji Uchiike
5 S Linden Ave., Ste. 6
South San Francisco, CA 94080-6419

John Day Golf Club

PO Box 176
John Day, OR 97845-0176

Junior Golf Association of Mobile

c/o Michael C. Thompson
PO Box 70106
Mobile, AL 36670-1106

Juniper Hill Golf Association

800 Louisville Rd.
Frankfort, KY 40601-3306

Kansas Golf Association

3301 Clinton Pkwy Ct., Ste. 4
Lawrence, KS 66047-2630
Phone: (913)842-4833

Kennedy-Wellshire Men's Golf Club

c/o Bart A. Skidmore
PO Box 24641
Denver, CO 80224-0641

Ketchikan Golf Association

2425 Tongass Ave.
Ketchikan, AK 99901-5927

Keystone Public Golf Association

PO Box 160
Murrysville, PA 15668
Phone: (412)468-8850

Koronis Hills Gulf Club

Box 55
Paynesville, MN 56362-0055

La Contenta Lakes Seniors Golf Club

PO Box 954
Valley Springs, CA 95252-0954

La Porte City Golf Club

9699 Bishop Ave.
La Porte City, IA 50651-2207
Phone: (319)342-2249

Ladies Charity Classic

c/o Sue King
1505 Highway 6 S, Ste. 101
Houston, TX 77077-1725

Ladies Professional Golf Association

2570 W. International Speedway Blvd., Ste. B
Daytona Beach, FL 32114

Phone: (904)254-8800
Fax : (904)254-4755
Contact: Charles S. Mechem, Commissioner
Description: Professional women golfers and educators. Compiles statistics on tournaments, money winnings, and scoring. Assists members in finding golfing positions. Provides major retirement program for members; maintains hall of fame.

Lago Vista Women's Golf Association

c/o Patricia A. Holt
PO Box 4527
Lago Vista, TX 78645-0007

Lago Vista Women's Golf Association

3309 Parliament Cove
Lago Vista, TX 78645
Phone: (512)267-2719

Lake View Country Club Charity Pro-Am Association

Box 468
North East, PA 16428-0408
Phone: (814)725-9561

Lakewood Golf Association

PO Box 543
Havana, IL 62644-0543

Lakewood Oaks Golf Club

c/o Fred Burns
651 NE St. Andrews Circle
Lees Summit, MO 64064-1356

Lampasas Golf Association

c/o Morris L. Ellis
PO Box 629
Lampasas, TX 76550-0629

Lawrence Golf Club

Causeway
Lawrence, NY 11559-1514

Lawrenceburg Golf & Country Club

PO Box 323
Lawrenceburg, TN 38464-0323

Lead Country Club

c/o Jackie Wilson
PO Box 633
Lead, SD 57754-0633

Lena Golf Club

621 West Lena St.
Lena, IL 61048-0000

Lenkota Golf Club

PO Box 495
Lennox, SD 57039-0495

Lighthouse Women's Golf Club

c/o Veronica R. Kersey
555 Douglas St., Apt. 16
West Sacramento, CA 95605-2527

Local No. 444 Golf Club

19476 Hathaway Ave., Apt. B
Hayward, CA 94541-2309
Phone: (510)276-8863

Long Island Golf Association

66 Magnolia Ave.
Garden City, NY 11530-6226

Los Angeles City Employees Golf Club

PO Box 574
Los Angeles, CA 90053-0574

Los Angeles Cougar Golf Club

827 Polynesian Dr.
Long Beach, CA 90805-2327

Los Angeles Fairways Golf Club

PO Box 431389
Los Angeles, CA 90043-9389
Phone: (213)737-0249

Lost Pines Golf Club

PO Box 900
Bastrop, TX 78602-0900

Luling Golf Association

c/o James E. Rougeou
106 South Cypress
Luling, TX 78648-2410

Mace Meadow Mens Golf Club

c/o William N. Talbott
25594 Meadow Dr.
Pioneer, CA 95666-9505

Madison County Golf Association

PO Box 522
Ennis, MT 59729-0522

Maryland State Golf Association

PO Box 16289
Baltimore, MD 21210
Phone: (410)467-8899

McLeansboro Golf Club

102 E Market
McLeansboro, IL 62859-1317

Meadow Creek Golf Club

c/o Virgil D. Newman
513 South St.
Volga, SD 57071-2113

Meadow Lark Country Club Women's Golf Association

300 County Club Blvd.
Great Falls, MT 59404

Menifee Lakes Womens Golf Association

c/o Uanita D. Lake
29875 Menifee Lakes Dr.
Menifee, CA 92584

Men's Golf Association of Brandermill County Club

c/o Donald M. Gerardi
PO Box 1846
Midlothian, VA 23113-1846

Merrimack River Golf Club

c/o Keith Bakaian
176 Webster St.
Hudson, NH 03051-3211

Mesquite Womens Golf Association

2700 E. Mesquite Ave.
Palm Springs, CA 92264-5050

Metropolitan Advertising Golf Association

c/o Harvey Oshinsky
PO Box 901, Murray Hill Sta.
New York, NY 10156-0901

Metropolitan Golf Association

c/o Jay Mottola
49 Knollwood Rd.
Elmsford, NY 10523
Phone: (914)347-4653

Middle Atlantic Golf Association

Box 635
Riderwood, MD 21139

Miniature Golf Association of America

P.O. Box 32353
Jacksonville, FL 32237
Phone: (904)781-4653
Fax : (904)781-4843
Contact: Skip Laun, Exec.Dir.
Description: Provides the sport, recreation, and entertainment industry with a network in which to keep up with the family sport and entertainment business. Conducts national promotions, purchasing, operational guidelines, and facts and figures about multi-faceted family fun centers covering miniature golf, driving ranges, arcades, alternative golf facilities, go-karts, and batting cages.

Minneapolis Golf Club

2001 Flag Ave.
Minneapolis, MN 55426-2300

Minnesota Golf Association

6550 York Ave. S., Ste. 211
Edina, MN 55435
Phone: (612)927-4643

Minority Golf Association of America

PO Box 1081
Westhampton Beach, NY 11978-7081
Phone: (516)288-8255

Missing Linksters Golf Club

c/o Michael H. Ikeda
4930 Elmwood Dr.
San Jose, CA 95130-1812

Mission Hills Womens Golf Auxiliary

34 600 Mission Hills Dr.
Rancho Mirage, CA 92270
Phone: (619)324-9400

Mississippi Golf Association

MGA
PO Box 684
Laurel, MS 39440
Phone: (601)649-0570

Missouri Womens Golf Association

c/o Marian Conner
1236 Arno Rd.
Kansas City, MO 64113-2011

Morrilton Country Club

PO Box 381
Morrilton, AR 72110-0381

Morris Williams Ladies Golf Association

3003 W. Terrace Dr.
Austin, TX 78731
Phone: (512)459-6115

Mountain Chapter of the Carolina Section of PGA of America

16 Sunset Dr.
Weaverville, NC 28787-9462

Musgrove Mill Golf Club

PO Box 1106
Clinton, SC 29325-1106

National Advertising Golf Association

PO Box 157
Cary, NC 27512-0157
Phone: (919)467-7401
Fax : (919)467-7401
Contact: David Pitkin, Exec.Dir.
Description: Comprises 16 advertising golf associations.

National Association of Left-Handed Golfers

1307 N. Orchard
Espanola, NM 87532
Phone: (800)844-6254
Contact: Dave McCall, Exec.Sec.-Treas.
Description: Golfers who play all shots left-handed. Purposes are: to organize the amateur and professional left-handed golfers of the U.S., Canada, and other countries into a recognized and accepted group; to foster closer acquaintances among all left-handed golfers and to work continuously for a spirit of goodwill and fellowship; to conduct a National Left-Handed Amateur Tournament, a National Lefty-Righty Amateur, one or more Lefty-Partner Tournaments, and any other tournaments approved by the board of governors; to recognize Open, Senior, and Women's champions

annually. Maintains hall of fame; compiles statistics. Sponsors annual golf tournaments.

National Association of Left-Handed Golfers—Alaska Chapter

101 E. 9th Ave. 9B
Anchorage, AK 99501-3651
Phone: (907)344-8528

National Association of Left-Handed Golfers—Carolina Chapter

546 Wilson Cornwell Rd.
Shelby, NC 28150
Phone: (704)482-3328

National Association of Left-Handed Golfers—Florida Chapter

4922 17th St. E
Bradenton, FL 34203
Phone: (813)756-9115

National Association of Left-Handed Golfers—Georgia Chapter

1807 Pine Forest Circle
Dublin, GA 31021
Phone: (912)272-0940

National Association of Left-Handed Golfers-Idaho Chapter

404 S Hall St.
Grangeville, ID 83530
Phone: (208)983-1183

National Association of Left-Handed Golfers—Illinois Chapter

1485 Haise Ln.
Elk Grove, IL 60007
Phone: (708)843-0707

National Association of Left-Handed Golfers—Indiana Chapter

6916 Broadway
Indianapolis, IN 46220
Phone: (317)253-9675

National Association of Left-Handed Golfers—Kentucky Chapter

5323 Westhall Ave.
Louisville, KY 40214
Phone: (502)964-0529

National Association of Left-Handed Golfers—Michigan Chapter

1485 Meadow
Walled Lake, MI 48390
Phone: (810)624-6997

National Association of Left-Handed Golfers—Missouri Chapter

6512 NW Blair
Kansas City, MO 64152
Phone: (816)587-1488

National Association of Left-Handed Golfers—NEALG Chapter

6 Park Ave.
Foxboro, MA 02055
Phone: (508)543-5246

National Association of Left-Handed Golfers—New Jersey Chapter

5 Tamarac Ln.
Medford, NJ 08055
Phone: (609)654-4528

National Association of Left-Handed Golfers-Oregon Chapter

PO Box 4323
Salem, OR 97302-8323
Phone: (503)364-6529

National Association of Left-Handed Golfers—Pennsylvania Chapter

136 Catskill Ave.
Pittsburgh, PA 15227
Phone: (412)882-5495

National Association of Left-Handed Golfers—Tennessee Chapter

4521 Priscilla Ave.
Memphis, TN 38128
Phone: (901)372-3074

National Association of Left-Handed Golfers—Texas Chapter

8561 Marina Dr.
Kempner, TX 75143
Phone: (903)498-7572

National Association of Left-Handed Golfers—Washington Chapter

294 Mantle Rd.
Sequim, WA 98382
Phone: (360)683-7907

National Association of Left-Handed Golfers—West Virginia Chapter

5657 Glen Carla Dr.
Huntington, WV 25705
Phone: (304)736-9639

National Association of Left-Handed Golfers—Wisconsin Chapter

N163 W 19400 Cedar Run Dr.
Jackson, WI 53037-9536
Phone: (414)677-1747

Needles Mens Golf Club

PO Box 845
Needles, CA 92363-0845
Phone: (619)326-3931

New England Professional Golfers Association of America

1 Audubon Rd.
Wakefield, MA 01880
Phone: (617)246-4653

New Hampshire Golf Association

c/o Robert H. Elliot
45 Kearney St.
Manchester, NH 03104-1814

19th Hole International

2050 Washington Rd.

Holt, MI 48841

Phone: (517)484-5107

Contact: Harold W. Schumacher, Mng. Dir.

Description: Promotes fellowship among golfers worldwide. Fosters exchange of information benefiting golfers, golf courses, and other golf organizations; encourages programs for senior golfers; perpetuates the game by establishing junior golf programs. Certifies awards for tournaments. Awards deserving golfers memberships in Honorable Kilted Shepherds of the Fairways and Greens and Royal Society of Hole-in-One Golfers. Others receive recognition for their actions on the golf course through memberships in such groups as Yak-a-Tee-Yak Foursome, Honorable Golfing Clan of Duffers and Diggers, Hookers, Hackers and Slicers in Roughs, and Sand Traps and Water Holes.

North Carolina Golf Council

c/o Ricky M. McKeel

4101 Lake Boone Trail, Ste. 201

Raleigh, NC 27607-7506

North Dakota Women's Golf Association

416 Shady Ln.

Bismarck, ND 58501-1782

Northern California Left-Handed Golfers Association

c/o Glenn Justice

572 Skyline Blvd.

San Bruno, CA 94066

Phone: (415)589-7177

Oak Hills Men's Golf Association

c/o Larry Andronaco

12 Lloyd Rd.

Norwalk, CT 06850-0000

Oaks North Mens Golf Club

c/o George W. Melbrod

17482 Plaza Cerado 94

San Diego, CA 92128-2210

Ocean County Golf Association

PO Box 126

Ship Bottom, NJ 08008

Phone: (609)698-2016

Ohio Golf Course Owners Association

5874 Moray Ct.

Dublin, OH 43017-9747

Phone: (614)761-1527

Okemah Golf Club

c/o Earl Phelan

PO Box 151

Okemah, OK 74859-0151

Oklahoma Golf Association

c/o Ross M. Coe

6217 N Classen Blvd.

Oklahoma City, OK 73118-5833

Orange Hills Country Club Mens Golf Association

389 Raebrook Rd.

Orange, CT 06477-1725

Phone: (203)795-4161

Oregon Golf Club

PO Box 331

Oregon, IL 61061-0331

Palmetto Golf Association—Sumter

c/o J. E. Eldridge, Jr.

PO Box 520

Sumter, SC 29151-0520

Pan American Golf Association of Odessa

PO Box 2244

Odessa, TX 79760-2244

Pan American Golf Association of Temple, Texas

PO Box 124
Temple, TX 76503-0124

Paradise Hills Mens Golf Association

10035 Country Club Ln. NW
Albuquerque, NM 87114-4201

Pennsylvania State Women's Golf Association

c/o Connie H. Shorb
830 Upland Rd.
York, PA 17403-4430

Perdido Bay Ladies Golf Association

1 Doug Ford Dr.
Pensacola, FL 32507-8707

Pittsburgh Youth Golf Foundation

c/o Robert Yeager
1500 Oliver Bldg.
Pittsburgh, PA 15222

Plantation Golf Club

PO Box 250
Rancho Mirage, CA 92270-0250

Poinciana Country Club Mens Golf Association

c/o A. Braverman
6991 Clover Ct.
Lake Worth, FL 33467-1455

Professional Businesswomen's Golf Network

c/o Marion Keener
PO Box 25518
Greenville, SC 29616-0518

Professional Golfers' Association of America

100 Ave. of Champions
Palm Beach Gardens, FL 33418
Phone: (407)624-8400
Fax : (407)624-8430

Contact: Jim Awtrey, CEO

Description: Golf professionals and apprentices associated with golf clubs, courses, and tournaments. Sponsors PGA Championship, PGA Seniors' Championship, Ryder Cup Matches, PGA Grand Slam of Golf, Club Professional Championship, National Golf Month Charities Event, and Senior Club Professional Championship; PGA Junior Championship; PGA Assistants Championship. Conducts Golf Professional Training Program; certifies college programs in golf management. Sponsors winter tournament program for club professionals including tournaments held in south Florida. Offers employment counseling; compiles statistics.

Professional Golfers' Association of America—Aloha Section

770 Kapiolani Blvd., No. 715
Honolulu, HI 96813
Phone: (808)593-2230

Professional Golfers Association of America—Connecticut

35 Cold Spring Rd., Ste. 212
Rocky Hill, CT 06067
Phone: (203)257-4653

Professional Golfers Association of America—Dixie Section

601 Vestavia Pkwy., Ste. 320
Birmingham, AL 35216
Phone: (205)822-0321

Professional Golfers Association of America—Kentucky

PO Box 18396
Louisville, KY 40261-0396
Phone: (502)499-7255

Professional Golfers Association of America—Minnesota Section

Bunker Hills Golf Club
Hwy. 242 and Foley Blvd.

Coon Rapids, MN 55448

Phone: (612)754-0820

Professional Golfers Association of America—New Jersey

Forest Gate Dr.
PO Box 200
Jamesburg, NJ 08831

Phone: (908)521-4000

Professional Golfers Association of America—Northern Ohio

38121 Euclid Ave.
Willoughby, OH 44094

Phone: (216)951-4546

Professional Golfers' Association of America—Southern Texas Section

1610 Woodstead Ct., No. 110
The Woodlands, TX 77380

Phone: (713)363-0511

Professional Golfers' Association of America—Southwest Section

5040 E. Shea Blvd., Ste. 250
Scottsdale, AZ 85254-4687

Phone: (602)443-9002

Professional Golfers' Association of America—Sun Country Section

5850 Eubank Blvd. NE, No. B-72
Albuquerque, NM 87111-6121

Phone: (505)260-0167

Professional Golfers' Association of America—Tennessee Section

400 Franklin Rd.
Franklin, TN 37064

Phone: (615)790-7600

Professional Golfers Association of America—Tri-State Section

221 Sherwood Dr.
Monaca, PA 15061-2559

Professional Golfers Association of America—Washington

4011 Yelm Hwy. SE
Olympia, WA 98501-5170

Phone: (360)456-6496

Professional Golfers Association of America—Western New York Section

PO Box 1728
Williamsville, NY 14231-1728

Phone: (716)626-0603

Professional Golfers Association of America—Wisconsin

4000 W. Brown Deer Rd.
Milwaukee, WI 53209

Phone: (414)365-4474

Professional Putters Association

P.O. Box 35237
Fayetteville, NC 28303

Phone: (910)485-7131

Fax : (919)485-1122

Contact: Joe Aboid, Dir.

Description: Persons over age 18 who compete in national putting tournaments sanctioned by the PPA; "putt putt" golf course franchise owners, managers, and suppliers. Seeks to recognize, develop, and reward the skills and abilities of America's putters. Sponsors competitions; compiles statistics; presents awards. Produces Putt-Putt Skins T.V. Series, a television sports show of three half-hour segments syndicated in the U.S.

Ranchland Hills Women's Golf Association

c/o Kathy A. Motley
4718 Cindy Pl.
Midland, TX 79707-5238

Remsen Golf Association

c/o Carl R. Anderson
Sunnyside Ave.
Remsen, IA 51050-0000

Riomar Country Club

c/o S. Farnum
2100 Club Dr.
Vero Beach, FL 32963-2154

River Island Country Club

31989 River Island Dr.
Porterville, CA 93257-9611
Phone: (209)781-2917

River Ridge Mens Golf Club

PO Box 7915
Oxnard, CA 93031-7915
Phone: (805)983-4653

Riverbend Men's Golf Club

c/o Greg Marks
PO Box 321
Kent, WA 98035
Phone: (206)854-3673

Robert Trent Jones Golf Club

c/o David C. Blivin
2200 W. Main St., Ste. 900
Durham, NC 27705-4643

Rocky Bayou Country Club

PO Box 577
Niceville, FL 32588-0577

Rolling Greens Golf Club

R 99 N Box 213
Mt. Sterling, IL 62353-0000

Rutland Country Club

PO Box 195
Rutland, VT 05702-0195

Sacramento Golf Club

PO Box 13721 A
Sacramento, CA 95853-3721

St. Louis District Golf Association

823 Cleveland
Kirkwood, MO 63122-3907
Phone: (314)821-1511

Salem Senior Golf Association

5227 Orchard Hgts. Rd. NW
Salem, OR 97304-9529

San Antonio Golf Association

70 NE Loop 410, Ste. 370
San Antonio, TX 78216
Phone: (210)341-0823

San Francisco Advertising Golf Association

PO Box 606
Fairfax, CA 94978-0606

Sand Hill River Golf Club

PO Box 115
Fertile, MN 56540-0115

Sandy Hollow Golf Club

3413 400th St.
Sioux Center, IA 51250-7557

Santa Barbara Mens Golf Club

PO Box 3033
Santa Barbara, CA 93130-3033

Santa Cruz Valley Seniors Golf

c/o Philip C. Stolp
PO Box 1376
Green Valley, AZ 85622-1376

Senior Golfers of Connecticut

c/o Richard W. Hawley
PO Box 1132
Stratford, CT 06497
Phone: (203)378-3831

Seymour Junior Golf Foundation

c/o Peter Demerath
753 Ivory St.
Seymour, WI 54165-1625

Silver Lake Golf Club

PO Box 94
Perry, NY 14530-0094

Southern California
Golf Association

3740 Cahuenga Blvd., West
North Hollywood, CA 91604
Phone: (818)980-3630

Southern California Professional
Golfer's Association

601 S Valencia Ave., Ste. 200
Brea, CA 92621-6346
Phone: (714)776-4653

Southern New England Women's
Golf Association

c/o Beverly A. Vigdor
16 Phelps Meadow
Windsor, CT 06095-0000

Southern Texas Professional
Golf Association

1610 Woodstead Ct., Ste. 110
The Woodlands, TX 77380
Phone: (713)367-3167

Springfield Golf Association

PO Box 1031
Springfield, OH 45501-1031

Summerland Golf Club

c/o Treasurer
PO Box 325
Ewing, NE 68735-0325

Sun City/Vistoso Ladies 18 Hole
Golf Club

1495 East Rancho Visto Blvd.
Tucson, AZ 85737-9120

Sun Valley Men's Golf Club

c/o Jim Henderson
2781 Country Club Dr.
Barstow, CA 92311-9760

Tamarack Women's 9 Hole
Golf Association

c/o Margaret Quirk
169 Prigmore St.
East Brunswick, NJ 08816-3177

Taos Country Club Men's
Golf Association

c/o Marcus Whitson
PO Box 254
Ranchos De Taos, NM 87557-0254

Tijeras Creek Mens
Golf Association

c/o Harold Trumble
29082 Tijeras Creek Rd.
Rancho Santa Margarita, CA 92688-3017
Phone: (714)589-9793

Tijeras Creek Womens
Golf Association

29082 Tijeras Creek
Rancho Santa Margarita, CA 92688-3017

Timber Oaks Golf
Club Association

8575 Ponderosa Ave.
Port Richey, FL 34668-2739

Toledo Minority Golf Association

c/o Charles Cohen
1943 Oakwood Ave.
Toledo, OH 43607-1521
Phone: (419)531-6535

Tournament Golf Foundation

6775 SW 111th Ave., Ste. 100
Beaverton, OR 97008-5378

Town and Country Golf Club

c/o Larry H. Aanenson
113 North St. and Paul Ave.
Fulda, MN 56131
Phone: (507)425-3328

Tucson National Men's Golf Association

9730 N Camino Del Grillo
Tucson, AZ 85741-9233

Tyler Community Golf Club

PO Box 447
Cty Rd. 7
Tyler, MN 56178-0447
Phone: (507)247-5895

United Golfers' Association

P.O. Box 5746
Evanston, IL 60204-5746
Contact: Harriett Powell, Pres.

Description: Golf clubs with predominantly, though not exclusively, black members. Promotes golf and encourages young people to participate in the sport. Sponsors annual tournament; offers scholarships.

U.S.A. Junior Golf Association

c/o George J. Theilemann
905 E Camp Mcdonald Rd.
Prospect Heights, IL 60070-2615

United States Golf Association

P.O. Box 708
Far Hills, NJ 07931
Phone: (908) 234-2300
Contact: David B. Fay, Exec.Dir.

Description: Regularly organized golf clubs and golf courses. Serves as governing body for golf in the United States. Turfgrass Visiting Service promotes scientific work in turf management. Provides data on rules, handicapping, amateur status, tournament procedure, turf maintenance, and golf balls and implements. Administers Golf House Museum, a collection of memorabilia including clubs of champions, the Moon Club, and paintings, insignia, and portraits of USGA champions. Sponsors USGA Research and Educational Fund. Con-

ducts 13 annual national championships and research programs; sponsors teams for international competitions.

USGA Green Section

P.O. Box 708
Far Hills, NJ 07931
Phone: (908)234-2300
Fax : (908)234-9488
Contact: James T. Snow, Dir.

Description: A department of United States Golf Association (see separate entry). Members are golf clubs and golf course superintendents. Aims to improve maintenance and management of golf courses. Maintains speakers' bureau, museum, and 8000 volume library of books and periodicals. Holds rules seminars.

Western Golf Association

1 Briar Rd.
Golf, IL 60029
Phone: (708) 724-4600
Fax: (708) 724-7133
Contact: Donald D. Johnson, Exec. Dir.

Description: Private country clubs. Conducts three national golf championships: the Western Open, Western Amateur, and Western Junior. Supports and administers the Evans Scholars Foundation, which awards four-year college scholarships to caddies on a competitive basis.

Western Lone Star Seniors Ladies Golf Association

PO Box 585
Farwell, TX 79325-0585

Western Pennsylvania Golf Association

1360 Old Freeport Rd., Ste. 1BR
Pittsburgh, PA 15238
Phone: (412)963-9806

William J. Stewart Memorial Golf Classic

1241 Adams St.
Dorchester, MA 02124-5766

Women's Central Pennsylvania Golf Association

c/o Florence A. Latawiec
401 Ruth Ridge Dr.
Lancaster, PA 17601-3633

Womens Texas Golf Association No. 113089

10 Artesian Frst
Conroe, TX 77304-2513
Phone: (713)947-9178

Women's Tidewater Golf Association

c/o Peggy H. Dorsk
10 Artesian Frst
Conroe, TX 77304-2513

Women's Western Golf Association

c/o Mrs. Walter Suberg
1331 Swainwood Dr.
Glenview, IL 60025-2841

World Amateur Golf Council

Golf House
P.O. Box 708
Far Hills, NJ 07931-0708
Phone: (908)234-2300
Fax: (908)234-2178
Contact: Michael F. Bonallack, Co-Sec.
Description: Multinational organization for amateur golf. Promotes high standards of amateur golf; fosters friendship and sportsmanship between members.

Young Minority Golf Association

15105 Rosemont
Detroit, MI 48223-0000

INTERNATIONAL ORGANIZATIONS

Association of Golf Club Secretaries

7A Beaconsfield Rd.
Weston-super-Mare, England
BS23 1YE
Phone: 44 1934 641166
Fax: 44 1934 644254
Contact: Ray Burniston, Sec.
Description: Golf club secretaries. Fosters cooperation with other golfing organizations and encourages the establishment of regional groups. Maintains an employment bureau and a benevolent fund for members; provides training facilities.

Austrian Golf Association

(Osterreichischer Golf-Verband)
Prinz-Eugen-Strasse 12
Vienna, Austria
A-1040
Phone: 43 1 5053245
Fax: 43 1 5054962
Contact: Mrs. Waltraud Neuwirth, Sec.Gen.
Description: Clubs representing the interests of 33,711 golfers. Organizes golfing events and championships in Austria. Arranges seminars for golf secretaries. Sponsors competitions; bestows award. Provides children's and placement services. Maintains speakers' bureau. Compiles statistics.

Canadian Ladies Golf Association (Association Canadienne des Golfeuses)

1333 Dorval Dr.
Oakville, ON, Canada
L6J 4Z3
Phone: (905)849-CLGA
Fax: (905)849-0188
Contact: Peggy Brown, Exec. Dir.
Description: Women interested in the sport of amateur golf in Canada. Promotes the game of

golf for women. Works to ensure understanding and maintainance of rules, regulations, handicapping, and course ratings.

China Golf Association

9 Tiyuguan Rd.
Beijing, People's Republic of China
100763
Phone: 86 1 7014994
Fax: 86 1 7015858
Contact: Li Pao, Sec.Gen.
Description: Golf clubs in the People's Republic of China. Promotes golf; fosters exchange between members and golf associations in other countries. Conducts research and educational programs. Offers consulting services.

English Golf Union

1-3 Upper King St.
Leicester, England
LE1 6XF
Phone: 44 116 2553042
Fax: 44 116 2471322
Contact: P. M. Baxter
Description: All male golfers who are members of one of the affiliated clubs. Concerned with the furtherance of men's amateur golf as its governing body.

English Ladies' Golf Association

Church Rd.
Birmingham, England
B15 3TB
Phone: 44 121 456 2088
Fax: 44 121 454 5542
Contact: Mrs. M. J. Carr
Description: Aims to further the interests of women's golf in England; to maintain, administer and enforce the LGU system of handicapping; to employ the funds of the Association in such a manner as shall be deemed best for the interest of women's golf in England; to maintain, administer and regulate the national championship and all

other competitions held under the auspices of the association.

Golfing Union of Ireland

Glencar House
81 Eglinton Rd.
Donnybrook, Ireland
4
Phone: 353 1 2694111
Fax: 353 1 2695368
Contact: Ivan E.R. Dickson, Gen.Sec.
Description: Men's golf clubs representing 135,000 members. Promotes and administrates men's amateur golf in Ireland. Arranges matches and tournaments. Provides advice, assistance, and coaching to selected candidates.

Hospitality and Outdoor Golf Society

7 Hamilton Way
Wallington, England
SM6 9NJ
Phone: 44 181 669 8121
Fax: 44 181 647 1128
Contact: John W. Barton
Description: Companies and individuals who play golf in the hospitality, outdoor events, leisure and entertainments industry. Members may play on some of the finest golf courses in the UK and abroad. Opportunities to entertain guests and enter regional and national competitions. Raise monies for public and trade charities.

Ladies' Golf Union

The Scores
St. Andrews, Fife, Scotland
KY16 9AT
Phone: 44 1334 475811
Fax: 44 1334 472818
Description: Amateur women golfers. Promotes and administers women's participation in amateur golf in Great Britain and Ireland. Organizes international matches.

National Association of Public Golf Courses

35 Sinclair Grove
London, England
NW11 9JH

Phone: 44 181 458 5433

Contact: Alan K. Witte

Description: Golf clubs playing on courses open to the general public and the course management authorities. To unite the clubs formed on public golf courses and their course managements, to provide competitive golf on a national and regional basis for members of all ages, gender and handicaps. To afford direct representation of public course interests in the national union.

Pitch and Putt Union of Ireland (Aontas Teilgin Agus Amais na h'Eireann)

House of Sport
Longmile Rd.
Dublin, Ireland
12

Phone: 353 1 4509299

Fax: 353 1 4502805

Contact: Peg Smith, Hon.Sec.

Description: Promotes the sport of pitch and putt, a short version of golf, in the Republic of Ireland, Northern Ireland, and internationally. Organizes championships, tournaments, and coaching classes. Maintains records of competition results and national register of handicaps.

Professional Golfers' Association— England

Apollo House
The Belfry
Sutton Coldfield
Birmingham, England
B76 9PT

Phone: 44 1675 470333

Fax: 44 1675 470674

Contact: Mike Gray

Description: Professional golfers. Aims to promote interest in the game of golf, to protect and advance the mutual and trade interests of its members, to hold meetings and tournaments periodically for members. It also institutes a benevolent fund for the relief of deserving members and acts as an agency to assist any professional to obtain employment.

Swiss Golf Association (Association Suisse de Golf)

19, place Croix Blanche
Case Postale
Epalinges, Switzerland
CH-1066

Phone: 41 21 7843531

Fax: 41 21 7843536

Contact: John C. Storjohann, Gen.Sec.

Description: Register of golf clubs in Switzerland.

Swiss Mini-Golf Association

(Schweizerischer Pistengolf-Sportverband)
Postfach G 365
Kloten, Switzerland
CH-8302

Phone: 41 1 8622131

Fax: 41 1 8622132

Contact: Erich Grubel, Exec. Officer

Description: Promotes the sport of miniature golf in Switzerland.

Women's Golf New Zealand

PO Box 11-187
Wellington, New Zealand

Phone: 64 4 4726733

Fax: 64 4 4226732

Contact: Anthea Black, Exec.Dir.

Description: Women golfers and followers of women's golf. Promotes increased participation by women in the sport of golf; works to increase public interest in women's golf.

VIDEOS

Approach Shot and Sand Play

Release Date: 1991

Run Time: 17 min.

Description: This video, fifth in a series, deals with the tricky shots encountered in the game of golf and how to approach them successfully.

Arnold Palmer Golf Series

Release Date: 1990

Run Time: 45 min.

Description: The great golf pro demonstrates his various methods and techniques for the viewer.

Arnold Palmer, Vol. 1: Mastering the Fundamentals

Release Date: 1983

Run Time: 53 min.

Description: Arnie lends all his knowledgable tips in an attempt to improve your game.

Arnold Palmer, Vol. 2: Course Strategy

Release Date: 1983

Run Time: 55 min.

Description: Arnie takes it to the green to see if you can apply your knowledge in the field of battle.

Arnold Palmer, Vol. 3: The Scoring Zone

Release Date: 1989

Run Time: 53 min.

Description: Arnie helps you put the finishing touches on your game, allowing you to crush all who would oppose you.

Arnold Palmer, Vol. 4: Practice Like a Pro

Release Date: 1989

Run Time: 52 min.

Description: The Master himself helps you improve your game and shares a little laughter along the way.

Automatic Golf

Release Date: 1975

Run Time: 46 min.

Description: The program shows how Nicklaus prepares for a practice session and how he approaches a shot with each club.

The Azinger Way

Release Date: 1992

Run Time: 55 min.

Description: Azinger and Redman demonstrate how to perform more consistently on the golf course.

Beginning Golf for Women

Release Date: 1988

Run Time: 40 min.

Description: Donna White of the Ladies' Professional Golf Association, demonstrates the proper techniques of playing golf.

Ben Crenshaw: The Art of Putting

Release Date: 1986

Run Time: 44 min.

Description: The renowned pro golfer demonstrates the nuances of putting.

The Best of the Drummer: Bob Drumm . . .The Andy Rooney of Golf

Run Time: 30 min.

Description: Collection of Bob Drumm's wackiest observations on golf.

Best of the Skins Game, the First Decade

Release Date: 1993

Run Time: 76 min.

Description: Four golfers compete with and against each other, sudden-death style, for big bucks. Highlights some of the top players, including Arnold Palmer, Jack Nicklaus, Lee Trevino, Tom Watson, Tom Kite, Fuzzy Zoeller, and others.

Better Golf with Gary Player

Release Date: 1996

Description: Legendary golf pro Gary Player provides tips to help improve all phases of ones golf game.

The Billy Casper Golf Video

Release Date: 1987

Run Time: 60 min.

Description: A basic golf primer by the seasoned teacher, expounding all of his preferred methods and practice techniques.

Billy Casper's Golf for Juniors

Release Date: 1992

Description: Veteran player Casper instructs young golfers on everything they need to know to play the game of golf.

Billy Casper's Golf Basics

Release Date: 1987

Run Time: 30 min.

Description: Your foes won't stand a "ghost" of a chance when Billy Casper describes the techniques he uses to play golf. He has won 51 PGA Tour events.

Birdies & Bloopers

Release Date: 1990

Run Time: 30 min.

Description: Gary McCord of CBS sports hosts this film of fantastic moments, unbelievable shots, and comedy. Coverage starting with the 1930's all the way up to the beginning of 1990. See celebrities from television, movies, and the game itself.

Birdies & Bloopers & Fun-damentals of Golf

Release Date: 1991

Run Time: 60 min.

Description: Two-tape set that exhibits the funny and hilarious mishaps in the game of golf.

Bob Anderson's Stretching For Better Golf

Release Date: 1990

Run Time: 40 min.

Description: This video offers golfers a stretching program designed to prevent injuries and lower their scores. Since the stretches are done on the course, they will not require additional time and will even help relax golfers between holes.

Bob Mann's Complete Automatic Golf Method

Release Date: 1990

Run Time: 80 min.

Description: Instructional golf video from the author of the #1 best-selling golf video ever, Bob Mann.

Bob Mann's Golf: The Specialty Shots

Release Date: 1988

Run Time: 30 min.

Description: The golf pro demonstrates how we amateur hackers can get out of a variety of bunkers.

Bob Toski Teaches You Golf

Release Date: 1984

Run Time: 40 min

Description: Divided into separate lessons, demonstrates the proper way to play golf.

Bobby Jones: How I Play Golf, Limited Collector's Edition

Release Date: 1987

Run Time: 180 min.

Description: Historic instructional shorts starring one of golf's legends. This two-tape presentation includes an approved biography of the golf champion. Includes an accompanying booklet on the golfing great.

Bobby Jones Instructional Series, Vol. 1: Full Swing

Release Date: 1988

Run Time: 60 min.

Description: This volume demonstrates golfing pre-swing fundamentals, proper backswing position, backswing energy in the downswing, hand and foot role and how to hook, slice and stop the ball at will.

Bobby Jones Instructional Series, Vol. 2: From Tee to Green

Release Date: 1988

Run Time: 60 min.

Description: Jones shows the basics of golf in an easy-to-understand approach.

Bobby Jones: Old Man Par

Release Date: 1954

Run Time: 15 min.

Description: The story of Bobby Jones' rise to golfing immortality. Classic newsreel footage.

Bobby Wadkins on Trouble Spots

Release Date: 1989

Run Time: 20 min.

Description: Pro Wadkins shares his technique for golf's basic fundamentals. He gives advice on club using, hitting height, and much more.

Break 90 in 21 Days: Bob Rosburg

Release Date: 1990

Run Time: 30 min.

Description: Bob Rosburg was better known for covering weekend TV golf for ABC Sports since 1975. He has been a professional on the golf course since 1953. Now he's active on the PGA Senior Tour. Bob shares his techniques for everyone to use.

Break 90 in 21 Days: Judy Rankin

Release Date: 1990

Run Time: 30 min.

Description: Judy Rankin was named LPGA Player of the Year in 1976 and 1977. Then in 1984 she became an on-course commentator for the golf broadcasting team of ABC Sports. In this video she gives tips and shares techniques that have helped her get to where she is today.

British Open Golf Championships

Release Date: 1989

Run Time: 416 min.

Description: A series of eight videos covering the British Open from 1977 to 1984. Featured players include Tom Watson, Jack Nicklaus, Steve Ballesteros (the youngest player to ever win at age 22), and Bill Rodgers.

Chi Chi's Bag of Tricks

Release Date: 1988

Run Time: 60 min.

Description: Rodriguez teaches practical golf to the viewer, and imitates many of his contemporaries on the green.

Chrysler American Great 18 Golf Championship

Release Date: 1994

Run Time: 180 min.

Description: Four of the world's best professional golfers go on a cross-country trek to play on the best courses in the U.S. and golf only the toughest holes at each of those courses. Fuzzy Zoeller, John Daly, Tom Kite, and Davis Love III compete for a purse of $500,000 on this four-day tour. Some of the 18 different famous courses include: Pebble Beach, Winged Foot, PGA West, and Merion Golf Club. Program also provides a behind-the-scenes look at the travel process, which involves golfers and their entourages, commentators, and a 25-member TV production crew.

Classic Golf Experiences, Vol. 1: TPC at Sawgrass

Release Date: 1988

Run Time: 40 min.

Description: CBS golf expert Gary McCord offers a thorough examination of one of the country's most beautiful and challenging courses.

Classic Golf Experiences, Vol. 2: Harbour Town Golf Links

Release Date: 1988

Run Time: 40 min.

Description: CBS golf expert Gary McCord takes an in-depth look at one of the pro's favorite courses.

Classic Golf Experiences, Vol. 4: Doral Country Club's Blue Course

Release Date: 1988

Run Time: 40 min.

Description: CBS golf analyst Gary McCord gives a hole by hole account of one of the country's most challenging courses.

The Complete History of Golf

Release Date: 1992

Run Time: 400 min.

Description: Provides a complete history of the sport of golf from 1100 to 1991, from its royal beginnings and the early golfing societies to innovations in equipment, professional golf tournaments, and televised games.

Courtesy on the Course

Release Date: 1975

Run Time: 18 min.

Description: This program colorfully depicts the game's etiquette procedures in the order of their natural occurrence during an afternoon round of golf.

Craig Stadler on the Short Game

Release Date: 1987

Run Time: 20 min.

Description: Craig Stadler, winner of the 1982 Masters, teaches the fundamentals of wedge play and offers advice on course strategy as well as proper attitude for those difficult shots.

Curtis Strange: How to Win & Win Again

Release Date: 1990

Run Time: 70 min.

Description: Strange uses slow-motion to illustrate proper swing technique in this excellent instructional video.

Dale Douglass on Rhythm, Tempo, Sand & Chip Shots

Release Date: 1989

Run Time: 25 min.

Description: Douglass advises the novice golfer on the influence rhythm and tempo have on one's game.

Dave Stockton Golf Clinic

Release Date: 1989

Run Time: 75 min.

Description: Stockton uses his training knowledge to lower scores with insightful explanations and tips for golf greatness.

Davis Love III on Driving

Release Date: 1987

Run Time: 20 min.

Description: Davis Love III is recognized as one of the PGA's top drivers. Here he offers advice on how to get the most from your swing.

Difficult Shots Made Easy with Hale Irwin

Release Date: 1987

Run Time: 60 min.

Description: U.S. Open Champion Hale Irwin offers this guide to dealing with shots from sandtraps, up-and downhill lies and obstacles.

Driving for Distance

Release Date: 1985

Run Time: 25 min.

Description: John Elliot demonstrates ways of improving tee shots.

The 18 Toughest Holes in Golf

Release Date: 1991

Description: Shoot the most difficult holes on any golf course with some of the greats in the game.

ESPN's Teaching Kids
Sports Series

Release Date: 1987

Run Time: 75 min.

Description: Experts in a variety of sports teach kids how to properly play sports. The tapes in this series can be purchased individually or as a set.

Exercise Fitness for Golf

Release Date: 1988

Run Time: 90 min.

Description: People who are in good shape are better golfers because they have more energy on the course.

Exercises for Better Golf

Release Date: 198?

Run Time: 74 min.

Description: Golf is a demanding sport that requires strength and endurance. This program features exercises designed to decrease scores and increase health. Developed by Dr. Frank Jobe, PGA Tour Medical Director.

Fabulous Putting

Release Date: 1988

Run Time: 30 min.

Description: Golfing's brightest stars are featured attempting their most difficult and unusual putts.

Fantastic Approaches:
The Pro's Edge

Release Date: 1989

Run Time: 38 min.

Description: All time greats of the game teach you how to use those tricky short-irons. With Sam Snead, Arnold Palmer and many others.

Feel Your Way to Better Golf

Release Date: 1988

Run Time: 52 min.

Description: Shows the golfer how to feel the power of the swing by using intuition instead of analysis.

50+ Seniors Golf

Release Date: 1990

Run Time: 60 min.

Description: This in-depth, comprehensive golf instruction video is dedicated to the millions of the male and female senior golfers in America, who are the fastest growing segment today within the golf community.

Find Your Own Fundamentals

Release Date: 1985

Run Time: 25 min.

Description: Jim Flick demonstrates pre-swing golf essentials.

Fit for Golf

Release Date: 1987

Run Time: 30 min.

Description: An instructional tape on eight basic exercises designed to augment your golf game.

Fit Fore Golf with Raymond Floyd

Run Time: 35 min.

Description: Professional golfer Raymond Floyd demonstrates his 30-minute exercise routine that helps him stay in shape and remain on top of his game.

Fitness for Golf

Release Date: 1990

Run Time: 30 min.

Description: Three programs designed to maximize golf play through physical fitness.

Fit Fore Golf with Raymond Floyd

Run Time: 35 min.

Description: Professional golfer Raymond Floyd demonstrates his 30-minute exercise routine that helps him stay in shape and remain on top of his game.

Fred Couples on Tempo

Release Date: 1989

Run Time: 20 min.

Description: Golf pro, Couples, emphasizes tempo as the element of golf to make or break your game.

Games Golfers, Hustlers and Cheaters Play

Release Date: 1991

Run Time: 30 min.

Description: Bob Kesler explains the types of scams that hustlers and cheaters run, and shows how to spot them and turn them to your advantage.

Gary Koch on Putting

Release Date: 1987

Run Time: 20 min.

Description: Gary Koch covers all putting fundamentals including blade position, grip and posture, and strategies on the green.

Gary Player on Golf

Release Date: 1985

Run Time: 90 min.

Description: Player instructs the viewer on the basics and nuances of the game.

Gene Sarazen: The Man Who Changed Golf

Run Time: 60 min.

Description: Gene Sarazen, along with Jack Nicklaus and Gary Player, recalls over 70 years of golfing highlights.

Get Rid of Back Problems and Play Better Golf

Run Time: 45 min.

Description: Exercise and conditioning program designed for golfers with back problems.

Golden Greats of Golf

Release Date: 1987

Run Time: 60 min.

Description: Provides a history and demonstration of the golf swing from its greatest practitioners.

Golden Tee

Release Date: 1985

Run Time: 60 min.

Description: Some of the PGA's legendary players offer their secrets of swinging on this tape.

Golf

Release Date: 1978

Run Time: 14 min.

Description: A two-part instructional program covering the grip and stance, pitching, chipping, putting, and trouble shots. The proper way to address the ball is also shown.

Golf

Release Date: 1988

Run Time: 30 min.

Description: Wally Armstrong presents easy-to-understand instruction in both basic and specialty golf shots, from driving to putting.

Golf: A Special Kind of Joy

Release Date: 1975

Run Time: 16 min.

Description: This program studies the joy and challenge of the game and its reflections in course design, and discusses its equipment.

Golf Basics Vol. 2

Release Date: 1988

Run Time: 30 min.

Description: The winner of 51 PGA events shows how to golf properly.

Golf Can Be Cruel: Play the Planet . . . Save the Par

Run Time: 45 min.

Description: Comical parody on the game of golf.

Golf Classic: The Golf Game & the Golfer

Release Date: 1955

Run Time: 51 min.

Description: Two episodes of "The Honeymooners" and "I Love Lucy," in which the respective casts go golfing.

Golf Course Equipment

Release Date: 1991

Run Time: 30 min.

Description: Learn all there is to know about golf course management, including maintenance of the greens, marking the course and fixing ball marks and divots.

Golf Digest School's Learning Library

Release Date: 1987

Run Time: 60 min.

Description: Golf Digest instructors show the golfer how to improve the quality of their game.

Golf for Kids of All Ages

Release Date: 1988

Run Time: 50 min.

Description: An easy-to-follow, instructional guide to golf for children.

Golf for Women

Release Date: 1992

Description: Beginning golf instruction hosted by golf pro Diane Barnard and instructional golf book author Nigel Blenkarne.

Golf Fundamentals

Release Date: 1973

Run Time: 30 min.

Description: The basic fundamentals of golf are explored in this visual lesson.

Golf Fundamentals with Ben Sutton Golf School

Release Date: 1990

Run Time: 60 min.

Description: World famous Ben Sutton teaches you how to dramatically improve your game. Different cassettes for men and women.

Golf Funnies

Release Date: 1991

Run Time: 35 min.

Description: A zany video composed of the scene shreds off of the editing room floor. The all-time golfing pros are exposed here at their worst. These are the clips that the sporting news forgets about.

Golf Gadgets & Gimmicks

Run Time: 30 min.

Description: Look at the many gadgets, doo-dads, and gimmicks available for the avid golfer.

Golf Greats

Release Date: 1991

Run Time: 25 min.

Description: Six golf legends offer helpful tips and relate stories of real-life golf situations intended to improve your game.

Golf in the Desert

Release Date: 1988

Run Time: 45 min.

Description: Great golf footage from the Palm Springs area is captured.

Golf Instructor's Curriculum Kit

Release Date: 1991

Description: A complete program for teaching golf to junior and senior high school students. Comes with manuals and booklets.

Golf: Its History & Traditions

Run Time: 30 min.

Description: Experts discuss the history of golf, from yesterday's longnose clubs to today's steel shafted blades.

Golf: Its History & Traditions & The Rules of Golf

Release Date: 1989

Run Time: 60 min.

Description: Two-tape set that begins with the history of golf and ends with explaining the rules of the game.

Golf Lessons from Sam Snead

Release Date: 1982

Run Time: 60 min.

Description: Golf champ Sam Snead demonstrates the proper grip and swing, how to use woods and irons, how to play on the fairway, in the sand trap, and over the water hazard, the fine art of putting and much more.

Golf Like a Pro with Billy Casper

Release Date: 1985

Run Time: 51 min.

Description: All-time golf great Billy Casper demonstrates basic techniques that will help to improve your game.

Golf Made Simple!

Release Date: 1990

Run Time: 60 min.

Description: PGA veteran Mike Schroeder the fundamentals of golf for all skill levels. S ten strokes off your game in just three weeks following Mike's advice, which covers both the mechanics and drills.

Golf: Mind Programming To Increase Your Skill

Release Date: 199?

Run Time: 30 min.

Description: Uses hypnosis and subliminal messages to promote a better golf swing through positive thinking, coordination and concentration.

Golf My Way 2

Release Date: 1983

Run Time: 128 min.

Description: Step-by-step instruction on every element of the game, highlighted in super-slow-motion.

Golf My Way with Jack Nicklaus

Release Date: 1984

Run Time: 120 min.

Description: Champion golfer Jack Nicklaus demonstrates step-by-step lessons on every element of golf for beginners or seasoned players. Crucial points are highlighted in super slow motion to highlight every detail. On three video-cassettes, each available separately.

Golf Shots Video Magazine

Release Date: 1988

Run Time: 90 min.

Description: A video magazine issued quarterly. Various equipment is shown; rules and terms of the game are discussed: swings and stances are illustrated and specific uses of various clubs are demonstrated.

Golf Swing

Release Date: 198?

Description: This six-part series is designed to cover all golf fundamentals for the beginning player.

Golf the Miller Way

Release Date: 1986

Run Time: 30 min.

Description: On the course clinic with Miller, the pro athlete teaches the nuances and basic techniques of golf. Guest appearance by Sean Connery.

Golf: The Perfect Passion

Release Date: 1991

Run Time: 30 min.

Description: Comments and anecdotes from famous golfers such as Arnold Palmer, Gerald Ford, Bob Hope and more!

Golf Tips from 27 Top Pros

Release Date: 1989

Run Time: 40 min.

Description: Some of the greatest men to ever play the game (Sam Snead, Gary Player, Don January . . .) share their triumphs and some helpful tips with the average golfer.

Golf 2000, Vol. 1: Bunkers, Every Golfer's Nightmare

Run Time: 100 min.

Description: Ross Herbert, head coach of the Australian Institute of Sport Golf Programme, demonstrates all aspects of greenside bunker play for beginners to advanced players. Looks at the modern strokes of golf from a biomechanical viewpoint.

Golf with Al Geiberger

Release Date: 1982

Run Time: 60 min.

Description: PGA champion Al Geiberger executes every fundamental golf shot, including a driver, fairway wood, chip and sand shot in SyberVision's inimitable style. Designed for men, this videotape uses neuromuscular training, a new sports science developed at Stanford University.

Golf with Patti Sheehan

Release Date: 1984

Run Time: 60 min.

Description: Patty Sheehan, 1983 LPGA Golfer of the Year, helps women improve their golf game with the SyberVision training technology.

Golf with the Super Pros

Release Date: 1991

Run Time: 42 min.

Description: This golf instruction video deals with sand traps, alignment, putting, course management and a whole lot more. Players include Nolan Henke, Hale Irwin, Arnold Palmer, Tom Kite, Sam Snead, Lee Trevino and others.

Golf with the Super Pros & Crash Course

Release Date: 1992

Run Time: 77 min.

Description: Two-tape set to help you improve your golf game. Includes lessons and advice from such pros as Arnold Palmer, Sam Snead and Lee Trevino.

Golf Without Ulcers

Release Date: 1992

Run Time: 28 min.

Description: Bill Findlay's maniacal approach to golf leads him to Fairway Farms, a golfers rehab center. After several months of therapy, Bill returns, renewed, to the game—hoping to actually finish a round of golf and maybe even break 115.

A Golfer's Paradise

Run Time: 40 min.

Description: View Hilton Head Island's golf courses designed by Pete Dye, George Fazio, Arthur Hills and others.

Golfoolery

Release Date: 1988

Run Time: 60 min.

Description: A combination of trick shots and great golf tips featuring Merlin Olsen, Sam Snead, and Erik Estrada.

Golf's Greats, Vol. 1

Release Date: 1990

Run Time: 30 min.

Description: Learn lots of tips from the early greats to improve your game of golf.

Golf's Gambling Games

Release Date: 1990

Run Time: 55 min.

Description: The foursome of Gene (2 Handicap), Joe (18 Handicap), Frank (18 Handicap) and Omar (36 Handicap) tee off and give funny but helpful advice on how to play, bet and win on golf at the Ojai Valley Inn and Country Club in California.

Golf's Greatest Moments

Release Date: 1989

Run Time: 77 min.

Description: Golf's centennial is celebrated here with a look at the finest and most memorable moments in its history. Some of the featured names include Sam Snead, Jack Nicklaus, Arnold Palmer, Patty Berg, Byron Nelson, Gene Sarazen and many more.

Golf's Greatest Trick Shots featuring Dennis Walters, introduced by Arnold Palmer

Release Date: 1996

Run Time: 60 min.

Description: World renowned trick shot master and paraplegic Dennis Walters demonstrates his skill of hitting shots from what he likes to call unusal lies with unusual clubs. He makes shots using such things as baseball bats, fishing rods, crutches, tennis rackets, and sometimes regular golf clubs.

Golf's One in a Million Shots

Release Date: 1987

Run Time: 60 min.

Description: This program features famous golfers making their greatest shots.

Good Grief! Golf?

Release Date: 1991

Run Time: 38 min.

Description: Features some of the craziest shots ever made by some of the greats of the game including Jack Nicklaus, Arnold Palmer and others.

Great Golf Courses of the World: Ireland

Release Date: 1991

Run Time: 58 min.

Description: Tour the Emerald Isle by way of its splendid golf courses, including Royal County Down, Lahinch and Ballybunion.

Great Golf Courses of the World: Pebble Beach

Release Date: 1991

Run Time: 70 min.

Description: View four of the best golf courses in the United States—Pebble Beach, Cypress Point Golf Club, Spyglass Hill Golf Club and the Links at Spanish Bay.

Great Golf Courses of the World: Scotland

Release Date: 1991

Run Time: 77 min.

Description: Jack Nicklaus hosts this program detailing the history of Scotland's best courses, including St. Andrews, Muirfield, Carnoustie, Gleneagles and Royal Troon.

Great Moments of the Masters

Release Date: 1989

Run Time: 53 min.

Description: This video is a one-of-a-kind collection of memories from the Masters over the years.

The Greater Golfer in You

Release Date: 1991

Run Time: 60 min.

Description: This two volume (untitled) video seminar demonstrates how to improve your swing technique, overcome those difficult situations and lower your golfing handicap.

Greg Norman: The Complete Golfer

Release Date: 1988

Run Time: 55 min.

Description: Tips for the ailing golfer from legendary pro Greg Norman.

Heroes of the Game

Release Date: 1995

Run Time: 90 min.

Description: Three-volume series of golf history commemorates the centennial of the United States Golf Association by looking at such players as Jack Nicklaus, Arnold Palmer, Ben Hogan, Bobby Jones, Byron Nelson, Patty Berg, Babe Didrikson, and Nancy Lopez. Tapes are available individually.

Highlights of the 1989 Masters Tournament

Release Date: 1989

Run Time: 60 min.

Description: Covers all four rounds of the tournament and tells the story of the biggest golfing event in the U.S. in 1989.

History and Traditions of Golf in Scotland

Release Date: 1990

Run Time: 30 min.

Description: Everyone who loves golf should see this video! You'll travel to Scotland which is the home and heart of golf. One of the things shown is a look inside the ancient and royal clubhouse at St. Andrews.

The History of the PGA Tour

Release Date: 1990

Run Time: 76 min.

Description: Review of the last seventy-five years of golf history. Profiles some of golf's greats such as Bobby Jones, Sam Snead, Ben Hogan, Arnold Palmer, Jack Nicklaus, and Tom Watson. Includes highlights from some of the greatest golf matches of all time. A must-see for the serious golf fan.

History of the Ryder Cup

Run Time: 81 min.

Description: A documentation of the passage of time from Sam Ryder's presentation of the gold cup for the first time, recognizing the winner of golf matches between the U.S. and Britain.

Hit it Farther with Betsy Cullen

Release Date: 1988

Run Time: 60 min.

Description: In this video presentation of golf for women, Betsy Cullen, a retired golf professional, teaches the body movements and positions that maximize power. Most women and many men are not approaching their power potential because they have not learned these movements through other sports.

Hot Shots: Trick Shot Golf

Release Date: 1989

Run Time: 40 min.

Description: Join Peter Longo as he performs a number of wacky golf tricks such as driving with a garden hose and using a half naked girl as a tee.

How Clubs Are Made

Release Date: 1991

Run Time: 30 min.

Description: Learn all there is to know about making a golf club as you enter a manufacturing plant.

How to Break 90 in 30 Days

Release Date: 1990

Run Time: 60 min.

Description: Comprehensive and successful methods for achieving your personal best in the game golf. Film covers sand traps, mental focus, slicing, scoring, your wedge, and much more.

How to Build a Golf Swing

Release Date: 1975

Run Time: 32 min.

Description: This program examines conditioning the mind and body to understand the swinging movements based upon six major concepts from flow of power to direction. In two parts.

How to Buy Golf Equipment

Release Date: 1989

Run Time: 5 min.

Description: Visits the famous Ping facility and shows how modern golf clubs are produced.

How to Golf

Release Date: 1986

Run Time: 50 min.

Description: Stephenson enacts a complete lesson in golf style, form and execution.

How to Win and Win Again with Curtis Strange

Release Date: 1990

Run Time: 70 min.

Description: Golf master Strange shares tips on how to compete effectively. Incorporates cutting edge video techniques that enable the viewer to see exactly what to do.

Ian Woosnam's Power Game

Release Date: 1989

Run Time: 55 min.

Description: Champion golfer Ian Woosnam gives the inside scoop on how to raise level of play and lower scores.

Imagine! All Eagles

Release Date: 1988

Run Time: 30 min.

Description: A look at those rare two-under-par moments that golfers cherish. With Arnold Palmer, Sam Snead, Billy Casper and others.

Improve Your Golf Game

Release Date: 1981

Run Time: 60 min.

Description: Slow motion and stop action photography are used to show the fundamentals of golf, including grip, stance, ball positioning, and the swing.

The Inside Look at the Game for a Lifetime

Release Date: 1983

Run Time: 60 min.

Description: Presents the fundamentals of golf.

Intermediate Golf

Release Date: 1991

Run Time: 30 min.

Description: PGA standout Jeff Thomsen offers advice and techniques on improving the game.

Intermediate Putting

Release Date: 1991

Run Time: 30 min.

Description: The finer points of putting a golf ball are explained to intermediate players.

Jack Nicklaus Shows You the Greatest 18 Holes of Major Championship Golf

Release Date: 1988

Run Time: 60 min.

Description: A compilation of golf trivia, tournament footage and Nicklaus's favorite putts and tees, featuring courses from around the world.

Jack Nicklaus Sports Clinic

Release Date: 1977

Run Time: 18 min.

Description: Golf pro Jack Nicklaus demonstrates proper golf techniques.

Jack Nicklaus: The Full Swing

Release Date: 1990

Run Time: 36 min.

Description: The legendary golfer examines the swings, technique, form and function of a well-tuned golf game.

Jay Golden's Fun-Damentals of Golf

Run Time: 30 min.

Description: Jay Golden examines golf from a humorous point of view.

The Jimmy Ballard Golf Connection

Release Date: 1987

Run Time: 90 min.

Description: The revised edition of the instructional program by the top PGA teacher, featuring his repetoire of shots and learning methods.

JoAnne Carner's Keys to Great Golf

Release Date: 1991

Run Time: 90 min.

Description: "Big Momma" shows how to take ten strokes off your golf game by concentrating on distance, accuracy, and consistency as priority goals.

John Jacobs' Golf

Release Date: 1983

Run Time: 60 min.

Description: A look at the fundamentals of the game, with answers to many of the questions asked by amateurs.

Judy Rankin Golf Tips

Release Date: 1987

Run Time: 60 min.

Description: A program of golf instruction for women, emphasizing the importance of a good short game.

Junior Golf: The Easy Way

Release Date: 1991

Run Time: 43 min.

Description: Pro golfer Mark Steinbauer explains the fundamentals of his sport in a simple language and manner for the younger player.

Just Missed. . .Dammit!

Release Date: 1988

Run Time: 40 min.

Description: Golf's greatest foul-ups and funnies by some of the most respected players in the sport. Hilarious sports fun!

Ken Venturi's Better Golf Now

Release Date: 1986

Run Time: 40 min.

Description: This video is a presentation of Ken Ventura's instructional analytical golf training.

Ken Venturi's Stroke Savers

Release Date: 1989

Run Time: 59 min.

Description: World famous golfer Ken Venturi shows how anyone can learn to take strokes off their game.

Keys to Consistency with Jack Grout

Run Time: 56 min.

Description: Jack Nicklaus's coach and teacher offers a method for bringing consistency to your golf game that leads to lower scores and greater confidence on the links.

Killer Golf

Release Date: 1991

Run Time: 45 min.

Description: Join Gary McCord and his zany golf pals as they show you excercises and techniques designed to improve your game.

Kinesthetic Golf

Release Date: 1987

Run Time: 60 min.

Description: A teaching program which endeavors to improve the viewer's golf swing simply by repetitive, unconsciously affecting visuals.

The King of Golf, Vol. 1

Release Date: 1993

Run Time: 60 min.

Description: Features the golf antics of Count Yogi.

The Last 100 Yards

Run Time: 50 min.

Description: From the man who taught the Golden Bear how to play golf, a step-by-step guide to chipping, pitching, putting, playing bunkers, bad lies, and more.

Lee Trevino

Release Date: 1991

Run Time: 30 min.

Description: The legendary golfer is honored in this collection of career highlights and interviews.

Lee Trevino's Golf Tips for Youngsters

Release Date: 1988

Run Time: 40 min.

Description: Lee Trevino gives helpful advice and tips to the younger golfer.

Lee Trevino's Priceless Golf Tips

Release Date: 1987

Run Time: 25 min.

Description: The peerless pro demonstrates for the viewer his basic techniques in chipping and putting.

Lee Trevino's Putt for Dough

Release Date: 1989

Run Time: 50 min.

Description: Putting tips fom all time great Lee Trevino.

Legacy of the Links

Release Date: 1987

Run Time: 90 min.

Description: A tour through St. Andrews and the history of the game of golf with several seasoned golf pros.

Leslie Nielsen's Bad Golf Made Easier

Release Date: 1993

Run Time: 40 min.

Description: Nielsen parodies golf instructional videos by allowing viewers to remain bad golfers and still improve their games (by bribery if necessary). With his caddie (Donner), Nielsen tutors the unassuming Billy (Hahn) in bending the rules of golf and having fun while doing it. Based on "Golf Your Way" by Henry Beard and John Boswell and "Mulligan's Laws," edited by Beard.

Leslie Nielsen's Bad Golf, My Way

Release Date: 1994

Run Time: 50 min.

Description: Bumbling, rule-bending sportsman Nielsen returns to the fairways to teach country club champion Brad van Courtlandt a few tricks of the game.

Lesson with Leadbetter: The Full Golf Swing

Run Time: 90 min.

Description: Avid golf coach of some of the world's most influencial personalities, David Leadbetter uses his specialized golf techniques to improve even the most twisted looking golf strokes.

Lon Hinkle's Driving for Distance

Release Date: 1987

Run Time: 30 min.

Description: A golf instruction program concentrating on longer drives for lower initial scores.

Mastering the Basics:
A Guide for the Woman Golfer

Release Date: 1987

Run Time: 60 min.

Description: The techniques of golf such as the swing and the grip are demonstrated by two professional golfers.

Master System to Better Golf, Vol. 1

Release Date: 1989

Run Time: 60 min.

Description: Four top-rated PGA pros reveal the methods that make them great. Featured are Davis Love III, Tom Purtzer, Craig Stadler and Gary Koch.

Master System to Better Golf, Vol. 2

Release Date: 1989

Run Time: 60 min.

Description: PGA pros share their practice hints with the novice golfer. A lesson to follow volume 1.

Master System to Better Golf, Vol. 3:
The Seniors

Release Date: 1989

Run Time: 60 min.

Description: Distinguished golfers get out on the green to offer the novice golfer an invaluable lesson.

The Masters' Tournament

Release Date: 1986

Run Time: 60 min.

Description: A collection of highlights from the 1986, 1987, and 1988 Masters Tournament.

The Medium and Long Iron Game

Release Date: 197?

Run Time: 60 min.

Description: Golf pros Dick Lawrence, John Ferrari, Joyce Ann Jackson, and Harry Offutt give pointers on how to develop a longer, stronger, fairway shot. From the "Name of the Game Is Golf" series.

Mid and Short Irons

Release Date: 1990

Run Time: 13 min.

Description: This video details the type of club selection necessary for improving your golf game.

Miller Barber on the Driver & the Wedge

Release Date: 1989

Run Time: 25 min.

Description: Video instruction designed to enlighten your golf game.

The Money Game

Release Date: 197?

Run Time: 16 min.

Description: The story of Jim Nelford, a young Canadian golfer who has experienced the intense competition and frustration encountered in the world of professional golf.

Murphy's Laws of Golf

Release Date: 1989

Run Time: 30 min.

Description: A hapless golfer falls victim to every trap and hazard known to the game, and a few new ones, too.

Name of the Game Is Golf:
Medium and Long Iron Game

Release Date: 1987

Run Time: 60 min.

Description: This instructional golf video can be used by anyone from the novice to the seasoned pro.

Name of the Game Is Golf: Putting for Beginner and Pro

Release Date: 1987

Run Time: 60 min.

Description: Established teaching golf pros give excellent tips and lessons in five phases of the game. Five one-hour lessons are included. Programs are available individually.

Name of the Game Is Golf: Sand Lessons and Special Shots

Release Date: 1987

Run Time: 60 min.

Description: This is a series devoted to instruction on specific golf swings and strategy, featuring an assortment of golf pros.

Name of the Game Is Golf: Short Iron Lessons

Release Date: 1987

Run Time: 60 min.

Description: An instructional golf video that can be used no matter the player's level.

Name of the Game Is Golf: Woods and Tee Shots

Release Date: 1987

Run Time: 60 min.

Description: Beginners and experts alike will be able to use this handy instructional golf video.

Nancy Lopez: Golf Made Easy

Release Date: 1988

Run Time: 48 min.

Description: Golf's grande dame demonstrates tips that can help make you a winner.

NCAA Instructional Videos

Release Date: 1992

Description: Famous college coaches teach about eighteen different sports. The instruction spans the range of ability from novice to expert. Winter and summer sports, men's and women's sports, land and water sports, and outdoor and indoor sports are covered. Available individually or by the sport or by the entire set.

Nice Shot!

Release Date: 1992

Run Time: 65 min.

Description: One of the aspects of golf instruction that most often goes unnoticed is the mental effort of concentration. That's why duffers who receive excellent instruction lapse back into old patterns. Learn the physical dynamics of golf as well as the mental concentration necessary to improve your game.

Nice Shot!

Release Date: 1995

Run Time: 60 min.

Description: Involves helping golfers of any ability level to dramatically improve their game.

Nick Faldo's Golf Course

Release Date: 1989

Run Time: 66 min.

Description: The man who is widely acknowledged as a leader in golf strategy offers advice on aspects of the game from grip and swings to driving and alignment.

Nick Faldo's Golf Course, Vol. 2

Release Date: 1990

Run Time: 61 min.

Description: Review golf basics with Nick Faldo and David Leadbetter.

Nick Faldo's Fixes

Release Date: 1995

Run Time: 62 min.

Description: Addresses the needs of the amateur golfer.

Nick Faldo's Tips and Drills

Release Date: 1995
Run Time: 55 min.
Description: Tips for the more seasoned golfer.

9 Tips from 9 Legends, Vol. 1: From Tee to Fairway

Release Date: 1991
Run Time: 60 min.
Description: Master golfers give you helpful hints on improving your swing, stance and other important aspects of golf.

From Tee to Fairway

Release Date: 1991
Run Time: 60 min.
Description: Key golf stategies from Billy Casper, Don January, and others.

1984 Liberty Mutual Legends of Golf

Release Date: 1984
Run Time: 27 min.
Description: Features many top golfers competing for top honors in the Liberty Mutual Legends of Golf Championship.

The 1986 Masters Tournament

Release Date: 1986
Run Time: 60 min.
Description: A record of the 1986 golf championship.

1989 Golf Digest Almanac

Release Date: 1989
Run Time: 60 min.
Description: Golfers can get all the essentials on the 1988 PGA tour with the 1989 Golf Digest Almanac. Purchase includes book "The Golf Digest Almanac: 1989."

1991 PGA Golf

Release Date: 1991
Run Time: 115 min.
Description: Two of 1991's best golf matches are featured. "Daly's . . . The Long Shot" highlights the exciting moments before John Daly became PGA champion. "The War by the Shore" shows how the United States won the Ryder Cup back from Europe.

The 1992 Masters

Release Date: 199?
Run Time: 52 min.
Description: Highlights from the Golf Masters tournament in Augusta, Georgia.

North Carolina: Golf State, U.S.A.

Release Date: 1975
Run Time: 15 min.
Description: A survey of North Carolina's golfing facilities, including the World Golf Hall of Fame in Pinehurst.

Official 1988 U.S. Open Golf Championship

Release Date: 1989
Run Time: 55 min.
Description: Highlights of this historic championship include Curtis Strange's exciting sudden-death play-off against Nick Faldo in his first of two back-to-back U.S. Open wins—the first golfer since Ben Hogan to do so. Jim McKay narrates.

Official Rules of Golf

Release Date: 198?
Run Time: 35 min.
Description: Every rule in the book of golf is covered by Tom Watson and Peter Alliss.

One Club Challenge, Vol. 1

Release Date: 1991
Run Time: 42 min.

Description: Lee Trevino and partner Steve Ballestros challenge Isao Aoki and Nick Faldo to a zany one club match at the historic St. Andrews Golf Course.

One Move to Better Golf

Release Date: 1989

Run Time: 30 min.

Description: This tape reveals the one simple "move" taught at secret PGA seminars that will immediately improve your game.

Orville Moody on Long Irons & Putting

Release Date: 1989

Run Time: 25 min.

Description: Hall-of Famer Moody teaches you his secret to winning in your own home.

Outrageously Funny Golf

Release Date: 1987

Run Time: 30 min.

Description: Paul Hahn Jr. shows you many trick shots that can improve your game.

Patty Berg: Fairway to Fame

Release Date: 1954

Run Time: 15 min.

Description: The story of the famed woman golfer, Patty Berg. Classic newsreel footage.

Paul Azinger on Fairway & Green Sand Traps

Release Date: 1989

Run Time: 20 min.

Description: Golf instruction focusing on the sand trap and how to get out of it.

PGA Tour Golf, Vol. 1: The Full Swing

Release Date: 1988

Run Time: 60 min.

Description: Improve the fundamentals of your swing by working on correct grip, setup, back swing and down swing.

PGA Tour Golf, Vol. 1: Tips from the Tour

Release Date: 1988

Run Time: 35 min.

Description: No less than fourteen professional golfers share their vast array of knowledge so that you may someday be King of the Green.

PGA Tour Golf, Vol. 2: The Short Game

Release Date: 1988

Run Time: 60 min.

Description: Five of the PGA's top pros offer advice on improving accuracy for those difficult "touch" shots.

PGA Tour Golf, Vol. 3: Course Strategy

Release Date: 1988

Run Time: 60 min.

Description: Five PGA pros review the variables that pop up during any given game and the methods for examining all possibilities of play.

A Picture's Worth 1000 Words

Run Time: 30 min.

Description: Companion to "Feel Your Way to Better Golf."

Play Better Golf, Vol. 1: The Basics

Release Date: 1989

Run Time: 30 min.

Description: Join Peter Alliss as he tackles every major problem confronting the novice golfer including grip, putting, driving and more.

Play Better Golf, Vol. 2: Shot Refinement

Release Date: 1989

Run Time: 30 min.

Description: This volume of the series deals with long irons, pitching wedge, calibrated putting and more.

Play Better Golf with Rip Collins

Release Date: 198?

Run Time: 60 min.

Description: In these two sessions you will learn the basics with Rip Collins as your instructor.

Play Senior Golf

Release Date: 1988

Run Time: 72 min.

Description: Several senior tour professional golfers explain how to correct the ten most common mistakes made by older golfers.

Play Your Best Golf, Vol. 1

Release Date: 198?

Run Time: 69 min.

Description: An instructional golf video in three chapters: Principles of the golf swing; woods and long irons; and mid and short irons.

Play Your Best Golf, Vol. 2

Release Date: 198?

Run Time: 69 min.

Description: An instructional golf video in four sections: The scoring shots; the trouble shots; playing the game and drills.

Power Driving with Mike Dunaway

Release Date: 1986

Run Time: 30 min.

Description: Accurate and powerful golf driving is demonstrated by Dunaway.

Precision Putting with Dave Stockton

Release Date: 1986

Run Time: 30 min.

Description: Stockton demonstrates optimum putting on the green.

Putting for the Beginner and the Pro

Release Date: 197?

Run Time: 60 min.

Description: Golf pros Toby Lyons, Carla Glasgow, Dick Lawrence, Neal Doyle, and Linda Craft teach the most deceptively simple shots in golf. From the "Name of the Game Is Golf" series.

Putting: Golf's End Game

Release Date: 1975

Run Time: 12 min.

Description: This program points out the geometric factors of putting and its demand for exactness.

Putting with Confidence

Release Date: 1989

Run Time: 30 min.

Description: Duff Lawrence and Barb Thomas give handy tips on how to putt more accurately

Putton: Wages War on the Rude Golfer

Release Date: 1993

Run Time: 35 min.

Description: Sports video spoofing "Patton" finds retired General George B. Putton invading a golf course to teach two obnoxious golfers the art of golf etiquette.

Quick Tips from Golf's Greats, Vol. 1

Release Date: 1987

Run Time: 30 min.

Description: Pick up some golfing tips from six of golf's greatest players—Billy Casper, Bobby Nichols, Jerry Barber, Orville Moody, George Bayer, and Charlie Sifford. Features tips on fairway woods, wedge play, the driver, and more.

Quick Tips from Golf's Greats, Vol. 2

Release Date: 1987

Run Time: 30 min.

Description: Get tips on recovery shots, putting, chipping, and more from some of golf's greatest players—Tommy Bolt, Charles Owens, Jack Fleck, Doug Ford, Dow Finsterwald, Harold Henning, and Billy Casper.

Ray Floyd's 60 Yards In

Release Date: 198?

Run Time: 60 min.

Description: Golfer Ray Floyd is here to help golfers' short game improve. He discusses difficult chipping, pitching, sand, and putting situations.

Reaching Your Golf Potential with Tom Kite & Friends

Release Date: 1989

Run Time: 50 min.

Description: Come to Ventana Canyon, the famed golf course in Tucson, Arizona, and play with the pros. Tom Kite and three friends show you tips and secrets of the pros. Tape 1 offers a short game clinic while tape 2 shows an entire round.

Rules and Etiquette of Golf

Release Date: 1992

Run Time: 60 min.

Description: Golf pro Derick Warwick is joined by Tommy Horton, a member of the PGA European Tour's Board of Directors, to teach golf rules and manners.

The Rules of Golf

Release Date: 1990

Run Time: 24 min.

Description: Your knowledge of the rules of golf can lower your score. As told by your hosts Julie Inkster, Tom Watson, and Peter Alliss.

Rules of Golf, Amen

Release Date: 1987

Run Time: 42 min.

Description: A comic, TV-gameshow satire of the rules of golf.

Sam Snead

Run Time: 30 min.

Description: A profile of one of golf's true legends, featuring interviews and career highlights.

Sam Snead: Secrets for Seniors

Run Time: 58 min.

Description: Golf's elder stsatesman offers tips for making tough shots, and reveals his physical and mental fitness program. Features a look at Snead's amazing career.

Sand Lessons and Special Shots

Release Date: 197?

Run Time: 60 min.

Description: Golf pros Toby Lyons, Harry Offutt, Penny Zavichas, and Dick Lawrence demonstrate bunker shots, showing how the sand trap can become a nicer place for the golfer to visit. Part of the series, "The Name of the Game Is Golf."

Saving Par from the Sand

Release Date: 1985

Run Time: 25 min.

Description: John Elliot demonstrates optimum bunker shots.

Secrets for Seniors

Release Date: 1991

Run Time: 58 min.

Description: Sam Snead shares his golf tips on shotmaking, physical and mental fitness, and his approaches to the game.

Senior Swinger

Release Date: 1991

Run Time: 90 min.

Description: Don January offers helpful hints for keeping Father Time away and saving strokes on the golf course.

Seniors Plus 50

Release Date: 1989

Description: Jay Overton of the Innisbrook Golf Institute demonstrates golf techniques for the mature individual.

Seve Ballesteros: The Short Game

Release Date: 1992

Run Time: 65 min.

Description: Players of all skill levels can learn how to improve their golf game from 100 yards and in.

75 Years of the PGA Championship: Great Champions, Great Moments

Release Date: 1994

Run Time: 65 min.

Description: Chronicles the first filmed PGA championship in 1916 to the sudden death playoff of 1993. Includes interviews and footage of some of golf's greatest legends, including Nicklaus, Daly, Norman, Trevino, Azinger, Hagen, Sarazen, Nelson, Snead, Hogan, Player, and others.

Sharpen Your Short Irons

Release Date: 1985

Run Time: 25 min.

Description: Jim Flick demonstrates optimum scoring club use.

Short Approach Shots

Release Date: 1975

Run Time: 9 min.

Description: Pitch and chip shots are identified and tips on the swing and club selection for these shots are demonstrated.

The Short Game with Phil Rodgers

Release Date: 1987

Run Time: 72 min.

Description: This is an instructional tape for semi-experienced golfers, concentrating on distance control, sand shots and other details.

Short Iron Lessons

Release Date: 197?

Run Time: 60 min.

Description: Golf pros Linda Craft, Toby Lyons, Penny Zavichas, Neal Doyle, and Harry Offutt teach the golfer how to play short iron shots well, which can save many agonizing strokes on the course. From the "Name of the Game Is Golf" series.

The Short Way to Lower Scoring

Release Date: 1986

Run Time: 60 min.

Description: A demonstration of the proper techniques of playing golf close to and on the green.

Simplify Your Circle

Release Date: 1991

Run Time: 60 min.

Description: Mike Schroder demonstrates proven methods that shave points off your score with drills and applied sciences.

Special Challenge Shots

Release Date: 1975

Run Time: 14 min.

Description: This program provides an overview of golf's architectural beauty, harboring the challenges that test a player's skill.

Sports Pages: Golf Bloopers

Release Date: 1992

Run Time: 30 min.

Description: See golf pros such as Jack Nicklaus, Payne Stewart and others have a bad day on the course.

Strange Reigns at Oak Hill: Highlights of the 1989 U.S. Open

Release Date: 1990

Run Time: 40 min.

Description: Curtis Strange's second victory is featured here, along with footage from past U.S. Open Tournaments.

Stratton Golf School's Crash Course

Release Date: 1991

Run Time: 35 min.

Description: Golf pro Keith Lyford provides easy drills and lessons for duffers, including posture, aiming, full swing, etiquette, stance, scoring, handicaps, and understaning the equipment.

Sudden Death and The Play-Offs

Release Date: 1992

Run Time: 59 min.

Description: Some of golf's most historic moments with some of the sport's best, including Seve Ballesteros, Nick Faldo, Jack Nicklaus, Greg Norman, Arnold Palmer, and Tom Watson.

Suntory World Match Play Championship

Run Time: 55 min.

Description: An exciting documentation of the tournament that gathers all the world's best golfers to play.

A Swing for a Lifetime

Release Date: 1985

Run Time: 25 min.

Description: Jim Flick demonstrates optimum golf swings.

Swing's the Thing

Release Date: 1987

Run Time: 40 min.

Description: A short instructional series on the golf swing, for experienced as well as novice players.

Sybervision Golf Video Series

Release Date: 1994

Description: Four-part golf training series that features tips from pro golfers Dave Stockton, Al Geiberger, Hale Irwin, and Patty Sheehan. Contains the SyberVision training approach, which centers on improvement of skills, concentration, and confidence by using repeated images, enhanced computer models, slow motion, rhythm, and specially composed music.

Teaching Kids Golf with Ben Sutton Golf School

Release Date: 199?

Run Time: 50 min.

Description: Kids learn to play golf from the instructors at the Ben Sutton School, where props, computer graphics and drills are used as a straight-forward approach to teaching.

Tee Off with Bob Kesler

Release Date: 1991

Run Time: 30 min.

Description: Bob Kesler addresses all aspects of the golf game and provides demonstrations for players of all levels.

Ten Fundamentals of the Modern Golf Swing

Run Time: 32 min.

Description: Two well-known golf instructors present 10 steps that can lead to longer straighter shots.

Ten Years of the British Open

Release Date: 1989

Run Time: 52 min.

Description: An interesting look at the shots that affected the outcome of ten open Championships spanning the 1980s. Featured players include Watson, Lyle, Faldo, and Ballesteros, as well as those not quite so famous.

This Price is Right: 1992 PGA Championship

Run Time: 58 min.

Description: Follows Nick Price as he wins his first major title at the 1992 PGA Championship.

Thom Sharp's Golf: I Hate this Game!

Release Date: 1988

Run Time: 40 min.

Description: Comedian Thom Sharp takes a wayward look at the genteel world of golf.

Three Men and a Bogey

Release Date: 1989

Run Time: 30 min.

Description: Spoof of a golf instructional tape.

Tiger-Shark Golf Series

Run Time: 15 min.

Description: Golf pro and club designer, Pat Simmons, shows how to improve every aspect of your golf game.

Tom Purtzer on Iron Accuracy

Release Date: 1989

Run Time: 20 min.

Description: Purtzer emphasizes the different techniques used with different irons.

Total Golf: Saving Strokes with Bruce Crampton

Release Date: 1987

Run Time: 75 min.

Description: The renowned pro demonstrates his own strategies in low-stroke golf.

Toughest 18 Holes in America

Description: Golfers can get a taste of how it might feel to shoot 18 of the most difficult holes on the PGA tour. Locations include Pebble Beach, Augusta National, Doral, and Oakmont.

Trick Shots

Release Date: 1991

Run Time: 30 min.

Description: Learn how to get out of those nasty situations with these trick golf shots and advice on swinging problems.

25 Great Pros' Second Shots

Release Date: 1987

Run Time: 30 min.

Description: Stars like Arnold Palmer and Tommy Bolt break par with astounding second shots.

The Ultimate Drive

Release Date: 1987

Run Time: 60 min.

Description: Arthur B. Sellinger, 1986 National Long Driving champion, shares his techniques for achieving the ultimate drive.

U.S. Open: Golf's Greatest Championship

Release Date: 1987

Run Time: 60 min.

Description: A history of professional golf, from Francis Ouimet's 1913 victory to the 1987 Open.

Wally Armstrong's Collection of Teaching Aids and Drills

Release Date: 1991

Run Time: 32 min.

Description: Using household items such as hula hoops and brooms, Wally gives a thorough demonstration of golf fundamentals in his own unique way. Reference guide sheets are included, but you'll have to supply your own hula hoop.

Wally Armstrong's Golf the Easy Way

Release Date: 1989

Run Time: 33 min.

Description: Wally Armstrong takes you step by step through some of the most bothersome shots. This video will help your game no matter what your skill level.

Wally Armstrong's Golf for Kids of All Ages

Release Date: 1991

Run Time: 40 min.

Description: Golf pro Wally Armstrong hosts this instructional golf video stressing the fundamentals of the sport.

The War by the Shore: 1991 Ryder Cup

Run Time: 62 min.

Description: Chronicles the 1991 Ryder Cup golf championship.

Water, Trees and Tall Grass . . . Or Where Did My Golf Ball Go?

Release Date: 1991

Run Time: 30 min.

Description: Learn how to escape from those unexplored regions that loom large on every golf course.

What's a Hazard

Release Date: 1991

Run Time: 30 min.

Description: Learn what to do when your golf ball gets wedged in an impossible angle.

Winner's Edge: Golf

Release Date: 198?

Run Time: 25 min.

Description: Join Kermit Zarley as he lends advice on all phases of the golfing game.

Winning at Golf with Amy Alcott

Release Date: 1991

Run Time: 37 min.

Description: Professional golfer Amy Alcott shares her secrets for successs on the green.

Winning Golf

Release Date: 198?

Run Time: 60 min.

Description: Join former PGA champion Al Geiberger as he demonstrates methods for improving swing, grip, stance, and other aspects of the game.

Women's Golf Fundamentals with the Ben Sutton Golf School

Release Date: 1989

Run Time: 60 min.

Description: Hostess Joyce Ann Jackson helps the lady golfer develop swing consistency and add power to her drive.

The Women's Guide to Golf

Release Date: 1995

Run Time: 60 min.

Description: Addresses questions from what kind of clubs to use, to the proper rules and golf course etiquette.

Woods and Tee Shots

Release Date: 197?

Run Time: 60 min.

Description: Golf pros Neal Doyle, Joyce Ann Jackson, and Linda Craft give lessons on how to straighten and lengthen your tee shots and fairway wood shots. Part of the series, "The Name of the Game Is Golf."

The World's Worst Avid Golfer

Release Date: 1991

Run Time: 30 min.

Description: A golfing foursome hacks up the couse but rarely comes into contact with the ball in the search for America's worst avid golfer.

WEB SITES

The First Tee!

URL: http://www.mindspring.com/~jwrogers /golf.html

Description: Here is a site that really catches the eye. It has a highly detailed grass background, that makes you think "golf course." This, accompanied by a competent selection of links and information, manages to appeal greatly to the internet golfer. It is worth the trip. Stop by this one—you won't be disappointed.

Golf by Nerd World Media

URL: http://www.nerdworld.com/nw268.html

Description: This site is a mass compilation of golf related information. The page's author, David Stein, must really know his way around the Internet to provide such a massive, detailed selection of sites throughout the web. If you cannot find the golf information you are looking for at this site, it possibly might not exist!

golf.com

URL: http://golf.com/

Description: The collaborative work of NBC Sports and Golf Digest, you'll find results from virtually every tournament including the PGA, LPGA and Nike challenges. Explore course maps and resorts, leafthrough the pages of leading golf publications or preview trendy new equipment leading-edge golfers areusing to win big prizes. With a live news ticker and a golfers chat area, each visit will be as unique as thelast. After you've polished up your clubs, par over for the latest occurring in the golf kingdom.

Golf Course Database

URL: http://www.traveller.com/golf

Description: The Golf Course Database provides information on more than 2000 golf clubs in the United States and Canada, including course ratings, course architect, tee information, and contact information.

Golf Links

URL: http://www.hut.fi/~kkontti/golf.html

Description: This site is one that is a definite eye-catcher when first opened, where you will find a photo of one of many tour professionals that is greatly regarded in the game of golf. This page was developed and is maintained by students at the University of Helsinki in Finland, which if nothing else makes it a novelty to peruse for its different view on the sport. This site is well worth a visit by all golf enthusiasts.

Golf Online

URL: http://www.golfonline.com/

Description: Like having Jack Nicklaus as your caddy! You almost need a golf cart to get around this forest full of golf news, tips, equipment ads and other golf stuff. The news section provide the latest details from all of the pro tours, including profiles of the hottest players, statistics, tournament schedules, and a primer on television coverage. A really great weather link provides four-day forecasts of playing conditions in golf hot spots around the United States. An instruction section provides the kind of personal attention most golfers have to buy from their club pro: "Tell us about your swing and we'll tell you how to improve," the site instructs. Plus, there's links to dozens of other golf sites.

Golf Pro

URL: http://www.cityscape.co.uk/users/fi28/shea/golfpro/home.html

Description: As the name indicates, this is all about professional golf. Timely results and recaps of previous tournaments and previews and predictions of upcoming tournaments. Also includes an exhaustive list of statistics from pro tours in both the United States and Europe. A world rankings section features the top pros.

Golf Resources

URL: http://www.kdcol.com/~enriko/golf.html

Description: Who ever decided to establish this site also decided to save all the glitz and glamour for you to discover in all the many links provided here. It has one of the most thorough golf resource directories available—there should be something here for everyone. Don't judge a book by its' cover, as the old adage goes. While not beautiful, it's certainly functional.

Golf World

URL: http://golf.com/golfworld/

Description: Designed for golfers who enjoy a good read. No media covers golf with a better writing style than the folks who put out this weekly magazine. Tournament recaps from the men's and women's pro tours make the matches come alive and big tournaments are profiled in great detail. The Masters coverage, for example, included a guide to handicapping picks for the office pool, and features on lesser-known and amateur entrants.

GolfData Web

URL: http:www.gdol.com

Description: This site is a virtual golf-fest. There is information on tournaments and results, courses and resorts, instruction and schools, equipment and merchandise, amateur golf and more. There are links to GolfDigest, Golf World, NBC Golf Tour and links to the best golf sites on the web. There also is info on the PGA, LPGA, Senior PGA and more. Also features this week in golf and recent updates. Is there anything else left? A great golf database for those who play the game or simply enjoy the sport from the gallery. Now, you an enjoy it from your chair in front of a computer screen.

Golf's.Greatest.Links

URL: http://users.aol.com/olanwade/www /glflinks.html

Description: This site is a marvel to the love of golf by an elder statesman of the game. He took a lot of time to compile this information, going so far as to play many courses in Arizona. He then jotted his opinions of these courses on this site so that you, the reader, can get advanced information if you are planning a golftrip to Arizona. It is amazing how much one man can love a sport, and this emotion shines through to the page. It is quite apparent that this is not just a sport to him, but rather a religion.

GolfWeb

URL: http://www.golfweb.com/cgi-bin/disp3.cgi?.

Description: Everything for the golfer. The best and most original feature is a nationwide, county-by-county listing of some 14,000 golf courses. The searchable list includes phone numbers, course characteristics such as length and par, and a super feature which allows lonely golfers to post e-mail messages in search of playing partners at individual courses. GolfWeb also includes extensive coverage of all the pro golf tours, a photo gallery, guides to miniature golf courses, weekly reader polls on a wide variety of golf topics, the rules of golf, an online pro shop and much, much more.

Great Lakes Golf Online

URL: http://iserve.bigweb.com/golf/

Description: All kinds of info on the area knowledgeable golfers are now calling Myrtle Beach of the North. Great Lakes Golf Online focuses on grass roots reporting of Michigan and Ohio golf trends, attractions and tournaments. A most refreshing angle is Great Lakes Golf Online's dedication to junior golf. An entire section of the web site is devoted not to the big name pros and their endorsements, but to youth tournament results and profiles of top-notch juniors. Plenty of first-hand, knowledgeable opinion here too, including course reviews, equipment reviews, book reviews, and travel tips to courses throughout North America. Resort package prices can be found here as well, along with an instruction tip or two.

Greenside

URL: http://www.golfball.com/green /greenmag.html

Description:An online magazine which covers golf and all of its aspects—equipment, courses, events, tournaments, players, and more. Stories from users and tips from professionals are also just some of the material found here. Great design overall, with links to resources such as golf equipment providers (complete with online purchase forms), lessons to help your game/swing, and the current schedules for the PGA, LPGA, or Senior PGA Tours.

Ladies Professional Golf Association

URL: http://www.golf.com/tour/lpga/

Description: Watch it, buster. These women could clean the wallets of every hacker everywhere, if they weren't so busy making such a bundle on their own pro golf tour. This is an intimate look at women's professional golf. Every current player is profiled in detail, including amateur and pro highlights and standings in every tournament of the year. The full LPGA schedule is listed here, along with an almanac of tournament results dating back to 1950.

National Golf Foundation

URL: http://www.gate.net/~ngf/ngf.html

Description: Created in 1995, the national Golf Foundation's web site functions primarily as a catalog of publications and services available from the Foundation. The various books and reports cover a vast array of topics of interest to the golf industry, from golf course operations to consumer habits. Ordering information is included but it is not possible to order directly from the web site.

Not Just Another Golf Page . . . The Golf Links

URL: http://www.sover.net/~sbound/golf1.html

Description: Do you find it hard to believe there is someone out there that loves golf to such an extent as to make a web page based around it? If you like golf you should really enjoy this page. The author provides links for all sorts of golf programs, from handicapping software to online golf gaming. Although the author hasn't seemed to updated this page in a while (at the time of review, the last update was in January of 1996), there is still plenty here to interest readers. This site is quite entertaining and worth a look.

101 Ways to Improve Your Golf

URL: http://www.compapp.dcu.ie/~c2aosul2 /golf.html

Description: If you're looking for a quick fix for your golf game, the tips contained within this site may help. There are 101 ways to improve your golf game, and they are arranged by categories such as Equipment, Preparation, Off the Tee, In the Rough, and Putting (to name just a few). There are even tips for the mental game, bad weather and the rules. Each tip is only a few sentences long and many are accentuated by photographs. The only drawback is the spelling. Hopefully Aidan O'Sullivan does not play golf like he spells.

Par Excellance

URL: http://golf.com/pub/parex/

Description: PAR Excellance is a quarterly publication about golf with news about golf and courses throughout the Midwest, golfer profiles, reviews of courses, and industry reports. The site also includes a group of other links links.

St. Andrews, The Home of Golf

URL: http://www.standrews.co.uk/

Description: The grand old game of golf began in Scotland, and this site takes every hacker back to the homeland. The Old Course at St. Andrews is the star of this show, but greens fees for it and others are all listed, along with instructions on how to make reservations. But before booking a flight and tee times, any respectable golfer would study the history, which is presented here in detail. The writing comes in a lucid British tone, like that of those British Open announcers: "The Old Course, in contrast, was modeled by the winds of God that formed the dunes into random and eccentrically complex shapes, indifferent then, as now, to the vanities of men."

South Carolina Golf Guide

URL: http://www.enews.com/magazines/golf/

Description: Travel-type of magazine designed to encourage and assist you in making plans for your next golf trip to the Palmetto state. The guide is divided into 10 sections that correspond to geographic regions in the state. Each section has two maps showing the location of the specific region and the golf courses within its boundaries. Each section also has a chart listing the public golf clubs and detailed information concerning each course. The name of the course and its architect, distance in yards, rating and slope (from the men's tee), phone number, pro's name, type of grass on the greens, whether or not golf packages are accepted, range in fees, whether or not walking is allowed, and the map number is charted for every public course inthe state. Several golf clubs have more than one course. These courses are grouped together on the charts by either a color band or a band of white.

Teeing up on the Web

URL: http://www.smoky.org/~mtyler/golf/

Description: When you first open this web site, you will find a picturesque photo a golf hole that is so inviting that you might want to go out and hit a few. The only problem is that this beautiful photo floats in the middle of a blinding white background. The high point of this site is that it provides weekly updates on all tournaments. Also provided is information on the mini-tours and links to other pages of interest. Enjoy this golfing splendor.

APPENDIX A

GOLF THROUGH THE AGES

PRE-1353   Variations on the game of field hockey are played in several western European countries, including Holland, France, Belgium, England, and Scotland; and it is from one of these variations that golf almost certainly derives. As trade increased between the western European nations, the game would have spread fairly quickly.

1353   The first recorded reference to chole, a field-hockey variation played in Flanders (Belgium) and a likely forerunner of modern golf.

1421   Chole is introduced to a Scottish regiment aiding the French against the English at the Siege of Bauge. Hugh Kennedy, Robert Stewart and John Smale, three of the players, are credited with introducing the game in Scotland.

1457   Along with football, golf is banned in Scotland by the Parliament of James II because it is interfering with military training for the wars against England.

1502   With the signing of the Treaty of Glasgow between England and Scotland, the ban on golf is lifted.

Scotland's James IV makes the first recorded purchase of golf equipment, a set of clubs from a bow-maker in Perth.

1552   The first recorded evidence of golf being played at St. Andrews.

1553   The Archbishop of St. Andrews issues a decree allowing the local populace to play golf on the links at St. Andrews.

1567   Mary, Queen of Scots is reported playing golf shortly after the death of her husband, Lord Darnley, and is the first known female golfer. She is also responsible for the word caddy; her French assistants (cadets in French, pages in English) carried her clubs for her.

1592   A decree by the Archbishop of St. Andrews in 1592 closes the courses at St. Andrews on the Sabbath. The final round of the British Open is an exception.

1618   The feathery ball is invented.

1637   Francis Brown is brought to trial in Banff, Scotland, for stealing two golf balls. He is found guilty and hanged.

1641   Charles II is playing golf at Leith, Scotland when he learns of the Irish rebellion, marking the beginning of the English Civil War. He finishes his round.

1659   The banning of golf from the streets of Albany, New York, is the first known reference to golf in America.

1682   In the first recorded international golf match, the Duke of York and John Paterstone of Scotland defeat two English noblemen on the links of Leith.

1687   A book by Thomas Kincaid, *Thoughts on Golve,* contains the first reference to how golf clubs are made.

1724   A match between Alexander Elphinstone and Captain John Porteous becomes the first golf match reported in a newspaper. Elphinstone fights and wins a duel on the same ground in 1729.

1743   Thomas Mathison's epic *The Goff* is the first literary effort devoted to golf.

1744   The first club of golfers, the Honourable Company of Edinburgh Golfers, is formed and plays at Leith links.

1754   The first codified *Rules of Golf* is published by the St. Andrews Golfers (later the Royal & Ancient Golf Club).

1759   The earliest reference to stroke-play, at St. Andrews. Previously, all golf was match-play.

1764   The first four holes at St. Andrews are combined into two, reducing the round from twenty-two holes to 18. St. Andrews thus becomes the first 18-hole golf course and sets the standard for future courses.

1766   England's Blackheath Club becomes the first golf club outside of Scotland.

1767 A score of 94 at St. Andrews, turned in by James Durham in the Silver Cup competition, sets a record unbroken for 86 years.

1768 The first clubhouse is constructed, the Golf House at Leith.

1774 The Edinburgh Burgess society hires the first golf course professional—a part-timer, who also serves as greenkeeper.

1786 The South Carolina Golf Club is formed in Charleston, becoming the first golf club in America.

1806 The St. Andrews Club changes its policy to begin electing its captains, rather than award captaincy to the winner of the Silver Cup. And thus begins the tradition of the Captain "playing himself into office," by hitting a single shot before the start of the annual competition.

1810 Earliest recorded reference to a women's competition, at Musselburgh.

1820 The Bangalore Club is formed in India, becoming the first club in Asia.

1826 Hickory imported from America is used to make golf shafts.

1833 King William IV confers the distinction of "Royal" on the Perth Golfing Society; as Royal Perth it is the first Club to hold the distinction.

The St. Andrews Golfers ban the stymie but rescind the ban one year later.

1834 William IV confers the title "Royal and Ancient" on the Golf Club at St. Andrews.

1836 At Elysian Fields, Samuel Messieux hits the longest drive ever recorded with a feathery ball—361 yards.

1848 The gutta-percha ball (or "guttie") is introduced, considerably increasing the popularity of the game. It flies farther than the feathery and is much less expensive.

1856 The Royal Curragh Golf Club, the first golf club in Ireland, is founded at Kildare.

The Pau Golf Club is founded in France, becoming the first on the European continent.

A rule is instituted mandating that, in match play, the ball must be played as it lies or the hole be conceded.

1857 The first book on golf instruction is published, *The Golfer's Manual*, by A. Keen Hand (H.B. Farnie).

1858 Allan Robertson shoots a 79 on the Old Course, the first golfer to break 80 at St. Andrews.

1859 The first British Amateur Championship is won by George Condie of Perth.

1860 The Prestwick Club hosts a Professionals Championship played at Prestwick. The first Championship Belt is won by Willie Park. The tournament is considered the first British Open.

1861 The Professionals Championship is opened to amateurs—becoming the first true British Open. The championship is won by Old Tom Morris.

1867 The Ladies' Golf Club at St. Andrews is founded, becoming the first golf club for women.

1869 At age 17, Young Tom Morris wins the first of four consecutive British Opens. His streak will include an 11-stroke victory in 1869 and a 12-stroke victory in 1870 (in a 36-hole format). His 149 over 36 holes in the 1870 British Open will not be equaled until the invention of the rubber-cored ball.

1870 The first golf club in Australia is founded, the Royal Adelaide Golf Club.

1871 The British Open is canceled. The tournament trophy, a red Moroccan belt, becomes the possession of Young Tom Morris for becoming a three-time winner, as stipulated in the rules of the Open.

1872 British Open resumes with a new trophy. Young Tom Morris wins his fourth Open Championship in succession.

1873 The Royal Montreal Golf Club is formed, becoming the first club in Canada.

For the first time, the British Open is held at the Old Course.

1875 The Oxford and Cambridge University Golf Clubs are founded.

1878 The first University Match, played at Wimbledon, is won by Oxford.

1880 Molds are used to dimple the gutta-percha ball. Golfers had long noticed that the guttie flew much better after it had been hit several times and scuffed up.

1884 The Oakhurst Golf Club is founded at White Sulphur Springs, West Virginia. The first hole at The Homestead, which survives from this course, is the oldest golf hole in America.

1888 The St. Andrews Golf Club is founded in Yonkers, New York, the oldest surviving golf club in America.

1890 John Ball, an English amateur, becomes the first non-Scotsman and the first amateur to win the British Open.

1892 Tournament admission is charged for the first time, at a match between Douglas Rollard and Jack White at Cambridge.

1893 The (British) Ladies' Golf Union is founded and its first Open Championship is won by Lady Margaret Scott, at St. Anne's.

1894 For the first time, the British Open is played in England and is won for the first time by an English professional, J.H. Taylor.

The Amateur Golf Association of the United States (later the United States Golf Association) is founded. Charter members are the Chicago Golf Club, The Country Club, Newport Golf Club, St. Andrews Golf Club, and Shinnecock Hills Golf Club.

1895 The first U.S. Open is won by Willie Anderson.

Chicago Golf Club opens the first 18-hole golf course in the United States.

The USGA bans the use of a pool cue as a putter.

The first U.S. Women's Amateur Championship is won by Mrs. Charles S. Brown.

1896 Harry Vardon wins his first British Open.

1897 The first NCAA golf championship is held, and Louis Bayard Jr. is the winner.

Golf, America's first golfing magazine, is published for the first time.

1898 The the first rubber-cored ball, the Haskell ball, is designed and patented by Coburn Haskell.

The term "birdie" is coined at Atlantic Country Club from "a bird of a hole."

1899 The Western Open is played at Glenview Golf Club, becoming the first tournament in what would evolve into the PGA Tour.

1900 Harry Vardon wins the U.S. Open and becomes the first golfer to win both the British and U.S. Opens.

Golf is placed on the schedule for the second Olympic Games in Paris.

Margaret Abbott becomes the first American woman to win an Olympic medal. She shot a 47 in the nine-hole final at the Olympic Games in Paris.

1901   Sunningdale, a course built on cleared forest land, opens for play, becoming the first course featuring grass grown completely from seed. Previously, golf courses were routed through existing meadows.

The first course at the Carolina Hotel (later the Pinehurst Resort & Country Club) in Pinehurst, North Carolina, is completed by Donald Ross. Ross will go on to design 600 courses in his legendary career as a golf course architect.

1902   The first grooved-faced irons are introduced.

1904   Walter J. Travis becomes the first American to win the British Amateur Championship.

Charlotte Dodd wins the Ladies' British Open; she had recently turned to playing golf, after having played tennis, where she won her first Wimbledon tennis championship in 1887 at the age of 15 and won five more Wimbledon singles titles between 1887 and 1893.

1905   The first dimple pattern for golf balls is patented, by William Taylor in England.

The Complete Golfer, by Harry Vardon, is published. It promotes and demonstrates the Vardon grip (also called the overlapping grip).

1906   Goodrich introduces the "Pneumatic," a ball filled with compressed air. When Willie Dunn hits the ball in a round at St. Andrews, it explodes in flight and injures a spectator.

1908   Mrs. Gordon Robertson, at Princes Ladies Golf Club, becomes the first female professional.

1909   The USGA rules that caddies, caddymasters, and greenkeepers over the age of sixteen are professional golfers. The rule is later modified and eventually rescinded in 1963.

1910   The R&A bans the center-shafted putter in Great Britain, while the USGA keeps it legal, marking the start of a 42-year period with two official versions of the Rules of Golf.

Steel shafts are patented by Arthur F. Knight.

1911   J.J. McDermott becomes the first native-born American to win the U.S. Open. And, at 17 years of age, he is the youngest winner to date.

1912   John Ball wins his eighth British Amateur Championship, a record not yet equaled.

1913   Francis Ouimet, age 20, becomes the first amateur to win the U.S. Open, defeating favorites Harry Vardon and Ted Ray in a play-off.

1914 The Tokyo Club at Komozawa is founded, starting a huge Japanese golf boom.

Harry Vardon wins his sixth British Open—a record that still stands. (Peter Thomson and Tom Watson have won five Opens each.)

1915 The British Open is discontinued for the duration of the First World War.

1916 The PGA of America is founded by 82 charter members and the PGA Championship is inaugurated. James Barnes is the first champion.

The first miniature golf course opens in Pinehurst, North Carolina.

Golf club head covers are designed by a Japanese student, Selchi Takahata, in Great Britain and sold at St. Andrews.

1917 The PGA Championship and the U.S. Open are discontinued as the United States enters World War I.

1919 The R&A assumes control over the British Open and the British Amateur.

Pebble Beach Golf Links opens as the Del Monte Golf Links in Pebble Beach, California.

1920 The first practice range is opened in Pinehurst, North Carolina.

The Professional Golfer of America (now known as *PGA Magazine*), is first published. It is now the oldest continuously published golf magazine in the United States.

1921 The R&A establishes standards for the size and weight of the ball.

1922 Walter Hagen becomes the first native-born American to win the British Open. He will later become the first professional golfer to open a golf equipment company under his own name.

The first Walker Cup Matches are held. The grandson of Walker Cup founder George Herbert Walker is former U.S. President George H.W. Bush.

Wooden tees are invented. Previously, golfers had used sand or dirt to build a mound to elevate the ball for a tee shot.

1924 The USGA legalizes steel shafted golf clubs. The R&A does not follow suit until 1929.

1925 The first fairway irrigation system is developed in Dallas, Texas.

Deeply grooved irons are banned by both the USGA and the R&A.

1926 In the final round of the British Open, the great amateur Bobby Jones has to pay admission to the course because he has forgotten his player's badge. He goes on to win the tournament.

For the first time, course admission fees are charged at the British Open.

1927 The inaugural Ryder Cup Matches are played between Britain and the United States.

Creeping bentgrass is developed for putting greens by the U.S. Department of Agriculture.

1930 Bobby Jones becomes the only golfer ever to complete the original Grand Slam, winning the U.S. and British Amateurs and the U.S. and British Opens in the same year. Since Jones is an amateur, however, the financial windfall belongs to professional Bobby Cruickshank, who bets on Jones to complete the Slam, and pockets somewhere between $10,000 and $100,000.

1931 Billy Burke defeats George Von Elm in a 72- hole playoff at Inverness to win the 1931 U.S. Open, in the longest playoff ever played. Burke is also the first golfer to win a major championship using steel-shafted golf clubs.

The USGA increases the minimum size of the golf ball from 1.62 inches to 1.68 inches, and decreases the maximum weight from 1.62 ounces to 1.55. The R&A does not follow suit. The lighter, larger "balloon ball" is universally despised and eventually the USGA raises the weight back to 1.62 ounces.

1932 The first Curtis Cup Matches are held at Wentworth, England.

The concave-faced wedge is banned.

The sand wedge is introduced by Gene Sarazen.

1933 Augusta National Golf Club, designed by Alister Mackenzie with advice from Bobby Jones, opens for play.

Craig Wood hits a 430-yard drive on the fifth hole at the Old Course in the British Open—the longest drive in a major championship.

Hershey Chocolate Company sponsors the Hershey Open and becomes the first corporate title sponsor of a professional golf tournament.

1933 The last amateur to win the U.S. Open was Johnny Goodman in 1933.

1934 The first Masters is played, and Horton Smith is the first champion. In this inaugural event, the present-day back and front nines were reversed.

1935 Glynna Collett Vare wins the U.S. Women's Amateur Championship a record sixth time.

1936 With his victory in the U.S. Amateur Championship, Johnny Fisher becomes the last golfer to win a major championship with hickory-shafted clubs.

1937 The Bing Crosby Pro-Am is inaugurated by the entertainer in San Diego, California. A few years later it moves to the Monterey Peninsula.

1938 At the Old Course, the British amateurs score their first victory over the United States in the Walker Cup Matches.

The USGA establishes 14 clubs as the maximum a player may legally carry.

1940 The British Open and British Amateur Championships are discontinued for the duration of World War II.

1942 The U.S. Open is discontinued for the duration of the war. A world-wide shortage of rubber, a vital military supply, results in a huge price increase in golf balls. Sam Snead manages to complete an entire four-day tournament with one ball, but the professional circuit is severely curtailed.

The U.S. government halts the manufacture of golf equipment for the duration of the war.

1943 The PGA Championship is canceled for the year, and the Masters is discontinued until war ends.

1945 Byron Nelson wins 18 tournaments in a calendar year to set an all-time PGA Tour record—including a record 11 in a row and a record 19 consecutive rounds under 70. His total prize earnings during his 11-win streak, $30,000, is less than last place money for today's PGA Championship.

1946 Patty Berg wins the first U.S. Women's Open instituted.

1947 Mildred "Babe" Didrikson Zaharias becomes the first American to win the British Women's Open, at Gullane.

The first televised broadcast of a golf tournament is the U.S. Open at the St. Louis Country Club in Clayton, Missouri.

1948 The U.S. Junior Amateur Championship is instituted. Ken Venturi loses to Dean Lind in the first final.

The *USGA Golf Journal* is founded.

1949 Marie Roke of Wollaston, Massachusetts, aces a 393-yard hole—the longest ace ever recorded by a woman.

Electric golf carts are used for the first time—the Thunderbird Golf Club is the site.

1950   The LPGA is founded, replacing the ailing Women's Professional Golf Association.

Just a few weeks after returning to the PGA Tour following a near-fatal auto accident, Ben Hogan wins the U.S. Open at Oakland Hills in Michigan.

1951   Francis Ouimet becomes the first American Captain of the R&A.

The USGA and the R&A hold a meeting to revise the Rules of Golf. Although the two organizations continue to differ over the size of the golf ball, all other conflicts are resolved in this momentous conference. The center-shafted putter is legalized world-wide; the out-of-bounds penalty is standardized at stroke-and-distance; and the stymie is finally and forever abolished.

Golf Digest is founded, with Bill Davis as editor.

1953   Ben Hogan wins the first three legs of the modern Grand Slam—The Masters, U.S. Open, and British Open—but fails to win the PGA Championship.

The Canada Cup is instituted and for the first time brings together teams from all over the world. (After 1966 the tournament is known as the World Cup.)

Japan issues the first golf-related postage stamp.

1954   With a victory in the British Open, Peter Thomson becomes the first Australian to win a major tournament.

Renowned course architect Robert Trent Jones receives complaints that he has made the par-3 fourth hole at Baltusrol too hard for the upcoming U.S. Open. He plays the hole to see for himself and records a hole-in-one.

The U.S. Open is nationally televised for the first time.

Babe Didrikson Zaharias returns to the LPGA Tour following cancer surgery and wins the U.S. Women's Open.

1955   Mike Souchak shoots 257 for 72 holes—a PGA Tour record 27 under par (with rounds of 60, 68, 64, and 65) at Brackenridge Park Golf Club in the Texas Open.

1956   The current yardage guides for par are adopted by the USGA.

1957   Great Britain wins the Ryder Cup matches at Lindrick, the first British victory since 1935.

At the 1957 Bing Crosby Pro-Am at Pebble Beach, Tony Lema jumps for joy after hitting a particularly good shot on the ninth hole. Unfortunately, he is standing near the edge of a cliff at the time and ends up going over the side. Luckily, he escapes serious injury.

1959   Bill Wright wins the U.S. Amateur Public Links Championship, becoming the first African-American to win a national championship.

Golf Magazine is founded, with Charles Price as the first editor.

1960   Arnold Palmer comes back from six shots down in the final round to win the U.S. Open. With his victory at the Masters, he completes the first two legs of the modern Grand Slam, the first to do so since Ben Hogan in 1953. His bid ends when he finishes second to Kel Nagle in the British Open.

The Rules of Golf are modified to allow lifting, cleaning, and repairing ballmarks on the putting green for the first time.

1961   Gary Player becomes the first foreign player to win the Masters.

Charlie Sifford plays the 1961 Greater Greensboro Open, the first time an African-American golfer competes in a PGA-sponsored event in the South. He placed fourth.

Arnold Palmer takes a 12 on the last hole of the 1961 Los Angeles Open at Rancho Park Golf Course. A bronze plaque commemorates the event.

1962   Jack Nicklaus wins his first professional tournament, the U.S. Open, becoming the last player to win the U.S. Open as his first pro victory.

Water hazards are marked with painted lines at the U.S. Open for the first time.

1963   Arnold Palmer becomes the first professional golfer to earn over $100,000 in prize money in one calendar year.

Irons are made with the casting method for the first time.

Bob Charles becomes the only left-handed golfer ever to win the British Open.

1964   Mickey Wright shoots a 62 at Hogan Park Golf Club in the Tall City Open, setting the LPGA 18-hole record.

Floyd Rood completes his swing of golf across the United States, from the Pacific coast to the Atlantic. He did it in 114,737 strokes, and it took 13 months. Along the way, Rood lost 3,511 balls.

1965   Sam Snead wins the Greater Greensboro Open, his record-setting 81st Tour victory. It is also Snead's eighth win in the Greensboro event, another record. Finally, the fact that he won at the age of 52 sets one more PGA Tour record.

Jack Nicklaus wins the Masters with a record-setting score of 271.

PGA Tour Qualifying School is inaugurated at PGA National, with 17 golfers of the 49 applicants winning their playing cards.

1967   Charlie Sifford, wins the Greater Hartford Open and becomes the first African-American to take a PGA Tour event.

Catherine Lacoste becomes the first amateur to win the U.S. Women's Open.

1968   Arnold Palmer passes the $1 million mark in career PGA earnings.

The PGA of America and the PGA Tour officially split, with the touring professionals forming a breakaway group known as the Association of Professional Golfers. The rift is eventually healed, and a Tournament Players Division of the PGA is founded. Joe Dey is elected the next year as the first PGA Tour commissioner.

1969   In Ryder Cup competition, Jack Nicklaus concedes Tony Jacklin's final putt and England ties the United States after five consecutive defeats. The gesture is cited as "the greatest act of sportsmanship in history."

Ken Nagle takes a 35-stroke penalty in the second round of the 1969 Alcan Golfer of the Year Tournament in Portland, Oregon. He was in second place in the tournament when he inadvertently entered his nine-hole total in the space for the ninth-hole score. After he signed the scorecard, he was forced to add 35 strokes to his score.

1970   Bill Burke, with a 57 at Normandie Country Club, sets the all-time official record for low 18-hole score.

1971   Astronaut Alan Shepard hits two shots with a six-iron on the moon and refuses to divulge what brand of ball he used.

1972   Spalding introduces the first two-piece ball, the Top-Flite.

Jack Nicklaus completes the first two legs of the modern Grand Slam, winning the Masters and the U.S. Open, but like Arnold Palmer in 1960, he comes in second in the British Open.

1973   Ben Crenshaw wins the NCAA title for a record third consecutive time. Later in the year, after earning his PGA Tour card, he wins the San Antonio Open, the first event he plays as a PGA Tour member.

The graphite shaft is invented.

Jack Nicklaus wins the PGA Championship, and with this 14th victory in a major, he breaks the record set by his idol, Bobby Jones.

1974   The Golf Hall of Fame is opened in Pinehurst, North Carolina.

At the National Seniors Open in Las Vegas, Mike Austin hits a 515-yard drive, the longest ever recorded in competition.

The Tournament Players Championship (TPC) is inaugurated.

1975   Lee Elder becomes the first African American golfer to play in the Masters.

Lee Trevino, Jerry Heard and Bobby Nichols are struck by lightning during the 1975 Western Open, an incident that prompts new safety standards in weather preparedness at PGA events.

The total tournament purse in the United States is $7,895,450. By 1984 it climbs to $21,251,382.

The record for throwing a golf ball around a regulation course is established by Joe "the Flinger" Flynn, who scores an 82 at the Port Royal Golf Course in Bermuda.

1976   Judy Rankin becomes the first LPGA professional to earn more than $100,000 in one season.

A new USGA rule bans golf balls that fly more than 280 yards during a standard test.

1977   Al Geiberger shoots 59 at Colonial Country Club in the second round of the Memphis Classic, setting a new PGA Tour record for 18 holes.

Bing Crosby dies after completing a round of golf in Spain. The Bing Crosby National Pro-Am will continue for several years, but eventually relations sour between the PGA Tour and the Crosby family, and AT&T takes over sponsorship of the event.

The "sudden-death" playoff format is used for the first time in a major championship, and Lanny Wadkins defeats Gene Littler in a playoff for the PGA Championship at Pebble Beach Golf Links.

In what has been described as the most exciting tournament in history, Tom Watson defeats Jack Nicklaus by one stroke in the British Open at Turnberry. They were tied after both the second and third rounds and were paired with each other during the final 36 holes.

1978   The Legends of Golf is inaugurated at Onion Creek Country Club in Austin, Texas. Its popularity will lead to the formation of the Senior Tour two years later.

1979   The Ryder Cup is reformatted to add European continent players to the British-Scottish-Irish side, making the event far more competitive.

Taylor Made introduces the first metal woods.

1980   Tom Watson is the first golfer to earn $500,000 in prize money in a single season.

The PGA Senior Tour is inaugurated with four official events.

Robert De Vincenzo is the winner of the first U.S. Senior Open.

Jack Nicklaus sets a record of 272 in the U.S. Open, at Baltusrol. His mark is equaled in 1993 by Lee Janzen, also at Baltusrol.

The USGA introduces the Symmetry Standard, banning balls like the Polaris which correct themselves in flight.

1981   Kathy Whitworth becomes the first woman golfer to earn $1 million in career prize money.

1982   Playing at the Guam Navy Golf Club, Chief Petty Officer Kevin W. Murray records the longest double eagle ever: a two on the 647-yard second hole.

1983   Hale Irwin loses the 1983 British Open by missing a 3-inch putt.

1984   Desert Highlands opens in Phoenix. Designed by Jack Nicklaus the course utilizes only 80 irrigated acres for 18 holes, instead of the typical 100-150. The success of Nicklaus' concept of "target golf" ushers in the era of environmentally-sensitive course design.

1985   Nancy Lopez shoots a 268 in the Henredon Classic, setting the LPGA 72-hole record.

For the first time since 1957, the United States loses the Ryder Cup matches—to the expanded European team.

The USGA introduces the Slope System to allow golfers to adjust their handicaps and compensate for the relative difficulty of a golf course.

1986   The Panasonic Las Vegas Invitational offers golf's first $1 million purse.

1987   Judy Bell becomes the first woman elected to the USGA Executive Committee.

The Nabisco Championships (later the Tour Championship) debuts as a season-ending event for the top 30 money winners. The first winner is Tom Watson, breaking his three-year drought.

1988   Square-grooved clubs such as the PING Eye2 irons are banned by the USGA, which claims that tests show the clubs give an unfair competitive advantage to PING customers. The next year, the PGA Tour also bans the clubs. Karsten Manufacturing, maker of the clubs, fights a costly two-year battle with both the USGA and the PGA

Tour. Eventually both organizations drop the ban, while Karsten acknowledges the right of the organizations to regulate equipment and pledges to make modifications to future designs.

When Curtis Strange wins the Nabisco Championships at Pebble Beach, the $360,000 prize takes his 1988 Tour earnings to $1,147,644, and thus he becomes the first player to win over $1,000,000 in a single season.

The U.S. Women's Open is playing so slow that at the 14th hole Lori Garbacz orders pizza to be delivered to the 17th tee. She ate the pizza and still hit in turn.

1989 On June 16, at the U.S. Open at Oak Hill Country Club in Rochester, New York, the impossible happens: four PGA players score holes-in-one in the same round on the same hole. In a span of less than two hours, Doug Weaver, Mark Wiebe, Jerry Pate, and Nick Price all ace the 159-yard sixth hole. The odds of this happening were later calculated at roughly 1.89 quadrillion to 1.

On the way to victory in the Masters, Nick Faldo sinks a 100-foot birdie putt on the second hole, the longest putt ever holed in a major tournament.

1990 Hall Thompson of Shoal Creek Golf Club, on the eve of the PGA Championship at Shoal Creek, defends his club's policy of not admitting African American members. Amidst public outcry, Shoal Creek is forced to change its policy, and both the PGA Tour and the USGA insist that in the future all clubs must submit to a standard set of guidelines on membership policies.

The R&A, after 38 years, adopts the 1.68 inch diameter ball, and for the first time since 1910 the Rules of Golf are standardized throughout the world.

1991 Ninth-alternate John Daly wins the PGA Championship at Crooked Stick after a slot in the tournament opens up on the night before the Championship begins. Phil Mickelson, an amateur, wins the PGA Tour's Northern Telecom Open.

Oversized metal woods are introduced, and Callaway Golf's Big Bertha quickly establishes itself as the dominant brand, becoming one of the biggest-selling clubs of all time.

Harvey Penick's *Little Red Book* becomes the all-time best selling golf book.

1993 An ownership group led by Joe Gibbs and Arnold Palmer announce plans for the Golf Channel, a 24-hour, 365-day cable service.

Monica Hannah wins the Greater Cincinnati Women's Amateur Championship while nine months pregnant.

1994 The PGA Tour announces that none of its member pros will be allowed to play in a World Tour proposed by an American-based group of entrepreneurs.

1995   The Golf Channel debuts on cable services nationwide.

1996   Eldrick "Tiger" Woods becomes the first golfer ever to win three consecutive U.S. Amateur Championships. He then joins the PGA Tour and wins 2 of his first 8 events, and earns over $780,000 to finish 24th on the money list.

APPENDIX B

MEN'S MAJOR CHAMPIONSHIP SUMMARIES

THE MASTERS

1934:   The Masters is organized by Bobby Jones as an invitation-only tournament. It is the only one of the Men's Majors played on the same course each year, the famed Augusta National—an Alister Mackenzie-designed course built on a plantation cultivated by a Belgian-born horticulturist. Jones, who retired in 1930, plays in the Masters to help generate publicity and attendance. Horton Smith wins the initial Masters by a stroke and becomes the first to don the Green Jacket awarded annually to the Masters champion.

1935:   Gene Sarazen ignites the golf world and helps make the Masters famous with his legendary albatross on the par 5 15th hole during the final round of the 1935 tournament. The albatross helps Sarazen make up a three-stroke deficit to Craig Wood, and he beats Wood by five strokes in a playoff.

1936-1939:   Great comebacks continue, as Horton Smith makes up a six-stroke deficit over the final two rounds and wins the 1936 Masters in a steady rain by a stroke over Harry Cooper. In 1937, Byron Nelson sets a record with a 66 opening round, then rapidly makes up a four-stroke final round deficit to Ralph Guldahl on the 12th and 13th holes (Nelson shoots 2 and 3 to Guldahl's 5 and 6) and wins by two strokes. After Henry Picard's steady play for victory in 1938, Ralph Guldahl, who eased past Sam Snead in the 1937 U.S. Open, shoots a back-nine 33 to beat Snead by one stroke in the 1939 Masters.

1940-1942:   Jimmy Demaret tees off his very successful decade with a 4-stroke victory in 1940, a Masters highlighted by Lloyd Mangrum's first round 64—the lowest score in a Major for several years and a total unmatched at Augusta until 1965 by Jack Nicklaus.

Craig Wood, runner-up in the first two Masters, breaks away from a tie with Byron Nelson on the final nine and wins by 3 strokes in 1941, the year when Wood also wins the U.S. Open. Nelson wins a thrilling playoff by one stroke over Ben Hogan in 1942. Nelson, who had been ahead of Hogan by 8 strokes after two rounds, falls behind in the playoff by 3 strokes after five holes. Hogan plays the 6th through 16th holes in one under par but falls behind by two strokes, as Nelson birdies his way through Amen corner while playing the 6th through the 13th in a whopping 6 under par.

1943-1945: Masters closed during World War II.

1946-1948: Hogan finishes second again in 1946, 3-putting the 18th to lose by a stroke to Herman Keiser, who began the final round five stokes ahead of Hogan and also 3-putted the closing hole. In 1947, Demaret joins Smith and Nelson as two-time Masters winners, and Claude Harmon ties the Masters' 4-round record with a 279 and a five-stroke victory in 1948.

1949-1950: Sam Snead wins his first of three Masters in 1949, catching Lloyd Mangrum in the third round, which Mangrum entered five strokes ahead. Snead shoots 134 over the final two rounds and collects 8 birdies during the closer after shooting 148 over the first two rounds in gusty spring winds. Jimmy Demaret becomes the first three-time Masters winner in 1950, exploding to a two-stroke victory highlighted by an astounding 7-stroke swing as he heats up and Jim Ferrier cools off during the final six holes.

1951-1955: The Masters is dominated by Ben Hogan and Sam Snead for four years. Hogan, who lost both the 1942 and 1946 Masters by a single stroke, wins in 1951 by two strokes over Skee Riegel, the only golfer to finish less than six strokes behind Hogan. Snead wins by four strokes in 1952, while Hogan plays his best golf ever in the 1953 Masters, winning by a record five strokes with a record low 274. Billy Joe Patton, a little-known amateur, leads the 1954 Masters after 36 holes, falls behind by five strokes after 54, recaptures the lead on the 12th hole of the final round, then falls away with a 7 on the 13th (he tried to clear the creek instead of laying up and ended up in the water) and a 6 on the 15th. Snead wins his third Masters in a playoff over Hogan, who finishes as runner-up by a stroke for the third time. Hogan finishes second again in 1955 and Snead third as Cary Middlecoff takes the green jacket with a record 7-stroke victory.

1956-1957: Amateur sensation Ken Venturi enters the 1956 final round with a 4-stroke lead over defending champ Middlecoff and 8 strokes over Jack Burke, Jr., but shoots a final-round 80 to Burke's 71 and loses by a stroke. Snead enters the final round of the 1957 Masters ahead by 3 strokes over Doug Ford, but Ford plays an amazing closing-round 66, a new record low, adds an exclamation point by holing out from a bunker on 18, and beats Snead by 3 strokes.

1958-1960: "Arnie's Army" is coined by sportswriter Johnny Hendrix to describe the swarm of fans cheering Arnold Palmer on to victory in the 1958 Masters. Palmer drives the green on 13 and finishes it off with an eight-foot eagle putt to highlight his one-stroke victory over defending champ Ford. Art Wall destroys Arnie and his army in the 1959 Masters, birdieing 5 of the last six holes and closing with a 66 to overcome a six-stroke final-round deficit to Palmer (who finishes third, two strokes back) and a five-stroke deficit to Cary Middlecoff (who finishes second, one stroke behind Wall). Palmer returns as champ in 1960, birdieing the final two holes to top Ken Venturi, who had a one-stroke lead but parred the last two holes. Of the nine Masters held between 1958 and 1966, eight would be won either by Palmer (4), Gary Player (1), or Jack Nicklaus (3); the threesome combined to finish in the top 3 fourteen times during that span; and overall they would combine for 13 Masters titles.

1961-1963:   South African Gary Player becomes the first foreign winner of the Masters with a thrilling one-stroke victory over Palmer and Charlie Coe, whose 281 is the best-ever showing by an amateur. Palmer and Player land in the same bunker on the final hole; Player saves with a 4, while Palmer can only manage a 6. Palmer comes back in 1961 with a best-ever Masters playoff round (68) to defeat Player by 3 strokes and Dow Finsterwald by 9. Jack Nicklaus wins his first Masters in 1963 by a stroke over Tony Lema.

1964-1966:   Palmer dominates in 1964 to win his fourth Masters and his last Major by six strokes. Nicklaus dominates in 1965 with a record low total 271 and ties the individual low round with a 64. Palmer and Player finish tied for second, 9 strokes back. Nicklaus becomes the first repeat winner in 1966, defeating Tommy Jacobs by 2 strokes and Gay Brewer, who bogeyed away victory on the final hole in regulation, by 8 in a three-man playoff. Brewer finishes the job in 1967 by one stroke over Bobby Nichols.

1968-1970:   In the most unfortunate of Masters, international great Roberto de Vicenzo enjoys an astonishing final-round—eight under par until a bogey at 18 drops him from the record book and also back into a tie for first with Bob Goalby. However, de Vicenzo signs an incorrect scorecard that credits him with a 4 instead of a 3 on the 17th hole, which places him in second, but the incorrect card disqualifies him anyway. George Archer makes the best late shot and prevails in 1969 as 25 different players lead at some point during the tournament and five players are in close contention going into the final four holes. Billy Casper has a terrible front nine in the final round, rallies to within one long putt on 18 for a tie, but he comes up short. Casper does tie for the lead in 1970 and whips Gene Littler in a playoff by five strokes.

1971-1973:   Charles Coody outduels Nicklaus and Johnny Miller for the 1971 championship on the final four holes, overcoming Miller's two-stroke lead. Nicklaus wins his fourth Masters in 1972 as the only one to finish under par. Georgian Tommy Aaron wins in 1973 by one stroke over J.C. Snead in a final round played on Monday—the third round was canceled because of rain.

1974-1975:   Two of the finest Masters are won by two golfing masters, Player and Nicklaus. Player emerges from a pack of seven vying for the lead on the final nine to win his second Masters; Tom Weiskopf finishes second for the third time (he was a runner-up in 1969 and 1972). Nicklaus emerges victorious for the fifth time in 1975 in an excellent showdown with Weiskopf and Johnny Miller. Weiskopf enters the final round ahead of Nicklaus by one and Miller by four, but Miller shoots an inspired 66 and Nicklaus a strong 68 to Weiskopf's impressive 70; Miller and Weiskopf both miss tournament-tieing birdie putts on the final hole. Neither Weiskopf (who finished second four times) nor Miller (who finished second three times) ever won the Masters.

1976-1978:   Raymond Floyd dominates the 1976 Masters, leading all the way, setting a record low with 131 after two rounds, tying Nicklaus' record low total 271, and winning by 8 strokes. Tom Watson begins a series of memorable duels in Majors with Jack Nicklaus, taking a three-stroke lead into the final round and shooting a 67 to withstand Nicklaus' 66 and win the 1977 Masters. Watson also beats Nicklaus late in the final rounds of the 1977 British Open, the 1981 Masters and the 1982 U.S. Open. Gary Player wins his third Masters with an amazing comeback in 1978: he starts the final round 7 strokes behind Hubert Green but birdies seven of the last ten holes, finishing the back 9 with a 30 to complete a record final-round 64 and win by a stroke.

1979-1980:   The first Masters to end with the sudden-death playoff format, the 1979 tournament features numerous nerve-wracking situations. Ed Sneed begins the final round with a safe 5-stroke lead over Watson and a six-stroke lead over Fuzzy Zoeller, but Sneed falters immediately, then rights himself in Amen corner, of all places, before bleeding strokes away on the final three holes and culminating the horror with a six-foot, tournament-winning putt that stops on the lip of the cup and refuses to fall. The sudden-death playoff begins on 10, where Sneed, Zoeller, and Watson all fail to make birdie putts. Zoeller ends the madness with a birdie on 11, becoming the first man to win a Masters on his first try (well, except for Horton Smith, who won the first Masters). There is seemingly no drama in 1980, just a dominant performance by Seve Ballesteros taking a huge 10-stroke lead into the final nine. Ballesteros then 3-putts on 10, double-bogeys the par 3 12th, and takes a 6 on the 13th hole before finishing the final five in one-under par for a four-stroke victory to become at 23 the youngest Masters champion. Tom Weiskopf also had trouble on that par 3 12th, taking a 13 in the first round by repeatedly failing to carry the water hazard and replaying shots from the fairway instead of dropping by the water.

1981-1982:   1981 features another Watson vs. Nicklaus duel: Nicklaus leads by four after two rounds, trails by four after 14 holes in the third round, and catches Watson at 17, only to three-putt 18 and finish the round a stroke behind. Watson plays a solid final round to edge Nicklaus and a late-charging Johnny Miller by two strokes. 1982 is an unseasonably cold Masters weathered by "The Walrus," Craig Stadler, who leads by six strokes after 11 holes in the final round before freezing and getting caught cold by Don Pohl (who had a third round sequence of two eagles followed by two birdies from the 13th hole to the 16th). Stadler wins the second sudden-death Masters playoff when Pohl bogeys the first playoff hole.

1983-1985:   Seve Ballesteros wins his second Masters in 1983, taking command at the start of the final round with two birdies (1 and 4) and an eagle (2) for a three-stroke lead, finishing the front nine in 31, one off of Johnny Miller's record pace, and cruising to a four-stroke victory over Ben Crenshaw and Tom Kite. Crenshaw wins a tight 1984 Masters, and Bernhard Langer prevails in 1985 with 68s in the final two rounds while strange things happen to Curtis Strange—leading by four with nine to play, he finishes in a tie for second, two strokes behind Langer.

1986-1987:   Jack Nicklaus just keeps getting better in 1986 and prevails in the Masters for the sixth time, improving from 1 over par after 36 holes to two-under after 54 and shooting a red-hot 65 final round, winning by a stroke over Greg Norman, whom he trailed by 4 going into the last round. Norman suffers greater agony in 1987 (with more to come) when he takes a one-stroke lead into the final round and finishes tied with two-time Masters champ Seve Ballesteros and little-known Larry Mize. Ballesteros 3-putts the first playoff hole and is eliminated, and Mize chips in from 140 feet on the second hole for a stunning triumph.

1988-1992:   Sandy Lyle becomes the first Englishman to win the Masters, as he builds a three-stroke lead in the final round, then loses it: he makes an excellent approach from a fairway bunker on 18, then sinks a winning eight-footer. The steely of nerves of Nick Faldo emerge in 1989 and 1990, as he wins in playoffs over Scott Hoch and Raymond Floyd, respectively. Ian Woosnam becomes the fourth straight British winner of the Masters in 1991, and Fred Couples shoots the best total (275) in twelve years to win in 1992.

1993-1996:   Bernhard Langer wins his second Masters in 1993, followed by a triumph by the unheralded Jose-Maria Olazabel in 1994. Ben Crenshaw wins an emotional 1995 Masters, played the day after the funeral of the beloved golf teacher and writer Harvey Penick, who was Crenshaw's mentor. Crenshaw's walk to the 18th green, which often affords the gallery a chance to salute the champion, was among the most moving Masters moments. Nick Faldo wins his third Master title in 1996, but the major story is the final round collapse of Greg Norman, who lost a six-stroke lead to Faldo by the 11th hole, and then finds water on the 12th and 15th holes in an agonizing fall from what seemed sure victory.

THE U.S. OPEN

1895:   The first U.S. Open and the first U.S. Amateur are held at the Newport Golf Club, Rhode Island, during the same week on the same course, each with four 9-hole rounds. Horace Rawlins, an English-born professional playing out of Newport, wins the first Open by two strokes.

1896-1899:   Jim Foulis takes the second Open and Joe Lloyd wins the third in dramatic fashion, shooting a 3 on the 465-yard final hole to win by one stroke. The Amateur and the Open are played separately beginning in 1898. The Open is expanded to 72 holes in four rounds played over three days, with the final 36 holes played on the third day— a format that lasts through 1964. Willie Smith wins the 1899 Open by 11 strokes, still the largest margin of victory.

1900-1901: Two members of Britain's Great Triumvirate, Harry Vardon and J.H. Taylor, battle it out in 1900, with Vardon winning by two strokes despite whiffing a putt on the last hole. Willie Anderson wins his first of four Opens in a 1901 with a one-stroke playoff victory over Alex Smith.

1902-1905: Laurie Auchterlonie, playing with the new Haskell rubber-cored ball, becomes the first man to break 80 in all four rounds in his 1902 victory, and then Willie Anderson wins three years in a row, beginning with his second straight playoff triumph in 1903.

1906-1908: Alex Smith becomes the first man to break 300 with a seven-stroke victory in 1906, and Fred McLeod, the smallest man (108 lbs.) ever to win the Open, defeats Willie Smith in a 1908 playoff by six strokes.

1909-1912: George Sargent sets a new Open low total at 290 with his 1909 win, and Alex Smith wins his second Open in 1910 with a playoff triumph over his brother, Mac-donald Smith, and eighteen-year-old Johnny McDermott. McDermott wins the next two Opens and seems headed for a phenomenal career but is beset by a series of misfortunes: he loses most of his money in the stock market in 1913, arrives late and is disqualified from the 1914 British Open, is involved in a shipwreck during his return to the U.S., suffers fainting spells later that year, and never plays tournament golf again—his career ending at age 23.

1913: The Ouimet Miracle: little known 20-year old amateur Francis Ouimet joins the U.S. Open being held across the street from his home at The Country Club in Brookline, Massachusetts, where he had practiced as a youngster by sneaking on the course in off-hours and played with golf balls he found while using the course as a shortcut on his way to school. Incredibly, he finishes in a tie for first with two great British golfing legends, Harry Vardon and Ted Ray, and then defeats them in a playoff by five and six strokes, respectively. He was caddied by ten-year old Eddie Lowery, who cried at the first playoff tee when Ouimet tried to replace him out of sympathy with a man better able to lug the clubs around the course. Eddie won out, wiped away the tears, and reminded Ouimet to keep his eye on the ball.

1914-1919: Walter Hagen wins his first of two Opens, but not before sweating out a thrilling finish by amateur Chick Evans, whose tournament-tying chip shot comes to rest within inches of the cup on the last hole of the 1914 Open. Amateurs Jerome Travers and Evans win the 1915 and 1916 Opens, respectively, with Evans carding a record 286 total that would stand for twenty years. The Open is cancelled in 1917 and 1918 because of World War I, and then Hagen wins a controversial playoff in 1919. Mike

Brady led Hagen by 5 strokes going into the final round, but shot an 80 and sweated the outcome in the clubhouse. Hagen reached the 18th hole tied with Brady and made a beautiful approach shot that stopped eight feet short of the cup. While he walked to the green Hagen sent word ahead to Brady, inviting him to watch the tournament-winning putt. As Brady watched, the putt lipped the cup, and Hagen settled for a tie. During the playoff Hagen proved very resourceful: at one point he recommended to Brady that he roll down his shirtsleeves because "everyone can see your forearms quavering"; later, when an errant shot lie mired in muck, Hagen claimed the right to identify the ball, picked it up, wiped it and placed it back softly for a more favorable lie.

1920-1922: Ted Ray, at 43 the oldest man to have won the Open until Raymond Floyd in 1986, claims the 1920 championship, as Harry Vardon loses a five stroke lead on a wind-whipped back nine and high-strung Leo Diegel loses his cool. Diegel was the final-round leader at 14 after Vardon and Ray bogeyed holes ahead. An excited friend broke Diegel's concentration as he prepared to drive on 14 by informing him of the good news and an exasperated Diegel fell apart, double-bogeying 14 and bogeying 16 and 17, finishing in a tie for second with Vardon, one stroke behind Ray. Jim Barnes, a two-time PGA champion, breezes to a 9-stroke win in 1921, and 20-year old Gene Sarazen shoots a final-round 68 in 1922 to overcome a 4-stroke deficit to Bobby Jones and edges Jones and John Black by a stroke.

1923-1926: Bobby Jones wins his first two of four Opens in 1923 and 1926. The 23 win comes in a playoff over Bobby Cruickshank, who made a spectacular final round comeback culminating with a birdie on the 72nd hole that Jones double-bogeyed earlier. Jones wins with a legendary shot on the 18th playoff hole. Englishman Cyril Walker wins the 1924 Open, and Willie Macfarlane defeats Jones in a marathon playoff in 1925, when the two tied after 72, were still tied after 18 more, and one stroke separated them after 108 holes. In 1926, Jones becomes the first man to win the British and U.S. Opens in the same year.

1927-1930: Tommy Armour wins a playoff over Harry Cooper in 1927, and Jones loses his second marathon playoff, this time to Johnny Farrell in 1928. In 1929, Jones blows a four-stroke lead over Al Espinosa with four holes to play and has to salvage a tie with a difficult 12-foot putt, but in the 36-hole playoff he whips Espinosa by 23 strokes. Jones wins again in 1930 as part of his grand slam year (U.S. and British Opens, U.S. and British Amateurs), helped when one shot skips off water and later by a beneficial ruling from USGA official Prescott Bush (later a U.S. Senator and father of President George Bush), who allows Jones to drop after a lost drive on the 71st hole rather than forcing him to hit again from the tee, as officials later conceded was the proper ruling.

1931-1934: Another marathon playoff in 1931, as Billy Burke tops George von Elm by one stroke after 72 extra holes. In 1932, Gene Sarazen becomes the second man to win the British and U.S. Opens in the same year. Johnny Goodman, the last amateur to win the Open, takes the crown in 1933, and Olin Dutra comes from 8-strokes behind second-round leader Bobby Cruickshank to win in 1934.

1935-1938: A virtual unknown, Sam Parks takes the 1935 Open at brutally tough Oakmont, while Tony Manero wins in 1936 with a record low total 282. Ralph Guldahl, who had quit professional golf in 1935 completes his comeback in 1937 with a record 281 and a two-stroke victory over Sam Snead and repeats his triumph with a whopping six-stroke win in 1938. Ray Ainsley sets a new one-hole record score of 19 when he takes 15 strokes to play out of a creek, not knowing he could have dropped at any time with a penalty stroke.

1939-1941: A legendary shot from a legendary golfer: Byron Nelson wins his only Open in 1939 with a 36-hole playoff victory over Craig Wood and Densmore Shute (who was eliminated after 18 playoff holes), highlighted by a double eagle on the 94th hole. Lawson Little edges Gene Sarazen in a 1940 playoff, and Wood, previously a three-time top five finisher in the Open, overcomes a bad back by wearing a corset to take the 1941 Open in fine fashion.

1942-1945: Open closed because of World War II.

1946-1947: In the classic and slapstick 1946 Open, where swarming crowds are a nuisance and a thunderstorm sweeps in to halt play, Lloyd Mangrum overcomes a three-stroke deficit to Vic Ghezzi and a two-stroke deficit to Byron Nelson with six holes left in the second playoff round to win by one; in the third round, Nelson loses a stroke when his caddy slips on the green and accidentally kicks Nelson's ball. Lew Worsham wins in 1947, as Sam Snead misses a three-footer on the 18th playoff hole. Worsham, who also faced a three-footer, requested a measurement to prove which golfer was away after Snead was set and prepared to putt. Snead was indeed away but was yipped by Worsham's strategic timeout.

1948-1951: The amazing story of Ben Hogan unfolds with the first of his four Open triumphs in 1948 with a record 278 total. Hogan suffers terrible injuries in a car crash and undergoes an arduous recuperation, then returns triumphant in the 50th Open in 1950, still showing the effects of his injuries but winning a playoff by four strokes over Mangrum (who was penalized two strokes on the 15th playoff hole for picking up his ball to blow away a fly) and six over George Fazio. The 1951 Open at Oakland Hills was controversial because of the remodeled course's great difficulty, as only runner-up Clayton Heafner (69) and champion Hogan (67) break par in the final round. In his famous victory speech, Hogan stated: "I'm glad I brought this course, this monster, to its knees."

1952-1953: Julius Boros, a 33-year-old third-year pro, plays consistently strong golf to take the 1952 Open, then Hogan totally dominates the 1953 tournament for his fourth Open win. Hogan leads all the way and wins by six strokes.

1954-1955: The first-ever nationally televised Open offers great human drama, as Ed Furgol, with a left arm permanently locked in a 45-degree angle after a playground injury when he was 12, wins by one stroke. A series of strategic choices on the final hole almost ruin his chances and then deliver his victory. More great drama in 1955, as municipal course pro Jack Fleck birdies the final two holes to tie Hogan, going for his unprecedented fifth Open championship, then beats Hogan by three strokes in the playoff.

1956-1959: Cary Middlecoff wins his second Open in 1956 (he first won in 1949), then, after making up 8 strokes during the final two rounds of the 1957 Open to tie Dick Mayer, he loses to Mayer by 7 strokes in a playoff. Tempestuous Tommy Bolt wins the 1958 Open, then refuses to attend post-tournament interviews because newspapers identified him as being 40 years-old; he claimed to be 39, but was actually 41. Middlecoff was also tempestuous: frustrated by his play and late tee time during the 1953 Open, he completely lost his cool when shooting into a second bunker on the 46th hole; he entered the bunker, turned away from the green, and shot the ball onto the Pennsylvania turnpike, then headed for the clubhouse. More mild-mannered Billy Casper wins the first of his two Opens in 1959.

1960: In one of the most famous Opens, Arnold Palmer overcomes a 7-stroke deficit after three rounds to win, recording birdies on 6 of the first 7 holes and finishing with a then-record 65 for a closing round. Jack Nicklaus finishes second by two strokes at 282, the best-ever Open total by an amateur.

1961-1963: Gene Littler, who lost by one stroke in the 1954 Open, wins by a stroke in 1961, and Nicklaus and Palmer battle it out in 1962, with Nicklaus winning his first of four Opens by three strokes in a playoff over Palmer. Palmer loses in another playoff in 1963, as Julius Boros wins his second Open by 3 strokes over Jacky Cupit and by 6 over Palmer.

1964-1965: The dramatic triumph of Ken Venturi, a one-time amateur phenom and a two-time runner-up at the Masters (1956 and 1960), whose career went downhill following a back injury. He had to play in a qualifying tournament to gain a spot in the Open. Trailing by six strokes going into the final day's 36 holes (the Open would switch to a four-day format in 1965), Venturi almost collapses from exhaustion during the final round and has to pass a medical examination in order to continue playing, but he steadies for a four-stroke win. In 1965, South African Gary Player becomes the first golfer outside of the United States and Great Britain to win the U.S. Open.

1966-1968: Arnold Palmer loses another tough playoff after having led Billy Casper by 7 strokes during the final round. Nicklaus tops Palmer in 1967 by four strokes with a new record low total of 275. Lee Trevino matches the 275 total in 1968 and becomes the first Open winner to record four sub-70 rounds.

1969-1971: Orville Moody, a retired army seargent and a Native American, wins the 1969 Open despite taking more putts than any previous winner with his cross-handed putting grip. Tony Jacklin becomes the first Englishmen to win the Open since 1920 by being the only player to break par on the notoriously rough and windy Hazeltine course in the 1970 Open. Jacklin's winning check is found stuffed in a sportcoat by a drycleaner a few days after the tournament, and Dave Hill, fined for complaining publicly about the course while others muttered their thoughts in private, has his runner-up paycheck placed on hold because a PGA official forgot to endorse it. In the 13th Open held at the Merion course in 1971, Lee Trevino tops Jack Nicklaus in a playoff by three strokes.

1972-1975:   Jack Nicklaus wins his third Open in 1972 at Pebble Beach, site of his 1961 U.S. Amateur championship. Johnny Miller, trailing by six strokes entering the final round, shoots a closing-round record 63 to win the 1973 Open by a stroke. Hale Irwin wins the first of his two Open championships in 1974 on the difficult Winged Foot course as the only golfer to finish under par. In 1975, Lou Graham wins by two strokes over John Mahhaffey in the 25th playoff in Open history.

1976-1979:   Jerry Pate wins dramatically in 1976 with an astounding approach shot on the 72nd hole. Hubert Green finishes ahead of a pack of 12 golfers all within two strokes going into the final round of the 1977 Open. No one beats par in the 1978 Open, but Andy North beats everyone else, and only Hale Irwin matches par in 1979, winning with 135 strokes in the middle rounds (68 and 67) compared with 149 strokes over his first and final rounds (74 and 75).

1980-1981:   Record low scoring returns to the Open in 1980, as Nicklaus and Weiskopf begin the festivities with opening-round 63s, tieing the all-time low score for a round, and Nicklaus and Isao "Jumbo" Ozaki share a three-round record total 204. Nicklaus' final round 68 establishes a new low total—272—and he wins his record-tying fourth Open (joining Willie Anderson, Ben Hogan, and Bobby Jones). In 1981, David Graham becomes the first Australian to win the Open.

1982-1984 :   Three magnificent Opens: Tom Watson makes a dramatic birdie chip on the 71st hole to break a tie with Nicklaus and wins the 1982 Open by two strokes. Larry Nelson sets a new record for the final 36 holes of an Open in 1983 and takes the lead with a monster birdie putt on the 70th hole. Greg Norman, who leads each of the four Majors at some time in 1984, makes up a three-stroke deficit to Fuzzy Zoeller on the final back nine, sinking a 45 footer on 18 to force a playoff; Zoeller prevails by eight strokes in one of several agonizing late losses in Majors that Norman will endure during his career.

1985-1986:   Andy North wins his second Open (and only his third professional tournament win of any kind) in a tournament highlighted by the spectacular rise and crash of T.C. Chen, who recorded an albatross on the par-5 2nd hole on the way to a first round Oakland Hills course-record 65. Chen was four strokes ahead after the 2nd hole of the final round, but his downfall is hastened by an 8, which includes a double-hit, on the 5th hole, and he finishes as one of three-runners up one stroke behind North. At age 43, Raymond Floyd becomes the oldest Open winner, shooting a final-round 66 in 1986 to best Lanny Wadkins and Chip Beck, who both shot 65s, by two strokes.

1987-1991:   Scott Simpson breaks from a pack of ten golfers bunched within three strokes in the final round and wins with a 68, the only one of the ten to break 70. Curtis

Strange and Nick Faldo battle it out in 1988, after Strange hits a potential winning putt 8 feet past the hole on 17, then makes a dramatic sand save on 18 to force a playoff, which he wins by four strokes. Strange becomes the first man since Ben Hogan in 1951 to defend the Open championship, as he ekes out a one-stroke victory over three others. He took the lead in the second round with a 64, then fell three strokes back to Tom Kite after the third round, before rising back to the top. Hale Irwin was granted a special exemption to enter the 1990 Open after the expiration of his ten-year privilege for winning the 1980 Open, and wins in a sudden-death playoff over Mike Donald. The two were still tied after 18 playoff holes. In another playoff in 1991, Payne Stewart edged 1987 winner Scott Simpson by two strokes.

1992-1993: Tom Kite struggles in heavy winds gusts during the final round to take the 1992 Open at Pebble Beach; after high scoring during the early rounds, the course and then the weather sent scores soaring. Lee Janzen shot four sub-70 rounds to take the 1993 Open, his first Major; in another first, 52-year-old Lil Drawdy became the first caddy-mom, hauling the clubs for her son, Oswald. John Daly reached the 630-yard 17th hole—longest ever hole in Major tournament play—in two, with a 325 yard drive followed by a 290-yard 1-iron.

1994-1996: 24-year old South African Ernie Els wins the marathon 1994 Open, finishing tied in a three-man playoff with Loren Roberts (while Colin Montgomery was eliminated), then triumphs on the second playoff hole. Corey Pavin wins dramatically in 1995 when his approach to the final hole lands within five feet of the cup, and he holes a tournament-winning birdie. Pavin shot an even 280 on the par-70 course, the first Open winner since Hale Irwin in 1979 to not break par. Steve Jones wins his first tournament in seven years by taking the closely fought 1996 Open. Jones had been sidelined for three years following a dirt bike injury.

THE BRITISH OPEN

1860: The British Open, the first organized golf competition, begins with a 36 hole format: 12 holes per round, 3 rounds, one day. Willie Park is the first Open champion, shooting a 174 to win by two strokes over Old Tom Morris. Charles Hunter takes 21 strokes on the 1st hole of the first Open, a record of futility that still stands.

1861-1862: Old Tom Morris wins the first two of his four Open championships; his 13-stroke victory margin in 1862 still stands as a record.

1863-1867: In 1863, Willie Park beats Old Tom by two strokes in the first Open ever played for prize money, and he wins his third of four Opens in 1866. Old Tom wins his final two Opens in 1864 and 1867, and Andrew Strath in 1865 becomes the first man other than Old Tom or Park to win an Open. Score cards were introduced in 1865.

1868-1870: Young Tom Morris succeeds his father as champion in 1868. He's only 17, and he also scored the first ace in Championship play (8th hole at Prestwick). The Morrises finish first and second in 69, well ahead of the field, as Young Tom beats Old Tom by two strokes; Young Tom shoots a record 149, which stands as the best ever with the gutty ball, in 1870 for his third straight win.

1871: No trophy, no championship. The Open was established with the provision that a belt of red, Moroccan leather with silver inlays was to be presented to the winner each year, and any man who won three straight Opens would win possession of the belt. Young Tom fulfilled this provision and claimed the belt as his property. With no trophy to award, the Open in 1871 was canceled.

1872-1875: A new trophy—a silver claret jug—is introduced, and Young Tom wins his fourth straight championship in 1872. The first Open at St. Andrews is held in 1873 and won by local golfer Tom Kidd. Field of 26 is largest-ever to that point. Musselburgh is added to form a three course rotation beginning in 1874, and local golfer Mungo Park takes the title. Willie Park, Mungo's brother is back as champion in 1875 after seven years and for the fourth and final time. The Park and Morris families take 13 of the first 15 Open championships.

1876-1879: Bob Martin and David Strath finish tied, but the 1876 title is awarded to Martin when Strath refuses to participate in a playoff while officials deliberate whether or not he should be disqualified over a technicality—his drive to the 17th green hit a golfer ahead who had not yet left the green. In 1877, Jamie Anderson begins a three-year reign as the Open champ. His 1878 win included late heroics at Prestwick: he holed a fairway shot on 15, made a tremendously long putt on 16, and aced the 17th. Fourteen-year-old John Ball, a later champion, finishes fifth in 1878.

1880-1882: Bob Fergus on wins three straight Opens. Several golfers leave the course and fail to finish the 1881 tournament due to the Great Storm, which hit on the last day of the Open. 180 fisherman were lost at sea during the storm.

1883-1885: First ever playoff is won in 1883 in dramatic fashion: Willie Fernie drives the green on the last hole and putts in to win by a stroke over Bob Fergus on, who had won the past three Opens. Bob Martin wins his second Open, both at the fabled St. Andrews, in 1885, a feat duplicated later by only three other golfers: James Braid, J.H. Taylor, and Jack Nicklaus are the only other two-time Open champs on the Old Course.

1886-1889: Willie Park, Jr., follows in dad's footsteps as a multiple Open winner, by a stroke in 1887 and in a playoff by two strokes over Andrew Kircaldy in 1889. The 1888 Open is won by Jack Burns, a plasterer by trade, in his only notable Open finish.

1890-1893: John Ball becomes the first Englishman, first non-Scot, and first amateur to win the Open (1890), and Hugh Kircaldy tops his brother, Andrew, by two strokes to win in 1891. British Open expands to 72 holes over two days, and Muirfield replaces

Musselburgh in the Open rotation in 1892. The 1893 Open is a wet one, and Harold Hilton's title defense drowns with a 10 on the first hole.

1894-1898:   In 1894 Royal St. George's Sandwich Course is added to the rotation as the first venue in England, and Royal Liverpool's Holyoke is added in 1897. J.H. Taylor wins the 1894 title, the first of five for him and the first of sixteen over the next twenty years by a member of the "Great Triumvirate"—Taylor, Harry Vardon, and James Braid. Taylor wins his second straight Open in 1895, Vardon wins in 1896 and 1898, the latter with a first-ever four sub-80 rounds. The "qualifying limit" (now known as the cut) is introduced in 1898 to eliminate players with the worst scores following the second round.

1899-1904:   Triumvirate members, Vardon, Taylor, and Braid, respectively, win the turn-of-the-century Opens, each handily. Sandy Herd switches from the gutty to the rubber-cored Haskel ball just before the 1902 Open and wins by a stroke over Vardon and Braid, though Braid makes up 7 strokes during the final round. The Vardon Bros.—Harry and Tom—finish first and second, respectively, in 1903, and records fall in 1904: Jack White is the first to win an Open with total strokes under 300 (296), and two others (Braid and Taylor) finish at 297; Taylor's 68 final round stands for 30 years; and Braid's third-round 69 was the first Open round ever under 70.

1905-1910:   Braid wins second and third of five titles in 1905 and 1906, and France's Arnaud Massy becomes the first winner from abroad in 1907. Braid wins again in 1908 and 1910, smoking the Prestwick course with a 291 in 08—beating the previous Open low total by five strokes. Taylor wins his fourth Open title in 1909.

1911-1914:   End of the reign of the Great Triumvirate, as Vardon wins in 1911 and 1914 and Taylor takes the 1913 crown. In 1912, Ted Ray becomes only the fifth non-Triumvirate winner since 1894.

1915-1919:   Open closed due to World War I.

1920:   The Royal and Ancient assumes full responsibility for the Open. George Duncan makes up a 13-stroke deficit in the third round to tie Abe Mitchell, who had been in the lead, for second, one behind Sandy Herd going into the final round; Duncan wins by two over Herd and four over Mitchell.

1921-1925:   The American Invasion begins when Jock Hutchison, an expatriate from St. Andrews, wallops hometown hero Roger Wethred of St. Andrews by nine strokes in a playoff. Hutchison aced the 8th hole and nearly aced the 9th during the first round—a two hole record of three strokes that still stands. Americans will win 11 of 12 Opens between 1921 and 1932. Walter Hagen becomes the first American-born Open winner in 1922, sweating out George Duncan's late charge, and Arthur Havers in 1923 is the last man born in Great Britain to win the Open until 1934. Hagen wins his second Open in 1924, and Jim Barnes wins in 1925, the last Open played at Prestwick.

1926-1927:   Bobby Jones wins two Opens in a row, the 1926 coming on a great shot on the 71st hole. John Ball makes his last Open appearance in 1927 at age 65, after competing for almost 50 years.

1928-1932:   Walter Hagen wins his third and fourth Opens in 1928 and 1929; Bobby Jones wins in 1930, the second win of his grand slam year; Tommy Armour makes up five strokes in the final round to defeat Argentina's Jose Jurado in 1931; and in 1932 Gene Sarazen leads all the way with a record 283, which stands until 1950.

1933-1937:   A classic at St. Andrews: Densmore Shute edges Craig Wood in a playoff when Wood's second shot lands deep in a bunker, described as the "side of a hill." Defending champ Sarazen fell back in the second round when he risked and failed to carry Hell's Bunker. Englishman Henry Cotton brings the Open championship back home in 1934 with a masterful five-stroke win that includes an opening 69 and a second-round 65 that stands as the Open record until 1977. Alfs (Padgham and Perry, respectively) win in 1935 and 1936, and Cotton wins again in 1937. Padgham, in 1936, had to break into a local clubmaker's shop before the final round, where his AWOL caddy left his clubs the night before.

1938-1939:   British golfers close out the 1930s with two more Open crowns, running a championship streak to six years before World War II halts the Open. The final round of the 1938 Open at Sandwich is played in terrible winds that blow down tents and rip off flags but also helps Alf Padgham drive the 11th green, 380 yards away. Dick Burton wins in 1939 and is the last victorious Englishman of an Open at St. Andrews.

1940-1945:   Open closed during World War II.

1946-1948:   Sam Snead wins his only Open in 1946, Irishman Fred Daly wins in 1947 despite a third-round 78, and Cotton is king again, winning his third Open in 1948 in the presence of King George VI.

1949-1952:   South African Bobby Locke wins his first two of four Opens, with a playoff victory over Henry Bradshaw in 1949 and in 1950 with the first-ever sub-280 four-round total. He wins again in 1952 by one stroke over Peter Thomson, with whom he will dominate the Open during the 1950s.

1953-1956:   Ben Hogan wins his third Major of the year by taking the 1953 Open, then Australian Peter Thomson takes over, winning three years in a row. The first Open to be televised live occurs in 1955.

1957-1958:   Locke wins his fourth and final Open in 1957; the tournament was moved from Murifield to St. Andrews because of a feared fuel shortage resulting from the Suez Canal crisis. Locke marked his ball on the final hole but mistakenly placed it in another spot; he wasn't cited for an infraction, and won by three strokes anyway. Thomson becomes the first man since Young Tom Morris to win four Opens in five years with a triumph in 1958.

1959-1960:   South Africa's Gary Player wins his first Major with the 1959 Open, and Australian Kel Nagle wins the 1960 Open, which finishes on Saturday after rain wipes out the final two rounds scheduled for Friday.

1961-1962:   Following a second-place finish (one-stroke behind Nagle) in his first Open in 1960, Arnold Palmer wins two straight. In 1961, he plays masterfully in strong winds at Royal Birkdale, where a plaque on the 15th hole commemorates an excellent second shot he made during the second round, and in 1962 he blows away the field by six strokes with an Open record 276.

1963-1964:   Bob Charles becomes the first lefty to win a Major, doing so in the last 36-hole playoff format (changed permanently in 1964 to 18 holes) in 1963. Tony Lema dominates the field by five strokes in 1964, but Jack Nicklaus makes his presence felt in the final two rounds, shooting a 66 and a 68. Lema died in a plane crash shortly after the 1966 Open.

1965-1968:   The end and the beginning of legends: Peter Thomson wins his fifth and final Open in 1965, joining Braid and Taylor (and, later, Tom Watson) as the only 5-time winners, and Jack Nicklaus win his first of three Opens in 1966. Longtime international favorite Roberto De Vicenzo breaks through in 1967 after 5 top-3 Open finishes dating back to 1948, and Gary Player wins his second Open in 1968.

1969-1970:   Tony Jacklin is a national hero by becoming the first Englishman to win the Open since 1948. Another St. Andrews classic occurs in 1970, and because of rain during the first round it becomes the first Open ever played on a Sunday. Jack Nicklaus wins an 18-hole playoff over Doug Sanders by driving the 18th green and becomes the first man to win the Open on a final-hole birdie. Sanders, who joined the field through a pre-tournament qualifying competition, 3-putted the 72nd hole to drop into a tie with Nicklaus.

1971-1975:   Lee Trevino wins two straight, beating Lu Liang Huan of Taiwan in 1971 by two strokes and holing 3 shots from outside the greens in 1972. Tom Weiskopf leads all the way in the 1973 Open, and Gene Sarazen aces the 8th hole of the first round— 50 years after competing in his first Open. Gary Player wins his third and final Open in 1974, and Tom Watson wins his first of five Opens with a one-stroke playoff victory over Jack Newton in 1975.

1976-1978:   Johnny Miller is almost as hot as the weather, winning by 6 strokes over Nicklaus and Severiano Ballesteros. The parched course catches on fire during the opening round. Watson wins his second Open in 1977 as records fall and the top eight finishers are all American. Watson's 279 total is an astounding 8 strokes under the previous record low. Over 125,000 attend the 1978 Open at St. Andrews, where Nicklaus wins his third Open, second at St. Andrews.

1979-1981:   Ballesteros survives shaky final two rounds, when he drives only two fairways but prevails to become the first winner from continental Europe since 1907. Nicklaus finishes second for the seventh time. In 1980, the first Open scheduled to conclude on a Sunday, Watson wins his third Open in Scotland as the Muirfield course proves generally accommodating to the field. In 1981, Bill Rogers has his day in the sun.

1982-1983: Watson wins his fourth and fifth Opens, playing steady in 1982 while young Bobby Clampett, in his first Open, experiences a spectacular rise and fall, leading by as many as 7 strokes in the third round before finding three bunkers and an eight on the sixth hole; his final two-round total was 23 strokes higher than his first two-round total. Craig Stadler sets the best first-round score ever in 1983 with a 64, but Watson prevails with a long approach shot on the 72nd hole that finds the green and sets up a tournament-winning putt.

1984-1986: Ballesteros wins his second Open in 1984, as the pursuing Watson is undone at the famous Road Hole of St. Andrews; Sandy Lyle becomes the first British golfer to win the Open in sixteen years in 1985; Greg Norman overcomes nasty wind and rough conditions with a record-tying 63 in the second round and wins in 1986, a year in which he led in all four Majors.

1987-1989: Nick Faldo wins his first of three Opens, Seve Ballesteros wins his third of three in 1988, and Mark Calcavecchia makes a series of amazing shots to tie Wayne Grady and Greg Norman, who shot a final-round 64. The threesome play a recently adopted (and quickly dispensed) 4-hole aggregate score playoff, which Calcavecchia wins.

1990-1993: Faldo wins his second and third opens (1990, 1992); relative unknown Ian Baker-Finch plays superbly to win in 1991, and Greg Norman shoots a new tournament low total 267 to edge out Nick Faldo for the 1993 crown.

1994-1996: Nick Price emerges as a leading pro with his 1994 Open win, which he follows up by taking the 1994 PGA Championship. Big-hitter John Daly rises above personal troubles to tame St. Andrews in 1995—consistently driving long into advantageous spots and showing brilliant command of the short game. Tom Lehman, the PGA Golfer of the Year in 1996, is in complete command of the 96 Open, taking a six-stroke lead into the final round and coasting to a two-stroke victory. Lehman had finished second in the U.S. Open that year.

THE PGA CHAMPIONSHIP

1916-1920: The PGA Championship is established in 1916 with criteria for invitation based on full PGA membership and success in American PGA Tour events. Winners receive lifetime exemptions from having to pre-qualify for PGA tournaments. From 1916 to 1957 the PGA Championship has a matchplay format. Jim Barnes defeats Jock Hutchison by one hole to become the first PGA champion, then, after the PGA is canceled for two years during World War I, Barnes repeats as champ in 1919. Hutchison, runner-up in the first PGA, wins in 1920.

1921-1927: Seven years of dominance by Walter Hagen and Gene Sarazen. Hagen wins in 1921 over two-time PGA champ Jim Barnes, and in 1922 twenty-year-old Sarazen, who won the U.S. Open that year, defeats Emmet French. Hagen and Sarazen meet in the final in 1923 and Sarazen wins on the second extra hole in the first PGA playoff. Hagen wins four straight PGAs from 1924 to 1927: he defeats four-time PGA finalist Jim Barnes (2 wins, 2 second-place finishes) in 1924; beats Al Watrous and Leo Diegel in playoffs during early rounds, then opens with an eagle in defeating Bill Melhorn in 1925; tops Diegel in the 1926 final, and though he was always one to seize any kind of advantage, he probably had nothing to do with the fact that Diegel's wayward drive on the 19th hole ended up under Hagen's parked car; and Hagen wins his fifth and final PGA in 1927, coming from behind to defeat Joe Turnsea during the final nine. During that back nine stretch in 1927, played under a glaring Texas sun, Hagen was lent a hat to wear by a fifteen-year-old spectator named Byron Nelson, who would later become a 5-time PGA finalist.

1928-1929: The quirky Leo Diegel ends Hagen's championship streak at 4 and consecutive match win streak at 22 during the third round, then Diegel defeats Gene Sarazen in the fourth round and wins the championship over Al Espinosa. Diegel repeats in 1929; during the back nine, he twice sets up a stymie—a legal maneuver until 1952—where his putt came to rest on a line between his opponent's ball and the cup, and both times Johnny Farrell, that year's U.S. Open champ, knocks Diegel's ball into the cup.

1930-1932: In a tight and dramatic final in 1930, Tommy Armour wins with a 14-foot putt on the last hole to beat Gene Sarazen. Dark horses win the next two PGAs: 20-year-old Tom Creavy, who caddied for Sarazen and Farrell, among others, carries the 1931 championship, and Olin Dutra goes red hot in 1932, playing 196 holes during the tournament in 19 under par. The 1932 championship features two amazing third-round matches, as Bobby Cruickshank comes from 9 down with 12 holes to play to defeat Al Watrous, and Johnny Golden beats Walter Hagen on the 7th extra hole—the longest playoff in PGA championship history.

1933-1938: Gene Sarazen wins his third and final PGA in 1933, Paul Runyan wins on the second playoff hole over Craig Wood to take the 1934 title, and Johnny Revolta begins a string of wins by masters of the short game with a 1935 triumph over Tommy Armour. Densmore Shute beats the heavy-hitting Jimmy Thomson in 1936, and Shute repeats in 1937 in a PGA marked by late heroics. Shute wins on the first playoff hole over Harold "Jug" McSpaden, who missed a short putt for victory on the final hole. McSpaden was involved in three playoffs during the 1937 PGA, winning early matches on the second and third playoff holes before losing in the final. In 1938, Paul Runyan shoots a 67 and goes up by 5 over Sam Snead en route to his second PGA title and the biggest match play victory margin in a PGA final, 8 and 7.

1939-1945: Byron Nelson appears in five finals in six years and dominates golf during the World War II years, when he was turned down for military service because of a blood condition. Henry Picard defeats Nelson late in the 1939 championship, but Nelson wins late in 1940 over Sam Snead, taking two of the final four holes. Vic Ghezzi turns the tables on Nelson in 1941, making up a three-hole deficit on the final nine. Sam Snead wins the 1942 championship over Jim Turnsea, who had defeated Ben Hogan, Jug McSpaden, and Nelson on his way to the final. After the 1943 PGA is postponed because of World War II, Nelson in 1944 loses for the third time in the PGA championship final round, this time to Bob Hamilton, who sinks a suspenseful birdie putt on the final hole to protect his one-hole lead. Nelson takes the 1945 PGA, as he wins almost everything that year during an astonishingly successful run that includes eleven-straight tournament wins and 19 tournament championships.

1946-1948:   Ben Hogan wins his first PGA in 1946, playing the final front nine in 30 and improving from down three to up by two. Jim Ferrier wins the 1947 tournament, and Hogan wins his second PGA in 1948, becoming only the second man to win the PGA and U.S. Open in the same year (Gene Sarazen, in 1922, was the other). 1948 marked the third time one of the Turnsea brothers lost to a future Hall of Famer in a PGA final: Joe, in 1927 to Hagen, Jim, in 1942 to Snead, and Mike, in 1948 to Hogan.

1949-1951:   Sam Snead becomes the third three-time PGA Championship winner (joining Hagen and Sarazen) with triumphs in 1949 and 1951, the 49 victory coming in front of a large group of enthusiastic supporters in his homestate of Virginia, and in devastating fashion in 1951 by taking five of the first six holes. Chandler Harper records his greatest victory in 1950, defeating contemporary greats Jimmy Demaret and Lloyd Mangrum in preliminary rounds and topping Henry Williams for the championship.

1952-1954:   The turning of the tide for the Turnsea family: Jim Turnsea makes up a three-hole deficit in the final round to bring the family its first PGA championship after he and his brothers, Joe and Mike, had all been previous PGA runners-up. Former runners-up also take the next two championships: Walter Burkemo, who was beaten by Snead in the 1951 PGA, has his greatest golfing moment before homestate fans in taking the 1953 championship held in Michigan. Burkemo returns to runner-up status in 1954, when Chick Harbert, himself a two-time runner-up, shoots 8 under par during the final round to ease the crown away from Burkemo.

1955-1957:   The final three PGAs played in the match format; matchplay loses out to stroke play, which is favored by pros and is better suited for presentation on network television. Doug Ford and Cary Middlecoff, who between them win 4 Majors from 1955 to 1957, battle for the PGA championship in 1955, with Ford's expert putting providing the slight edge. Jack Burke comes back late in a semifinal round and in the final round to defeat Ted Kroll in 1956, and in the final matchplay PGA, Lionel Hebert wins his first tournament, defeating Dow Finsterwald.

1958-1961:   Recurring PGA themes—runners-up become champions and "we are family" —play again. Dow Finsterwald, the 1957 runner-up, wins the first PGA stroke play championship in 1958, shooting opening- and closing-round 67s to charge in front early and charge to victory late. The 1960 PGA is won by Jay Hebert, whose brother, Lionel, was the 1957 champ. Bob Rosburg comes from back in the pack to edge Jerry Barber and Doug Sanders for the 1959 championship. Rosburg trails Barber by 9 after two rounds and trails Barber by 6 and Ford by 5 after three rounds, but he prevails with a sizzling 66 in the final round to win by one stroke. Runner-up Barber becomes the PGA champ in 1961, holing from just off the green three times during the tournament and defeating Don January (now a runner up, later a champion) by one stroke in a playoff.

1962-1963: Not surprisingly, the 1962 and 1963 PGAs are won by Gary Player and Jack Nicklaus, respectively. Together with Arnold Palmer, who never won the PGA, the threesome win 6 of the 8 Majors held in 1962-63, win at least 2 Majors every year from 1960 through 1966 (except for one in 1964), accumulate 15 total Majors from 1960 through 1966 and win five in row from the 1962 sweep through the 1963 Masters. Player adds the 1962 PGA to his British Open (1959) and Masters (1961) crowns in a tight match: he leads Bob Goalby by two strokes after 36 holes; by two over George Bayer, four over Goalby, and six over the charging Nicklaus after three rounds; and finishes victorious by a stroke over Goalby and by three over Nicklaus and Bayer. Nicklaus charges early and late in 1963 to win his third Major in his second year as a professional.

1964-1966: Bobby Nichols starts strong with a first-round 64 in 64 and never looks back, winning by 3 strokes over Arnold Palmer (who shoots four sub-70 rounds) and Jack Nicklaus, setting the all-time PGA low total at 271. Dave Marr wins in 1965, shooting in and out of danger on the final five holes as Nicklaus and Billy Casper pursue but finish 2 strokes behind. Marr admits that on the par three 14th, where he lost a stroke on a weak tee shot, he had begun rehearsing his victory speech; on the 15th, where he made an excellent approach shot to a small green, he thought of family, friends, and his coach; on 16, he explodes out of a bunker to within two feet of the hole, then misses the putt ("I told myself to be careful") and loses a stroke; then on 18, his approach lands within a yard of the cup as he recalls his coach's advice—"trust your swing." In 1966, Al Geiberger wins by four strokes, the largest victory margin in PGA history.

1967-1970: Don January, runner-up in a playoff in the 1961 PGA, wins the 1967 PGA by 2 strokes in a playoff over Don Massengale. In 1968, Julius Boros at age 48 becomes the oldest player to win a Major; always excellent with the short game, Boros recovers from a poor tee shot on 18 with strong iron and wedge shots to save his one-stroke margin. Raymond Floyd builds a five stroke lead going into the final round of the 1969 Open, but Gary Player makes a charge and falls one stroke short of catching Floyd. In a sign of the times, the tournament is disrupted by demonstrators, who target Player, a South African, and Jack Nicklaus. In 1970, Dave Stockton takes command of the tough Southern Hills, Oklahoma, course with a third-round 66 and cruises to a two-stroke victory over Bob Murphy, who made up seven of a nine-stroke deficit he faced going into the round, and Arnold Palmer, who finishes second in the PGA for the third time.

1971-1973: Jack Nicklaus wins his second and third PGAs (1971 and 1973) and Gary Player his second (1972). Player was slipping late in 1972 until a daring stroke on the final-round 16th hole at Oakland Hills—over trees and water to a tightly-bunkered green with a dangerous runoff—stops within four feet of the cup; he birdies the hole and finishes with a two-stroke victory. In 1971 Nicklaus begins a second brilliant PGA tournament run: from 1962 through 1965, he recorded a win, two seconds, and a third, and from 1971 through 1977 he records three wins, a second, and a third. Nicklaus becomes the first man to win each of the Majors at least twice with his 1971 PGA win, and his 1973 triumph (tying the largest PGA victory margin of 4 strokes) is his 14th Major, putting him ahead of Bobby Jones for most wins in the Majors.

1974-1976: Lee Trevino wins his third Major of 1974, adding the PGA to his British and U.S. Open crowns, by taking command in the third round and winning a tight battle over Nicklaus and four others. In 1975, Nicklaus contends with Bruce Crampton, who sets the early pace with a PGA record 63 in the second round and a two-round 134 to match Jerry Barber's 1959 record two-round total. Nicklaus reverses a 4-stroke deficit to Crampton into a 4-stroke lead by the end of the third round and coasts to a two-stroke win. Crampton also finished second to Nicklaus in 1973. Past PGA champions clash to the end of the 1976 tournament, as Dave Stockton (1970 winner) holes a 10-footer to stave off a playoff with Raymond Floyd (1969 winner) and Don January (1967 winner) to win his second PGA.

1977-1980: Pebble Beach plays a tough host in 1977. Gene Littler, leader since the first round, is up by five with 9 to play, but Lanny Wadkins is hot, having scored two eagles on the front nine, and Littler finds trouble coming in: he loses the five stroke lead by the 15th, as Jack Nicklaus takes the lead, but Nicklaus suffers a bogey on 17; Littler hangs on, but Wadkins ties him with a birdie on the sublime 18th hole. Wadkins stays alive with a tough 20-foot putt on the first playoff hole, then wins the PGA on the third playoff hole. It's sudden death again in 1978, as John Mahaffey prevails over Tom Watson and Jerry Pate, who miss their opportunities for victory: Watson led Pate by 4 and Mahaffey by 5 with nine to play, and Pate fails to negotiate a short tournament-winning putt on 18. Mahaffey's long comeback—he was down by 8 strokes after the first round—ends in victory with a birdie on the second playoff hole. It's sudden death again in 1979, with a tremendous finish. Ben Crenshaw is steady with four sub-70 rounds but David Graham stays close and gets hot on the final day: Graham has a shot at a record-low total for a PGA Championship, but his tee shot on 18 fades right and his approach sails over the green, followed by two chips to the green and two putts, and he ends tied with Crenshaw. In the playoff, Graham stays alive with tricky putts from 20 and 10 feet, respectively, then birdies the third playoff hole for victory.

1981-1983: Larry Nelson shoots a pair of 66s in the middle rounds to build a four stroke lead in the 1981 PGA and maintains that lead through to victory, and in 1982 Raymond Floyd starts hot, with a PGA-low first round 63, and leads all the way; his second-(132) and third- (200) round totals are also record lows, and he has a chance at the all-time tournament low score, but like Graham in a similar situation in 1980 he double-bogeys the final hole. Floyd's 36-hole record lasts a year, as Hal Sutton shoots 131 over the first two rounds in 1983 and builds a large lead to withstand late charges by Nicklaus, who makes up 6 strokes over the final two rounds to finish second by a stroke, and Peter Jacobsen, who makes up 10 strokes over the final two rounds, during which he totals a 133.

1984-1986:   Lee Trevino captures his second PGA in 1984 by becoming the first winner with four sub-70 rounds, and he leads the 1985 PGA by two strokes at the midway point but falters with a 75 in the third round. Hubert Green takes a three-stroke lead into the final round and shoots par for a two-stroke win over Trevino and by three over the late charging Andy Bean and T.C. Chen, who shoot 68 and 65, respectively, in the final round. Stormy weather shortened the first round and delayed the final. Greg Norman, who is almost as well known for his crushing losses late in Majors as he is for enormous successes as the PGA's all-time money winner, suffers a stunning reversal of fortune in the 1986 PGA. Norman leads safely after two rounds, including a 9-stroke advantage over Bob Tway. After the third round is moved to Sunday because of a rain postponement, Norman shoots a strong 69, but Tway makes up 5 strokes with a sterling 64. Tway, playing the final round with Norman, whittles away Norman's lead and they reach 18 tied. Norman's approach on 18 lies safely while Tway finds a bunker, but Tway holes out from the bunker for an incredible victory.

1987-1991:   Former PGA champs Lanny Wadkins (1977) and Larry Nelson (1981) battle in a playoff, with Nelson becoming the two-time winner. Jeff Sluman wis in 1988, and beknickered Payne Stewart wins his first Major in 1989. Wayne Grady outduels Fred Couples late in 1990, and the 1991 tournament is highlighted by the arrival of John Daly, who learned he was invited to play as the ninth alternate near the midnight hour that would turn into Thursday. He shoots an opening round 69, then takes the lead with a second-round 67. Because of his unlikely story and booming drives he becomes the big story and keeps on playing his game even in the limelight, finishing with a three-stroke victory.

1992-1996:   Nick Price wins twice (1992 and 1994), with playoffs deciding the 1993 and 1995 Championships. In 1993, Paul Azinger wins his first Major by defeating Greg Norman, who finishes as runner-up in a Major for the seventh time), and Steve Elkington outduels Colin Montgomerie for the 1995 title. Mark Brooks wins a sudden death playoff over Kenny Perry in 1996.

APPENDIX C

U.S. AMATEUR CHAMPIONSHIP SUMMARIES

U.S. MEN'S AMATEUR CHAMPIONSHIP

1894: Two clubs, the Newport (Rhode Island) Golf Club and the St. Andrews Golf Club of New York, each hold tournaments and proclaim the winner to be the national amateur champion, creating a monumental controversy. Recognizing the need for a single national champion, representatives of five major golf clubs found the United States Golf Association (USGA) on December 22, 1894.

1895: The USGA conducts its first tournaments, the Open, the Amateur Championship, and the Women's Amateur Championship. The winner of the first Amateur Championship, a match-play tournament held at the Newport Golf Club, is Charles Blair Macdonald of Chicago.

1896-1908: Interest in the Championship increases, and it becomes necessary to limit participation in the tournament. Qualifying is introduced in 1896. Walter Travis, who took up the game of golf at age 35, wins the first of three Amateurs in 1900 (winning again in 1901 and 1903). Jerome D. Travers wins the first of his four Amateurs in 1907 (winning again 1908, 1912 and 1913).

1909-1915: In 1909, Robert A. Gardner becomes the youngest winner at 19 years, 5 months, a record that stands until 1994, when it is broken by Tiger Woods. Harold Hilton becomes the first man to win the British and American Amateurs in the same year, taking the American Amateur with an incredible shot on the final hole (see a description of the shot in the Taming the Monsters section). In 1912 a method of handicapping is instituted, which will become the model for today's USGA handicapping system. Francis Ouimet, who shocked the golf world with his stunning victory in the U.S. Open in 1913, wins the Amateur in 1914, as four-time Amateur winner Travers suffers his first finals defeat.

1916-1918: A noteworthy year. Charles "Chick" Evans becomes the first golfer to win the Amateur and the Open in the same year. And a precocious 14-year-old named Bobby Jones competes in his first U.S. Amateur Championship, winning two rounds. The Amateur is canceled for two years during World War I.

1919-1923: Competition resumes after World War I. In 1920, due to an increase in the number of participants, two courses are used for qualifying for the first time. The 1921 Amateur at St. Louis Golf and Country Club marks the first time the Championship is held west of the Mississippi.

1924-1930: The Jones Era. Bobby Jones scores his first victory, at Merion, defeating Francis Ouimet in the semi-final and George von Elm in the final. Jones goes on to win a total of five Amateur Championships before his retirement in 1930. That year marks his unprecedented and unequaled Grand Slam, victories in the British Open, the British Amateur, the U.S. Open, and the U.S. Amateur. Von Elm defeated Jones in the 1926 final.

1931-1941: In 1931 sectional qualifying begins, with competition held at 20 different courses. Francis Ouimet takes the 1931 Amateur after a 17-year gap. In 1935 Lawson Little takes both the U.S. and British Amateur Championships, and wins the U.S. Amateur again in 1936. The Amateur is held in the Pacific northwest for the first time as Oregon's Alderwood Country Club hosts the tournament in 1937.

1946-1952: When competition resumes after World War II, Skee Riegel sets a qualifying record of 136 (69, 67), and the 1946 Amateur at Baltusrol Golf Club in New Jersey is won by S.E. Bishop. The year 1948 sees the largest field to date: 1220 golfers. In 1952 Jack Westland, a finalist against Ouimet in 1931, becomes the oldest winner of the Amateur at age 47.

1953-1958: Gene Littler takes the 1953 Championship while serving in the U.S. Navy. In a memorable final in 1954 at the Country Club of Detroit, Arnold Palmer defeats Robert Sweeney on the 36th green; Palmer turns pro immediately after the victory. Hillman Robbins sets a new qualifying record of 132 (66, 66) in 1955, and wins the Amateur in 1957.

1959-1964: In 1959, competing in his second U.S. Amateur, Jack Nicklaus becomes the second-youngest winner in tournament history when he defeats Charles Coe, the defending champion. The two were tied on the 36th tee, and Nicklaus sank an eight-foot putt to take the tournament. In 1960, Deane Beman becomes the ninth player in history to win both the U.S. and British Amateur Championships. In 1961 Nicklaus wins the Amateur at Pebble Beach and then turns pro. In 1962, at Pinehurst, Charles Evans, Jr., makes a record 50th appearance in the U.S. Amateur. Beman wins again in 1963, then William C. Campbell wins in 1964. Campbell competes in 37 U.S. Amateurs.

1965-1972: The stroke-play years. After seventy years of match-play competition, the USGA switches to stroke-play in 1965. That year, Robert Murphy defeats Bob Dickson by one stroke. Dickson comes back in 1967 to win both the U.S. and British Amateurs. In the 1969 Championship, won by Steve Melnyk, Vinny Giles finishes runner-up for the third year in a row. Lanny Wadkins' winning score of 279 in 1970 is the lowest ever recorded during the eight years of stroke play.

1973-1980: Match play is restored in 1973. That year Craig Stadler beats David Strawn at Inverness. Jerry Pate wins at Ridgewood in 1974, the first year he qualifies for the Amateur. In 1979 John Cook, the defending champion, talks a reluctant, 22-year-old Mark O'Meara into entering the championship. O'Meara defeats Cook in the final.

1981-1986: A great sentimental victory in 1981, as Nathaniel Crosby (son of entertainer and World Golf Hall of Fame member Bing Crosby) wins the Amateur at the Olympic Club in San Francisco, only a few miles from the Crosby home. It is the first final to go to extra holes since 1950. In 1982, the same year he wins the British Amateur, Jay Sigel wins his first U.S. Amateur after 16 tries. The next year Sigel becomes the first back-to-back winner since Harvie Ward in 1955-56. Buddy Alexander's win at Shoal Creek, Alabama, marks the first time a reinstated amateur takes the Championship. A golf coach at Louisiana State University, Alexander had regained amateur status only a month earlier.

1987-1993: Billy Mayfair wins the 1987 Amateur, and two other future stars of the PGA, lefty Phil Mickelson and Justin Leonard, are champs in 1990 and 1992, respectively. Leonard was the top ranked amateur in both 1992 and 1993, but John Harris takes the title in 1993.

1994-1996: Tiger, Tiger, burning bright. In 1994 Eldrick "Tiger" Woods becomes the youngest U.S. Amateur champion in history as he defeats Trip Kuehne at TPC Sawgrass in Florida. Woods repeats as champion in 1995, the first player in 12 years to successfully defend a the title, with his victory over George "Buddy" Marucci, Jr., at Newport Country Club. In 1996, with large media coverage and fan interest, Woods becomes the only golfer ever to win three consecutive U.S. Amateur Championships when he edges out Steve Scott at Pumpkin Ridge Golf Club in a tense, 38-hole final that stretches over nine hours.

U.S. WOMEN'S AMATEUR CHAMPIONSHIP

1895: A month after staging its first U.S. Amateur and U.S. Open Championships, the fledgling USGA holds the inaugural Women's Amateur, a stroke-play event, at the Meadow

Brook Club in Hempstead, New York. The title is taken by Mrs. C.S. Brown, who wins over a field of thirteen competitors.

1896-1899: In 1896 the Women's Amateur changes format to a match-play final preceded by 18-hole stroke-play qualifying. At a time when few clubs encourage women to play golf, Long Island's Shinnecock Hills Club is a notable exception. When Brown decides not to defend her title, Shinnecock Hills sends another member, Beatrix Hoyt—only 16 years, 3 months old—to compete in the 1896 Championship. Hoyt wins the first of three consecutive Women's Amateurs.

1900-1918: The 1907 final is contested by sisters Margaret Curtis and defending champion Harriot Curtis. Margaret wins the tournament, 7 and 6. Margaret previously finished as runner-up in 1900 and 1905, and she wins the championship again in 1911 and 1912. In 1909 Dorothy Campbell becomes the first player to win both the U.S. and British Women's Amateur Championships in the same year. She repeats as champion in 1910. The 1916 Amateur is won by Alexa Stirling, then the tournament is canceled in 1917 and 1918 because of World War I.

1919-1924: Play resumes after World War I, with Alexa Stirling repeating as the first postwar champion; she competes a three-peat in 1920, and later becomes a three-time runner-up (1921, 1923, 1925), In 1924 Dorothy Campbell Hurd becomes the oldest golfer ever to win the Championship at 41 years, 4 months; she also tallies the longest span between victories, 14 years (1910-1924). Glenna Collett wins in 1922 and will become the most successful female American amateur as well as a popular athlete. She later becomes Glenna Collett Vare, and the Vare Trophy, awarded annually to the LPGA golfer with the best scoring average, is named in honor of her accomplishments and contributions to women's golf.

1925-1931: Glenna Collett dominates the Amateur in 1925 then wins three year in succession (1928-1930), before falling in the 1931 finals to Helen Hicks.

1932-1935: Virginia van Wie takes three consecutive Championships, 1932-1934, defeating Collett in the 1932 final. In 1935 Glenna Collett Vare wins her unprecedented sixth Women's Amateur with a thrilling victory over 18-year old Patty Berg at Interlachen Country Club, in Berg's hometown (see a description of Berg's heroics en route to the finals in the Taming the Monsters section. Collett Vare's record of six Amateur titles still stands.

1936-1945: Nineteen-year-old Londoner Pam Barton wins both the U.S. Women's and British Women's Amateurs in 1936, and she repeats as champion in the British Women's Amateur in 1939. Barton joined the WAAF as a Flight-Officer during World War II and was killed in a airplane crash in 1943 at an air force base in Kent. Patty Berg finishes as runner up again in 1937, then wins the 1938 Amateur and turns professional. Another future great of the LPGA, Betty Jameson, wins the last two Amateurs before they are canceled because of World War II.

1946-1952: Babe Zaharias adds to her formidable list of athletic achievements with a resounding victory in the 1946 Amateur. With her victory at the British Women's Amateur in 1947 she becomes the first American to win both tournaments. In 1948 she turns professional and, with Patty Berg, organizes the American Women's Professional Tour. Louise Suggs follows Babe in the winner's circle in 1947, defeating Dorothy Kirby, who wins the title in 1951. Hawaiian Jacqueline Pung wins the 1952 Amateur.

1953-1956: In 1953 the tournament format is changed from stroke-play qualifying rounds to an all-match-play format. The 1954 final, halted by storms, lasts 29 hours, 15 minutes. The great Mickey Wright finishes runner-up in 1954, turns pro and becomes the dominant player on the LPGA tour over the next decade, and Joanne Gunderson, runner-up in 1956, emerges as the next dominant amateur.

1957-1968: The Gunderson years. JoAnne Gunderson (later Carner) wins five Amateur championships (1957, 1960, 1962, 1966, 1968) and finishes twice more as a runner-up. Anne Quast wins three times (1958, 1961, 1963) during the same period, and the two finally meet in the 1968 finals, which Gunderson Carner takes 5 and 4. Quast was a runner-up on three occasions. Quast's victory in 1961 is the largest margin of victory in U.S. Women's Amateur history, as she defeats Phyllis Preuss, 14 and 13 at Tacoma Golf and Country Club. In 1962 Jean Trainor wins over her daughter, Anne Trainor, in the fourth round. The longest final in tournament history (and the longest of any USGA event) takes place in 1966, when it requires 41 holes for Gunderson Carner to beat Marlene Stewart Streit at Sewickley Heights Golf Club in Pennsylvania.

1969-1980: French Amateur Catherine Lacoste, daughter of Wimbledon tennis champion Rene Lacoste and six-time French Women's golf champion, wins the 1969 Amateur, two years after becoming the only amateur to have won the U.S. Women's Open. In 1971 Laura Baugh establishes a new record for youngest tournament winner at 16 years, 2 months, 21 days, when she defeats Beth Barry at Atlanta Country Club. Beth Daniel becomes a two time champion (1975 and 1977.

1980-1985: The Amateur format is changed in 1980 to 36-hole stroke-play qualifying, followed by an 18-hole match-play final. With her 1982 victory over Cathy Hanlon at Broadmoor Country Club in Colorado, Juli Simpson Inkster ties the Women's Amateur record for three consecutive wins (1980-1982).

1986-1992: Kay Cockerill wins back-to-back Amateurs in 1986-1987, and Vicki Goetz is a two-time winner, taking the 1989 tournament and winning again in 1992, when she was also the top-ranked Amateur player—the first time in four years that the top-ranked amateur won the title, and the last time it has happened.

1993-1996: Jill McGill and Wendy Ward win the 1993 and 1994 titles, respectively, and Kelli Kuehne, the 1994 Junior Girls' Amateur champion, wins the 1995 Amateur at the fabled course in Brookline, Massachusetts, The Country Club.

APPENDIX D

THE RYDER CUP: FROM PAST TO PRESENT

1926: An unofficial match takes place in Wentworth, England, between a group of American professional golfers and a team from England and Ireland. The home side racks up a resounding victory, but all the participants agree that such international competition is great fun and should be continued. A British seed merchant and avid golfer, Samuel Ryder, is so taken with the idea that he donates a cup to be awarded biennially at a match between golfers from both sides of the Atlantic.

1927-1931: First official Ryder Cup match is played at Worcester Country Club in Massachusetts, consisting of four foursomes and eight singles matches. This format will remain until 1961. The first four Ryder Cups are won by the home team. The U.S., Captained by Walter Hagen, wins in 1927 by a whopping 9.5 to 2.5 margin, taking 3 of the 4 foursome matches and six of eight singles. Great Britain wins 7-5 in 1929 at Moortown Golf Club in Leeds, as Henry Cotton leads the way with two singles victories and British Captain George Duncan defeats U.S. Captain Walter Hagen in the pivotal match. At Scioto Country Club in Ohio, the U.S. team wins easily in 1931, 9-3; Gene Sarazen is victorious in his singles match, taking one hole when he plays out from inside a concession stand, chipping through an opening under the canopy and over the bar, reaching the green and putting for a par while his opponent, Fred Robson, three-putts after landing his tee shot within twenty-five feet of the cup on the par 3 hole. Billy Burke, whose solid career is punctuated by an excellent 1931 season, when he captures the U.S. Open, reaches the semi-finals of the PGA Championship, and wins three other tournaments, is victorious in both of his Ryder Cup matches.

1933-1937: One of the great Ryder Cups is decided at the very end in 1933 at Southport & Ainsdale Golf Club in front of a large crowd. The British team is Captained by J.H.

Taylor, who has the golfers running on the beach at 6:30 each morning as part of a regular physical regimen. Syd Easterbrook of Great Britain defeats Desmond Shute of the U.S. in the final singles match with a short but swiftly curling putt on the 18th hole, as Great Britain takes a 6.5 to 5.5 win. Shute misses a four-footer on that hole, but he rebounds a few weeks later and wins the British Open. Captains Walter Hagen and J.H. Taylor play a game of one-upsmanship in a pre-match drama, as Hagen fails to show up at two lineup-exchange meetings and Taylor threatens to call the whole thing off. A long American winning streak begins in 1935 at Ridgewood Country Club with a 9-3 win in 1935, and in 1937, in the second Ryder Cup to be played at Southport & Ainsdale Golf Club, the U.S. breaks the home team domination of the Cup with an 8-3 victory. Ed Dudley, Ralph Guhldal, and Henry Picard each win two singles. The next four Cup competitions are canceled because of World War II.

1947-1949: The Ryder Cup resumes at the Portland Golf Club, with local businessman Robert Hudson helping finance the match. The U.S. totally dominates the competition, winning the first 11 matches before Sam King wins the final single for Great Britain. Ben Hogan, only just recovering from a severe automobile accident, Captains the U.S., squad in 1949 and the team responds with its own great comeback. After falling behind 3-1, the U.S. wins six of the eight singles matches to take a 7-5 victory. Sam Snead, enjoying one of his finest years, is a member of the winning team (he will be a member of a record 7 Ryder Cup champs); he also wins the Vardon Trophy, his first Masters, and second PGA Championship in 1949.

1951-1955: Led by a Hall of Fame roster and playing at fabled Pinehurst, the U.S. wins its fifth straight Ryder Cup, 9.5 to 2.5. Ben Hogan, Captain Sam Snead, Jimmy Demaret and Lloyd Mangrum win their singles matches. Jack Burke, Jr. is the star, however, with two lopsided victories; he will also play on the 1953 and 1955 teams, Captains the squad in 1957, and serves as a non-playing Captain in 1973. The score is much closer at Wentworth in 1953, as the British team fails to make several short putts and falls to the U.S., 6.5 to 5.5. At Thunderbird Golf & Country Club in 1955, the U.S. wins its seventh straight Cup, taking the match 8 to 4.

1957-1961: Great Britain wins for the third time and ends a 24-year drought with a 7.5 to 4.5 victory, taking six of eight singles matches before cheering throngs at Lindrick. At Eldorado in 1959, the British team endures a harrowing plane trip in a sudden storm while traveling from Los Angeles to Palm Springs, then loses the match 8.5 to 3.5. Eric Brown finishes his Ryder Cup participation for Great Britain with a perfect 4-0 singles record. In 1961, the Cup format changes from 12 matches (four foursomes, eight singles, all 36 hole competitions) to 24 matches (two sets of four foursomes playing 18 holes, two sets of eight singles matches, each 18 holes). Arnold Palmer and Billy Casper lead the American team, which wins the foursomes, 6-2, and the singles, 8.5 to 7.5, en route to a 14.5 to 9.5 victory at Royal Lytham & St. Annes.

1963-1967: The format changes again, as play is extended over three days and 32 matches: two series of 18-hole foursomes the first day, fourballs (8 matches between two teams of two players) the second day, and singles the third day. The U.S. wins easily, 23-9, at East Lake Country Club in 1963. The 1965 match at Royal Birkdale is closer, 19.5 to 12.5, as the U.S. wins the Cup for the fourth straight time and runs its record over Great Britain to 13-3. The domination continues at the Champions Golf Club in Houston in 1967, as the U.S. wins 23.5 to 8.5. The '67 squad includes veterans Julius Boros (4 Cups, 9-3-4 singles record), Billy Casper (8 Cups, 20-10-7 record), and Gene Littler (7 Cups, 14-5-8 singles record), and first-timers Gardner Dickinson (3 Cups, 9-1 singles record) and Bobby Nichols, who goes 4-0-1 in the '67 competition.

1969-1971: A thrilling tie occurs in 1969 at Royal Birkdale, as the two sides are never more than a point apart and 18 of the 32 matches are decided on the final hole. British Open champion Tony Jacklin defeats Jack Nicklaus 4 and 3 to tie the score going into the final afternoon. Appropriately, match-tying putts become the most memorable shots of the competition. Brian Huggett of Great Britain culminates a great comeback tie against Billy Casper with a tough five-footer on the 18th hole, just after he backs away from the putt because of a tremendous roar from the crowd at the 17th hole, where Jacklin is battling Nicklaus again. Thinking the roar means that Jacklin has clinched his match, Huggett falls into a victory swoon after holing his putt. But, Jacklin had tied Jack Nicklaus there on 17 with a tremendous, long putt. On 18, Nicklaus holes a tough short putt, then in a consummate act of sportsmanship, concedes Jacklin's three-footer to tie the competition. Nicklaus tells Jacklin, "I didn't think you would miss but I didn't want to give you the chance." The U.S. runs its unbeaten streak to 7 in 1971 at Old Warson Country Club in St. Louis, taking an 18.5 to 13.5 victory.

1973-77: The format is altered again in 1973, with the first two days consisting of 18 hole foursomes and fourballs and the third day featuring two series of singles matches. The U.S. wins 19-13 in 1973 and 21-11 in 1975. The 1977 match at Royal Lytham & St. Anne's is shortened to 18 holes each day in hopes of turning up the intensity, but the format proves unpopular and the U.S. triumphs again, taking a large lead then settling for a 12.5 to 5.5 victory, as Jack Nicklaus (losing for the fourth time in five Ryder Cup singles matches), Tom Watson, and Hale Irwin lose their singles matches. Nicklaus still managed a 17-8-3 lifetime mark in Ryder singles, while Irwin enjoyed an 11-4-1 mark and Watson went 9-3.

1979-1981: The competition changes to a United States vs. Europe match and a three day format—with foursomes and fourballs the first two days and twelve singles on the final day. The U.S. takes a first-day lead, 5.5 to 2.5, Europe comes back to close the second day trailing by one, 8.5 to 7.5, then the U.S. runs away with victory by taking the singles, 8.5 to 3.5. Larry Nelson goes 5-0 in 1979 and follows with a 4-0 record in 1981 at Walton Heath in England. The U.S. wins in 1981 to run its Ryder Cup record to 20-3-1.

1983-1987: Three great Ryder Cup matches. In 1983 at PGA National in Palm Beach Florida, the teams are tied at 13 with two singles matches remaining. Tom Watson wins late over Bernard Gallagher to give the U.S. a 14-13 advantage, but Lanny Wadkins comes to the final hole trailing Jose Maria Canizares by one. Wadkins outdrives Canizares, and Canizares' approach falls short of the green. Wadkins then hits a marvelous chip shot that bounces on the green, teases the cup, and settles within a foot of the hole. His tap in halves the match and gives the U.S. a thrilling 14.5 to 13.5 victory. U.S. Captain Jack Nicklaus runs out to the fairway, falls to his knees, and kisses the divot left from Wadkins' remarkable approach. The 1985 Europe squad includes Seve Ballesteros, Bernhard Langer, and Nick Faldo. Nevertheless, the U.S. jumps out to a 3-1 lead, but the match is tied at the end of the second day when Curtis Strange and Craig Stadler, two up with two to play, can't complete a victory in fourball over Bernhard Langer and Sandy Lyle. Lyle wins the 17th hole for Europe with a long putt, then Stadler misses a two-footer on 18 that would have halved the hole and clinched a U.S. point for the match. Then the Europe team wins the singles, 7.5 to 4.5, with Sam Torrance snaking in a tough putt for jubilant victory in front of a wildly enthusiastic crowd. In 1987 at Muirfield Village, the European team takes a commanding 5 match lead going into the singles competition, then hangs on for a 15-13 victory, with Seve Ballesteros performing the heroics. It is the first time the U.S. is defeated on its home greens and the first time the Europe/Great/Britain/Ireland side wins back-to-back Ryder Cups.

1991:   The 1991 Ryder Cup is played at the Kiawah Island Ocean Course in South Carolina, which plays extremely tough and humbles the players. The U.S. wins 14.5 to 13.5, but it comes as a result of shots not made, as opposed to brilliant play. Mark Calcavecchia seems to be wrapping up the U.S. victory, leading Colin Montgomerie by four with four to play. Calcavecchia promptly bogeys 15 and 16 to Montgomerie's uneventful pars, but Montgomerie fails to carry the sprawling pond fronting the par 3 17th green, giving Calcavecchia a chance to end the match. But Calcavecchia hits his tee shot into the water as well, then hits a second tee shot into the water, proceeding to lose the hole, and then he loses the 18th as well. In the final singles match, Hale Irwin bogeys 18, but Bernhard Langer misses a six-foot putt and a chance to tie the match.

1993-1995:   The third straight home-greens Ryder Cup at Belfry is the stage for a late great U.S. comeback, with a parade of singles wins turning a 8.5 to 7.5 deficit into a 15-13 victory, as Raymond Floyd outduels Jose Maria Olazabal on the 18th hole to clinch victory. Payne Stewart, Davis Love III, Jim Gallagher, and Tom Kite, who upped his Ryder Cup record to 5-0-2, won their matches as well. The European team comes back in 1995 at Oak Hill, winning 14.5 to 13.5 led by the emotional Constantino Rocco. The European team has registered a 3-2-1 mark over the past six Ryder Cups, and the renewed competitiveness, emotion, and brilliant play during this period have made the Ryder Cup as popular as ever.

INDEX

T his index lists courses as well as golfers profiled in this book who have regularly competed in tournaments. For further information, chapter 16 features celebrity golfers and golf
movies, literature, and songs. Chapter 17 includes a glossary of golf terms, and terms
specifically relating to golf architecture can be found in Chapter 14. Chapter 18 has extensive
lists of golf resources,and brief summaries of major tournaments appear as Appendices.